Managing Human Resources

19th Edition

Snell • Morris

Cengage

Australia • Brazil • Canada • India • Mexico • Singapore • United Kingdom • United States

Cengage

Managing Human Resources,
19th Edition

Scott Snell and
Shad Morris

For product information and technology assistance, contact us at
asia.infoindia@cengage.com

For permission to use material from this text or product, submit all requests online at
www.cengage.com/permissions

ISBN-13: 978-93-6660-688-0
ISBN-10: 93-6660-688-1

Cengage Learning India Pvt. Ltd.
T-303, 3rd Floor
DAV Complex, Plot 3
Mayur Vihar Phase 1
Delhi 110091

Cengage is a leading provider of customized learning solutions with employees residing in nearly 40 different countries and sales in more than 125 countries around the world. Find your local representative at: **www.cengage.com.**

Cengage is committed to creating inclusive and diverse products, including perspectives that represent the diversity of people across all backgrounds, identities, opinions, and experiences. If you have any feedback related to this, please contact us at **support.cengage.com.**

To learn more about Cengage products, platforms and services, visit **www.cengage.co.in.**

Disclaimer:
This book contains link to resources which are a part of the imported edition. The same may not be available with the Indian edition. The buyer needs to purchase a copy of the imported edition to have full access to those resources. In no event the publisher shall be liable for any limitation or performance due to unavailability of these resources.

Printed by:
B.B Press
C-23, Sector-A-7, Phase-1
Tronica City, Ghaziabad (U.P)

Printed in India
Print Number: 01 Print Year: 2025

Contents

Brief Contents

Preface

The 19th edition of *Managing Human Resources* will place your students at the forefront of understanding how organizations can gain a sustainable competitive advantage through people. Today's HR managers play an active role in the strategic planning and decision making within their organizations. Great managers elevate the importance of their organization's human resources to C-suite levels and have a major impact on the success of their firms. But human resource management is not limited to the HR staff. The best organizations recognize that managing people is the job of every manager, working in partnership with HR.

As human resource management continually changes, each edition of the book is updated to highlight these changes. Even so, this book reveals that the goal of utilizing an organization's talent in the best way possible never changes. Consequently, the purpose of this book is always twofold: (1) to equip students with the tools and practices of HR management and give them an appreciation for the changes they can make by understanding how best to manage people, and (2) to present the most current challenges and opportunities graduating students will face when it comes to today's human resource management environment. These challenges exist both for those who will become HR managers and those who will go on to become other types of managers.

Toward that end, the first chapter of the book lays out in broad terms the key challenges in HRM today. It includes a discussion of the HR strategies pursued by firms and the importance of retaining and motivating employees in the process. Other aspects broached include the strategies companies are using to continue to try to control health care costs; how social media is affecting hiring, human resources management, and employees' privacy rights; and how good human resources practices can help a firm achieve its corporate social responsibility and sustainability goals and make it an employer of choice. The chapter also discusses the important partnership with line managers and the competencies required of HR management. The textbook continues with the introduction, explanation, and discussion of the individual practices and policies that make up HRM. We understand the role of managers is continually adjusting; therefore, we emphasize current issues and real-world problems to discuss changes to policies and practices of HRM.

Strategy and talent have become such central concerns of HR today that we continue to emphasize the topic in this edition of the book in Chapter 2. Chapter 5 focuses on expanding and managing the talent pool in organizations. Employee diversity, equity and inclusion, and how firms can leverage all types of differences among their workers to their strategic advantage, are examined.

Organizations in today's competitive world are discovering that it is *how* the individual HR topics are combined that makes all the difference. Managers typically don't focus on HR issues such as staffing, training, and compensation in isolation from one another. Each of these HR practices should be combined into an overall system—one that furthers a firm's strategy by enhancing employee involvement and productivity. *Managing Human Resources* ends with a final chapter that focuses on how high-performance work systems (HPWSs) are used to implement these strategies. We outline the strategic processes used to implement HPWSs, including workflow design, HR practices, management processes, and supporting technologies as well as the outcomes of an HPWS that benefit both the employee and the organization as a whole.

Streamlined Coverage

Today's students are extremely busy. They want to know what they need to learn and how to learn it as quickly as possible. Instructors want to be able to cover all of the material they want to teach during a semester. To help both groups, we made a special effort to streamline our coverage in this edition.

New Cutting-Edge Content

As with other editions, a great deal of new information is provided in this revision to accurately reflect HRM in today's business world and help the reader understand today's HRM issues more effectively. Examples include the concerns of Millennial and Generation Z employees, and how Big Data, HR analytics, remote work, and social media are profoundly affecting the field, and the effects artificial intelligence and automation are having. Ever-changing international HR concerns are covered, including the work-visa challenges facing U.S. firms, immigration, human rights issues, global rights issues such as data protection, and intellectual property rights. The Coronavirus pandemic had staggering consequences and resulted in numerous updates in the workplace and, therefore, this edition. Of course, the 19th edition also includes a complete update of all laws, administrative rulings and guidelines, and court decisions governing HRM. We have previously shown that Millennials are seeking collective action through unions. We now also discuss how Generation Z believes in labor movements to motivate change, without the help of unions.

Lastly, to help instructors incorporate the new material discussed into their courses, the following is a list of chapter-by-chapter additions:

Chapter 1

- Updated discussion on international trade, Brexit, and the H-1B visa debate.
- The loss of middle-class jobs in the United States and new technology affecting HR, such as robotics and automation.
- New coverage on the employee experience.
- New coverage on Generation Z.
- Updated information on workforce demographic trends and the progress of under-represented groups in the workplace.

Chapter 2

- New real-life examples throughout the text.

Chapter 3

- New legal interpretations on what reasonable accommodation means for employees with disabilities.
- Updated information on how Title VII is being interpreted to prohibit discrimination based on gender identity or sexual orientation.
- A look at discrimination due to race-based natural hair and hairstyles.
- The lifting of the ban on transgender individuals from serving in the military.
- A discussion of how the #MeToo movement changed the perception and dealings of sexual harassment.
- New research about companies' efforts to make diversity, equity, and inclusion a priority amidst the Black Lives Matter movement.
- Steps to increase diversity in your workplace.

Chapter 4

- New discussion of the change continually happening for workflow.
- New discussion of the need for flexible work arrangements.
- Term change from "telecommuting" to "working remote."
- New section considering the recent spike in remote work.

Chapter 5

- Expanded discussion about the benefits and challenges of having open-ended application collection.
- New facts related to online recruiting and social media examination.
- Language adjustments to focus on inclusivity.
- New information about veteran job seekers and the VETS agency which helps place veterans in jobs.

Chapter 6

- New information regarding remote and virtual interviews, particularly in response to the COVID-19 pandemic.
- New tips for conducting effective interviews.

Chapter 7

- Another learning objective added to highlight the evaluation of training programs.
- New paragraph about the training benefits of special assignments.
- Simplified section to focus on only the most important content.

Chapter 8

- Additional tips for minimizing criticism when conducting performance evaluations.
- Clarifications about information systems and databases.
- Edits to improve information flow including one-word descriptions of performance review guidelines.

Chapter 9

- New coverage of systems and websites, such as Glassdoor and Buffer, to collect salary and other related data used especially in job evaluation.
- A list of the highest paying jobs for 2019 in the United States.
- An updated discussion of the minimum age required for employment.
- Updated salary rates for the fastest growing jobs in the United States.

Chapter 10

- New research shows that unless done correctly and carefully, pay for performance can hurt the company.
- Spot bonuses were found to be a great way to encourage employees during the COVID pandemic.
- Recognition at work is extremely important to employees and frequent public recognitions are the preferred method by employees.
- Are CEOs still being paid too much even in the face of a global pandemic?

Chapter 11

- Updated information on the current status of the Patient Protection and Affordable Care Act (PPACA).
- An analysis of the increase in Employee Assistance Programs focused on mental health due to the Coronavirus pandemic.
- Expanded discussion on how the Mental Health Parity and Addiction Equity Act of 2008 requires mental health care benefits yet still does not help.
- New discussions about domestic partnership and fertility benefits.

Chapter 12

- Updated research on preventing employee burnout.
- Updated information on U.S. employee injury and safety statistics today.
- New research on the proven success of computer game safety trainings.
- Updated information on enforcing safety rules and the importance of crisis management teams.
- Updated information on the prevalence of workplace violence.

Chapter 13

- New information on employee privacy rights at their place of employment and at home due to remote work.
- New examples related to monitoring off-duty conduct.
- Updated information on how employees are protected for blowing the whistle.
- New discussions and statistics of social media and how it is used and abused by employees.

Chapter 14

- Discussion of how the last presidential election impacted unions and their traditional allegiance to the Democratic Party.
- New research showing the decrease in union membership but certainly not a decrease in labor movements.
- New examples of how unionizing successfully raised employees' starting salary.
- Adjustment of learning outcomes organization.

Chapter 15

- New example of two countries working towards economic development.
- Simplified and clearer Learning Objectives.

Chapter 16

- A look at how companies created remote work data access in response to the COVID-19 pandemic.
- Edited and updated case study on Whole Foods' HPWS and the challenges the company faces sustaining it and regaining a competitive advantage.

Features of the Book

Designed to facilitate understanding and retention of the material presented, each chapter contains the following pedagogical features:

- **Learning Outcomes** listed at the beginning of each chapter provide the basis for the Integrated Learning System. Each outcome is also listed in the margin of the chapter in which it appears. The outcomes are revisited in the chapter summary and discussion questions and in all of the book's ancillaries.
- **Small Business Application Boxes.** The boxes are designed to help entrepreneurs, small business owners, and managers think about how to organize, implement, and leverage talent and to draw attention to resources designed especially for them to do so. We feel the coverage is very important because many students today are very interested in entrepreneurship and will go on to found their own businesses. Moreover, small businesses provide most of America's jobs to workers.
- **Highlights in HRM.** This popular boxed feature provides real-world examples of how organizations perform HR functions. The highlights are introduced in the text discussion and include topics such as small businesses and international issues.
- **Key Terms** appear in boldface and are defined in margin notes next to the text discussion. The Key Terms are also listed at the end of the chapter and appear in the glossary at the end of the book.
- **Figures.** An abundance of graphic materials and flowcharts provides a visual, dynamic presentation of concepts and HR activities. All figures are systematically referenced in the text discussion.
- **Summary.** A paragraph or two for each Learning Outcome provides a brief and focused review of the chapter.

- **Discussion Questions** following the chapter summary offer an opportunity to focus on each of the Learning Outcomes in the chapter and stimulate critical thinking. Many of these questions allow for group analysis and class discussion.
- **HRM Experience.** An experiential activity designed to simulate HR activities is included in each chapter.
- **End-of-Chapter Cases.** Two case studies per chapter present current HRM issues in real-life settings that allow for student consideration and critical analysis.
- **Extended Cases.** Ten extended cases are provided at the end of the main text. These cases use material covered in more than one chapter and provide capstone opportunities.

Mindtap's Innovative Digital Features

Today's leading digital platform, MindTap, gives you complete control of your course—equipping you to craft unique learning experiences that challenge students, build confidence and elevate performance.

Use MindTap as-is or customize it to meet your specific needs. You can even integrate it easily into your institution's Learning Management System (LMS). A MindTap presents complex concepts using a blend of engaging narrative and media assets clearly linked to assessments. So, students can start applying concepts to real-world situations from the beginning of your course with content that pogresses from understanding core concepts to critical thinking and, ultimately, application.

Product Features

MindTap's outcome-based learning design propels students from memorization to mastery. It's the only platform today that gives you complete ownership of your course. With MindTap you can challenge every student, build confidence, and empower today's learners to be unstoppable.

Anchor Learning With Improved Learning Path Design.

MindTap helps students focus by dividing the Learning Path into groups of bite-size activities that are anchored to a single concept.

Access Everything You Need In One Place.

Cut down on prep with preloaded, organized course materials in MindTap. Teach more efficiently with interactive multimedia, assignments, quizzes and focused resources all on one screen.

Control Your Course, Your Content.

Only MindTap gives you complete control of your course. You have the flexibility to reorder textbook chapters, add your own notes and embed a variety of content, including OER. Personalize course content to your students' needs by editing question text or answer choices. They can even read your notes, add their own and highlight key text to aid their progress.

Count On Our Dedicated Team, Whenever You Need Them.

MindTap is not simply a comprehensive tool—it's a network of support from a personalized team eager to further your success. We're ready to help—from setting up your course to tailoring MindTap resources to meet your specific objectives. You'll be ready to make an impact from day one. And, we'll be right here to help you and your students throughout the semester—and beyond.

Mindtap Table of Contents

MindTap brings together quality learning and convenience through seamless, LMS integrated access to a curated set learning tools designed intentionally for the Principles of Management learner. Each MindTap follows a "Learn It, Apply It, Study It" structure that guides students through bite sized learning exercises, followed by authentic scenario-based application opportunities and then gives them the necessary tools to prepare for quizzes and exams.

Chapter-Level Ebook

Dynamic eBook brings the value, concepts and applications of the printed text to life. Stu- dents open an active learning experience as each chapter provides opportunities to interact with content using the approach that's best for the individual learner.

Learn It Activities

New "Learn It" modules aligned to each learning objective and are designed to help students learn the basics of theories and concepts presented in a chapter through digestible summaries and randomized questions that help check their comprehension of the chapter material.

Apply It

"Apply It" Chapter Assignments and Case Activities bridge the understanding of concepts with their real-world applications in the practice of management.

Study It

The "Study It" module for each chapter includes Practice Tests powered by A+ Test Prep, a student-powered practice exam tool that allows them to tailor practice tests to fit their needs, and receive immediate feedback and links back to the material they need to review. The "Study It" module also contains digital flashcards to help students practice key terminology and a student-facing version of the PowerPoint slides that accompany the text.

Additional Resources

Concept Clips: These short concept videos bring to life concepts from the text.

On the Job Videos: These videos enhance the learning experience by giving students the chance to hear from real-world business leaders so they can see the direct application of the management theories they have learned.

You Make The Decision

You Make the Decision mini-simulation activities build critical thinking and deci-sion- making skills by challenging students to use what they know about concepts and theories in the context of a scenario as it unfolds. Throughout the scenario, the stu-dent would be provided with information and subsequently faced with decisions. The scenario can change dynamically based on the decisions the students make throughout the short simulation, resulting in different end points that showcase the consequences of the decisions made along the way.

Of Special Interest to Instructors

Instructors will find a number of valuable resources available on our Cengage Instructor Center, accessed through your instructor account (www.cengage.com.) These include the following:

Instructor's Manual. Designed to provide support for instructors new to the course, as well as innovative materials for experienced professors, the Instructor's Manual includes activities and assessments for each chapter and their correlation to specific learning objectives, an outline, key terms with definitions, a chapter summary, and ideas for engaging with students—such as discussion questions, ice breakers, case studies, and social learning activities that may be conducted in an on-ground, hybrid, or online modality.

PowerPoint Lecture Presentation. The PowerPoint Lecture Presentations provide ample opportunities for generating classroom discussion and interaction. They offer ready-to-use, visual outlines of each chapter, which may be easily customized for your lectures.

Guide to Teaching Online. This guide presents technological and pedagogical con-siderations and suggestions for teaching the Management course when you can't be in the same room with students.

Transition Guide. This guide highlights all of the changes in the text and in the digital offerings from the previous edition to this edition.

Educator Guide: This guide walks you through what the unique activities are in the MindTap, where you'll find them and how they're built for easier curriculum integration.

Acknowledgments

Because preparation of manuscript for a project as large as *Managing Human Resources* is a continuing process, we would like to acknowledge the work of those colleagues who provided thoughtful feedback and invaluable content expertise for this and the previous editions of the text. Our appreciation and thanks go to:

Ryan Hall, Chatfield College
Loren Kuzuhara, University of Wisconsin
Kim Fox-Marchetti, Lone Star College
Dale King, Lenoir-Rhyne University
Carol Decker, Tennessee Wesleyan University
Christie Hovey, Lincoln Land Community College
Tony Hunnicutt, College of the Ouachitas
Debra Moody, Virginia Commonwealth University
Dave Quirk, Northwest Christian University
Greg Berezewski, Robert Morris University of Illinois
Avan Jassawalla, SUNY Geneseo School of Business
Jeffrey Moser, Valley City State University
Jonathan Biggane, Fresno State University
Niesha Geoffroy, Golden Gate University
Julia Levashina, Kent State University
Jaime Simmons, Marlboro College Graduate School
Zhaoquong Qin, Langston University
Justin Wareham, Oklahoma City University
Kiristen Jefferson, Southern New Hampshire University
LaSondra Banks, Triton Community College
Misty Resendez, Ivy Tech
Neeley Shaw, Waynesburg University
Rimjhim Banerjee-Batist, Schenectady County Community College
Rhoda Sautner, University of Mary
Robin Sawyer, University of Maryland
Sandra Obilade, Bresica University
Shirley Rijkse, Central Carolina Community College
Weichu Xu, East Stroudsburg University
Steve Ash, University of Akron
Michael Bedell, California State University, Bakersfield
Brad Bell, Cornell University
Katherine Clyde, Pitt Community College
Mary Connerley, Virginia Tech University
Susie Cox, McNeese State University
Paula S. Daly, James Madison University
Sharon Davis, Central Texas College
Douglas Dierking, University of Texas, Austin
Suzanne Dyer-Gear, Carroll Community College
Joe J. Eassa, Jr., Palm Beach Atlantic University
Summer Zwanziger Elsinger, Upper Iowa University
Robert E. Ettl, SUNY Stony Brook
Diane Fagan, Webster University
Angela L. Farrar, University of Nevada, Las Vegas

Lou Firenze, Northwood University
Olene L. Fuller, San Jacinto College
Judith Gordon, Boston College
Rita G. Greer, Spalding University
Mike Griffith, Cascade College
Daniel Grundmann, Indiana University
Adrian Guardia, Texas A&M University, San Antonio
Xuguang Guo, University of Wisconsin, Whitewater
Sally Hackman, Central Methodist College
Kevin Hale, Lonestar College
Mike Hashek, Gateway Technical College
Rich Havranek, SUNY Institute of Technology
Kim Hester, Arkansas State University
Stephen Hiatt, Catawba College
Alyce Hochhalter, St. Mary Woods College
Madison Holloway, Metropolitan State College of Denver
David J. Hudson, Spalding University
Karen Jacobs, LeTourneau University
Avan Jassawalla, SUNY at Geneseo
Michelle Jetzer, Madison College
Nancy M. Johnson, Madison Area Technical College
Jeffrey Johnston, Alpena Community College
Pravin Kamdar, Cardinal Stritch University
Cheryl L. Kane, University of North Carolina, Charlotte
Jordan J. Kaplan, Long Island University
Steve Karau, Southern Illinois University at Carbondale
Joseph Kavanaugh, Sam Houston State University
John Kelley, Villanova University
Dennis Lee Kovach, Community College of Allegheny County
Kenneth Kovach, University of Maryland
Trudy Kroeger, Wisconsin Indianhead Technical College
Chalmer E. Labig, Jr., Oklahoma State University
Alecia N. Lawrence, Williamsburg Technical College
Scott W. Lester, University of Wisconsin, Eau Claire
J. Jonathan Lewis, Texas Southern University
Corinne Livesay, Bryan College
Beverly Loach, Central Piedmont Community College
L. M. Lockhart, Penn State Greater Allegheny
Gloria Lopez, New Mexico Highlands University
Barbara Luck, Jackson Community College
Larry Maes, Davenport University
Jennifer Malfitano, Delaware County Community College
Michael Matukonis, SUNY Oneonta
Doug McCabe, Georgetown University
Lee McCain, Seminole Community College
Marjorie L. McInerney, Marshall University
Veronica Meyers, San Diego State University
Robert T. Mooney, Texas State University
Julia Morrison, Bloomfield College

Jim Nichols, Crown College
Harold Nolan, Georgian Court University
Sue Norton, University of Wisconsin Parkside
David Nye, Kennedy-Western University
Paul Olsen, Saint Michael's College
Donald Otto, Lindenwood University
Charles Parsons, Georgia Institute of Technology
Dane Partridge, University of Southern Indiana
Bryan J. Pesta, Cleveland State University
Theodore Peters, Hartwick College
David Pitts, Delaware Technical and Community College
Amy Pogue, Valencia College
Alex Pomnichowski, Ferris State University
Victor Prosper, University of the Incarnate Word
Michael Raphael, Central Connecticut State University
Charles Rarick, Barry University
Eladio D. Reid, University of Houston Downtown
June Roux, Salem Community College
Robert Rustic, University of Findlay
Laura L. Sankovich, Capella University
Machelle Schroeder, University of Wisconsin–Platteville
Kelli Schutte, Calvin College
Mike Sciarini, Michigan State University
Tom Sedwick, Indiana University of Pennsylvania
Jim Sethi, University of Montana Western
Patricia Setlik, William Rainey Harper College
William L. Smith, Emporia State University
Norman Solomon, Fairfield University
Emeric Solymossy, Western Illinois University
Carol Spector, University of North Florida
Howard Stanger, Canisius College
Scott L. Stevens, Detroit College of Business
Michael Sturman, Cornell University
Nanette Swarthout, Fontbonne College
Michael T. Korns, Indiana University of Pennsylvania
Karen Ann Tarnoff, East Tennessee State University
Thomas Taveggia, University of Arizona
Donna Testa, Herkimer County Community College
Alan Tillquist, West Virginia State College
Sue Toombs, Weatherford College
Richard Trotter, University of Baltimore
William Turnley, Kansas State University
Catherine L. Tyler, Oakland University
Melissa Waite, The College at Brockport, SUNY
Harvell Walker, Texas Tech University
Barbara Warschawski, Schenectady County Community College
Steve Werner, University of Houston
Liesl Wesson, Texas A&M University
JoAnn Wiggins, Walla Walla University

Jim Wilkinson, Stark State College
L. A. Witt, University of New Orleans
Evelyn Zent, University of Washington, Tacoma
Ryan Zimmerman, Texas A&M University

In the manuscript for this edition, we have drawn not only on the current literature but also on the current practices of organizations that furnished information and illustrations relating to their HR programs. We are indebted to the leaders in the field who have developed the available heritage of information and practices of HRM and who have influenced us through their writings and personal associations. We have also been aided by students in our classes; by research assistants like Katie Bahr, Claire Bird, Lameck Muaka, and Connor Peterson, and by former students; by the participants in the management development programs with whom we have been associated; by HR managers; and by our colleagues. We appreciate the efforts of everyone at Cengage who helped develop and produce this text and its supplements. They include: Heather Mooney and Michael Worls, Product Directors; Julia Chase, Senior Content Manager; Courtney Wolstoncroft, Learning Designer; Beth Ross, Digital Delivery Lead; Chris Doughman, Art Director; and Adam Graber, Product Assistant.

We are also so grateful to our wives—Marybeth Snell and Mindi Morris—who have contributed in so many ways to this book. They are always sources of invaluable guidance and assistance. Furthermore, by their continued enthusiasm and support, they have made the process a more pleasant and rewarding experience. We are most grateful to them for their many contributions to this publication, to our lives, and to our families.

Scott A. Snell
University of Virginia

Shad S. Morris
Brigham Young University

About the Authors

Scott A. Snell

Scott Snell is the Frank Sands, Sr. Chair of business administration and former senior associate dean for executive education at the University of Virginia's Darden Graduate School of Business. Scott teaches courses in leadership and strategic management and works with senior executives on aligning their human resource investments to better execute their strategies. Scott is the author of four books and was listed among the top one hundred most-cited authors in scholarly journals of management. He currently serves on the board of directors for SHRM, and has served on the boards of HR People + Strategy, and previously has served on the boards of the Strategic Management Society's Human Capital Group, the Society for Human Resource Management Foundation, the Academy of Management's Human Resource Division, the *Academy of Management Journal,* and the *Academy of Management Review.*

Prior to joining the Darden faculty, Scott was professor and director of executive education at Cornell University's Center for Advanced Human Resource Studies and a professor of management in the Smeal College of Business at Pennsylvania State University. He received a BA from Miami University, as well as an MBA and PhD in business from Michigan State University. Originally from Ohio, Scott now lives in Charlottesville, Virginia.

Shad S. Morris

Shad Morris is the William F. Edwards Distinguished Fellow and professor of management at the Marriott School of Business at Brigham Young University. He teaches courses in the areas of human resources management and international business. Prior to joining the Marriott School, Shad was an assistant professor of management and human resources at The Ohio State University and has held appointments at the Sloan School of Management at MIT, Copenhagen Business School in Denmark, China Europe International Business School (CEIBS) in China, Indian School of Business in India and SKK Graduate School of Business in South Korea.

Shad's research focuses on strategic human resource management in a global environment. His research has been published in a number of journals, such as the *Harvard Business Review, MIT Sloan Management Review, Academy of Management Review, Academy of Management Journal, Journal of International Business Studies, Strategic Management Journal, Journal of Management,* and *Human Resource Management.* He has worked for the World Bank, Management Systems International, and Alcoa. He has consulted with numerous companies on their HR and knowledge practices. He is the recipient of the International HRM Scholarly Research Award from the Academy of Management and has been a faculty fellow at Cambridge University's Centre for International Human Resource Management. In addition, Shad is currently an Associate Editor at the Academy of Management Review and serves on the board of the *International Journal of Human Resources Management.* He received a BS in psychology and a masters in organizational behavior from Brigham Young University, as well as a PhD in human resources management from Cornell University.

CHAPTER 1

The Opportunities and Challenges of Human Resources Management

Learning Outcomes

After studying this chapter, you should be able to

LO 1 Explain how human resource (HR) managers and other managers can have rewarding careers by helping their firms gain a sustainable competitive advantage through the strategic utilization of people.

LO 2 Explain how good human resource practices can help a firm address strategic challenges such as globalization, competition, and sustainability efforts.

LO 3 Describe how technology can improve how people perform and how they are managed.

LO 4 Explain the dual goals HR managers have in terms of increasing productivity and controlling costs.

LO 5 Discuss how firms can leverage employee differences to their strategic advantage and how educational and cultural changes in the workforce are affecting how human resource managers engage employees.

LO 6 Provide examples of the roles and competencies of today's HR managers and their relationship with other managers.

We use a lot of words to describe how important people are to organizations. The terms *human resources* (*HR*), *human capital, intellectual assets,* and *talent management* imply that it's people who drive the performance of their organizations (along with other resources such as money, materials, and information). Successful organizations are particularly adept at bringing together different kinds of people to achieve a common purpose. This is the essence of **human resources management (HRM)**. HRM involves a wide variety of activities, including analyzing a company's competitive environment and designing jobs and teams so that a firm's strategy can be successfully implemented to beat the competition. This, in turn, requires identifying, recruiting, and selecting the right people for those jobs and teams; training, motivating, and appraising these people; developing competitive compensation policies to retain them; grooming them to lead the organization in the future—and the list goes on.

human resources management (HRM)
The process of managing human talent to achieve an organization's objectives.

1.1 Why Should You Study Human Resources Management? Will It Pay Off?

LO1
Think of a firm you do business with that is facing the prospect of undergoing dramatic changes just to survive. (Traditional bricks-and-mortar retailers such as Target and Macy's, which are facing stiff competition from online retailers, are an example.) How do you think the firm's personnel can help it adapt? What role will the company's HR staff play in helping the firm achieve that goal?

Which of these activities would you like to engage in your career?

- Establishing the strategic direction your firm should take
- Attracting top-notch people to come to work for you and your firm
- Determining the right people to hire so your team and company are a success
- Helping and coaching people so they become top-notch performers

If these activities appeal to you, a job managing people might be a rewarding career for you and an excellent reason why you should study HRM. Having a good understanding of HRM is important for managers and entrepreneurs of all types—not just HR personnel. All managers are responsible for at least some of the activities that fall into the category of management. Managers play a key role in selecting employees, training and motivating them, appraising them, promoting them, and so forth. It's a job that can be incredibly rewarding—like a gardener helping their crops to grow. But what if you do a poor job of these activities? Believe it or not, many businesspeople with great business strategies, business plans, and products and services fail because they do not fully grasp the importance of HRM. Laments one entrepreneur:

> My first year after investing in a small business that was failing, I tripled the amount of business the company did and made a lot of money. But I didn't pay my personnel enough or motivate them. They eventually abandoned me, and a larger competitor muscled me out of the marketplace. I now understand the important role personnel play in a business. They can make or break it.

In addition, while great business plans and products and services can easily be copied by your competitors, great personnel cannot. Their knowledge and abilities are among the most distinctive and renewable resources upon which a company can draw.

If an employer requested your Facebook login credentials, what would you do?

Rawpixel.com/ Shutterstock.com

As Thomas J. Watson, founder of IBM, said, "You can get capital and erect buildings, but it takes people to build a business."[1]

Lastly, even if you never become a manager, understanding HRM can help you understand your responsibilities and rights as an employee. For example, what if your employer asks for the passwords to your accounts on Facebook or other social media sites? Do you need to provide the manager with that information? This textbook can help you answer questions such as these.

1.1a Human Capital and Organizational Culture

The idea that organizations "compete through people" highlights the fact that achieving success increasingly depends on an organization's ability to manage its *human capital.* The term **human capital** describes the employees' knowledge, skills, abilities, and other attributes (KSAOs) that have economic value to the firm. Although the value of these assets might not show up directly on a company's balance sheet, it nevertheless has a tremendous impact on an organization's performance. The following quotations from notable CEOs and former CEOs illustrate this point[2]:

human capital
The knowledge, skills, and capabilities of individuals who have economic value to an organization.

- "The key for us, number one, has always been hiring very smart people." (Bill Gates, Microsoft)
- "In technology, it's about the people. Getting the best people, retaining them, nurturing a creative environment, and helping to find a way to innovate." (Marissa Mayer, former CEO, Yahoo)
- "You gotta build a team that is so talented, they almost make you uncomfortable." (Brian Chesky, Airbnb)

Companies that *do* "win" because of the talent they find, hire, and manage include:

- Publix, which empowers its employees to make decisions—decisions that are good for an individual store, its customers, area growers, community, and the firm as a whole.
- Nordstrom, which empowers its employees to go through near-heroics to satisfy customers.
- The Martin Agency, a Virginia-based advertising agency whose talented and creative personnel generate award-winning advertising campaigns like those for insurer Geico and cable-TV network Nickelodeon.
- Sewell Automotive, a family-owned business of 16 automobile dealerships, which emphasizes that building long-term relationships, not selling cars and trucks, is key to its success. The company seeks to hire only the best employees, and develop them as stewards of the company to create long-term "customers for life."

Unlike physical capital and resources, human capital is intangible—so it cannot be managed the same way that organizations manage jobs, products, and technologies. One reason why this is so is because employees, *not* the organization, own their own human capital. If valued employees leave a company, they take their human capital with them, and any investment the company has made in training and developing these people is lost.

To build human capital in organizations, managers must continue to develop superior knowledge, skills, and experience within their workforces and retain and promote top performers.[3] Beyond the need to invest in employee development, organizations have to find ways to better utilize the knowledge of their workers. Too often employees have knowledge that goes unused. HR managers and programs are often the conduit through which knowledge is developed and transferred among employees. As Dave Ulrich, a noted expert in human resources, notes: "Learning capability is *g* times *g*—a business's ability to *generate* new ideas multiplied by its adeptness at *generalizing* them throughout the company."[4]

Why does knowledge go unshared and unused in organizations? Oftentimes it's because of a firm's organizational culture. **Organizational culture** refers to the shared values, beliefs, assumptions, and expectations that permeate an organization. Organizational culture affects how people in an organization work and treat each other and their customers. A negative organizational culture stifles employees and leads to lower productivity and morale. In contrast, a positive organizational culture not only helps employees acquire knowledge and skills, but also fosters curiosity among employees, allows them to grow and thrive, and creates mission-driven teams that actually achieve success.

organizational culture
The shared values, beliefs, and assumptions people in an organization have.

You probably understand organizational culture more than you realize. Are there businesses you like to shop with because they perform better and you enjoy the atmosphere and people? Are there other businesses that are similar but that you don't like to shop with? The difference is likely due to organizational culture. For example, Marriott's culture is critical to its success. The hotel chain takes care of its employees. They, in turn, take care of the customers, who come back time and again.

Although "competing through people" and "organizational culture" are major themes of HRM, on a day-to-day basis, managers of all types have to carry out the specific activities for a company to effectively do so. Figure 1.1 provides an overall framework of these activities.

What do you think are the biggest human resource–related challenges you would have to face as a manager or team leader? Professional organizations such as the Society for Human Resource Management (SHRM) conduct ongoing studies of the most pressing competitive issues facing firms. The top trends, or challenges, firms name today include those outlined in the sections that follow.

Figure 1.1 Overall Framework for Human Resources Management

> **LO2**
> Name a company you hope to work for someday. What makes it special? How does it create an advantage in the marketplace? Does it put people at the center of their strategy?

1.2 Strategic and Global Challenges

When the COVID-19 pandemic devastated economies, businesses, jobs, and families around the world, the challenges of HRM took center stage. Never had senior leaders depended more on their HR colleagues to keep people safe, get them back to work, and help bolster the culture of collaboration and mutual support. There was an initial phase of crisis management, and the challenges of HR extended to longer-term reinvention of work and employment during a time of transformation.

The COVID-19 pandemic highlighted the fact that organizations can rarely stand still for long. Being able to adapt has become the key to capturing opportunities and overcoming obstacles both domestically and abroad. In fact, it is often the key to the very survival of organizations. Since 2000, more than half of the firms in the *Fortune* 500 have either gone bankrupt, been acquired, or ceased to exist as a result of industry disruption (Constellation Research, 2014).[5]

Not surprisingly, a recent IBM study of more than 1,500 executives showed that managing disruption ranked among the top concerns of CEOs. According to these executives, their need to lead change is growing, but their ability to do so is shrinking.[6]

1.2a Responding Strategically to Changes and Disruptions in the Marketplace

Products and markets are evolving at a breakneck pace, transforming what businesses produce, how they produce, and for whom. Changes in the stock market, world economic conditions, labor markets, and technology are making "business as usual" a thing of the past. So how do HR managers help their firms cope with ever-changing business conditions? One way is by helping redesign their firms to achieve agility.

Agility is a firm's ability make quick changes to gain a competitive advantage. Achieving agility often involves eliminating managerial layers that can slow down decision-making and make an organization less nimble. It means project teams that can gear up fast, make their own decisions, and disband quickly are utilized to develop and get new products out the door while they're "hot." Many tech companies operate this way, and other firms are finding that the model can work for them as well.

agility
A firm's ability make quick changes to gain a competitive advantage.

The online shoe company Zappos (owned by Amazon) went so far as to eliminate its entire hierarchy of managers. Employees at Zappos aren't told how to work, but instead "self-manage" and belong to voluntary employee teams. The company adapted its internal operations to resemble a market-based system, where teams function like independent small businesses—even managing their own individual profit-and-loss statements. Employees are motivated to develop new skills and capabilities so they can join multiple teams and work on new projects at a moment's notice. Successful companies, says Harvard Business School professor Rosabeth Moss Kanter, develop a culture that just keeps moving all the time.[7] It's been said that "No change means no chance." The change applies to HR managers, too.

Human Resources Managers and Business Strategies

In decades past, HR departments were often focused on performing administrative tasks, dealing with unions, and complying with labor laws. While these remain potentially important issues for many firms, HR management is vastly different today. Astute executives know that HR professionals can help them improve, comply with the law, and boost the bottom line by streamlining employment costs. HR professionals can improve the top line by redesigning work to foster innovation, by forecasting labor trends, by recruiting and motivating employees, and by measuring their effectiveness. HR managers also help their firms with business strategies, as well as mergers, acquisitions, and ways to enter new and global markets. "If you look at the evolution going back to when we called HR 'personnel,' it's come a long way as a function," says Art Mazor, with Deloitte Consulting. New HR tools and technologies are allowing the HR function to look outside the tactical, administrative reporting, and data gathering tasks that were once its purview, so as to bring insights and to drive business strategy and results.[8]

Sometimes changing a firm's strategy requires adjusting the composition of the workforce, the number of employees, the skills they require, or the way they approach their work. Growth strategies often require increasing the size of the workforce. Transition or retrenchment strategies may involve reducing the workforce through **downsizing**—the planned elimination of jobs. Innovation strategies often focus on changing the design of work and the way employees approach it, empowering behavior, or cultivating creativity and collaboration. There are many different possibilities when it comes to changing strategy, and we will discuss them further throughout the book.

downsizing
The planned elimination of jobs.

A common denominator of all these strategies is that they require companies to engage in bringing about and managing both organizational changes and changes on the individual level. Although most employees understand that change is continuous—responsibilities, job assignments, and work processes may all change over time—people often resist it because it requires them to modify or abandon ways of working that have been successful or at least familiar to them. Successful change rarely occurs naturally or easily.

Some of the strategic changes companies pursue are reactive changes that result when external forces, such as the competition, a recession, a law change, or an ethical crisis (such as the backlash Volkswagen experienced in 2016 for cheating on its vehicles' emissions tests), have already affected the organization's performance. Other strategic changes are proactive changes, initiated by managers to take advantage of targeted

Some changes are reactive, such as those experienced by Volkswagen when it was revealed the company had cheated on its vehicles' emission tests.

opportunities, by innovating and doing things in a new way. These approaches can be particularly important, especially in fast-changing industries in which leaders rule the roost and followers are not successful.

Good HR managers know that they can be key players when it comes to driving the business strategies of their organizations to make changes. That is why forward-looking CEOs, including those of Marriott, Microsoft, UPS, and Vail Resorts, make certain their top HR executives report directly to them and help them address key issues.

A rapidly growing number of companies are assigning HR representatives to their core business teams to make certain they are knowledgeable about core business issues. In addition, companies are increasingly rotating non-HR managers *into* HR positions, and vice versa, to give them exposure to different areas of the organization. Rather than emphasizing the administrative aspects of HR, these companies develop and promote their HR personnel and provide them with key business statistics and numbers they can use to measure the effectiveness of the workforce.

We will discuss competitive HR strategies and HR in more depth in Chapter 2. Meanwhile, keep in mind that HR's role is not all about providing advice to CEOs and supervisors. In addition to serving as strategic partners to management, HR managers are responsible for listening to and advocating on behalf of employees to make sure their interests are aligned with those of the firm, and vice versa. A good deal of evidence suggests that this is one of the toughest parts of an HR manager's job. We will discuss this aspect of the job more thoroughly later in the chapter.

1.2b Competing, Recruiting, and Staffing Globally

Have you ever thought about working abroad or learning a second (or third) language? Doing so could give you a big advantage in today's workplace. Why? Because the strategies companies are pursing today increasingly involve one or more elements of globalization. The integration of world economies and markets has sent businesses abroad to look for opportunities, fend off foreign competitors domestically, and find the right kind of employees to help them do so. Consumers around the world today want to be able to buy "anything, anytime, anywhere," and companies are making it possible for them to do so. Want to buy a Coke in Pakistan? No problem. Coca-Cola has an elaborate delivery system designed to transport its products to some of the remotest places on the planet. In fact, the company has long generated more of its revenues abroad than it does in the United States.

Importing and exporting goods and services is the easiest way to "go global." India has the world's second-largest population (1.2 billion people) and a growing middle class, so firms are increasingly trying to expand their exports to that country.[9] Apple is one of those companies. Although the iPhone dominates the U.S. market, only 5 percent of smartphones in India are iPhones. Partnerships, mergers, and takeovers are other ways companies are preparing for globalization.

Many American and foreign firms have partnered with Chinese firms to expand in China, which is the world's most populous country, with 1.3 billion people. In turn, Chinese and other foreign companies are merging with American firms, sometimes in industries you wouldn't expect. For example, in 2016, the Chinese firm Dalian Wanda Group bought U.S. film company Legendary, which produced *The Dark Knight, Jurassic World*, and *Straight Outta Compton*.[10]

As a result of globalization, the national identities of products are blurring, too. BMW is a German brand, but the automaker builds cars in the United States, China, and elsewhere. Likewise, you probably think of Budweiser as an American beer, but its maker (Anheuser-Busch) is owned by a Belgian company called InBev. Like many other companies, Anheuser-Busch InBev has been purchasing or partnering with factories and brands in other countries such China and Mexico to expand its sales.[11] After buying Legendary, Dalian Wanda Group produced *The Great Wall* starring Matt Damon, which was released in both China and the United States.

Numerous free-trade agreements forged between nations in the last half century have helped quicken the pace of globalization. The first major trade agreement of the modern era was reached in 1948, following World War II. Called the General Agreement on Tariffs and Trade (GATT), it established rules and guidelines for global commerce between nations and groups of nations. Since GATT began, the growth in world trade has far outpaced the growth in the world's overall output. GATT paved the way for the formation of many major trade agreements and institutions, and these are continuously changing. Recently, the United Kingdom decided to exit—"Brexit"—the European Union, and the North American Free Trade Agreement (NAFTA) was revised to establish the United States–Mexico–Canada Agreement (USMCA).

Although they have come under fire from people and politicians around the world, new free-trade agreements continue to be forged. As China continues to gain prominence on the world stage, trade agreements will be an important challenge. Even the United Kingdom's most vocal opponents of global trade are anxious to complete a new free-trade deal with India so that U.K. firms can do more business with that nation.[12]

How Globalization Affects HRM

Due to globalization, firms have to balance a complicated set of issues related to different geographies, including different cultures, employment laws, and business practices, and the safety of employees and facilities abroad. Human resource issues underlie each of these concerns. They include such things as dealing with employees today who, via the Internet and social media, are better informed about global job opportunities and are willing to pursue them, even if it means working for competing companies or foreign companies. Gauging the knowledge and skill base of workers worldwide and figuring out how best to hire and train them is also an issue for firms. Relocating managers and training foreign managers abroad to direct the efforts of an international workforce is a challenge as well. In Chapter 15, we will explain how these challenges are tackled.

At times, firms to decide to respond to their global challenges through outsourcing and offshoring. **Outsourcing** simply means hiring someone outside the company to perform business processes that were previously done within the firm. **Offshoring**, also referred to as "global sourcing," involves shifting work to locations abroad.

outsourcing
Contracting outside the organization to have work done that formerly was performed by internal employees.

offshoring
The business practice of sending jobs to other countries.

1.2c Setting and Achieving Corporate Social Responsibility and Sustainability Goals

Globalization has led to an improvement in people's living standards in the last half century. As a result of free trade, Americans are able to buy products made abroad more cheaply. Meanwhile, people in low-wage countries that make those goods and services are becoming wealthier and are beginning to buy American-made products. Nonetheless, globalization stirs fierce debate—especially when it comes to jobs. Since the turn of the century, millions of U.S. jobs—both white collar and blue collar—have been exported to low-wage nations all around the world. Other people worry that free trade is creating a "have/have not" world economy, in which the people in developing economies and the world's environment are being exploited by companies in richer, more developed countries. This has sparked anti-free-trade protests in many nations.

Concerns such as these, coupled with corporate scandals over the years, including the use of sweatshop labor in developing countries, have led to a new focus on **corporate social responsibility**, or good corporate citizenship. Many firms and professional associations also have ethics codes, or codes of conduct. Such codes are written guidelines that clarify right and wrong behaviors that an organization endorses or prohibits, respectively. Highlights in HRM 1 shows the codes of ethics adopted by SHRM. Other firms have gone so far as to appoint "chief ethics officers" to try to ensure that ethical breaches by employees don't adversely affect their companies. Chief ethics officers and ethics are discussed in more detail in Chapters 7 and 13.

corporate social responsibility
The responsibility of the firm to act in the best interests of the people and communities affected by its activities.

Companies are learning (sometimes the hard way) that being ethical and socially responsible both domestically and abroad can not only help them avoid lawsuits but also improve their earnings. For example, researchers at Boston College's Center for Corporate Citizenship found that as a company's reputation improved, so did the percentage increase in the number of people who would recommend that firm. Nearly two-thirds of the members of the 80-million-strong Millennial generation (people born in the 1980s and 1990s) consider a company's social reputation when deciding where to shop, and 9 of 10 say they would switch brands based on their perceptions of a company's commitment to social responsibility.[13] Moreover, many prospective workers now say that corporate responsibility is important to their job selection. They want to work for companies that are concerned not only with making a profit but also making the world a better place for everyone, both rich and poor.

Corporate social responsibility is often framed within the larger context of **sustainability**—a company's ability to produce goods or services without depleting the world's resources and while doing the least amount of harm to the environment as

sustainability
Doing business in a way that does as little harm to the environment and depletes as few natural resources as possible.

Munir Uz Zaman/AFP/Getty Images

After an unsafe factory collapsed, killing hundreds of textiles workers in Bangladesh in 2013, approximately 70 retailers, mostly European, signed an agreement to inspect factories they offshore work to and finance safety upgrades for them.

possible. Unilever, for example, developed its Sustainable Living Plan with a vision to improve the health and well-being of 1 billion people, cut its environmental impact by 50 percent, and enhance the livelihood of those in its value chain. The company established rigorous standards on seven criteria, which were translated to more than 50 metrics related to its "carbon footprint," greenhouse gas emissions, water usage, sustainable agriculture, and the like. Within several years, Unilever achieved its goals and expanded its vision to "do well by doing good."

More recently, firms have begun to embrace their view of sustainability to include **environmental, social, and governance (ESG)** criteria. These factors are seen as leading to—rather than detracting from—the long-term financial performance of organizations, and investors are taking notice of them. Top-rated ESG firms include Nvidia, Salesforce, Best Buy, Microsoft, and Boise Cascade.[14]

environmental, social, and governance (ESG)
Factors used to evaluate an organization's collective conscientiousness for social and environmental sustainability.

One of HR's leadership roles is to spearhead the development and implementation of corporate citizenship throughout their organizations, especially the fair treatment of workers.[15]

1.3 Technology Challenges

LO3
Will technology eliminate the need for human resource managers?

Advancements in information technology have enabled organizations to take advantage of the information explosion. Computer networks and "cloud computing" (Internet computer services and data storage) have made it possible for nearly unlimited amounts of data to be stored, retrieved, and used in a wide variety of ways to improve decision-making. Software that allows workers to collaborate and share information with one another electronically anywhere, anytime—for example, social media,

1 Highlights in HRM

SHRM Code of Ethical and Professional Standards in Human Resource Management

Code Provisions

Professional Responsibility

Core Principle

As HR professionals, we are responsible for adding value to the organizations we serve and contributing to the ethical success of those organizations. We accept professional responsibility for our individual decisions and actions. We are also advocates for the profession by engaging in activities that enhance its credibility and value.

Intent

- To build respect, credibility, and strategic importance for the HR profession within our organizations, the business community, and the communities in which we work.
- To assist the organizations we serve in achieving their objectives and goals.
- To inform and educate current and future practitioners, the organizations we serve, and the general public about principles and practices that help the profession.
- To positively influence workplace and recruitment practices.
- To encourage professional decision making and responsibility.
- To encourage social responsibility.

Guidelines

1. Adhere to the highest standards of ethical and professional behavior.
2. Measure the effectiveness of HR in contributing to or achieving organizational goals.
3. Comply with the law.
4. Work consistent with the values of the profession.
5. Strive to achieve the highest levels of service, performance, and social responsibility.
6. Advocate for the appropriate use and appreciation of human beings as employees.
7. Advocate openly and within the established forums for debate in order to influence decision making and results.

Professional Development

Core Principle

As professionals we must strive to meet the highest standards of competence and commit to strengthen our competencies on a continuous basis.

Intent

- To expand our knowledge of human resource management to further our understanding of how our organizations function.
- To advance our understanding of how organizations work ("the business of the business").

Guidelines

1. Pursue formal academic opportunities.
2. Commit to continuous learning, skills development, and application of new knowledge related to both human resource management and the organizations we serve.
3. Contribute to the body of knowledge, the evolution of the profession, and the growth of individuals through teaching, research, and dissemination of knowledge.
4. Pursue certification where available, or comparable measures of competencies and knowledge.

Ethical Leadership

Core Principle

HR professionals are expected to exhibit individual leadership as a role model for maintaining the highest standards of ethical conduct.

Intent

- To set the standard and be an example for others.
- To earn individual respect and increase our credibility with those we serve.

Guidelines

1. Be ethical; act ethically in every professional interaction.
2. Question pending individual and group actions when necessary to ensure that decisions are ethical and are implemented in an ethical manner.

3. Seek expert guidance if ever in doubt about the ethical propriety of a situation.
4. Through teaching and mentoring, champion the development of others as ethical leaders in the profession and in organizations.

Fairness and Justice

Core Principle

As human resource professionals, we are ethically responsible for promoting and fostering fairness and justice for all employees and their organizations.

Intent

- To create and sustain an environment that encourages all individuals and the organization to reach their fullest potential in a positive and productive manner.

Guidelines

1. Respect the uniqueness and intrinsic worth of every individual.
2. Treat people with dignity, respect, and compassion to foster a trusting work environment free of harassment, intimidation, and unlawful discrimination.
3. Ensure that everyone has the opportunity to develop their skills and new competencies.
4. Assure an environment of inclusiveness and a commitment to diversity in the organizations we serve.
5. Develop, administer, and advocate policies and procedures that foster fair, consistent, and equitable treatment for all.
6. Regardless of personal interests, support decisions made by our organizations that are both ethical and legal.
7. Act in a responsible manner and practice sound management in the country(ies) in which the organizations we serve operate.

Conflicts of Interest

Core Principle

As HR professionals, we must maintain a high level of trust with our stakeholders. We must protect the interests of our stakeholders as well as our professional integrity and should not engage in activities that create actual, apparent, or potential conflicts of interest.

Intent

To avoid activities that are in conflict or may appear to be in conflict with any of the provisions of this Code of Ethical and Professional Standards in Human Resource Management or with one's responsibilities and duties as a member of the human resource profession and/or as an employee of any organization.

Guidelines

1. Adhere to and advocate the use of published policies on conflicts of interest within your organization.
2. Refrain from using your position for personal, material, or financial gain or the appearance of such.
3. Refrain from giving or seeking preferential treatment in the human resources processes.
4. Prioritize your obligations to identify conflicts of interest or the appearance thereof; when conflicts arise, disclose them to relevant stakeholders.

Use of Information

Core Principle

HR professionals consider and protect the rights of individuals, especially in the acquisition and dissemination of information while ensuring truthful communications and facilitating informed decision making.

Intent

To build trust among all organization constituents by maximizing the open exchange of information, while eliminating anxieties about inappropriate and/or inaccurate acquisition and sharing of information.

Guidelines

1. Acquire and disseminate information through ethical and responsible means.
2. Ensure only appropriate information is used in decisions affecting the employment relationship.
3. Investigate the accuracy and source of information before allowing it to be used in employment-related decisions.
4. Maintain current and accurate HR information.
5. Safeguard restricted or confidential information.
6. Take appropriate steps to ensure the accuracy and completeness of all communicated information about HR policies and practices.
7. Take appropriate steps to ensure the accuracy and completeness of all communicated information used in HR-related training.

wikis, document-sharing platforms such as Google Docs, online chat, and instant messaging—have changed how and where people and companies do business. For example, BNSF Railway uses the social media site Yammer to help employees collaborate on ideas and provide each other with praise and feedback. The COVID-19 pandemic made Web and videoconferencing applications like Zoom, Skype, and Microsoft Teams everyday necessities.

Social media networking has also become the way workers find jobs and employers recruit and screen candidates today. Companies are hiring firms such as Social Intelligence, which combs through Facebook, LinkedIn, Twitter, Instagram, YouTube, and "thousands of other sources" to create reports about the "real you"—not the "you" you have presented in your resume.[16] (Care to change your Facebook page, anyone?)

HR managers are often responsible for developing Internet and social media policies for employees, including policies related to how much time employees should be allowed to spend online, the sites they should be allowed to visit, and whether employees can use their own electronic devices (e.g., mobile phones, tablets) for work purposes. Other issues include which apps employees can use. Deutsche Bank doesn't allow its employees to use unapproved apps such as Google Talk and What's App for business purposes on either their work or personal phones.[17]

The Digitalization of Work: From Touch Labor to Knowledge Workers

Technology—and automation in particular—has reduced the number of jobs that require routine tasks and little skill and increased the number of jobs that require considerable skill. In 1979, approximately 40 percent of Americans held routine-task type jobs. Today, only about 30 percent do because of the trends toward automation, robotics, and digitalization of work.[18] This change in workforce requirements has been referred to as a shift from "touch labor" to **knowledge workers**, in which employee responsibilities expand to include a richer array of activities that involve analyzing information and problem solving.[19]

knowledge workers
Workers whose responsibilities extend beyond the physical execution of work to include planning, decision making, and problem solving.

This transformation has brought both good news and bad news. On the positive side, technology investments can lead to "upskilling" and the chance to enrich the nature of work. On the downside, technology often leads to worker displacement. Fewer good, traditional "middle class" type jobs are available to U.S. workers today as a result, disrupting the labor market. "One of our retail utility customers in the U.K. has about 300 robots doing 600 people's worth of work," says Alistair Bathgate, co-founder of Blue Prism, a company that helps automate business functions. "Before you needed a building to house 600 people, but all that gets crushed down to one cabinet in the corner of a data center."[20]

But it's not just routine jobs and blue-collar jobs that are affected by technology. Automation, robotics, and artificial intelligence, are affecting white-collar work as well. For example, news organizations are using Web robots ("bots") to gather information and write basic stories about corporate earnings and sports recaps. Many of the entries on Wikipedia aren't written by people, but rather by bots that comb the Web for information and compile the information you see on the site. Or consider the IBM robot Jill Watson. In 2016, Georgia Institute of Technology used Jill as an online teaching assistant in an experiment with an artificial intelligence class. Most students never figured out Jill wasn't human—although some of them said they suspected she was because she seemed to answer their questions way too fast.[21]

Clearly, no one is immune to the changes that technology bring. But that doesn't mean that all jobs are going away because of it. A recent study found that about

Sorbis/Shutterstock.com

Ordering kiosks like this one in a New York City store are likely to replace some workers.

50 percent of workers' *tasks* today could be eliminated with current technology and technology now under development—but only 5 percent of *jobs* could be.[22] More likely, humans will work in this new environment with the help of virtual assistants similar to Siri, Cortana, and Amazon's Echo device.

Knowledge-based training is critical to the business model of Manpower, the largest employment agency in the United States. Manpower offers free information technology training to its employees through its online university. The site features thousands of hours of instruction in technology applications, along with professional development, business skills, and telecommunications courses, seminars, and chat rooms with mentors. "Just-in-time" learning is delivered via the Internet to Manpower employees' mobile phones, tablets, and computers.

Firms and their employees are also taking advantage of the massive open online courses (MOOCs) created by colleges and educational firms. A MOOC is a noncredit, often low-cost course anyone can take online, and enrollment is unlimited. MOOCs can help employees get training quickly as well as stretch a company's training budget.

Virtual learning is taking place as well, using both synchronous tools (everyone collaborating online live) and asynchronous methods (materials that learners can access on demand at their convenience). In 2016, Microsoft acquired LinkedIn Learning, a Web-based portal offering video courses taught by industry experts. The company has curated more than 16,000 courses, and has generated more than 17 million users. Its system also uses advanced analytics to customize recommended courses for each user. When the COVID-19 pandemic created an economic crisis in 2020–2021, throwing millions of people out of work, Microsoft launched an initiative to help those hardest hit by job loss—including people with lower incomes, women, and underrepresented groups—by offering them free access to LinkedIn Learning so they could gain the digital skills they needed to reboot their careers. The program, which aimed to help 25 million people worldwide, shows the power and scope of virtual learning.[23]

Augmented reality devices such as Google Glass and "wearables" such as the Apple Watch are helping employees get information when and where they need it, too. At AGCO, a manufacturer of agricultural equipment, factory workers wear augmented reality glasses, which display diagrams and instructions to help them conduct quality checks.[24]

Technology's Effect on HRM

human resources information system (HRIS)
A computerized system that provides current and accurate HR-related data for the purposes of control and decision making.

Perhaps the most central use of technology in HRM is an organization's **human resources information system (HRIS)**. HR functions affect the entire workforce—everyone who works for the company must be hired, trained, paid, and promoted, usually through the HR staff efforts. HRIS are used for everything from automating payroll processing to administering benefits programs. These systems allow managers to access employee records for administrative purposes and allow employees to engage in "self-service" when they need to access and change their own benefits and other personal information, via either an intranet or a secure website.

Firms use HRIS to recruit, screen, and pretest applicants online before hiring them, as well as to train, track, and promote employees once they have been hired. The pharmaceutical company Merck's HRIS "applicant tracking" software captures information from job recruiting sites and social network sites like LinkedIn, scans applicants' resumes, and makes the information immediately accessible to managers so they can search systematically for the people whose skills they want. Managers can search online for internal and external talent by running searches of candidates who have been categorized by skill set.[25] The HRIS of the consumer-products giant Procter and Gamble (P&G) makes good internal candidates visible to managers, instead of forcing the managers to scour the company to find them. The system contains information about P&G's 100,000-plus employees worldwide for promotion purposes at the country, business category, and regional levels.

Corning Inc. uses HR software, among other things, to set the developmental goals of its employees once they have been hired and to gauge how well they are meeting those goals. Employees can look online to see their own goals and mark their progress as well as see everyone else's goals in the command chain, from the CEO down to their immediate supervisors. This "cascading" of goals has helped Corning's employees align their personal goals with the organization's overall objectives, as well as reach higher levels. "Like any large company, we tended to get 'silo-ed' and fragmented the more we grew," said one vice president at a company using a system similar to Corning's. "We needed a better way to pull our global team together and get people focused on what the priorities are for our business."[26]

One of the newer HRIS applications involves the use of big data. *Big data* is a buzzword that describes the massive amounts data available online and offline today that can be "crunched" to make decisions. Marketing departments have very successfully used big data to detect people's buying patterns. By analyzing its customers' buying habits, Target was able to predict which customers were pregnant, sometimes before they had even told their families. The company then sent the customers ads and coupons for baby products.

workforce (HR) analytics
The process of gathering and analyzing data to improve a firm's human resources management.

Now companies are doing the same thing to analyze HR information, a process referred to as **workforce (HR) analytics**. Using HR data, such as employee demographic information, performance ratings, pay, employee surveys, academic history, years of service, and so on, a firm can definitely do a better job with workforce planning, and answer questions like the following:

- Do employees with degrees from Ivy League schools perform better—or not?
- Where is the hidden talent within pockets of the organization going unnoticed?
- Exactly how much more do top performers need to be paid to stay with our firm?
- Which job applicants are likely to perform better?
- Which employees are most likely to quit?

Traditionally, questions such as these have been answered based on anecdotal evidence or the "gut" feelings of HR professionals. But workforce analytics can provide more definitive answers. For example, a major customer service provider analyzed more than 7,000 of its employees and found that "relevant job experience" in the customer service area had no impact on how well they performed and stayed with the company. As a result, the company altered its hiring criteria.[27] Gathering and analyzing HR data might sound like a daunting task, but HR software providers are including data analysis tools in their programs that make it easier to collect and visualize HR data in a meaningful way.

So what sort of HRIS should HR professionals choose among the many options available to them? One of the first steps in choosing a HRIS is for HR personnel to evaluate the biggest "headaches" they experience, or the most time-consuming tasks, and then choose the applications that can have the strongest impact on the firm's financial measures—that is, the ones that get the "biggest bang for the buck" Off-the-shelf HR Web-based solutions are as commonly used as custom-designed systems. Free open-source HRIS software is also available on the Web; OrangeHRM is an example. Open-source software can be a good solution for startup and small businesses looking for a low-cost HRIS solution. Highlights in HRM 2 shows the other factors that need to be evaluated.

Ultimately, the HRIS selected should provide HR personnel with analytical information—statistics, metrics, and so forth—that helps them analyze, refine, and better implement a firm's strategic direction. This can include forecasting personnel needs (especially for firms planning to expand, contract, or merge), planning for career and employee promotions, and evaluating the impact of the firm's policies—both those related to HR functions and those pertinent to other functions.

1.4 Productivity and Cost Challenges

> **LO4**
> Do cost-containment pressures work against the effective management of people? Why or why not?

Labor costs are often the largest expenditures companies make, particularly in service and knowledge-intensive firms. How can companies actually spend more money on employees and still drive overall costs lower? The answer: via higher employee productivity. Employee productivity is the result of a combination of employees' abilities, motivation, and work environment, and the technology they use to work.

1.4a Maximizing Productivity

Productivity can be defined as "the output gained from a fixed amount of inputs." Organizations can increase their productivity either by reducing their inputs (the cost approach) or by increasing the amount that employees produce by adding more human and/or physical capital to the process. Companies such as Southwest Airlines, Nucor, and the manufacturing and technology firm Danaher achieve low costs in their industries not because they scrimp on employees but because they are the most productive.

2 Highlights in HRM

Factors to Consider When Evaluating a Human Resources Information System

- *Fit of the application to the firm's employee base.* If many of the firm's employees work on a factory floor, is the system appropriate, or does HR need to install kiosks in employee areas? Will employees be able to access the HRIS offsite on the Internet or on their mobile phones? How will the information be secured? Will employees need to be assigned passwords?
- *Ability to upgrade or customize the application.* What sorts of costs will be involved to upgrade the application in the coming years?
- *Compatibility with current systems.* Does the HRIS link into existing, or planned, information systems easily and inexpensively?
- *User friendliness.* Does the application provide additional features such as links to learning resources or help for managers or employees who might need it?
- *Collaboration.* Does the system connect employees and allow them to collaborate on solutions to problems and projects?
- *Workforce analytics.* Does the system make it easy to gather HR data and visualize its implications?
- *Survey capabilities.* Does the system have an app that allows employees to be surveyed electronically?
- *Recruiting and applicant tracking.* Does the system make it easy to find, recruit, and track applicants and a company's current employees for hiring purposes?
- *Scheduling.* Does the system have scheduling ability to ensure employees are in the right places, working at the right times, and on the right projects?
- *Availability of technical support.* Should the HRIS be supported internally, or should the vendor host it? Will it be cloud based?
- *Time required to implement and train staff members to use the HRIS, including HR and payroll personnel, managers, and employees.* Who is responsible for training employees, and how will it be done?
- *Initial costs and annual maintenance costs.* Is a "suite" of apps needed or just a few key apps? Experts advise HR managers to price each application separately and then ask vendors for a "bundled" price.[28]

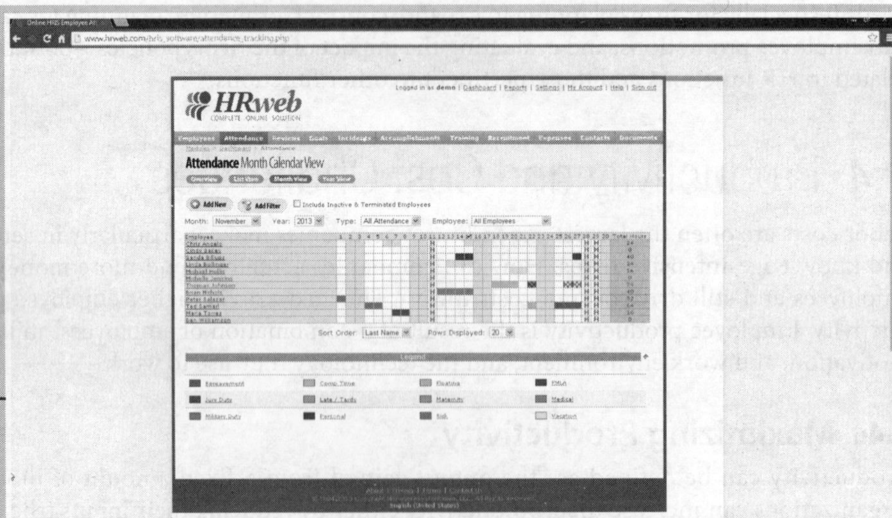

HRweb (shown here) is an example of one of the many HRIS available for firms to manage HR-related tasks.

Source: HRWeb.com

United States is still by far the world's most productive nation in terms of the total value of all goods and services it produces, even when it comes to manufacturing. China ranks second. Apparel and textile manufacturing are far smaller industries in the United States than what they once were, but they have been replaced by industries that rely more on technological precision and brainpower than on low-skilled labor—industries for aircraft, sophisticated machinery, medical devices, and so on.[29] However, the growth in output per worker is now climbing fast in countries such as China that in the past have lacked the amount of technology available to U.S. workers. When the investment in faster computers and more efficient machine tools levels off, this limits how much assistance technology can offer employees in terms of their productivity. Any additional productivity will have to come from the enhanced ability of employees, their motivation, and their work environment, which makes the job of the HR manager in the coming years all the more crucial.[30]

1.4b Managing the Size of the Workforce

Part of managing productivity is matching the size of the workforce to the demand requirements of a firm given its technology, the firm's strategic direction, and global competition. Sometimes this task entails hiring additional personnel to expand a firm's capacity. At other times, offshoring is used to increase capacity. Offshoring can help a firm deliver products more quickly if people across the globe are working around the clock on them. For example, to keep up with demand as well as to lower costs, some U.S. clinics and hospitals have offshored the task of reading X-rays to radiologists in other countries such as India. X-rays taken in the day are read at night abroad and the results delivered the next day to the hospitals and clinics.[31] Offshoring is also used when companies want to expand to other countries and capture market share there. Apple is trying to do this by opening an iPhone manufacturing facility in India.

Outsourcing can help a firm manage the size of its workforce, reduce costs, and focus on the activities it does best. For example, companies hire advertising firms to handle their promotions, software firms to develop data-processing systems for them, and law firms to handle their legal issues rather than perform these functions in-house. Likewise, maintenance, security, catering, and payroll (and in small companies, sometimes entire HR departments) may be outsourced to increase the organization's flexibility and manage the size of the workforce.

Despite the advantages that offshoring and outsourcing offer, in recent years a growing number of firms have begun moving jobs back to their domestic markets or in-house. Delta Air Lines is among the firms that returned its call-center operations to the United States after customers complained about the service they received from personnel in foreign countries. Other companies are **nearshoring**, which is the practice of bringing jobs closer to domestic countries, and **homeshoring**, which is the practice of outsourcing work to domestic workers who work out of their homes.

Downsizing is, of course, another way to manage the size of the workforce, as is furloughing. **Furloughing** is the practice of requiring employees to take time off for either no pay or reduced pay. More diligent workforce planning may be a better solution than either downsizing or furloughing, says John Sullivan, an HR expert and consultant. Business revenues seldom fall off overnight. According to Sullivan, the best managers develop a process that pinpoints skills the company no longer needs, low-impact jobs, and poor performers in advance of a crisis. Then, part-time or contract employees can be hired based on this analysis, and their hours of service adjusted as needed.[32]

nearshoring
Occurs when a firm relocates jobs abroad to nations closer to its domestic market.

homeshoring
The practice of outsourcing work to domestic workers who work out of their homes.

furloughing
A situation in which an organization asks or requires employees to take time off for either no pay or reduced pay.

1.4c Managing Pay and Benefits

Most firms closely monitor employee pay and benefit programs. Skyrocketing health care costs are perhaps the biggest concerns companies are facing when it comes to compensation and benefits. Companies are taking many different approaches to try to keep health care costs in check, including charging employees higher premiums for covering their spouses if they are able to obtain insurance through their own employers. Yet another approach is giving employees a set amount of money they can use to purchase health insurance on their own. Walgreen's and Darden Restaurants, which operates the Olive Garden and Red Lobster chains, have taken this approach. A more proactive approach is to offer employees incentives to get healthy—for example, by quitting smoking, losing weight, or exercising.[33]

employee leasing
The process of eliminating the jobs of employees, who are then hired by a leasing company (which handles all HR-related activities), and contracting with that company to lease back the employees.

Another way firms are managing benefits is by using employee leasing. When **employee leasing** is used, a firm signs an agreement with a professional employer organization (PEO). The PEO—typically a larger company—takes over the management

Small Business Application

A Small Business Built on Helping Small Businesses

As experienced and highly respected HR professionals, Delise West and Tonya Rochette could have easily furthered their careers by pursuing positions in large corporations or academia. Instead, they chose to forge a new path for themselves by founding Human Resource Partners, a small HR consulting firm located in Dover, New Hampshire. Friends and family thought they were both a little crazy to enter the "risky" world of owning a small business, but since joining forces 12 years ago, they have been very successful at serving other small, entrepreneurial businesses just like theirs.

West and Rochette both recognized early on that small businesses need to address HR issues just as much as larger businesses do, yet small-business owners usually do not have the time or expertise to devote to these issues themselves and often do not have the financial resources to hire a full-time, knowledgeable HR manager. This pair of entrepreneurs saw that reality as an opportunity to provide a full spectrum of HR services to companies in need.

"There are so many companies who don't have the right HR infrastructure in place," said West, whose firm works mostly with companies having fewer than 70 employees. "Oftentimes, an owner of a growing business will come to me and simply say, 'I can't do it anymore because it has become too time consuming.'" Some of the companies that have turned to West and Rochette for help with HR functions and strategy include a major car dealership, a regional construction company, and a local nursery.

Work with a new client typically begins with an evaluation of the firm's level of HR compliance and best practices, such as job description documentation, payroll systems, and legal interviewing practices. From there, Human Resource Partners develops strategies for the client to implement in the areas of recruiting, screening, interviewing, and hiring new staff; evaluating and recognizing current employee performance; and improving employee relations and developing supervisory skills.

By giving small firms the tools, services, and training they need, West and Rochette allow their clients to focus on their core business. According to West, Human Resource Partners lets small firms "realize the return on their investments in their greatest assets—their people."

Outsourcing a firm's HR functions isn't a new strategy for firms, big or small. Many companies have outsourced their pay and benefits functions for years. What is new is the growth in HR outsourcing. Currently, it's a $42.6 billion industry. By 2020, that number was expected to grow to $53.9 billion, a 25 percent increase.

The growth of HR outsourcing has been good news for West and Rochette. Human Resource Partners expanded quickly and now serves larger, midsize businesses as well. To help meet demand in Dover and other New Hampshire towns, the two entrepreneurs also brought on additional HR professionals as partners. Because the outsourcing model gives small and midsize businesses senior-level HR expertise, West says she believes Human Resource Partners will only continue to grow.

Sources: Mark Feffer, "Meet the People behind Your Outsourcing," *HR News* (July 1, 2016), https://www.shrm.org; Kim Murdoch, "Celebrating 10 Years: Concord- and Dover-Based HRP Marks Milestone," *Concord Patch* (May 24, 2013), http://concord-nh.patch.com; Michael McCord, "Outsourcing Frees Owners from Time Consuming Tasks," Sea-Coastonline.com (January 10, 2011), http://www.seacoastonline.com; company website: h-rpartners.com.

of the smaller company's HR tasks and becomes a coemployer to its employees. The PEO performs all the HR duties of an employer—hiring, payroll, and performance appraisal. Because PEOs can coemploy a large number of people working at many different companies, they can provide employees with benefits that small companies cannot afford, such as 401(k) and health care plans, workers' compensation, and even adoption assistance.

Another strategy to manage pay and benefits is to hire freelancers, part-time employees, independent contractors, and consultants, who work in what's called the "gig economy." In the gig economy, people earn income from various nonpermanent "gigs," or jobs, and work independently, rather than full time for a single employer. An Uber driver is an example of a person participating in the gig economy. The gig economy isn't new, but it's definitely a growing trend. Its greater visibility in recent years has also generated controversies, particularly regarding whether these workers should be classified as employees, with all the rights and benefits associated with that status.

Some companies, such as Google, are able to hire talented employees by offering them great pay and fantastic benefits. However, most companies, especially small ones or ones that are struggling, find it hard to compete with bigger firms like Google with deluxe benefit packages. What can small companies do to attract employees yet still contain costs? Many companies are finding that providing work flexibility is a good way to improve the productivity and motivation of valuable employees, especially when giving them larger benefit packages is not an option. For example, when gasoline prices shot up to more than $4/gallon during the last recession, most small companies weren't able to increase their employees' pay because they were facing higher transportation costs themselves for the goods and services they had to buy. But some companies began letting employees telecommute (work from home) or, as the state of Utah did, work 10 hours per day, 4 days a week.

1.5 Employee Challenges

> **LO5**
> What are the pros and cons of having a more diverse workforce? Is the United States in a better position to compete globally because of its diverse population?

On the one hand, we have discussed how HR focuses on the business, playing a role as a strategic partner to help ensure its success. On the other hand, HR focuses on being an "employee advocate," making sure that the needs of workers are met. For example, do you think a company has a moral obligation to take care of its workforce? What kind of company would you like to work for? These are questions you are probably asking yourself as you prepare for your career. Clearly, in addition to the strategic challenges that companies face, they must attend to some very important employee concerns. Those challenges span a wide range of pressing concerns such as job security, health care, diversity, and employee rights.

1.5a Responding to the Demographic and Diversity Challenges of the Workforce

To forecast trends to support the strategies of their organizations, HR managers frequently analyze the capabilities of different demographic groups and how well each is represented in both fast-growing and slow-growing occupations. Women, for example, are fairly well represented in fast-growing occupations such as health services, but are also amply represented in some slow-growth occupations such as administrative jobs and computer and financial records processing jobs. Blacks and Hispanics have been heavily concentrated in several of the slow-growth and declining occupations. The U.S. labor force also grew more slowly in the last decade than it did in the previous one, a trend that is projected to continue. The labor force participation rate—that is, the percentage of the population 16 years and older that is currently employed or actively looking for work—is also declining in the United States. Figure 1.2 shows the U.S. labor force participation rate. This rate peaked in 2000 at about 67 percent; however, during the last recession, many people dropped out of the job market. The rate continued to decline until 2016, when it began rising again to 63.4 percent—only to drop again when the COVID-19 pandemic hit.

But even with economic recovery, the labor participation rate is predicted to fall because of declining birth rates and the aging U.S. population. The U.S. Bureau of Labor Statistics (BLS) predicts the labor force participation rate will be about 60.2 percent in 2050. To accommodate shifts such as these demographic trends, find qualified talent, and broaden their customer bases, businesses know it is absolutely vital to increase their efforts to recruit and train a more diverse workforce. Of course, with a more diverse workforce comes more diverse expectations on the part of employees that their employers to meet.

Ethnic and Racial Diversity in the Workforce

Traditionally underrepresented groups in the United States are increasing in size relative to the total population. U.S. workers are becoming more diverse as well. Even so, there is growing concern that organizations are not doing enough to ensure equitable treatment, access, and employment of people from underrepresented groups. Following the widespread protests associated with the death of George Floyd (a Black man killed by a White police officer in Minneapolis) and the Black Lives Matter movement, many companies have worked to address this important issue. We will discuss these efforts in more depth in Chapter 3, which focuses on equal opportunity.

Much of the growth in the non-White U.S. workforce is due to immigration. Immigrants account for more than 17 percent of the total U.S. labor force. At times, firms have been criticized for hiring immigrant workers—both legal and illegal—because some people believe they prevent U.S. citizens from getting jobs. In recent years, there has been pressure to limit the number of work visas issued to foreigners by the U.S. government. Many American employers say this policy is a problem, however, because

Figure 1.2 U.S. Labor Force Participation Rates over Time

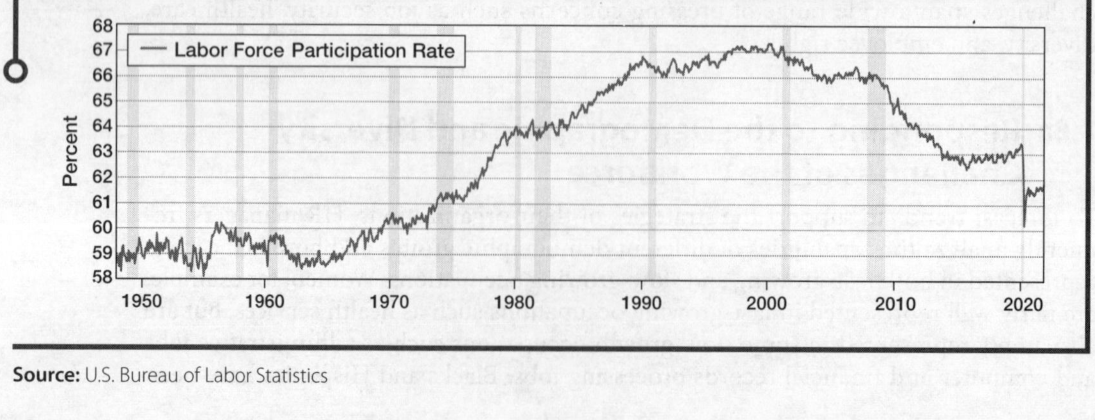

Source: U.S. Bureau of Labor Statistics

Figure 1.3 New Temporary Work Visa Approvals, 2010–2019

Visa Category	Type of Worker	Skilled or Unskilled	2010	2014	2019
E	Treaty Investors and Workers[1]	Skilled	33,954	49,971	59,001
H-1B	Professional	Skilled	117,828	162,239	189,847
H-2A	Seasonal Agricultural	Unskilled	55,921	89,274	204,801
H-2B	Seasonal Non-Agricultural	Unskilled	47,403	68,102	97,623
J	Exchange Program Worker	Both	258,935	216,558	230,000[3]
L	Intra-Company Transfer	Skilled	74,719	71,513	76,988
O	"Extraordinary" Ability	Skilled	13,024	18,957	26,494
P	Athletes/Entertainers	Skilled	32,496	31,721	25,601
Q	Cultural Exchange Visa	Skilled	1,589	2,036	2,029
R	Religious Workers	Both	3,390	4,599	4,583
TN[2]	NAFTA Professionals	Skilled	3,392	11,207	21,193
Total			642,651	726,177	916,967

[1]Total includes some family members.
[2]Includes only Mexicans; does not include Canadians, who are not tracked by DHS.
[3]Estimate of work exchange participants (filtering out students and other short-term exchanges) based on 2018 statistics.

Source: State Department.

they lack the highly qualified workers they need for key positions. Figure 1.3 shows the number of new temporary work visa approvals issued from 2010 to 2019 by the U.S. government.[34] To bring in the talent it needs from abroad, Microsoft opened a facility in Canada, across from its Redmond, Washington, headquarters. However, critics of work visas claim there isn't a shortage of qualified workers and that employers use the program to hire foreign workers they can pay less. The United States has long been able to attract the best and brightest of the world's talent, which has fueled the country's success. For example, in 2016, all American Nobel laureates were immigrants. But as you will learn in Chapter 15, that situation is changing.[35]

It is not just the most highly educated immigrant workers who are in demand. Some businesses, including those in the agricultural business, face labor shortages that would be even more severe without less-skilled immigrants willing to work for low pay and few or no benefits. The jobs these people do are often labor intensive, must be performed in bad weather or in agricultural facilities in less-than-pleasant conditions, and involve work that many Americans don't want to do. Nonetheless, there is a concern that immigrants (both documented and undocumented) are taking away jobs from Americans. An estimated 8 million undocumented workers are part of the U.S. labor force (or about 5 percent of the total workforce). They are concentrated in certain jobs, such as farming (26%), cleaning and maintenance (17%), and construction (14%).[36]

In recent years, the federal government and state and local governments have tried to make it harder for firms to hire undocumented workers and passed laws making it more difficult for them to live, work, and drive in the United States. After Arizona, Georgia, and Alabama did so, crops rotted in the fields in those states because of a lack of workers to harvest them. Those states subsequently relaxed their rules. Later in this book, we will discuss in more detail what companies are doing in response to minority and immigration challenges and opportunities.[37]

Age Distribution of the Workforce

The newest generation entering the workplace is Generation Z. The members of Generation Z were born in the mid-1990s and early 2000s. Today, they make up approximately one-third of the workforce. These workers have never known life without smartphones and social media, and they expect to be trained and managed with digital tools. They are also more comfortable with racial, cultural, and sexual diversity than other generations and want to change the world for the better. A large number of members of this generation say they want to start their own businesses. Others, having grown up during the last recession, want to go straight to work rather than incurring the cost of college.

The Millennial generation (Generation Y) is having a big impact on the labor market right now. The group includes an estimated 75 to 80 million people, making it the largest generation ever. Millennials are generally regarded as having good technological know-how and initiative, especially when it comes to starting their own businesses. (Facebook founder Mark Zuckerberg is a notable example.) Like Generation Z, they are also interested in meaningful work that will improve the world around them and want a good work–life balance. Neither generation wants to be pigeonholed into jobs: They want to try new jobs and new tasks, and they are quite willing to job hop to do so.

People in Generation X were born between 1964 and 1979. Many members of Generation X watched their baby-boomer parents get downsized at some point in their lives. Now that they are raising children themselves, Generation Xers value job security. However, they are less likely to think of themselves as being as tightly wed to one employer as their parents were. The members of Generation X are also independent: They like challenging work rather than repetitive work, and dislike supervisors who look over their shoulders.

A relatively large number of people were born after World War II (between 1946 and 1964); they are members of the baby-boom generation. A significant proportion of baby-boomers have now hit retirement age. Not all baby-boomers are retiring, though. Due to advances in medicine, people are staying healthier as they age, and many are remaining in the labor force longer. Other factors—including an increase in the official retirement age in the United States from 65 to 67—are also keeping baby-boomers working.

So are economic factors: Many baby-boomers have not saved enough to retire, or their 401(k) retirement accounts have not grown as well as expected. Older workers tend to be dependable and remain on the job longer than younger workers, who operate more like free agents. Because their kids are grown up, older workers are also often willing to work flexible hours.

So, what will the workforce look like in years to come in terms of ages? Figure 1.4 shows that older Americans—those hitting the 55-and-older age bracket—are the fastest-growing segment of the workforce and will claim this title for decades as the U.S. workforce continues to age. By contrast, the average annual growth rate of 16- to 24-year-olds in the labor force is projected to decline.

Managers can find themselves challenged in terms of getting the four generations to work well together. Baby-boomers sometimes categorize younger workers as having a poorer work ethic. Some younger workers have the perception that older workers are set in their ways and technologically challenged. The presence of multiple generations in

Figure 1.4 Labor Force Participation Rates of Workers in the Labor Force by Age

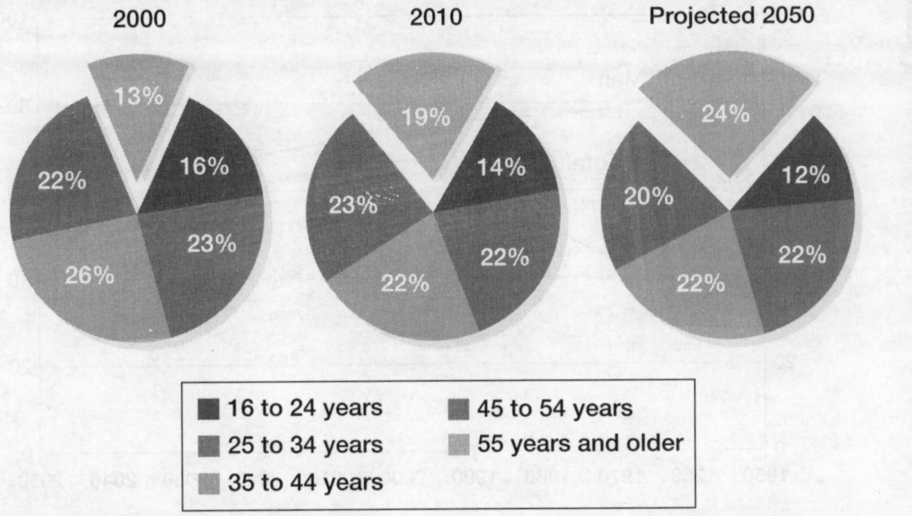

Source: U.S. Bureau of Labor Statistics

the workplace can also create supervisory issues. How will a 55-year-old react to being managed by someone in their 20s or 30s? To help companies overcome these obstacles, HR departments and experts are developing programs to help the generations understand one another better so they can capitalize on one another's strengths rather than preying on one another's weaknesses.

Keep in mind that our descriptions of the four generations of workers are generalizations. Individual employees are vastly different from one another and motivated by different factors, even if they belong to the same generation. It is up to managers to figure out what drives each person so as to best utilize their talents and to meet the person's employment demands and career aspirations.

Gender Distribution of the Workforce

Following World War II, fewer than one-third of all U.S. women were in the workforce. Currently, women constitute a little less than half of the U.S. workforce. About 60 percent of women age 16 and older are in the labor force, and approximately 70 percent of mothers with school-age children are employed in some capacity. As Figure 1.5 shows, the number of women joining the U.S. labor force has tapered off to some extent in recent years (as it has for men) and is expected to continue to do so.[38]

The educational attainment of women is also increasing relative to men. Today, three of every five college graduates are women. Women's wages have increased, too. In 1979, on average, women made 62 percent of what men made. Although this gap has not fully closed, it has narrowed. Women who are employed full time today make about 83 percent of what men employed full time make.[39]

Notably, some studies have found that younger women in urban areas make more than their male counterparts. One market research firm analyzing census data found that in 47 of the 50 biggest U.S. metropolitan areas, the median full-time salaries of young women were 8 percent higher than for men in their peer group.[40] Top executive positions are still dominated by men, though.

Figure 1.5 Labor Force Participation Rates by Gender

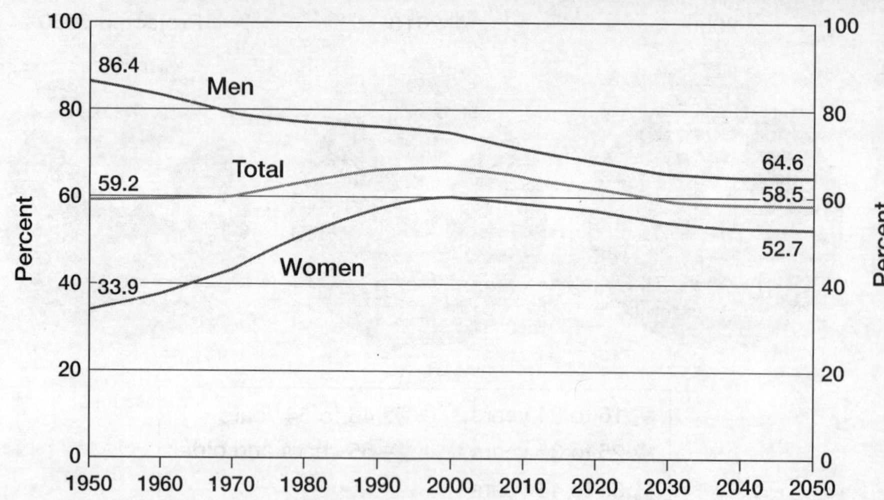

Source: U.S. Bureau of Labor Statistics

Employers wanting to attract the talent that women have to offer are taking measures to ensure they are treated equally in the workplace in terms of their advancement opportunities and compensation. In addition, more companies are accommodating working parents by offering them parental leave, part-time employment, flexible work schedules, job sharing, telecommuting, child and elder care assistance, and adoption assistance. Following the COVID-19 pandemic, these trends came into sharper focus, as some companies made special efforts to address the challenges and setbacks that working women experienced.

As we have suggested, harnessing a company's talent means being aware of characteristics *common* to employees while also managing these employees as *individuals.* It means not just tolerating or accommodating all sorts of differences, but actively supporting, nurturing, and utilizing these differences to the organization's advantage—in other words, strategically leveraging them rather than simply managing them so that people are treated equitably and "everyone gets along." This also extends to recognizing gender-nonconforming and transgender employees who are part of the organization. Evidence suggests that many organizations lag behind addressing these demographic and cultural shifts.[41]

HR managers have to ask themselves the following questions: What is it about the experiences, mindsets, and talents of different groups of people that can be utilized in a strategic way? After all, despite our similarities, *all* of us are different in one way or another, aside from the obvious differences we have outlined in this section. These differences, too, can be the source of organizational strength. Later in the book, we will explore the steps firms can take to leverage employee differences.

1.5b Educational Shifts Affecting the Workforce

Over the years, the educational attainment of the U.S. labor force has risen dramatically.[42] Figure 1.6 shows that a college education results in higher wages and lower unemployment rates. Despite the fact the educational attainment of the labor force has risen

Figure 1.6 Earnings and Unemployment Rates of Full-Time U.S. Workers by Education

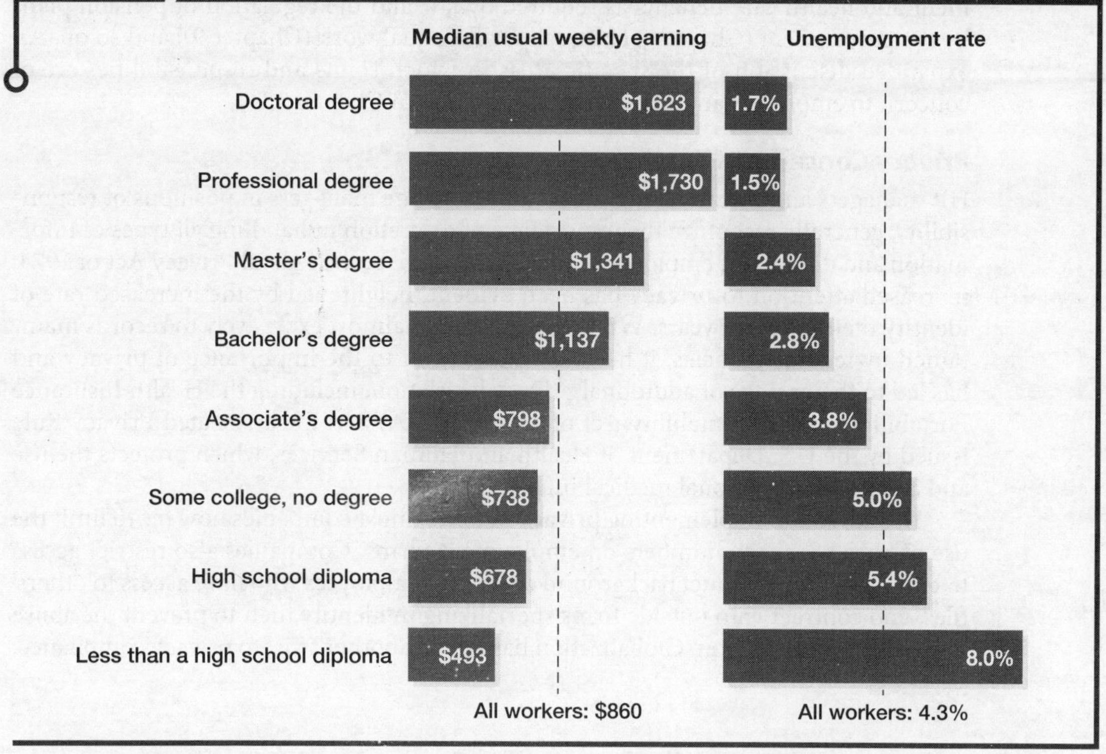

Source: U.S. Department of Labor.

in general, American students' math and science test scores lag behind those of students in China, Japan, Singapore, Finland, and several other nations. The U.S. Department of Education has found that fewer than half of all high school seniors can handle mathematics problems involving fractions, decimals, percentages, elementary geometry, and simple algebra. American adults are struggling, too. In survey of adults in 24 developed countries, Americans scored below the average on literacy, math, and computer skills tests.[43] What does this mean for the United States? What will HR managers do? The best ones will find strategies to help their firms compete, despite these challenges.

1.5c Adapting to Cultural and Societal Changes Affecting the Workforce

The attitudes, beliefs, values, and customs of people in a society are an integral part of their culture. Naturally, their culture and society affect their behavior on the job and the environment within the organization, influencing their reactions to work assignments, leadership styles, and reward systems. Cultural and societal changes are ongoing. HR policies and procedures therefore must be adjusted to cope with these changes.

Changing Employee Rights

Laws affecting employee rights are continually changing. In this book we will discuss the major laws affecting companies today. Among them are laws granting employees the right to equal employment opportunities (Chapter 3); union representation if they desire it (Chapter 14); a safe and healthful work environment (Chapter 12); unemployment and health care benefits as required by law and the regulation of pension plans by the government (Chapter 11); equal pay for equal work (Chapter 9); and so on. An expanded discussion of the specific areas in which rights and responsibilities are of concern to employers and employees is presented in Chapter 13.

Privacy Concerns of Employees

HR managers and their staff members, as well as line managers in positions of responsibility, generally recognize the importance of discretion in handling all types of information and data about employees. Since the passage of the federal Privacy Act of 1974, increased attention to privacy has been evident, heightened by the increased rate of identity theft in recent years. While the act applies almost exclusively to records maintained by federal agencies, it has drawn attention to the importance of privacy and has led to the passage of additional privacy legislation, including the Health Insurance Portability and Accountability Act of 1996 (HIPAA) and the associated Privacy Rule issued by the U.S. Department of Health and Human Services, which protects the use and disclosure of personal medical information.

In addition to implementing privacy policies, most companies now try to limit the use of Social Security numbers on employment forms. Companies also restrict access to employee files, conduct background checks on employees who have access to others' files, and contract with outside firms specializing in identity theft to prevent the abuse of employee information. Globalization has added another twist to privacy compliance.

Tracking Software and mobile apps are becoming more popular as ways for employers to remotely track employees' actions on their cell phones or computer and monitor their whereabouts and activities while on the job.

chombosan/Shutterstock.com

For example, EU countries prohibit the transfer of personal data to countries with inadequate data protection laws.[44]

The Electronic Communications Privacy Act of 1986 protects people's electronic communications, such as their email. However, employers have a right to monitor their employees' emails, phone calls, texts, and Internet use while on the job. Camera surveillance in the workplace is also an issue, as is the use of the global positioning system (GPS) to monitor employees' behavior. The nonprofit organization Workplace Fairness reports that employers are using GPS in company cars to track where workers are, how fast they are driving, and the length of their breaks based on how long their vehicles have not moved. Employers are also using applications installed on workers' smartphones and employee ID cards to see where they are, to see if they have arrived at jobsites on time, and to dispatch the closest employees to jobs.[45] In addition, employers are scrutinizing information that employees post on the Web and social media. Some employers have gone so far as to demand that job applicants give them their passwords to social media sites.

Is it legal to do these things? In many cases, yes. In most U.S. states, it's legal for employers to require their employees to provide passwords to their social networking accounts, and to ask job applicants what they earned at their previous jobs, despite efforts by some legislators to prohibit the practice. Likewise, in most states, it's legal to monitor your employees without telling them.

But although legislators have not addressed all privacy situations, some of them are being decided in court. Firms that have disciplined or fired employees for making disparaging remarks about their organizations on the Internet have found themselves sued by the employees and labor organizations claiming the workers' rights to communicate and congregate freely were violated. Intrusive practices can also seriously erode employee morale and a firm's ability to attract top talent. In Chapter 13, we discuss employer-implemented privacy programs and guidelines and consider the privacy employees can expect while on the job.

Changing Attitudes toward Work and How They Relate to Employee Engagement

Employees today are less likely to define their personal success only in terms of financial gains. Many employees, especially younger ones, believe satisfaction in life is more likely to result from balancing their work challenges and rewards with those in their personal lives. Although most people still enjoy work and want to excel at it, they tend to be focused on finding interesting work and are more inclined to pursue multiple careers. In fact, in a survey of more than 3,000 workers, 86 percent said work fulfillment and work–life balance were their top priorities. Only 35 percent of workers said being successful at work and moving up the ladder were their top priorities. Remaining with a single employer is no longer a top priority, either. People also appear to be seeking ways of living that are less complicated but more meaningful.

These new lifestyles are clearly having an impact on the way employees must be motivated, managed, and engaged. **Employee engagement** can be defined as the extent to which employees are enthused about their work and committed to it. Employee engagement is not easy to achieve. Many studies show that far fewer employees are engaged with their jobs than their firms would like.

employee engagement
The extent to which employees are enthused about their work and committed to it.

Consequently, firms are rethinking what employee engagement means and how it can be achieved. A growing number of them are thinking about the "employee experience" like they do the "customer experience." For example, how can a firm excite its employees about their jobs and gain their loyalty like Apple does its iPhone customers?

In other words, firms are using some of the insights of consumer marketing and applying them to HR.

To improve the employee experience, firms such as Whole Foods are allowing their workers to vote on firmwide initiatives and rate their company's HR practices—much in the same way that people rate restaurants, hotels, and movies on Yelp.[46] Improving the employee experience also includes allowing employees to test-drive new roles and jobs, much as customers test-drive different products. One HR manager predicts there will come a time when, after completing projects, workers will get computer messages that say something like: *If you enjoyed this type of work, you might also enjoy X type of work*—just like you get alternate product selections when you're shopping on the Web.

Balancing Work and Family

Even though new Census Bureau figures show couples postponing marriage and parenthood, balancing work and family continues to be a major concern for firms and their employees. Employees are already working more hours than they have at any time since 1973, and increasingly they are tethered to their companies around the clock via communication technologies. Complicating the task is the fact that today's families are also more diverse. They can consist of two-wage-earner families, single-parent families, families headed by same-sex couples, and families in which multiple generations of adults are living under one roof.

Competitive organizations are finding it advantageous to provide employees with more family-friendly options. Those options include telecommuting, flexible work hours, day care, elder care, part-time work, job sharing, parental leave, adoption assistance, spousal involvement in career planning, and assistance with family problems. Most *Fortune* 500 companies, including Walmart and Exxon-Mobile, now provide same-sex-partner health-insurance benefits.[47]

Companies with programs such as these calculate that accommodating their employees' individual needs and circumstances is a powerful way to attract and retain top-caliber people. Aetna Life and Casualty, for example, cut its turnover by 50 percent after it began offering 6-month parental leaves, coupled with an option for part-time work when employees return to the job. Bank of America encourages all its employees to visit their children's schools or volunteer at any school—on company time.[48]

Family-friendly companies have to balance the benefits they provide to families versus their single employees, though. The majority of employees have no children younger than age 18. A Conference Board survey of companies with family-friendly programs found that companies acknowledge that childless employees sometimes harbor resentment against employees with children who are able to take advantage of these programs when they cannot.[49]

LO6

In your opinion, what is the most important role HR managers play?

1.6 The Role HR Managers Play and Their Partnership with Other Managers

So far in this chapter, we have outlined a number of challenges faced by firms. HR managers can play a key role in helping their firms meet these challenges. For example, utilizing business statistics and surveys, HR managers can measure the engagement and effectiveness of their firms' workforces. How do employees think, learn, work, solve problems, manage their time, and deal with other people? By first seeing differences such as these, exploring them, and then discovering how they can provide value to the organization, HR managers can leverage those differences.

Similarly, by staying abreast of workforce trends and developments and gathering and analyzing data, HR managers can help their firms choose the best strategies when it comes to competing globally, selecting HR systems that are ideal for the firm and its workers, maximizing productivity, managing benefits, and so on. For example, rather than cutting its health care benefits, HR personnel at Cerner Corporation, a midsize Kansas City–based technology company, looked at statistics and other data to find out which diseases its workers were most likely to suffer from and adjusted its employee health-and-wellness programs accordingly. The company has been able to lower its health care costs as a result.

HR managers also serve as valuable partners to other managers, including **line managers**. Line managers are non-HR managers who are responsible for overseeing the work of other employees. Successful organizations combine the experience of line managers with the expertise of HR managers to develop and utilize the talents of employees to their greatest potential. HR programs in particular tend to more successful if they are "owned" by line managers *and* HR. When employees see HR as the sole owner of a program, they sometimes interpret it as an administrative or back-office program rather than a strategic initiative.

line managers
Non-HR managers who are responsible for overseeing the work of other employees.

Just as there are different types of line managers who specialize in different functions—operations, accounting, marketing, and so forth—there are different types of HR managers who specialize in different functions. Some of these workers specialize in employee training and development, recruitment, or compensation. Others specialize in studying the effects of industry and occupational trends, or concentrate on labor relations and prepare information for managers to use during negotiations with labor unions. By contrast, an HR generalist might handle all aspects of human resources work depending on the employer's needs. Figure 1.7 shows salary information for some of the HR positions we have discussed. The median pay for HR managers in 2019 was $116,720.

The Bureau of Labor Statistics has predicted that the number of HR managers needed will grow by 6 percent between 2019 and 2029, which is faster than the average for all occupations. Nonetheless, we understand that most readers of this book will be line managers and supervisors rather than HR specialists. The text is, therefore, oriented to *helping people lead and manage people more effectively,* whether they become team leaders, first-line supervisors, HR managers, or chief executive officers.

Figure 1.7 Positions in HR and Their Median Annual Wages

Position	Annual Wage
Training and development specialists	$ 58,210
Labor relations specialists	$ 58,820
Training and development managers	$ 60,850
Training and development managers	$ 102,640
Compensation and benefits managers	$ 111,430

Source: U.S. Bureau of Labor Statistics.

1.6a Responsibilities of Human Resource Managers

HR managers are typically responsible for the following major activities:

1. *Strategic advice and counsel.* HR managers often serve as in-house consultants to supervisors, managers, and executives. Given their knowledge of internal employment information and productivity metrics, as well as their awareness of external trends such as economic and unemployment data and new legal and regulatory issues, HR managers are an invaluable resource for making decisions. In some companies, generally larger ones, chief compliance or ethics officers help employees wade through gray areas when it comes to right and wrong and ensure personnel comply with the laws and regulations that affect their industries. The firm's top HR manager is in a good position to handle this responsibility. HR managers are also being relied on more heavily to advise compensation committees, which are more closely scrutinizing executives' pay than they have in years past.
2. *Service.* HR managers perform a host of service activities, such as recruiting, selecting, testing, and planning/conducting training programs. Technical expertise in these areas is essential for HR managers as they design and implement talent-management programs.
3. *Policy formulation and implementation.* HR managers generally propose and draft new policies or policy revisions to cover recurring problems or to prevent anticipated problems. Ordinarily, these policies are proposed to the senior executives of the organization, who actually issue them. HR managers also monitor the firm's managers and employees to ensure they follow established HR policies, procedures, and practices. Perhaps more important, they serve as a resource to whom managers can turn for policy interpretation.
4. *Employee advocacy.* One of the enduring roles of HR managers is to serve as an employee advocate—listening to employees' concerns and representing their needs to managers—to make certain that the interests of employees and the interests of the organization are aligned with one another.

1.6b Competencies Human Resource Managers Require

As top executives expect HR managers to assume a broader role in overall organizational strategy, many of these managers will need to acquire a complementary set of competencies. These competencies are summarized in the SHRM model, which is shown graphically in Figure 1.8.

- Leadership and navigation: The ability to direct and contribute to initiatives and processes within the organization.
- Ethical practice: The ability to integrate core values, integrity, and accountability throughout all organizational and business practices.
- Business acumen: The ability to understand and apply information with which to contribute to the organization's strategic plan.
- Relationship management: The ability to manage interactions to provide service and to support the organization.

Figure 1.8 Human Resource Competency Model

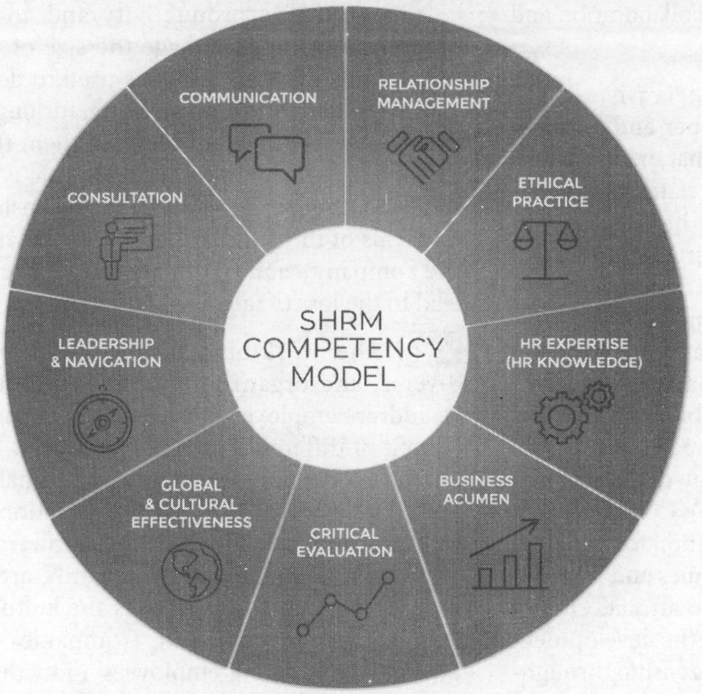

Source: Society for Human Resource Management, 1800 Duke Street, Alexandria, VA 22314.

- Consultation: The ability to provide guidance to organizational stakeholders.
- Critical evaluation: The ability to interpret information with which to make business decisions and recommendations.
- Global and cultural effectiveness: The ability to value and consider the perspectives and backgrounds of all parties.
- Communication: The ability to effectively exchange information with stakeholders.
- HR expertise (HR knowledge): The knowledge of principles, practices, and functions of effective HR management.

Summary

LO 1 Understanding human resource management practices and issues can help you better compete in the marketplace—as an employee, manager, or HR manager. Employees and managers who have a good understanding of their firm's business can help it achieve its strategies—whatever they may be—through the effective utilization of people and their talents.

An organization's success increasingly depends on the knowledge, skills, and abilities of its employees. To "compete through people," organizations must do a good job of fostering and managing human capital: the knowledge, skills, and capabilities that have value to organizations. Managers must develop strategies for identifying, recruiting, and hiring the best talent available; developing these employees in firm-specific ways; helping them generate new ideas and generalize those ideas throughout the company; encouraging information sharing; and rewarding collaboration and teamwork among employees.

LO 2 Globalization has become pervasive in the marketplace. It influences the number and kinds of jobs that are available and requires that organizations balance a complicated set of issues related to managing people working under different business conditions in different geographies, cultures, and legal environments. HR strategies and functions must be adjusted to account for these differences.

The fast pace of globalization and a number of corporate scandals over the years have led to a new focus on corporate social responsibility (good citizenship) and sustainability (a company's ability to produce a good or service without damaging the environment or depleting a resource). Companies are finding out that having a good reputation for pursuing these efforts can enhance their revenues and improve the caliber of talent they are able to attract. One of HR's leadership roles is to spearhead the development and implementation of corporate citizenship throughout their organizations, especially the fair treatment of workers.

LO 3 Technology has tended to reduce the number of jobs that require little skill and to increase the number of jobs that require considerable skill, a shift we refer to as moving from touch labor to knowledge work. This transition is displacing some employees and requiring that others be retrained. In addition, information technology has influenced HRM through human resources information systems (HRIS) that streamline HR processes, make information more readily available to managers and employees, and enable HR departments to focus on the firm's strategies. The Internet and social media are also affecting how employees are hired, work, and are managed.

LO 4 Productivity can be defined as "the output gained from a fixed amount of inputs." Organizations can increase their productivity either by reducing their inputs (the cost approach) or by increasing the amount that employees produce by adding more human and/or physical capital to the process. Companies such as Southwest Airlines, Nucor, and the manufacturing and technology firm Danaher achieve low costs in their industries not because they scrimp on employees but because they are the most productive.

To maximize productivity and contain costs, organizations must manage the size of their workforce. Some of the techniques used to do so are offshoring, outsourcing, downsizing, furloughing, using part-time employees, and leasing them from professional employment agencies. HR's role is to not only implement these programs but also consider the pros and cons of the programs and how they might affect the company's ability to compete, especially if they lead to the loss of talented staff members.

LO 5 The workforce is becoming increasingly diverse, and organizations are having to do more to address employee concerns and to maximize the benefit of different kinds of employees. HR managers must keep abreast of the educational abilities of the talent available to their organization. Employee rights, privacy concerns, attitudes toward work, and efforts to balance work and family are becoming more important to workers as the cultural dynamics in the labor force shift. Companies are finding that accommodating employees' individual needs as a result of these shifts is a powerful way to attract and retain top-caliber people and improve employee engagement.

LO 6 HR managers play a number of important roles when it comes to meeting the challenges their firms face; they are called for strategic planning, advice and ethics counsel, various service activities, policy formulation and implementation, and employee advocacy. To perform these roles effectively, HR managers must have a deep understanding of their firm's operational, financial, and personnel capabilities and work with line managers and executive managers above and below them. HR managers who do and are creative and innovative can help shape a firm's strategies so that the company can respond successfully to changes in the marketplace. Ultimately, managing people is rarely the exclusive responsibility of the HR function; rather, every manager's job involves managing people. Consequently, successful companies combine the expertise of HR specialists with the experience of line managers and executives to develop and use the talents of employees to their greatest potential.

Key Terms

agility
corporate social responsibility
downsizing
employee engagement
employee leasing
environmental, social, and governance (ESG)
furloughing
homeshoring
human capital
human resources information system (HRIS)
human resources management (HRM)
knowledge workers
line managers
nearshoring
offshoring
organizational culture
outsourcing
sustainability
workforce (HR) analytics

Discussion Questions

LO 1 Are people always an organization's most valuable asset? Why or why not? Suppose your boss asked you to summarize the major people-related concerns related to opening an office in India. What issues would be on your list?

LO 2 Name a company you hope to work for someday. What is its track record in terms of corporate social responsibility and sustainability? Are these factors important to you? Why or why not?

LO 3 Will technology eliminate the need for HR managers?

LO 4 Do cost-containment pressures work against the effective management of people? Why or why not?

LO 5 What are the pros and cons of having a more diverse workforce? Is the United States in a better position to compete globally because of its diverse population?

LO 6 In your opinion, what is the most important role HR managers play?

CASE STUDY 1 New HR Strategy Makes Lloyd's a "Best Company"

After more than 300 years in business, a few years ago, the global insurer Lloyd's of London finally set out to establish its first true HR strategy, starting with the hiring of HR Director Suzy Black. "I was brought in to transform the HR function from one modeled on an old-style personnel office to a function that is more cutting edge, business focused, and value adding," says Black.

Black's first order of business was to evaluate the current state of affairs, particularly how the corporation's senior managers perceived the HR role. With this information in hand, Black and her team began to develop an overarching strategic agenda as well as specific tactics, addressing everything from recruitment to performance management to basic policies to rewards and compensation.

Changing longtime employees' perception of HR took a bit of convincing, but employees quickly began to recognize the value of Black's actions. Gradually, they could see how the HR strategies were effectively creating conditions in which they could develop in their careers, be successful, and find meaning and value in their work. Today, Lloyd's employees list the company's challenging work environment, healthy incentive programs, and meaningful community outreach programs among the key reasons they enjoy working for the insurance giant.

Black's efforts also enhanced Lloyd's position as a desirable place to work. The average tenure of employees at the company is, incredibly, 21 years. The insurer has been named one of the "Top 100 Best Companies to Work For" (in the United Kingdom) by the *Sunday Times* and hailed as one of the United Kingdom's Top 40 Business Brands by an independent researcher.

Each year, new graduates scramble to get hired by Lloyd's. These new hires rotate through three to four different assignments within Lloyd's so they get a perspective of the company and the insurance market as well as a better idea of the departments in which they would like to ultimately work. Lloyd's also offers a graduate program in insurance, apprenticeships, and internships.

Work–life balance at the company is good. Although sometimes extra hours have to be worked, that's not the norm. Working mothers can choose to work part or full time. In addition, the company offers employees time to do charity and non-work-related activities to further their personal growth. "Employees are very sophisticated people, and they have more drivers than just wanting to earn money," Black notes.

Ironically, Black's position was the first HR position she had ever held, having risen through the ranks in other arenas in business. But her experience has given her a clear definition of the ideal characteristics of the HR professionals. "They must understand change and transformation, excel at operations, and balance tactical and strategic thinking and acting," she says. "They will have to be able to manage and navigate organizational complexity and ambiguities and not be afraid to say no occasionally in order to establish appropriate boundaries with the business."

Questions

1. What skills does Black think employees need to work successfully in the HR area?
2. What are some of the outcomes of the company's new HR strategy?
3. What do you think might be some of the challenges of establishing HR policies for a global company?
4. What types of situations do you think might require an HR manager to say "no"?

Sources: "Lloyd's of London Says India Reinsurance Branch to Open by April," *Reuters* (January 18, 2017), http://uk.reuters.com; "Careers," Lloyds.com (January 17, 2017), http://www.lloyds.com; "Lloyd's: A Top Place to Work," Lloyds.com (March 16, 2011), http://www.lloyds.com; Helen William, "City Slicker," *Personnel Today* (August 11, 2009): 10–11; *Digby Morgan Human Resourcefulness Newsletter* (February 2010), http://www.digbymorgannewsletter.com/story04_HR_02_10.htm; company website: www.lloyds.com.

CASE STUDY 2 Shell's Top Recruiter Takes His Cues from Marketing

When Navjot Singh joined the global oil-and-gas company Shell, the company was facing an extraordinary challenge: The rate at which Shell's engineers were retiring meant the global firm needed to more than triple the number of new recruits it hired, from approximately 2,500 to nearly 8,000. Yet at the time, Shell was not considered an employer of choice. The company needed to project a new image—and fast. Says Singh, "In the same way marketers know they need to advertise to be a market leader, HR had to know how to create an employer brand. Marketing is the only way to ensure customers buy products. It was also the only way to ensure Shell got the best people coming to us first."

"Wait! Why would Shell's HR guy be talking about marketing?" you might be wondering. As both an HR and marketing expert, Singh saw a powerful synergy between the two. "I'm 50 percent a marketer—the rest is HR, communications, and recruitment," says Singh. Singh initially started out as vice president of customer relationship management, but quickly joined the HR team when he recognized Shell's emerging need for new talent and the immense potential for him to use classic marketing techniques to help the company achieve its objectives. His vision, skill sets, and experience were a perfect match for the company's situation.

So in Singh's mind, addressing the company's need for new talent meant building a brand as an employer, which in turn meant creating a cohesive message. But Shell's global recruiting approach was anything but cohesive. "At the time we had 1,200 recruitment systems, 35 recruitment companies, and 400 executive search companies working for us," he recalls. "I attended a careers event at Cambridge University where there were three Shell stands beside each other—one from the UK, one from Malaysia, and another from Nigeria. This was a fragmented approach and tough for candidates to understand." Shell needed to create a unified outreach program if it was going to meet its need for numbers while fulfilling its desire for a global talent pool. The company recruits from among 90 different nationalities each year because it recognizes the benefits of cultural diversity.

"It's not enough to tell candidates why they should join Shell. We needed to demonstrate such reasons through the interviewing process and the whole candidate experience," explains Singh. "A motivating candidate experience—from the moment someone hears about Shell to the moment they have joined us—requires a coordinated approach across all the recruitment disciplines: marketing, operations, recruiters, and line managers all need to work together." It also necessitated that personnel take less of a more Shell-concentric perspective and adopt one that focused instead on candidates.

Singh and his team set about applying various marketing techniques to the recruitment process, which have since resulted in an 80 percent decrease in the company's recruitment costs and a 20 percent reduction in the time to hire new staff. To attract talented graduates, Shell annually sponsors a popular competition that challenges student teams around the world to solve various food, water, and alternative energy problems. About a thousand teams compete annually.

The efforts have paid off. Shell has won more than 75 awards for its unique HR strategy. Better yet, in a recent global survey of 8,400 people in the oil-and-gas sector, Shell received the most mentions from respondents who were asked to name the employers they would most like to work for.

Despite Shell's recruiting success, Singh believes the war for talent will be ongoing: "In the future, companies will have to apply for skilled people to work for them rather than candidates applying to work at an organization. HR must still realize the strategic value it can bring."

Questions

1. What functions of HRM are similar to marketing functions? How can thinking about "marketing" a company's jobs improve the strategic focus of HR personnel?
2. If you were planning to use marketing strategies to "brand" a company as an employer of choice, what are some of the factors you would consider?
3. Do you agree with Singh's statement that in the future, companies will have to apply for skilled people to work for them rather than candidates applying to work at an organization? Why or why not?

Sources: Jon Mainwaring, "Shell Q&A: What Makes an Ideal Employer in Oil, Gas?" *Rigzone* (November 16, 2016), http://www.rigzone.com; Jon Mainwaring, "Shell Takes First Place in Rigzone's Inaugural Ideal Employer Survey," *Rigzone* (November 16, 2016), http://www.rigzone.com; Don Wood, "Lateral Thinking," *Human Resources* (January 2010): 12–13; Christopher Van Mosseveld, "Views from the Top," *Employer Branding Today* (April 16, 2009), http://www.employerbrandingtoday.com; Peter Crush, "Shell UK Combines HR and Marketing to Sell the Brand," *HR Magazine* (August 25, 2009), http://www.hrmagazine.co.uk; Navjot Singh and Ana Maria Santos, "How Shell Recruited More for Less," *Marketing Society* (July 9, 2012), https://www.marketingsociety.co.uk.

Notes and References

1. T. J. Watson, Jr. *A Business and Its Beliefs: The Ideas That Helped Build IBM* (New York: McGraw-Hill, 1963).
2. Donald C. Busi, "Assignment Reviews (ARs): Moving toward Measuring Your Most Valuable Asset," *Supervision* 66, no. 1 (January 2005): 3–7.
3. David Lepak and Scott Snell, "Managing the Human Resource Architecture for Knowledge-Based Competition," in S. Jackson, M. Hitt, and A. DeNisi (eds.), *Managing Knowledge for Sustained Competitive Advantage: Designing Strategies for Effective Human Resource Management,* Scientific Frontiers Series (San Francisco: John Wiley & Sons, 2003), 127–154; David Lepak and Scott Snell, "Examining the Human Resource Architecture: The Relationship among Human Capital, Employment, and Human Resource Configurations," *Journal of Management* 28, no. 4 (2002): 517–543; Steve Bates, "Study Links HR Practices with the Bottom Line" *HR Magazine* 46, no. 12 (December 2001): 14; Ann Pomeroy, "Cooking up Innovation: When It Comes to Helping Employees Create New Products and Services, HR's Efforts Are a Key Ingredient," *HR Magazine* 49, no. 11 (November 2004): 46–54.
4. Dave Ulrich, Steve Kerr, and Ron Ashkenas, *The GE Work-Out: How to Implement GEs Revolutionary Method for Busting Bureaucracy and Attacking Organizational Problems* (New York: McGraw-Hill Professional Publishing, 2002).
5. R Wang. 2014. "Constellation's 2014 Outlook on Dominating Digital Business Disruption," Constellation Research. https://www.constellationr.com/research/constellations-2014-outlook-dominating-digital-business-disruption

6. Wang, R. "Research Summary: Sneak Peaks From Constellation's Futurist Framework and 2014 Outlook On Digital Disruption," *Constellation,* February 18, 2014; "Capitalizing on Complexity: Insights from the Global Chief Executive Officer Study," *IBM,* 2010. https://www.ibm.com/downloads/cas/1VZV5X8J https://www.constellationr.com/blog-news/research-summary-sneak-peeks-constellations-futurist-framework-and-2014-outlook-digital
7. Cameron Albert-Deitch, "Zappos CEO Tony Hsieh's Biggest Management Experiment Is Evolving Again (in a Very Intriguing Way)," *Inc.* January 30, 2020; John P. Kotter, "Ten Observations," *Executive Excellence* 16, no. 8 (1999): 15–16. https://www.inc.com/cameron-albert-deitch/zappos-tony-hsieh-holacracy-market-system.html
8. Jared Lindzon, "Welcome to a New Era of Human Resources," *Fast Company* (May 20, 2015), https://www.fastcompany.com.
9. "Best Countries," *U.S. News & World Report* (2016), http://worldnews.com.
10. Ellen Sheng, "The Five Biggest Chinese Investments in the U.S. in 2016," *Forbes* (December 21, 2016), http://www.forbes.com.
11. Candice Choi and Bruce Schreiner, "Beam Being Acquired by Japan's Suntory," *Associated Press* (January 13, 2014), http://ap.org; "Beermaker Eyes Chinese Factories," *Fort Worth Star Telegram* (December 28, 2010): 3C; Susan Meisinger, "Going Global: A Smart Move for HR Professionals," *HR Magazine* 49, no. 3 (March 2004): 6; "AB InBev Completes ModeloGrupo Deal," *St. Louis Post-Dispatch* (June 4, 2013), http://www.stltoday.com.
12. "USMCA Takes Effect But North American Trade Tensions Remain," *Wall Street Journal,* July 1, 2020; "U.K. Expresses Keenness to Have Free Trade Agreement with India," *The Tribune* (January 18, 2017), http://www.tribuneindia.com.
13. Laura McKnight, "For Companies, Doing Good Is Good Business," *Kansas City Star* (December 26, 2010), http://www.kansascity.com.
14. C. A. Bartlett, "Unilever's New Global Strategy: Competing through Sustainability," Harvard Business Publishing (9-916-414), 2016; "Best ESG Companies: Top 50 Stocks for Environmental, Social and Governance Values," *Investor's Business Daily,* October 26, 2020.
15. Nancy R. Lockwood, "Corporate Social Responsibility: HR's Leadership Role," *HR Magazine* 49, no. 2 (December 2004): S1–11.
16. Carol Carter, *Keys to Business Communication* (Upper Saddle River, NJ: Pearson, 2012), 414.
17. "Text Messaging Curtailed at Bank," *Wall Street Journal* (January 14–15, 2017): B3.
18. M. Muro, S. Liu, J. Whiton, and S. Kulkarni, "Digitalization and the American Workforce," *Brookings,* November, 2017; Lauren Webber, "'Routine Jobs' Are Disappearing," *Wall Street Journal* (January 3, 2017), http://www.wsj.com.
19. "China Engineers Next Great Leap with Wave of 'Knowledge Workers,'" *Milwaukee Journal Sentinel* (December 31, 2003), http://www.jsonline.com; "Edward Yourdon's New Book Helps 'Knowledge Workers' Put Emotion aside to Look at the Facts of the New Economic Reality," *PR Newswire* (October 4, 2004); Marshall Goldsmith, "Supervisors of the Smart," *BRW* 30, no. 20 (May 22, 2008): 57–57.
20. Christopher Mims, "Technology's Long-Term Toll on the Middle Class," *Wall Street Journal* (January 23, 2017): B1-B4.
21. Melissa Korn, "Imagine Discovering Your Teaching Assistant Is a Robot," *Wall Street Journal* (May 6, 2016), http://wsj.com.
22. Steve Lohr, "Robots Will Take Jobs, But Not as Fast as Some Fear, New Report Says," *New York Times* (January 12, 2017), https://www.nytimes.com.
23. Brad Smith, "Microsoft Launches Initiative to Help 25 Million People Worldwide Acquire the Digital Skills Needed in a COVID-19 Economy," Microsoft Blog, June 30, 2020.
24. Sarah Castellanos, "Augmented Reality in the Workplace," *Wall Street Journal* (December 13, 2016): B4.
25. Scott A. Snell, Donna Stueber, and David P. Lepak, "Virtual HR Departments: Getting out of the Middle," in R. L. Heneman and D. B. Greenberger (eds.), *Human Resource Management in Virtual Organizations* (Columbus, OH: Information Age Publishing, 2002): 81–99; Samuel Greengard, "How to Fulfill Technology's Promise," *Workforce, HR Software Insights* (February 1999): S10–18.
26. Drew Robb, "Building a Better Workforce: Performance Management Software Can Help You Identify and Develop High-Performing Workers," *HR Magazine* 49, no. 10 (October 2004): 86–92.
27. "Nine Benefits of Embracing Big Data in Human Resources," *Forbes,* January 2, 2020. Josh Bersin, "The Datification of Human Resources," *Forbes* (July 19, 2013), http://www.forbes.com.
28. Robb, "Building a Better Workforce," 86–92; "How to Implement an Effective Process for a New HR Management System," *HR Focus* (January 2005): 3–4; "New Study Finds HRIS Key to Reducing Costs," *Payroll Managers Report* 7, no. 5 (May 2007): 13.
29. Bruce Stokes, "Is There a Future for 'Made in America,'" *The Atlantic* (December 9, 2010), http://www.theatlantic.com.
30. Patrick Barta and Andrew Caffrey, "Productivity Leap Shows Potential of U.S. Economy—Rise at 8.6 Percent Pace, Positive for Profits, Doesn't Bode Very Well for Employment," *Wall Street Journal* (May 8, 2002): A1; Jon E. Hilsenrath, "The Economy: Big U.S. Service Sectors Boosted Late 1990s Surge in Productivity," *Wall Street Journal* (April 22, 2002): A2; Karen Lowry Miller, "Economy: Out of Steam—A Dip in U.S. Productivity Provokes Anxious Questions," *Newsweek International* (February 21, 2005): 34; Milan Yager, "Outsource to Gain Human Resources Expertise," *Hotel & Motel Management* 223, no. 7 (April 21, 2008): 14.
31. "Future Outsourcing Trends for 2020," Flatworld Solutions, 2021; Pete Engardio, Michael Arndt, and Dean Foust, "The Future of Outsourcing," *Business Week* (January 30, 2006): 50–58.

32. John Sullivan, "Employee Furloughs Can Be a Bad Alternative to Layoffs," ere.net (February 9, 2009), http://www.ere.net/.
33. Mike Stobbe, "Dieting Like It's Your Job: Does Paying for Healthy Habits Work?" *USA Today* (June 1, 2010), http://www.usatoday.com; Tom Murphy, "To Cut Health Costs, Firms Target Spousal Benefits," *Fort Worth Star-Telegram* (September 16, 2013): 1D.
34. Daniel Costa. "Temporary work visa programs and the need for reform: A briefing on program frameworks, policy issues and fixes, and the impact of COVID-19." Economic Policy Institute, February 3, 2021
35. Ibid.
36. Miriam Jordan, "Alabama Immigrant Law Irks Business," *Wall Street Journal*, August 24, 2011; Jeffrey S. Passel and D'Vera Cohn, "Share of Unauthorized Immigrant Workers in Production Construction Jobs Falls, since 2007," Pew Research Center (March 26, 2015), www.pewhispanic.org.
37. Irwin Speizer, "Diversity on the Menu: Rachelle Hood, Denny's Chief Diversity Officer, Has Boosted the Company's Image. But That Hasn't Sold More Breakfasts," *Workforce Management* 83, no. 12 (November 1, 2004): 41; Patrick Purcell, "Older Workers: Employment and Retirement Trends," *Journal of Pension Planning & Compliance* 34, no. 1 (Spring 2008): 32–48.
38. U.S. Bureau of Labor Statistics, "Occupational Employment," *Occupational Outlook Quarterly Online* (Winter 2013–2014), http://www.bls.gov.
39. Ibid.
40. U.S. Bureau of Labor Statistics, "Women in the Labor Force: A Databook," *BLS Reports* (December 2015), http://www.bls.gov.
41. Lily Zheng, "Transgender, Gender-Fluid, Nonbinary, and Gender-Nonconforming Employees Deserve Better Policies, *Harvard Business Review,* November 20, 2020; Alison Fogarty and Lily Zheng, *Gender Ambiguity in the Workplace: Transgender and Gender-Diverse Discrimination* (Santa Barbara, CA: Praeger, 2018); Kathleen Iverson, "Managing for Effective Workforce Diversity," *Cornell Hotel and Restaurant Administration Quarterly* 41, no. 2 (April 2000): 31–38; Gail Johnson, "Time to Broaden Diversity Training," *Training* 41, no. 9 (September 2004): 16.
42. The U.S. Department of Labor's Bureau of Labor Statistics keeps up-to-date projections and percentages on educational requirements for different kinds of jobs. Interested readers can access this information at http://www.bls.gov; Josh Mitchell, "College Still Pays off, But Not for Everyone," *Wall Street Journal,* August 9, 2019; Louis Uchitelle, "College Degree Still Pays, But It's Leveling off," *The New York Times* (January 13, 2005): C1.
43. Lyndsey Layton, "U. S. Adults Lag Most Countries in Literacy and Computer Skills," *Washington Post* (October 8, 2013), http://washingtonpost.com.
44. Avoiding Identity Theft," *Aftermarket Business* 114, no. 12 (December 2004): 10.
45. "Your Rights: Surveillance at Work," *Workplace Fairness* (December 2010), http://www.workplacefairness.org.
46. Jeanne Meister, "The Employee Experience Is the Future of Work," *Forbes* (January 5, 2017), http://www.forbes.com; Rachel Emma Silverman, "Workplace Democracy Catches On, *Wall Street Journal* (March 28, 2016): B5.
47. Ashley Surdin, "Benefits for Same-Sex Couples Expanding," *Washington Post* (November 27, 2009), http://www.washingtonpost.com.
48. Todd Raphael, "The Drive to Down-Shifting," *Workforce* 80, no. 10 (October 2001): 23; Jim Olsztynski, "Flexible Work Schedules May Make More Sense: One in Six Americans Qualifies as a Caregiver Who May Benefit from Flextime," *National Driller* 26, no. 2 (February 2005): 16–19; Karen Springen, "Cutting back Your Hours," *Newsweek,* 151, no. 19 (May 12, 2008): 60.
49. Leah Carlson, "Flextime Elevated to National Issue," *Employee Benefit News* (September 15, 2004): 1–16.

Rawpixel.com/Shutterstock.com

CHAPTER 2

Strategy and Human Resource Planning

Learning Outcomes

After studying this chapter, you should be able to

- **LO 1** Explain how human resource planning and a firm's mission, vision, and values are integrally linked to its strategy.
- **LO 2** Describe how an organization's external environment influences its strategic planning.
- **LO 3** Summarize why it is important for an organization to do an internal resource analysis.
- **LO 4** Explain the linkages between competitive strategies and human resources.
- **LO 5** Classify what is required for a firm to successfully execute a strategy and assess its effectiveness.
- **LO 6** Describe how firms evaluate their strategies and HR execution.

One of the clichés about corporate annual reports is that they often begin with a claim that "people are our most important asset." Do you believe this is true? Historically, many managers have not acted as though they themselves really believed it. All too frequently, the focus has been on minimizing the number of a firm's employees rather than strategically utilizing their talents. Managers, it seems, have treated employees as costs to be minimized rather than assets to be valued.

But for many firms, this is changing. Surveys show that 92 percent of chief financial officers now believe human capital affects an organization's customer service, 82 percent believe it affects profitability, and 72 percent believe it affects innovation.[1] In a survey by the consulting firm Deloitte, nearly 80 percent of corporate executives said the importance of HRM in their firms has grown substantially over the years, and two-thirds said that HR expenditures are now viewed as a strategic investment rather than simply a cost to be minimized.

Forward-thinking companies are asking their human resource groups to push past short-term projections, and to provide detailed forecasts of personnel needs and associated costs over a 2- to 3-year horizon. Even small companies are realizing that their employees are the key to creating and ensuring their ability to compete in the future. As Apple's legendary founder Steve Jobs put it: "Hiring the best is your most important task."

2.1 Strategic Planning and Human Resource Planning

LO1 Identify the three key elements of the human resources planning model and discuss the relationships among them.

As we explained in Chapter 1, "competing through people" is a theme emphasized throughout this book. But the idea remains only a premise for action until put it into practice. To deliver on this promise, we need to understand some of the systems and processes in organizations that link human resources management with strategic management. A few definitions may be helpful upfront.

First of all, **strategic planning** involves a set of procedures for making decisions about the organization's long-term goals and ways to achieve those goals. Strategic plans have a strong external orientation that covers major portions of the organization. These plans especially focus on how the organization will position itself relative to its competitors so as to ensure its long-term survival, create value, and grow. **Human resource planning (HRP)**, by comparison, is the process of anticipating and providing for the movement of people into, within, and out of an organization. Its overall purpose is to help managers deploy their human resources as effectively as possible, where and when they are needed, to accomplish the organization's goals. **Strategic human resource management** combines strategic planning and HRP. It can be thought of as the pattern of human resource activities and investments that enable an organization to achieve its strategic goals.

HRP is an essential activity of organizations. Consider CNA Financial Corporation, a Chicago-based insurance company. CNA Financial discovered via HRP that it would run short of underwriters—a key skill pool in the company—in just 2 years' time if their turnover rates continued at their current pace.

strategic planning
Procedures for making decisions about the organization's long-term goals and strategies.

human resource planning (HRP)
The process of anticipating and providing for the movement of people into, within, and out of an organization.

strategic human resource management
The pattern of human resources deployments and activities that enable an organization to achieve its strategic goals.

According to Walt Cleaver, an HR strategist and president of the Cleaver Consulting Group, increased global competitiveness in many industries has led to the commoditization of products based on price, which is making talent the "great differentiator" among firms. As we explained in Chapter 1, it is relatively easy for competitors to copy your product and make it more cheaply. But duplicating the talents of your employees is much more difficult.[2] Globalization and shifts in the composition of the labor force require that HR managers become more heavily involved in planning because these changes affect the full range of a company's HR practices, such as employee recruitment, selection, training, compensation, and motivation.

2.1a Strategic Planning and HR Planning: Linking the Processes

Good HR managers "marry" HRP to the strategic planning for their organizations as a whole. Although HRP connects to strategic planning in several ways, at a fundamental level we can focus on two issues: strategy formulation and strategy execution. HRP provides inputs into the strategic *formulation* process in terms of what is possible—that is, whether a firm has the types and numbers of people available to pursue a given strategy. For example, when Walmart executives contemplated their company's move into Web-based commerce to compete with Amazon, one of the issues they had to address was whether they had the talent needed to succeed in that arena. Walmart had to go through the same exercise again prior to launching its business in India.

In addition to strategy formulation, HRP is important in terms of strategy *execution*. In other words, once the firm has devised its strategy, the company's executives must make resource allocation decisions to implement that strategy, including decisions related to the firm's structure, processes, and human capital.[3] 3M's managers have the two aspects of HRP down to a science. Not only does the company engage in elaborate workforce planning, but it has also figured out how to utilize its employees to expand into markets worldwide. Once primarily a domestic company, today most of 3M's products are sold abroad. The company is able to project the demand for any workforce category, in any business, in any part of the world.[4]

Figure 2.1 will serve as a map for this chapter's discussion. It shows how companies align their HRP and strategic planning. This logic works this way: A firm's business strategy, along with its overall purpose, goals, and values, establishes the context for its HR strategy and the number and types of people the firm needs, the skills they must have, and the like. In other words, the firm's HR strategy follows the business strategy and helps to execute it. For example, Marriott's business strategy is to grow globally by offering efficient hotel operations and great customer service. Its HR strategy supports this business strategy by focusing on attracting and developing employees all over the world who work hard and take care of the company's customers. Marriott's selection, training, and reward systems all support this approach.

Although the firm's business strategy affects its HR strategy, it is not a one-way street. The type of people an organization has, and the culture and climate of the company, in turn will *constrain* what the firm is able to achieve strategically. Ultimately, HRP and strategic planning are integral to each other: Strategic planning decisions affect—and are affected by—HR concerns. As James Walker, a noted HRP expert, put it, "Today, virtually *all* business issues have people implications; *all* human resource issues have business implications."

Figure 2.1 Linking Strategic Planning and Human Resources

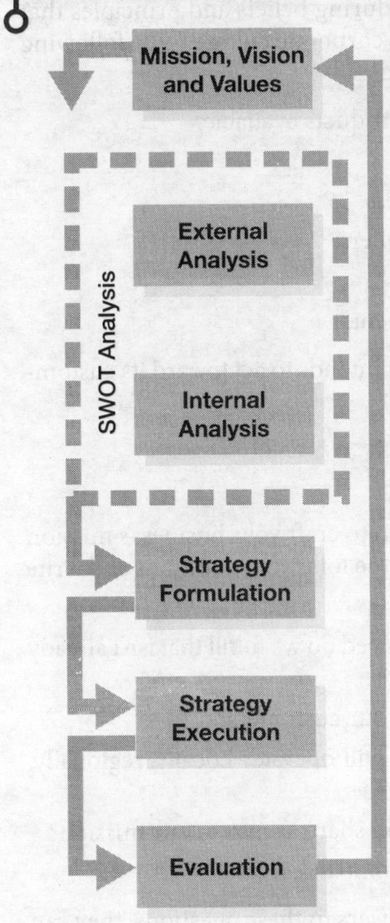

	STRATEGIC PLANNING	HR PLANNING
Mission, Vision and Values	• Identify purpose and scope of organization • Clarify its long-term direction • Establish its enduring beliefs and principles	• Capture underlying business philosophy • Establish cultural foundation • Guide ethical codes of conduct
External Analysis	• Assess its opportunities and threats (OT) • Conduct environmental scanning (legal, etc.) • Analyze the industry and competitors	• Gauge demographic trends • Gauge the external supply of labor • Benchmark competitors' HR metrics
Internal Analysis	• Analyze firm's strengths and weaknesses (SW) • Analyze firm's core competencies • Analyze firm's resources: people, process, and systems	• Analyze workforce's culture, competencies, and composition • Forecast the demand for employees • Forecast the supply of employees
Strategy Formulation	• Develop corporate strategy • Develop business strategy	• Establish productivity and efficiency goals • Establish quality, service, speed, and innovation goals for workforce • Reconcile supply and demand via hiring, downsizing, layoffs, etc.
Strategy Execution	• Design structure, systems, and so on • Allocate resources • Functional strategy: ensure alignment	• Ensure vertical and horizontal fit • Use staffing, training, rewards, and so on to motivate employees to achieve the strategy
Evaluation	• Evaluate benchmarking efforts • Ensure alignment is achieved • Encourage workforce agility and flexibility	• Maintain human capital metrics • Utilize balanced scorecard

2.2 Step One: Mission, Vision, and Values

Let's begin with purpose. When you entered college, you probably thought a lot about what you wanted to do with your life. Believe it or not, firms go through the same sort of search process when they develop their strategic plans. The first step in strategic planning is establishing a mission, vision, and values for the organization. The **mission** is the basic purpose of the organization, as well as its scope of operations. It is a statement of the organization's reason for existing and the shared purpose of the people in the organization. The mission is often described in terms of the customers the firm serves. Depending on the scope of the organization, the mission may be broad or narrow. For example, the mission of Google is "to organize the world's information and make it universally accessible and useful."[5]

mission
The basic purpose of the organization as well as its scope of operations.

strategic vision
A statement about where the company is going and what it can become in the future.

The **strategic vision** of the organization moves beyond the mission statement to provide a perspective on where the company is headed and what the organization can become in the future. Although the terms *mission* and *vision* are often used interchangeably, the vision statement ideally clarifies the long-term direction of the company and its strategic intent.

core values
The strong and enduring beliefs and principles that guide a firm's decisions and are the foundation of its corporate culture.

The organization's **core values** are the strong enduring beliefs and principles that guide a firm's decisions and form the foundation of its corporate culture.[6] The following are the core values for the organic grocer Whole Foods:

- We sell the highest-quality natural and organic products available.
- We satisfy and delight our customers.
- We promote team members' growth and happiness.
- We practice win–win partnerships with our suppliers.
- We create profits and prosperity.
- We care about our community and the environment.

Core values such as these indicate how a company intends to act toward its customers, employees, and the public in general.

2.2a Developing a Mission Statement

As a manager or business owner, how would you begin to craft your business's mission statement? One way to begin would be to ask yourself the following questions and write down your answers to them:

- What is my organization's reason for being? What need do we fulfill that isn't already being met by another firm or could be met better?
- For whom will the firm fulfill the need? Who are our customers?
- Where is our market and our customers? Where will operate? Locally, regionally, nationally, or globally?
- What core values do the people in my organization share as part of our mission?
- How do these values differentiate us from other companies?

Once an organization or entrepreneur has the answers to these questions, they can begin to draft a mission statement that synthesizes the information.

2.2b HR's Role in Establishing and Reinforcing a Firm's Mission, Vision, and Values

HR managers play a key role when it comes to formulating, vetting, and fine-tuning a firm's mission, vision, and values. Does the mission statement accurately reflect employees' beliefs and aspirations, or only those of upper management? Does it inspire both employees and managers? If not, how should it be changed? A firm's mission statement keeps everyone on the "same page" and heading in the same direction. Hence, it needs to be accurate.

HR managers help embody the firm's mission, vision, and values within the organization by what they say and what they do:

- By communicating the mission, vision, and values frequently, both informally and formally, via verbal and written communications such as employee meetings, emails, newsletters, bulletins boards, the firm's website, the annual report, and employee orientations. Nordstrom asks its employees to describe to new hires work incidents that demonstrate how they put the retailer's mission, vision, and values into action. Doing so is more powerful and motivating than merely stating them or putting them into print.

- By recruiting and hiring employees whose values are consistent with the organization. This can also help organizations attract Generation Z and Millennial workers, who place a high priority on finding employment meaningful to them and aligned with their own goals and values in life.
- By translating the mission, vision, and values into job descriptions and specific behaviors and recognizing and rewarding employees based on them.

Just as the organization itself may evolve over time, firms have to be prepared to change their mission statements as conditions change. Monitoring those changes requires a firm to continually scan the environment for threats and opportunities, which we discuss next. Following the financial crisis and Great Recession, SunTrust Bank adapted and reinvigorated its mission, vision, and values so that employees would be proud to work for the firm. Its company mantra became "lighting the way to financial freedom." This statement reminded employees why they were there, and how they could help their communities.[7]

2.3 Step Two: External Analysis

LO2 What external forces influence a firm's strategy?

Let's take the next step. Before you selected your major, you probably looked at information about possible careers—whether there were many opportunities in those careers or relatively few. Were certain fields becoming hotter than others or more rewarding? As you looked at these options, you probably compared them to your interests and capabilities. Firms do something similar. On an ongoing basis, they analyze external opportunities and threats, and they compare them to their strengths and weaknesses. This comparison is called SWOT (*strengths, weaknesses, opportunities,* and *threats*) analysis. A SWOT analysis is a simple way to summarize the major facts and forecasts derived from external and internal analyses. We'll discuss how to do a SWOT analysis later in the chapter.

Environmental scanning is the systematic monitoring of major external forces influencing the organization, including forces in the business environment—which is sometimes called the remote environment—and the competitive environment. Changes in the external environment directly impact the way organizations are run and people are managed. Some of these changes represent opportunities, and some of them represent real threats to the organization. By continuously scanning the environment for changes, managers can anticipate their impact and make adjustments early.

environmental scanning Systematic monitoring of the major external forces influencing the organization.

2.3a The Business Environment

A firm's **business environment** consists of all of the external factors in the general environment—factors that a firm cannot directly control but that can affect its strategy. The business environment includes forces that generally affect most, if not all, firms—forces over which they have virtually no control. Economic changes, technological changes, demographic changes, and legal and regulatory changes are examples. By and large, a firm can only adapt to these changes rather than influence them. For example, when the

business environment Factors in the external environment that a firm cannot directly control but that can affect its strategy and performance.

COVID-19 pandemic struck, the global economy stopped, the stock market crashed (at least for a little while), unemployment increased, supply chains were shut down, and employees' health and safety were put at risk. Companies had little choice but to react as best they could to manage the crisis. Although this was an extreme event, it illustrates the challenges that firms can face. Let's look at more specific factors to better understand the business environment.

Economic Changes

All firms must react to local, regional, and global economic conditions. During good times, firms can more easily expand; during bad times, they often contract. But this isn't true for all businesses—it depends upon their strategies. During the COVID-19 pandemic, when people were sheltering in place, sales of home improvement stores like Home Depot and Lowe's actually grew. Meanwhile, many other retailers scaled back their operations.[8]

Ecological Changes

Closely related to the economy are ecological conditions in the natural environment. To deal with climate change, farmers around the globe have had to adopt environmentally conscious techniques to combat erosion and depleted aquifers. No-till farming is one such technique: With this method, farmers don't ever till up the soil. Doing so depletes it of moisture and nutrients. Instead, growers just plant over any old plants from the year before.[9]

The catastrophic earthquake and subsequent tsunami that struck Japan in 2011 is another example of an ecological change that affected thousands of different types of businesses and supply chains worldwide. One Japanese semiconductor manufacturer recovered more quickly than its peers from the tsunami, thanks to a strategy it had developed in the aftermath of an earlier earthquake: The company had created flexible manufacturing capabilities that allowed it to shift production to unaffected facilities in other parts of Japan and Asia.[10]

Technological Changes

Like economic and ecological changes, technological changes such as the Internet have a broad effect on businesses—changes to which they must adapt strategically. For example, in manufacturing, technologies like 3D printing, the Internet of Things (IoT), nanotechnology, cloud computing, and other advances are dramatically changing which products get made, how they get made, and by whom. The Internet, of course, has disrupted nearly every industry, affecting businesses all over the world. Just think of the many examples of Web-based businesses: hotels (Airbnb), transportation (Uber), retail (Amazon), movies (Netflix), music (Spotify), advertising (Google)—and the list goes on. While some firms adapt their strategies to take advantage of technological change, others are slower to react and may fall victim to the change and faster-moving competitors.

Demographic and Social Changes

Chapter 1 discussed demographic and labor market trends, including the age, education, diversity, and composition of the workforce. From a strategic standpoint, changes in the labor supply can limit the strategies available to firms. High-growth companies, in particular, may find it difficult to find the talent they need to expand their businesses. Unemployment rates vary by sector, but the shortage of talent in high-skill jobs continues to create strategic challenges for firms. The U.S. Department of Labor indicates that 11 of the 15 fastest-growing occupations between now and 2024 will require some level of postsecondary education. These labor force trends illustrate the importance of monitoring demographic changes as a part of environmental scanning—a core responsibility of human resource managers.

Likewise, societal attitudes are constantly changing the business landscape for firms in all industries. We talked about social changes in Chapter 1 such as people's changing priorities toward work, job security, or environmental and sustainability concerns. How do these changes affect a firm's strategies, and its HR strategies in particular?

Consider the auto industry. In response to both environmental sustainability concerns and technological innovation, Ford and GM have been doubling down on their investments in electric vehicles (EVs), and forecast that they will move away from internal combustion engines in the coming decades.[11]

Legal and Regulatory Changes

Finally, government and legislative issues, including laws and administrative rulings, have a broad effect on the business environment. Any one change can require firms and entire industries to dramatically adjust their strategic directions. For example, the U.S. government banned the slaughtering of horses in 2006. U.S. horse slaughterhouses were forced to exit this line of business or move their plants abroad, such as to Mexico—not an inexpensive proposition. And it's not just U.S. laws and regulations that are a part of the business environment: The laws of other countries also affect businesses.

2.3b The Competitive Environment

The competitive environment is narrower than the business environment, and firms have a greater ability to affect it. As Figure 2.2 shows, the **competitive environment** consists of a firm's specific industry, including the industry's customers, rival firms, new entrants, substitutes, and suppliers. Firms analyze their competitive environment so that they can adapt to or influence the nature of competition. A general rule of thumb about

competitive environment
Consists of a firm's specific industry, including the industry's customers, rival firms, new entrants, substitutes, and suppliers.

Figure 2.2 The Five Forces Framework

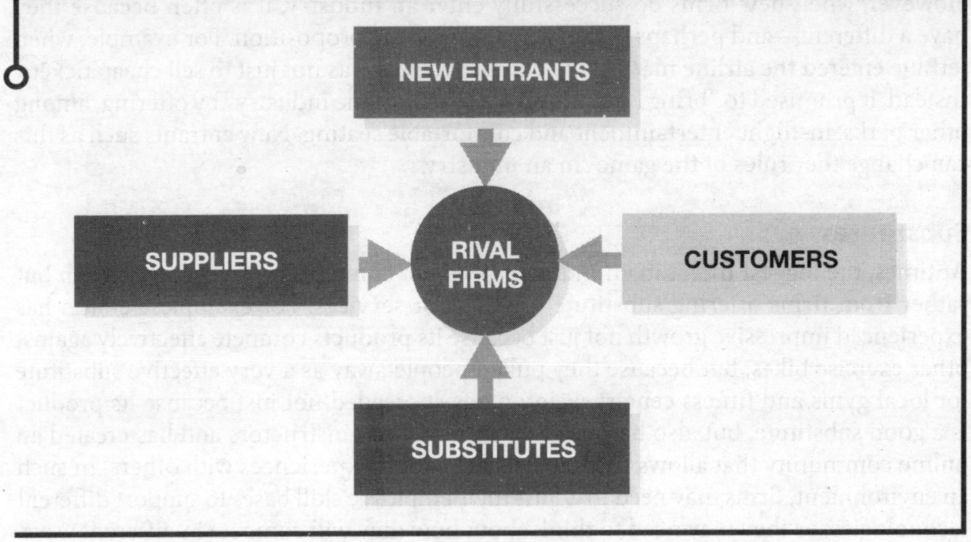

this analysis is: The more power each of these forces has, the less profitable (and therefore attractive) the industry will be. Let us look at each of the five forces in turn.

Customers

A firm's strategy should focus on creating value for customers, who often want different things. For example, in the hotel industry, business travelers may want convenient locations with meeting facilities. Vacationers may want resort locations with swimming pools, golf courses, and luxury spas. Other travelers may just want an inexpensive room next to the highway. The point is that increasingly "one size does not fit all," so organizations need to know how they will provide value to their customers. That is the foundation for strategy, and it influences the kinds of skills and behaviors needed from employees.

Rival Firms

Perhaps the most obvious element of industry analysis is examining the nature of competition. We can think of many examples of intense rivalries, such as between Coke and Pepsi. Sometimes firms compete head to head, with almost identical strategies, in what researchers have indelicately called a "red ocean." Often a more successful approach is to search out "blue oceans," which are pure and uncontested. Cirque du Soleil, for example, is widely recognized as developing a blue ocean strategy in the entertainment world that combines elements of a circus with aspects of a Broadway show. The result gives the company a unique position relative to its rivals.[12]

New Entrants

New companies can sometimes enter an industry and compete well against established firms, and sometimes they cannot. Think of the beer industry. Every year, a substantial number of micro-brews and craft breweries spring up with unique characteristics that give them a chance to compete against the big players like Anheuser Busch (AB InBev) and MillerCoors. Some make it and some don't. To protect their positions, established firms try to create entry barriers that will keep new firms out of their industries. Sometimes the barriers are erected through effective branding, and at other times through scale, which gives bigger companies cost advantages over their smaller competitors. However, when new firms do successfully enter an industry, it is often because they have a different—and perhaps better—customer value proposition. For example, when JetBlue entered the airline market, the company's goal was not just to sell cheap tickets. Instead, it promised to "bring humanity back to the airline industry" by offering, among other perks, in-flight entertainment and comfortable seating. New entrants such as this can change the "rules of the game" in an industry.

Substitutes

At times, the biggest threat in an industry does not come from direct competition but rather from firms offering substitute products or services. For example, Peloton has experienced impressive growth not just because its products compete effectively against other exercise bikes, but because they pulled people away as a very effective substitute for local gyms and fitness centers. Peloton has succeeded not just because its product is a good substitute, but also because it has world-class instructors and has created an online community that allows users to co-create their experiences with others. In such an environment, firms may need to adjust their employee skill bases to support different technologies, or they may need to think about how they will compete in different ways.

Suppliers

Organizations rarely create everything on their own, but instead have suppliers that provide them with key inputs. These inputs can include raw materials for production, money (from banks and stockholders), information, and people. This last factor—people, or labor as it is historically called—has direct implications for strategic planning and HRP.

Stakeholders

Stakeholders are the key people and groups that have an interest in a firm's activities and can either affect them or be affected by them. A firm's primary stakeholders include its investors, employees, customers, suppliers, and creditors. Primary stakeholders have a direct stake in the firm and its success. A firm's *secondary stakeholders* have less of a stake but can nonetheless affect or be affected by the company. Secondary stakeholders include the community in which the firm operates, the government, business groups, and the media.

stakeholders
Key people and groups that have an interest in a firm's activities and that can either affect them or be affected by them.

Firms have to analyze and balance the interests of their various stakeholders. For example, laying off employees will often result in lower costs for a firm, at least in the short term. But if the cuts are too severe and affect a firm's service, for instance, customers are likely to suffer, as will investors and creditors. The community could suffer as well.

One way a firm attempts to balance the interests of its shareholders is by determining how a strategic action is likely to impact each group. For which group is the action critical? For which group is the action less critical? As Figure 2.3 shows, the firm may want to involve or at least consult primary shareholders in major strategic actions. In contrast, secondary stakeholders can be monitored and informed. So, for example, if a firm is considering developing a new product, its suppliers, creditors, and employees should definitely be involved and consulted about the move. Secondary stakeholders, such as the community and the media, can merely be informed about the new strategy when appropriate and their responses monitored.

Figure 2.3 Primary Stakeholders versus Secondary Stakeholders

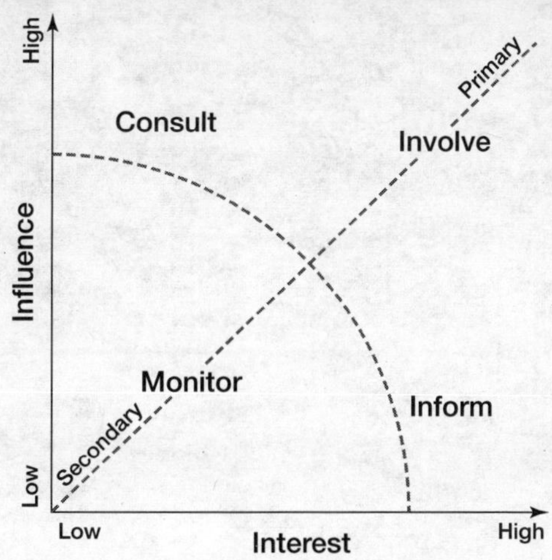

2.3c HR's External Analysis

benchmarking
The process of looking at your practices and performance in a given area and comparing them with those of other companies.

Because strategic management is ultimately aimed at creating a competitive advantage, many firms also evaluate their performance against other firms. **Benchmarking** is the process of looking at your practices and performance in a given area and comparing them with those of other companies. To accomplish this, a benchmarking team collects metrics on its own company's performance and those of other firms to uncover any gaps. These gaps help determine the causes of performance differences the team can use to map out a set of best practices.

The target company for benchmarking does not need to be a competitor. For example, when Xerox wanted to learn about excellent customer service, it benchmarked L.L. Bean. By working with noncompeting companies, Xerox was able to get access to information that a competitor would not divulge.

Sources of information about the changes in a firm's external environment, particularly the external supply of labor, are invaluable for both operational and strategic reasons. HRP, in turn, has to focus on both. At an operational level, changes in the labor supply directly affect hiring plans in the area where the organization is located or plans to locate. To be closer to younger, educated workers, who will lead them into the digital future, many companies have moved to "tech hubs" like Silicon Valley; Austin, Texas; or Boston.[13]

Similarly, with a "maturing" workforce, HRP must consider the implications for their recruitment and replacement policies. Other "barometers" of the labor market include migration in and out of the area and the mobility of the population, the firm's demand for specific skills, unemployment rates, the educational level of the workforce, government labor regulations, and so on.

The analysis of the external labor market is aided by published documents. In the United States, the U.S. Department of Labor reports a variety of data, including unemployment rates, labor force projection figures, and population characteristics.[14] The *Monthly Labor Review* and *Occupational Outlook Handbook,* both published by the Bureau of Labor Statistics (BLS), contain information on jobholder characteristics and predicted changes in the workforce. In addition, local chambers of commerce and individual state development and planning agencies can assist both large organizations

Amazon.com has tested technology to deliver small packages to people's houses via drones. How might drone delivery change Amazon's competitive environment? Which changes in customers, new entrants, substitutes, and suppliers might result? How would it affect the firm's HR practices?

Amazon/UPI/Newscom

and new business ventures by providing them with a labor market analysis of their target areas.

Conducting an external labor analysis also includes gauging the talent in your own industry—in other words, looking at the competitive environment for labor. From which schools are the top candidates being recruited? Which firms are attracting the most candidates, and why? Which firms end up hiring the best candidates, and why? Astute HR managers who track their firms' hiring and recruiting metrics relative to the competition are invaluable sources of this kind of external labor "intelligence." Attending industry conventions and talking to your company's suppliers about business and employment trends are other informal ways of gathering competitive intelligence. So are interviews with job candidates. Simply asking candidates who turned down job offers why they did so can yield a great deal of information. We will talk more about this aspect of HR in Chapter 5.

The HR benchmarks, or metrics, a firm collects fall into two basic categories: human capital metrics and HR metrics. Human capital metrics assess aspects of the workforce, whereas HR metrics assess the performance of the HR function itself. For its clients, the management consulting company PwC publishes monthly and annual human capital benchmarking information, which includes metrics from almost 900 companies.

Highlights in HRM 1 shows some of the basic HR metrics that companies use. Most larger companies rely on software to track their HR metrics over time. Figure 2.4 shows

Figure 2.4 An Example of an HR Dashboard

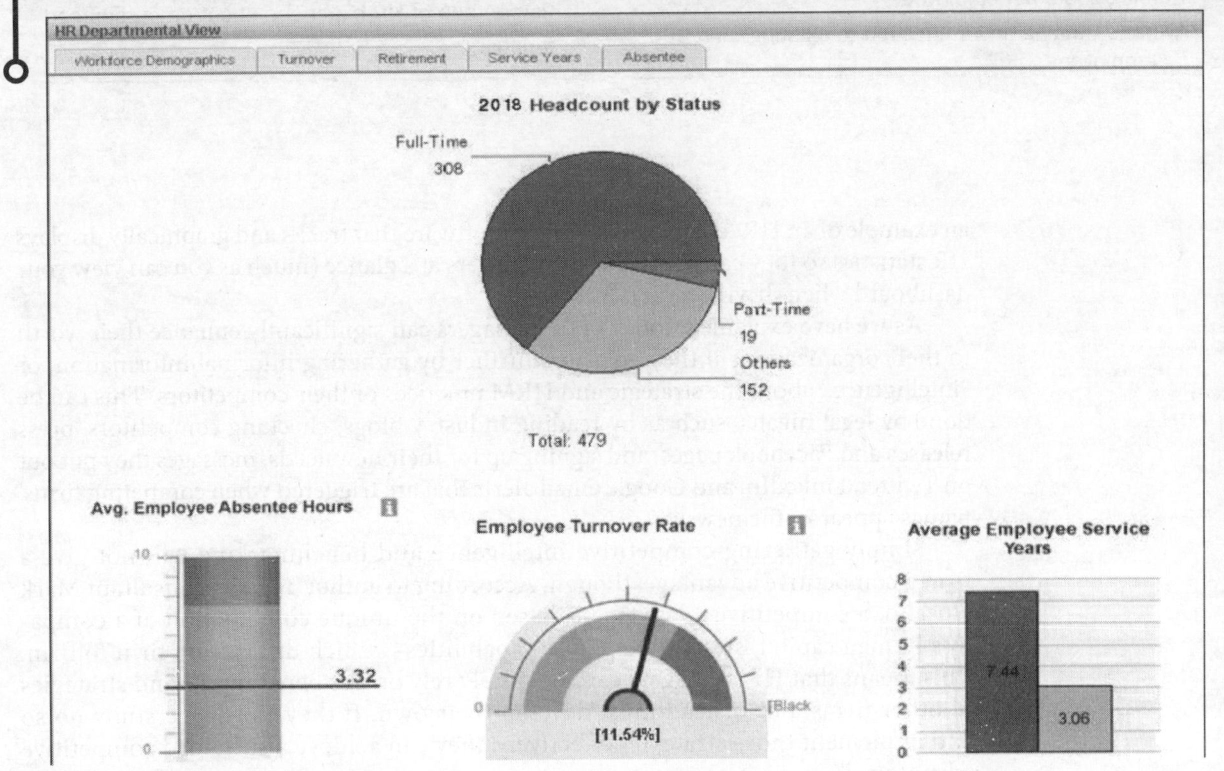

HRM Metrics

Different companies rely on different HRM metrics, depending on their strategic objectives. The following are some of the metrics mostly commonly used by firms:

General

- Total payroll and benefits costs
- Payroll and benefits costs per employee
- Revenue earned per employee
- Average salary per employee
- Total employee hours worked
- Hours worked per employee
- Employees per department
- Average employee tenure
- Average employee age
- Employee absenteeism rate

Training and Development

- Total training costs
- Training costs per employee
- Average training hours provided to existing employees
- Average training hours provided to new hires

Hiring and Turnover

- Total separation costs (severance, etc.)
- Separation costs per employee
- Average time to fill (a position)
- Quality of fill
- Cost per fill
- Percentage of positions filled internally
- Percentage of new hires retained for 90 days
- Employee turnover rate
- Voluntary turnover rate
- Involuntary turnover rate

HR Department Metrics

- Number of employees per HR professional
- Total HR expenses
- HR expenses per employee
- Percentage of HR expenses spent on outsourced functions

an example of an HR "dashboard"—that is, software that tracks and graphically displays HR statistics so they can be viewed by managers at a glance (much as you can view your dashboard when driving a car).

As we have explained, today's HR managers can significantly enhance their worth to their organizations if they go a step further by gathering informal information, or "intelligence," about the strategic and HRM practices of their competitors. This can be done by legal means, such as by reading industry blogs, checking competitors' press releases and Facebook pages, and signing up for their newsfeeds, messages they put out on Twitter, LinkedIn, and Google email alerts that are triggered when competing firms' names appear in the news.

Simply gathering competitive intelligence and benchmarking will not give a firm a competitive advantage, though. According to author and HR consultant Mark Huselid, a competitive advantage is based on the unique combination of a company's human capital, strategy, and core capabilities—which differ from firm to firm. This means that HR managers cannot simply rely on the benchmarks and strategies of other firms, but instead must develop their own. If they can successfully do so and implement those strategies effectively, they can achieve a sustained competitive advantage.[15]

2.4 Step Three: Internal Analysis

LO3

What criteria must be met if firms are to achieve a competitive advantage through their employees?

Now let's take the next step in strategic planning. When you decided on your major, you not only had to look at careers that were in demand, but also had to take a hard look at yourself and what you're good at relative to other people. For example, software engineers make a lot of money and are in great demand. But do you have what it takes to become one? Similarly, organizations analyze their own strengths and weaknesses, and compare these with external opportunities and threats.

2.4a Core Capabilities

A growing number of experts now argue that the key to a firm's success is establishing a set of **core capabilities**—abilities that distinguish an organization from its competitors and create value to customers. You can think of **value creation** as a cost-benefit scenario: Value = benefits − costs. For example, why would customers buy from your firm versus another? What benefits do customers get from your firm relative to the costs they incur? In what areas does your organization excel as far as potential customers are concerned? Most firms recognize that there is a small set of three to six core capabilities that are most critical to differentiating them from competitors. Core capabilities can consist of a combination of three resources: (1) processes, (2) systems (technologies), and (3) people.

core capabilities
Integrated knowledge sets within an organization that distinguish it from its competitors and that deliver value to customers.

value creation
What a firm adds to a product or service by virtue of making it; the amount of benefits provided by the product or service once the costs of making it are subtracted.

Processes are standard ways of working or routines for how work will be done and results will be accomplished. For example, when Intermountain Healthcare (IHC), a hospital and clinic chain in Utah, analyzed the firm's capabilities, it found that less than 10 percent of its processes accounted for more than 90 percent of the cost, time, and quality of its health care. Consequently, IHC chose to focus on these processes to enhance its core capabilities.

Top-notch systems are also part of the core capabilities equation. They include information systems, databases, proprietary technologies, and the like. Great systems and technologies are a core capability of Amazon .com—one that has resulted in a significant competitive advantage for the firm. UPS's Orion system is another example of a great system. The Orion system takes into account all of the packages a UPS driver has to deliver and determines out the fastest route for doing so.

Last, but certainly not least, people are a key resource that underlies a firm's core capabilities. Particularly in knowledge-based industries such as the software and information services industries, success depends on "people-embodied know-how." Know-how includes the knowledge, skills, and

AP Images/Ben Margot

FedEx's workers support their employer's core capabilities. That helps FedEx stand out from its competitors and deliver added value to its customers.

abilities of employees that are most critical for executing the firm's plan to create the most value for customers and whose skills are difficult to replicate or replace.

In recent years, a number of companies that previously relied on standard plans for recruiting and managing their employees have sought to design more tailored plans to address the individual needs of employees so they will be in a better position to help execute their firms' strategies. Microsoft enables certain types of employees to design their own career paths. For example, the company offers software engineers both management-focused and technical specialist career tracks, and allows them to move back and forth between the two.

2.4b Sustaining a Competitive Advantage through People

Organizations can achieve a sustained competitive advantage if they have resources—particularly people—that meet the following criteria[16]:

1. *The resources must be valuable.* People are a source of competitive advantage when they improve the efficiency or effectiveness of the company. Value is increased when employees find ways to decrease costs, provide something unique to customers, or some combination of the two. To improve the bottom line, REI and Southwest Airlines are among the companies that empower and motivate their workers to spark their creativity.
2. *The resources must be rare.* People are a source of competitive advantage when their knowledge, skills, and abilities are not equally available to competitors. Companies such as Facebook, Four Seasons Hotels, and Virgin America therefore invest a great deal to hire and train the best and the brightest employees to gain an advantage over their competitors.
3. *The resources must be difficult to imitate.* People are a source of competitive advantage when the capabilities and contributions of a firm's employees cannot be copied by others. Disney and Starbucks are both known for creating unique cultures that get the most from their employees (through teamwork) and are difficult to imitate.
4. *The resources must be organized.* People are a source of competitive advantage when their talents can be combined and deployed to work on new assignments at a moment's notice. As you learned in Chapter 1, companies such as IBM, GE, and Procter & Gamble closely "track" employees and their talents. As a result, these firms are able to quickly reassign talent to different areas of their companies and around the world as needed.

These four criteria highlight the importance of people and show the closeness of HRM to strategic management.

2.4c Types of Talent and Their Composition in the Workforce

A related element of internal analysis for organizations that compete on capabilities is determining the types of talent needed and their composition of a firm's current workforce. As we have indicated, managers need to determine whether people are available internally to execute their organization's strategy. Managers have to make tough decisions about whom to employ internally, whom to contract externally, and how to manage different types of employees with different skills who contribute in different ways to the organization.

As shown in Figure 2.5, different skill groups in any given organization can be classified according to the degree to which they create strategic value and are unique to the organization. This figure depicts the departments for an Australian biotechnology firm and the quadrants in which those groups fall. As a general rule, managers often consider contracting externally (or outsourcing) skill areas that are not central to the firm's core capabilities. HRP plays an important role in helping managers weigh the costs and benefits of using one approach to employment versus another. Evidence from research suggests that employment relationships and HR practices for different employees vary according to which segment they occupy in a matrix like that shown in Figure 2.5.

Strategic Knowledge Workers

Strategic knowledge workers tend to have unique skills directly linked to the company's strategy and are difficult to replace, such as research and development scientists in a pharmaceuticals company or computer scientists in a software development company.

Figure 2.5 Mapping Human Capital

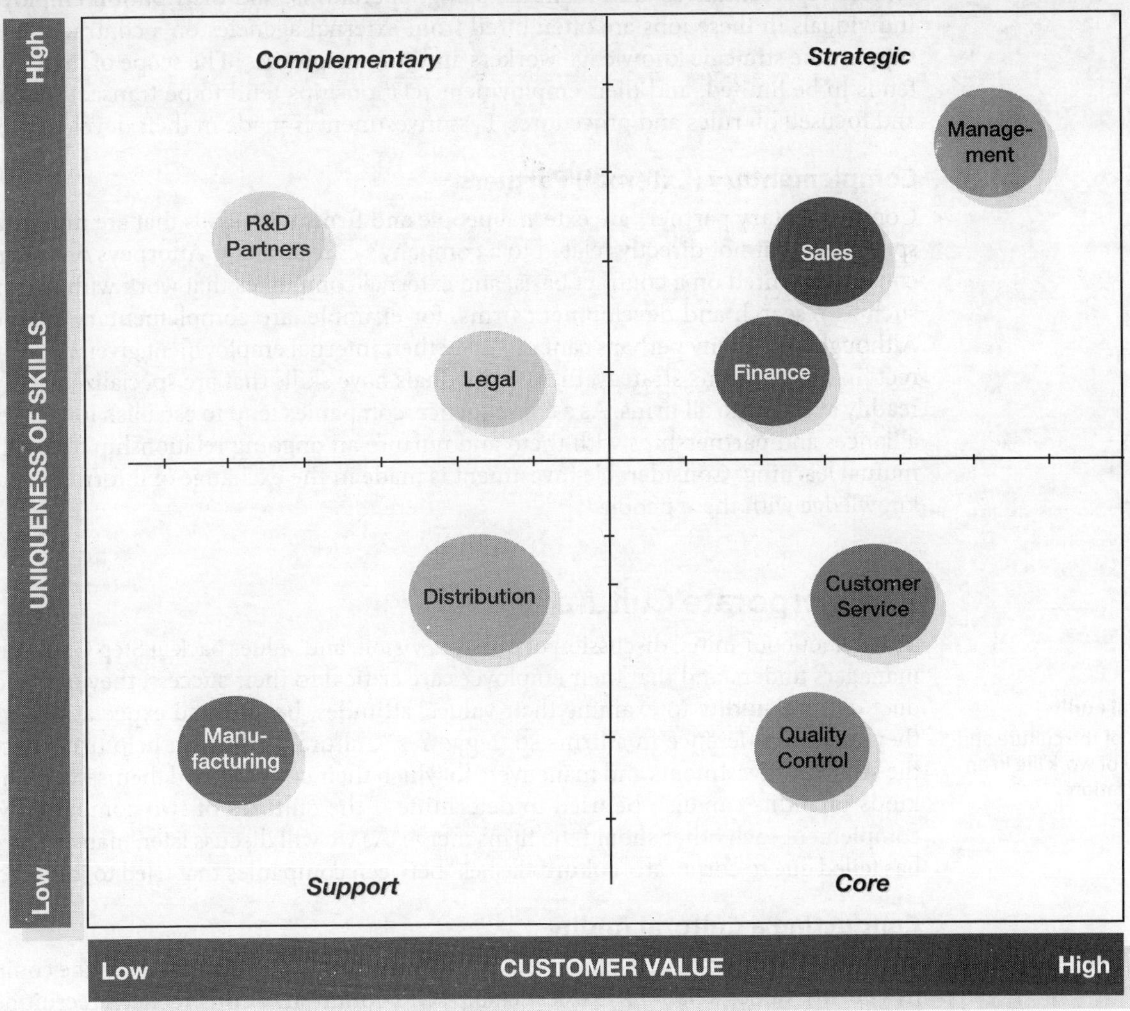

These employees typically engage in knowledge work that involves considerable autonomy. Companies tend to make long-term commitments to these employees, investing in their continuous training and development, and perhaps giving them an equity stake in the organization.

Core Employees

Core employees have skills that are quite valuable to a company but not particularly unique or difficult to replace; examples are salespeople in a department store or truckdrivers for a courier service. These workers tend to be employed in traditional types of jobs. Because their skills are transferable, it is quite possible that they could leave to go to another firm. As a consequence, managers frequently invest less to train and develop these employees and focus more on paying them for their short-term performance achievements.

Supporting Workers

Supporting workers typically have skills that are less central to creating customer value and generally available in the labor market; examples are clerical workers, customer service representatives, and manufacturing, operations, and distribution employees. Individuals in these jobs are often hired from external agencies on a contract basis to support the strategic knowledge workers and core employees. The scope of their duties tends to be limited, and their employment relationships tend to be transaction based and focused on rules and procedures. Less investment is made in their development.

Complementary (External) Partners

Complementary partners are external people and firms with skills that are unique and specialized but not directly related to a company's core strategy. Attorneys on retainer, consultants hired on a contract basis, and external companies that work with the firm, such as research and development firms, for example, are complementary partners. Although a company perhaps cannot justify their internal employment given their indirect link to the firm's strategy, these individuals have skills that are specialized and not readily available to all firms. As a consequence, companies tend to establish longer-term alliances and partnerships with them and nurture an ongoing relationship focused on mutual learning. Considerable investment is made in the exchange of information and knowledge with these people.[17]

2.4d Corporate Culture

Think about our initial discussion of mission, vision, and values back at Step One. When managers understand that their employees are critical to their success, they often conduct **cultural audits** to examine their values, attitudes, beliefs, and expectations. Can they make a difference in a firm's strategy? Yes. Cultural audits can help firms decide the strategic investments and maneuvers to which their cultures lend themselves. These kinds of audits can also be used to determine if the cultures of two companies will complement each other should the firms merge. As we will discuss later, many a merger has failed due to corporate "culture clashes" between companies that tried to join forces.

cultural audits
Audits of the culture and quality of work life in an organization.

Conducting a Cultural Audit

To conduct a cultural audit, employees can be surveyed about such things as the company's norms, values, relationships, leadership style, communication practices, recruitment and evaluation practices, measurements, pay and benefit programs, and the like. The survey may also include a series of open-ended questions about the company's practices.

The goal is to determine whether these practices hinder or support the organization's purpose.[18] In addition, cultural audits can be used to determine whether there are different groups, or subcultures, within the organization that have distinctly different views about the nature of the work and how it should be done. To prevent legal and ethical breaches, some firms conduct cultural audits that ask employees questions about the degree of fear associated with meeting their firms' revenue goals and incentive plans that could encourage unethical or illegal behavior.[19]

According to author James Clawson, leaders who focus on employees' values, attitudes, beliefs, and expectations are more effective than those who simply focus on workers' behaviors or thought processes. This makes sense. Recall from Chapter 1 the story about the entrepreneur who tripled his sales but, because he took his staff for granted, was then muscled out of the market by a competitor. If a firm lacks a clear idea of how employees view the organization, no matter how great the organization's plans are, those plans might never be successfully executed and sustained.

2.4e Forecasting

An internal analysis of an organization can reveal a great deal about where it stands today. However, things change. In an important sense, strategic planning is about managing that change. Managers must continually forecast both the needs and the capabilities of the firm in the future to do an effective job at strategic planning. As Figure 2.6 shows,

Figure 2.6 Model of HR Forecasting

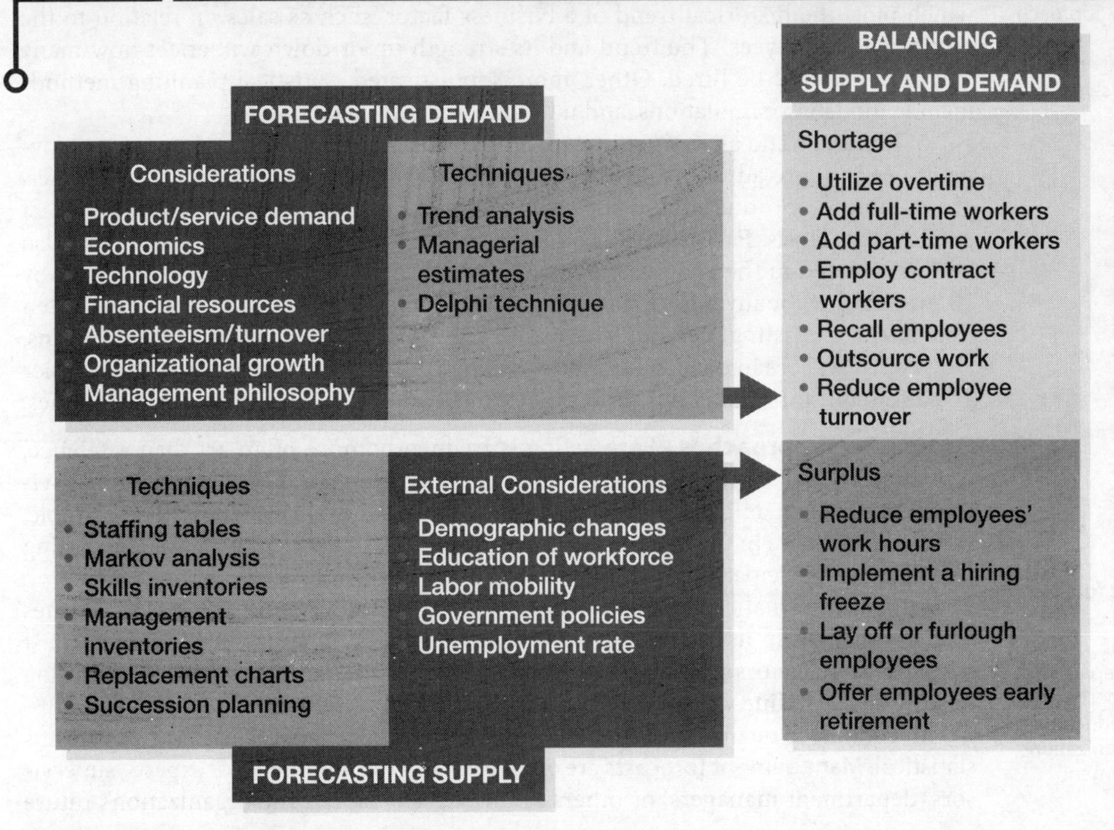

managers focus on (at least) three key elements: (1) forecasting the demand for talent, (2) forecasting the supply of talent, and (3) balancing supply and demand considerations.

Consider for a moment the high costs of not forecasting—or of forecasting poorly. If job vacancies are left unfilled, the resulting loss in productivity can be very costly, particularly when you consider the amount of time it takes to hire and train replacement employees. As pointless as it may sound, it's not uncommon for employees to be laid off in one department while applicants are hired for similar jobs in another department. Poor forecasting that leads to unnecessary layoffs also makes it difficult for employees to accurately assess their own career prospects and development. When this happens, a firm's more competent and ambitious workers will be inclined to seek employment at other firms where they perceive better career opportunities.[20]

On the plus side, accurate forecasting provides the kind of information managers need to make sound decisions. It can help them ensure that they have the right number and right kinds of people in the right places at the right times, doing things that provide value to both the organization and the employees.

Forecasting a Firm's Demand for Employees

As we have indicated, a variety of factors, including a firm's competitive strategy, technology, structure, and productivity, will affect its demand for talent, including both the number of employees and the types of skills and knowledge they bring. There are two approaches to HR forecasting—quantitative and qualitative—which we discuss next.

trend analysis
A quantitative approach to forecasting labor demand based on a factor such as sales.

Quantitative Approaches. Quantitative forecasting approaches involve the use of statistical or mathematical techniques. One commonly used method is a **trend analysis**, which plots the historical trend of a business factor, such as sales, in relation to the number of employees. The trend and its strength up or down will affect how many employees should be hired. Other, more sophisticated statistical planning methods include modeling, simulations, and multiple predictive techniques.

Whereas a trend analysis relies on a single factor (such as sales) to predict employment needs, more advanced methods combine several factors, such as interest rates, gross domestic product, the disposable income of consumers, and sales, to predict employment levels. Factors such as a firm's strategy and "what if" scenarios can also be incorporated in the analysis. For example, if the firm wants to increase its sales by 10 percent, how many additional salespeople should it hire? Larger companies often implement forecasting methods such as these with the help of analysts and statisticians. However, advances in data collection technology and software have also made it easier and affordable for smaller businesses to use more sophisticated forecasting techniques.

Qualitative Approaches. Forecasting is frequently more of an art than a science, providing inexact approximations rather than absolute results. The ever-changing environment in which an organization operates contributes to this situation. For example, estimating changes in the demand for a firm's products or services is a basic forecasting concern, as is anticipating economic changes.

management forecasts
The opinions (judgments) of supervisors, department managers, experts, or others knowledgeable about the organization's future employment needs.

A firm's internal changes are critical, too. A community hospital that anticipates internal changes in its technology or how the facility is organized or managed must consider these factors when it forecasts its staffing needs. Also, the forecasted staffing needs must be in line with the organization's financial resources.

In contrast to quantitative approaches, qualitative approaches to forecasting are less statistical. **Management forecasts** are often based on the judgments of experts, supervisors, department managers, or others knowledgeable about the organization's future employment needs. For example, at Souplantation and Sweet Tomatoes, a national soup, salad, and bakery chain, each restaurant manager is responsible for their store's employment forecasts. Another qualitative forecasting method, the Delphi technique, attempts to decrease the subjectivity of forecasts by soliciting and summarizing the judgments of a preselected group of individuals. HR personnel can apply this method by developing a list of questions to ask the managers in their companies. Highlights in HRM 2 lists some good questions to ask.

Ideally, forecasting should include the use of both quantitative and qualitative approaches. Numbers without context—including the context supplied by skilled HR professionals who understand the business and can analyze and interpret the data—are less useful. "The most important software is the one running between your ears," explains one HR director in regard to qualitative forecasting.[21]

Forecasting the Supply of Employees

Just as an organization must forecast its future requirements for employees, so it must also determine whether sufficient numbers and types of employees are available to staff the openings it anticipates having. As with demand forecasts, this process involves both tracking current employee levels and making future projections about those levels.

staffing table
A table that shows a firm's jobs, along with the numbers of employees currently occupying those jobs and future (monthly or yearly) employment requirements.

markov analysis
A method for tracking the pattern of employee movements through various jobs in a firm.

Staffing Tables and Markov Analyses. An internal supply analysis can begin with staffing tables. A **staffing table** shows a firm's jobs, along with the numbers of employees currently occupying those jobs (and perhaps future employment requirements derived from demand forecasts). Another technique, called a **Markov analysis**, shows the percentage and actual number of employees who remain in each of a firm's jobs from year to year and the proportions of those promoted, demoted, transferred, or who have quit. As Figure 2.7 shows, a Markov analysis can be used to track the pattern of employee movements through various jobs and to develop a transition matrix for forecasting the labor supply.

Figure 2.7 Hypothetical Markov Analysis for a Retail Company

2018 → 2019	Store Managers	Asst. Store Managers	Section Managers	Dept. Managers	Sales Associates	Exit
Store Managers (n = 12)	90% 11					10% 1
Assistant Store Managers (n = 36)	11% 4	83% 30				6% 2
Section Managers (n = 96)		11% 11	66% 63	8% 8		15% 14
Department Managers (n = 288)			10% 29	72% 207	2% 6	16% 46
Sales Associates (n = 1440)				6% 86	74% 1066	20% 288
Forecasted Supply	15	41	92	301	1072	351

Transition percentage / Actual number of employees

2 Highlights in HRM

HR Planning and Strategy Questions to Ask Business Managers

- What are our pressing business issues today? What are our competitors' organizational strengths? How do we compare?
- What core capabilities do we need to win in our markets?
- What are the required knowledge, skills, and abilities we need to execute the winning strategy?
- What are the barriers to achieving the strategy?
- What types of skills and positions will be required or no longer required?
- Which skills should we have internally versus contract with outside providers?
- What actions need to be taken to align our resources with our strategy priorities?
- What recognition and rewards are needed to attract, motivate, and retain the employees we need?

Sources: Adapted from Agilent Technologies for The Conference Board and the Society for Human Resource Management.

Forecasting the supply of human resources available to a firm requires managers to have a good understanding of employee turnover and absenteeism. We have included formulas for computing turnover and absenteeism rates in an appendix to this chapter. Also included in the appendix is a formula for calculating a metric called **quality of fill**. It was developed because managers understand that simply having "bodies" in place is not enough. The quality-of-fill metric attempts to measure how well new hires are performing so the company will have enough top performers to propel it toward its strategic objectives. We will show you how it is calculated in Chapter 5, when we discuss recruiting metrics.

quality of fill
A metric designed to measure how well new hires who fill positions are performing on the job.

Skill Inventories and Management Inventories. Staffing tables, a Markov analysis, turnover rates, and the like tend to focus on the *number* of employees in particular jobs. Other techniques are more oriented toward the *types* of employees and their skills, knowledge, and experiences. **Skill inventories** can be prepared either manually or using a human resources information system that lists each employee's education, past work experience, vocational interests, specific abilities and skills, compensation history, and job tenure. The inventories allow an organization to quickly match job openings with existing employees' backgrounds. When data are gathered on managers, these inventories are called *management inventories.*

skill inventories
Files of personnel education, experience, interests, skills, and so on that allow managers to quickly match job openings with employee backgrounds.

Replacement Charts and Succession Planning. Skill and management inventories (talent inventories) can be used to develop employee **replacement charts**, which list current jobholders and identify possible replacements should openings occur. Figure 2.8 shows an example of how an organization might develop a replacement chart for the managers in one of its divisions. The chart provides information on the current performance and promotability of possible replacements.

replacement charts
Listings of current jobholders and people who are potential replacements if an opening occurs.

A replacement chart can be used side by side with other pieces of information for **succession planning**—the process of identifying, developing, and tracking talented individuals so that they can eventually assume top-level positions in the firm. The strategy and consulting firm Accenture has developed an application listing its employees, where they are based, and their individual areas of expertise. This application helps managers with deployment decisions. It also makes it easier for Accenture's employees who do not necessarily know each other or work together to collaborate with one

succession planning
The process of identifying, developing, and tracking key individuals for executive positions.

Figure 2.8 An Executive Replacement Chart

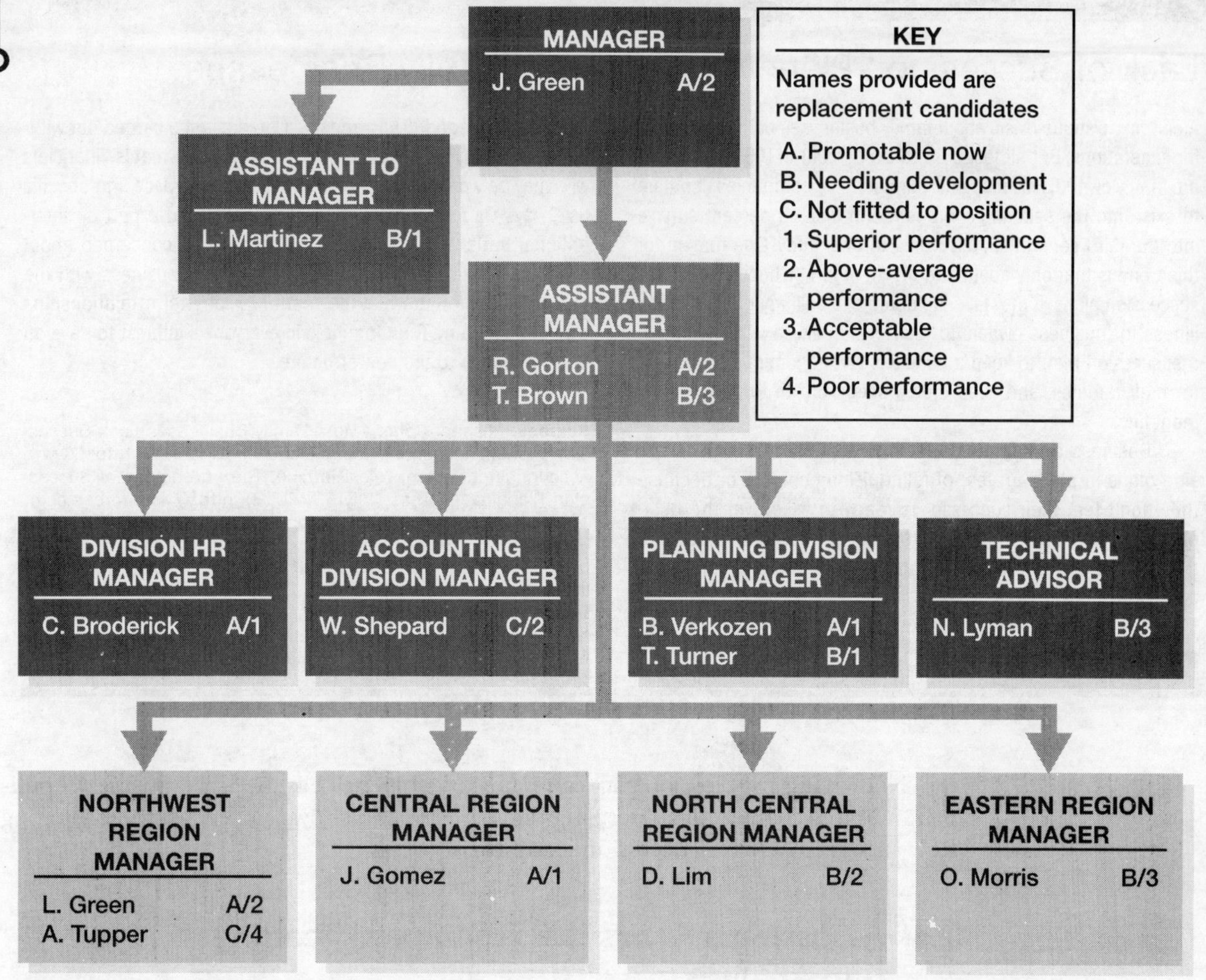

another. Succession planning and replacement charts are often developed in conjunction with **talent reviews**—strategic meetings to determine if a company has the human resources it needs to compete in the future.

talent reviews
Strategic meetings to determine if a company has the human resources it needs to compete in the future.

Human resource managers frequently lament that they have trouble keeping managers, including CEOs, focused on succession planning. It's possible that because CEOs are increasingly being recruited from outside the firm, they are less concerned with internal succession planning than they are with "bringing in their own people." And, of course, because the workforce is becoming increasingly mobile, some managers wonder why they should develop employees internally, only to see those individuals eventually leave the organization, when they can recruit qualified talent from the outside. Managers may also get distracted by putting out immediate fires, especially in tough times, explains Ranjay Gulati, a Harvard Business School professor. Instead of planning for succession, they look externally for "savior" types of employees to rescue their organization because they have been unable to adapt to the competition.[22]

Small Business Application

Lack of Succession Planning Threatens Family Businesses

A certain mystique exists about family businesses being carried on for generations, But although 80 to 90 percent of U.S. businesses are family owned, less than one-third of these companies continue to exist into the second generation, and just 10 percent survive into the third generation, according to one study. One reason for this trend is that only about one-fourth of family businesses have succession plans. It may take the death of a colleague or a sudden illness for business owners to realize that, like a will, they need a succession plan to keep a business going, continue to provide for their families, and keep their workers out of the unemployment line.

Business owners are sometimes reluctant to put succession plans in place for fear of relinquishing control, or because they don't feel their successor is ready to take over the business. In some cases, there is no clear successor. Sometimes the next generation just is not enthusiastic about joining the family business.

Even with a business owner willing to relinquish the reins and a well-chosen successor waiting in the wings, an actual transition plan is still needed. "[Any transition] needs to be carried out without causing any alarm to the other stakeholders—that is, financiers who may be worried that such a change may increase firm-specific risk," says Dr. Ashraf Mahate, an economist and expert on international trade and finance. "Suppliers may be concerned about providing future credit facilities or even doing business with the company. Customers may be fearful of long-term relationships with the company. Therefore, it is in everyone's interest to have an orderly change to the new structure."

Sources: Michael Cohn, "Most Family Businesses Lack Succession Plans," *Accounting Today* (January 14, 2017), http://www.accountingtoday.com; "Next in Line: The Advantages of Succession Planning," *Forbes* (July 30, 2013), http://www.forbes.com; "Canada's Banks Eye Succession Plans for Boomers," Reuters (December 20, 2012), http://www.reuters.com; Manoj Nair, "Succession Planning Is the Key," gulfnews.com (January 19, 2011), http://gulfnews.com; Ernesto J. Poza, *Family Business* (Boston: South-Western/Cengage Learning, 2010), 85–89; Don Schwerzler, "Family Succession Plan First," http://www.family-business-experts.com/family-succession-plan.html.

Not having a succession plan can imperil a small firm, as the Small Business Application in this chapter illustrates. Highlights in HRM 3 shows a checklist for evaluating how successful a firm's succession planning is.

2.4f Assessing a Firm's Human Capital Readiness: Gap Analysis

human capital readiness
The process of evaluating the availability of critical talent in a company and comparing it to the firm's supply.

Once a company has assessed both the supply and demand for employee talent, it can begin to understand its **human capital readiness**. Any difference between the quantity and quality of employees required versus the quantity and quality of employees available represents a gap that needs to be bridged.

Figure 2.9 shows how a pharmaceutical company, "PharmaCo" (a pseudonym), approached its assessment of human capital readiness. Similar to our discussion in the preceding sections, managers began by identifying the company's core capabilities and the key people and processes critical to those capabilities. The company identified nine key job "families." For each of these critical job families, managers identified the critical knowledge, skills, and behaviors necessary to build the core capabilities. They then determined the number of people required for these positions, as well as the number who were currently qualified for them. As the lower portion of the figure shows, the company's human capital (HC) readiness ranged between 63 percent for bioscientists and 100 percent for chemical and mechanical engineers. Once such an assessment of a firm's human capital readiness is complete, managers have a much better foundation for establishing their strategy going forward and the specific requirements for developing the talent needed to execute the strategy.[23]

Succession-Planning Checklist

RATE THE SUCCESS OF YOUR SUCCESSION PLANNING

For each characteristic of a best-practice succession-planning and management program appearing in the left column below, enter a number to the right to indicate how well you believe your organization manages that characteristic. Ask other decision makers in your organization to complete this form individually. Then compile the scores and compare notes.

Characteristics of a Best-Practice Succession-Planning and Management Program		How Would You Rate Your Organization's Succession-Planning and Management Program on the Characteristic?				
Your organization has successfully...		Very Poor (1)	Poor (2)	Neither Poor Nor Good (3)	Good (4)	Very Good (5)
1	Clarified the purpose and desired results of the succession-planning and management program.					
2	Determined what performance is required now for all job categories in the organization by establishing competency models.					
3	Established a means to measure individual performance that is aligned with the competencies currently demonstrated by successful performers.					
4	Determined what performance is needed in the future by establishing future competency models for all job categories.					
5	Created an ongoing means by which to assess individual potential against future competency models.					
6	Established a means by which to narrow gaps through the use of individual development plans (IDPs).					
7	Created a means to follow up and hold people accountable.					
8	Created a means by which to document competence and find organizational talent quickly when needed.					
9	Created and sustained rewards for developing people.					
10	Established a means by which to evaluate the results of the succession planning and management program.					

Total (add up the scores for items 1–10 and place in the box on the right)

SCORES

50–40	Congratulations. The succession-planning and management program in your organization conforms with best practices.
39–30	Pretty good. Your organization is on the way toward establishing a first-rate succession-planning and management program.
29–20	Okay. While your organization could make improvements, you appear to have some of the major pieces in place for a succession-planning and management program.
19–10	Not good at all. Your organization is probably filling positions on an as-needed basis.
9–0	Give yourself a failing grade. You need to take steps immediately to improve the succession-planning and management practices of your organization.

Source: From William J. Rothwell, "Putting Success into Your Succession Planning," *Journal of Business Strategy* 23, no. 3 (2002): 32–37. Republished with permission—Thomson Media, One State Street, 26th Floor, New York, NY 10004.

Figure 2.9 Assessing a Firm's Human Capital

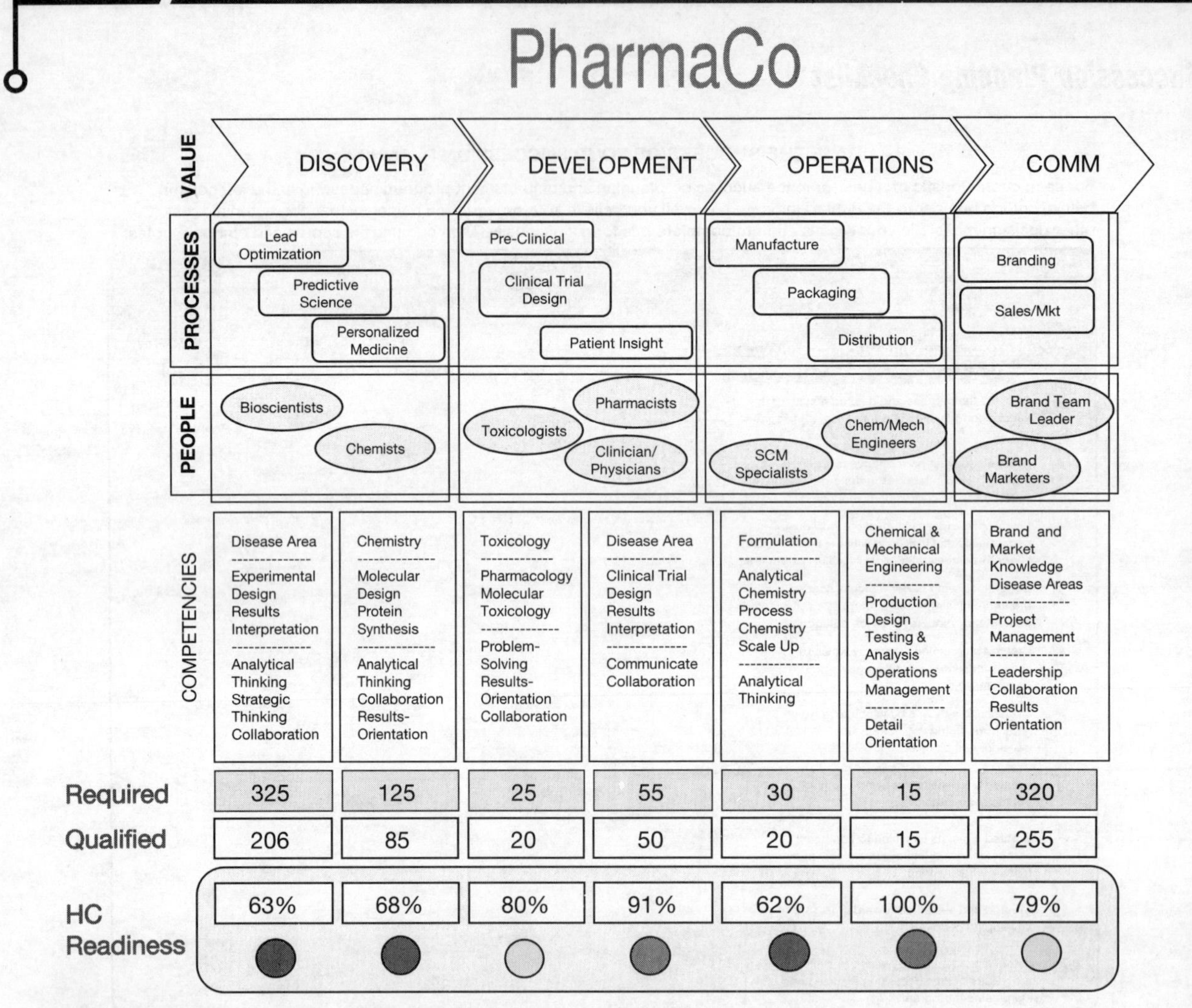

LO4 Explain the difference between a firm's corporate strategy and business strategy. Why do firms need to look at both aspects?

2.5 Step Four: Formulating a Strategy

Think once again about your education, your major, and career choices. After you looked at possible careers, the opportunities they presented, and your ability and desire to do them, you probably had to formulate a strategy for pursuing one of them by choosing a college. When you graduate, you will have to formulate a strategy for successfully landing a job in your field. Similarly, after managers have analyzed the internal strengths and weaknesses of a firm, as well as its external opportunities and threats, they have the information they need to formulate corporate, business, and HR strategies for the organization.

Strategy formulation builds on a SWOT analysis, discussed earlier in the chapter. A SWOT analysis can help a company move from formulating a strategy, to devising a plan, to capitalizing on opportunities, to counteracting threats, to alleviating internal weaknesses. Figure 2.10 is an example of a SWOT analysis done for the women's clothing brand Liz Claiborne.

Figure 2.10 An Example of a SWOT Analysis for Liz Claiborne

Strengths	Weaknesses
• Brand recognition • Understanding customer needs • New product lines • Advertising scheme • Product diversification strategy • Tailor to changing needs • Preferences and lifestyles	• Changing consumer needs • Highly competitive market • Long lead time for bringing new styles to market • Clothing line is complete success or costly mistake
Opportunities	**Threats**
• Overseas markets • Worldwide advertising • Entering the large-size consumer market • Designing mix-and-match outfits • Men's sportswear	• Key competitors • Strict government regulations • Changing shopping patterns • Quota restrictions

Source: "Liz Claiborne SWOT Analysis," WikiSWOT, http://www.wikiswot.com.

2.5a Corporate Strategy

A firm's corporate strategy addresses the question of "where" the company should compete, its markets and business segments, as well as its sets of customers, partners, and competitors. Some firms choose a concentration strategy that focuses on only a portion of the industry. Visteon Corporation specializes in electronics, climate, and powertrain technologies for the automotive industry. In contrast, Henry Ford at one time owned everything from the ore mines needed to make steel for his cars, all the way down to the showrooms in which they were sold.

Growth and Diversification

Emerging and growing companies execute their strategies differently than mature companies or those in decline. As companies grow, they often formulate geographic, volume, and product-expansion strategies. HR planning is vital to these decisions because achieving growth requires three related elements: (1) increased employee productivity, (2) a larger number of employees, and (3) employees developing or acquiring new skills. Thus, a firm's staffing, training, employee motivation efforts, and the like can either enable the company to grow or limit its potential.

As companies diversify into new businesses, managers are faced with a "make or buy" decision, just as Henry Ford was. That is, should they develop the capabilities in-house to produce their products, or should they contract externally for them, or at least parts of them? When IBM entered the personal computer market in the early 1980s, it contracted with (then startup companies) Intel and Microsoft to make the hardware and operating systems for its PCs. This decision did not rest solely on HR issues, but they were certainly an important part of the equation.

Eventually IBM got out of the PC business altogether by selling its PC product lineup to the Chinese computer manufacturer Lenovo. Today IBM develops custom technology services for businesses, which it believes will be more profitable in the long run and a harder product for competitors to imitate. To help accomplish the strategy, IBM bought up dozens of business-service–related companies and hired their talent.

Some companies diversify far beyond their core businesses. Danaher, for example, is a widely diversified global company with businesses in life sciences and diagnostics, dental, test and measurement, environmental, and industrial technologies. To manage such a diverse portfolio, Danaher has invested heavily in developing its general managers, who have the talent and leadership abilities needed to manage such a diverse portfolio.

Mergers and Acquisitions

As we have explained, the world has seen a host of mergers and acquisitions in recent years. Examples of firms that joined forces in this way include AT&T and TimeWarner, CVS and Aetna, and Dow Chemical and DuPont, among others. When companies merge, they can often streamline their costs by eliminating duplicate staff functions, such as duplicate accounting, finance, and HR departments, for example.

However, many mergers end up being risky transactions because they do not go well (measured by return on investment, shareholder value, and the like). Often the failure is due to cultural inconsistencies, as well as conflicts among the managers of each firm. The failed merger between the German firm Daimler-Benz (manufacturer of Mercedes Benz vehicles) and Chrysler in 1998 is an example. Although the German portion of the firm had superior technology, reportedly it was less than eager to share its know-how with its American counterparts. Problems like this one point directly to the importance of effective HR planning prior to—and during—the merger process.

Strategic Alliances and Joint Ventures

Sometimes firms do not acquire or merge with another firm but instead pursue cooperative strategies such as a strategic alliance or joint venture. Especially when firms enter into international joint ventures, the issues of culture (both company culture and national culture) become paramount. On the front end, HR plays a vital role in assessing the compatibility of the would-be partners' cultures and potential problems. As the alliance is formed, HR helps select key executives and develops teamwork across the respective workforces. In addition, HR is typically involved in the design of performance assessment and mutual incentives for the alliance.

2.5b Business Strategy

While we often think about corporate strategy as selection of a domain to target, business strategy is viewed in terms of domain navigation. It focuses more keenly on how the company will compete against rival firms to create value for customers. Companies can increase the value they offer customers by decreasing the costs of their goods and services or by increasing the benefits their products provide (or some combination of the two). Their business strategies reflect these choices.

Low-Cost Strategy: Compete on Productivity and Efficiency

A low-cost strategy means keeping your costs low enough that you can offer an attractive price to customers relative to your competitors. Organizations such as Walmart, TJ Maxx, and Spirit Airlines have been very successful in competing based on a low-cost strategy by focusing on efficiency, productivity, and minimizing waste. These types of companies often are large enough to take advantage of economies of scale in the production and distribution of goods and services so they can sell them at lower prices, which leads to higher market shares, volumes, and (hopefully) profits. However, even a low cost leader must offer a product or service that customers find valuable. As one CEO put it, "You can make a pizza so cheap that no one will buy it."[24] Ultimately, organizations need to use a cost strategy to increase value for customers, rather than to take it away.

A low-cost strategy is linked to HR planning in several ways. The first connection has to do with productivity. A common misconception about low-cost strategies is that they inevitably require cutting labor costs. On the contrary, many companies pay their employees "top dollar" but gain back cost advantages because of those workers' excellent productivity. That is, they get a terrific "bang for the buck": Either they produce more with the workforce they have, or they produce the same amount with a smaller workforce.

According to Peter Cappelli, who heads the Center for Human Resources at the Wharton School at the University of Pennsylvania, the productivity of the best-performing staffs can be 5 to 20 *times* higher than the productivity of the worst-performing staffs, depending on the industry. Both Costco and Sam's Club have low-cost, high-volume strategies. However, one study found that the pay and benefits to Costco's employees far outstripped those earned by Sam's Club employees—but so do Costco's profits per employee. In addition, employee turnover and the costs associated with it are much lower for Costco.[25] Similarly, Billy Beane, the general manager of Major League Baseball's Oakland A's, became famous for making the most of the A's small payroll. Beane did so by carefully choosing and developing players and using them more strategically than other teams with bigger payroll budgets.

The second way that low-cost strategies are linked to HR pertains to outsourcing. Companies may consider contracting with complementary (external) partners that can perform particular activities or services equally well (or better) at a lower cost. However, to do so effectively, organizations need to have a clear understanding of their core processes and skills. All too often, a firm bases outsourcing decisions on costs alone. This can lead to detrimental effects if the skills base of the firm's employees suffers and its core capabilities erode.

Differentiation Strategy: Compete on Unique Value Added

Another way to compete is by providing something unique and distinctive to customers, such as a high-quality product, innovative features, speed to market, or superior service. The Ritz-Carlton's commitment to quality and luxury, FedEx's focus on speed and flexible delivery, and Apple's emphasis on innovation and product development are all easily recognized examples of differentiation strategies.

Each of these strategies is rooted in HRM. Companies that focus on service, for example, need to identify and support ways to empower employees to serve customers better. Relative to companies that emphasize low cost and efficiencies, differentiating companies will bend the rules a bit more and customize products and services to let the customer "have it their way." In place of rigid rules, Starbucks looks for prospective employees with the ability to make good decisions on their own. Similarly, Nordstrom is legendary for an employee handbook consisting of just a single 5×8 index card that reads: "Welcome to Nordstrom. Rule #1. Use your good judgment in all situations. There will be no additional rules."

Loyal shoppers crowd Nordstrom's because of the company's excellent service.

2.5c HR Strategy

A firm's HR strategy must work in tandem with its corporate and business strategies. For example, decisions must be made about the composition of the workforce. Getting the right number and the right kinds of people in the right places at the right times doing things that will benefit both them and the firm is no small task. Too often firms focus on their most prominent employees, such as their strategic knowledge workers, because they are in the best position to implement a firm's strategies. But these workers alone can't make or break a company. Engineering may develop a great product, but if the firm's customer service representatives do a poor job of helping customers with the good or service, its sales will suffer—as will the company.

Instead, the firm must focus on all of its talent, including support employees, contractors, temporary employees, and complementary partners and how they mesh with one another. Each group of workers differs in terms of the human capital they bring, the expectations placed on them, the extent to which they are trained and developed, and so on. Subcultures will also emerge from the various groups. The firm's engineers may have a whole different way of working and viewing the firm than, say, the company's customer representatives. HR managers have to examine and analyze these differences. They and line managers must then formulate a plan that blends the firm's structure, culture, operations, technology, and "people management" practices in ways that facilitate a firm's competencies and drive its strategies forward.[26]

LO5

Why is it often difficult for a firm to match its strategy to HR deliverables?

2.6 Step Five: Executing a Firm's Strategy

As the old saying goes, "Well begun is half done"—but only half. Like any plan, formulating the appropriate strategy is not enough. You can't be successful by just planning to go to college and formulating a strategy to get a career. You have to actually do it. As you know, this is easier said than done.

Similarly, strategy alone does not differentiate high-performing firms from their low-performing counterparts. The true differentiator between winners and losers turns out to be not what their strategies were, but how well the strategy was executed. Yet half of managers in one survey said there is a substantial gap between their organization's ability to develop a vision and strategy, and then actually execute it. Former Honeywell

CEO Larry Bossidy noted in his book *Execution* that people believe they understand the concept—"it's about getting things done"—but when asked *how* they get things done, "the dialogue goes rapidly downhill."

Figure 2.11 shows the "4As" required to successfully execute a strategy. They are as follows:

- *Alignment.* Alignment occurs in an organization when it has a clear strategic intent, its staff has shared performance expectations, and they are accountable for the results. We will talk about alignment more later in the chapter.
- *Agility.* Execution is not a "one and done event." It's also about competing tomorrow. The key to execution increasingly depends on being agile, nimble, and proactive in the face of change. As the great former hockey player Wayne Gretsky used to say, "I don't skate to where the puck is. I skate to where the puck is going to be."
- *Architecture.* A firm's architecture consists of its structures, processes, and systems. Ideally, they should be simple and streamlined so as to propel the firm to success. But too often a firm's architecture can end up being overly complicated and stifle its capacity to function effectively.
- *Ability.* As we have explained, products and processes are easy to duplicate. Talent is not. Strategy execution (and ultimately growth and profitability) depend on a firm's talent capacity—a talented group of leaders, managers, and employees working together in an engaged and collaborative way.

As Figure 2.11 shows, execution is the process of combining these four elements of human capital and organizational capital.

Figure 2.11 The 4As Framework of Execution Capability

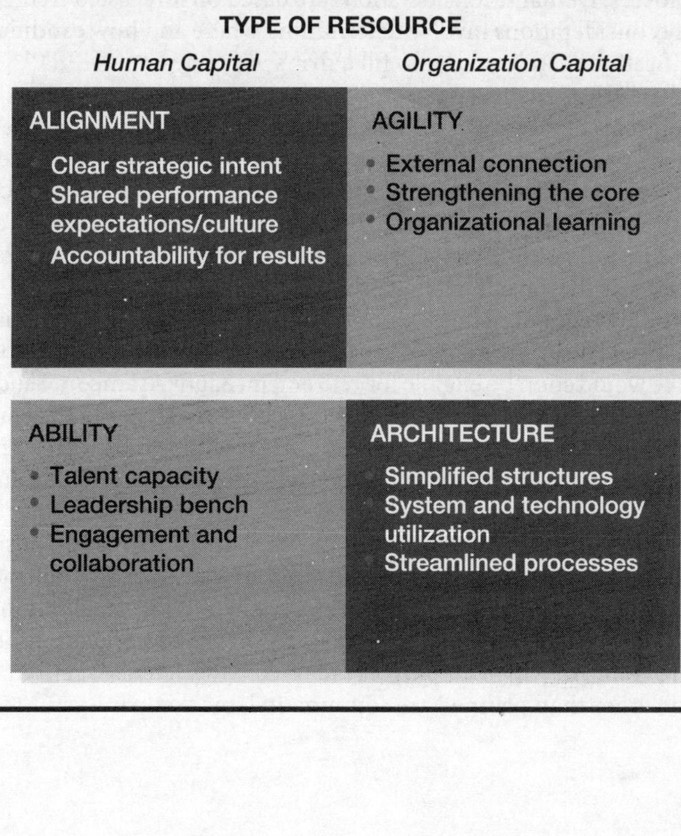

2.6a HR's Role in Strategy Execution

In addition to formulating corporate- and business-level strategies, managers need to "translate" strategic priorities into functional areas of the organization (such as marketing, manufacturing, human resources, and the like). Human resources management is instrumental to almost every aspect of strategy execution, whether it pertains to the organization's structure, systems, style, skills, staff, or shared values.

Remaining Agile

Like the firm as a whole, HR has to focus on ensuring agility when the environment changes. HR agility can be achieved in two primary ways: coordination agility and resource agility.

Coordination agility is the ability to rapidly reallocate resources to new or changing needs. Through HRP, managers can anticipate upcoming events, keep abreast of changes in legal regulations, forecast economic trends, spot competitors' moves, and the like. With enough advance notice, managers can move people into and out of jobs, retrain them for new skill requirements, and modify the kinds of incentives they use. The use of a contingency workforce composed of part-timers, temporary employees, and complementary partners also helps achieve coordination flexibility.[27]

Resource agility, in contrast, results from having resources that can be used in different ways and people who can perform different functions in different ways. Cross-training employees, rotating them into different jobs, and using teams are all efforts that focus on building a flexible workforce.

Reconciling Supply and Demand

Part of remaining agile includes reconciling the firm's demand for its products with its supply of employees. Demand considerations are based on forecasted trends in business activity. Supply considerations involve determining where and how candidates with the required qualifications can be found to fill a firm's vacancies.

To meet their HR demands, organizations have many staffing options at their disposal. For example, they can recruit and hire full-time employees as well as reduce their turnover, have employees work overtime, recall laid-off workers, use temporary or contract employees, and outsource or offshore some of their business processes. Some of the ways firms say they are, or will, attract and retain baby-boomers to avoid future labor shortages include offering employees flexible scheduling, health care, and long-term care benefits as they eventually retire.[28]

If its labor shortages are acute, a company may have to make special efforts to develop talent from the ground up. For example, knowing that nearly 40 percent of its aging workforce would soon be eligible for retirement, Saudi Aramco, a Saudi-owned oil company, developed a system of hiring top high school graduates in the country, sponsoring their college educations, and providing them with job training. The company employs 400 planners to analyze its workforce needs for the next decade and beyond.[29]

When forecasts show a surplus of employees, organizations often restrict their hiring, reduce their employees' work hours or furlough them, and consider layoffs. Across-the-board pay cuts are sometimes utilized in lieu of or in addition to layoffs. Some organizations try to reduce their workforces by relying on attrition, which is a gradual reduction of employees that occurs due to employee resignations, retirements, and deaths. Programs in which employees are offered "sweetened" retirement benefits to leave a firm earlier than planned are common in large companies.

As we have discussed, organizations must be constantly prepared to exit and enter new lines of business, restructure, outsource, offshore, and sometimes downsize either because they have too many employees or because their employees have the wrong skill sets. Decisions about employee layoffs are usually based on seniority and/or performance. In some organizations, especially in Japanese firms, seniority is more likely to be the primary consideration. In other organizations, factors such as an employee's ability and productivity take precedence over seniority. In the case of unionized organizations, the criteria for determining who will be laid off are typically set forth in union agreements and based on seniority. Unions recognize seniority because they feel that their members deserve certain rights proportionate to the years they have invested in their jobs.

Employers also often recognize the seniority of employees who are not unionized, though. But one disadvantage of doing so is that the less-competent employees can end up receiving the same rewards and security as the more-competent employees. Also, the practice of using seniority as the basis for deciding which workers to lay off can inadvertently have a disparate impact on women and people from other underrepresented groups, who often have less seniority than other groups of workers.

When firms are downsizing, HR managers must ensure that the decision-making process does not violate any laws, of which there are many. They range from laws designed to protect employees from underrepresented groups and older employees from being unfairly targeted to laws requiring companies of a certain size laying off a certain number of employees to give them ample warning, ranging from 60 days to 6 months. Firms must also comply with government provisions, giving some workers who have been laid off and their families the right to purchase temporary health care coverage at group rates. We will talk more about these laws in Chapter 13.

2.7 Step Six: Evaluation

LO6 What steps does the firm need to take to execute its strategy and measure the results?

You probably know someone who graduated, went to work in a particular field, assessed their success (or lack of it) in that field, and then decided to do something else for a living. The same sort of reevaluation and assessment is an important function for businesses as well. At one level, it might seem that assessing a firm's effectiveness is the final step in the planning process. In reality, it is also the first step. Planning is cyclical, of course, and while we have somewhat conveniently placed evaluation at the end of this chapter, the information it provides actually gives firms inputs they need for the next cycle in the planning process.

To evaluate their performance, firms need to establish a set of "desired" objectives as well as the metrics they will use to monitor how well their organizations delivered against those objectives. These objectives can include achieving a certain level of productivity, revenue, profit, market share, market penetration, customer satisfaction, and so forth. For example, after Barnes and Noble saw lackluster sales for its Nook e-reader, the company reevaluated its strategy and began contemplating selling its Nook division or partnering with another company to produce it. Today the firm develops different tablets in conjunction with Samsung and Lenovo.

2.7a Evaluating a Firm's Strategic Alignment

Evaluation involves all aspects of the business, but in particular there needs to be a clear alignment between HR and the requirements of an organization's strategy. HR policies and practices need to achieve two types of fit: vertical and horizontal.[30]

Vertical Fit/Alignment

Vertical fit (or *vertical alignment*) focuses on the connection between the business's objectives and the major initiatives undertaken by HR. On the one hand, as we noted earlier, if a company's strategy focuses on achieving low cost, its HR policies and practices need to encourage employees to work more efficiently and be more productive. On the other hand, if the organization competes through innovation and development of new products, then its HR policies and practices should be more aligned with the notion of fostering creativity and flexibility.

When ensuring alignment, firms have to ask themselves whether their capabilities, including those of the employees, are truly aligned with their value proposition. Most observers would agree that Tom Monahan, founder of Domino's, was able to change the pizza industry not because he created a better product, but because he was able to offer a different value proposition—delivery in 30 minutes or the pizza was free—and then created the capability to "deliver" against that promise. Case Study 2 discusses Domino's alignment in more detail.

Horizontal Fit/Alignment

In addition to vertical fit (alignment), managers need to ensure that their HR practices are all aligned with one another internally to establish a configuration that is mutually reinforcing. The entire range of the firm's HR practices—from its job design to staffing, training, performance appraisal, and compensation—need to focus on the *same* objectives. Too often, one HR practice will emphasize one objective, whereas another HR practice will emphasize another. Charles Schwab & Co. faced this situation. The company has a reputation in the financial services industry for developing a culture of teamwork that has been important to its strategy. However, when it changed its compensation strategy to provide more rewards to its high-performing brokers, the firm sent mixed signals to its employees. Which is more important: teamwork or individual high flyers?[31]

Figure 2.12 shows an example of how organizations can assess the horizontal fit among their HR practices. There are essentially three steps. First, managers need to identify the key workforce objectives they hope to achieve. These objectives might include loyalty, customer service, productivity, and creativity. Second, managers must identify each of the HR practices used to elicit or reinforce those workforce objectives (job design, staffing, training, appraisal, compensation, and so on). Third, managers need to evaluate each HR practice on a scale of –5 (not supportive) to +5 (supportive). By tallying up the ratings across managers, organizations can get a very clear idea of which HR practices are working together to achieve the workforce objectives and which are not.

Keep in mind that horizontal fit is a necessary, but insufficient, cause of strategic alignment. A company could have nearly perfect alignment among its HR practices, and they still might not be aligned with the competitive strategy. For that reason, it is important for managers to assess both vertical and horizontal fit.

Strategic Alignment and the Balanced Scorecard

balanced scorecard (BSC)
A measurement framework that helps managers translate strategic goals into operational objectives.

One tool for mapping a firm's strategy to ensure strategic alignment is the **balanced scorecard (BSC)**. Developed by Harvard professors Robert Kaplan and David Norton, the BSC is a framework that helps managers translate their firms' strategic goals into operational objectives. The model contains four related cells: (1) financial, (2) customer, (3) processes, and (4) learning. The logic of the BSC is firmly rooted in HRM. People management and learning help organizations improve their internal processes (and

Figure 2.12 Assessing Horizontal Fit

ORGANIZATION	WORKFORCE OBJECTIVES: SALES PRODUCTIVITY	CUSTOMER SERVICE	MERCHANDISE INFORMATION	STOCK MAINTENANCE	TOTAL
Structure/Workflow					
• Cross-functional teams	3	2	0	−1	4
• Rotation (Depts.)	3	3	−1	−1	4
Staffing					
• Test battery	2	2	1	1	6
• Select for experience	5	3	2	2	12
Training					
• Retail selling skills	4	5	1	1	11
Rewards					
• Results appraisal	5	−4	−2	−5	−6
• Individual incentives	5	−5	−3	−5	−8
Leadership					
• Corporate	3	3	1	0	7
• Store manager	4	2	2	2	10
Technologies					
• Merchandise IS	5	2	5	1	13
• Daily postings	4	−3	4	−1	4
	43/55	10/55	10/55	26/55	57/220
			SYSTEM COHERENCE		26%

FUNCTIONAL COHESION

5 = Strongly supports the priority
0 = Neutral
−5 = Strongly counterproductive

capabilities), enabling them to provide excellent customer service. Internal processes—product development, service, and the like—are critical for creating customer satisfaction and loyalty, and for ensuring efficient productivity that contains costs for better financial performance. Customer value creation, in turn, drives up revenues, which enhances profitability.

Figure 2.13 shows how this might work at Starbucks. In each cell, Starbucks would identify the key metrics that help translate its strategic goals to operational imperatives. For example, under customer metrics, Starbucks might look at the percentage of repeat customers, number of new customers, growth rate, and so forth. Under people metrics, managers might measure the number of suggestions provided by employees, participation in the Starbucks stock-purchase program, employee turnover, training hours spent, and the like. Each of these cells links vertically. People management issues such as rewards, training, and suggestions can be linked to efficient processes (such as brewing the perfect cup and delivering top-notch customer service). These processes then lead to higher customer loyalty and better growth. Growth and customer loyalty, in turn, lead to higher profitability and market value.

Figure 2.13 Building the Metrics Model

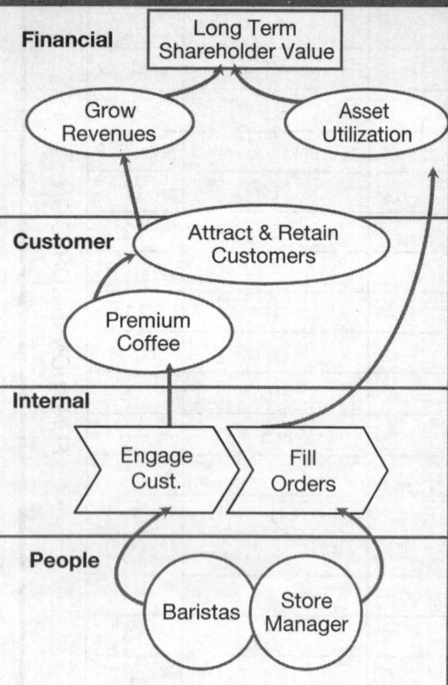

Strategic Theme: "The Third Place"	Objectives	Measures	Targets	Initiatives
Financial	• Profitability • Grow revenues • Improve cost structure	• Market value • Revenue • General and administrative costs as % of Sales	• 20% Compound annual growth rate (CAGR)	• Intl. growth • U.S. growth
Customer	• New customers • More value to current (now) customers	• Number of customers • New stores • Repeat customers • Same store sales	• 20 mill/week • 1500/yr • 15% 2/wk • 13% growth	• Store develop • New products • Customer loyalty program • New partners
Internal	• Friendly service • Accurate orders • Fast fulfillment	• Customer feedback • First time right • Order fulfillment	• 90+ satisfaction • 99+% accurate • <3 minutes	• Customer engagement • Automation
People	• Store manager stability • Barista engagement	• Average tenure • Voluntary turnover • Engagement survey	• Mgr >3 yrs • Barista 80% • 85% rating	• 40 hrs. training • Employee awards

Summary

LO 1 Strategic human resources management (SHRM) integrates strategic planning and HR planning. It can be thought of as the pattern of HR deployments and activities that enable an organization to achieve its strategic goals. The firm's mission, vision, and values provide a perspective on where the company is headed and what the organization can become in the future. Ideally, they clarify the long-term direction of the company and its strategic intent.

LO 2 Analyzing the firm's external environment is central to strategic planning. Benchmarking is the process of looking at the firm's practices and performance and then comparing them to those of the competitors. Environmental scanning is the systematic monitoring of major external forces influencing the organization, including forces in the business environment and the competitive environment. Changes in the external environment have a direct impact on the way organizations are run and people are managed. Some of these changes represent opportunities, and some of them represent real threats to the organization.

LO 3 Conducting an internal analysis to gauge the firm's strengths and weaknesses involves looking at a firm's core capabilities, its talent and composition in the firm, and the firm's corporate culture. An internal analysis enables strategic decision makers to assess the organization's workforce—its skills, cultural beliefs, and values.

An organization's success increasingly depends on the knowledge, skills, and abilities of its employees, particularly as they help establish a set of core capabilities that distinguish the organization from its competitors. When employees' talents are valuable, rare, difficult to imitate, and organized, a firm can achieve a sustained competitive advantage through its people. HRP is a systematic process that involves forecasting the demand for labor, performing supply analysis, and balancing supply and demand considerations. Quantitative and qualitative methods help a firm identify the number and type of people needed to meet the organization's goals.

LO 4 After managers have analyzed the internal strengths and weaknesses of the firm, as well as its external opportunities and threats, they have the information they need to formulate corporate, business, and HR strategies for the organization. A firm's corporate strategy identifies the markets in which it will compete, against whom, and how. The firm's business strategy is viewed in terms of domain navigation—that is, how the company will compete against rival firms to create value for customers. A firm's HR strategies and practices should be aligned with its corporate and business strategies.

LO 5 Formulating an HR strategy is only half of the HR battle: The strategy must also be executed. HRM is instrumental to almost every aspect of strategy execution, whether it pertains to the organization's structure, systems, style, skills, staff, or shared values. Like the firm as a whole, HR has to focus on ensuring agility when the environment changes. Employment forecasts must also be reconciled against the internal and external labor supplies the firm faces. Executing the HR strategy may involve having current employees work overtime; hiring full-time, part-time, or contract employees; downsizing employees; furloughing them; and outsourcing or offshoring. In the face of a labor shortage, the firm might have to reformulate its long-term and short-term strategic plans or find ways to develop employees "from the ground up."

LO 6 To evaluate their performance, firms need to establish a set of "desired" objectives as well as the metrics they will use to monitor how well their organizations delivered against those objectives. The objectives might include achieving certain levels of productivity, revenue, profit, market share, market penetration, customer satisfaction, and so forth. Issues of measurement, alignment, fit, and agility are central to the evaluation process. Firms use strategy mapping, the balanced scorecard (BSC) tool, and various HR-related metrics for these purposes.

Key Terms

balanced scorecard (BSC)
benchmarking
business environment
competitive environment
core capabilities
core values
cultural audits
environmental scanning
human capital readiness
human resource planning (HRP)
management forecasts
Markov analysis
mission
quality of fill
replacement charts
skill inventories
staffing tables
stakeholders
strategic human resource management
strategic planning
strategic vision
succession planning
talent reviews
trend analysis
value creation

Discussion Questions

LO 1 Identify the three key elements of the human resources planning model and discuss the relationships among them.

LO 2 Which external forces influence a firm's strategy?

LO 3 Which criteria must be met if firms are to achieve a competitive advantage through their employees?

LO 4 Explain the difference between a firm's corporate strategy and business strategy. Why do firms need to look at both aspects?

LO 5 Why is it often difficult for a firm to match its strategy to HR deliverables?

LO 6 What steps does the firm need to take to execute its strategy and measure the results?

HRM Experience

Customizing HR for Different Types of Human Capital

Part of strategic planning is mapping an organization's human capital. When we look at the strategic value of a person's skills as well as their uniqueness, we soon discover that organizations include many different kinds of workers who have very different kinds of skills. Some are core knowledge workers; some are more traditional job-based employees; some are contract workers; and some are external partners. It is unlikely that a firm would manage all of these employees the same way; there are differences in HR practices for different groups. That is not bad, but it makes the job of HR managers more difficult.

Assignment

Following are descriptions of three different employees. How would you characterize each worker? What role does each play when it comes to the organization's strategy?

Sobadia Bascomb is a highly talented computer programmer for Applied Software Solutions. She is among an elite set of engineers in the computer industry doing leading-edge work on advanced computer modeling. The firm's CEO, Bill Ding, believes the future of the company rests on the innovative work that Sobadia and her team are doing. He worries that someone might lure her away to work for them, so he wants to give her all the room she needs to grow and stay committed to the firm.

Calvin Duff is a salesperson on the retail side of the firm. He has daily contact with customers and is responsible for making sales and communicating with service personnel. Make no mistake: To many customers, Calvin and his coworkers are the "face" of the company. Always on the lookout for a better position, Calvin has thought about working for PeachTree Computing, Applied Software Solutions' main competitor. Other salespeople have found that they can leave Applied Software Solutions and get "up to speed" easily at other firms. Their skills are very transferable, and the transition is not difficult. Bill Ding and other managers at the company recognize this fact, so they try to keep salespeople loyal and productive, while recognizing that many of them will eventually leave.

Chandra Singh is a part-time administrative assistant for Applied Software Solutions. She handles routine typing and filing work for the company, particularly in peak periods in the summer and around the holidays. She usually works for a few weeks at a time and then takes time off. The executives at the company have considered either outsourcing her job to an agency or automating it through a new computer system. But for now things are steady.

CASE STUDY 1 How a Strategy Change Led to Nike's Formation

Nike, the world's most famous athletic company, didn't start out by making Air Jordans. In fact, it didn't make shoes at all. It distributed them.

Nike actually began as company called Blue Ribbon. It was founded in 1964 by Phil Knight, a runner from Oregon, along with his former college track coach, Bill Bowerman. At the time, the running shoe market was dominated by the German firms Adidas and Puma. However, Knight and Bowerman had become intrigued by new lighter, lower-cost running shoes made in Japan. Bowerman had always tinkered with shoe designs to try to make his runners faster. Meanwhile, Knight had just earned an MBA from Stanford University and was looking for a way to combine what he loved— sports—with work. So, the two men each chipped in $500, and began importing and selling Tiger-brand shoes (now Asics) made by the Japanese company Onitsuka.

Blue Ribbon's start wasn't glamorous. Bowerman and Knight began by selling the shoes out of their cars at local track meets. But runners liked the new lighter shoes, and the company started earning a profit. Eventually the business did well enough it was able to hire some employees, most of whom were passionate runners like the owners.

For about a decade Blue Ribbon's strategy worked well. Business grew, and the company even opened its own store in Santa Monica, California. But by 1971, the firm was facing a crisis. Bowerman wanted Onitsuka to make a lighter shoe he had designed; Onitsuka wasn't interested. Moreover, Knight believed Onitsuka was looking for other distributors to cut Blue Ribbon out of the business.

What did Knight and Bowerman do? They designed their own shoe called "the Nike" and began selling it. Executives at Onitsuka were enraged by the move. They immediately stopped selling shoes to Blue Robbin and sued it to boot.

At that point, it looked like it might be the end of the road for Blue Ribbon. There wasn't much of a market for the Nike shoes yet. The company was still young and in debt, and a lawsuit would be expensive to fight.

Knight gave Blue Ribbon's employees the bad news. But instead of throwing in the towel, he laid out a new vision and mission for the firm: "This is the moment we've been waiting for," Knight recounts telling them in his bestselling book, *Shoe Dog*. "No more selling someone else's brand. No more working for someone else. Onitsuka has been holding us down for years. Their late deliveries, their mixed-up orders, their refusal to hear and implement our design ideas—who among us isn't sick of dealing with all that? . . . If we're going to succeed, or fail, we should do so on our own terms, with our own ideas—our own brand."

After the initial shock wore off, relief swept across Blue Ribbon's employees. Not only were they undaunted by the new mission, but they were energized and excited about it. Their future lay in their own hands, and they would find a way to achieve it. They immediately began formulating new strategies and plans.

Knight thinks the culture and agility of the company were major reasons why Nike became the success it is today. Most, if not all, of its employees were scrappy competitive types. "Each of us was willing to do whatever was necessary to win," he says. "And if 'whatever was necessary' fell outside our area of expertise, no problem. Not that any of us thought we wouldn't fail. In fact, we had every expectation that we would. But when we did fail, we had faith we'd do it fast, learn from it, and be better for it . . . Taking a chance on people—you could argue that's what it's all been about."

Questions

1. Who is ultimately responsible for formulating a firm's strategy—its managers, its employees, or both?
2. What strategy execution problems do you think Knight and Bowerman might have faced in their effort to make Nike successful?

Sources: Frank Kaiman, "Nike, Phil Knight and the Power of Shared Purpose," *Talent Economy* (January 26, 2017), http://wwwtalenteconomy.com; Andy Gould, "Three Lessons for Entrepreneurs from Nike 'Shoe Dog' Phil Knight," *Motley Fool* (January 17, 2017), http://fool.com; Lara O'Reilly, "Eleven Things Hardly Anyone Knows about Nike," *Business Insider* (November 4, 2014), http://www.businessinsider.

CASE STUDY 2 Domino's Tries to Get Its Strategic Recipe Right

Believe it or not, it was once normal for people to have wait an hour or more to get their pizzas delivered. But those were the years B.D.—before Domino's. Started by Tom Monahan and his brother in Ypsilanti, Michigan, in the 1960s, Domino's created a value proposition that people were hungering for: pizza delivered in 30 minutes or less. Better yet, if a Domino's pizza *wasn't* delivered in 30 minutes, it was free. That was unheard of in the pizza business.

Monahan changed the pizza industry not because Domino's created a better product, but because it was able to offer a different value proposition than anyone else had and to align its people, processes, and systems to deliver against that promise. Domino's used assembly line–based systems and standardized processes to improve efficiency and reduce pizza preparation times. For example, it was the first to use conveyor-belt oven technology to ensure uniform temperatures and reduce baking times. Domino's also translated its strategy into HR deliverables by emphasizing and encouraging fast pizza-making and delivery. Each year, the company holds a "World's Fastest Pizza Maker" competition in which its pizza makers compete for cash and other prizes.

As important as what Domino's did is what it did *not* do. Strategy is about making choices. Domino's did not focus on great pizza—it focused on fast pizza. It didn't customize every order, but rather prepared them all in advance. It didn't hire premiere pizza chefs who tossed pizza dough into the air to make lighter crusts. It didn't use the wood-fired stoves to give the pizza an old-world taste. And it didn't offer in-store dining.

Each of the ingredients in Monahan's formula was aligned around its value proposition of fast delivery—a strategy that worked well for Domino's for decades. This strategy and a franchise model helped the company grow by leaps and bounds. Today there are more than 13,000 Domino's pizza stores, which are located in 80-plus countries around the world. India is currently the company's hottest market.

Over time, however, Domino's competitive environment changed. Other companies began delivering pizzas in about 30 minutes, and consumers began wanting more than fast pizza: They wanted good pizza. The problem was that Domino's wasn't delivering on that score. In taste tests, customers complained Domino's pizzas tasted like cardboard. At one point, the firm's customer-satisfaction scores in terms of its food and service were lower than those of any other pizza chain. Perhaps not surprisingly, the firm's stock price reflected that position.

To turn things around, the company had to rethink its value proposition. That included revamping its food. The company developed a new recipe for its pizza crusts; began using fresher, gourmet types of ingredients; and began offering new products, such as artisan pizzas, pasta, and desserts. It also remodeled its stores and added in-store dining. But Domino's had to revamp its HR strategies and policies, too. One problem was employee turnover. Domino's turnover rate was 158 percent annually. In other words, for every employee hired during a year, another 1.5 employees quit.

Domino's CEO at the time, David Brandon, wasn't convinced that higher pay for hourly-wage employees was the solution, though. "If we could have increased everybody's pay 20 percent, could we have moved the needle a little bit to buy some loyalty? Maybe, but that's not a long-term solution." Moreover, because most of Domino's stores are individually owned rather than corporate owned, it is the individual owners of the stores who have to decide for themselves whether to increase hourly wages.

Instead, the company focused on the quality of store managers—choosing better ones, finding ways to retain good ones, and coaching them to train and motivate employees by being respectful and polite. It's store managers who cause employees to stick around—or not, said Rob Cecere, a regional manager for Domino's. Employees can go to McDonald's or Pizza Hut and make as much as they make at Domino's. "You've got to make sure they are happy to come to work for you," Cecere explained. Domino's also worked harder to promote a culture of "fun" via its World's Fastest Pizza competition and other initiatives.

Despite these changes, Domino's chief strength still lies in its systems and technology. The biggest department at the firm's headquarters in Ann Arbor, Michigan, is its technology department. The department has built novel applications over the years, such as an online ordering system that allows customers to "build" their pizzas online and track their preparation, cooking, and delivery times. Customers can also use a mobile app for ordering, an emoji to text a standard order, or simply tell "Dom," Domino's chatbot, what they want. In Australia and New Zealand, the company is experimenting with robot and drone delivery.

Has Domino's new recipe worked? By most accounts, yes. Turnover dropped by more than 100 percent following the initiative, and customer satisfaction scores jumped up, too. In 2016, Domino's sales growth was the best among the 25 largest restaurant chains in the United States. Its stock price has rocketed upward as well.

Even so, strategy changes and their implementation are continually evolving challenges for firms, and Domino's is no exception. "We need to understand what's going on and create competitive advantage by being ahead of the curve," says the company's current CEO, J. Patrick Doyle. For one thing, the company still faces issues with its HR piece of the puzzle and ensuring its strategy is aligned all the way down the food chain. Recently, a group of franchise owners in New York agreed to pay $1.5 million to settle cases for minimum-wage and overtime violations. Clearly, there's still work to be done on the HR front.

Doyle says the firm *has* to start paying higher wages. Minimum-wage laws are rising in some states, and employers like Walmart and Target are raising their minimum wages. "The reality is the labor market is tightening up, and we've got to respond to that. It's getting harder to hire people," says Doyle. "We've got to do what the market demands to get the right people for our business," he explains.

Will paying hourly-wage employees a little more buy Domino's a little more loyalty and prevent negative publicity for the company? And if so, would the costs have been worth the benefits? And who should incur these costs, given that most of the stores are privately owned? These questions are food for thought—ones that Domino's will have to resolve.

After all, even with the best technologies and systems, pizzas don't cook and deliver themselves. People do.

Questions

1. Explain how Domino's strategy differed from its competitors.
2. Has the firm been able to achieve a long-term strategic fit between its strategy and HR practices in your opinion? Why or why not?

Sources: Dave Buss, "What Matters to Domino's: Five Questions with CEO J. Patrick Doyle," *Brandchannel* (January 23, 2017), http://brandchannel.com; Kevin McCoy, "N.Y. Sues Domino's Pizza for Alleged Wage Theft," *USA Today* (May 24, 2016), http://www.usatoday.com; "Domino's Pizza Will Have to Raise Wages to Stay Competitive," *Reuters* (April 6, 2015), http://www.reuters.com; William James, David Kretzman, "Why Domino's Digital Component Is Important," *Motley Fool* (December 10, 2013), http://motleyfool.com; Erin White, "To Keep Employees, Dominos Decides It's Not All about Pay," *The Wall Street Journal* (February 17, 2005), http://online.wsj.com.

Notes and References

1. Christopher Rees and Hasanah Johari, "'Senior Managers' Perceptions of the HRM Function during Times of 'Strategic Organizational Change,'" *Journal of Organizational Change Management* 23, no 2. (2010): 517. See also Y. Wang, S. Kim, A. Rafferty, and K. Sanders, "Employee Perceptions of HR Practices: A Critical Review and Future Directions," *International Journal of Human Resource Management* (November 2019): 128–173.
2. Scott A. Snell, Mark Shadur, and Patrick M. Wright, "Human Resources Strategy: The Era of Our Ways," in M. A. Hitt, R. E. Freeman, and J. S. Harrison (eds.), *Handbook of Strategic Management* (Oxford, UK: Blackwell, 2002), 627–649; Patrick M. Wright, Benjamin Dunford, and Scott A. Snell, "Human Resources and the Resource-Based View of the Firm," *Journal of Management* 27, no. 6 (2002): 701–721; "What's Affecting HR Operations? Globalization, Sustainability, and Talent," *HR Focus* 84, no. 8 (August 2007): 8; Doris Sims, "Do You Know Where Your Talent Is?" *Training* 45, no. 1 (January 2008): 46.
3. K. Carrig, S. Snell, and A. Onozuka, "In Search of Execution," in P. M. Wright, D. Ulrich, R. Antione, and E. Sartaine, eds., *View from the Top: Leveraging Human and Organizational Capital to Create Value* Alexandria, VA: SHRM Publishing, 2016).
4. Patrick Kiger, "Serious Progress in Strategic Workforce Planning," *Workforce Management* (July 1, 2010), http://workforce.com.
5. Bala Iyer, "Deconstructing Google," *Computerworld* 42, no. 15 (April 7, 2008): 32–33.
6. "Core Values and the Companies That Do Them Well, Grapper," *Grasslands: The Entrepreneurial Blog* (April 4, 2010), http://grasshopper.com.
7. Carrig, K.J. & Snell, S.A. 2019. *Strategic execution: Driving breakthrough performance in business*. Palo Alto, Stanford University Press.
8. P. Wahba, "How Lowe's and Home Depot Plan to Keep Growing Even after the COVID Home Improvement Boom," *Fortune*, November 2020.
9. Hiroko Tabuchi, "In America's Heartland, Discussing Climate Change without Saying 'Climate Change,'" *New York Times* (January 28, 2017), https://www.nytimes.com.
10. Kelly Marchese, Siva Paramasivam, Michael Held, and Deloitte Consulting, "Bouncing Back: Supply Chain Risk Management Lessons from Post-Tsunami Japan," *Industry Week* (March 9, 2012), http://www.industryweek.com.
11. A. Trivedi, "Getting Real about Electric Cars, Batteries and Hype," *Bloomberg*, September 29, 2020.
12. R. Bauborgne and W. C. Kim, *Blue Ocean Strategy* (Boston: Harvard Business Press, 2004).
13. "US Tech Hubs: Top Tech Cities in the US," *Built In*, https://builtin.com/tech-hubs.
14. For example, see U.S. Department of Labor, Bureau of Labor Statistics, *Geographic Profiles of Employment and Unemployment*. The data and information are accessible via the Office of Employment Protections home page at http://www.bls.gov/emp.
15. Ray Brillinger, "Best Practices: Human Resources Benchmarking," *Canadian HR Reporter* 14, no. 12 (2001): 12; Chris Mahoney, "Benchmarking Your Way to Smarter Decisions," *Workforce* 79, no. 10 (2000): 100–103; Brian E. Becker and Mark A. Huselid, "Strategic Human Resources Management: Where Do We Go from Here?" *Journal of Management* 32, no. 6 (January 2006): 898–925.
16. For more information on methods to identify a firm's core capabilities, see Khalid Hafeez, YanBing Zhang, and Naila Malak, "Core Competence for Sustainable Competitive Advantage: A Structured Methodology for Identifying Core Competence," *IEEE Transactions on Engineering Management* 49, no. 1 (2002): 28–35; J. B. Quinn, "The Intelligent Enterprise: A New Paradigm," *Academy of Management Executive* 6, no. 4 (2002): 48–63; Jane Wollman Rusoff, "Outsourced Solutions: Brokerage Firms Looking to Focus on Their Core Competencies Find the Most Value in a Resource-Rich Clearing Partner," *Research* 27, no. 11 (2004): 37–40.
17. Snell, Shadur, and Wright, "Human Resources Strategy," 627–649; Wright, Dunford, and Snell, "Human Resources and the Resource-Based View of the Firm," 701–721; David Collis and Cynthia Montgomery, "Competing on Resources," *Harvard Business Review* 86, no. 7/8 (2008): 140–150; Susan Cantrell, "The Work Force of One," *Wall Street Journal* 249, no. 140 (June 16, 2007): R10.

18. "20 Questions to Ask in a Culture Audit," *Thought Famer* (July 2020), https://www.thoughtfarmer.com/blog/shout-it-out-loud/.
19. Joseph F. Castellan and Susan S. Lightle, "Using Cultural Audits to Assess Tone at the Top," *CPA Journal* 75, no. 2 (2005): 6–11.
20. Peter Louch, "Workforce Planning Is Essential to High-Performing Organizations," Society for Human Resource Management (October 3, 2014), https://www.shrm.org/resourcesandtools/hr-topics/technology/pages/louch-workforce-planning.aspx.
21. Carolyn Hirschman, "Putting Forecasting in Focus," *HRMagazine* 52, no. 3 (2007): 44–49.
22. Leslie Kwoh, "Are Firms Neglecting Succession Planning?" *Wall Street Journal* (September 5, 2012), http://www.wsj.com.
23. Robert Kaplan and David Norton, *Strategy Maps: Converting Intangible Assets into Tangible Objectives* (Boston: Harvard Business School Press, 2006).
24. John Huey, "Outlaw Flyboy CEOs," *Fortune* 142, no. 11 (2000): 237–250; "Visions of the Future," *Human Resources* (January 2008): special section, 22.
25. Patrick Wright, "Human Resource Strategy: Adapting to the Age of Human Resources Management," SHRM Foundation (2008), http://www.shrm.org/foundation.
26. Scott A. Snell, Mark A. Shadur, and Patrick M. Wright, *Human Resources Strategy: The Era of Our Ways* [Working paper] (Ithaca, NY: Center for Advanced Human Resource Studies: November 1, 2000), 23–29.
27. R. Sanchez, "Strategic Flexibility in Product Competition," *Strategic Management Journal* 16 (1995): 135–159; Wright and Snell, "Toward a Unifying Framework," 756–772.
28. "Poll Shows Concern about Aging Workforce," *Credit Union Management* 32, no. 6 (2011): 36.
29. Patrick Kiger, "Serious Progress in Strategic Workforce Planning," *Workforce Management* (July 1, 2010), http://workforce.com.
30. Brian Becker, Mark Huselid, and Dave Ulrich, *The HR Scorecard: Linking People, Strategy, and Performance* (Cambridge, MA: Harvard Business School Press, 2001); see also Shari Caudron, "How HR Drives Profits," *Workforce* 80, no. 12 (2001): 26–31.
31. "A Singular Sensation for Schwab Brokers," *Businessweek* (January 24, 2002), http://www.businessweek.com.

Appendix

Calculating Employee Turnover and Absenteeism

Throughout this chapter, we have emphasized that HRP depends on having an accurate picture of both the supply of and the demand for employees. Two factors, employee turnover and absenteeism, have a direct impact on HRP strategy and recruitment processes. In this appendix, we provide a detailed discussion of turnover and absenteeism, methods for measuring them, and suggestions for managing their impact.

A.1 Employee Turnover Rates

Employee turnover refers simply to the movement of employees out of an organization. It is often cited as one of the factors behind the failure of U.S. employee productivity rates to keep pace with those of foreign competitors. It is also one of the chief determinants of labor supply. Even if everything else about an organization stays the same, as employees leave, its supply of labor goes down. This involves both direct and indirect costs to the organization.

A.1a Computing the Turnover Rate

The U.S. Department of Labor suggests the following formula for computing turnover rates:

$$\frac{\text{Number of separations during the month}}{\text{Total number of employees at midmonth}} \times 100$$

So, if there were 25 separations during a month and the total number of employees at midmonth was 500, the turnover rate would be:

$$\frac{25}{500} \times 100 = 5 \text{ percent}$$

Turnover rates are computed on a regular basis to compare specific units such as departments, divisions, and work groups. In many cases, comparisons are made with data provided by other organizations. The Bureau of Labor Statistics' *Job Openings and Labor Turnover Survey* (https://www.bls.gov/jlt/) is a very good source of comparative turnover data.

Another method of computing the turnover rate is one that reflects only the avoidable separations (S). This rate is computed by subtracting unavoidable separations (US)—for example, due to pregnancy, return to school, or death—from all separations. The formula for this method is as follows:

$$\frac{S - US}{M} \times 100 = T(\text{turnover rate})$$

where *M* represents the total number of employees at midmonth. For example, if there were 25 separations during a month, 5 of which were *US*, and the total number of employees at midmonth (*M*) was 500, the turnover rate would be:

$$\frac{25 - 5}{500} \times 100 = 4 \text{ percent}$$

A.1b Determining the Costs of Turnover

Replacing an employee is time consuming and expensive. Costs can generally be broken down into three categories: separation costs for the departing employee, replacement costs, and training costs for the new employee. These costs are conservatively estimated at two to three times the monthly salary of the departing employee, and they do not include indirect costs such as low productivity prior to quitting and lower morale and overtime for other employees because of the vacated job. Consequently, reducing turnover could result in significant savings to an organization. Highlights in HRM 4 details one organization's costs associated with the turnover of a single computer programmer. Note that the major expense is the cost involved in training a replacement.

A.2 Employee Absenteeism Rates

How frequently employees are absent from their work—the absenteeism rate—is also directly related to HRP and recruitment. When employees miss work, the organization incurs direct costs of lost wages and decreased productivity. It is not uncommon for organizations to hire extra workers just to make up for the cumulative number of absences across all employees. In addition to these direct costs, indirect costs may underlie excessive absenteeism. A certain amount of absenteeism is, of course, unavoidable. There will always be some people who must be absent from work because of sickness, accidents, serious family problems, or other legitimate reasons. However, chronic absenteeism may signal deeper problems in the work environment.

A.2a Computing Absenteeism Rates

Managers should determine the extent of the absenteeism problem, if any, by maintaining individual and departmental attendance records and by computing absenteeism rates. Although there is no universally accepted definition of "absence" or a standard formula for computing absenteeism rates, the method most frequently used is that recommended by the U.S. Department of Labor.

$$\frac{\text{Number of worker} - \text{days lost through job absence during period}}{\text{Average number of employees 3 number of workdays}} \times 100$$

If 300 worker-days are lost through job absence during a month having 25 scheduled working days at an organization that employs 500 workers, the absenteeism rate for that month is:

$$\frac{300}{300 \times 25} \times 100 = 2.4 \text{ percent}$$

The U.S. Department of Labor defines job absence as the failure of employees to report to work when their schedules require it, whether or not such failure to report

Costs Associated with the Turnover of One Computer Programmer

Turnover costs = Separation costs + Replacement costs + Training costs

Separation Costs

1. Exit interview = cost for salary and benefits of both interviewer and departing employee during the exit interview = $30 + $30 = $60
2. Administrative and record-keeping action = $30
   Separation costs = $60 + $30 = $90

Replacement Costs

1. Advertising for job opening = $2,500
2. Preemployment administrative functions and record-keeping action = $100
3. Selection interview = $250
4. Employment tests = $40
5. Meeting to discuss candidates(salary and benefits of managers while participating in meetings) = $250
   Replacement costs = $2,500 + $100 + $250 + $40 + $250 = $3,140

Training Costs

1. Booklets, manuals, and reports = $50
2. Education = $240/day for new employee's salary and benefits × 10 days of workshops, seminars, or courses = $2,400
3. One-to-one coaching = ($240/day per new employee + $240/day per staff coach or job expert) × 20 days of one-to-one coaching = $9,600
4. Salary and benefits of new employee until they get "up to par" = $240/day for salary and benefits × 20 days = $4,800
   Training costs $50 + $2,400 + $9,600 + $4,800 = $16,850
   Total turnover costs = $90 + $3,140 + $16,850 = $20,080

Sources: Adapted from Michael Mercer, *Turning Your Human Resources Department into a Profit Center* (Barrington, IL: Castlegate Publishers, 2002). Copyright 2002 Michael Mercer. Reproduced with permission from Michael Mercer, PhD, http://www.DrMercer.com.

is excused. Scheduled vacations, holidays, and prearranged leaves of absence are not counted as job absences.

A.2b Comparing Absenteeism Data

The Bureau of Labor Statistics of the U.S. Department of Labor obtains data on job absences from the Current Population Survey of Households conducted by the Bureau of the Census, and analyses of these data are published periodically. These analyses help identify problem areas—industries, occupations, or groups of workers with the highest incidence of absence or with rapidly increasing rates of absence. Comparison with other organizations may be made by referring to Bureau of Labor Statistics data reported in the *Monthly Labor Review.*

A.2c Costs of Absenteeism

The cost of each person-hour lost to absenteeism is based on the hourly weighted average salary, costs of employee benefits, supervisory costs, and incidental costs. For example, XYZ Company, with 1,200 employees, has 78,000 person-hours lost to absenteeism; the total absence cost is $560,886. When this figure is divided by 1,200 employees, the cost per employee is $467.41. (In this example, we are assuming the absent workers are paid. If absent workers are not paid, their salary figures are omitted from the computation.)

A.2d Absenteeism and HR Planning

While an employer may find that the overall absenteeism rate and costs are within an acceptable range, it is still advisable to study the statistics to determine whether the data show any patterns. Rarely does absenteeism spread itself evenly across an organization. It is very likely that employees in one area (or occupational group) may have nearly perfect attendance records, while others in a different area may be absent frequently. By monitoring these differences, managers can assess where problems might exist and, more important, begin planning ways to resolve or improve the underlying causes. For example, incentives could be provided for perfect attendance. Alternatively, progressive discipline procedures might be used with employees having a record of recurring absenteeism.

By establishing a comprehensive absenteeism policy, Allen-Bradley (which is now a part of Rockwell Automation) cut its absenteeism by 83.5 percent in a 25-month period. This reduced the strain on the company due to labor costs and increased productivity.

Yuri_Arcurs/Getty Images

CHAPTER 3

Equal Employment Opportunity and Human Resources Management

Learning Outcomes

After studying this chapter, you should be able to

LO 1 Identify the three factors that influence equal employment opportunity (EEO) legislation.

LO 2 Determine how the major EEO laws related to age, gender, religion, disability, weight, sexual orientation, and genetic information affect you and others within companies.

LO 3 Demonstrate how to prevent other forms of discrimination that are of particular interest to managers.

LO 4 Explain how the Uniform Guidelines on Employee Selection Procedures are used by firms and how they relate to the issues of adverse impact and disparate treatment.

LO 5 Describe how EEO recordkeeping and posting requirements work, including how discrimination charges are processed by the Equal Employment Opportunity Commission (EEOC).

LO 6 Explain what affirmative action is and how companies today are seeing the value of voluntarily having diverse workforces.

One of the most important topics that must be discussed in any human resources management textbook is **equal employment opportunity (EEO)**. Equal employment opportunity, or the employment of individuals in a fair and nonbiased manner, commands the attention of the media, courts, legislators, HR managers, and their firms alike. On average, approximately 80,000 employment discrimination charges are filed each year with the **Equal Employment Opportunity Commission (EEOC)**, the federal agency that enforces the nation's fair employment laws. These charges made by individuals result in nearly $400 million of benefits paid out on a yearly basis. Less than 10 percent of these charges ever make it to court; the majority of them end up settling with some benefits being paid to the individuals who filed the charges.[1]

equal employment opportunity (EEO)
The treatment of individuals in all aspects of employment—hiring, promotion, training, and so on—in a fair and nonbiased manner.

Equal Employment Opportunity Commission (EEOC)
The EEOC's work consists of formulating EEO policy and approving all litigation involved in maintaining equal employment opportunity. The EEOC's guidelines are not federal law but administrative rules and regulations published in the *Federal Register.*

When managers ignore or are unaware of fair employment laws, they and their firms run the risk of incurring costly and time-consuming litigation, negative public attention, potentially lower sales, lower employee morale, and even damage to their own individual careers.[2] Because even unintentional discrimination can be illegal, supervisors need to be aware of their personal biases and how they can affect their dealings with their subordinates.[3] Employment discrimination is not just a legal issue, but an emotional one. It concerns all individuals, regardless of their gender, race, religion, age, national origin, color, sexual orientation, physical condition, and position in an organization. Fortunately, it is a problem that can be minimized with good HR practices.

iStock.com/Portra

The CROWN Coalition is working hard to ensure protection against discrimination due to race-based hairstyles.

This chapter will help you better understand how to minimize employment discrimination. It also discusses the diversity efforts that companies are actively pursuing as a way to gain a strategic edge. HR professionals agree that when all functions of HRM comply with the law, the organization becomes a fairer place to work and a more effective competitor.

LO1 Identify the three factors that influence equal employment opportunity (EEO) legislation.

3.1 Historical Perspective on EEO Legislation

Equal employment opportunity as a national priority has emerged slowly in the United States. Three factors seem to have influenced the growth of EEO legislation: (1) changing attitudes toward employment discrimination; (2) published reports highlighting the economic problems and injustices experienced by underrepresented workers; and (3) a growing body of disparate discrimination laws and regulations at different levels of government that legislators feel should be standardized (see Figure 3.1). Although the United States has progressed substantially in improving business practices and public attitudes about discrimination, problems still persist.

3.1a Changing National Values

The United States was founded on the principles of individual merit, hard work, and equality. In spite of these values, employment discrimination has a long history in the United States and still exists to this day. Organizations that claim to offer fair treatment to their employees have intentionally or unintentionally engaged in discriminatory practices. As a result, laws have been passed to ensure equality and reward individual merit and hard work.

Figure 3.1 Three Factors Come Together to Influence EEO Legislation

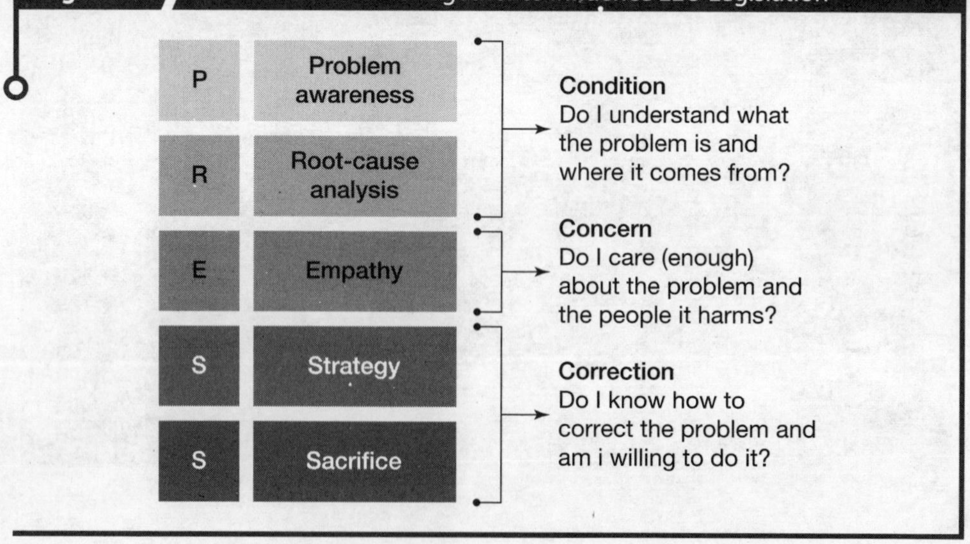

Small Business Application

The Perils of Noncompliance

Owners and managers of growing small businesses should consider conducting routine HR compliance assessments, either annually or perhaps each time the company reaches another significant increase in employees—for example, from fewer than 5 employees to closer to 15 employees.

There are other occasions when a small firm should check its compliance as well. Eric A. Marks, a partner in charge of the Human Resources Consulting Practice at the New York accounting firm Marks Paneth & Shron, explains:

> Significant changes to the business, such as mergers; the retirement of senior managers; newly hired or promoted supervisors or managers who may lack HR experience; creation or revision of an employee handbook; changes in employee morale, turnover, attendance, or disciplinary problems; taking on government contracts where compliance requirements are often stricter; and major changes in state or federal regulations—any of these are danger signs. They signal that the business has a fresh need to address compliance and make sure its house is in order.

In short, an HR compliance assessment reviews how well an employer is following employment, benefits, and safety laws. Fortunately, small-business owners do not have to remain in the danger zone. Numerous HR consulting firms can not only conduct a compliance assessment, but also assist the owner with rectifying any noncompliant systems and procedures and train the company's managers and supervisors to maintain them. There are even HR compliance self-assessment forms available online. Help is only a mouse-click away.

Source: "New Risks to Small Businesses" *Marketwire* (February 28, 2011), http://www2.marketwire.com; "HR Compliance Assessment Overview," http://www.the-arnold-group.com/hr-assessment.cfm; "HR Challenges: Compliance," http://www.strategic-workplace-solutions.com/services/compliance.

3.1b Early Legal Developments

Litigation concerning discriminatory practices has been prevalent since the nineteenth century. In 1866, Congress passed the Civil Rights Act, which extended to all people the right to enjoy full and equal benefits of all laws, regardless of race. In 1933, Congress enacted the Unemployment Relief Act, which prohibited employment discrimination on account of race, color, or creed (religious beliefs). Then in 1941, President Franklin D. Roosevelt issued Executive Order 8802, which sought to ensure that every American citizen, "regardless of race, creed, color, or national origin," would be guaranteed equal employment opportunities at firms awarded World War II defense contracts. Over the next 20 years a variety of other legislative efforts were promoted to resolve inequities in employment practices.

Unfortunately, these early efforts did little to correct employment discrimination. First, nondiscrimination laws gave no enforcement powers to agencies. Second, these laws did not specify which discriminatory practices or methods needed correction and employers were not required to comply with EEO legislation.

LO2 Determine how you and your fellow employees might be affected by major EEO laws related to age, gender, religion, disability, weight, sexual orientation, and genetic information.

3.2 Government Regulation of Equal Employment Opportunity

Despite their shortcomings, the laws and executive orders discussed in Section 3.1 laid the groundwork for a significant number of laws that have since been passed barring employment discrimination.

Part of the reason why it is so critical for managers and supervisors to understand and apply EEO laws is that employees act as agents of their employers. If a manager or supervisor violates the law, *both* that individual and their organization can face legal consequences. The organization cannot claim that it is not legally responsible for what the manager or supervisor did.

Figure 3.2 shows the various prohibited HR activities related to hiring, promoting, compensating employees, and so forth covered by EEO laws. If you think you already know what constitutes a legal or illegal employment practice, you might be surprised. Highlights in HRM 1 will test your current understanding of how EEO laws are applied in the workplace.

protected classes
Individuals of an underrepresented race, women, older people, and individuals with disabilities who are covered by federal laws on equal employment opportunity.

3.2a Major Federal Laws

Major federal EEO laws have been enacted to prevent discrimination against the groups of workers most often affected by unfair employment practices. These groups are referred to as **protected classes** (see Figure 3.3).[4]

Defined broadly, protected classes include employees of a particular race, color, religion, national origin, sex (including distinctions based on pregnancy, gender identity, and sexual orientation), age, disability (mental and physical), and genetic information.

Figure 3.2 Prohibited Discriminatory Employment Practices

It is illegal to discriminate in any aspect of employment, including:

- Hiring and firing
- Compensation, assignment, or classification of employees
- Transfer, promotion, layoff, or recall
- Job advertisements
- Recruitment
- Testing
- Use of company facilities
- Training and apprenticeship programs
- Fringe benefits
- Pay, retirement plans, and disability leave
- Other terms and conditions of employment

Discriminatory practices under these laws also include:

- Harassment on the basis of race, color, religion, sex, national origin, disability, genetic information, or age.
- Retaliation against an individual for filing a charge of discrimination, participating in an investigation, or opposing discriminatory practices.
- Employment decisions based on stereotypes or assumptions about the abilities, traits, or performance of individuals of a certain sex, race, age, religion, or ethnic group, or individuals with disabilities, or based on myths or assumptions about an individual's genetic information.
- Denying employment opportunities to a person because of marriage to, or association with, an individual of a particular race, religion, national origin, or an individual with a disability. Title VII also prohibits discrimination because of participation in schools or places of worship associated with a particular racial, ethnic, or religious group.

1 Highlights in HRM

Test Your Knowledge of Equal Employment Opportunity Law

The following questions have been used as "icebreakers" by employers and consultants when training supervisors and managers in EEO legislation. What is your knowledge of EEO laws? Answers are found at the end of this chapter.

1. Two male employees tell a sexually explicit joke. The joke is overheard by a female employee, who complains to her supervisor that this is sexual harassment. Is her complaint legitimate?

   ________ Yes ________ No

2. To be covered by Title VII of the Civil Rights Act, an employer must be engaged in interstate commerce and employ 25 or more employees.

   ________ True ________ False

3. People addicted to illegal drugs are classified as disabled under the Americans with Disabilities Act of 1990.

   ________ Yes ________ No

4. The Equal Pay Act of 1963 allows employers to pay different wages to men and women who are performing substantially similar work. What are the three defenses for paying a different wage?

   1. ____________________
   2. ____________________
   3. ____________________

5. A person applies for a job as a janitor at your company. During his interview with you, the person mentions that since birth he has sometimes experienced short periods of memory loss. Must you consider this individual a disabled person under the Americans with Disabilities Act of 1990?

   ________ Yes ________ No

6. On Friday afternoon, you tell Nancy Penley, a computer analyst, that she must work overtime the next day. She refuses, saying that Saturday is her regular religious holiday and she can't work. Do you have the legal right to order her to work on Saturday?

   ________ Yes ________ No

7. You have just told an applicant that she will not receive the job for which she applied. She claims that you denied her employment because of her age (she's 52). You claim she is not protected under the age discrimination law. Is your reasoning correct?

   ________ Yes ________ No

8. As an employer, you can select those applicants who are the most qualified in terms of education and experience.

   ________ Yes ________ No

9. As a manager, you have the legal right to mandate dates for pregnancy leaves.

   ________ True ________ False

10. State and local fair employment practice laws cover smaller employers that are not covered by federal legislation.

    ________ True ________ False

Figure 3.4 lists the major federal laws targeting workplace discrimination and their provisions governing equal employment opportunity.

Equal Pay Act of 1963

The Equal Pay Act makes it illegal to discriminate against people in terms of the pay, employee benefits, and pension they earn based on their gender when they do equal work.[5] Jobs are considered "equal" when they require substantially the same skill, effort, and responsibility under similar working conditions and in the same establishment. However, a company does not violate the Equal Pay Act when the differences in the wages it pays to men and women for equal work are based on seniority systems, merit considerations, or

Figure 3.3 Protected Classes of Employees

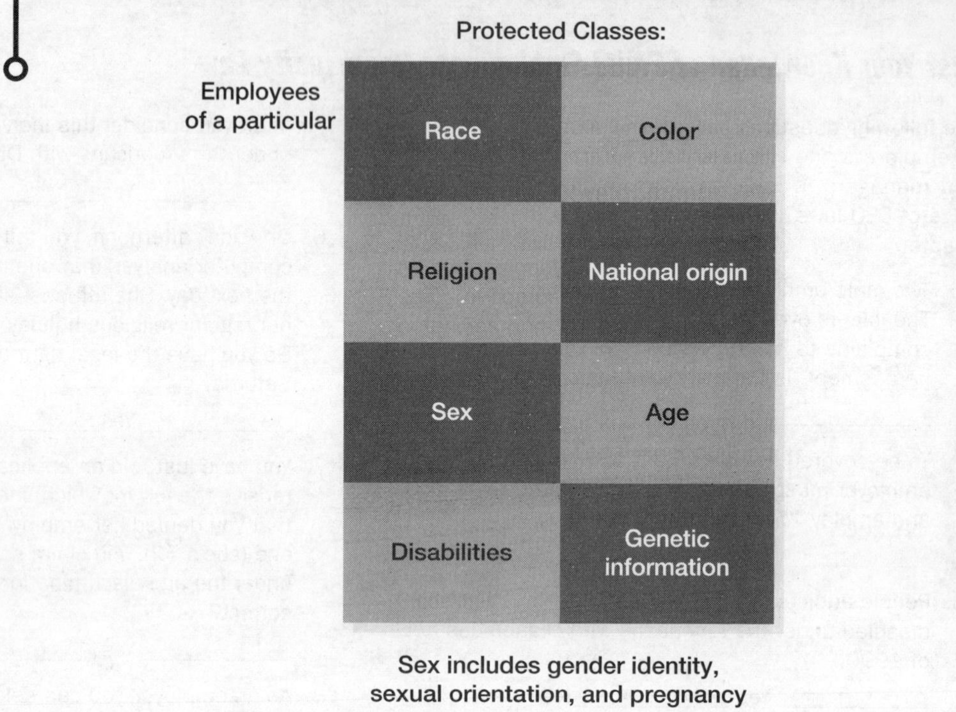

the workers' quantity or quality of production. Also, if a pay disparity between employees of different genders exists, employers cannot legally lower the wages of one gender to comply with the law; rather, they must raise the wages of the gender being underpaid.

Civil Rights Act of 1964

The Civil Rights Act of 1964 is a landmark law that addresses discrimination in society. Title VII of the act specifically bars employment discrimination in all HR activities, including hiring, training, promotion, transfers, pay, employee benefits, and other conditions of employment. Discrimination is prohibited on the basis of race, color, religion, sex, or national origin. Title VII of the Civil Rights Act also created the EEOC to administer the law and thereby promote equal employment opportunity.

In response to the growing number of immigrant workers and increasing workplace cultural and ethnic awareness, the EEOC has issued important guidelines on national origin discrimination.[6] A "national origin group" is defined as a group of people sharing a common language, culture, ancestry, and/or similar social characteristics. This definition includes people born in the United States who are not in racially or ethnically underrepresented groups. Also prohibited under the act is discrimination based on pregnancy or a medical condition related to it or childbirth. The Civil Rights Act of 1964 covers a broad range of organizations. Specifically, the law includes under its jurisdiction the following types of organizations:

1. All private employers in interstate commerce that employ 15 or more employees for 20 or more weeks per year
2. State and local governments

Figure 3.4 Major Laws Affecting Equal Employment Opportunity

Law	Provisions
Equal Pay Act of 1963	Requires all employers covered by the Fair Labor Standards Act and others to provide equal pay for equal work, regardless of sex.
Title VII of Civil Rights Act of 1964 (amended in 1972, 1991, 1994, and 2009)	Prohibits discrimination in employment on the basis of race, color, religion, sex, or national origin; created the EEOC to enforce the provisions of Title VII.
Age Discrimination in Employment Act of 1967 (amended in 1986 and 1990)	Prohibits private and public employers from discriminating against people age 40 or older in any area of employment because of age; exceptions are permitted when age is a bona fide occupational qualification.
Equal Employment Opportunity Act of 1972	Amended Title VII of Civil Rights Act of 1964; strengthens the EEOC's enforcement powers and extends coverage of Title VII to government employees, employees in higher education, and other employers and employees.
Pregnancy Discrimination Act of 1978	Broadens the definition of sex discrimination to include pregnancy, childbirth, or related medical conditions; prohibits employers from discriminating against pregnant women in employment benefits if they are capable of performing their job duties.
Americans with Disabilities Act of 1990 (amended in 2008)	Prohibits discrimination in employment against people with physical or mental disabilities or the chronically ill; enjoins employers to make reasonable accommodations to the employment needs of the disabled; covers employers with 15 or more employees.
Civil Rights Act of 1991	Provides for compensatory and punitive damages and jury trials in cases involving intentional discrimination; requires employers to demonstrate that job practices are job-related and consistent with business necessity; extends coverage to U.S. citizens working for U.S. companies overseas.
Uniformed Services Employment and Reemployment Rights Act of 1994 (amended in 1998, 2004, and 2008)	Protects the employment rights of individuals who enter the military for short periods of service.
Don't Ask, Don't Tell Repeal Act of 2010	Bars discrimination against military personnel based on their sexual orientation.

3. Private and public employment agencies
4. Joint labor–management committees that govern apprenticeship or training programs
5. Labor unions having 15 or more members or employees
6. Public and private educational institutions
7. Foreign subsidiaries of U.S. organizations employing U.S. citizens

Certain employers are excluded from coverage of the Civil Rights Act. Broadly defined, these organizations include (1) U.S. government-owned corporations; (2) bona fide, tax-exempt private clubs; (3) religious organizations employing people of a specific religion; and (4) organizations hiring Native Americans on or near a reservation.

bona fide occupational qualification (BFOQ)
Suitable defense against a discrimination charge only when age, religion, sex, or national origin is an actual qualification for performing the job.

Bona Fide Occupational Qualification. Under Title VII of the Civil Rights Act, employers are permitted limited exemptions from antidiscrimination regulations if the employment preferences are based on a bona fide occupational qualification. A **bona fide occupational qualification (BFOQ)** permits discrimination when employer hiring preferences are a reasonable necessity for the normal operation of the business. Courts

business necessity
A work-related practice that is necessary to the safe and efficient operation of an organization.

have ruled that a **business necessity** is a practice that is necessary for the safe and efficient operation of the organization.

However, a BFOQ is a suitable defense against a discrimination charge only when *age, religion, gender*, or *national origin* is an actual qualification for performing the job (see Figure 3.5). For example, an older person could legitimately be excluded from consideration for employment as a model for teenage designer jeans. It is also reasonable to expect the Chicago Bears of the National Football League to hire male locker-room attendants or for Abercrombie and Fitch Clothing Store to employ women as models for women's fashions. Religion is a BFOQ in organizations that require employees to share a particular religious doctrine. National origin can also be a BFOQ if it is an actual qualification for a job. For example, to ensure the "authenticity" of the dining experience, an Asian restaurant could use the business-necessity defense to support its preference for hiring Asian American servers. Notably, the BFOQ exception does *not* apply to discrimination based on race or color.

Religious Preference. Title VII of the Civil Rights Act prohibits employment discrimination based on a person's religion. Title VII does not, however, require employers to grant complete religious freedom in employment situations. Employers need only make a *reasonable accommodation* for a current employee's or job applicant's religious observance or practice without incurring undue hardship in the conduct of the business. Managers or supervisors may have to accommodate an employee's religion in the specific areas of (1) holidays and observances, such as scheduling; (2) personal appearance, such as wearing beards, veils, or turbans; and (3) religious conduct on the job, such as missionary work among other employees.

What constitutes "reasonable accommodation" can be difficult to define. For example, in the 2018 case *Tabura v. Kellogg USA*, the Kellogg company had tried to resolve scheduling conflicts with Richard Tabura and Guadalupe Diaz by offering them the option to use their paid time off to not work on Saturdays, which was their religious Sabbath. Eventually their paid time off ran out, and Kellogg fired Diaz and Tabura for not fulfilling their work responsibilities. Diaz and Tabura sued their employer, claiming religious discrimination. Kellogg was granted summary judgment before the case went

Figure 3.5 BFOQ Bona Fide Occupational Qualification

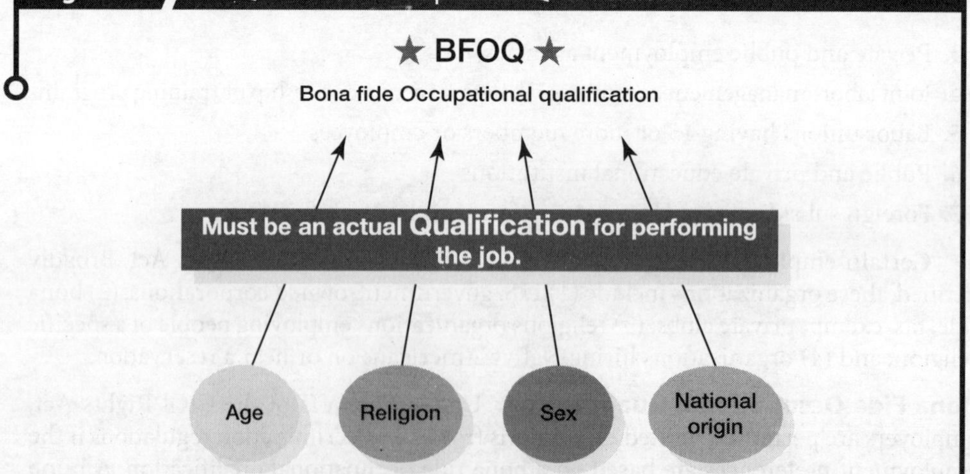

FS-Stock/Alamy Stock Photo

Title VII of the Civil Rights Act requires employers to make reasonable accommodations for an employee's religious practices and observances.

to trial, as the judge concluded that Kellogg provided reasonable accommodation until doing so would have incurred undue hardship on the company.[7] Reasonable accommodation doesn't mean an employer must accommodate at all costs, but rather is meant to provide a possible benefit to the employee.

Employer–employee cooperation and flexibility is often the key when it comes to employment accommodations, including those extended for religious reasons. The EEOC's position is not that firms need to quash religious expression in the workplace, but rather that they need to make a reasonable effort to accommodate people with different belief systems.

Amendments to the Civil Rights Act of 1964

Equal Employment Opportunity Act of 1972. The Equal Employment Opportunity Act of 1972 amended the Civil Rights Act of 1964, making two important changes to this law. First, the act's coverage was broadened to include state and local governments and public and private educational institutions. Second, the law strengthened the enforcement powers of the EEOC by allowing the agency itself to sue employers in court.

Civil Rights Act of 1991. The Civil Rights Act of 1991 was enacted to allow employees who can prove they were intentionally discriminated against to seek compensatory monetary damages. Compensatory damages include money for emotional pain, suffering, mental anguish, and so forth.

The Civil Rights Act of 1991 also states that employees who are sent abroad to work for U.S.-based companies are protected by U.S. antidiscrimination legislation governing age and disability and Title VII of the Civil Rights Act of 1964.

Glass Ceiling Act of 1991. The Glass Ceiling Act of 1991 was passed jointly with the Civil Rights Act of 1991. The term "glass ceiling" represents an invisible barrier that hinders protected class members from reaching top organizational positions. The act created the Glass Ceiling Commission to study and report on the status of and obstacles faced by members of underrepresented groups as they strive for top-level management jobs.

Lilly Ledbetter Fair Pay Act (2009). The Lilly Ledbetter Fair Pay Act states that the 180-day statute of limitations for filing an equal-pay lawsuit with EEOC resets with each new discriminatory paycheck an employee receives—not the date the employee received the first discriminatory paycheck, as the U.S. Supreme Court had previously ruled. From a practical standpoint, this means that employees can claim discrimination after years of getting unfair pay and demand to be compensated for the lost wages. Therefore, organizations need to diligently and regularly examine their pay systems to be sure they are equitable.

Age Discrimination in Employment Act of 1967

The Age Discrimination in Employment Act (ADEA) prohibits specific employers from discriminating against employees and applicants age 40 or older in any employment area. Employers affected are those with 20 or more employees; unions with 25 or more members; employment agencies; and federal, state, and local governments. Managers or supervisors discriminate against older employees if they:

- Exclude older workers from important work activities.
- Make negative changes in the performance evaluations of older employees.
- Deny older employees job-related education, career development, or promotional opportunities.
- Select younger job applicants over older, better-qualified candidates.
- Pressure older employees into taking early retirement or terminate them.
- Reduce the job duties and responsibilities of older employees.[8]

Exceptions to the law are permitted when age is a bona fide occupational qualification. For example, an airline may choose not to hire pilots who are older than a certain age to ensure the safety of passengers.

Amendments to the ADEA

The Older Workers Benefit Protection Act of 1990 specifically prohibits employers from denying benefits to older employees except in limited circumstances. This law also allows employers to ask older employees to waive their legal rights under the ADEA in exchange for compensation such as severance packages or court settlements. As a result of the act, many firms that have downsized have been able to legally offer older employees early-retirement severance packages. However, to be valid, an ADEA waiver must be in writing, clear, and understandable, and the recipients need to be given a certain amount of time to consider the offer in the waiver.

Pregnancy Discrimination Act of 1978

The Pregnancy Discrimination Act amended the Civil Rights Act of 1964 by stating that pregnancy is a disability and that pregnant employees in covered organizations must be treated on an equal basis with employees having other medical conditions. Specifically, the Pregnancy Discrimination Act affects employee benefit programs including (1) hospitalization and major medical insurance, (2) temporary disability and salary continuation plans, and (3) sick leave policies.[9] The law also prohibits discrimination in the hiring, promotion, transfer, or termination of women because of pregnancy.

Americans with Disabilities Act of 1990

In 1990, Congress passed the Americans with Disabilities Act (ADA), which prohibits employers from discriminating against individuals with physical and mental disabilities and against chronically ill individuals.[10] In a notable trend, disability discrimination charges from employees almost doubled from 2005 to 2019, from 14,893 to 24,238.[11]

The ADA defines a disability as "(a) a physical or mental impairment that substantially limits one or more of the major activities; (b) a record of such impairment; or (c) being regarded as having such an impairment." Note that the law specifically protects people "regarded" as having a disability—for example, individuals with disfiguring burns.

Not every mental or physical impairment is considered a disability under the ADA. For example, significant personality disorders are covered under the EEOC's "Enforcement Guidance on the Americans with Disabilities Act and Psychiatric Disabilities."[12] Covered personality disorders include schizophrenia, bipolar disorders, major affective disorders, personality disorders, and anxiety disorders. These impairments are characterized by aberrant behavior, self-defeating behavior, manipulation of others, and troublesome manners of behavior. However, mental impairments described as "adjustment disorders" or attributed to stress have generally not been subject to ADA coverage. Therefore, employees who claim to be "stressed" over marital problems, financial hardships, demands of the work environment, job duties, or harsh and unreasonable treatment from a supervisor would not be classified as disabled.

The ADA requires employers to make a reasonable accommodation for disabled people who are otherwise qualified to work, unless doing so would cause undue hardship to the employer.[13] "Undue hardship" refers to unusual work modifications or excessive expenses that might be incurred by an employer in providing an accommodation. **Reasonable accommodation** "includes making facilities accessible and usable to disabled persons, restructuring jobs, permitting part-time or modified work schedules, reassigning to a vacant position, changing equipment, and/or expense." One example of a reasonable accommodation legal case is *Barbuto v. Advantage Sales & Marketing, LLC.* Cristina Barbuto worked in an entry-level position with Advantage Sales and Marketing, contingent upon her passing a drug test. Barbuto informed Advantage that she would test positive on the test because she used lawfully prescribed marijuana to help treat her Crohn's disease. Her supervisor first told her that this use should not be a problem with the company, then later called to confirm that it would not be a problem. However, after Barbuto's drug test results came back positive for marijuana, Advantage terminated her employment. Barbuto filed suit on the ground that the mandatory drug test was an invasion of her privacy and that her termination was unlawful. The court found that Barbuto qualified as a person with a disability and that she was qualified to perform the essential functions of the position with reasonable accommodation, with that accommodation being a waiver of the company's policy barring employment of any person who tested positive for marijuana. Advantage had a duty to engage in an interactive process to determine if alternative accommodations would be possible; if the accommodations were not feasible, the company needed to prove that the use of medicinal marijuana would cause an undue burden on its business. Its refusal to engage in the interactive process alone was sufficient to support the claim of discrimination.[14]

reasonable accommodation
An attempt by employers to adjust, without undue hardship, the working conditions or schedules of employees with disabilities or religious preferences.

In addition to making reasonable accommodations, employers cannot use selection procedures that screen out or tend to screen out disabled people unless the selection procedure "is shown to be job-related for the position in question and is consistent with business necessity" and acceptable job performance cannot be achieved through

ESB Professional/Shutterstock.com

The ADA prohibits employers from discriminating against individuals regarded as having physical or mental disabilities.

reasonable accommodation. Information and forms related to the health of employees must be kept confidential and separate from their regular personnel files.

Giving disabled individuals an equal opportunity to be hired is not only a legal mandate, but also good business. Employers subject to the ADA and those who value the varied skills and abilities of the disabled approach the law as a proactive business requirement. Hiring the disabled emphasizes what these individuals *can* do rather than what they *cannot* do. Two of the most comprehensive studies conducted on the ADA show that the law has had a positive effect on both business outcomes and disabled employees. Conducted by the National Council on Disability (NCD), the studies reported positive gains regarding the ADA's four major goals: equal opportunity, full participation, independent living, and economic self-sufficiency for people with disabilities.[15] Figure 3.6 identifies specific ways to make the workplace more accessible to the disabled.

Figure 3.6 Americans with Disabilities Act Suggestions for an Accessible Workplace

- Install easy-to-reach switches.
- Provide sloping sidewalks and entrances.
- Install wheelchair ramps.
- Reposition shelves for the easy reach of materials.
- Rearrange tables, chairs, vending machines, dispensers, and other furniture and fixtures.
- Widen doors and hallways.
- Add raised markings on control buttons.
- Provide designated accessible parking spaces.
- Install hand controls or manipulation devices.
- Provide flashing alarm lights.
- Remove turnstiles and revolving doors or provide alternative accessible paths.
- Install holding bars in toilet areas.
- Redesign toilet partitions to increase access space.
- Add paper cup dispensers at water fountains.
- Replace high-pile, low-density carpeting.
- Reposition telephones, water fountains, and other needed equipment.
- Add raised toilet seats.
- Provide a full-length bathroom mirror.

Amendments to the ADA

The Americans with Disabilities Act Amendments Act (ADAAA) was enacted in 2008 in response to court rulings that had weakened the ADA. The ADAAA broadened the definition of what constitutes a disability. In doing so, the act made it less likely that a person will be denied protection because their condition does not seem severe enough or because the person's symptoms are minimized by drugs, prosthetic devices, and so forth.

After the passage of the ADAAA, the EEOC filed a number of suits against companies, including one that alleged a longtime cashier with severe arthritis was denied reasonable accommodation—a stool. The woman had used the stool for seven years, but a new manager did not like that practice and had terminated her.[16]

Genetic Information Nondiscrimination Act of 2008

The Genetic Information Nondiscrimination Act of 2008 (GINA) was passed to alleviate people's fears that their genetic information would be misused. Under Title II of the act, employers are prohibited from requesting, requiring, or purchasing the genetic information of workers or their family members. Employers that happen to possess genetic information as a result of health insurance records must keep the information confidential and separate from an employee's personnel files.[17]

In 2016, this act was supported by the court's decision in *EEOC v. Joy Mining Machinery*, a case in which the employer was denied the ability to require post-offer medical examinations after asking prospective employees if they had a family medical history of tuberculosis, cancer, epilepsy, and heart disease.[18]

Uniformed Services Employment and Reemployment Rights Act of 1994

The Uniformed Services Employment and Reemployment Rights Act of 1994 (USERRA) covers all military personnel, including National Guard members, reservists, and active-duty military personnel, who enlist either voluntarily or involuntarily during peace or wartime. Under this act, people who enter the military for a total of five years can return to their private-sector jobs without risk of loss of seniority or benefits.[19] The act protects against discrimination on the basis of military obligation in the areas of hiring, job retention, and advancement. The law does not require employers to pay the workers' wages while they are enlisted.

Amendments to the USERRA

In 2004, the USERRA was amended by the Veterans Benefits Improvement Act, which required employers to provide a notice of rights, benefits, and obligations of both employees and employers under USERRA.[20] For their part, service members must provide their employers with advance notice of their military obligations so that they will be protected by the reemployment rights statute.

3.2b Other Federal Laws and Executive Orders

Executive orders are used to ensure equal employment opportunities for individuals employed by government contractors. Since many large employers—such as General Dynamics, Intel, Dell Computer, and Motorola—and numerous small companies have contracts with the federal government, managers are expected to know and comply with the provisions of executive orders and other laws. The federal laws and executive orders that apply to government agencies and government contractors are summarized in Figure 3.7.

Figure 3.7 EEO Rules Applicable to Federal Contractors and Agencies

Law	Provisions
Vocational Rehabilitation Act of 1973 (amended in 1974)	Prohibits federal contractors from discriminating against disabled individuals in any program or activity receiving federal financial assistance; requires federal contractors to develop affirmative action plans to hire and promote disabled people.
Executive Order 11246 (1965), as amended by Order 11375 (1966)	Prohibits employment discrimination based on race, color, religion, sex, or national origin by government contractors with contracts exceeding $10,000; requires contractors employing 50 or more workers to develop affirmative action plans when government contracts exceed $50,000 per year.
Executive Order 11478 (1969)	Obligates the federal government to ensure that all personnel actions affecting applicants for employment be free from discrimination based on race, color, religion, sex, or national origin.

Vocational Rehabilitation Act of 1973

The Vocational Rehabilitation Act of 1973 required private employers with federal contracts valued at more than $2,500 to take action to hire individuals with mental or physical disabilities. Recipients of federal financial assistance, such as public and private colleges and universities, are also covered by this act. In applying the safeguards of this law, the term **disabled individual** means "any person who (1) has a physical or mental impairment which substantially limits one or more of such person's major life activities, (2) has a record of such an impairment, or (3) is regarded as having such an impairment." Employment is not required when some aspect of the employee's disability prevents that person from carrying out essential parts of the job, nor is it required if the disabled person is not otherwise qualified for the job.

disabled individual
Any person who (1) has a physical or mental impairment that substantially limits one or more of the person's major life activities, (2) has a record of such impairment, or (3) is regarded as having such an impairment.

In cases when people with contagious diseases are "otherwise qualified" to do their jobs, the law requires employers to make a reasonable accommodation to allow the disabled employees to perform their jobs.[21] Individuals with AIDS or HIV are also considered disabled within the meaning of the Rehabilitation Act. However, the Rehabilitation Act does not require employers to hire or retain a disabled person if he or she has a contagious disease that poses a direct threat to the health or safety of others and the individual cannot be accommodated.

Executive Order 11246

Federal agencies and government contractors with contracts valued at $10,000 or more must comply with the antidiscrimination provisions of Executive Order 11246. This order prohibits discrimination based on race, color, religion, sex, sexual orientation, or national origin in all employment activities. Furthermore, it requires that government contractors or subcontractors having 50 or more employees with contracts in excess of $50,000 develop affirmative action plans—such plans are discussed later in this chapter.

Don't Ask, Don't Tell Repeal Act of 2010. On September 20, 2011, the Don't Ask, Don't Tell Repeal Act was implemented to end the ban on gay, lesbian, or bisexual persons openly serving in the U.S. military. More recently, on January 25, 2021, President Joe Biden signed an executive order that lifted the previous restriction on transgender individuals serving in the military.[22]

3.2c Fair Employment Practice Laws

In addition to federal laws and executive orders, almost all states and many local governments have passed laws barring employment discrimination. Referred to as **fair employment practices (FEPs)**, these statutes are often more comprehensive than the federal laws.

fair employment practices (FEPs)
State and local laws governing equal employment opportunity that are often more comprehensive than federal laws and apply to small-business employers.

3.3 Other Equal Employment Opportunity Issues

LO3
Demonstrate how to prevent other forms of discrimination that are of particular interest to managers.

Federal laws, executive orders, court cases, and state and local statutes provide the broad legal framework for dealing with EEO concerns. Within these major laws, specific issues are of particular interest to supervisors and managers.

3.3a Sexual Harassment

sexual harassment
Unwelcome advances, requests for sexual favors, and other verbal or physical conduct of a sexual nature in the working environment.

Sexual harassment refers to unwelcome sexual advances, requests for sexual favors, and other verbal or physical harassment of a sexual nature. It can also include offensive remarks, vulgar or obscene gestures, and language or comments related to one's sex, an individual's body, or sexual activity. Both the victim and the harasser can be of any gender, and harassment can occur between individuals of the same or different genders. The harasser can be the victim's supervisor, a supervisor in another area, a coworker, or someone who is not an employee of the employer, such as a client or customer.[23]

The EEOC recognizes two forms of sexual harassment as being illegal under Title VII. The first, *quid pro quo harassment*, occurs when "submission to or rejection of sexual conduct is used as a basis for employment decisions."[24] This type of harassment involves a tangible or economic consequence, such as a demotion or loss of pay. For example, if a supervisor promotes an employee only after the person agrees to an after-work date, that conduct is clearly illegal.

The second type of harassment, *hostile environment*, can occur when unwelcome sexual conduct "has the purpose or effect of unreasonably interfering with job performance or creating an intimidating, hostile, or offensive working environment."[25] In 2021, New York Governor Andrew Cuomo was confronted with multiple accounts of women who accused him of sexual harassment, claiming that he had created a hostile environment at work through inappropriate touching and/or asking uncomfortable questions about their romantic relationships.[26]

Dirty jokes, vulgar slang, nude pictures, swearing, and personal ridicule and insult create a hostile environment when an employee finds them offensive. Email, instant and text messages, and posts on social networking sites have become convenient ways for employees to sexually harass their coworkers electronically.

Via a questionnaire, it is possible to test the understanding of your employees about what is and what is not sexual harassment. Highlights in HRM 2 shows some examples of questions that firms can ask their employees to gauge their knowledge of the topic.

The EEOC considers an employer guilty of sexual harassment when the employer knew or should have known about the unlawful conduct and failed to remedy it or to take corrective action. Employers are also guilty of sexual harassment when they allow nonemployees (customers or salespeople) to sexually harass employees.[27] When charges of sexual harassment have been proved, victims forced out of their jobs can be awarded back pay, lost benefits, attorney's fees, and interest charges, and they may be reinstated in

Questions Used to Audit Sexual Harassment in the Workplace

ACTIVITY	IS THIS SEXUAL HARASSMENT?			AWARE OF THIS BEHAVIOR IN THE ORGANIZATION?	
• Employees post cartoons on bulletin boards containing sexually related material.	Yes	No	Uncertain	Yes	No
• A male employee says to a female employee that she has beautiful eyes and hair.	Yes	No	Uncertain	Yes	No
• A male manager habitually calls all female employees "sweetie" or "darling."	Yes	No	Uncertain	Yes	No
• A manager fails to promote an employee of a different gender for not granting sexual favors.	Yes	No	Uncertain	Yes	No
• Male employees use vulgar language and tell sexual jokes that are overheard by, but not directed at, female employees.	Yes	No	Uncertain	Yes	No
• A male employee leans and peers over the back of a female employee when she wears a low-cut dress.	Yes	No	Uncertain	Yes	No
• A supervisor gives a subordinate of a different gender a nice gift on their birthday.	Yes	No	Uncertain	Yes	No
• Two male employees share a sexually explicit magazine while observed by a female employee.	Yes	No	Uncertain	Yes	No
• Female office workers are "rated" by male employees as they pass the men's desks.	Yes	No	Uncertain	Yes	No
• Revealing female clothing is given as a gift at an office birthday party.	Yes	No	Uncertain	Yes	No
• A sales representative from a supplier makes suggestive sexual remarks to a receptionist.	Yes	No	Uncertain	Yes	No

their jobs. Sexual harassment involving physical conduct can invite criminal charges, and punitive damages can be assessed against both the employer and the individual offender.[28]

In October 2017, the #MeToo movement emerged and quickly gained momentum, shining a brighter light on sexual harassment in the workplace. Research has shown many positive changes as a result of this movement: Nearly one-third of executives said they have changed their behaviors to avoid behavior that could be perceived as sexual harassment, companies have changed how complaints are handled and implemented new trainings, and sexual harassment lawsuits filed by the EEOC increased by 50 percent in 2017 and another 14 percent in 2018.[29]

However, since the #MeToo movement quieted down, reporting of sexual harassment has started to decrease again. In 2017, 55 percent of harassed women reported the hostile incident, but in 2020 that share dropped to 45 percent.[30] While many recognize the positive impact that the #MeToo movement has had in emboldening targets of sexual harassment to come forward, it is important not to become complacent.

Sexual harassment includes any type of behavior, comments, gestures, and actions of a sexual nature that create a hostile work environment for an employee.

David Pereiras/Shutterstock.com

3.3b Sexual Orientation

The Employment Non-Discrimination Act (ENDA) proposed by the U.S. Congress would extend the federal employment discrimination protection currently provided based on race, religion, gender, national origin, age, and disability to include sexual orientation and gender identity. Despite equality advocates' and politicians' efforts since 1994, this act has not been passed yet. Nevertheless, in *Bostock v. Clayton County* (2020), the U.S. Supreme Court held that Title VII of the Civil Rights Act of 1964 protects employees against discrimination because of their sexual orientation or gender identity.[31] Until this time, individual states had acted on their own accord to extend employment discrimination protections to explicitly cover lesbian, gay, bisexual, transgender, and queer (LGBTQ) employees. Because of the 2020 ruling, it is now considered illegal to discriminate based on sexual orientation or transgender status.

In addition to this ruling by the Supreme Court, the EEOC interprets and enforces Title VII's prohibition of sex discrimination in many additional ways. Some examples of LGBTQ-related claims that EEOC views as unlawful gender discrimination include the following:

- Failing to hire an applicant because they are transgender
- Firing an employee because they are planning to make or have made a *gender transition*
- Denying an employee equal access to a common *restroom* corresponding to the employee's gender identity
- Harassing an employee because of a gender transition, such as by intentionally and persistently *failing to use the name and gender pronoun that correspond to the gender identity with which the employee identifies*, and which the employee has communicated to management and employees
- Denying an employee a promotion because of sexual orientation

- Discriminating in *terms, conditions,* or *privileges of employment*, such as providing a lower salary to an employee because of sexual orientation, or denying spousal health insurance benefits to a female employee because her legal spouse is a woman, while providing spousal health insurance to a male employee whose legal spouse is a woman
- *Harassing* an employee because of their sexual orientation—for example, by using derogatory terms, sexually oriented comments, or disparaging remarks for associating with a person of the same or different genders

Figure 3.8 States with Laws Prohibiting Sexual Orientation and Gender Identity Discrimination

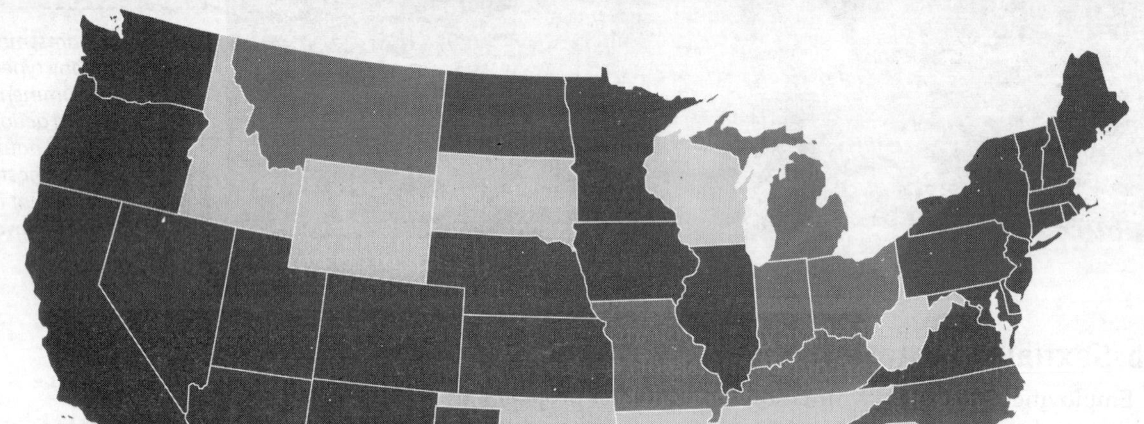

- Prohibit discrimination against public employees based on sexual orientation only
  1 state*
- Prohibit discrimination against public employees based on sexual orientation and gender identity
  6 states
- Prohibit discrimination based on sexual orientation only
  1 state
- Enforcement authorities are accepting complaints on the basis of sexual orientation and gender identity because the state has adopted the Bostock rationale into state law**
  8 states
- Prohibit discrimination based on sexual orientation and gender identity
  22 states & DC

*North Carolina's executive order enumerates sexual orientation and gender identity. However, this order has a bathroom carve out for transgender employees making the executive order not fully inclusive.

**On June 15, 2020, the U.S. Supreme Court ruled in *Bostock v. Clayton County*, Georgia that sexual orientation and gender identity discrimination are prohibited under federal sex-based employment protections.

Source: Human Rights Campaign, "State Equality Index 2020," https://www.hrc.org/resources/state-equality-index.

- Discriminating against or harassing an employee because of their sexual orientation or gender identity, in combination with another unlawful reason—for example, on the basis of transgender status and race, or sexual orientation and disability[32]

Regardless of how companies may feel about sexual orientation discrimination, studies have shown that prohibiting sexual orientation and gender discrimination can increase company performance. For example, one study points out that patent-based innovation increases by 8 percent in states after they adopt the federal ENDA guidelines to ban sexual orientation and gender identity discrimination in the workplace.[33]

3.3c Immigration Reform and Control

Good employment is the magnet that attracts many people to the United States. However, unauthorized immigration is an issue of national concern at the federal, state, and local legislative levels and among employers, unions, and civil rights groups alike.[34]

Employers must comply with the requirements of the Immigration Reform and Control Act (IRCA). This law includes two employer mandates. First, all employers covered by the law are prohibited from knowingly hiring or retaining undocumented individuals on the job.[35] Second, employers with four or more employees are prohibited from discriminating in hiring or termination decisions on the basis of national origin or citizenship.[36]

To comply with the IRCA, employers must verify and maintain records on the legal rights of applicants to work in the United States. The *Handbook for Employers*, published by the U.S. Department of Justice, lists five actions that employers must take to comply with the law:

1. Have employees fill out their part of Form I-9.
2. Check documents establishing an employee's identity and eligibility to work.
3. Complete the employer's section of Form I-9.
4. Retain Form I-9 for at least three years.
5. Present Form I-9 for inspection to an Immigration and Naturalization Service officer or to a Department of Labor officer upon request.[37]

Employers with sizable contracts with the federal government must also use its E-Verify system. E-Verify provides an automated link to federal databases to help employers determine the legal eligibility of workers and the validity of their Social Security numbers. Employers that do not conduct business with the government can also use E-Verify, if they choose.

Employers found to have violated IRCA's discrimination provisions will be ordered to cease the discriminatory practice. They may also be directed to hire, with or without back pay, individuals harmed by the discrimination and to pay a fine of up to $1,000 for each of those individuals. Charges of discrimination based on national origin or citizenship are filed with the Office of Special Counsel in the Department of Justice.

3.3d Emerging Employment Discrimination Issues

Weight Discrimination

Some studies show that weight discrimination, especially against women, is not only increasing but has become almost as common as racial discrimination.[38] No federal laws prohibit weight discrimination, although the EEOC has said that morbid obesity is a protected disability under the ADA. At some point, it is not out of the realm of possibility that overweight/obesity could become a protected class.[39]

IF YOU HAVE THE RIGHT TO WORK

DON'T LET ANYONE TAKE IT AWAY

If you have the skills, experience, and legal right to work, your citizenship or immigration status shouldn't get in the way. Neither should the place you were born or another aspect of your national origin. A part of U.S. immigration laws protects legally-authorized workers from discrimination based on their citizenship status and national origin. You can read this law at 8 U.S.C. § 1324b.

The Immigrant and Employee Rights Section (IER) may be able to help if an employer treats you unfairly in violation of this law.

The law that IER enforces is 8 U.S.C. § 1324b. The regulations for this law are at 28 C.F.R. Part 44.

Call IER if an employer:

Does not hire you or fires you because of your national origin or citizenship status (this may violate a part of the law at 8 U.S.C. § 1324b(a)(1))

Treats you unfairly while checking your right to work in the U.S., including while completing the Form I-9 or using E-Verify (this may violate the law at 8 U.S.C. § 1324b(a)(1) or (a)(6))

Retaliates against you because you are speaking up for your right to work as protected by this law (the law prohibits retaliation at 8 U.S.C. § 1324b(a)(5))

The law can be complicated. Call IER to get more information on protections from discrimination based on citizenship status and national origin.

Immigrant and Employee Rights Section (IER)
1-800-255-7688 **TTY 1-800-237-2515**
www.justice.gov/ier
IER@usdoj.gov

U.S. Department of Justice, Civil Rights Division, Immigrant and Employee Rights Section, January 2019

This guidance document is not intended to be a final agency action, has no legally binding effect, and has no force or effect of law. The document may be rescinded or modified at the Department's discretion, in accordance with applicable laws. The Department's guidance documents, including this guidance, do not establish legally enforceable responsibilities beyond what is required by the terms of the applicable statutes, regulations, or binding judicial precedent. For more information, see "Memorandum for All Components: Prohibition of Improper Guidance Documents," from Attorney General Jefferson B. Sessions III, November 16, 2017.

https://www.e-verify.gov/sites/default/files/everify/posters/IER_RightToWorkPoster%20Eng_Es.pdf

Employers using E-Verify must display a copy of this poster for employees to see.

Attractiveness and Discrimination

There are no federal laws prohibiting discrimination in the workplace based on people's attractiveness, although it undoubtedly occurs. In a survey of hiring managers conducted by *Newsweek*, 57 percent of them said that qualified but unattractive job candidates would have a harder time landing a job. This discriminatory treatment of people who are considered physically unattractive is known as "lookism."[40] Part of the problem with implementing a law making it illegal to discriminate based on a person's appearance would be deciding who is unattractive enough to be protected by such a law. Moreover, in some instances, good looks can be a BFOQ. The modeling business is one example of this.[41]

Natural Hair Discrimination

In the workplace, Black women often find themselves discriminated against when they wear their natural hair. Black women are 80 percent more likely to change their natural hair to conform to social norms or expectations at work, such as by straightening (processing) it; they are also 1.5 times more likely to be sent home or know of a woman sent home from the workplace due to her hairstyle.[42] In July 2019, California became the first state to ban discrimination against natural hair—a legislative policy referred to as the CROWN Act.[43] Other states and cities have followed California's example, and many advocates are pushing for the U.S. Congress to implement national legislation against such discrimination.

Caregivers and Discrimination

In 2007, the EEOC issued new enforcement guidelines to help prevent discrimination against workers with caregiving responsibilities. There are no federal statutes that prohibit discrimination based "solely" on a person being a caregiver. However, disparate

g-stockstudio/
Shutterstock.com

The EEOC provides guidelines to help prevent discrimination against caregivers.

treatment arises when an employee with caregiving responsibilities is subjected to discrimination based on a protected characteristic under equal opportunity laws (such as gender, race, or age).[44] The EEOC has outlined numerous scenarios it says could constitute discrimination against a caregiver. Denying women with young children an employment opportunity available to men with young children is an example. So is refusing to hire a worker who is a single parent of a child with a disability based on the assumption that caregiving responsibilities will make the worker unreliable.

3.4 Uniform Guidelines on Employee Selection Procedures

LO4 Explain how the Uniform Guidelines on Employee Selection Procedures are used by firms and how they relate to the issues of adverse impact and disparate treatment.

Employers are often uncertain about the appropriateness of specific selection procedures, especially those related to testing and selection. To remedy this concern, the EEOC, along with three other government agencies, adopted the current **Uniform Guidelines on Employee Selection Procedures.**[45] The *Uniform Guidelines* is a very important procedural document for managers because it applies to employee selection procedures in the areas of hiring, retention, promotion, transfer, demotion, dismissal, and referral. It is designed to help employers, labor organizations, employment agencies, and licensing and certification boards comply with the requirements of federal laws prohibiting employment discrimination.

Uniform Guidelines on Employee Selection Procedures
A procedural document published in the *Federal Register* to help employers comply with federal regulations against discriminatory actions.

Validity

When using a test or other selection instrument to choose individuals for employment, employers must be able to prove that the selection instrument bears a direct relationship to success on the job. This proof is established through validation studies that show how related the test is to the job.

Adverse Impact and Disparate Treatment

adverse impact
A concept that refers to the rejection of a significantly higher percentage of a protected class for employment, placement, or promotion when compared with the successful, non protected class.

For an applicant or employee to pursue a discrimination case successfully, the individual must establish that the employer's selection procedures resulted in an adverse impact on a protected class. **Adverse impact** refers to the unintentional rejection for employment, placement, or promotion of a significantly higher percentage of members of a protected class when compared with members of nonprotected classes.[46] The *Uniform Guidelines* does not require an employer to conduct validity studies of its selection procedures when they have not resulted in adverse impact on a protected class. However, organizations that validate their selection procedures on a regular basis, and that use interviews, tests, and other procedures in such a manner so as to avoid adverse impact, will generally be in compliance and avoid costly litigation.

disparate treatment
A situation in which protected class members receive unequal treatment or are evaluated by different standards.

In EEO cases, it is important to distinguish between adverse impact and disparate treatment discrimination. Adverse impact cases deal with unintentional discrimination; **disparate treatment** cases involve instances of purposeful discrimination. Allowing men to apply for craft jobs, such as carpentry or electrical work, but denying this opportunity to women would qualify as disparate treatment. To win a disparate treatment case, the plaintiff must prove that the employer's actions intended to discriminate, which is often difficult.

There are two basic ways to show that adverse impact exists.

four-fifths rule
A rule of thumb followed by the EEOC in determining adverse impact for use in enforcement proceedings.

Adverse Rejection Rate (Four-Fifths Rule). According to the *Uniform Guidelines*, a selection program has an adverse impact when the selection rate for any racial, ethnic, or sex class is less than four-fifths (or 80 percent) of the rate of the class with the highest selection rate. The EEOC has adopted the **four-fifths rule** as a rule of thumb to determine adverse impact in enforcement proceedings. The four-fifths rule is not a legal definition of discrimination, but rather a method by which the EEOC or any other enforcement agency can monitor serious discrepancies in hiring, promotion, or other employment decisions.

As an example of how the four-fifths rule is applied, suppose a company wants to fill 50 positions, and it interviews 60 men and 250 women for those positions. If the company hires 20 men and 30 women, women are adversely impacted, because the selection rate for women (30/250) is 12 percent while that for men (20/60) is 33.3 percent. Dividing 12 by 33.3 gives us 36.36 percent, which is less than 80 percent (or four-fifths). In this scenario, significantly more women were interviewed, so significantly more women should be hired. One potential bias with the four-fifths rule may come if the company decides to count gender based on anatomic sex at birth rather than how the individual self-identifies, which may not squarely be as a man or a woman.[47] The appendix at the end of this chapter further explains how adverse impact is determined and gives another realistic example of how the four-fifths rule is applied.

An alternative to the four-fifths rule, and one frequently used in discrimination lawsuits, is to conduct a standard deviation analysis of a firm's applicant data. The US. Supreme Court, in *Hazelwood School District v. United States*, set forth a standard deviation analysis that determines whether the difference between the expected selection rates for protected groups and the actual selection rates could be attributed to chance. If chance is eliminated as an explanation for the lower selection rates of the protected class, it is assumed that the employer's selection technique has an adverse impact on the employment opportunities of that group.

Restricted Policy. Any evidence that an employer has a selection procedure that excludes members of a protected class, whether intentional or not, constitutes adverse impact. For example, hiring individuals who must meet a minimum height or appearance standard (at the expense of protected class members) is evidence of a restricted policy.

The benchmark case in employment selection procedures is *Griggs v. Duke Power Company* (1971). Willie Griggs, who was Black, had applied for the position of coal handler with the Duke Power Company. His request for the position was denied because he was not a high school graduate, a requirement for the position. Griggs claimed the job standard was discriminatory because it did not relate to job success and because the standard had an adverse impact on a protected class. When employers use educational, physical, or intelligence standards as a basis for hiring or promotion, they must be absolutely necessary for job success.

Workforce Utilization Analysis

As you have learned, employers must be aware of how their selection procedures affect protected class members. Part of this process involves analyzing the composition of their internal workforce when compared with their external labor market. The EEOC refers to this comparison as **workforce utilization analysis**. This type of analysis simply compares an employer's workforce by race and gender for specific job categories against the surrounding labor market. The employer's relevant labor market is the area from which employees are drawn who have the skills needed to successfully perform the job. For example, if Squarespace, the website maker, is hiring computer technicians from a labor market composed of 10 percent B lack workers, 8 percent Hispanic workers, and 2 percent Native American workers, all of whom possess the qualifications for the job, the employer's internal workforce should reflect this racial composition. When this occurs, the employer's workforce is said to be *at parity* with the relevant labor market. If the employer's racial workforce composition in terms of one or more underrepresented groups does not match the external figures, then the protected class is said to be *underutilized*, and the employer should take steps to correct the imbalance.

workforce utilization analysis
A process of classifying protected-class members by number and by the type of job they hold within the organization.

3.5 Enforcing Equal Employment Opportunity Legislation

LO5

Describe how EEO recordkeeping and posting requirements work, including how discrimination charges are processed by the Equal Employment Opportunity Commission (EEOC).

As the federal government's leading civil rights agency, the EEOC is responsible for ensuring that covered employers comply with EEO legislation. It accomplishes this goal primarily by (1) issuing various employment guidelines and monitoring the employment practices of organizations and (2) protecting employee rights through the investigation and prosecution of discrimination charges.[48]

3.5a Record-Keeping and Posting Requirements

Organizations subject to Title VII are required by law to maintain specific employment records and reports. Those failing to comply with record-keeping and posting requirements or willfully falsifying records can incur penalties, including fines and imprisonment. Highlights in HRM 3 provides a recent example of one of the posters that companies are required by law to display in prominent places such as the cafeteria, by time clocks, or by the water cooler. These placements allow for employees to easily find and read the posters. If requirements are not posted, then the EEOC could allow an employee to file a discrimination charge late (past the 180-day filing deadline).

EEOC Poster Supplement for 2016

"EEO is the Law" Poster Supplement

Employers Holding Federal Contracts or Subcontracts Section Revisions

The Executive Order 11246 section is revised as follows:

RACE, COLOR, RELIGION, SEX, SEXUAL ORIENTATION, GENDER IDENTITY, NATIONAL ORIGIN

Executive Order 11246, as amended, prohibits employment discrimination based on race, color, religion, sex, sexual orientation, gender identity, or national origin, and requires affirmative action to ensure equality of opportunity in all aspects of employment.

PAY SECRECY

Executive Order 11246, as amended, protects applicants and employees from discrimination based on inquiring about, disclosing, or discussing their compensation or the compensation of other applicants or employees.

The Individuals with Disabilities section is revised as follows:

INDIVIDUALS WITH DISABILITIES

Section 503 of the Rehabilitation Act of 1973, as amended, protects qualified individuals with disabilities from discrimination in hiring, promotion, discharge, pay, fringe benefits, job training, classification, referral, and other aspects of employment. Disability discrimination includes not making reasonable accommodation to the known physical or mental limitations of an otherwise qualified individual with a disability who is an applicant or employee, barring undue hardship to the employer. Section 503 also requires that Federal contractors take affirmative action to employ and advance in employment qualified individuals with disabilities at all levels of employment, including the executive level.

The Vietnam Era, Special Disabled Veterans section is revised as follows:

PROTECTED VETERANS

The Vietnam Era Veterans' Readjustment Assistance Act of 1974, as amended, 38 U.S.C. 4212, prohibits employment discrimination against, and requires affirmative action to recruit, employ, and advance in employment, disabled veterans, recently separated veterans (i.e., within three years of discharge or release from active duty), active duty wartime or campaign badge veterans, or Armed Forces service medal veterans.

Mandatory Supplement to EEOC P/E-1(Revised 11/09) "EEO is the Law" Poster.

If you believe that you have experienced discrimination contact OFCCP: 1-800-397-6251 | TTY 1-877-889-5627 | www.dol.gov.

3.5b Processing Discrimination Charges

Figure 3.9 summarizes the process of filing a discrimination charge with the EEOC.[49] (Note that the process is slightly different for federal employees and job applicants.) Employees or job applicants who believe they have been discriminated against first file a discrimination complaint, or **charge form**, with the EEOC. This charge must be filed within 180 days of the alleged unlawful practice occurring.[50] When the EEOC processes a charge, it notifies the employer that a charge of employment discrimination has been filed. Employers will receive a copy of the charge within 10 days of it being filed. Both parties—the plaintiff (employee) and the defendant (organization)—must be prepared to support their beliefs or actions as the investigation proceeds.

charge form
A discrimination complaint filed with the EEOC by employees or job applicants.

Retaliation

Managers and supervisors must not retaliate against individuals who invoke their legal rights to file charges or to support other employees during EEOC proceedings.[51] Retaliation can include any punitive action taken against employees who elect to exercise their legal rights before any EEO agency.[52] These actions can include terminating employees, giving them unjustified negative appraisals, subjecting them to more supervision,

Figure 3.9 Filing a Charge of Employment Discrimination

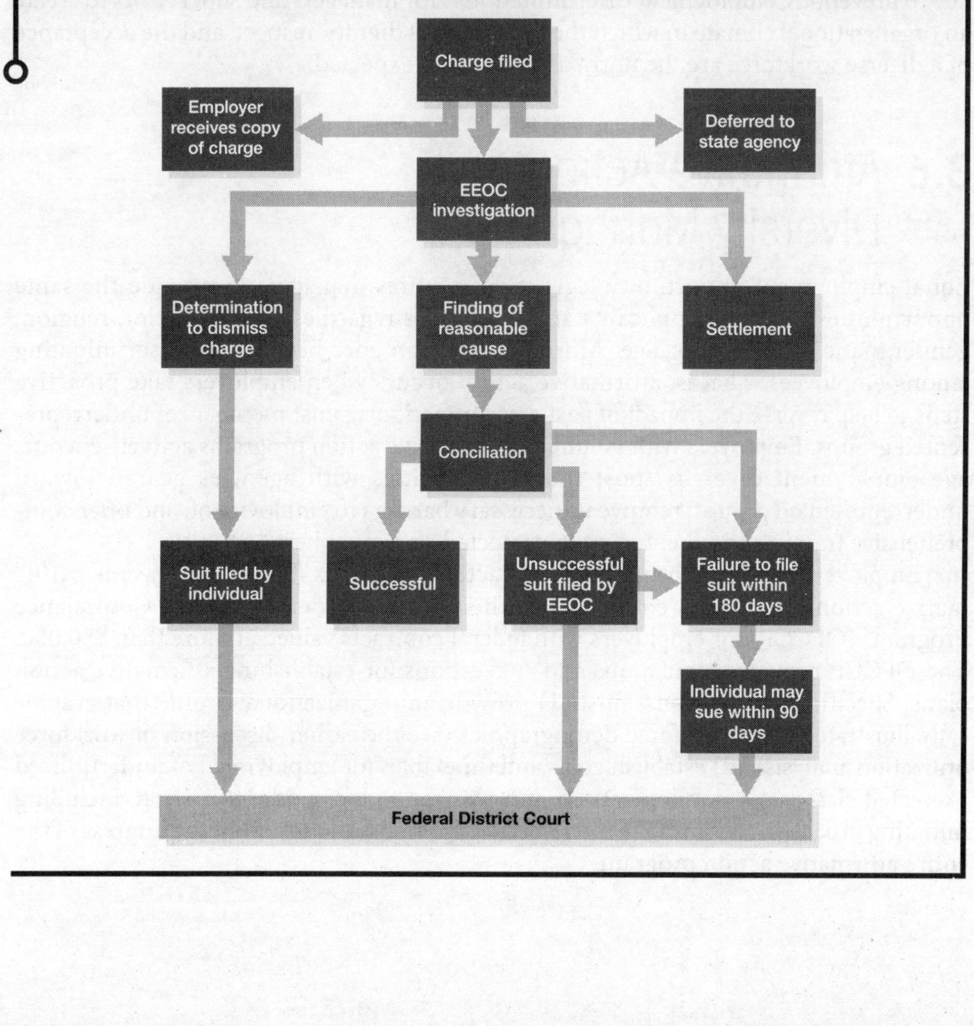

demoting them, reducing their salaries and work responsibilities, and transferring them to a less desirable job.[53] Of course, employees are not excused from continuing to perform their jobs or following their company's legitimate workplace rules just because they have filed a complaint with the EEOC or opposed discrimination.

3.5c Preventing Discrimination Charges

Both large and small employers understand that the foundation to preventing any form of discrimination is having a comprehensive EEO policy. Employers that do not have an EEO policy are legally vulnerable. Antidiscrimination policy statements must be inclusive; they must cover all applicable laws and EEOC guidelines and contain practical illustrations of specific inappropriate behavior. For the policy to have value, it must be widely disseminated to managers, supervisors, and all nonmanagerial employees. A complete policy will include specific consequences for those found guilty of engaging in discriminatory behavior.[54]

Because managers and supervisors are key to preventing and correcting discrimination, they, in particular, must be trained to understand employee rights and managerial obligations.[55] A comprehensive training program will include (1) the prohibitions covered in the various EEO statutes and executive orders, (2) guidance on how to respond to complaints of discrimination, (3) procedures for investigating complaints (see Chapter 13), and (4) suggestions for remedying inappropriate behavior. Perhaps the ultimate key to preventing employment discrimination is for managers and supervisors to create an organizational climate in which the principles of dignity, respect, and the acceptance of a diverse workforce are the norm and therefore expected.

LO6 Explain what affirmative action is and how companies today are seeing the value of voluntarily having diverse workforces.

3.6 Affirmative Action and Diversity Management

affirmative action
A policy that goes beyond equal employment opportunity by requiring organizations to comply with the law and correct any past discriminatory practices by increasing the numbers of underrepresented groups in specific positions.

Equal employment opportunity legislation requires managers to provide the same opportunities to all job applicants and employees regardless of race, color, religion, gender, national origin, or age. **Affirmative action** goes beyond not discriminating among employees. That is, affirmative action occurs when employers take proactive steps to help reverse the impact of past discrimination against members of underrepresented groups. Employers with voluntary affirmative action programs actively encourage employment diversity, post job opportunities with agencies geared toward underrepresented groups, remove unnecessary barriers to employment, and offer comprehensive training and mentoring to protected class members.

Employers may establish affirmative action programs for several reasons. Affirmative action programs are required by the Office of Federal Contract Compliance Programs (OFCCP) for employers with federal contracts valued at more than $50,000. The OFCCP provides regulations and suggestions for establishing affirmative action plans. Specifically, employers must (1) provide an organizational profile that graphically illustrates their workforce demographics (see the earlier discussion of workforce utilization analysis); (2) establish goals and timetables for employment of underutilized protected classes; (3) develop actions and plans to reduce underutilization, including initiating proactive recruitment and selection methods; and (4) monitor progress of the entire affirmative action program.

Courts will sometimes mandate employers that have been found guilty of past discrimination to establish affirmative action programs, particularly when the discrimination has been pervasive and a long-held organizational practice. A court-ordered program, often implemented through a *consent decree* between the court and employer, will require the setting of hiring and promotional goals along with stated timetables for compliance. When the requirements of the consent decree are met, the employer is no longer bound by the court order.

Sometimes employers voluntarily develop their own affirmative action programs to ensure that protected class members receive fair treatment in all aspects of employment. For example, some companies have designated chief diversity officers. A **chief diversity officer (CDO)** is a top executive responsible for the implementation of a firm's diversity efforts. In 2016, Salesforce, Dropbox, Pinterest, and Twitter all hired a CDO, following the footsteps of tech giants like Google, Microsoft, and Facebook. Today, about one in five *Fortune* 1000 companies has a CDO.

chief diversity officer (CDO)
A top executive responsible for implementing a firm's diversity efforts.

When the coronavirus pandemic struck the United States in mid-March 2020, CDO jobs were affected more than any other job. Between March and June of 2020, job postings for CDO and similar job titles fell by 60 percent, more than double the 28 percent by which job openings decreased overall. This large gap sent a message that diversity and inclusion were not priorities for many businesses and companies. In June 2020, just after the death of George Floyd, a Black man, at the hands of a White Minneapolis police officer, and at the height of the Black Lives Matter movement, diversity and inclusion job postings rose 50 percent.[56] By August 2020, they were more than 40 percent higher than the number available 8 months earlier.[57] Employers felt the pressure of the controversies circulating in the current society, and have begun to make equality and diversity a priority in an effort to remedy perceived injustices.

Many companies have announced initiatives to increase the diversity of their workforces. Merck, GM, and Walmart have pledged $100 million as part of an effort to hire 1 million Black workers by 2030. Pinterest interviewed hundreds of its employees and created a committee to improve workplace culture and diversity. Starbucks is now mandating antibias training for executives and tying their compensation to increasing minority representation. Salesforce, Nasdaq, PepsiCo, and many others are following suit in these efforts to build a diverse and inclusive workforce.[58]

A number of studies have demonstrated how having a diverse workforce can increase a company's revenue.[59] In fact, one study showed that having a diverse set of leaders can improve a company's likelihood of improving market share by 45 percent. As HR professionals readily note, the success of any voluntary affirmative action program or diversity effort largely depends on the support it receives from senior managers and supervisors at all organizational levels.[60] The EEOC recommends that organizations developing affirmative action programs follow specific steps, as shown in Highlights in HRM 4.

One of the drawbacks of implementing an affirmative action program is that an employer may sometimes be accused of **reverse discrimination**—that is, giving preference to members of protected classes to such an extent that unprotected individuals believe they are suffering from discrimination. For example, a male employee may feel as if he was more qualified for a promotion than the female employee who received it. He might claim reverse discrimination, saying that he was denied the position solely because he was not in a protected class. When charges of reverse discrimination are made, organizations encounter a "Catch-22" situation—they are caught between attempting to correct past discriminatory practices and handling present complaints from unprotected members alleging that HR policies are unfair.

reverse discrimination
The act of giving preference to members of protected classes to the extent that unprotected individuals believe they are suffering discrimination.

Basic Steps in Developing an Effective Affirmative Action Program

Filing a Charge of Employment Discrimination

1. Issue a written equal employment opportunity policy and an affirmative action commitment statement.
2. Publicize the policy and the organization's affirmative action commitment.
3. Appoint a top official within the organization to direct and implement the program.
4. Survey underrepresented race, ethnic background, or gender employment by department and job classification.
5. Develop goals and timetables to improve utilization of those of underrepresented groups (such as race, ethnicity, and gender) in each area in which underutilization has been identified.
6. Develop and implement specific programs to achieve goals.
7. Establish an internal audit and reporting system to monitor and evaluate progress in each aspect of the program.
8. Develop supportive in-house and community programs.

Source: U.S. Equal Employment Opportunity Commission.

3.6a Court Decisions

In the 1970s, in two major cases dealing with reverse discrimination, the U.S. Supreme Court ruled that applicants must be evaluated on an individual basis and that race can be one factor used in the evaluation process as long as other competitive factors are considered (*University of California Regents v. Bakke* and *United States Steelworkers of America v. Weber*[61]). The Court stated that affirmative action programs were not illegal as long as rigid quota systems were not specified for different protected classes. Also, voluntary affirmative action programs are permissible where they attempt to eliminate racial or gender imbalances in traditionally segregated job categories.

The judicial support for affirmative action programs has eroded over the decades, however. During the mid-1990s, federal courts increasingly restricted the use of race and when awarding scholarships, determining college admissions, making layoff decisions, selecting employees, promoting employees, and awarding government contracts. Then in 2009, the Supreme Court heard *Ricci vs. DeStafano*, a lawsuit brought against the City of New Haven, Connecticut, by 19 city firefighters. The firefighters alleged that the city discriminated against them by invalidating a test for a promotion because no Black firefighters had passed it with a score high enough to warrant promotion. The firefighters, 17 of whom were White and 2 of whom were Hispanic, claimed they were denied the promotions because of their race.

In a split decision, the Court ruled in the firefighters' favor. The ruling did not question the fire department's efforts to ensure that members of underrepresented races were fairly promoted. However, it said that throwing out the test in midstream (that test, incidentally, had been designed by an outside consulting firm to be nondiscriminatory) was unfair to those who had passed it. In its ruling, the Court said: "once that process

Rawpixel.com/Shutterstock.com

One of the ways companies can foster diversity within their organizations is by getting employees to talk about their differences. For example, the Mallon Group Training and Management has developed a series of Know Me games that enable participants of different cultures, races, sexual orientations, and so forth to explore issues of diversity together.

has been established and employers have made clear their selection criteria, they may not then invalidate the test results, thus upsetting an employee's legitimate expectation not to be judged on the basis of race."

The *Ricci vs. DeStafano* ruling underscores the importance of carefully designing selection procedures as well as diligently following them once they are designed. It also shows how tricky it can be to implement an affirmative action program.[62]

3.6b Beyond Affirmative Action: Leveraging Diversity

The future of affirmative action might not rest on judicial decisions or laws, but rather depend on managers' attitudes and voluntary actions to make the workplace fairer and more competitive. Managers who embrace a diverse workforce know that individual employee differences and the contributions made by people of varied abilities are one way to develop a competitive advantage. For example, some studies have found that companies with more progressive nondiscrimination policies outperform competing firms that lack them.[63] Other studies have shown that the more diverse a company's executive team, in terms of both gender and ethnic diversity, the more likely it is to outperform its less diverse peer companies.[64] As more companies expand around the globe either physically or on the Web, they are recognizing that they need to employ diverse people with different talents to better understand and compete in various markets abroad.

Investors are also pushing companies to be more diverse. John Hoeppner, head of U.S. stewardship for Legal and General Investment Management, manages approximately $1.5 trillion in assets worldwide and has begun to invest more heavily in companies with greater diversity. His firm, he reports, is not just investing in diversity for diversity's sake. "It is absolutely about financial performance," Hoeppner says. "More diversity has higher probability of better results." Recognizing this relationship, an increasing number of companies have begun reporting diversity data to the public.

Today, more than one-third of publicly listed companies include diversity disclosures in their annual reports.[65]

Robert Livingston, a lecturer at Harvard University, created a five-step plan for organizations to develop policies and promote equity and diversity. These five stages, which are illustrated in Figure 3.10, are (1) problem awareness; (2) root-cause analysis; (3) empathy, indicating its level of concern about the problem and the people it affects; (4) strategies for addressing the problem; and (5) sacrifice, or willingness to invest the time, energy, and resources necessary for strategy implementation.[66] Organizations and leaders can use these steps to increase the diversity of their workforces.

After promoting diversity and equity overall, organizations can also take steps to leverage each person's individual differences. According to Martin Davidson, a professor and researcher at the Darden School of Business at the University of Virginia, these steps focus on seeing not only the more obvious differences between people, such as their ethnic backgrounds, sexes, ages, religions, and so forth, but also how they think, learn, work, and interact with each other. Thus, the three specific steps toward leveraging people's differences are seeing, understanding, and valuing people. Highlights in HRM 5 identifies some specific activities that individuals and organizations can undertake to facilitate each of these steps. We will discuss diversity in more detail in Chapter 5 and throughout this textbook.

Figure 3.10 Steps to Leveraging Employee Differences

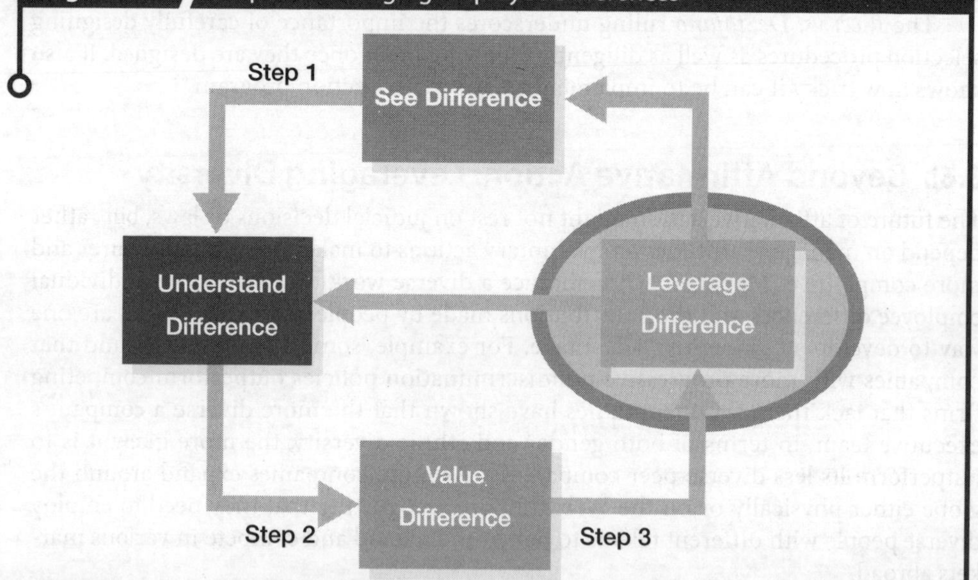

Source: Martin N. Davidson, *The End of Diversity as We Know It: Why Diversity Efforts Fail and How Leveraging Difference Can Succeed* (San Francisco: Berrett-Kohler Press, 2011).

5 Highlights in HRM

Embracing Diversity and Leveraging Employee Differences

Practices for Individuals

Seeing

- Openly acknowledge that relevant differences are common.
- Address points of conflict. Observe while remaining silent.

Understanding

- Seek sources of information that bring understanding about the differences.
- Acquire data through listening, asking questions, and sharing your story.
- Involve people who are different from you in your network.

Valuing

- Avoid being overly careful in dealing with differences.
- Accept that there will be conflict and discomfort that require perseverance.
- Use data to develop a new perspective.

Practices for Organizations

Seeing

- Openly address tension among members. Encourage members to avoid secrecy.

Understanding

- Seek sources of information that bring understanding about the differences.
- Gather data through surveys and other techniques. Establish inclusive structures.

Valuing

- Reward members for engaging in activities that address and diminish differences.
- Hold employees accountable for employing new behaviors. Actively seek diversity when recruiting.

Source: Adapted from Martin N. Davidson, *The End of Diversity as We Know It: Why Diversity Efforts Fail and How Leveraging Difference Can Succeed*. (San Francisco: Berrett-Kohler Press, 2011).

Summary

LO 1 Three factors have influenced the growth of EEOC legislation: (1) changing attitudes toward employment discrimination; (2) published reports highlighting the economic problems and injustices experienced by minority workers; and (3) a growing body of disparate discrimination laws and regulations.

LO 2 Government reports show that wages and job opportunities for underrepresented groups typically lag behind those for White men. The EEOC was originally set up to ensure fair employment practices regardless of race, gender, or age. Being fair requires knowing the legal aspects of the employment relationship, including the laws and various executive orders mentioned in this chapter. Other areas that have more recently become a concern include discrimination based on disabilities, sexual orientation, weight, appearance, or status as a caregiver.

LO 3 Other bases on which employees can be discriminated against include (1) sexual harassment, (2) sexual orientation, (3) immigrant status, (4) weight, (5) appearance, and (6) caregiver status. Many federal laws, executive orders, court cases, and state and local statutes have provided a broad legal framework for addressing these areas of discrimination, and managers should become familiar with this framework.

LO 4 The *Uniform Guidelines on Employee Selection Procedures* is a document designed to help employers comply with federal bans against employment practices that discriminate on the basis of race, color, religion, gender, or national origin. The *Uniform Guidelines* provides employers with a framework for making legally enforceable employment decisions. Employers must be able to show that their selection procedures are valid when it comes to predicting a person's job performance.

LO 5 To ensure that organizations comply with antidiscrimination legislation, the EEOC was established to monitor employers' actions. Employers subject to federal laws must maintain certain records and report certain employment statistics where mandated. Employees or applicants for employment who believe they have been discriminated against may file a discrimination complaint (a charge form) with the EEOC. If an agreement is not reached, the EEOC may elect to sue the employer in federal court. Figure 3.9 illustrates the steps in filing a discrimination charge.

LO 6 Affirmative action goes beyond providing equal employment opportunities to employees. Firms with federal contracts and firms that have been found guilty of past discrimination can be required to implement affirmative action programs. This is accomplished by employing protected classes in jobs in which they are underrepresented. The employer's goal is to have a balanced internal workforce representative of the employer's relevant labor market. The future of affirmative action might not rest on judicial decisions or laws, but rather depend on the efforts of managers to voluntarily embrace and foster diversity. Differences of all sorts among people are ubiquitous in the workforce. Managers need to leverage these differences because they can be the source of organizational strength.

Key Terms

adverse impact
affirmative action
bona fide occupational qualification (BFOQ)
business necessity
charge form
chief diversity officer (CDO)
disabled individual
disparate treatment
equal employment opportunity (EEO)
Equal Employment Opportunity Commission (EEOC)
fair employment practices (FEPs)
four-fifths rule
protected classes
reasonable accommodation
reverse discrimination
sexual harassment
workforce utilization analysis
Uniform Guidelines on Employee Selection Procedures

Discussion Questions

LO 1 Given that the United States was founded on the principles of individual merit, hard work, and equality, how have people's perceptions of these values changed the way they see discrimination in the workplace?

More recent events, such as the tragic killings of George Floyd, Breonna Taylor, Ahmaud Arbery, and others, have laid bare the brutal costs of systemic discrimination. How would you advise a manager to root out system discrimination in an organization?

LO 2 EEO legislation was prompted by significant social events. List those events and describe how they influenced the passage of various EEO laws. Cite and describe the major federal laws and court decisions that affect the employment process of both large and small organizations.

After receiving several complaints of sexual harassment, the HR department of a city library decided to establish a sexual harassment policy. What should be included in the policy? How should it be implemented?

LO 3 List specific behaviors that may be considered sexual harassment in terms of either *quid pro quo* or *hostile environment* harassment.

Discuss some examples of LGBTQ-related claims that the EEOC might view as unlawful discrimination.

LO 4 What is the *Uniform Guidelines on Employee Selection Procedures?* To whom do the guidelines apply? What do they cover?

Joe Alverez has filed a complaint with the EEOC alleging that his employer, Universal Mortgage Company, promotes more Whites than Hispanics into managerial positions. Explain the statistical methods used by the EEOC to investigate this adverse impact claim.

LO 5 How does the EEOC affect companies? What must you do as a manager to appropriately respond to the administrative rules and regulations published in the *Federal Register?*

As a marketing manager, you have recently turned down Nancy Conrad for a position as sales supervisor. Nancy believes the denial was due to her gender, and she has filed a sex discrimination charge with the EEOC. Explain the steps the EEOC will use to process the charge; include Nancy's options during the process.

LO 6 Affirmative action is both a legal and emotional issue affecting employees and employers. Develop as many arguments as you can both supporting and opposing affirmative action as an employer policy. If you were asked to implement such a program, what steps would you follow?

CASE STUDY 1 Going to the Dogs

Let's admit it: With very few exceptions, we all love dogs. We love to be with our dogs, and our dogs love to be with us. So it is only natural, then, to want to keep our dogs with us as much as possible, even when we go to work. Pet Sitters International thinks this is such a good idea that it has instituted "Take Your Dog to Work Day," a once-a-year event designed to raise awareness of the benefits of dog ownership and to encourage pet adoption.

But maybe you would like something a bit more regular, like having the option to bring Fido to work every day? According to a survey by the American Pet Products Manufacturers Association, it should not be too hard to find an opportunity: Nearly one in five companies already allows pets in the workplace. You can even find a list of employers that allow canines at work on DogFriendly.com. Fans of the dogs-at-the-office policy say it increases employee morale and decreases stress.

Before we go too far with this idea, however, perhaps we should take note of some arguments against bringing dogs to work. First, some HR experts like Ethan Winning have cautioned that dogs can be messy, placing an unfair burden on employers to clean up after they have been present in the office. Dogs can also be a distraction, and other employees may be allergic or otherwise disturbed by them. And what happens when two or more employees bring their dogs to work on the same day, and Fido and Fifi don't want to play nice?

Of course, some people actually need to bring their dogs to work, which is why the Americans with Disabilities Act permits the use of "service animals" to assist persons with disabilities. For example, guide dogs are allowed to accompany blind individuals at work. The EEOC guideline is reasonable because guide dogs are necessary to blind individuals and, furthermore, these dogs are trained not to be a nuisance.

It can be challenging for employers to know where to draw the line. Take the case of Elizabeth Booth, a quadriplegic individual hired by Case Services Corporation as an accountant in the billing department. Booth, who uses a wheelchair for mobility, has trained her small, well-behaved dog to pick up small items that Booth has dropped. Along with a formal request to be allowed to bring her dog to work to assist her, Booth submitted to her employer a letter from her doctor stating that the dog would help relieve Booth's stress. When Case Services' HR director denied the request, Booth immediately filed a discrimination charge with the EEOC, claiming the company did not provide a reasonable accommodation to her disability or her health needs.

When it comes to establishing a pet policy, as is so often the case, balancing the employer's needs and responsibilities with the employees' needs and wants presents something of a dilemma.

Questions

1. What is your position on this issue? Provide two or three reasons to support your argument.
2. If you were an HR manager of a company, what pet policy would you set and how would you implement it?
3. How would you decide the case of Elizabeth Booth, and which laws would you base your decision on? Explain.

Sources: James J. McDonald, Jr., "Take Your Dog to Work Every Day," *Employee Relations Law Journal* 32, no. 3 (Winter 2006): 86; "Has Your Organization Gone to the Dogs?" http://www.hrwebcafe.com/2007/06/has_your_organization_gone_to.html; Ethan A. Winning, "Pets at the Corporate Zoo," http://www.ewin.com/arch/pets.htm; "About Take Your Dog to Work Day," http://www.takeyourdog.com/About/; "Take Your Dog to Work Every Day," http://www.dogfriendly.com/server/general/workplace/.

CASE STUDY 2 Misplaced Affections: Discharge for Sexual Harassment

Peter Lewiston was terminated on July 15, 2021, by the governing board of the Pine Circle Unified School District (PCUSD) for violation of the district's sexual harassment policy. Prior to Lewiston's termination, he was a senior maintenance employee with an above-average work record who had worked for the PCUSD for 11 years. He had been a widower since 2016 and was described by his coworkers as a friendly, outgoing, but lonely individual. Beverly Gilbury was a fifth-grade teacher working in the district's Advanced Learning Program. She was 28 years old and married and had worked for PCUSD for 6 years. At the time of the incidents, Lewiston and Gilbury both worked at Simpson Elementary School, where their relationship was described as "cooperative." The following sequence of events was reported separately by Lewiston and Gilbury during the district's investigation of this sexual harassment case.

Gilbury reported that her relationship with Lewiston began to change during the last month of the 2020–2021 school year. She believed that Lewiston was paying her more attention and that his behavior was "out of the ordinary" and "sometimes weird." He began spending more time in her classroom talking with the children and with her. At the time she did not say anything to Lewiston because "I didn't want to hurt his feelings since he is a nice, lonely, older man." However, on May 25, when Lewiston told Gilbury that he was "very fond" of her and that she had "very beautiful eyes," she replied, "Remember, Peter, we're just friends." For the remainder of the school year, there was little contact between them; however, when they did see each other, Lewiston seemed "overly friendly" to her.

June 7, 2021. On the first day of summer school, Gilbury returned to school to find a dozen roses and a card from Lewiston. The card read, "Please forgive me for thinking you could like me. I played the big fool. Yours always, P.L." Later in the day Lewiston asked Gilbury to lunch. She replied, "It's been a long time since anyone sent me roses, but I can't go to lunch. We need to remain just friends." Gilbury told another teacher that she was uncomfortable about receiving the roses and card and that Lewiston would not leave her alone. She expressed concern that Lewiston might get "more romantic" with her.

June 8, 2021. Gilbury arrived at school to find another card from Lewiston. Inside was a handwritten note that read, "I hope you can someday return my affections for you. I need you so much." Later in the day, Lewiston again asked her to lunch, and she declined, saying, "I'm a happily married woman." At the close of the school day, when Gilbury went to her car, Lewiston suddenly appeared. He asked to explain himself but Gilbury became agitated and shouted, "I have to leave right now." Lewiston reached inside the car, supposedly to pat her shoulder, but touched her head instead. She believed he meant to stroke her hair. He stated that he was only trying to calm her down. She drove away, very upset.

June 9, 2021. Gilbury received another card and a lengthy letter from Lewiston, stating that he was wrong in trying to develop a relationship with her and he hoped they could still remain friends. He wished her all happiness with her family and job.

June 11, 2021. Gilbury obtained from the Western Justice Court an injunction prohibiting sexual harassment by Lewiston. Shortly thereafter Lewiston

HRM Experience

Sexual Harassment: A Frank Discussion

Over the past decade, the problem of sexual harassment has captured the attention of all managers and employees. While it is widely known that sexual harassment is both unethical and illegal, incidents of sexual harassment continue to plague business. Unfortunately, when these cases arise, they cause morale problems among employees, embarrassment to the organization, and costly legal damages. Consequently, all managers and supervisors play a central role in preventing sexual harassment complaints. It is important that managers understand the definition of sexual harassment, who is covered by sexual harassment guidelines, and how to prevent its occurrence. This skill-building exercise will provide you with knowledge in each of these areas.

Assignment

1. Working in teams (ensure they are mixed teams including people of another gender), develop a list of behaviors that could be classified as quid pro quo harassment or hostile environment. Explore the possibility that some sexual harassment behaviors might be viewed differently by employees of another gender. Give examples.
2. Many sexual harassment incidents go unreported. Fully discuss why this can occur and what might be done to reduce this problem.
3. The cornerstone of addressing sexual harassment is achieving organizational awareness through training. Develop a sexual harassment training program for a company of 250 employees that covers, at a minimum, the following: (1) who should attend the training sessions, (2) the content outline for the training program (the list of materials your team wants to teach), (3) specific examples to illustrate the training materials, and (4) how to investigate sexual harassment complaints.
4. This chapter will assist you with this assignment. You can obtain additional materials from EEOC offices and from various HR magazines.
5. Be prepared to present your training outline to other class members.

appealed the injunction. A notice was mailed to Gilbury giving the dates of the appeal hearing. The notice stated in part, "If you fail to appear, the injunction may be vacated and the petition dismissed." Gilbury failed to appear at the hearing, and the injunction was set aside. Additionally, on June 11 she had filed with the district's EEOC officer a sexual harassment complaint against Lewiston. After the investigation, the district concluded that Lewiston's actions created an "extremely sexually hostile" environment for Gilbury. The investigative report recommended dismissal based upon the grievous conduct of Lewiston and the initial injunction granted by the Justice Court.

Questions

1. Evaluate the conduct of Peter Lewiston against the EEOC's definition of sexual harassment.
2. Should the intent or motive behind Lewiston's conduct be considered when deciding sexual harassment activities? Explain.
3. If you were the district's EEOC officer, what would you conclude? What disciplinary action, if any, would you take?

Sources: This case is adapted from an actual arbitration hearing conducted by George Bohlander. The background information is factual. All names and dates are fictitious.

Answers to Highlights in HRM 1

1. Yes
2. False
3. No
4. Merit, seniority, incentive pay plans
5. Yes
6. Yes, if no reasonable accommodation can be made
7. No
8. Yes, except if under a court order
9. False
10. True

Notes and References

1. U.S. Equal Employment Opportunity Commission, "Enforcement and Litigation Statistics," USA.gov (January 7, 2021), https://www.eeoc.gov/statistics/enforcement-and-litigation-statistics.
2. A. Kalev and F. Dobbin, "Companies Need to Think Bigger Than Diversity Training," *Harvard Business Review*, October 20, 2020; J. B. Becton, J. B. Gilstrap, and M. Forsyth, "Preventing and Correcting Workplace Harassment: Guidelines for Employers," *Business Horizons* 60, no. 1 (2017): 101–111; Darla Mercado, "Morgan Stanley Settles $46 Million Discrimination Suit," Workforce.com (October 16, 2007), http://www.workforce.com/articles/morgan-stanley-settles-46-million-discrimination-suit.
3. Michael Orey, "White Men Can't Help It," *Business Week* (May 15, 2006): 54.
4. For a practical overview of EEO law, see David J. Walsh, *Employment Law for Human Resource Practice*, 3rd ed. (Mason, OH: South-Western, 2010).
5. Dennis Cauchon, "Gender Pay Gap Is Smallest on Record," *USA Today* (September 14, 2010), http://www.usatoday.com.
6. For information on national origin discrimination, go to http://www.justice.gov/crt/publications/natorigin2.php.
7. *Tabura vs. Kellogg USA*, No. 16-4135 (10th Cir. [January 17, 2018]).
8. Lynn D. Lieber, "As Average Age of Workforce Increases, Age Discrimination Verdicts Rise," *Employment Relations Today* 34, no. 1 (Spring 2007): 105.
9. Maria Greco Danaher, "Include Pregnancy Leave in Pension Credit," *HR Magazine* 52, no. 11 (November 2007): 98.
10. U.S. Department of Justice, Civil Rights Division, "The Americans with Disabilities Act of 1990 and Revised ADA Regulations Implementing Title II and Title III," ADA.gov (January 2014), http://www.ada.gov/2010_regs.htm.
11. For more on these statistics, see https://www.eeoc.gov/statistics/charge-statistics-charges-filed-eeoc-fy-1997-through-fy-2019.
12. U.S. Equal Employment Opportunity Commission, "EEOC Enforcement Guidance on the Americans with Disabilities Act and Psychiatric Disabilities," EEOC (1997; January 2014), http://www.eeoc.gov/policy/docs/psych.html.
13. Jonathan R. Mook, "Accommodation Paradigm Shifts," *HR Magazine* 52, no. 1 (January 2007): 115; see also James J. McDonald, Jr., "Take Your Dog to Work Everyday," *Employee Relations Law Journal* 32, no. 3 (Winter 2006): 86.
14. *Barbuto v. Advantage Sales & Mktg., LLC*, 148 F. Supp. 3d 145, 2015 U.S. Dist. LEXIS 162922 (D. Mass., December 4, 2015)
15. Sandy Murillo, "Top 5 Benefits of Hiring People with Disabilities," *The Chicago Lighthouse*, October 7, 2016; Bill Leonard, "Studies: ADA Makes Business Better," *HR Magazine* 52, no. 10 (October 2007): 22.
16. "Broadening the Coverage of the ADA: The 2008 Amendments to the Americans with Disabilities Act," *INSIGHT into Diversity* (November 2010): 32–35.
17. "Genetic Information Nondiscrimination Act: A Primer on Title II," *Venulex Legal Summaries* (Winter 2010): special section, 1.
18. "Joy Mining Machinery Settles EEOC Genetic Information Non-Discrimination Act Lawsuit," U.S. Equal Employment Opportunity Commission, https://www.eeoc.gov/eeoc/newsroom/release/1-7-16.cfm.
19. Gary L. Tidwell, Daniel A. Rice, and Gary Kropkowski, "Employer and Employee Obligations and Rights under the Uniformed Services Employment and Reemployment Rights Act," *Business Horizons* 52, no. 3, (May 2009): 243–250, DOI: 10.1016/j.bushor.2009.01.003. Find additional information on the law, visit the USERRA Advisor at the Department of Labor's website, http://www.dol.gov/elaws.
20. *Veterans Benefits Improvement Act of 2004, Public Law 108-454* (December 20, 2004).
21. As currently defined, an "otherwise qualified" employee is one who can perform the "essential functions" of the job under consideration.
22. Lisa Nagele-Piazza, "White House Lifts Restrictions on Transgender Troops," Society for Human Resource Management, January 26, 2021.
23. *Oncale v. Sundowner Offshore Services, Inc.* 72 PED 45, 175; WL 88039 (U.S. 11998), http://www.eeoc.gov/laws/types/sexual_harassment.cfm.
24. *Guidelines on Discrimination Because of Sex, 29 C.F.R. Sec. 1604.11(a)* (1955).
25. *Guidelines on Discrimination*, Sec. 1605.11(a).
26. Luis Ferre-Sadurni and Mihir Zaveri, "Sexual Harassment Claims Against Cuomo: What We Know So Far," *The New York Times*, March 9, 2021.
27. Jeffrey I. Chasen, "Discrimination and Harassment in the Workplace: Five Essential Strategies for Smarter Risk Management," *Risk Institute PERI* (January 2014), http://www.riskinstitute.org/.
28. Margaret Bryant, "Harassment Lawsuits and Lessons," *Security Management* 60, no. 4 (April 2006): 50.
29. Khadija Murad, "Sexual Harassment in the Workplace," National Conference of State Legislators, February 17, 2020; "EEOC Data Confirms #MeToo's Impact: Six Keys for Employers in the Wake of This Powerful Cultural Moment," *National Law Review*, October 21, 2018; Kathy Gurchiek, "One Year after #MeToo and 'Weinstein Effect': What's Changed?", Society for Human Resource Management, August 16, 2019.
30. "Has the #MeToo Movement Had Any Impact on the Tech Workplace?", Allred, Maroko & Goldberg, January 19, 2021.

31. *Bostock v. Clayton County*, No. 17-1618, 590 U.S. (2020).
32. *Kadel v. Folwell*, No. 1:19CV272, --- F.Supp.3d ---, (M.D.N.C. March 11, 2020); "What You Should Know: The EEOC and Protections for LGBT Workers," U.S. Equal Employment Opportunity Commission (March 7, 2017), https://www.eeoc.gov/eeoc/newsroom/wysk/enforcement_protections_lgbt_workers.cfm.
33. Huasheng Gao and Wei Zhang, "Non-Discrimination Laws Make U.S. States More Innovative," *Harvard Business Review* (August 17, 2016).
34. Ali Vitali, "President Trump Signs New Immigration Executive Order," *NBCNews* (March 6, 2017); Mark Schoeff, "DHS Rule Rankles Employer Groups," *Workforce Management* 86, no. 14 (August 20, 2007): 1.
35. 8 U.S.C.A. § 1324a (a) (1), (2) (2005).
36. 8 U.S.C.A. § 1324B (1) (2005).
37. U.S. Department of Justice, Immigration and Naturalization Service, *Handbook for Employers: Instructions for Completing Form I* (Washington, DC: U.S. Government Printing Office, 2005).
38. Jacqueline Howard, "Weight Bias Is Bigger Problem Than You May Think, Experts Say," CNN.com; Svetlana Shkolnikova, "Weight Discrimination Could Be as Common as Racial Discrimination," *USA Today* (May 28, 2008), http://www.usatoday.com.
39. Donna Ballman, "Is Weight Discrimination at Work Illegal?", *AOL Jobs* (November 6, 2012), http://jobs.aol.com/articles/2012/11/06/is-weight-discrimination-illegal/.
40. Kai Wang and Yuanlu Niu, "Reducing Lookism in the Workplace, in *Implementation Strategies for Improving Diversity in Organizations* (Hershey, PA: IGI Global, 2021), 110–132.
41. Tomas Chamorro-Premuzic, "Attractive People Get Unfair Advantages at Work; AI Can Help," *Harvard Business Review* (October 31, 2019); Enbar Toledano, "May the Best (Looking) Man Win: The Unconscious Role of Attractiveness in Employment Decisions," *Cornell (University) HR Review* (February 14, 2013), http://www.cornellhrreview.org.
42. The Crown Coalition, "New Dove Study Confirms Workplace Bias against Hairstyles Impacts Black Women's Ability to Celebrate Their Natural Beauty," *PR Newswire*, May 1, 2019.
43. "California Becomes First State to Ban Discrimination against Natural Hair," CBS News, July 4, 2019.
44. Gerald E. Calvasina, Richard V. Calvasina, and Eugene J. Calvasina, "Caregiver Responsibility Discrimination and EEOC Guidelines," *Journal of Legal, Ethical & Regulatory Issues* 13, no. 2 (June 2010): 1–2.
45. The guidelines themselves and examples of their application can be found at www.uniformguidelines.com.
46. *Uniform Guidelines*, Sec. 40. Adverse impact need not be considered for groups that constitute less than 2 percent of the relevant labor force.
47. Footnote content to come.
48. The primary website for the EEOC is http://www.eeoc.gov. This website contains a wealth of information about the EEOC, including the agency's history and administration, how discrimination charges are filed and processed, training and outreach programs, litigation statistics, and various pamphlets and posters offered free of charge to interested parties.
49. Howard S. Lavin and Elizabeth E. DiMichele, "The Time for Filing Charges of Discrimination: The Supreme Court's Decision and Its Aftermath," *Employee Relations Law Journal* 33, no. 3 (Winter 2007): 113; see also Reynolds Holding, "Stumble on the Bench," *Time* (June 18, 2007): 56.
50. The time period is 300 days in states in which the charge is deferred to a state agency.
51. David Sherwyn, Zev Eigen, and Gregg Gilman, "Retaliation: The Fastest Growing Discrimination Claim," *Cornell Hotel and Restaurant Administration Quarterly* 47, no. 4 (November 2006): 350.
52. Rebecca M. Archer and Stephen T. Lanctot, "Are Your Hands Tied? A Practical Look at Employee Claims of Retaliation," *Employee Relations Law Journal* 33, no. 1 (Summer 2007): 53; see also Mary Price Birk, "Walking on Eggshells: Avoiding Retaliation Claims When the Employee Does Not Leave," *Employee Relations Law Journal* 32, no. 3 (Winter 2006): 10; and Martin K. LaPointe, "The Supreme Court Sets the Standard for Title VII Retaliation Claims: Burlington Northern and *Santa Fe Railway v. White*," *Labor Law Journal* 57, no. 4 (Winter 2006): 205.
53. Jathan Janove, "Retaliation Nation," *HR Magazine* 51, no. 10 (October 2006): 62.
54. Heather J. Broadwater, "Preventing Workplace Sexual Harassment," *Rural Telecommunications* 25, no. 5 (September/October 2006): 34.
55. Michael W. Johnson, "Harassment and Discrimination Prevention Training," *Labor Law Journal* 55, no. 2 (Summer 2004): 119.
56. Jena McGregor, "Diversity Job Openings Fell Nearly 60% after the Coronavirus. Then Came the Black Lives Matter Protests," *The Washington Post*, July 15, 2020.
57. Denise Hamilton, "Don't Let Chief Diversity Officer Be a Dead-End Job," *Crain's Chicago Business*, January 18, 2021.
58. Kathy Gurchiek, "Businesses Respond to Demand to Put Muscle into DE&I Efforts," Society for Human Resource Management, December 18, 2020.
59. Alison DeNisco, "Does Your Company Need a Chief Diversity Officer?", *TechRepublic*, September 28, 2016.
60. Voluntary Diversity Plans Can Lead to Risk," *HR Focus* 84, no. 6 (June 2007): 2.
61. *University of California Regents v. Bakke*, 438 U.S. 265 (1978) and *United Steelworkers of America v. Weber*, 443, U.S. 193 (1979).
62. Daniel A. Biddle and Richard E. Biddle, "Ricci v. Destefano: New Opportunities for Employers to Correct Disparate Impact," *Labor Law Journal* 61, no. 3 (Fall 2010): 123–141.

63. Shaun Pichler, Jannel L. Blazovich, Kirsten A. Cook, Janet M. Huston, and William R. Strawser, "Do LGBT-Supportive Corporate Policies Enhance Firm Performance?", *Human Resource Management* 57, no. 1 (August 2017): 263–278; Peng Wang and Joshua L. Schwarz, "Stock Price Reactions to GLBT Nondiscrimination Policies," *Human Resource Management* 49, no. 2 (March-April 2010): 195.
64. Sudiatu Dixon-Fyle, Kevin Dolan, Vivian Hunt, and Sara Prince, *Diversity Wins: How Inclusion Matters* (McKinsey & Company, May 19, 2020).
65. Theo Francis, Inti Pacheco and Thomas Gryta, "Big Companies Disclose Details on Gender, Race in Workforces," *The Wall Street Journal*, March 1, 2021.
66. Robert Livingston, "How to Promote Racial Equity in the Workplace," *Harvard Business Review*, November 10, 2020.

Appendix

Determining Adverse Impact

A.1 The Four-Fifths Rule

Employers can determine adverse impact by using the method outlined in the interpretive manual for the *Uniform Guidelines on Employee Selection Procedures.*

1. Calculate the rate of selection for each group (divide the number of people selected from a group by the number of total applicants from that group).
2. Observe which group has the highest selection.
3. Calculate the impact ratios by comparing the selection rate for each group with that of the highest group (divide the selection rate for a group by the selection rate for the highest group).
4. Observe whether the selection rate for any group is substantially less (usually less than four-fifths, or 80 percent) than the selection rate for the highest group. If it is, adverse impact is indicated in most circumstances.

Example

	Job Applicants	Number Hired	Selection Rate Percent Hired
Step A	Whites 100	52	52/100 = 52%
	Blacks 50	14	14/50 = 28%
Step B	The group with the highest selection rate is White, 52%.		
Step C	Divide the B lack selection rate (28%) by the White selection rate (52%). The Black rate is 53.8% of the White rate.		
Step D	Since 53.8% is less than four-fifths, or 80%, adverse impact is indicated.		

Source: "Adoption of Questions and Answers to Clarify and Provide a Common Interpretation of the Uniform Guidelines on Employee Selection Procedures," *Federal Register* 44, no. 43 (March 2, 1979): 11998.

rozdemir/Shutterstock.com

CHAPTER 4

Job Analysis and Job Design

Learning Outcomes

After studying this chapter, you should be able to

LO 1 Explain what a job analysis is and how it is used in conjunction with a firm's HRM functions.

LO 2 Explain how the information for a job analysis is collected and incorporated into various sections of a job's description.

LO 3 Provide examples illustrating the various factors that must be taken into account when designing a job, including what motivates employees.

LO 4 Describe the different types of teams and work arrangements used to enhance the contributions of employees.

Organizations exist because people can accomplish more together than they can on their own. However, the actions of an organization need to be coordinated, and each person within it needs to do the things they do best. This coordination is achieved in part by creating individual jobs. A **job** can be defined as an activity people do for which they get paid, particularly as part of the trade or occupation they occupy. But how exactly should the work be divided, and which people should do which tasks or jobs? These are questions businesspeople such as Henry Ford and scientific management researchers such as Frederick Winslow Taylor sought to answer at least a century ago, and ones managers still ask today.

job
An activity people do for which they get paid, particularly as part of the trade or occupation they occupy.

The answers to the questions about which jobs an organization should have stem from a firm's strategy. What good or service does the firm intend to provide, and how much of it will the firm offer? What does the firm believe its competitive advantage is? Is the company trying to capture market share based on a new product it has developed? A lower-priced product? A higher-quality product? How and where will the product be produced, and distributed, and with what technology? Which types of people and skills will be needed to accomplish these tasks and how should they be organized?

A *workflow analysis* can help a company answer these questions. A workflow analysis helps a firm determine the best processes, types, and mix of jobs, and identify how they should ideally be organized to execute the firm's mission. For example, both Apple and Lenovo make computers. However, Apple focuses on producing innovative products, whereas Lenovo has traditionally focused on producing low-priced products. As a result, how the companies are organized, their workflows, and the numbers and types of jobs they support differ in significant ways. To develop and improve their workflows, large organizations often hire outside business analysts and operations management specialists who work in conjunction with the firm's top managers and HR personnel to fine-tune their operations. The resulting workflow analysis outlines the division of labor among employees, the degree to which they are specialized, the people to whom they report, and each supervisor's authority, or span of control over his or her subordinates.

However, as the competitive environment changes, these elements also have to change to keep pace. As an example, in the past Lenovo had a typical hierarchical organizational structure. (Recall from your introduction to business and management classes that tall organizational structures are characterized by many managerial levels with narrow spans of control and jobs that are narrowly focused.) That structure worked well for the firm's PC business, but to remain competitive, the company needed to improve its innovation capabilities and expand its product lineup to attract new types of customers.

So, a few years ago, Lenovo flattened its organization by dividing its PC-focused division into four separate business units: PCs, mobile devices, servers and storage, and cloud computing systems. It also classified its country markets as either emerging or mature, and developed different strategies and personnel for each type. Today, Lenovo is the biggest seller of PCs in the world.

What will workflows and jobs look like in the near future? In recent years, the big game changer was the rapid shift to "virtual work" required by the COVID-19 pandemic. As people began working remotely, many found it surprisingly advantageous in terms of their productivity. Companies such as Expedia, Adobe, and Prudential Financial found that most employees enjoyed working remotely but missed the planning, ideation, and collaboration that takes place in person. As people began going back to the office, companies had to adapt their jobs and workflows to a "hybrid model," in which some employees were physically present in the workplace while others worked remotely.[1]

More generally, technology continues to change the nature of work. As we discussed in Chapter 1, some of these changes are positive and some are potentially negative. Information technology, for example, can bring better data to our fingertips more quickly, which then leads to better decision making. Automation can lead to upskilling of jobs as it takes over routine or repetitive work, but can also leave some workers vulnerable to losing their jobs. There is an old joke: "The factory of the future will be so automated that it will be staffed by just one worker and a dog. The worker will be there to feed the dog, and the dog will be there to make sure the worker doesn't touch anything." But for those who lose their jobs to machines, this trend no laughing matter.

LO1

Assume you are the general manager of a service department. How might formally written job requirements help you manage your work unit?

job analysis
The process of obtaining information about a job by determining its duties, tasks, or activities.

4.1 What Is a Job Analysis and How Does It Affect Human Resources Management?

Think about an organization you worked for or a job or position you have held. Did you ever think about ways to make things flow more smoothly? If so, you were doing an informal work analysis. Likewise, did you analyze the tasks you were doing and conclude they should be done by someone else, or vice versa? If so, you were doing an informal analysis of your job. A **job analysis** is the systematic process of collecting information about all of the parameters of a job—its basic responsibilities, along with the behaviors, skills, and the physical and mental requirements of the people who do it.

A job analysis should also outline the tools needed to do the job, the environment and times at which it needs to be done, with whom it needs to be done, and the outcome or performance level it should produce.[2] Normally, a manager or an HR manager such as a job analyst is responsible for collecting the information for a job analysis. These people rely on the cooperation of employees and their supervisors to gather the information needed for the analysis.

How does a job analysis help facilitate a firm's human resources efforts? As Figure 4.1 shows, the information in a job analysis is crucial to a number of human resources management (HRM) functions, including the following:

- *Strategic HR planning.* A job analysis is used to examine a company's organizational structure and strategically position it for the future. Does the firm have the right numbers and types of jobs and skills needed to cover the scope of its activities both now and in the future? Are the jobs aligned with one another, or do their purposes or duties conflict? Are there tasks that need to be done in the organization but are not clearly assigned to a particular job? Conducting a job analysis helps ensure alignment.

Figure 4.1 Job Analysis: The Cornerstone of HRM Functions

Alignment of:	Job Description (TDRs)	Job Specification (KSAOs)
• HR strategy and planning	Nature of structure and work to achieve business results and goals	Supply and demand of labor, number and kinds of people needed to fill open positions
• Workflow analysis and job design	Sequencing or grouping of related jobs, and the nature of interdependence	Enriching or expanding jobs to develop and motivate employees further
• Recruitment and selection	Posting advertisements and other information about jobs to fill and the nature of their responsibilities	Hiring criteria for evaluating candidates who apply for open positions
• Performance appraisal process	Setting goals, duties, and activities that define the desired performance	Attributes and demonstrated qualities used to assess performance and give feedback
• Compensation and benefits	Evaluation of the job in terms of responsibilities and working conditions	Evaluation of the job in terms of the skills, effort required, and other aspects that are rewarded
• Legal compliance	Equal employment requirements	Fair treatment and valid employment practices

- *Workflow analysis and job design.* The information generated by a job analysis can be used to analyze a company's work processes—that is, how work is done. Would rearranging an organization's workflow or jobs help the company compete more effectively? Can the nature of the jobs be redesigned to improve the firm's performance?
- *Recruitment and selection.* Some of the information provided in a job analysis is contained in job advertisements. The information and qualifications in such ads provide a basis for attracting qualified applicants and discouraging unqualified ones.
- *Training and development.* Any discrepancies between the abilities of jobholders and the firm's job descriptions provide clues about the training jobholders need to succeed and advance into different jobs as well as the training the firm needs to provide.
- *Performance appraisal and compensation.* A job analysis provides the criteria for evaluating what constitutes good performance versus poor performance by employees; the firm can then take steps to improve the latter.
- *Compensation management.* Conducting a job analysis helps HR managers figure out the relative worth of positions so the compensation for them will be fair and equitable, and employees will want to remain with the firm rather than search for other jobs.
- *Legal compliance.* If the criteria used to hire and evaluate employees are not job related, employers may find themselves being accused of discrimination. In decades past, before firms regularly analyzed jobs, non-job-related criteria were quite prevalent. For example, laborers were often required to have high school diplomas; plumbers, electricians, and machinists were sometimes required to be male. As you learned in Chapter 3, these kinds of job specifications are discriminatory.

4.1a Major Parts of the Job Analysis

Let's look at the two major pieces of information that come out of a job analysis:

job description
A statement of the tasks, duties, and responsibilities of a job to be performed.

1. A **job description** is a written document that describes the overall purpose of the job; its tasks, duties, and responsibilities (TDRs); and the qualifications needed to do it. The following is an excerpt of the purpose and TDRs for a firefighter's position posted by the city of Del Mar, California.

   Purpose

   Responds to emergency calls to protect life and property; participates in training, drill, and independent study activities; participates in the maintenance of fire department apparatus, equipment, and facilities; performs various staff support assignments; and performs related work as assigned.

   Tasks, Duties, and Responsibilities

   - Responds to a wide variety of emergency alarms, such as structural and environmental fires, traffic accidents, natural gas leaks, medical emergencies, and hazardous material spills.
   - Provides first-responder medical emergency response at the basic life support level, including initial patient and situation assessment, cardiopulmonary resuscitation, and trauma emergency medical care; prepares patients and assists paramedics in advanced life support emergency medical care.

job specifications
A statement of the specific knowledge, skills, and abilities that a person who is to perform a job needs.

2. **Job specifications**, or qualifications, are a part of the written job description and outline the specific knowledge, skills, abilities, and other attributes (KSAOs) required of the person performing the job. *Knowledge* refers to what you know. Your education is an example of knowledge. For example, some cities require firefighters to be certified paramedics; other cities don't. *Skills* are things you have learned to do. If you're a firefighter, that experience could include knowing how to make minor repairs to fire equipment. *Abilities* are your innate aptitudes; you don't have to be taught them or learn them on a job. Examples for a firefighter would include the ability to lift firefighting equipment and stay calm during an emergency. *Other attributes* refer to your personality, values, and so on. Helpfulness and a predisposition toward teamwork are examples of "other attributes" firefighters need.

Are you thinking you want to go into human resources management? If so, Highlights in HRM 2 later in this chapter will give you an idea of what a job description for an entry-level position in this field would look like. Note that a job description isn't necessarily the information you would see in a job posting, which is used for advertising a job opening. The job description in Highlights in HRM 2 is an internal document used by the firm and its HR personnel to define their planning and staffing needs. For example, note that the job analyst who compiled the information and the date the job was analyzed are included at the top of the document. We will take a closer look at the parts of the document later in the chapter.

For now, as an exercise, answer the questions in Highlights in HRM 1 based on the job you currently hold or most recently held. Then organize the information into the various job sections of a job description.

1 Highlights in HRM

Job Analysis Interview Questions

The following are examples of interview questions HR professionals use to gather information for a job analysis.

1. Job's purpose
   - What work do you essentially do? What is the job's overall purpose?
   - How do you see your work contributing to the overall mission or purpose of the organization, now and in the future?
2. Job's duties
   - Describe your duties in terms of what they are, how you do them, how often you perform them, and how long each of them takes.
   - Does the job have to be done in the way you were trained to do it, or do you see ways to improve it?
   - Are you performing duties not presently included in your job description? Describe them.
   - Are the instructions you receive from your supervisor clear and consistent with your job description?
3. Job criteria and results
   - Have work standards for the job been established (errors allowed, time taken for a particular task, etc.)? If so, what are they?
   - Describe the successful completion and/or end results of the job.
4. Background and knowledge
   - What personal attributes are needed to be successful in this position?
   - Describe the level, degree, and breadth of knowledge required for this position.
   - Indicate the education, certification, and license requirements for the job.
5. Training
   - Describe the orientation you received when you first began this job and its effectiveness.
   - What sort of on-the-job training and training period is needed for the position?
   - What tools, equipment, or other resources are needed to train people for this position?
   - What assessment tests are needed to determine if someone is competent in this position?
6. Abilities required
   - Do you use special software tools, equipment, or machines? If so, list them.
   - What manual skills are needed to operate the machines, tools, and equipment to do the job?
   - What reasoning or problem-solving ability must you have?
   - Are any supervisory or managing abilities required?
   - What physical abilities such as strength, coordination, or visual acuity must you have?
7. Working conditions
   - Describe your working conditions.
   - Describe the frequency and degree to which you encounter working conditions such as these: contact with hazardous materials, strenuous physical labor, cramped quarters, moving objects, vibration, and inadequate ventilation.
8. Authority
   - What is the job's level of authority, and to whom are you accountable?
   - What kinds of independent action are you allowed to take?
9. Responsibilities
   - Are you responsible for any confidential material? If so, describe how you handle it.
   - Are you responsible for any money or things of monetary value? If so, describe how you handle it.
10. Evaluation and compensation
    - In what ways and how often is your performance evaluated and feedback provided?
    - What criteria do you think should be used in the evaluation process?
    - Considering your level of productivity and the skill level required to fulfill your responsibilities, do you think you are compensated adequately?
    - Describe the criteria that should be used to determine the compensation for the position: responsibilities, skills, experience, knowledge, work environment, safety hazards, and so forth.

Sources: Michael G. Aamodt, *Industrial/Organizational Psychology: An Applied Approach*, 7th ed. (Mason, OH: Cengage Learning, 2012); David Ngo, "Job Analysis Questions" (March 3, 2011), http://www.humanresources.hrvinet.com; "Job Analysis: Overview," HR Guide to the Internet, http://www.job-analysis.net/G000.htm; "Job Analysis: Asking Questions," Department for Business Innovation & Skills, http://www.bis.gov.uk.

LO2

Discuss the various ways in which a job analysis can be completed. Compare and contrast these methods, noting the pros or cons of each.

4.2 Sources of Job Analysis Information

You have learned that a job analysis is an important HR building block. What you are probably wondering now is how a person conducts such an analysis. The first step is to collect the information needed to analyze jobs. The methods most commonly used to collect this information are interviews, questionnaires, observation, and diaries.

- *Interviews.* A job analyst or supervisor interviews individual employees and their managers about the parameters of the job. Highlights in HRM 1 shows the types of questions asked as part of job analysis interviews. When a job is particularly complex, firms sometimes interview a panel of *subject matter experts (SMEs)*. SMEs are job experts who actually do the job or train and supervise others to do the job.
- *Questionnaires.* The job analyst or supervisor circulates standard questionnaires for jobholders to fill out individually. These forms contain questions similar to those asked in an interview.
- *Observation.* The job analyst or supervisor learns about the job by observing and recording the activities associated with it on a standardized form.
- *Diaries.* Jobholders are asked to keep diaries of their work activities for an entire work cycle. The diaries are typically filled out at specific times of the work shift (such as every half-hour or hour) and maintained for a 2- to 4-week period.

Job analysis software and templates available on the Web have greatly facilitated the job analysis process. They usually contain task statements that can apply to many different jobs. Managers and employees select those statements that best describe the job under review, indicating the importance of the task to the job.

Figure 4.2 shows the job analysis process. As illustrated in the figure, the information analyzed is collected and feeds back into the HRM functions we discussed in Figure 4.1.

4.2a Controlling the Accuracy of the Job Data Collected

When interviewing employees or reviewing their questionnaires, job analysts should look for any responses that contradict other facts or impressions they have received about the job. Sometimes employees exaggerate the difficulty of their positions to inflate their egos and their paychecks.[3] Inflating a job's responsibilities can also occur unintentionally. For example, people who have been in their jobs for a long time and are good at them sometimes mistakenly believe that the skills needed for those jobs are higher than they really are. As one job analyst noted, "When in doubt about the accuracy of employee responses, always double-check the data with others."[4] In other words, collect information from a representative sample of individuals doing the same job, not just one or two jobholders. Also, once a job analysis is done, it should be checked for accuracy by both the jobholders and their managers.[5]

4.2b Other Sources of Job Analysis Information

Do managers and job analysts have to start from scratch when it comes to designing questionnaires to gather job information and analyzing it? No, not necessarily, even if a position is a new one. Several different quantitative job analysis approaches already exist. Each has its own advantages and disadvantages.[6] Five of the more popular methods are the functional job analysis, the position analysis system, the critical incident method, the task inventory analysis, and the competency-based job analysis.

Figure 4.2 The Job Analysis Process

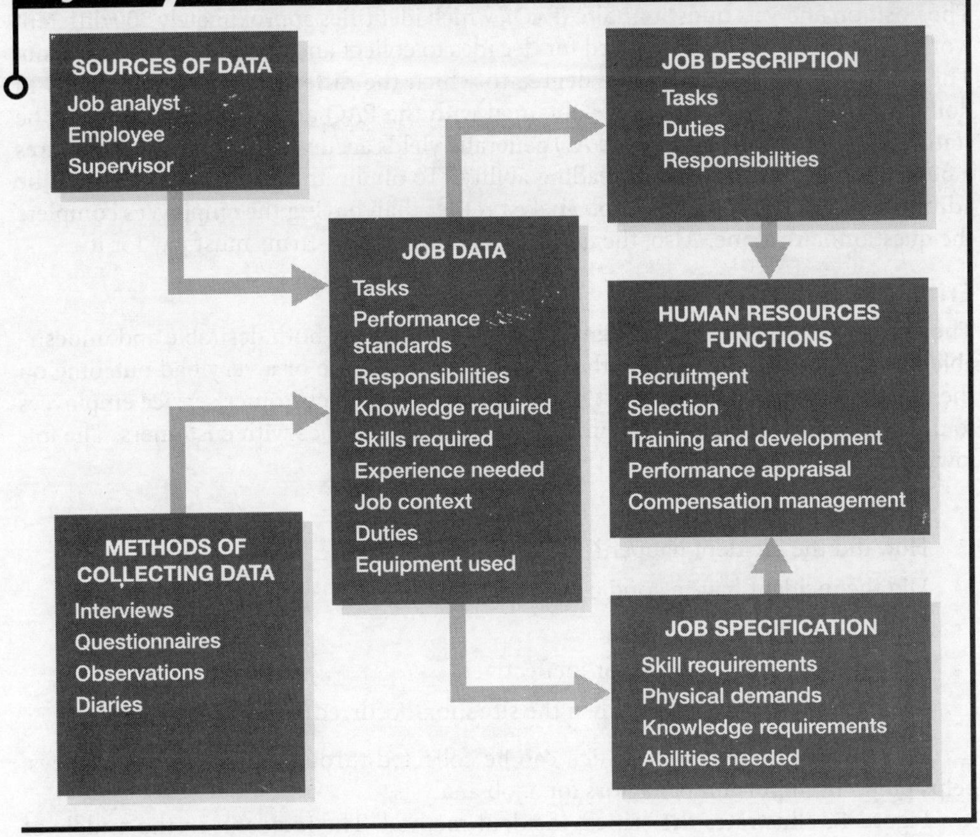

Source: U.S. Bureau of Labor Statistics

Functional Job Analysis System

Developed by the U.S. Training and Employment Service, the **functional job analysis (FJA)** approach utilizes an inventory of the various types of work activities that can constitute any job. Basic activities, called worker functions, are used to describe what workers do with regard to "information, people, and things" as part of this system. For example, when it comes to people, the basic functions of a job might include coordinating and supervising them. Each job function is assigned a percentage in terms of its importance to the job. For example, supervising might be 75 percent of the job.

functional job analysis (FJA)
A job analysis approach that utilizes an inventory of the various types of work activities that can constitute any job.

The U.S. Department of Labor has a comprehensive occupation-information website called O*NET Online that contains thousands of free job descriptions, which can help match people's interests and abilities with occupations as well as serve as a starting point for analyzing a job. The jobs on the site are classified into broader functional areas, from entry level to advanced, and across various specialties. The descriptions include comprehensive information about the tasks, tools and technology, KSAOs, education, interests, work styles, wages, and employment outlook associated with the jobs. Free job analysis questionnaires can also be downloaded from O*NET. Although they are generic, these templates can be customized and used to collect occupational information from jobholders and their managers.

Position Analysis Questionnaire System

position analysis questionnaire (PAQ)
A questionnaire that identifies approximately 300 different tasks to determine the degree to which each is involved in doing a job.

The **position analysis questionnaire (PAQ)**, which identifies approximately 300 different worker tasks, has been widely used for decades to collect and analyze job information. The PAQ seeks to determine the degree to which the different tasks are involved in doing a particular job. The results obtained with the PAQ are quantitative and can be statistically analyzed. Although a PAQ generally yields accurate information, it requires a person to have a high level of reading ability.[7] To obtain the best results, it should be administered to employees by a job analyst rather than having the employees complete the questionnaire alone. Also, the questionnaire isn't free—firms must pay for it.

Critical Incident Method

critical incident method
A job analysis method used to identify both desirable and undesirable behaviors that resulted in either a very good outcome or a very bad outcome on the job.

The objective of the **critical incident method** is to identify both desirable and undesirable behaviors that resulted in either a very good outcome or a very bad outcome on the job. For example, a job analyst might ask a company's customer service employees to describe incidents that led to either good or bad outcomes with customers. The following are examples of questions that might be asked:

- What happened?
- How did the incident happen?
- Did the incident have a good or bad outcome?
- What led to the outcome?
- What actions were effective or ineffective?
- What would you do differently if the situation occurred again?

This kind of information, which can be collected through interviews or surveys, helps pinpoint important behaviors for a job analysis.

Figure 4.3 illustrates the critical incident method. The incidents in the middle of the figure are associated with neutral outcomes. Most of the outcomes will fall into

Figure 4.3 The Critical Incident Method Illustrated

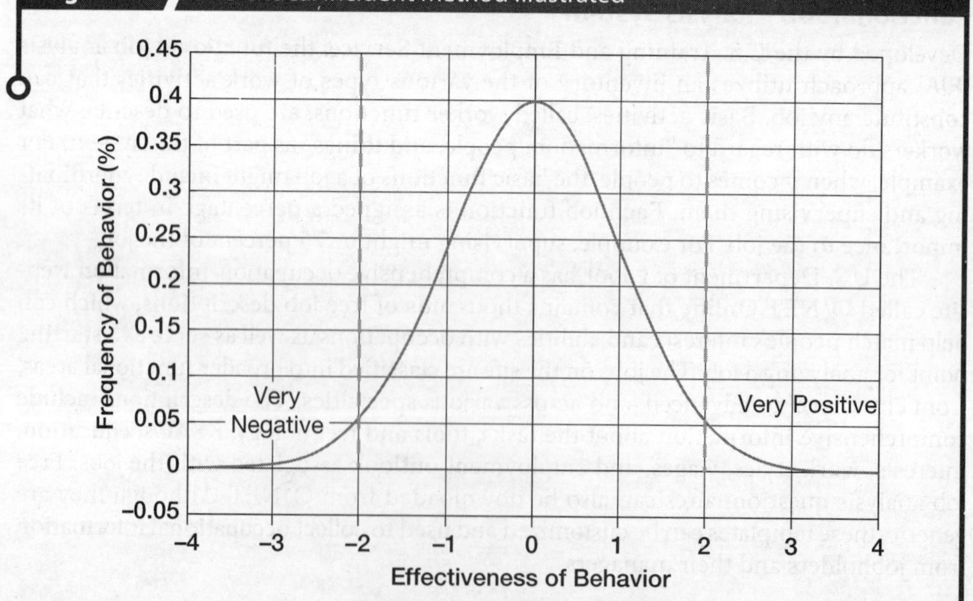

this area. The incidents on the ends of the figure are extremely good or bad outcomes, respectively. Although relatively few of the incidents will occur in these areas, examining them is important because they can reveal critical job behaviors.

Task Inventory Analysis

The **task inventory analysis** method was pioneered by the U.S. Air Force. Unlike the PAQ, which uses a standardized form to analyze jobs in different organizations, a task inventory questionnaire can be tailored to a specific organization. With the help of employees and their managers, a list of tasks and their descriptions are developed for different jobs and then rated based on how important they are. The goal is to produce a comprehensive list of task statements applicable to all jobs. These task statements are then listed on a task inventory survey form to be completed by the person analyzing the job under review. For example, a task statement might be: "Monitors current supplies to maintain stock levels." The job analysis would also note the importance of the task, the frequency of its occurrence, and the time spent on the task to the successful completion of the job.

task inventory analysis
An organization-specific list of tasks and their descriptions used as a basis to identify components of jobs.

Competency-Based Approach

The approaches to job analysis we have discussed so far focus on the tasks employees do, but not what they are capable of doing. The following statement by a HR professional highlights this concern: "Typically, job analysis looks at how a job is currently done. But the ever-changing business market makes it difficult to keep a job analysis up-to-date. Also, companies are asking employees to do more, so there is a question of whether 'jobs' as we know them are obsolete." The risk is that in a dynamic environment where job demands change rapidly, obsolete job analysis information will hinder an organization's ability to adapt to change.

When organizations operate in a fast-moving environment, managers often adopt a competency-based approach to job analysis.[8] This method relies on building job profiles that look at not only the responsibilities and activities of the job a worker does currently but also the competencies or capabilities the worker needs to do them well and to adapt to new job challenges. *How* the work is done (and, therefore, how it can be improved) becomes more of the focus than simply *what* work is done.[9]

The objective is to identify key competencies for the organization's success. Competencies can be identified through focus groups, surveys, or interviews, and might include such things as interpersonal communication skills, decision-making ability, conflict resolution skills, adaptability, or self-motivation. Figure 4.4 shows a form used to gather information for a competency-based job analysis.

4.2c Parts of a Job Description

Most job descriptions contain at least three parts: (1) the job's title and location; (2) a job identification section, which contains administration information such a numerical code for the job, to whom the jobholder reports, and wage information; and (3) a job duties section. The other important outcome of the job analysis is the job specification, or the description of KSAOs. If the job specification is not prepared as a separate document, it is usually stated in the concluding section of the job description, as Highlights in HRM 2 shows. Next, let's look at these sections in more detail.

Job Title

Selecting a job's title serves several purposes. First, the job title is psychologically important because it provides status to the employee. For instance, "sanitation engineer" is a more appealing title than "garbage collector." Second, if possible, the title provides

Figure 4.4 Form Used to Gather Information for a Competency-Based Job Analysis

Part B: Skill Matrix in a Dejobbed Organization

Job Title: XYZ

8	8	8	8	8	8
7	7	7	7	7	7
6	6	6	6	6	6
5	5	5	5	5	5
4	4	4	4	4	4
3	3	3	3	3	3
2	2	2	2	2	2
1	1	1	1	1	1
Technical Expertise	Communication & Interpersonal Ability	Business Acumen & Decision Making	Leadership & Guidance	Planning & Organizing	Initiative & Problem Solving

- The numbers in the matrix describe each skill level. For example, for technical expertise (1) might read: basic knowledge of handling machine, while (8) might read: conducts and supervises complex tasks requiring advanced knowledge of a range of skills.
- The shaded boxes indicate the minimum level of skill required in each skill category for the position XYZ.
- The jobholder is required to move from the minimum level to higher levels. The appraisal and rewards are tied to this movement.

Source: Feza Tabassum Azmi, "Job Descriptions to Job Fluidity: Treading the Dejobbing Path," *EBS Review*, no. 23 (2007): 8. Reprinted by permission.

an indication of which duties the job entails. Titles such as *meat inspector*, *electronics assembler*, *salesperson*, and *engineer* obviously hint at the nature of the duties associated with these jobs. In addition, the job title should indicate the level of the job within the organization. For example, the title *junior engineer* implies that this job occupies a lower level than that of *senior engineer*.

Job Identification Section

The job identification section usually follows the job title. It includes such items as the department and location of the job, the person to whom the jobholder reports, and the date the job description was last revised. In addition, it sometimes contains a payroll or code number, the number of employees performing the job, the number of employees in the department where the job is located, and the code assigned to the job using the O*NET system. A "Purpose" statement usually appears at the bottom of this section and distinguishes this job from other jobs in the organization—something the job title might fail to do. Working conditions may also be listed.

Tasks, Duties, and Responsibilities Section

Statements covering job duties are typically arranged in order of their importance. Sometimes the statements indicate the percentage of time devoted to each duty. The Civil Rights Act of 1991, the American with Disabilities Act (ADA), and landmark court rulings require employers to show that the job criteria they use to select employees for a particular position are valid and relate specifically to the duties for that job. Moreover, the duties must be *essential functions* for success on the job. For example, if

2 Highlights in HRM

An Example of a Job Description

Title: Employment Assistant

Job Identification

Division:	Southern Division
Department:	Human Resources
Job Analyst:	Antonio Floros
Date Analyzed:	1/3/22
Wage Category:	Exempt
Report to:	HR Manager
Job Code:	1117
Date Verified:	1/17/22

Purpose

Performs professional human resources work in the areas of employee recruitment and selection, testing, orientation, transfers, and maintenance of employee human resources files. May handle special assignments and projects related to EEO/affirmative action, employee grievances, training, or classification and compensation. Works under general supervision. Incumbent exercises initiative and independent judgment in the performance of assigned tasks.

Working Conditions: This job is done in a professional office environment with the use of equipment such as laptop computers, photocopiers, and smartphones. Working hours are Monday through Friday, 8:30 a.m. to 5:00 p.m. Evening, weekend work, and travel may be required occasionally.

Tasks, Duties, and Responsibilities

1. Maintains a daily working relationship with division managers on human resources matters, including recruitment concerns, retention or release of probationary employees, and discipline or discharge of permanent employees. (25%)
2. Schedules and conducts personal interviews to determine applicants' suitability for employment. Includes reviewing applications and resumes. Supervises the administration of the applicant testing program. Responsible for developing or improving testing instruments and procedures. (20%)
3. Presents orientation program to all new employees. Reviews and develops all materials and procedures for the orientation program. (15%)
4. Coordinates the division job posting and transfer program. Establishes job posting procedures. Responsible for reviewing transfer applications, arranging transfer interviews, and determining effective transfer dates. (10%)
5. Distributes new or revised human resources policies and procedures to all employees and managers through email, the company's intranet, meetings, memorandums, or personal contact. (10%)
6. Prepares recruitment literature and job advertisements. (10%)
7. Performs related duties as assigned by the human resources manager. (10%)

Job Specifications

- Four-year college or university degree with major course work in human resources management, business administration, or industrial psychology; OR a combination of experience, education, and training equivalent to a four-year college degree in human resources management.
- Detailed knowledge of the principles of employee selection and assignment of personnel.
- Ability to express ideas clearly in both written and oral communications.
- Ability to independently plan and organize one's own activities.
- Knowledge of HRIS applications desirable.

Physical Requirements: The employee is regularly required to talk and hear. Occasionally the employee is required to stand, walk, sit, and use hands and figures to control objects. Occasional lifting or movement of office products and supplies, up to 10 pounds is required.

the job requires the jobholder to categorize materials or memorize stock codes, these requirements should be stated within the job description. Criteria that are vague or not job related are increasingly and successfully challenged in the courts as unfair and potentially sources of discrimination.

Job Specifications Section

Typically, a job specifications section covers two areas of qualifications: (1) the skills required to perform the job and (2) the job's physical demands. Skills relevant to a job include the education, experience, and specialized training it requires, and the personal traits or abilities and manual dexterities it requires. To comply with Equal Employment Opportunity Commission (EEOC) requirements, the physical demands of a job should refer to how much walking, standing, reaching, lifting, bending, or talking must be done on the job. Recall from Chapter 3 that an organization is legally required to make a reasonable accommodation for disabled individuals who would be able to do the functions if they were accommodated. The condition of the physical work environment and the hazards an employee might encounter in the position are also considered part of the physical demands of a job.

The job specifications section should include interpersonal skills if a competency-based job analysis approach is used. For example, behavioral competencies might include the ability to make decisions based on incomplete information, handle multiple tasks, and resolve conflicts.

LO3

Why is employee motivation such an important aspect of designing today's jobs? The job characteristics model has five components—skill variety, task identity, task significance, autonomy, and feedback. Provide an example of how each component can be used to improve an organization and the job of an employee. (Suggestion: Consider your present or a recent job to answer this question.)

4.2d Writing Clear and Specific Job Descriptions

Several problems are frequently associated with job descriptions, including the following:

1. If they are poorly written, using vague rather than specific terms, they provide little guidance to the jobholder.
2. They are sometimes not updated as job duties or specifications change.
3. They may violate the law or union agreements and lead to employee grievances.
4. They can limit the scope of activities of the jobholder, reducing an organization's flexibility.

When writing a job description, keep the items on it direct and simply worded. Unnecessary words or phrases should be eliminated. The term "occasionally" is used to describe duties that are performed once in a while. The term "may" is used in connection with duties performed only by some workers on the job.

To help alleviate the problem of employees claiming that a task "is not my job," organizations often include language in their job descriptions stating that the jobholder will perform "other duties" as needed. Notice that the job duties section in Highlights in HRM 2 contains the following language: *Performs related duties as assigned by the human resources manager.*

job design
An outgrowth of job analysis that improves jobs through technological and human considerations so as to enhance organization efficiency and employee job satisfaction.

4.3 Job Design

Job design, which is an outgrowth of job analysis, focuses on reconfiguring jobs to capture the talents of employees, improve their work satisfaction, and enhance an organization's performance.[10] Many organizations routinely review the design of work and adjust it to meet technological and organizational requirements as well as the social and personal requirements of work. As Figure 4.5 shows, four basic approaches can be used to design jobs. Top-down approaches—that is, industrial engineering and ergonomics—focus on the tasks of a job and how they can be done better or more efficiently. Bottom-up approaches—that is, enrichment and empowerment—are more person focused. The idea behind them is to design jobs so that the people doing them are more motivated to do them well. Because each approach tackles job design in a different way, all four may work together.

4.3a Industrial Engineering

industrial engineering A field of study concerned with analyzing work methods and establishing time standards.

Industrial engineering, a top-down job design approach, is the study of work to determine which, if any, elements of work can be modified, combined, rearranged, or eliminated to reduce the time needed to complete the work cycle. Time standards are then established by recording the time required to complete each element in the work cycle, using a stopwatch or work-sampling technique. Industrial engineering dramatically changed how people worked around the beginning of the twentieth century and for decades to come, and continues to do so today.

For example, consider the jobs done by pit crews in NASCAR races. In the past, the members of NASCAR pit crews were mechanics who worked at the races on weekends, and changing the tires on a vehicle took about 30 seconds. Today, pit crews need to change the tires in less than 12 seconds for their teams to win. The jobs are now done by former athletes who are stronger and faster, work out, and watch tapes to speed up the 70-plus moves they need to make during a pit stop.[11]

Figure 4.5 Top-Down versus Bottom-Up Job Design Approaches

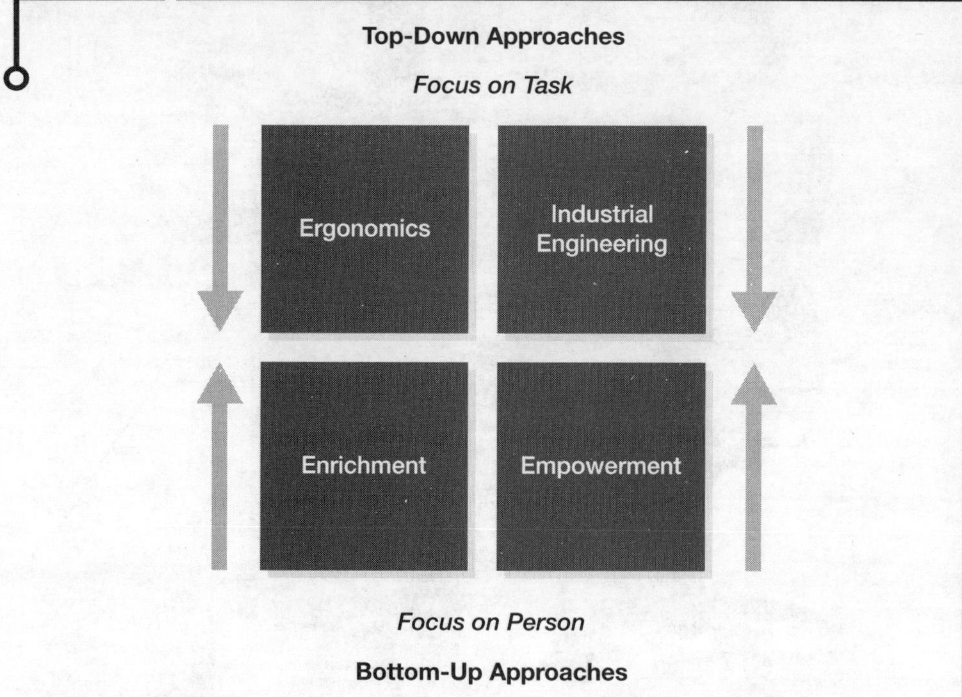

4.3b Ergonomics

ergonomics
The process of studying and designing easy-to-use equipment and systems so the physical well-being of employees is not compromised and work gets done more efficiently.

Ergonomics, another top-down approach, is the process of studying and designing equipment and systems that are easy and efficient for employees to use so that their physical well-being isn't compromised and work gets done more efficiently in the organization. Thus, in contrast to industrial engineering, which focuses on time and efficiency, ergonomics focuses on the well-being of workers so as to improve efficiency. Factors such as the climate in which employees work, the temperatures of facilities, noise and lighting conditions, and the length of schedules and fatigue factors are examined. For example, UPS developed an ergonomic simulator to help train its drivers to walk on ice without injuring themselves.[12] Even just sitting for long periods of time, as office workers often do, can be hazardous to one's health. Prolonged sitting slows down a person's metabolism and can lead to diabetes and heart problems. Standing desks and treadmill desks have been developed to help alleviate this problem.

Ergonomics efforts need not be that complicated, though. They can be as simple as rearranging the flow of work so workers need to take fewer steps or organizing items so they are within easier reach of workers. Part of ergonomics involves looking at the design of equipment and the physical abilities of the different operators who use it. That could include lowering shelves so workers can more easily reach items or redesigning hand controls to make them more comfortable. Or it could mean encouraging employees to wear fitness trackers that electronically prompt them to move around after sitting for long periods of time. Fitbit Inc. has partnered with more than a thousand firms, including Target, IBM, and Gonzaga University, to outfit their employees with Fitbit trackers.[13] Ergonomics is discussed in more detail in Chapter 12.

Although not inexpensive, standing desks and treadmills can improve a workplace's ergonomics.

GARO/PHANIE/ Alamy Stock Photo

4.3c Enrichment

Would you find it motivating if your supervisor timed to the minute each of the tasks associated with your job and then asked you to meet those times? Probably not. Such an approach would get mind-numbing. After a while, you would begin to feel like a machine. In an effort to counter the motivational problems that occur when workers do standardized, repetitive tasks, researchers began identifying ways to improve both the efficiency of organizations and the job satisfaction of employees.[14]

Any effort that makes work more rewarding or satisfying by adding more variety and meaning to a job is called **job enrichment**. Job enrichment was pioneered by Frederick Herzberg in the 1960s.[15] Its goal is to enrich a job so that it is *intrinsically motivating* to employees versus *extrinsically motivating*. Extrinsic motivators consist of external rewards such as money and bonuses. But most employers want their employees to do more than just work for a paycheck. When people are intrinsically motivated, they are energized by the work itself. They may take pride in their work, want to do a good job because it's interesting, and feel they are making a difference by doing it.

job enrichment
Enhancing a job by adding more meaningful tasks and duties to make the work more rewarding or satisfying.

The **job characteristics model** is a more recent theory developed by Richard Hackman and Greg Oldham.[16] According to this model, the following three psychological states of a jobholder result in improved work performance, internal motivation, and lower absenteeism and turnover:

job characteristics model
A job design theory that purports that three psychological states (experiencing meaningfulness of the work performed, responsibility for work outcomes, and knowing the results of the work performed) result in a jobholder's improved work performance, internal motivation, and lower absenteeism and turnover.

1. Experiencing the meaningfulness of the work performed
2. Experiencing responsibility for work outcomes
3. Knowing the results of the work performed[17]

Hackman and Oldham believe that five core job dimensions produce these three psychological states. The five job characteristics are as listed here and illustrated in Figure 4.6:

1. *Skill variety.* The degree to which a job includes a variety of activities, which demand that the jobholder use a number of different skills and talents.
2. *Task identity.* The degree to which a jobholder is able to complete a whole and identifiable piece of work—that is, do a job from beginning to end with a visible outcome.
3. *Task significance.* The degree to which the job has a substantial impact on the lives or work of other people in the jobholder's organization or elsewhere.
4. *Autonomy.* The degree to which the job provides a person with the freedom and discretion to schedule their work and determine how to do it.
5. *Feedback.* The degree to which a person is given direct and clear information about the effectiveness of their job performance.

Other techniques to enrich jobs include job enlargement and job rotation. **Job enlargement** is the process of adding a greater variety of tasks to a job. Maytag, IBM, and AT&T are some of the firms that have used job enlargement to motivate their employees.[18] **Job rotation** is a process whereby employees switch in and out of different jobs.

Job enlargement
The process of adding a greater variety of tasks to a job.

Job enlargement and job rotation help prevent the boredom people experience where they perform narrow, specialized jobs. There is an old saying that "change is as good as a rest," and often it is true. Rotating people to different jobs can also help employees who do repetitive physical tasks avoid health problems and on-the-job injuries. For instance, after a number of hours on their feet, sales people in a clothing store might rotate to the stock room to process inventory or update data records while sitting down.

Job rotation
The process whereby employees rotate in and out of different jobs.

Figure 4.6 Job Characteristics Model

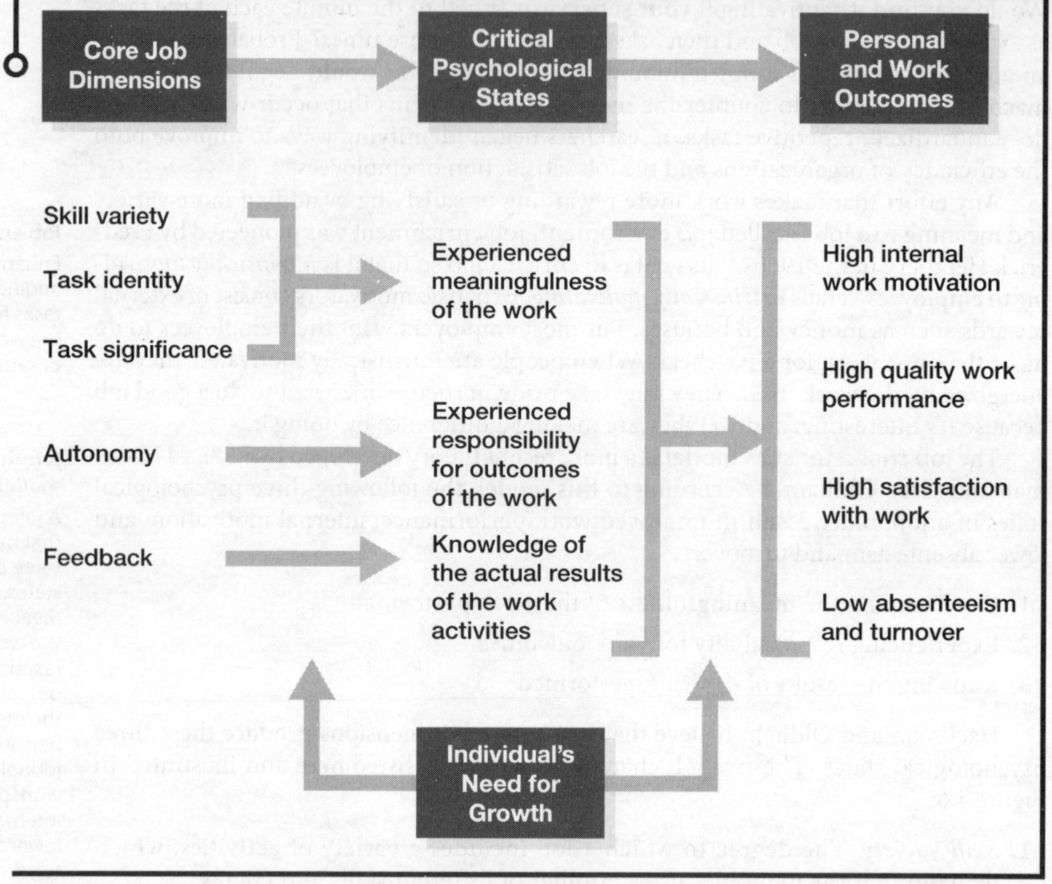

Source: Richard Hackman and Greg R. Oldham, "Motivation through the Design of Work: Test of a Theory," *Organizational Behavior and Human Performance* 16, no. 2: 250–279 (1976).

4.3d Empowerment

employee empowerment
Giving employees the power to initiate change, thereby encouraging them to take charge of what they do.

The techniques we have described so far are ones in which managers change the jobs of employees. A less-structured method is to allow employees to initiate their own job changes through the concept of empowerment. **Employee empowerment** encourages workers to become innovators and managers of their own work, and it involves them in their jobs in ways that give them more control and autonomous decision-making capabilities.

Walt Disney Parks and Resorts is well known for empowering its "cast members" to deliver extraordinary service to every guest. In fact, Walt Disney himself once said, "You can dream, create, design, and build the most wonderful place in the world . . . but it requires people to make the dream a reality."[19] The objective is to develop jobs and basic work units that are adaptable and to allow employees discretion to respond in a world of high-velocity change. See Highlights in HRM 3 for more examples of employee empowerment.

Employee empowerment succeeds when the culture of an organization is open and receptive to change.[20] Workers with innovative ideas need to be encouraged to explore

3 Highlights in HRM

Empowered Employees Achieve Results

By empowering their employees, Home Depot, Walmart, Cigna HealthCare, Costco, AutoZone, Disney, and Applebee's have reduced costs, successfully modified products, and created new ones.

- Kraft Foods employees at the company's Sussex, Wisconsin, food plant redesigned their work, which increased the plant's productivity, reduced its overhead, and cut assembly times.
- Employees at Ford Motor Company's assembly plant in Wayne, Michigan, saved $115,000 a year on protective gloves used to handle sheet metal and glass. The group figured out how to have the gloves washed so they could be used more than once.
- Home Depot's Special Project Support Teams (SPST) improved the company's business and information services. Employees with a wide range of backgrounds and skills collaborated to address a variety of strategic and tactical business needs.
- The American Airlines "Rainbow Team" of employees brought in $192 million in annual revenue by targeting the gay community.

new paths and take reasonable risks at reasonable costs. An empowered environment is created when curiosity is as highly regarded as technical expertise. For this approach to have the intended effects, employees must also have access to a wide range of information within their firms and be held accountable for the results of their empowerment.

Employee empowerment won't work without the support of an organization's senior managers, though. They set the tone of the organization. If they are honest, confident, trusting, and receptive to new ideas, and if they respect employees as partners in the organization's success, it's more likely the firm will be able to empower its employees.

Source: http://www.microsoft.com/en-us/news/stories/garage/index.html138

To help spark innovation at Microsoft, the company created "Microsoft Garage" by renovating an older building. The building has whiteboards, 60 touchscreen monitors, comfortable chairs, 3D printers, laser cutters, and other gadgets. The goal is to encourage employees as well as people from the community to hang out and to tinker at Microsoft on their own time, much as they would in their own garages at home.

Closely related to employee empowerment is workplace democracy. *Workplace democracy* is the utilization of democratic principles such as voting and debate to give employees more say on how an organization is run and the direction it will take. The grocer Whole Foods allows its employees to vote on issues both large and small. W. L. Gore & Associates, which makes Gore-Tex fabric, surgical, aerospace, and other products, asked its employees to help choose its current CEO. But as with empowerment initiatives, workplace democracy requires managers to be willing to give up some decision-making authority.[21]

job crafting
A naturally occurring phenomenon in which employees mold their tasks to better fit their individual strengths, passions, and motives.

Another type of empowerment technique that occurs at the individual level is **job crafting**. In this naturally occurring phenomenon, employees mold their tasks to better fit their individual strengths, passions, and motives.[22] Dorothy Galvez, an administrative assistant at the W. P. Carey School of Business at Arizona State University is an example. Galvez found a way to make her job more meaningful by doing a lot more than traditional administrative work. She expanded her role by planning college activities and events, preparing special college reports, and serving as the dean's representative at college and business events.

employee engagement
A situation in which workers are enthusiastic and immersed in their work to the degree that it improves the performance of their companies.

One study found that employees who are proactive, as Galvez is, are more likely to job craft.[23] But whether their managers want them to or not, employees of all types often reshape their jobs. And in many cases, job crafting results in significantly more employee engagement, which we briefly discussed in Chapter 1. **Employee engagement** is a situation in which workers are enthusiastic and immersed in their work to a degree that improves the performance of their companies.

LO4 ///
Figure 4.8 shows the different forms of employee teams. Provide an example of where each type of team can be used. How do teams create synergy?

4.4 Employee Teams and Flexible Work Schedules

Do you enjoy working teams? Increasingly, teams are how work gets done in organizations. There's a sense among firms that the traditional ways of organizing can be too rigid for today's dynamic marketplace and that they don't meet employees' needs. In addition, companies are seeing the advantages of tinkering with and redesigning work schedules to make them more flexible, and adding flexibility to where employees can work.

4.4a Employee Teams

employee team
A group of employees working together toward a common purpose, in which members have complementary skills, members' work is mutually dependent, and the group has discretion over tasks performed.

An **employee team** can be defined as a group of employees working together toward a common purpose, in which members have complementary skills, members' work is mutually dependent, and the group has discretion over tasks performed. Organizations of all types—for example, Federal Express, LinkedIn, Tesla, and Martin Agency (the advertising firm behind the clever commercials for Geico, DoorDash, and Buffalo Wild Wings)—are using employee teams to solve unique and complex problems and improve the collaboration among workers and their morale.[24] Even the U.S. Army has turned to teams to improve its operations. Early on in the Iraq War, the army's hierarchical structure hindered its operations. General Stanley McChrystal's solution was to learn something from the insurgents whom the army was fighting: decentralize authority to self-organizing teams.[25]

Part of the reason why employee teams exist is that employees—not managers—are closest to the work that's actually being done in an organization. Thus, they are often in a better position to see how the work can be done better. Teamwork can also result in synergy. Synergy occurs when the interactions and outcomes of team members are greater than the sum of their individual efforts.[26] Synergy in teams does not automatically happen, though. Figure 4.7 lists the behaviors that can help a team develop synergy.

Teams can operate in a variety of structures, each with different strategic purposes or functional activities. Figure 4.8 describes some common team forms, including cross-functional teams, project teams, self-directed teams, taskforce teams, process-improvement teams, and virtual teams. Self-directed teams are often championed as being the highest form of teams. Also called *autonomous work groups*, *self-managed teams*, or *high-performance teams*, they consist of groups of employees who are accountable for an entire work process or segment that delivers a product or service to an internal or external customer. For example, in a manufacturing environment, a team might be responsible for a whole product such as a computer screen or a clearly defined segment of the production process, such as the building of an engine for a passenger car.

Figure 4.7 Synergistic Team Characteristics

Team synergy is heightened when team members engage in the following behaviors.

- *Support.* The team exhibits an atmosphere of inclusion. All team members speak up and feel free to offer constructive comments.
- *Listening and clarification.* Members honestly listen to others and seek clarification on discussion points. The team members summarize discussions held.
- *Disagreement.* Disagreements are seen as natural and are expected. The members' comments are nonjudgmental and focus on factual issues rather than personality differences.
- *Consensus.* The team's members reach agreements through consensus. Proposals that are acceptable to all team members are adopted, even if they are not the first choice of some of the individual members. Common ground among ideas is sought.
- *Acceptance.* The team members value one another as individuals. They recognize that each person brings a valuable mix of skills and abilities to the team.
- *Quality.* Each team member is committed to excellence. There is emphasis on continuous improvement and attention to detail.

Figure 4.8 Forms of Employee Teams

Cross-Functional Team. A group staffed with a mix of employees from an organization's marketing, production, engineering departments, and so forth, which is formed to accomplish a specific objective.
Project Team. A group formed specifically to design a new product or service. The members are assigned by their managers on the basis of their ability to contribute to the team's success. The group normally disbands after the task is completed.
Self-Directed Team. A group of highly trained individuals performing a set of interdependent job tasks within a natural work unit. The team members rely on consensus-type decision making to perform their work duties, solve problems, or deal with internal or external customers.
Taskforce Team. A group formed by management to immediately resolve a major problem.
Process-Improvement Team. A group made up of experienced people from different departments or functions. The group is charged with improving quality, decreasing waste, or enhancing the productivity of processes that affect all departments or functions. The members are normally appointed by management.
Virtual Team. A team that utilizes telecommunications technology to link team members who are geographically dispersed—often worldwide, across cultures and across time zones.

Similarly, in a service environment, a team is usually responsible for an entire group of products and services, or it might be responsible for serving clients in one particular geographic area.

Typical team functions include setting work schedules, dealing directly with external customers, training team members, setting performance targets, budgeting, inventory management, and purchasing equipment or services. To operate efficiently, team members generally acquire multiple skills so that they are able to perform a variety of tasks as part of the team. In addition, job rotation is often used in work teams so members can trade off doing different tasks as needed.

dejobbing
The process of structuring organizations not around jobs, but rather around projects that are constantly changing.

Closely associated with teams is dejobbing. **Dejobbing** refers to a process of structuring organizations not around jobs, but rather around projects that are constantly changing and have different team members. In a dejobbed organization, a skills matrix like the one shown in Figure 4.4 is likely to be used instead of a traditional job description that defines specific work. Current trends suggest that this type of organizational structure will be the norm in the future.[27]

To be sure, it is hard to imagine a world without jobs. Nonetheless, dejobbed organizations do exist. There are no traditional bosses at W. L. Gore or traditional jobs per se. All employees are hired as "associates" and assigned to "sponsors" in the functional groups in which they work. This structure has helped create a culture of innovation within the company that has repeatedly landed it on *Fortune* magazine's annual list of the U.S. "100 Best Companies to Work For." Zappos, the online shoe seller, is an extreme example of dejobbing. A few years ago, the company took the extreme step of eliminating all of its hierarchical structures, jobs, and roles. Zappos wanted to give its employees the flexibility to take on various tasks and move between teams freely. Case Study 1 at the end of the chapter explains what Zappos did and how well it's working.

virtual teams
Teams that utilize telecommunications technology to link team members who are geographically dispersed— often worldwide, across cultures and across time zones.

Virtual Teams

Virtual teams utilize technology to link team members who are geographically dispersed—often worldwide, across cultures and across time zones. It has become commonplace for virtual teams to use wikis, document sharing platforms such as Google Docs, online chat and instant messaging, web- and videoconferencing, and electronic calendar systems, to name a few communication technologies. People and firms working virtually in hundreds of countries worldwide helped design the U.S. Defense

Online services such as Skype and iMeet allow virtual workers to get better acquainted with one another and have face-to-face conversations across any distance.

Fizkes/Shutterstock.com

Department's latest fighter jet, the F-35. Microsoft used a virtual team of top scientists around the world to improve the functionality of its Windows 10 Cortana product.[28]

Virtual teams do not have to work for just one organization, though. Many virtual teams consist of members from different organizations. For example, to improve workflows in supply chains, it is not uncommon for manufacturers to have their employees team up with the employees of their suppliers and the employees of the retailers who buy the manufacturers' products.

Although virtual teams have many benefits, they are not without their challenges.[29] These sources of potential difficulties include language and cultural barriers, unclear objectives, time conflicts due to diverse geographic locations, and members' ability to work in a collaborative setting.[30] NASA encountered an extreme problem of this type when it lost a $125 million space probe as a result of its team members around the world using different units of measurement—the English system versus the metric system.

Navi Radjou, an expert in network innovations, notes, "One problem with distributing work is that you lose the intimacy of talking things through at the local café." To help virtual teams "gel," more companies are beginning to use online collaborative meetings to allow members of a team to share more personal information such as photos and links to social media, and engage with one another via private chat. Gathering the members of a team together, especially when the team is first launched but also at regular intervals, can help a team build more intimacy and trust among the members.

Facilitating Teams

Regardless of the structure or purpose of the team, the following characteristics are associated with successful teams:

- A commitment to shared goals and objectives
- Motivated and energetic team members
- Open and honest communication
- Shared leadership
- Clear role assignments
- A climate of cooperation, collaboration, trust, and accountability
- The recognition of conflict and its positive resolution

Unfortunately, not all teams succeed or operate at their full potential. Richard Hackman (who helped develop the job characteristics model discussed earlier in the chapter) once said, "I have no question that when you have a team, the possibility exists that it will generate magic, producing something extraordinary . . . But don't count on it."[31] Power struggles, uncertainty about the roles members should play, a lack of resources, conflicts of interest, and personality differences are common team problems. Another difficulty with work teams is that they alter the traditional manager–employee relationship. Managers sometimes feel threatened by the growing power of the team and the reduced power of management.

Organizations can help prevent some of the problems that a team might experience. First, the firm should determine when a team is, and is not, needed. It's not unusual for teams to be assembled for tasks that could be better done by individuals working alone or by working separately and collaborating only occasionally with one another. To determine whether a team is appropriate, researcher Jeffrey Polzer suggests that firms conduct a *process analysis* to evaluate the work by looking at its complexity and the interdependence of the tasks that need to be done. Complex tasks include projects

Small Business Application

Building Teams in the Small Business Environment

Specialization and employees solely dedicated to well-defined tasks may work well in large corporations, but small businesses can't really afford that luxury. In an entrepreneurial business setting, employees typically wear multiple hats. They need to understand what their coworkers do and how they do it so that the business can always continue to function, regardless of the circumstances. That's why a team environment—where a small number of employees are cross-trained to perform a variety of roles—is an ideal strategy for the small-business owner.

In some ways, establishing a team environment within a small business may be easier because it's so obvious how individuals are contributing to the whole—a key component of success in team building. Adds human resources and management development consultant Susan M. Heathfield, "Fostering teamwork is creating a work culture that values collaboration. In a teamwork environment, people understand and believe that thinking, planning, decisions, and actions are better when done cooperatively." To nurture this kind of environment, Heathfield recommends holding regular discussions about collaboration and its purpose, recognizing and rewarding teamwork both publicly and privately, and finding ways to build some fun into team activities in addition to doing the hard work.

Of course, a successful team starts with an effective leader. Some teams have a single leader, whereas others are structured so that members take turns leading. Business strategist Rick Johnson says that team managers need to know how to communicate expectations clearly, how to avoid micromanaging, and how to build confidence in team members, which empowers them to perform well. This means team leaders will need to learn how to act as facilitators. "Coaching is a skill set that should be required training for all managers to improve team management," adds Johnson.

Craig Wagganer, a speaker and trainer who specializes in team building, has developed an easy-to-remember method for effectively leading teams, which he calls the CARE method. He suggests that team leaders:

- **Consider** each team member's strengths, goals, and relationship to the team. A good leader will not only capitalize on what the team member has to offer, but also help the member realize his or her potential.
- **Appreciate** each team member's gifts and contributions, and express that appreciation often.
- **Respect** differences among team members so that conflicts can be resolved fairly and impersonally and mistakes can be handled with grace, not blame.
- **Encourage** team members, individually and as a group, in their efforts.

Wagganer goes on to describe the ripple effect of a healthy team environment under expert leadership: "When the heart of each team member is encouraged first by the team leader, then the team will be poised to cheer on each other. It starts at the top. And when a person feels encouraged, their outlook changes and becomes one of enthusiasm for the cause and excitement for the team making a positive difference and being successful in its endeavors." That kind of optimism goes a long way in the small business environment.

Sources: Stephane Kasriel "Three Team-Building Secrets of Successful Small-Business Owners," *Entrepreneur* (May 2, 2016), https://www.entrepreneur.com; "Building a High-Performance Sales Team," *Atlanta Journal-Constitution* (January 30, 2014), http://ajc.com; Chuck Stinnett, *Evansville Courier Press* (February 26, 2011), http://www.courierpress.com; Rick Johnson, "The Six Principles of Effective Team Management," http://www.teambuildingtips.com; Susan M. Heathfield, "How to Build a Teamwork Culture," http://humanresources.about.com; Craig Wagganer, "Team Building Starts with Team Member Building," http://www.leadershipinstitute.com.

that are large, uncertain, and for which there are no standard procedures for completing. Interdependent tasks require people to rely closely on one another to execute them. Teams are ideal for projects that are *both* highly complex and require a high degree of interdependence.[32]

Once it's been determined a team is a needed, a company can help it succeed by designing the compensation so that the team's members individually and jointly work for its achievements and by having the members undergo team training. Complete training for the team would cover important skills in (1) team leadership, (2) mission/goal setting, (3) conducting meetings, (4) team decision making, (5) conflict resolution, (6) effective communication, and (7) diversity awareness.[33] In addition, research shows that teams are more effective when they initially establish "ground rules" for how they should operate and how their members should behave. HRM Experience, at the end of the chapter, presents an exercise to set team ground rules.

4.4b Flexible Work Arrangements

The COVID-19 pandemic upended most traditional work arrangements, as employees needed to adjust both to the closing of their worksite facilities and to working at home. But even before the pandemic hit, many employers had adapted the standard workday or workweek to improve their productivity and the morale of their employees by giving those employees more control over the hours they work.[34] As far back as 2006, more than half of companies surveyed by the Society for Human Resource Management offered their employees flexible working options.[35] One reason is that such policies helped companies attract and retain employees when they were unable to offer the benefits or pay a competitor would. In one survey, 42 percent of employers who were unable to provide raises to their employees said they were willing to offer them flexible hours instead.[36] Especially common flexible work arrangements include remote work (or telecommuting), the compressed workweek, flextime, and job sharing.

Working Remotely

In the past, companies allowed some employees to work from home or an alternative location, at least some of the time. **Telecommuting**, as it is often called, entails the use of smartphones, tablets, personal computers, and other communication technology to do work traditionally performed in the workplace.[37] But what used to be an exception, or a perk, or a special benefit, is fast becoming the norm for many organizations. Perhaps not surprisingly, big technology companies are leading the way. Following the COVID-19 pandemic, Twitter CEO Jack Dorsey told employees that they could work from home indefinitely. Facebook CEO Mark Zuckerberg told his company's employees the same thing. In contrast, some other companies, such as large banks, returned to normal working arrangements. Jamie Dimon, CEO of JPMorgan Chase, noted that only perhaps 10 percent of his workforce "in very special roles" would work from home every day.[38]

telecommuting
Working remotely; the use of personal computers, networks, and other communications technology to do work in the home that is traditionally done in the employer's workplace.

Recent surveys show that most workers believe that working remotely at least some of the time is the ideal work situation. A recent Gallup survey revealed that three out of five respondents said that they prefer to work remotely as much as possible. One reason is that telecommuting may reduce stress. According to a study conducted by the University of Wisconsin–Milwaukee, employees who telecommute are often more satisfied with their jobs because they experience fewer interruptions and less office politics. Evidence suggests that employees can be as productive—or even more productive—when working from home. However, remote workers often end up working a few more hours per week than people who don't telecommute.[39]

How does remote work help firms? The better work–life balance that employees experience can help firms attract and retain valuable employees who otherwise might quit. Remote work can also dramatically lower a firm's real estate costs by reducing the amount of office space it needs and restructuring it. However, the importance (and cost) of cyber-security increases dramatically with remote work.

Not all employees have the self-discipline to work alone at home, however. In addition, collaboration and communication within an organization can suffer because employees are not interacting face to face with one another on a regular basis. For reasons such as these, some companies are moving to "hybrid" work arrangements in which some employees work from a central location, while others connect remotely.[40]

Figure 4.9 summarizes some of the keys to remote working.

Flextime

flextime
Flexible working hours that give employees the option of choosing their daily starting and quitting times, provided that they work a set number of hours per day or week.

Flextime, or flexible working hours, gives employees the option of choosing their daily starting and quitting times, provided they work a certain number of hours per day or week. With flextime, employees have considerable latitude in scheduling their work. Often there is a "core period" during the morning and afternoon when all employees are required to be on the job.

Flextime provides both employees and employers with several advantages. By allowing employees greater flexibility in work scheduling, employers can reduce some of the traditional causes of tardiness and absenteeism.[41] Employees can adjust their work to accommodate their particular lifestyles and, in doing so, gain greater job satisfaction. Employees can also schedule their working hours for the time of day when they are most productive. In addition, variations in arrival and departure times can help reduce traffic congestion at the peak commuting hours, so employees spend less time on the road.

Younger workers, in particular, want flexibility on the job. A lack of it was making it difficult for PricewaterhouseCoopers, a Big-4 accounting firm, to retain Millennial workers, especially during the busy tax auditing season. So, the company implemented a program that encourages employees to customize their schedules to avoid burnout. Kathie Lingle, national director of work/life at KPMG, a competing Big-4 accounting firm, says flextime is the number-one driver of retention for her firm.[42]

Besides being a good employee recruiting and retention tool, flextime allows organizations that want to improve their service to customers or clients to extend their operating hours. CenturyLink, a telecommunications company, uses flextime to keep its business offices open for customers who cannot get there during the day. Research demonstrates that flextime can have a positive impact on performance measures such as reliability, quality, and quantity of the employee's work.

Figure 4.9 Keys for Successful Remote Working

- *Determine the jobs suitable for remote work.* Jobs that require face-to-face contact with customers, the use of specialized equipment, or a physical presence (such as security guards) aren't candidates. Also, determine eligibility criteria to assess who is or who is not eligible to telecommute based on their types of jobs or collective bargaining agreements, for example.
- *Establish formalized guidelines for remote work.* The guidelines could cover hours of availability, office reporting periods, performance expectations, and weekly progress reports or email updates.
- *Identify the needed resources.* The technology and equipment needed for working remotely should be specified. What equipment is the firm providing? What equipment is the worker providing? Who provides technical assistance in the event of equipment disruption?
- *Keep everyone informed.* Physical separation can make remote workers feel isolated and invisible. Department and staff updates that include remote workers on project teams, required attendance at meetings, and "chat room" discussions can keep everyone "in the loop."
- *Recognize when remote working is not effective.* State in written policies that the arrangement can be terminated when it no longer serves the company's needs or if the employee's performance declines.

Sources: Greg Kratz, "Twelve Tips to Help You Work from Home Successfully," *Flexjobs*, October 298, 2020; Barbara Hemphill, "Telecommuting Productivity," *Occupational Health and Safety* 73, no. 3 (2004): 16; U.S. Office of Personnel Management, "Guide to Telework in the Federal Government" (April 2011), I.D. No.: ES/WLW-04-11, http://www.telework.gov.

Even so, flextime also has some disadvantages. First, it is not suited to some jobs, such as those that require specific workstations to be staffed at all times. Second, it can create problems for managers trying to supervise and schedule meetings with employees who aren't onsite when the managers are. To keep in closer touch with employees when they are working offsite, some firms utilize work-oriented social media tools such as Slack, Yammer, and Workplace by Facebook.

Compressed Workweek

A compressed workweek is one in which the number of days in the workweek is shortened by lengthening the number of hours worked per day. For example, employees might work 10 hours a day for 4 days a week. Alternatively, they might work 80 hours over 9 days and take 1 day off every other week.

Compressed workweeks have been shown to reduce absenteeism and make it easier to recruit and retain employees.[43] Many workers like the arrangement because it lengthens their weekends and decreases the time and money they spend getting ready for work and commuting back and forth to the job. The major disadvantage of the compressed workweek involves federal laws regarding overtime. The Fair Labor Standards Act has stringent rules requiring the payment of overtime to nonsupervisory employees who work more than 40 hours a week (see Chapter 9). Another disadvantage of the compressed workweek is that it can increase the stress employees experience—the long workdays can be exhausting.

Job Sharing

An arrangement whereby two part-time employees do a job normally held by one full-time employee is called **job sharing**. People who have families or want to work part-time, and older workers who want to phase into retirement by shortening their workweeks, often find job sharing desirable.[44] After her doctor warned that the stress of her 100-mile roundtrip daily commute could shorten her life, Mary Kaye Stuart decided to pursue a job-sharing situation. "I had been wanting more balance in my life, and this was the answer," says Stuart, 63, an account executive in Austin, Texas.[45] Job sharing can also reduce layoffs in hard economic times. Companies with job sharing programs include Sprint, American Express, and Kaiser Permanente, one of the nation's largest health organizations.

job sharing
An arrangement in which two part-time employees do a job normally held by one full-time employee.

Summary

LO 1 A job analysis is the systematic process of collecting information about all of the parameters of a job—its basic responsibilities, along with the behaviors, skills, and physical and mental requirements of the people who do it. A job analysis should also outline the tools needed to do the job, the environment and times at which it needs to done, with whom it needs to be done, and the outcome or performance level it should produce. The information a job analysis collects serves many HRM functions, including a firm's workflow and design of jobs, its legal compliance efforts, and the recruitment, selection, training and development, performance appraisal, and compensation of employees. To comply with the law, human resources decisions must be based on criteria objectively collected by analyzing the requirements of each job.

LO 2 Job analysis information can be gathered in several ways—via interviews, questionnaires, observations, and diaries. Other more quantitative approaches include the U.S. Department of Labor's job analysis system, the position analysis questionnaire system, the critical incident method, the task inventory analysis, and the competency-based analysis. The format of job descriptions varies widely, often reflecting the needs of the organization and the expertise of the writer. At a minimum, job descriptions should contain a job title; a job identification section; the purpose of the job; the tasks, duties, and responsibilities of the job; and the job's specifications (KSAOs). Job descriptions should be written in clear and specific terms with consideration given to their legal implications.

LO 3 Job design, which is an outgrowth of job analysis, focuses on restructuring jobs so as to capture the talents of employees, improve their work satisfaction, and enhance an organization's performance. Top-down job design techniques such as industrial engineering and ergonomics focus more on tasks; bottom-down techniques such as enrichment and empowerment focus more on workers and seek to motivate them to do their jobs better. In the job characteristics model, five job factors affect employees' satisfaction: job skill variety, task identity, task significance, autonomy, and feedback. All of these factors should be built into jobs, since each affects the psychological state of employees.

LO 4 Increasingly, firms are using employee teams to solve unique and complex problems, enhance collaboration among workers, improve their morale and performance, and make the most of the firm's scarce resources. An employee team is a group of individuals working together toward a common purpose, in which members have complementary skills, members' work is mutually dependent, and the group has discretion over the tasks it performs. Types of teams commonly used in today's business environment include cross-functional teams, project teams, self-directed teams, taskforce teams, process-improvement teams, and virtual teams. In recent years, employers have been adapting traditional work arrangements to create alternative approaches that improve productivity and the morale of their employees by giving them more control over where, when, and how they work. Remote work, compressed workweeks, flextime, and job sharing allow employees to adjust their work arrangements to accommodate their particular lifestyles.

Key Terms

- **critical incident method**
- **dejobbing**
- **employee empowerment**
- **employee engagement**
- **employee team**
- **ergonomics**
- **flextime**
- **functional job analysis (FJA)**
- **industrial engineering**
- **job**
- **job analysis**
- **job characteristics model**
- **job crafting**
- **job description**
- **job design**
- **job enlargement**
- **job enrichment**
- **job rotation**
- **job sharing**
- **job specification**
- **position analysis questionnaire (PAQ)**
- **task inventory analysis**
- **telecommuting**
- **virtual teams**

Discussion Questions

LO 1 Assume you are the general manager of a service department. How might formally written job requirements help you manage your work unit?

LO 2 Discuss the various ways in which a job analysis can be completed. Compare and contrast these methods, noting the pros or cons of each.

LO 3 Why is employee motivation such an important aspect of designing today's jobs? The job characteristics model includes five components—skill variety, task identity, task significance, autonomy, and feedback. Provide an example of how each component can be used to improve an organization and the job of an employee. (Suggestion: Consider your present or a recent job to answer this question.)

LO 4 Figure 4.8 shows the different forms of employee teams. Provide an example of where each type of team can be used. How do teams create synergy?

HRM Experience

Establishing Ground Rules for a Team's Success

Ground rules—or team norms—are agreed-on formal rules that guide the behavior of a team's members, including how they want to be treated and agree to treat others. Ground rules help teams maintain order, promote positive behavior, and can be used to correct undesirable actions.

Assignment

1. Divide your class into teams.
2. Using the following list, have each team member silently select 10 behaviors they believe are most critical for a team's success. The first list of 10 behaviors (each person's A list) should consist of those most important for group conduct. The second list of 10 behaviors (each person's B list) should consist of those that are desirable.
3. Have the members of your team select a final list of 10 behaviors from both lists. These will become your team's ground rules. The items can be modified or combined to meet your team's specific needs.

Behaviors List

While working in our team, individuals should:

1. Do their fair share of the work.
2. Check to ensure that everyone clearly understands what is to be done.
3. Encourage planning, including short-range agendas as well as long-range goals.
4. Encourage open and candid opinions about issues.
5. Listen willingly and carefully to other people's ideas, even if those people have a different viewpoint.
6. Prepare thoroughly before meetings.
7. Make team members feel at ease during discussions.
8. Encourage members to ask questions when they do not clearly understand tasks or procedures.
9. Outline the pros and cons of decisions faced by the team.
10. Follow through on task assignments.
11. Help other members when they need assistance.
12. Treat all team members as equals.
13. Paraphrase or restate what someone else says to check its meaning.
14. Openly voice opinions and share ideas.
15. Be flexible in arranging meeting schedules.
16. Compliment others for things they have said or done.
17. Be willing to meet whenever it is necessary to discuss a problem.
18. Bring conflicts to the attention of the team and deal with them directly.
19. Express enthusiasm about what the team is doing.
20. Encourage budgeting of the team's time.
21. At the end of a meeting, have members restate their own responsibilities to check for agreement.
22. Be serious about the team's work.
23. Arrive on time for regularly scheduled meetings.
24. Be willing to listen to other team members' ideas.
25. Get the team's approval on important matters before proceeding.

CASE STUDY 1 The Zappos Experiment

There are many different ways in which firms can organize themselves. There are flat organizations and there are tall organizations. There are organizations structured by products, divisions, and geography. But one thing nearly all structures have in common is a chain of command, or hierarchy.

But do companies have to be set up that way? As founder and CEO of Zappos, Tony Hsieh didn't think so. Hsieh was a guy who thought outside the box. When he started Zappos in 1999, no one was selling shoes online. It seemed like a crazy idea—you couldn't try on shoes online to see if they fit. But Zappos made the business work by offering good products, free shipping and returns, and great customer service.

Hsieh believed it was not just the Zappos business model that led to its success. Employees and their satisfaction were essential, too. To keep workers happy and passionate about their jobs, the company offered top-of-the-line and unusual perks: good pay, free health care, and employees could bring their dogs to work if they were well socialized. Quirky celebrations and parties were the norm at the company, which routinely made it a candidate for *Fortune*'s "Best Places to Work" list.

Happy Zapponians and a booming business weren't enough for Hsieh, though. He had noticed that most companies on the *Fortune* 500 list in 1955 were no longer on the list by the end of the millennium. In fact, many of them no longer existed.

Hsieh figured it was because as firms grow, they become slow and lose touch with their customers. Executives at the top make the decisions, but they don't really understand what customers want, know how products can be improved, or have a lot ideas for transforming the business. Lower-level employees—the people closest to the work—often do, but their suggestions rarely make it up the food chain. He didn't want that to happen at Zappos.

So what did Hsieh do? In 2014, he instituted a new type of self-management system. Managers were eliminated at Zappos. Everyone became an equal, and no one could tell anyone else what to do.

Job titles were also eliminated at the company. Instead, employees had "roles" and their coworkers were "partners." They worked together in "circles" (or teams) of their choosing. The members of a circle could meet regularly to talk about improvements and ideas. Each meeting began with a "chit chat," where everyone was required to speak. The idea was to ensure that even the quietest employee was heard. A software system was installed to track the circle's goals and who agreed to do what and when. The goal was to turn each employee into a "mini-entrepreneur" with the ability to sense ideas and do something about it.

Performance appraisals were also eliminated at Zappos. Instead, the new system had coworkers distribute 100 "people points" to the members in their circles. Those employees who didn't get enough points might get booted from a circle—much as contestants get voted off of the island in *Survivor.* Ultimately, if the person had no circle to work in, they lost their job. Pay raises were based on new skills a person developed, a system called "badging." For example, a person might earn a badge for Java coding or merchandising.

If ditching the old corporate structure for something new sounds simple, it turned out to be anything but that for Zappos. First, all kinds of rules and meetings were required to set up the system: "tactical" meetings focused on the workflows, and "governance" meetings focused on hashing out processes and eliminating roadblocks. Second, employees had trouble understanding the new system and weren't sure what they were supposed to be doing. Former managers felt diminished. They no longer had any power or status, and they never would; so much for having climbed the corporate ladder. Writer/editor Roger Hodge referred to Zappos' new organizational structure as "a radical experiment . . . to end the office workplace as we know it."

Hsieh knew the transition wouldn't be easy, so he offered employees who didn't like the new system a buyout, which amounted to about 5 months' pay. Eighteen percent of the workforce, or 1,600 employees, took the company up on its offer. Another 15 percent or so quit later. Morale fell, and Zappos dropped off of *Fortune*'s "Best Companies to Work for" list for the first time in its history.

Hsieh admitted that he was surprised how hard it was for people to leave their bureaucratic baggage behind. "In retrospect, I would have probably ripped off the Band-Aid sooner," he said. Even so, things improved after coworkers who didn't like the system left. Not surprisingly, the company also implemented a program to better screen and prepare new employees to manage themselves. Reportedly, the firm's profit margins held up during the change.

Derek Noel, an employee with Zappos, put it this way. "My worst day at Zappos is still better than my best day anywhere else," he says. "I can't imagine going back to traditional hierarchy anymore." The new system helped ensure his ideas would be heard and allowed him to take on a more substantive role in the company.

Following Hsieh's retirement and premature death in 2020, some say that Zappos quietly began returning to a more traditional approach.

Discussion Questions

1. Is a self-managing organization a good idea? Why or why not?
2. Could Zappos have done anything to make the transition to the new system smoother? If so, what?

Sources: Diana Ransom, "Tony Hsieh Is Leaving Zappos after 20 Years," *Inc.*, August 25, 2020; Aimee Groth, "Zappos Has Quietly Backed Away from Holacracy," *Quartz at Work*, January 29, 2020; Zack Guzman, "Zappos CEO Tony Hsieh on Getting Rid of Managers: What I Wish I'd Done Differently," *CNBC* (September 13, 2016), http://www.cnbc.com; Yuki Noguchi, "Zappos: A Workplace Where No One and Everyone Is the Boss," *NPR* (July 21, 2015), http://npr.org; Jennifer Reingold, "How a Radical Shift Left Zappos Reeling," *Fortune* (March 4, 2017), http://fortune.com; Camille Sweeney and Josh Gosfied, "No Managers Required: How Zappos Ditched the Old Corporate Structure for Something New," *Fast Company* (January 6, 2014), https://www.fastcompany.com.

CASE STUDY 2 Apple's Design Team[1]

In a surprise notice issued late on Thursday, June 20, 2019, Apple announced that its chief design officer, Jonathan "Jony" Ive, would be leaving the company later in the year. Ive was the man behind the design team that created Apple's most iconic products—the iMac, the MacBook, the iPod, the iPhone, the iPad, and the Apple Watch. Working side by side with Apple's founder, Steve Jobs, Ive led what was arguably the most successful design team in the history of business, and the inspiration for a whole new generation of consumer electronics. It was not an exaggeration to say that the work of his design team had rescued Apple from the edge of the abyss, and made it one of the most highly valued companies in the world. And now Ive was moving on.

Apple's Renaissance

Apple's storied history is fairly well known. Steve Jobs and Steve Wozniak founded Apple Computer in 1976. After disrupting the industry and setting a new course for personal computing, the company struggled, and Jobs and Wozniak left the company in 1985. Jobs returned to Apple in 1997 and put the company on a different trajectory, increasing Apple's emphasis on innovation and design.

Jobs began searching for talent, and he wanted A+ players he could use to build his design team. Up until that time, the company had partnered with firms outside of Apple to design its products. But Jobs wanted to bring the work in-house. Jobs and Ive had a remarkable first meeting; the two just clicked. "I can't really remember that happening really ever before," Ive said. "It was the most bizarre thing, where we were both perhaps a little—a little bit odd. We weren't used to clicking."

The iMac was Jobs's and Ive's first big hit in 1998. Both men knew they were redesigning not just Apple's flagship computer, but the company itself. As Steven Levy put it, the iMac "was the beginning of a succession of products that changed the expectations not just of technology design but the role of design in consumer products."

Jobs and Ive had complementary styles and complementary strengths. "Ive could translate futuristic concepts into physical objects with simplicity and sophistication. . . . Jobs was the inspiration and the editor needed to bring these ideas to life." Ive was generally reserved, while Jobs was famously charismatic. His reputation was "one of almost maniacal micromanagement when it came to creating a new product and of almost Barnum-like mastery of hoopla and razzmatazz when it came to selling."

But Jobs and Ive were alike in their design philosophies: both put beauty before everything else. As Ive described it, "We think alike about how products should be made to look pure and seamless." For both, less was more. "In so many ways, we're trying to get the object out of the way," Ive said. Both Jobs and Ive were equally passionate about big ideas and small details. They didn't just care about how a product looked from the outside; they were focused on the complete picture, inside and out.

Their offices were right next to each other, and they often ate lunch and took walks together, discussing new projects and plans. Ive recalled, "Steve used to say to me—and he used to say this a lot—'Hey, Jony, here's a dopey idea.' And sometimes they were: really dopey. Sometimes they were truly dreadful. But sometimes they took the air from the room, and they left us both completely silent. Bold, crazy, magnificent ideas.

Or quiet, simple ones which, in their subtlety, their detail, they were utterly profound." Matt Rogers, who developed software for the iPhone and iPad between 2007 and 2010, said, "Most of the greatest debates at Apple happened between those two as they walked together."

The Design Team

Ive's 20-person design team was the epicenter of Apple's great run of iconic products. An eclectic group, the team members included Eugene Whang, who moonlighted as a DJ; Julian Hönig, who previously had designed Lamborghinis; Jody Akana, who specialized in color; and Bart André, who had more design patents than any other Apple employee.

Although the group expanded somewhat over the years, it remained very loyal. In almost two decades, only two designers had ever left the studio. Given that special mix of talent, losing an individual designer was a big loss. Three recruiters were specifically assigned to identify and recruit new designers; they were uber-selective, onboarding only about one new member per year.

As a rule, the design team worked apart from the rest of the company: it was fairly insular from others, even secretive. Team members were not allowed to discuss their work with friends, but shared virtually everything with each other. Although each designer had a specialty, and each project had a team leader, they cross-pollinated continuously, and everyone contributed to one another's work, sharing the credit. The team typically worked long 12-hour days, obsessing over elements of design—the shape of curves, the angle of displays, even the color palette of package materials. The team described itself as a family, socialized together after work, and created a "work hard, play hard" culture that continued for years.

Ive described his role as lying between two extremes of design leadership: he was not the source of all creativity, nor did he merely assess the proposals of colleagues. The big ideas were often his, and he had an opinion about every detail. Team meetings were held two or three times a week, and Ive encouraged candor. "We put the product ahead of anything else," he said.

Reflecting Ive's style, the design team members worked quietly and brilliantly, and rarely gained public recognition. By all accounts, they liked it that way. They liked the creative work, not the hype. As designer Richard Howarth described it, "It's not like the weight of the world's on our shoulders. Jony set it up so that it's a little—it's freer than you might imagine."

However, the design team enjoyed a level of influence at Apple unimaginable at other firms. At most tech companies, engineering dictates product development. At Apple, it was the other way around. "Ive often gave concepts to Apple's engineering department, telling them to make the product design possible." Designers reigned supreme.

Ive also changed the process by which design was created. As Brunner put it, design had been "a vertical stripe in the [value] chain of events" in a product's creation. But at Apple, Ive shaped it to become "a long horizontal stripe, where design is part of every conversation."

The team obsessed over the designs, understanding the importance of iteration. "Everything we make I could describe as being partially wrong, because it's not perfect. . . . We get to do it again. That's one of the things Steve and I used to talk about: 'Isn't this fantastic? Everything we aren't happy about, with this, we can try and fix.'"

The End of an Era

Steve Jobs died in October 2011, succumbing to a rare form of pancreatic cancer. Ive was by his side when he passed away. Ive remained the creative soul of Apple, and in the absence of Jobs, he had more responsibility. Ive's role expanded "from strictly physical industrial design to digital user interface as well." In other words, he was in charge of both hardware and software design. He had a much bigger team reporting to him, and his impact was immense.

But something had changed within Apple, and within Ive himself. The pace of work, and the cadence within the design studio, slowed. Ive acknowledged the change, too. To regain momentum, Ive began pushing to make a watch, intrigued by miniaturization of the iPhone's powerful technology. "He met with the team almost daily and immersed in detail, helping dream up the distinctive, hexagonal grid of apps that morphed as people scrolled."

After the Apple Watch launched in 2015, Ive met with his team. He "thanked them for their work, and said 2014 had been one of his most challenging years at Apple. In an interview with *The New Yorker*, Ive confessed to being "deeply tired." The staff beneath him had ballooned to hundreds of people. He wanted "time and space to think."

In the summer of 2015, Tim Cook, Apple's new CEO, promoted Ive to chief design officer, in recognition of his expanded design responsibilities, including hardware, human interface, packaging, retail stores, and the company's new spaceship-inspired campus in Cupertino, California. Day-to-day responsibilities were assumed by two veterans from Ive's team.

Apple said little publicly about the change. But internally, it proved disruptive. As part of the deal, Cook agreed that Ive would be less present at the company. He traveled to headquarters only a day or two per week, and he often set up meetings closer to his homes. People noticed. "The team craved being around him," said a person close to Apple leadership. "He's engaging. [His] being around less was disappointing." Indeed, designers viewed approval from their new leaders as merely tentative; they had looked forward to Ive's promised monthly "design weeks," but Ive rarely showed up.

When the company was preparing for the 10th anniversary of the iPhone, the designers gathered in a San Francisco penthouse chosen specifically for its proximity to Ive's home, so that they could demonstrate planned features of the new iPhone to Ive. For nearly three hours, the team waited for Ive to show up. After he finally arrived, he listened to the presentations, but left without answering their key questions. The team was frustrated. "Many of us were thinking: How did it come to this?" said a person at the meeting. "There was a sense that Jony was gone but reluctant to hand over the reins."

For his part, Tim Cook worked to keep Ive engaged and committed to the organization, in part with a pay package that far exceeded that of other top Apple executives—a point of friction for others on the executive team. And cracks started to show in his design team as well. Several members left over the next few years. Their departures heralded a new era.

The Announcement

On June 20, 2019, Ive gathered his design team in their new headquarters at Apple Park. He explained that he was leaving the company, and answered their questions. Just like old times, the gathering felt like family, and it was a fitting way for the design chief to say goodbye.

Discussion Questions

1. What made Apple's design team so unique? How did the members work together? What made it so successful
2. What happened to the team? How could Apple have prevented its decay?
3. Now that there is a new team, what should Apple do to recreate the magic?

Source: Adapted from S. A. Snell, *Apple's Design Guru: Jony Ive*, UVA-S-0320 (Charlottesville, VA: Darden Business Publishing, 2019).

Notes and References

1. Emily Glazer and Chip Cutter, "Companies Wrestle with Hybrid Work Plans," *Wall Street Journal*, March 21, 2021.
2. Rehman Safdar, Ajmal Waheed, and Khattak Hamid Rafiq, "Impact of Job Analysis on Job Performance: Analysis of a Hypothesized Model," *Journal of Diversity Management* 5, no. 2 (2010): 17–36.
3. Frederick P. Morgeson, Kelly Delaney-Klinger, Melinda S. Mayfield, Philip Ferrara, and Michael A. Campion, "Self-Presentation Processes in Job Analysis: A Field Experiment Investigating Inflation in Abilities, Tasks, and Competencies," *Journal of Applied Psychology* 89, no. 4 (2004): 674.
4. Interview with job analyst Carol Tucker, Mesa, AZ, May 10, 2006.
5. Angela R. Connell and Satris S. Culbertons, "Eye of the Beholder: Does What Is Important about a Job Depend on Who Is Asked?" *Academy of Management Perspectives* 24, no. 2 (2010): 83.
6. A detailed description of different job analysis techniques is beyond the scope of this text. For those interested in more comprehensive information or job analysis tools, see Frederick P. Morgeson, Michael T. Bannick, and Edward L. Levine, *Job and Work Analysis: Methods, Research, and Applications for Human Resource Management*, 2nd ed. (Thousand Oaks, CA: Sage, 2020).
7. V. S. Rama Rao, "Quantitative Job Analysis Techniques," *The Cite Man Network* (March 4, 2011), http://www.citeman.com.
8. Piers Steel and John Kammeyer-Mueller, "Using a Meta-Analytic Perspective to Enhance Job Component Validation," *Personnel Psychology* 62, no. 3 (2009): 533.
9. Eric Klas, Alexandros Papalexandris, George Ioannou, and Gregory Prastacos, "From Task-Based to Competency-Based," *Personnel Review* 39, no. 3 (2010): 325–346, doi: 10.1108/0048348101103052.

10. Gensheng Liu, Rachna Shah, and Roger G. Schroeder, "Linking Work Design to Mass Customization: A Socio-technical Systems Perspective," *Decision Sciences* 37, no. 4 (2006): 519; Nicolai J. Foss, Dana B. Minbaeva, Torben Pedersen, and Mia Reinholt, "Encouraging Knowledge Sharing among Employees: How Job Design Matters," *Human Resource Management* 48, no. 5 (2009): 871.
11. Jay Heizer and Barry Render, *Operations Management*, 11th ed. (Upper Saddle River, NJ: Pearson, 2013), 396.
12. Ibid.
13. Christina Farr, "How Fitbit Became the Next Big Thing in Corporate Wellness," *Fast Company* (April 18, 2016), http://fastcompany.com.
14. Pooja Garg and Renu Rastogi, "New Models of Job Design: Motivating Employees' Performance," *Journal of Management Development* 25, no. 6 (2006): 572.
15. For Herzberg's classic article on job enrichment, see Frederick Herzberg, "One More Time: How Do You Motivate Employees?" *Harvard Business Review* 46, no. 2 (1968): 53–62.
16. For the original article on the job characteristics model, see J. Richard Hackman and Greg R. Oldham, "Motivation through the Design of Work: Test of a Theory," *Organizational Behavior and Human Performance* 16, no. 2 (1976): 250–279.
17. Jed DeVaro, Robert Li, and Dana Brookshire, "Analyzing the Job Characteristics Model: New Support from a Cross-Section of Establishments," *International Journal of Human* 31. *Resource Management* 18, no. 6 (2007): 986.
18. O. C. Ferrell, Geoffrey Hirt, and Linda Ferrell, *Introduction to Business* (Burr Ridge, IL: McGraw-Hill, 2008), 309.
19. Bruce Jones, "How Disney Empowers Its Employees to Deliver Exceptional Customer Service," *Harvard Business Review*, February 2018.
20. Boris Groysberg, J. Lee, J. Price, and Y.J. and Cheng. 2018. The Leader's Guide to Corporate Culture. *Harvard Business Review*. January-February, 2018.
21. Rachel Emma Silverman, "Workplace Democracy Catches On," *Wall Street Journal* (March 28, 2016): B5.
22. Amy Wrzesniewski, Nicholas LoBuglio, Jane Dutton, and Justin Berg, "Job Crafting and Cultivating Positive Meaning and Identity at Work," *Advances in Positive Organizational Psychology* 1 (2013): 281–302; Fangfang Zhang and Sharon Parker, "Reorienting Job Crafting Research: A Hierarchical Structure of Job Crafting Concepts and Integrative Review," *Journal of Organizational Behavior* 40, no. 2 (2019): 126–146.
23. Judith Plomp, Maria Tims, Svetlana Khapova, Paul Jansen, and Arnold Baker, "Proactive Personality and Well-Being: The Mediating Role of Job Crafting and Career Competencies," *Academy of Management Proceedings* (January 2016), 37. doi: 10.5465/AMBPP.2016.11411abstract.
24. Feza Tabassum Azmi, "Job Descriptions to Job Fluidity: Treading the Dejobbing Path," *EBS Review* 2, no. 23 (2007): 8.
25. Stanley McChrystal, Chris Fussell, David Silverman, and Tantum Collins, *Team of Teams* (New York: Penguin Publishing Group, 2015); "Team Spirit," *The Economist* (March 19, 2016), http://www.economist.com.
26. Brian Hindo, "The Empire Strikes at Silos," *Business Week* (August 20, 2007): 63.
27. Leigh Thompson, "Improving the Creativity of Organizational Work Groups," *Academy of Management Executive* 17, no. 1 (2003): 96.
28. Matt Weinberger, "How the Forgetfulness of One of Microsoft's Top Scientists Inspired a Killer New Feature for Windows 10," *Business Insider* (February 9, 2017), http://www.businessinsider.com.
29. Laura A. Hambley, Thomas A. O'Neil, and Theresa J. B. Klien, "Virtual Team Leadership: The Effects of Leadership Style and Communication Medium on Team Interaction Styles and Outcomes," *Organizational Behavior and Human Decision Processes* 103, no. 1 (2007): 1.
30. Interview with Paulette Tichenor, Arizona State University, Tempe, AZ, January 18, 2007.
31. "Team Spirit," *The Economist* (March 19, 2016), http://www.economist.com.
32. Jeffrey T. Holzer, *Leading Teams* (HBS 9-403-094) (Cambridge, MA: Harvard Business School), 1–23.
33. Jay F. Nunamaker Jr., Bruce A. Reinig, and Robert O. Briggs, "Principles for Effective Virtual Teamwork," *Communications of the ACM* 52, no. 4 (2009): 113; Stephen B. Knouse, "Building Task Cohesion to Bring Teams Together," *Quality Progress* 40, no. 3 (2007): 49.
34. Michelle Conlin, "Smashing the Clock," *Businessweek* (December 11, 2006): 60.
35. Mark Fadden, "Workplace Trends," *Fort Worth Star-Telegram* (February 19, 2017): E1.
36. "Employers Willing to Negotiate Salary," *OfficePro* 7, no. 1 (2011): 4.
37. Caroline Castrillon, "This is the Future of Remote Work," *Forbes*, December 27, 2020; "Remote Work," https://en.wikipedia.org/wiki/Remote_work.
38. Marie Beaudette, "Jamie Dimon Says JPMorgan Won't Go Remote after the Pandemic," *Wall Street Journal*, April 7, 2021.
39. Megan Brenan, "U.S. Workers Discovering Affinity for Remote Work," *Gallup*, April 3, 2020; Wendell Joice, "Implementing Telework: The Technology Issue," *Public Manager* 36, no. 2 (2007): 64; Megan Scudellari, "The Downsides of Telecommuting," *Boston Globe* (February 10, 2017), http://bostonglobe.com.
40. Kathy Gurchiek, "Hybrid Work Model Likely to Be New Norm in 2021," Society for Human Resource Management, January 21, 2021.
41. Rita Zeidner, "Bending with the Times," *HR Magazine* 53, no. 7 (2008): 10.

42. Mark Fadden, "Workplace Trends," *Fort Worth Star-Telegram* (February 19, 2017): E1.
43. Lori L. Wadsworth and Rex L. Facer, "Work-Family Balance and Alternative Work Schedules," *Public Personnel Management* 45, no. 4 (2016): 42; Kathy Gurchiek, "Good News for Moms Reconsidering Work," *HR Magazine* 51, no. 7 (2006): 39.
44. "Have You Considered Job Sharing as a Retention Tool?" *HR Focus* 83, no. 9 (2006): 10.
45. Vivian Wagner, "Take This Job and Share It," *AARP* (January 27, 2017), http://www.aarp.org.

ImageFlow/Shutterstock.com

CHAPTER 5

Expanding the Talent Pool: Recruitment and Careers

Learning Outcomes

After studying this chapter, you should be able to

LO 1 Describe how a firm's strategy affects its recruiting efforts, and the elements that are part of a strategic recruiting strategy.

LO 2 Describe the methods firms use to recruit externally and internally.

LO 4 List some of the ways firms can improve their recruiting and the metrics they use to do so.

LO 4 Explain how career management programs integrate the needs of individual employees and their organizations.

LO 5 Explain why recruitment and career development activities focused on diversity and inclusion are important to companies.

In this chapter, we discuss the many strategies and techniques organizations use both internally and externally to acquire the talent they need. The competition for top talent requires firms not only to look for talented pools of employees, but also to figure out what they want, determine how to develop relationships with them, and establish the firm as an employer of choice. In this chapter, we also discuss the approaches organizations take to help employees manage their careers over time. This issue is important because, unlike physical assets, human assets (employees) can decide to leave the firm. Finally, at the end of the chapter, we devote special attention to the recruitment and career development of diverse employees.

5.1 Business Strategies and Their Link to Strategic Recruiting

> **LO1** Name some companies with whom you have done business. Then discuss how you view their employer brands. Would you want to work for them or not? How might these firms improve their employer brands?

Suppose you're an entrepreneur trying to capitalize on the next "big idea." You have developed a strategic vision for your firm, analyzed its workflows, and determined which jobs you will need and how many of them will be required. Now where do you begin to find the talent you'll need for success?

The decisions you make about talent—regardless of whether they pertain to recruiting, transferring, promoting, developing, or deploying people—need to be considered within the context of your business's strategies and priorities. Consider the decision to outsource and offshore work. In the last few decades, most American clothing makers have outsourced or offshored work because labor costs are cheaper outside the United States. (Nearly all of the clothing purchased in the United States today is imported. Just check your clothing labels.) But that's not the strategy Round House Workwear, based in Oklahoma, and All American Clothing, based in Ohio, have pursued. These companies have managed to carve out a niche by selling products with the "Made in America" label, which appeal to people who see it as a sign of prestige or national pride. However, that decision means that the firms need to identify and recruit capable workers who have the skills to realize their strategy. The point of this story is that strategy and recruiting are closely connected.

5.1a Elements of a Recruiting Strategy

Figure 5.1 shows the various elements a firm has to consider as part of its recruitment strategy. These elements include the strength of the firm's employment "brand," the types of positions the company is recruiting for, where it needs them, when it needs them, and who is responsible for doing the recruiting and making the recruiting decision. We will talk about each of these factors next.

At any given time, a firm might use multiple recruiting strategies—that is, different approaches for different jobs. Moreover, a strategy that works for one firm or one job might not work for another firm (or job). For example, an engineering firm might place a premium on finding highly qualified applicants, whereas an amusement park ramping up for a new season might place a premium on hiring quickly. Recruiting strategies and their effectiveness can change over time as well. As a result, firms need to continuously

Figure 5.1 Elements of a Recruitment Strategy

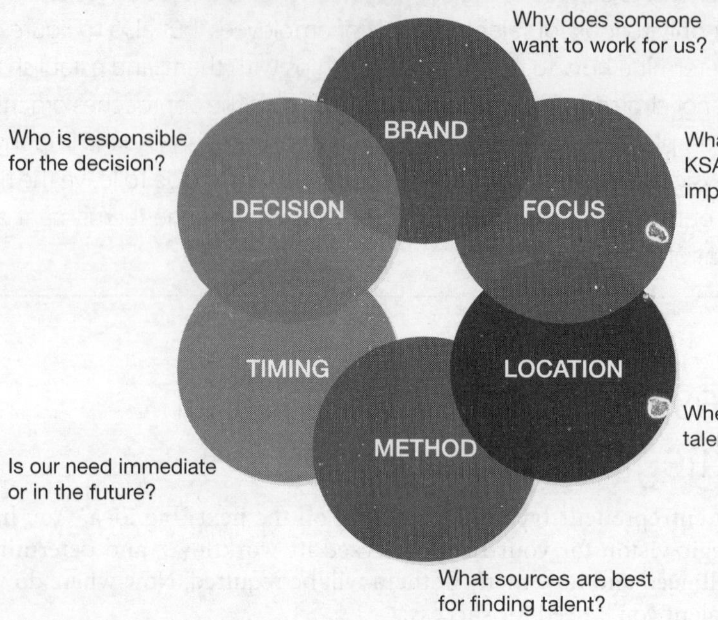

examine their recruiting efforts and refine them. So, for example, if the engineering firm landed a huge construction contract, being able to hire engineers quickly could become a priority.

Brand: How Do We Attract Talent?

branding
A company's efforts to help existing and prospective workers understand why it is a desirable place to work.

Whomever and wherever a firm is recruiting, it wants to be *the* employer of choice to attract and hire top candidates before its competitors do. Branding can help organizations achieve this goal. **Branding** refers to a company's efforts to help existing and prospective workers understand why it is a more desirable place to work compared to its competitors. It helps communicate the overall purpose or mission of the firm, its shared values and culture, what it is like to work for the firm, and the overall work environment. A good employment brand can make all the difference. A LinkedIn survey found that the hiring costs for firms with strong employer brands are two times lower than those for firms with weaker employer brand rankings. Companies with strong employer brands also experience less turnover. In contrast, negative stories about a firm can have just the opposite effect. For example, Glassdoor is a website where current and former employees anonymously review their companies, sharing both positive and negative experiences that influence those firms' employment brand.[1]

So how does a company "burnish" its employment brand? One way is to think of applicants as consumers and focus on what they want in terms of jobs and careers as opposed to what an organization has to "sell" them. Diane Delich, from recruiting firm Executive Pursuits, advises companies to listen and reach out to applicants just as they do to consumers. In fact, some firms turn their customers into their employees. A high percentage of the people whom The Container Store recruits are customers who like doing business with the storage-solution company. "Basically we have mini human resources departments in each of our stores. We challenge each of our 4,000 employees to be recruiters and refer us to great people," says The Container Store's Director of Recruiting Karyn Maynard.[2]

Another way to improve the firm's employer brand is by reaching out to people via social networks. Firms often create pages on websites like LinkedIn and Facebook to promote their organizations and careers they have to offer. The sites allow recruiters to strike up conversations with potential applicants on those pages and give them a preview of what it is like to work for their firms. Writing blogs and articles for industry publications is another way to shed light on the company's employer brand and find new employees.

Using the Internet and social networks is an inexpensive way to brand and recruit. This strategy can be particularly effective for small companies that can't afford to pay for a lot of job advertising to promote their firms and attract candidates. Luke's Lobster, a chain that began as a small restaurant in New York City, uses all the social media tools it can—Facebook, LinkedIn, YouTube, Twitter, Tumblr, Pinterest, and Vimeo—to post photos and videos about the restaurant and its employees and make announcements about specials, contests, and job openings. This strategy has made it easy to recruit great employees, each of whom is featured in a colorful profile on the company's website. We will talk more about social networks as a recruiting tool later in the chapter.

In the global arena, branding can be enormously helpful because local residents are often unfamiliar with foreign firms. In India, the firms people work for are very important to applicants and their families. U.S. firms often set up "storefronts" in major Indian cities to promote their employment brands. Candidates can walk in and chat with company representatives about what these firms do and the kinds of opportunities they offer.

Online games can also be a good branding and recruiting tool. Barclays Investment Bank has a free online stock-trading game that uses real-time market data. More than 4,500 people, mostly college students, have played the game, and about 8 percent of them have applied for jobs with the company.[3] Philanthropic activities can help burnish a company's employer brand, too, especially among Generation Z and Millennial employees, who want more out of life than just a job and a paycheck. The accounting firm Deloitte sponsors volunteer spring-break programs for undergraduate students, who work alongside the firms' employees to help communities in need. Highlights in HRM 1 shows how Marriott lives up to its top ranking in the *Fortune* 500 employment brands list, enabling this company to recruit the best talent.

Focus: What Types of Positions Are Needed?

As you learned in Chapter 2, a major responsibility of human resources managers is knowing which jobs a firm needs now and in the future as well as the KSAOs required for those jobs. Given those needs, the condition of the labor market can have a big effect on a firm's recruiting plans. During periods of high unemployment, an organization might be able to maintain an adequate supply of qualified candidates by accepting unsolicited resumes and applications and from internal labor markets. By contrast, a tight labor market (one with low unemployment) might force the employer to advertise heavily and/or seek assistance from recruiting and employment agencies. Keep in mind that the actual labor market a company faces depends on the industry in which the firm operates and the types of positions it is seeking to fill. In one industry, the supply of qualified individuals might be plentiful for a particular position. In another industry, they may not be.

1 Highlights in HRM

Marriott's Recruitment Principles: Living up to the Employment Brand

1. *Build the employment brand.* Marriott attracts employees the same way it attracts customers. Just as consumers buy experiences, not just products, so potential employees are looking for a great work experience when they shop for jobs. As the company's founder, J. W. Marriott, put it: "For more than 70 years, we've lived by a simple motto: If we take care of our associates, they'll take care of our guests."
2. *Get it right the first time.* Marriott "hires friendly" and "trains technical." It is better to hire people with "the spirit to serve" and train them to work than to hire people who know business and try to teach them to enjoy serving guests. Marriott hires cooks who love to cook and housekeepers who love to clean. The company has learned that this approach works both for delivering excellent service and for retaining its employees.
3. *Money is a big thing, but. . . .* The top concern of Marriott associates is total compensation. But intangible factors taken together, such as work–life balance, leadership quality, opportunity for advancement, work environment, and training, far outweigh money in their decisions to stay or leave. From flexible schedules to tailored benefit packages and development opportunities, Marriott has built systems to address nonmonetary factors.
4. *A caring workplace is a bottom-line issue.* When employees come to work, they feel safe, secure, and welcome. Managers are accountable for associate satisfaction ratings and for turnover rates. Every day, associates in each of Marriott's full-service hotels participate in a 15-minute meeting to review basic values such as respect and encourage associates to raise their personal concerns. They take the time to celebrate birthdays and anniversaries. Practices such as these build loyalty among associates and repeat business from customers.
5. *Promote from within.* More than 50 percent of Marriott's current managers have been promoted from within. All associates are given the opportunity to advance as far as their abilities will carry them. Elevating employees who have continually served the company to positions of leadership helps Marriott pass on the soul of its business—its corporate culture—from one generation to the next.

Sources: Aman Kidwai, "Marriott Tops Ranking of *Fortune* 500 Employment Brands," *HR Drive*, March 10, 2020; J. W. Marriott, "Competitive Strength," *Executive Excellence* 18, no. 4 (2001): 3–4; J. W. Marriott, "Our Competitive Strength: Human Capital," *Executive Speeches* 15, no. 5 (2001): 18–21.

Fortune ranked Marriott the #1 employer brand in 2020.

Lets Design Studio/Shutterstock.com

Location: Where Do We Need the Talent, and Where Will We Find It?

The two primary locations in which to find candidates are those internal to the firm (internal candidates) and those external to the firm (external candidates). Members of each of these groups are recruited somewhat differently.

Internal versus External Recruiting Markets. Recruiting internally—that is, finding candidates for jobs from among those employees who already work for the firm—is generally easier, faster, and less expensive. It can also help nurture and strengthen the company culture. **Internal labor markets** are associated with "promotion within" policies, where workers are hired into entry-level jobs and higher-level jobs are filled from within.[4] However, not all positions can be filled internally. Jobs that require specialized training and experience or new skills cannot always be easily filled from within and, therefore, may need to be filled from the outside. This is especially common in small organizations in which the existing talent pool is limited. Moreover, in rapidly changing industries, there may not be time for a company's employees to develop completely new skill sets. Consequently, hiring from the outside makes sense.

internal labor markets
Labor markets in which workers are hired into entry-level jobs and higher-level jobs are filled from within.

Applicants hired externally can also be a source of new ideas and creativity, and may bring with them the latest knowledge acquired from their previous employers. It is not uncommon for firms to attempt to learn their competitors' secrets by hiring away their employees. Amazon.com was sued by Walmart, which accused the online retailer of hiring away or "poaching" employees who had in-depth knowledge about Walmart's sophisticated inventory systems. Tesla Motors sued a former employee for allegedly stealing its self-driving car technology and trying recruit dozens of the company's engineers for a startup firm.[5]

Some applicants bring more than knowledge to their new employers—they bring revenue. Talented salespeople, doctors, accountants, lawyers, and hair stylists are examples. When these people leave their organizations, their clients often go with them. Recruiting externally in this case makes sense. Reaching an employer's diversity goals is another factor that can lead a firm to recruit externally.

Regional Recruiting Markets. Have you ever noticed that competing firms are often located in the same areas? Oil and gas companies are plentiful in the Houston area. Film and television companies are clustered around Los Angeles. This is not a coincidence. These "business clusters" occur because the resources these firms need—both human and natural—are located in some areas and not others. Many manufacturers have located their plants in the South because lower-cost labor is plentiful there and unions are less prevalent than they are in the North. Likewise, because nearby Stanford University has one of the top computer science schools in the country, high-tech companies have flocked to Silicon Valley in California.[6] The upshot from these business clusters is that firms have a concentrated regional market for talent, and it is not uncommon for "knowledge spillovers" to occur as firms recruit employees from one another.

Global Recruiting Markets. To stay apace of their competitors and expand their operations around the world, companies look globally for not only goods and services, but also talent. Firms aren't doing this just to save on labor costs; they are doing it to attract the best workers wherever they may be. Firms in countries such as China and India have heated up the competition for talent to staff the growing high-tech industries in these nations.

Recruiting abroad can be very complicated, however. In addition to having to deal with a myriad of local, national, and international laws, as well as immigration requirements such as visas and work permits, employers must take into account the different labor costs, preemployment and compensation practices, and cultural differences associated with the countries in which they are recruiting. In volatile areas of the world, security is also a concern. To help them navigate these kinds of challenges, many companies utilize the services of firms such as Genpact and Robert Half International, which specialize in global recruiting.

Timing: When Do We Need the Talent?

You have probably heard the saying "Timing is everything." This is especially true for recruiters. HR professionals shouldn't engage in recruiting only when a position comes open. Instead, they need to understand their firm's business strategies, recognize the talent the company currently has, and study succession plans and determine what the company will need in the future—and then translate that understanding into ongoing recruiting plans. Is the firm rapidly expanding? If so, how many positions will be needed and in which areas? How many applicants will need to be recruited to result in a single hire? If a firm waits too long to hire, its competitors may capitalize on emerging business opportunities before it can.

In addition, HR managers must consider which jobs have the biggest impact on the firm's financial results and prioritize filling them. It may be possible for a firm to leave an administrative position unfilled for a few months by assigning some of the job's duties to other people. By contrast, leaving open a salesperson's position in a sales territory that generates a lot of revenue and is highly competitive could take a serious toll on a company's revenues.

Timing also comes into play in terms of the recruiting process. Some jobs, such as the job of an administrative assistant, can be advertised and filled relatively quickly. Other jobs, such as that of the CEO, can take months to fill. These factors have to be taken into consideration when recruiting and moving applicants through the various hiring stages.

Method: How Do We Find the Talent?

Firms use different methods to try to recruit different types of people for different jobs. The methods also change over time as technology changes and the sources of candidates change. In recent times, recruitment ads on Internet and social media sites such as LinkedIn have replaced the bulk of print advertisements.

For example, UPS typically needs to recruit more than 50,000 temporary workers to help deliver the millions of extra packages the company ships during the holiday season. By using mobile apps, the company can reach a broader talent pool. City youths who used to have to go to a library or school to search for UPS can now do so on their mobile devices.

Decision: Who Does the Recruiting and Makes the Final Hiring Decision?

The size of an organization often affects who performs the recruitment function. Most large firms have full-time, in-house HR recruiters. In smaller organizations, the recruiting might be done by an HR generalist. If the organization has no HR function, managers and supervisors may recruit their own employees. At companies such as Macy's and Williams-Sonoma, the members of work teams help select new employees for their groups.

recruitment process outsourcing (RPO)
The practice of outsourcing an organization's recruiting function to an outside firm.

Organizations that want to focus on their core functions, including small businesses that lack time or HR personnel, sometimes outsource their recruiting functions to outside firms. This practice is known as **recruitment process outsourcing (RPO)**. Organizations also sometimes use RPO providers when they need to hire a lot of employees or hire employees quickly. RPO providers can also be useful when a firm has had trouble finding suitable candidates in the past or needs a different way to tap different talent pools, perhaps to find more diverse candidates.

Regardless of who does the recruiting, those people must have a good understanding of the knowledge, skills, abilities, experiences, and other characteristics required for the job and be personable, enthusiastic, and competent. Recruiters can often enhance the perceived attractiveness of a job and an organization—or detract from it. They are often a major reason why applicants select one organization over another.

5.2 External and Internal Recruiting Methods

LO2 Think of a new type of business you would like to start up or manage. Which sources would you use to recruit employees who could help you make it a success?

When you graduate, what sources do you expect to use to search for a job? Conversely, what is the best source, or method, a firm should use to find talented people like you to hire? In essence, these two questions are really different sides of the same coin. Employers are searching for the right employees and the right places to find them. Conversely, people searching for work are looking for the best companies they can find and ways to connect with them.

5.2a External Recruiting Methods

Figure 5.2 shows the major external recruitment methods. The "active" and "passive" labels indicate that some methods take more effort on the part of the applicant and/or the recruiting firm than others do. The sources from which employers recruit externally

Figure 5.2 Sources of External Recruitment

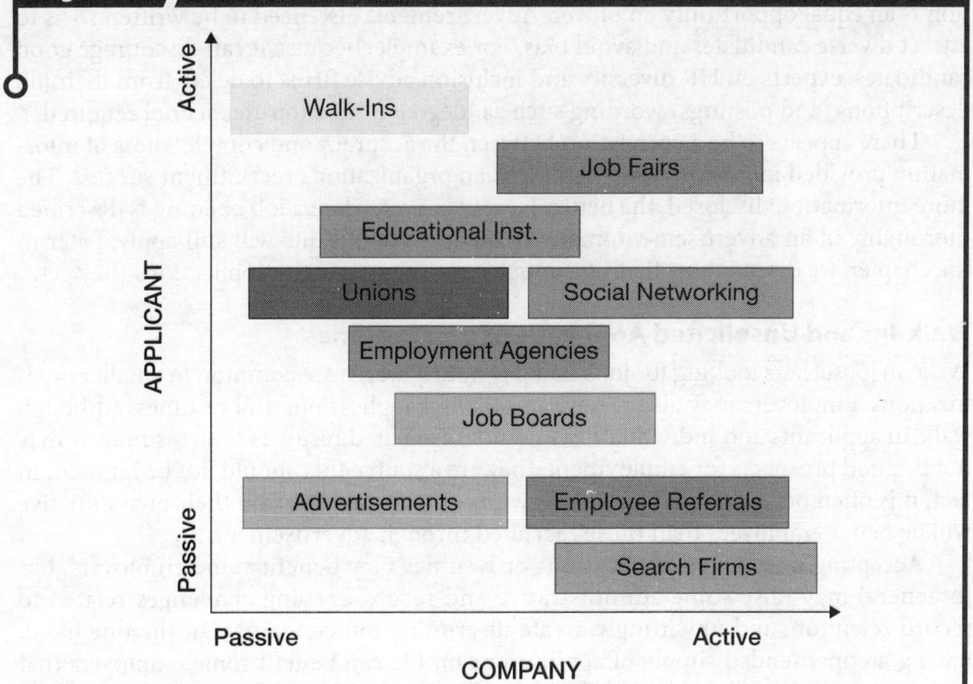

will vary with the type of position to be filled. A computer programmer, for example, is not likely to be recruited from the same source as a machine operator. Trade schools can be a good source of applicants for entry-level positions.

Firms also keep detailed statistics by job type on the sources from which their employees are hired. This helps HR managers make better decisions about the places to begin recruiting when different job openings arise. We will talk more about recruiting statistics later in the chapter.

Advertisements

Advertising job openings on websites, on social media, and in newspapers and trade journals is a common way to attract candidates. But help-wanted signs, billboards, and even Craigslist are sometimes used for this purpose. In countries in which literacy rates are lower, radio and television ads can be more effective. Amazon.com places ads on bus stop benches to alert prospective applicants to job openings at its distributions center. Job postings that include videos describing the firm and the positions it offers are particularly effective. According to the job website CareerBuilder, ads such as these get viewed more frequently and generate significantly more applicants.[7]

Advertising has the advantage of reaching a large audience of possible applicants. However, some degree of selectivity can be achieved by choosing among the sources to use. Professional and trade journals, blogs, the professional social networking groups on LinkedIn, and the publications of unions and various fraternal or nonprofit organizations will attract different types of candidates than help-wanted signs, for example.

Preparing recruiting advertisements is not just time consuming, but also requires creativity in terms of developing their design and message content. Well-designed advertisements highlight the major assets of the position while showing the responsiveness of the organization to the job, career, and lifestyle needs of applicants. Among the information typically included in advertisements is a statement that the recruiting organization is an equal opportunity employer. Advertisements also need to be written so as to attract diverse candidates and avoid bias. For example, because it can discourage good candidates, experts on HR diversity and inclusion advise firms to delete from their job descriptions (and postings) wording such as "degree from a top-tier school required."

There appears to be a correlation between the accuracy and completeness of information provided in job advertisements and an organization's recruitment success. The more information disclosed, the better. However, even when a job opening is described thoroughly in an advertisement, many unqualified applicants will still apply. Later in the chapter, we discuss how firms go about screening the many applications they get.

Walk-Ins and Unsolicited Applications and Resumes

Walk-in jobseekers looking for jobs that pay hourly wages are common in smaller organizations. Employers may also receive unsolicited applications and resumes. Although walk-in applicants and individuals who send unsolicited resumes to firms may or may not be good prospects for employment, they are a source that should not be ignored. In fact, it is often believed that individuals who contact employers on their own initiative will be better employees than those recruited through advertisements.

Accepting unsolicited applications or resumes may benefit some employers, but in general may raise some administrative and record-keeping challenges related to record retention, and unwittingly create discrimination concerns. On the one hand, having an open-ended supply of applications on file can benefit some employers that have high turnover, allowing positions to be filled quickly—think fast-food chains. On

Rawpixel.com/Shutterstock.com

Textio is a Web-based product that checks job postings for bias. You paste in a post, and the software suggests how to rephrase it to attract a more diverse candidate pool.

the other hand, both state and federal employment laws require employers to retain employment applications for at least one year and possibly longer. When an employer reviews unsolicited applications, those applications are seen as having been considered for employment, thereby triggering an obligation to retain the document, which can be time-consuming and costly. In addition, the practice of accepting and reviewing unsolicited applications, when applied inconsistently, may open up the organization to claims of unlawful discrimination. The bottom line: if an employer decides to accept unsolicited resumes or applications, it should accept all unsolicited resumes or applications, and it should have a consistently followed written policy for handling them.[8]

The Internet: Recruiting Online

Online recruiting is the most commonly used search tactic by jobseekers and recruiters to connect with one another. Both companies and applicants find this approach to be cheaper, faster, and potentially more effective. Tens of thousands of independent job boards can be found on the Web. Widely used jobs boards include Monster, CareerBuilder, Indeed, GlassDoor and Google for Jobs. Staffing experts say it is also a good idea to post your firm's jobs at free association and trade group sites, where your specific talent pool is most likely to congregate.[9]

Specialty Internet recruiting sites such as Medzilla (for the pharmaceutical industry), AMFMJobs (for radio personnel), and JobsInLogistics (for supply-chain jobs) are common, too. "Niche job boards are particularly useful for cutting through the clutter and finding talent for hard-to-fill roles, specialized positions, specific industries—or to tap into unique candidate audiences, such as military veterans," says Susan Vitale, the chief marketing officer at Matawan, a New Jersey–based recruitment software provider.[10] Of course, most large companies also post job openings on their own corporate websites, usually under a "careers" link, along with information about the benefits of working for their firms.

Other companies are taking Internet recruiting to a whole new level. Instead of recruiters trying to figure out where to place individual ads and when to take them down, they are using big data, robots, and artificial intelligence (AI) software to do the job. Appcast is software that trolls the Internet looking for candidates who are well suited for positions based on the interests they express, where they go on the Web, and whether they appear to be looking for jobs. Job ads then appear on their screens—just like ads for products do when you are shopping online. The software recruiting company FirstJob has developed a chatbot named "Mya" to help recruit candidates for jobs. Mya converses with candidates online to encourage them to apply—or not to apply—for certain jobs, reviews their applications, and can even schedule interviews with them, among other things.[11]

Social Media

As we indicated, to help establish their employer brands as well as recruit talent, firms are utilizing social media websites, where they can create company pages, post and advertise jobs, showcase their company's attractive features, and join groups that target certain types of professionals. Potential applicants can then "follow" companies they are interested in working for. The online shoe seller Zappos no longer accepts resumes, but instead uses social media to recruit applicants. By using social media, recruiters at UPS say they were able to access a new applicant pool—namely, Millennials—and significantly increase the number of them applying to work at the company. UPS engages potential candidates with conversations with other UPS employees, unscripted "day in the life" videos of employees, and interviews with senior managers explaining how they first started with the company and possible career paths.[12]

When companies use social media for recruitment, the top three tools they most often utilize are LinkedIn (68 percent), Facebook (32 percent), and Twitter (15 percent). LinkedIn has become the social media site of choice for recruiters—so much so that it's disrupting the market for job boards, advertisers, recruitment service firms, and recruitment software companies. For a subscription fee, firms can use LinkedIn Recruiter to search its 400-million-plus member database for talented passive jobseekers. **Passive jobseekers** are people who are not looking for jobs but could be persuaded to take new ones given the right opportunity. Software developers such as TalentBin and ZoomInfo have created applications that search the Web for passive job candidates based on information they post on industry blogs, social networking sites, and so forth.

passive jobseekers
People who are not looking for jobs but could be persuaded to take new ones given the right opportunity.

Facebook has also made it easier to find passive jobseekers. Recruiters can create job postings targeted at certain types of people's newsfeeds and contact them via Messenger if they want. Those who are interested in the job can simply click on the "Apply Now" button, and their applications are automatically populated with information from their Facebook profiles.[13]

Interestingly, despite more organizations using social media to recruit employees, 65 percent of employers report they do not review the social media profiles of job candidates during the hiring process. Sixteen percent of employers list the hiring manager as the individual who is responsible for performing this review, when it takes place.

A potential drawback of using social media, and the Internet in general, is that some groups of people, including older adults and people with less than a high school education, are less likely to go online. A study by the Kessler Foundation and National Organization on Disability (NOD) found that only a little more than half of adults with disabilities go online. As a result, relying too heavily on electronic recruiting could hurt a company's diversity efforts.[14]

Mobile Recruiting

Mobile recruiting is the process of recruiting candidates via their mobile devices. People around the world are glued to their mobile phones. For this reason, whatever social networking or Internet platform an organization uses should have a mobile application tied to it that people can use to search for jobs and apply for them.

mobile recruiting The process of recruiting candidates via their mobile devices.

Recruiters are also using text messages, sometimes to announce job openings and to communicate information about interview schedules and speed up the recruitment process. Text messages work well because they are inexpensive, easy to send, and fast. Plus, because most people have their mobile devices on all of the time, they get the messages immediately instead of having to launch applications on their phones to get to a site such as Facebook or LinkedIn.

Job Fairs

Job fairs can be a good way to cast a wide net for diverse applicants in a certain region. At a job fair, companies and their recruiters set up booths, meet with prospective applicants, and exchange employment information. Often the fairs are industry specific.

Although job fairs often attract a lot of applicants, many of them might not be qualified. Another problem is that they attract applicants only in the regional area in which they are held.

One way to get around the latter problem is to hold an online **virtual job fair** and use networks such as LinkedIn, Facebook, and Twitter to inform potential candidates about it. During a virtual job fair, recruiters man "virtual booths" online, where they provide links to their career resources, collect resumes, and talk with candidates via online chat functions and webcams. Holding a virtual job fair can also be cost effective for both recruiters and attendees because they do not have to pay travel costs.

virtual job fair Job fairs conducted online.

Some larger companies, such as Procter & Gamble, host virtual fairs on their own websites. Others, including Boeing and Citigroup, join virtual job fairs hosted by other companies such as the job board Monster and Unicruit.com, a company that hosts virtual job fairs designed to attract new graduates.[15]

Employee Referrals

One of the great "unsung heroes" of effective recruiting is employee referrals. The reality is that the recruitment efforts of organizations are greatly aided when its employees nominate potential candidates. In fact, word-of-mouth recommendations are the way most job positions are filled. (Apparently there is truth to the phrase, "It is not what you know, but who you know.") A number of studies have found that employee referrals are the best source of applicants. According to one study, referred employees have much higher retention rates than employees who are not referred, and they are hired in less than half the time as other candidates. Research also shows that once hired, applicants referred by an employee also tend to remain with the organization longer.[16]

Some firms have created referral pages on their intranets to make it easier for employees to refer candidates and to track their progress through the hiring process.[17] Highlights in HRM 2 shows some additional ways firms can encourage employee referrals.

There are some negative factors associated with employee referrals and profiles, though. They include the possibility of corporate "inbreeding" or workforce homogenization. Because employees and the people they refer tend to have similar

2 Highlights in HRM

Making Employee Referral Programs Work

- Educate employees about the kinds of people the organization wants to hire.
- Acknowledge referrals promptly. Not doing so makes employees feel as if their suggestions are poor ones or are being ignored. Let the candidate and the referring employee know right away when a referral has entered the system.
- Reward employees with something they value, such as bonuses and recognition within the company, for referrals. Small rewards can be given for candidates who meet the company's requirements but are not selected and larger rewards for successful matches. Consider offering larger rewards for referrals that improve a firm's diversity.
- Give employees the right tools. Make it easy for employees to post or tweet information about job openings to their online network of associates.
- Measure results after the program is implemented and study them in terms of the volume of referrals, qualifications of candidates, and success of new hires on the job.

Sources: J. R. Pieper, J. M. Greenwald, and S. D. Schlachter, "Motivating Employee Referrals: The Interactive Effects of the Referral Bonus, Perceived Risk in Referring, and Affective Commitment," *Human Resource Management* 57, no. 5 (2017): 1159–1174; Stephen V. Burks, Bo Cowgill, Mitchell Hoffman, and Michael Housman, "The Value of Hiring through Employee Referrals," *Quarterly Journal of Economics* 130, no. 2 (2015): 805–839; "How a Talent Management Plan Can Anchor Your Company's Future," *HR Focus* 81, no. 10 (2004): 7–10; Susan M. Heathfield, "You Can Inspire Great Employee Referrals," http://humanresources.about.com; John Sullivan, "Advanced Employee Referral Programs: Best Practices You Need to Copy," http://www.drjohnsullivan.com.

backgrounds, firms that rely heavily on referrals may intentionally or unintentionally screen out, and thereby discriminate against, protected classes. In 2016, the U.S. Labor Department sued Plantir, a Silicon Valley data-mining company, for not hiring enough Asians. It wasn't that Plantir had intentionally discriminated against Asians; rather, it had simply relied too heavily on applicants its employees had referred, most of whom weren't Asian.

Some researchers have found that workforce homogenization occurs gradually as part of a three-stage trend: According to the attraction–selection–attrition (ASA) model, in the first stage (attraction) people with values similar to those of an organization are attracted to it and become employees. In the second stage (selection), these employees then choose applicants similar to themselves. In the final stage (attrition), employees who do not fit in leave. The result is an organization in which employees think alike, act alike, and maybe even look alike.[18] One way to remedy this problem is by offering employees larger referral bonuses if they bring in candidates from underrepresented groups. Intel, for example, was able to increase the proportion of women in its workforce this way.[19]

nepotism
A preference for hiring the relatives of current employees.

Nepotism, which is the preference for hiring the relatives of employees, can invite charges of favoritism. Various anti-nepotism laws exist at the local, state, and federal levels. However, in some other cultures, including Asia and the Middle East, nepotism is the norm, and hiring managers need to be aware of it. But even in the United States, nepotism gets mixed reviews, in part because family members are in an ideal position to pass job knowledge and skills on to one another. Many corporate dynasties (Ford Motor Company and the Rockefeller Foundation, among them) have been built on nepotism. Labor unions would not have flourished without it. In recent years, a number of law firms and universities have dropped restrictions against hiring spouses on the basis that they are prejudicial.[20]

Re-recruiting or Boomerang

Re-recruiting is the process of keeping track of and maintaining relationships with former employees to see if they would be willing to return to the firm. Former employees who return to their former firms are sometimes referred to as "boomerang" employees. At the accounting and consulting firm Deloitte, more than 75,000 former employees are tracked via an online alumni network. Alumni networks are often hosted on Facebook and LinkedIn or on the employees' former firms' websites.

re-recruiting
The process of keeping track of and maintaining relationships with former employees to see if they would be willing to return to the firm.

Re-recruiting is an attractive option for recruiters. They don't have to sift through scores of resumes to find qualified applicants and have a better idea of how boomerang employees will perform. Boomerang employees also tend to have better retention rates.[21]

Executive Search Firms

In contrast to public and private employment agencies, which help jobseekers find the right job, executive search firms (often called "headhunters") help employers find the right person for a job. Firms such as Korn Ferry International, N2Growth, and Heidrick & Struggles are top recruiting firms for executives. Executive search firms do not advertise in the media for job candidates, nor do they accept a fee from the individual being placed. The fees charged by search firms can range anywhere from 25 to 40 percent of the annual salary for the position to be filled. A large number of CEOs are hired with the help of executive search firms. However, newer data suggest that CEOs who are promoted from within their organizations actually outperform those hired from the outside.

Educational Institutions and Career Centers

Educational institutions typically are a source of young applicants with formal training but little full-time work experience. High schools often prepare employees for clerical and blue-collar jobs. Community colleges, with their various types of specialized training, can provide candidates for technical jobs. These institutions can also be a source of applicants for a variety of white-collar jobs, including those in the sales and retail fields and some management trainee jobs. For technical and managerial positions, companies generally look to colleges and universities. Campus recruiting is a win-win for companies that need talent and schools trying to place students.

Rather than recruiting students from dozens of schools, which can be expensive, more companies are targeting smaller numbers of colleges and forming closer partnerships with them. Employees give guest lectures at the schools and develop relationships with instructors, who then recommend students for jobs. Some companies are sending their CEOs to campus because they have found that it puts a "face" on the company and attracts more applicants.[22] Figure 5.3 shows some of the steps firms can take to strengthen their on-campus recruiting relationships.

Work-Study Programs and Internships. To attract graduates in high-demand fields, in addition to offering higher pay, firms sometimes establish work-study (co-op) programs and offer low-interest loans for promising recruits, scholarships, and internships. Internships can be a great way for firms to "try out" college students who want to work

Figure 5.3 Steps for Strengthening a Firm's On-Campus Recruiting Relationships

- Invite professors and advisers to visit your office and take them to lunch.
- Invite them to bring a student group to the office.
- Send electronic press releases to students and bring them up to date on the firm's latest news and innovations.
- Provide guest speakers for classes.
- Conduct mock interviews, especially in years when not interviewing for full-time or internship positions.
- Provide scholarships to students.
- Attend the campus career fair, even when the firm will not be hiring, so that its name becomes known by the faculty and students.
- Offer job-shadowing programs for students.

Sources: Bruce Busta, D'Arcy Becker, and Jane P. Saly, "Effective Campus Recruiting: The Faculty Perspective," *CPA Journal* 77, no. 7 (2007): 62–65; Deborah J. Sessions, "Recruiting Made Easy," *Journal of Accountancy* 201, no. 5 (2006): 31–34.

in their fields and for students to decide if they want to work for an organization on a long-term basis.

Unfortunately, many internships are not as successful as they should be because the sponsoring firms haven't thought through how to effectively utilize their interns. This can lead to bored interns, who can in turn become disillusioned about their fields. Highlights in HRM 3 shows steps companies can take to ensure their internships are successful.

Firms also have to be careful when deciding whether their internships should be paid positions. In recent years, interns have sued companies for wages, claiming they did the work of employees and should have been compensated as such, or were promised full-time jobs once their internships ended but were not hired. Figure 5.4 shows the criteria that must be met if an intern is not to be paid, according to the U.S. Department of Labor.

Professional Associations and Labor Unions

Many professional associations and societies offer placement services to their members as one of their benefits. For the mutual benefit of employers and jobseekers, placement centers are usually available at the national meetings of professional associations.

Figure 5.4 Unpaid Internship Guidelines

1. The internship, even though it includes actual operation of the facilities of the employer, is similar to training that would be given in an educational environment.
2. The internship experience is for the benefit of the intern.
3. The intern does not displace regular employees but works under close supervision of existing staff.
4. The employer that provides the training derives no immediate advantage from the activities of the intern, and on occasion its operations may actually be impeded.
5. The intern is not necessarily entitled to a job at the conclusion of the internship.
6. The employer and the intern understand that the intern is not entitled to wages for the time spent in the internship.

3 Highlights in HRM

Making Your Internship Program a Success

- Build relationships with colleges and universities. Let the career advisors at these schools know what you are looking for and what you have to offer the interns on an ongoing basis.
- Make it clear the type of candidate you're looking for—for example, the required GPA, preferred or required major, specific skills, attributes, and other experience.
- Develop a work-learning plan for each intern. Give interns actual work related to their majors. Create an internship handbook or website that includes information on intern orientation, mentoring, executive engagement, project work, and cross-functional activity opportunities. Provide this to all of the supervisors and mentors in the program as well as the interns.
- Set up a system for providing interns with feedback on their performance, preferably at the midpoint of their internship and again at the conclusion.
- Survey interns and conduct interviews with them after their internships to find out what went well and what could be improved.

Sources: Michelle Bradford, "Follow Practical Advice to Limit Legal Challenges Regarding Internship Programs," *Campus Legal Advisor* 16, no. 5 (2016): 6; "Getting the Most from Internship Programs," *Supply Chain Management Review* 13, no. 8 (2009): 34; Audrey Watters, "5 Tips for Creating an Internship Program for Your Startup," http://www.readwriteweb.com; Jean Scheid, "Designing Internship Programs," http://www.brighthub.com; Penny Loretto, "Developing an Internship Program," http://internships.about.com.

The Society for Human Resource Management (SHRM), for example, helps employers and prospective HR employees come together.

Labor unions have been a principal source of applicants for blue-collar and some professional jobs. Some unions, such as those in the maritime and construction industries, maintain hiring halls that can provide a supply of applicants, particularly for short-term needs. Unions also offer their members training and in some cases apprenticeship programs, making these organizations a good source of candidates.

Public Employment Agencies

Each of the 50 U.S. states maintains an employment agency that administers its unemployment insurance program. These agencies work with employers to post their openings in online job banks, such as America's Job Exchange and America's Career InfoNet (ACINet), and match unemployed qualified workers to the jobs so they can apply for them. In addition to matching unemployed applicants with job openings, public employment agencies sometimes assist employers with apprenticeship programs, employment testing, job analysis, evaluation programs, and community wage surveys.

Private Employment Agencies

Private employment agencies are companies that, for a fee, match people with full-time jobs. The fee may be paid by the employer, the jobseeker, or both. It is not uncommon for private employment agencies to charge an employer a 25 to 30 percent fee, based on the position's annual salary, if the employer hires an applicant found by the agency.

Private employment agencies often specialize in serving specific occupational or geographic areas. When recruiting abroad, companies frequently use local employment agencies because they understand the country's culture, its labor market, and the best ways to recruit workers there. Companies also sometimes use private employment agencies when they are trying to recruit many people or when they have had trouble in the past recruiting enough applicants, finding applicants with the right skills, finding diverse applicants, or finding the time or personnel needed to recruit, screen, and hire applicants.

Staffing Agencies

Staffing agencies are firms that hire and place workers in temporary positions. Adecco, ManpowerGroup, and Kelly Services are among the major U.S. staffing agencies. "Temps" are typically used for short-term assignments or to help when managers cannot justify hiring a full-time employee, such as for vacation fill-ins, for peak work periods, or during an employee's pregnancy leave or sick leave. A firm contracts with a staffing agency, and the employees hired are then paid by the staffing agency itself and are available to work for multiple organizations.

Temps give organizations added flexibility because they can be used only when needed. In addition, the employment costs of temporary workers are often lower than those of permanent employees because temps are not provided with benefits and can be let go without the firm having to file unemployment insurance claims. Many temporary employees are eventually hired on a full-time basis. Temping allows them and the firms they contract with to try each other out before making a permanent commitment.

One concern related to using temps is that they have less of an incentive to be loyal to an employer and its clients or to go the extra mile to help a company achieve success. Instead of hiring temps, the Hilton hotel chain sends full-time employees from one hotel to another to address temporary spikes in demand. This strategy not only makes efficient use of the hotel chain's staff, but also has helped the firm develop an agile workforce.[23]

Independent Contractors

independent contractors
Workers who are self-employed and do project work on a contract basis for different organizations.

Independent contractors are workers who are self-employed and do project work on a contract basis for organizations. We discussed these types of "contingency workers" in Chapter 1, along with the growth of the "gig economy." Often these workers are referred to as "freelancers" because they are "free" to work for multiple organizations on multiple projects at the same time. Independent contractors can be found on freelance job boards, staffing agencies, and websites such as elance.com. Former and retired employees who want to work on a freelance basis are also a good source of independent contractors for a firm because they are familiar with its business, its personnel, and how work gets done in the organization. Employers face similar concerns with contractors as they do temporary workers. Indeed, some experts believe the national security leaks the United States has experienced in the past were due to independent contractors and not actual employees of the agencies they worked for. Consequently, they were less loyal to the agencies.

As with temps, a firm can use independent contractors as needed, and those workers don't receive benefits. In addition, companies don't pay Social Security, unemployment, or workers' compensation taxes when they hire independent contractors; the independent contractors must pay these taxes themselves. However, numerous companies, including Lowe's, Lufthansa, Microsoft, and FedEx, have been fined millions of dollars for misclassifying permanent workers as independent contractors in an effort to cut employment-related costs. Uber and Lyft, in particular, have faced some high-profile legal challenges to their practice of classifying drivers as independent contractors. To prevent such abuses, Congress and the U.S. Department of Labor have established criteria that companies should follow when deciding how to characterize their workers. Highlights in HRM 4 offers some guidance firms can use to make this determination.

Highlights in HRM

Is a Worker an Independent Contractor—or Not?

Signs of independent contractor status include a person who:

- Is free from direct supervision and control
- Has an established business
- Keeps a place of business and invests in facilities, equipment, and supplies
- Pays their own expenses
- Assumes the risk for profits or losses
- Sets their own schedule
- Sets or negotiates their own pay rate
- Offers services to other businesses (competitive or noncompetitive)
- Is free to refuse work offers
- May choose to hire help
- Carries insurance
- Advertises in the electronic and/or print media
- Uses business cards, stationery, and billheads

Source: Adapted from "Independent Contractor," New York Department of Labor, http://www.labor.ny.gov.

However, the U.S. Supreme Court has ruled that there is no single test to determine whether an employee is an independent contractor or not. To avoid any hint of impropriety, companies are increasingly requiring independent contractors to sign up with staffing agencies and then hiring the contractors through them.

Employee Leasing

The practice of **employee leasing** by professional employer organizations (PEOs) has grown rapidly since the passage of the Tax Equity and Fiscal Responsibility Act of 1982. As we explained in Chapter 1, more than 150,000 businesses and roughly 3 million U.S. workers are involved in PEO arrangements, according to the National Association of Professional Employer Organizations (NAPEO). Basically, a PEO—typically a larger company—takes over the management of a smaller company's HR tasks and becomes a coemployer to its employees. The PEO performs all the HR duties of an employer—recruiting, background checks, hiring, payroll, performance appraisal, benefits administration, and other day-to-day HR activities—and in return is paid a placement fee of normally 4 to 8 percent of payroll cost plus 9 to 20 percent of gross wages. Unlike temporary agencies, which supply workers only for limited periods, employee leasing companies place their employees with subscribers on a permanent basis.

employee leasing
The process of dismissing employees, who are then hired by a leasing company (which handles all HR-related activities), and contracting with that company to lease back the employees.

Because PEOs can coemploy a large number of people working at many different companies, they can provide employees with benefits such as 401(k) and health plans that small companies cannot afford. (The average client of a PEO is a business with 19 employees.) SHRM reports that companies with fewer than 50 employees can save anywhere from $5,000 to $50,000 in time and labor costs annually by hiring a PEO.[24]

5.2b Internal Recruiting Methods

Oftentimes firms do not post job openings to the outside world, but instead seek prospects internally. Internal recruitment involves promoting or transferring individuals into new positions from within the organization. Think about this for a moment: Why would firms choose one approach over another? What would be the advantages, and which drawbacks could result?

Most companies try initially to fill job vacancies above the entry-level position through promotions and transfers. Internal candidates are readily available and get up to speed faster, and there is less uncertainty about how they will perform. Firms also do not have to run advertisements to find them, which can be costly.

By filling vacancies internally, an organization can capitalize on the investment it has made in recruiting, selecting, training, and developing its current employees. Promoting employees rewards them for their past performance and encourages them to continue their efforts. This can improve morale within the organization and support a culture of employee engagement. For example, promotion-from-within policies at Marriott, Nordstrom's, Nucor Steel, and Whole Foods have contributed to these companies' overall growth and success.[25]

However, at least one research study has found that managers often hire external candidates rather than promote their current employees because they have a tendency to overvalue unfamiliar candidates and undervalue known ones.[26] This may be because the managers are not yet as familiar with the external candidates' flaws as they are with internal candidates' flaws. At other times, extremely good employees are prevented from being promoted to other departments because their current managers are reluctant to lose them.

Research by Matthew Bidwell suggests that internal candidates are likely to outperform external candidates. Bidwell looked at seven years of data and 5,300 employees in different jobs in the financial industry. Even though external hires got paid nearly 20 percent more, they received significantly lower marks on their performance reviews for their first two years on the job. External hires were also 61 percent more likely to be fired. In addition, the productivity of business units and groups with new hires suffered because it took time for the groups to help the new employees learn their jobs and become proficient at them.[27]

When qualified employees are passed over for external candidates (whom they are often asked to train), a firm's current employees can become disillusioned to the point that they begin looking elsewhere for jobs, even when the external candidates hired end up being very qualified for their positions. Employee surveys and other research show that a lack of career advancement is a major reason why people quit their jobs.[28]

When experienced employees leave an organization, they take with them years of corporate know-how that is hard to replace. Some signs that the firm needs to work harder at grooming internal talent are shown in Figure 5.5. To lessen the chances of losing top performers, some managers actively identify "at risk" employees and take steps to retain these people.

Figure 5.5 Warning Signs of a Weak Talent "Bench"

1. It takes a long time to fill key positions.
2. Key positions can be filled only by hiring from the outside.
3. Key positions cannot be filled with confidence in the abilities of those chosen for them.
4. Replacements for positions often are unsuccessful in performing their new duties.
5. Promotions are made on the basis of whim, favoritism, or nepotism.

Sources: Adapted from William Rothwell, *Effective Succession Planning* (New York: AMACOM, 2000); Victor Lipman, "Why Employee Development Is Important, Neglected, and Can Cost You Talent," *Forbes* (January 29, 2013), https://www.forbes.com.

Internal Job Postings

Internal job postings are a quick way to find qualified employees interested in a position. A small business might simply post a notice on a bulletin board in its break room. Larger companies generally post their openings on their intranet sites. The intranets of some companies alert specific employees about jobs in which they may be interested. As a position becomes available, a list of employees interested in that position is retrieved, and the records of these employees are reviewed to select possible candidates for interviews. The employees can be electronically notified about interview schedules and track their progress electronically through the various hiring stages.[29]

Identifying Talent through Performance Appraisals

Successful performers are often good candidates for a promotion. Identifying and developing all employees is a role that all managers should take seriously. A tool called a **nine-box grid** is helping firms such as General Electric, Novartis, and others do this. The grid helps managers by compiling appraisal and assessment data into a single visual reference so they can see both an employee's actual performance and their potential performance. This can then help managers determine the developmental needs of the employee and predict what the person's next steps within the organization might be. Figure 5.6 is an example of a nine-box grid.

nine-box grid
A comparative diagram that includes appraisal and assessment data to allow managers to easily see an employee's actual and potential performance.

Skills Inventories, Replacement Charts, and Succession Plans

Recall from Chapter 2 that firms utilize talent reviews, or strategic meetings, to determine whether a company has the human resources it needs to compete in the future. That chapter also discussed skills inventories, which help track an employee's education, past work experience, vocational interests, specific abilities and skills, compensation history, and job tenure to see how they can best be used. Procter & Gamble and HSBC are among the firms that track their employees this way to locate capable employees who can be recruited to fill open positions. Along with skill inventories, replacement charts

Figure 5.6 An Example of a Nine-Box Grid

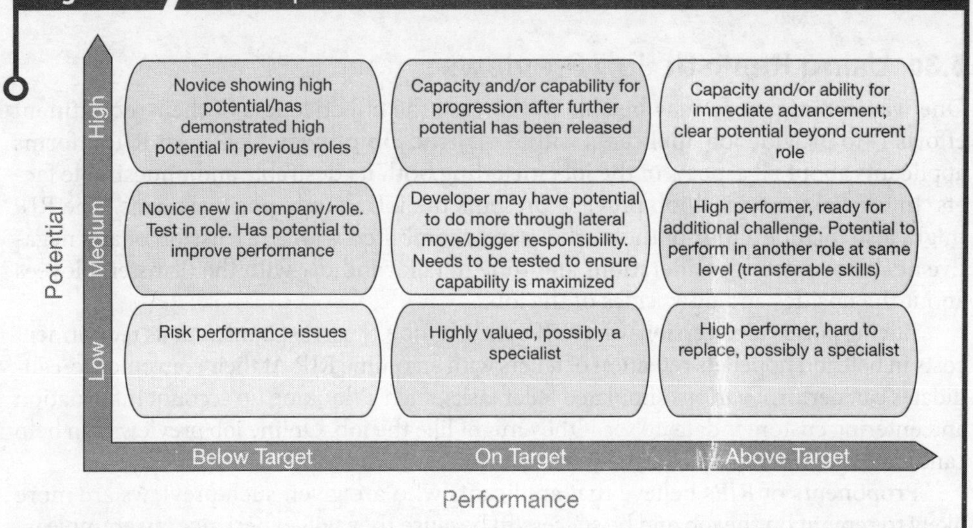

Source: © RapidBI.com 2000–2008

are an important tool for succession planning. At GE, for every position at or above a director level, two or three people are usually identified who can easily step in when the current jobholder moves on.[30]

As we also discussed in Chapter 2, more firms are electronically capturing the qualifications of each of their employees. Companies such as Oracle and SAP have developed automated staffing and skills management software that allow an organization to rapidly screen its entire workforce to locate suitable candidates to fill an internal opening. These data can also be used to predict the career paths of employees and to anticipate when and where promotion opportunities might arise.[31]

LO3

Explain how realistic job previews (RJPs) operate. As a manager or business owner, would you use them?

5.3 Improving the Effectiveness of Recruiting

How can a firm improve its effectiveness when it comes to recruiting? First, recruiters need an accurate job analysis. Which skills and abilities are they truly recruiting for? Have they been precisely defined? Firms often neglect to update their job descriptions, which in turn results in job postings that aren't accurate and the wrong candidates applying for jobs. Second, line managers and employees need to be intimately involved in the process. Without their input, the hiring process is far more likely to fail. Third, a job-starting date that works for both the organization and the potential new hire needs to be established. Fourth, after the person has been hired, the firm should conduct a "debrief" and identify any lessons learned to improve the recruiting process.

Other questions a firm needs to ask itself are the following: How well is the company doing when it comes to recruiting talent from all sources? Are some sources more effective than others? Have the firm's recruiters been able to hire enough employees to meet the company's needs, including key personnel? Are the recruiters slow or fast when it comes to filling positions? Are line managers happy with the process and the quality of the people hired? Are the people who have been hired happy with their jobs and likely to remain with the firm and advance in the organization? HR managers have many tools available to them to gauge their efforts and improve their recruiting. Let's now look at a few of them.

5.3a Using Realistic Job Previews

realistic job preview (RJP)
Informing applicants about all aspects of the job, including both its desirable and undesirable facets.

One way organizations may be able to increase the effectiveness of their recruitment efforts is to provide job applicants with a **realistic job preview (RJP)**. An RJP informs applicants about all aspects of the job, including both its desirable and undesirable facets. In contrast, a typical job preview presents the job in only positive terms. The RJP might also include a tour of the working area, combined with a discussion of any negative health or safety considerations and time to talk candidly with the firm's employees about the upsides and downsides of the job.

Boeing posts video versions of its RJPs on YouTube. SunTrust Banks cut its recruitment costs in half and upped its retention of tellers with an online RJP. At their convenience, candidates can perform various simulated teller tasks, such as looking up account information and entering customer data, to see if they might like the job. Online job previews can help candidates get a better feel for the work than a written description provides.[32]

Proponents of RJPs believe that applicants who are given such previews are more likely to remain on the job and be successful because they will experience fewer unpleasant surprises. Yet some companies avoid RJPs because they worry that presenting both the positive and negative aspects of a job could discourage applicants. In reality, downplaying the negative aspects is likely to be counterproductive, because (1) it is more likely to result in turnover, and (2) postings on social media sites such as Glassdoor and LinkedIn enable applicants to research what current and ex-employees are saying about companies and the jobs.

5.3b Surveys and Employee Profiles

Another way to improve a company's recruiting is to survey managers about how satisfied they are with the process. Are managers happy with the time it takes to hire new employees, the degree to which they need to be involved in the process, and the overall quality of the people recruited? Why or why not? To find ways to reach out to and recruit the right kinds of candidates, some companies develop **employee profiles** by surveying their top performers about what they like to do, what events they attend, what websites they visit, and how they like to be contacted and recruited. New hires can also be surveyed to see how satisfied they are. In addition, candidates who turned down jobs often can provide valuable information about why they did not accept the firm's offer.

employee profiles
Profile of workers developed by studying an organization's top performers to recruit similar types of people.

5.3c Recruiting Metrics

As we explained earlier in the chapter, recruiters should keep statistics on the sources from which candidates are recruited and hired as well as the costs of each source. The time it takes to recruit various employees from various sources as well as the quality of employees are other statistics recruiters collect and study. Doing so helps them understand which recruiting sources work best for different employees, which then allows them to find better employees faster and at a lower cost. The following are some of the metrics used.

Time to Fill

Time-to-fill metrics refer to the number of days from when a job opening is approved to the date a person accepts and/or begins the job. Figure 5.7 shows how time-to-fill metrics are calculated. Generally speaking, lower time-to-fill statistics are better. However, a trade-off has to be made between the time to fill a position and the quality of the candidates needed for that position.

time-to-fill
Metrics that refer to the number of days from when a job opening is approved to the date a person accepts the job and begins it.

Figure 5.7 Time-to-Fill Calculations

Position	Date Position Approved	Date Offer Accepted	Date Started Work	Selection Time	Time to Start
Engineer	10/10/22	11/30/22	12/15/22	51	15
Marketing manager	10/11/22	11/24/22	12/16/22	44	22
Salesperson	10/12/22	11/13/22	11/20/22	32	7
Administrative Assistant	10/13/22	11/7/22	11/14/22	25	7
Clerk	10/13/22	10/30/22	11/14/22	17	15
Averages				**33.8**	**13.2**

Quality of Fill

quality-of-fill
A metric that measures how well new hires have gotten "up to speed," are performing, and are being retained.

Hiring quality employees is also a primary concern of recruiters. Firms have attempted to develop a **quality-of-fill** metric that measures how well new hires have gotten "up to speed," are performing, and are being retained. The quality-of-fill metric can be calculated as follows:

$$\text{Quality of fill} = (PR + HP + HR) \div N$$

where

PR = Average job performance rating of new hires

HP = Percentage of new hires achieving acceptable productivity within an acceptable time frame

HR = Percentage of new hires retained after 1 year

N = Number of performance indicators

Example:

PR = Average 3.5 on a 5.0 scale = 70%

HP = Of 100 new hires, 75 are meeting acceptable productivity levels = 75%

HP = 80% of new hires have been retained

N = 3

$$\text{Quality of fill} = (70 + 75 + 80) \div 3 = 75\%$$

Yield Ratio

yield ratio
The percentage of applicants from a particular source who make it to the next stage in the selection process.

Yield ratios help indicate which recruitment sources are most effective at producing qualified job candidates. A **yield ratio** is the percentage of applicants from a particular source who make it to the next stage in the selection process. For example, if 100 resumes were obtained from an employment agency and 17 of the applicants submitting those resumes were invited for an onsite interview, the yield ratio for that agency would be 17 percent (17 ÷ 100).

Yield ratios help firms determine which sources produce the most qualified applicants. They can also be used to determine how many total applicants a firm typically needs to attract and advance to different stages in the hiring process to fill different jobs.

Acceptance Rate

acceptance rate
The percentage of applicants who accept a firm's jobs after being offered them.

The **acceptance rate** is the percentage of applicants who accept a firm's jobs after being offered them. For example, if over the course of a year a firm offers jobs to 100 applicants, 90 of whom accept those offers, the firm's acceptance rate is 90 percent. A firm can track its acceptance rate for the company overall or for particular jobs. Normally, high acceptance rates are better.

If a firm has lower acceptance rates or declining acceptance rates, the firm and its HR personnel must determine why employees are declining offers. Is the pay not competitive? Does the firm have a problem with its branding? Are its recruiters, managers, and employees doing a good job of "selling" the firm to potential applicants? Is the firm looking toward the right sources to recruit applicants? If acceptance rates are low, a firm may want to consider hiring a private employment agency to help improve its recruiting.

Cost of Recruitment

The average cost of recruiting a new hire can be computed rather simply. The firm's total recruiting costs from all sources—including advertising, travel expenses, referral bonuses, and so on—are summed up and then divided by the number of people hired:

Total recruiting costs ÷ Number of people hired = Average recruiting cost per hire

The same calculation can be used to determine the cost of recruiting from a single source, such as employee referrals. To calculate this metric, the firm would divide the total referral bonuses it paid employees by the number of people hired. For example, if the firm spent $10,000 on referral bonuses and hired 40 people in a given year, the average cost of recruitment in terms of referral bonuses paid that year would be:

10,000 ÷ 40 = $250 per hire

When combined with information about yield ratios, these calculations can provide valuable information to managers about the usefulness of different approaches and sources of recruitment. For example, although both ads and employee referrals may yield qualified applicants, managers may find that referral bonuses are a more economical alternative.

An **applicant tracking system (ATS)** enables recruiters to electronically post job openings, screen the uploaded profiles and/or resumes of applicants, rank them, and contact them via email for interviews. An ATS also tracks the sources of applicants—that is, the various websites they use to apply for jobs and how far they got in the process—and the time and costs related to hiring people. Looking at these data can help recruiters fine-tune where and how they are recruiting.[33]

applicant tracking system (ATS)
A system recruiters use to post job openings, screen resumes and uploaded profiles, contact (via email) potential candidates for interviews, and track the time, costs, and other metrics related to hiring people.

Rather than employing an ATS, Google has used reams of data and analytics to figure out why it was having problems recruiting diverse candidates, particularly women engineers. The company also developed an algorithm to predict which candidates would have the highest probability of succeeding once hired. Spokespeople for Google say the company is determined to bring the same level of rigor to personnel decisions as it does its engineering decisions.[34] Moreover, Google isn't waiting for great candidates to come to the firm. After all, it's a search-engine company. The company is using machine learning and big data to suggest opportunities at Google aligned to a jobseeker's skill sets and interests.[35]

5.3d Retention: How Do We Keep Our Talent?

The flipside of recruiting is retaining employees. Once you've burnished your brand and enticed people to join your organization, what will make them remain with your firm? Turnover drags down morale among a firm's staff and takes a toll on productivity. Replacing employees is extremely costly and time consuming. Yet even in the post–COVID-19 pandemic environment, when the labor market was still uncertain, research suggested that somewhere between 40 percent and 50 percent of U.S. employees were planning to look for new jobs in the coming year.[36]

Why do so many employees think about leaving their jobs? And, what, if anything, can be done about it? Many managers believe employees leave their organizations for better pay and benefits they can't match. Google offers employees free massages and rides back and forth to work. Some organizations are attracting and retaining employees by offering them student-loan repayment assistance. The insurer Aetna is one of them: Aetna will match $2,000 per year of an employee's payments, up to a maximum of $10,000 total. Programs such as these are helping companies retain Generation Z and Millennial workers, who tend to switch employers frequently.

For many firms, especially smaller ones, matching these kinds of generous pay and benefits packages isn't possible. Perks that don't cost a lot can go a long way toward retaining employees, though. Flextime, telecommuting, relaxed dress codes or no dress codes, summer hours, and modest performance bonuses are examples. Requiring employees to shut off their mobile phones after hours is another work–life balance perk that firms are increasingly giving their employees.

In fact, contrary to what managers believe, factors other than pay and benefits are usually what prompt employees to quit. Workers more often quit their jobs because they think their input isn't valued, they were a poor fit for the job in the first place, or they have too few growth and advancement opportunities.

The Carnegie study found that leadership is the key reason for turnover. There's an old adage, "People join a company and quit a boss." Supervisors have to demonstrate interest in and empathy toward their employees, but unfortunately too few do. Supervisors also need to help employees grow and develop, a topic that's discussed in the next section.

Some firms conduct "stay" interviews with longtime employees to determine why they have remained with the firm for as long as they have. What do they like about it, and what needs improving? HR managers can then use that information to develop retention strategies.

LO4 ///

How can a career management program help an organization forced to downsize its operations?

5.4 Career Management: Developing Talent over Time

Why should both employees and their employers be concerned about career management programs? As a manager or owner of firm, why might you want to help employees develop their careers over time when you can just hire people from the outside as you need them, especially since they can quit their jobs at any time? Too often, firms do just that. Their career development and recruiting are reactive processes in which they engage periodically, when a position needs to be filled.

Proactive companies see career development and recruiting functions as strategic imperatives and, therefore, as an ongoing process designed to maximize the talents of their employees and retain them. These companies study their strategies in conjunction with their organizational charts, job analysis information, and external factors such as the labor market and the competition, and then recruit proactively and continually. At The Container Store, which regularly tops *Fortune*'s "100 Best Companies to Work For" list, store managers spend a couple of hours a week identifying potentially good candidates for future potential openings.

Regardless of the source from which employees are recruited—internally or externally—managers play a key role in expanding their firms' talent pools. And make no mistake, they continue "recruiting" talented employees over time to help build the future of the firm. Good managers "grow" talent by listening to their employees' aspirations, act as coaches, identify their strengths and areas for improvement, and offer them continual feedback. Good managers also ensure employees receive training, self-assessment tools, and information about the organization and possible career paths within it. As you have learned, internal recruiting is highly effective. It also builds loyalty between firms and their employees, something that seems to be in short supply in today's transaction-based labor market.

Figure 5.8 Steps in the Career Management Process

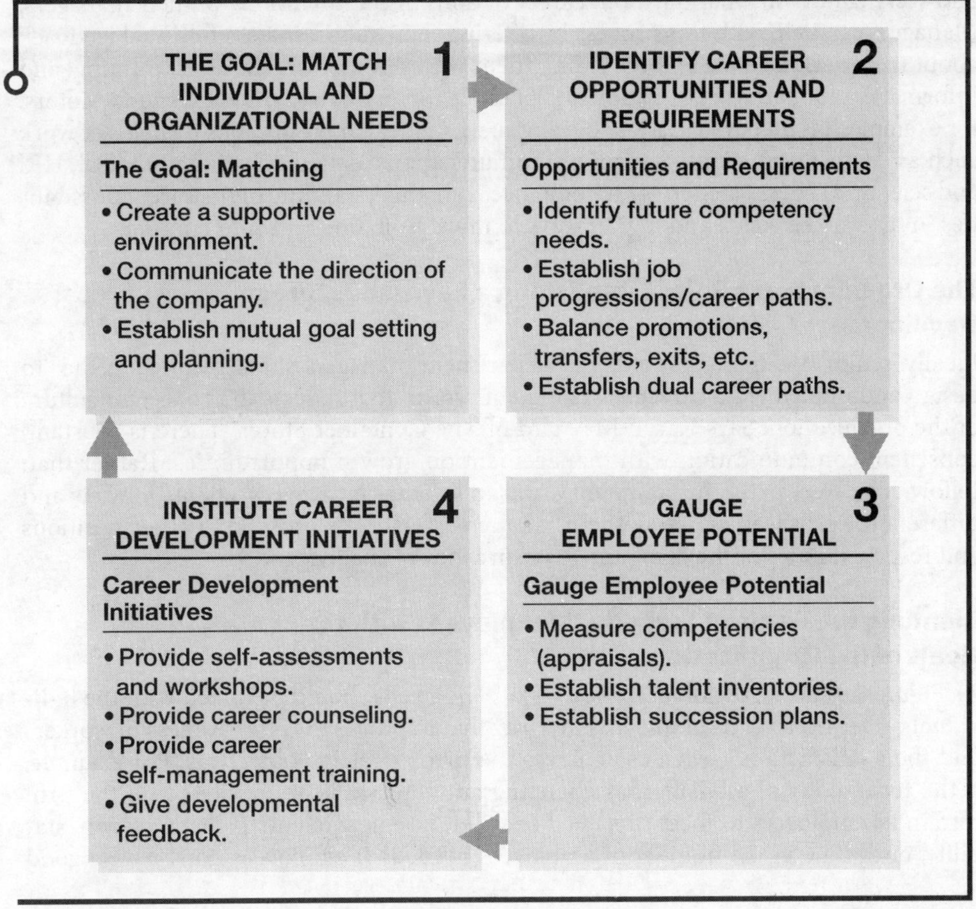

Figure 5.8 shows the steps in the career management process. For example, to plan their careers, employees need organizational information—information that strategic planning, forecasting, succession planning, and skills inventories can provide. Similarly, as they obtain information themselves and use it to plan their careers, employees need to know what the career paths within their organizations are and how managers view their performance.

5.4a The Goal: Matching the Needs of the Organization to the Needs of Employees

A career development program should be viewed as a dynamic process that matches the needs of the organization with the needs of employees as those needs change. Each party has a distinct role to play in the process.

The Employee's Role

Because having a successful career involves creating your own career path—not just following a path that has been established by the organization—employees need to take an active role in planning their careers, especially in light of how fast the world of work is changing. This includes identifying their knowledge, skills, abilities, interests, and values and seeking out information about career options in conjunction with their managers. Managers can help with this process by offering their subordinates continual feedback about their performance and providing them with self-assessment tools, training, and information about the organization and possible career paths within it. General Motors, for example, has prepared a career development guide that groups jobs by fields of work such as engineering, manufacturing, communications, data processing, financial, HR, and scientific. These categories give employees an understanding of the career possibilities in the various fields and logical ways to move from one area into another.

The Organization's Role: Establishing a Favorable Career Development Climate

Ideally, senior line managers and HR department managers should work together to design and implement a career development system that reflects the goals and culture of the organization. Says Karyn Maynard of The Container Store: "There is constant, consistent communication with management on growth opportunities. Rather than follow one career path, the company works to leverage employees' talents for new and different roles, as well as giving them as much exposure as possible to other positions and responsibilities in the company to ensure they're challenged."[37]

Blending the Goals of Individual Employees with the Goals of the Organization

As Figure 5.9 shows, the organization's goals and needs should be linked with the individual career needs of its employees in a way that improves the effectiveness of workers and their satisfaction as well as achieves the firm's strategic objectives. For example, if the technology of a business is changing and new skills are needed, will the firm retrain its employees to meet this need or will it hire new talent? Is there growth, stability, or decline in the number of employees needed? If employees don't have a good

Figure 5.9 Blending the Needs of Individual Employees with the Needs of Their Organizations

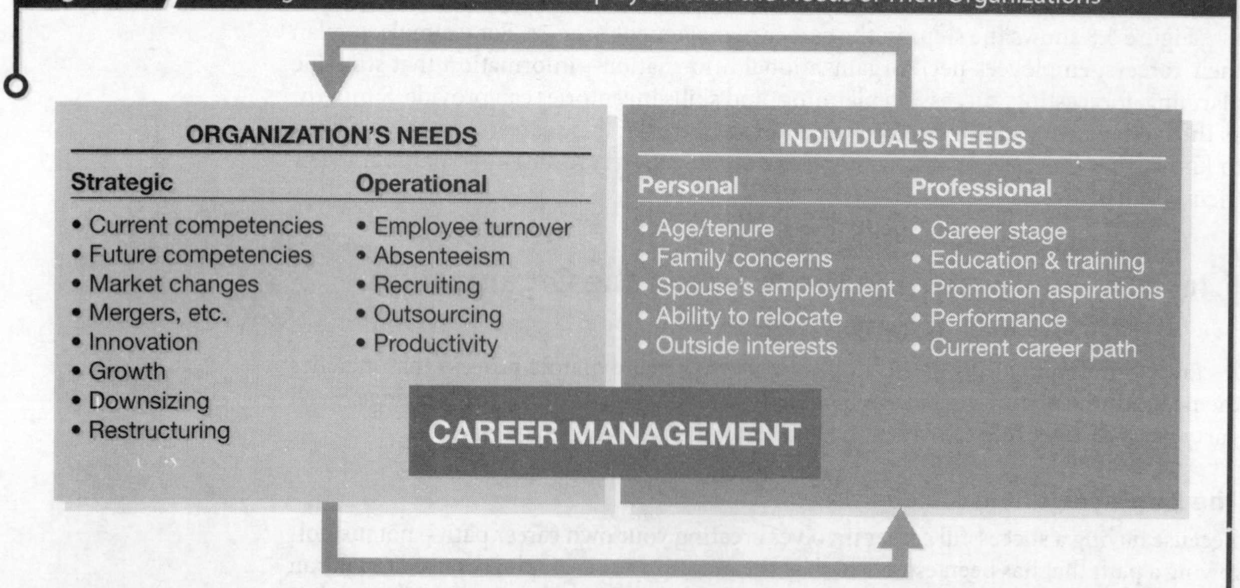

understanding the goals of their firms, they could end up setting career goals that are a poor match for the firm.

5.4b Identifying Career Opportunities and Requirements

To identify career opportunities and requirements, managers have to continually analyze the competencies required for jobs, the progression among related jobs, and the supply of ready (and potential) talent available to fill those jobs. In Chapter 4, we discussed a variety of ways this can be done, such as via questionnaires and interviews. Informal discussion with different groups, such as new employees, managers, longtime employees, minority employees, and technical and professional employees, is another way. Identifying the needs and problems of these groups provides the starting point for the organization's career development efforts.

Begin with a Competency Analysis

In Chapter 4, we also discussed how firms analyze jobs carefully to identify and assign weights to the knowledge and skills that each requires. The system that one major retailer uses measures three basic competencies for each job: know-how, problem solving, and accountability. Know-how is broken down into three types of job knowledge: technical, managerial, and human relations. Problem solving and accountability also have several dimensions. Scores for each of these three major competencies are assigned to each job, and a total value is computed for each job. This information is then used to make certain that a transfer to a different job provides an employee with the following experiences: (1) an increase in at least one skill area on each new assignment, (2) an increase of at least 10 percent in total points on each new assignment, and (3) assignments in several different functional areas.[38]

Identify Job Progressions and Career Paths

Once the skill demands of jobs are identified and weighted according to their importance, it then becomes possible to plan **job progressions**. A new employee with no experience is typically assigned to a "starting job." After a period of time in that job, the employee can be promoted to one that requires more knowledge and/or skill. While most organizations concentrate on developing job progressions for managerial, professional, and technical jobs, progressions can and should be developed for all categories of jobs.

Job progressions can serve as a basis for developing **career paths**—the lines of advancement within an organization—for individuals. Figure 5.10 illustrates a typical advancement for an HR associate for a large multinational corporation.

Career development and planning systems were once primarily focused on promotions. However, in today's flatter organizations and more dynamic work environment, an individual's career advancement can move along several different paths via promotions, transfers, demotions, and even exits. A **promotion** is a change of assignment to a job at a higher level in the organization. The new job normally provides an increase in pay and status and demands more skill or carries more responsibility. To retain employees and improve their promotability, many larger firms offer to reimburse employees for getting advanced degrees and remaining with the company for a certain period of time. "Corporate universities"—special facilities where employees receive training—are also utilized. (We will talk more about these programs in Chapter 7.)

Flatter organizations offer fewer promotional opportunities, so many individuals find career advancement through lateral moves. A **transfer** occurs when an employee is placed in another job for which the duties, responsibilities, status, and pay and benefits are

job progressions
The hierarchy of jobs new employees might experience, ranging from a starting job to jobs that successively require more knowledge and/or skill.

career paths
Lines of advancement in an occupational field within an organization.

promotion
A change of assignment to a job at a higher level in the organization.

transfer
The placement of an employee in another job for which the duties, responsibilities, status, and pay and benefits are approximately equal to those of the previous job the person held.

Figure 5.10 Typical Line of Advancement in HR Management

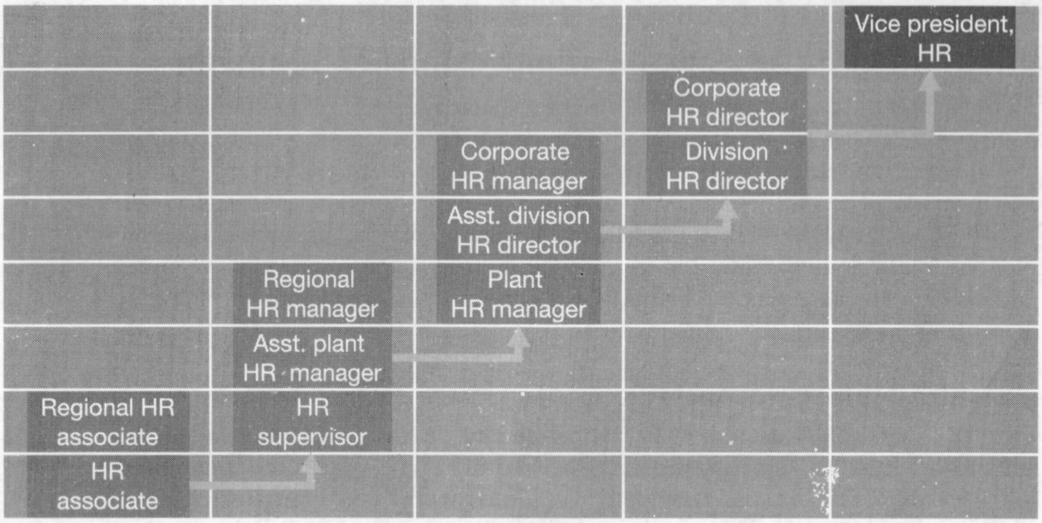

approximately equal to those of the previous job that individual held (although as an incentive to make a transfer, organizations sometimes offer transferred employees small pay increases). Individuals who look forward to change or want a chance to learn more about their organizations and obtain different skills often seek out transfers. In many cases, these employees do so to augment their skills so they will be more promotable in the future.

A transfer sometimes requires the employee to change work group, workplace, work shift, or organizational unit; it may even necessitate moving to another geographic area. Thus, transfers make it possible for an organization to place its employees in jobs where there is a greater need for their services and where they can acquire new knowledge and skills.

demotion
A downward transfer that moves an individual into a lower-level job that can provide developmental opportunities.

A downward transfer, or **demotion**, moves an individual into a lower-level job that can provide developmental opportunities. Although a demotion is ordinarily considered unfavorable, some individuals actually may request it to return to their "technical roots." Engineers and computer programmers who get promoted to management positions but end up missing their former jobs are examples. It is also not uncommon for organizations to appoint temporary leaders (especially in team environments) to positions with the understanding that they will eventually return to their former jobs.

Transfers, promotions, and demotions require individuals to adjust to new job demands and usually to a different work environment. A transfer that involves moving to a new location within the United States or abroad requires the person to adapt to not only a new work environment but also new living conditions. Employees with families have the added responsibility of helping family members adjust to the new living arrangements. Even though some employers provide various types of relocation services—including covering moving expenses, help selling a home, and providing cultural orientation and language training—there is always some loss in the employee's productivity during the relocation process. Pretransfer training, whether it's related to job skills or to the lifestyle changes required, is one of the most effective ways to reduce lost productivity.

Of course, many employees choose to exit their organizations as part of their career development. When a person's career opportunities within a firm are limited and their skills are in demand externally, the best career options could be for the individual to switch companies or to work as a freelancer, consultant, or entrepreneur. Although some employees leave voluntarily, other employees are forced to leave. Larger organizations often provide **outplacement services** to help terminated employees find jobs elsewhere.

outplacement services
Services provided by organizations to help terminated employees find a new job.

Scripps Health, a California-based hospital group, has created a career center for workers who might otherwise lose their jobs through layoffs.[39] (See Case Study 1 at the end of the chapter.) However, even with the best career planning, it is almost impossible for people to have perfect certainty about where their careers are going. People change over time, so their needs and interests also change. Moreover, successful career paths often do not proceed in a lockstep manner. As Highlights in HRM 5 mentions, before founding Amazon.com, Jeff Bezos spent a number of years in the financial industry. In terms of their career advancements, many people note that they were either "in the right place at the right time" or carved out entirely new career paths for themselves.

Track Employees' Career Stages

A person's knowledge, skills, abilities, and attitudes as well as career aspirations change with age and maturity. The challenges and frustrations people face at the same stages in their careers are remarkably similar. A model describing these stages—(1) preparation for work, (2) organizational entry, (3) early career, (4) midcareer, and (5) late career—is shown in Figure 5.11. The typical age range and the major tasks of each stage are also presented in the figure.

Figure 5.11 Stages of Career Development

Stage 5: Late Career (age 55–retirement):
Continue to improve one's productivity, mentor other employees, and prepare for retirement.

Stage 4: Midcareer (ages 40–55):
Reappraise early career and early adulthood goals, reaffirm or modify goals, continue to improve one's productivity, and mentor other employees.

Stage 3: Early Career (ages 25–40):
Learn the job, learn organizational rules and norms, fit into the chosen occupation and organization, increase competence, pursue goals.

Stage 2: Organizational Entry (ages 18–25):
Obtain job offer(s) from the desired organization(s), select an appropriate job based on complete and accurate information.

Stage 1: Preparation for Work (ages 0–25):
Develop an occupational self-image, assess alternative occupations, develop an initial occupational choice, pursue necessary education.

Career Path of Jeff Bezos, Founder of Amazon.com

1986—Graduated from Princeton University with a B.S. in electrical engineering and computer science

1986—Hired by Fitel, a telecommunications and information technology firm that created software for tracking international stock trades

1988—Hired by Bankers Trust, Co., a financial firm that specialized in risk management utilizing new sophisticated computer systems

1990—Promoted to vice president

1990—Hired by D. E. Shaw, an investment and hedge fund company

1992—Promoted to senior vice president

1995—Founded Amazon.com

The first stage, preparation for work, encompasses the period prior to entering an organization, often extending until age 25. It is a period in which individuals must acquire the knowledge, abilities, and skills they need to compete in the marketplace. The second stage, typically from ages 18 to 25, is devoted to soliciting job offers and selecting appropriate jobs. During this period, a person might also be involved in preparing for work. The next three stages entail fitting into a chosen occupation and organization(s), modifying one's goals, continuing to improve one's productivity, helping groom other employees, and finally preparing for retirement.

Offer Different Career Paths

As we have indicated, in many organizations, people in technical careers—successful engineers, scientists, and so on—are often promoted right out of their area of specialization into management. Instead of doing what they are good at, they end up in jobs they aren't well suited for or don't enjoy.

The solution to this dilemma has been to develop *dual career paths*, or tracks, that provide for progression in special areas such as information technology, finance, marketing, and engineering, with compensation that is comparable to that received by managers at different levels. As we explained in Chapter 2, Microsoft offers software engineers both management-focused and technical-specialist career tracks and allows them to move back and forth between the two.

Fast-track programs are another way to give employees exposure to different types of jobs, particularly younger employees with high potential who seek meaningful training assignments and whom a firm is trying to retain. In fast-track programs, "HIPOs" (high-potential employees) progress rapidly through a number of managerial positions designed to expose them to different functions within the organization. General Electric has an intensive two-year program of this type. Employees in the program might, for example, spend a number of months in the company's energy division in Atlanta, its aviation division in Cincinnati, and its oil and gas division in Brazil.

However, proactive companies try to make the most of *all* of their talent rather than just their high-potential employees. It's not uncommon for an employee to do poorly in one position but be an excellent fit for another role, or an employee who is burned out to be reinvigorated by a different job.

Small Business Application

Small Companies Often Offer Big Rewards

Many new grads and seasoned professionals alike are choosing to work for less-than-500-employee firms because of the many advantages they offer, and smaller firms are welcoming these workers with open arms. For midterm and advanced career professionals, a smaller company often means jumping straight into the limelight. Such a change can be rejuvenating because they may find themselves taking on more diverse responsibilities, getting involved in new arenas, and seeing more clearly how their own efforts impact the company's results. "You are more likely to be listened to, and to feel that you are an important part of the company and that your ideas really matter," says Lindsey Pollak, a management expert of next-generation career trends. That's what happened to Mike Barnes, a logistics executive who went to work at Halton Company, a construction equipment provider in Portland, Oregon. Barnes says the closer connection to the mission of the business gave him a level of job satisfaction he had not felt in a long time.

However, employees who opt for working in a small firm cannot expect to find everything they might get in a larger corporation. Tighter budgets mean smaller companies sometimes cannot afford to pay salaries equal to those of big firms, and they often cannot provide the same support systems or perks, such as generous expense accounts, hefty bonuses, and company-paid smartphones. But many small employers provide alluring trade-offs such as shorter workweeks, less travel, and work–life balance incentives, including telecommuting and flextime.

Where people decide to work really comes down to determining how they are going to meet their career and life goals. Notes management author and analyst Tony Jacowski, "Your choice of organization should be based on the quality of work experience you will gain rather than the size of the organization."

Sources: Michael Mazzeo, Paul Oyer, and Scott Schaefer, "What Small Businesses Do Better than Corporate America," *Fortune* (June 10, 2014), http://www.fortune.com; Sarah E. Needleman, "Moving to a Small Company Can Lead to Big Rewards," *Wall Street Journal* (March 5, 2008), http://online.wsj.com; Lindsey Pollak, "The Advantages of Working for a Small Company," http://www.lindseypollak.com; Tony Jacowski, "Benefits of Working in a Small Company vs a Corporation," http://ezinearticles.com; Jacqueline Parks, "The Benefits of Working for a Small Business," http://www.associatedcontent.com.

One way to help rank-and-file employees learn new skills, identify new roles they might aim for in the future, and retain them is by allowing them to exchange or swap jobs. Virgin America and PricewaterhouseCoopers have programs that allow flight attendants and junior staffers, respectively, to swap jobs with their counterparts in the United States and Australia. BNSF Railway allows employees to switch jobs in different areas and in different locales. Such swaps are referred to as "career development moves."[40]

5.4c Career Development Initiatives

Workers today are not waiting to get laid off. They are taking charge of planning their career paths and getting the skills and development they need to go from one job (and employer) to the next. Employers who understand this trend can take preemptive action by having career conversations with their employees and implementing career management programs to prevent them from leaving. Let's look at some of these efforts.[41]

Career Counseling

A key part of developing your talent pool is talking to your employees about their current job activities and performance, personal and career interests and goals, personal skills, and suitable career development objectives. This kind of discussion can be initiated by HR staff members, managers and supervisors, or outside consultants. Often it is done as part of the performance appraisals. Once the conversation has begun, how those goals can be achieved and fit in with the organization's goals can be discussed and a career "action" plan for the employee established. The telecommunications company Verizon, for example, has rolled out a program in which career advisors both offer employees one-on-one counseling and hold periodic webinars and workshops about the career and education opportunities the company offers. The firm also has an online career center with career maps to help employees chart possible job progressions.[42]

Some organizations have instituted "career self-management" programs to help employees learn to continuously gather feedback and information about themselves and their careers. Employees typically undertake self-assessments to increase their awareness of their own career attitudes and values and attend workshops. In addition, they are encouraged to widen their viewpoint beyond the next company promotion to broader opportunities in the marketplace, attend conferences, and develop good long-term relationships with their bosses and colleagues. General Electric has developed an extensive set of career development programs to help employees explore life issues that affect career decisions.[43]

Mentoring Programs

People often mention coworkers who positively influenced them early on in their careers. Individuals who coach, advise, and encourage employees of a lesser rank are called **mentors**. Millennials consistently say they want coaching and feedback. When Deloitte surveyed Millennials, it found the ones who planned to stay with their employers more than 5 years were twice as likely to have a mentor as those who did not.[44]

mentors
Individuals who coach, advise, and encourage employees of a lesser rank.

reverse mentoring
A program whereby younger employees are called on to mentor older employees and executives about social media trends, new technology, and marketplace trends.

Mentors need not be more senior employees, however. **Reverse mentoring** is a program whereby younger employees are called on to mentor older employees and executives about social media trends, new technology, and marketplace trends. Hewlett-Packard, Cisco, and the advertising agency Ogilvy & Mather are among the companies that have implemented reverse mentoring. Spencer Osborn, an executive with Ogilvy and Mather, said his younger mentors helped him jazz up his Twitter posts, which had a reputation for being boring. At Cisco, when the word got out that some executives had younger mentors, other executives wanted mentors, too. Reverse mentoring programs help younger employees feel valued and "heard" and can increase their retention.[45]

Mentoring relationships don't have to be formal, though. Informal mentoring goes on daily within every type of organization. Generally, the mentor initiates the relationship, but sometimes an employee will approach a potential mentor for advice. Most mentoring relationships develop over time on an informal basis. They frequently end that way, too. A study of 15 high-ranking executive women found that although many of them lacked formal mentors, they had successfully engaged in a kind of "360-degree" networking: the women made it a point to form and maintain relationships with people above, below, and at the same level as themselves, which helped advance their careers.[46] Highlights in HRM 6 shows some of the myths about mentoring relations. Highlights in HRM 7 shows how as an employee, you can take the initiative to form a relationship with a mentor, even if your firm doesn't have a formal mentoring program.

Not surprisingly, mentoring and networking are being done electronically. "A lot of our people work virtually, and [electronic] mentoring can erase geographic and business-unit borders," explained one IBM manager.[47] At Rockwell Collins, a communication and aviation electronics company, nearly 6,000 employees utilize an e-mentoring

6 Highlights in HRM

Myths about Mentors

- *Mentors exist only for career development.* Sometimes the mentor focuses on formal career development. Sometimes the mentor is teacher, counselor, and friend.
- *You need only one mentor.* We can have multiple mentors in our lives. Different mentors provide different things.
- *Mentoring is a one-way process.* Learning flows both ways. The mentor often learns from the protégé, so the growth is reciprocal.
- *A mentor has to be older than the protégé.* Age does not matter. Experience and wisdom matter.
- *A mentor has to be the same gender and race as the protégé.* Seek mentors who are different from you.
- *Mentor relationships just happen.* Being in the right place at the right time can help, but don't be afraid to actively seek a mentor.
- *High-profile people make the best mentors.* Prestige and success can help, but good mentors are people who challenge you according to your needs, readiness, and aspirations.
- *Once a mentor, always a mentor.* Over time, the mentor should let the protégé go their own way but maintain contact. The relationship changes over time.

software solution. The software can connect to a firm's existing talent management software, gauge competency gaps, and match mentors and mentees based upon their knowledge and learning needs.[48]

Tuition Assistance Programs

Large corporations often offer their employees tuition assistance to help them further their careers if they take courses related to the firms' businesses. For example, managers or would-be managers might be reimbursed for taking postgraduate classes such as MBA courses or other courses related to their professional development. The terms of the programs vary, as do the amounts employees are reimbursed annually. Sometimes the amount of reimbursement depends on the grade an employee earns in class. Companies often require employees who are reimbursed for courses to remain with their firms for a certain amount of time after completing the courses.

Career Plateau Initiatives

Career plateaus are common obstacles in the career development of employees. A **career plateau** is a situation in which, for either organizational or personal reasons, the probability of moving up the career ladder is low. Three types of plateaus are possible: structural, content, and life. A *structural plateau* marks the end of promotions. A *content plateau* occurs when a person has learned a job too well and is bored with day-to-day activities. A *life plateau* is more profound and may feel like a midlife crisis. People who experience life plateaus often have allowed work or some other major factor to become the most significant aspect of their lives, and they experience a loss of identity and self-esteem when they are no longer advancing in their careers. Figure 5.12 lists some probing questions managers can ask themselves if they think their employees are experiencing a career plateau.

career plateau
A situation in which for either organizational or personal reasons the probability of moving up the career ladder is low.

Organizations can help individuals cope with plateaus by providing them with opportunities for lateral growth or allowing them to choose their own assignments when

Highlights in HRM

Establishing a Relationship with a Mentor

1. *Research the person's background.* The more you know about your potential mentor, the easier it will be to approach that person and establish a relationship that will work for both of you.
2. *Make contact with the person.* Introduce yourself or have a mutual friend or acquaintance do it. Alternately, get involved with your potential mentor in business settings. That will help the mentor see your skills in action.
3. *Request help on a particular matter.* Let the mentor know that you admire them, and ask for help in that arena. For example, you might say, "You're good at dealing with customers. Would it be okay if I came to you for advice on my customers from time to time?"
4. *Consider what you can offer in exchange.* Mentoring is a two-way street. If you can do something for your potential mentor, then, by all means, tell them.
5. *Arrange a meeting.* Prepare a list of questions for the meeting. Listen closely.
6. *Follow up.* Try some of your potential mentor's suggestions and share the results.
7. *Ask to meet on an ongoing basis.* Express appreciation and suggest that you meet with your mentor regularly, or ask permission to get help on an ad hoc basis.

Sources: Mattia Martin and Dario Cavenago, *International Journal of Training & Development* 21, no. 1 (2017), 18–34; Jeff Barbian, "The Road Best Traveled," *Training* 39, no. 5 (2002): 38–42; Kathleen Barton, "Will You Mentor Me?" *Training and Development* 56, no. 5 (2002): 90–92.

sabbatical
An extended period of time in which an employee leaves an organization to pursue other activities and later returns to their job.

opportunities for advancement do not exist. Companies with international divisions can encourage employees to take assignments abroad to expand their horizons, lead philanthropic and volunteer activities for their firms, or take sabbaticals. A **sabbatical** is an extended period of time during which an employee leaves an organization to pursue other activities before returning to the firm. A sabbatical can help prevent employee burnout and increase a person's loyalty to a company. Some, but not all, sabbaticals are paid. Approximately 20 percent of the companies on *Fortune*'s "100 Best Companies to Work For" list offer paid sabbaticals. Some smaller companies do, too. The convenience-store chain QuickTrip does for employees with 20 years of service.[49] That might sound like a long time to wait, but due its great employment practices, many QuickTrip employees end up working for the firm for decades.

Figure 5.12 Career Plateau Questions

"No" answers may indicate an employee is facing a career plateau.
1. Does the employee accept high-visibility assignments?
2. Has the employee continued to advance their education, both formal and vocational?
3. Is the employee recognized by leaders in the organization, routinely promoted, and rewarded?
4. Does the employee get high performance ratings and larger-than-normal raises?
5. Does the employee have a career plan with measurable objectives that has been updated recently?

Source: John Rosche, "Who's Managing Your Career?" *Contract Management* 44, no. 2 (2004): 20–22.

5.5 Developing a Diverse and Inclusive Talent Pool

LO5
What barriers to career advancement do women and minorities face?

As an employer, would you like to hire people who are extremely loyal to your firm and likely to remain with it? Are there groups of employees you might have overlooked but who could help you grow your business? Firms look to diverse talent not only for these reasons but also to meet their legal obligations to provide equal employment opportunities. Employers often develop formal equal employment opportunity (EEO)/ affirmative action policies to recruit and promote members of protected classes so that their representation at all levels within the organization approximates their proportionate numbers in the labor market.

However, the reasons to develop a diverse talent pool go far beyond merely legal obligation. Today, underrepresented ethnic groups account for approximately 30 percent of the total U.S. population. In 2060, they are expected to make 60 percent of the population. These groups have a growing amount of buying power. Some researchers predict that companies that fail to diversify their talent pools will have a hard time identifying with their target customers and competing with firms that do. Perhaps most importantly, as companies face tougher competition in the United States and abroad, they need all the leadership, productivity, innovation, and creativity the talent pool has to offer. A diverse talent pool increases the range of human capital available to the firm.

5.5a Women

Women make up a little less than half of the total U.S. labor force and are the largest of the legally protected classes. A major employment obstacle for women, both skilled and unskilled, is the stereotyped thinking that persists within our society. Women traditionally have been at a disadvantage because they have not been part of the "good old boys' network." That network comprises an informal web of interpersonal relationships that has traditionally provided a way for senior (male) members of the organization to pass along news of advancement opportunities and other career tips to junior (male) members as well as to recommend them.

In the past, women were not as likely as men to have professional training and preparation for entrance or advancement into management positions. But that's not the case today. Now, three of every five U.S. college graduates are women, and according to the U.S. Census Bureau, more women hold bachelor's degrees than do men. Women also hold 51.5 percent of management, professional, and related positions. At IBM, scores of women run $100-million-plus divisions.

Even so, the entire picture is not necessarily a rosy one. Women still make less than men, on average, and sometimes feel as if the workplace is a "man's world." In addition, the proportion of women in the top echelons of management, although growing, remains extremely low.[50] In 2020, only 39 of the companies in the *Fortune* 500 were run by women—though that is 36 more than there were in 2000. Although these data suggest that there has been some progress, there is much left to do to break the "glass ceiling."

Eliminating Women's Barriers to Advancement

Glass ceiling audits are conducted by the U.S. Department of Labor to identify practices that appear to hinder the upward mobility of both qualified women and members of underrepresented groups. As the name suggests, a "glass ceiling" is an invisible barrier

Mary Barra broke through many barriers on her way to becoming the CEO of General Motors.

Pete Marovich/Bloomberg/Getty Images

that keeps women from moving higher in the organization. Black women, in particular, are at risk of not being promoted relative to other groups, say labor economists.

Organizations are increasingly conducting their own glass ceiling audits prior to government review to avoid fines and externally imposed corrective actions. These audits can document any ceilings and the reasons they exist. Self-audits are one step toward tapping the potential of a diversified workforce. Following the largest class-action suit ever brought in the United States, Walmart began conducting self-audits. The company now has certain promotion goals for women and other underrepresented groups. For example, if 40 percent of the qualified people who apply for assistant store manager positions are women, 40 percent of those hired should be women. JCPenney created advisory teams to help increase the number of members of underrepresented groups at the senior management level and to find ways to make the company's affirmative action plan more effective. Each team is composed of 16 to 18 management associates. Firms are establishing professional groups within their organizations to help members of underrepresented groups connect with one another and combat their difficulty in advancing in organizations. At BNSF Railway, a women's network serves as a system for encouraging and fostering women's career development and for sharing information, experiences, and insights. Women in lower levels of the company are mentored by women at higher levels. Corporate officers are invited to regularly scheduled network meetings to discuss such matters as planning, development, and company performance.

People from underrepresented groups are also breaking through the glass ceiling by starting their own businesses. As one entrepreneur put it, "It's not hard to break through the glass ceiling when you own it."

Accommodating Families

One of the major problems women have faced is balancing their careers with their families. After the grip of the COVID-19 pandemic slackened, working mothers came back to work at a slower rate than other women, and significantly more slowly than men returned to the workforce. This is particularly true of single mothers, who are a growing segment of the population. Women with young children often experience conflict between their responsibility to the children and their duty to the employer. If the conflict becomes too painful, they may decide to forgo their careers, at least temporarily, and leave their jobs.

In recent years, many employers, including AFLAC, SunTrust Banks, Quaker Oats Company, Abbott Labs, Bristol-Myers Squibb, IBM, and the accounting firm KPMG, have launched family-friendly programs that are designed to be mutually advantageous to the career-oriented woman and the employer. The programs, which include alternative career paths, extended leave, flextime, job sharing, and telecommuting, provide new ways to balance career and family. AFLAC offers families hot take-home meals at its onsite cafeterias to ease the burden that employees face in having to prepare dinner after leaving the office for the day. The company also subsidizes babysitting for parents on Saturday nights so they can spend some free time together.[51] These efforts are paying off. Both IBM and KPMG, for example, report that their programs have helped them retain and increase their numbers of women workers.

Retaining employees who are part of dual-career couples can also be a challenge, especially if an employee needs to be relocated or travel extensively. To help make the transition easier, some organizations now offer job-finding assistance for spouses of employees who are relocated, including payment of fees charged by employment agencies, job counseling firms, and executive search firms.

Organizations are also developing networking relationships with other employers to find jobs for the spouses and partners of their relocating employees. These networks can provide a way to "share the wealth and talent" in a community while simultaneously assisting in the recruitment efforts of the participating organizations.[52]

Relocating dual-career couples to foreign facilities is a major issue that international employers face. Fewer employees are willing to relocate without assistance for their spouses. Many employers have developed effective approaches for integrating the various allowances typically paid for overseas assignments when two partners work for the same employer. Far more complex are the problems that arise when couples work for two different employers. The problems associated with overseas assignments of dual-career couples are examined in greater detail in Chapter 15.

5.5b Minorities

Since the passage of the Civil Rights Act of 1964, many members of underrepresented groups have substantially improved their economic well-being. However, for many members of these groups, employment opportunities remain limited because of educational and societal disadvantages. The unemployment rates for underrepresented youths are particularly high.

Diversity Employers is an online job board geared toward underrepresented-group jobseekers and companies that want to hire them. Facebook and LinkedIn have functions that allow recruiters to create targeted advertising campaigns designed to reach underrepresented groups. Community action agencies, civil rights organizations, and church groups within communities can help recruiters reach inner-city residents.

Internships are another way in which organizations are building relationships with prospective employees from underrepresented groups. *The Chicago Tribune* offers a newsroom training program for aspiring journalists from these groups who want to work as news reporters. ABC, NBC, CBS, and Fox networks work with the Emma L. Bowen Foundation to provide internships, college scholarships, and postgraduate employment for underrepresented groups. The defense contractor Lockheed Martin teamed up with Operation Enterprise, the American Management Association's summer program for high school and college students, to offer 10-week paid internships to students from America's historically Black colleges and universities.[53]

Larger firms often have networks, or groups, that members of underrepresented groups can join to help them advance their careers, akin to the women's networks frequently found in such organizations. General Electric's African-American Forum (AAF) began informally but has grown into a major initiative.[54] The company also has forum networks for employees who are Asian and Pacific Americans, women, Latinx, and the LGBTQ+ community. Highlights in HRM 8 shows how to design a tailored approach to diversity and inclusion planning.

5.5c People Who Are Disabled

If someone told HR managers where they could find millions of working-age people who are proven problem solvers, provide a tax benefit for their companies, and have higher retention rates than average employees, they likely would ask: "What's the catch?" Not only is there no catch, but such a group of potential employees already exists: individuals with disabilities.[55]

According to the U.S. Census Bureau, more than 50 million Americans of working age have a disability. Currently, about 18 percent of working-age people with a disability are unemployed, according to the Bureau of Labor Statistics.[56] Of those who do not work, most would like to. They often aren't working because employers mistakenly believe there are no jobs they might be able to do.

The Job Accommodation Network (JAN), sponsored by the U.S. Department of Labor, is a site that connects jobseekers who have disabilities with potential employers. JAN also provides information about how to accommodate different types of disabilities in the workplace. According to data from the U.S. Department of Labor's Office of Disability Employment, 15 percent of accommodations cost nothing; 51 percent cost between \$1 and \$500; 12 percent cost between \$501 and \$1,000; and 22 percent cost more than \$1,000.[57] Many managers are unaware of how low cost most accommodations can be overall.

IBM hired its first employee with a disability in 1914. This is not surprising, since the company makes software and other products that help eliminate workplace barriers for individuals with disabilities. IBM's viewpoint is that no employee should be overlooked because of a disability, because that person might potentially develop the next generation of hardware or software from which the company will profit. Several of the company's researchers have a hearing impairment; they are responsible for world-class work with innovations such as voice recognition technology.

IBM also participates in mentoring and internships for people with disabilities. The Workforce Recruitment Program for College Students with Disabilities (WRP) is one internship organization. WRP puts together profiles of thousands of college students and recent graduates seeking summer internships or permanent employment nationwide with federal agencies. These profiles are then made available free of charge to business owners. Similarly, the American Association for the Advancement of Science has a program called Entry Point, which has placed hundreds of science and engineering students with disabilities in internships in the public and private sectors.

5.5d Veterans

Approximately 200,000 trained and work-ready veterans transition out of the U.S. military each year. That is a big number, and it represents a significant talent pool. The trick for employers is to figure out how best to use this talent. Perhaps surprisingly, there is

Tips for Enhancing a Firm's Diversity

- Ascertain whether diversity is adequately represented in the firm's workforce by comparing company data to the statistics on diversity within the general workforce in the region. Diversity data within a firm should be broken down and measured across various specific categories, such as management, customer service, accounting, and so forth.
- Clearly define the goals of the diversity recruitment and retention program, and ensure managers at all levels understand its significance and support its motives.
- Understand the demographic changes in the workforce.
- Build long-term relationships with organizations for underrepresented groups, colleges, and other strategic resources.
- Become the employer of choice for an inclusive workforce by developing a diversity-friendly corporate culture and fostering a culturally sensitive work environment. Showcase this with a diversity and inclusion statement on your social media pages and your website. Include diversity statistics and photos, and testimonial videos that show the breadth of inclusion across all levels of your organization.
- Establish a presence among underrepresented groups by participating in job fairs, targeting recruitment advertising to publications such as Diversity Inc., and monitoring websites where a diverse range of candidates are likely to be found.
- Use internal employee resource groups. Demonstrate the organization's commitment to diversity and inclusion by making it a formal part of the employee referral program.
- Train hiring managers to ensure no applicant is discounted in the interviewing process because they are different.
- Measure the efficacy of these recruitment efforts, and use the results to improve the program.

Sources: Condensed from Patricia Digh, "Getting People in the Pool: Diversity Recruitment That Works," *HR Magazine* 44, no. 10 (1999): 94–98; Sungjoo Choi, "Workforce Diversity and Job Satisfaction of the Majority and the Minority," *Review of Public Personnel Administration* 37, no. 1 (2017): 84–107; John Sullivan and Sally Baack, "Diversity Recruiting Is a Failure: It's Time to Raise the Bar," http://www.multiculturaladvantage.com; Aaron Green, "Diversity Recruiting: Getting It Right," http://www.boston.com.

a gap between companies' intentions to hire veterans and their actual track records of doing so. Research by SHRM suggests that much of the general public is unaware of how skilled, trained, and educated modern military service members are. A study by the Center for New American Security found that 68 percent of employers reported that veterans perform "better than or much better than" regular employees do. A study by the Call of Duty Endowment and ZipRecruiter found that veterans also stay on the job longer than regular employees do.

Even so, nearly one-third of veteran job seekers are underemployed. The Department of Labor has an agency, VETS, tasked with boost veteran hiring efforts. The mission of VETS is to enable veterans to reach their full potential in the workplace. To achieve this mission, the agency is seeking to improve transition programs, promote apprenticeships, and leverage benevolent organizations designed to help veterans transition out of the military. The federal government requires firms that do business with it to hire a certain percentage of workers who are veterans.

But firms aren't recruiting military personnel just because they do business with the government and have to, but because it's good business. AT&T, Boeing, Starbucks, Amazon, Capital One, and Lowe's are among the many companies that have found veterans to be a valuable source of job candidates. Employers say veterans have a good work ethic, are disciplined, follow the chain of command, and make good decisions in different situations, such as mission types of operations. According to a study by CareerBuilder.com, 65 percent of employers said that, given the choice between two equally qualified applicants, they are more likely to hire the veteran.[58]

Numerous websites are dedicated to recruiting veterans, including Veterans.gov, Hireourheros.org, and Recruitmilitary.com. These organizations hold virtual job fairs, which can help vets apply for jobs while they are still enlisted, if they are disabled, or if they are otherwise unable to travel to a regular job fair. Contacting and forming a relationship with a military base is another way. Most military bases have career centers for people leaving the military. These are often the first place military personnel turn to when they are transitioning into civilian lives. The U.S. Department of Labor's VETS program, mentioned earlier, is another good source. VETS has local veterans' employment representatives across the country dedicated to increasing the employment of former military members.[59]

5.5e Older Employees

Many people continue to work after they reach age 65—a trend that is likely to become more pronounced as more baby-boomers reach retirement age. Conversely, the COVID-19 pandemic led many older workers to retire early.[60] These trends are shaped by changing workforce demographics, rising health care costs, and baby-boomers spending down their retirement savings.

Why should a company hire older workers? For one thing, such individuals have proven employment experience, are reliable, and are more likely to remain with a firm than job hop. They are also an excellent recruitment source to staff part-time and full-time positions that are otherwise hard to fill. Independent contracting or consulting, on-call work (such as substitute nursing or teaching), and temporary work in administrative or IT roles are examples. Some retirees return to or stay in the workforce at

During annual meetings of shareholders in 2017, Starbucks announced a new goal to hire 25,000 veterans by 2025.

Stephen Brashear/Getty Images News/Getty Images

the request of their employers, who cannot afford to lose the knowledge accumulated by longtime employees or their reliable work habits that have a positive effect on the entire work group.

But even though age discrimination (or "ageism") is illegal, it is still a problem. Managers may wonder whether older employees are adaptable enough to learn new processes and technologies. Younger workers are more likely to get interviews than older people, studies have shown. To counter problems such as these, the AARP, an advocacy group for retired people, offers virtual job fairs and online videos to help its members assess, brush up on, and learn new tech skills. This organization also partners with firms that recruit older workers and offer them flexible work schedules and health benefits. General Mills, Kimberly Clark, Dominion Resources, and Pfizer are featured on the AARP site. The AARP will even pay an older worker's wages and workers' compensation costs as part of a "try before you hire" program it has with companies. After a trial period of working for a company, the firm can decide whether it wants to commit to hiring the worker.

Summary

LO 1 The decisions a company makes about talent need to be considered within the context of the business's strategies: which types of positions are needed; where the talent is needed and where can it be found; the strength of the firm's employment "brand"; how the talent can be attracted; and who will recruit the talent and make the final hiring decision. Which internal and external sources and methods are used in recruiting will depend on the strategy and goals of the organization, conditions of the labor market, and specifications of the jobs to be filled.

LO 2 Outside candidates are recruited when internal talent is lacking or a firm wants to hire employees with expertise from other organizations for competitive reasons and to prevent the inbreeding of ideas within their organization. To help meet their EEO requirements and diversify their talent pools, firms also look externally for candidates. Advertisements, the Internet, social networks, mobile recruiting, employment agencies, tapping educational institutions and professional associations, and re-recruiting are among the many ways firms recruit external candidates.

Employers usually find it advantageous to use internal promotions and transfers to fill as many openings as possible above the entry level. Doing so is faster, less expensive, and more likely to result in a successful hire. It also builds loyalty among workers. Internal job postings, performance appraisals, skills inventories, and replacement charts are ways in which firms identify internal talent.

LO 3 HR managers have many tools available to them to gauge their efforts and improve their recruiting. Using realistic job reviews, surveying managers and applicants about the process, and examining metrics such as the cost per hire, time to fill a position, yield ratios, and acceptance rates are some of the ways in which firms evaluate their recruiting efforts. An applicant tracking system (ATS) can help a firm automatically track and calculate many of these statistics. The flipside of recruiting is retaining employees. Pay and benefits are important, but nonmonetary aspects, such as the support of their supervisor and the ability to further their career in an organization, can ultimately lead to employees' retention.

LO 4 Identifying and developing talent is a responsibility of all managers. A career development program is a dynamic process that should integrate the career goals of employees with the goals of the organization. Job opportunities can be identified by studying jobs and determining the knowledge and skills each requires. Once that is accomplished, key jobs can be identified and job progressions can be planned. These progressions can then serve as a basis for developing the career paths of employees. Employees need to be made aware of the organization's philosophy and its goals; otherwise, they will not know whether their goals match those of the organization. Firms can "grow" their internal talent by offering employees different career paths and programs, counseling them about their careers, establishing mentoring and tuition assistance programs, and helping them overcome career plateaus.

LO 5 The first step toward facilitating the career development of women and underrepresented groups is to eliminate barriers to their advancement. Creating professional networks, providing these employees with managerial training and mentors, and accommodating families have been found to be effective ways to facilitate more effective career development.

A diversified workforce is composed of many different groups. To capture the advantages of a diverse and inclusive workforce, many organizations have special programs such as internships that provide hands-on experience as well as special training opportunities to develop and celebrate people in underrepresented groups.

Key Terms

acceptance rate
applicant tracking system (ATS)
branding
career paths
career plateau
demotion
employee leasing
employee profiles
independent contractors
internal labor markets
job progressions
mentors
mobile recruiting
nepotism
nine-box grid
outplacement services
passive jobseekers
promotion
quality of fill
realistic job preview (RJP)
recruitment process outsourcing (RPO)
re-recruiting
reverse mentoring
sabbatical
time to fill
transfer
virtual job fair
yield ratio

Discussion Questions

LO 1 Name some companies with whom you have done business. Then discuss how you view their employer brands. Would you want to work for them? How might these firms improve their employer brands?

LO 2 Think of a new type of business you would like to start up or manage. Which sources would you use to recruit employees who could help you make it a success?

LO 3 Explain how realistic job previews (RJPs) operate. As a manager or business owner, would you use them?

LO 4 How can a career management program help an organization forced to downsize its operations?

LO 5 What barriers to career advancement do women and members of underrepresented groups face?

HRM Experience

Career Management

Do successful people plan their careers in advance and then work toward their goals in a logical and sequential way? Or does a career occur as a result of a person's preparedness, insight, and taking advantages of opportunities as they arise?

Assignment

1. Form teams of four to six members. Identify three different people to interview about their careers. One person should be in the early stages of their career, one should be in midcareer, and one should be in the final stages of their career.
2. Ask each person to identify their career goals and how they have changed or are expected to change over time.
3. Ask each person to describe the sequence of events that led to where they are.
4. Ask each person what (if anything) they would do differently. Ask what advice they have for you about how to approach your career.

CASE STUDY 1 A Life-Cycle Approach to Talent

To build a workforce that can respond to the health care industry's rapid transformation, Scripps Health, in San Diego, accommodates the needs of employees at the beginning, middle, and later stages in their careers. The result is higher morale and impeccable performance. "One-size-fits-all HR practices don't work when you want a diverse, knowledge-based workforce," says Victor Buzachero, corporate senior vice president for innovation, human resources, and performance management. "Originally many HR practices were designed primarily to be consistent and to avoid legal issues. Today our focus is on HR practices that engage people and encourage a higher contribution."

For example, Scripps has implemented daily "huddles," where workers can offer input and affect decisions—something especially prized by Millennial employees. "In the past workers wanted a supervisor who acted like a 'boss.'" Buzachero say, "Today they want a supervisor who acts like a coach, and we're educating our supervisors to be strong coaches."

In one program, seasoned nurses are trained to mentor recent nursing graduates to improve their critical-thinking skills; as a result, the graduates indicate they feel more prepared for their roles as nurses. Scripps currently offers more than 1,870 skills-building, leadership training, and continuing education units.

Scripps also encourages movement across the organization to remain a career destination for talent at the mid-career stage. For example, workers in medical–surgical units can receive 26 weeks of training to shift into areas where skilled workers are in short supply, such as operating rooms.

Traditional retirement packages that max out at age 60 can encourage these experienced workers to leave, even if they want to continue working. Scripps lets retirement plans continue to grow past age 65, while supporting staged retirement programs such as job sharing. "One of our most successful clinical nursing units is managed by two women who job share," Buzachero says. "If we didn't offer that kind of flexibility, they may have gone somewhere else."

This life-cycle approach creates a diverse workforce able to address the health care industry's mandate to improve outcomes while cutting costs. "As patients ask for more and more from us, we need a workforce with all-encompassing view and innovative approach," Buzachero says. "But we can only build a highly skilled, varied workforce if we satisfy the many career needs of a varied workforce."

Questions

1. In what ways does the Scripps life-cycle approach lead to a more diverse workforce?
2. Why are managers increasingly being encouraged to act as coaches? Do you see any problems with a manager acting as both a coach and a supervisor?

Source: Scripps Health.

CASE STUDY 2 Homegrown Talent: Mary Barra Rises to GM's Top Post

When Mary Barra was a kid, she used to hang out in the garage with her dad, tinkering on cars. Little did her father, a lifelong die-maker for GM's Pontiac division, know that his daughter would one day become the CEO of the company and the first woman ever to lead a major U.S. car manufacturer. But that's what happened in 2013. Barra was unanimously chosen by the board members of General Motors to lead the company—a decision employees cheered when they heard the news over the loudspeakers at corporate headquarters. Maybe they cheered because unlike GM's previous two CEOs, Barra was one of them. Having worked in multiple departments at GM since she was 18, she knows the car business through and through. "There's nobody with more years of honest 'car guy' credentials than she has," says Ross Gordon in the Ross School of Business at the University of Michigan.

Barra, who grew up in a Detroit suburb, initially began working for GM in the 1980s as part of a work-study program. In this program, which is also referred to as a co-op program, students alternate working full-time (for pay) and going to college. Barra earned an undergraduate degree in electrical engineering, and GM later sent her to Stanford University, where she got an MBA. During her career, she has rotated through various positions at GM. Besides working in engineering and design, she managed one GM's manufacturing plants and most recently was the senior vice president for global product development and quality control. Under her watch, the company has rolled out successful models that have helped bring the company back from its bankruptcy during the latest economic recession.

Barra has a reputation for getting results. When she took the CEO job in early 2014, she inherited a company that for decades was both large and unwieldy, so much so that executives sometimes didn't know whether parts of the business were making or losing money. She trimmed excess operations to create a more agile organization, improving profitability along the way. Today, Barra is adamant that GM can still grow, but in a different way than in the past—that is, through new businesses built on electric and driverless cars. These are big transformational bets, and Barra is a courageous leader.

Sue Meisinger, formerly the president and CEO of the Society of Human Resources Management, says that Barra's being named CEO underscores the importance of HR personnel working in and understanding different areas of their firms. "If you're interested in a career path that extends beyond HR, you need to have experience in multiple facets of the business," Meisinger says. She notes that for many HR professionals, their crowning achievement is to be the head of HR. Barra's rise to CEO, however, will have many of these professionals shifting their career goals.

Questions

1. Mary Barra's father worked at General Motors. Was her hiring an example of nepotism? If you were a business owner, would you want to hire relatives of your employees? What are the pros and cons of doing so be?
2. What role did Barra play in advancing her career? What role did GM play in "growing" her career?

Sources: Mike Colias, "The Incredible Shrinking GM: Mary Barra Bets That Smaller Is Better," *Wall Street Journal*, September 28, 2020; Tom Beaman, "CEO Mary Barra Revs Things up at General Motors," *Costco Connection* 32, no 4 (2017): 45; Dee Ann Durbin and Tom Krisher, "Barra Inherits a Stronger GM," Associated Press (December 29, 2013), http://www.ap.org; Dee Ann Durbin and Tom Krisher, "GM Picks Woman CEO," Associated Press (December 29, 2013), http://www.ap.org; Chris Woodyard, "Who Is Mary Barra, the Next CEO of GM?" *USA Today* (December 10, 2013), http://www.usatoday.com; Mary Pyrillis, "Mary Barra, General Motors' Next CEO Breaks Ground for Women and HR," *Workforce* (December 11, 2013), http://www.workforce.com.

Notes and References

1. Sam Acuna and Shannon Mullen O'Keefe, "Leaders, Take Control of Your Employment Brand," *Gallup Workplace*, August 25, 2020; R. Bruab and David G. Allen, "Third Party Employment Branding: Human Capital Inflows and Outflows following 'Best Places to Work' Certifications," *Academy of Management Journal* 59, no. 1 (2016): 90–112. For more information about Glassdoor employment branding, see https://www.glassdoor.com/employers/solutions/employer-branding/.

2. Blake Landua, "The Uncontained Culture of the Container Store," *Human Resources IQ* (March 6, 2008), http://www.humanresources.iqu.com.
3. Sarah E. Needleman, "Play This Game and Win a Job," *Wall Street Journal* (March 14, 2016): R2.
4. Damali Curry Edwards, "People and Technology: A Winning Recruiting Combination," *Career Planning and Adult Development Journal* 32 no. 3 (2016): 45; Edward P. Lazear and Paul Oyer, *Internal and External Labor Markets: A Personnel Economics Approach* [Working paper], (National Bureau of Economic Research, 2003), http://www.nber.org/papers/w10192.
5. Chip Cutter and Patrick Thomas, "Looking for a Job? Big Tech Is Still Hiring," *Wall Street Journal*, April 14, 2020; Daisuke Wakabayashi and Mike Ramsey, "Apple Gears up to Challenge Tesla in Electric Cars," *Wall Street Journal*, February 13, 2015; Debbie Mack, "P&G Fights to Protect Its Bounty," *Corporate Legal Times* 13, no. 135 (2003): 64; Alexandria Sage, "Tesla Sues Ex-Autopilot Head over Recruiting," *Reuters* (January 27, 2017), http://reuters.com.
6. Jeff Tanner and Mary Anne Raymond, *Principles of Marketing* (Washington, DC: FlatWorld Knowledge, 2016): 79.
7. Kazim Ladimeji, "Five Ways to Significantly Increase Recruiting Effectiveness," *Recruiter* (September 28, 2012), https://www.recruiter.com.
8. "HR Q&Qs: Should an Employer Accept Applications and Resumes When It Has No Open Positions?" Society for Human Resource Management, https://www.shrm.org/resourcesandtools/tools-and-samples/hr-qa/pages/whatstheprosandconsofacceptingresumeswhenanemployer-hasnopositionsopen.aspx.
9. "25 Online Recruiting Tools and Strategies Making It Cheaper and Faster to Recruit," *GlassDoor for Employers*, August 30, 2019; Henry S. Faber, Dan Silverman, and Till Von Wachter, "Determinants of Callbacks to Job Applications: An Audit Study," *American Economic Review* 106 no. 5 (2016): 314–318; Douglas P. Shuit, "Monster Board Games," *Workforce Management* 82, no. 2 (2003): 37–42; Joe Dysart, "New Directions in Internet Recruiting," *Contractor Magazine* 53, no. 7 (2006): 33–36.
10. Roy Maurer, "Niche Job Boards Muscle into Recruiting Marketplace," Society for Human Resource Management (February 24, 2017), https://www.shrm.org.
11. Allan Schweyer, "Robots in Recruiting: The Implications of AI on Talent Acquisition," Webinar, 2017, http://info.appcast.io.
12. Mike Vangel, "Social Recruitment Delivers Results for UPS," *Talent Management* (August 13, 2013), http://www.talentmgt.com.
13. "Five Popular Recruitment Sources Used by Employers," ERC, June 16, 2015; John E. Dunn, "Facebook's New Job Service Sparks Privacy Fears," *Naked Security* (February 20, 2017), https://nakedsecurity.sophos.com.
14. "Five Popular Recruitment Sources Used by Employers," ERC; Monica Anderson and Andrew Perri, "13% of Americans Don't Use the Internet. Who Are They?" Pew Research (September 7, 2016); http://www.pewresearch.org.
15. Emily Glazer, "Virtual Fairs Offer Real Jobs," *Wall Street Journal* (October 31, 2011): B9.
16. J. R. Pieper, J. M. Greenwald, and S. D. Schlachter, "Motivating Employee Referrals: The Interactive Effects of the Referral Bonus, Perceived Risk in Referring, and Affective Commitment," *Human Resource Management* 57, no. 5 (2017): 1159–1174; Kazim Ladimeji, "Five Ways to Significantly Increase Recruiting Effectiveness," *Recruiter* (September 28, 2012), https://www.recruiter.com.
17. Stephen V. Burks et al., "The Value of Hiring through Employee Referrals," *Quarterly Journal of Economics* (2015): qjv010; Jennifer Salopek, "Employee Referrals Remain a Recruiter's Best Friend," *Workforce Management* (December 2010), http://www.workforce.com.
18. Sara Stockman and Greet Van Hoye, "Rewarding Employee Referrals: Effects on Organizational Attractiveness," 9th Dutch HRM Network Conference, 2016; Jennifer Taylor Arnold, "Employee Referrals at a Keystroke," *HRMagazine* 51, no. 10 (October 2006): 82–88; Victoria Furnes, "The New Frontier," *Personnel Today* (January 22, 2008): 13–16.
19. Greg Patrick Haudek, "A Longitudinal Test of the Attraction–Selection–Attrition Model," Paper AAI3010091, *ETD Collection for Wayne State University* (January 1, 2001), http://digitalcommons.wayne.edu.
20. Joshua Brustein, "Plantir Case Draws Attention to Discriminatory Potential of Referral Programs," *Bloomberg* (September 28, 2017), https://www.bloomberg.com.
21. S. Firfiray, C. Cruz, I. Neacsu, and L. R. Gomez-Mejia, "Is Nepotism So Bad for Family Firms? A Socioemotional Wealth Approach," *Human Resource Management Review* 28, no. 1 (2018): 83–97; Joanne B. Ciulla, "In Praise of Nepotism?" *Business Ethics Quarterly* 15, no. 1 (2005): 153–161; Richard Reeve and Gavin Sheridan, "Nepotism: Is It Back?" *New Statesman* 135 (September 29, 2003): 22–25.
22. Abbie J Shipp et al., "Gone Today But Here Tomorrow: Extending the Unfolding Model of Turnover to Consider Boomerang Employees," *Personnel Psychology* 67, no. 2 (2014): 421–462; Melissa Korn, "Boomerang Employees," *Wall Street Journal Online* (October 24, 2011), http://wjsonline.com; Madeline Laurano, "Best Practices in Re-recruiting Top Talent," Bersin & Associates [Blog], (August 6, 2009), http://www.bersin.com.
23. Rachel Feintzeig, "CEOs Head Back to School," *Wall Street Journal* (February 2, 2017): B4.
24. Paul Benjamin Lowry and David Wilson, "Creating Agile Organizations through IT," *Journal of Strategic Information Systems* 25 no. 3 (2016): 211–226; Ed Frauenheim, "Companies Focus Their Attention on Flexibility," *Workforce Management* (February 2011): 3–4.

25. Chris Pentilla, "Got It Covered: If You Can't Afford to Offer Employee Benefits on Your Own, Why Not Join Forces with a PEO?" *Entrepreneur* 32, no. 2 (2004): 66–68; Bill Leonard, "Small Firms Prepare for Aging Workforce," *HR Magazine* 53, no. 5 (May 2008): 32.
26. Robert Rodriguez, "Filling the HR Pipeline," *HR Magazine* 49, no. 9 (2004): 78–84; James W. Walker, "Perspectives," *Human Resource Planning* 25, no. 1 (2002): 12–14.
27. "Heading for the Fast Track: New Studies Examine Who Gets Promoted and Why," *Knowledge@Wharton* (August 10, 2005), http://www.knowledge.wharton.upenn.edu.
28. Matthew Bidwell, "Paying More to Get Less: Specific Skills, Matching, and the Effects of External Hiring versus Internal Promotion," *Administrative Science Quarterly* (2011): 369–407.
29. Pamela Tate, "Calling on Career Development," *Talent Management* (January 7, 2014), http://www.talentmgt.com.
30. Pandey Smita and Mishra Sarika, "Analysis of the Pros and Cons of Online Recruitment Methods in India," *International Journal of Engineering and Management Sciences* 6, no. 2 (2015): 65–67; "The Pros and Cons of Online Recruiting," *HR Focus* 81 (April 2004): S2.
31. D. J. Schepker, A. J. Nyberg, M. D. Ulrich, and P. M. Wright, "Planning for Future Leadership: Procedural Rationality, Formalized Succession Processes, and CEO Influence in CEO Succession Planning," *Academy of Management Journal* (April 2018); <AU: Please give volume/page numbers> Bidwell <AU: Please give Bidwell's first initials> and J. R. Keller, "Within or Without? How Firms Combine Internal and External Labor Markets to Fill Jobs," *Academy of Management Journal* 57, no. 4 (2014): 1035–1055; Stanley Ragalevsky, "CEO Succession: Five Best Practices for Internal Candidates," *Community Banker* 17, no. 2 (2008): 24–25.
32. S. A. Shibly, "Mapping the Holistic Impact of Realistic Job Preview: Pre-recruitment Phase, Post-recruitment Phase and Marketing Spillover Effect," *Journal of Organizational Psychology* 19, no. 1 (2019): 70–78; "How to Implement an Effective Process for a New HR Management System," *HR Focus* 82, no. 1 (2005): 3–4; Connie Winkler, "Job Tryouts Go Virtual," *HR Magazine* 51, no. 9 (2006): 131–134.
33. Colin Lee, "The Potential of Computer-Aided Applicant Prescreening," *RSM Discovery-Management Knowledge* 26, no. 2 (2016): 21–22; "Applicant Tracking System," *SearchCIO.com* (March 18, 2011), http://searchcio.techtarget.com.
34. Bruce Fecheyr-Lippens, Bill Schaninger, and Karen Tanner, "Power to the New People Analytics," *McKinsey Quarterly* 51, no. 1 (2015): 61–63; John Sullivan, "How Google Is Using People Analytics to Completely Reinvent HR," *TLNT* (February 26, 2013), http://www.tlnt.com.
35. R. D. Adams, "Survey: 49% of Employees Plan to Land a New Position in 2021," *TechRepublic*, March 26, 2021; Sunil Bagai, "Google Brings Machine Learning to the Staffing Industry" *B2C* (November 18, 2016), http://www.business2community.com.
36. H. Mitchell, "Study: 52% of Employees Are Looking for a New Job plus Reasons They Are Leaving," *Hospital Review*, March 30, 2021; M. Schwantes, "A New Study Reveals 70 Percent of Workers Day They Are Actively Looking for a New Job," *Inc.*, December 18, 2018; "Dale Carnegie Training Global Leadership Study: USA 2016," http://www.dalecarnegie.com.
37. Blake Landau, "The Uncontained Culture of The Container Store," *Human Resources IQ* (March 6, 2008), http://www.humanresourcesiq.com.
38. Jos Akkermans et al., "It's All about CareerSKILLS," *Human Resource Management* 54, no. 4 (2015): 533–551; Peg O'Herron and Peggy Simonsen, "Career Development Gets a Charge at Sears Credit," *Personnel Journal* 74, no. 5 (1995): 103–106; Jules Abend, "Behind the Scenes at: Sears," *Bobbin* 39, no. 11 (1998): 22–26; Shari Caudron, "The De-jobbing of America," *Industry Week* 243, no. 16 (1994): 30–36; Edward E. Lawler III, "From Job-Based to Competency-Based Organizations," *Journal of Organizational Behavior* 15, no. 1 (1994): 3–15; Douglas T. Hall, "Accelerate Executive Development—At Your Peril!" *Career Development International* 4, no. 4 (1999): 237–239.
39. Akkermans et al., "It's All about CareerSKILLS," 2015; O'Herron and Simonsen, "Career Development Gets a Charge at Sears Credit," 1995; Abend, "Behind the Scenes at: Sears," 1998; Caudron, "The De-jobbing of America," 1994; Lawler, "From Job-Based to Competency-Based Organizations," 1994; Hall, "Accelerate Executive Development—At Your Peril!" 1999.
40. Erika Fry, "An Ex-Cop Comes to the Rescue," *Fortune* (March 18, 2013): 38.
41. "Coworkers Get a Chance to Change Places," *Wall Street Journal* (February 21, 2012), http://online.wsj.com.
42. Hank Boyer, "Emerging Trends in Career Management," LinkedIn (February 2, 2016), https://www.linkedin.com.
43. Elaine Farndale et al., "Balancing Individual and Organizational Goals in Global Talent Management," *Journal of World Business* 49, no. 2 (2014): 204–214; "How a Talent Management Plan Can Anchor Your Company's Future," *HR Focus* 81, no. 10 (2004): 7–10; "Heading for the Fast Track? New Studies Examine Who Gets Promoted and Why," *Knowledge@Wharton* (August 10, 2005), http://knowledge.wharton.upenn.edu.
44. Dona Dezube, "How a Workplace Mentoring Program Can Benefit Your Company," *Tampa Bay Times* (January 18, 2017), http://www.tampabay.com.
45. Leslie Kwoh, "Reverse Mentoring Cracks Workplace," *Wall Street Journal* (November 28, 2011): B7.
46. Tory Paez, "My Friend, My Mentor: The Benefits of Peer Mentoring in the Workplace," *Catalyst* (2016); Suzanne C. de Janasz, Shery E. Sullivan, and Vicki Whiting, "Mentor Networks and Career Success: Lessons for Turbulent Times," *Academy of Management Executive* 17, no. 4 (2003): 78–92; Kate Walsh and Judith Gordon, "Creating an Individual

Work Identity," *Human Resource Management Review* 18, no. 1 (2008): 46–61.

47. Paez, "My Friend, My Mentor: The Benefits of Peer Mentoring in the Workplace," 2016; de Janasz, Sullivan, and Whiting, "Mentor Networks and Career Success," 2003; Walsh and Gordon, "Creating an Individual Work Identity," 2008.
48. Akkermans et al., "It's All about CareerSKILLS," 2015; Larry Cambron, "Career Development Pays," *Far Eastern Economic Review* 164, no. 42 (25, 2001): 83.
49. Paez, "My Friend, My Mentor: The Benefits of Peer Mentoring in the Workplace," 2016; de Janasz, Sullivan, and Whiting, "Mentor Networks and Career Success," 2003; Walsh and Gordon, "Creating an Individual Work Identity," 2008.
50. Heidi Hartmann, Jeffrey Hayes, and Jennifer Clark, *How Equal Pay for Working Women Would Reduce Poverty and Grow the American Economy*, Briefing paper IWPR# C411 (Washington, DC: Institute for Women's Policy Research, January 10, 2014); Hope Yen, "Women Gain Ground against Salary Disparity," *Fort Worth Star-Telegram* (December 11, 2103): 6A.
51. K. Riley and S. Stamm, "Nearly 1.5 Million Mothers Are Still Missing from the Workforce," *Wall Street Journal*, April 27, 2021; Eunmi Chang, Hyun Chin, and Jieun Ye, "Organizational Work–Family Culture and Working Mothers' Affective Commitment," *Human Resource Management* 53, no. 5 (2014): 683–700; Alison Stein Wellner, "Welcoming Back Mom," *HR Magazine* 49, no. 6 (2004): 76–83; "Mothers' Labor Force Participation," *Monthly Labor Review* 137, no. 5 (2004): 2; Brian Braiker and Anna Kuchment, "Just Do Not Call Me Mr. Mom," *Newsweek* 150, no. 15 (2007): 52–55; Melissa Fletcher, "Working Moms Fully in Favor of Going Part-Time," *Fort Worth Star-Telegram* (August 30, 2007): E1, E9.
52. Courtney R. Masterson and Jenny M. Hoobler, "Care and Career: A Family Identity-Based Typology of Dual-Earner Couples," *Journal of Organizational Behavior* 36, no. 1 (2015): 75–93; Janice Rosenberg, "Dual Career Couples Face Expensive Choices," Bankrate.com (July 2, 2007); Erin White, "Help Increases for Partners of Relocated Workers," *Wall Street Journal* (March 25, 2008): D4.
53. C. Cutter, "Employers Want More Diversity. They May Need to Open Offices in New Places," *Wall Street Journal*, February 21, 2021; "Why Black Workers Are Still Underrepresented in Management Roles," *Wall Street Journal*, February 24, 2021; "Recruiting Minorities," *Black Enterprise* 35, no. 6 (2005):53; Debbie Smith, "Building a New Diversity Road Map," *Multichannel News* 25, no. 38 (2004): 82.
54. TK
55. Kathleen C. Brannen and Terrence M. Begley, "The Americans with Disabilities Act: What It Means to Small Business Owners," *Journal of Small Business Strategy* 6, no. 1 (2015): 79–92; Joe Mullich, "Hiring without Limits," *Workforce Management* 83, no. 6 (2004): 53–60; Julie Hotchkiss, "Growing Part-Time Employment among Workers with Disabilities," *Economic Review* 89, no. 3 (2004): 25–42; "Entry Point Interns Top 400 in Seventh Year," *Science* 301, no. 5637 (2003): 1195; Kelly Butler, "Ten Million Ways to Fill the Talent Gap," *Employee Benefit News* 21, no. 3 (2007): 22–24.
56. "Persons with a Disability: Labor Force Characteristics Summary," U.S. Bureau of Labor Statistics (June 21, 2016), https://www.bls.gov; Sam Hananel, "New Rules Boost Hiring of Vets, Disabled," Associated Press (August 28, 2013), http://www.ap.org.
57. Nabanita Datta Gupta, Mona Larsen, and Lars Stage Thomsen, "Do Wage Subsidies for Disabled Workers Reduce Their Nonemployment?" *IZA Journal of Labor Policy* 4 no. 1 (2015): 10; "As ADA Turns 20, Harris Interactive Survey Finds Lifestyle and Economic Gaps Still Remain between Americans with and without Disabilities" [Press release], Kessler Foundation and National Organization on Disability, July 26, 2010.
58. "Veterans at Work Initiative Builds Business Case for an Untapped Talent Pool," SHRM Foundation, 2021, https://www.shrm.org/foundation/about/pages/vaw-psa-hr-article.aspx; Kimberly Curry Hall et al., "Connecting Veterans and Employers," <AU: please give publisher/URL/other source info> (2015); Jessica Miller-Merrell, "How to Recruit Veterans," *GlassDoor* (June 20, 2013), http://glassdoor.com.
59. TK
60. "Pandemic Accelerates Retirements, Threatening Economic Growth," *Wall Street Journal*, March 28, 2021; Christopher Reynolds, "Boomers, Act II," *American Demographics* 27, no. 8 (2004): 10–12; Theresa Minton Eversole, "Senate Forum Explores Ways to Keep Aging Workforce Working," *HR Magazine* 48, no. 10 (2003): 30; Carly Foster, "Rehiring Retirees among 2008's Top Recruiting Trends," *Employee Benefit News* (January 8, 2008): 5.

Appendix

Personal Career Development

Because you are likely to spend more time working during your life than doing anything else, it makes sense to plan your career. Although organizations can be a positive force in the career development process, the primary responsibility for shaping your career is yours.

A.1 Developing Personal Skills and Competencies

Planning for a career involves more than simply acquiring specific job knowledge and skills. You must also develop other skills to be successful as an employee. To succeed as a manager, you must achieve still higher-level skills in the areas of communication, time management, self-motivation, interpersonal relationships, and leadership. Highlights in HRM 9 shows the competencies candidates "must have" today to successfully embark on a career in any field.

It's never too early to start planning your career.

Sindlera/Shutterstock.com

"Must Have" Career Competencies

The following are "must have" career competencies according to the National Association of Colleges and Employers.

- *Critical thinking/problem solving.* Exercise sound reasoning to analyze issues, make decisions, and overcome problems. The individual is able to obtain, interpret, and use knowledge, facts, and data in this process, and may demonstrate originality and inventiveness.
- *Oral/written communications.* Articulate thoughts and ideas clearly and effectively in written and oral forms to persons inside and outside of the organization. The individual has public speaking skills; is able to express ideas to others; and can write/edit memos, letters, and complex technical reports clearly and effectively.
- *Teamwork/collaboration.* Build collaborative relationships with colleagues and customers representing diverse cultures, races, ages, genders, religions, lifestyles, and viewpoints. The individual is able to work within a team structure, and can negotiate and manage conflict.
- *Digital technology.* Leverage existing digital technologies ethically and efficiently to solve problems, complete tasks, and accomplish goals. The individual demonstrates effective adaptability to new and emerging technologies.
- *Leadership.* Leverage the strengths of others to achieve common goals, and use interpersonal skills to coach and develop others. The individual is able to assess and manage their emotions and those of others; use empathetic skills to guide and motivate; and organize, prioritize, and delegate work.
- *Professionalism/work ethic.* Demonstrate personal accountability and effective work habits (e.g., punctuality, working productively with others, and time workload management), and understand the impact of nonverbal communication on professional work image. The individual demonstrates integrity and ethical behavior, acts responsibly with the interests of the larger community in mind, and is able to learn from their mistakes.
- *Career management.* Identify and articulate one's skills, strengths, knowledge, and experiences relevant to the position desired and career goals, and identify areas necessary for professional growth. The individual is able to navigate and explore job options, understands and can take the steps necessary to pursue opportunities, and understands how to self-advocate for opportunities in the workplace.
- *Global/intercultural fluency.* Value, respect, and learn from diverse cultures, races, ages, genders, sexual orientations, and religions. The individual demonstrates openness, inclusiveness, sensitivity, and the ability to interact respectfully with all people and understand individuals' differences.

A.2 Choosing a Career

People often have to do a lot of searching and changing of jobs before they find a career that suits them. Counselors at colleges and universities, as well as those in private practice, can help individuals evaluate their aptitudes, abilities, interests, and values as they relate to selecting careers. Placement offices and continuing education centers also offer career planning assistance.

Critical to your career planning is determining the long-term opportunities and salaries in the occupational fields you are considering. Most job-related websites, including those operated by Monster, CareerBuilder, Indeed, and LinkedIn, contain free information about careers and wages. Government sources include O*Net OnLine, America's Career InfoNet, and Career Outlook.

A.3 Self-Evaluation

Successful career development depends in part on an individual's ability to conduct an accurate self-evaluation. When you are doing a self-evaluation, you need to consider factors that are personally significant to you. What activities do you like to do? Do you like working alone or with other people? Do you like technical work or creative work? Do you think you would like working in an office, or would you prefer another setting? What have you always dreamed of doing?

A.3a Interest Inventories

Psychologists who specialize in career counseling typically administer a battery of tests. The *Strong Interest Inventory,* developed by E. K. Strong Jr., was among the first of the interest tests.[1] Strong found people's interests vary from occupation to occupation. Strong's assessment tool can help you learn the degree to which your interests correspond with those of successful people in a wide range of occupations. Another inventory that measures both interests and skills is the *Campbell Interest and Skill Survey* (*CISS*). Occupations are identified with advice about whether each of the occupations should be "pursued," "explored," or "avoided" by the person who took the test. Both tests can be taken online for a fee. About.com offers a number of free self-assessments, as do other sites such as MyPlan.com, CareerPath, and LiveCareer. The *O*Net Interest Profiler* is a free online interest assessment tool offered by the U.S. Department of Labor.

Of course, many people have taken interest and skills inventories that dissuaded them from their chosen careers, pursued them anyway, and become extremely successful. If you find yourself in such a situation, do not be discouraged about your career choice. Consider exploring the career further via internships, informational interviews, and job shadowing (discussed next). Also, keep in mind that most people change careers multiple times during their lives. If your first choice of a career is not what you hoped it would be, you are always free to pursue another.

A.3b Informational Interviews, Job Shadowing, and Internships

informational interview
A conversation you have with someone in a career you are interested in to gather information about it.

job shadowing
The process of observing someone in their work environment to see if the job is of interest to you.

An **informational interview** is a conversation you have with someone in an occupation that you are interested in. You invite the person to lunch or for coffee and ask the individual what the job is really like—the good and the bad, the qualifications needed, the outlook for the career, and so forth. Most people are flattered to be asked to provide career information and like to talk about what they do. However, make it clear that you are not soliciting the person for a job—just seeking information.

Job shadowing is the process of observing someone in their own work environment to better understand what they do. Generally this is done for a few hours to a half-day. The website Virtualjobshadow.com provides videos of professionals in approximately 100 different careers who explain their jobs. The site also contains information about the earnings and outlook of various professions, their educational requirements, and a search function that lists colleges that offer degrees for specific professions. People who sign up for the site can also ask a professional question they might have.

As explained earlier in this chapter, internships can also be a great way to experience a particular field of work, as is volunteering. Check with your college advisor and career placement center to find opportunities such as these.

Networking is a way to find out about not only different professions but different employers you might be interested in working for. Some of the best places to network include the following:

- Social media websites
- Your college alumni association or career office networking lists
- Your own extended family
- Your friends' parents and other family members
- Your professors, advisors, coaches, tutors, and clergy
- Your former bosses and your friends' and family members' bosses
- Members of clubs, religious groups, and other organizations to which you belong
- All of the organizations near where you live or go to school[2]

A.4 Choosing an Employer

Once you've made a career choice, even if only tentatively, the next major step is deciding which employer you think you might want to work for and where. Numerous company directories containing information about privately and publicly held companies are available. D&B Hoovers is one online source, as is Vault.com. Corporate websites are another source. Under the "Investors" or "Media" tabs of these sites, you can often find press releases issued by the companies in which you are interested. Such releases may highlight the initiatives companies are pursuing and the directions in which they are taking their business. You can also sign up for Google Alerts to get news on companies you are researching. Knowing something about an employer and an industry can give you a competitive edge in terms of getting an interview, landing a job, and negotiating a good salary.

Once you have landed an interview, you have the opportunity to learn more about an employer, including the type of people who work there, its corporate culture, benefits, and so forth. If you are offered a job with the firm, a website such as Salary.com can help you determine whether the firm's offer is acceptable to you. Several cost-of-living calculators are available online that can help you figure out whether it is monetarily feasible to relocate for a job. Highlights in HRM 10 shows the questions you should ask yourself before you accept a job offer with a particular company.

A.5 Consider the Boundaryless Career

A generation ago, career success was synonymous with ascending a corporate hierarchy over the course of a lifetime spent in a single firm. Today, however, individuals pursuing *boundaryless careers* prefer to see themselves as self-directed "free agents" who develop a portfolio of employment opportunities by proactively moving from employer

10 **Highlights in HRM**

Questions to Ask Yourself before You Accept a Job

- Have I been offered a fair salary? Is it comparable to what other people in the same position are making? Will it work with my budget?
- What is the benefit package, and when am I eligible for it?
- Do I like my potential boss? Does this person seem like someone with whom I can have a good working relationship?
- Do I like my potential coworkers?
- Will I be comfortable in this office environment?
- Is the corporate culture in line with my own values, attitudes, and goals?
- Am I genuinely excited about the job?
- Can I handle the commute to this job?

Sources: Liz Ryan, "Five Questions to Ask before You Accept a Job Offer," *Forbes* (January 1, 2015), https://www.forbes.com; Dawn Rosenberg McKay, About.com,

to employer, simultaneously developing and utilizing their marketable skills. Employees pursuing boundaryless careers develop their human capital along dimensions of industry and occupational knowledge. That is, they may be experts in computer programming or have great insights into trends in the banking industry. In contrast, individuals pursuing more traditional careers develop their knowledge in ways specific to a given firm.

entrepreneur
Someone es, manages, and assumes responsibility for a business or other enterprise.

Alternately, you might want to become an entrepreneur. Being an **entrepreneur**—someone who starts, organizes, manages, and assumes responsibility for a business or other enterprise—offers a personal challenge that many individuals prefer over being an employee.[3]

A.6 Keeping Your Career in Perspective

For most people, work is a primary factor in the overall quality of their lives. Nevertheless, it is advisable to keep one's career in perspective so that other important areas of life are not neglected.

A.6a Developing Off-the-Job Interests

How satisfied you are with your life is a product of many forces. When people complain about not having a good work–life balance, often the problem is not too much work but too little "life."[4] Some of the more important ingredients of "life" are physical health, emotional well-being, harmonious interpersonal relationships, financial security, freedom from too much stress, and achievement of one's goals. While a career can provide some of the satisfaction that an individual needs, most people find it necessary to turn to interests and activities outside their career. Off-the-job activities not only provide a respite from daily work responsibilities, but also offer satisfaction in areas unrelated to work. With that said, it is up to you to decide what is important to you and how to spend your work and off-the-job time. Your life is yours to live, and it is shorter than you think.

A.6b Balancing Marital and/or Family Life

As we have said, the one event that often poses the greatest threat to a family is relocation. Families often experience conflicts between the desire to advance the careers of different parents and settling down in one place. If an employee is experiencing ambiguity and/or conflict with their work role, a low level of supervisory support, or disappointment due to unfulfilled work expectations, this can affect family life as well. Other conflicts include work–life balance problems, such the need to spend time with a person's family members and to care for children, aging elders, or a spouse. The different employment patterns in a family and dissimilarity in a couple's career orientations can take a toll on employees.

A number of employers are doing more today to help their employees cope with these problems via alternative work options. Employees are also actively looking for companies that have family-friendly policies. *Working Mother* magazine annually publishes a survey of the 100 top companies in the United States for working parents. Understand that "to be a success in the business world takes hard work, long hours, persistent effort, and constant attention. To be a success in marriage or partnership takes hard work, long hours, persistent effort, and constant attention. The problem is giving each its due and not shortchanging the other."[5]

A.6c Planning for Retirement

Although you might be many years from retirement right now, it is never too early to plan for it. In your 20s, you will want to begin a savings plan and start paying off your student loans. As you get older, your goals will probably change. Perhaps you will want to buy a home, and you will need money for a down payment. No matter what your current stage of life, you should never neglect saving for your retirement throughout your working years. A small sum of money saved early, compounded with interest over years, can amount to millions of dollars. But if you wait until later, you will have to save a lot of money for it to amount to as much.

Your employer can help you with some aspects of retirement planning by providing you with information about tax-advantaged employer and individual savings plans. But although employer-sponsored preretirement programs can be helpful (as we will see in Chapter 11), planning for your own retirement is up to you. Do you want to travel or live in another state or country? What kind of retirement does your spouse envision? How much money will all of this require?

Your employer will not be able to answer these questions. However, by reading about the subject of retirement and taking it seriously while you are young, you will be able to answer these questions yourself. Planning early will help you set the stage for a healthy and satisfying retirement as free as possible from worries—especially worries that could have been avoided or minimized had you taken a few easy steps earlier in life.

Key Terms

entrepreneur **informational interview** **job shadowing**

Notes and References

1. E. K. Strong Jr., of Stanford University, was active in the measurement of interests from the early 1920s until his death in 1963. Since then his work has been carried on by the staff of the Measurement Research Center, University of Minnesota. The *Strong Interest Inventory* is distributed by Consulting Psychologists Press, Inc., to qualified people under an exclusive license from the publisher, Stanford University Press.
2. Carol Carter, *Keys to Business Communication* (Upper Saddle River, NJ: Pearson, 2012), Chapter 15.
3. R. Rodrigues, C. Butler, and D. Guest, "Antecedents of Protean and Boundaryless Career Orientations: The Role of Core Self-Evaluations, Perceived Employability and Social Capital," *Journal of Vocational Behavior* 110 (2019): 1–11; Julie Rose, "The New Risk Takers," *Fortune Small Business* 12, no. 2 (2002): 28–34; Jack Howard, "Balancing Conflicts of Interest when Employing Spouses," *Employee Responsibilities & Rights* 20, no. 1 (2008): 29–43.
4. Jamie Eckle, "Randall Craig," *Computerworld* 42, no. 26 (2008): 36.
5. Maria Malik et al., "The Role of Work–Life Balance in Job Satisfaction and Job Benefit," *Journal of Applied Business Research* 30, no. 6 (2014): 1627; Christopher Caggiano, "Married . . . with Companies," *Inc.* 17, no. 6 (1995): 68–76; Sue Shellenbarger, "Sustaining a Marriage when Job Demands Seem to Be Endless," *Wall Street Journal* (December 8, 1999): B1; Johan A. Turner, "Work Options for Older Americans: Employee Benefits for the Era of Living Longer," *Benefits Quarterly* 24, no. 3 (2008): 20–25.

Dimitri Otis/DigitalVision/Getty Images

CHAPTER 6

Employee Selection

Learning Outcomes

After studying this chapter, you should be able to

LO 1 Explain what the objectives of the employee selection process are, its steps, and why the information gathered during the process must be reliable and valid.

LO 2 Describe the tools used to screen applicants, the types of employment interviews and methods to administer them, and the post-interview screening tools firms use.

LO 3 Compare the value of different types of employment tests and how to assess their reliability and validity.

LO 4 Explain how firms evaluate the information they collect on candidates and the decision strategies they use to select employees.

Regardless of whether a company is large or small, it wants to hire the best employees. In addition, equal employment opportunity (EEO) legislation, court decisions, and the *Uniform Guidelines* (discussed in Chapter 3) make it critical for the selection process to be done well and fairly. One group of researchers found that employers lose approximately 90 percent of all hiring discrimination suits, and the average payout per case is $1.5 million. The bottom line: good selection decisions make a difference—and so do bad ones.[1]

6.1 Overview of the Selection Process

LO1 Is there a "best" employment process stepwise? What steps must come first and last?

Suppose you have started a small business, and a number of people have expressed interest in working for you. Now you have to pick the right employees and avoid the wrong ones. But how should this be done? And what happens if it is not done correctly?

Selection is the process of choosing individuals who are qualified to fill existing or projected job openings. Figure 6.1 shows that the overall goal of selection is to maximize "hits" and avoid "misses." Hits are accurate predictions, and misses are inaccurate ones. The cost of one type of miss, called a false positive, would be the expense of hiring an employee who turns out to be unsuccessful on the job. The cost of the other type of miss, called a false negative, is an opportunity cost—someone who could have done a great job but did not get the chance to do so.

selection
The process of choosing individuals who are qualified to fill existing or projected job openings.

Figure 6.1 The Goal of Selection: Maximize "Hits"

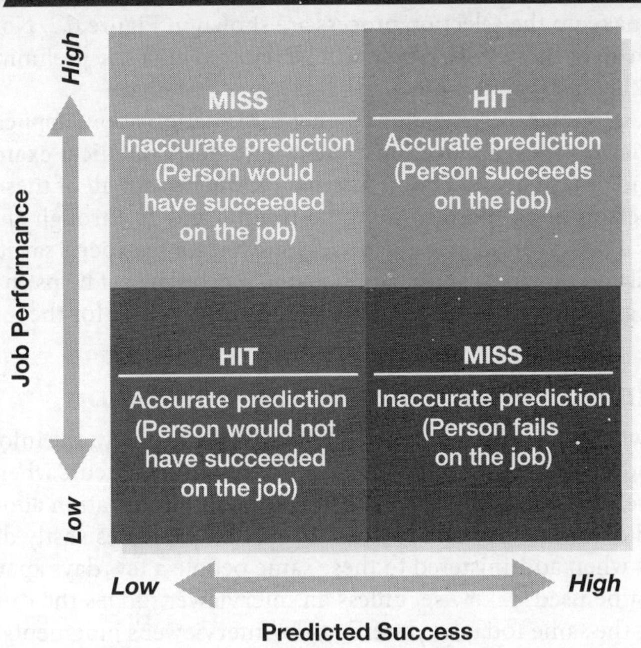

6.1a Begin with a Job Analysis

As discussed in Chapter 4, job specifications help identify the competencies employees need for success—the knowledge, skills, abilities, and other factors (KSAOs) that lead to superior performance. Managers then use selection methods such as interviews, reference checks, and preemployment tests to measure applicants' KSAOs against the competencies required for the job. Complete and clear job specifications help interviewers differentiate between qualified and unqualified applicants and reduce the effect of an interviewer's biases and prejudices. Applicants whose KSAOs are well matched to the jobs they are hired for typically perform better and are more satisfied. This relationship is often referred to generally as "person–job fit."[2]

Ordinarily, line managers are well acquainted with the skills, physical demands, and other characteristics of the jobs in their organizations. Interviewers and members of the HR department who participate in the selection process should become familiar with the jobs and competencies needed to perform them as well. In addition to matching candidates to the requirements of the specific job, many organizations, including Morgan Stanley, Merck, Southwest Airlines, and Starbucks, try to hire individuals who match their values and cultures. Recall from Chapter 2 that this process is referred to as values-based hiring. It is designed to achieve better "person–organization fit." Zappos and Salesforce.com are firms that give their employees the power to veto candidates they don't think will fit in with their cultures. In contrast, Facebook discourages hiring for cultural fit because it can result in a lack of diversity. Recall from Chapter 5 that this undesirable outcome can occur because of the cycle of "attraction–selection–attrition."[3]

6.1b Steps in the Selection Process

The selection process follows a logical sequence, although the specific steps may vary depending on the type of organization and the type of job being filled. Each step should be evaluated in terms of its contribution to the process and the final decision. The steps that typically make up the selection process are shown in Figure 6.2. Not all applicants will go through all of these steps. Some will be rejected after the preliminary interview, others after taking tests, and so on.

As Figure 6.2 shows, organizations gather information about applicants in a number of ways: via resumes, applications, interviews, tests, medical examinations, and background and other checks. For an internal candidate, not all of these steps may be needed. The person might need to submit a resume and go through an interview but not necessarily a background investigation. However, some experts say it is a good idea to treat internal and external candidates the same way because it helps ensure no special treatment was given to any one candidate, and the best person for the job is chosen.

6.1c Obtaining Reliable and Valid Information

reliability
The degree to which an interview, test, or other selection procedures result in consistent information about a candidate.

Regardless of whether a position is filled internally or externally, the information gathered about candidates must be reliable and valid. **Reliability** occurs when an interview, test, or other selection procedure results in consistent information about a candidate when repeated over time or across raters. A test that produces vastly different scores for individuals when administered to these same people a few days apart is unreliable and should not be used. Likewise, unless an interviewer judges the capabilities of an applicant to be the same today as yesterday, the interviewer's judgments are unreliable (i.e., unstable). *Interrater reliability*—agreement among two or more raters—is one

Figure 6.2 Steps in the Selection Process

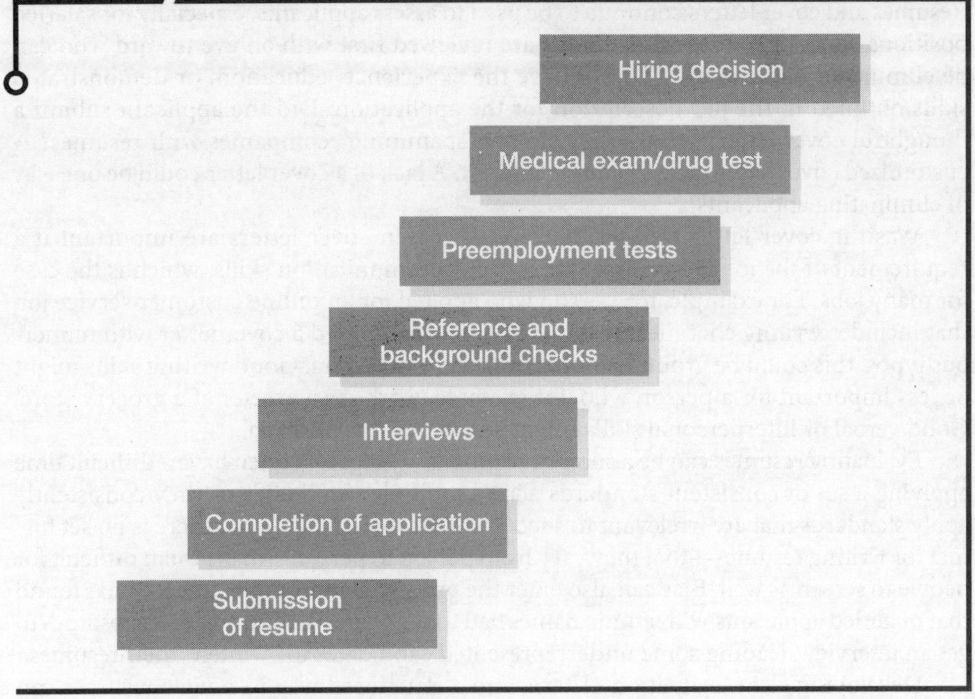

Note: Steps may vary. An applicant may be rejected after any step in the process.

measure of a method's consistency. Reliability also refers to the extent to which two or more methods (e.g., interviews and tests) yield similar results or are consistent with one another.

Validity refers to the degree to which a test or selection procedure accurately measures what it intends to, and accurately predicts how well a person performs on the job. Equal Employment Opportunity Commission (EEOC) regulations require selection procedures to be valid. Like a new medicine, a selection procedure must be validated before it is used. We will discuss ways to determine validity later in the chapter.[4]

validity
The degree to which a test or selection procedure actually measures or predicts a person's ability to do a job.

6.2 Initial Screening

LO2
Compare briefly the major types of employment interviews described in this chapter. Which type would you prefer to conduct? Why?

As an employer, would you want to interview all applicants who applied for one of your jobs? Probably not. Doing so would be very time consuming, and expensive. Instead you would first want to screen out all those people who aren't qualified for the job. As the old adage goes, you have to open a lot of oysters to find a pearl. Next, let's look at the tools you can use to make this job easier.

6.2a Initial Screening Methods

Employers use many different pieces of information to try to determine if an applicant will be successful on the job. The initial information tools for screening candidates include resumes, cover letters, the Internet, phone screening, and application forms.

Cover Letters and Resumes

Resumes and cover letters continue to be used to assess applicants, especially for salaried positions. Generally, these documents are reviewed first with an eye toward who can be eliminated because they do not have the experience, education, or demonstrated skills outlined in the job description for the application. Did the applicant submit a thoughtful cover letter? Or are they simply "spamming" companies with resumes? A customized cover letter shows genuine interest. A lack of a cover letter could be one way of eliminating applicants.

Was the cover letter well written? Well-written cover letters are important if a requirement of the job is having good written communication skills, which is the case for many jobs. For example, if a person who applied for an online customer service job that includes writing chat messages to customers submitted a cover letter with numerous typos, this could be grounds for passing over the person. Good writing skills might be less important for a person who, for example, works as a greeter at a grocery store. Good verbal or interpersonal skills might suffice for this position.

Evaluating resumes can be a subjective process. Evaluators often have a difficult time applying a set of consistent standards across multiple candidates or they consistently apply standards that are irrelevant to success on the job. The fact that there is no set format for writing resumes—that they vary from person to person—make them difficult for people to screen as well. Bias can also enter the process. For example, research has found that qualified applicants with ethnic names had to send out significantly more resumes to get an interview, leading some underrepresented candidates to "whiten" their resumes.[5]

Developing clear evaluation criteria and a structured way to review resumes can help make the process less biased. Using an assessment grid like the one shown in Figure 6.3 can take some of the guesswork out of this process. Job description criteria

Figure 6.3 Application/Resume Assessment Grid

Rate each candidate on a scale of 1–5, with 5 being the highest rating.

Quantitative requirements	**Applicant A**	**Applicant B**	**Applicant C**	**Applicant D**
Business degree and/or MBA	5			
Two years' managerial experience	5			
Ability to develop strategies	2			
Ability to manage budgets	2			
Qualitative requirements				
Demonstrated interpersonal skills	4			
Demonstrated coaching and development skills	4			
Ability to manage diverse teams and work with other departments	4			
Flexibility	3			
Writing and verbal skills	4			
Presentation skills	4			
Level of integrity	4			
Totals	**41**			

are placed in the left-hand column of the grid, and candidates are then ranked based on a scale as to whether the skills outlined in their resumes and cover letters match the job. The totals for the candidates are then compared.

The downside of manually screening and assessing cover letters is that firms can get hundreds of them for a single position. As you learned in Chapter 5, some companies use software such as applicant tracking systems to screen resumes. For example, a hiring manager or HR representative will specify the educational and experience levels a job requires and keywords that indicate experience. The software then scans the resumes collected for that position, pulls a list of qualified candidates, and ranks them according to how closely they match the job criteria. Some of the systems also prescreen people who submit resumes by first asking them to take a short questionnaire to determine how qualified they are. Resume screening software isn't perfect, though.[6] Case Study 2 at the end of the chapter takes a closer look at the pros and cons of resume screening.

Internet Checks

According to a survey by the website CareerBuilder, approximately 60 percent of employers research candidates using the Internet and social media sites, a practice that's grown exponentially in recent years.[7] However, doing so can be problematic for a number of reasons:

1. It can be difficult to verify the authenticity of information posted online (i.e., did the candidate really post the information, or did someone else?) and easy to confuse an applicant with someone else who has the same name, which could result in a lawsuit. Some federal courts have ruled that employers *must ensure* the information they collect online is verified by multiple sources.
2. Much of the information people post online isn't job related. For example, recruiters need to ensure they don't screen out applicants because they discovered they smoke or drink alcohol or engage in other activities that are not job related and are, in fact, legal.[8]
3. Scouring the Internet and social media sites can inadvertently lead to discrimination against members of protected classes.[9]

Another CareerBuilder survey found the biggest factor influencing an employer's decision not to hire an applicant was provocative photos on social media, an issue that may be more likely to affect women than men. Religious discrimination can be a problem, too. Researchers at Carnegie Mellon University found that applicants whose online profiles indicated they were Muslim were less likely to get called for interviews than Christian applicants.[10]

Many companies are still in the process of developing policies related to social media and Internet searches—that is, what information should be searched for and when, how it should be documented, and by whom. To avoid discrimination, most HR experts advise firms to not conduct any searches until after an applicant has been interviewed, and to use the same search process for all candidates. Candidates should also be told during their interviews that their public (not private) online profiles may be checked. Not all applicants realize that such checking occurs and could feel their privacy is violated without such notice. At a minimum, advance notice gives candidates a chance to review and edit their profiles or make them private, if they want.

Phone and Video Screening

Short phone interviews, or screening interviews, are often conducted, many times by HR personnel, to narrow down the field and save managers time by eliminating candidates who are not likely to be hired. Video is being used to prescreen applicants

video resumes
Short video clips that highlight applicants' qualifications beyond what they can communicate on their resumes.

as well. To give employers a "preview" of themselves, some candidates post **video resumes** on YouTube and include links to them in their resumes and LinkedIn profiles.[11] Video resumes are short video clips that highlight applicants' qualifications beyond what they can communicate via their resumes and cover letters. The videos allow employers to see how well they present themselves and decide whether they should be interviewed.

However, not all employers accept video resumes, and there is a concern they can result in employers screening people based on their looks, gender, or ethnicity rather than their qualifications. To eliminate bias and recruit more diverse workforces, some companies actually strip out names and photos from resumes before reviewing them. The recruiting software Hired does this automatically. Mehul Patel, the CEO of Hired, says he can envision a day when virtual-reality programs disguise the appearances and voices of candidates, forcing recruiters and interviewers to focus on their experience and skills.[12]

Application Forms

Application forms provide a fairly quick and systematic means of obtaining a variety of information about the applicant, such as whether the applicant meets the minimum requirements for experience, education, and so on. Even when applicants come armed with elaborate resumes, they should complete application forms because it is a way to gather consistent information about candidates. People, even those in high positions, frequently exaggerate their qualifications on their resumes and omit unflattering information.[13]

Far fewer people lie on application forms relative to their resumes, a survey by the job board CareerBuilder found. Most forms require an applicant to sign a statement verifying the information on the form is true and granting the employer the right to terminate the candidate's employment if any of the information is found to be false.[14]

However, the EEOC and the courts have found that many questions on application forms discriminate against women and other underrepresented groups and often are not job related. Highlights in HRM 1 offers firms some guidelines about the types of questions that should and should not be asked on an application form if a firm wants to stay out of court.

Because of differences in state laws, organizations operating in more than one state will find it difficult to develop one form that can be used nationally. For example, roughly two-thirds of U.S. states and more than 150 cities have banned boxes applicants must check about their criminal history because this information can adversely affect members of underrepresented groups. Although it's not a federal mandate, the EEOC supports "banning the box" (also call "fair chance" legislation) because it helps ex-offenders reenter the workforce instead of being sidelined for life.[15] When the boxes are present, virtually anyone with even a minor conviction that may have occurred years ago will get screened out.

That doesn't mean a company can't check a candidate's criminal record later in the hiring process for job-related reasons, though. If someone applying for a bookkeeper's job was recently convicted of embezzlement, a firm needs to be able to check that history. Some state laws require firms to delay asking about an applicant's criminal history until after an interview or after a provisional offer has been made to the candidate.

1 **Highlights in HRM**

What to Include—and Not to Include—on a Job Application Form

- *Application date.* This helps managers know when the form was completed and gives them an idea of how long (e.g., one year) the form should remain on file.
- *Educational background.* Include blanks for high school, college, and post-college attendance—but not the dates attended, since that can be connected with age.
- *Experience.* Virtually any questions that focus on work experience related to the job are permissible.
- *Arrests and criminal convictions.* Don't ask questions about arrests. Questions about convictions and guilty pleadings can be problematic if they are not related to the job. Some states prohibit conviction questions, and the EEOC has indicated that they can have a disparate impact on African American and Hispanic workers.
- *Marital status and dependents.* Don't ask questions about marital status or whether a person has dependents or children.
- *National origin.* Don't ask questions about an applicant's national origin. However, it is acceptable to ask whether the person is legally prevented from working in the United States.
- *References.* Most applications include blanks for the names, addresses, and phone numbers of references provided by applicants.
- *Disabilities.* Don't ask applicants questions designed to elicit information about the existence, nature, or severity of a disability. Inquiries about the ability of the person to perform job functions, however, are acceptable. Under the most recent guidelines issued by the EEOC, employers can ask whether an applicant needs reasonable accommodation—*if* the disability is obvious or *if* the applicant has voluntarily disclosed the disability.

Disclaimers

- *EEOC and at-will statements.* State on the application form that the firm does not discriminate and is an EEOC employer. If your state allows it, the form should state that all employees are hired *at will.* This gives both employer and employee the right to end the employment relationship at any time without reason.
- *Reference checks.* Include language that gives the hiring firm the right to contact the applicants' previous employers listed on the form and their resumes.
- *Employment testing.* List any tests the applicant may have to take and ask the applicant to sign the application consenting to their use.
- *Information falsification.* Notify applicants that any falsification of the information they provide could result in their disqualification or termination should they be hired.

6.3 Employment Interviews

Even though they are plagued by subjectivity and have shown to be poor predictors of performance, employment interviews are almost always utilized in the selection process. As Figure 6.4 shows, situational factors and candidate characteristics, such as a person's race and gender, can affect the perceptions of an interviewer and ultimately the interview's outcome. Nonetheless, firms continue to use interviews because (1) they are practical when there are only a small number of applicants; (2) they serve other purposes, such as public relations; and (3) interviewers trust their judgments when it comes to making decisions about which candidates to choose. Even a limited understanding of the variables in Figure 6.4 and periodic training, however, have been shown to dramatically improve the effectiveness of interviewers.[16]

Figure 6.4 Variables in the Employment Interview

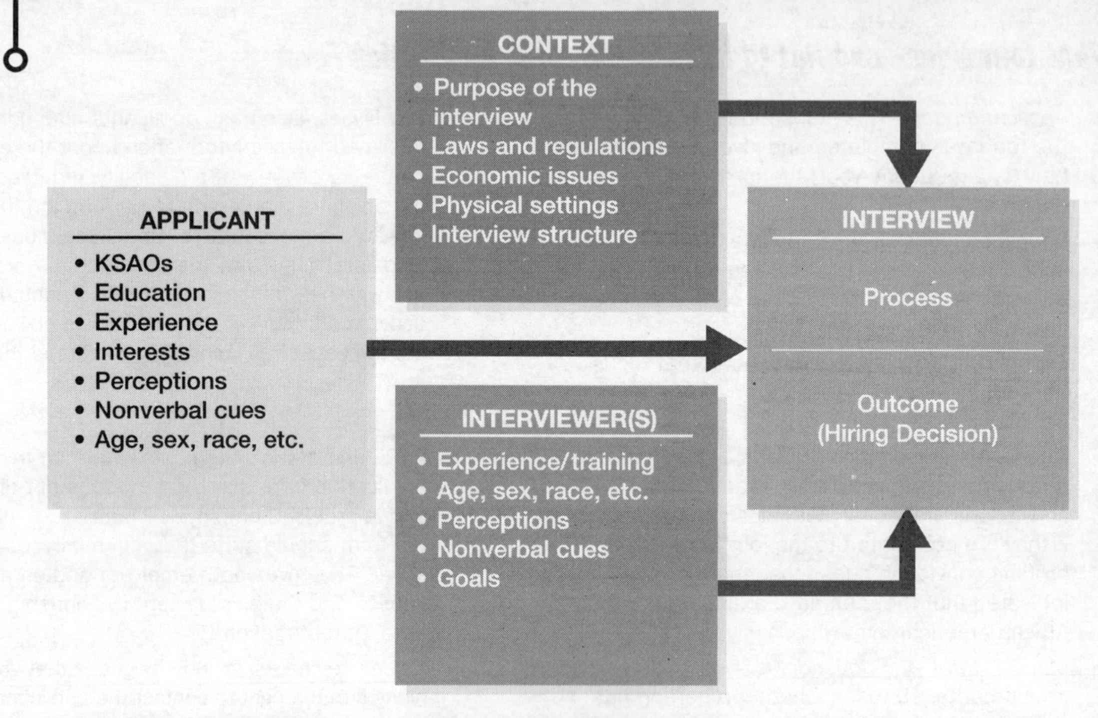

We will review different types of interview methods next. But first, regardless of which type you use, here are a few tips to keep in mind to make things go more smoothly:

- *Be prepared.* Too many interviewers just skim resumes prior to the interview. If you prepare for the interview, though, you'll have more substance to talk about. Also, make sure you've done your homework on the job requirements.
- *Be respectful.* Everyone is busy these days, so be punctual, and begin and end on time. Be an active listener. Put the candidate at ease. The interview questions should flow like a conversation, not an interrogation.
- *Build rapport.* Begin the relationship building before the person is hired. Express enthusiasm. If you haven't built a good vibe with the candidate, it will be difficult to convey the positive message of the organization.
- *Communicate well and often.* Don't just interview and forget about the candidate. Follow up with them and keep them in the loop.
- *Review your work.* With so many interviews and so little time, we often neglect the very important step of summarizing our notes and thinking through what just happened. This step not only helps you identify one or two key points to remember, but helps you consider how you can continuously improve the process.

6.3a Types of Interviews

Interviewing methods differ in several ways. In highly structured interviews, the interviewer determines the course that the interview will follow as each question is asked. In a structured interview, the applicant plays a larger role in determining the course the discussion will take. Next, let's look at the different types of interviews from the least structured to the most structured. Note that the various types of interview styles and questions they utilize can be mixed and matched to yield a more complete picture of candidates.

Nondirective Interviews

In a **nondirective interview**, the interviewer asks broad, open-ended questions—such as "Tell me more about your experiences on your last job"—and allows the applicant to talk freely with a minimum of interruption. The freedom afforded to the applicant helps uncover information a candidate might not disclose during more structured questioning. However, because the applicant determines the course of the interview, the information gathered on one applicant can be vastly different from the information gathered on another. Thus, the reliability and validity of these interviews are not likely to be high.

nondirective interview
An interview in which the applicant is allowed the maximum amount of freedom in determining the course of the discussion, while the interviewer carefully refrains from influencing the applicant's remarks.

Structured Interviews

A **structured interview** includes a set of standardized questions (based on a job analysis) and an established set of answers against which applicant responses are rated. Thus, it provides a more consistent basis for evaluating job candidates and predicting their on-the-job performance. Weyerhaeuser Company, a forest products firm, has developed a structured interviewing process. Candidates' responses are rated on a five-point scale relative to those answers, and the interviewers take notes for future reference and in case of a legal challenge. Structured interviews are also less likely than nondirective interviews to be attacked in court.[17]

structured interview
An interview in which a set of standardized questions having an established set of answers is used.

Situational Interviews

A **situational interview** is a variation of a structured interview. Candidates are given a hypothetical incident and asked how they would respond to it. Each candidate's response is then evaluated relative to a preestablished standard. Many organizations use situational interviews to select new college graduates because they may lack actual situations in the workplace they can describe. Highlights in HRM 2 shows a sample question from a situational interview used to select systems analysts at a chemical plant.

situational interview
An interview in which an applicant is given a hypothetical incident and asked how they would respond to it.

Behavioral Description Interviews

A **behavioral description interview (BDI)** focuses on actual work incidents in the interviewee's past and what the applicant did in response. For example, to assess a potential manager's ability to handle a problem employee, an interviewer might ask, "Tell me about the last time you disciplined an employee."

A BDI assumes that past performance is the best predictor of future performance. This format also may be somewhat less susceptible to applicant faking. In addition, research indicates that the BDI is more effective than the situational interview for hiring employees to fill higher-level positions such as general managers and executives.[18]

behavioral description interview (BDI)
An interview in which an applicant is asked questions about what they actually did in a given situation.

Sequential and Panel Interviews

In a **sequential interview**, a candidate is interviewed by multiple people, one right after another. Sequential interviews are very common. They allow different interviewers who have a vested interest in the candidate's success to meet and evaluate the person on a one-on-one basis. The interviewers later get together and compare their assessments of the candidates.

sequential interview
A format in which a candidate is interviewed by multiple people, one right after another.

Sample Situational Interview Question

Question:

It is the night before your scheduled vacation. You are all packed and ready to go. Just before you get into bed, you receive a call from the plant. A problem has arisen that only you can handle. You are asked to come in to take care of things. What would you do in this situation?

Record Answer:

____

____

____

Scoring Guide:

Good: "I would go in to work and make certain that everything is okay. Then I would go on vacation."
Good: "There are no problems that *only* I can handle. I would make certain that someone qualified was there to handle things."
Fair: "I would try to find someone else to deal with the problem."
Poor: "I would go on vacation."

panel interview
An interview in which a board of interviewers questions and observes a single candidate.

In a **panel interview**, the candidate meets with a group of interviewers, who take turns asking questions. After the interview, the interviewers pool their observations and their scores of the candidate. Because these interviews involve input from multiple people, they tend to be more reliable and accepted as fair by candidates. If the panels are composed of a diverse group of interviewers, they may minimize the risk of discrimination in the hiring process.[19] A panel interview also results in a shorter decision-making period than if each applicant has to be interviewed by each interviewer separately.

6.3b Methods for Administering Interviews

Most interviews take place in person. However, they can be administered in other ways to broaden the talent pool and make interviewing easier, faster, and less costly.

Remote or Virtual Interviews

remote or virtual interviews
Interviews conducted via videoconferencing or over the Web.

A recent Gartner study, conducted after the COVID-19 pandemic, found that 86 percent of companies are now utilizing **remote or virtual interviews**, using Zoom or some other videoconferencing platform.[20] Remote interviews via video are convenient, carry a low cost, and make it easier to interview people in different geographic areas, thereby expanding the talent pool. However, the results can be mixed.

On the one hand, a study by DeGroote School of Business at McMaster University in Ontario, Canada, found that candidates interviewed via video came across as less likable. Some candidates may be more comfortable on camera or using the technology than other candidates. The researchers suggested that, at a minimum, all candidates be treated the same in terms of the methods by which they are interviewed.[21]

On the other hand, evidence suggests that remote interviews have the potential to minimize the power differential between the interviewer and the interviewee. Instead

3 Highlights in HRM

Hiring Managers Reveal Mistakes Candidates Make during Job Interviews

The following are some memorable blunders that have caused managers to not hire candidates.

- "The candidate spoke no English, so he brought his mother to translate for him during the interview. It was for a customer-service position."
- "She kept telling me about her marital problems."
- "The candidate knew nothing about the job being offered or our organization."
- "One guy ate a sandwich."
- "The candidate asked me to hurry up because she left her child in the car."
- "He told me the only reason he was here was because his mother wanted him to get a job. He was 37."
- "One candidate did not wear shoes to the interview."
- "Body odor so bad I had to excuse myself mid-interview and put lip gloss in my nose in order to get through the rest."
- "One guy asked if we drug-tested and if we gave advance notice (we are a drug treatment facility)."

Sources: CareerBuilder.com, *Reader's Digest*.

of the interviewer sitting high behind a big desk and the interviewee sinking low in a chair, each person is on a more level playing field. The effect can be that the interview is more of a conversation between equals.[22]

automated interview Interviews in which the questions are administered to applicants via computers. The interviews can be conducted at a firm's facilities, using kiosks, online, or via phone.

Automated Interviews

Nike, Safeway Cigna Insurance, and Pinkerton Security are among the many companies that have used automated interviews (also known as "on-demand" or asynchronous interviews) to gather information as well as to compare candidates. An **automated interview** uses a set of prerecorded questions that interviewees need to answer, typically on video. The interviews can be conducted at a firm's facilities, using kiosks, via phone, or online.

martin-dm/E+/Getty Images

Video interviews make it easy and cost-effective to interview candidates from different geographic areas.

A drawback of automated interviews is that recruiters and managers can't immediately ask candidates follow-up questions based on their answers. Consequently, organizations use automated interviews mainly as a complement to, rather than as a replacement for, live interviews. Automated interviews can also be perceived as impersonal.[23]

When the grocer Giant Eagle needed to hire 1,000 employees, it utilized computer-administered interviews at a Pittsburgh-area convention center. People who passed them were then led to group interviews, where HR personnel worked with as many as 20 applicants at a time.[24] Some firms use automated video interviewing services like HireVue and VidCruiter.com. Applicants are invited to interview by email, provided with passwords to log onto the sites, and given questions to answer; their answers are recorded by their webcams and then sent to the hiring firm. HireVue uses machine learning to analyze the video, audio, and language metrics in the interviews and then rank candidates based on previous top and bottom performers.

6.3c Diversity Management: Could Your Questions Get You into Legal Trouble?

Which questions should be or should not be asked in an interview? The EEOC discourages direct or indirect questions related to race, color, age, religion, sex, gender identity, sexual orientation, national origin, caregiver status, and other factors discussed in Chapter 3. Some questions that interviewers once felt free to ask are now problematic. Asking people if they are married or have children are examples. Several states have fair employment practice laws that are more restrictive than federal legislation. In general, if a question is job related, is asked of everyone, and does not discriminate against a certain class of applicants, it is likely to be acceptable.

Employers should provide their interviewers with instructions on how to avoid potentially discriminatory questions in their interviews. The examples of appropriate and inappropriate questions shown in Highlights in HRM 4 can serve as guidelines for application forms as well as preemployment interviews. Complete guidelines can be developed from current information available from district and regional EEOC offices and from state fair-employment practice offices.

6.4 Post-Interview Screening

After a candidate has been interviewed and appears to be a good potential new hire, information about the person's previous employment as well as other information provided by the applicant is investigated.

6.4a Reference Checks

Organizations check the references of employees in a number of ways. Phone checks are fast and make it easy for references to elaborate on a candidate. Prescient InfoTech, a software development company in Fairfax, Virginia, first calls references to establish contact and then emails them a two-page questionnaire, asking them to numerically rank the applicant's various job-related attributes. There is room at the end of the questionnaire for comments and recommendations.

The most reliable information usually comes from supervisors, who are in the best position to report on an applicant's work habits and performance. Verification related

4 Highlights in HRM

Appropriate and Inappropriate Interview Questions

	APPROPRIATE QUESTIONS	INAPPROPRIATE QUESTIONS
National origin	What is your name? Have you ever worked under a different name? Do you speak any foreign languages that may be pertinent to this job?	What is the origin of your name? What is your ancestry?
Age	Are you older than age 18? If hired, can you prove your age?	How old are you? What is your date of birth?
Sex	(Say nothing unless it involves a bona fide occupational qualification.)	Are you a man or a woman?
Race	(Say nothing.)	What is your race?
Disabilities	Do you have any disabilities that may inhibit your job performance? Are you willing to take a physical exam if the job requires it?	Do you have any physical defects? When was your last physical exam?
Height and weight	(Not appropriate unless it is a bona fide occupational qualification.)	How tall are you? How much do you weigh?
Residence	What is your address? How long have you lived there?	What are the names and relationships of those with whom you live?
Religion	(You may inform a person of the required work schedule.)	What church do you go to?
Military record	Did you have any military education/experience pertinent to this job?	What type of discharge did you receive?
Education and experience	Where did you go to school? What is your prior work experience? Why did you leave? What is your salary history?	Is that a church-affiliated school? When did you graduate?
Criminal record	Have you ever been convicted of a crime? (May not be appropriate unless not being convicted is a bona fide occupational qualification.)	Have you ever been arrested?
Citizenship	Do you have a legal right to work in the United States?	Are you a U.S. citizen?
Marital/family status	What is the name, address, and telephone number of a person we may contact in case of an emergency?	Are you married, divorced, single? Do you prefer Miss, Mrs., or Ms.? Do you have any children? How old are they?

to an applicant's job title, duties, and pay level from a former employer's HR office is also very helpful. Highlights in HRM 5 includes a list of helpful questions to ask about candidates when checking their references.[25]

Prior to checking a candidate's references, the candidate must complete forms permitting information to be solicited from former employers and other reference sources. Even with these safeguards, organizations are often reluctant to put into writing an evaluation of a former employee for fear of being sued by that person. Many employers

5 Highlights in HRM

Sample Reference-Checking Questions

- What is your relationship to the applicant? Are you the person's supervisor, peer, or subordinate? What were the start and end dates of the applicant's employment?
- What were the applicant's title and responsibilities? In what areas did the applicant excel? What unique, or exceptional, talents does the applicant have?
- In what areas did the applicant need improvement? What was the applicant's biggest accomplishment at your organization?
- How well does the applicant communicate with and get along with others?
- How does the applicant deal with conflicts and stress?
- To what extent is the applicant driven to succeed?
- Was the applicant punctual?
- For what reason did the applicant leave your organization?
- Would you rehire the applicant?
- Are there any serious problems with the applicant we should know about?
- Is there any additional information about the applicant you would like to share with me?

Sources: Rebecca Knight, "The Right Way to Check Someone's References," *Harvard Business Review*, July 29, 2016; "Four Reasons Why You Should Always Check References," *Human Resources Today* (December 29, 2015), http://www.humanresourcestoday.com; Alison Doyle, "Reference Check Questions," About.com (March 24, 2011), http://www.about.com; Carolyn Hirschman, "The Whole Truth," *HRMagazine* 45, no. 6 (June 2000): 86–72.

will only verify former employees' employment dates and positions. Even firms that have refused to give an employee a recommendation have found themselves sued. Other firms have been sued for knowing a former employee posed a danger to others but failing to disclose it. Recognizing this predicament, a number of states have enacted statutes called "reference immunity" legislation, which offer protection from liability for employers who give references in good faith.[26]

6.4b Background Checks

negligent hiring
The failure of an organization to discover, via due diligence, that an employee it hired had the propensity to do harm to others.

Background investigations, which require the consent of applicants, have become standard procedure for many companies. Moreover, state courts have ruled that companies can be held liable for **negligent hiring** if they fail to do adequate background checks. Federal law requires comprehensive background checks for all child care providers, for example. It also prohibits convicted felons from engaging in financial and security-oriented transactions. According to the Society of Human Resources Management, companies are increasingly background-checking contingent workers given the growth of the "gig" economy. Uber and Lyft drivers are examples. Some employers, but certainly not all, rescreen their employees when they change jobs within their companies.

Among the checks are Social Security number verification, past employment, education, and certification and license verification. A number of other checks can be conducted if they pertain to the job for which one is being hired. They include a driving-record check (for jobs involving driving), a credit check (for money-handling jobs), a military records check, and criminal records check.

To run background checks, firms must obtain clear and conspicuous written consent from applicants beforehand (usually on a separate form). Applicants must also be told if the information uncovered will be used to deny them employment; they must be given a copy of the report(s), the right to dispute it (them), and time to do so. This is important because it's not uncommon for background checks to be inaccurate or even include information about the wrong applicant. To comply with various laws, many companies hire firms that specialize in background checks to conduct them for them or use the Department of Homeland Security's free e-Verify system.[27]

Criminal Records Checks

According to the Society of Human Resources Management, most major firms check candidates' backgrounds for criminal records. However, as we have indicated, the EEOC has found that they can have a disparate impact on candidates from underrepresented groups, who, relative to other groups of people, have higher conviction and incarceration rates.

Federal law does not prohibit employers from asking job candidates about their criminal history. However, EEO laws do prohibit employers from discriminating when they use criminal history information. If criminal histories are taken into account, employers must also consider the nature of the job. For example, it may make sense to disqualify an applicant who was convicted of theft for a clerk's position, but not one who was convicted drunk driving. Even if the person were convicted of theft, the EEOC requires the employer to consider mitigating factors, such as the individual's age at the time of conviction, how long ago it occurred, whether the person has been successfully rehabilitated, and whether the person has worked successfully in the same type of work following the conviction.[28]

Credit Checks

In the past, credit checks were conducted primarily to screen applicants who handled money, such as banking employees. However, the number of companies performing credit check tests has risen in recent years—even though the evidence is mixed as to whether there is a clear correlation between good employees and good credit scores.[29] Too often credit checks are used when they are not really needed, and candidates tend to view them as invasive and question their job relatedness. Eight of ten companies surveyed by the Society of Human Resource Management have gone ahead and hired job candidates with negative credit scores.[30]

Credit checks can also adversely affect qualified applicants who have been unemployed for long periods of time or faced bankruptcies or home foreclosures—problems that became more common among workers during the last recession. The EEOC has also warned employers that credit checks can have an adverse impact on some protected groups. For reasons such as these, a number of states, including Washington, California, Connecticut, Maryland, Illinois, and Hawaii, prohibit credit checks; many other states and U.S. lawmakers are considering similar action.

LO3 What characteristics do job knowledge and job sample tests have that often make them more acceptable to candidates than other types of tests?

6.5 Preemployment Tests

What if you have narrowed down the list of candidates you're considering hiring but still can't decide among them? Is there a test you could use that would tell you which one would perform better than the others? That's what people have wondered for years—and hence the development of preemployment tests.

preemployment test An objective and standardized test used to gauge a person's knowledge, skills, abilities, and other characteristics relative to those of other individuals.

A **preemployment test** is an objective and standardized device used to gauge a person's KSAOs relative to other individuals.[31] Not all companies conduct preemployment tests, but many do. One of the drawbacks of preemployment tests is that they create the potential for legal challenges by applicants claiming the tests they took were

Small Business Application

Adding Structure to the Employee Selection Process in Small Businesses

How do small businesses go about selecting employees to work at their firms? Not very systematically, some HR professionals and researchers say. "All too often, employees are relatives or friends who lack the basic skills to augment the organization's ability to be profitable/successful," says an executive who coaches other businesspeople to help them achieve superior results.

Sometimes a small firm will make poor selections because it is anxious to get someone hired when the firm is short staffed. But if the wrong person is hired, that only compounds the problem. Another pitfall is being too confident about the right "type" of person for the job, which can cause hiring managers to make snap judgments about candidates based on casual conversations, before examining the candidates' qualifications for the job. Properly vetting candidates can not only lead to better employees, but also help a company defend itself should it be accused of discriminatory practices. And at least one research study has found that the use of formal recruitment and selection techniques gives employees a positive perception of their firms and their bosses and results in greater loyalty to their organizations.

Adding structure to the selection process doesn't have to be difficult. You can map out the qualifications for the job on a form similar to the one shown in Figure 6.3. Then develop a series of open-ended and situational questions designed to elicit information about the candidate's job knowledge, conscientiousness, interest in the work, and how well his or her personality squares with the job.

Once you have the questions drafted, ask the same questions of all candidates. Last, embezzlement and theft can be particularly devastating to small businesses, so *do* run background checks on employees and check their references, even if you know the candidates. You might be surprised by what you find.

Sources: Robert N. Lussier and Joel Corman, "There Are Few Differences between Successful and Failed Small Businesses," *Journal of Small Business Strategy* 6, no. 1 (2015): 21–34; "Selecting the Best," *Elitefts* (November 9, 2010), http://www.elitefts.com/; Barbara Reda and Linda Dyer, "Finding Employees and Keeping Them: Predicting Loyalty in the Small Business," *Journal of Small Business & Entrepreneurship* 23, no. 3 (2010): 445.

discriminatory. In the past, FedEx administered a basic skills test for the purposes of promoting employees, but it dropped the test following a lawsuit that alleged it was discriminatory. Some of these circumstances were discussed in Chapter 3 (for example, recall the *Griggs vs. Duke Power* case).

The cost, time, and ease of administering and scoring the tests must also be considered. For some jobs, the costs of testing may outweigh the benefits. Some evidence also indicates that the more tests that are required, the higher the likelihood of a lawsuit, and the more important it is for companies to demonstrate their reliability and validity in their procedures.[32]

It is the test developer's responsibility to ensure the test meets accepted standards of validity and reliability.[33] The data about a test's reliability are ordinarily presented in the manual for the test. However, a firm should not just take a developer's word that its tests are reliable and valid. One source of information about commercially available tests—the *Mental Measurements Yearbook* (*MMY*)—contains descriptive information plus critical reviews by experts of various types of tests. The firm should also confirm that the test was professionally validated in compliance with the *Uniform Guidelines on Employee Selection Procedures*, that it has been vetted for disparate impact, and that it has not been contested in court or by the EEOC.

Keep in mind that even if a test is reliable and valid for positions in other organizations, it might not be reliable and valid for the positions in your organization, because they may be somewhat different. Managers therefore need to do a thorough job analysis to determine the skills candidates actually need to be tested for and then eliminate any unnecessary or duplicate tests.

6.5a Types of Tests

We will talk more about what the EEOC demands as far as the validity of preemployment tests goes later in this section. First, let's look at the different types of preemployment tests.

Job Knowledge Tests

Job knowledge tests are achievement tests designed to measure people's level of understanding, or knowledge, about a particular job. The Uniform CPA Examination used to license certified public accountants is one such test. Most civil service examinations are used to determine whether an applicant possesses the information and understanding to do the job without further training.[34] Job knowledge tests are also used by the U.S. Armed Forces.

Work Sample Tests

Work sample tests, or job sample tests, require the applicant to perform tasks that are actually a part of the work required on the job. Examples include a map-reading test for traffic control officers, a lathe test for machine operators, and a test to determine if an administrative assistant understands Microsoft Office. Computer simulations are sometimes used, particularly when testing a candidate might prove dangerous. Anyone who wants to become a pilot in the armed services and fly multimillion-dollar jets, for example, must undergo this type of testing. (Case Study 1 looks at different simulations firms are using.) Like job knowledge tests, when work sample tests are constructed from a carefully developed outline that experts agree includes the major job functions, the tests are considered effective, reliable, valid, and fair.[35]

Assessment Center Tests

An **assessment center test** is used to evaluate candidates, often as a group, as they participate in a series of situations that resemble what they might be called on to handle on the job. AT&T was the first company to use assessment centers. Some assessment centers, where the tests are professionally conducted, take a "day in the life" approach. Candidates "report to work" at the assessment center and receive the usual steady diet of emails and other interruptions, meet with various role-players who play different characters, and handle manufactured events while they are observed and recorded.[36] Because they are costly, assessment centers are often used to select managers and executives.

assessment center test
A process by which managerial candidates are evaluated at an assessment center as they participate in a series of situations that resemble what they might need to handle on the job.

Cognitive Ability Tests

A growing body of research suggests general cognitive ability may be the best predictor of job performance. Cognitive ability tests measure mental capabilities such as general intelligence, verbal fluency, numerical ability, and reasoning ability. The Scholastic Aptitude Test (SAT) and Graduate Management Aptitude Test (GMAT) are examples. The Wonderlic Personnel Test is a cognitive ability test also used by many organizations, including the National Football League. Figure 6.5 shows some items that could be used to measure different cognitive abilities.

Although cognitive ability tests can be developed to measure very specialized areas such as reading comprehension and spatial relations, many experts believe that the validity of cognitive ability tests simply reflects their connection to general intelligence. Past studies of general intelligence, such as IQ, have been shown to be very good predictors of performance across a wide variety of jobs. However, newer studies suggest that this may be more of a perception in Western cultures, and that choosing people with the

Figure 6.5 Examples of Questions on a Cognitive Ability Test

Verbal	1. What is the meaning of the word "surreptitious"? a. covert c. lively b. winding d. sweet
Quantitative	2. Divide 50 by 0.5 and add 5. What is the result? a. 25 c. 95 b. 30 d. 105
Reasoning	3. ________ is to *boat* as *snow* is to ________. a. Sail, ski c. Water, ski b. Water, winter d. Engine, water
Mechanical	4. If gear A and gear C are both turning counterclockwise, what is happening to gear B? a. It is turning counterclockwise. c. It remains stationary. b. It is turning clockwise. d. The whole system will jam.

Answers: 1. a, 2. d, 3. c, 4. b

highest IQs might not always lead to hiring the best candidates.[37] Cognitive ability tests also have to be job related and carefully validated. Ford Motor Co. settled a $1.6 million case with the EEOC for having implemented a cognitive ability test that had a disparate impact on Black applicants.

Biographical Data (Biodata) Tests

Biographical data tests (biodata tests) collect biographical information about candidates that has been shown to correlate with on-the-job success. Candidates are questioned about events and behaviors that reflect attitudes, experiences, interests, skills, and

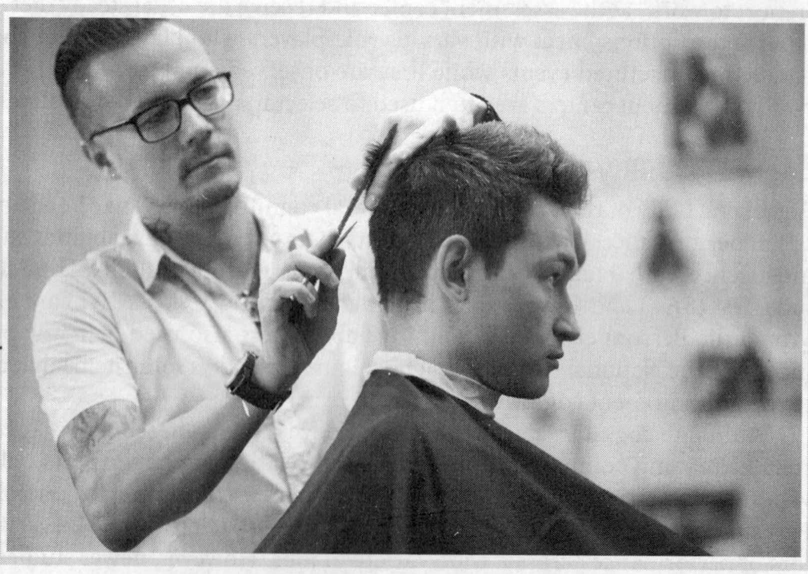

fizkes/Shutterstock.com

With jobs that require specific skills, it is quite common for employers to ask candidates to demonstrate their abilities through work sample tests.

abilities. Typically the questions relate to events that occurred in a person's life and ask what the person did in those situations. The idea is that past behavior is the best predictor of future behavior. For example, a question on a biodata test might ask, "How do you handle stressful situations?" or "How often have you put aside tasks to complete another, more difficult assignment?" Test takers choose one of several predetermined alternatives to best match their past behavior and experiences. Because it costs approximately $100,000 to train an air-traffic controller, in 2014 the Federal Aviation Administration (FAA) instituted a biodata test to identify people who can handle the high-stress, high-stakes work without quitting.[38]

A response to a single biodata question is of little value. Rather, it is the pattern of responses across several different situations that give biographical data the power to predict future behavior on the job. Although biodata tests have been found to be good predictors of on-the-job success, they are sophisticated and must be professionally developed and validated. Another drawback is that the questions might not appear to be clearly related to the job being tested for, so applicants might question the test's validity. For example, so many people with aviation experience failed the FAA test that it came under fire. The personal nature of biodata questions can also lead applicants to believe the tests invade their privacy.[39]

Personality and Interest Inventories

During the 1990s, testing by the U.S. Army found that cognitive ability tests were the best predictors of how well soldiers were able to acquire job knowledge and, ultimately, of their technical proficiencies. But personality tests were the better predictors of their motivation, such as their leadership efforts and propensity to adhere to rules. In years since then, employers also began using personality tests with increased frequency to identify the candidates best equipped to perform certain jobs (and to eliminate those least likely to succeed).

Years of research show that personality traits can be classified into five dimensions. The "Big Five" factors are as follows:

1. *Extroversion*—the degree to which someone is talkative, sociable, active, aggressive, and excitable.
2. *Agreeableness*—the degree to which someone is trusting, amiable, generous, tolerant, honest, cooperative, and flexible.
3. *Conscientiousness*—the degree to which someone is dependable and organized and perseveres in tasks.
4. *Neuroticism*—the degree to which someone is secure, calm, independent, and autonomous.
5. *Openness to experience*—the degree to which someone is intellectual, philosophical, insightful, creative, artistic, and curious.[40]

Well-known personality tests include the California Psychological Inventory (CPI); the 180-question Caliper test, whose users range from FedEx to the Chicago Cubs; and the Predictive Index, which complies with EEOC guidelines.

Although some evidence shows that personality tests can help predict how well a person will perform on the job, historically the connection between the two has been quite low. There is also some concern that the tests can easily be "faked" by applicants trying to give hiring firms the answers they think they want to hear. Personality tests can also be problematic if they inadvertently discriminate against individuals who would otherwise perform effectively, which is why several states severely restrict their usage.[41] In addition, personality tests that reveal anything about a person's mental impairment or a psychological condition, even inadvertently, violate the Americans with Disabilities Act (ADA). Rather than being used to make hiring decisions, personality and interest inventories may be most useful for helping people with their occupational selection and career planning.

Polygraph Tests

The polygraph, or lie detector, is a device that measures changes in the breathing, blood pressure, and pulse of a person who is being questioned. Questions asked in a polygraph test for employment typically cover such items as whether a person uses drugs, has stolen from an employer, or has committed a serious undetected crime. The growing swell of objections to the use of polygraphs in employment situations culminated in the passage of the federal Employee Polygraph Protection Act of 1988. This act generally prohibits using lie detectors for prehire screening and random testing of a firm's current employees; it applies to all private employers except pharmaceutical companies and security service firms.[42] Federal, state, and local governments can use polygraphs to screen applicants, but normally they are used only for law-enforcement personnel and high-security Central Intelligence Agency– and Federal Bureau of Investigation–type jobs.

Honesty and Integrity Tests

In response to the restrictions imposed by the Employee Polygraph Protection Act, employers have begun using honesty and integrity tests. Questions that might appear on an integrity test include the following:

- How likely would you be to report a coworker you discovered was stealing office supplies?
- Should an employee who lied on the application be fired if the falsification is uncovered?

Kansas-based Payless ShoeSource used an honesty test that reduced employee theft by 20 percent, the company claims.[43]

Although some studies have shown that honesty tests are valid means of predicting job performance as well as a wide range of disruptive behaviors such as theft, disciplinary problems, and absenteeism, other studies have questioned their validity.[44] It is possible that the tests "work" not because they predict behavior, but rather because they deter less-than-honest applicants from joining a company. Evolv, an assessment company, is one of a number of firms attempting to improve the accuracy of honesty and integrity tests by using big data and other analysis technology in the process.[45]

Physical Ability Tests

For some jobs, employers need to assess a person's physical abilities. Particularly for demanding and potentially dangerous jobs such as those held by firefighters and police officers, physical abilities such as strength and endurance tend to be good predictors of not only performance but also accidents and injuries.[46]

Physical ability tests must be used cautiously, however. In the past, requirements for physical characteristics such as strength, agility, height, and weight were often determined by an employer's unvalidated notion of what should be required. This often put women and job applicants with disabilities at a disadvantage. After a Dial Corporation

iStock.com/xavieramau

Like other organizations, fire departments have had to ensure their physical abilities tests are job-related.

plant in Fort Madison, Iowa, began using a strength test, the company was sued. Prior to the test's use, nearly 50 percent of the people hired at the plant were women. Once the test was implemented, the percentage dropped dramatically. An appeals court ruled the test had a disparate impact on women because, although injuries at the plant fell, they only did so after the company instituted new safety rules, which happened years before the strength test was implemented.[47] Because of situations such as these, physical requirements have been questioned and modified so as to represent typical job demands.

Medical Examinations

A medical examination is one of the later steps in the selection process because the law prohibits it from being administered to an applicant before an individual has been made a conditional employment offer and agreed to undergo the test. A medical examination can be given only to ensure that an applicant is fit for duty.[48] The ADA limits the types of medical inquiries and examinations employers may use and states that all exams must be directly related to the requirements of the job. Furthermore, the ADA prohibits companies from screening out a prospective employee because an individual has an elevated risk of on-the-job injury or a medical condition that could be aggravated because of job demands.

Drug Tests

In the United Sates, not only do employers have the right to use drug tests to screen candidates for use of illegal substances, but roughly half of them actually do so. Different states have different laws regarding drug testing. In some states, drug tests can be given to candidates only after they have been extended job offers conditional upon their passing the tests. A candidate can refuse to take the test, but that is tantamount to turning down the job.[49] As with other background checks, candidates must be given the results of the tests and the right to dispute them.

However, some studies have failed to show that drug testing makes the workplace safer or leads to improvements in the performance of workers. Relatively few applicants test positive for drugs (about 4 percent). In fact, legal drugs such as alcohol and prescription painkillers such as opioids appear to create more problems than illegal drugs in the workplace.[50] Marijuana is legal for recreational use in a number of states, which complicates the issue of which drugs can be tested for, and it can be medically prescribed. It is also not uncommon for "false positives" to occur—that is, for a test to mistakenly show someone has used illegal drugs when they haven't. Some over-the-counter drugs can also lead to false positives.

For reasons such as these and because candidates view them as invasive, some companies no longer conduct drug tests on job candidates. In other cases, should a candidate fail a drug test, the companies allow the candidate to retake it to ensure its accuracy. Other companies say drug testing has saved them thousands of dollars in workers' compensation and other costs. The weight of the evidence suggests that testing is most appropriate for high-risk and safety-critical positions and those required by state and federal laws.

The U.S. Department of Labor suggests that if a company wants to implement drug testing, it should seek legal advice and follow the same testing standards that federal agencies follow—namely, the procedures established by the Substance Abuse and Mental Health Services Administration (SAMHSA). Of course, not testing job candidates for drugs doesn't mean firms can't continue to have drug-free workplace policies requiring employees to come to work sober.

6.5b Determining the Validity of Tests

The *Uniform Guidelines* (see Chapter 3) recognizes and accepts different approaches to validating tests (and selection procedures in general): criterion-related validity, content validity, and construct validity.

Criterion-Related Validity

criterion-related validity
The extent to which a selection tool predicts, or significantly correlates with, important work behaviors.

concurrent validity
The extent to which the test scores of current employees correlate with their job performance.

The extent to which a test significantly correlates with important work behaviors is known as **criterion-related validity**. How well a person performs on a test, for example, is compared with their actual production records, supervisor's ratings, training outcomes, and other measures of on-the-job success. Sales figures are commonly used to measure success in sales jobs. In production jobs, the quantity and quality of output are likely to be the best indicators of job success.

Two types of criterion-related validity exist: concurrent and predictive. **Concurrent validity** is the extent to which the test scores of a firm's current employees correlate with their job performance. To test concurrent validity, a firm obtains data from its current employees at about the same time that test scores (or other predictor information) are obtained. For example, a supervisor would rate a group of clerical employees on the quantity and quality of their performance. These employees would then be given a clerical aptitude test, and their scores would be compared with the supervisor's ratings to determine the degree of relationship between them. Establishing the concurrent validity of a test prior to administering it to candidates can be quick and convenient because the firm has employees readily available to take the test. The drawback of this approach is that current employees have a great deal more experience, so their scores may not be comparable to candidates' scores.

Predictive validity involves testing candidates and obtaining criterion data after the individuals have been hired and on the job for a period of time. For example, candidates would be given clerical aptitude tests, which would then be filed away for later study. After the individuals have been on the job for several months, supervisors (who should not know the employees' test scores) are asked to rate them on the quality and quantity of their performance. The test scores are then compared with the supervisors' ratings. If the scores and supervisors' ratings are in line with each other, the test has predictive validity and can be used to test subsequent job candidates. Obviously, this approach to testing will take longer to develop than the concurrent validity approach.

predictive validity The extent to which candidates' test scores match criterion data obtained from them after they have been hired and on the job for a period of time.

Regardless of the method used, cross-validation is essential. **Cross-validation** is a process in which a test or battery of tests is administered to a different sample of people (drawn from the same population) for the purpose of verifying the results obtained from the original validation study. One way to measure a test's validity is to administer it to an organization's current employees and create a benchmark score against which candidates' scores can be compared. This is what FedEx has agreed to do before administering any new tests.

cross-validation Verifying the results obtained from a validation study by administering a test or test battery to a different sample (drawn from the same population).

Correlation methods are generally used to determine the relationship between predictor information such as test scores and criterion data. The correlation scatterplots in Figure 6.6 illustrate the difference between a selection test with zero validity (A) and one with high validity (B). Each dot represents a person.

In scatterplot A, there is no relationship between test scores and success on the job; in other words, the validity is zero. In scatterplot B, people who score low on the test tend to have low success on the job, whereas those who score high on the test tend to have high success on the job, indicating high validity. In actual practice, we would apply a statistical formula to the data to obtain a coefficient of correlation referred to as a *validity coefficient*. Correlation coefficients range from 0.00, denoting a complete absence of relationship, to +1.00 and to −1.00, indicating a perfect positive and a perfect negative relationship, respectively.

Figure 6.6 Correlation Scatterplots

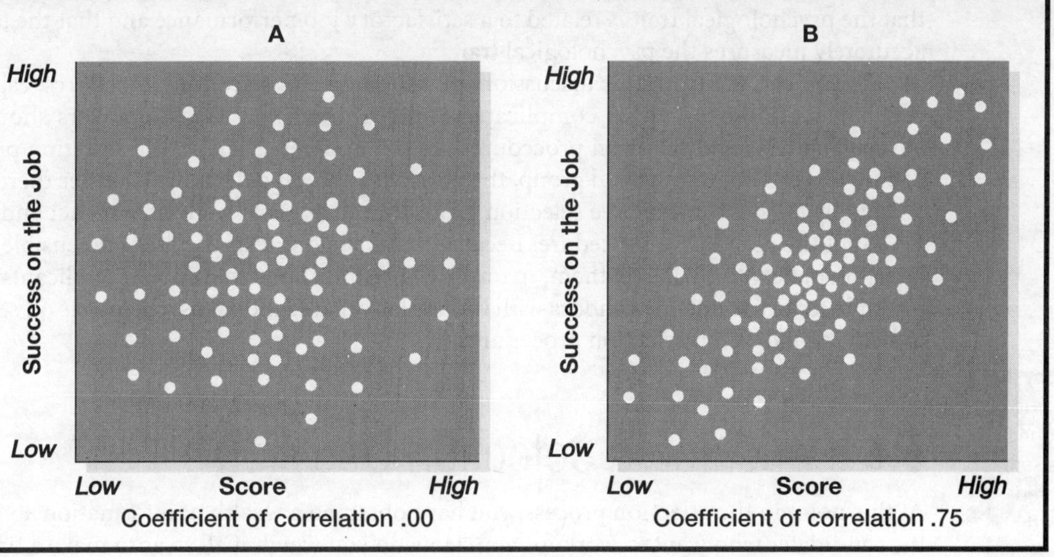

Combining two or more procedures, such as an interview and a test, can improve the validity of a firm's selection process. The higher the overall validity is, the greater the chances are of hiring individuals who will be better performers.

Content Validity

When it is not feasible to use the criterion-related approach, perhaps because of limited samples of employees or applicants available for testing, the content method is used. **Content validity** is assumed to exist when a test adequately samples the knowledge and skills a person needs to do a particular job. The closer the content of the selection instrument is to actual work samples or behaviors, the higher its content validity is. For example, a test for accountants has high content validity when it requires applicants to solve accounting problems representative of those found on the job. Asking an accountant to lift a 60-pound box, however, is a selection procedure that has content validity only if the job description indicates that accountants must be able to meet this requirement.

content validity
The extent to which a selection instrument, such as a test, adequately samples the knowledge and skills needed to do a particular job.

Content validity is the most direct and least complicated type of validity to assess. It is generally used to evaluate job knowledge and skills tests. Unlike the criterion-related method, content validity is not expressed as a correlation. Instead, an index is computed (based on the evaluations of an expert panel) that indicates the relationship between the content of the test items and a person's performance on the job.[51] Although content validity does have its limitations, it has made a positive contribution to job analysis procedures and the role expert judgments play in sampling and scoring procedures.

Construct Validity

The extent to which a test measures a theoretical construct, or trait, is known as **construct validity**. Examples of constructs include intelligence, mechanical comprehension, and anxiety. Constructs are, in effect, broad, general categories of human functions that are based on the measurement of many discrete behaviors. For example, the Bennett Mechanical Comprehension Test consists of a wide variety of tasks that measure the construct of mechanical comprehension. Measuring construct validity requires showing that the psychological trait is related to a satisfactory job performance and that the test accurately measures the psychological trait.[52]

construct validity
The extent to which a selection tool measures a theoretical construct or trait.

As you can tell from this discussion, developing valid selection procedures, especially selection tests, can be complicated and requires expertise. Employers should ensure that tests and selection procedures are not adopted casually. If a selection procedure screens out a protected group, the employer should determine whether there is an equally effective alternative selection procedure that has less adverse impact and, if so, adopt the alternative procedure. Because valid custom tests are more defensible in court if applicants challenge them, many large organizations that subject applicants to multiple tests hire outside vendors with industrial-organizational psychologists on staff to help them develop selection procedures.

LO4
What is meant by the term criterion as it is used in personnel selection? Give some examples of criteria used for jobs with which you are familiar.

6.6 Reaching a Selection Decision

At this point in the selection process, you have obtained a wealth of information about the candidates who want to work for you. How do you weigh it all so as to make a final decision? In this section, we'll look at the various approaches you might use.

6.6a Summarizing Information about Applicants

Once you have gathered relevant information about multiple applicants, you have to systematically organize and evaluate it. Summary forms and checklists such as the one shown in Figure 6.7 can be used to ensure that all of the pertinent information about applicants has been included. Fundamentally, an employer is interested in what an applicant can do and will do. Evaluating candidates on the basis of information you have assembled should focus on these two factors, as Figure 6.8 shows. The "can-do" factors include a candidate's knowledge and skills, as well as the aptitude (potential) for acquiring new knowledge and skills. The "will-do" factors include the candidate's motivation, interests, and other personality characteristics. Both factors are essential to successful performance on the job. The employee who has the ability (can do) but is not motivated to use it (will not do) is little better than the employee who lacks the necessary ability.

It is much easier to measure what individuals can do than what they will do. The can-do factors are readily evident from test scores and verified information. What the

Figure 6.7 Candidate Evaluation Form

Position:
Candidate Name:
Interviewer Name:
Interview Date:

Complete the comments section as you interview the candidate. After the interview, circle your ratings for each section, and then add them together for a final score. The ratings scale is as follows:

RATINGS SCALE

1. Negligible or doesn't meet requirements
2. More needed
3. Adequate
4. Exceeds requirements

Education
Comments:
Rating: ____________

Experience
Comments:
Rating: ____________

Job Knowledge
Comments:
Rating: ____________

Job Skills
Comments:

Interest in Position
Comments:
Rating:

Problem-Solving Ability
Comments:
Rating: ____________

Communication Skills
Comments:
Rating: ____________

Leadership Skills
Comments:
Rating: ____________

____________ TOTAL POINTS

Rater's Recommendation:

Figure 6.8 "Can-Do" and "Will-Do" Factors in Selection Decisions

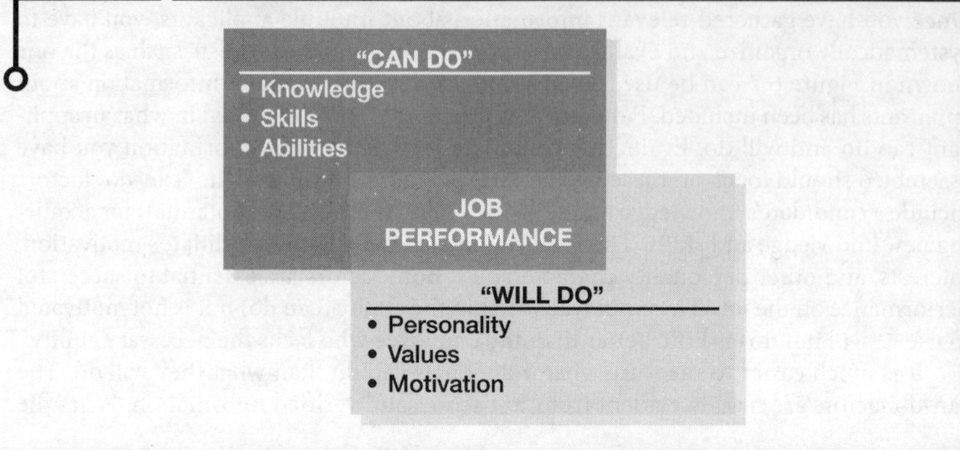

individual will do can only be inferred. Employers can use the responses to interview and application form questions and references to obtain information for making inferences about what an individual will do once on the job.

6.6b Decision-Making Strategy

The strategy used to make personnel decisions for one type of job, such as a manager, will differ from those used to make decisions for other types of jobs, such as a clerk or a technician. Although many factors must be considered, the following are some of the questions firms must consider when deciding who to hire:

1. Should the individuals be hired according to their highest potential or according to the needs of the organization?
2. At what grade or wage level should the individual be hired?
3. Should the selection be based on finding an ideal employee to match the job currently open, or should a candidate's potential for advancement in the organization be considered?
4. Should individuals who are not qualified but trainable be considered?
5. Should overqualified individuals be considered?
6. What effect will the decision have on the firm's affirmative action plans and diversity and inclusion goals?

In addition to these factors, a firm must decide which selection approach to use: the clinical (personal judgment) approach or the statistical approach. These approaches are discussed next.

Clinical Approach

With the clinical approach, the people making the selection decision review all the data on the applicants. Then, based on their understanding of the job and the individuals who have been successful in that job, they make a holistic assessment of the information to reach a decision. Different evaluators may make different decisions about an applicant when they use the clinical approach because each may have different insights or judgments about the applicant's strengths and weaknesses. Unfortunately, personal biases and stereotypes are frequently covered up by what appear to be rational reasons for either accepting or rejecting a candidate. The clinical approach can also lead to a homogenous workforce because, as you learned in Chapter 5, according to the attraction–selection–attrition (ASA) model, people are often tempted to hire applicants like themselves.

Statistical Approach

The statistical approach to decision making is more objective. It involves identifying the most valid predictors and weighting them using statistical methods such as multiple regression.[53] Quantified data such as scores or ratings from interviews, tests, and other procedures are then combined according to their weighted value, and individuals with the highest combined scores are selected. Compared to the clinical approach, the statistical approach has been shown to be superior in a wide variety of situations.

With a strictly statistical approach, a candidate's high score on one predictor (such as a cognitive ability test) may make up for a low score on another predictor (such as the interview). For this reason, the model produced with this approach is a **compensatory model**. However, it is frequently important for applicants to achieve some minimum level of proficiency on *all* selection dimensions. When this is the case, a **multiple cutoff model** can be used, in which only those candidates who score above the minimum cutoff on all dimensions are considered. A selection from that subset of candidates is then made.[54]

compensatory model
A selection decision model in which a high score in one area can make up for a low score in another area.

multiple cutoff model
A selection decision model that requires an applicant to achieve some minimum level of proficiency on all selection dimensions.

multiple hurdle model
A selection decision model in which only those applicants with the highest scores at an initial test stage go on to subsequent stages.

A variation of the multiple cutoff model is the **multiple hurdle model**. After candidates go through an initial evaluation stage, those who score well advance to the next stage. The process continues through several stages (hurdles) until a final decision is made. This approach is especially useful when either the testing or training procedures are lengthy and expensive.

Each of the statistical approaches requires that a decision be made about where the cutoff lies—that point in the distribution of scores above which a person should be considered and below which the person should be rejected. The score that the applicant must achieve is the cutoff score. Depending on the labor supply and diversity and inclusion considerations, it may be necessary to lower or raise the cutoff score.

The effects of raising and lowering the cutoff score are illustrated in Figure 6.9. Each dot in the center of the figure represents the relationship between the test score (or a weighted combination of test scores) and a criterion of success for one individual. The elliptical pattern of the dots indicates the test has a fairly high validity. Note that the high-scoring individuals are concentrated in the satisfactory job success category, whereas the low-scoring individuals are concentrated in the unsatisfactory category.

If the cutoff score is set at A, only the individuals represented by areas 1 and 2 will be accepted. Nearly all of them will be successful. If more employees are needed, the cutoff score can be lowered to point B. In this case, a larger number of potential failures will be accepted, as shown in quadrants 2 and 4. Even if the cutoff is lowered to C, the total number of satisfactory individuals selected (represented by the dots in areas 1, 3, and 5) exceeds the total number selected who are unsatisfactory (areas 2, 4, and 6). Thus, the test serves to maximize the selection of probable successes and to minimize the selection of probable failures. This is all we can hope for in terms of predicting on-the-job success: the probability of selecting a greater proportion of individuals who will be successful rather than unsuccessful.

Figure 6.9 Test Scores Scatterplot with Hypothetical Cutoffs

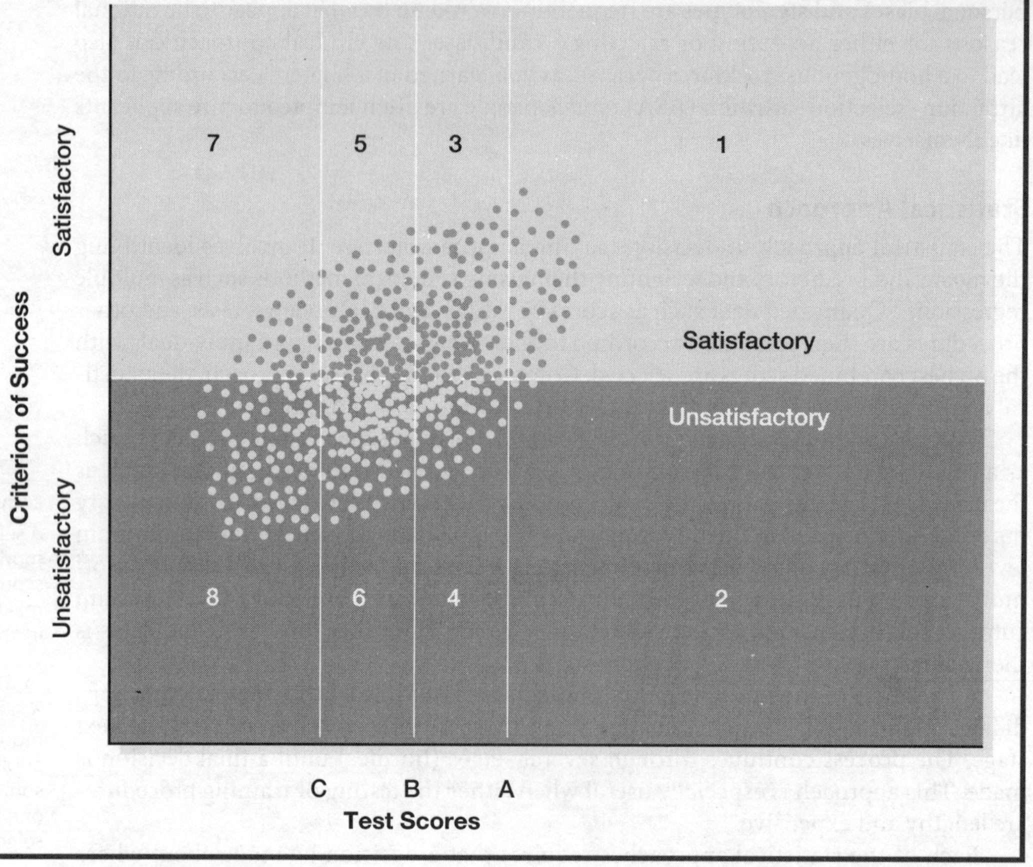

selection ratio
The number of applicants compared with the number of people to be hired.

A related factor helps ensure the best-qualified people are selected: having an adequate number of candidates from which to make a selection. This factor is typically expressed in terms of a **selection ratio**, which is the ratio of the number of applicants to be selected to the total number of applicants. A ratio of 0.10, for example, means that 10 percent of the applicants will be selected. A ratio of 0.90 means that 90 percent will be selected. If the selection ratio is low, only the most promising applicants will be hired. When the ratio is high, very little selectivity will be possible because even applicants with mediocre abilities will have to be hired to fill the firm's vacancies. When this is the situation, a firm's managers can fall prey to what some experts call the "desperation bias"—choosing someone just because you are in a pinch. It is a common problem among managers because of the many time and operating constraints they face.

6.6c Final Decision

In large organizations, managers or supervisors usually make the final decision about who to hire, and communicate it to the HR department. HR personnel then notify the candidate about the decision and make a job offer. The HR department should confirm the details of the job, working arrangements, hours, wages, and so on, and specify a deadline by which the applicant must reach a decision. If, at this point, findings from the medical examination or drug test are not yet available, an offer is often made contingent on the applicant passing the examination. This information can be verbally communicated initially. It is commonplace to first contact candidates by phone to inform them of the offer. The offer should then be put in writing, generally in a letter to the candidate.

The process of notifying internal candidates is slightly different. Generally, the hiring manager contacts the candidates personally and informs them of the decision. However, it is still important to put the offer in writing if an internal candidate is chosen so there is no ambiguity or dispute about its terms.

Rejecting both internal candidates and external candidates is a difficult task, but rejecting internal candidates can be particularly tricky. Most internal candidates seeking a promotion are valuable employees their firms would rather not lose. The manager delivering the bad news should explain to the employee that the person who got the job has skills more closely aligned with the firm's needs, but that the process has given the organization a better understanding of their background when future job openings arise. The manager should also explain that while the decision was made in a systematic way based on objective criteria, it was nonetheless a hard one to make.[55]

Last, organizations should not fail to notify candidates who are not chosen for the position. This happens too often with both internal candidates and external candidates. It is not uncommon for external candidates to be customers of the firms to which they apply. Not letting them know about the employment decision can jeopardize that relationship. The same is true for internal candidates. One employee lamented that after applying internally for a job, no one contacted him or the other candidates to tell them they did not get the job. They learned the news only after a manager sent out an email about the new hire. "After 10-plus years of working for the company, I felt I deserved better treatment than that," says the employee.

Summary

LO 1 The employee selection process should start with a job analysis. The steps in the selection process and their sequence will vary not only with the organization, but also with the type and level of jobs to be filled. The employee selection process should provide reliable and valid information about applicants so that their qualifications can be carefully matched with the job's specifications. The information that is obtained should be clearly job related, predict success on the job, and be free from discrimination. Reliability refers to the consistency of test scores over time and across measures. Validity refers to what a test or other selection procedure is supposed to measure and how well it actually measures it.

LO 2 Initial applicant screening tools include resumes and cover letters, application forms, references, Internet checks and phone screening, and sometimes short electronic questionnaires. Despite problems with its validity, the employment interview remains central to the selection process. Depending on the type of job, applicants could be interviewed by one person, members of a work team, or other individuals in the organization. Structured interviews have been found to be better predictors of the performance of job applicants than nonstructured interviews. Some interviews are situational and can focus on hypothetical situations or actual behavioral descriptions of a candidate's previous work experiences. Most interviews are conducted in person, but they can also be conducted via video, phone, or a computer (automated). Post-interview screening tools include reference and background checks, including criminal, drug, and credit checks.

LO 3 Preemployment tests are more objective than interviews and can give managers a fuller sense of the capabilities of different candidates. A wide range of tests exist. Cognitive ability tests are especially valuable for assessing verbal, quantitative, and reasoning abilities. Personality and interest-inventory tests are perhaps best used for placement or career development. Job knowledge and work sample tests are achievement tests that are useful for determining whether a candidate can perform the duties of the job without further training. Physical ability tests can be used to prevent accidents and injuries, particularly for physically demanding work. However, they must not be used if they will have a disparate impact on candidates in protected classes. Medical examinations and drug tests should be administered only after a conditional offer of employment has been made. A test's validity can be assessed in terms of whether the measurement is based on a job specification (content validity), whether test scores correlate with performance criteria (predictive validity), and whether the test accurately measures what it purports to measure (construct validity).

LO 4 In the process of making decisions, all "can-do" and "will-do" factors should be assembled and weighted systematically so that the final decision can be based on a composite of the most reliable and valid information. Although the clinical approach to decision making is used more than the statistical approach, the former lacks the accuracy of the latter. Compensatory models allow a candidate's high score on one predictor to make up for a low score on another aspect. When the multiple cutoff model is used, only those candidates who score above a minimum cutoff level remain in the running for the job. A variation of the multiple cutoff is the multiple hurdle model, which involves several stages and cutoff levels. Organizations should not fail to notify candidates who are not chosen for jobs. Those who are chosen should receive their offers in writing so the terms are clearly agreed upon and be given a time limit to either accept or reject the offer.

Key Terms

assessment center test
automated interview
behavioral description interview (BDI)
compensatory model
concurrent validity
construct validity
content validity
criterion-related validity
cross-validation
multiple cutoff model
multiple hurdle model
negligent hiring
nondirective interview
panel interview
predictive validity
preemployment test
reliability
remote or virtual interviews
selection
selection ratio
sequential interview
situational interview
structured interview
validity
video resumes

Discussion Questions

LO 1 Is there a "best" employment process from a stepwise perspective? Which steps must come first? Which must come last?

LO 2 Compare briefly the major types of employment interviews described in this chapter. Which type would you prefer to conduct? Why?

LO 3 What characteristics do job knowledge and job sample tests have that often make them more acceptable to candidates than other types of tests?

LO 4 What is meant by the term *criterion* as it is used in personnel selection? Give some examples of criteria used for jobs with which you are familiar.

HRM Experience

Designing Selection Criteria and Methods

Making hiring decisions is important but difficult. Without good information, managers have almost no chance of making the right choice. They may as well randomly choose a candidate.

The information-gathering process begins with a sound understanding of the job: the tasks, duties, and responsibilities associated with it, and the knowledge, skills, and abilities needed to do it. A job analysis should be done to make certain that all managers have assembled all of the information they need to ensure a good person–job fit. However, this information may not be enough. Other information about the company's values and philosophy are likely to be required to ensure that a good person–organization fit results.

Assignment

1. Working in teams of four to six individuals, choose a job with which you are familiar and identify the KSAOs needed to do it well.
2. Identify how you would evaluate candidates with these qualities. Which tools would you use (applications, interviews, cognitive or ability tests, work samples, etc.) and why? Justify the cost and time required to conduct each.
3. After you have identified your selection criteria and methods, do a "reality check" in a real organization. Interview a manager who employs someone in that job. For example, if the job you selected is salesperson, go to a local business to learn how they select individuals for sales jobs. Compare what you thought would be a good selection approach with what you learned from the company you visited.
4. Identify the reasons for any discrepancies between your approach and the approach used by the company. Which approach do you think is better?

CASE STUDY 1 Job Candidate Assessment Tests Go Virtual

A growing number of preemployment tests simulate a job's functions and are being conducted via computer or on the Web. You can liken them to video games but within a work setting. Toyota, Starbucks, the paint maker Sherwin Williams, and numerous financial firms such as SunTrust Banks, KeyBank, and National City Bank have successfully used virtual job simulations to assess applicants.

At Toyota, applicants participating in simulations read dials and gauges, spot safety problems, and use their ability to solve problems as well as their general ability to learn as assessed. The candidates can see and hear about the job they're applying for from current Toyota employees. National City Bank has used virtual assessments to test call-center candidates and branch manager candidates. Call-center candidates are given customer-service problems to solve, and branch manager candidates go through a simulation that assesses their ability to foster relationships with clients and make personnel decisions.

These kinds of virtual assessment tools, which are produced by companies such as Shaker Consulting Group, Profiles International, and others, do not come cheap. But although they can cost tens of thousands of dollars, larger companies that can afford them are saying they are worth it. The benefits? Better-qualified candidates, faster recruiting, and lower turnover among employees hired. KeyBank says that by using virtual testing tools, it realized savings of more than $1.75 million per year due to lower turnover.

Candidates also seem to like the assessments because they provide a more realistic job preview and make them feel as if they are being chosen for jobs based on more than just their personalities or how they performed during an interview. "It was a very insightful experience that made you think about what exactly you like and dislike in the workplace and if you really enjoy helping customers and have patience to do so," says one candidate tested for a customer service job.

And it is not just younger candidates who play a lot of video games who like the tests—older candidates do as well. "We haven't seen any adverse impact," says Ken Troyan, chief staffing officer for SunTrust Banks.

"There's some mythology—if you will—about older people not being computer-savvy, and that's just not so." One study found that the simulations also tend to result in less of a gap between people in underrepresented groups and White candidates than when paper-and-pencil tests are used.

A handful of software companies have developed games that don't mirror work tasks but are actual video games you would play for fun. "Bomba Blitz" and "Meta Maze" are two mobile games developed by the preemployment-testing company Knack. According to Knack, the games utilize behavioral neuroscience and big data—in this case, the game scores and decision-making traits of thousands of different types of workers—to match people with jobs.

HR experts warn that companies need to be sure they aren't simply buying glitzy simulations that don't translate well to the jobs for which they are hiring. Games like those produced by Knack are just now starting to be used, and firms generally aren't solely relying on them to make hiring decisions. Also, the tools could potentially eliminate candidates who have trouble with simulations, games, or computers but might make good employees. You should still use the U.S. Department of Labor's "whole-person approach" to hiring, says one HR professional. The whole-person approach factors in the results of a variety of accepted tests along with prior actual performance and interview results to get the most complete picture of an employee or candidate.

Questions

1. What do you think are the prime advantages and disadvantages of "virtual tryouts"?
2. Do you think there would be any EEOC concerns regarding this system?
3. Do you think virtual job tryouts might be better suited for some jobs than others? If so, which ones?

Sources: Sarah Needleman, "Play This Game and Win a Job!" *Wall Street Journal* (March 14, 2016): R2; Karen Vilardo, "KeyBank's Success with the 'Virtual Job Tryout,'" *Journal of Corporate Recruiting Leadership* 5, no. 4 (2010): 24; Ira S. Wolfe, "Success Performance Solutions," *The Total View Newsletter* (May 12, 2010); Connie Winkle, "HR Technology: Job Tryouts Go Virtual," *HR Magazine* (September 1, 2006), http://www.shrm.org/; Gina Ruiz, "Job Candidate Assessment Tests Go Virtual," *Workforce Management Online* (January 2008), http://www.workforce.com; "Clients and Case Studies," *Shaker Consulting Group* (March 27, 2011), http://www.shakercg.com.

CASE STUDY 2 Pros and Cons of Cleaning up the "Resu-mess"

HR and hiring managers often find themselves swamped by resumes because they are so easy to send with a click of a button. Some large retailers can get a million or more resumes a year. Even small businesses get flooded with them. When Raising Cain, a Louisiana-based fast-food chain, opened an office in Dallas, the firm needed to hire 35 people. It received 10,000 resumes and had to hire an outside firm to help sort through them.

Applicant tracking systems and resume screening software are helping harried HR personnel, managers, and business owners cope with the problem. After resumes are screened and reviewed, interviews can be scheduled automatically using a firm's email system and electronic calendar, and job offers sent to candidates to sign electronically and return. Many job boards have resume screening capabilities and algorithms to recommend candidates, similar to the way Amazon.com recommends products based on what a person has purchased in the past.

Not all HR professionals are fans of resume screening software, however. Managers tend to use huge numbers of key words so that very few applicants can make it past the screen. Different kinds of software can have different kinds of glitches. The software might not read certain types of fonts or might reject a resume of a good candidate if it contains a single typo. Unqualified applicants have also learned to "pepper" their resumes with a job's keywords to get past resume-screening software.

In his book *Why Good People Can't Get Jobs,* Peter Cappelli relates an incident in which an HR manager put his own resume through his company's screening process and got rejected. In another instance, an engineering firm received more than 25,000 resumes for a job but none of the candidates made it past electronic screening.

There is also a lack of the human touch and judgment in the process. Resume-screening software can't easily pick up on candidates' "soft" skills, such as a person's ability to interact well with other people. And managers don't end up seeing interesting resumes—resumes from people who have different skills or life experiences that would translate well to the job. Consequently, a lot of people who would make excellent employees never get even a first glance.

Some recruiters have found ways to avoid the downsides of automatic resume screening altogether. Kevin Mercuri, president of Propheta Communications, a public relations firm in New York City, got tired of being swamped by resumes. Now when he needs to recruit personnel, he posts a message about job openings on his LinkedIn page. "I get people vouching for each applicant, so I don't have to spend hours sorting through resumes," he says.

Questions

1. What impact do you think resume screening tools are having on HR departments? What about line managers? Would you use the software to screen resumes?
2. How might the drawbacks associated with resume screening software be addressed?

Sources: Ryan Craig, "Blame Bad Applicant Tracing for the Soft Skills Shortage at Your Company," *TechCrunch* (March 5, 2017), https://techcrunch.com; Dave Wessel, "Software Raises the Bar for Hiring," *Wall Street Journal* (May 31, 2012), http://online.wsj.com; Darren Dahl, "Tapping the Talent Pool … without Drowning in Résumés," *Inc.* 31 no. 3 (2009): 122; Anne Kadet, "Did You Get My Résumé?" *Smart Money* (February 27, 2009), http://www.smartmoney.com; Drew Robb, "Screening for Speedier Selection," *HR Magazine* 49, no. 9 (2004): 143–147.

Notes and References

1. Philip L. Roth et al., "Social Media in Employee-Selection-Related Decisions: A Research Agenda for Uncharted Territory," *Journal of Management* (2013), 0149206313503018; Kate Z. Williams, Meline M. Schaffer, and Lauren E. Ellis, "Legal Risk in Selection: An Analysis of Processes and Tools," *Journal of Business & Psychology* 28, no. 4 (2013), doi: 10.1007/s10869-013-9299-4.
2. D. T. A. M. Kooij, M. van Woerkom, J. Wilkenloh, L. Dorenbosch, and J. J. A. Denissen, "Job Crafting towards Strengths and Interests: The Effects of a Job Crafting Intervention on Person–Job Fit and the Role of Age," *Journal of Applied Psychology* 102, no. 6 (2017): 971–981; Misty L. Loughry, Matthew W. Ohland, and D. Dewayne Moore, "Development of a Theory-Based Assessment of Team Member Effectiveness," *Educational & Psychological Measurement* 67, no. 3 (2007): 505–524; Patrick D. Converse, Fredrick L. Oswald, Michael A. Gillespie, Kevin A. Field, and Elizabeth B. Bizot, "Matching Individual to Occupations Using Abilities and the O*NET," *Personnel Psychology* 57, no. 2 (2004): 451–488.
3. Murray R. Barrick and Laura Parks-Leduc, "Selection for Fit," *Annual Review of Organizational Psychology and Organizational Behavior* 6 (2019): 171–193; A. L. Kristof-Brown and K. J. Jansen, "Issues of Person–Organization Fit," in C. Ostroff and T. A. Judge, eds., *The Organizational Frontiers Series: Perspectives on Organizational Fit* (Oxfordshire, UK: Lawrence Erlbaum Associates, 2012), 123–153; Rachel Feintzeig, "Cultural Fit Plays Role in Hiring," *Wall Street Journal* (October 12, 2006), https://www.wsj.com.
4. Nathaniel M. Voss, Christopher J. Lake, and Cassandra Chlevin-Thiele, "Effectively Communicating Validity Information about Personnel Selection Tools," *Personnel Psychology*, July 29, 2020; Joe Williams, "Bringing the Human Touch to Recruitment," *Bloomberg Businessweek* (January 24, 2011), http://bx.businessweek.com.
5. Dina Gerdeman, "Minorities Who 'Whiten' Job Resumes Get More Interviews," *Working Knowledge* (Harvard Business School, May 17, 2017); Sonia K. Kang, Katherine A. DeCelles, and András Tilcsik, "Whitened Résumés: Race and Self-Presentation in the Labor Market," *Administrative Science Quarterly* 61, no. 3 (2016): 469–502; Mary-Kathryn Zachary, "Discrimination without Intent," *Supervision* 64, no. 5 (2003): 23–29; Neal Schmitt, William Rogers, David Chan, Lori Sheppard, and Danielle Jennings, "Adverse Impact and Predictive Efficiency of Various Predictor Combinations," *Journal of Applied Psychology* 82, no. 5 (1997): 719–730.
6. Amy Elisa Jackson, "Can Your Resume Beat the Bots? How to Make It ATS-Friendly," *GlassDoor*, April 25, 2018; Gary N. Burns et al., "Effects of Applicant Personality on Résumé Evaluations," *Journal of Business and Psychology* 29, no. 4 (2014): 573–591; Michael Luo, "'Whitening' the Résumé," *New York Times* (December 5, 2009), http://www.nytimes.com.
7. Roy Mauer, "Know before You Hire: 2017 Employment Screening Trends," Society of Human Resources Management (January 25, 2017), https://www.shrm.org.
8. Roy Mauer, "Know before You Hire," 2017.
9. Alexander Reicher, "The Background of Our Bing: Internet Background Checks in the Hiring Process," *Berkeley Technology Law Journal* 28, no. 1 (2013): 115–153.
10. Rachel Feintzeig and Vanessa Fuhrmans, "Past Social-Media Posts Upend Hiring," *Wall Street Journal*, August 8, 2018; Jennifer Valentino DeVries, "Bosses May Use Social Media to Discriminate against Job Seekers," *Wall Street Journal* (November 20, 2013), https://www.wsj.com.

11. "How to Make a Video Resume: Tips and Examples," Indeed: Career Guide (December 29, 2020), https://www.indeed.com/career-advice/resumes-cover-letters/how-to-make-a-video-resume; Lisa Takeuchi Cullen, "It's a Wrap: You're Hired," *Time* (February 22, 2007, http://time.com.
12. Hanna Kuchler, "Silicon Valley Tactics for Waging War on Biases in the Workplace" (March 7, 2017), https://www.ft.com.
13. Tessa West, "The Lies We Tell at Work—and the Damage They Do," *Wall Street Journal*, March 27, 2020.
14. "75% of HR Managers Have Caught a Lie on a Resume, According to a New CareerBuilder Survey," CareerBuilder, September 14, 2017; Scott Bennet, *The Elements of Résumé Style: Essential Rules for Writing Résumés and Cover Letters That Work* (New York, NY: AMACOM, 2014); "Busted," *Training Development* 60, no. 12 (2006): 19; Pamela Babock, "Spotting Lies," *HRMagazine* 48, no. 10 (2003): 46–51; Tammy Prater and Sara Bliss Kiser, "Lies, Lies, and More Lies," *A.A.M. Advance Management Journal* 67, no. 2 (2002): 9–14.
15. Ben Leubsdorf, "'Ban the Box' Laws May Worsen Hiring Discrimination, New Research Finds," *Wall Street Journal*, October 3, 2016; Max Mihelich, "Check on Background Checks," Workforce.com (September 23, 2013), http://www.workforce.com.
16. Roy Maurer, "Recruiting 101: 5 Tips for Better Interviews," Society for Human Resource Management, January 28, 2020; Barbara Bruno, "6 Things Every Recruiter Can Do to Make Interviews More Effective," LinkedIn, July 5, 2018; Amy Maingault, John Sweeney, and Naomi Cossack, "Interviewing, Management Training, Strikes," *HRMagazine* 52, no. 6 (2007): 43; James Bassett, "Stop, Thief!" *Gifts & Decorative Accessories* 104, no. 1 (2003): 130–134; Richard A. Posthuma, Frederick Morgeson, and Michael Campion, "Beyond Employment Interview Validity: A Comprehensive Narrative Review of Recent Research and Trends over Time," *Personnel Psychology* 55, no. 1 (2002): 1–8.
17. Robert Gatewood, Hubert S. Feild, and Murray Barrick, *Human Resource Selection* (Nelson Education, 2015); Yen-Chun Chen, Wei-Chi Tsai, and Changya Hu, "The Influences of Interviewer-Related and Situational Factors on Interviewer Reactions to High Structured Job Interviews," *International Journal of Human Resource Management* 19, no. 6 (2008): 1056–1071; Jesus F. Salgado and Silvia Moscoso, "Comprehensive Meta-Analysis of the Construct Validity of the Employment Interview," *European Journal of Work and Organizational Psychology* 11, no. 3 (2002): 299–325.
18. S. Culbertson, W. S. Weyhrauch, and A. I. Huffcutt, "A Tale of Two Formats: Direct Comparison of Matching Situational and Behavior Description Interview Questions," *Human Resource Management Review* 27, no. 1 (2017): 167–177; Julia Levashina et al., "The Structured Employment Interview: Narrative and Quantitative Review of the Research Literature," *Personnel Psychology* 67, no. 1 (2014): 241–293; Allen Huffcutt, Jeff Weekley, Willi Wiesner, Timothy Degroot, and Casey Jones, "Comparison of Situational and Behavior Description Interview Questions for Higher-Level Positions," *Personnel Psychology* 54, no. 3 (2001): 619–644.
19. Allen I. Huffcutt, Satoris S. Culbertson, and William S. Weyhrauch, "Employment Interview Reliability," *International Journal of Selection and Assessment* 21, no. 3 (2013): 264–276; Peter Herriot, "Assessment by Groups: Can Value Be Added?" *European Journal of Work & Organizational Psychology* 12, no. 2 (2003): 131–146; Salgado and Moscoso, "Comprehensive Meta-Analysis," 2002; Amelia J. Prewett-Livingston, John G. Veres III, Hubert S. Field, and Philip M. Lewis, "Effects of Race on Interview Ratings in a Situational Panel Interview," *Journal of Applied Psychology* 81, no. 2 (1996).
20. M. Baker, "Gartner HR Survey Shows 86% of Organizations Are Conducting Virtual Interviews to Hire Candidates during Coronavirus Pandemic," Gartner, April 30, 2020.
21. Julia Thomas, "Video Killed the Interview Star," *DeGroote School of Business* (July 29, 2013), http://www.degroote.mcmaster.ca.
22. Lynda Speigel, "How to Ace the Remote Job Interview," *Wall Street Journal*, March 23, 2021.
23. P. Rubinstein, "Asynchronous Video Interviews: The Tools You Need to Succeed," BBC, November 5, 2020; Darren Dahl, "Tapping the Talent Pool . . . without Drowning in Résumés," *Inc.* 31, no. 3 (2009): 122.
24. Joe Smydo, "Giant Eagle Job Fairs Attract Hundreds," *Pittsburgh Post-Gazette* (September 21, 2014), http://www.postgazette.com.
25. Rebecca Knight, "The Right Way to Check Someone's References," *Harvard Business Review*, July 29, 2016.
26. Lisa Nagele-Piazza, "Can Employers Give a Bad Reference for a Former Employee?" Society for Human Resource Management, February 28, 2018; Kira Vermond, "References Done Right," *Profit* 26, no. 2 (2007): 101; Kathleen Samey, "A Not-So-Perfect Fit," *Adweek* 44, no. 47 (2003): 34; Ann Fisher, "How Can We Be Sure We're Not Hiring a Bunch of Shady Liars?" *Fortune* 147, no. 10 (2003).
27. "Verify Employment Eligibility (E-Verify)," Department of Homeland Security, March 26, 2019, https://www.e-verify.gov.
28. "Pre-employment Inquiries and Arrest & Conviction," U.S. Equal Employment Opportunity Commission, https://www.eeoc.gov/; Katherine Erdel, "Changes May Prompt Review of Background Check Policies," *Corporate Counsel Guide* 24 (2014): 12B–13B.
29. Marsha Nielsen and Kristine Kuhn, "Late Payments and Leery Applicants: Credit Checks as a Selection Test," *Employee Responsibilities & Rights Journal* 21, no. 2 (2009): 115.
30. Beth Braverman, "Employers Running Credit Checks on Job Applicants Must Tread Carefully," CreditCards.com (July 25, 2016), http://www.creditcards.com.

31. Elizabeth D. MacGillivray, Juanita H. Beecher, and Diedre M. Golden, "Employment Testing: The New Hot Button Issue for Federal Agencies—and Other Legal Developments," *Global Business & Organizational Excellence* 27, no. 3 (2008): 68–78.
32. "EEOC Clarifies the Definition of Who Is an 'Applicant' in the Context of Internet Recruiting and Hiring," *Fair Employment Practices Guidelines* 587 (April 1, 2004): 3–13; Kathryn Tyler, "Put Applicants' Skills to the Test," *HRMagazine* 45, no. 1 (2000): 74–80.
33. Standards that testing programs should meet are described in *Standards for Educational and Psychological Tests* (Washington, DC: American Psychological Association, 2014).
34. Hershey H. Friedman, Linda Weiser Friedman, and Chaya Leverton, "Increase Diversity to Boost Creativity and Enhance Problem Solving," *Psychosociological Issues in Human Resource Management* 4, no. 2 (2016): 7–33; John Bret Becton, Hubert S. Feild, William F. Giles, and Allison Jones-Farmer, "Racial Differences in Promotion Candidate Performance and Reactions to Selection Procedures: A Field Study in a Diverse Top-Management Context," *Journal of Organizational Behavior* 29, no. 3 (2008): 265–285.
35. Rachel Suff, "Testing the Water: Using Work Sampling for Selection," *IRS Employment Review* 802 (June 18, 2004): 44–49; Leonard D. Goodstein and Alan D. Davidson, "Hiring the Right Stuff: Using Competency-Based Selection," *Compensation & Benefits Management* 14, no. 3 (1998): 1–10.
36. P. R. Sackett, O. R. Shewach, and H. N. Keiser, "Assessment Centers versus Cognitive Ability Tests: Challenging the Conventional Wisdom on Criterion-Related Validity," *Journal of Applied Psychology* 102, no. 10 (2017): 1435–1447; Stuart Crandell, "Assessment Centers in Talent Management: Strategies, Use, and Value," *Talent Management* (January 7, 2008), http://www.talentmgt.com.
37. Ken Richardson and Sarah H. Norgate, "Does IQ Really Predict Job Performance?" *Applied Development Science* 19, no. 3 (2015): 153–169; Shanna Lebowitz, "Why Your IQ May Have More Influence on Your Success Than You Think," *Inc.*, October 9, 2017; Matthew Night, "Does IQ Predict Performance at Work?" *CNN* (February 28, 2011), http://edition.cnn.com; Noelle Murphy, "Testing the Waters: Employers' Use of Selection Assessments," *IRS Employment Review* 852 (August 4, 2006): 42–48.
38. Candice Rudd, "FAA's Bid to Expand Air Traffic Hiring Pool Hits Turbulence," *Newsday* (April 24, 2016), http://www.newsday.com.
39. Personnel Selection and Resource Center, *Biographical Data (Biodata) Tests* (Washington DC: U.S. Office of Personnel Management, 2011), http://apps.opm.gov.
40. Julie Furr Yougman, "The Use and Abuse of Pre-employment Personality Tests," *Business Horizons* 60, no. 3 (2017): 261–269; Jesús F. Salgado and Gabriel Táuriz, "The Five-Factor Model, Forced-Choice Personality Inventories and Performance," *European Journal of Work and Organizational Psychology* 23, no. 1 (2014): 3–30; Timothy Judge and Joyce Bono, "Five Factor Model of Personality and Transformational Leadership," *Journal of Applied Psychology* 85, no. 5 (2000): 751–765.
41. Jason L. Huang et al., "Personality and Adaptive Performance at Work," *Journal of Applied Psychology* 99, no. 1 (2014): 162; Frederick P. Morgeson, Michael A. Campion, Robert L. Dipboye, John R. Hollenbeck, Kevin Murphy, and Neal Schmitt, "Reconsidering the Use of Personality Tests in Personnel Selection Contexts," *Personnel Psychology* 60, no. 3 (2007): 683–729; Gregory Hurtz and John Donovan, "Personality and Job Performance: The Big Five Revisited," *Journal of Applied Psychology* 85, no. 6 (2000): 869–879.
42. Lawrence Peikes and Meghan D. Burns, "Polygraph Test Request Unlawful," *HRMagazine* 50, no. 7 (2005): 110; "Pretext for Discrimination: How to Avoid Looking Like a Liar," *Fair Employment Practices Guidelines* 592 (September 1, 2004): 1–3; Gillian Flynn, Diane D. Hatch, and James E. Hall, "Know the Background of Background Checks," *Workforce* 81, no. 9 (2002): 96–98.
43. Josh Speraneo, "Does Payless Hire Felons in 2020?" *Successful Release* (2021), https://successfulrelease.com/does-payless-hire-felons/; "If the Shoe Fits," *Security Management* 40, no. 2 (1996): 11; Michelle Cottle, "Job Testing: Multiple Choices," *The New York Times* (September 5, 1999): 3, 10.
44. Y. Lee, C. M. Berry, and E. Gonzalez-Mulé, "The Importance of Being Humble: A Meta-Analysis and Incremental Validity Analysis of the Relationship between Honesty–Humility and Job Performance," *Journal of Applied Psychology* 104, no. 12 (2019): 1535–1546; R. J. Karren and L. Zacharias, "Integrity Tests: Critical Issues," *Human Resource Management Review* 17, no. 2 (2007): 221–234; Taya R. Cohen et al., "Moral Character in the Workplace," *Journal of Personality and Social Psychology* 107, no. 5 (2014): 943; Thomas J. Ryan, "Nerves of Steal," *SGB* 37, no. 6 (2004): 8–10; D. S. Ones, C. Viswesvaran, and F. L. Schmidt, "Comprehensive Meta-Analysis of Integrity Test Validities: Findings and Implications for Personnel Selection and Theories of Job Performance," *Journal of Applied Psychology* 78 (1993): 679–703.
45. Steve Lorh, "Big Data, Trying to Build Better Workers," *New York Times* (April 20, 2013), http://www.nytimes.com.
46. Paul Zielbauer, "Small Changes Could Improve Police Hiring, Panel Says," *New York Times* (January 7, 1999): 8; Lynn McFarland and Ann Marie Ryan, "Variance in Faking across Noncognitive Measures," *Journal of Applied Psychology* 85, no. 5 (2000): 812–821.
47. "Screening by Means of Pre-employment Testing," Society for Human Resource Management, September 10, 2018; Robert Gatewood, Hubert S. Feild, and Murray Barrick, *Human Resource Selection* (Nelson Education, 2015); Maria Greco Danaher, "Strength Test Falls," *HRMagazine* 52, no. 2 (2007): 115–116; M. S. Sothmann, D. L. Gebhardt, T. A. Baker, G. M. Kastello, and V. A. Sheppard, "Performance

Requirements of Physically Strenuous Occupations: Validating Minimum Standards for Muscular Strength," *Ergonomics* 47, no. 8 (2004): 864.

48. Kenneth G. Dau-Schmidt, Matt Finkin, and Robert Covington, *Legal Protection for the Individual Employee* (West Academic, 2016); Michael Adams, Ben Van Houten, Robert Klara, and Elizabeth Bernstein, "Access Denied?" *Restaurant Business* 98, no. 2 (1999): 36–48; "Medical Screening: Are Employers Going Too Far?" *Employee Benefit Plan Review* 53, no. 11 (1999): 42–43.
49. "News Briefs," *Security Directors Report* 13, no. 18 (2013): 6.
50. Ibid.
51. Philip Bobko, Philip L. Roth, and Maury A. Buster, "The Usefulness of Unit Weights in Creating Composite Scores: A Literature Review, Application to Content Validity, and Meta-Analysis," *Organizational Research Methods* 10, no. 4 (2007): 689–709.
52. Deniz S. Ones, Chockalingam Viswesvaran, and Frank L Schmidt, "No New Terrain: Reliability and Construct Validity of Job Performance Ratings," *Industrial & Organizational Psychology* 1, no. 2 (2008): 174–179; D. Brent Smith and Lill Ellingson, "Substance versus Style: A New Look at Social Desirability in Motivating Contexts," *Journal of Applied Psychology* 87, no. 2 (2002): 211–219; Ken Craik et al., "Explorations of Construct Validity in a Combined Managerial and Personality Assessment Programme," *Journal of Occupational and Organizational Psychology* 75, no. 2 (2002): 171–193.
53. Multiple regression is a statistical method for evaluating the magnitude of effects of more than one independent variable (e.g., selection predictors) on a dependent variable (e.g., job performance) using principles of correlation and regression.
54. Patricia M. Buhler, "Managing in the New Millennium," *Supervision* 68, no. 11 (2007): 17–20; Ann Marie Ryan, Joshua Sacco, Lynn McFarland, and David Kriska, "Applicant Self-Selection: Correlates of Withdrawal from a Multiple Hurdle Process," *Journal of Applied Psychology* 85, no. 2 (2000): 163–179.
55. "Considering and Evaluating Internal Candidates for Senior-Level Nonprofit Positions," *Bridgestar* (March 27, 2011), http://www.bridgestar.org.

Monkey Business Images/Shutterstock.com

CHAPTER 7

Training and Development

Learning Outcomes

After studying this chapter, you should be able to

LO 1 Discuss the scope of training and development and its strategic aspects.

LO 2 Describe how a training needs assessment should be done.

LO 3 Describe the factors that must be taken into account when designing a training program.

LO 4 Identify the types of training-delivery methods used by organizations.

LO 5 Describe some of the additional training programs conducted by firms, and explain why they are important.

LO 6 Explain how the effectiveness of training programs is evaluated.

Workplace training used to be rather boxlike. It focused on teaching employees to do particular activities—operate machines, process work, and so forth. However, as the workplace has shifted from "touch labor" to "knowledge workers" (see Chapter 1), the focus of training has shifted as well. Companies are realizing that workers need not only operational knowhow, but also superior job expertise; knowledge about competitive, industry, and technological trends; and the ability to continually learn, adapt, seek out, and utilize new information. These characteristics help an organization innovate more effectively and be more agile—capabilities that are essential to compete in today's fast-paced global business world. Because training plays a central role in nurturing, strengthening, and expanding the capabilities of a firm in this way, it has become part of the backbone of strategic management.

7.1 The Scope of Training

LO1 What economic, social, and political forces have made employee training even more important today than it was in the past?

Think of some organizations you know well. How much importance do they place on training? Many new employees come equipped with most of the knowledge, skills, and abilities needed to start work. Others require extensive training before they are ready to make much of a contribution to the organization. The term *training* is often used casually to describe almost any effort initiated by an organization to foster learning among its members. However, many experts distinguish between *training*, which tends to be more narrowly focused and oriented toward short-term performance concerns, and *development*, which, as you learned in Chapter 5, tends to be oriented more toward broadening an individual's skills for future responsibilities. The two terms are often combined into a single phrase—*training and development*—to recognize the combination of activities that organizations use to increase the knowledge and skills of their employees.

Research shows that an organization's revenues and overall profitability are positively correlated to the amount of training it gives its employees. According to *Training* magazine's ongoing industry report, U.S. businesses provide each of their employees between 45 and 55 hours of training, on average, annually.[1] By contrast, the 100 best U.S. companies to work for, as cited by *Fortune* magazine, provide their employees with approximately double that amount of training, and sometimes even more. New employees hired by the Ritz Carlton hotel chain get more than 300 hours of training. The greatest proportion of training is devoted to rank-and-file employees and supervisors.

Source: McDonald's Corporation

Hamburger University, located at the company's headquarters in Oak Brook, Illinois, is McDonald's management training center.

It's not unusual for large corporations to have their own "universities" where they train their employees and future managers. Hamburger University, operated by

McDonald's Corporation near Chicago, is probably the best-known corporate university. General Electric has a 53-acre training campus north of New York City, in Crotonville, where approximately 10,000 people attend classes each year. The Campbell's Soup Company operates Campbell University, which offers a 2-year program focused on personal leadership development for both aspiring and seasoned managers.

So how much does all of this corporate training cost? More than $80 billion annually. That's a significant amount of money, so firms want to ensure it's well spent.

U.S. businesses spend nearly four times as much on informal instruction as they do formal instruction, however. Such informal instruction ranges from simple, on-the-job instruction to sophisticated skills training conducted on multimillion-dollar simulators. Other types of training include orientation training given to new hires, customer service and communication-skills training, and compliance training—that is, training employees must receive as a result of various legal mandates, such as Equal Employment Opportunity (EEO) requirements or Occupational Safety and Health Administration (OSHA) requirements. Airline attendants must undergo mandatory safety training designated by the Federal Aviation Administration. Train crews must annually undergo training mandated by the Federal Railroad Administration.

7.1a A Strategic Approach to Training

Managers should keep a close eye on their firm's goals and strategies and orient their training accordingly. Is it the firm's goal to develop new product lines or to implement new technologies? If so, how should this affect its training initiatives? Is the firm trying to lower its costs of production so it can utilize a low-cost strategy to capture new business? If so, can training initiatives be undertaken to help the company deliver on this strategy?

Unfortunately, some organizations fail to make the connection between training and their organizational goals. Instead, they do whatever the competition is doing or just fall in line with the latest trend. As a result, training programs are often misdirected, poorly designed, and inadequately evaluated—not to mention a waste of money. Because business conditions change rapidly, especially with technology and the digitalization of work, staying current with the types of training a firm's employees need to remain competitive can be a challenge. If organizations consistently fail to achieve their productivity objectives, this might be a signal that employee training is needed. Likewise, if organizations receive an excessive number of customer complaints, this, too, might suggest a firm's training is inadequate. Larger firms typically have **chief learning officers**, who are high-ranking executives responsible for ensuring a company's training and development initiatives are timely, well designed, and focused on the firm's strategic issues.

chief learning officer
A high-ranking executive who is responsible for fostering employee learning and development within the firm.

To ensure a firm's training and development investment has the maximum impact possible, a strategic and systematic approach should be used that involves four phases:

1. Needs assessment: Based on the firm's competitive objectives, what training does the firm really need?
2. Program design: Given those needs, how should the training program best be designed or structured?
3. Implementation: How should the program be delivered—that is, by what methods?
4. Evaluation: How can the firm tell if the training program is really working?

Figure 7.1 presents these elements. We will use it as a framework for organizing the material in this chapter.

Figure 7.1 Strategic Model of Training and Development

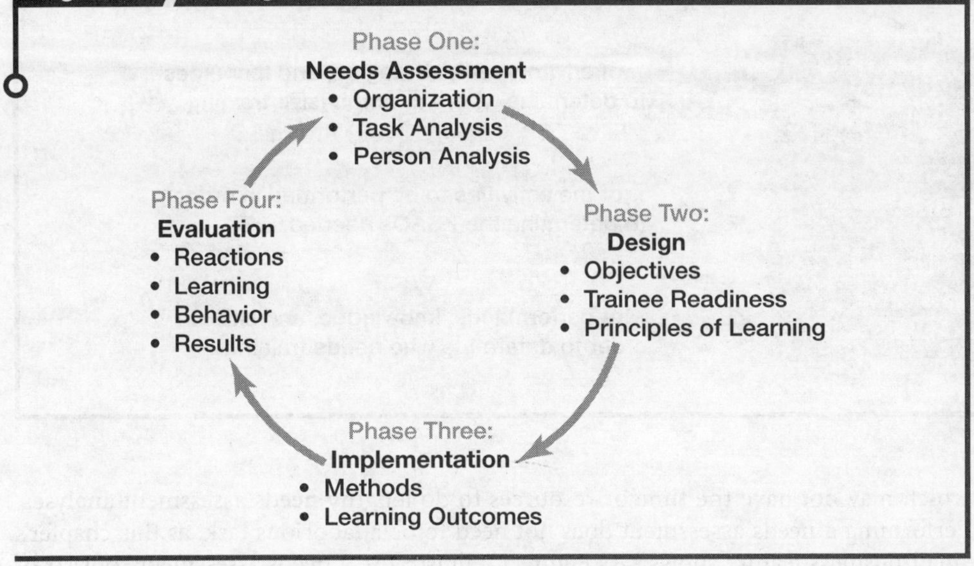

7.2 Phase 1: Conducting the Needs Assessment

> **LO2**
> What analyses should be done to determine the training needs of an organization? After the needs are determined, what is the next step?

If you own or manage a business, how would you figure out what types of training your employees need and how much of it? The following are some of the most common types of training employees are given. "Hard skills" refer to the tangible and teachable skills needed to do a job. Learning to operate a machine is an example. "Soft skills" refer to subjective skills that are more difficult to measure; they often require more discretion or judgment, but are just as valuable as hard skills in the workplace. Working well with other people is an example of a soft skill.

Hard-Skills Training

- On-the-job training for new hires
- Basic skills training
- Budgeting and accounting training
- Machinery operating training
- Technology training
- Customer service training
- Compliance (regulations) training

Soft-Skills Training

- Ethics training
- Diversity training
- Leadership training
- Communications training
- Team training
- Time management training
- Interpersonal skills training

To determine what type of training your firm needs, you must conduct a training needs assessment. Unfortunately, a study conducted a few years ago by the American Society for Training and Development found that organizations conduct needs assessments less than 50 percent of the time before they jump into training. This situation has improved somewhat, in part because tighter training budgets have forced firms to ensure that their training is well aligned with their objectives. Being able to quickly assess the training your employees need is especially important for small businesses,

Figure 7.2 Needs Assessment for Training

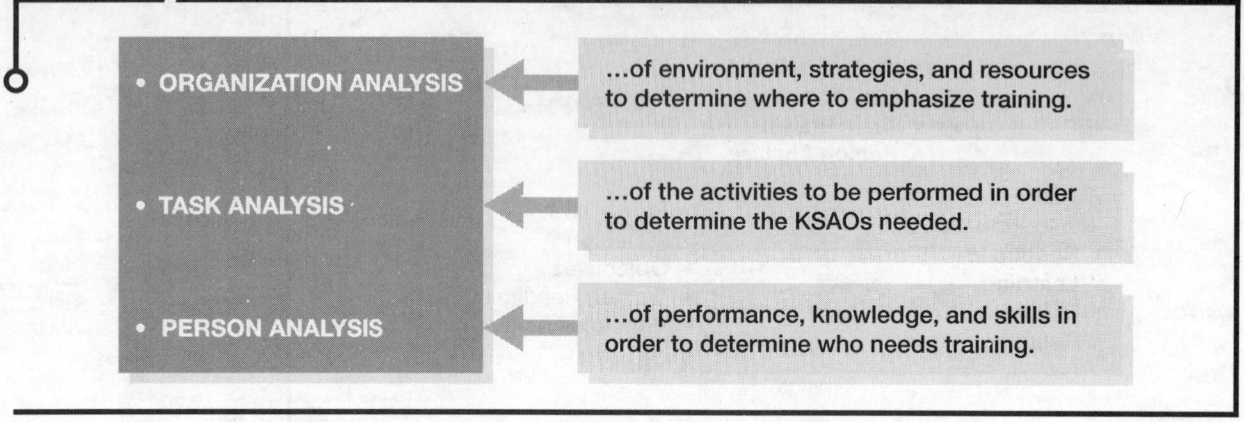

which may not have the time or resources to do lengthy needs assessment analyses. Performing a needs assessment does not need to be a laborious task, as this chapter's small-business feature shows.[2] As Figure 7.2 illustrates, a needs assessment consists of three parts: an organization analysis, a task analysis, and a person analysis. Each of these steps is discussed next.

7.2a Organization Analysis

organization analysis
An examination of an organization's environment, goals, strategies, performance, and resources so as to determine what training it should do.

An **organization analysis** is an examination of a firm's environment, goals, strategies, performance, and resources to determine what training it should do. For this purpose, HR personnel typically collect data such as information on the quality of a firm's goods or services and its absenteeism, turnover, and number of accidents. The availability of potential replacements and the time required to train them are important factors in organization analysis. Other issues include technological change, innovation, globalization, quality and process improvement, mergers and acquisition, and restructuring—all of which necessitate training. Why? Because these broad organizational changes frequently require employees and managers to take on new roles and responsibilities and adjust to new cultures and ways of doing business.

The COVID-19 pandemic placed many organizations in crisis mode, as they had to rapidly train employees on methods of remote working. Economic and public policy issues influence corporate training needs as well. For example, cybersecurity concerns, the shift to sustainable energy, and diversity and inclusion are all public policy issues that influence the training needed in organizations.[3] Finally, trends in the workforce itself affect a firm's training needs. As older workers near retirement, younger workers need the training and knowledge to take their place.

Conducting an organization analysis also involves examining a firm's resources—technological, financial, and human—available to conduct the training. HR departments are under constant pressure to make the most of their limited training dollars. When budgets are tight, training and development are usually the first programs to be cut. Companies such as Darden Restaurants, Ford, and Merck have used information technology to significantly improve the efficiency of their training investments. When Microsoft acquired LinkedIn in 2016, it inherited LinkedIn Learning, which gave employees access to a vast repository of video courses taught by industry experts. Other

Small Business Application

A Small Business's Guide to Quickly Assessing Its Training Needs

Do environmental scanning. Continually look at what is happening in your industry and organization to anticipate upcoming training needs. Enlist the help of employees and managers in this process. Question managers about their strategic goals and their impact on the organization, and gear your analysis accordingly.

Do internal scanning. Determine which skills are most important to acquire in terms of your organization's current and future needs. Which ones will provide the biggest payback?

Gather organizational data. Performance data for your firm (such as errors, sales, and customer complaints) and staffing data (such as turnover and absenteeism) can be very helpful as a starting point.

Develop a plan. Once the training need has been identified, identify various ways to deliver the necessary training and consider the costs and benefits of each option. Determine what kind of growth or other measure is a reasonable result of the training.

Utilize state and local government programs. Many state and local governments have programs to help small businesses train their employees. For example, the Texas Workforce Commission will pay small businesses in Texas up to $1,800 annually in tuition and fees for each new full-time employee hired and trained at a local college. (For a current employee, the program covers tuition and fees up to $900 annually.)

Make the needs-assessment process ongoing. Repeat these activities as your business needs change.

Sources: Patti Greene, "Five Affordable and Effective Ways Small Business Owners Could Better Train Employees," *Forbes* (October 21, 2016), https://www.forbes.com; "TWC Launches Small Business Employee Training Program," *Your Houston News* (November 20, 2010), http://www.yourhoustonnews.com; "Employee Training Tips," D&B.com, http://smallbusiness.dnb.com; Ron Zemke, "How to Do a Needs Assessment When You Think You Don't Have Time," *Training* 35, no. 3 (1998): 38–44.

companies outsource their training programs, or at least part of them, to external firms to cut costs or to take advantage of expertise the firm lacks. Still other organizations purchase "off the shelf" course materials developed by training companies rather than develop their own. Another trend is for companies to partner with firms in their supply chains to jointly train their employees more cost effectively.[4]

7.2b Task Analysis

The second step in training-needs assessment is task analysis. A **task analysis** involves reviewing the job description and KSAOs of a particular position, including the specific actions and behaviors required to do it. In other words, a task analysis goes beyond just the "what" of a job to include the "how."

task analysis
The process of determining a training program's content by studying the tasks and duties a job involves.

Task analysis is especially important if the job is new or jobs are changing. The first step in a task analysis is to list all the tasks or duties included in the job. The second step is to list the steps the employee needs to take to complete each task effectively. The type of performance required, along with the skills and knowledge necessary to do it, can then be identified. Sometimes this information can be very detailed, even sequenced. For example, in the task of taking a chest X-ray, a radiologist correctly positions the patient, gives special instructions, and checks the proper distance of the X-ray tube from the patient. The types of skills and knowledge that trainees need can be determined by observing and questioning skilled jobholders or by reviewing job descriptions. This information helps trainers select program content and choose the most effective training methods.

competency assessment
An analysis of the sets of skills and knowledge needed for decision-oriented and knowledge-intensive jobs.

Jobs are changing so quickly today that instead of focusing on a fixed sequence of tasks, firms are finding that their employees need more flexible sets of competencies to adapt. A **competency assessment** focuses on the sets of skills and knowledge employees need to be successful, particularly for decision-oriented and knowledge-intensive jobs that require critical thinking and good judgment. A competency assessment goes beyond simply describing the traits employees must have to successfully perform the work: It also captures elements of how those traits should be used within an organization's context and culture. That might include the motivation levels of employees, their interpersonal skills, and so on.[5]

Instead of offering a laundry list of training plans as it once did, Amway has established job competencies for its employees around the world. These competencies denote the particular skills each employee needs for their job and a training "road map" to get them there.[6] Highlights in HRM 1 shows an example of a partial competency assessment tool used for evaluating a manager.

7.2c Person Analysis

person analysis
The process of determining the specific individuals who need training in an organization.

A **person analysis** is the process of determining which employees require training and, equally important, which do not. This helps organizations avoid providing all employees with training when some do not need it. In addition, a person analysis helps managers determine what prospective trainees are able to do currently so that the programs can be designed to provide training that will benefit them.

Performance appraisal information can also be used to conduct a person analysis. However, although performance appraisals might reveal which employees are not meeting the firm's expectations, they typically do not reveal why. If the performance gap is due to ability problems, training is likely to be a good solution. If the performance problems are due to poor motivation or factors outside an employee's control, however, training might not be the answer. Conducting a deeper performance diagnosis is discussed in Chapter 8, which covers performance appraisals. Ultimately, managers have to sit down with employees to talk about areas for improvement so that they can jointly determine the training or other development approaches that will have maximum benefit.[7] A person analysis along with appraisal information can also be used to determine the training someone needs for a new position, a promotion, or to take on new responsibilities.

LO3
Which principles of learning do you see demonstrated in your own classes? In what ways might you bring other principles into them?

7.3 Phase 2: Designing the Training Program

Once you have assessed your firm's training needs, the next step is to design the training program. Think of your own experience in college: What characteristics lead to the best learning? Experts believe that the design of training programs should focus on at least four related issues: (1) the training's instructional objectives, (2) readiness of trainees and their motivation, (3) principles of learning, and (4) characteristics of instructors.

7.3a Developing Instructional Objectives

instructional objectives
The desired outcomes of a training program.

After conducting the organization, task, and person analyses, managers should have a more complete picture of their firms' training needs. On the basis of this information, they can more formally state the desired outcomes of training via written **instructional objectives**, which describe the skills or knowledge to be acquired and/or the attitudes to be changed. The learning objectives at the beginning of this chapter are examples of instructional objectives.

1 Highlights in HRM

A Competency Assessment for a Managerial Position

For each item, select the number that best describes the manager's characteristics. For items that do not apply, select **NA** (not applicable). For other items for which you lack sufficient observations or documentary evidence, select **DK** (don't know).

4: Exemplary

3: Proficient

2: Progressing

1: Needs assistance

NA: Not applicable

DK: Don't know

Competency 1: Behaves professionally and encourages other staff members to do likewise.

4 3 2 1 NA DK

Evidence:____________

Competency 2: Behaves ethically and encourages staff members to do likewise.

4 3 2 1 NA DK

Evidence:____________

Competency 3: Uses a variety of modes of communication and conveys information fully and clearly.

4 3 2 1 NA DK

Evidence:____________

Competency 4: Seeks input from all levels and demonstrates fairness and consistency.

4 3 2 1 NA DK

Evidence:____________

Competency 5: Engages in an open style of management and is open to criticism from supervisors and subordinates.

4 3 2 1 NA DK

Evidence:____________

Competency 6: Searches for and embraces innovative solutions to improve the department's programs and products.

4 3 2 1 NA DK

Evidence:____________

The objectives should be performance centered. Performance-centered objectives typically include precise terms, such as "to calculate," "to repair," "to adjust," "to construct," "to assemble," and "to classify."[8] For example, the stated objective for one training program might be "Employees trained in team methods will be able to perform the different jobs of their team members within six months."

7.3b Assessing the Readiness and Motivation of Trainees

Two preconditions for learning affect the success of those who are to receive training: readiness and motivation. *Trainee readiness* refers to whether the prerequisite experience and knowledge of trainees have made them ready to absorb the training. Do they have the background knowledge and the skills necessary to absorb what will be presented?

It is often desirable to group individuals according to their readiness, as determined by test scores or other assessment information, and to provide alternative types of instruction for those who need it. The receptiveness and readiness of participants in training programs can be increased by having them complete questionnaires about why they are attending training and what they hope to accomplish as a result of it.

The other precondition for learning is *trainee motivation*. The organization needs to help employees understand the link between the effort they put into training and the payoff. Why is the training important? What will happen if it does not occur? Moreover, what is in it for the individual employee? By focusing on the trainees themselves, managers can create a training environment that is conducive to learning. Unless they are nearing retirement, most employees are motivated by training if it can help them perform better, advance their careers, or both.

7.3c Incorporating Effective Principles of Learning

What makes some types of training more effective than others? Training has to build a bridge between employees and the organization. One important step in this transition is giving full consideration to the psychological principles of learning—that is, the characteristics of training programs that help employees grasp new material, make sense of it in their own lives, and transfer it back to their jobs. All things considered, training programs are likely to be more effective if they incorporate the principles of learning shown in Figure 7.3.

Goal Setting

In some cases, goal setting can simply take the form of a "road map" of the course or program, its objectives, and its learning points.[9] When trainers take the time to explain the training's goals and objectives to trainees—or when trainees are encouraged to set goals on their own—the level of interest, understanding, motivation, and effort directed

Figure 7.3 Principles of Learning

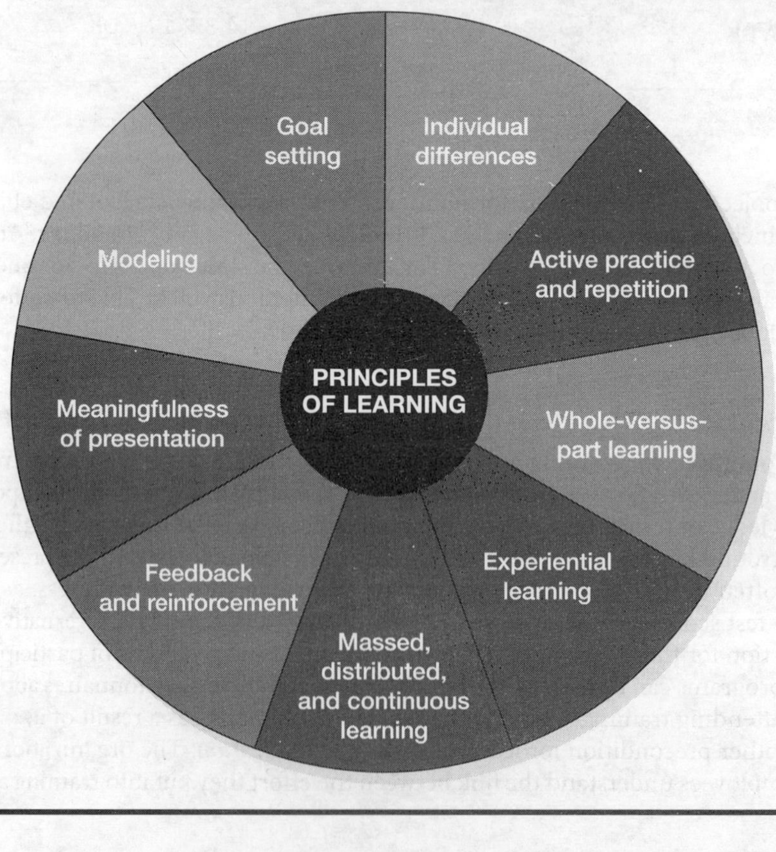

toward the training is likely to increase. Allowing employees to undergo training in areas that they want to pursue can be very motivating, as can enlisting employees to train other employees with the information they learn. Who in an organization does not want to be called upon for their expertise?

Meaningfulness of Presentation

Trainees will be better able to learn new information if it is presented using terminology they can understand and the training is connected with things already familiar to them. This is the reason why trainers frequently use colorful examples to which trainees can relate. Such examples make the material meaningful. In addition, material should be arranged so that each experience builds on preceding ones. In this way, trainees are able to integrate the experiences into a usable pattern of knowledge and skills.

Modeling

The old saying "A picture is worth a thousand words" applies to training. Just as examples increase the meaningfulness of factual material or new knowledge in a training environment, modeling increases the salience of behavioral training. In other words, people learn by mimicking other people. For example, if you were learning to ride a horse, it would be much easier to watch someone do it—and then try it yourself—than to read a book or listen to a lecture and hope you can do it right.[10]

Modeling can take many forms. Real-life demonstrations and recorded demonstrations, visual aids, pictures, and drawings can get the message across. In some cases, even modeling the wrong behavior can be helpful if it shows trainees what not to do and then clarifies the right behavior.

Individual Learning Differences

People learn at different rates and in different ways. Visual learners absorb information best through pictures, diagrams, and demonstrations. Verbal learners absorb information best through spoken or written words. Similarly, some learners who do horribly in large lecture settings excel in small discussion groups.

Trainers can help accommodate the different learning styles found among trainees in a variety of ways. The key is to avoid delivering the material in only one way. So, for example, instead of delivering a monologue, trainers should incorporate variety into their presentations. They should use visual aids, encourage the participation of learners by including them in demonstrations, and ask them questions about their own experiences. Hands-on activities and breaking large groups into smaller groups for specific activities can also help trainers accommodate trainees' different learning styles.[11]

Active Practice and Repetition

Trainees should be given frequent opportunities to practice what they will ultimately be expected to do. An individual being taught how to operate a machine should have an opportunity to practice on it. A manager being taught how to train should be given supervised practice in training.

Practice causes behaviors to become second nature. For example, when you first learned to drive a car, you focused a great deal on the mechanics: "Where are my hands? Where are my feet? How fast am I going?" As you practiced driving, you began to think less about the mechanics and more about the road, the weather, and the traffic. Other forms of learning are no different—by practicing, a trainee can forget about distinct behaviors and concentrate on the subtleties of how they are used.

Experiential Learning

experiential learning
The process of learning by "doing," reflecting on it, critically analyzing it, and applying it in new situations or settings.

Experiential learning refers to the process of learning by experience or "doing," often outside the classroom and without traditional ready-made learning content. Experiential learning might sound like hands-on learning, which can be a part of experiential learning, but it is more than that. This process involves not only engaging in an activity, but also reflecting on it, critically analyzing it—and potentially improving upon it—and then applying it in new situations or settings. Benjamin Franklin once said, "Tell me and I forget; teach me and I remember; involve me and I will learn." Experiential learning corresponds to the "involve me and I will learn" part of Franklin's statement. Simulations, games, and special assignments—which we will discuss later in the chapter—fall into the category of experiential learning.

Whole-versus-Part Learning

Most jobs and tasks can be broken down into parts that lend themselves to further analysis. Learning to sell a product is an example. This process can essentially be broken down into a few discrete steps: finding customer opportunities; uncovering a prospective customer's needs by learning the proper questions to ask; presenting the firm's product in a way that meets those needs; and finally, learning how and when to ask the customer to buy the product (closing the deal). If the task can be broken down successfully, it probably should be to facilitate learning; otherwise, it should probably be taught as a unit.

Programmed instruction, also referred to as *self-paced learning*, is often used to break down learning into sequences for employees to learn at their own pace. After being presented with a small segment of information, the trainee is required to answer a question, either by writing in a response or selecting one on a computer. If the response is correct, the trainee is presented with the next step (or screen) in the material. If the response is incorrect, further explanatory information is given, and the trainee is told to try again.

Massed, Distributed, and Continuous Learning

Another factor that determines the effectiveness of training is the amount of time devoted to practice in one session. Should trainees be given training in five 2-hour periods or in ten 1-hour periods? In most cases, spacing out the training has been found to result in faster learning and longer retention. This is the principle of *distributed learning.* Rather than a serious of events, *continuous learning* is an ongoing process whereby employees are continually acquiring new skills and knowledge via training, observing more experienced workers, collaborating with others, or simply performing the job itself.

A person's training progress, measured in terms of either mistakes or successes, can be plotted on a learning curve like the one in Figure 7.4. In many learning situations, there are times when progress does not occur. Such periods show up on the curve as a fairly straight horizontal line called a *plateau.* A plateau can occur because of reduced motivation or because a person gets discouraged when they do not always perform a new task as well as hoped. It is a natural phenomenon, and learners usually experience a spontaneous recovery later, as Figure 7.4 shows.

Feedback and Reinforcement

Can any learning occur without feedback? Some feedback comes from the task itself as trainees self-monitor their performance, whereas other feedback comes from trainers, fellow trainees, and the like. Feedback can help individuals focus on what they are doing right and what they are doing wrong. Think about when you first learned how to throw a baseball, ride a bicycle, or swim. Someone, perhaps a parent, told you what

Figure 7.4 A Typical Learning Curve

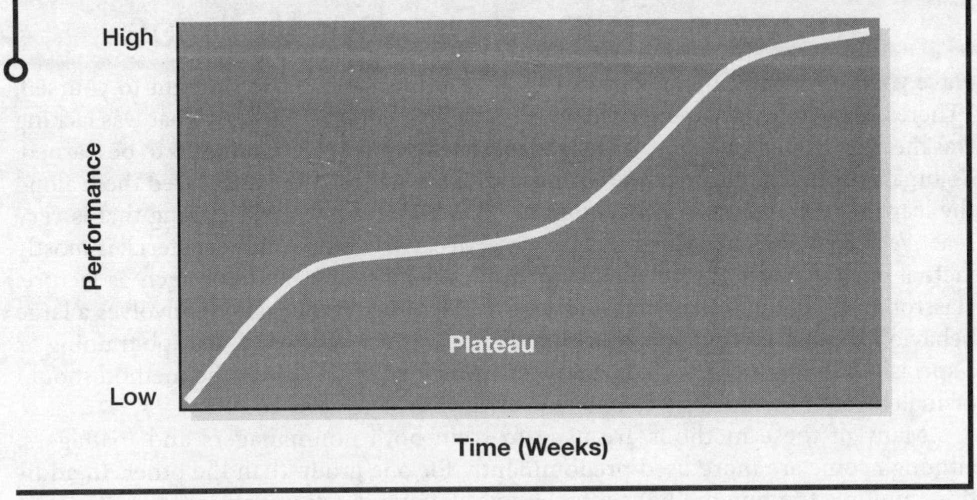

you were doing right and what things to correct. As you corrected those things, you perhaps got better.

As a follow-up to training or as part of the training itself, managers can use relatively simple rewards to discourage undesired behaviors and encourage and maintain desired behaviors. This kind of reward system is a form of behavior modification. **Behavior modification** operates on the principle that behavior that is rewarded, or positively reinforced, will occur more frequently, whereas behavior that is penalized or unrewarded will decrease in frequency. The retailer Nordstrom has found that nothing more than words of encouragement and feedback are needed to strengthen employee behaviors. This approach is often used in smaller companies that don't have particularly formal or sophisticated rewards systems. However, more tangible rewards such as prizes, awards, and ceremonies can also help reinforce desirable behaviors.

behavior modification
A technique that operates on the principle that behavior that is rewarded, or positively reinforced, will be exhibited more frequently in the future, whereas behavior that is penalized or unrewarded will decrease in frequency.

Encouragement is most effective when it is given immediately after a trainee successfully accomplishes a certain task. This is why some employers, including Nordstrom and Whole Foods, have instituted **spot rewards** programs, which award employees "on the spot" when they do something particularly well during training or on the job. The awards can consist of cash, gift cards, time off, or anything else employees value.

spot rewards
Programs that award employees on the spot when they do something particularly well during training or on the job.

7.3d Characteristics of Instructors

The success of any training effort will depend in large part on the teaching skills and personal characteristics of the people doing the training. What separates good trainers from mediocre ones? Often a good trainer is one who shows a little more effort or demonstrates more instructional preparation. However, training is also influenced by the trainer's personal manner and characteristics such as their knowledge of the subject, enthusiasm and sincerity, interest in trainees, sense of humor, ability to communicate clearly, and willingness to provide individual assistance to trainees. Because they can have a huge impact on the workforce, organizations should reward managers who are excellent trainers. Too often managers are not recognized for their contributions to this important aspect of HRM.

LO4

Suppose that you are the manager of an accounts receivable unit in a large company. You are switching to a new system of billing and record-keeping and need to train your three supervisors and 28 employees in the new procedures. What training method(s) would you use? Why?

7.4 Phase 3: Implementing the Training Program—Training Delivery Methods

Have you ever sat through a less-than-great training session and thought to yourself, "There has got to be a better way to get this material across"? Perhaps what was lacking was the right training method. The right approach depends on the KSAOs to be learned. To organize our discussion of the various training methods, we have placed them along the learning continuum shown in Figure 7.5, which ranges from learning that is very reactive and passive to learning that is very active. For example, if the material is mostly factual or designed to create a shift in employee attitudes, methods such as lecture, classroom, or online instruction may be fine. However, if the training involves a large behavioral or skill component, more hands-on methods such as on-the-job training or a special job assignment are likely to work better.[12] In other words, the method should be matched to the learning outcome you are trying to achieve.

Many of these methods are used to train both nonmanagers and managers, although some are more used predominantly for one group than the other. In addition, multiple training methods often are used in conjunction with different types of learners. The practice of using multiple methods is referred to as blended learning. As Figure 7.6 shows, traditional classroom instruction delivered by lecturers continues to be the number-one training delivery method for formally training employees. However, its popularity has been steadily dropping relative to technology-enabled methods, which we will discuss shortly.

on-the-job training (OJT)
A method by which employees are given hands-on experience with instructions from their supervisor or other trainer.

On-the-Job Training

By far, the most common informal method used to train employees is **on-the-job training (OJT)**. By some estimates, 80 to 90 percent of employee learning occurs via OJT. OJT has the advantage of providing hands-on experience under normal working conditions and

Figure 7.5 Learning Outcomes Differ by Training Method

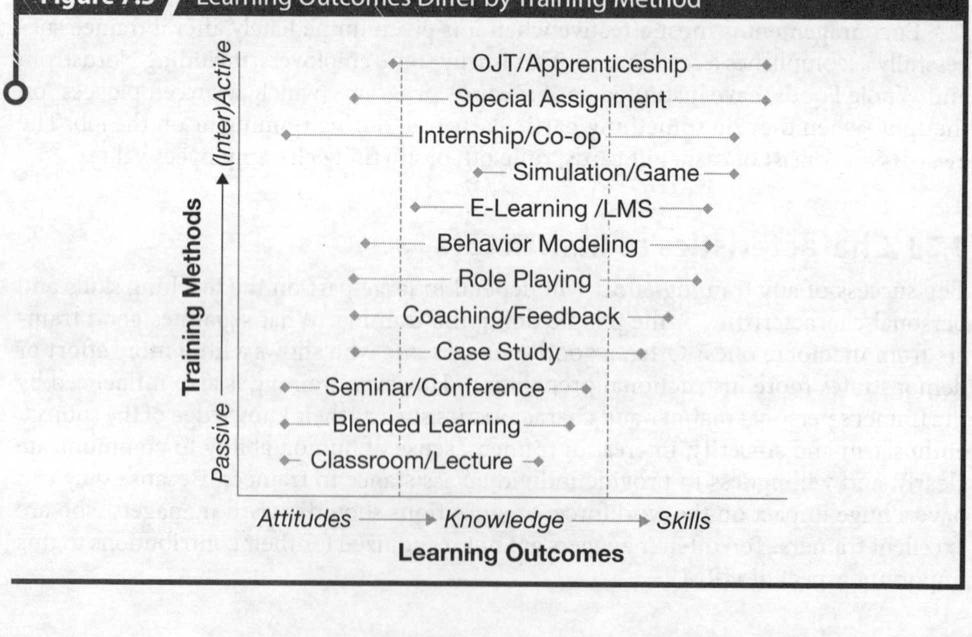

Figure 7.6 Training Delivery Methods

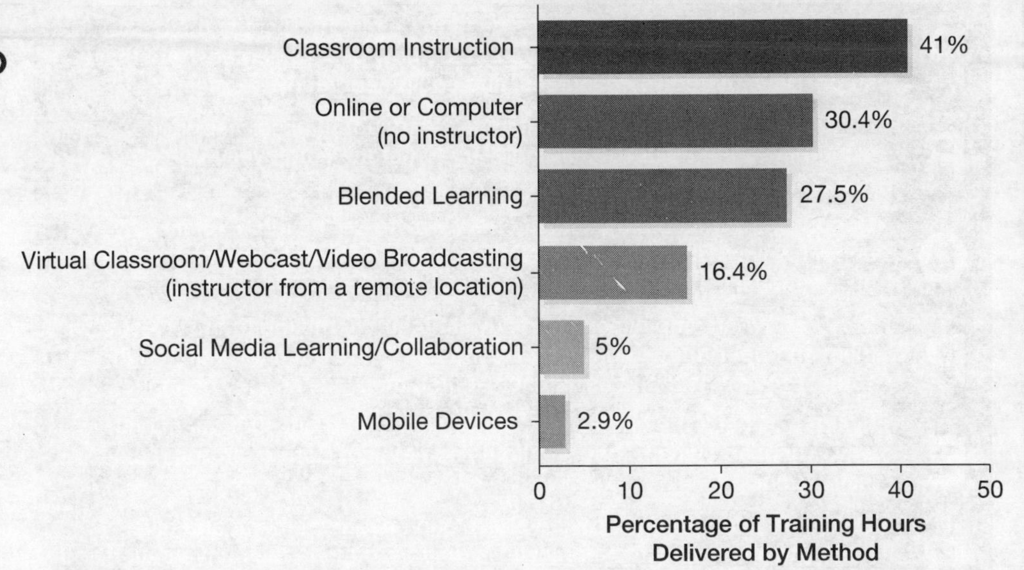

Source: Adapted from "2016 Training Industry Report," *Training* (November–December 2016): 36.

an opportunity for the trainer—a manager or senior employee—to build good relationships with new employees. Figure 7.7 shows the basic steps of an OJT program.

Although it is used by all types of organizations, OJT is sometimes poorly implemented because of its informal nature. To overcome these problems, training experts suggest firms develop realistic goals and measures for the training as well as plan a specific training schedule for each trainee. Conducting periodic evaluations after the training is completed can help ensure employees have not forgotten what they learned.

Indigo Airlines, based in India, uses OJT to train its flight attendants. The airline places trainees in the classroom for a certain period and then gives them additional training during evaluation flights. On these flights, experienced flight attendants provide OJT based on a list of identified job tasks. Some tasks, such as serving meals and snacks, are demonstrated during the actual delivery of services to passengers.[13]

An extension of OJT is **apprenticeship training**. With this method, individuals entering the skilled trades are given thorough instruction and experience, both on and off the job. Machinists, aviation mechanics, and electricians are examples of people who hold skilled-trade jobs. Generally, an apprentice is initially paid 50 percent of a skilled journey worker's wage, but the wage increases at regular intervals as the apprentice's job skills increase. An apprentice who successfully completes the apprenticeship becomes a certified journey-level worker earning full pay.[14] Case Study 2 at the end of the chapter explains how Whirlpool Corporation is utilizing apprenticeships to hire new employees.

apprenticeship training
A system of training in which a worker entering the skilled trades is given thorough instruction and experience, both on and off the job, in the practical and theoretical aspects of the work.

Apprenticeship programs originated in Europe centuries ago and still are used extensively there. In the United States, tens of thousands of organizations have registered their programs with the U.S. Department of Labor's Office of Apprenticeships and state agencies. Apprenticeships are available in a wide range of industries, including construction and manufacturing and the telecommunications, arts, and health fields.

Figure 7.7 The PROPER Way to Do On-the-Job Training

P — **Prepare.** Decide what employees need to be taught. Identify the best sequence or steps of the training. Decide how best to demonstrate these steps. Have materials, resources, and equipment ready.

R — **Reassure.** Put each employee at ease. Learn about his or her prior experience, and adjust accordingly. Try to get the employee interested, relaxed, and motivated to learn.

O — **Orient.** Show the employee the correct way to do the job. Explain why it is done this way. Discuss how it relates to other jobs. Let him or her ask lots of questions.

P — **Perform.** When employees are ready, let them try the job themselves. Give them an opportunity to practice the job and guide them through rough spots. Provide help and assistance at first, then less as they continue.

E — **Evaluate.** Check the employees' performance, and question them on how, why, when, and where they should do something. Correct errors; repeat instructions.

R — **Reinforce and Review.** Provide praise and encouragement, and give feedback about how the employee is doing. Continue the conversation and express confidence in his or her doing the job.

Source: Scott Snell, University of Virginia.

Cooperative Training, Internships, and Governmental Training

cooperative training
A training program that combines practical on-the-job experience with formal educational classes.

Similar to apprenticeships, **cooperative training** programs combine practical on-the-job experience with formal classes. For example, a student might alternate between working at an organization for one semester (for pay) and then going to school the next semester. Many organizations, including Fannie Mae, General Motors, Burger King, Champion International, Cray, and the insurance company UNUM, have invested millions of dollars in educational cooperative training programs in conjunction with high schools and colleges.

Internship programs, which we discussed in Chapter 5, are jointly sponsored by colleges, universities, and a variety of organizations. These programs offer students the chance to get real-world experience while finding out how they will perform in work organizations. Organizations benefit by getting student-employees with new ideas, energy, and eagerness to accomplish their assignments. Some universities and community colleges allow students to earn college credits for successfully completing internships.

The federal government and various state governments work together with private employers to sponsor training programs for new and current employees at career centers nationwide that take place at American Job Centers, which are also known as "Career One Stop" centers or "Workforce Development" centers. The centers help workers find jobs, help employers find qualified workers, and provide job training and other employment services all under one roof (hence the name One Stop). 3M, Honeywell, and General Mills are just a few of the companies involved in the One Stop program.[15]

Monkey Business Images/ Shutterstock.com

Apprenticeships are a good way to recruit and train employees.

Special Assignments

Special job assignments (discussed in Chapter 5) involve assigning trainees, who are often but not always on managerial tracks, to different jobs in different areas of a firm, often in different regions and countries. In some cases, these trainees are groomed by other managers in *understudy assignments* to do important job functions. Job rotation and lateral transfers also provide trainees with a variety of hands-on work experiences. Special projects, task forces, and *junior boards* give trainees an opportunity to study an organization's challenges, make decisions about them, discuss which aspects of the projects went right and wrong, and plan and work on new initiatives.

Simulations

Simulations are used when it is either impractical or unwise to train employees on the actual equipment used on the job. An obvious example is training employees to operate aircraft, spacecraft, and other highly technical and expensive equipment. Southwest Airlines has 10 full-motion 737 flight simulators at its training center adjacent to Southwest's headquarters at Dallas's Love Field. During each 4-hour training situation in a simulator, a flight crew faces more abnormal flight situations than it would in a lifetime. The Federal Aviation Administration developed a simulator to dramatically speed up the training of air traffic controllers, a process that used to take as long as 5 years. Variables such as wind speed, precipitation, and the number of airplanes to be guided can be adjusted on the simulator to test trainees' abilities.

The distinction between simulators like the cockpits at Southwest Airlines that move/jostle flight crews about and computer-based simulations has blurred in recent years. To train its forklift operators, the aluminum company Alcoa uses a computer simulation called Safedock. In the simulation, trainees perform common tasks such as moving loads from one end of a loading area to the other. If a trainee makes a wrong move, they instantly see the consequences: The forklift might end up driving off the dock or crashing into another forklift.[16] Medical students and doctors are putting on virtual reality headsets to train for different types of trauma care, too.[17]

Pilots are trained with flight simulators to help them make the right decisions in critical situations without the risk.

Monty Rakusen/MediaBakery

Simulations can also be used to help employees and managers make tactical decisions. Marriott International uses a computer program called Business Acumen to train its managers on the finer points of hotel operation. The program simulates hotel operation scenarios such as budgetary decisions.[18] The Federal Emergency Management Agency has used simulations to help managers better respond to crises. In one computer simulation, a chemical cloud engulfs a city, and managers attempt to respond dynamically to the various problems it creates.

Games

Games are becoming more popular for training purposes, a phenomenon referred to as the "gamification" of learning. Sometimes, the games resemble actual tasks done in the workplace. At other times, the games communicate principles that can be transferred to the job. Because games have a competitive component and are fun, trainers have found people are more likely to want to engage with them as well as to remember what they learned from them. In particular, Generation Zers and Millennials tend to like them. To train its retail employees, many of whom are younger, Bloomingdales uses games that employees can load on a wide variety of devices and play during slow times on the job. Employees report that the games have given them more confidence in their selling skills and increased their desire to participate in corporate training.[19]

Games (and simulations) do not always require a computer, however. Motorola developed a non-computer-based simulation called "Equal Employment Opportunity: It's Your Job" to teach the basic principles of equal employment opportunity to managers. Trainees get caught up in the competitive spirit of the game and at the same time absorb and remember government regulations. They also become aware of how their own daily decisions affect their employer's compliance with these regulations.

E-Learning

e-learning
Learning that takes place via electronic media.

The training methods we just discussed are evolving into what trainers today refer to as e-learning or virtual learning. **E-learning** covers a wide variety of electronic applications, such as computer-based training (CBT), online resources, and social networks. It includes the delivery of content via the Internet, intranets and extranets, mobile

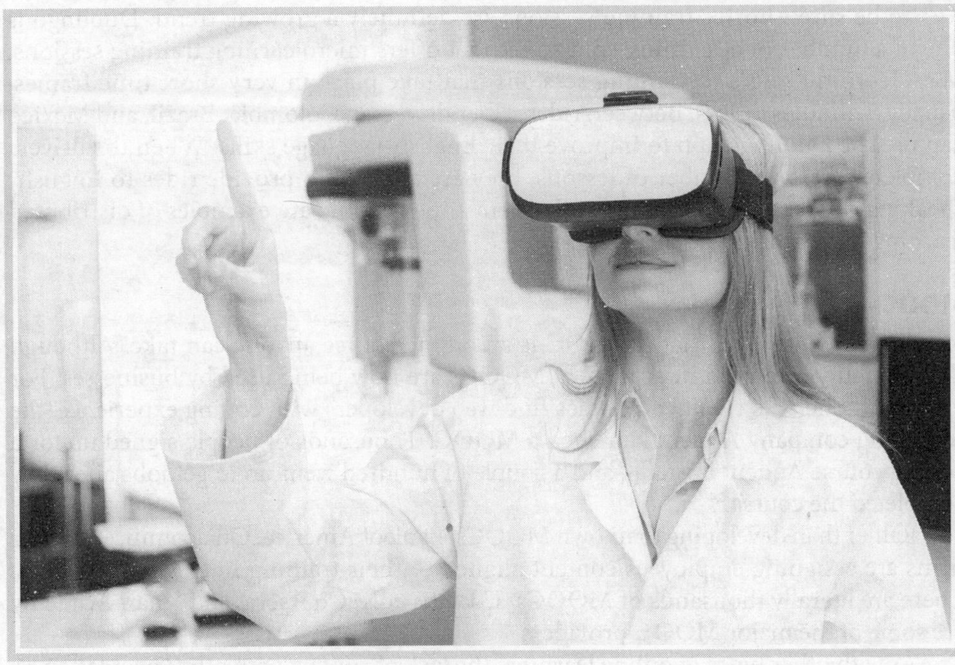

iStock.com/yoh4nn

Virtual reality headsets are being used to train people in different occupations, including people in medical occupations.

devices, podcasts, and other virtual spaces powered by platforms like Zoom and WebEx.[20] E-learning need not be expensive. Many e-learning training programs use existing applications with which employees are already familiar, such as PowerPoint, Word, Adobe Acrobat, and audio and video files that can be easily uploaded and viewed or listened to online using computers and mobile devices.

A major advantage of e-learning is that it allows the firm to bring the training to employees, which is generally more efficient and cost effective than the other way around.

Increasingly, e-learning involves the use of a **learning management system (LMS)**, which combines a company's e-learning, employee assessment tools, resources, and other training functions into one electronic tool, often custom built for the firm by software vendors. Using this software, managers can assess the skills of employees, register them for courses, deliver interactive learning modules directly to employees' desktops when they need or want them, evaluate and track their progress, and determine when they are ready to advance. You are very likely use an LMS for this course or others in your educational curriculum.[21]

learning management system (LMS)
Online system that provides a variety of assessment, communication, teaching, and learning opportunities.

Just-in-Time Training and Microlearning

E-learning also allows companies to offer individual training to employees exactly when and where they need it, on demand—a practice known as **just-in-time training**. Just-in-time training helps alleviate the boredom that trainees sometimes experience during full-blown training courses, and employees are more likely to retain the information when they can immediately put it to use.

just-in-time training
Electronic training delivered to trainees when and where they need it to do their jobs.

Just-in-time learning is used in manual labor positions, safety training, and sales and customer service roles. Notably, it counteracts some of the disadvantages of traditional training. For example, long training courses can pull people away from making sales, and with so many products continually being launched, it is difficult for employees to keep up to date if they have to take frequent training sessions. Also, employees are unlikely to remember the content of the training if they cannot put it to use immediately.[22]

To be sure, shorter training sessions are definitely a growing trend. Duolingo is one of a number of e-learning companies that offers microlearning training sessions. **Microlearning** refers to training sessions that take place in very short time frames, usually 5 minutes or less. Between rides, Uber drivers in Colombia, Brazil, and Mexico can use the Duolingo app to improve their English-language skills. When the drivers complete a certain number of lessons, they are allowed to provide rides to English-speaking riders.[23] Microlearning and just-in-time training are examples of distributed learning rather than mass learning.

microlearning
Training sessions that take place in a very short time frame, usually 5 minutes or less.

MOOCs

Recall from Chapter 1 that a MOOC is an online course anyone can take. Although they initially were used in academia, MOOCs are now being used by businesses. For example, to help its client companies find web developers with coding experience, the recruiting company Aquent launched a MOOC. Thousands of people signed up for a coding course Aquent hosted—and a couple of hundred went on to get jobs after they completed the course.[24]

Rather than developing their own MOOCs, Bank of America, Qualcomm, and other firms are assigning employees content aligned to their training in existing MOOCs. There are literally thousands of MOOCs. Udacity, edX, Coursera, and Khan Academy are some of the major MOOC providers.

As with other types of online learning, the lack of contact with other people can be a problem for some learners enrolled in MOOCs. To eliminate this sense of isolation, some MOOCs allow students to have classroom discussions virtually with other people. Others include application assignments and projects. Still others allow instructors to record audio comments or videos about what's going on in the course each week, which can help keep learners engaged.[25]

Social Media

About 5 percent of the training hours delivered to employees involve social media sites, blogs, and wikis (sites where people can post information, as they can on Wikipedia).[26] When U.S. soldiers were having problems using a grenade launcher, a unit commander posted a question on one of the Army's internal social media sites. Shortly thereafter, someone who had experienced a similar problem posted a simple solution. The Cheesecake Factory restaurant chain trains employees by letting them upload and share video snippets on job-related topics, including how best to prepare certain foods and provide good customer service.[27]

Workplace by Facebook and Yammer are two corporate social media tools that firms can use. However, even a basic community page on LinkedIn or Facebook will work: A trainer can set up a page to provide information about an upcoming training session, post materials for it, and engage participants by allowing them to ask questions, volunteer answers, and collaborate with one another before and after the session.[28]

Behavior Modeling

Behavior modeling training is an approach in which work behaviors are modeled, or demonstrated, and trainees are asked to mimic them. Behavior modeling consists of four basic components:

behavior modeling
A learning approach in which work behaviors are modeled, or demonstrated, and trainees are asked to mimic them.

1. *Learning points.* For example, the learning points might describe the skill, why it's important for trainees to learn, and when it should be utilized.

2. *Modeling.* Participants might view a video in which a manager deals with an employee in an effort to improve his or her performance. The manager would model how specifically to deal with the situation and demonstrate the learning points.
3. *Practice.* Trainees practice the behaviors modeled.
4. *Feedback and reinforcement.* The trainer and other trainees reinforce the behavior with praise, approval, encouragement, and attention. Digitally recording the sessions can also be very instructive.

Behavior modeling seems to work, according to various studies. Examples of its use range from teaching dance to coaching sports to learning to paint. Military training is a classic example of how behavior modeling can work. Drill sergeants model the behavior expected of new recruits; by emulating them, the recruits develop discipline, positive habits, and confidence.[29]

Role-Playing

Role-playing consists of playing the roles of others—often a supervisor and a subordinate who are facing a particular problem, such as a disagreement or a performance problem. Role-playing is used not only for managers, but also to train salespeople to question customers to understand their needs for goods and services. Health care professionals also use role-playing to learn to question patients and be empathetic and sensitive to their concerns. Singapore Airlines uses role-playing exercises to help its employees learn how to deal with difficult or unruly passengers.

Computer programs that simulate role-playing also have been developed. Virtual Leader, a product by SimuLearn, is one such program. In this program, management trainees interact with animated "employees"—some of whom are more cooperative than others. The trainees are then given feedback as to how well they applied their managerial skills to each situation.

Coaching

Coaching is growing in popularity as a method to improve learning and development. It consists of a continuing flow of instructions, comments, and suggestions from the manager to a subordinate. Coaching is more than just a flow of instruction, though. It is an ongoing stream of encouragement and support meant to help people not just do their jobs right and get ahead, but become leaders.

Part of coaching involves personalized learning—that is, talking to one's employees about what their goals are and being excited about their achievement of those goals, even if it means good employees will ultimately leave your department and you will have to replace them with new ones and begin the process anew. Once a manager understands employees' goals, the manager can customize a plan to help them grow their skills by taking on new leadership responsibilities, training and mentoring other employees, and spearheading projects; the manager then provides feedback on their performance.[30]

One way to coach employees who are being groomed as managers is to allow them to participate in managers' staff meetings. This can help them become more familiar with the problems and events occurring outside their immediate areas and how they are handled by exposing those employees to the ideas and thinking of other managers. Note, however, that coaching is important for all employees to receive—not just employees who are on managerial tracks. Many top managers as well as rank-and-file employees say that without coaching, they would never have accomplished as much for their organizations as they did.

Case Studies

A particularly useful method used in classroom learning situations is the case study. The FBI's Integrated Case Scenario method is used as part of a multiweek training program for all new FBI agents. Using documented examples, case-study participants learn how to analyze (take apart) and synthesize (put together) facts, become conscious of the many variables on which management decisions are based, and, in general, improve their decision-making skills.[31] Figure 7.8 provides a set of guidelines for when and how to conduct case studies.

Seminars and Conferences

Seminars and conferences, like classroom instruction, are useful for bringing groups of people together for training and development. These gatherings can be used to communicate ideas, policies, or procedures, but they are also good forums for raising points of debate and discussing issues (usually with the help of a qualified leader) that have no set answers or resolutions. For this reason, seminars and conferences often are used when an organization's goal focuses on change.

Many outside seminars and conferences are conducted jointly with universities and consulting firms. Associations and third-party organizations, such as the American Management Association, the Conference Board, and the Center for Creative Leadership, also offer many different types of management seminars. The construction and mining equipment manufacturer Caterpillar is one company that, in conjunction with an outside consulting firm, has developed a training program to groom new managers so it will have enough of them to effectively run the company in the coming decade. Caterpillar began with a series of high-level meetings and strategy sessions. During those meetings, 11 characteristics were identified that the company seeks in its managers and leaders, including communication, teamwork, and developing talent. These characteristics are used as a foundation for evaluating the potential of future managers, as well as providing a focus for their development.

Classroom (Lecture) Instruction

You might wonder why firms still use classroom training when so many other interactive and virtual methods are available. Some of the advantages of classroom instruction relate to participants' motivation and attendance. Have you ever taken a self-paced course outside a classroom setting? If so, you might have had a hard time completing

Figure 7.8 Case Studies

When Using Case Studies . . .

- Decide which goals can best be achieved by using case studies.
- Identify available cases that might work or consider writing your own.
- Set up the activity—including the case materials, the room or place, and the schedule.
- Give all participants a chance to take part in the discussions and activities and try to keep the groups small.
- Bridge the gap between the theories presented in case studies and how they can actually be put into practice in your organization.

Source: Adapted from Albert A. Einsiedel Jr., "Case Studies: Indispensable Tools for Trainers," *Training and Development* (August 1995): 50–53.

it. As one professor put it, "When it comes to learning, just getting to class is half the battle." In addition, if a trainee experiences problems, a live instructor is generally in the best position to help the trainee.

Classroom training need not necessarily take place in a classroom per se. Electronic Data Systems uses videoconferencing to train its employees wherever they are in the world rather than having them travel to one location. For example, the company conducted a "coaching skills for leaders" program for 1,500 managers in 41 countries via videoconferencing.

Blended Learning

Blended learning incorporates the use of both in-person classroom learning and online learning. Blended learning is effective because different people learn better in different ways, and because it breaks up the tedium of relying on a single learning technique. For example, to instruct flight crew trainees, airlines play actual cockpit audio recorded on airplanes involved in accidents. After listening to the recordings, the trainees discuss the behavior of the crew during the crisis. Recordings of trainees themselves also can be used. Golf and tennis coaches frequently record their students to let them see their mistakes and then provide them with verbal instructions for improvement. As shown in Figure 7.6, blended learning is the third most common way that firms deliver training to their employees.

blended learning
The use of both in-person classroom learning and online learning.

7.5 Additional Training and Development Programs

LO5
Discuss some of the special training and development programs that you have seen. Why were they implemented and what outcomes did they hope to achieve?

In addition to training to address the demands of a particular job, many employers develop training programs to meet the special needs of employees. In this section, we summarize some of these programs, including orientation training and onboarding, basic skills training, team training, cross-training, and ethics and diversity training. Intercultural training is covered in Chapter 15.

7.5a Orientation and Onboarding

Orientation is the formal process of familiarizing new employees with the organization, their jobs, and their work units. Whereas training typically emphasizes the *what* and the *how*, orientation often stresses the *why*. It outlines the organization's philosophy and is designed to influence employees' attitudes about their role and the work they will be doing.

orientation
The formal process of familiarizing new employees with the organization, their jobs, and their work units.

An organization's HR department ordinarily is responsible for coordinating orientation activities and providing new employees with information about their conditions of employment, pay, benefits, and other areas not directly under a supervisor's direction. Those responsible for conducting the orientation often use checklists so no aspect of the orientation is overlooked. This checklist would include such things as (1) an introduction to other employees; (2) an outline of training; (3) attendance, conduct, and appearance expectations; (4) the conditions of employment, such as hours and pay periods; (5) an explanation of job duties, standards, and appraisal criteria; (6) safety regulations; (7) a list of the chain of command; and (8) an explanation of the organization's purpose and strategic goals. Highlights in HRM 2 shows the types of materials new hires can be given and the various steps that can ease their transition into the workplace.[32] To be sure no materials are forgotten, companies often post orientation materials on their intranets and then provide new hires with passwords to access the sites.

2 Highlights in HRM

Checklist for Orienting New Employees

Orientation Items

- Welcome information outlining the company's background, corporate vision, and mission statement
- Map of the facility, including parking information
- Computer passwords, security cards, and parking decals
- Current organizational chart
- Information about where to find the firm's corporate news, intranet sites, and bulletin boards
- Phone numbers, email addresses, and locations of key personnel and help desk personnel
- A copy of the employee's specific job goals and job description
- Lists of unique terms in the industry, company, and job
- Training class schedules
- Safety and emergency procedures
- The organization's policy handbook, including the firm's EEOC policies, office hours, dress code, vacation, and email and Internet rules
- List of employee benefits, including insurance plans
- Holiday schedule

Follow-Up Activities

- Ensure that employee has completed the required paperwork, including benefit enrollment forms
- Revisit the employee's performance standards
- Schedule the employee's first performance appraisal meeting

Some organizations combine orientation programs with online training. Macy's cut its orientation training time in half this way, orienting 2,500 new employees in just 6 weeks. During the COVID-19 pandemic, many companies, including Accenture, took their orientation programs online. New hires at SumTotal Systems, an e-learning company based in Bellevue, Washington, take virtual tours of the company's various departments with introductions to company leaders sprinkled throughout. Of course, ideally these programs *supplement*—but do not replace—the face-to-face orientations.[33]

onboarding
The process of systematically socializing new employees to help them get "on board" with an organization.

Onboarding is the process of systematically socializing new employees to help them get "on board" with an organization. Onboarding goes beyond just orienting new employees to their new environment—it brings them into the organization's fold so that they truly feel as if they are a part of it. This is important because new hires are at a high risk of quitting.

Many new hires quit their jobs not because they can't handle the job tasks, but rather because they are going through culture shock within the new organization. When new employees quit soon after being hired, companies are then forced to begin recruiting, interviewing, and screening candidates all over again. Ultimately, the best recruiting and selection processes are of little value if a firm is not able to retain the people it hires.

To help new hires avoid culture shock, some companies make videos and podcasts available to them before they even begin work. These introductions typically describe the mission and goals of the organization, provide a mini-tour of its facilities, and include interviews with current employees talking about what they like about the organization. Executives often are featured as well, which helps new hires develop an early understanding of who's who in the organization.

In some firms, experienced coworkers serve as volunteer "sponsors," or buddies, for incoming employees. In addition to providing the new hires with practical help, they are an important source of information about the culture of the organization, different workgroups, and expectations for employees. These relationships help with the socialization of new employees and contribute significantly to their long-term success within the organization. PepsiCo has a buddy system for new hires. The company's Barcelona unit created a YouTube video explaining where these newbies need to go on their first day and what to expect. They also get a set of written information, and a box of PepsiCo chips and sodas as a welcome gift.

Southwest Airlines approaches onboarding as a welcoming party. "It was so much fun and so informative," remarked one eager new employee after Southwest's onboarding process.[34] New employees always start on Fridays at CityMax.com, a build-your-own-website service in Vancouver, British Columbia. On Fridays, people are in a better mood, more relaxed, and are more willing to spend time getting to know new hires.[35]

7.5b Basic Skills Training

Remedial, or basic skills, training for adults has grown to be a full-blown educational industry on which businesses now spend billions of dollars annually. A report by the National Endowment for the Arts recently concluded that employers ranked the lack of reading and writing skills as the top deficiencies in new hires. Although literacy levels today are similar to what they were in 1970, the economy has changed drastically since then. The basic skills employees need in addition to reading, writing, and computing include speaking, listening, problem solving, working in teams, and leading other people.[36]

Smith & Wesson, Hewlett-Packard, Motorola, and the City of Phoenix instituted basic skills assessment programs to teach reading, math, and communication skills to employees who show some level of deficiency in these areas. Ford, Polaroid, United Technologies, and AT&T are among the many companies that now offer remedial courses to their employees, many of which are conducted in-house.

7.5c Team Training

As we discussed earlier in the book, organizations rely on teams to help them attain their strategic and operational goals. Whether the team is an aircrew, a research team, or a manufacturing or service unit, the contributions of the individual members of the team

David Pereiras/Shutterstock.com

AdVenture Games is a San Diego–based company that provides companies with adventure-based games. The games are designed to improve employees' strategic leadership and creativity, among other things.

are a function of not only the KSAOs of each individual but also the interactions among the team members. The teamwork behaviors of effective teams are shown in Figure 7.9. Team training focused on team roles, group dynamics, and problem-solving provides skills needed to function effectively as a team.[37]

adventure-based learning
The use of adventures, such as games, trust activities, and problem-solving initiatives, to further the personal and social development of participants.

Games often are used in team training, as is adventure-based learning. **Adventure-based learning** is the use of adventures, such as games, trust activities, and problem-solving initiatives, to further the personal and social development of participants.[38] Combine the TV shows *The Amazing Race* and *Survivor* with corporate training, and you will get an idea of what adventure-based learning is. Adventure-based learning is a type of experiential learning (learning by experience). Facebook, Google, Reebok, Coca-Cola, and Dell are among the companies that have utilized adventure-based learning for team-building purposes.

How effective is the adventure-based learning method? It depends. “The most creative way to teach valuable lessons of leadership and communication is to engage employees in an unexpected activity that is carefully designed and backed by parallels to real-life situations,” says Chad Michael, the founder of AdVenture Games, a San Diego company that provides corporate training. “If the team building activity does not come with lessons learned and a creative way to instill valuable skill sets, the investment is no more effective than an afternoon at the park.”

Figure 7.9 Team Training Skills

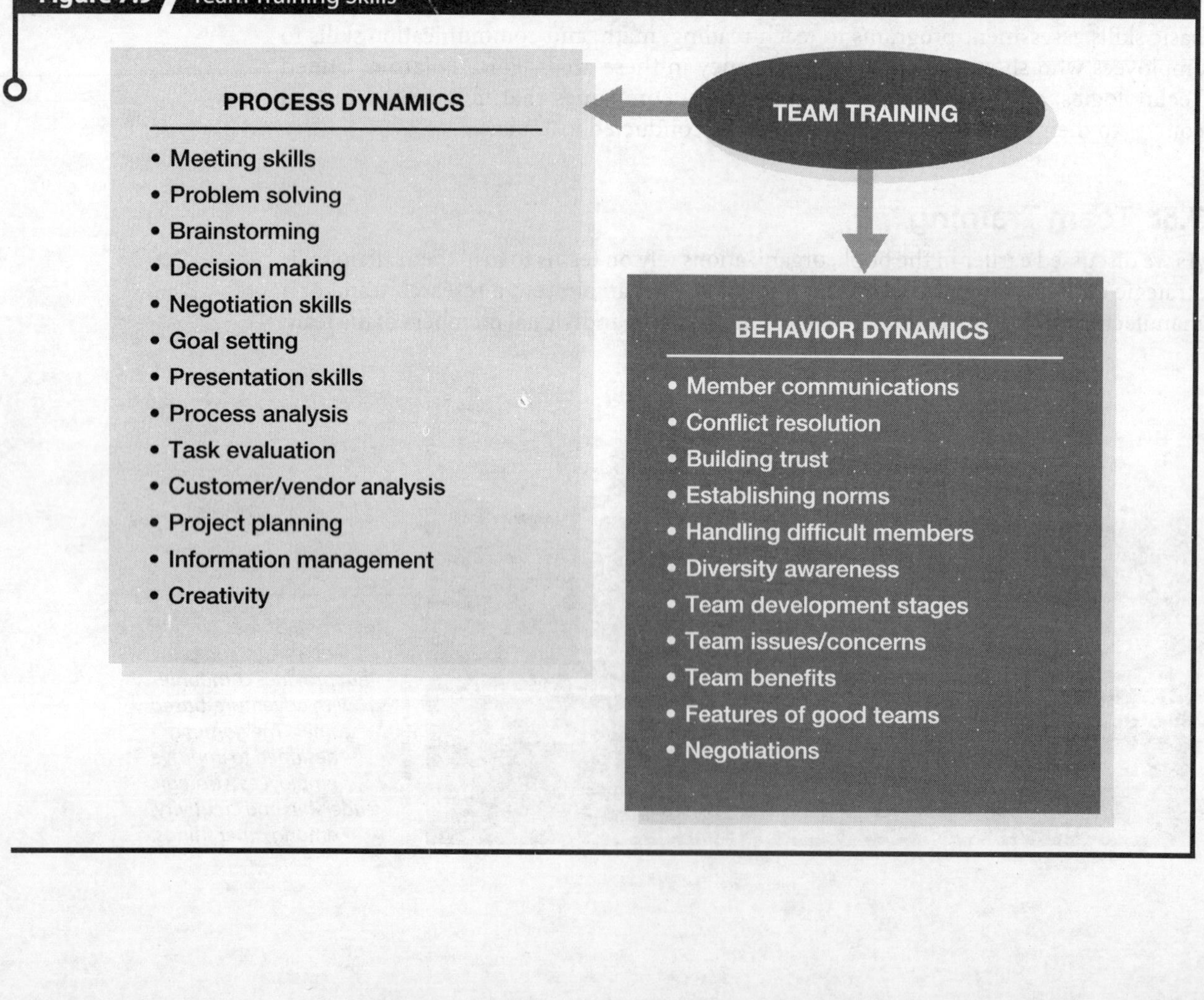

7.5d Cross-Training

Closely related to team training is **cross-training**. Cross-trained employees learn how to do different jobs within an organization as well as their own. "It's easy for top performers to become experts in a certain niche, but 'talent factories' focus on creating generalists," explains one HR consultant. "To get the most from talented employees, they should know how to handle a wide range of functions."

cross-training
The process of training employees to do multiple jobs within an organization.

Part of the motivation for cross-training is that it gives firms flexible capacity. Workers can be shifted when and where they are needed. Cross-training represents a move away from Henry Ford's assembly line production to the world of flexible production. Coca-Cola's Fountain Manufacturing Operation (which makes the syrups for Coke and Diet Coke) developed team training for its manufacturing employees. Its program focuses on three skill categories: (1) technical, (2) interpersonal, and (3) team action. The technical component, called Four-Deep Training, requires each individual to learn four different jobs to allow for team flexibility.

Some companies have used cross-training to keep their workers and plants in the United States versus offshoring them. Pace Worldwide, a Maryland-based company that sells soldering equipment, watched all of its competitors move offshore. To compete with its low-cost rivals abroad, Pace grouped workers into teams and trained each team to build an entire product as well as different products. "Some of the people could only do certain things, and if they had no work, they would just sit and wait," said one Pace manager. "Now they have ownership of it all." Employees have an incentive to learn because their hourly wages get bumped up as they master more skills. Today Pace builds products to meet actual customer demand rather than storing inventory, which is more costly, and it has been able to shorten its production times and move its operations into one building versus two.

By keeping workers interested and motivated, cross-training can cut turnover, increase productivity, pare down labor costs, and lay the foundation for careers rather than dead-end jobs. At Boston's The Gourmet Pizza, employees begin cross-training their first day on the job. They cycle through every function in the back and front of the restaurant and then plot their own course. If they are interested in the bar, they have the opportunity to work there in various positions; those who want to become managers or franchise owners learn the entire operation, a process that takes 8 to 12 months.[39] In addition to making them more productive, research shows that cross-training gives employees the "big picture," making them more creative and better problem solvers.[40]

7.5e Ethics Training

Ethics training became more prevalent in companies following a number of high-profile corporate scandals in the early 2000. Corporate scandals are, of course, neither new nor confined to the twenty-first century. The most common forms of ethics violations, such as harassment, health and safety, and wage-and-hour violations, are related to employment laws.

Government contractors and subcontractors with contracts that last for 120 days or longer and amount to more than $5 million are required by law to have business ethics codes and compliance policies and procedures. Other organizations are not legally required to do so. However, in the event of a violation, those that have "effective programs to prevent and detect violations of law" will face reduced penalties under U.S. federal sentencing guidelines.

Workers who are responsible for areas that expose them to ethical lapses are likely to require special training. Employees who do the purchasing for their firms are one example. Likewise, some firms offer special training to their overseas personnel who work in countries in which corruption and bribery are prevalent. (We will talk more about bribery in Chapter 15, which covers international topics.) Bringing in an outside expert trained in ethics or values-based management can be helpful in increasing ethical awareness, as can surveying employees, managers, and sometimes even customers about what they believe the ethical state of their companies is and where improvements could be made. Other efforts a firm can take to ensure employees at all levels are behaving ethically and legally include establishing toll-free ethics hotlines and secure email addresses where employees can confidentially report violations they have noticed.

chief ethics officers
A high-ranking manager who is directly responsible for fostering the ethical climate within the firm.

Some firms have **chief ethics officers**—high-ranking managers directly responsible for fostering the ethical climate within their firms and ensuring compliance. The Business Roundtable Institute for Corporate Ethics, the Ethics Resource Center, and Ethics & Compliance Officer Association are some additional sources human resource managers can consult to develop ethics training programs. Keep in mind, however, that employees take their cues from top managers and mirror their behavior. If these people don't behave ethically, no ethics training program within a company can be effective.

7.5f Diversity and Inclusion Training

Diversity training programs were designed in response to an increase in globalization, an awareness of the varied demographics of the workforce, challenges of affirmative action, dynamics of stereotyping, changing values of the workforce, and potential competitive payoffs from bringing different people together for a common purpose. There are basically three types of diversity training: (1) awareness building, which helps employees appreciate the benefits of diversity; (2) training to prevent discrimination, harassment, and associated lawsuits, which for some firms is a major reason why they conduct them; and (3) skill building, which provides employees with the KSAOs necessary for working with people who are different from them.[41]

Starbucks is one company that has gained special recognition for its proactive efforts to improve diversity, equity, and inclusion, even to the point of closing stores for antibias training. The San Francisco 49ers football team underwent diversity training after Lindsey McLean, a retired gay trainer with the team, admitted publicly that he was gay and stated that he had endured taunts and humiliation from players at times during his 24 years with the 49ers. "We're trying to create an environment where we can talk about these things and eliminate the problems and violence that can take place and help them understand that they can create an environment that people can work in, even if they are different," said one 49ers manager.[42]

The effectiveness of diversity training continues to be debated, however. A comprehensive review of 31 years of data from 830 midsize to large U.S. workplaces found that following diversity training, even fewer minorities and women were being promoted into management at firms. But that does not necessarily mean that diversity training in and of itself has led to fewer promotions for women and minorities. Moreover, not all diversity training was ineffective, the review found. Rather, it showed that mandatory programs—those instituted solely for the purpose of avoiding liability in discrimination lawsuits—were the problem. When diversity training is voluntary and undertaken to increase awareness of the problem and advance a company's business goals, it can be quite effective.[43] This is one reason why companies are increasingly focusing on *inclusion.* An inclusive workplace is one in which people are treated fairly and with respect, and are supported and encouraged to participate in all aspects of the organization.

7.6 Phase 4: Evaluating the Training Program

> **LO6** Participants in a training course are often asked to evaluate the course by means of a questionnaire. What are the pros and cons of this approach? Are there better ways of evaluating a course?

How can you figure out whether the training program you conducted was successful? A variety of methods are available to assess the extent to which a firm's training programs improve learning, affect behavior on the job, and impact the bottom-line performance of an organization. Figure 7.10 shows that four basic criteria are available to evaluate training: (1) reactions, (2) learning, (3) behavior, and (4) results. Some of these criteria are easier to measure than others, but each is important because it provides different information about the success of the training. The combination of these criteria can give a total picture of a training program to help managers decide where problem areas lie, what to change about the program, and whether to continue it.

7.6a Criterion 1: Reactions

One of the simplest approaches to evaluating a training program is to assess participants' reactions to it. In addition to indicating whether they enjoyed the training, they can give insights into the content and techniques they found most useful. They can critique the instructors, suggest ways to improve the training, and indicate whether it should be continued.

However, positive reactions to a training session are no guarantee it has been successful. Trainees might offer up glowing comments, but as gratifying as this information is, it may not be useful to the organization unless it translates into tangible, improved on-the-job performance based on the firm's strategic goals. Reaction measures should not stop with assessing the training's entertainment value.[44]

Figure 7.10 Criteria for Evaluating Training

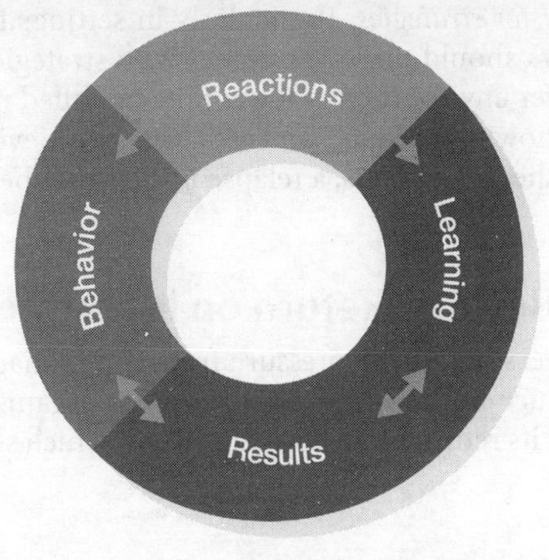

7.6b Criterion 2: Learning

Beyond what participants *think* about the training, did they actually learn anything? Testing the knowledge and skills of trainees before and after a training program will help determine their improvement. The skill and knowledge levels of employees who have undergone a training program also can be compared to employees who have not. Federal Express took this approach. The company studied 20 van drivers who attended a weeklong new-hire training program. The company then compared the performance of these drivers with a control group of 20 drivers who had received only OTJ training. FedEx found that the drivers who had been formally trained made fewer package processing errors, saving the company about $500 per trained driver.[45]

7.6c Criterion 3: Behavior

transfer of training
The effective application of principles learned to what is required on the job.

The **transfer of training** refers to how well employees apply what they have learned to their jobs. There are several ways to assess the transfer of learned skills back to the job. At Xerox, trainers observe trainees once they return to their regular positions, interview the trainees' managers about their progress later on, and examine their post-training performance appraisals.

You might be surprised to learn that much of what is learned in a training program never gets used back on the job. To maximize the transfer of training, managers and trainers can take several approaches:

1. *Feature identical elements.* Have conditions in the training program come as close as possible to those on the job. For example, instead of verbally explaining a manufacturing process, it is better to demonstrate it on a factory floor.
2. *Focus on general principles, if necessary.* When jobs change or the work environment cannot be matched exactly, trainers often stress the general principles behind the training rather than focusing on rote behavior. This approach helps trainees learn how to apply the main learning points to varying conditions on the job.
3. *Establish a climate for transfer.* In some cases, trained behavior is not implemented because old approaches and routines are still reinforced by people within the organization. To prevent this kind of problem, firms need to encourage their managers to embrace the strategic changes their organizations are seeking to implement and reinforce and reward trainees for applying the new skills or knowledge.
4. *Give employees transfer strategies.* Particularly in settings that are not conducive to transfer, managers should provide trainees with strategies and tactics for dealing with their transfer environment. One approach, called *relapse prevention (RP)*, teaches individuals how to anticipate and cope with the inevitable setbacks they will encounter back on the job—that is, a relapse into former behaviors.[46]

7.6d Criterion 4: Results (Return on Investment)

Human resource managers are under pressure from top managers to show that their training programs produce bottom-line results.[47] Most organizations today measure their training in terms of its return on investment (ROI), which sometimes is referred to as the *utility* the firm gets for its training dollars. A company's ROI refers to the benefits it derives from training compared to what that training costs.

The benefits of training can include higher revenues generated, increased productivity, improved quality, lower costs, more satisfied customers, higher job satisfaction, lower employee turnover, and greater innovation. To put a dollar value on these benefits, HR managers use various types of data, such as sales data, human resources and financial data, and employee survey and control group data gathered from various sources within the organization.

To put a dollar value on the firm's training costs, the company calculates the direct costs of the programs (materials, software, employee travel and meals, meeting site costs, equipment, trainers' salaries or fees, etc.) as well as the indirect costs of the programs (participants' salaries and the productivity they lose while they are attending the training).

Recall that benchmarking is the practice of comparing data and statistics from your operations, such as training, against those of recognized leaders in your industry. The American Society of Training has developed training benchmarks from hundreds of different companies to which other firms can compare the data on their training costs, staffing, administration, design, development, and delivery of training programs. Benchmarks such as these can help organizations evaluate their current and future training programs. Highlights in HRM 3 shows several aspects of training that can be benchmarked.

As e-learning continues to change training, the benchmarks for it are changing as well. Measures such as the extent to which learning content has been accessed and downloaded, and the ratings given it by users are likely to become new measures of how well a firm's training programs are working.[48]

Some HR experts think managers are overly preoccupied with ROI calculations and benchmarking for their training programs. Why? Because often the benefits of training can be intangible or take a long time to appear. Measuring participants' reactions can be done immediately, of course. Measuring improved employee skills, customer satisfaction, and other outcomes can take somewhat longer, and factors other than training can also affect these measures. Finally, the development of groundbreaking products or new processes can be sparked by training but take years to develop, making it more difficult to attribute these accomplishments to training. Developments such as these nonetheless can transform organizations.

The key to improving a training program's effectiveness is continually evaluating it. The information generated by the evaluations then feeds back into Phase 1 of the training process, as shown in Figure 7.1. By tying the training closely to key performance metrics and then measuring the training's impact against them, a firm will be in a better position to improve its programs over time.[49]

3 Highlights in HRM

Benchmarking HR Training

MEASUREMENT	HOW TO CALCULATE
Percentage of payroll spent on training	Total training expenditures ÷ total payroll
Training dollars spent per employee	Total training expenditures ÷ total employees served
Average training hours per employee	Total number of training hours (hours × participants) ÷ total employees trained
Percentage of employees trained per year	Total number of employees receiving training ÷ total employee population
HRD staff per 1,000 employees	Number of human resource development staff ÷ total employee population × 1,000
Cost savings as a ratio of training	Total savings in scrap or waste ÷ dollars invested expenses in training
Profits per employee per year	Total yearly gross profits ÷ total number of employees
Training costs per student hour	Total costs of training ÷ total number of hours of training

Summary

LO 1 The types of training given to employees range from simple, on-the-job instruction to sophisticated skills training conducted on multimillion-dollar simulators. Training programs cover a broad range of subjects and involve personnel at all levels. The goal of training is to contribute to an organization's overall strategic goals. To be effective, training programs need to be developed systematically. This approach consists of four phases: (1) needs assessment, (2) program design, (3) implementation, and (4) evaluation.

LO 2 The needs assessment phase begins with an organization analysis. Managers must establish a context for training by deciding where training is needed, how it connects with their firms' strategic goals, and how their companies' resources can best be used in terms of training. A task analysis is used to identify the knowledge, skills, and abilities employees need. A person analysis is used to identify which people need training.

LO 3 When designing a training program, managers need to consider the two preconditions for learning: the readiness and motivation of trainees. In addition, the principles of learning should be considered to create an environment that is conducive to learning. These principles include goal setting; the meaningfulness of the presentation; modeling; individual differences; active practice and repetition; experiential learning; whole-versus-part learning; massed, distributed, and continuous learning; and feedback and reinforcement.

LO 4 A wide variety of methods are available to train personnel. On-the-job training is one of the most commonly used methods. Apprenticeship training and internships are especially effective. On-the-job experiences include coaching, understudy assignments, job rotation, lateral transfers, project and committee assignments, and staff meetings. Off-the-job experiences include analysis of case studies, role-playing, and behavior modeling.

Classroom training remains the most popular way to train employees, but e-learning methods, such as simulations, games, just-in-time learning, microlearning, and social media, are rapidly growing in popularity. Using multiple methods, an approach called blended learning, has been found to be most effective.

LO 5 Employers develop different training programs for various purposes. Orientation training allows new hires to more quickly acquire the knowledge, skills, and attitudes that increase the probability of their success within the organization. Onboarding programs help new hires feel as if they truly are a part of a firm—something that is important because new hires are at a high risk of quitting. Basic skills training, team and cross-training, ethics training, and diversity training are other programs commonly conducted by organizations.

LO 6 The effectiveness of training can be evaluated against several criteria: participants' reactions, the amount of learning they have acquired, their behavioral changes on the job, and bottom-line results such as the program's return on investment. The transfer of training is measured via examination of the degree to which trained skills are demonstrated back on the job. Benchmarking and utility analysis help evaluate the impact of training and provide the information for further needs assessment.

Key Terms

adventure-based learning
apprenticeship training
behavior modeling
behavior modification
blended learning
chief ethics officer
chief learning officer
competency assessment
cooperative training
cross-training
e-learning
experiential learning
instructional objectives
just-in-time training
learning management system (LMS)
microlearning
on-the-job training (OJT)
onboarding
organization analysis
orientation
person analysis
spot rewards
task analysis
transfer of training

Discussion Questions

LO 1 What economic, social, and political forces have made employee training even more important today than it was in the past?

LO 2 What analyses should be done to determine the training needs of an organization? After the needs are determined, what is the next step?

LO 3 Which principles of learning do you see demonstrated in your own classes? In what ways might you bring other principles into them?

LO 4 Suppose that you are the manager of an accounts receivable unit in a large company. You are switching to a new system of billing and record-keeping and need to train your 3 supervisors and 28 employees in the new procedures. What training method(s) would you use? Why?

LO 5 Participants in a training course are often asked to evaluate the course by means of a questionnaire. What are the pros and cons of this approach? Are there better ways of evaluating a course?

HRM Experience

Training and Learning Principles

Even though it is not difficult to do so, a surprising number of training programs don't explicitly incorporate the principles of learning (goal setting, modeling, individual differences, and feedback). To prove incorporating them is not difficult to do, complete the following assignment for building a paper airplane.

Assignment

1. Form teams of four to six members. Identify someone on the team who knows how to make a paper airplane. That person will be the trainer.
2. Identify someone who will be the observer/recorder. That person will not participate in the training but will write down how many (and how effectively) principles of learning are used in the instruction:
   a. Goal setting
   b. Modeling
   c. Meaningfulness
   d. Individual differences
   e. Whole-versus-part learning
   f. Mass versus distributed learning
   g. Active practice
   h. Feedback
   i. Experiential learning
3. Give the trainer 10 to 15 minutes to train the group in making a paper airplane. The observer/recorder will keep notes of effective and ineffective training techniques (demonstrated learning principles).
4. Have someone from each team—not the trainer—volunteer to come before the class for a friendly competition. The instructor will give each team member 2 minutes to make a paper airplane. Then, just for fun, they can compete by seeing which one flies the farthest. (No wagering, please.)
5. To finish the exercise, the observers/recorders will lead a discussion of the learning principles that were demonstrated. If the principles were incorporated for this activity, discuss why they might not be incorporated in other training settings.

CASE STUDY 1 Whirlpool Mixes up Its Managerial Training: Closed-Looped Method Brings Learning Full Circle

Most Americans are familiar with Whirlpool. Whirlpool, which is based in Benton Harbor, Michigan, has been in business for more than century and is perhaps best known for the washers and dryers it makes. In addition, the company makes refrigerators, freezers, and cooking appliances that it sells under various other brand names around the world (Amana, Maytag, KitchenAid, and Roper are some of them).

During the last economic recession, appliance sales plummeted, and Whirlpool was forced to lay off thousands of workers. Although budgets were being slashed, Whirlpool needed to develop managers who could lead the company through the downturn as well as provide training that would have a measurable impact at a lower cost.

Previously Whirlpool University, the company's 100-acre learning division located at its corporate headquarters, had used mainly classroom learning. The university now has a learning management system and conducts online training. A series of 30-minute modules are used to help familiarize and onboard new hires. In addition, Whirlpool now takes a "closed-loop" approach to training. Instead of just doing the popular types of training that other companies have adopted, it surveys managers to find out what types of training Whirlpool truly needs and what types it doesn't, and then designs training programs based on those specific needs.

Because managers are central to the training and development of their employees and are in the best position to observe and coach rank-and-file employees, Whirlpool utilizes a 12-month-long intermittent training program for its managers called Leading People. The program consists of blended learning, including prework modules managers do online, followed by classroom training, business projects, and seminars with top managers. A manager's direct reports provide an initial baseline assessment of the manager's skills, and then the manager is assessed again following the training. James Crawford, in Whirlpool's Chicago division, said the training helped him become a better leader: "It helped me pinpoint weak spots in my leadership practices and then gave me a strategy for turning those weaknesses into strengths." The managers are later surveyed on how well the training is working and what can be done to improve it. In other words, there is a feedback system in place—hence the "closed-loop" moniker. With this approach, the design, delivery, and redesign of the training is a continuous circle and constantly being improved over time.

Its closed-loop feedback system has helped Whirlpool continue to assess and alter its training to adapt to new conditions. For example, today Whirlpool isn't laying off employees; it's trying to hire more of them as its older workers retire. To attract Millennials, the company has partnered with high school and colleges to offer an on-site apprenticeship program called "Work, Earn, and Learn." In 2017, Whirlpool's CEO, Jeff Fettig, was one of a number of corporate executives who met with President Donald Trump to talk about saving American jobs and encourage government support for the vocational training that today's high-tech skills manufacturers today. "The jobs are there, but the skills are not," said one executive at the meeting.

Questions

1. Why are a needs assessment and ongoing training important for firms like Whirlpool to conduct?
2. How do you think Whirlpool's training strategy will need to change in the future?

Sources: Greg Sowinski, "Manufacturers Prep to Replace Retiring Workforce," *LimaOhio.com* (March 5, 2017), http://limaohio.com; Christopher S. Rugaber, "U.S. Factory CEOs to Trump: Jobs Exist; Skills Don't," *Chicago Tribune* (February 24, 2017), http://www.chicagotribune.com; Garry Kranz, "Whirlpool Adopts E-Learning for Leadership," *Workforce* (November 14, 2012), http://www.workforce.com; Tamara Patrick, "Unleashing a Learning Partnership with Managers," *ATD* (August 16, 2012), http://www.astd.org; Tamara Patrick, "Whirlpool University Re-invents in the Face of the Recession," *Management Innovation Exchange* (September 16, 2011), http://www.managementexchange.com.

CASE STUDY 2 Loews Hotels: Training for Four-Diamond Service and More

Most people expect to receive great service at four-diamond hotels. But that's not good enough for Loews. The New York–based hotel chain, which has properties in 16 cities across the United States and Canada, tries to "wow" every one of its guests with high-quality accommodations, impressive surroundings, personalized service, and thoughtful amenities for a luxurious experience.

A key element of success at Loews is the extensive training it provides to its employees. Whether they work at the front desk or as housekeepers, accountants, or marketing managers, all employees learn about the big-picture goals of the company and how the quality of service differentiates one company from another in the hotel business. "The key is to train *all* departments of your organization to be customer-centric," says Jon Tisch, the company's co-chairman. "Thinking about customers can't be left to marketing and sales alone. Manufacturing, R&D, strategy, management, all have to be focused on the needs and desires of the customer."

Customer-facing employees at Loews undergo classroom training, including role-playing and simulations to learn how to deal with customers. "Living Loews," a 2-day training program, teaches employees not only the finer points of etiquette but how to really sell the Loews experience—even when things go wrong. "We're all human, so mistakes can happen," Tisch explains. "But when they do, we train our coworkers to impress our guests with an extraordinary recovery that we hope they'll remember even more."

Training sessions such as "Green" training, "Loews Meeting Experience," "Loews Pool Concierge" program, "Spa 101," and the "YouFirst" guest loyalty program ensure that customers of all types who use the hotel's various services get top-notch service.

The training does not end with the sessions, though. Once the sessions are over, training managers go out on the front lines to do spot checks and offer feedback to employees to make sure the training really "sticks." A train-the-trainer program and other managerial workshops such as "Communicating Loews" help managers promote the hotel brand and inspire their employees to do so as well. A comprehensive executive training program covers topics ranging from communication and salesmanship to public speaking and presentation skills.

Loews also tries to "grow" its own talent. Most training managers, for example, are promoted from line-level jobs or from operations, so they know the company's processes and culture firsthand. The company also has a tuition assistance program.

To recruit undergraduates, Loews offers paid summer internships. Interns work in a variety of areas such as the rooms division, food and beverage department, sales and marketing, and human resources. Each intern is assigned a mentor and given opportunities to network by attending operational meetings. At the conclusion of their internships, they complete a report on their experience. Successive-year internships give them exposure to additional functional areas, project work, supervisory experience, and ultimately the opportunity to join the company's management training program.

To keep things interesting, Lowes recently began using gamification to create quick-burst mobile games to upskill, onboard, and improve the productivity of employees. The games are used to translate existing training materials—manuals, tests, and videos—into a platform that is engaging and fun. So successful is the training at Loews that even trainers are impressed. Douglas Kennedy, the founder and president of the Kennedy Training Network, which specializes in hospitality training, says he was knocked out by his experience while conducting training at Loews's various properties. Kennedy says he's gotten very spoiled during his overnight stays at Loews hotels: "I'm sure it will be a rude awakening next month when I return to staying in more typical upscale hotels."

Questions

1. How do the training programs at Loews relate to the company's business strategy?
2. Why does the company encourage its employees to focus on the customers' needs versus other metrics?

Sources: Corris Little, "Using Mobile Gamification to Enhance Hotel Training," *Hotel Business*, October 11, 2018; Amy Freifeld, "Loews Hotels' Secret to Being a Good Neighbor," *Training Magazine*, November 12, 2012; Amy Bertrand, "Luxury Hotel Trends to Watch," *St. Louis Today* (February 4, 2014), http://www.stltoday.com; Jill Busch, "Training Reveals Rankings for 2011 Top 125," *Training Magazine* (February 8, 2011), http://www.trainingmag.com; Ann LaGreca, "Loews Hotels CEO Jonathan Tisch on the Essence of Customer Service: Experience, Service and Quality," *Knowledge@Emory* (July 11, 2007), http://knowledge.emory.edu; "Loews Hotels Named among 'Top 125' by Training Magazine," *Hotel and Motel Management* (March 9, 2009), http://www.hospitalityworldnetwork.com; Holly Dolezalek, "We Train to Please," *Training* 45, no. 3 (2008): 34–35.

Notes and References

1. "2020 Training Industry Report," *Training* (November–December 2020): 35.
2. Jean Barbazette, *Training Needs Assessment: Methods, Tools, and Techniques* (San Francisco, CA: Pfeiffer Publishing, 2006); Peter Franks, Stephen Hay, and Tim Mavin, "Can Competency-Based Training Fly?: An Overview of Key Issues for AB Onitio Pilot Training," *International Journal of Training Research* 12, no. 2 (2014): 132–147; Lori Freifeld, "Best of the Best," *Training* 45, no. 2 (February 2008): 8; David Dubois and William Rothwell, "Competency-Based or a Traditional Approach to Training?" *Training and Development* 58, no. 4 (April 2004): 46–59; see also Irwin L. Goldstein and J. Kevin Ford, *Training in Organizations: Needs Assessment, Development and Evaluation*, 4th ed. (Belmont, CA: Wadsworth, 2002). For the classic citation on needs assessment, see William McGehee and Paul W. Thayer, *Training in Business and Industry* (New York: John Wiley and Sons, 1961).
3. Roz Brooks, Scott McCandless, Joseph Nocera, and Kevin O'Connell. "Top Policy Trends 2021," PWC (2021), https://www.pwc.com/us/en/services/consulting/risk-regulatory/library/top-policy-trends.html; Mackenzie Adams and Maged Makramalla, "Cybersecurity Skills Training: An Attacker-Centric Gamified Approach," *Technology Innovation Management Review.* 5, no. 1 (2015); Liam Lahey, "RFIDs Touted as Standard for Airport Security" *Computing Canada* 28, no. 13 (2002): 21; Caroline Wilson, "Ensuring a Smooth Ride," *Security Management* 46, no. 8 (2002): 92.
4. Lauren Weber, "Microsoft Aims to Train 25 Million Workers Free in 2020," *Wall Street Journal*, June 30, 2020; Laurie Bassi and Daniel McMurrer, "How's Your Return on People?"

Harvard Business Review 8, no. 3 (March 2004): 18; Tracy Mauro, "Helping Organizations Build Community," *Training and Development* 56, no. 2 (2002): 25–29.

5. Sanghamitra Chaudhuri and Kenneth R. Bartlett, "The Relationship between Training Outsourcing and Employee Commitment to Organization," *Human Resource Development International* 17, no. 2 (2014): 145–163; Brad Long, "Strategic Human Resource Management and the Worker's Experience," *Journal of Individual Employment Rights* 12, no. 3 (2007): 265–282; "E-Learning and Teleconferencing Join Needs Assessment to Control Training Costs," *Managing Training & Development*, no. 3 (December 2003): 1; Thomas Gainey, Brian Klaas, and Darla Moore, "Outsourcing the Training Function: Results from the Field," *Human Resource Planning* 25, no. 1 (2002): 16; Sarah Fister Gale, "Creative Training: Doing More with Less," *Workforce* 80, no. 10 (2001): 82–88.
6. J. L. Callahan and C. E. Watkins, "The Science of Training III: Supervision, Competency, and Internship Training," *Training and Education in Professional Psychology* 12, no. 4 (2018): 245–261; Peter Franks, Stephen Hay, and Tim Mavin, "Can Competency-Based Training Fly?"; Patty Davis, Jennifer Naughton, and William Rothwell, "New Roles and New Competencies for the Profession: Are You Ready for the Next Generation," *Training and Development* 58, no. 4 (2004): 26–38; David Dubois and William Rothwell, "Competency-Based or a Traditional Approach to Training?" *Training and Development* 58, no. 4 (2004): 46–59.
7. "How to Identify Training Needs of Employees: 8 Ways To Start," *eLearning Industry*, June 12, 2019; "Using Feedback to Improve the Employee Training Experience," Designing Digitally, November 28, 2018; Allison S. Gabriel et al., "The Supervisor Feedback Environment Is Empowering, But Not All the Time: Feedback Orientation as a Critical Moderator," *Journal of Occupational and Organizational Psychology* 87, no. 3 (2014): 487–506; Gary Kranz, "Special Report: More to Learn," *Workforce Management* (January 2011), http://www.workforce.com/.
8. Nima Jafari Navimipour and Batool Zareie, "A Model for Assessing the Impact of E-Learning Systems on Employees' Satisfaction," *Computers in Human Behavior* 53 (2015): 475–485; Thomas Hoffman, "Motivation: These IT Leaders Keep Staffers Upbeat during Lean Times by Targeting What Drives Them: Technology and Training," *Computerworld* 38, no. 1 (2004): 39; Elwood Holton, Reid Bates, and Sharon Naquin, "Large-Scale Performance-Driven Training Needs Assessment: A Case Study," *Public Personnel Management* 29, no. 2 (2000): 249–267.
9. Alice Hsiaw, "Goal-Setting and Self-Control," *Journal of Economic Theory* 148, no. 2 (2013): 601–626; Debbie Schachter, "How to Set Performance Goals: Employee Reviews Are More Than Annual Critiques," *Information Outlook* 8, no. 9 (2004): 26–30; "Burger Olympics," *Training* 41, no. 7 (2004): 20; Jason A. Colquitt and Marcia J. Simmering, "Conscientiousness, Goal Orientation, and Motivation to Learn during the Learning Process: A Longitudinal Study," *Journal of Applied Psychology* 83, no. 4 (1998): 654–665.
10. Leroy Hannes et al., "Mindfulness, Authentic Functioning, and Work Engagement: A Growth Modeling Approach," *Journal of Vocational Behavior* 82 no. 3 (2013): 238–247; Annette Towler and Robert Dipboye, "Effects of Trainer Expressiveness, Organization, and Trainee Goal Orientation on Training Outcomes," *Journal of Applied Psychology* 86, no. 4 (2001): 664–673; Steve Kozlowski, Stanley Gully, Kenneth Brown, and Eduardo Salas, "Effects of Training Goals and Goal Orientation Traits on Multidimensional Training Outcomes and Performance Adaptability," *Organizational Behavior and Human Decision Processes* 85, no. 1 (2001): 1–31.
11. The classics by Albert Bandura include *Social Foundations of Thought and Action: A Social Cognitive Theory* (Englewood Cliffs, NJ: Prentice Hall, 1986) and *A Social Learning Theory* (Englewood Cliffs, NJ: Prentice Hall, 1977). See also Melesa Altizer Bolt, Larry Killough, and Hian Chye Koh, "Testing the Interaction Effects of Task Complexity in Computer Training Using the Social Cognitive Model," *Decision Sciences* 32, no. 1 (2001): 1020; Rose M. Marra et al., "Why Problem-Based Learning Works," *Journal on Excellence in College Teaching* 25, no. 3/4 (2014): 221–238; Susan Pedersen and Min Liu, "The Transfer of Problem-Solving Skills from a Problem-Based Learning Environment: The Effect of Modeling an Expert's Cognitive Processes," *Journal of Research on Technology in Education* 35, no. 2 (2002): 303–321.
12. Chadwick Reese and Debra Hunter, "What about the Middle Man? The Impact of Middle Level Managers on Organizational Learning," *Journal of Management* 4, no. 1 (2016): 17–25; Joe M. Ricks, Jacqueline A. Williams, and William A. Weeks, "Sales Trainer Roles, Competencies, Skills, and Behaviors: A Case Study," *Industrial Marketing Management* 37, no. 5 (2008): 593–609; John L. Bennett, "Trainers as Leaders of Learning," *Training and Development* 55, no. 3 (2001): 42–45; Ruth Palombo Weiss, "Deconstructing Trainers' Self-Image," *Training and Development* 55, no. 12 (2001): 34–39.
13. G. Yemen and E. Weiss, *The Indigo Story: On Time, Hassel Free* (Darden Business Publishing, 2018); Josep-Maria Batalla-Busquets and Carmen Pacheco-Bernal, "On-the-Job e-Learning: Workers' Attitudes and Perceptions," *The International Review of Research in Open and Distributed Learning* 14, no. 1 (2013): 40–64; "Eight Steps to Better On-the-Job Training," *HRFocus* 80, no. 7 (2003): 11; Alison Booth, Yu-Fu Chen, and Gylfi Zoega, "Hiring and Firing: A Tale of Two Thresholds," *Journal of Labor Economics* 20, no. 2 (2002): 217–248.
14. For more information on apprenticeship programs, opportunities, and benefits, see Apprenticeship.gov (https://www.apprenticeship.gov/).
15. Yeonsoo Kim, "Use of Career One Stop and Career Network in US," *Talent Management Monthly* 121 (2015): 83; "Workforce Investment Act: One-Stop Centers Implemented Strategies to Strengthen Services and Partnerships, But More Research and

Information Sharing Is Needed," *General Accounting Office Reports & Testimony* 2003, no. 7 (2003).

16. Dominic Gorecky, Mohamed Khamis, and Katharina Mura, "Introduction and Establishment of Virtual Training in the Factory of the Future," *International Journal of Computer Integrated Manufacturing* 30, no. 1 (2017): 182–190; Sarah Fister Gale, "Virtual Training with Real Results," *Workforce Management* (December 2008), http://www.workforce.com.
17. Joanne Viviano, "Ohio Doctors Employ Virtual Reality to Train for Trauma Care," *Columbus Dispatch* (March 26, 2017), http://www.dispatch.com; "Soup to Nuts: Simulator Manufacturing Is a Lucrative But Risky Business, Which Is Why Market Leader CAE Has Tapped into the More Stable World of Flight Training," *Air Transport World* 40, no. 5 (2003): 69–71; "SimsSir: Modeling and Simulation Are Leading the Assault on New Learning Technologies That Are Winning Favor with the U.S. Military," *Training and Development* 57, no. 10 (2003): 46–52.
18. Erika Darling et al., "Effective Game-Based Training at the Point of Need," in *Advances in Human Factors, Business Management, Training and Education* (New York: Springer International Publishing, 2017): 677–685; Adam Kirby, "Guest Service Is Fun and Games," *Hotels* 42, no. 5 (2008): 71–72; Dan Heilman, "Putting Games to Work: Game-Based Training Is Shaping up to Be One of This Generation's Primary Teaching Tools, in Business and Elsewhere," *Computer User* 22, no. 2 (2004): 14–16.
19. Judy Mottl, "Bloomingdales, Altar'd State Share Associate Training Success Stores," *Retail Customer Experience* (February 28, 2017), https://www.retailcustomerexperience.com.
20. Anjali Bal et al., "Second Best in Second Life: Teaching Marketing Cases in a Virtual World Environment," *Proceedings of the 2010 Academy of Marketing Science (AMS) Annual Conference* (Springer International Publishing, 2015); Aili McConnon, "The Games Managers Play," *BusinessWeek* (June 25, 2007): 12.
21. Phil Britt, "E-Learning on the Rise in the Classroom: Companies Move Content Online: Cisco Systems' Employees and Partners Routinely Watch Videos on the Internet," *EContent* 27, no. 11 (2004): 36–41; Heather Johnson, "The Whole Picture: When It Comes to Finding out How Employees Feel about Training, Many Companies Fail to Get a Clear Picture," *Training* 47, no. 7 (2004): 30–35.
22. Ravi Rajputh et al., "Interactive Materials Development Using the Rapid e-Learning Method: Examples from the Field" (2016); "What to Do Now That Training Is Becoming a Major HR Force," *HRFocus* (February 2005): 5–6; Tammy Galvin, "The Delivery," *Training* 38, no. 10 (2001): 66–72; Kenneth G. Brown, "Using Computers to Deliver Training: Which Employees Learn and Why?" *Personnel Psychology* 54, no. 2 (2001): 271–296; Bill Roberts, "E-Learning New Twist on CBT," *HRMagazine* 46, no. 4 (2001): 99–106.
23. Lara Kolodny, "A New Way to Train Workers, One Small Bite at a Time," *Wall Street Journal* (May 13, 2016), https://www.wsj.com.
24. Garry Kranz, "Online Learning Gets Massive, Open," *Workforce Management* (August 13, 2013), http://www.workforce.com.
25. David Ong et al., "Reducing Employee Learning and Development Costs: The Use of Massive Open Online Courses (MOOC)," *Development and Learning in Organizations: An International Journal* 30, no. 5 (2016): 18–21; Geoffrey Fowler, "An Early Report Card e-ln MOOCs," *Wall Street Journal* (October 8, 2013), http://online.wsj.com.
26. "2016 Training Industry Report" *Training* (November–December 2016): 31.
27. "Learning 2.0: Improving Workforce Productivity," *Workforce Management* (April 2010), http://www.workforce.com.
28. Bill Leonard, "Social Media Can Enhance Employee Learning," *HR Today* (May 20, 2015), https://www.shrm.org.
29. T. L. Stanley, "Be a Good Role Model for Your Employees," *Supervision* 65, no. 5 (2004): 5–8; Gary May and William Kahnweiler, "The Effect of a Mastery Practice Design on Learning and Transfer in Behavior Modeling Training," *Personnel Psychology* 53, no. 2 (2000): 353–373.
30. Jason J. Dahling et al., "Does Coaching Matter? A Multilevel Model Linking Managerial Coaching Skill and Frequency to Sales Goal Attainment," *Personnel Psychology* (2015); Avery Augustine, "How to Coach Your Really Good Employees," *Forbes* (January 22, 2014), http://www.forbes.com.
31. Amir Elnaga and Amen Imran, "The Effect of Training on Employee Performance," *European Journal of Business and Management* 5, no. 4 (2013): 137–147; Chris Whitcomb, "Scenario-Based Training to the F.B.I.," *Training and Development* 53, no. 6 (1999): 42–46; Anne Hoag, Dale Brickley, and Joanne Cawley, "Media Management Education and the Case Method," *Journalism and Mass Communication Educator* 55, no. 4 (2001): 49–59.
32. M. Srimannarayana, "Designing New Employee Orientation Programs: An Empirical Study," *Indian Journal of Industrial Relations* 51, no. 4 (2016): 620–633; Mike Frost, "Creative New Employee Orientation Programs," *HRMagazine* 47, no. 8 (2002): 120–121; Marilyn Moats Kennedy, "Setting the Right Tone, Right Away," *Across the Board* 36, no. 4 (1999): 51–52.
33. Kathryn Dill, "It's Not Just Working Remotely; Hiring and Onboarding Go Virtual, Too," *Wall Street Journal*, April 15, 2020; Vurain Tabvuma, Yannis Georgellis, and Thomas Lange, "Orientation Training and Job Satisfaction: A Sector and Gender Analysis," *Human Resource Management* 54, no. 2 (2015): 303–321; Emmanuella Plakoyiannaki, Nikolaos Tzokas, Pavlos Dimitratos, and Michael Saren, "How Critical Is Employee Orientation for Customer Relationship Management? Insights from a Case Study," *Journal of Management Studies* 45, no. 2 (2008): 268–293.
34. Kathryn Tyler, "Take New Employee Orientation off the Back Burner," *HRMagazine* 43, no. 6 (1998): 49–57; Noel Tichy, "No Ordinary Boot Camp," *Harvard Business Review* 79, no. 4 (2001): 63–70.
35. Gail B. Caldwell and Cam Caldwell, "Ten Classic Onboarding Errors: Violations of the HRM–Employee Relationship,"

Business and Management Research 5, no. 4 (2016): 47; Leigh Buchanan, "How to Make New Hires Feel at Home," *Inc.* (June 8, 2010), http://www.inc.com.

36. "Workplace Readiness: Job Candidates Lack Writing Skills," *Washington Post*, August 22, 2017; "Corporate America Can't Write," *Work & Family Newsbrief* (January 2005): 4; Matt Bolch, "School at Work," *Training* 39, no. 2 (2002); Slav Kanyba, "Community Colleges React to Job-Training Request," *San Fernando Valley Business Journal* 9, no. 2 (2004): 1–2.
37. Eduardo Salas, Deborah DiazGranados, Cameron Klein, "Does Team Training Improve Team Performance? A Meta-Analysis," *Human Factors*, December 1, 2008; "Behavior-Based Sales Team Training Produces a 56% Increase in Revenues," *Managing Training & Development* (April 2004): 1.
38. Peter Loftus, "Latest Medical-School Trend: Wilderness Training," *Wall Street Journal*, March 21, 2017; Marg Cosgriff, "Walking Our Talk: Adventure-Based Learning and Physical Education," *Journal of Physical Education (New Zealand)* 33, no. 2 (2000): 90.
39. Caroline Miller, "Cross-Training Employees: Ensure You're Ready for the Unexpected," *Biz Library*, October 27, 2020; J. K. Winch, X. Cai, and G. L. Vairaktarakis, "Cyclic Job Scheduling in Paced Assembly Lines with Cross-Trained Workers," *International Journal of Production Research* 45, no. 4 (2007): 803–828; Lisa Bertagnoli, "The Ten-Minute Manager's Guide to . . . Cross-Training Staff," *Restaurants & Institutions* 114, no. 18 (2004): 26–28; Wallace J. Hopp and Mark P. Van Oyen, "Agile Workforce Evaluation: A Framework for Cross-Training and Coordination," *IIE Transactions* 36, no. 10 (2004): 919–941.
40. Tomislav Hernaus, Matej Cerne, and Miha Škerlavaj, "Going the Extra Mile: Cross-Training, Relational Job Design, and Extra-Role Behavior of High-Skilled and Low-Skilled Workers," *International HRM Workshop* (2016); Lorraine Mirabella, "Productivity Gains in Maryland Mean Less Hiring But More Job Cross-Training," *The Baltimore Sun* (via *Knight-Ridder/Tribune Business News*), April 17, 2004.
41. Krithika Varagur, "The Unfinished Business of Office Diversity Training," *Wall Street Journal*, December 20, 2020; Gary Stern, "Small Slights Bring Big Problems," *Workforce* 81, no. 8 (2002): 17.
42. Heather Haddon, "Starbucks Ties Executive Pay to 2025 Diversity Targets," *Wall Street Journal*, October 14, 2020; "49ers Decide to Add Diversity to Training Camp," *The New York Times* (July 8, 20014): D3.
43. Zachary T. Kalinoski, Debra Steele-Johnson, Elizabeth J. Peyton, Keith A. Leas, Julie Steinke, and Nathan A. Bowling, "A Meta-Analytic Evaluation of Diversity Training Outcomes," *Journal of Organizational Behavior* 34, no. 8 (2013): 1076–1104; Frank Dobbin and Alexandra Kalev, "Why Doesn't Diversity Training Work? The Challenge for Industry and Academia," *Anthropology Now* 10, no. 2 (2018): 48–55; Shankar Vedantam, "Most Diversity Training Ineffective, Study Finds," *Washington Post* (January 19, 2008), http://www.washingtonpost.com.
44. Jolyn Gelens et al., "Talent Management and Organizational Justice: Employee Reactions to High Potential Identification," *Human Resource Management Journal* 24, no. 2 (2014): 159–175; Heather Johnson, "The Whole Picture: When It Comes to Finding out How Employees Feel about Training, Many Companies Fail to Get a Clear Picture," *Training* 47, no. 7 (2004): 30–35; Martin Delahoussaye, "Show Me the Results," *Training* 39, no. 3 (2002): 28–29; Reinout van Brakel, "Why ROI Isn't Enough," *Training and Development* 56, no. 6 (2002): 72–74.
45. "Dissatisfaction with Job Training Contributes to Low Job Satisfaction," *Managing Training & Development* (November 2003): 8; James Pershing and Jana Pershing, "Ineffective Reaction Evaluation," *Human Resource Development Quarterly* 12, no. 1 (2001): 73–90.
46. Anna Grohmann and Simone Kauffeld, "Evaluating Training Programs: Development and Correlates of the Questionnaire for Professional Training Evaluation," *International Journal of Training and Development* 17, no. 2 (2013): 135–155; Andreas Putra, "Evaluating Training Programs: An Exploratory Study of Transfer of Learning onto the Job at Hotel A and Hotel B, Sydney, Australia," *Journal of Hospitality and Tourism Management* 11, no. 1 (2004): 77–78.
47. Delahoussaye, "Show Me the Results," 28–29; van Brakel, "Why ROI Isn't Enough," 72–74.
48. Richard J. Wagner and Robert J. Weigand, "Can the Value of Training Be Measured? A Simplified Approach to Evaluating Training," *Health Care Manager* 23, no. 1 (2004): 71–79; "Why ROI Isn't Enough," 72–74; Sarah Fister Gale, "Measuring the ROI of E-Learning," *Workforce* 81, no. 8 (2002): 74–77; Earl Honeycutt, Kiran Karande, Ashraf Attia, and Steven Maurer, "A Utility-Based Framework for Evaluating the Financial Impact of Sales Force Training Programs," *Journal of Personal Selling and Sales Management* 21, no. 3 (2001): 229–238.
49. Bradford S. Bell et al., "100 Years of Training and Development Research: What We Know and Where We Should Go" (2017); "Three Quick and Easy Ways to Gauge Your Training Outcomes," *IOMA's Report on Managing Training & Development* (January 2005): 4–5; "Use This Eight-Step Process to Predict the ROI of Your Training Programs," *IOMA's Human Resource Department Management Report* (December 2004): 4–5; Ellen Drost, Colette Frayne, Keven Lowe, and J. Michael Geringer, "Benchmarking Training and Development Practices: A MultiCountry Comparative Analysis," *Human Resource Management* 41, no. 1 (2002): 67–86; Daniel McMurrer, Mark Van Buren, and William Woodwell, "Making the Commitment." Training and Development, v54 n1 (2000) p41–48 January

CHAPTER 8

Performance Management

Learning Outcomes

After studying this chapter, you should be able to

LO 1 Explain what performance management is and how the establishment of goals, ongoing performance feedback, and the evaluation process are part of it.

LO 2 Describe the different sources of performance-management information, as well as the strengths or limitations of each.

LO 3 Explain the various methods used to evaluate the performance of employees, and their potential trade-offs.

LO 4 Outline the characteristics of effective performance review meetings and feedback sessions, and describe ways to improve the performance of employees.

8.1 Performance Management Systems

LO1 Describe how the performance management process is linked to employee selection, training, and development.

We have discussed some of the ways that you as a manager can acquire top-notch employees and train and develop them. But how do you know if your efforts are really paying off in terms of what the employees are contributing once they are on the job?

Performance management is the process of creating a work environment in which people can perform to the best of their abilities so as to meet a company's goals. It is an entire work system that flows from a company's goals. Figure 8.1 shows the elements of a performance management process.

performance management
The process of creating a work environment in which people can perform to the best of their abilities.

Performance reviews are the result of the process in which a manager evaluates an employee's performance relative to the requirements of their job and the goals set collaboratively with the manager, and then uses this information to show the person where improvements can be made and how. Such reviews are a tool organizations can use to develop employees. Performance reviews are also referred to as *performance appraisals* and *performance evaluations.*

Figure 8.1 Steps in the Performance Management Process

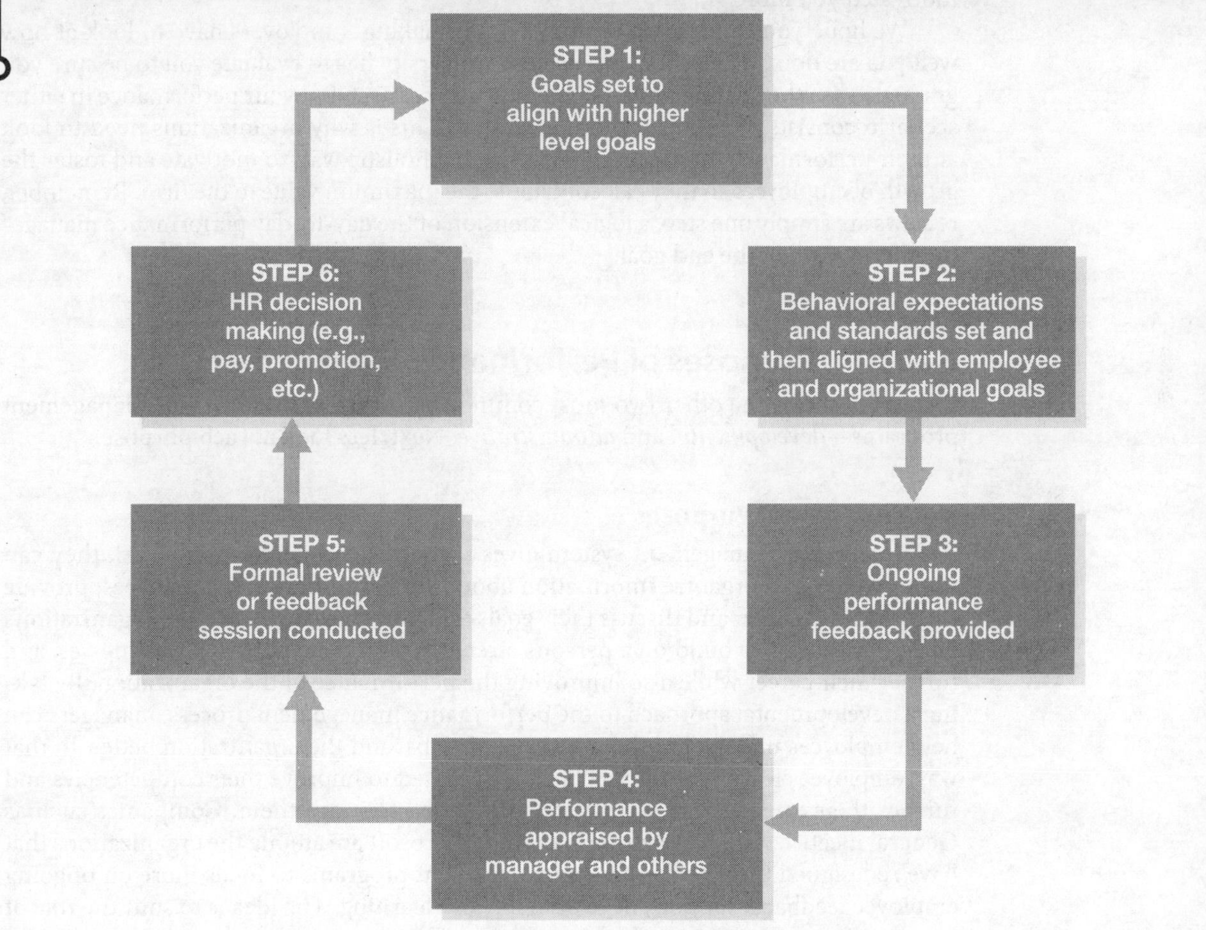

performance reviews
A process in which a manager evaluates an employee's performance relative to the requirements of their job and uses the information to show the person where improvements can be made and how.

Typically performance reviews are delivered annually, biannually, or sometimes on a quarterly basis. However, firms are finding that more frequent short reviews that provide employees with regular feedback are actually more effective. In a rapidly changing world, "once a year" performance reviews may be hopelessly outdated, as new requirements continuously arise within today's dynamic work environment. Many companies are discovering that giving employees ongoing feedback and coaching has clear benefits. At RoundPegg, a hiring startup that develops social applications, all employees have quarterly reviews, or "feedback sessions," that last just 20 minutes. "My job here isn't just to make sure everyone is crossing their T's and dotting their I's," says Brent Daily, RoundPegg's cofounder and chief operating officer. "My job is to remove the obstacles they face and allow them to do what they do best."[1]

In Figure 8.1, the performance review is just part of the performance management process. Aligning the goals of employees with those of the firm, providing workers with continual on-the-job feedback, and encouraging and rewarding them for a job done well are critical, too.

You might compare a performance review to receiving grades in college. Do grades motivate you? Do they make you want to truly excel, or do you just want to get by? But what if your instructor also talked with you about your career plans, complimented you on your performance, and offered you suggestions for improving it? That probably motivated you more.

We hope you can see the analogy we are making. Employers have to look at how well you are doing on the job, just as your university has to evaluate you to be sure you graduate with the qualifications people in society expect. But your performance in either scenario consists of so much more than that. This is why organizations need to look at their performance management systems in a holistic way, to motivate and foster the growth of employees so they can contribute the maximum value to the firm. Remember, reviews are simply one step, a logical extension of the day-to-day performance management process, not the end goal.[2]

8.1a The Purposes of Performance Management

Figure 8.2 shows the other two most common purposes of performance management programs—*developmental* and *administrative*. Next, let's look at each purpose.

Developmental Purposes

A performance management system gives managers a concrete framework they can use to gather and organize information about the performance of employees, provide them with feedback, and discuss their goals and how they align with the organization's goals. The idea is to build on a person's strengths, eliminate potential weaknesses, and further their career while also improving the performance of the organization. By taking a developmental approach to the performance management process, managers can help employees understand themselves, their jobs, and the organization better. In that way, employees learn that the feedback is designed to improve their competencies and further their careers, and is not simply intended to judge them. Companies such as General Electric (GE), Adobe, the Gap, and Microsoft are among the organizations that have redesigned their performance management programs to focus more on ongoing employee feedback, support, development, and learning. The idea is to shift the role of manager from that of "judge" to one of "coach."[3]

Figure 8.2 Purposes of a Performance Review

DEVELOPMENTAL

- Provide performance feedback
- Identify individual strengths and weaknesses
- Recognize individual performance achievements
- Help employees identify goals
- Evaluate goal achievement of employees
- Identify individual training needs
- Determine organizational training needs
- Allow employees to discuss concerns
- Improve communication
- Provide a forum for leaders to help employees

ADMINISTRATIVE

- Document personnel decisions
- Promote employees
- Determine transfers and assignments
- Identify performance problems and develop ways to correct them
- Make retention, termination, and layoff decisions
- Validate selection criteria
- Meet legal requirements
- Evaluate training programs/progress
- Assist with human resources planning
- Make reward and compensation decisions

Administrative Purposes

Performance management programs provide input that can be used for the entire range of HRM activities, such as determining the relative worth of jobs, recruiting criteria, validating selection tests, promotions, transfers, layoffs, and pay decisions. "Pay-for-performance" systems—that is, basing employees' pay on their achievements—are found in all types of organizations. Studies have shown that employees who earn performance-based pay are more satisfied.[4] Performance management programs also provide input for talent reviews: strategic meetings to determine if a company has the human resources it needs to compete in the future. Performance data can also be used for HR planning.

Yet another purpose of having a performance management system is to document human resources management (HRM) actions that can result in legal action. Equal employment opportunity and affirmative action directives require employers to maintain accurate, objective employee performance records. Without them, firms will be unable to defend themselves against possible discrimination charges when it comes to promotions, salaries, or terminations. Finally, the success of the entire HR program depends on knowing how the performance of employees compares with the goals established for them. Taken together, you can see the importance of an effective performance management system. Unfortunately, as we discuss next, these systems sometimes fail.

8.1b Why Performance Management Systems Sometimes Fail

Performance reviews often fall short of their potential. But why? According to a survey by the Society for Human Resource Management, only half of HR professionals say annual performance reviews are an accurate appraisal of an employee's performance. Forty-nine percent believe their firms' performance-review process needs to be reevaluated.[5] Employees and managers alike often dread appraisals, and complain that they are time consuming and ineffective.

Many people fault the formal review process. They believe it discourages teamwork and breeds unhealthy competition by focusing on workers' individual achievements rather than on what their teams or firms accomplish. (Who gets the best rating and the biggest raise? Who does not?) This is what happened at Microsoft, and one of the key reasons the company changed its approach.

Others contend that reviews are useful only at the extremes—for highly effective or highly ineffective employees—and are not as useful for the majority of employees in the middle. Other people point out that reviews often focus on short-term achievements rather than on long-term improvement and learning. Still others complain that the only feedback they get is during formal reviews, or they aren't done at all (sometimes we call this the "disappearing performance appraisal"). This can especially be a problem in small businesses, as this chapter's Small Business Application feature shows. A more complete list of the reasons why formal reviews fail is shown in Figure 8.3.

Figure 8.3 Let Me Count the Ways ... Reasons Why Performance Reviews Can Fail

- Inadequate preparation on the part of the manager
- The employee is not given clear objectives at the beginning of the performance period
- The manager may not be able to observe performance or have all the information
- The performance standards may not be clear
- Inconsistent ratings among supervisors or other raters
- The manager rates the employee's personality rather than performance
- The halo effect, contrast effect, or some other perceptual bias
- Inappropriate time span for review (either too short or too long)
- Overemphasis on uncharacteristic performance
- Inflated ratings because managers do not want to deal with "bad news"
- Subjective or vague language in written reviews
- Organizational politics or personal relationships cloud judgments
- No thorough discussion of causes of performance problems
- The manager is not trained in evaluation or giving feedback
- No follow-up and coaching after the review

Sources: Patricia Evres, "Problems to Avoid during Performance Evaluations," *Air Conditioning, Heating & Refrigeration News* 216, no. 16 (2002): 24–26; Clinton Longnecker and Dennis Gioia, "The Politics of Executive Appraisals," *Journal of Compensation and Benefits* 10, no. 2 (1994): 5–11; "Seven Deadly Sins of Performance Appraisals," *Supervisory Management* 39, no. 1 (1994): 7–8.

Small Business Application

Does a Small Business Need to Formally Evaluate Its Employees?

So now you have your own business. That means you can dispense with those pesky, time-consuming performance reviews everyone dreads, right? You never liked them as an employee. In fact, maybe they helped solidify your desire to work for yourself. Why would you like them any more as a manager, entrepreneur, or small business owner?

Don't be so fast to dump formal performance reviews. Without them, you might end up "flying blind" when it comes to some important performance metrics. "In a small business in particular, the performance review is like a dashboard—it gives you all kinds of gauges about quality, job knowledge, and customer service," says Robert Chanin, the director of client services for the Alcott

HR Group. "If there isn't any gauge, you don't know if your business is doing well or not."

By contrast, put a good performance management system in place and the sky is the limit, says Barrie Gross, an HR expert and employment law attorney. "They're one of the tools businesses can use to get employees more involved, increase their motivation, and help them achieve success," Gross explains. Evaluating your employees also lets them know they are not just human cogs in the production process—it tells them that you care about them, their involvement in the firm, and their personal goals. This can help a small business retain its top employees rather than losing them to big companies, where they are often treated more impersonally. The feedback can be verbal, if the reviews are for development purposes only. However, if the reviews are used in conjunction with raises and promotions, they should be written to provide a firm with greater legal protection.

Small businesses can utilize off-the-shelf systems consisting of either printed forms or software. Featherlight and Halogen's Performance product are two Web-based systems. Generally, a manager can customize the review forms by selecting elements from a list of attributes and behaviors that describe on-the-job success for a position.

Performance reviews are not about the forms, though. They should be a two-way discussion. In addition to your employees learning how they can improve their performance, the reviews can help you learn how to improve yours.

Sources: Leanne Hoaglund-Smith, "Small Business Roles and Responsibilities, Require Clarity, Documentation," *Chicago Tribune* (February 10, 2017), http://www.chicagotribune.com; Amy Linn, "Boost Performance with Performance Reviews," *Small Business Review*, http://smallbusinessreview.com; David Javitch, "How to Survive Employee Appraisals," Entreprenur.com, http://www.entrepreneur.com.

For reasons such as these, a substantial number of organizations have reconceived and redesigned their performance reviews to focus on continuous feedback and coaching.[6] Adobe has an ongoing "check-in" system that employees and their managers use to give each other feedback; written reviews aren't requried.[7] (See Case Study 1 at the end of the chapter.) But although many people have predicted that formal performance reviews will one day become obsolete, firms continue to use them, often for legal reasons such as justifying promotions and pay decisions.

8.2 Developing an Effective Performance Management System

LO2

What sources could be used to evaluate the performance of people working in the following jobs?
- Sales representative
- Robotics engineer
- Director of nursing in a hospital
- HR manager
- Air traffic controller

A firm's HR department ordinarily has the primary responsibility for overseeing and coordinating the performance management system. However, managers from the company's operating departments must also be actively involved, particularly when it comes to helping establish the objectives for the program, ensure they are aligned with a company's strategic goals, and actually translate to on-the-job efforts. More than one manager has told us, if performance management is seen as primarily run by the HR department, it will not be successful. Managers need to "own it."

Employees are more likely to accept and be satisfied with a performance management system when they have the chance to participate in its development. Asking experienced employees to help identify important job behaviors and SMART goals also helps ensure the system accounts for all of the tasks that need to be done in an organization, especially when major changes in the firm and its jobs are taking place.[8]

8.2a What Are the Performance Standards?

Performance standards describe the accepted level of performance to be achieved by an employee. These standards should be based on job-related requirements derived from a job analysis and reflected in an employee's job description and job specifications. In

SMART goals can help improve the performance of employees as well as remove the vagueness and subjectivity of performance reviews.

marekuliasz/Shutterstock.com

this sense, performance standards are based on the position, not the individual. They describe the specific indicators of success for each skill within a competency map. In essence, they illustrate "what a good job looks like." For example, "the ability and willingness to handle customer orders" is not as good a performance standard as "all customer orders will be filled in 4 hours with a 98 percent accuracy rate in 2021." When the standard is expressed in specific, measurable terms, comparing an employee's performance against it results in more accurate feedback. The ultimate goal is to create effective goals that will work for your employees, says Gary Foster, customized training program manager at Minnesota's Ridgewater College. "It's not an easy task; it's not a short task, but it can be done."[9]

As Figure 8.4 shows, four basic elements must be considered when establishing performance standards: strategic relevance, criterion deficiency, criterion contamination, and reliability.

Strategic Relevance

Strategic relevance refers to the extent to which the performance standards relate to or serve the organization's strategic objectives. For example, if an organization has established a standard that "95 percent of all customer complaints are to be resolved in one day," then it is relevant for the firm's customer service representatives to be held to this standard when evaluated. Companies such as 3M and Buckman Laboratories have established strategic objectives stating that a certain percentage of their sales are to be generated from recently developed products. These objectives are then translated into performance standards for their employees. General Motors and Whirlpool's strategic objectives include cost, quality, and speed, and the two companies have developed metrics to identify and compare their performance around the world on these measures.

Figure 8.4 Establishing Performance Standards

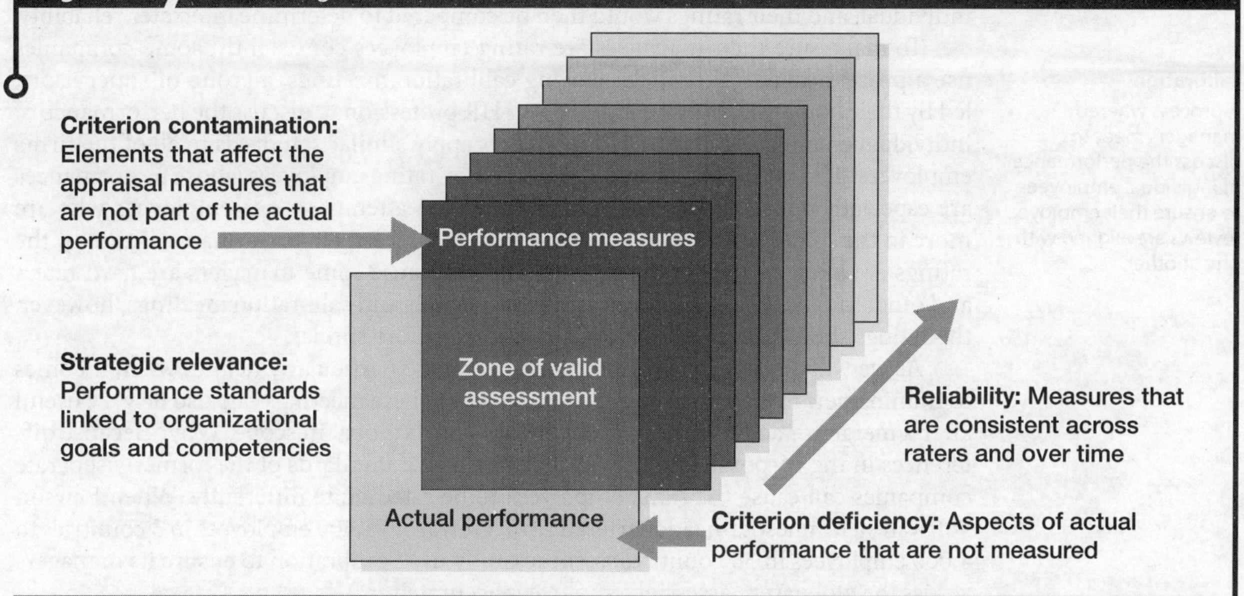

A strategy-driven review process also provides the documentation HR managers require to justify training expenses needed to close any gaps between employees' current skills and those they will need in the future to execute the firm's strategy. Moreover, because they provide evidence of a person's performance, review metrics based on a firm's strategy are more defensible in court. Perhaps most importantly, strategic relevance helps employees know how they are contributing to the overall success of the firm. That can be very motivating.[10]

Criterion Deficiency

The performance standards should capture the entire range of an employee's performance, not just one part. When they focus on a single criterion (such as sales revenues) to the exclusion of other important, but less readily quantified performance dimensions (such as customer service), then the performance management system is said to suffer from criterion deficiency.[11]

Criterion Contamination

Just as performance criteria can be deficient, they can also be contaminated. Factors outside of employees' control may often influence their performance. A comparison of performance of production workers, for example, should not be contaminated by the fact that some work with newer machines than others do. A comparison of the performance of traveling salespeople should not be contaminated by the fact that their territories differ in terms of their sales potential.[12]

Reliability

As we discussed in Chapter 6, reliability refers to the stability or consistency of a standard or the extent to which individuals tend to maintain a certain level of performance over time. Reliability can be measured by correlating two sets of ratings made by a single rater or by two different raters. For example, two managers would rate the same individual, and their ratings would then be compared to determine interrater reliability.

calibration
A process whereby managers meet to discuss the performance of individual employees to ensure their employee reviews are aligned with one another.

To make sure their managers are rating employees consistently, some companies use a process called **calibration**. During calibration meetings, a group of supervisors, led by their managers and facilitated by an HR professional, discuss the performance of individual employees to ensure all managers apply similar standards to all of the firm's employees. The supervisors begin the process by rating employees whose performances are especially good or especially poor. They then attempt to rate employees who are more in the middle and try to achieve a consensus on their performance. Initially, the ratings are likely to vary considerably simply because some managers are hard raters and others are not. Over subsequent review periods and calibration meetings, however, the ratings should begin to converge, or become more similar.

As we will discuss, calibration meetings can be particularly helpful when it comes to training new managers to appraise employees. These meetings can also be very useful after a merger or acquisition—especially one that is global in scope. Why? Because differences in the corporate cultures and performance standards of the formerly separate companies can cause the same employees to be rated quite differently. When Lawson Software, a Minnesota-headquartered firm, grew from 1,400 employees in 3 countries to 4,000 employees in 30 countries, it successfully used calibration to ensure its managers across the globe were assessing employees accurately.[13]

Fairness and Acceptability

One of the main concerns employees have about performance management systems in general and reviews is fairness. Organizational politics, a firm's culture, the orientation of its managers, history, and current competitive conditions can all affect how managers view their employees' performance on the job as well as rate that performance.[14] Sometimes managers inflate reviews because they want to obtain higher salaries for their employees or because higher ratings for their subordinates make them look good as supervisors.

Even when reviews are supposed to be confidential, employees often have a keen sense about whether the process is fair, or at least they think they do. Those impressions may not always be accurate, but they do matter. Employees who believe the system is unfair are likely to consider the process a waste of time or feel frustrated and cynical. As we discussed earlier in the section on developing a management performance system, if employees are allowed to provide input on what constitutes good performance and how the performance management system operates, they are more likely to believe the resulting system is fair, and the program is more likely to be successful.

Acceptability relates to how hard or difficult it is to administer and use the performance management system. If using it is time consuming or difficult, or if it's hard to see how the system is really helping the organization, managers and employees won't go to the trouble, and the system is likely to fail.

8.2b Do Your Performance Reviews Comply with the Law?

Importantly, because they can have a significant impact on employees, performance reviews must meet certain legal requirements, just as selection procedures do.[15] Carefully defined and measurable performance standards are required. In one landmark case, the U.S. Supreme Court found that employees had been ranked against a vague standard, open to each supervisor's own interpretation.[16] The Court's decision prompted organizations to try to eliminate vagueness in their descriptions of attitudes, cooperation, dependability, initiative, and leadership. For example, the trait "dependability" can be made much less vague if it is spelled out in terms of employee tardiness and/or unexcused absences.

Other court decisions have suggested that employers might face legal challenges when reviews indicate an employee's performance is acceptable or above average but the person is later passed over for promotion, disciplined for poor performance, discharged, or laid off from the organization. In another U.S. Supreme Court case, an employee claimed she was terminated because the company she worked for said she had a poor attitude. The problem? Her reviews stated that she was "a pleasure to work with and handles herself in a professional manner," and that she "hit the ground running in eastern and is doing an excellent job for that department. The staff in eastern is enjoying her presence." The Court ruled in her favor.[17]

Other companies have faced legal battles because their performance reviews discriminated against underrepresented groups such as older workers, racial and ethnic minorities, and women. A researcher who studied 250 reviews of high-achieving tech workers found that women received far more critical reviews than men did.[18]

So, from a legal perspective, performance reviews can be a double-edged sword. You need them to help employees perform better and document your actions as a manager, but if they are poorly done or inaccurate, or if you don't make decisions based on them, you can find yourself in legal trouble. To avoid problems such as these, performance reviews should meet the following legal guidelines:

- *Relevance.* Performance ratings must be job related, with performance standards developed through a job analysis. Only evaluate those areas that are necessary for effective job performance.
- *No surprises.* Employees must be provided with clear, written job standards in advance of their reviews so they understand what they need to do to get top ratings.
- *Avoid subjectivity.* Managers who conduct the reviews must be able to observe the behavior they are rating. This implies having measurable standards with which to compare employee behavior.
- *Timeliness.* Do not allow performance problems to continue unchecked. Document problems when they occur and refer to them in employees' reviews. This information may prove decisive should an employee take legal action. Supervisors should be trained to use review forms correctly and to apply the review standards when making judgments.
- *Avoid bias in the process and the outcomes.* A firm's HR department should review the evaluations to see if underrepresented groups are being adversely impacted.
- *Transparency.* The reviews should be discussed openly with employees and counseling or corrective guidance should be offered to help poor performers improve their performance. Be open to the possibility that employees could be transferred to other positions that better suit their abilities.
- *Fairness.* An appeals procedure should be established to enable employees to express their disagreement with the evaluations.[19]

HR professionals should also review supervisors' reviews for comments that could indicate the firm is not complying with the law. Consider the following comments: "Ted was absent for several weeks in 2017, which adversely affected operations." If some of Ted's absences were taken in conjunction with the Family Medical Leave Act, the comment could be used in court to show Ted was deprived of his right to take leave under the act without being retaliated against.[20] Having a supervisor's superior examine the reviews can also reduce the chance of biased reviews and evaluations that could prove legally problematic.

8.2c Sources of Performance Review Information

Given the complexity of today's jobs, it's unrealistic to presume that one person can fully observe and evaluate an employee's performance. At IBM, employees are regularly reviewed by a broad cross section of the company's leaders, not just their immediate bosses. As Figure 8.5 shows, inputs can come from supervisors, peers, team members, employees themselves, their subordinates, customers, vendors, and suppliers.

Manager/Supervisor

manager and/or supervisor evaluation
A performance evaluation done by an employee's manager and often reviewed by a manager one level higher.

The **manager and/or supervisor evaluation** has traditionally been used to evaluate the performance of employees. Supervisors are in the best position to perform this function, although it may not always be possible for them to do so. Managers with many subordinates often complain they don't have enough time to fully observe the performance of each of them. The managers must then rely on the employees' performance records. In today's environment, where more of our work is digitized, performance data are often available from databases and information systems. However, if reliable and valid performance data are not available, the review is likely to be less than accurate as a result. (Recall our earlier discussion of criterion deficiency and criterion contamination.) In addition, research has shown that the ratings managers give employees they have known for less than one year are less reliable, which can be a drawback of relying solely on information from managers.[21]

Figure 8.5 Alternative Sources of Reviews

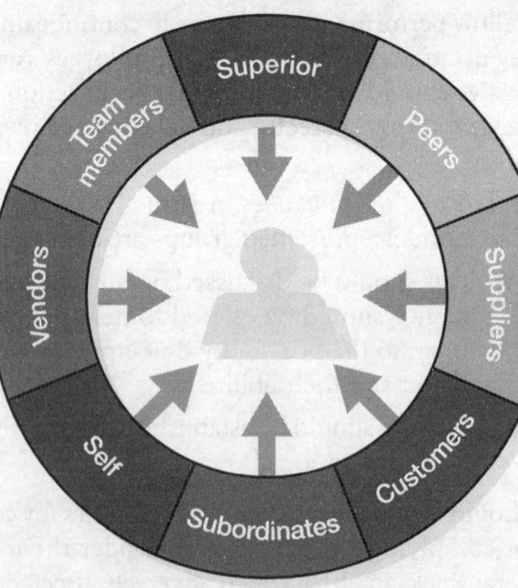

The Employee

In many firms, employees are asked to provide feedback on self-evaluation forms. A **self-evaluation** can increase an employee's involvement in the review process and get the employee thinking about their strengths and weaknesses. In other words, self-evaluations serve as a catalyst for self-awareness and discussion. The employee and their manager can then compare notes about the employee's job performance and agree on a final evaluation.

self-evaluation
A performance evaluation done by the employee being evaluated, generally on an evaluation form completed by the employee prior to the evaluation meeting.

A word of caution: self-appraisals are notoriously inflated. It's not uncommon for employees to present themselves highly favorably in self-evaluations or believe such appraisals will give them more influence over their performance ratings. If that expectation is not met, an employee can become frustrated. For this reason, self-evaluations are often best used for developmental purposes rather than for administrative decisions.[22]

Subordinates

Subordinate evaluations have been used by both large and small organizations to give managers feedback on how their subordinates view them.[23] Subordinates are in a good position to provide feedback to their managers because they are in frequent contact with their superiors and occupy a unique position from which to observe many performance-related behaviors, such as their leadership ability, ability to delegate, support for their employees, and so on. However, many managers resist subordinate appraisals, believing that such evaluations give their employees too much power. For that reason, in most cases the information gathered is used for developmental rather than administrative purposes. Evidence suggests that when managers heed the advice of their subordinates, their own performance can improve substantially. To avoid any problems with retaliation, subordinate evaluations should be submitted anonymously and the results combined in a single report. The manager's supervisor then uses the information as part of the person's final evaluation.[24]

subordinate evaluations
A performance evaluation of a superior by an employee, which is often used for developmental rather than for administrative purposes.

Peers

Individuals of equal rank who work together are increasingly being asked to evaluate each other using a **peer evaluation**. With peer evaluations, coworkers complete a review on the employee. The information from the coworkers is then usually combined and given to the employee's supervisor for use in that person's final evaluation. One advantage of peer evaluations is that they can sometimes provide more accurate and valid information about employees. Supervisors often see employees putting their best foot forward. Those who work together on a regular basis may see a more realistic picture. Peers can readily identify the leadership and interpersonal skills of their coworkers along with their other strengths and weaknesses. For example, a police superior asked to rate a patrol officer on a dimension such as "dealing with the public" might not have had much opportunity to observe it. Fellow officers, however, likely would have.

peer evaluation
A performance evaluation done by one's fellow employees, generally on forms compiled into a single profile for use in the evaluation meeting conducted by the employee's manager.

For employees who have trouble confronting their coworkers about problems, the reviews provide a forum in which to address issues and resolve conflicts. They also provide an opportunity to hand out praise.[25] However, peer evaluations alone should not be used to make administrative decisions related to salaries, bonuses, promotions, and other major decisions about an employee. They should also be kept confidential, so interpersonal rivalries or hurt feelings don't arise among coworkers. Instead of listing individual comments and ratings from an employee's peers, the ratings should be tallied to arrive at a composite score, and the comments summarized by the worker's supervisor.

Team Members

team evaluation
A performance evaluation that recognizes team accomplishments rather than individual performance.

An extension of the peer evaluation is the **team evaluation.** In a team setting, it may be nearly impossible to distinguish one individual's contribution. To address this issue, organizations such as Google, Boeing, and Apple have used team evaluations to evaluate the performance of their teams as a whole.[26] These companies believe that team evaluations can help break down barriers between individual employees and encourage a joint effort on their part.

Frequently, this kind of system is complemented by the use of team incentives or group variable pay (see Chapters 10 and 16). When Apple developed the iOS 10 (operating system), it used team rewards to encourage better performance. No one member of the 600-person team could receive an exceptional performance review unless the entire team did.[27]

Customers

customer evaluations
A performance evaluation that includes evaluations from a firm's external and internal customers.

Customer evaluations are another source of performance review information. FedEx, Best Buy, and Isuzu are among the companies that have utilized external customers to provide feedback for their employees' evaluations. Other companies survey their vendors and suppliers as part of the review process. By including the firm's business partners in the performance reviews, managers hope to produce more objective reviews, more effective employees, more satisfied customers, and better business performance.[28]

In contrast to external customers, internal customers include anyone inside the organization who depends on an employee's work output. For example, managers who rely on the HR department for selecting and training employees would be candidates for conducting internal customer evaluations of employees in that department or the department as a whole. For both developmental and administrative purposes, internal customers can provide extremely useful feedback about the value added by an employee or team of employees.

8.2d Putting It All Together: 360-Degree Evaluations

360-degree evaluation
A performance evaluation done by different people who interact with the employee, generally on forms compiled into a single document for use in the evaluation meeting conducted by the employee's manager.

Companies such as Google, Morgan Stanley, and Disney are among the many organizations that have used a multiple-rater approach—or **360-degree evaluation**—that combines various sources of performance review information.[29] Jobs are multifaceted, and different people see different things. As the name implies, 360-degree feedback is intended to provide employees with as accurate a view of their performance as possible by getting input from all angles: supervisors, peers, subordinates, customers, and the like. This information is then compiled into a single document, which is synthesized by the employee's manager as part of the overall evaluation. Information systems and databases make the curation and synthesis of these inputs much easier. Figure 8.6 shows a list of the advantages and disadvantages of a 360-degree review.

8.2e Training Appraisers

Training appraisers can vastly improve the performance review process. A weakness of many performance review programs is that raters are not adequately trained for the task, so the feedback they provide their subordinates is not as accurate or useful as it might be, or is actually destructive According to one HR manager, "What's not important is the (review) form or the (measuring) scale. What's important is that managers can objectively observe people's performance and objectively give feedback on that performance." Nonetheless, in a survey of 55 HR managers from medium and large companies,

Figure 8.6 Pros and Cons of 360-Degree Reviews

PROS
• The system is more comprehensive because feedback is gathered from multiple perspectives. • It may lessen bias and prejudice since feedback comes from more people, not one individual. • The feedback from peers and others may improve an employee's self-development.
CONS
• The system is complex in combining all the responses. • The feedback can be intimidating and cause resentment if employees feel the respondents have "ganged up" on them. • There may be conflicting opinions, though they may all be accurate from the respective standpoints. • Raters must undergo some training. • Employees may collude or "game" the system by giving invalid evaluations to one another. • Raters may not feel accountable if their reviews are anonymous.

Sources: Compiled from David A. Waldman, Leanne E. Atwater, and David Antonioni, "Has 360-Degree Feedback Gone Amok?" *Academy of Management Executive* 12, no. 2 (1998): 86–94; Bruce Pfau, Ira Kay, Kenneth Nowak, and Jai Ghorpade, "Does 360-Degree Feedback Negatively Affect Company Performance?" *HRMagazine* 47, no. 6 (2002): 54–59; Maury Peiperl, "Getting 360-Degree Feedback Right," *Harvard Business Review* 79, no. 1 (2001): 142–147; Joyce E. Bono and Amy E. Colbert, "Understanding Responses to Multi-Source Feedback: The Role of Core Self-Evaluations," *Personnel Psychology* 58, no. 1 (2005): 171–205.

more than half said their companies did either little or no assessment of how well their supervisors conduct reviews.[30] In addition to providing supervisors with training, firms should make accurately evaluating and developing their subordinates a standard by which the supervisors themselves will be evaluated.

Establishing a Review Plan

A training program for raters is most effective when it follows a systematic process that begins by explaining the objectives of the firm's performance management system and its philosophy on reviews. For example, the rater needs to know the purpose for which the review is to be used. Using the review for compensation decisions rather than development purposes can affect how the rater evaluates the employee, and it may change the rater's opinion of how the review form should be completed. The mechanics of the rating system should also be explained, including how managers keep performance records and review them, how frequently the reviews are to be conducted, who will conduct them, what the standards of performance are, and how to go about preparing for reviews. In addition, evaluation training should alert raters to the weaknesses and problems of reviews, so raters can avoid them.

Eliminating Rating Errors

Eliminating the subjective errors made by managers in the rating process is an extremely important part of evaluating the performance of an employee. The "halo error," which we discussed in Chapter 6 when we looked at selecting employees, can also occur during the review process if raters do not have carefully developed descriptions of the employee behaviors being rated. The "horn error" is the opposite of the halo effect. It occurs when a manager focuses on one negative aspect when reviewing an employee and generalizes it into an overall poor rating. A personality conflict between a manager and an employee increases the probability of the horn effect, which can lead to a high level of frustration on the employee's part if it is not corrected.[31]

Distributional Errors. A *distributional rating error* occurs when a single rating is skewed toward an entire group of employees. For example, raters who are reluctant to assign either extremely high or extremely low ratings commit the **error of central tendency**. In this case, all employees are rated about average. It is also common for some raters to give unusually high or low ratings. For example, a manager might erroneously assert, "All my employees are excellent" or "None of my people are good enough." These beliefs give rise to what is called **leniency or strictness error**, respectively.[32]

error of central tendency
A performance rating error in which all employees are rated about average.

leniency or strictness error
A performance rating error in which the appraiser tends to give employees either unusually high or unusually low ratings.

One way to reduce distributional errors is to explain to raters that when you are looking at large groups of employees, you should generally expect to find significant differences among them. Using clearly defined characteristics or dimensions of performance and providing meaningful descriptions of behavior on the scale, known as "anchors," can help raters determine how individual employees should be rated. Another approach is to require ratings to conform to a **forced distribution**, sometimes referred to as *forced ranking*. Managers appraising employees under a forced distribution system are required to place a certain percentage of employees into various performance categories. For example, a firm may require that 10 percent of ratings be poor (or excellent). This is similar to the requirement in some schools that instructors grade on a curve. For many years, GE used such a system, which the firm called "the vitality curve"; it reserved the top category for only 20 percent of employees, and forced 10 percent into the bottom. A variation of this is *peer ranking*, whereby employees in a work group are ranked against one another from best to worst, and the rankings are then used to determine pay raises. Some companies go so far as to terminate low-ranking employees. As you can probably tell, ranking systems can be controversial and divisive.

forced distribution
A performance ranking system whereby raters are required to place a certain percentage of employees into various performance categories.

Although forced distribution and peer ranking may solve leniency and strictness errors, they can create other rating errors—particularly if most employees are performing above the standard, in the middle, or below the standard. Similarly, with

Andrey_Popov/Shutterstock.com

Performance evaluation programs are most effective when managers have been properly trained to adequately observe and give feedback to their employees.

peer ranking, three employees all performing at nearly the same level would have to be ranked one, two, and three. That process creates a misleading picture of how well the individuals are performing, which in turn affects their pay, promotability, and so forth. Moreover, if the system has a disparate impact on a legally protected group, such as members of underrepresented groups or older employees, it can result—and has resulted—in discrimination lawsuits. GE, which pioneered forced ranking, discovered this firsthand. Other companies, including Ford, Goodyear, and Microsoft, abandoned their forced ranking systems after lawsuits, lower morale, decreased teamwork, and destructive employee competition ensued following their use. Eventually even GE discontinued the practice. The company now has a mobile app employees and managers can use to request feedback and provide each other with performance-related comments.[33]

Of course, not all corporate cultures are conducive to forced ranking systems. For example, at Starbucks, which fosters a corporate climate based on teamwork, using a forced ranking system would probably be counterproductive.

Because teamwork is so important in organizations today, companies are starting to use crowdsourcing as part of their performance management systems. In an HR context, *crowdsourcing* involves continually gathering feedback, compliments, and suggestions from the different people who work with an employee using "social recognition" software and mobile apps. (You can think of the applications as being somewhat analogous to "liking" something someone posts on Facebook.) Achievers and Globoforce are two such brands. Hey Taco and Growbot are two crowdsourcing add-ons that can be used with the popular chat platform Slack. When employees are recognized by other workers for doing a good job, they get points that translate into monetary and other rewards, such as time off or gift cards. 3M, Marriott hotels, and the pharmaceutical company Eli Lilly are using this type of software.

To track the performance of its sales agents and motivate them, the Home Shopping Network (HSN) uses a game module that enables agents to earn badges of increasing difficulty that reflect their performance.[34] Badgeville is a performance-management game that Samsung and the accounting firm Deloitte have used to motivate their call center representatives and salespeople. The games make attaining one's performance goals more fun. Digital "leaderboards" that show at a glance who is "winning" in various areas can spark competition without hampering teamwork.

Temporal Errors. Some rating errors are *temporal* in that the performance review is biased either favorably or unfavorably depending on the way performance information is selected, evaluated, and organized by the rater over time. For example, when the evaluation is based largely on the employee's recent behavior, good or bad, the rater has committed the **recency error**. Managers who give higher ratings because they believe an employee is "showing improvement" may unwittingly be committing recency error. Having the rater routinely document the employee's accomplishments and failures throughout the whole review period can minimize the recency error. One way for managers to do this is by keeping a diary or a log.

recency error
A performance rating error in which the evaluation is based largely on the employee's most recent behavior rather than on their behavior throughout the evaluation period.

Contrast Error. A **contrast error** occurs when an employee's review is biased either upward or downward because of another employee's performance. For example, an average employee may appear very productive when compared with a poor performer. However, that same employee could appear unproductive when compared with a star performer. Contrast errors are most likely when raters are required to rank employees in order from the best to the poorest.[35]

contrast error
A performance rating error in which an employee's review is biased either upward or downward because that employee is compared with another employee just previously evaluated.

A dashboard in Achievers allows managers to see which employees are being recognized by other people for their contributions.

Fallen Knight/Shutterstock.com

similar-to-me error
A performance rating error in which an appraiser inflates the review of an employee because of a mutual personal connection.

Similar-to-Me Error. The **similar-to-me error** occurs when a supervisor inflates the reviews of people with whom they have something in common. For example, if both the manager and the employee are from the same state or went to the same schools, the manager may unwittingly have a more favorable impression of the employee. The similar-to-me error can be powerful, and when the similarity is based on race, religion, sex, or some other protected category, it can result in discrimination.

Furthermore, raters should be aware of any stereotypes they may hold toward particular groups. For example, one study found that men who experienced conflicts between family and work received lower overall performance ratings than men who did not experience such conflicts. Women, by contrast, were judged no differently whether they experienced family–work conflicts or not.[36]

Holding "mock" calibration meetings can help trainers improve the accuracy of their ratings. This kind of training can pay off, particularly when participants have the opportunity to (1) observe other managers making errors, (2) actively participate in discovering their own errors, and (3) practice job-related tasks to reduce the errors they tend to make.[37] Google, which often conducts performance reviews with input from employee groups, has compiled a "cognitive biases" list for employees to refer to as they discuss ratings.[38] Other companies, including the consulting firm Accenture and the software developer SAP, are experimenting with *machine learning* to collect data on employees' work and analyze it to get an unbiased picture of a person's performance.[39] Machine learning is a type of artificial intelligence that allows computers to discover new insights from data without being programmed where to look for it.[40]

Feedback Training

A training program for raters should provide some pointers that managers can use to provide better performance feedback to employees on an ongoing basis and during formal reviews and feedback sessions. During formal reviews in particular, many managers are as nervous about giving feedback as employees are about receiving it. Oftentimes they just want the "ordeal" to be over. When this happens, managers do not engage employees in much of a conversation during the reviews, which is a major drawback.

Managers need to understand that employees want to know how they are doing and how they can improve. They are less eager to be appraised or judged. This is why it is important for their managers to provide employees with ongoing feedback, and not just "dump on them" during a review. If an employee is doing something wrong, waiting for a formal evaluation later in the year to communicate that information is the wrong approach. The person's behavior needs to be addressed immediately.

Even when appraising an outstanding employee, managers are often reluctant to evaluate an employee's performance. Sometimes the source of this hesitancy is as simple as the manager lacking the skills to execute an effective performance review session; sometimes there is never enough money to recognize even the top performer. The result: reviews are postponed or handled poorly, and even the organization's best performers are left frustrated, angry, disillusioned, and demotivated.

Conflicting purposes of the review can also hamper the effectiveness of the feedback employees receive. For example, if a review program is used to simultaneously determine an employee's future pay and motivate the person to perform better, the two purposes can end up conflicting with each other. Often when salary decisions are discussed during a performance review, they tend to become the dominant topic of conversation, and managers spend a lot of time justifying their pay decisions. As a result, ways to improve the employee's future job performance get lost in the discussion.

Feedback training should cover at least three basic areas: (1) communicating effectively so as to gain the employee's support, (2) diagnosing the root causes of performance problems, and (3) setting goals and objectives for the employee to achieve in conjunction with the feedback. A checklist like the one in Highlights in HRM 1 can be used to help supervisors prepare for performance review meetings. We will discuss this topic further later in the chapter.

1 Highlights in HRM

Supervisor's Checklist for a Formal Performance Review Meeting

Scheduling

1. Schedule the meeting and notify the employee 10 days to 2 weeks in advance.
2. Ask the employee to prepare for the session by reviewing their performance, job objectives, and development goals.

Preparing

1. Review the performance documentation collected throughout the year. Concentrate on work patterns that have developed.
2. Be prepared to give specific examples of above- or below-average performance.
3. If the performance meets or exceeds expectations, discuss this and ways to reinforce it. When the performance falls short of expectations, determine which changes need to be made.
4. After the review is written, set it aside for a few days and then review it again.

Conducting the Review

1. Select a private location that is comfortable and free of distractions.
2. Discuss each area of performance one at a time and address both the employee's strengths and shortcomings in that area.
3. Be specific and descriptive, not general and judgmental. Report occurrences rather than evaluating them.
4. Discuss your differences and resolve them.
5. Jointly discuss and design plans for taking corrective action, if necessary, as well as plans for growth and development.
6. Maintain a professional and supportive approach to the discussion.

LO3

Three types of review meetings are described in this chapter. What different skills are required for each? What reactions can one expect from using these different skills? How can a manager develop the skills needed to conduct a problem-solving type of meeting? Which method do you feel is the least desirable? Why?

8.3 Performance Review Methods

Now that you understand more about performance management, the question is, How do you go about measuring, or appraising, it? Performance review methods can be broadly classified as measuring traits, behaviors, or results. Trait approaches based on people's characteristics continue to be used despite their subjectivity. Behavioral approaches provide more action-oriented information to employees and may be best suited to development. The results-oriented approach has become more popular because it focuses on the measurable contributions that employees make to the organization.

8.3a Trait Methods

Trait approaches are designed to measure the extent to which an employee possesses certain characteristics—such as dependability, reactivity, initiative, and leadership—that are viewed as important for the job and the organization in general. Trait methods became popular because they are easy to develop. However, if not designed carefully on the basis of job analysis, trait evaluations can be notoriously biased and subjective.

graphic rating scale method
A trait approach to performance rating whereby each employee is rated according to a scale of characteristics.

Graphic Rating Scales

Perhaps the most well-known approach to evaluation is the **graphic rating scale method**, where each trait or characteristic is represented by a scale on which a rater indicates the degree to which an employee possesses that trait or characteristic.

2 Highlights in HRM

A Graphic Rating Scale with Comments

Appraise employee's performance in PRESENT ASSIGNMENT. Check (✔) most appropriate square. Appraisers are *urged to freely use* the "Remarks" sections for significant comments descriptive of the individual.

Factor	Scale	Rating	Remarks
1. KNOWLEDGE OF WORK: Understanding of all phases of his/her work and related matters	Needs instruction or guidance / Has required knowledge of own and related work / Has exceptional knowledge of own and related work	☐ ☐ ☐ ☑ ☐	*Is particularly good on gas engines.*
2. INITIATIVE: Ability to originate or develop ideas and to get things started	Lacks imagination / Meets necessary requirements / Unusually resourceful	☐ ☑ ☐ ☐ ☐	*Has good ideas when asked for an opinion, but otherwise will not offer them. Somewhat lacking in self-confidence.*
3. APPLICATION: Attention and application to his/her work	Wastes time Needs close supervision / Steady and willing worker / Exceptionally industrious	☐ ☐ ☑ ☐ ☐	*Accepts new jobs when assigned.*
4. QUALITY OF WORK: Thoroughness, neatness, and accuracy of work	Needs improvement / Regularly meets recognized standards / Consistently maintains highest quality	☐ ☐ ☐ ☐ ☑	*The work he turns out is always of the highest possible quality.*
5. VOLUME OF WORK: Quantity of acceptable work	Should be increased / Regularly meets recognized standards / Unusually high output	☐ ☐ ☑ ☐ ☐	*Would be higher if he did not spend so much time checking and rechecking his work.*

An example of this type of scale is shown in Highlights in HRM 2. In HRM 2, the dimensions are defined briefly, and some attempt is made to define the points on the scale. Defining them precisely helps reduce subjectivity.[41]

mixed-standard scale method
A trait approach to performance rating that is similar to other scale methods but based on a comparison with (better than, equal to, or worse than) a standard.

Mixed-Standard Scales

Rather than evaluating traits according to a single scale, with a **mixed-standard scale method**, the rater is given three specific randomly sequenced descriptions of each trait: superior, average, and inferior. As Highlights in HRM 3 shows, supervisors evaluate employees by indicating whether their performance is better than, equal to, or worse than the standard for each behavior.

3 Highlights in HRM

Example of a Mixed-Standard Scale

Directions: Indicate whether the individual's performance is above (1), equal to (0), or lower than (2) each of the following standards.

1. ________ Employee uses good judgment when addressing problems and provides workable alternatives; however, at times does not take actions to prevent problems. *(medium PROBLEM-SOLVING)*
2. ________ Employee lacks supervisory skills; frequently handles employees poorly and is at times argumentative. *(low LEADERSHIP)*
3. ________ Employee is extremely cooperative; can be expected to take the lead in developing cooperation among employees; completes job tasks with a positive attitude. *(high COOPERATION)*
4. ________ Employee has effective supervision skills; encourages productivity, quality, and employee development. *(medium LEADERSHIP)*
5. ________ Employee normally displays an argumentative or defensive attitude toward fellow employees and job assignments. *(low COOPERATION)*
6. ________ Employee is generally agreeable but becomes argumentative at times when given job assignments; cooperates with other employees as expected. *(medium COOPERATION)*
7. ________ Employee is not good at solving problems; uses poor judgment and does not anticipate potential difficulties. *(low PROBLEM-SOLVING)*
8. ________ Employee anticipates potential problems and provides creative, proactive alternative solutions; has good attention to follow-up. *(high PROBLEM-SOLVING)*
9. ________ Employee displays skilled direction, effectively coordinates unit activities, is generally a dynamic leader, and motivates employees to high performance. *(high LEADERSHIP)*

Forced-Choice Method

forced-choice method
A trait approach to performance rating that requires the rater to choose from statements designed to distinguish between successful and unsuccessful performance.

The **forced-choice method** requires the rater to choose from statements, often in pairs, that appear equally favorable or equally unfavorable but are designed to distinguish between successful and unsuccessful performance. For example, forced-choice pairs might include the following:

1. ____________ (a) Works hard ____________ (b) Works quickly
2. ____________ (a) Shows initiative ____________ (b) Is responsive to customers
3. ____________ (a) Work is reliable ____________ (b) Performance is good

The rater then selects one statement from the pair without knowing *which* statement correctly describes successful job behavior. Because it's not immediately clear which response results in a higher rating, this approach results in less bias.

Essay Method

essay method
A trait approach to performance rating that requires the rater to write a statement describing an employee's behavior.

The **essay method** requires the rater to write a description of the employee's performance and make recommendations for their development. Often this method is combined with other rating methods because it provides additional descriptive information about an employee's performance that can't be obtained with a rating scale. Essays also provide an excellent opportunity for supervisors to point out the unique characteristics of employees, including their promotability, special talents, skills, strengths, and weaknesses. A limitation of the essay method is that it can be subjective.

8.3b Behavioral Methods

As the preceding section suggested, trait-oriented performance reviews can be vague and subjective. In contrast, behavioral methods specifically describe which actions should (were or were not) be exhibited on the job. Let's look at some behavioral methods.

Critical Incident Method

Recall from Chapter 4 that a critical incident occurs when employee behavior results in unusual success or failure. The manager keeps a log or diary for each employee throughout the review period and notes specific critical incidents related to how well they perform. The critical incident method can also help a manager counsel employees when they are having performance problems. In addition, it increases the objectivity of the review by requiring the rater to use job performance criteria to justify the ratings.[42]

Behavioral Checklist Method

The behavioral checklist method requires the rater to check statements on a list that describe characteristics of the employee's behavior. A checklist developed for salespeople who sell electronic products might include the following items:

- Questions customers about their needs
- Identifies products that meet customers' needs
- Keeps abreast of new developments in technology
- Processes orders correctly

Behaviorally Anchored Rating Scale

A **behaviorally anchored rating scale (BARS)** consists of a series of 5 to 10 vertical scales—one for each important dimension of performance. These dimensions are "anchored" by behaviors identified through a critical incident job analysis. The critical incidents are placed along the scale and are assigned point values based on the opinions of experts. A BARS for a job dimension for firefighters is shown in the upper portion of Highlights in HRM 4.

behaviorally anchored rating scale (BARS)
A behavioral approach to performance rating that consists of a series of vertical scales, one for each important dimension of job performance.

A BARS is typically developed by a committee, whose members include both subordinates and managers. Employee participation can lead to greater acceptance of the performance review process and of the performance measures that it uses. The procedures followed in developing a BARS also result in scales that have a high degree of content validity.

Behavior Observation Scale

A **behavior observation scale (BOS)** is similar to a BARS in that both are based on critical incidents. However, the lower portion of Highlights in HRM 4 shows that rather than asking the evaluator to choose the most representative behavioral anchor, a BOS is designed to measure how frequently each of the behaviors has been observed.

behavior observation scale (BOS)
A behavioral approach to performance rating that measures the frequency of observed behavior.

8.3c Results Methods

Rather than looking at employees' traits or on-the-job behaviors, many organizations evaluate employees' accomplishments—such as the sales and output results they achieve. Employees are responsible for their outcomes but also have discretion over the way they accomplish them (within limits). Advocates of results-based reviews argue that they are more objective and empowering for employees.

4 Highlights in HRM

BARS and BOS Examples

Example of a BARS for Firefighters

FIREFIGHTING STRATEGY: Knowledge of Fire Characteristics. This area of performance assesses the ability of a firefighter to understand fire characteristics to develop the best strategy for fighting a fire.

HIGH	7	—Finds the fire when no one else can
	6	—Correctly assesses the best point of entry for fighting fire
	5	—Uses the type of smoke as an indicator of the type of fire
AVERAGE	4	—Understands basic hydraulics
	3	—Cannot tell the type of fire by observing the color of flame
	2	—Cannot identify the location of the fire
LOW	1	—Will not change the firefighting strategy in spite of flashbacks and other signs that accelerants are present

Source: Adapted from Landy, Jacobs, and Associates. Reprinted with permission.

Sample Items from Behavior Observation Scales

For each behavior observed, use the following scale:

5 represents *almost always*	95–100% of the time
4 represents *frequently*	85–94% of the time
3 represents *sometimes*	75–84% of the time
2 represents *seldom*	65–74% of the time
1 represents *almost never*	0–64% of the time

SALES PRODUCTIVITY	**NEVER**				**ALWAYS**
1. Reviews individual productivity results with manager	1	2	3	4	5
2. Suggests to peers ways of building sales	1	2	3	4	5
3. Uncovers specific needs for each contact	1	2	3	4	5
4. Keeps account plans updated	1	2	3	4	5
5. Follows up on customer leads	1	2	3	4	5

Sales, Productivity, and Quality Measures

Salespeople are evaluated on the amount of revenue they bring in. Production workers are evaluated on the number of units they produce and perhaps the scrap rate or number of defects detected in their work. Executives are frequently evaluated on the basis of a company's profits or growth rate. Each of these measures directly links what employees accomplish to results that benefit the organization. In this way, results-based reviews can directly align an employee and an organization's goals.

Nevertheless, some problems may arise with results-based reviews. For jobs that are more service oriented, it is not enough to simply look at production or sales figures. Factors such as cooperation, adaptability, initiative, and concern for human relations are important to the job success of employees, too. If these factors are important job standards, they should be included in the evaluation review. Thus, to be realistic, both the results and the methods or processes used to achieve them should be considered.[43]

management by objectives (MBO)
A philosophy of management that rates the performance of employees based on their achievement of goals set mutually by them and their managers.

Management by Objectives

One method that attempts to overcome some of the limitations of results-based reviews is **management by objectives (MBO)**. With this approach, employees establish objectives (such as production costs, sales per product, quality standards, and profits) in consultation with their managers and are then evaluated based on whether they have met those objectives.[44] In an MBO system (Figure 8.7), the cycle begins with setting the

Figure 8.7 Performance Review under an MBO Program

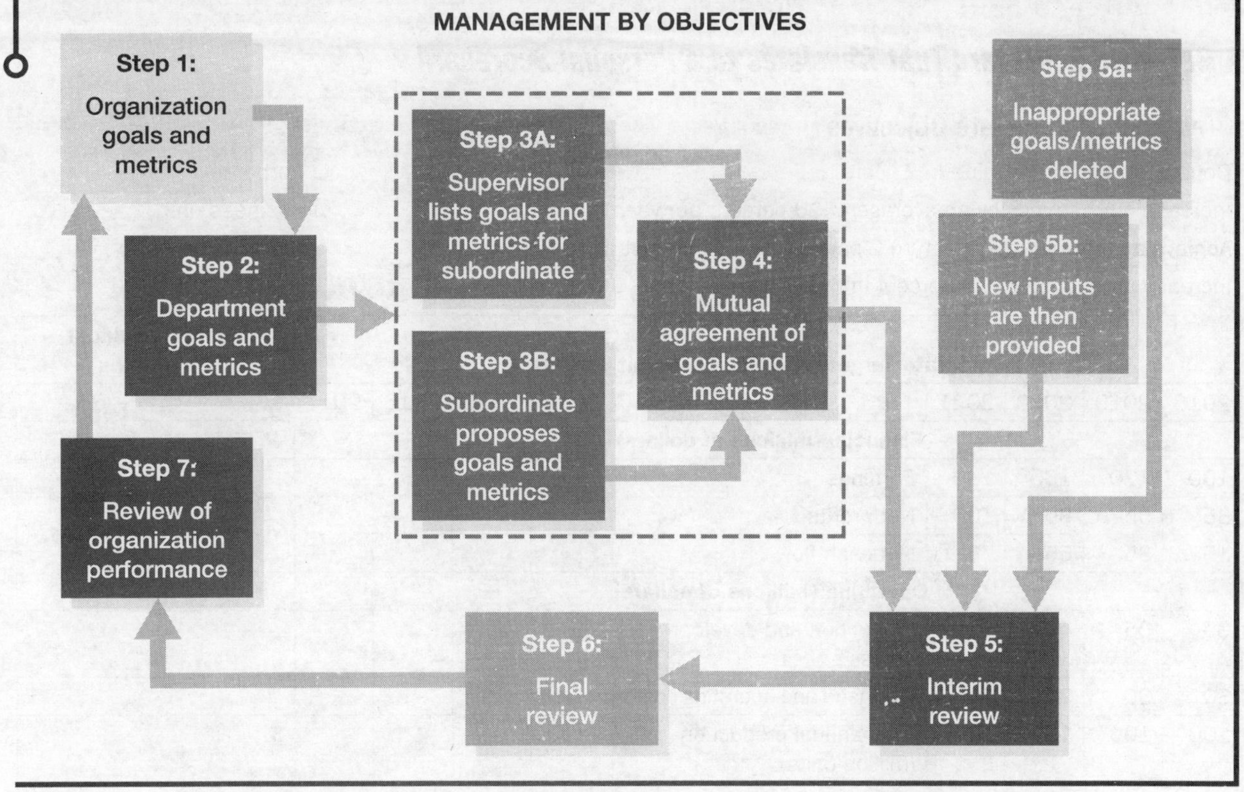

organization's common goals and objectives and ultimately returns to that step. The system acts as a goal-setting process whereby objectives are established for the organization (Step 1), departments (Step 2), and individual managers and employees (Step 3).

As Figure 8.7 shows, employees help establish specific goals, but those goals are based on a broad statement of an employee's responsibilities prepared by the person's supervisor. The employee-established goals are then discussed with the supervisor and jointly reviewed and modified until both parties are satisfied with them (Step 4). The goal statements are accompanied by a detailed account of the actions the employee proposes to take to reach the goals and how they will be measured (the metrics).

During periodic reviews, the progress the employee makes toward the goals is assessed (Step 5). The goals and metrics may be changed at this time as new or additional information is received. After a period of time, the employee does a self-evaluation and documents what they have accomplished. The employee and their manager then jointly review and discuss the self-evaluation (Step 6). The final step (Step 7) is reviewing the connection between the employee's performance and the organization's performance. Notice how the steps in an MBO program are similar to, but more specific than, the steps in Figure 8.1, which depicts the elements of the performance management process.

The Balanced Scorecard

The balanced scorecard (BSC), which we first discussed in Chapter 2, can be used to appraise individual employees, teams, business units, and the corporation itself. A BSC review takes into account four related categories: (1) financial measures,

5 Highlights in HRM

A Balanced Scorecard That Translates to a Personal Scorecard

Corporate Objectives

Double our corporate value in 7 years.
Increase our earnings by an average of 20 percent per year.
Achieve an internal rate of return 2 percent above the cost of capital.
Increase production by 20 percent in the next decade.

❑ Corporate
❑ Business unit
❑ Team/individual

Corporate Targets and Business-Unit Targets									**Team/Individual Objectives**
2018	2019	2020	2021		2014	2015	2016	2017	**1.**
				Financial (millions of dollars)					
100	120	160	180	Earnings					
35	55	85	100	Net profits					
15	35	65	75	Net cash flow					**2.**
				Operating (millions of dollars)					
35	35	40	50	Production and development costs					
30	30	35	30	Overhead and operating costs					
100	105	108	110	Total annual production (million units)					**3.**
Team/Individual Measures					**Targets**				
1.									
2.									**4.**
3.									
4.									

Source: Adapted from Robert Kaplan and David Norton, "Using the Balanced Scorecard as a Strategic Management System," *Harvard Business Review* (January–February 1996): 75–85.

(2) customer measures, (3) process measures, and (4) learning measures. Highlights in HRM 5 shows how a balanced scorecard in the financial category translates to a personal scorecard for an employee. The corporation's financial objectives have already been spelled out on the top of the scorecard. The business unit targets are then added, followed by the target objectives of the firm's teams and individual employees. The scorecard helps employees see clearly how their performance ties in to the overall performance of the firm.

The BSC review method is similar to an MBO system in that it translates broad corporate goals into divisional, departmental, team, and individual goals in a cascading way. This ensures that implementing the firm's strategy becomes "everyone's" job.

Figure 8.8 A Summary of Various Review Methods

	Advantages	Disadvantages
Trait Methods	1. Are inexpensive to develop 2. Use meaningful dimensions 3. Are easy to use	1. Have a high potential for rating errors 2. Are not useful for employee counseling 3. Are not useful for allocating rewards 4. Are not useful for promotion decisions
Behavioral Methods	1. Use specific performance dimensions 2. Are acceptable to employees and superiors 3. Are useful for providing feedback 4. Are fair for reward and promotion decisions	1. Can be time consuming to develop and use 2. Can be costly to develop 3. Have some potential for rating error
Results Methods	1. Have less subjectivity bias 2. Are acceptable to employees and superiors 3. Link individual performance to organizational performance 4. Encourage mutual goal setting 5. Are good for reward and promotion decisions	1. Are time consuming to develop and use 2. May encourage a short-term perspective 3. May use contaminated criteria 4. May use deficient criteria

8.3d Which Performance Review Method Should You Use?

Figure 8.8 lists some of the strengths and weaknesses of the trait, behavior, and results approaches to appraising employees. Although traditionally researchers and HR managers believed that the more sophisticated and time-consuming methods offer more useful information, that view has since been called into question. No system will be effective if it is too complicated to use, or if managers avoid the cumbersome process. Conversely, even a simple system, when used properly, can initiate a discussion between managers and employees that leads to genuinely better performance—and that is what's most important. Says Ronald Gross, an industrial psychologist and human resources consultant: "I've seen many systems fail miserably because they're too complex, too time consuming, and too burdensome. I've never seen a system fail because it was too simple."[45]

The accounting firm Deloitte uses a review form with only four measures that it administers quarterly. For example, one measure asks evaluators to use a five-point scale to answer the following question: "Given what I know of this person's performance, I would always want him or her on my team."[46] One way to assess whether an organization's review system is effective is by doing an annual, or at least periodic, audit of the process using a survey instrument that both managers and employees complete on a periodic basis. This should give HR personnel a better sense of whether the review process is improving.

8.4 Performance Review Meetings and Feedback Sessions

LO4

Discuss how you would go about diagnosing an employee's performance problems. List several factors to consider.

After you have evaluated how well your employees are doing using one or more review methods, how should you begin to present the information to them in a review meeting or feedback session? The format for this meeting or session will be determined in large part by its purpose, the type of performance management system used, and the organization of a firm's review form. A formal performance evaluation should be scheduled far enough in advance to allow both the subordinate and the manager to prepare for the discussion. Usually 10 days to 2 weeks is a sufficient amount of lead time.

Sometimes discussing an employee's past performance and future development goals can make for a meeting or feedback session that is too long. It can also be difficult for a supervisor to perform the role of both evaluator and counselor in the same review period. Dividing the meeting into two sessions, one for the performance review and the other for the employee's growth plans, can be helpful.

8.4a Types of Performance Review Meetings and Feedback Sessions

There are three basic formats for providing feedback during a performance review meeting or feedback session: tell-and-sell, tell-and-listen, and problem solving. No one format is best for every review session. Rather, managers can use one or more of the formats depending on the purpose of the session, the topic being discussed, and the receptiveness of the employee.

- *Tell-and-sell.* The skills required in the tell-and-sell format include the ability to persuade an employee to change their behavior in a certain way. This requires a manager to skillfully use motivational and persuasive techniques to try to change the behavior. But because there is less communication on the part of the employee with this format, it is less than ideal when used for this purpose. However, the tell-and-sell format may be used if other formats haven't worked, the employee is resistant to change, or the employee is reluctant to participate in the discussion.
- *Tell-and-listen.* In the tell-and-listen format, the appraiser or supervisor communicates the strong and weak points of an employee's job performance during the first part of the session. During the second part of the session, both participants thoroughly explore the employee's feelings about the review. The tell-and-listen method gives both managers and employees the opportunity to release and iron out any frustration or negative feelings they might have.
- *Problem solving.* This format is the most proactive. Listening, accepting, and responding to feelings are certainly essential elements of the problem-solving approach, but this format goes beyond addressing the employee's feelings. It seeks to obtain the employee's buy-in for a mutually agreed-upon way to overcome obstacles and improve the person's actual performance. One way in which a problem-solving format is implemented is by beginning with the employee's self-evaluation. That way, the manager and employee can compare where they agree and disagree, and focus on problem solving instead of the manager trying to convince the employee that the manager's viewpoint is right.

8.4b Conducting the Performance Review Meeting or Feedback Session

There are no hard-and-fast rules for how to conduct a review, but the guidelines that follow can increase the willingness of employees to accept feedback, discuss their performance and improve it, and increase their overall satisfaction with the feedback process.

Ask for a Self-Evaluation

Research shows that employees are more satisfied and perceive review systems as more fair when they have input into the process. A self-evaluation can be used to discuss areas in which managers and employees have reached different conclusions—not so much to resolve the "truth," as to work toward the resolution of problems. A self-evaluation also ensures that employees know against what criteria they are being evaluated, eliminating any potential surprises.

Invite Participation

Communication is a two-way street. Most experts advise supervisors to encourage their employees to speak freely and listen closely to what they have to say. When an employee is an active participant in the discussion, it becomes more likely that any root causes and obstacles to the employee's performance will be uncovered and constructive ideas for improvement developed. In addition, research suggests that an employee's ability to participate in the discussion is strongly related to the person's satisfaction with the feedback delivered, the extent to which the person believes it is fair and useful, and the desire to improve their performance. As a rule of thumb, supervisors should spend only about 30 to 35 percent of the time talking. They should spend the rest of the time listening to the information their employees volunteer and their responses to questions.

Express Appreciation

Because praise is a powerful motivator and employees are seeking positive feedback, it is frequently beneficial to start the session by expressing appreciation for what the employee has done well. Surprisingly, not all supervisors actually think to do this—but they should. A performance review is the perfect time to tell people—and top performers in particular—that they are valued, so they feel encouraged and motivated to continue to come to work day after day and remain with the firm.

Starting the meeting by talking about what the employee is doing well will also make the person less defensive and more likely to talk about aspects of the job that are not going so well. But don't deliberately "sandwich" positive statements with negative ones, which are then followed by positive statements. If you do, the individual will be less likely to take the praise seriously and may view it instead as a way to soften the bad news. Furthermore, if employees are given feedback on their performance on a regular basis, there will be no need to sandwich bad news between good news.

Be Supportive and Demonstrate That You Care

One of the better techniques for engaging an employee is for the manager to ask: "What can I do to help?" Employees frequently attribute performance problems to either real or perceived obstacles (such as bureaucratic procedures or inadequate resources). By being open and supportive, the manager conveys to the employee that they will try to eliminate roadblocks and will work with the employee to achieve a higher standard of performance. Good managers also demonstrate during reviews and on the job that not only do they support their employees' work efforts and ways to improve them, but they also care about them personally and want to help them get what they want out of life. No one wants to be just a "cog in the machine."

Minimize Criticism

Even the most stoic employees can absorb only so much criticism before they start to get defensive. If an employee has many areas in need of improvement, managers should focus on the issues that are most problematic or most important to the job. In other words, criticism should be given in small doses.

Some tips for using criticism constructively include the following:

- *Consider whether it's really necessary.* Sometimes a manager's frustration with a performance problem is little more than "letting off steam." Be sure that the criticism focuses on a recurrent problem or a consistent pattern of behavior over which the employee has control.
- *Consider the person's ability to handle it.* Everyone handles criticism differently. Some people are able to handle it well; others react very negatively to even the slightest criticism.
- *Be specific and don't exaggerate.* Sometimes we overstate problems in an effort to be convincing or to demonstrate our concern. Try to keep criticism simple, factual, and to the point. Avoid using "absolute" terms such as *always*, *completely*, and *never*.
- *Watch your timing.* Properly timed criticism can often mean the difference between success and failure. Even good criticism given late in the day, for example, can touch a raw nerve if the employee is tired. Take a break or save it for another day.
- *Focus on the problem behavior, not the person.* It is often easier and more effective to describe the behavior you have observed, rather than to characterize the person's attitude or personality (or traits). For example, if the employee has a tardiness or absentee problem, you might say, "I've noticed that you arrive to work late," rather than attributing this behavior to a lack of commitment or laziness.
- *Make improvement your goal.* It's hard to change a person's behavior with a single conversation, so "laying it on the line" is not probably a good idea. Instead of getting into a "blame game" in which both manager and employee enter into a potentially endless discussion of why a situation has occurred, focus on the problem and come up with a solution to it.[47]

Establish Mutual Goals

The final step is establishing goals for the next performance management cycle. Jointly establishing goals and then revisiting and revising them at the end of the cycle is a critical part of the review process. Revisiting goals during a performance review also emphasizes the ongoing nature of the process. Because one of the major purposes of the review meeting or feedback session is to improve an employee's future performance, their manager should focus the person's attention on the future rather than the past:

- Emphasize strengths on which the employee can build rather than weaknesses to overcome.
- Drop unproductive tasks.
- Limit improvement plans to a few important items that can be accomplished within a reasonable period of time and spell out how they will be achieved. The plans might include a list of resources, contact information for people who can help the employee achieve the goals, and timetables for following up to ensure they are met.
- Highlight how both the employee and the firm will excel if the goals are achieved.

- Establishing SMART goals can be very helpful for this purpose. **SMART goals** are specific, measurable, attainable, realistic, and time based—hence, the acronym. Realistic and specific goals that are actually attainable in a certain amount of time (given the firm's current resources and the employee's abilities), measurable, and written down communicate precise information to employees.

SMART goals
Goals that are specific, measurable, achievable, realistic, and time-based.

Follow Up on a Day-to-Day Basis

Often both managers and employees are happy to finish formal performance reviews and file away the review form. As we have emphasized, a better approach than the "disappearing appraisal" is to have informal talks periodically to follow up on the issues that were discussed in the review. This puts managers in more of a coaching role versus that of a judge.

For example, as a sales manager, should you wait to appraise your employees once or twice a year? Probably not. Most likely you would want to monitor their sales on a weekly and monthly basis. Has a particular salesperson met their customer-contact numbers this week? Why or why not? Is the salesperson closing deals with the people contacted? If the salesperson isn't making their goals at the 6-month mark, how can you help them if you haven't provided ongoing feedback? The lack of sales will be hard to make up at this point.

It's not just salespeople who need continual feedback. All types of employees can benefit from ongoing performance conversations with their managers. "Millennials and Gen Z-ers don't want hierarchy, formal feedback processes and appraisals," says Nicholas Greschner, the Canadian director of human resources for the consulting firm Accenture. "They demand real-time, in-person feedback, forward-looking conversations and support to grow their careers."[48] Once the manager and employees have a series of discussions, there is an ebb and flow of ideas, some with the potential to serve as catalysts for improvement within the company.[49] The ultimate purpose is to better both parties.

Providing employees with feedback on a continuous basis also helps them know where they stand if and when they receive formal reviews. As a result, the anxiety they experience is often alleviated, and a more meaningful conversation with them and their supervisors can take place. If employees are surprised by their reviews, it is probably safe to say that their supervisors have not been providing them with much ongoing feedback.

8.4c Improving Performance

What if one of your employees is performing poorly? What can you do to help that person perform better? This requires some diagnosis of the situation. But although performance management systems can often tell us who is not performing well, they typically cannot reveal why.

Identifying the Sources of Ineffective Performance

A person's performance is a function of several factors, but perhaps it can be boiled down to three primary concerns: ability, motivation, and environment. Each individual has a unique pattern of strengths and weaknesses that play a part in their performance. But talented employees with low motivation are not likely to succeed. In addition, other factors in the work environment—or even in the external environment, which includes personal, family, and community concerns—can affect a person's performance either positively or negatively. To diagnose a poor performance, managers should focus on

Figure 8.9 Factors That Affect an Employee's Performance

ABILITY	MOTIVATION	ENVIRONMENT
• Technical skills • Interpersonal skills • Problem-solving skills • Analytical skills • Communication skills • Physical limitations	• Career ambition • Goals and expectations • Job satisfaction and frustrations • Fairness perceptions • Relations with coworkers	• Equipment/materials • Job design • Economic conditions • Unions • Rules and policies • Managerial support • Laws and regulations

these three interactive elements. Figure 8.9 provides a better picture of how these three factors (ability, motivation, and environment) can influence employees' performance.

As Figure 8.10 shows, if an employee's performance is not up to standards, the cause could be a skill problem (a lack of knowledge, abilities, or technical competencies), an effort problem (a lack of motivation to get the job done), or some problem in the external conditions of work (poor economic conditions, worker shortages due to downsizing, difficult sales territories, etc.). Problems in any one of these areas could cause the person's performance to suffer.

Too often, however, managers assume that poor performance is due first to lack of ability, second to poor motivation, and third to external conditions the employee faces. Ironically, research suggests that we tend to draw exactly the opposite conclusion about our own performance. We first attribute poor performance to external constraints such as bad luck or factors out of our control. If the problem is internal, then we typically attribute it to temporary factors such as low motivation or energy ("I had a bad day"). Only as a last resort are we likely to admit our poor performance might be due to our abilities or lack of them.

This difference in opinion between the two parties can result in a negative feedback cycle if it's not handled properly. A manager who assumes an employee isn't motivated or not capable may begin to treat the person differently, perhaps by supervising the individual too closely or watching for the employee's next mistake. This reaction is likely to decrease the employee's motivation and result in an even lower performance level. Seeing this might confirm the manager's initial belief that the employee does not "measure up." As you can probably tell, this "set-up-to-fail" syndrome can be self-fulfilling and self-reinforcing.[50]

Performance Diagnosis

So what can be done to diagnose the *real* reasons for poor performance? More specifically, how can managers identify the root causes and get to work on a solution that improves performance? By comparing different performance measures, managers can begin to get an idea of the underlying causes of performance problems.

For example, as Figure 8.10 shows, results measures cannot distinguish between ability, motivation, and the situational determinants of performance. So if someone is not achieving the desired results, it could be due to one or more of these factors. In contrast, behavioral measures are less affected by external constraints. So if someone is demonstrating all the desired behaviors but is not achieving the desired results, logic

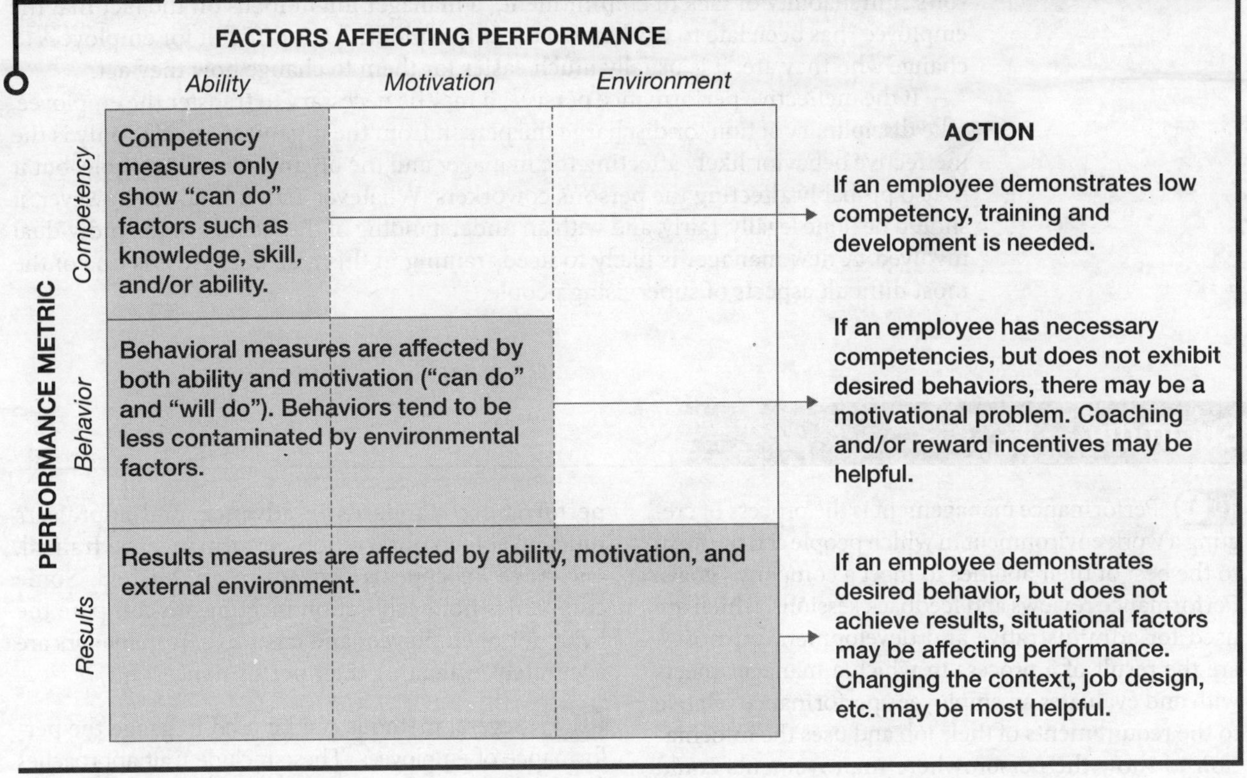

Figure 8.10 Performance Diagnosis

suggests that outcome might be due to factors beyond the person's control. Similarly, other kinds of diagnoses are possible by comparing other measures of performance. Only by correctly diagnosing the causes of performance problems can managers—and employees—hope to improve them.

Managing Ineffective Performance

Once the sources of performance problems are known, a course of action can be planned. This might involve providing training in areas that would increase the knowledge and skills the employee needs to perform effectively. A transfer to another job or department might give an employee a chance to become a more effective member of the organization. In other instances, different ways to motivate the individual might have to be found. Sometimes underperformers simply do not understand exactly what is expected of them. However, once their responsibilities are clarified, they are in a position to take the corrective actions needed to improve their performance.

Focus on Changing the Behavior, Not the Person

Bad performance on the part of an employee is likely to make their supervisor's job harder. As difficult as it might be to do, the supervisor must try to separate the employee from the behavior—it is not the employee who is bad, but rather their actions exhibited on the job. One way to communicate this information to employees is to not make suggestions about personal traits they should change but instead to suggest more acceptable ways of performing. For example, as we noted earlier, instead of focusing on a person's "unreliability or lack of commitment," a manager might focus on the fact that the employee "has been late to work seven times this month." It is difficult for employees to change who they are; it is usually much easier for them to change how they act.

If the ineffective performance persists, it may be necessary to transfer the employee, take disciplinary action, or discharge the person from the organization. Not only is the ineffective behavior likely affecting the manager and the organization as a whole, but it is also probably affecting the person's coworkers. Whatever action is taken, however, it should be done legally, fairly, and with an understanding of the feelings of the individual involved. A new manager is likely to need training in this area because it is one of the most difficult aspects of supervising people.

Summary

LO 1 Performance management is the process of creating a work environment in which people can perform to the best of their abilities to meet a company's goals. Performance reviews and feedback sessions, which are used for administrative and development purposes, are the result of a process in which a manager meets with and evaluates an employee's performance relative to the requirements of their job and uses the information to show the person where improvements could be made and why. Such reviews are just part of the performance management process, however. Aligning the goals of employees with the goals of the firm, providing employees with continual on-the-job feedback, and rewarding them are critical as well.

Although some firms believe performance reviews are ineffective and no longer use them, most organizations continue to do so. The ultimate success or failure of a performance review program depends on its underlying philosophy, its connection with the firm's business goals, and the attitudes and skills of those responsible for its administration.

LO 2 Information about how well employees are performing can be derived from a variety of sources, including the employees as well as their supervisors, peers, customers, suppliers, and subordinates. Using multiple sources is frequently a good idea because different individuals see different facets of an employee's performance.

Performance management systems must comply with the law and, like selections tests, be job related, valid and reliable, and free from criterion deficiency and contamination. Employees must understand their performance standards in advance, and appraisers must be able to observe job performance, be trained, and have an appeals procedure established. Some companies hold calibration meetings to compare the behavior of employees and ensure their managers are accurately evaluating their performance.

LO 3 Several methods can be used to gauge the performance of employees. These include trait approaches (such as graphic rating scales, mixed-standard scales, forced-choice forms, and essays), behavioral methods (such as critical incident ratings, checklists, BARS, and BOS), and results methods (MBO). The choice of method depends on the purpose of the review. Trait methods are simple to develop and complete, but they are more subjective and less useful for providing feedback. Behavioral methods provide more specific information for giving feedback but can be time consuming and costly to develop. Results methods are more objective and can link an employee's performance to the organization as a whole. However, they may promote a short-term perspective (such as meeting annual goals) but not encourage subtle yet important aspects of performance.

LO 4 Although various approaches to review meetings are possible, research suggests that employee participation and goal setting lead to higher satisfaction and improved performance. Discussing problems with employees, showing support for them, minimizing criticism, and rewarding them when they perform well are critical. During the meeting, performance deficiencies can be discussed and plans for improvement can be made.

Key Terms

behavior observation scale (BOS)
behaviorally anchored rating scale (BARS)
calibration
contrast error
customer evaluation
error of central tendency
essay method
forced-choice method
forced distribution
graphic rating scale method
leniency or strictness error
management by objectives (MBO)
manager and/or supervisor evaluation
mixed-standard scale method
peer evaluation
performance management
performance review
recency error
self-evaluation
similar-to-me error
SMART goals
subordinate evaluation
team evaluation
360-degree evaluation

Discussion Questions

LO 1 Describe how the performance management process is linked to employee selection, training, and development.

LO 2 What sources could be used to evaluate the performance of people working in the following jobs?

a. Sales representative
b. Robotics engineer
c. Director of nursing in a hospital
d. HR manager
e. Air traffic controller

LO 3 Three types of review meetings are described in this chapter.

a. What different skills are required for each? What reactions can one expect from using these different skills?
b. How can a manager develop the skills needed to conduct a problem-solving type of meeting?
c. Which method do you feel is the least desirable? Why?

LO 4 Discuss how you would go about diagnosing an employee's performance problems. List several factors to consider.

CASE STUDY 1 Adobe Ditches Formal Performance Reviews—And Wants to Help Other Companies Do So, Too

As noted in the chapter, an increasing number of companies are no longer conducting formal performance reviews. However, most still do. In a recent survey of 1,500 U.S. office workers, 88 percent of them reported receiving formal written reviews—often with rankings—usually on an annual basis.

The survey, which was conducted by Adobe Systems, the maker of Acrobat, Photoshop, and Flash software, also revealed the following bad news about formal performance reviews:

- More than half of office workers feel that formal performance reviews have no impact on how they do their jobs (59 percent) and are a needless HR requirement (58 percent).
- Eighty percent of office workers would prefer feedback in the moment rather than a progress review after a certain number of months. Performance reviews are extremely stressful for both managers and employees. Rankings and ratings create competition among employees and result in even more stress.

HRM Experience

Performance Diagnosis

Managing the performance of employees is a vital—yet delicate—responsibility. One of the toughest aspects of performance management is assessing why someone is not performing well. Although it may be easy to spot who is not performing well, it is not always easy to diagnose the underlying causes of that person's poor performance (such as their motivation, ability, and external constraints). But without a correct diagnosis, it is nearly impossible to fix the problem. Managers also need to coach employees to improve their performance.

Assignment

Following are descriptions of three different employees. Describe what the potential causes of poor performance for each of the following employees might be and solutions that could enhance the person's performance.

1. ***Carl Spackler*** is the assistant greenskeeper at Bushwood Country Club. Over the past few months, members have been complaining that gophers are destroying the course and digging holes in the greens. Although Carl has been working evenings and weekends to address the situation, the problem persists. Unfortunately, his boss is interested only in results, and because the gophers are still there, he contends that Carl is not doing his job. He has accused Carl of "slacking off" and threatened his job.
2. ***Clark Griswold*** works in research and development for a chemical company that makes non-nutritive food additives. His most recent assignment has been the development of a non-nutritive aerosol cooking spray, but the project is far behind schedule and seems to be going nowhere. CEO Frank Shirley is decidedly upset and has threatened that if things do not improve, he will suspend bonuses again this year, as he did last year. Clark feels dejected because without the bonus he will not be able to make a down payment on the family's swimming pool.
3. ***Tommy Callahan Jr.*** recently graduated from college after 7 years and returned home to Sandusky, Ohio. His father, Big Tom Callahan, the owner of Callahan Motors, offers Tommy a job in the auto parts factory that makes brake pads. The factory is in severe danger of going under unless sales of the company's new brake pads increase dramatically. Tommy must go on the road with Richard (Big Tom's right-hand man) in a last-ditch effort to save the company. But Tommy proves to be unfocused, inexperienced, and lacking in confidence. In sales call after sales call he meets with rejection, even when the prospect looks promising. Customers express some concern about a warranty on the brake pads, but Richard believes that Tommy's inexperience and awkward approach are the big problems.

- A surprisingly large number of workers, across genders, reported actually crying after a performance review and either looked for another job or quit their jobs shortly afterward.
- Nearly two-thirds of Millennials (61 percent) would switch jobs to a company with no formal performance reviews even if the pay and job level were the same.

For reasons such as these, Adobe stopped doing formal reviews in 2012. The effort to ditch them began somewhat haphazardly: Donna Morris, then a senior vice president of human resources for Adobe, believed the firm's 360-degree employee review and ranking process was too complex and bureaucratic, and ate up massive amounts of time for which the company saw little or no return. She also believed they created barriers to teamwork and innovation because being ranked for compensation seemed to pit employees against one another.

The problem was something Morris had been thinking about at Adobe's offices in India while being interviewed for a major business publication in that country. The reporter conducting the interview asked Morris what new cutting-edge HR practices Adobe was implementing. Suffering from jetlag, she offhandedly responded: "We plan to abolish the annual performance review format."

Quickly Morris's announcement made headlines. There was just one problem with it: she had only been contemplating ending formal performance reviews. and hadn't actually cleared the idea with her CEO. Needless to say, when she got back to Adobe's office in the United States, she had some explaining to do.

Morris wrote her case for ending performance reviews and posted it on the company's intranet.

She encouraged employees and managers to examine Adobe's current review practice to figure out how to improve it, which they subsequently did. What they discovered was troubling. Adobe's managers were spending in excess of 80,000 hours annually on the reviews. Worse yet, feeling demoralized by their reviews and rankings, a high number of Adobe employees quit after having them. That was making it hard for Adobe to retain talent, especially because the company's headquarters is located in Silicon Valley, where the demand for tech employees is high.

Instead of formal performance reviews, today Adobe employees have periodic "check-ins" with their managers, who offer them feedback, help with on-the-job problems, and ideas for their growth and development. No written review is required.

So does the new check-in system work? Yes. In surveys, employees say the check-ins make performance conversations easier and less stressful, and that they get better feedback. Voluntary turnover has dropped dramatically.

In fact, Adobe believes its check-in system works so well that it is helping other companies adopt it—for free. No software purchase necessary. The company has posted information about the system and all of its associated documents on its public website. Among the items posted are worksheets and discussion guides for managers and employees and FAQs (frequently asked questions) about how the check-in process works and how to implement it.

"We love talking to other companies that are considering a move away from structured performance reviews, and many have adopted some form of check-in already," says Morris. "Now we want to make it easier to share our experience with people who are exploring a model like this—whether they're in technology or a totally different industry."

Questions

1. Why did Adobe need a new performance management system? What drawbacks might there be to the company's check-ins?
2. Are formal performance reviews always bad? Why or why not?

Sources: David Burkus, "How Adobe Scrapped Its Performance Review System and Why It Worked," *Forbes* (June 1, 2016); Kate Samuelson, "Twenty-Five Percent of Men Cry after a Progress Review, Study Shows," *Forbes* (January 13, 2017); "Adobe Study into Performance Reviews Shows Office Workers Waste Time and Tears," *Which-50*, https://which50.com; "About Adobe Check-in," Adobe.com (April 2, 2017).

CASE STUDY 2 "Project Oxygen" Resuscitates Google's Poor-Performing Bosses

When it comes to gathering data and analyzing it to build new and better products, few companies handle that challenge as well as Google. Recently Google decided to use its info-tech expertise to answer an important question: Since people make the difference between good and great companies, could a data-driven, analytical approach be used to improve Google's HRM function? Such an approach worked for Billy Beane, so surely it could work for Google, couldn't it? Recall from Chapter 1 that Beane, the manager of the baseball's Oakland A's, dramatically improved players and the team using data and statistics. (Actor Brad Pitt dramatized Beane's efforts in the movie *Moneyball.*)

One thing Google wanted to know was if it could "build" better bosses. Why? Despite the many job perks enjoyed by Google's workers, the company's employee turnover rate was surprisingly high. It's been said that the number 1 reason people leave their jobs is because of their bosses. Could this be true at Google? And if so, could the behaviors of good bosses be pinpointed and used to improve the performance of not-so-good bosses? The researchers at Google wanted to find out. They also wanted to answer these questions using data from their own organization to find out precisely what would work for Google rather than other organizations.

To answers these questions, a team of 25-plus Google researchers and scientists began studying the company's supervisors using their performance reviews, surveys from their employees, interviews, and observations of their behaviors. More than 10,000 observations were collected on 100 variables to determine how well the supervisors were performing. Initially, not all supervisors were thrilled to be evaluated by their subordinates and "put under the microscope." Consequently, the effort took some "selling" to Google's top management. The fact that the researchers could point to dramatic differences in the overall ratings employees gave different managers and that some teams performed much better than others helped fuel the fire to get "Project Oxygen" off the ground. (Presumably a good boss gives you room to breathe, whereas a bad boss can suck the life right out of you—hence the project's name.)

Once concluded, Project Oxygen yielded a wealth of information, some which mirrored conventional wisdom and some which did not: Teams with higher-rated managers performed better, the employees in them were happier, and they stayed with the company longer. Their managers had more impact on how the employees felt about their jobs than any other factor. However, it turned out that the best bosses weren't the ones with the greatest technical expertise, as Google had anticipated. Instead, the truly great bosses were those who were even tempered, helped their employees think through problems without micromanaging them, and cared about them as people. Google then used the information it gathered to implement training and coaching programs to quickly improve the managerial skills of its worst-performing managers.

Specifically, Google identified eight behaviors you should engage in if you want to be a good boss—at least at Google:

1. Be a good coach.
2. Empower your team and don't micromanage.
3. Express interest in team members' success and personal well-being.
4. Be productive and results oriented.
5. Be a good communicator and listen to your team.
6. Help your employees with career development.
7. Have a clear vision and strategy for the team.
8. Have key technical skills so you can help advise the team.

Questions

1. Why isn't having the greatest amount of technical expertise the key to being a good supervisor at Google?
2. Does Google's research on the performance of its managers surprise you? Why or why not?

Sources: Brad Hall, "Google's Project Oxygen Pumps Fresh Air into Management," *The Street* (February 11, 2014), https://www.thestreet.com; Adam Bryant, "Google's Quest to Build a Better Boss," *New York Times* (March 12, 2011), http://www.nytimes.com; Meghan Casserly, "Google's Failed Quest to Find Managers Are Evil, and Why You Should Care," *Forbes* (July 17, 2103), http://www.forbes.com; Judith Aquino, "Eight Traits of Stellar Managers as Defined by Googlers," *Business Insider* (March 15, 2011), http://www.businessinsider.com.

Notes and References

1. Peter Cappelli and Anna Travis, "The Performance Management Revolution," *Harvard Business Review*, October 2016; Ladan Nikravan, "A Needed Change: Make Reviews Proactive, Not Reactive," *Forbes* (September 29, 2013), http://forbes.com.
2. Rebecca Knight, "Delivering an Effective Performance Review," *Harvard Business Review*, November 2011; Susan Scherreik, "Your Performance Review: Make It Perform," *Businessweek* 3762 (December 17, 2001): 139; Dick Grote, "Performance Evaluations: Is It Time for a Makeover?" *HRFocus* 77, no. 11 (2000): 6–7; "Employers Need to Do a Better Job of Performance Management," *Managing Training & Development* (April 2003): 8; Christopher D. Lee, "Feedback, Not Appraisal," *HRMagazine* 51, no. 11 (2006): 111–114; R. L. Cardy and B. Leonard, *Performance Management: Concepts, Skills, and Exercises* (Armonk, NY: M. E. Sharpe, 2011).
3. Graham Kenny, "Fixing Performance Appraisal Is about More Than Ditching Annual Reviews," *Harvard Business Review*, February, 2016; Jason J. Dahling et al., "Does Coaching Matter?" *Personnel Psychology* (2015); Donna Doldwasser, "Me a Trainer?" *Training* 38, no. 4 (2001): 60–66; Rebecca Ganzel, "Mike Carter," *Training* 38, no. 7 (2001): 28–30; Carla Joinson, "Making Sure Employees Measure Up," *HRMagazine* 46, no. 3 (2001): 36–41; Morton D. Rosenbaum, "Gratitude Adjustment: When a Pat on the Back Isn't Enough," *Meetings & Conventions* 39, no. 7 (2004): 20; James W. Smither, Manuel London, and Richard R. Reilly, "Does Performance Improve Following Multisource Feedback?" *Personnel Psychology* 58, no. 1 (2005): 33–67.
4. Sharon Koss, "How a Pay-for-Performance Compensation Strategy Pays Off," Society for Human Resource Management (January 3, 2008), https://www.shrm.org/resourcesandtools/hr-topics/compensation/pages/payforperformancepaysoff.aspx); Janet Wiscombe, "Can Pay for Performance Really

Work?" *Workforce* 80, no. 8 (2001): 28–34; Charlotte Garvey, "Meaningful Tokens of Appreciation: Cash Awards Aren't the Only Way to Motivate Your Workforce," *HRMagazine* 49, no. 8 (2004): 101–106; Lisa D. Sprenkle, "Forced Ranking: A Good Thing for Business?" Workforce.com.

5. Heather R. Huhman, "Five Ways HR Technology Can Improve Performance Reviews," *Entrepreneur* (July 23, 2014), https://www.entrepreneur.com; Don Pontefract, "Only 55 Percent of Employees Feel as Though Performance Management Appraisals Are Effective," *Forbes* (March 31, 2015), https://www.forbes.com; Drew Robb, "Building a Better Workforce: Performance Management Software Can Help You Identify and Develop High-Performing Workers," *HRMagazine* 49, no. 10 (2004): 86–93.
6. Bill Fotsch and John Case, "Why Performance Management Fails," *Forbes*, May 1, 2018; Sunnie Giles, "Turning Performance Reviews into a Vehicle for Radical Innovation," *Forbes* (March 28, 2017), https://www.forbes.com; Jonathan A. Segal, "86 Your Appraisal Process?" *HRMagazine* 45, no. 10 (2000): 199–206; Barry Witcher and Rosie Butterworth, "Honshin Kanri: How Xerox Manages," *Long-Range Planning* 32, no. 3 (1999): 323–332.
7. Graham Kenny, "Fixing Performance Appraisal Is about More Than Ditching Annual Reviews," *Harvard Business Review*, February, 2016; Jeff Kauflin, "Hate Performance Reviews? Good News? They're Getting Shorter and Simpler," *Forbes* (March 9, 2017), http://https://www.forbes.com.
8. David Javitch, "How to Survive Employee Appraisals," Entrepreneur.com (April 23, 2011), http://www.entrepreneur.com.
9. Juliana Thill, "Set Goals to Get Results," Crow River Media (April 5, 2017), http://www.crowrivermedia.com.
10. Mahmoud Javidmehr and Mehrdad Ebrahimpour, "Performance Appraisal Bias and Errors: The Influences and Consequences," *International Journal of Organizational Leadership* 4, no. 3 (2015): 286; Doug Cederblom, "From Performance Appraisal to Performance Management: One Agency's Experience," *Public Personnel Management* 31, no. 2 (2002): 131–140; "Anonymous 360-Feedback Drives Vauxhall Strategy," *Personnel Today* (August 19, 2003): 16; Cindy Romaine, "Staying Relevant: Competencies and Employee Reviews," *Information Outlook* 8, no. 7 (2004): 21–25; Jerry K. Palmer and James M. Loveland, "The Influence of Group Discussion on Performance Judgments: Rating Accuracy, Contrast Effects, and Halo," *Journal of Psychology* 142, no. 2 (2008): 117–130; "When Promotions Are on the Line, Follow Your Criteria and Beware Supervisor Bias," *HR Specialist: Ohio Employment Law* 3, no. 12 (2009): 2.
11. Jason D. Shaw and Nina Gupta, "Let the Evidence Speak Again! Financial Incentives Are More Effective Than We Thought," *Human Resource Management Journal* 25, no. 3 (2015): 281–293; "Job Complexity, Performance, and Well-Being: When Does Supplies–Values Fit Matter?" *Personnel Psychology* 57, no. 4 (2004): 847–880.
12. Joel Lefkowitz, "The Role of Interpersonal Affective Regard in Supervisory Performance Ratings: A Literature Review and Proposed Causal Model," *Journal of Occupational and Organizational Psychology* 73, no. 1 (2000): 67–85; Scott Highhouse, "Assessing the Candidate as a Whole: A Historical and Critical Analysis of Individual Psychological Assessment for Personnel Decision Making," *Personnel Psychology* 55, no. 2 (2002): 363–397.
13. "Dear *Workforce*: How Should We Conduct Performance-Appraisal 'Calibration' Meetings with Managers?" *Workforce*, September 7, 2011; Joanne Sammer, "Calibrating Consistency," *HRMagazine* 53, no. 1 (2008): 73–75; Jennie Sumelius et al., "What Determines Employee Perceptions of HRM Process Features?" *Human Resource Management* 53, no. 4 (2014): 569–592.
14. Silva Karkoulian, Guy Assaker, and Rob Hallak, "An Empirical Study of 360-Degree Feedback, Organizational Justice, and Firm Sustainability," *Journal of Business Research* 69, no. 5 (2016): 1862–1867; Kathryn Bartol, Cathy Durham, and June Poon, "Influence of Performance Evaluation Rating Segmentation on Motivation and Fairness Perceptions," *Journal of Applied Psychology* 86, no. 6 (2001): 1106–1119; Anne P. Hubbell, "Motivating Factors: Perceptions of Justice and Their Relationship with Managerial and Organizational Trust," *Communication Studies* 56, no. 1 (2005): 47; Rebecca M. Chory-Assad, "Room for Improvement," *Training* 40, no. 11 (2003): 18–20; Deanna M. Merritt, "Appraising the Performance Appraisal," *Supervision* 68, no. 4 (2007): 3–5.
15. *Brito v. Zia Company*, 478 F.2d 1200 (10th Cir. 1973); Treena L. Gillespie and Richard O. Parry, "Fuel for Litigation? Links between Procedural Justice and Multisource Feedback," *Journal of Managerial Issues* 18, no. 4 (2006): 530–546; Suzanne Tsacoumis and Michelle Davis King, "Litigation Driven Human Resource Management Changes," *Advancing Human Resource Project Management* (2014): 48–72.
16. *Albemarle Paper Company v. Moody*, 422 U.S. 405 (1975); Terry Gillen, "Appraisal: When Best Practice Is Bad Practice," *People Management* 11, no. 19 (2005): 58.
17. Ladan Nikravan, "It's Not Just about Performance: Time to Think Differently," *Forbes* (September 29, 2013), http://www.forbes.com.
18. Kieran Snyder, "High Achieving Men and Women Are Described Differently in Reviews," *Fortune* (August 26, 2014), http://fortune.com.
19. Rebecca Hastings, "Legal Expert Gives Performance Appraisal Advice," Society for Human Resource Management, February 2010; Gillian Flynn, "Getting Performance Reviews Right," *Workforce* 80, no. 5 (2001): 76–78; David C. Martin, Kathryn M. Bartol, and Patrick E. Kehoe, "The Legal Ramifications of Performance Appraisal: The Growing Significance," *Public Personnel Management* 29, no. 3 (2000): 381; Deanna M. Merritt, "Appraising the Performance Appraisal," *Supervision* 68, no. 4 (2007): 3–5; Kevin R. Murphy, "Perspectives on the Relationship between Job Performance and Ratings of Job Performance," *Industrial & Organizational Psychology* (June 2008): 197–205;

Cindy Miller, "Performance Appraisals in a Legal Context," *HR Info* (July 8, 2008), http://cindymiller.wordpress.com/.

20. Tsacoumis and King, "Litigation Driven Human Resource Management Changes," 2014; "Loose Lips Lose Lawsuits: Screen Performance Reviews for FMLA Comments," *Business Management Daily* (August 31, 2010), http://www.business-managementdaily.com.
21. Karkoulian, Assaker, and Hallak, "An Empirical Study of 360-Degree Feedback, Organizational Justice, and Firm Sustainability," 2016; Joan Brett and Leanne Atwater, "360-Degree Feedback: Accuracy, Reactions, and Perceptions of Usefulness," *Journal of Applied Psychology* 86, no. 5 (2001): 930–942; Bruce Pfau, Ira Kay, Kenneth Nowak, and Jai Ghorpade, "Does 360-Degree Feedback Negatively Affect Company Performance?" *HRMagazine* 47, no. 6 (2002): 54–59; Maury Peiperl, "Getting 360-Degree Feedback Right," *Harvard Business Review* 79, no. 1 (2001): 142–147; Robert Gandossy and Tina Kao, "Talent Wars: Out of Mind, Out of Practice," *Human Resource Planning* 27, no. 4 (2004): 15–20; Nima Jafari Navimipouret et al., "Expert Cloud: A Cloud-Based Framework to Share the Knowledge and Skills of Human Resources," *Computers in Human Behavior* 46 (2015): 57–74.
22. Corey E. Miller and Carl L. Thornton, "How Accurate Are Your Performance Appraisals?" *Public Personnel Management* (Summer 2006): 153–162; Edward J. Inderrieden, Robert E. Allen, and Timothy J. Keaveny, "Managerial Discretion in the Use of Self-Ratings in an Appraisal System: The Antecedents and Consequences," *Journal of Managerial Issues* 16, no. 4 (2004): 460–484.
23. Michael C. Campion, Emily D. Campion, and Michael A. Campion, "Improvements in Performance Management through the Use of 360 Feedback," *Industrial and Organizational Psychology* 8, no. 1 (2015): 85–93; Jeffrey Seglin, "Reviewing Your Boss," *Fortune* 143, no. 12 (2001): 248; Ann Harrington, "Workers of the World, Rate Your Boss!" *Fortune* 142, no. 6 (2000): 340–342; Robert Thompson, "Management Lite: Less Control, More Innovation," *HRMagazine* 44, no. 8 (1999): 10.
24. Brett and Atwater, "360-Degree Feedback," 930–942; Paula Silva and Henry L. Tosi, "Determinants of the Anonymity of the CEO Evaluation Process," *Journal of Managerial Issues* 16, no. 1 (2004): 87–103.
25. Alessandro Di Fiore and Marcio Souza, "Are Peer Reviews the Future of Performance Evaluations?" *Harvard Business Review*, January 12, 2021; Angelo S. DeNisi and Kevin R. Murphy, "Performance Appraisal and Performance Management: 100 Years of Progress?" (2017); John Drexler Jr., Terry Beehr, and Thomas Stetz, "Peer Appraisals: Differentiation of Individual Performance on Group Tasks," *Human Resource Management* 40, no. 4 (2001): 333–345.
26. Tammy L. Rapp et al., "The Role of Team Goal Monitoring in the Curvilinear Relationship between Team Efficacy and Team Performance," *Journal of Applied Psychology* 99, no. 5 (2014): 976; Scott and Einstein, "Strategic Performance Appraisal in Team-Based Organizations," 107–116; Debbie Kibbe and Jill Casner-Lotto, "Ralston Foods: From Greenfield to Maturity in a Team-Based Plant," *Journal of Organizational Excellence* 21, no. 3 (2002): 57–67; Simon Taggar and Mitchell Neubert, "The Impact of Poor Performers on Team Outcomes: An Empirical Examination of Attribution Theory," *Personnel Psychology* 57, no. 4 (2004): 935–969.
27. Stephanie Vozza, "Why Employees at Apple and Google Are More Productive," *Fast Company* (March 13, 2017), https://www.fastcompany.com.
28. Michael Cohn, "Best Buy Beefs up Customer Value at the Call Center," *Internet World* 8, no. 6 (2002): 42–43; Joe Kohn, "Isuzu Has IDEA for Boosting Sales," *Automotive News* 76, no. 5973 (2002): 41; D. L. Radcliff, "A New Paradigm of Feedback," *Executive Excellence* 19, no. 4 (2002): 20; Neeraj Bharadwaj and Anne Roggeveen, "The Impact of Offshored and Outsourced Call Service Centers on Customer Appraisals," *Marketing Letters* 19, no. 1 (2008): 13–23.
29. Jack Zenger and Joseph Folkman, "What Makes a 360-Degree Review Successful? *Harvard Business Review*, December 2020; Kenneth M. Nowack, "360 Feedback: From Insight to Improvement," *Public Manager* 44, no. 2 (2015): 20; Pfau, Kay, Nowak, and Ghorpade, "Does 360-Degree Feedback Negatively Affect Company Performance?" 54–59; Peiperl, "Getting 360-Degree Feedback Right," 142–147; Jack Kondrasuk and Matt Graybill, "From Paper to Computer," *The Human Resource Professional* 13, no. 6 (2000): 18–19.
30. Seymour Adler et al., "Getting Rid of Performance Ratings: Genius or Folly? A Debate," *Industrial and Organizational Psychology* 9, no. 2 (2016): 219–252; Gary E. Roberts, "Perspectives on Enduring and Emerging Issues in Performance Appraisal," *Public Personnel Management* 27, no. 3 (1998): 301–320; William Hubbartt, "Bring Performance Appraisal Training to Life," *HRMagazine* 40, no. 5 (1995): 166, 168; Filip Lievens, "Assessor Training Strategies and Their Effects on Accuracy, Interrater Reliability, and Discriminant Validity," *Journal of Applied Psychology* 86, no. 2 (2001): 255–264; Dick Grote, "Performance Appraisals: Solving Tough Challenges," *HRMagazine* 45, no. 7 (2000): 145–150; Leslie A. Weatherly, "Performance Management: Getting It Right from the Start," *HRMagazine* 49, no. 3 (2004): S1–S12.
31. E. Deepa, R. Palaniswamy, and S. Kuppusamy, "Effect of Performance Appraisal System in Organizational Commitment, Job Satisfaction and Productivity," *Journal of Contemporary Management Research* 8, no. 1 (2014): 72; Gary P. Latham and Kenneth N. Wexley, *Increasing Productivity through Performance Appraisal*, 2nd ed. (Reading, MA: Addison-Wesley, 1994), 137.
32. Jeffrey R. Spence and Lisa M. Keeping, "The Road to Performance Ratings Is Paved with Intentions," *Organizational Psychology Review* 3, no. 4 (2013): 360–383; Lefkowitz, "The Role of Interpersonal Affective Regard in Supervisory Performance Ratings," 67–85; Edwin Arnold and Marcia Pulich,

"Personality Conflicts and Objectivity in Appraising Performance," *Health Care Manager* 22, no. 3 (2003): 227; Krista Uggersly and Lorne M. Suksy, "Using Frame-of-Reference Training to Understand the Implications of Rater Idiosyncrasy for Rating Accuracy" *Journal of Applied Psychology* 93, no. 3 (2008): 711–719.

33. "Times Are Changing: The Future of Performance Management and Reviews," Business.com (February 22, 2017), https://www.business.com; Christopher Bartlett and Andrew McLean, "GE's Talent Machine," Case # 9-304-049 (Harvard Business School, 2006).
34. "HSN Enhances Employee Engagement with Nice Performance Management," *BusinessWire* (March 8, 2017), http://www.businesswire.com.
35. Sue H. Moon, Steven E. Scullen, and Gary P. Latham, "Precarious Curve Ahead: The Effects of Forced Distribution Rating Systems on Job Performance," *Human Resource Management Review* 26, no. 2 (2016): 166–179; Gail Johnson, "Forced Ranking: The Good, the Bad, and the Alternative," *Training* 41, no. 5 (2004): 24–31; Christine A. Amalfe and Eileen Quinn Steiner, "Forced Ranking Systems: Yesterday's Legal Target?" *New Jersey Law Journal* (March 28, 2005); Jessica Marquez, "Is GE'S Ranking System Broken?" *Workforce Management* 86, no. 12 (2007): 1–3.
36. Andrew Li, Jessica Bagger, and Russell Cropanzano, "The Impact of Stereotypes and Supervisor Perceptions of Employee Work–Family Conflict on Job Performance Ratings," *Human Relations* 70, no. 1 (2017): 119–145; Adam B. Butler and Amie Skattebo, "What Is Acceptable for Women May Not Be for Men: The Effect of Family Conflicts with Work on Job-Performance Ratings," *Journal of Occupational and Organizational Psychology* 77, no. 4 (2004): 553–564; Cheri Ostroff, Leanne E. Atwater, and Barbara J. Feinberg, "Understanding Self–Other Agreement: A Look at Rater and Ratee Characteristics, Context, and Outcomes," *Personnel Psychology* 57, no. 1 (2004): 333–337; Mike Schraeder and Jim Simpson, "How Similarity and Liking Affect Performance Appraisals," *Journal for Quality & Participation* 29, no. 1 (2006): 34–40.
37. Lisa Keeping and Paul Levy, "Performance Appraisal Reaction: Measurement, Modeling, and Method Bias," *Journal of Applied Psychology* 85, no. 5 (2000): 708–723.
38. Adam Bryant, "Google's Quest to Build a Better Boss," *New York Times* (March 12, 2011), http://www.nytimes.com.
39. Braveteta Hassell, "Machine Learning Could Mean a Lot for People Management," *Chief Learning Officer* (November 30, 2016), http://www.clomedia.com.
40. "Machine Learning: What It Is and Why It's Important," SAS.com (April 2, 2017), https://www.sas.com.
41. S. Black, D. G. Gardner, J. L. Pierce, and R. Steers, "Techniques of Performance Appraisal," *Organizational Behavior*, 2019; <AU: please give volume/page numbers> Kristina E. Chirico, M. Ronald Buckley, Anthony R. Wheeler, Jeffrey D. Facteau, H. John Bernardin, and Danielle S. Beu, "A Note on the Need for True Scores in Frame-of-Reference (FOR) Training Research," *Journal of Managerial Issues* 16, no. 3 (2004): 382–398; Christopher D. Lee, "Feedback, Not Appraisal," *HRMagazine* 51, no. 11 (2006): 111–114.
42. Patrick Kampkötter, "Performance Appraisals and Job Satisfaction," *International Journal of Human Resource Management* (2016): 1–25; Stephen C. Behrenbrinker, "Conducting Productive Performance Evaluations in the Assessor's Office," *Assessment Journal* 2, no. 5 (1995): 48–54; Aharon Tziner, Christine Joanis, and Kevin Murphy, "A Comparison of Three Methods of Performance Appraisal with Regard to Goal Properties, Goal Perception, and Rate Satisfaction," *Group & Organization Management* 25, no. 2 (2000): 175–190.
43. Daniel Bachrach, Elliot Bendoly, and Philip Podsakoff, "Attributions of the 'Causes' of Group Performance as an Alternative Explanation of the Relationship between Organizational Citizenship Behavior and Organizational Performance," *Journal of Applied Psychology* 86, no. 6 (2001): 1285–1293; Susan Leandri, "Measures That Matter: How to Fine-Tune Your Performance Measures," *Journal for Quality and Participation* 24, no. 1 (2001): 39–41.
44. Peter F. Drucker, *The Practice of Management* (New York: Harper & Brothers, 1954), reissued by HarperCollins in 1993; Janice S. Miller, "High Tech and High Performance: Managing Appraisal in the Information Age," *Journal of Labor Research* 24, no. 3 (2003): 409–425.
45. Deloris McGee Wanguri, "A Review, an Integration, and a Critique of Cross-Disciplinary Research on Performance Appraisals, Evaluations, and Feedback," *Journal of Business Communications* 32, no. 3 (1995): 267–293; Tziner, Joanis, and Murphy, "A Comparison of Three Methods of Performance Appraisal," 175–190; "Good Appraisal Is Simple, Happens Often, Experts Say"; Joanna Haworth, "Measuring Performance," *Nursing Management—UK* 15, no. 3 (2008): 22–28.
46. Jeff Kauflin, "Hate Performance Reviews? Good News? They're Getting Shorter and Simpler," *Forbes* (March 9, 2017), https://www.forbes.com.
47. Kwok Leung, Steven Su, and Michael Morris, "When Is Criticism Not Constructive? The Roles of Fairness Perceptions and Dispositional Attributions in Employee Acceptance of Critical Supervisory Feedback," *Human Relations* 54, no. 9 (2001): 1155–1187; Ted Pollock, "Make Your Criticism Pay Off," *Electric Light & Power* 81, no. 1 (2003): 31; "Five Ways to Tackle Poor Performers," *Law Office Management & Administration Report* 6, no. 12 (2006): 9.
48. Virginia Galt, "Is It Time to Retire the Employee Ranking System?" *Globe and Mail* (March 10, 2017), http://www.theglobeandmail.com.
49. "Focus on Success," *Aftermarket Business* 115, no. 2 (2005): 1.
50. Helen Wilkie, "The Tricky Art of Criticism," *HRMagazine* 49, no. 12 (2004): 77–83.

PORTRAIT IMAGES ASIA BY NONWARIT/Shutterstock.com

CHAPTER 9

Managing Compensation

Learning Outcomes

After studying this chapter, you should be able to

LO 1 Explain the three main components of a person's compensation.

LO 2 Distinguish between a strategic compensation program and a non-strategic compensation program.

LO 3 Determine how to design pay systems.

LO 4 Evaluate which jobs should be paid more.

LO 5 Estimate whether a pay system is consistent within an industry.

LO 6 Estimate whether a pay system is aligned with government laws.

LO 7 Design a compensation scorecard.

Compensation is a way to increase employee loyalty and to decrease the likelihood that employees will be hired away by competitors. It reflects a strategic move on the part of the company to show that its employees are the most important component for success.[1] So why focus on compensation to retain talent? Why not just hire employees who will be more loyal? Why not just improve the training programs or evaluation systems? The answer is simple: Compensation is directly linked to an employee's livelihood. Employees can receive stellar training, have copious growth opportunities, and be completely satisfied with their work and environment, but they will not show up to work if there is no paycheck in return.

9.1 What Is Compensation?

LO1 Explain the three main components of a person's compensation.

Compensation consists of three main components: (1) *direct compensation,* which encompasses employee wages and salaries, incentives, bonuses, and commissions; (2) *indirect compensation,* which comprises the many benefits supplied by employers; and (3) *nonfinancial compensation,* which includes employee recognition programs, rewarding jobs, organizational support, work environment, and flexible work hours to accommodate personal needs (see Figure 9.1).

Figure 9.1 Compensation Components

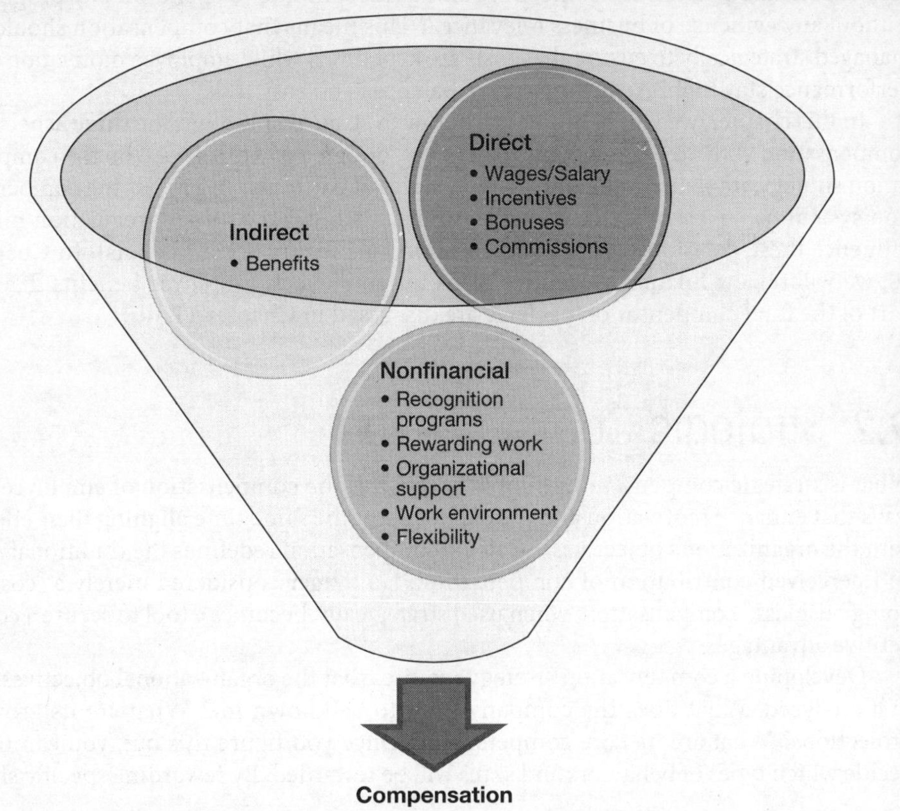

Figure 9.2 Compensation Alignment

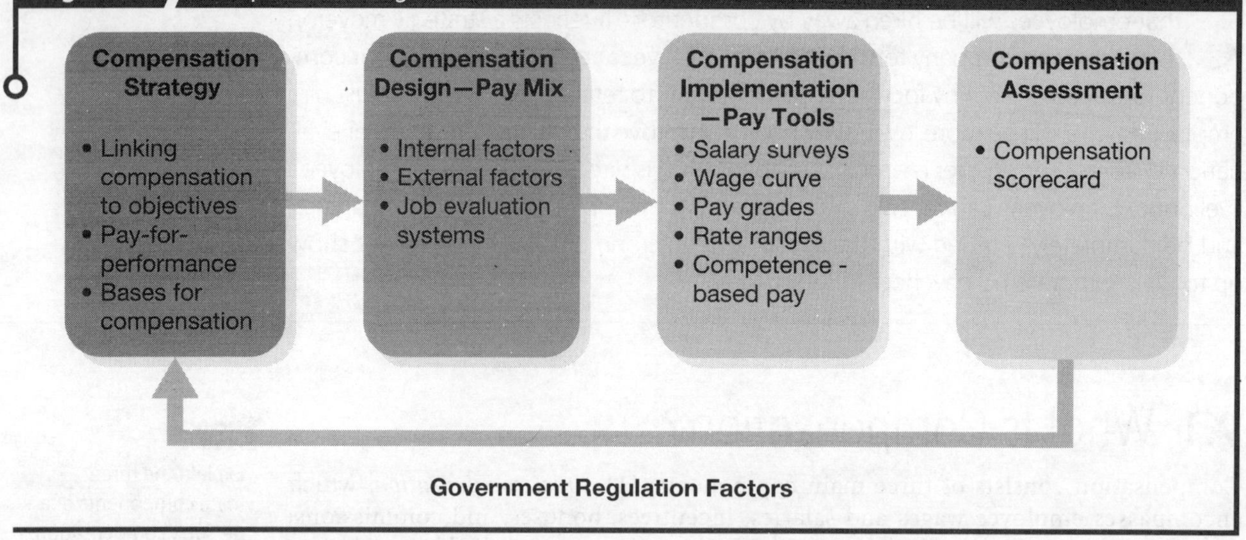

The way these three components of compensation are allocated sends a message to the employees about what management believes is important and the types of activities the organization encourages.[2] However, for an employer, compensation constitutes a sizable operating cost. Ravin Jesuthasan, a compensation specialist at Towers Perrin, notes, "Labor costs are a significant portion of expenses for any organization and a very substantial portion for some, but companies continue to spend on pay programs without any evidence of business relevance."[3] This means that compensation should be managed strategically to ensure that costs are kept down while employee motivation and performance stay high. Achieving such a balance is no easy task.

In this chapter, we will help you learn how to strategically align the three aspects of compensation with an organization's objectives, design a pay mix based on the compensation strategy, implement that mix using a series of pay tools, and assess the compensation system using a scorecard. We will also discuss how government regulation might influence these decisions about compensation (see Figure 9.2 for details). In Chapter 10, we will review financial incentive plans for employees. Employee benefits that are part of the total compensation package are discussed in Chapter 11.

9.2 Strategic Compensation

LO2

Distinguish between a strategic compensation program and a non-strategic compensation program.

What is strategic compensation? Simply stated, it is the compensation of employees in ways that enhance motivation and growth, while at the same time aligning their efforts with the organization's objectives. Strategic compensation redefines the traditional role and perceived contribution of compensation. No longer considered merely a "cost of doing business," compensation, when used strategically, becomes a tool to secure a competitive advantage.

Developing a compensation strategy requires that the organizational objectives are first analyzed. What does the company want to be known for? What are its growth projections? What are its core competencies? Once you figure this out, you can then decide which types of behaviors and skills will be rewarded. By rewarding specific skills and behaviors, you demonstrate that you are willing to pay for performance, rather than just for showing up to work. Then, as part of your strategy you need to decide on the compensation base most appropriate for the types of jobs in your company. For example, you might want to base the pay for a sales representative more on commissions and the pay for a manager more on a yearly salary.

Strategic compensation goes beyond determining the appropriate market rates to pay employees, although market rates are one element of compensation planning. Strategic compensation should also purposefully link compensation to the organization's mission and general business objectives. For example, while a company's decision to increase base pay for all its employees is a strategic move to be more competitive with market rates, companies should also recognize that base pay is not everything. For example, one product development manager stated, "I could be making much more than I'm getting at Google, but I chose Google because of the flexibility to grow and work on exciting new products . . . plus, where else can you get a chef making you breakfast, lunch, and dinner anytime you want?"[4] In this regard, Google has not only aligned its compensation strategy with the external market, but also aligned it with its desire to be a flexible and innovative company that capitalizes on the creativity of its people. Commenting on the importance of strategic compensation to organizational success, compensation specialists Gerald Ledford and Elizabeth Hawk note, "Companies throughout the economy have begun to rethink their compensation systems in search for competitive advantage."

Additionally, strategic compensation serves to mesh the monetary payments made to employees with other HR initiatives, such as recruitment, selection, training, retention, and performance appraisal. For example, starting pay can make a difference in whether someone will apply for the job. A compensation specialist speaking to one of the authors noted, "The linkage of pay levels to labor markets is a strategic policy issue because it serves to attract or retain valued employees while affecting the organization's relative payroll budget." For example, colleges such as University of Arkansas, Fayetteville; Bridgewater State University, Monroe College; and Brown Mackie College know that they cannot attract or retain qualified professors unless their pay strategy is linked to competitive market rates.

Many fast-food restaurants, such as Burger King and Blimpie's—traditionally low-wage employers—have needed to raise their starting wages to attract a sufficient number of job applicants to meet their staffing requirements. High pay rates create a large applicant pool from which organizations raise their selection standards and hire better-qualified employees. This, in turn, can reduce employer training costs. When employees perform at exceptional levels, their performance appraisals may justify an increased pay rate. In 2020, Taco Bell, another low-wage fast-food employer, decided to try paying its general managers $100,000 to see if greater pay would incentivize managers to devote themselves to the business and its success. This higher salary was also intended to decrease turnover, attract better applicants, and help Taco Bell remain competitive in the fast-food industry.[5]

For these reasons and others, an organization needs to develop a formal program to manage employee compensation. Step one of this program is to develop a compensation strategy that is linked to the organization's objectives.

9.2a Linking Compensation to Organizational Objectives

In a radical reconsideration of its compensation strategy, Zappos moved toward paying employees based on their skills rather than their position. This move emerged from the company's ongoing transition from a traditional management structure to a holacracy, a system where work is organized around roles rather than titles and employees report to teams instead of to individual supervisors. When this transition was completed, Zappos began using a system of badges to represent roles rather than job titles to determine compensation. Employees are free to earn badges as they wish, with a chance to earn more and plot a unique path in the company. The idea behind the badges is similar to leveling up in a video game— Zappos was hoping the badge-based compensation system would encourage employees to focus on building skills rather than climbing the corporate ladder, and to explore different aspects of the company rather than adhering to a strict hierarchy of roles. This idea is in line with some of Zappos' basic cultural values, such as pursuing growth and learning; being adventurous, creative, and open-minded; and embracing and driving change.[6]

The new compensation landscape requires that Zappos managers be more strategic about their compensation decisions. Managers must first and foremost understand the strategic objectives of the organization in relation to the industry in which it operates. Next, they need to move away from paying for a specific position or job title, and toward rewarding employees on the basis of their individual competencies or work contributions to the organizational objectives, similar to the Zappos pay strategy. In fact, studies have shown that pay for performance that is linked to organizational objectives is a primary component of most compensation systems.[7]

As part of linking compensation systems to company objectives, managers need to consider what kinds of compensation create value. To do so, managers must ask questions such as "How will this pay program help to retain and motivate valued employees?" and "Does the benefit or pay practice affect the administrative cost?" If a component of the compensation package—whether benefits, base pay, incentives, or something else—doesn't advance either the employee or the organization, it should be removed from the compensation program. It is not uncommon for organizations to establish very specific goals for linking their organizational objectives to their compensation program.[8]

a katz/Shutterstock.com

The #Fightfor15 movement started in 2012, advocating for a minimum wage of $15 per hour. Many states heeded this call, including California, New York, and Maryland. In January 2021, a $15 minimum wage bill was reintroduced into Congress.

Formalized compensation goals serve as guidelines for managers to ensure that wage and benefit policies achieve their intended purpose.

For instance, tech companies such as Google, Oracle, Twitter, LinkedIn, and MX have adopted what is known as an Objectives and Key Results (OKR) system to tie compensation to objectives. The OKR system, which originally came from Intel, offers a simple way to link compensation to performance. Here's how it works:

1. Set up an *objective* for your team and the individuals within the team. Your objective should be definitive and measurable. For instance, don't say, "I want my website to be faster." Say, "I want my website to load 30 percent quicker."
2. Set up a number of *key results* that are quantifiable that your team and each member of the team must complete by a specific time period.

To be successful at the OKR system, you need to have quarterly check-ins. The check-ins should be at the team level, at the manager level, and at the individual team member level. Collectively, they aim to keep the company on track toward its objectives. At Google, all OKRs are public, from Sundar Pichai on down. Posting the OKRs helps people know what everyone is working on.[9]

While not all companies tie OKRs to compensation, there are a few things you must remember if you adopt this system:

1. Clarify expectations. If you intend to reward contributors who go above and beyond to complete their objectives, you must first identify the criteria for outstanding performance versus just completing your OKRs on time.
2. Balance aspirational with operational. Some OKRs can be big stretch goals, while others can be more operational in nature. Once you've determined how many of the goals are stretch goals as opposed to routine responsibilities, you can determine a ratio and increase people's performance based on work that they did that was a stretch.
3. Consider additional performance factors. Hitting your objectives demonstrates hard work, but it does not cover everything that should be rewarded. For example, you may want to reward people for developing their skills, attitudes, and professionalism, as well as based on the difficulty of the OKRs.
4. Drive collaboration, not competition. One of the biggest dangers associated with rewarding people based on reaching their OKRs is that they may focus too much on their individual OKRs at the expense of those of a team or group. To avoid this problem, you might want to provide bonuses or pay raises based on a combination of individual-level and group-level OKRs.[10]

9.2b The Pay-for-Performance Standard

In a study from the Institute for Corporate Productivity, researchers found that nearly half of the high-performing organizations surveyed recognized that their long-term competitive advantage came from motivating and rewarding their top talent.[11] The **pay-for-performance standard** in these companies serves to raise productivity and lower labor costs in today's competitive economic environment—a relationship that will be discussed in more depth in Chapter 10.

pay-for-performance standard
A standard by which managers tie compensation to employee effort and performance.

The term "pay-for-performance" refers to a wide range of compensation options, including merit-based pay, bonuses, salary commissions, job and pay banding, team/group incentives, and various gainsharing programs. (Gainsharing plans are discussed in Chapter 10.) Each of these compensation systems seeks to differentiate between the pay of average performers and that of outstanding performers. For example, the Bridges to Excellence program seeks to increase performance of health care professionals by switching to a pay-for-performance system rather than using a traditional salary-based compensation strategy. This means doctors are rewarded based on quality of care instead of quantity, thus increasing motivation and performance. Today, more than half of health care organizations utilize some form of pay-for-performance scheme, and studies have even shown that pay-for-performance plans for physicians lead to improved performance, better patient health, and reduced cost of care.[12]

Motivating Employees through Compensation

Pay constitutes a quantitative measure of an employee's relative worth. For most employees, pay has a direct bearing not only on perceived fairness, but also on the status and recognition they may be able to achieve both on and off the job. Because pay represents a reward received in exchange for an employee's contributions, it is essential, according to the equity theory, that the pay be equitable in terms of those contributions. It is also essential that an employee's pay be equitable in terms of what other employees are receiving for their contributions.

Pay Equity

Simply defined, equity embraces the concept of fairness. Equity theory, also referred to as *distributive fairness,* is a motivation theory that explains how people respond to situations in which they feel they have received less (or more) than they deserve.[13]

pay equity
An employee's perception that compensation received is equal to the value of the work performed.

For employees, **pay equity** is achieved when the compensation received is equal to the value of the work performed. There are three kinds of pay equity:

1. External equity—people in similar jobs compare themselves to what others are making in different organizations.
2. Internal equity—people compare themselves to peers in different jobs in the same organization.
3. Individual equity—people compare themselves to others in their organization with the same job.

Research clearly demonstrates that employees' perceptions of pay equity, or inequity, can have dramatic effects on their motivation for both work behaviors and productivity. Managers must, therefore, develop strategic pay practices that are both internally and externally equitable.

Expectancy Theory and Pay

Another tool to help determine your compensation strategy is expectancy theory. The expectancy theory of motivation predicts that a person's level of motivation depends on the attractiveness of the rewards sought and the probability of obtaining those rewards.[14] In other words, employees should exert greater work effort if they have reason to expect that it will result in a reward that is valued.[15] To motivate this effort, the value of any monetary reward should be attractive. Employees also must believe that good performance is valued by their employer and will result in them receiving the expected reward.

Figure 9.3 shows the relationship between pay-for-performance and the expectancy theory of motivation. The model predicts, first, that high effort will lead to high performance (expectancy). For example, if employees believe they have the skills and abilities

Figure 9.3 Pay-for-Performance and Expectancy Theory

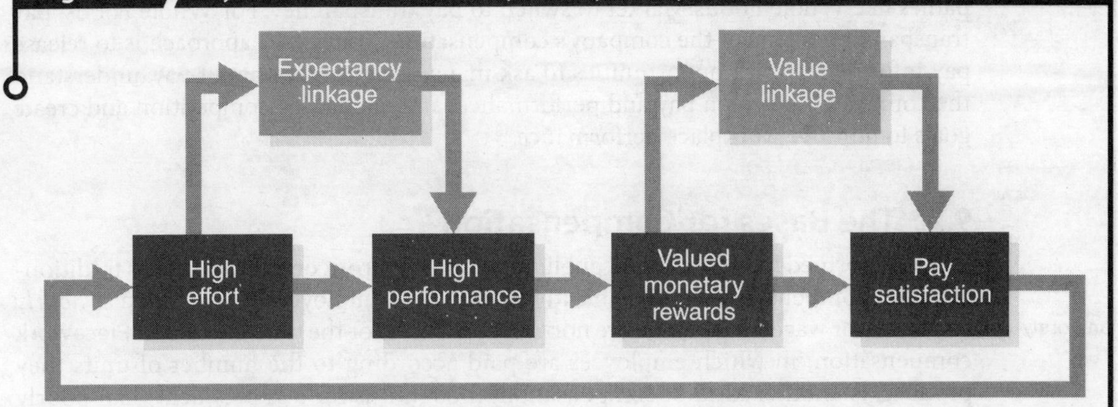

to perform their job and if they work hard (effort), then their performance will improve or be high. Second, high performance should result in rewards that are appreciated by the employee (valued). Elements of the compensation package are said to have *instrumentality* when an employee's high performance leads to monetary rewards that are valued. As previously stated, pay-for-performance leads to a feeling of pay satisfaction, and this feeling should reinforce one's high level of effort.

Thus, how employees view compensation can be an important factor in determining the motivational value of compensation. Furthermore, the effective communication of pay information together with an organizational environment that elicits employee trust in management can contribute to employees' having more accurate perceptions of their pay. The perceptions that employees develop concerning their pay are influenced by the accuracy of their knowledge and understanding of the compensation program's strategic objectives.

Pay Secrecy

Misperceptions by employees concerning the equity of their pay and its relationship to performance can be created by secrecy about the pay that others receive. Secrecy can generate distrust in the compensation system, reduce employee motivation, and inhibit organizational effectiveness. Despite these drawbacks, pay secrecy seems to be an accepted practice in many organizations. A U.S. survey found that about half of all workers say they work in a place where discussions of pay are "either explicitly prohibited or strongly discouraged."[16]

There are a few reasons why management might refuse to divulge salary information. Managers may want to reduce conflicts between people about their pay, especially if an employee makes less than someone they consider an inferior.[17] Secrecy can also cover up inequalities in the internal pay structure, such as in the epic employment discrimination case *Ledbetter v. Goodyear Tire & Rubber Co.* In that case, if she had been allowed to ask about other workers' pay, the plaintiff might have found out that she was being paid less than men doing the same job and remedied the problem much earlier.

Today, it is harder for managers to maintain pay secrecy among employees, given the widespread availability of salary survey data on Internet sites such as Glassdoor. Ready access to free online salary surveys gives employees an approximate idea of how their salary compares to others nationally or locally, which has been encouraging companies like Whole Foods Market to switch to pay transparency. For Whole Foods, pay transparency is part of the company's compensation strategy. Its approach is to release pay information with opportunities to ask managers questions about pay, understand the connection between pay and performance, and encourage competition and create goals to improve workplace performance.[18]

9.2c The Bases for Compensation

hourly work
Work paid on an hourly basis.

piecework
Work paid according to the number of units produced.

Work performed in most private, public, and not-for-profit organizations has traditionally been compensated based on **hourly work**. These employees are classified as *hourly employees*, or wage earners, and are normally paid only for the time they work. **Piecework** compensation, in which employees are paid according to the number of units they produce, is another kind of compensation, though it is far less prevalent than hourly work as a basis for paying employees.

Workers whose compensation is computed on the basis of weekly, biweekly, or monthly pay periods are classified as *salaried employees*. Salaried employees, unlike hourly employees, are generally paid the same amount for each pay period, even though they occasionally may work either more or fewer hours than the regular number of hours in a period. They also usually receive certain benefits not provided to hourly employees.

nonexempt employees
Employees covered by the overtime provisions of the Fair Labor Standards Act.

exempt employees
Employees not covered by the overtime provisions of the Fair Labor Standards Act.

Another basis for compensation centers on whether employees are classified as *nonexempt* or *exempt* under the Fair Labor Standards Act (FLSA).[19] **Nonexempt employees** are covered by the act and must be paid at a rate of one and a half times their *regular* pay rate for time worked in excess of 40 hours in their workweek. Most hourly workers employed in interstate commerce are considered nonexempt workers under the FLSA. Employees not covered by the overtime provision of the FLSA are classified as **exempt employees**. The U.S. Department of Labor (DOL) considers employees to be exempt when their primary duty includes "the exercise of discretion and independent judgment with respect to matters of significance."[20] This group includes managers, supervisors, and a large number of white-collar employees. Other classifications for exemption also exist, so employers should check the exact terms and conditions of exemption before classifying employees as either exempt or nonexempt. (see "Exemption from Overtime Provisions" in Figure 9.4).

To help in making these types of decisions, larger companies will often obtain the services of a compensation consultant. One study showed that about 86 percent of large U.S. companies use a compensation consultant to help them with their compensation strategy and pay mix.[21]

LO3

Determine how to design pay systems.

9.3 Compensation Design: The Pay Mix

An employee may ask, "How is my pay determined?" In practice, a combination of *internal* and *external* factors can directly or indirectly influence the rates at which employees are paid. The interaction of these factors constitutes the pay mix, as shown in Figure 9.5. For example, the pay rate for administrative assistants in a particular area might be $16.50 per hour. However, one employer may elect to pay its administrative assistants $19.25 per hour because of their excellent performance. The influence of government legislation on the pay mix is discussed later in this chapter.

Figure 9.4 Six Excluded Employee Groups

Category	Job Duties Required
Executive	Primary duty must be managing the enterprise, or managing a customarily recognized department or subdivision of the enterprise; must customarily and regularly direct the work of at least two or more other full-time employees or their equivalent; and must have the authority to hire or fire other employees, or the employee's suggestions and recommendations as to the hiring, firing, advancement, promotion, or any other change of status of other employees must be given particular weight.
Administrative	Primary duty must be the performance of office or nonmanual work directly related to the management or general business operations of the employer or the employer's customers; and includes the exercise of discretion and independent judgment with respect to matters of significance.
Learned	Primary duty must be the performance of work requiring advanced knowledge, defined as work that is predominantly intellectual in character, and which includes work requiring the consistent exercise of discretion and judgment; the advanced knowledge must be in a field of science or learning; and the advanced knowledge must be customarily acquired by a prolonged course of specialized intellectual instruction.
Creative	Primary duty must be the performance of work requiring invention, imagination, originality, or talent in a recognized field of artistic or creative endeavor.
Computer	Must be employed as a computer systems analyst, computer programmer, software engineer, or other similarly skilled worker in the computer field. The primary duty must consist of (1) the application of systems analysis techniques and procedures, including consulting with users, to determine hardware, software, or system functional specifications; (2) the design, development, documentation, analysis, creation, testing, or modification of computer systems or programs, including prototypes, based on and related to user or system design specifications; (3) the design, documentation, testing, creation, or modification of computer programs related to machine operating systems; or (4) a combination of the aforementioned duties, the performance of which requires the same level of skills.
Outside sales	Primary duty must be making sales (as defined in the FLSA), or obtaining orders or contracts for services or for the use of facilities for which a consideration will be paid by the client or customer; and must be customarily and regularly engaged away from the employer's place or places of business.
Highly compensated	The regulations contain a special rule for "highly compensated" workers who are paid total annual compensation of \$100,000 or more. A highly compensated employee is deemed exempt under Section 13(a)(1) if the employee earns total annual compensation of \$100,000 or more, which includes at least \$455 per week paid on a salary basis; the employee's primary duty includes performing office or nonmanual work; and the employee customarily and regularly performs at least one of the exempt duties or responsibilities of an exempt executive, administrative, or professional employee.
Other	Teachers are exempt if their primary duty is teaching, tutoring, instructing, or lecturing in the activity of imparting knowledge, and if they are employed and engaged in this activity as a teacher in an educational establishment. *Practice of law or medicine:* An employee holding a valid license or certificate permitting the practice of law or medicine is exempt if the employee is actually engaged in such a practice. An employee who holds the requisite academic degree for the general practice of medicine is also exempt if he or she is engaged in an internship or resident program for the profession.

Source: Adapted from Vicki M. Lambert, "The Top Three FLSA Violations and How to Avoid Them," ADP, 2008.

Figure 9.5 Factors Affecting the Pay Mix

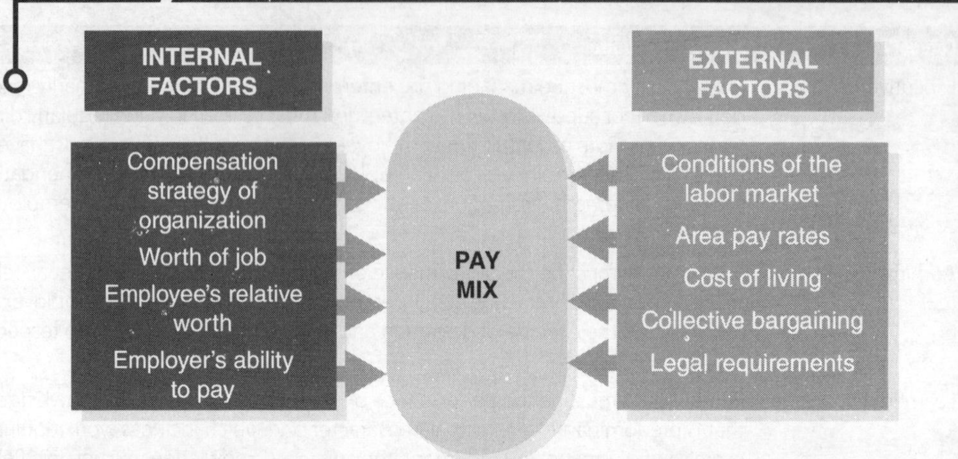

Jim West/Alamy

9.3a Internal Factors

The internal factors that influence pay rates include the organization's compensation strategy, the worth of a job, an employee's relative worth in meeting job requirements, and an employer's ability to pay.

Compensation Strategy

Highlights in HRM 1 illustrates the compensation strategies of two organizations, Tri Star Performance and Preventive Health Care. The strategy of Preventive Health Care is to be an industry pay leader, while Tri Star Performance seeks to be pay competitive. Both employers strive to promote a compensation policy that is internally fair.

Tri Star Performance and Preventive Health Care, like other employers, will establish numerous compensation objectives that affect the pay employees receive. At a minimum, both large and small employers should set pay policies reflecting (1) the internal wage relationship between jobs and skill levels; (2) the external competition, or an employer's pay position relative to what competitors are paying; (3) a policy of rewarding employee performance; and (4) administrative decisions concerning elements of the pay system such as overtime premiums, payment periods, and short- or long-term incentives.

Worth of a Job

Organizations without a formal compensation program generally base the worth of jobs on the subjective opinions of people who are familiar with those jobs. In such instances, pay rates may be influenced heavily by the labor market or, in the case of unionized employers, by collective bargaining. Organizations with formal compensation programs, however, are more likely to rely on a system of *job evaluation* to aid in rate determination. (This topic is covered later in this chapter in the discussion of pay structure.) Job evaluation can assist the organization in maintaining some degree of control over its pay structure, even when rates are subjected to collective bargaining. The use of job evaluation is widespread in both the public and the private sectors. The cities of Chicago and

1 Highlights in HRM

Comparison of Compensation Strategies

Compensation strategies and objectives can differ widely across large and small employers as well as across employers in the private and public sectors. Here are the compensation strategies at Tri Star Performance and Preventive Health Care.

Tri Star Performance

- Promote pay-for-performance practices
- Pay market-competitive compensation
- Achieve internal and external pay equity
- Achieve simplicity in compensation programs
- Strive for employee commitment and a collaborative work environment
- Promote gender fairness in pay and benefits
- Comply with all governmental compensation regulations
- Minimize increased fixed costs

Preventive Health Care

- Be a pay leader in the health care industry
- Promote open and understandable pay practices
- Ensure fair employee treatment
- Offer benefits promoting individual employee needs
- Offer compensation rewarding employee creativity and achievements
- Offer compensation to foster the strategic mission of the organization
- Obtain employee input when developing compensation practices
- Emphasize performance through variable pay and stock options

Miami use job evaluation in establishing pay structures, as do Google, Goldman Sachs, and GM. The jobs covered most frequently by job evaluation are clerical, technical, and various nonmanagerial groups, as well as managerial and top executive positions.

In today's competitive environment, compensation professionals believe that the worth of a job should be based on more than market prices or job evaluation programs. More specifically, a job's value should be based on *the total value* delivered to the organization. Some jobs may simply be more important to organizational success than others, regardless of how they are internally evaluated.[22] Valuing work properly not only enables organizations to price "important" jobs effectively, but also provides insights into how a job relates to the organization's objectives and can help the company attract and retain the right talent to drive organizational performance.[23]

Employee's Relative Worth

In both hourly and salary jobs, employee performance can be recognized and rewarded through promotion and with various incentive systems. (The incentive systems used most often are discussed in Chapter 10.) Superior performance can also be rewarded by granting merit raises on the basis of the person's job classification. If merit raises are to have their intended value, however, they must be determined by an effective performance appraisal system that differentiates between employees who deserve the raises and those who do not. Moreover, this system must rely on a visible and credible relationship between performance and any raises received. Unfortunately, too many so-called merit systems provide for raises to be granted automatically. As a result, employees tend to be rewarded more for merely being present than for being productive on the job.

Frances Roberts/Alamy Stock Photo

Several factors, such as the worth of the job and the worth of an employee for nonmanagerial jobs, are taken into consideration when determining how much an employee should be paid.

Employer's Ability to Pay

Pay levels are limited by earned profits and other financial resources available to employers. Competition and recessions can force prices down and reduce the income from which compensation payments are derived. In such situations, employers have little choice but to reduce wages and/or lay off employees or, even worse, to go out of business. This is especially true for small businesses. In a survey of small businesses about performance and financial decisions, half of the respondents stated that they didn't hire more employees because of high wages and benefit costs, and almost one-third cited the uncertain economic climate as the reason for their reluctance to increase their workforce.[24]

Furthermore, an organization's ability to pay is determined in part by the productivity of its employees. The level of productivity achieved in a company reflects not only employee performance, but also the amount of capital the organization has invested in labor-saving equipment. Generally, increases in capital investment reduce the number of employees required to perform the work and increase an employer's ability to provide higher pay for employees.

9.3b External Factors

The major external factors that influence pay rates include labor market conditions, area pay rates, the cost of living, collective bargaining if the employer is unionized, and legal requirements. The legal requirements related to compensation are discussed later in the chapter.

Labor Market Conditions

The labor market reflects the forces of supply and demand for qualified labor within an area. These forces, in turn, influence the pay rates required to recruit or retain competent employees. It must be recognized, however, that counterforces can reduce the full impact of supply and demand on the labor market. The economic power of unions, for example, may prevent employers from lowering pay rates even when unemployment is high among union members. Government regulations also may prevent an employer from paying employees at a market rate that is less than an established minimum.

Area Pay Rates

A formal pay structure should provide rates that are in line with those being paid by other employers for comparable jobs within the area. Data pertaining to area pay rates may be obtained from local wage surveys. Wage survey data may be obtained from a variety of sources, including the American Management Association, Administrative Management Society, U.S. Department of Labor, and Federal Reserve Banks. Smaller employers, such as the Woodsmith Corporation and Golden State Container, use government surveys to establish rates of pay for new and senior employees. Many organizations, such as the City of Atlanta, Delta Airlines, and Progress Energy, conduct their own surveys. Others engage in a cooperative exchange of wage information or rely on various professional associations for these data. The results of many wage data surveys can be obtained inexpensively—for less than $100—and are therefore available to all employers, regardless of size.

Small Business Application

Compensation for Small Businesses

Big businesses can woo job candidates by offering comprehensive compensation packages that include stock options, consistent pay raises, security, and sometimes even a Starbucks in the lobby. While small businesses cannot offer these perks, they can often customize pay packages to deal with employees' individual needs. For example, not having a complex and bureaucratic compensation system means a small company can more readily adjust its employees' wages to match those of the external market.

If the small business is private, there are many opportunities to attract and retain top talent by padding lower salaries with stock in the company. By offering shares of the company as a form of compensation, small, private companies can lure employees with the possibility of making larger sums of money in the future. Offering shares or options to buy shares as a form of compensation can be extremely attractive, as employees can make a lot of money when their young company finally goes public and its shares are sold on the stock market. For example, when Snap, owner of Snapchat, became a public company in 2017, hundreds of the employees who were with the company early on made enough to become instant millionaires.[26]

Following is a list of specific things small businesses can do to compete with the compensation packages of big business:

1. **Tailor the pay mix to individual employee needs and wants.** For example, one employee may place a higher value on bonus opportunities than base pay, while another may want the money the company would spend on health insurance to be paid in salary.
2. **Provide stock options in high-growth environments.** Potential employees will find the opportunity to be part of a high-growth company to be an exciting and potentially lucrative risk.
3. **Provide faster promotions.** Express how the smallness of your company allows people to move into new and exciting positions quickly, without the bureaucratic red tape found in big business.
4. **Provide frequent contact with top management.** Not being able to interact with and receive mentoring from top management is a major concern for young talent. Smaller companies are abie to offer more of these types of growth opportunities than their larger competitors can.
5. **Provide a greater sense of personal involvement.** One advantage of a small company is that it can treat its employees like family. In an age of depersonalized billion-dollar companies, a sense of belongingness, where you know the company cares about you, can go a long way in compensating for lower pay.

Wage surveys (discussed fully later in the chapter) serve the important function of ensuring external pay equity between the surveying organization and other organizations competing for labor in the surrounding labor market. Importantly, data from area wage surveys can be used to prevent the pay rates for a company's jobs from drifting too far above or below those of other employers in the region.

In addition, many companies are proactive in accessing external market pay rates by having their employees tell them when they get outside offers from competing firms. This information is often used by the current employer to ensure that it is paying market pay rates. For example, Netflix encourages its employees to get salary estimates from recruiters trying to poach them and then relay that information back to their boss. If the boss wants to keep an employee, then the boss is encouraged to give that employee a raise to make sure the employee doesn't leave for the competing firm. As Netflix CEO Reed Hastings points out, "It costs more to lose people and to recruit replacements than to overpay a little in the first place."[25]

Cost of Living

Because of inflation, compensation rates have to be adjusted upward periodically to help employees maintain their purchasing power. Employers make these changes by applying the **consumer price index (CPI)**. The CPI is a measure of the average change in prices over time in a fixed "market basket" of goods and services. The Bureau of Labor Statistics collects price information on a monthly basis and calculates the CPI for the nation as a whole and as various U.S. city averages.

consumer price index (CPI)
A measure of the average change in prices over time in a fixed "market basket" of goods and services.

CPI figures can have important consequences for organizational morale and productivity. Granting wages based largely on "cost-of-living" figures will not inspire higher

Employee wages may be based in part on how much money people in that area need for day-to-day living.

Stokkete/Shutterstock.com

employee performance because then pay is unrelated to individual performance and may cause valued employees to leave the organization. Furthermore, should cost-of-living increases be discontinued, managers can expect disgruntled employees who may be less likely to receive merit raises.

Employees who work under a union contract may receive wage increases through **escalator clauses** found in their labor agreement. These clauses provide for cost-of-living adjustments (COLA) in wages based on changes in the CPI. The most common adjustments are 1 percent per hour for each 0.3- or 0.4-point change in the CPI. COLAs are favored by unions during particularly high periods of inflation.

escalator clauses
Clauses in labor agreements that provide for quarterly cost-of-living adjustments in wages, basing the adjustments on changes in the consumer price index.

Collective Bargaining

One of the primary functions of a labor union is to bargain collectively over conditions of employment, the most important of which is compensation.[27] The union's goal in each new agreement is to achieve increases in **real wages**—wage increases larger than the increase in the CPI—thereby improving the purchasing power and standard of living of its members.

real wages
Wage increases larger than rises in the consumer price index; that is, the real earning power of wages.

9.4 Job Evaluation Systems

LO4 Evaluate which jobs should be paid more.

As we discussed earlier, one important component of the pay mix is the worth of the job. Organizations formally determine the value of jobs through the process of job evaluation. **Job evaluation** is the systematic process of determining the *relative* worth of jobs to establish which jobs should be paid more than others within the organization; in this way, it helps establish internal equity between various jobs. The relative worth of a job may be determined by comparing it with others within the organization or by comparing it with a scale that has been constructed for this purpose.

job evaluation
A systematic process of determining the relative worth of jobs to establish which jobs should be paid more than others within an organization.

Three traditional methods of comparison provide the basis for the principal systems of job evaluation:

1. Rank the value of jobs from highest to lowest.
2. Classify jobs so they can be benchmarked internally and externally.
3. Award points to each job based on its link to organizational objectives.

Such a job valuation system can prove effective not only in designing employee compensation, but also in determining whether a job can be contracted to a local or offshore company—a major decision that should always take into account the value of the job. For example, Delta Airlines brought back more than 4,500 customer service jobs from overseas to the United States. The company reported that "customers weren't happy with the service they got from operators based [overseas]." Even Walmart brought back more than 30 manufacturing plants from China, with the hope of creating more than 300,000 jobs in the United States.[28]

We will begin by discussing the simpler nonquantitative approaches to job evaluation and conclude by reviewing the more popular quantitative system and work evaluation. Regardless of the methodology used, it is important to remember that all job evaluation methods require varying degrees of managerial judgment. Also, those involved in evaluating jobs must consider the impact of the Americans with Disabilities Act on the process (see Chapter 3).

9.4a Job Ranking System

job ranking system
The simplest and oldest system of job evaluation, in which jobs are arrayed on the basis of their relative worth.

The simplest and oldest system of job evaluation is the **job ranking system**, which ranks jobs on the basis of their relative worth. Job ranking can be done by a single individual who is knowledgeable about all jobs or by a committee of management and employee representatives. In one technique, the ranker arranges cards, one for each job with a list of its duties and responsibilities, in order of the importance of the jobs.

The basic disadvantages of the job ranking system are that it does not measure precisely each job's worth, it can be used for just a small number of jobs, and it indicates only the relative importance of the job, not the differences in the degree of importance that may exist between jobs. Its simplicity, however, makes it ideal for small businesses.

9.4b Job Classification System

job classification system
A system of job evaluation in which jobs are classified and grouped according to a series of predetermined wage grades.

In a **job classification system**, jobs are classified and grouped according to a series of predetermined grades. Successive grades require increasing amounts of job responsibility, skill, knowledge, ability, or other factors selected to compare jobs. Job classification systems are widely used by municipal and state governments.[29] For example, Grade GS-1 from the federal government grade descriptions reads as follows:

> GS-1 includes those classes of positions the duties of which are to perform, under immediate supervision, with little or no latitude for the exercise of independent judgment (A) the simplest routine work in office, business, or fiscal operations; or (B) elementary work of a subordinate technical character in a professional, scientific, or technical field.

The descriptions of each of the job classes constitute the scale against which the specifications for the various jobs are compared. Managers then evaluate jobs by comparing job descriptions with the different wage grades to "slot" the job into the appropriate grade. While this system has the advantage of simplicity, the point system (discussed next) is more precise.

9.4c Point System

point system
A quantitative job evaluation procedure that determines the relative value of a job based on the total points assigned to it.

The **point system** is a quantitative job evaluation procedure that determines a job's relative value by calculating the total points assigned to it.[30] The principal advantage of this job evaluation approach is that it provides a more refined basis for making judgments than either the ranking or classification system, so it can produce results that are more valid and more difficult to manipulate. Point systems have been successfully used by high-visibility organizations such as Digital Equipment Company, MetLife, Johnson Wax, Prudential Financial, TransAmerica, and many other public and private organizations, large and small. Although point systems are rather complicated to establish, once in place they are relatively simple to understand and use.

A point system permits jobs to be evaluated quantitatively on the basis of factors or elements—commonly called *compensable factors*—that constitute the job.[31] For example, compensable factors might include fiscal accountability, leadership, teamwork, and project accountability. The number of compensable factors an organization uses depends on the nature of the organization and the jobs to be evaluated. Once selected, compensable factors are assigned weights according to their relative importance to the organization. For example, if responsibility is considered extremely important to the organization's objectives, it could be assigned a weight of 40 percent. Next, each factor is divided into a number of degrees. Degrees represent different levels of difficulty associated with each factor.

The Point Manual

The point system requires the use of a *point manual.* The point manual is, in effect, a handbook that contains a description of the compensable factors and the degrees to which these factors may exist within the jobs. The point value assigned to a job represents the sum of the numerical degree values of each compensable factor that the job possesses.

Using the Point Manual

Job evaluation under the point system is accomplished by comparing the job descriptions and job specifications, factor by factor, against the various factor-degree descriptions contained in the manual. Each factor within the job being evaluated is then assigned the number of points specified in the manual. When the points for each factor have been determined from the manual, the total point value for the job as a whole can be calculated.

9.4d Work Valuation

Work valuation is a relatively new job evaluation system championed as being able to meet the demands of a dynamic business environment. The cornerstone of this approach is that work is valued relative to the business goals of the organization rather than by an internally applied point-factor job evaluation system.[32] As one compensation specialist noted, "Valuing work properly enables organizations to not only price individual jobs effectively, but provides insight into how jobs relate to overall organizational goals and objectives and how roles ultimately contribute to organizational success."[33] Additionally, work valuation serves to direct compensation dollars to the type of work that is pivotal to organizational goals.

work valuation
A job evaluation system that seeks to measure a job's worth through its value to the organization.

9.4e Job Evaluation for Management Positions

Because management positions are more difficult to evaluate and involve certain demands not found in lower-level jobs, some organizations do not attempt to include them in their job evaluation programs for hourly employees. Rather, they employ either a standardized (purchased) program or customize a point method to fit their particular jobs. However, regardless of the approach adopted, point plans for executive and managerial employees operate similarly to those for other groups of employees.

One of the better-known standardized job evaluation programs for evaluating executive, managerial, and professional positions is the **Hay profile method**, developed by Edward N. Hay. In this approach, the three puzzle pieces that constitute the evaluation in the "profile" are knowledge (or knowhow), mental activity (or problem solving), and accountability (see Figure 9.6). These factors represent the most important aspects of all executive and managerial positions. The profile for each position is developed by determining the percentage value to be assigned to each of the three factors. Jobs are then ranked on the basis of each factor, and the point values that make up the profile are assigned to each job on the basis of the percentage-value level at which the job is ranked.

Hay profile method
A job evaluation technique using three factors—knowledge, mental activity, and accountability—to evaluate executive and managerial positions.

Figure 9.6 Hay Evaluation Profile

Hay Evaluation Profile

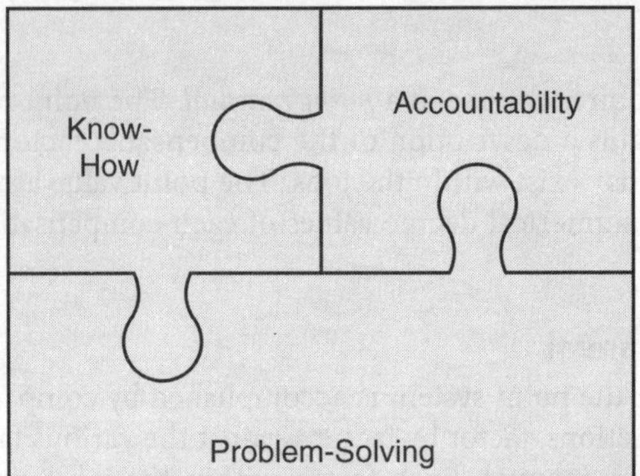

LO5

Estimate whether a pay system is consistent within an industry.

9.5 Compensation Implementation: Pay Tools

Compensation design systems, such as job evaluations, provide for internal equity and serve as the basis for pay rate determination. Nevertheless, they do not in themselves determine the pay rate. Instead, the evaluated worth of each job in terms of its rank, class, points, or monetary worth must be translated into an hourly, daily, weekly, or monthly pay rate. To appropriately implement compensation, specific tools must be incorporated into the pay system. The primary compensation tool used to set pay is the wage and salary survey.

9.5a Wage and Salary Surveys

wage and salary survey A survey of the wages paid to employees of other employers in the surveying organization's relevant labor market.

A **wage and salary survey** is a survey of the wages paid by employers in an organization's relevant labor market—local, regional, or national—depending on the job. The labor market is frequently defined as the area from which employers obtain certain types of workers. The labor market for office personnel would be local, whereas the labor market for engineers would be national and even global. It is the wage and salary survey that permits an organization to maintain external equity—that is, to pay its employees wages equivalent to the wages that similar employees earn in other establishments.

When job evaluation and wage survey data are used jointly, they increase the likelihood of achieving both internal and external equity. Although surveys are conducted primarily to gather competitive wage data, they can also collect information on employee benefits or organizational pay practices (such as overtime rates or shift differentials).

Collecting Survey Data

Conducting surveys and collecting information may take both time and resources, but the resulting survey data let HR professionals stay aware of the employment market and help the organization continue to attract and retain top talent.[34] Many organizations conduct their own wage and salary surveys, and a variety of "preconducted" pay

2 Highlights in HRM

Bureau of Labor Statistics National Compensation Survey

NCS data are used by managers and compensation specialists in large and small organizations to answer such questions as the following:

- How much must I pay accountants in Atlanta, Georgia?
- Is a 3 percent benefits increase comparable to that of other employers in the manufacturing industry?
- Is vision coverage a prevalent benefit among large employers in the Northeast?
- How have wage costs changed over the past year?

How the NCS Works

The National Compensation Survey is an area-based survey. Wage and benefit data are collected from a predetermined set of 154 metropolitan and nonmetropolitan areas throughout the 50 states and the District of Columbia to represent the United States. Compensation information is collected from such diverse locations as Knoxville, Tennessee; Pittsburgh, Pennsylvania; Reno, Nevada; and Richland–Kennewick–Pasco, Washington. All areas are selected to produce regional estimates for nine broad geographic divisions and four broad regions.

Within each area, a scientific sample of establishments represents all area establishments. An "establishment" is a single physical location, such as a plant, warehouse, corporate office, or retail outlet. State and local government offices are also included in the survey.

Once an establishment has been chosen for inclusion in the survey, a BLS economist selects occupations within that establishment to represent all occupations in the establishment. The BLS limits the selection to a small number of occupations to reduce the survey burden for employers. Data are collected for all incumbents in a selected occupation.

The selected occupations are then classified based on the Census Bureau's occupation classification system. The census classification categorizes approximately 450 individual occupations into 10 major groupings such as sales, professional specialty, technical and machine operators, assemblers, and inspectors. For the occupations selected, wage and benefit data are collected. Items included in the collection of wages are time-based payments, piece rates, commissions, hazard pay, and other items directly related to the work being performed. A variety of benefit data are collected, including paid vacations, paid holidays, paid sick leave, shift differentials, and nonproduction bonuses.

surveys are available to satisfy the requirements of most public and not-for-profit or private employers. In the United States, the Bureau of Labor Statistics (BLS) is a major publisher of wage and salary data. The BLS publishes data from the National Compensation Survey (NCS), a statistically valid and comprehensive compensation program of wage, salary, and benefit information[35] (see Highlights in HRM 2).

Salary Surveys

Wage and benefits survey data can be found on numerous websites. The National Compensation Survey, mentioned previously, is an example. Also readily available are commercial products such as those offered at Salary.com or Glassdoor. Other, less well-known sources of salary information include Payscale, Buffer, and Salary List. Buffer is a website that offers not only salary data, but also free resources that anyone can access and use. It provides a transparent salary calculator, offers examples and explanations of job levels, and shows users how to create a career framework. While relatively few resources for finding salary data once existed, now there are many sites and options available for companies to discover how to pay their employees.

Let's look at Glassdoor as an example. In the past, Glassdoor provided a safe platform where people could anonymously share information about their pay and company in return for free information about other companies and salaries. Glassdoor's current

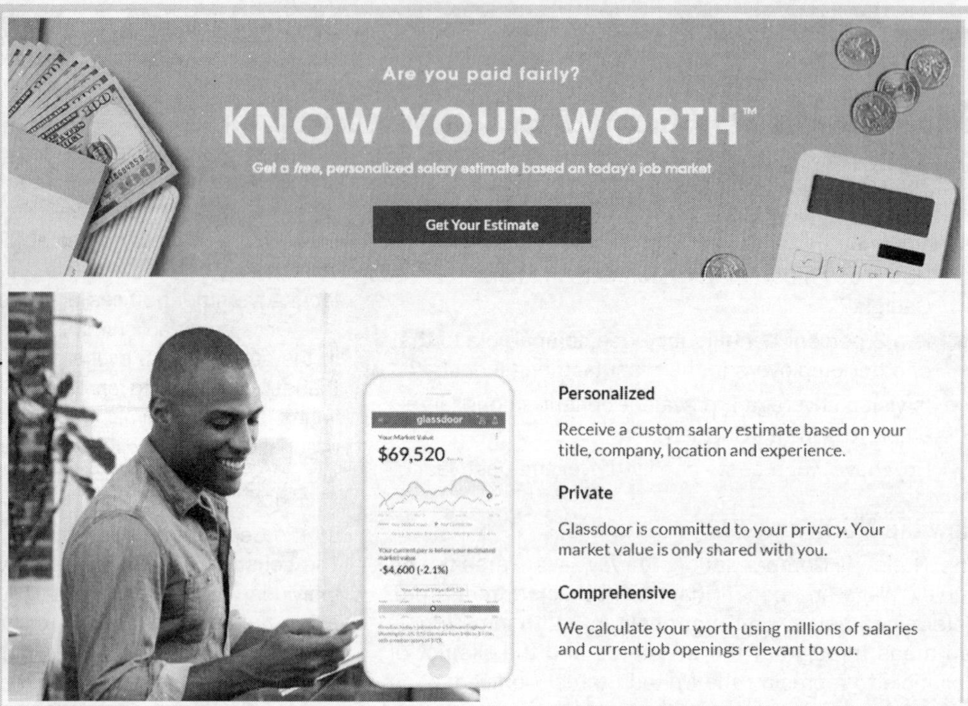

Glassdoor collects salary data from employees who anonymously volunteer salary information and comments about employers in return for access to salary and company information about other companies.

Source: Glassdoor.com

platform enables users to view salary information, company reviews, and job postings. You can even identify the top-paying companies and target your search accordingly. For example, in 2019 Glassdoor listed the 25 highest-paying companies in the United States. Looks like health care, technology, and consulting are all the best options . . . if you're interested in high pay.

1. Palo Alto Networks
   - Median total compensation: $170,929
   - Industry: Technology
2. NVIDIA
   - Median total compensation: $170,068
   - Industry: Health care
3. Twitter
   - Median total compensation: $162,852
   - Industry: Technology
4. Gilead Sciences
   - Median total compensation: $162,210
   - Industry: Biotechnology and pharmaceuticals
5. Google
   - Median total compensation: $161,254
   - Industry: Technology
6. VMware
   - Median total compensation: $158,063
   - Industry: Technology
7. LinkedIn
   - Median total compensation: $157,402
   - Industry: Technology
8. Facebook
   - Median total compensation: $152,962
   - Industry: Technology

9. Salesforce
   - Median total compensation: $150,379
   - Industry: Technology
10. Microsoft
   - Median total compensation: $148,068
   - Industry: Technology
11. Juniper Networks
   - Median total compensation: $146,781
   - Industry: Technology
12. ServiceNow
   - Median total compensation: $145,529
   - Industry: Technology
13. McKinsey & Company
   - Median total compensation: $145,367
   - Industry: Consulting
14. PlayStation
   - Median total compensation: $143,229
   - Industry: Technology
15. Autodesk
   - Median total compensation: $142,083
   - Industry: Technology
16. Workday
   - Median total compensation $141,893
   - Industry: Technology
17. Synopsys
   - Median total compensation: $140,577
   - Industry: Technology
18. eBay
   - Median total compensation: $140,056
   - Industry: Technology
19. BNP Paribas
   - Median total compensation: $140,056
   - Industry: Banking
20. Qualcomm
   - Median total compensation: $139,754
   - Industry: Technology
21. Tableau Software
   - Median total compensation: $138,043
   - Industry: Technology
22. Western Digital
   - Median total compensation: $137,527
   - Industry: Technology
23. Veritas
   - Median total compensation: $137,244
   - Industry: Technology
24. Adobe
   - Median total compensation: $135,027
   - Industry: Technology
25. Genentech
   - Median total compensation: $133,605
   - Industry: Technology[36]

9.5b The Wage Curve

The relationship between the relative worth of jobs and their pay rates can be represented by means of a **wage curve**. This curve may indicate the rates currently paid for jobs within an organization, new rates resulting from job evaluation, or rates for similar jobs currently being paid by other organizations within the labor market. A curve may

wage curve
A curve in a scattergram representing the relationship between relative worth of jobs and pay rates.

be constructed graphically by preparing a scattergram consisting of a series of dots that represent the current pay rates. As shown in Figure 9.7, a freehand curve is then drawn through the cluster of dots in such a manner as to leave approximately an equal number of dots above and below the curve. The wage curve can be relatively straight or curved. This curve can then be used to determine the relationship between the value of a job and its pay rate at any given point on the line.

9.5c Pay Grades

pay grades
Groups of jobs within a particular class that are paid the same rate.

From an administrative standpoint, it is generally preferable to group jobs into **pay grades** and to pay all jobs within a particular grade the same rate or rate range. When the classification system is used for job evaluation, jobs are grouped into grades as part of the evaluation process. When the point system is used, however, pay grades must be established at selected intervals that represent either the point or the evaluated monetary value of these jobs. The graph in Figure 9.8 illustrates a series of pay grades designated along the horizontal axis at 50-point intervals.

The grades within a pay structure may vary in number.[37] The number is determined by such factors as the slope of the wage curve, the number and distribution of the jobs within the structure, and the organization's wage administration and promotion policies. The number or grades utilized should be sufficient to permit difficulty levels to be distinguished but not so great as to make the distinction between two adjoining grades insignificant.

Figure 9.7 Freehand Wage Curve

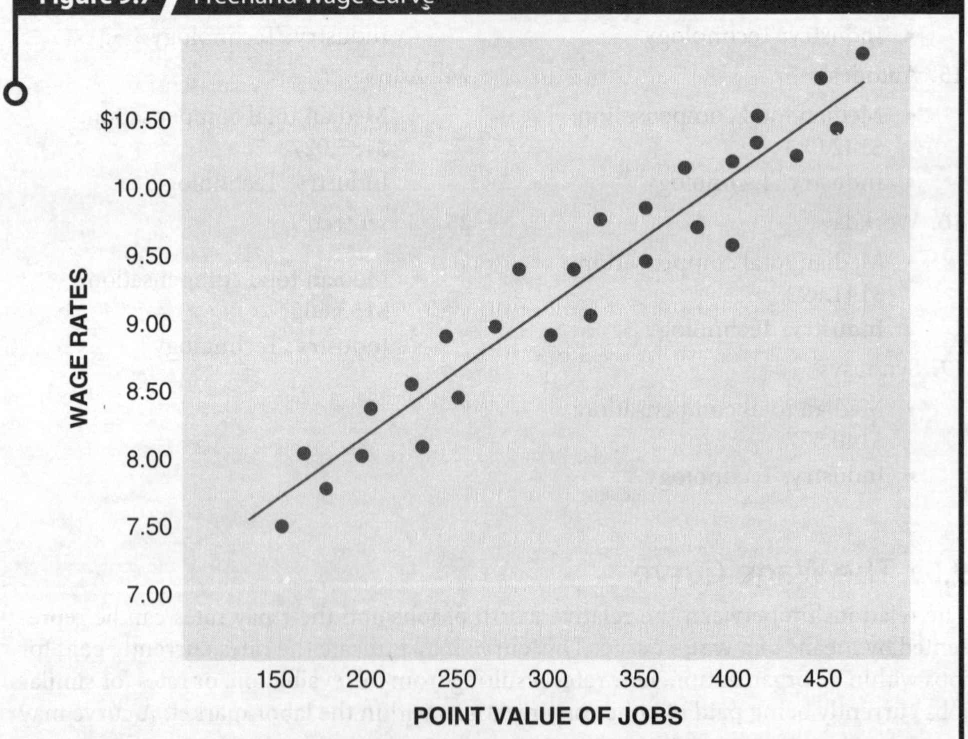

9.5d Rate Ranges

Although a single rate may be created for each pay grade, as shown in Figure 9.8, a more common practice is to provide a range of rates for each pay grade. The rate ranges may be the same for each grade or proportionately greater for each successive grade, as shown in Figure 9.9. Rate ranges constructed on the latter basis provide a greater incentive for employees to accept a promotion to a job in a higher grade.

Rate ranges generally are divided into a series of steps that permit employees to receive increases up to the maximum rate for the range on the basis of merit or seniority, or a combination of the two. In most salary structures, the ranges of adjoining pay grades overlap. Such an overlap permits an employee with greater experience to earn as much as or more than a person with less experience in the next higher job classification.

The final step in setting up a wage structure is to determine the appropriate pay grade into which each job should be placed on the basis of its evaluated worth. Traditionally, this worth is determined on the basis of job requirements without regard to the performance of the person in that job. Under this system, the performance of those employees who exceed the requirements of a job may be acknowledged by merit increases within the grade range or by promotion to a job in the next higher pay grade.[38]

Figure 9.8 Single Rate Structure

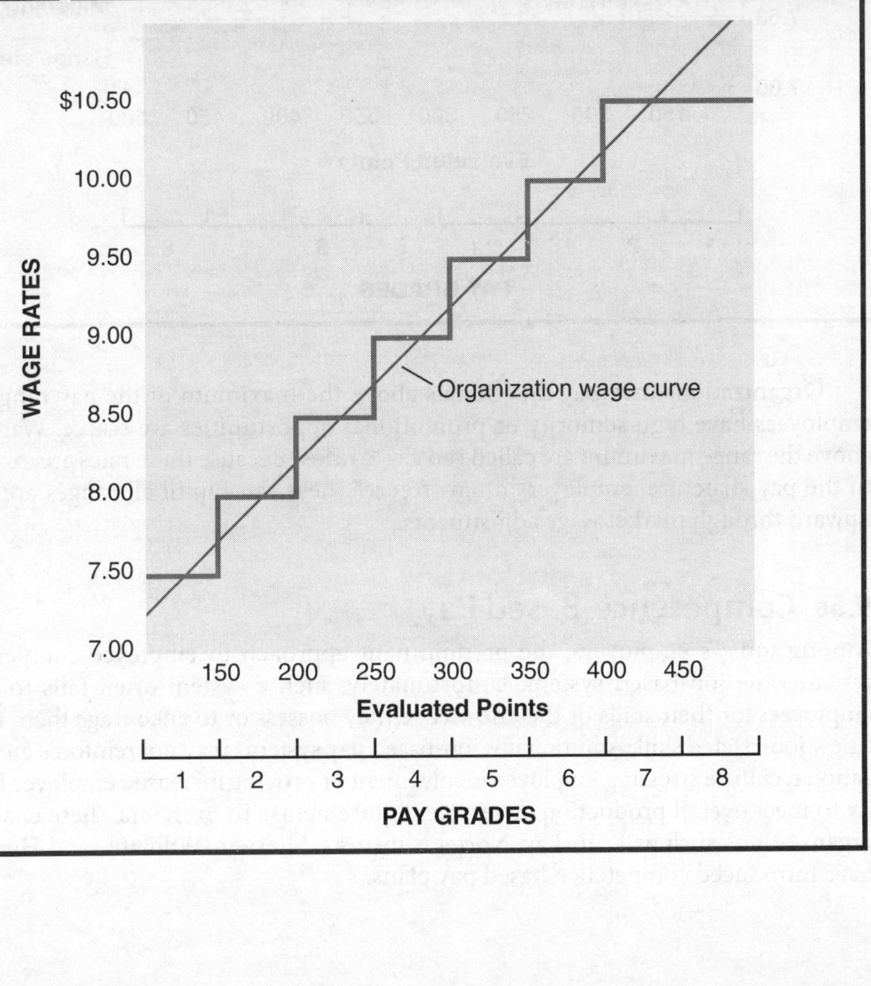

Figure 9.9 Rate Range Structure

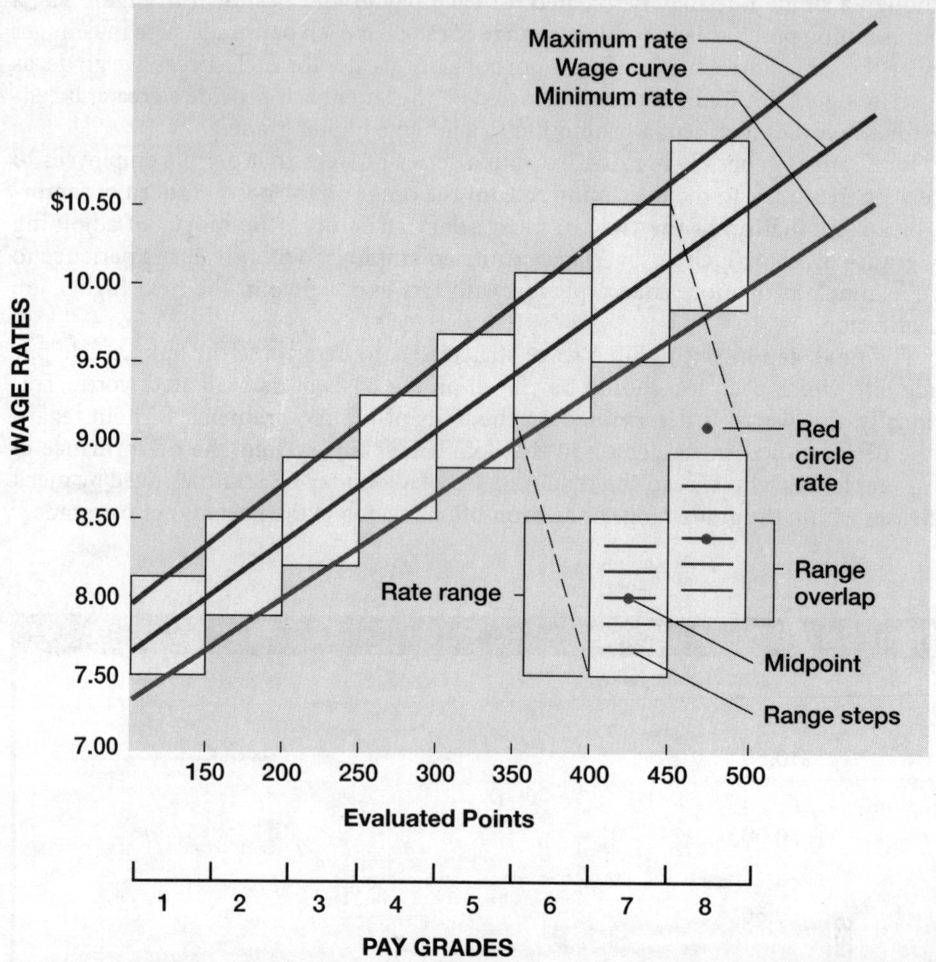

red circle rates
Payment rates above the maximum of the pay range.

Organizations may pay individuals above the maximum of the pay range when employees have high seniority or promotional opportunities are scarce. Wages paid above the range maximum are called **red circle rates**. Because these rates are exceptions to the pay structure, employers often "freeze" these rates until all ranges are shifted upward through market wage adjustments.

9.5e Competence-Based Pay

Among today's employers, the predominant approach to employee compensation remains the job-based system. Unfortunately, such a system often fails to reward employees for their skills or the knowledge they possess or to encourage them to learn a new job-related skill. Additionally, job-based pay systems may not reinforce an organizational culture stressing employee involvement or provide increased employee flexibility to meet overall production or service requirements. To overcome these challenges, organizations such as Frito-Lay, Nortel Networks, Sherwin-Williams, and Honeywell have introduced competence-based pay plans.

Competence-based pay, also referred to as skill-based pay or knowledge-based pay, compensates employees for the different skills or increased knowledge they possess rather than for the job they hold in a designated job category.[39] Regardless of the name, these pay plans encourage employees to earn higher base wages by learning and performing a wider variety of skills (or jobs) or by developing an array of competencies that can be applied to a variety of organizational requirements. For example, in a manufacturing setting, new tasks might include various assembly activities carried out in a particular production system or a variety of maintenance functions. Within service organizations, employees might acquire new knowledge related to advanced computer systems or accounting procedures. Organizations will grant an increase in pay after each skill or knowledge has been mastered and can be demonstrated according to a predetermined standard.

competence-based pay
Pay based on an employee's skill level, variety of skills possessed, or increased job knowledge.

Competence-based pay systems represent a fundamental change in the attitude of management regarding how work should be organized and how employees should be paid for their work efforts. The most frequently cited benefits of competence-based pay include greater productivity, increased employee learning and commitment to work, improved staffing flexibility to meet production or service demands, and reduced effects of absenteeism and turnover, because managers can assign employees where and when needed. Competence-based pay also encourages employees to seek out training when new or updated skills are needed by an organization.

Unfortunately, competence-based plans bring some long-term difficulties. Some plans limit the amount of compensation employees can earn, regardless of the new skills or competencies they acquire. Thus, after achieving the top wage, employees may be reluctant to continue their educational training. Perhaps the greatest challenge in paying individuals for their skills, knowledge, and competencies is developing appropriate measures. It is difficult to write specific knowledge and skill descriptions for jobs that employees perform and then establish accurate measures of acquired skills or knowledge.

Broadbanding

Organizations that adopt a competency-based or skill-based pay system frequently use broadbanding to structure their compensation payments to employees. **Broadbanding** simply collapses many traditional salary grades into a few wide salary bands. These bands may include midpoints and quartiles, or they may have extremely wide salary ranges or no ranges at all. Banding encourages lateral skill building while addressing the need to pay employees for performing multiple jobs with different skill level requirements. Additionally, broadbands help eliminate the obsession with grades and, instead, encourage employees to move to jobs in which they can develop in their careers and add value to the organization. Paying employees through broadbands enables organizations to consider job responsibilities, individual skills and competencies, and career mobility patterns when assigning employees to bands.[40] Overall, such pay tools help the organization more effectively implement a compensation strategy.

broadbanding
A pay system that collapses many traditional salary grades into a few wide salary bands.

LO6

Estimate whether a pay system is aligned with government laws.

9.6 Government Regulation of Compensation

In addition to reflecting data from salary surveys and competence-based assessments, compensation implementation is subject to state and federal regulations. A majority of states have established minimum wage laws or wage boards that fix minimum wage rates on an industry-by-industry basis. When an employee is subject to both the state and federal minimum wage laws, that person is entitled to the higher of the two minimum wages (see Highlights in HRM 3 for state minimum wage laws and Highlights in HRM 4 for worldwide minimum wages). Most states also regulate hours of work and overtime payments.

Wage and Hour Provisions

It's important to understand the differences between a minimum wage, overtime, and compensatory time and to be familiar with the details of each.

Minimum wage rate	• The minimum wage prescribed by federal law has been raised many times, from an original figure of $0.25 per hour to $7.25 per hour on July 24, 2009. This is where the minimum wage stands today (see Highlights in HRM 5 for the federal minimum wage poster that employers are required to display). • Assessed every few years and adjusted for cost-of-living factors (e.g., consumer price index). • Applies to the actual earning rate *before* any added overtime premiums.
Overtime wage rate	• 1.5 times the base rate must be paid for all hours worked over 40 during a given week. • Base wage rate must include incentive payments or bonuses received during that period. • Employees paid on a piecework basis must receive a premium for overtime work.
Compensatory time (comp time)	• When employees are given time off in return for overtime work. • Granted at 1.5 times the number of hours worked as overtime.

Note: The FLSA does not require severance pay, sick leave, vacation, or holidays.

Under the FLSA, an employer must pay an employee for whatever work the employer "suffers or permits" the employee to perform, even if the work is done away from the workplace and even if it is not specifically expected or requested. This condition could likely occur when employees work away from headquarters and are unsupervised or when they telecommute on a frequent basis.

Minimum Wage and Pay Compression

pay rate compression
Compression of pay between new and experienced employees caused by the higher starting salaries of new employees; also the differential in pay between hourly workers and their managers.

In 2021, members of the U.S. Congress reintroduced a bill to gradually raise the minimum wage to $15 over a period of four years.[41] Such legislation forces the consideration of both sides of the minimum wage argument. Some argue that increases in the minimum wage may lead to pay compression. **Pay rate compression** means that differences between low- and high-paying jobs decrease. It occurs when less experienced, often junior employees, earn as much or more than experienced employees due to high starting salaries for new employees. It also occurs when the minimum wage requirements push up salaries for lower-tier jobs but not for higher-tier jobs. Both lower- and

Minimum Wage Laws in the States

Note: Where federal and state law have different minimum wage rates, the higher standard applies.

2017 MINIMUM WAGE BY STATE

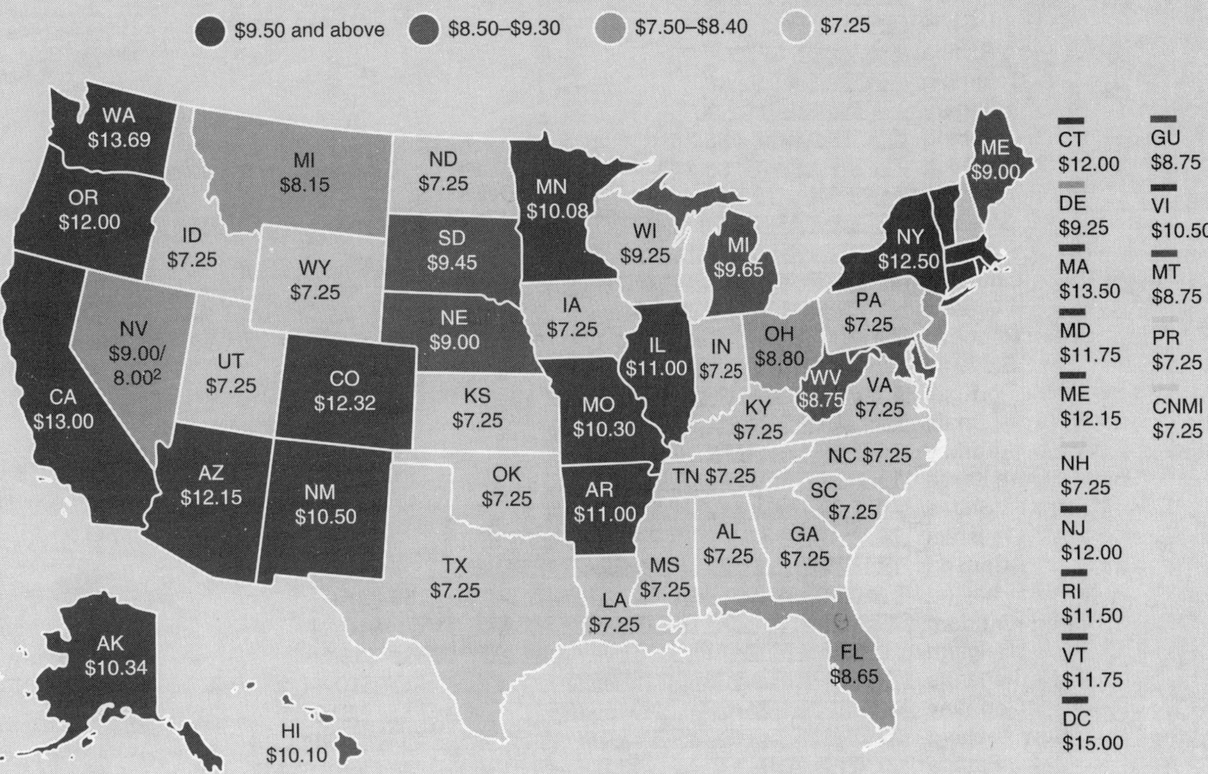

higher-paid jobs can experience pay compression. For example, if the starting hourly wage for preschool teachers is $10.00 and that for preschool teacher aides is $7.25, a minimum wage increase to $10.00 would bring both groups of employees to essentially the same starting wage (the U.S. median salary for preschool teachers is actually $13.00, while the bottom 10 percent make $9.78).[42]

The reasons why pay compression occurs are usually more market based than government based. For example, the scarcity of qualified applicants in computer science, engineering, and other professional and technical fields has forced starting salaries for these occupations to be at or near the salaries paid employees with considerable experience and seniority. Pay compression can also occur when hourly employees, at the top of their pay grades, earn only slightly less than managers at the low end of their pay grades.

4 Highlights in HRM

Worldwide Minimum Wages

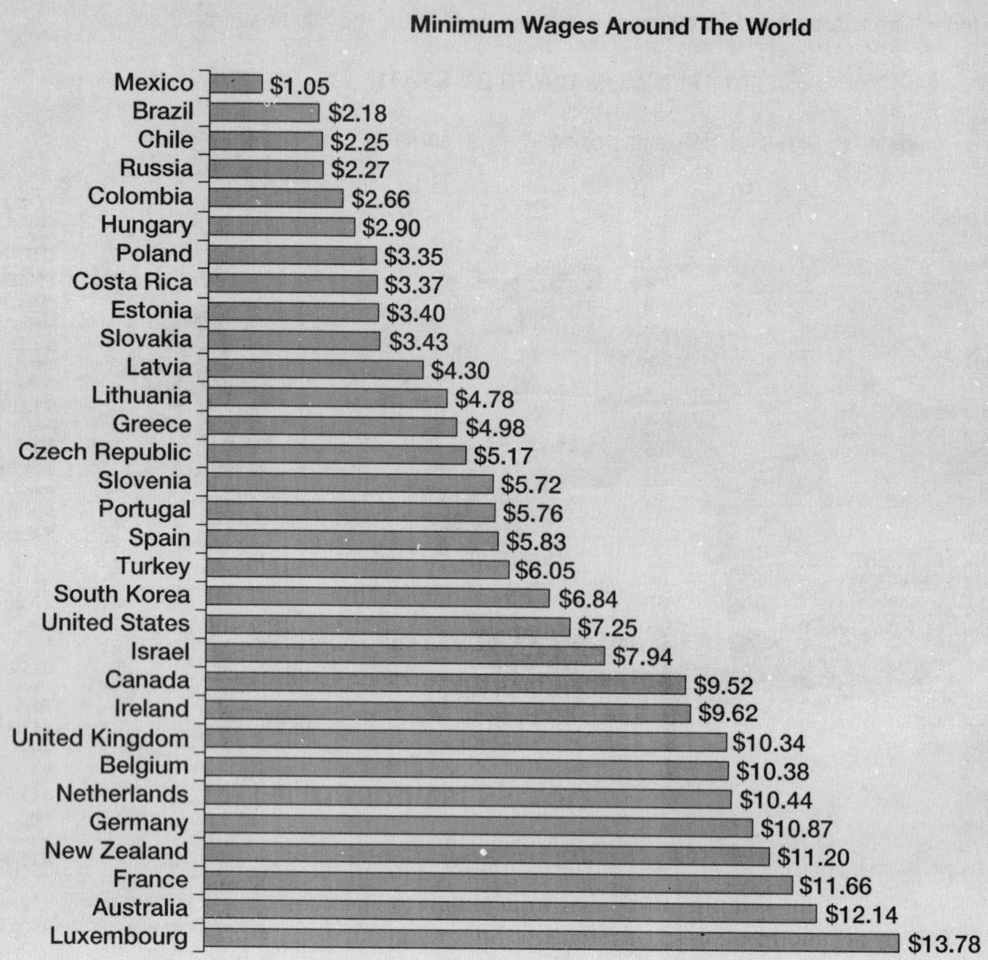

Identifying pay rate compression and its causes is far simpler than implementing organizational policies to alleviate its effects. Organizations wishing to minimize this problem may incorporate the following ideas into their pay policies:

- Reward high-performance and merit-worthy employees with large pay increases.
- Design the pay structure to allow a wide spread between hourly and supervisory employees.
- Prepare high-performing employees for promotions to jobs with higher salary levels.
- Provide equity adjustments for selected employees who are hardest hit by pay compression.[43]

The Federal Wage Poster

EMPLOYEE RIGHTS
UNDER THE FAIR LABOR STANDARDS ACT

THE UNITED STATES DEPARTMENT OF LABOR WAGE AND HOUR DIVISION

FEDERAL MINIMUM WAGE

$5.85 PER HOUR — BEGINNING JULY 24, 2007

$6.55 PER HOUR — BEGINNING JULY 24, 2008

$7.25 PER HOUR — BEGINNING JULY 24, 2009

OVERTIME PAY At least $1\frac{1}{2}$ times your regular rate of pay for all hours worked over 40 in a workweek.

YOUTH EMPLOYMENT An employee must be at least **16** years old to work in most non-farm jobs and at least **18** to work in non-farm jobs declared hazardous by the Secretary of Labor.

Youths **14** and **15** years old may work outside school hours in various non-manufacturing, non-mining, non-hazardous jobs under the following conditions:

No more than

- **3** hours on a school day or **18** hours in a school week;
- **8** hours on a non-school day or **40** hours in a non-school week.

Also, work may not begin before **7 a.m.** or end after **7 p.m.**, except from June 1 through Labor Day, when evening hours are extended to **9 p.m.** Different rules apply in agricultural employment. For more information, visit the YouthRules! Web site at **www.youthrules.dol.gov.**

TIP CREDIT Employers of "tipped employees" must pay a cash wage of at least $2.13 per hour if they claim a tip credit against their minimum wage obligation. If an employee's tips combined with the employer's cash wage of at least $2.13 per hour do not equal the minimum hourly wage, the employer must make up the difference. Certain other conditions must also be met.

ENFORCEMENT The Department of Labor may recover back wages either administratively or through court action, for the employees that have been underpaid in violation of the law. Violations may result in civil or criminal action.

Civil money penalties of up to $11,000 per violation may be assessed against employers who violate the youth employment provisions of the law and up to $1,100 per violation against employers who willfully or repeatedly violate the minimum wage or overtime pay provisions. This law prohibits discriminating against or discharging workers who file a complaint or participate in any proceedings under the Act.

ADDITIONAL INFORMATION

- Certain occupations and establishments are exempt from the minimum wage and/or overtime pay provisions.
- Special provisions apply to workers in American Samoa and the Commonwealth of the Northern Mariana Islands.
- Some state laws provide greater employee protections; employers must comply with both.
- The law requires employers to display this poster where employees can readily see it.
- Employees under 20 years of age may be paid $4.25 per hour during their first 90 consecutive calendar days of employment with an employer.
- Certain full-time students, student learners, apprentices, and workers with disabilities may be paid less than the minimum wage under special certificates issued by the Department of Labor.

For additional information:

1-866-4-USWAGE

(1-866-487-9243) TTY: 1-877-889-5627

WHD U.S. Wage and Hour Division

WWW.WAGEHOUR.DOL.GOV

U.S. Department of Labor | Employment Standards Administration | Wage and Hour Division

WHD Publication 1088 (Revised June 2007)

Since pay rate compression is largely an internal pay equity concern, if not addressed fairly, it can cause low employee morale, leading to issues of reduced employee performance, hard feelings between employees, higher absenteeism and turnover, and even delinquent behavior such as employee theft.

Child Labor Provisions

Another concern with the minimum wage is that the "floor" it imposes makes it more difficult for high school students and young adults to find jobs. Many employers who might otherwise be willing to hire these individuals are unwilling to pay them the same rate as adults because of their lack of experience.

Age 16 is the basic minimum age required for employment. At age 16, youth can be employed for unlimited hours in any occupation that is not declared hazardous by the U.S. Secretary of Labor. For example, a 16-year-old could not work as a coal miner, but she could work at the local snow-cone shack. Children ages 14 and 15 can also be hired in specified jobs outside of school hours for limited periods of time each day and each week. Employees younger than age 20 can be paid $4.25 per hour during their first 90 calendar days with an employer. Such pay is considered training pay. Finally, employers of "tipped employees" must pay at least $2.13 per hour if they claim a tip credit against their minimum wage obligations. If an employee's tips combined with the employer's pay of at least $2.13 do not equal the minimum hourly wage, the employer must make up the difference.[44]

Pay Equity Provisions

Laws exist to protect employees against pay discrimination, yet pay discrimination remains a persistent problem among companies today. For example, in 2017 Wells Fargo paid $35.5 million as part of a settlement of a putative class-action lawsuit that alleged discrimination against African American advisors. A group of African American brokers and trainees alleged that they had been excluded from certain business opportunities and higher-up teams because of race. In addition to the monetary settlement, Wells Fargo agreed to set up resources to focus on recruiting more diverse trainees and hire from a more diverse applicant pool, along with other changes to its management training.[45] Figure 9.10 further examines pay inequality based on race and gender.

Figure 9.10 Race and Gender Pay Inequality

Race and Ethnicity	Male Weekly Income	Female Weekly Income	Women's Earnings as % of Male Earnings
All races	1,082	891	82.4 %
White alone, not Hispanic	1,110	905	81.5%
Black or African American only	830	764	92 %
Asian only	1,447	1,143	79 %
Hispanic or Latino (any race)	797	705	88.5%

Source: Bureau of Labor Statistics, Current Population Survey, "Table 37: Median Weekly Earnings of Full-Time Wage and Salary Workers by Selected Characteristics, 2020," Annual Averages (2021), https://www.bls.gov/cps/cpsaat37.htm.

9.7 Compensation Assessment

LO7 Design a compensation scorecard.

Getting your compensation system up and running is not the end of your tasks as a manager. Once it has been implemented, assessing the effectiveness of your compensation system is vitally important to linking compensation with strategy. With the right measures, you can (1) help the company detect potential compensation problems, (2) make compensation decisions more transparent, and (3) improve the alignment of compensation decisions with organizational objectives. The **compensation scorecard** collects and displays the results for all the measures that a company uses to monitor and compare compensation among internal departments or units. While different companies will use different measures of compensation, the scorecard creates a comparative tool within the organization that can reinforce desired outcomes that are unique to the company's strategy.

compensation scorecard
Displays the results for all the measures that a company uses to monitor and compare compensation among internal departments or units.

Managers in companies without compensation scorecards often struggle to know if the promotions, raises, bonuses, and pay adjustments they make are in line with the rest of the organization and its strategy. A scorecard improves transparency regarding how people are rewarded and makes managers responsible for how they spend company money. Most compensation scorecards are completed once a year by HR personnel.

Figure 9.11 provides an example of a compensation scorecard. In this example, each functional department in the company reports the average performance rating received by its employees on a scale of 1 (low) to 5 (high). This measure helps to show managers where they are in terms of evaluating their employees. Average merit increases are also gathered. The company had budgeted enough money for a 4 percent increase, on average. If the average merit increase you give your employees is greater than 4 percent, then the additional money needed to compensate the employees in your function will need to be drawn from elsewhere in the company. Grade inflation is the growth or decline of the average salary grade distribution; it shows whether pay raises are changing on a year-to-year basis. The compa ratio is a measure of the appropriateness of the salaries given by a function. In essence, it is an internal benchmark of salaries. Functions with a compa ratio less than 100 percent are considered to be paying their employees below the company norm. Finally, a measure of the percentage of annual incentives in relation to organizational targets helps managers assess whether a function is meeting its targets and paying its employees in accordance with those objectives.[46]

Figure 9.11 Sample Compensation Scorecard

Function	Average Performance Rating (1–5)	Average Merit Increase (4% Budget)	Grade Inflation*	Compa Ratio**	Annual Incentive (% of Target)
Marketing	3.4	4.3%	−3%	101%	100%
R&D	3.2	4.4%	0%	98%	102%
Production	4.0	4.2%	12%	96%	105%
Sales	4.1	3.4%	8%	99%	100%
Customer Service	3.6	3.6%	17%	88%	110%

*__Grade inflation__ is determined by calculating the percentage change in the number of employees in each grade in comparison to the year befores.
**__Compa ratio__ is actual salary divided by the midpoint of the salary range. It is a gauge of the appropriateness of the organization's salary ranges.

Source: Reprinted by permission of The Segal Group, Inc., parent of The Segal Company and its Sibson Consulting Division. © 2011. All rights reserved.

Summary

LO 1 Compensation consists of (1) direct compensation, which includes wages, salary bonuses, and commissions; (2) indirect compensation, which includes benefits such as health care and vacation days; and (3) nonfinancial compensation, which includes recognition programs, rewards, support, flexibility and the work environment. Collectively, these three forms of compensation represent a major cost to the company. If managed strategically, these costs can also represent investments.

LO 2 Establishing strategic compensation programs requires an assessment of organizational objectives in relation to specific employment goals—employee retention for continued growth, compensation distribution to ensure employees feel treated fairly, communication of compensation methods to increase employee understanding of organizational objectives, and adherence to a budget for cost efficiencies, for instance. Compensation must reward employees for past efforts (pay-for-performance) while simultaneously motivating employees' future performance. The internal and external equity of the pay program affect employees' concepts of fairness. Organizations must balance each of these concerns while still remaining competitive. The ability to attract and retain qualified employees while controlling labor costs is a major factor in allowing organizations to remain viable in their domestic and/or international markets.

LO 3 The basis on which compensation payments are determined and the way they are administered can significantly affect employee productivity and the achievement of organizational goals. Internal influences include the employer's compensation policy, worth of the job, performance of the employee, and employer's ability to pay. External factors influencing pay rates include labor market conditions, area pay rates, cost of living, outcomes of collective bargaining, and legal requirements.

LO 4 Job evaluation is a system to help determine the relative worth of a job in comparison to other jobs within the organization. It consists of three steps: (1) ranking the value of jobs from highest to lowest, (2) classifying jobs, and (3) awarding points to each job based on its link to organizational objectives.

LO 5 Wage surveys determine the external equity of jobs. Data obtained from surveys will facilitate establishing the organization's wage policy while ensuring that the employer pays neither more nor less than needed for jobs in the relevant labor market. The wage structure is determined based on wage surveys, but will vary based on job function and individual skill differences. Companies may use wage curves, pay grades, and rate ranges to group jobs together and to allow for individual employee differences within each type of job.

LO 6 Wage structures will also depend on the legal requirements stipulated for wages. A majority of states have passed laws that fix minimum wage rates. The federal government has also established a minimum wage, which is currently set at $7.25 per hour. When employees are subject to both the state and federal minimum wage laws, they are entitled to the higher of the two minimum wages. Most states also regulate how many hours per week a person can work and how old an employee must be to avoid violating child labor laws. Laws also exist to protect employees from pay discrimination.

LO 7 The effectiveness of a compensation system can be assessed by using a compensation scorecard. Such a scorecard collects and displays where all departments and functions sit in terms of their relative compensation. It increases the transparency of compensation systems, promotes accountability of managers, and helps companies align their compensation decisions with organizational objectives.

Key Terms

broadbanding
compensation scorecard
competence-based pay
consumer price index (CPI)
escalator clauses
exempt employees
Hay profile method
hourly work
job classification system
job evaluation
job ranking system
nonexempt employees
pay equity
pay-for-performance standard
pay grades
pay rate compression
piecework
point system
real wages
red circle rates
wage and salary survey
wage curve
work valuation

Discussion Questions

LO 1 MX, the fintech company, offers the following benefits to its employees: free lunches and dinners twice a week, discounted massages from an on-site masseuse, comprehensive health care insurance, unlimited vacation days, competitive salaries, bonuses if the company meets targets, and an open and transparent work environment that embraces diversity and inclusion. Identify which of these compensation components would be classified as (1) indirect, (2) direct, or (3) nonfinancial compensation.

LO 2 Tomax Corporation has 400 employees and wishes to develop a compensation policy to correspond to its dynamic business strategy. The company wants to employ a high-quality workforce capable of responding to a competitive business environment. Suggest different compensation objectives to match Tomax's business goals.

LO 3 Since employees may differ in terms of their job performance, would it be more feasible to determine the wage rate for each employee on the basis of their relative worth to the organization? Explain.

LO 4 Which job evaluation system would you use as an HR manager? Explain your answer.

LO 5 Describe the basic steps in conducting a wage and salary survey. What are some factors to consider?

One of the objections to granting wage increases on a percentage basis is that the lowest-paid employees, who are having the most trouble making ends meet, get the smallest increase, while the highest-paid employees get the largest increase. Is this objection a valid one? Explain.

LO 6 According to the Living Wage Calculator developed by Amy Glasmeier, Professor of Economic Geography and Regional Planning at MIT, the living wage rate for a family of four (two working adults, two children) is $16.54 per hour. What are the implications of raising the minimum wage rate to a livable wage? Do you think the government should increase the federal minimum wage? Explain your answer.

LO 7 What is a compensation scorecard and how does it help align a company's strategy with its compensation system?

HRM Experience

Why This Salary?

A question frequently asked is, "Why is that person paid more than I am when we both perform the same job?" The answer to this question lies in understanding the components of the pay mix, as discussed in this chapter. While we may disapprove of the idea that someone is paid more or less than we are for similar work, factors both internal and external to the organization influence the final salary paid to a job or a specific person. Often we have little control over the pay mix factors. At other times, we can improve our wage by gaining additional job experience or seniority or by increasing our job knowledge or skills. This project is designed to give you experience in understanding why jobs are paid different salaries.

Assignment

Shown here are the annual median salaries paid in some of the fastest-growing occupations in the United States based on expected growth rates from now until 2024. Study the salaries paid to these workers and then answer the questions that follow as to why the differences in salaries exist. Relate these reasons to the internal and external factors of the pay mix that are discussed in the text.

Occupation	***Median Annual Salary***
Wind turbine service technician	$51,050
Physical therapist	$84,020
Statistician	$80,110
Ambulance driver	$23,740
Genetic counselors	$72,090
Interpreter and translator	$44,190
Optometrist	$103,900

1. What factors may account for the wide differences among salaries for different occupations?
2. What factors may account for the differences among salaries for the identical occupation in the same organization?
3. What factors may account for the differences among salaries for the identical occupation in different organizations?

You may work individually or in teams to complete this skill building exercise. The *Occupational Outlook Handbook* published by the U.S. Bureau of Labor Statistics can be found at http://www.bls.gov.

CASE STUDY 1 Pay Decisions at Performance Sports

Katie Perkins's career objective while attending Rockford State College was to obtain a degree in small business management and to start her own business after graduation. Her ultimate desire was to combine her love of sports and a strong interest in marketing by starting a mail-order golf equipment business aimed specifically at beginning golfers.

After extensive development of a strategic business plan and a loan in the amount of $75,000 from the U.S. Small Business Administration, Performance Sports was launched. Based on a marketing plan that stressed fast delivery, error-free customer service, and hefty discount pricing, Performance Sports grew rapidly. Currently, the company employs 16 people: 8 customer service representatives earning between $11.25 and $13.50 per hour; 4 shipping and receiving associates paid between $8.50 and $9.50 per hour; 2 clerical employees each earning $8.25 per hour; an assistant manager earning $15.25 per hour; and a general manager with a wage of $16.75 per hour. Both the manager and the assistant manager are former customer service representatives.

Perkins intends to create a new managerial position, purchasing agent, to handle the complex duties of purchasing golf equipment from the company's numerous equipment manufacturers. Also, the mail-order catalog will be expanded to handle a complete line of tennis equipment. Since the position of purchasing agent is new, Perkins is not sure how much to pay this person. She wants to employ an individual with 5 to 8 years of experience in sports equipment purchasing.

While attending an equipment manufacturers' convention in Las Vegas, Nevada, Perkins learns that a competitor, East Valley Sports, pays its customer service representatives on a pay-for-performance basis. Intrigued by this compensation philosophy, Perkins asks her assistant manager, George Balkin, to research the pros and cons of this payment strategy. This request has become a priority because only last week two customer service representatives expressed dissatisfaction with their hourly wage. Both complained that they felt underpaid relative to the large amount of sales revenue each generates for the company.

Questions

1. What factors should Perkins and Balkin consider when setting the wage for the purchasing agent position? What resources are available for them to consult when establishing this wage?
2. Suggest advantages and disadvantages of a pay-for-performance policy for Performance Sports.
3. Suggest a new payment plan for the customer service representatives.

CASE STUDY 2 An In-N-Out Pay Strategy: Costa Vida's Decision to Boost Pay

For many businesses in today's belt-tightening economy, decisions on pay need to be strategic to ensure that employees are treated fairly, yet the business can remain viable. This requires knowing what your competitors pay their employees and knowing your own salary budget. But knowing what your competitors are paying can be both valuable and painful.

As a primary stakeholder and former CEO of Costa Vida, a fast-growing chain of fresh Mexican restaurants, Nathan Gardner knew he was competing against some restaurant chains with competitive compensation systems. Costa Vida is a fresh Mexican grill featuring Baja-inspired foods that are made from scratch daily. Following a trip to Cabo San Lucas on the Baja Coast in Mexico, Costa Vida founders JD and Sarah Gardner were inspired with a vision: bring the freshly made local cuisine and the vibrant lifestyle to the United States. They started their first restaurant in 2001, and now Costa Vida has more than 100 franchises in Arizona, California, Colorado, Florida, Idaho, Illinois, Nevada, New Mexico, Missouri, Oklahoma, Oregon, Texas, Washington, Wyoming, and Utah, and 3 locations in Canada. One of the main challenges Costa Vida faces is the fierce competition for customers as well as employees. "You'd be surprised how much of a difference having good employees in all areas of the business makes," commented Nathan.

"For the fast-casual food industry," remarked Nathan, "you are dependent upon your people. If you don't treat your people well, they won't treat your customers well. If your customers aren't treated well, you have no business." For months, Nathan agonized over how he could develop a competitive compensation plan that matched the organization's objectives, but that fell in line with the tight budget of each individually owned franchise unit. He stated, "We, of course, leave the final compensation decision to the franchise owner, but we do all we can to educate and persuade our franchisees to be competitive and fair. In the long run, this is how they can maintain a superior level of customer satisfaction."

According to Nathan, a strong benchmark for Costa Vida has been In-N-Out Burger. In-N-Out started in California and is known for its great compensation package. All new "associates" (employees) start at a minimum of $14 per hour. The company also offers flexible schedules to accommodate school and other activities, paid vacation, free meals, and a 401(k) retirement plan. Full-time associates are eligible for medical, dental, vision, life, and travel insurance coverage. The company's reason for offering such generous compensation is based on its strategy—namely, that lower turnover and more committed workers will lead to better service. "What In-N-Out does for its employees is truly amazing," commented Nathan. "We often see employees moving from one fast-food chain to another, but we rarely see employees coming from In-N-Out."

Nathan had a tough challenge ahead in trying to convince his franchise owners and managers to think more strategically about their pay systems. He needed to help them realize that paying wages and offering other compensation benefits that were better than their competitors' compensation packages might mean lower profit margins initially, but that the returns would be greater in the long run. He also needed to offer evidence to show that this approach was not just about being fair, but also about being strategic. The restaurant business is a fast and fierce industry, and companies come and go all the time. What was it going to take for Costa Vida to survive and thrive over the long haul?

Questions

1. Why is it important for pay to be externally fair?
2. Why is it important for pay to be internally fair?
3. What should Costa Vida's compensation strategy look like? Hint: What are the company objectives and how can employee pay help to achieve those objectives?
4. What should the pay structure look like? What pay mix would you recommend?
5. How should Nathan communicate a new compensation strategy to his franchisee owners and managers?
6. What effect will paying higher wages have on Costa Vida in the short term? What effect will it have in the long term? Explain.

Notes and References

1. S. Morris, S. A. Alvarez, and J. Barney, "Dancing with the Stars: The Practical Value of Theory in Managing Star Employees," *Academy of Management Perspectives* (2021); and D. Kryscynski and S. Morris, "Human Capital in Strategy 2008–2018," *Strategic Management Journal*, Virtual Special Issue (2020).
2. Jennifer M. George and Gareth R. Jones, *Understanding Organizational Behavior*, 6th ed. (Boston, MA: Prentice Hall, 2012), Chapter 3; Debra L. Nelson and James Campbell Quick, *Organizational Behavior: Science, the Real World, and You*, 8th ed. (Mason, OH: South-Western, Cengage Learning, 2013), Chapter 16.
3. For a frequently referenced book on strategic compensation planning, see Edward E. Lawler III, *Strategic Pay: Aligning Organizational Strategies and Pay Systems* (San Francisco: Jossey-Bass, 1990). See also Susan E. Jackson and Randall S. Schuler, *Managing Human Resources: Through Strategic Partnerships*, 9th ed. (Mason, OH: South-Western, 2006), Chapter 9.
4. Personal interview with a product development manager at Google.
5. Derrick Bryson Tyler, "Taco Bell to Test Paying Managers $100,000 a Year," *The New York Times* (January 11, 2020), https://www.nytimes.com/2020/01/10/business/taco-bell-manager-salary.html.
6. George Hancock Jr., "Zappos Employees Might Set Their Own Salaries," *Best Company* (February 24, 2020), https://bestcompany.com/ecommerce/blog/zappos-employees-set-salaries; Daniel Rothberg, "With No Bosses, How Do Zappos Employees Get Raises?", *Las Vegas Sun*,(July 15, 2015), https://lasvegassun.com/news/2015/jul/15/no-bosses-how-dozappos-employees-get-raises/; Zappos, "Why Us? Our Core Values" (March 2017), http://jobs.jobvite.com/zappos/p/why#values.
7. M. J. Bloomfield, "Compensation Disclosures and Strategic Commitment: Evidence from Revenue-Based Pay" (2020), SSRN 2862069; Jonathon Trevor, *Can Pay Be Strategic: A Critical Exploration of Strategic Pay in Practice* (London: Palgrave Macmillan, 2011).
8. Hai-Ming Chen and Yi-Hua Hsien, "Key Trends in the Total Reward System of the 21st Century," *Compensation and Benefits Review* 38, no. 6 (November–December 2006): 64.
9. Jay Yarow, "This Is the Internal Grading System Google Uses for Its Employees—and You Should Use It Too," *Business Insider* (January 6, 2014).
10. Nick Ushkoff, "Can OKRs Be Tied to Compensation?", Atiim (March 27, 2017).
11. Stephen Miller, "Study: Pay for Performance Pays Off," Society for Human Resource Management (September 14, 2011), https://www.shrm.org/resourcesandtools/hr-topics/compensation/pages/paysoff.aspx#:~:text=The%20study%20report%2C%20Tying%20Pay,lower%2Dperformers%20do%20the%20same.
12. Health Care Incentives Improvement Institute, "Pay-for-Performance: Will the Latest Payment Trend Improve?", http://www.hci3.org/thought-leadership/why-incentives-matter/pay-performance.
13. For a classic article on equity theory, see J. Stacey Adams, "Integrity in Social Exchange," in *Advances in Experimental Social Psychology*, L. Berkowitz, ed. (New York: Academic Press, 1965), 276-299.
14. Victor H. Vroom, *Work and Motivation* (San Francisco: Jossey-Bass, 1994). This landmark book, originally published in 1964, integrates the work of hundreds of researchers seeking to explain choice of work, job satisfaction, and job performance.
15. Joseph E. Champoux, *Organizational Behavior: Integrating Individuals, Groups, and Organizations*, 5th ed. (New York: Routledge, 2017), Chapter 8.
16. Julie Cook Ramirez, "The End of Pay Secrecy?", *Human Resource Executive Order* (February 4, 2016), http://resources.ehscareers.com/directory/the-end-of-pay-secrecy-article-339.aspx.

17. Ariane Hegewisch, Claudia Williams, and Robert Drago, "Pay Secrecy and Wage Discrimination Fact Sheet," Institute for Women's Policy Research, ((January 2014).
18. Catherine Clifford, "Whole Foods CEO John Mackey: Store Managers Could Be Making 'Well over $100,000,' without a College Degree," https://www.cnbc.com/2020/11/05/ceo-john-mackey-on-how-much-you-can-make-working-at-whole-foods.html.
19. A detailed discussion of the exempt and nonexempt rules under the FLSA can be found at http://www.dol.gov.
20. U.S. Department of Labor, "Exemption for Executive, Administrative, Professional, Computer & Outside Sales Employees Under the Fair Labor Standards Act (FLSA)," https://www.dol.gov/whd/overtime/fs17a_overview.pdf.
21. David Lepak and Scott Snell, "The Human Resource Architecture: Toward a Theory of Human Capital Allocation and Development," *Academy of Management Review* 24, no. 1 (1999): 31-48.
22. Konrad Reiher, "Compensation and Benefits: Job Evaluation," in *Handbook of Human Resources Management*, Matthias Zeuch, ed. Berlin, Springer 2016): 1-14. See also Robert L. Heneman, Peter V. LeBlanc, and Tim L. Reynolds, "Using Work Valuation to Identify and Protect the Talent Pool," *WorldatWork* 11, no. 2 (2002): 31-41.
23. James R. Bowers, "Valuing Work: An Integrated Approach," *WorldatWork* 12, no. 2 (2003): 28-39.
24. Federal Reserve Bank of New York, "Spring 2014 Small Business Credit Survey" (2014), https://www.newyorkfed.org/smallbusiness/Spring2014/index.html.
25. R. Hastings and E. Meyer, *No Rules Rules: Netflix and the Culture of Reinvention* (New York: Penguin Press, 2020).
26. Tracy Lien, "Snap's IPO Could Make Some Employees Millionaires while Others Are Left Out," *LA Times* (February 28, 2017).
27. Lynn Rinehart and Celine McNicholas, "Collective Bargaining beyond the Worksite," Economic Policy Institute (May 4, 2020), https://www.epi.org/publication/collective-bargaining-beyond-the-worksite-how-workers-and-their-unions-build-power-and-set-standards-for-their-industries/.
28. Strategic Economic Consortium, "Reshoring in the United States," January 16, 2020.
29. For information on the federal job classification system, visit http://www.opm.gov.
30. Emin Kahya, "Revising the Metal Industry Job Evaluation System for Blue-Collar Jobs," *Compensation and Benefits Review* 38, no. 6 (November–December 2006): 49.
31. "Performing Job Evaluations," *Society for Human Resource Management* (October 27, 2016).
32. Lance A. Berger and Dorothy R. Berger, *The Compensation Handbook: A State-of-the-Art Guide to Compensation Strategy and Design*, 5th ed. (New York: McGraw-Hill, 2015). See also Robert L. Heneman, Peter V. LeBlanc, and Howard Risher, "Work Valuation Addresses Shortcomings of Both Job Evaluation and Market Pricing," *Compensation and Benefits Review* 35, no. 1 (January–February 2003): 7-11.
33. Pawel Fiedor, "Job Evaluation for Knowledge-Based Organizations," *European Conference on Knowledge* (September 2013): 860-867.
34. Pawel Fiedor, "Job Evaluation for Knowledge-Based Organizations," *European Conference on Knowledge* (September 2013): 860-867.
35. The Bureau of Labor, http://www.bls.gov.
36. Amanda Stansell, "Searching for a Career Paying Top Dollar? These Are the Highest Paying Jobs and Highest Paying Companies in 2019," Glassdoor (September 18, 2019), https://www.glassdoor.com/research/jobs-companies-2019/.
37. John H. Davis, *Statistics for Compensation: A Practical Guide to Compensation Analysis* (Hoboken, NJ: Wiley, 2011). See also Curt Finch, "How to Create an Effective Pay Structure," *Employee Benefit Plan Review* 61, no. 10 (April 2007): 26.
38. Some organizations may establish a compensation program that pays a differential based on geographic location. See Thomas J. Atchison, "Branch Office Salary Structure," *Compensation and Benefits Review* 39, no. 3 (June 2007): 35; and James R. Guzak, Barbara Crandall, and Hoda Alavinejad. "Compensation and Culture: A Configurational Fit between Systems and Culture Types," *Southwest Academy of Management Proceedings* (2017): 88-97, http://www.swamfbd.org/uploads/SWAM_Proceedings_2017.pdf#page=88.
39. Mirta Diaz-Fernandez, Alvaro Lopez-Cabrales, and Ramon Valle-Cabrera, "What Companies Pay For: The Strategic Role of Employee Competencies," *European Journal of International Management* 3, no. 4 (2009): 439-456.
40. PayScale, "The Advantages of Broadbanding" (April 28, 2011), http://www.payscale.com/compensation-today/2011/04/advantages-of-broadbanding.
41. Raise the Wage Act of 2021, H.R. 601, 117th Cong. (2021).
42. Payscale.com (February 3, 2021), https://www.payscale.com/research/US/Job=Preschool_Teacher%2C_(but_not_Special_Education)/Hourly_Rate.
43. Stephen Bruce, "The 9 Steps to Solving Pay Compression," HR Daily Advisor (January 9, 2012), http://hrdailyadvisor.blr.com/2012/01/09/the-9-steps-to-solving-pay-compression/.
44. U.S. Department of Labor, Wage and Hour Division, "Child Labor Bulletin 101 WH-1330," April 4, 2017.
45. Paul Tassin, "Wells Fargo Will Pay $35.5M to Settle Race Discrimination Class Action," Topclassaction.com (May 5, 2017), https://topclassactions.com/lawsuit-settlements/lawsuit-news/661027-wells-fargo-will-pay-35m-settle-race-discrimination-class-action/.
46. Petr Snapka and Andrea Copikova, "Balanced Scorecard and Compensation," *International Conference on Business and Economics Research* 16 (2011), https://images.template.net/wp-content/uploads/2016/06/30090322/Cost-Based-Performance-Scorecard.pdf.

Fuse/Getty Images

CHAPTER 10

Pay-for-Performance: Incentive Rewards

Learning Outcomes

After studying this chapter, you should be able to

- LO 1 Give examples of a strategic incentive program, including aligning incentives with company objectives.
- LO 2 Identify clear and quantifiable performance measures.
- LO 3 Summarize performance measures that incentivize employees.
- LO 4 Differentiate between individual incentive programs such as piecewise, sales commission, and standard hourly rates.
- LO 5 Differentiate between team incentive programs such as gainsharing, Scanlon, and improshare.
- LO 6 Differentiate between enterprise-wide incentive programs that involve stock options, profit sharing, and stock ownership.
- LO 7 Compare how incentives for professional employees might differ from incentives for other types of employees.
- LO 8 Explain how compensation for executives impacts a firm.

Studies show that pay-for-performance plans can increase job satisfaction, commitment to the company, and trust in management—if handled correctly.[1] The process of (1) choosing the right incentive plans based on organizational objectives, (2) setting up performance measures, and (3) administering those incentive plans may seem a bit daunting—especially since so much can go wrong.

In this chapter, we will discuss incentive plans in terms of the objectives they hope to achieve and the various factors that may affect their success. Because many organizations have implemented broad-based incentive programs to differentiate employees and their performance, for discussion purposes we have grouped incentive plans into three broad categories: individual incentive plans, group incentive plans, and enterprise incentive plans (see Figure 10.1).[2] At the end of the chapter, we also discuss some special incentive plans for professional employees and executives.

10.1 Strategic Reasons for Incentive Plans

LO1 Give examples of a strategic incentive program, including aligning incentives with company objectives.

A major element of strategic compensation management is the use of incentive plans, also called **variable pay** programs. Variable pay programs consist of bonuses, incentives, or recognition for good work. They allow organizations to reward employees for making continued contributions to the enterprise. The majority of companies are increasing the variable pay proportion of their payroll budget to compensate for low increases in base pay.[3] Variable pay is more flexible than fixed pay (salaries, hourly wages) because variable pay is attached to fixed costs, which gives the organization flexibility to increase, decrease, or maintain future payments to employees as business conditions warrant.[4] Most HR managers see variable pay as strategic because it allows the organization to align its employees' interests and outcomes with those of the organization.

variable pay
Tying pay to some measure of individual, group, or organizational performance.

However, an additional strategic component that HR managers seem to forget is that variable pay can be used to exercise fairness and equity within the organization. As a result, variable pay not only motivates employees to do what the organization wants

Figure 10.1 Types of Incentive Plans

Individual	Group	Enterprise
Piecework	Team compensation	Profit sharing
Standard hour plan	Scanlon plan	Stock options
Bonuses	Improshare	Employee stock ownership plans (ESOPs)
Merit pay		
Lump sum merit pay		
Incentive awards		
Sales incentives		
Professional employee incentive plans		
Executive incentive plans		

them to do, but also ensures that employees feel the organization is fair and responsive to their individual contributions.

For example, it has been said that "no good deed goes unpunished." Sometimes for employees who make valuable contributions, this cliché is not far from the truth. Professors James Oldroyd and Shad Morris pointed out that employees with "high potential" are more likely to get burned out and leave their organization than their more average-performing peers. The reason? Feelings of pay inequity. Many high-performing employees perceive that because of their high performance they are asked to take on additional work and are bombarded with overwhelming numbers of requests for help without additional pay. As a result, challenges meant to be energizing can feel like punishment for being successful if they are not attached to additional rewards.[5]

One of the key challenges that companies face during difficult times is asking everyone to tighten their belts—yet high performers know they can receive more competitive compensation from the market. Even employees who are not high performers work harder (and seem happier) when they work for a company that adequately rewards people who deserve it.[6] Incentive rewards are based entirely upon a pay-for-performance philosophy (see Chapter 9). Incentive pay plans establish a performance "threshold" (a baseline performance level) that an employee or group of employees must achieve to qualify for incentive payments (see Figure 10.2).

Incentive plans create an operating environment that champions a philosophy of shared commitment through the belief that every individual contributes to organizational performance and success.

10.1a Incentive Plans as Links to Organizational Objectives

Contemporary arguments for incentive plans focus on linking both individual and group compensation rewards to organizational goals. Specific company goals or objectives might be to lower labor costs, improve customer satisfaction, expand product markets, or maintain high levels of productivity and quality. By matching compensation with organizational objectives, managers anticipate that employees will assume "ownership" of their jobs, thereby improving their effort and overall job performance. Incentive pay is highly valued as a compensation strategy to attract and retain top-performing employees.[7] Figure 10.3 summarizes the major advantages of incentive pay programs as noted by researchers and HR professionals.

Figure 10.2 Pay-for-Performance Philosophy

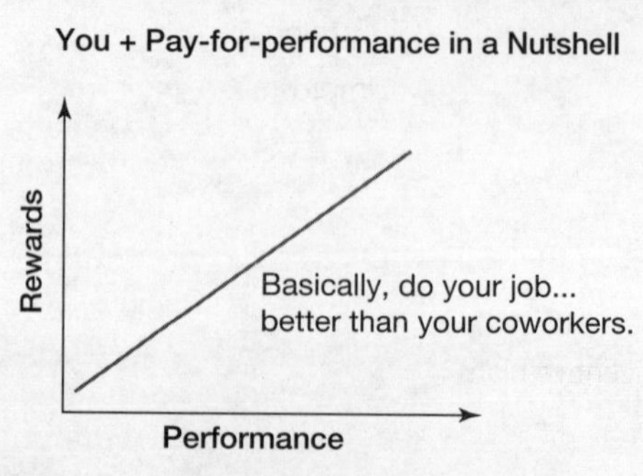

Figure 10.3 Advantages of Incentive Pay Programs

- Incentives focus employee efforts on specific performance targets. They provide real motivation that produces important employee and organizational gains.
- Incentive payouts are variable costs linked to the achievement of results. Base salaries are fixed costs largely unrelated to output.
- Incentive compensation is directly related to operating performance. If performance objectives (quantity and/or quality) are met, incentives are paid. If objectives are not achieved, incentives are withheld.
- Incentives foster teamwork and unit cohesiveness when payments to individuals are based on team results.
- Incentives are a way to distribute success among those responsible for producing that success.
- Incentives are a way to increase equity and justice in an organization.
- Incentives are a means to reward or attract top performers when salary budgets are low.

Do incentive plans work? The answer is both yes and no. Various studies, along with reports from individual organizations, show a measurable relationship between incentive plans and improved organizational performance.[8] However, the degree of success attained depends on several factors, including (1) identifying important organizational metrics to measure employee performance and (2) a customized incentive plan that effectively measures employee output and rewards exceptional employee performance.[9] For example, the U.S. Department of Defense now requires better linking of performance to rewards such as bonuses and promotions. This approach to compensation suggests the Department of Defense is now more interested in aligning an individual's work quality to organizational objectives.[10]

Conversely, other studies are calling into question the underlying assumptions of pay-for-performance systems. First, companies assume pay-for-performance increases equity. However, because measuring performance is difficult, the relationship between one's performance and rewards can be obscured. As a result, employees may question the equity of the system. Indeed, research has shown that if companies make idiosyncratic deals with some employees and not others, then the performance of the peers who do not get these special deals decreases, hurting the organization's overall performance.[11] Second, organizations hope that paying for performance will motivate employees. Considering that the connection between extrinsic rewards and performance is unclear, and sometimes even negative, employees might not be as motivated by variable pay incentives as managers assume. Thus, the challenge lies in how confident an organization can be in its ability to measure performance, tie that performance to organizational goals, and effectively connect employees' behavior to the resulting reward.[12]

10.1b Requirements for a Successful Incentive Plan

For an incentive plan to succeed, employees must be able to clearly connect the incentive payments they receive and their job performance. This connection becomes more visible when the organization has established objective standards by which workers can judge their performance. Management should guard against incentive payments being seen as an *entitlement*. Instead, these payments should be viewed as a reward that must be earned through effort. This perception can be strengthened if the incentive money is distributed to employees in a separate check. Compensation specialist Joanne Sammer notes the following steps as characteristics of a successful incentive plan[13]:

- Identify important organizational metrics that encourage employee behavior.
- Involve employees. Incentive programs should seem fair to employees.
- Find the right incentive payout. Payout formulas should be simple and understandable.
- Establish a clear link between performance and payout.

LO2 Identify clear and quantifiable performance measures.

10.2 Setting Performance Measures

As we discussed in Chapter 7 on appraising and managing performance, measuring and differentiating performance among employees is one of the most difficult tasks you will face as a manager. This is especially the case when your assessments are used to distribute rewards.[14] You will need to be able to distinguish between individual contributions and those made by a group. You must also avoid biases based on who you like and dislike, different personalities, and political agendas. At the group level, you will need to distinguish how much one group contributed relative to another group, even if the work they do is highly interdependent.[15] In sum, measuring individual-, group-, and enterprise-level contributions can be extremely complex. Measuring in a way that makes employees feel they are being treated unfairly can lead to serious problems. See Figure 10.4 for details on the do's and don'ts of measuring performance for incentives.

If done correctly, however, measurement can communicate the importance of established organizational goals. For example, if the organization desires to be a leader in quality, then performance indexes may focus on customer satisfaction, timeliness, or

Figure 10.4 Measurement Dos and Don'ts

	Individual Pay	Group Pay	Enterprise Pay
Do	• Measure things that are quantitative and simple • Measure work that is independent of others' contributions • Measure in a way that shows a relationship between work and performance	• Measure when work is group interdependent • Measure in a way that shows a relationship between work and performance	• Measure when work is organizationally interdependent • Measure results that employees can control • Measure in a way that shows a relationship between work and performance
Don't	• Measure based on who you like and dislike • Measure based on personalities • Measure based on political preferences • Measure without considering the contributions of peers	• Measure without considering the contributions of other teams • Measure unless there is a mechanism for teams to discipline their "slackers"	• Measure unless employees can see how their work actually contributes to the enterprise • Measure without considering effects of the environment (e.g., economic downturns)

1 Highlights in HRM

Setting Performance Measures—The Keys

Establishing meaningful performance measures is one of the important, yet difficult challenges facing management today. Before managers or supervisors develop and implement organizational measures, they should consider the following guidelines:

- *Performance measures—at all organizational levels—must be consistent with the strategic goals of the organization.* Avoid nonrelevant measures or metrics that are not closely linked to the business or what employees do in their work.
- *Define the intent of performance measures and champion the cause relentlessly.* Demonstrate that performance measures are, in fact, good business management, and hold managers and employees accountable for their success.
- *Involve employees.* A critical step in any measurement program is the development of an employee involvement strategy outlining the nature of employee participation, implementation, and ongoing management of the performance management program. Segment the workforce based on the nature of the work and the potential for impact. Consider which metrics require customization. Acceptance of a performance measurement program is heightened when employees "buy into" the process.
- *Consider the organization's culture and workforce demographics when designing performance measures.* For example, organizations with a more traditional hierarchical structure may need more time to introduce performance metrics compared to flatter organizations, which are more fluid and less steeped in control-and-command characteristics.
- *Widely communicate the importance of performance measures.* Performance messages are the principles and guidelines that communicate to employees what the required performance levels are and why the organization needs to achieve those levels of success.

error-free performance. If being a low-priced producer is the goal, then the incentive plan should emphasize cost reduction or increased productivity with lower acceptable levels of quality. While a variety of performance options are available, most focus on quality, cost control, or productivity. Highlights in HRM 1 provides five proven guidelines on how to establish and maintain an effective performance measurement program.

10.3 Administering Incentive Plans

> **LO3** Summarize performance measures that incentivize employees.

While incentive plans based on productivity can reduce direct labor costs, to achieve their full benefits they must be carefully thought out, implemented, and maintained. A cardinal rule is that thorough planning must be combined with a "proceed with caution" approach. Three of the more important points when administering such plans are highlighted here:

1. Allowing incentive payments to become pay guarantees defeats the motivational intent of the incentive. Poor performance must go unrewarded.
2. Annual salary budgets must be large enough to reward and reinforce exceptional performance.
3. The overhead costs associated with plan implementation and administration must be determined.

Small Business Application

Administering Incentive Plans for Small Businesses

For small businesses, incentive plans can be both a blessing and a curse. They provide a great way to align the employees' interests directly with the owner's interests, but managing them can also be time consuming and lead to feelings of inequity.

While the potential pitfalls of incentive systems in small businesses are great, the potential benefits are often worth the risk. The key is to understand these risks and then to manage them. Following are some things small businesses can do to help administer incentive plans:

1. *Keep incentive plans simple.* The easier it is for employees to know how they will be rewarded, the more likely they are to buy into the incentive system.
2. *Treat the plan as a work in progress.* Small business owners need to be open with their employees by communicating that they are trying to reward employees in a fair and equitable manner.
3. *Set a minimum requirement regarding what constitutes average performance.* Employees need to know that it is only after the employee exceeds general expectations that the additional rewards begin to kick in.
4. *Decide when the rewards will be provided to the employee.* The more closely you can tie incentives to performance, the more likely you will be able to sustain that behavior.
5. *Separate rewards from employees' regular pay.* When employees can see that they are actually being given something extra based on their performance, they will make a clearer distinction between showing up for work and actually contributing. It is also important to ensure that these bonuses are visible to others in the organization, because this public recognition acts as a reward in and of itself.
6. *Refine your measures and make sure employees are happy with them.* Communicating with your employees is key to making sure incentive plans do not end up being scrapped the month after they are administered.

LO4

Differentiate between individual incentive programs such as piecewise, sales commission, and standard hourly rates.

10.4 Individual Incentive Plans

One word—*flexibility*—describes the design of individual incentive plans.[16] For example, technology, job tasks and duties, and organizational goals (such as being a low-cost producer) impact the organization's choice of incentive pay programs. Incentive payments may be determined by the number of units produced, achievement of specific performance goals, or productivity improvements in the organization as a whole.

straight piecework
An incentive plan under which employees receive a certain rate for each unit produced.

differential piece rate
A compensation rate under which employees whose production exceeds the standard amount of output receive a higher rate for all of their work than the rate paid to those who do not exceed the standard amount.

10.4a Piecework

One of the oldest incentive plans is based on piecework. Under a **straight piecework** system, employees receive a certain rate for each unit produced. Their compensation is determined by the number of units they produce during a pay period. At Steelcase, an office furniture maker, employees can earn more than their base pay, often as much as 35 percent more, through piecework for each slab of metal they cut or each chair they upholster. Under a **differential piece rate**, employees whose production exceeds the standard output receive a higher rate for all of their work than the rate paid to those who do not exceed the standard.

The piecework system is more likely to succeed when units of output can be measured readily, the quality of the product is less critical, the job is fairly standardized, and a constant flow of work can be maintained.

Computing the Piece Rate

The incentive rates must be based on hourly wage rates that would otherwise be paid for the type of work being performed. For example, the standard time for producing one unit of work in a job paying $12.75 per hour was set at 12 minutes. The piece rate would be $2.55 per unit, computed as follows:

$$\frac{60(\text{minutes per hour})}{12(\text{standard time per hour})} = 5 \text{ units per hour}$$

$$\frac{\$12.75(\text{hourly rate})}{5(\text{units per hour})} = 2.55 \text{ per unit}$$

Piecework: The Drawbacks

Despite their obvious advantages—including their direct tie to a pay-for-performance philosophy—piecework systems have a number of disadvantages that offset their usefulness. One of the most significant weaknesses of piecework, as well as of other incentive plans based on individual effort, is that it may not always be an effective motivator. If employees believe that an increase in their output will provoke disapproval from fellow workers (often referred to as "rate busting"), they may avoid exerting maximum effort because their desire for peer approval outweighs their desire for more money.[17] Also, jobs in which individual contributions are difficult to distinguish or measure or in which the work is mechanized to the point that the employee exercises very little control over output may be unsuited to piecework. Piecework may also be inappropriate in the following situations:

- When quality is more important than quantity
- When technology changes are frequent
- When productivity standards on which piecework must be based are difficult to develop

Importantly, piecework incentive systems can work against an organizational culture promoting workforce cooperation, creativity, or problem solving, because each of these goals can infringe on employee' time and productivity and, therefore, total pay earned.

10.4b Standard Hour Plan

Another common incentive technique is the **standard hour plan**, which sets incentive rates on the basis of a predetermined "standard time" for completing a job. If employees finish the work in less than the expected time, their pay is still based on the standard time for the job multiplied by their hourly rate. However, while standard hour plans can motivate employees to produce more, employers must ensure that equipment maintenance and product quality do not suffer as employees strive to do their work faster to earn additional income.

standard hour plan
An incentive plan that sets rates based on the completion of a job in a predetermined standard amount of time.

10.4c Bonuses

A **bonus** is an incentive payment given to employees beyond their normal base wage. It is frequently given at the end of the year and does not become part of base pay.

bonus
An incentive payment that is supplemental to the base wage.

Bonuses can be a powerful tool to increase future performance. For instance, if the link between pay and performance is clearly established, bonuses can be one of the most effective means to increase future performance. For example, a study on bonuses versus actual pay raises showed that improving one's pay through merit increases by 1 percent would increase future performance by 2 percent. However, if the same amount of money was applied to pay-for-performance bonuses, the employee's performance would increase by 15 percent. Indeed, providing a strong pay-for-performance link for bonuses can dramatically improve employee productivity.[18]

A great example of a company that uses bonuses effectively is One Week Bath. One Week Bath maintains a weekly spreadsheet showing the up-to-date profits an employee is making for the company. Employees can see the bonus they have earned so far, and view a forecasted profit for the company and their personal bonus for the remainder of the year. The bonuses are effective because they are objective, rather than being dependent on some manager's performance assessment. They are also transparent: people know in advance how big their bonus will be.[19]

spot bonus
An unplanned bonus given for an employee's effort unrelated to an established performance measure.

When some special employee contribution warrants a reward, a spot bonus may be used. A **spot bonus**, as the name implies, is given "on the spot," usually for some employee's effort not directly tied to an established performance standard. Lauren Sejen, compensation expert with Watson Wyatt Worldwide, notes, "I think spot bonuses are one of the most underutilized forms of rewards, given how well employees respond to them. These plans make perfect sense."[20] These impromptu rewards can also be beneficial in difficult times. For example, during the economic slowdown in 2020 and 2021 due to the COVID-19 pandemic, many companies found that spot bonuses were an inexpensive way to encourage employees while their morale was low.[21]

10.4d Merit Pay

A merit pay program (merit raise) links an increase in base pay to how successfully employees perform their job. Unlike bonuses, merit increases, once they are given, become part of base pay, regardless of future performance. Merit raises can serve as effective motivators if employees perceive the raise to be related to the performance required to earn it.[22] If incentive plans become too complex, however, they can act as a disincentive (see Figure 10.5).

Research shows that a merit increase must be in the range of 7 to 9 percent if it is to serve as a pay motivator.[23] Employees may welcome lower percentage amounts, but low salary increases may not lead to significantly greater effort on the part of employees to drive business results. Consequently, if they have low salary budgets (see Chapter 9),

Figure 10.5 Merit Pay

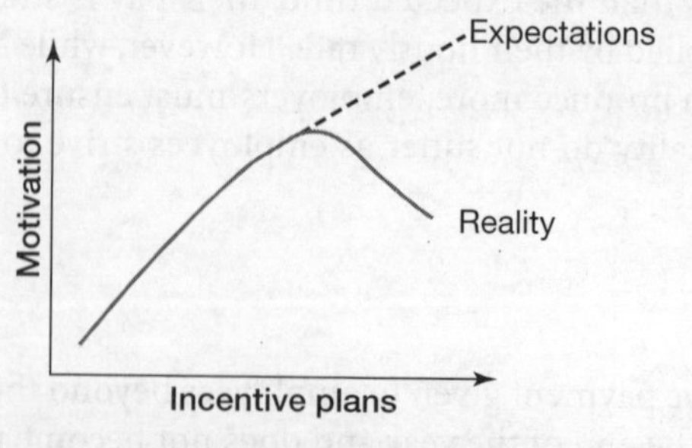

The more you base people's pay on merit, the better they perform. However, as incentive plans become more complex and are less associated with daily performance, they tend to decrease employee motivation.

organizations wishing to reward top performers will be required to distribute a large portion of the compensation budget to these individuals.[24] A meaningful merit increase will catch the attention of top performers while sending a signal to poor-performing employees. To achieve this goal, a strategic compensation policy *must differentiate* between outstanding and good or average performance.

Problems with Merit Raises

Merit raises may not always achieve their intended purpose. As CEO of BetterWorks, Kris Duggan, stated: "It doesn't make sense to only give employees one numeric, formal review. Imagine if your Fitbit gave you your step count at the end of each year. It'd have absolutely no impact on the way you work. Managers should be reviewing employees' work at least quarterly and convening to discuss progress frequently, in some cases weekly or monthly."[25]

Compensation specialists recognize the following problems with merit pay plans:

1. The money available for merit increases may be inadequate to satisfactorily raise all employees' base pay.
2. Managers may have no guidance in how to define and measure performance; the merit award criteria may suffer from vagueness.
3. Employees may not believe that their compensation is tied to effort and performance; they may be unable to differentiate between merit pay and other types of pay increases.
4. Employees and their managers may hold different views of the factors that contribute to job success.
5. Merit pay plans may create perceptions of pay inequity.[26]

While there are no easy solutions to these problems, organizations using a true merit pay plan often base the percentage pay raise on **merit guidelines** tied to performance appraisals. For example, a certain pay increase, such as "3 percent," will be tied to a certain performance evaluation, such as "above average." These percentages may change each year, depending on various internal or external concerns, such as profit levels or national economic conditions as indicated by changes in the consumer price index. To prevent all employees from being rated as outstanding or above average, managers may be required to distribute the performance rating according to some preestablished formula (such as "only 10 percent of employees can be rated as outstanding"). Additionally, when setting merit percentage guidelines, organizations should consider individual performance along with such factors as training, experience, and current earnings.

merit guidelines
Guidelines for awarding merit raises that are tied to performance objectives.

10.4e Incentive Awards and Recognition

Incentive awards and employee recognition are an important part of an employer's pay-for-performance compensation strategy. Employees often feel they receive inadequate and infrequent recognition for their contributions to the organization. To help remedy this potential problem, symbolic awards and recognition—interventions such as congratulatory cards, public recognition, and certificates—can significantly increase employees' motivation, performance, and retention. One study found that most employees prefer to be recognized daily or at least weekly, and they prefer to be recognized publicly via social media instead of privately or in person with smaller numbers of people present.[27]

For example, if you have ever worked in a restaurant as a server, you know that a little recognition goes a long way. One popular app used to recognize servers for

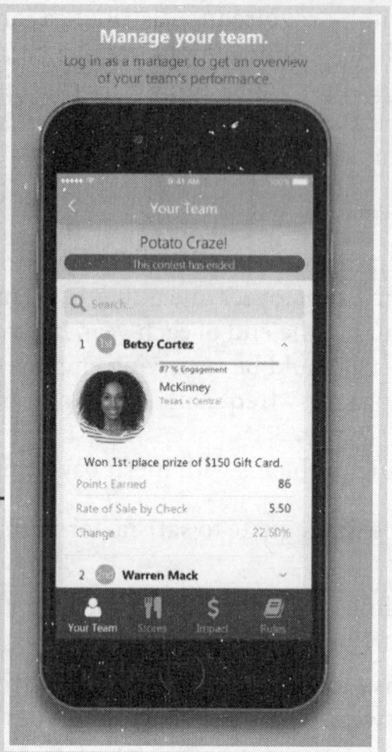

Source: IncentivizeMe.com

IncentivizeMe app provides performance-based rankings and built-in contests to show how servers are doing at upselling rather than just comparing number of sales they have.

upselling is called "IncentivizeMe." IncentivizeMe gamifies the sometimes daunting task of upselling food. Employees can choose to compete with one another to see who can upsell the most. This app provides performance-based rankings aimed at normalizing sections worked and different shifts, so that employees are judged on their upselling rather than their total sales volume. It has been especially effective for Millennial workers, who see fairness in ratings as key to their motivation.[28]

Awards may be given to recognize productivity gains, special contributions or achievements, and service to the organization. Popular noncash incentive awards include merchandise, personalized gifts, theater or sports tickets, vacations, dining out, gift certificates or gift cards, and personalized clothing. Employers should take care to tie awards to performance and deliver awards in a timely, sincere, public, and specific way. Most importantly, noncash incentive awards should support business goals and objectives.

A great example of a company that excels at offering noncash incentives is Atlassian, a software company based in Sydney, Australia, that focuses on making products for developers and project managers. Every quarter, on "ShipIt Day," Atlassian hosts a 24-hour hackathon where any employee can innovate however they want.[29]

The most effective recognition programs tie incentives to organizational objectives. An SHRM employee recognition survey found that 78 percent of HR professionals rated their recognition programs highly when the recognition was clearly connected with the organization's values (see Figure 10.6).[30] For example, if quality improvement is a business goal, then recognition needs to be tied to those behaviors that further the achievement of quality. Highlights in HRM 2 provides suggestions for noncash incentive awards based on the generational grouping of employees.

Figure 10.6 Employee Incentives Should Align with Organizational Objectives

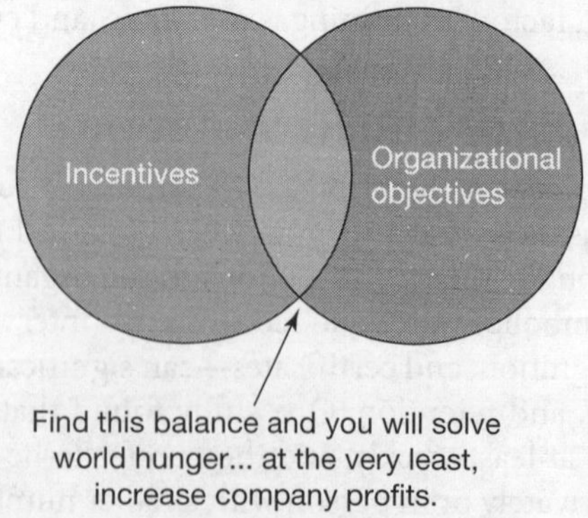

2 Highlights in HRM

Lessons Learned: Designing Effective Team Incentives

Will your team incentive program be successful? While there are no exact keys to success, team compensation specialists cite the following as important components of a meaningful team incentive plan:

- Are organizational members—employees and managers—predisposed to a team incentive reward system? Is there a cultural readiness for team compensation? If change is indicated, what information needs to be given to all organizational employees?
- Enlist total employee and managerial support for the incentive effort. While top management support is critical, without the encouragement of employees and middle- and lower-level managers (those directly involved in the program implementation), team incentive programs will invariably fail.
- When developing new programs, include representatives from all groups affected by the incentive effort—labor, management, and employees. Inclusion (not exclusion) serves to build trust and understanding of the program's intent, and its overall importance to organizational success.
- Establish effective, fair, and precise measurement standards. Selected performance measures should be key indicators of organizational success. Do not attempt to measure everything. Employees should be able to directly influence the performance measures selected. Furthermore, those performance measures should be challenging but realistic and obtainable. Standards must encourage increased effort without becoming entitlements.
- Incentive payout formulas must be seen as fair, be easy for employees to calculate, offer payouts on a frequent basis, and be large enough to encourage future employee effort. The goal is to create a pay-for-performance environment. When standards are not met, explain why the reward was not earned.
- Determine how incentive rewards will be distributed. Will team members receive equal dollar awards, or will team members receive differential payments based on such factors as seniority, skill levels, rates of pay, member contributions, and so forth?
- Communicate, communicate, communicate. Constantly champion the benefits of the incentive awards to employees and their contribution to organizational success.

Caiaimage/Paul Bradbury/OJO+/Getty Images

Nonmonetary rewards let employees know they are valued, which is why an increasing number of companies are using incentives like these to recognize high performance.

10.4f Sales Incentives

The enthusiasm and drive required in most types of sales work demand that sales representatives be highly motivated. Incentive plans must provide a source of motivation that will elicit cooperation and trust.

Unique Needs of Sales Incentive Plans

Incentive systems for salespeople are complicated by the wide differences in the types of sales jobs. These range from department store clerks who ring up customer purchases to the industrial salespeople at McGraw-Edison who provide consultation and other highly technical services. Sales associates' performance may be measured by the dollar volume of their sales and by their ability to establish new accounts. Other measures include the ability to promote new products or services and to provide various forms of customer service and assistance that do not produce immediate sales revenues.[31] Performance standards for sales employees are difficult to develop, but if done right can motivate them to improve their performance.

Gamification is one fun way to motivate sales teams. Approximately 50 percent of all sales organizations run sales competitions multiple times throughout the year.[32] For example, when companies use games to have employees and teams compete with one another or even teams outside of the office, they tend to see improvements in performance. According to one study, 71 percent of companies that use gamification for their sales associates see anywhere from 11 percent to 50 percent increases in measured sales performance.[33]

But successful gamification of sales teams involves much more than simply announcing contests. It consists of doing these six things well:

1. **Reward behaviors immediately.** For example, create an immediate contest between two sales members to see who can make a sale within the next 20 minutes. Immediately provide a $25 Amazon gift card to the person who wins. The idea is to reward behavior immediately after it is performed.
2. **Reward behaviors consistently.** Sales reps are enthusiastic about competitions that align with their goals and that set challenging but realistic benchmarks. Consistency changes gamification from gimmicky, one-off events to a strategic part of team culture.
3. **Reward the correct behaviors.** Sometimes sales contests can reinforce the wrong behaviors, such as not helping colleagues with their own sales. Sometimes you can create a contest within a team based on the highest number of sales assists. Consider the example of John Stockton, the former Utah Jazz player, who is still remembered for having the highest number of point assists in National Basketball League history.[34]
4. **Use data-driven gamification.** Knowing when employees are most likely to succeed or when lulls may occur in sales can help you strategically start a game or contest between teams when the time is right. Maybe you have a slow hour at 4 p.m., when everyone is gearing up to go home. Use this time to start a sales competition between teams to boost sales.
5. **Use team games.** When one team is competing against another team or office, that helps drive motivation through camaraderie. Reps will work hard not to let their teammates down and feel motivated by a cause greater than themselves.
6. **Use public recognition more often than money.** Sales reps are more strongly motivated by public recognition than they are by prizes and money. As a result, some

companies communicate game outcomes via email and "cc" the boss as well. This may even lead to the boss reaching out to congratulate the employee in a public setting—something that drives employee loyalty.[35]

Types of Sales Incentive Plans

Compensation plans for sales employees may consist of a straight salary plan, a straight commission plan, a combination salary and commission plan, or a sales plus bonus plan.[36] A **straight salary plan** permits salespeople to be paid for performing various duties that are not reflected immediately in their sales volume. It enables them to devote more time to providing services and building up goodwill with customers without jeopardizing their income. The principal limitation of the straight salary plan is that it may not motivate salespeople to exert sufficient effort in maximizing their sales volume.

straight salary plan
A compensation plan that permits salespeople to be paid for performing various duties that are not reflected immediately in their sales volume.

The **straight commission plan**, which is based on a percentage of sales, provides the maximum incentive and is easy to compute and understand. For example, total cash compensation might equal total sales volume times some percentage of total sales, perhaps 2 percent. Straight commission plans encourage aggressive selling, which might be needed in highly competitive industries. Under such a plan, salespeople may be allowed a salary draw. A *draw* is a cash advance that must be paid back as commissions are earned.[37]

straight commission plan
A compensation plan based on a percentage of sales.

However, the straight commission plan is limited by the following disadvantages:

1. Salespeople will stress high-priced products when making their pitches to customers.
2. Customer service after the sale is likely to be neglected.
3. Earnings tend to fluctuate widely between good and poor periods of business, and turnover of trained sales employees tends to increase in poor periods.
4. Salespeople are tempted to grant price concessions.

The **combined salary and commission plan** is the most widely used sales incentive program. For example, the most common pay mix (see the discussion in Chapter 9) for salespersons responsible for *new* accounts is 50 percent base pay and 50 percent variable pay. For salespersons servicing *existing* accounts, the pay distribution will lean more toward base pay and less toward commission. The ratio of base salary to commission can be set to fit the organizational objectives.

combined salary and commission plan
A compensation plan that includes a straight salary and a commission.

Another type of sales incentive plan is a **salary plus bonus plan**, where the payout can occur on a monthly, quarterly, or yearly schedule contingent based on the salesperson achieving targeted sales goals, such as number of sales calls made, account servicing, or quality of sales.

salary plus bonus plan
A compensation plan that pays a salary plus a bonus achieved by reaching targeted sales goals.

10.5 Group Incentive Plans

LO5
Differentiate between team incentive programs such as gainsharing, Scanlon, and improshare.

The emphasis on cost reduction and productivity has led many organizations to implement a variety of group incentive plans. Group plans enable employees to share in the benefits of improved efficiency realized by major organizational units or various individual work teams. These plans encourage a cooperative—rather than individualistic—spirit among all employees and reward them for their total contribution to the organization.

10.5a Team Compensation

team incentive plan
A compensation plan in which all team members receive an incentive bonus payment when production or service standards are met or exceeded.

The **team incentive plan** rewards team members with an incentive when agreed-on performance standards are met or exceeded. Team incentives seek to establish a psychological climate that fosters team member cooperation and a collective desire to fulfill organizational goals and objectives.

One catch with setting team compensation is that not all teams are alike (see Chapter 4). For example, the same type of team incentive plan will not be appropriate for cross-functional teams, self-directed teams, and taskforce teams. When the organization includes a variety of teams, managers find it difficult to adopt uniform measurement standards or payout formulas for team pay.[38]

After deciding on their team compensation model, organizations typically use a three-step approach to establish team incentive payments. First, the organization sets the performance measures on which incentive payments are based. Improvements in efficiency, product quality, or reduction in materials or labor costs are common benchmark criteria. For example, if labor costs for a team represent 30 percent of the organization's sales dollars and the organization pays a bonus for labor cost savings, then whenever team labor costs are less than 30 percent of sales dollars, those savings might be paid as an incentive bonus to team members. Second, the organization determines the size of the incentive bonus. For example, at Thrivent Financial for Lutherans, health insurance underwriters can receive team incentive bonuses of up to 10 percent of base salary. However, the exact level of incentive pay depends on overall team performance and the company's performance over a year. Third, the organization establishes a payout formula and fully explains it to employees. For instance, the team bonus may be distributed to employees equally, in proportion to their base pay or on the basis of their relative contribution to the team.

The following are some problems associated with team compensation:

- Individual team members may perceive that "their" efforts contribute little to team success or to the attainment of the incentive reward.
- Team members may be afraid that one individual may make the others look bad, or that one individual may put in less effort than others but share equally in team rewards—the "free-rider" effect.
- Complex payout formulas or insufficient payout rewards may diminish employees' motivation.

10.5b Gainsharing Incentive Plans

gainsharing plans
Programs under which both employees and the organization share financial gains according to a predetermined formula that reflects improved productivity and profitability.

Gainsharing plans are organizational programs designed to increase productivity or decrease labor costs and share monetary gains with employees. These plans are based on a mathematical formula that compares baseline performance with actual productivity during a given period. When productivity exceeds the baseline, an agreed-upon amount of savings is shared with employees. Inherent in gainsharing is the idea that involved employees will improve productivity through more effective use of organizational resources.

Many variations of gainsharing plans exist, such as the Scanlon plan and improshare plans. The Scanlon plan emphasizes participative management and encourages cost reductions by sharing with employees any savings resulting from those reductions. Improshare plans are based on the number of finished goods that the work teams complete in an established period.

The Scanlon Plan

The **Scanlon plan** is a specific type of gainsharing plan. Its underlying philosophy is that employees should offer ideas and suggestions to improve productivity and, in turn, be rewarded for their constructive efforts. Improvement or gains largely come from "working smarter, not harder." Figure 10.7 illustrates the Scanlon plan suggestion process, including the duties and responsibilities of two important groups—the *shop* and the *screening* committees.

Scanlon plan
A bonus incentive plan managed by employee and management committees, with the aim of attaining cost-reduction improvements.

Financial incentives under the Scanlon plan are ordinarily offered to all employees (a significant feature of the plan) on the basis of an established formula. This formula reflects increases in employee productivity as determined by the designated norm for labor costs.

Improshare

Improshare—or, more formally, improved productivity through sharing—is another type of gainsharing program. Whereas individual production bonuses are typically based on how much an employee produces above some standard amount, improshare bonuses are based on the overall productivity of the *work team*. Improshare output is measured by the number of finished products that the team produces in a given period. Both production (direct) employees and nonproduction (indirect) employees are included in the determination of the bonus.[39]

improshare
A gainsharing program under which bonuses are based on the overall productivity of the work team.

Under an improshare plan, the bonus is based on the productivity gains that result from reducing the time it takes to produce a finished product. The employees and the

Figure 10.7 Scanlon Plan Suggestion Process

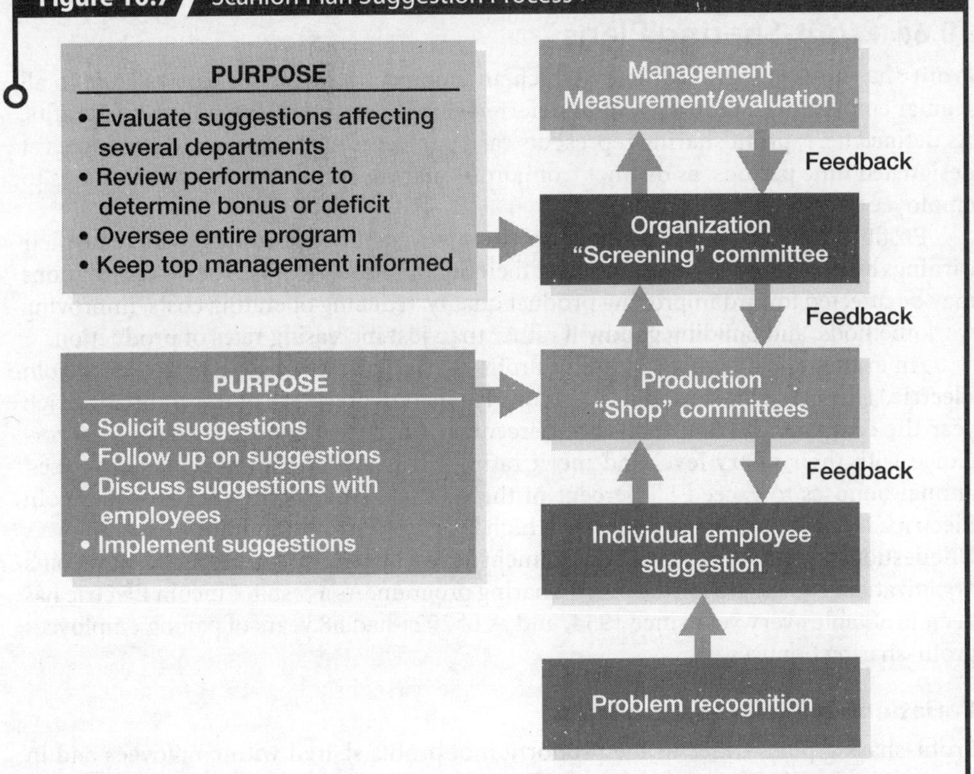

company each receive payment for 50 percent of the improvement. Since maintaining a cooperative environment benefits all parties under this system, improshare promotes increased interaction and support between employees and management.

Lessons from the Scanlon Plan and Improshare

Perhaps the most important lesson to be learned from the Scanlon plan and improshare—or any gainsharing program—is that if management expects to gain the cooperation of employees in improving efficiency, it must allow them to become involved in the organization both psychologically and financially. If employees are to contribute maximum effort, they must have a feeling of involvement and identification with their organization—something that does not flow from the traditional manager–subordinate relationship.

LO6 Differentiate between enterprise-wide incentives programs that involve stock options, profit sharing, and stock ownership.

10.6 Enterprise Incentive Plans

Do you believe that individual employees can actually impact a firm's performance?

Enterprise incentive plans differ from individual and group incentive plans in that all organizational members participate in the plans' compensation payout. They reward employees on the basis of the organization's success over an extended time period—normally a year, although the period can be longer. Enterprise incentive plans seek to create a "culture of ownership" by fostering a philosophy of cooperation and teamwork among all organizational members. Common enterprise incentive plans include profit sharing, stock options, and **employee stock ownership plans (ESOPs)**.

employee stock ownership plans (ESOPs)
Stock plans in which an organization contributes shares of its stock to an established trust for the purpose of stock purchases by its employees.

profit sharing
Any procedure by which an employer pays, or makes available to all regular employees, special current or deferred sums based on the organization's profits.

10.6a Profit-Sharing Plans

Profit sharing is any procedure by which an employer pays, or makes available to all regular employees, special current or deferred sums based on the organization's profits. As defined here, profit sharing represents cash payments made to eligible employees at designated time periods, as distinct from profit sharing in the form of contributions to employee pension funds.

Profit-sharing plans are intended to give employees the opportunity to increase their earnings by contributing to the growth of their organization's profits. These contributions may be directed toward improving product quality, reducing operating costs, improving work methods, and building goodwill rather than just increasing rates of production.

An example of a highly successful profit-sharing plan is the one in use at Lincoln Electric. This plan was started in 1934 by J. F. Lincoln, president of the company. Each year the company distributes a large percentage of its profits to employees in accordance with their salary level and merit ratings. It is not uncommon for employees' annual bonuses to exceed 50 percent of their annual wages. The success of Lincoln Electric's incentive system depends on a high level of contribution from each employee. Unquestionably, employees and management have a high degree of respect for Lincoln's organizational goals and for the profit-sharing program. As a result, Lincoln Electric has been profitable every year since 1934, and as of 2021 had 88 years of paying employees profit-sharing bonuses.[40]

Variations in Profit-Sharing Plans

Profit-sharing plans differ in the proportion of profits shared with employees and in the distribution and form of payment. The amount shared with employees may range from 5 to 50 percent of the net profit. In most plans, however, approximately 20 to 25 percent of the net profit is shared. Profit distributions may be made to all employees on an equal basis, or they may be based on regular salaries or some formula that takes into account seniority and/or merit. The payments may be disbursed in cash, be deferred, or combine the two forms of payments.

Weaknesses of Profit-Sharing Plans

Despite their potential advantages, profit-sharing plans are prone to certain weaknesses. The profits shared with employees may be the result of inventory speculation, climatic factors, economic conditions, national emergencies, or other factors over which employees have no control. Conversely, losses may occur during years when employee contributions have been at a maximum. The fact that profit-sharing payments are made only once a year or deferred until retirement may reduce their motivational value. If a plan fails to pay off for several years in a row, this can have an adverse effect on productivity and employee morale.

10.6b Stock Options

Apple, Google, Coca-Cola, Starbucks, Nike, Quaker Oats, and Sara Lee—what do these successful companies have in common? The answer: Each of these diverse organizations offers a stock option program to its employees.[41] Stock option plans grant to employees the right to purchase a specific number of shares of the company's stock at a guaranteed price (the option price) during a designated time period.

Organizations that offer stock option programs to employees do so with the belief that they are creating an incentive that will drive higher performance. When allowed to purchase stock, employees are expected to increase their productivity, assume a partnership role in the organization, and thus cause the stock price to rise.[42] Highlights in HRM 3 explains how stock option plans work.

Unfortunately, in the wake of various corporate scandals, employee stock option plans have come under attack from stockholder groups, government officials, and the general public. Criticism largely focuses on the extravagance of executive stock option plans and dubious corporate accounting procedures.[43] Nevertheless, despite these faults, stock options remain a popular and efficient way to pay for the performance of employees and managers. When stock prices rise, employee stock plans can prove financially rewarding to employees.

10.6c Employee Stock Ownership Plans

According to the National Center for Employee Ownership, in 2018 nearly 7,000 organizations had ESOPs for their employees.[44] Columbia Forest Products, Hy-Vee, Publix Super Markets, Herff Jones, the Tribune Co., U.S. Sugar, the Bureau of National Affairs, and Scheels All Sports are some of the many organizations with established ESOPs. W. L. Gore and Associates also decided that employee stock ownership was an effective and innovative way to give employees a share of the company's success.

An ESOP is an employer-established trust that qualifies as a tax-exempt employee trust under Section 401(a) of the Internal Revenue Code. Under an ESOP, employees do not actually buy shares. Instead, the company contributes its own shares to the plan, contributes cash to buy its own stock (often from an existing owner), or, most commonly, has the plan borrow money to buy stock, with the company repaying the loan. All of these approaches have significant tax benefits for the company, the employees, and the sellers. The ESOP holds the stock for employees, and they are routinely informed of the

How Stock Option Plans Work

Here is an example of a typical employee stock option plan. An employee is granted the option to purchase 1,000 shares of the company's stock at the current market price of $5 per share (the "grant" price). The employee can exercise the option at $5 per share—typically the exercise price will be equal to the price when the options are granted. Such plans allow employees to exercise their options after a certain number of years or when the company's stock reaches a certain price. If the price of the stock increases to $20 per share, for example, the employee may exercise the option to buy 1,000 shares at $5 per share and then sell the stock at the current market price of $20 per share.

Companies sometimes revalue the price at which the options can be exercised. This may happen, for example, when a company's stock price has fallen below the original exercise price. Companies revalue the exercise price as a way to retain their employees.

Source: Adapted from "Employee Stock Options Fact Sheet, National Center for Employee Ownership," http://www.nceo.org/.

value of their accounts. Stock allocations can be based on employee wages or seniority. When employees leave the organization or retire, they can sell their stock back to the organization, or they can sell it on the open market if it is traded publicly.

Advantages of Employee Stock Ownership Plans

Encouraged by favorable federal income tax provisions, employers often use ESOPs to provide retirement benefits for their employees. These tax incentives permit a portion of earnings to be excluded from taxation if that portion is assigned to employees in the form of shares of stock. Employers can therefore provide retirement benefits for their employees at relatively low cost because stock contributions are, in effect, subsidized by the federal government. ESOPs can also increase employees' pride of ownership in the organization, providing an incentive for them to increase productivity and help the organization prosper and grow.

Problems with Employee Stock Ownership Plans

Generally, ESOPs are more likely to serve their intended purposes in publicly held companies than in privately held ones. A major problem with the privately held company is its potential inability to pay back the stock of employees when they retire. These employees do not have the alternative of selling their stock on the open market. Thus, if these private organizations suffer financial difficulties and the value of their stock falls, so does the value of the employees' retirement plan.

Other problems with ESOPs include the following:

- The more retirement income comes from these plans, the more dependent a pensioner becomes on the price of company stock. Future retirees are vulnerable to stock market fluctuations as well as to management mistakes.
- Unlike traditional pension plans, ESOP contributions are not guaranteed by the federally established Pension Benefit Guaranty Corporation (see Chapter 11). This poses a major threat to employees' investments should their employer face serious financial setbacks or closure.

10.7 Incentives for Professional Employees

LO7 Compare how incentives for professional employees might differ from incentives for other types of employees.

When it comes to individual, team, and enterprise incentives, professional employees—engineers, scientists, and attorneys, for example—are no different than anyone else. They want to be rewarded for good work. However, where many companies often mess up is by applying the same individual and team-based pay-for-performance principles used in traditional jobs (e.g., manufacturing, clerical) to compensation for these professionals. For example, many companies offer cash bonuses to professionals who complete projects on or before deadline dates. They also pay individuals for new patents, for publications, or for completing certain tasks within a given time frame. Unfortunately, the compensation systems that often work for employees engaged in more narrowly specified tasks may not be effective for employees whose work is ambiguous and complex and requires creative thought.[45]

It turns out that individual incentives narrow a person's focus; they concentrate the mind. That explains why they work in so many circumstances. However, when the task is complex and the solution is not easy to figure out—as is the case with professional employees—it is important to motivate employees to be more creative. Pay-for-performance, unless it is a longer-term incentive, can prove problematic in this case. As an example, in the nineteenth century, Delhi, India, was infested with cobra snakes. To help get rid of the snakes, the city government created an incentive plan for people to turn in cobra skins. At first, the incentives worked, and the cobra population in the city began to decrease. Over time, however, as it became more difficult to catch cobras in the city, people found a way to game the system. They started to farm cobra snakes. When the government discovered this plot, it stopped paying for cobra skins—and the farmers released the snakes back into the city. As this example illustrates, short-term incentives to solve a problem can often have unintended consequences that create other problems.

So how should you incentivize your professional workers? Pay is still important, but it should be based more on overall performance over time, and it should not limit these employees to a set of certain tasks. In other words, make sure your incentives are based on the impact of someone's work, and not just on whether a certain task was completed. Such rewards should provide (1) autonomy to the worker, (2) opportunity to master a skill, and (3) purpose (e.g., helping to build a better organization, curing cancer, alleviating poverty).[46] Figure 10.8 indicates which areas incentive plans need to cover.

Figure 10.8 Things to Consider When Managing Professionals

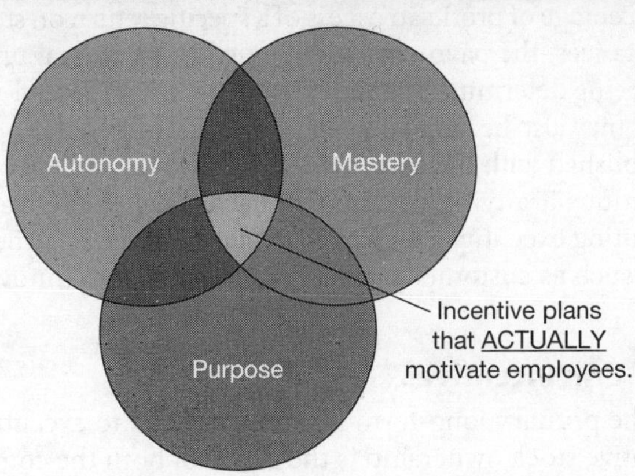

LO8

Explain how compensation for executives impacts a firm.

10.8 Incentives for Executives

10.8a The Executive Pay Package

Executive compensation plans consist of five basic components: (1) base salary, (2) short-term incentives or bonuses, (3) long-term incentives or stock plans, (4) benefits, and (5) perks.[47] Each of these elements may receive different emphasis in the executive's compensation package depending on various organizational goals and executive needs.[48]

Executive Base Salaries

Executive base salaries represent between 30 and 40 percent of these employees' total annual compensation.[49] An analysis of executive salaries revealed that the largest portion of executive pay takes the form of long-term incentive rewards and bonuses. Regardless, executives of *Fortune* 500 firms routinely earn annual base salaries in excess of $500,000, with executives in very large corporations earning considerably more. The levels of competitive salaries in the job market exert perhaps the greatest influence on executive base salaries. To determine the appropriate pay level, an organization's compensation committee—usually made up of members of the board of directors—will order a salary survey to find out what executives earn in comparable enterprises.[50] For example, by one estimate, more than 90 percent of companies in the Standard & Poor's 500 stock index use a technique called *competitive benchmarking* when setting executive pay or to remain competitive for executive talent.[51] Company boards reason that CEOs who do not earn as much as their peers are likely to "take a hike." Comparisons may be based on organization size, sales volume, or industry groupings. Thus, by analyzing the data from published studies, along with self-generated salary surveys, the compensation committee can determine the equity of the compensation package outside the organization.

Executive Short-Term Incentives

Annual bonuses represent the main element of executive short-term incentives.[52] Most organizations pay short-term incentive bonuses in cash (in the form of a supplemental check), in keeping with their pay-for-performance strategy. By providing a reward soon after the performance and thus linking it to the effort on which it is based, they can use cash bonuses as a significant motivator. Deferred bonuses are used to provide a source of retirement benefits or to supplement a regular pension plan.

Incentive bonuses for executives should be based on the contribution the individual makes to the organization. These bonuses may be based on a percentage of a company's total profits or a percentage of profits in excess of a specific return on stockholders' investments. In other instances, the payments may be tied to an annual profit plan, with the exact amount paid being determined by the extent to which an agreed-upon profit level is exceeded. Payments may also be based on performance ratings or the achievement of specific objectives established with the agreement of executives and the board of directors.

More organizations are tying operational yardsticks to the traditional financial gauges when computing executive pay. Called *balanced scorecards*, these yardsticks may measure outcomes such as customer satisfaction, the ability to innovate, or product or service leadership.[53]

Executive Long-Term Incentives

Stock options are the primary long-term incentive offered to executives.[54] The principal driver for executive stock ownership is the desire of both the company and outside investors for senior managers to have a significant stake in the success of the business. Figure 10.9 highlights several common forms of long-term incentives.

Figure 10.9 Types of Long-Term Incentive Plans

Stock options	Rights granted to executives to purchase shares of their organization's stock at an established price for a fixed period of time. The stock price is usually set at the market value at the time the option is granted.
Stock appreciation rights (SARs)	Cash or stock award determined by an increase in the stock price during any time chosen by the executive in the option period; does not require executive financing.
Stock purchase	Opportunities for executives to purchase shares of their organization's stock valued at the full market price or a discount price, often with the organization providing financial assistance.
Phantom stock	Grant of units equal in value to the fair market value or book value of a share of stock; on a specified date the executive will be paid the appreciation in the value of the units up to that time.
Restricted stock	Grant of stock or stock units at a reduced price with the condition that the stock not be transferred or sold (by risk of forfeiture) before a specified employment date.
Performance units	Grants analogous to annual bonuses except that the measurement period exceeds one year. The value of the grant can be expressed as a flat dollar amount or converted to a number of "units" of equivalent aggregate value.
Performance shares	Grants of actual stock or phantom stock units. Value is contingent on both predetermined performance objectives over a specified period of time and the stock market.

Short-term incentive bonuses are often criticized for causing top executives to focus on quarterly profit goals, to the detriment of the organization's long-term survival and growth objectives. Outcomes important to stockholders include performance results such as growth in earnings per share, return on stockholders' equity, and, ultimately, stock price appreciation. To promote the desired outcomes, a variety of incentive plans have been developed to tie rewards to these performance results, particularly over the long term. Additionally, stock options can serve to retain key executive personnel when exercising the options is linked to a specified vesting period, perhaps two to four years—a type of incentive called "golden handcuffs."

Executive Benefits

The benefits package offered to executives may parallel one offered to other groups of employees. Various programs for health insurance, life insurance, retirement plans, and vacations are common. However, unlike other employee groups, the benefits offered to executives are likely to be broader in coverage and free of charge. Additionally, executives may be given financial assistance in the form of trusts for estate planning, payment of mortgage interest, and legal help.[55]

Executive Perks

perquisites
Special nonmonetary benefits given to executives; often referred to as *perks*.

Perquisites (or perks) are nonmonetary rewards given to executives that are intended to demonstrate the executive's importance to the organization. Examples of perks include use of a company plane/car, large insurance policies, financial planning, income tax preparation, and chauffeur service, along with family perks such as children's education, spouse travel, and estate planning. However, perks have a dark side: they are viewed as wasteful spending and overly lavish. Even so, these rewards may save executive time or improve executive health.

Highlights in HRM 4 shows the more common perks offered to executives.

4 **Highlights in HRM**

The "Sweetness" of Executive Perks

Compensation consulting firms such as Price Waterhouse Coopers, World at Work, and Aon Hewitt regularly survey companies nationwide to identify the perks they provide for executives and other top managers. The following are popular executive perks.

- Company car
- Company plane
- Executive eating facilities
- Financial consulting
- Company-paid parking
- Personal liability insurance
- Estate planning
- First-class air travel
- Home computers
- Chauffeur service
- Children's education
- Spouse travel
- Physical exams
- Mobile phones
- Large insurance policies
- Income tax preparation
- Country club membership
- Luncheon club membership
- Personal home repairs
- Loans
- Legal counseling
- Vacation cabins

10.8b Executive Compensation: Ethics and Accountability

In 2019, the chief executives of American companies got a collective raise of 14 percent, which is 320 times as much as a typical worker.[56] Almost three in four Americans think CEOs and top-level executives are overpaid. Yet at the same time, most Americans still underestimate how much CEOs make. When asked how much the average CEO is paid in the largest 500 U.S. companies, the median guess was about $1 million per year.[57]

So what is the real answer? The median compensation for the CEOs of the biggest 500 U.S. companies is $12.3 million—10 times what most Americans think.[58] As examples of these enormous rewards, consider the total compensation drawn by the executives shown in Figure 10.10.[59]

While the average American may believe executives are overpaid, corporate compensation committees justify big bonuses in the following ways[60]:

1. Large financial incentives are a way to reward superior performance.
2. Business competition is pressure-filled and demanding.
3. Good executive talent is in great demand.
4. Effective executives create shareholder value.

Others justify high compensation as a fact of business life, reflecting market compensation trends.

Given the large compensation packages awarded to top-level executives, cries for performance accountability and openness abound. Many argue that such exorbitant pay gaps are not only bad for the reputations of the firms that pay them, but also create discontent in the general population, threatening the very foundation on which pay-for-performance was established. While not all executive pay is exorbitant and not all

Figure 10.10 CEO Pay

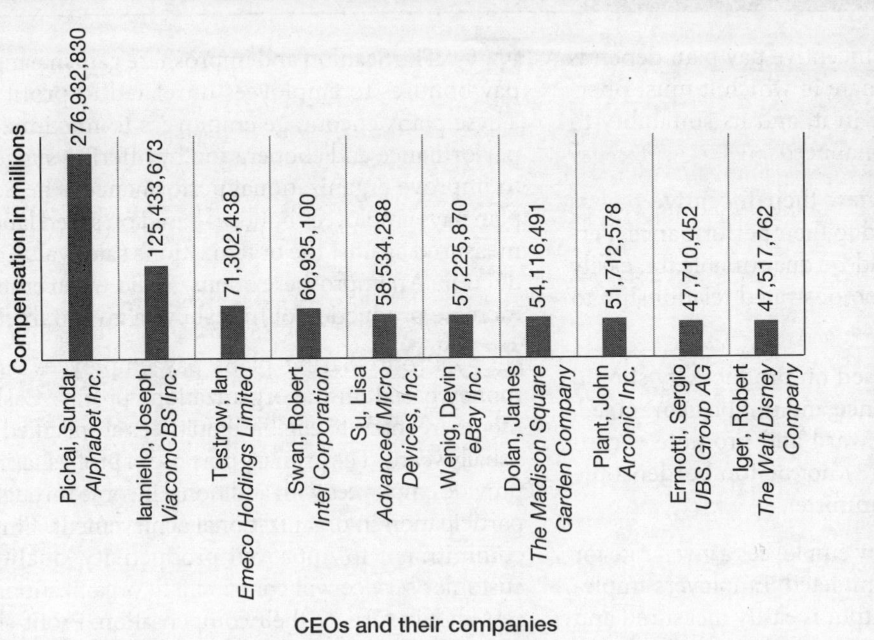

"2020 CEO Pay Review: The Top 50 Highest Paid CEOs," *CGLytics*, https://cglytics.com/2020-ceo-pay-review-the-top-50-highest-paid-ceos/.

executive performance is poor, angry employees, union groups, government officials, and stockholders may nevertheless argue for change.

10.8c Executive Compensation Reform

Several important changes will impact future executive compensation. First, the Internal Revenue Service (IRS) always looks for tax code violations in connection with hefty executive pay packages. The IRS makes executive pay a part of every corporate audit.[61]

Second, the Securities and Exchange Commission has disclosure rules that require companies listed on the New York Stock Exchange and NASDAQ to disclose the true size of their top executive pay packages. Companies must reveal details of accumulated pension benefits, deferred compensation, and perks that exceed more than $10,000 in total value. Also, companies must provide a plain-English table that summarizes executives' various forms of compensation.[62]

Third, the Financial Accounting Standards Board (FASB) requires that stock options be recognized as an expense on income statements. Companies and compensation committees must now weigh the benefits provided by stock options programs against the potential charge to earnings.[63]

Finally, the Dodd-Frank Wall Street Reform and Consumer Protection Act (Pub. L. 111–203) requires companies to disclose the median total compensation of all their employees in comparison to the total CEO compensation. It also gives shareholders of a company a "say on pay," which means that voting shareholders of a company must ultimately approve executive salaries.

Summary

LO 1 The success of an incentive pay plan depends on the organizational climate in which it must operate, employee confidence in it, and its suitability to employee and organizational needs.

LO 2 Employees must view their incentive pay as being equitable and related to their performance. Performance measures should be quantifiable, be easily understood, and bear a demonstrated relationship to organizational performance.

LO 3 Incentive plans based on productivity should (1) only reward performance and not be guaranteed, (2) be large enough to reward and promote exceptional performance, and (3) not be too burdensome for the organization to administer.

LO 4 Piecework plans pay employees a given rate for each unit satisfactorily completed. Employers implement these plans when output is easily measured and when the production process is fairly standardized. Bonuses are incentive payments above base wages paid on either an individual or team basis. A bonus is offered to encourage employees to exert greater effort. Standard hour plans establish a standard time for job completion. An incentive is paid for finishing the job in less than the preestablished time. These plans are popular for jobs with a fixed time for completion.

Paying employees a straight salary allows them to focus on tasks other than sales, such as providing service and encouraging customer goodwill. A straight commission plan causes employees to emphasize sales goals. A combination of salary and commission or bonus provides the advantages of both the straight salary and the straight commission forms of payment.

LO 5 The Scanlon and improshare gainsharing plans pay bonuses to employees unrelated to profit levels. These plans encourage employees to maximize their performance and cooperation by offering suggestions to improve organizational performance. The Scanlon plan pays employees bonuses based on saved labor cost measured against the organization's sales value of production. An improshare bonus is paid when employees increase production output above a given target level.

LO 6 Profit-sharing plans pay employees sums of money based on the organization's profits. Cash payments are made to eligible employees at specified times, usually yearly. The primary purpose of profit sharing is to provide employees with additional income through their participation in organizational achievement. Employee commitment to improved productivity, quality, and customer service will contribute to organizational success and, in turn, to their compensation. Profit-sharing plans may not achieve their stated gains when employee performance is unrelated to organizational success or failure, such as when economic conditions, other competition, or environmental conditions play a larger role in the organization's outcomes. Profit-sharing plans can also have a negative effect on employee morale when they fail to consistently reward employees.

LO 7 Professional pay should be based more on overall performance over time, and it should not limit these employees to a set of certain tasks.

LO 8 Executives are often offered very elaborate incentives based on how well the company does. Because executives stand to gain more from the decisions they make, they also often stand to lose more.

Key Terms

bonus
combined salary and commission plan
differential piece rate
employee stock ownership plans (ESOPs)
gainsharing plans
improshare
merit guidelines
perquisites
profit sharing
salary plus bonus plan
Scanlon plan
spot bonus
standard hour plan
straight commission plan
straight piecework
straight salary plan
team incentive plan
variable pay

HRM Experience

Awarding Salary Increases

Because pay-for-performance is an important factor governing salary increases, managers must be able to defend the compensation recommendations they make for their employees. Merit raises granted under a pay-for-performance policy must be based on objective appraisals if they are to achieve their intended purposes of rewarding outstanding employee performance. As managers know, however, they must deal with other factors that can affect salary recommendations. These may include the opinions of the employee's peers or extenuating circumstances such as illness or family responsibilities. The purpose of this exercise is to provide you experience in granting salary increases to employees based on their work performance and other information.

Assignment

Following are the work records of five employees. As their supervisor, you have just completed their annual appraisal reviews, and it is now time to make recommendations for their future salary. Your department budget has $5,780 allocated for salary increases. Distribute the $5,780 among your employees based on the descriptions for each subordinate.

a. Janet Jenkins currently earns $41,000. Her performance appraisal rating was very high. She is respected by her peers and is felt to be an asset to the work group. She is divorced and has three young children to support.

b. Russell Watts earns a salary of $36,000. His annual performance appraisal was average. Several members of the work group have spoken to you about the difficulty involved in Russell's job. They feel that it is a tough and demanding job and that he is doing his best.

c. Jack Perkins earns $31,250. His performance appraisal was below average, and he seems to have difficulty adjusting to his coworkers. Jack has had a difficult time this past year. His wife passed away early in the year, and his father has recently been diagnosed as terminally ill.

d. Rick Jacobson earns $28,000. His performance appraisal was above average. He is respected by his peers and is generally considered to be a "good guy."

e. Paula Merrill earns $28,850. Her performance appraisal was very high. Her peers are upset because they feel that she is working only to provide a second income. Moreover, her peers see her as trying to "show them up."

Share your results with other class members. Be prepared to explain your allocation of money.

Discussion Questions

LO 1 Working individually or in groups, identify key factors for a successful incentive plan.

LO 2 Assume you are being asked to measure the individual pay, group pay, and enterprise pay for a new software engineering position at Adobe. Write down how you would measure this person's performance as it relates to these three areas of pay.

LO 3 Based on the performance measures you put together for a new software engineering position at Adobe, what is your biggest concern in administering this incentive plan? Explain your answer.

LO 4 Contrast the straight piecework, differential piece rate, and standard hour plans. Explain where each of these plans might best be used. What are the reasons behind the different payment methods used for sales employees?

LO 5 A frequently heard complaint about merit raises is that they do little to increase employee effort. What are the causes of this belief? Suggest ways in which the motivating value of merit raises might be increased. What are the reasons for the success of the Scanlon and improshare plans?

LO 6 Because of competitive forces within your industry, you have decided to implement a profit-sharing plan for your employees. Discuss the advantages of profit sharing and identify specific characteristics that will ensure success for your plan.

LO 7 What are three types of rewards professionals are interested in?

LO 8 Do you believe executives are overpaid? Discuss this issue with someone else and try to understand a different perspective.

CASE STUDY 1 CEO Pandemic Pay . . . Taking One for the Team or Window Dressing?

During the 2020–2021 global COVID-19 pandemic, many executives' pay was stifled, reduced, or even withheld. In an effort to build unity and keep people in jobs, some executives decided to make personal sacrifices. For example, Ronald Rittenmeyer, CEO of Tenet Healthcare Corporation, gave up three months' pay—roughly $390,000—to a fund that was set up to help struggling employees.

While this may seem quite generous, even after the pay cut Rittenmeyer's salary, including bonuses, was close to $2 million. This amount does not include his stock awards, which were worth more than $11 million. Little wonder, then, that one of the largest U.S. unions said Rittenmeyer's donation amounted to little more than "a gesture."

A study examining companies during the COVID-19 pandemic found that 762 companies issued some type of action to reduce executive compensation during the crisis. However, as the study points out, "The average amount of base salary reduction for the CEOs only makes up about 7.8% of their total granted compensation." This may not be much of a sacrifice when you consider that the typical pay package for CEOs at the largest U.S. companies tops $12 million per year. To put this number in perspective, companies in the S&P 500 stock index pay executives, on average, 264 times as much as median employees. Is it too much?

That depends on who you ask. To most people, it seems unreasonable that a boss would make 264 times the pay of the average worker. However, if you ask workers who have seen their CEOs steer their companies back from the edge of bankruptcy and weather the storm of a pandemic, they might not complain too much.

Questions

1. Are CEOs and key corporate executives worth the large pay packages they receive? Explain.
2. Do you agree with Peter Drucker that corporate executives should receive compensation packages no larger than a certain percentage of the pay of hourly workers? Explain.
3. Has the Dodd-Frank Wall Street Reform and Consumer Protection Act giving shareholders the right to vote on executive pay influenced the size of these packages? Explain.

Sources: Adam Shapiro, "New Study Calls CEOs Pandemic Pay Cuts 'Window Dressing,'" Yahoo! Finance (February 10, 2021); Anders Melin and Bloomberg, "Some CEOs Are Keeping Those Massive Bonuses—Even after Cutting Thousands of Jobs," *Fortune* (May 18, 2020); Peter Eavis, "As the Pandemic Forced Layoffs, CEOs Gave up Little," *The New York Times* (July 29, 2020).

CASE STUDY 2 Team-Based Incentives: Not Your Usual Office

Done-Deal Paper Inc. operates throughout central Pennsylvania with offices in Scranton, Harrisburg, and Altoona. Providing paper and paper needs to most of Central Pennsylvania, Done-Deal is one of the top two competitors in the area.

In January 2022, Conner Carell, office manager of one of the branch offices for Done-Deal, somehow convinced company president and CEO Bailey Zucker that they needed to change the way their sales representatives were incentivized. He argued, "Putting our sales reps into teams will not only increase cooperation, but it will increase sales. Right now there are too many sales being lost that could have been won through a team effort." Most of the time, sales made to clients required multiple interactions by multiple reps anyway. Bailey agreed with Conner and pointed out that teamwork can also improve morale and synergy. Based on these assessments, Conner organized his 20 sales reps into 4 teams of 5 reps. Sales teams would pool their commissions regardless of who initiated and worked on the sale. After the first year of this team-based incentive program, sales commissions across the four groups varied dramatically. For instance, the highest-paid employees in a team made, on average, $50,000 more than the lowest-paid team members.

During August 2023, Conner sent to all 20 sales reps a survey requesting feedback on the satisfaction with teams and, specifically, the team-based incentive rewards program. While survey results were generally positive, not everyone was happy in the office. Problems could be grouped into the following categories:

1. Some sales representatives believed that various team members did not "buy into" the team concept and were simply "free riding"—benefiting from the efforts of higher-performing reps.
2. There was a general feeling that some teams were assigned difficult regions that prevented them from achieving higher sales.
3. Teams did not always display the motivation and synergy expected, since "bickering" was prevalent between stars and their lesser-performing peers. Average performers complained that star reps made them look bad.
4. At least a third of the sales staff felt the incentive rewards program was unfair and asked for a return to individual sales incentives.[64]

Questions

1. Do results from the survey illustrate typical complaints about teams and specifically about team incentive rewards? Explain.
2. If appropriate, what changes would you recommend to improve the incentive reward program? Be specific.
3. Would management have benefited from employee involvement in the initial design and implementation of the program? Explain.

Notes and References

1. Chidiebere Ogbonnaya, Kevin Daniels, and Karina Nielsen, "Research: How Incentive Pay Affects Employee Engagement, Satisfaction, and Trust," *Harvard Business Review* (March 15, 2017).
2. Patricia K. Zingheim and Jay R. Schuster, "Designing Pay and Rewards in Professional Service Companies," *Compensation and Benefits Review* 39, no. 1 (January–February 2007): 55.
3. Connor Harrison, "77% of Organizations Offering Variable Pay Plans," Salary.com (January 8, 2019), https://www.salary.com/blog/compensation-trends-organizations-embracing-variable-pay/.
4. Kerry Chou, "Hedge Your Bets with Variable Pay," *WorldatWork* (2011), http://www.worldatwork.org/adimComment?id=48615.
5. James Oldroyd and Shad Morris, "Catching Falling Stars: A Human Resource Response to Social Capital's Detrimental Effect of Information Overload on Star Employees," *Academy of Management Review* (July 2012): 396–418.
6. Jean Martin and Conrad Schmidt, "How to Keep Your Top Talent," *Harvard Business Review* (May 2010): 54–61.
7. Gary Charness, Michael Cooper, and J. Lucas Reddinger, "Wage Policies, Incentive Schemes, and Motivation," *Handbook of Labor, Human Resources and Population Economics* (2020): 1–33; John A. Menefee and Ryan O. Murphy, "Rewarding and Retaining the Best," *Benefits Quarterly* 20, no. 3 (2004): 13–21; Anthony Nyberg, "Retaining Your High Performers: Moderators of the Performance–Job Satisfaction–Voluntary Turnover Relationship," *Journal of Applied Psychology* 95, no. 3 (2010): 440–453.
8. Enno Siemsen, Sridhar Balasubramanian, and Aleda V. Roth, "Incentives That Induce Task-Related Effort, Helping, and Knowledge Sharing in Workgroups," *Management Science* 53, no. 10 (October 2007): 1533.
9. Ann Bares, "Incentive Plan Design Begins with Good Questions," *Workforce Management* (October 2008); Fay Hansen, "Control and Customization," *Workforce Management* 86, no. 19 (November 5, 2007): 42, http://www.workforce.com/articles/14112; Luis R. Gomez-Mejia Pascual Berrone, and Monica Franco-Santos, *Compensation and Organizational Performance: Theory, Research and Practice* (Armonk, NY: M. E. Sharpe Publishing, 2010).
10. Joe Abusamra, "Here Comes Pay for Performance!" *Federal Times* (March 8, 2017).

11. Dhuha Abdulsalam et al., "Individualized Pay-for-Performance Arrangements: Peer Reactions and Consequences," *Journal of Applied Psychology* (2020), Vol. 106, pg. 1202–1223.
12. Shonna Waters, "Should Organizations Pay for Performance?" Society for Human Resource Management (August 16, 2019), https://www.shrm.org/hr-today/news/hr-magazine/1117/pages/should-organizations-pay-for-performance.aspx.
13. Joanne Sammer, "Weighing Pay Incentives," *HR Magazine* 52, no. 6 (June 2007): 64.
14. M. Franco-Santos, "Performance Measurement Issues, Incentive Application and Globalization," in L. R. Gomez-Mejia and S. Werner (eds.), *Global Compensation: Foundations and Perspectives* (London: Routledge, 2008), 41–56.
15. J. M Welbourne and L. R. Gomez-Mejia, "Team-Based Incentives," in L. A. Berger and D. R. Berger (eds.), *The Compensation Handbook: A State of the Art Guide to Compensation Strategy and Design* (New York: McGraw-Hill, 2008).
16. George T. Milkovich and Jerry M. Newman, *Compensation*, 10th ed. (Boston: McGraw-Hill Irwin, 2010).
17. Monica Torres, "Study: Need for Peer Approval Is the Biggest Motivator at Work," Ladders (January 24, 2018), https://www.theladders.com/career-advice/study-need-for-peer-approval-is-the-biggest-motivator-at-work.
18. Michael C. Sturman, "Using Your Pay System to Improve Employees' Performance: How You Pay Makes a Difference," *Cornell Hospitality Report* 6, no. 13 (2006): 4–20.
19. Bill Fotsch and John Case, "How to Build Incentive Plans That Actually Work," *Forbes* (August 24, 2015).
20. Chris Taylor, "On-the-Spot Incentives," *HR Magazine* 49, no. 5 (May 2004): 80–84.
21. Sanjiv Das, "Reward Your Employees—Without Breaking the Bank," *Harvard Business Review* (August 7, 2020), https://hbr.org/2020/08/reward-your-employees-without-breaking-the-bank; Stephen Miller, "More Companies Offer Bonuses as a Challenging Year Ends," Society for Human Resource Management (December 3, 2020), https://www.shrm.org/resourcesandtools/hr-topics/compensation/pages/more-companies-offer-bonuses-as-a-challenging-year-ends.aspx.
22. Don Hellriegel and John W. Slocum, Jr., *Organizational Behavior*, 12th ed. (Mason, OH: South-Western, 2009), Chapter 6.
23. Employee perceptions of appropriate pay raises likely depend on the employer's ability to pay and the economics of the period. For example, if an employer's ability to pay is great and the economics of the industry are strong, then employees will expect larger percentage merit raises.
24. Susan J. Wells, "No Results, No Raise," *HR Magazine* 50, no. 5 (May 2005): 76.
25. Dana Wilkie, "Instead of Rating Performance with Numbers, How about Adjectives?" *Society for Human Resource Management* (July 6, 2016).
26. Stephen Miller, "Employers Seek Better Approaches to Pay for Performance," Society for Human Resource Management (February 8, 2016); David E. Terpstra and Andre L. Honoree, "Employees' Responses to Merit Pay Inequity," *Compensation and Benefits Review* 37, no. 1 (January–February 2005): 51.
27. Bimal Chandra Nayak, Gopal Krishna Nayak, and Debasish Jena, "Social Recognition and Employee Engagement: The Effect of Social Media in Organizations," *International Journal of Engineering Business Management* 12 (2020): 1847979020975109; Shibeal O'Flaherty, Michael T. Sanders, and Ashley Whillans, "Research: A Little Recognition Can Provide a Big Morale Boost," *Harvard Business Review* (March 29, 2021).
28. Ward Olgreen, "Modern-Day Motivation for Restaurant Employees," *IncentiveMag* (March 10, 2017).
29. Dominic Price and Philip Braddock, "'24 Hours of Opportunity': Behind the Scenes of ShipIt," Atlassian Blog (October 14, 2019), https://www.atlassian.com/blog/inside-atlassian/atlassians-shipit-hackathon-for-technical-and-non-technical-teams.
30. "Employee Recognition Programs Tied to Organizational Goals More Likely to Be Rated Highly, SHRM–Globoforce Survey Shows," Society for Human Resource Management (June 22, 2015). https://www.shrm.org/about-shrm/press-room/press-releases/pages/employee_recognition_survey.aspx
31. L. S. Beitelspacher, T. L. Baker, A. Rapp, and D. Grewal, "Understanding the Long-Term Implications of Retailer Returns in Business-to-Business Relationships," *Journal of the Academy of Marketing Science* (2017): 1–21.
32. Miller Heimen Group, Inc., "Sales Performance Optimization Study: 2016 Key Trends Analysis," *CSO Insights* (2016).
33. Bob Marsh, "Gamification and Sales: Is It Working?" Salesforce Blog (March 21, 2017), https://www.salesforce.com/blog/2013/08/gamification-and-sales.html.
34. http://www.espn.com/nba/history/leaders/_/stat/assists (March 21, 2017).
35. Jonathan Lautaha, "7 Sales Gamification Secrets to Drive Productivity," Insidesales.com Blog (February 5, 2016).
36. Jim Stockmann, "Change on the Horizon: An Analysis of Sales Compensation Practices," *Workspan* (April 2007): 41.
37. Amy Lyman, "Nordstrom—Great Service for Over 100 Years: Best Company for 25 Years," *2009 Great Place to Work Institute*, https://www.greatplacetowork-conference.com.
38. J. Delfgaauw, R. Dur, and M. Souverijn, "Team Incentives, Task Assignment, and Performance: A Field Experiment," *Leadership Quarterly* 31, no. 3 (2020): 101241; George T. Milkovich and Jerry M. Newman, *Compensation*, 10th ed. (Boston: McGraw-Hill Irwin, 2010).
39. The foundation for improshare's measurement system is the base productivity factor (BPF), defined as the ratio of standard direct labor hours produced to total actual hours worked

in a base period. The productivity of subsequent periods is then measured by enlarging the standard direct labor hours earned by the BPF ratio to establish improshare hours (IH). IH is then compared with the actual hours worked in the same period. If earned hours exceed actual hours, 50 percent of the gain is divided by actual hours worked to establish a bonus percentage for all employees in the plan.

40. https://www.glassdoor.com/Reviews/Lincoln-Electric-Reviews-E3658.htm (September 17, 2021).
41. Jason Kovac, "Stock Options," *Workspan* (August 2006): 23. See also Seymour Burchman and Blair Jones, "The Future of Stock Options: From Starring Role to Ensemble Player," *WorldatWork* 13, no. 1 (2004): 29–38.
42. Mamdough Farid, Vincent Conte, and Harold Lazaus, "Toward a General Model for Executive Compensation," *Journal of Management Development* 30, no. 1 (2011): 67–86; Ira T. Kay and Steve Seelig, "Revising the Use of a Management Stock Purchase Plan to Increase Management Ownership," *Journal of Deferred Compensation* 11, no. 3 (2006): 24.
43. Chris Matthews and Matthew Heimer, "The 5 Biggest Corporate Scandals of 2016," *Fortune* (December 28, 2016); Raquel Meyer Alexander, Mark Hirchey, and Susan Scholz, "Backdating Employee Stock Options: Tax Implications," *CPA Journal* 77, no. 10 (2007): 24. See also T. Thomas Cottingham III, "The Stock Options Backdating Scandal: Critical First Response," *Risk Management* 54, no. 6 (2007): 12.
44. "Employee Ownership by the Numbers," National Center for Employee Ownership (September 2020), https://www.nceo.org/articles/employee-ownership-by-the-numbers#. Based on research conducted by the National Center for Employee Ownership (NCEO) in 2016. NCEO is a private, nonprofit membership and research organization that serves as the leading source of accurate, unbiased information on ESOPs, broadly granted employee stock options and related programs, and ownership culture. It can be reached at http://www.nceo.org or by phone at (510) 208–1300.
45. Dan Ariely, Anat Bracha, and Stephan Meier, "Doing Good or Doing Well? Image Motivation and Monetary Incentives in Behaving Prosocially," *American Economic Review* 99, no. 1 (2009): 544–555; Karl Duncker and Lynne Lees, "On Problem Solving," *Psychological Monographs* 58, no. 5 (1945).
46. D. H. Pink, *Drive: The Surprising Truth about What Motivates Us* (New York: Penguin, 2011).
47. Mark Reilly and Brian Enright, "A New Approach to Executive Compensation," *Workspan* (August 2007): 45.
48. Seymour Burchman and Blair Jones, "Executive Compensation as a Support for Growth Strategy," *WorldatWork* 15, no. 3 (2006): 39.
49. Total annual compensation is the sum of an executive's annual and long-term compensation. Annual compensation consists of salary, bonus, and other yearly pay. Long-term compensation consists of stock awards, the value of any stock options exercised during the year, and any other long-term compensation (such as payouts from long-term incentive plans, director's fees, and special bonuses).
50. Edward E. Lawler III and David Finegold, "CEO Compensation: What Board Members Think," *WorldatWork* 16, no. 3 (2007): 38.
51. "2017 Salary Guide," *CEO Update*, 2017; Mercedes Erickson, "Peer Benchmarking and Trends in Executive Compensation: 2016 Update," *Audit Analytics*, http://www.auditanalytics.com/blog/peer-benchmarking-and-trends-inexecutive-compensation-2016-update/.
52. Brandon Cherry, "Executive Bonus Plans: Recent Trends in Equity Compensation," *Workspan* (January 2007): 22.
53. Darrell Rigby and Barbara Bilodeau, "Selecting Management Tools Wisely," *Harvard Business Review* 85, no. 12 (December 2007): 20.
54. Brad Hill and Christine Tande, "What's Next for Executive Incentives Now That Options Are Limited?" *Workspan* (September 2007): 47.
55. Pam Delaney, "Filling the Executive Benefits Gap," *Workspan* (November 2007), 69.
56. Lawrence Mishel and Jori Kandra, "CEO Compensation Surged 14% in 2019 to $21.3 Million," Economic Policy Institute (Ithaca, NY: Cornell University Press, August 18, 2020).
57. Kara Brandeisky, "Most Americans Can't Guess the Average CEO's Salary. Can You?" *Money* (February 5, 2016).
58. Stan Choe, "On Average, Top CEOs Make Over $12.3 Million. Can That Continue after the Coronavirus?" *Fortune* (May 27, 2020).
59. "200 Highest-Paid CEOs 2016," *New York Times*, http://www.equilar.com/reports/38-2-new-york-times-200-highestpaid-ceos-2016.html.
60. Steven N. Kaplan, "Are CEOs Overpaid?" *WorldatWork* 16, no. 3 (2007): 22. See also Ira Kay and Steve Van Putten, *Myths and Realities of Executive Pay* (Cambridge, MA: Cambridge University Press, 2007); Jessica Marquez, "5 Questions: In Defense of CEO Pay," *Workforce Management* 86, no. 16 (2007): 8.
61. Louis Lavelle, "Everybody Should Be a Little Nervous," *Business Week* (December 22, 2003): 42.
62. Seymour Burchman and Blair Jones, "A New Day for Executive Compensation," *Workspan* (January 2007): 15. See also "Out at Home Depot," *Business Week* (January 15, 2007): 56.
63. Mark Gimein, "The Bottom Line on Options," *Business Week* (April 3, 2006): 32. See also Peter Burrows, "Is Steve's Job Untouchable?" *Business Week* (January 15, 2007): 28.
64. Fictional case adapted from the Network Cable, Inc. case.

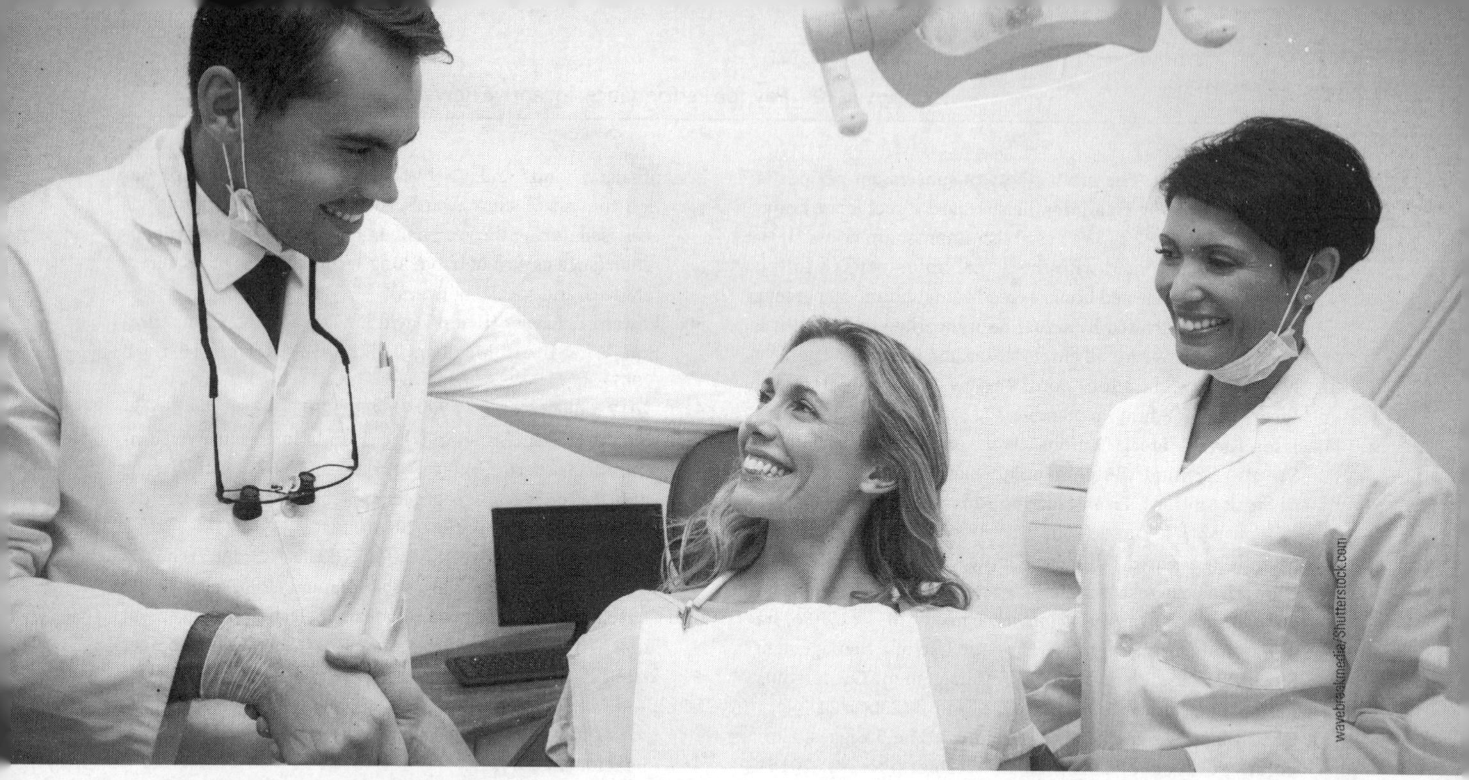

CHAPTER 11

Employee Benefits

Learning Outcomes

After studying this chapter, you should be able to

LO 1 Detect cost-effective strategies companies use to develop benefits plans.

LO 2 Summarize the employee benefits required by U.S. law.

LO 3 Describe the types of work–life benefits, retirement programs, and pension plans, as well as the regulations related to them.

Approximately three in five people report that benefits and perks are among their top considerations when thinking about accepting a job.[1] Maybe this is why companies like Netflix provide one paid year of parental leave to new parents, or why Spotify covers the costs for egg freezing and fertility assistance, or why Airbnb gives its employees an annual stipend of $2,000 to travel and stay in an Airbnb listing anywhere in the world.[2] Despite how cool many of these benefits may be, the cost of providing them has been climbing sharply. Due to increased access to employer information through social media and search engines, employees are increasingly aware of the benefits they receive and how they compare to what other companies are offering. Hence, benefits act as a key source of advantage (or disadvantage) for companies.

11.1 Elements of a Successful Benefits Program

LO1 Detect cost-effective strategies companies use to develop benefits plans.

Benefits can represent more than 50 percent of the total payroll costs an employer pays, depending on the types of benefits it offers. Some benefits are required by law, whereas others are voluntarily granted by employers. Figure 11.1 shows the proportion of employees' total compensation that U.S. organizations, on average, pay in the form of benefits, and a breakdown of how much goes to each.

Benefits are expensive, so companies must pay close attention to them. The cost of benefits for employers has increased more than 300 percent in the last decade.[3] Health care costs, which have been growing at double and triple the rate of inflation, are of

Figure 11.1 Where a Dollar of Employee Compensation Goes in the United States

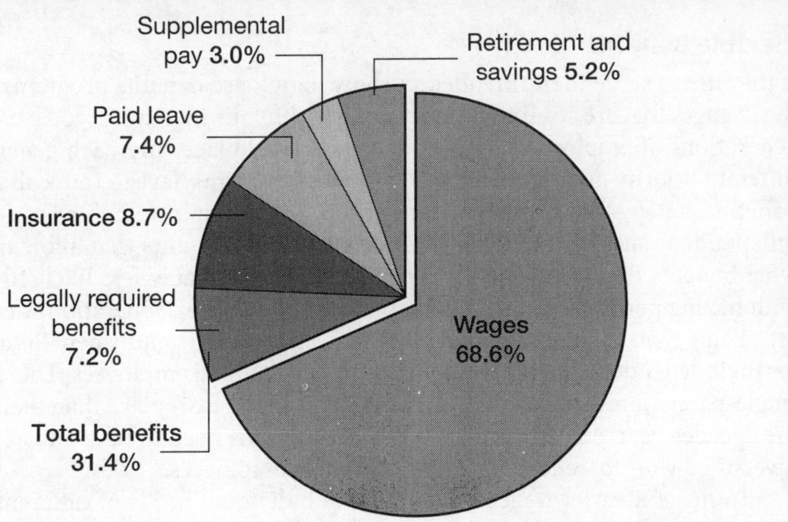

Source: *Employer Costs per Hour Worked* (Washington, DC: U.S. Bureau of Labor Statistics: 2021), http://www.bls.gov/news.release/ecec.t01.htm.

particular concern. We will discuss health care reform in more depth later in the chapter, along with the various health care cost-containment measures firms are implementing.

Many forces must be kept in balance for a benefits program to succeed. For example, a firm's managers must consider how to fund its benefits program and sustain it, as well as the tax consequences related to it. The needs of a company's employees also must be considered, because they can differ significantly from firm to firm. If the firm's industry is unionized, that fact will affect the types of benefits the firm is likely to have to offer. So will the benefits its competitors are offering and the organization's strategic objectives. Microsoft, for example, picks up the full tab for medical care for all of its U.S. employees and their dependents, which is unusual.[4] Microsoft does so because one of its strategic objectives is to attract the top talent in the country. An employer's benefits plan also needs to be compatible with the organization's strategic compensation plan (see Chapter 9), including its total rewards strategy.[5]

11.1a Selecting Benefits

In designing a benefits program, a firm can purchase detailed compensation data or hire outside firms to help it construct the most appropriate program. Before a new benefit is introduced, the need for it should first be determined through consultation with employees. Designing benefits programs with employee participation will likely mean that employees are more satisfied with the final benefits plan. Employees who are satisfied with their benefits are, in turn, more likely to be satisfied with their jobs. Opinion surveys are also a common method for obtaining employee input.

Many organizations establish committees composed of managers and employees to administer, interpret, and oversee their benefits policies. The Leadership and Learning Center in Salem, Massachusetts, a professional development organization, has decreased turnover from 40 percent in the 1990s to the single digits in recent years. The reason? A benefits committee. Twice a year, employees break into committees to administer benefits surveys and revise the benefits plan, giving employees much more responsibility and say in their own benefits packages.[6]

Flexible Benefits

If they are to serve their intended purpose, employee benefits programs must adapt to the changes that are continually occurring within our society. As you have learned, four generations of employees are part of today's workplace, and each generation places a different priority on their benefits. Consequently, firms have to think about designing a benefits strategy that appeals to each group. For example, members of Gen Z are more independent and tend to want lifestyle spending accounts that allow them to decide what benefits they get. Millennial employees are probably less likely to be concerned with having pensions than are baby boomers. Likewise, Generation X employees who are raising their families are more likely to want family-friendly benefits and health care for their dependents than baby boomers and Millennial employees. There are also more single-parent families and two-earner couples in the workplace than there have been in the decades past. As you can see, benefits programs need to take into account a highly diversified workforce to attract highly capable employees.

flexible benefits plans (cafeteria plans)
Benefit plans that enable individual employees to choose the benefits that are best suited to their particular needs.

To make it easier to accommodate the individual needs of different employees, a wide range of organizations have begun offering **flexible benefits plans**, also known as **cafeteria plans**. Rather than being one-size-fits-all plans, these plans allow individual employees to choose the benefits that are best suited to their particular needs. They also prevent certain benefits from being wasted on employees who have no need for them. Furthermore, companies realize they can get a better return on investment by tailoring benefits to an employee's stage of life or family status.[7] Compensation specialists often see flexible benefits plans as the ideal solution to ensure good employee–benefits matching. Employees select the benefits of greatest value to them, while employers manage benefits costs by limiting the dollars employees have to spend.

Typically, employees are offered a basic or core benefits package of life and health insurance, sick leave, and vacation. Requiring a core set of benefits ensures that employees have a minimum level of coverage to protect against unforeseen financial hardships. Employees are then given a certain amount of funds to purchase whatever other benefits they need through the plan. Other benefit options might include prepaid legal services, financial planning, dental insurance, and long-term care insurance. Elder care, public transportation vouchers, and even pet insurance are often options as well, but are less commonly offered because they depend on stage of life or current situation.

11.1b Administering Benefits

With the wide variety of benefits offered to employees today, administering an organization's benefits program can be both costly and time-consuming. Even for small employers with 30 to 40 employees, keeping track of each employee's use of a benefit or request for a change of benefits can be cumbersome. Fortunately, online employee benefit systems have become mainstream practice for both large and small employers. Employees are provided with passwords that allow them to get information about their benefits plans, enroll in their plans of choice, change their coverage, or simply inquire about the status of their various benefit accounts without contacting a HR representative. Online benefits systems, which are often referred to as *employee self-service (ESS) systems*, can result in significant cost savings in benefits administration, improve the accuracy of decisions, decrease processing time, and increase employee satisfaction.[8] Such systems are so successful because they give employees the information and responsibility of personalizing and tracking their own benefits.

As with the benefits themselves, it can be helpful to obtain feedback on the different online systems a firm is investigating for adoption by asking employees to "test drive" them. If a system is difficult to navigate, employees will end up calling the HR department for assistance, defeating the purpose of the system.

11.1c Communicating Employee Benefits

Communicating the costs of benefits is a key part of an effective benefits strategy. One survey from a research and consulting firm found that 4 of 10 U.S. employees lack any knowledge of the costs of their benefits, and of the 60 percent who think they know the cost of their benefits, only 15 percent could provide a reasonable estimate.[9]

Communication of employee benefits information improved significantly with the passage of the Employee Retirement Income Security Act (ERISA) in 1974. This act requires that employees be informed about their pension and certain other benefits in a manner calculated to be understood by the average employee. Additionally, employees can sue their employers for misleading them about their health and welfare benefits under ERISA.

In one settlement, Providence Health & Services, a nonprofit hospital chain, paid $352 million to settle a proposed class-action suit accusing the organization of using its religious affiliation as a church exemption to avoid the ERISA requirements of minimum funding and of failing to protect employees' retirement plans.[10] This and other settlements underscore the importance of communicating benefit information accurately and unambiguously.

When communicating employee benefits, the best advice is to use multiple media techniques. Different employee groups have different ways of learning and distinct preferences for how they receive information, so a one-size-fits-all strategy will not work. Also, the level of complexity of the benefit information being communicated is likely to determine the media selected for communicating this information.[11] Because about one-third of IKEA's employees are Millennials, the company was worried if it only mailed out benefits information to these employees, many of them would not bother to open the packages. So, in addition to mailing information, the company used Twitter to send a weblink to its benefits site and remind employees about the firm's benefits enrollment deadline. "We wanted to talk to our co-workers in a way they are talking," says Beth Gleba, former corporate information manager for IKEA, North America.[12]

Some general pointers for designing benefits information regardless of the medium include the following:

- Avoid complex language when describing benefits. Clear, concise, and understandable language is a must.
- Explain the purpose behind a benefit and the value it offers employees. Be upfront about the pros and cons of different benefit plans.
- Use graphics whenever possible to make the information understandable at a glance.
- Provide numerous examples to illustrate how a benefit choice might affect different types of employees, depending on their personal circumstances.

Even if employees can access their benefits information online, most firms periodically mail out printed benefits statements that detail the status of an employee's benefits. See Highlights in HRM 1 for an example of how to calculate your total compensation based on salary and benefits. Notice how the employee's total compensation is highlighted so that the full value of the benefits received is easier to see.

Cost Containment Strategies

Many firms have either begun requiring employees to pay part of the cost of their benefits or, if they were already doing so, increasing the amounts employees pay in the form of premiums, copayments, and deductibles. In addition, it is not uncommon for larger companies to cut the health care plans they once provided their retirees.

Containing Medical Benefits Costs

high-deductible health insurance plans (HDHPs)
A medical insurance plan characterized by high deductibles but lower premiums for workers and a health spending account to which employers contribute funds employees can keep should they leave the organization.

What is causing the growth in health care costs? This rise has been attributed to many factors. One factor is the overuse of costly health care services by consumers. This is part of the reason why firms have turned to health savings accounts and **high-deductible health insurance plans (HDHPs)**. In conjunction with HDHPs, employees are provided with a *health care spending account (HSA)* to which they and their employers can contribute on a pretax basis. In addition, employees can deduct the amounts they contribute to their HSAs from their earnings when they pay their income taxes. An advantage of HSAs is that the funds remaining in the account at the end of the year belong to the employee, even if he or she leaves the company. Employees often like HDHPs for this reason, and because the regular premiums deducted from their paychecks for insurance

A Personalized Statement of Benefits Costs

ABC Corporation

Your Total Compensation Report

Enclosed is a personalized Statement prepared specifically for you. This statement shows the contributions made by your company toward your total compensation package. As you review this statement, you will see that the value of your benefits, added to your annual pay, produce your total compensation. The statement is designed to show how much your service is valued by your company.

Thank you for your service,

Jonathan Bigg, President

Department: Marketing

Chris Smith
123 Maple Street
Pittsburgh, PA 15212

Base Pay		Other Cash Benefits		Company-Paid Benefits		Total Compensation
$40,000	+	$1,600	+	$19,579	=	$61,179

Pay		
Base Pay Total	$	40,000
Salary	$	40,000
Other Income Total	$	1,600
Holiday Bonus	$	200
Annual Bonus	$	500
Performance Bonus	$	900

Total Compensation Package
(Your Base Pay and Company-Paid Benefits)

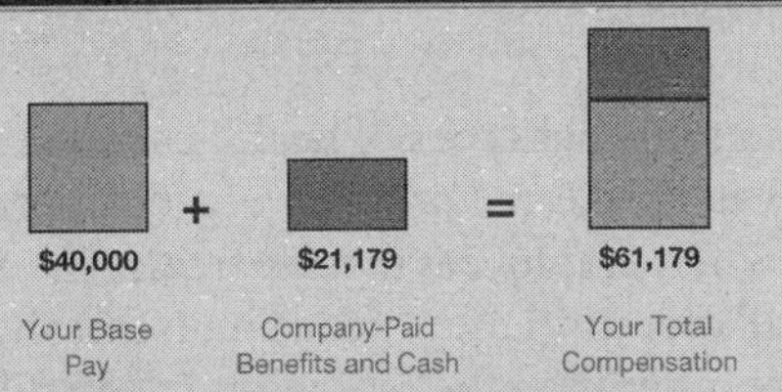

53% **Your Company-Paid Benefits and Cash represent an additional 53% of Your Base Pay!**

Additional Company Perks
Free Coffee Service
Annual Holiday Gala
Annual Company Picnic

Benefits	Company Contribution		Your Contribution	
Insurance Benefits Total	$	6,917	$	4,703
Health Insurance	$	5,770	$	2,885
Dental Insurance	$	577	$	288
Vision Insurance	$	344	$	--
Short-Term Disability	$	133	$	--
Long-Term Disability	$	93	$	--
Aflac Short-Term Disability	$	--	$	680
Aflac Personal Accident	$	--	$	522
Aflac Cancer	$	--	$	328
Retirement Benefits Total	$	3,425	$	4,175
Social Security	$	2,579	$	2,579
Medicare	$	596	$	596
401K	$	250	$	1,000
Time Off Benefits Total	$	3,320	$	--
PTO	$	3,320	$	--
Mandated Benefits Total	$	1,747	$	--
Federal Unemployment	$	56	$	--
State Unemployment	$	179	$	--
Worker's Compensation	$	1,512	$	--
Special Benefits Total	$	4,170	$	--
Free Parking	$	2,400	$	--
Fun Fridays Food Fests	$	250	$	--
Cell/PC/Technology	$	600	$	--
Education/Training	$	920	$	--
Benefits Total	$	19,579	$	8,878

69% **Your Company-Paid Benefits represent 69% of your Total Benefits!**

Disclaimer: Neither ComPackage Corp. nor your employer shall be liable for any errors or omissions in this report generated using the ComPackage softwareThe contents of this report are for illustrative purposes only and are not intended to be, nor shall they constitute, a definitive statement of your compensation packageCalculation totals may differ on account of roundingAny questions regarding your compensation package should be directed to your employer.

COMPackage Corp © 2010 This Total Compensation Report was created by© COMPackage Corp. http://www.compackage.cor

Employers must use a variety of techniques to communicate the complexities of benefits programs to their employees.

Source: http://blogs.intel.com/jobs/

are generally lower than the premiums paid for other types of health care plans, such as health maintenance organizations (HMOs) and preferred provider organizations (PPOs).

The downside is that with an HDHP, when employees receive treatment, they have to pay either a percentage of their care or all of it until they meet a high threshold called a deductible. These expenses are generally higher than the copays and deductibles associated with other types of health care insurance plans. As a consequence, employees are more conscious of medical costs. They have an incentive to spend their health care funds wisely and over time to increase the value of their HSAs. For this reason, HDHPs are sometimes referred to as *consumer-driven plans.*

HDHPs do seem to help control costs. However, because they work differently and require higher out-of-pocket costs for employees, HR managers need to carefully explain how they work and show employees how much long-term savings they can accumulate for their long-term medical care. Also, some studies have shown that employees with HSAs tend to put off preventive care in favor of growing their HSAs. This can be a mistake if an employee later develops a serious and costly disease that could have been prevented with early screening and treatment.

health maintenance organizations (HMOs)
Organizations of physicians and health care professionals that provide a wide range of services to subscribers and their dependents on a prepaid basis.

Because HMOs and PPOs offer discounted rates for health care services, they have become another vehicle for reducing costs. **Health maintenance organizations (HMOs)** are organizations of physicians and other health care professionals that provide a wide range of services to subscribers and their dependents on a prepaid basis. Employees pay a small fixed fee called a copay (copayment), often $25 or $30, whenever they get medical treatment. Employers pay a fixed annual fee to the HMO to cover the majority of their employees' medical costs. Because they must provide all covered services for a fixed dollar amount, HMOs generally emphasize preventive care and early intervention. Employees who sign up for the plan must choose a general-practice physician, called a *primary care physician*, from the HMO's list of doctors. Their primary care physicians provide employees with basic medical care. However, to see a specialist, employees need a referral from their primary care physicians. This helps keep costs down as well, because specialists charge fees that are generally higher than those charged by primary care physicians. The copays employees pay to see specialists are also slightly higher, which gives employees an incentive to see their primary care physicians first.

A **preferred provider organization (PPO)** is a group of physicians who establish an organization or a network of doctors who guarantee lower costs to the employer through lower service charges or agreed-on utilization controls (such as a reduced number of diagnostic tests per employee). Unlike HMOs, where employees may have limited choices when it comes to the doctors they can see, PPOs allow employees to select their doctor from a wider list of physicians (participating doctors). Usually, a number of physicians are available to choose from for different medical needs, and employees do not need a referral to see a specialist. Small copays are a common feature of PPOs as well. Employees also have the option of using a doctor outside of the PPO, although that causes them to pay higher costs.

preferred provider organization (PPO)
A network of physicians who establish an organization that guarantees lower health care costs to employers and their employees.

Employers sometimes couple PPOs and HMOS with different types of tax-advantaged accounts employees can use to pay their out-of-pocket health care expenses such as their copays, the cost of prescription drugs, and so forth. A *health reimbursement account (HRA)* allows employees to be reimbursed by their companies for their out-of-pocket expenses. Employees do not have to pay taxes on the amounts they are reimbursed, unlike if the reimbursements were made through their paychecks. A *flexible spending account (FSA)* is another type of account employees can use to pay for their health-related expenses. Employees fund these accounts by having money deducted from their paychecks. The money deducted is not subject to taxes, so workers have more to spend on their health care than they would without the accounts. Companies can make contributions to employees' FSAs as well. A disadvantage of FSAs is that any funds not used by the end of the plan year revert back to the employer.

In addition, many companies—even *Fortune* 500 companies—are limiting the plans available to employees to all but the least expensive ones and conducting audits to be sure non-eligible dependents of employees are not being covered.

Containing Dental, Optical, and Mental Health Benefits Costs

Dental plans are designed to help pay for dental care costs and to encourage employees to receive regular dental attention. Like medical plans, dental care plans may be operated by insurance companies, dental service corporations, organizations administering Blue Cross/Blue Shield plans, HMOs, and groups of dental care providers. Typically, the insurance pays a portion of the charges incurred by the employee, and the subscriber pays the remainder. Optical benefits work in a similar way. These benefits generally cover or offset the cost of seeing an optometrist once or twice a year as well as the costs of contact lenses and glasses purchased periodically.

Almost all workers with health coverage receive mental health benefits as part of their plans.[13] However, prior to 2009, most plans placed limits on inpatient hospital stays and outpatient visits, and the copays were often higher than the copays for medical care.

The Mental Health Parity and Addiction Equity Act of 2008 changed that. In terms of the costs and access to care, this law requires group health plans to treat mental health benefits the same way they do medical and surgical benefits.[14] However, even with the passage of this law, there are some significant issues around insurance coverage of mental health issues that make it typically much more expensive than other types of care. This is due in part to inadequate provider networks, fueled by a shortage of mental health professionals and the fact that many mental health professionals do not accept insurance at all because insurance companies do not compensate them fairly.[15]

Containing Additional Costs

An aging U.S. population, high obesity rates, and the health problems associated with them are three other reasons cited for rising health care costs. To combat these problems, companies are offering employees lower health care premiums for adopting healthy habits and activities. Wellness programs (discussed shortly) are a part of this effort. Conversely, some firms are also penalizing employees who engage in unhealthy habits such as smoking by charging them higher health care premiums.[16] To help cope with the rising costs of drugs, companies are encouraging their employees to use generic drugs and buy 90-day supplies through designated mail-order pharmacies that provide them at a discount.

One of the more dramatic moves companies are making in an effort to save on their health care expenditures is waiving the deductibles and copays for medical tourism. This means employees can pay less if they are willing to travel abroad for medical procedures to countries where they often cost only a fraction of what they do in the United States.[17] Figure 11.2 shows the countries Americans most often utilize for treatment abroad and the approximate cost of procedures in these countries as a percentage of U.S. costs.

Value-Based Health Initiatives

A small but growing number of employers are turning to *value-based health initiatives.* Value-based initiatives focus on more than cost-cutting. Companies pursuing this strategy look at the medical care that their employees most use and need—such as treatment for asthma, high blood pressure, or diabetes—and target benefits and health programs toward them. For example, Cerner Corporation, an electronic health record system

Figure 11.2 The Cost of Medical Procedures Abroad as a Percentage of U.S. Costs

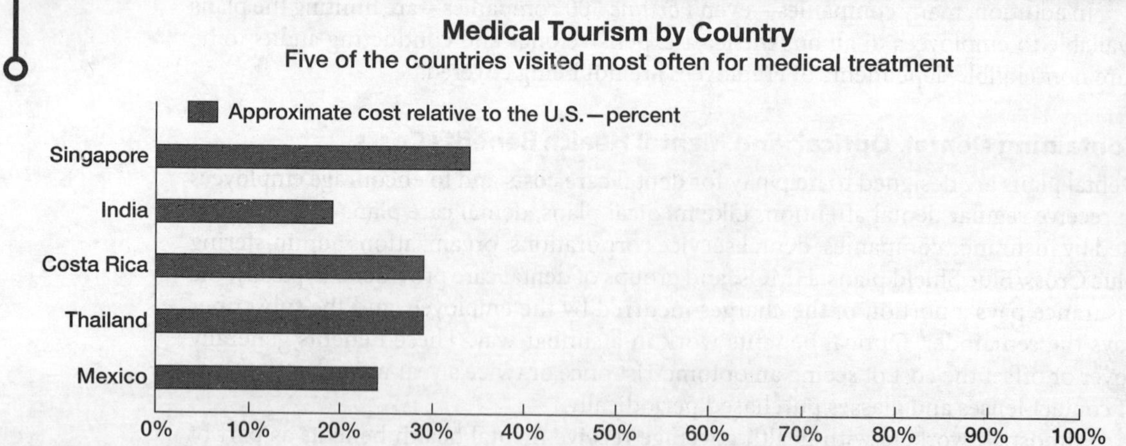

Source: Adapted from *Reuters*, Deloitte, and the research findings of Joseph Woodman, the author of *Patients without Borders*.

for health care providers like hospitals and clinics, noticed that many of its employees didn't purchase the medicine they needed to handle their anxiety or depression. So the company reduced the out-of-pocket costs and waived copays for antidepressant prescriptions for employees and their families. Following this policy change, Cerner Corporation employees were more likely to use or start a new medication for anxiety or depression and reported positive health outcomes.[18]

Lucky Business/Shutterstock.com

Many employers offer incentives for employees who take care of their health, such as discounts on health club memberships.

Wellness Programs

Wellness programs are employer-sponsored programs designed to encourage employees to maintain and improve their health and well-being by getting regular checkups, eating properly, exercising, and managing their stress levels so as to prevent costly and protracted illnesses. The Home Depot has a broad corporate wellness program to prioritize employee health and demonstrates the kinds of strategies other firms can use when formulating their own wellness programs. The Home Depot offers resources such as healthy cooking and physical fitness programs, including resources like cookbooks, discounts to health club chains, and chats with coaches to set goals and create a 12-week journey to better health; health challenges every summer for a chance to win cash prizes; smoking cessation programs with free one-on-one coaching and nicotine patches; free on-site flu shots; and wellness recognition programs where employees nominate one employee who sets and achieves their wellness goal for a prized patch to wear on their apron and recognition from The Home Depot.[19]

wellness programs
Employer-sponsored programs designed to encourage employees to maintain and improve their health and well-being by getting regular checkups, eating properly, exercising, and managing their stress levels so as to prevent costly and protracted illnesses.

Disease Management Programs

Using medically trained personnel, **disease management programs** provide patients and their caregivers with information on monitoring and treating medical conditions, while coordinating communication between them, their health care providers, employers, and insurers. Bank One Corporation of Chicago developed such a program when managers noticed high absenteeism among employees with diabetes, asthma, and depression. Disease management programs can also be used in conjunction with the rehabilitation of employees who are injured on the job to help them recover more quickly and return safely to work.

disease management programs
Programs that provide patients and their caregivers with information on monitoring and treating medical conditions, while coordinating communication between them, their health care providers, their employers, and insurers.

Employee Assistance Programs

To help workers cope with a wide variety of problems that may interfere with the way they perform their jobs, all kinds of organizations, including the New York Mets, USAA, the Los Angeles Police Department, and Levi Strauss, have developed **employee assistance programs (EAPs)**. An employee assistance program typically provides diagnosis, counseling, and referral for advice or treatment when necessary for problems related to alcohol

employee assistance programs (EAPs)
Services provided by employers to help workers cope with a wide variety of problems that interfere with the way they perform their jobs.

Richard Sennott/Tribune Content Agency LLC/Alamy Stock Photo

Walk while you work? To combat obesity and other health problems, GlaxoSmithKline, Humana, Mutual of Omaha, and Best Buy have begun utilizing treadmill desks like the one shown here. The treadmills move at a slow speed so employees do not get hot, sweaty, or out of breath.

or drug abuse, emotional difficulties, and financial or family difficulties.[20] The main goal is to help employees solve their personal problems, or at least to prevent problems from turning into crises that affect their ability to work productively. To handle crises, many EAPs offer hotlines, available around the clock, that employees can call for help. After Cerner Corporation offered its employees an EAP, the company's outpatient mental health care costs declined by nearly 41 percent.[21]

Mental Health

In recent years, EAPs have earned the nickname "emotional assistance programs" because of an increase in their use by employees seeking mental and emotional health services. Such services can include access to yoga and meditation services and apps, and counseling sessions. The counseling services it provides to employees is an important part of an EAP. While most organizations expect managers to counsel subordinates, some employees may have problems that require the services of professional counselors. Most organizations refer such individuals to outside counseling services, such as family counseling services, marriage counselors, and mental health clinics. Some organizations have a clinical psychologist, counselor, or comparable specialist on staff to whom employees may be referred.

Following the COVID-19 pandemic, this focus on mental health increased even more. When the pandemic hit in early March 2020, 62 percent of employees said that they were more stressed than they had been in their entire careers.[22] Companies began to roll out mental health assistance as soon as April 2020. Starbucks gave access to 20 free therapy sessions to its employees and their families. Research from the National Alliance of Healthcare Purchaser Coalitions shows that 56 percent of employers studied are now providing mental and emotional health support to their employees.[23]

LO2 Summarize the employee benefits required by U.S. law.

11.2 Employee Benefits Required by Law

Legally required employee benefits constitute 19 percent of the benefits package that employers provide. These benefits include employer contributions to Social Security, unemployment insurance, and workers' compensation insurance. We will discuss each of these benefits.

11.2a Social Security Insurance

The Social Security Act was designed to protect workers against the loss of earnings resulting from old age and unemployment. The act was later amended to include disability, or, in the case of dependents, the death of the worker supporting them. Collectively, these programs are now referred to as Old Age, Survivors, and Disability Insurance (OASDI). According to the Social Security Administration, more than 64 million people received retirement benefits from Social Security in 2020.[24]

OASDI has become nearly universal for work performed in the United States, covering approximately 96 percent of the American workforce. Workers excluded from coverage include railroad workers and civil service employees covered by their own systems, as well as farmers, domestic workers, and the self-employed whose earnings do not meet certain minimum requirements.[25] The Social Security program is supported by means of a tax levied against an employee's earnings, which must be matched by the employer in each pay period. In 2021, the tax was 6.2 percent, although the percentage can vary depending on economic conditions.[26] The tax revenues are used to pay three major types of benefits: (1) retirement benefits, (2) disability benefits, and (3) survivors' benefits.

Because of the continual changes that result from legislation and administrative rulings related to this system, as well as the complexities of making determinations of an individual's rights under Social Security, we will describe these benefits only in general terms.

Retirement Benefits

To qualify for retirement benefits, a person must have reached retirement age and be fully insured. A *fully insured person* has earned 40 credits—a maximum of 4 credits a year for 10 years, based on annual earnings, a figure adjusted annually. The amount of monthly Social Security retirement benefits is based on earnings, adjusted for inflation, over the years an individual is covered by Social Security. Under Social Security guidelines, an individual's *full retirement age* depends on the year of their birth. Workers born after 1928 can collect full benefits once they have earned 40 credits, about 10 years of work.[27] Because of longer life expectancies, for those born after that date, the age to collect full benefits has been gradually raised to age 67.

Disability Benefits under Social Security

Social Security pays benefits to people who cannot work because they have a medical condition that is expected to last at least a year or result in death. Although some government programs provide money to people with partial disabilities or short-term disabilities, Social Security does not.[28] In addition to disability payments to the worker, certain members of an employee's family, such as spouses older than age 62 and dependent children, may qualify for benefits based on the person's work history. The Social Security Administration uses a five-step process to decide if a worker is disabled and eligible to collect benefits. Highlights in HRM 2 outlines this process.

Survivors' Benefits

Survivors' benefits represent a form of life insurance paid to members of a deceased person's family who meet the eligibility requirements.[29] Survivors' benefits can be paid only if the deceased worker had credit for a certain amount of time spent in work covered by Social Security. The exact amount of work credit needed depends on the worker's age at death. As with the other benefits discussed earlier, the *amount* of benefit survivors receive is based on the worker's lifetime earnings doing work covered by Social Security.

2 **Highlights in HRM**

Who Is Eligible to Collect Disability Payments under the Social Security Act?

If you experience a disability, the Social Security Administration, in conjunction with a state agency, will use the following five-step process to determine if you are eligible to collect benefits.

1. **Are you working?** If you are working and your earnings average more than a certain amount each month, you will generally not be considered disabled. The amount changes each year. If you are not working, or your monthly earnings average this amount or less, a state agency will then look at your medical condition.
2. **Is your medical condition "severe"?** For the state agency to decide that you are disabled, your medical condition must significantly limit your ability to do basic work activities—such as walking, sitting, and remembering—for at least one year. If your medical condition is not that severe, the state agency will not consider you disabled. If your condition is that severe, the state agency goes on to step 3.
3. **Is your medical condition on the List of Impairments?** The state agency has a list of impairments that describes medical conditions that are considered so severe that they automatically mean that you are disabled as defined by law. If your condition (or combination of medical conditions) is not on this list, the state agency looks at whether your condition is as severe as a condition that is on the list. If the severity of your medical condition meets or equals that of a listed impairment, the state agency will decide that you are disabled. If it does not, the state agency goes on to step 4.
4. **Can you do the work you did before?** At this step, the state agency decides if your medical condition prevents you from being able to do the work you did before. If it does not, the state agency will decide that you are not disabled. If it does, the state agency goes on to step 5.
5. **Can you do any other type of work?** If you cannot do the work you did in the past, the state agency considers whether you would be able to do other work. It evaluates your medical condition, age, education, past work experience, and any skills you may have that could be used to do other work. If you cannot do other work, the state agency will decide that you are disabled. If you can do other work, the state agency will decide that you are not disabled.

Source: *Disability Benefits*, SSA Publication No. 05-10029 (Washington, DC: U.S. Social Security Administration, 2019), https://www.ssa.gov/pubs/EN-05-10029.pdf.

Medicare

The Social Security Administration also administers the Medicare program, which is funded by a separate payroll tax. Retired people age 65 or older are eligible for Medicare, which includes both medical and hospital insurance and prescription drug coverage.[30] The program helps with the cost of health care, but it does not cover all medical expenses or the cost of most long-term care.[31] A portion of the payroll taxes is paid by workers and matched by their employers. In 2021, workers and their employers each paid 1.45 percent on every dollar of salary or wages paid to fund the Medicare program.[32] Medicare is also financed in part by monthly medical premiums deducted from Social Security recipients' checks.

11.2b Unemployment Insurance

Unemployment insurance is part of a national program administered by the U.S. Department of Labor under the Social Security Act and coordinated with the states. It protects workers who lose their jobs through no fault of their own. Employers entirely foot the bill for this benefit via a payroll tax, though this tax rate varies widely by state. The rates firms pay also depend on their layoff records, or what is referred to as their *experience ratings*. Generally speaking, a firm with a record of laying off large numbers of employees will have to pay a higher rate than a firm that does not. In consequence, the companies most likely to lay people off will have to pay a larger share of the unemployment taxes that ultimately end up going to their former workers. As you can see, unemployment taxes are something HR managers must consider when they make decisions about where to locate their operations and hire employees as well as lay them off.

Employees who are laid off are generally eligible for up to 26 weeks of unemployment insurance benefits during their unemployment. During periods of high unemployment, such as during the COVID-19 pandemic, the federal government has sometimes passed legislation extending the amount of weeks employees can collect benefits.

Workers eligible for unemployment benefits must submit an application for unemployment compensation with their state employment agencies, register for available work, and be willing to accept any suitable employment that may be offered to them. However, the term "suitable" gives individuals considerable discretion in accepting or rejecting job offers. The amount of compensation workers are eligible to receive, which also varies by the state, is determined by a worker's previous wage rate and length of employment.

11.2c Workers' Compensation Insurance

Workers' compensation insurance is a system whereby employers purchase private or state-funded insurance to cover employees who become injured at work. Workers' compensation law is governed by statutes in every state, so the specific laws vary depending on the jurisdiction. For example, each state has different regulations governing the amount and duration of lost income benefits, including provisions for medical and rehabilitation services and how the state system is administered. Workers' compensation laws also provide death benefits to surviving spouses and dependents.

workers' compensation insurance
State-mandated insurance provided to workers to defray the loss of income and cost of treatment due to work-related injuries or illness.

Workers' compensation insurance covers workers who are injured on the job, whether they become injured on the workplace premises, elsewhere, or in an auto accident while traveling on business. It does not matter if the employee was at fault. In addition, workers who collect such compensation cannot sue their employers for their injuries unless gross negligence by the employer led to the injury or the employer lacked the level of insurance required by law. Workers' compensation insurance also covers certain work-related illnesses. Before any workers' compensation claim will be allowed, the work-related nature of the disability must be established. Also, the evaluation of the claimant by a physician trained in occupational medicine is an essential part of the claim process.

While employers in all states pay "workers' comp" insurance, the amount they pay—through payroll taxes—varies. As with unemployment insurance rates, the rate an employer pays depends on its experience rating, which is based on factors including the company's frequency and severity of employee injuries (referred to as the company's experience rating). Not surprisingly, organizations will strive to have good safety records (see Chapter 12 on creating a safe work environment) so that they can pay a lower payroll tax rate.

11.2d COBRA Insurance

The Consolidated Omnibus Budget Reconciliation Act (COBRA) mandates that employers make health care coverage—at the same rate the employer would pay—available to employees, their spouses, and their dependents on termination of employment, death, or divorce.[33] This coverage must be offered for 18 to 36 months, depending on the qualifying guidelines.

11.2e Benefits Provided by the Patient Protection and Affordable Care Act

In 2010, the Patient Protection and Affordable Care Act (PPACA) became law. This act, along with the Health Care and Education Reconciliation Act of 2010, comprises the health care reform platform that went into effect in 2014.

The key provisions related to the PPACA that all employers need to consider are the following:

- Firms that employ 50 or more people who work 30 or more hours per week but that do not offer these employees health insurance will have to pay a penalty to the government. Also, firms with 200 full-time employees are required to automatically enroll new full-time employees in their health care plans.
- Employers must offer coverage for their employee's children until they turn 26.
- No copays or deductibles can be charged to employees and their dependents for certain "essential" health care services, which are generally related to preventive care.
- Lifetime dollar limits on key health care benefits are not allowed.
- Employees cannot lose their insurance coverage solely because of an honest mistake they or their employers made on their insurance applications.

The PPACA has been under scrutiny with the party transitions between Republican and Democrat congresses and presidents. In 2021, President Joe Biden took major steps to strengthen the PPACA by increasing the subsidy amounts available to help consumers purchase health insurance and widening the range of people eligible to receive the subsidies.[34]

11.2f Benefits Provided under the Family and Medical Leave Act

The Family and Medical Leave Act (FMLA) applies to employers having 50 or more employees during 20 or more calendar workweeks in the current or preceding year.[35] A covered employer must grant an eligible employee up to a total of 12 workweeks of unpaid leave in a 12-month period for one or more of the following reasons:

- Birth of and care for a newborn child
- Adoption or foster care placement of a child
- Care for an immediate family member (spouse, child, or parent) with a serious medical condition
- Serious health condition of the employee[36]

Under the FMLA, employees are eligible to take leave if they have worked for their employers for at least 12 months, have at least 1,250 hours of service, and work in organizations that have 50 or more employees within a 75-mile radius. An employer can require that the need for medical leave be supported by a certification issued by a health care provider. Highlights in HRM 3 shows the federally required poster for the FMLA. In studying the poster, note the other important stipulations, such as enforcement and unlawful acts, which are of direct concern to managers.

Your Rights under the Family and Medical Leave Act

Employers are required to provide employees, at their worksite (or electronically), information about FMLA in an employee general notice, which must be posted in the handbook or given to new employees upon hire.

EMPLOYEE RIGHTS AND RESPONSIBILITIES UNDER THE FAMILY AND MEDICAL LEAVE ACT

Leave Entitlement

Eligible employees who work for covered employers can take up to 12 weeks of unpaid, job-protected leave in a 12-month period for the following reasons:

- The birth of a child or placement of a child for adoption or foster care
- To bond with a child (leave must be taken within 1 year of the child's birth or placement)
- To care for the employee's spouse, child, or parent, who has a qualifying serious health condition
- For the employee's own qualifying serious health condition that makes the employee unable to perform the employee's job
- For qualifying exigencies related to the foreign deployment of a military member who is the employee's spouse, child, or parent

An eligible employee who is a covered servicemember's spouse, child, parent, or next of kin may also take up to 26 weeks of FMLA leave in a single 12-month period to care for the servicemember with a serious injury or illness.

An employee does not need to use leave in one block. When it is medically necessary or otherwise permitted, employees may take leave intermittently or on a reduced schedule.

Employees may choose, or an employer may require, use of accrued paid leave while taking FMLA leave. If an employee substitutes accrued paid leave for FMLA leave, the employee must comply with the employer's normal paid leave policies.

Benefits and Protections

While employees are on FMLA leave, employers must continue health insurance coverage as if the employees were not on leave.

Upon return from FMLA leave, most employees must be restored to the same job or one nearly identical to it with equivalent pay, benefits, and other employment terms and conditions.

An employer may not interfere with an individual's FMLA rights or retaliate against someone for using or trying to use FMLA leave, opposing any practice made unlawful by the FMLA, or being involved in any proceeding under or related to the FMLA.

Eligibility Requirements

An employee who works for a covered employer must meet three criteria to be eligible for FMLA leave. The employee must:

- Have worked for the employer for at least 12 months
- Have at least 1,250 hours of service in the 12 months before taking leave*
- Work at a location where the employer has at least 50 employees within 75 miles of the employee's worksite

*Special "hours of service" requirements apply to airline flight crew employees.

Requesting Leave

Generally, employees must give 30-day advance notice of the need for FMLA leave. If it is not possible to give a 30-day notice, an employee must notify the employer as soon as possible and, generally, follow the employer's usual procedures.

Employees do not have to share a medical diagnosis, but must provide enough information to the employer so it can determine if the leave qualifies for FMLA protection. Sufficient information could include informing an employer that the employee is or will be unable to perform their job functions, that a family member cannot perform daily activities, or that hospitalization or continuing medical treatment is necessary. Employees must inform the employer if the need for leave is for a reason for which FMLA leave was previously taken or certified.

Employers can require a certification or periodic recertification supporting the need for leave. If the employer determines that the certification is incomplete, it must provide a written notice indicating what additional information is required.

Employer Responsibilities

Once an employer becomes aware that an employee's need for leave is for a reason that may qualify under the FMLA, the employer must notify the employee if he or she is eligible for FMLA leave and, if eligible, must also provide a notice of right and responsibilities under the FMLA. If the employee is not eligible, the employer must provide a reason for ineligibility.

Employers must notify its employees if leave will be designated as FMLA leave, and if so, how much leave will be designated as FMLA leave.

Enforcement

Employees may file a complaint with the U.S. Department of Labor, Wage and Hour Division, or may bring a private lawsuit against an employer.

The FMLA does not affect any federal or state law prohibiting discrimination or supersede any state or local law or collective bargaining agreement that provides greater family or medical leave rights.

For additional information or to file a complaint:
1-866-4US-WAGE (1-866-487-9243) TTY: 1-877-889-5627
www.dol.gov/whd

U.S. Wage and Hour Division

U.S. Department of Labor | Wage and Hour Division
WHD Publication 1420 Revised April 2016

WHD Publication 1420 Revised January 2009

Note: Other federally required posters are reproduced in Chapters 3, 9, and 12.

Parents of newborn children are guaranteed 12 weeks of unpaid leave under the provisions of the Family and Medical Leave Act.

OJO Images Ltd/Alamy Stock Photo

This law affects an organization's benefits program through several of its provisions: It mandates continuation of medical coverage, it prohibits loss of accrued benefits, it provides for restoration of benefits after leave, it permits substitution of paid leave and vacation during leave, it makes communication and notice compulsory, and it prohibits waiver of benefits. On return from FMLA leave, an employee must be restored to their original job or to an "equivalent" job. Equivalent jobs are those identical to the original job in terms of pay, benefits, and other employment terms and conditions.

Employers need to check their state employee-leave laws as well. Some states provide rights to employees that are greater than those provided by the FMLA. Wisconsin is an example. A few states—California, Colorado, Connecticut, the District of Columbia, Massachusetts, New Jersey, New York, Oregon, Rhode Island, and Washington—require employers to provide paid leave to parents following childbirth or adoption.[37]

In January 2008, Congress passed the National Defense Authorization Act, which amended the FMLA to provide eligible employees working for covered employers with new leave rights related to military service. Specifically, an eligible employee who is the spouse, son, daughter, parent, or next of kin of a covered service member who is recovering from a serious illness or injury sustained in the line of duty on active duty is entitled to up to 26 weeks of leave in a single 12-month period to care for the service member. Importantly, managers or supervisors with legal or administrative questions regarding the FMLA are advised to seek assistance from HR professionals before proceeding with an employee's FMLA leave request. Also, employers cannot penalize employees for requesting or taking FMLA leave through an employment action including hiring, promotion, transfer, training, disciplinary action, or awards for attendance (not missing work).

11.3 Work–Life Discretionary Benefits

LO3 Describe the types of work–life benefits, retirement programs, and pension plans, as well as the regulations related to them.

Zoom, the video conferencing company whose value shot up more than 300 percent on a quarterly basis during the COVID-19 pandemic, provides a generous time-off policy and a buddy-up new-hire initiative where the buddy takes the new hire out to coffee, lunch, and other events known in the company as "happiness events." Eddie Bauer, an outdoor clothing and equipment supplier, offers its employees takeout dinners and one paid "balance day" off a year. eBay sets aside spaces at its San Jose, California, campuses as prayer and meditation rooms where employees can "decompress" during the workday. Ben & Jerry's employees have access to a nap room. At Mitre, a nonprofit researcher, employees can take up to a week of paid time off to help with scouting trips or volunteer projects.[38] These organizations, like many others, are seeking to create a work–life organizational climate that allows employees to balance their work with their personal needs. Why? One research report shows that 60 percent of employees prefer to have work–life balance benefits, and that employees are 20 percent more engaged in and satisfied with their job when they've hit the right work–life balance.[39]

Work–life balance programs not only retain talent, but can also be a factor in attracting and recruiting potential employees. As Millennials trend toward dominating the job market, attracting this demographic means adjusting programs to include the kinds of benefits they want, such as 401(k) matching, on-site nutritionists, corporate-wide community events and challenges, the ability to work from home, and opportunities to volunteer or contribute to social causes.[40] To appeal to this broad demographic group and other employees concerned about the environment, some companies have begun offering their employees "green" benefits. Clif Bar & Company gives employees $6,500 toward the purchase of a hybrid car.

11.3a Child and Elder Care

Consider this: Every week, child care providers in the United States look after nearly 12.5 million children younger than the age of 6 whose parents are working.[41] This fact, combined with the increased employment of women with dependent children, illustrates the unprecedented demand for child care arrangements. Some employers, such as Fel-Pro, Merck, Syntex, Baptist Hospital of Miami, and Ben & Jerry's, promote on-site or near-site child care centers. Employer-sponsored dependent care spending accounts allow employees to set aside a portion of their pay before taxes to care for a dependent child. If a mother has to travel with a breastfeeding child, Zillow will pay for them to ship their breast milk back home; and Facebook provides $4,000 in "Baby Cash" to employees with a newborn.[42]

Similarly, according to a study conducted by AARP and the National Alliance for Caregiving, today more than 42 million Americans are caring, unpaid, for an older parent. The term **elder care**, as used in the context of employment, occurs when an employee provides care to an older person while remaining actively at work. The majority of these caregivers are women.[43]

elder care
Care provided to an elderly person by an employee who remains actively at work.

Beyond the loss of organizational productivity and higher employee costs, a growing concern of employers is the negative effects of caregiving on employee health. Not surprisingly, caregivers in the workforce suffer higher levels of physical, emotional, and financial stress because they find it difficult to respond to the demands of balancing work and family.[44] To help employees meet the challenges of caregiving, organizations may offer elder care counseling, educational fairs and seminars, printed resource materials, support groups, and special flexible schedules and leaves of absence.[45] Employers may also band together to provide for better elder care. The Partnership for Elder Care—a consortium formed by American Express, JPMorganChase, Philip Morris, and other companies—uses the resources of the New York City Department of Aging, a public information and aging support agency. In addition, an increasing number of employers supply or subsidize temporary care for employees' elders and children when their regular arrangements fall through so that these employees can come to work. This kind of benefit is referred to as a **backup care program**. The Home Depot, for example, offers a backup care program to its employees. Its program provides a 24/7 back-up care service that is available to employees who need spur-of-the-moment care so they can come to work.[46]

backup care program
A benefit program whereby an employer provides or subsidizes temporary care for its employee's elders or children when their regular arrangements fall through.

11.3b Payment for Time Not Worked

The "payment for time not worked" category of benefits includes paid vacations, bonuses given in lieu of paid vacations, payments for holidays not worked, paid sick leave, military and jury duty, and payments for absence due to a death in the family or other personal reasons. Figure 11.1 showed that these benefits constitute another large component of an employer's total payroll costs—7 percent on average.[47]

Paid time off is not mandatory in the United States, though. This contrasts sharply with the policies of other countries around the world, including Brazil, France, Niger, Mali, Libya, and Kuwait, where employees must be given 30 paid days off annually.[48] When he was mayor of New York City, Bill de Blasio attempted to pass a bill requiring two weeks of paid vacation for all employees, but its failure left the United States as still the only advanced economy that does not offer paid time off.[49]

Vacations with Pay

Despite the fact that vacation pay is not required in the United States, most employers generally agree that vacations are essential to the well-being of an employee. Research shows that workers who use their vacation time are more productive and less prone to job-related burnout.[50] Exactly how much paid vacation time firms provide to their employees varies by a firm's industry, locale, size, and other factors. Employees in the United States who work for large companies often get 10 paid days of vacation per year. To qualify for longer vacations of 3, 4, or 5 weeks, an employee may expect to work for the same company for 7, 15, and 20 years, respectively.

Most companies require their employees to take their vacation days by the end of the year or forfeit them ("use it or lose it"). An increasing number of employees say they are too busy at work to take all the vacation days they are allotted. According to one survey, Americans hand back more than $21 billion in unused vacation dollars to their employers each year.[51] Some companies, however, let their employees "roll over" at least some of their vacation days to the following year. Of those that do, the average they allow workers to roll over is 20 days, according to a survey by the Society for Human Resources Management.[52]

Paid Holidays

The federal government recognizes 10 legal public holidays, which are shown in Figure 11.3. However, private employers are not required to offer employees these days off or pay employees for them. Many companies do, though. Organizations that have to remain open during holidays (emergency services providers such as hospitals,

Figure 11.3 Federally Recognized Holidays in the United States

- New Year's Day, January 1
- Martin Luther King, Jr. Day, the third Monday in January
- President's Day, the third Monday in February
- Memorial Day, the last Monday in May
- Independence Day, July 4
- Labor Day, the first Monday in September
- Columbus Day, the second Monday in October
- Veterans Day, November 11
- Thanksgiving Day, the fourth Thursday in November
- Christmas Day, December 25

transportation companies, etc.) often pay employees who work on holidays extra for doing so. Many organizations also give workers an additional 2 or 3 days off at their discretion for personal use.

Of course, not all employees celebrate all the holidays their companies recognize, particularly Christian holidays. A variety of arrangements can be made for these employees. For example, they might be allowed to work the holidays and then take off other days as a substitute. Or they might be allowed to use personal days or vacation days, or, as a last resort, take the holidays they do not want to work off without pay. Another trend is to give all employees a certain number of paid days they can use as holidays whenever they want.

Sick Leave

There are several ways in which employees may be compensated during periods when they are unable to work because of illness or injury. Most public employees, as well as many employees of private firms, receive a set number of sick leave days each year to cover such absences. Where permitted, sick leave that employees do not use can be accumulated to cover prolonged absences. Accumulated vacation leave may sometimes be used as a source of income when sick leave benefits have been exhausted. Some employers also make group insurance that provides income protection during a long-term disability available. As discussed earlier in the chapter, workers' compensation partially reimburses the income employees lose during absences resulting from job-related injuries.

Sabbaticals

A **sabbatical** is paid (or unpaid) time away from a job for 4 or more weeks that employees take off to renew themselves before returning to work. Historically, sabbaticals have been associated with academia, but in the 1960s, companies, including McDonald's, began to adopt them. *Fortune* magazine has added sabbaticals to its criteria for naming the 100 Best Companies to Work For.[53] For example, Epic Systems Corporation, a Wisconsin-based health care software company, offers employees a paid 4-week sabbatical to pursue their creative talents after 5 years at the company. For small businesses that need to temporarily cut their payroll costs, unpaid sabbaticals can be a short-term alternative to layoffs and a way to reward valuable employees who never previously imagined they would be able to take a significant amount of time off to pursue other activities.

sabbatical
Paid (or unpaid) time away from a job for 4 or more weeks; employees take this time off to renew themselves before returning to work.

Small Business Application

Creative Benefit Strategies Can Help Small Businesses Compete

Although competing with large companies on the basis of benefits might seem impossible, small business owners still have some other "cards" they can play that bigger companies might not offer. For example, if they cannot offer extensive benefits, it is not uncommon for small businesses to offer stock or shares in the company to their employees. Flexible work hours and arrangements are also a low-cost strategic benefit that small businesses can offer their employees without first having to cut through a lot of corporate red tape.

Another way small businesses can augment their benefits programs is by partnering with companies that offer discount programs to employers' workers. Price Optical offers a discount program for employers that are not able to provide vision benefits for their employees. Discounts for homeowners, automobile and group life insurance, dental and chiropractic care, health club memberships, and weight-control programs are other benefits that small businesses can procure on behalf of their employees, as well as tickets to entertainment events and product discounts.

Finally, if a small business wants its employees to have benefits but does not want to either provide or administer them, it can contract with a professional employer organization (PEO). Recall from Chapter 1 that a PEO is typically a larger company that, for a fee, takes over the management of a smaller company's HR tasks and can provide employees with benefits that small companies cannot afford.

Sources: J. Dickler, "Why Small Businesses Are Banking on Better Benefits," CNBC (January 2020), https://www.cnbc.com/2020/01/24/why-small-businesses-are-banking-on-better-benefits.html; J. Stowers, "How PEOs Are Behind Companies with the Best Benefits," business.com (March 17, 2020), https://www.business.com/articles/companies-with-best-benefits/; Theresa Agovin, "The Green Wave," Society for Human Resource Management (April 13, 2019), https://www.shrm.org/hr-today/news/all-things-work/pages/greening-your-company.aspx; Will Rumsey, "What Are Cost Containment Strategies?" First Stop Health (December 3, 2020), fshealth.com/blog/what-are-cost-containment-strategies-plus-3-solutions-for-your-clients.

Severance Pay

severance pay
A one-time payment sometimes given to an employee who is being involuntarily terminated.

Severance pay is a one-time payment sometimes given to an employee who is being involuntarily terminated. The severance pay may cover only a few days' wages, or it may amount to the employee's wages for several months. The pay received usually depends on the employee's years of service. Employers that are downsizing often use severance pay as a means of lessening the negative effects of unexpected termination of employees. Other triggers for severance pay include job elimination, voluntary separation programs, or refusal of a reassignment or relocation. Employees who quit do not ordinarily receive severance pay. An employee who accepts severance pay is generally required to sign a release agreement waiving their right to take any kind of legal action against the company. To avoid legal action, companies sometimes offer severance pay to employees who are fired for cause.

Supplemental Unemployment Benefits

supplemental unemployment benefits (SUBs)
A plan that enables an employee who is laid off to draw weekly benefits from the employer, which draws from a fund created for this purpose, in addition to state unemployment compensation.

While not required by law, in cyclical industries, unemployment compensation is augmented by **supplemental unemployment benefits (SUBs)** paid for by employers. The mining industry is an example. If the price of a metal being mined falls sharply (which is not an uncommon occurrence), the firms mining the metal often slow down production until the price rises again. SUBs help attract employees to these kinds of industries, where full-time employment is not always certain. The amount of the benefits is generally determined by an employee's length of service and wage rate.

11.3c Life Insurance

One of the oldest and most popular employee benefits is group term life insurance, which provides death benefits to beneficiaries and may also provide accidental death and dismemberment benefits. The premium costs are normally paid by the employer, with the face value of the life insurance being equal to two times the employee's yearly wages. These programs frequently allow employees to purchase additional amounts of insurance for nominal charges. In addition, many companies allow employees to purchase life insurance for their spouses and dependents via their company plans. This is an attractive benefit because the rates employees pay for the insurance is often lower when it is purchased through their company plans.

11.3d Long-Term Care Insurance

Long-term care insurance is designed to pay for nursing home and other medical-related costs during old age. Because the overall workforce is aging and people are living longer, a small but growing number of employers are finding that long-term care insurance can be a strategic benefit to attract and retain employees, particularly workers caring for older parents and relatives. Many of these employees have experienced firsthand the challenges of caring for aging loved ones who were unable to prepare properly for their long-term needs.

11.3e Other Benefits and Services

Credit Unions

Credit unions exist in many organizations to serve the financial needs of employees and attract potential employees. They offer a variety of deposits as well as other banking services and make loans to their members. Although the employer may provide office space and a payroll deduction service, credit unions are operated by the employees under federal and state legislation and supervision. Because credit unions are owned by their members, they often charge lower banking fees and offer loans at lower rates. Generally, credit unions are located near an employer's facility, making it fast and convenient for employees to do their banking there. The service employees receive is also often more personal at their credit union than the service they would get from bigger banks.

Educational Assistance

Proactive employers view educational assistance programs, also called tuition aid, as a strategic business tool to support talent management and develop leadership.[54] To be eligible for tuition aid, an employee may have to meet a length of service requirement and show that classes taken relate to job performance or organizational career development. Employers may pay full or partial tuition costs plus related expenses such as books and supplies. For example, PwC offers its employees $1,200 per year for student loan debt reimbursement.[55]

Figure 11.4 shows some of the other benefits firms are offering employees that we have not already mentioned in this chapter. In summary, although benefits are expensive, they can be a good way for a company to differentiate itself, strengthen its employer "brand" to attract top talent, and retain that talent. However, both small and large employers need to implement their benefit plans strategically as well as continually monitor their effectiveness and costs.

Retirement Programs

Airline pilots are required by law to retire at age 65. However, for most other professions in the United States there is no law mandating a retirement age. Therefore, whether an employee elects to retire depends on various factors such as personal and financial

Figure 11.4 Other Benefits Organizations Offer Employees

- Mental health support
- Business travel insurance
- Time off for children's school activities
- Work-at-home arrangements/telecommuting
- On-site cafeterias and take-home food
- Onsite laundry, dry cleaning, and hair-dressing services
- Employee referral bonuses
- Donation-gift matching
- Adoption assistance
- On-site nurses and doctors
- Shuttle services for commuters
- Onsite massage services
- College scholarships

condition and health, other family obligations, the extent to which they receive satisfaction from work, and the ability to meet changing job demands.

Preretirement and Phased Retirement Programs

Although most people eagerly anticipate retirement, many of them find that it requires a major adjustment in their financial lifestyle. Employers sometimes offer preretirement planning seminars and workshops to help make employees aware of the kinds of adjustments they may need to make when they retire. The topics covered can include pension plans, health insurance coverage, Social Security and Medicare, personal financial planning, wellness and lifestyles, and the process of adjusting to being around one's spouse 24/7!

To help older workers get used to the idea of retirement, some organizations experiment with "retirement rehearsal." Polaroid, for example, offers employees an opportunity to try out retirement through an unpaid 3-month leave program and allows its employees to gradually cut their hours before retirement. This kind of program is referred to as **phased retirement**. Formal phased retirement programs are common in other countries, but are rarer in the United States because employees often need to get their health care coverage through their employers until they turn 65. At that point, they are eligible for Medicare coverage. However, as more baby-boomers want to continue to work and employers seek to retain them, the number of phased retirement programs is expected to grow.

phased retirement
A program that allows employees to gradually cut their hours at work before retiring.

11.3f Pension Plans

Pensions reward employees for their years of service with a company by providing them with income when they retire. However, like with other discretionary benefits, the decision whether to offer a pension plan is up to the employer.

Types of Pension Plans

There are two major ways to categorize pension plans: (1) according to contributions made by the employer and (2) according to the amount of pension benefits to be paid. In a **contributory plan**, contributions to a pension plan are made jointly by employees and employers. In a **noncontributory plan**, the contributions are made solely by the

contributory plan
A pension plan in which contributions are made jointly by employees and employers.

noncontributory plan
A pension plan in which contributions are made solely by the employer.

employer. When pension plans are classified by the amount of pension benefits to be paid, there are two basic types: the defined benefit plan and the defined contribution plan. Under a **defined benefit plan,**[56] the amount an employee is to receive on retirement is specifically set forth. The amount employees collect is usually based on their years of service, average earnings during a specific period of time, and age at time of retirement. While a variety of formulas exist for determining pension benefits, the one used most often is based on the employee's average earnings (usually over a 3- to 5-year period immediately preceding retirement), multiplied by the number of years of service with the organization. A deduction is then made for each year the retiree is younger than age 65. For example, an employee with a 4-year preretirement annual salary of $55,000 and 30 years of service may receive a yearly retirement payment of $23,000.

defined benefit plan
A pension plan in which the amount an employee is to receive on retirement is specifically set forth.

A **defined contribution plan** establishes the basis on which an employer will contribute to the pension fund. These contributions may be made through profit sharing, thrift plans, matches of employee contributions, employer-sponsored individual retirement accounts (IRAs), and various other means. The amount of benefits employees receive on retirement is determined by the funds accumulated in their accounts and how well the investments purchased with the funds have grown over time. In other words, the amount employees get is not certain. As a result, defined contribution plans pose more financial risk for employees than defined benefit plans do. However, employers have come to prefer them because they do not have to shoulder all of the responsibility of funding them. In 1989, 39 percent of private sector employees were covered by defined benefit pension plans; today, only 11 percent are.[57] Even *Fortune* 100 firms are scrapping their defined benefit plans. According to a survey by the HR consulting firm Watson Wyatt, today most *Fortune* 100 companies now offer their new salaried employees only a defined contribution plan.

defined contribution plan
A pension plan that establishes the basis on which an employer will contribute to the pension fund.

401(k) Savings Plans

401(k) plans started to become extremely popular as an employee-savings vehicle beginning in the 1980s. This type of defined contribution plan is named after section 401(k) of the Internal Revenue Code. It allows employees to save through payroll deductions that reduce their taxable income and have their contributions matched by the employer.

Vladimir Vladimirov/ Getty Images

Many baby-boomers in the United States are continuing to work long past the traditional retirement age of 65.

Usually the employer matches the employee contributions at the rate of 25 to 50 cents for every worker dollar contributed.

401(k) plans have been widely embraced by companies as a replacement for the costly defined benefit pension funds. Today, about 60 percent of households nearing retirement have 401(k)-type of accounts.[58] However, unlike defined benefit pension plans, which guarantee payments based on years of service, the 401(k) plan guarantees nothing. The return depends entirely on how much money goes into the plan, the rate of return on the investments purchased with the funds contributed, and, with stock-funded plans, the price of the company's stock. Thus, economic downturns and stock market crashes take a heavy toll on 401(k) accounts.

Cash Balance Pension Plans

Along with 401(k) saving plans, a significant development in pension planning has been cash balance saving plans.[59] With cash balance plans, the employer makes a yearly contribution into an employee's retirement savings account.[60] These contributions are based on a percentage of the employee's pay—typically 4 percent. Additionally, the employee's account earns annual interest, often tied to the 30-year Treasury bill rate. For example, an employee earning $35,000 per year would receive a yearly contribution of $1,400 to their account. After a year, the account would receive an interest credit of around 5 percent. Employees can usually roll their account balances into a personal IRA should they change jobs.

Federal Regulation of Pension Plans

Vesting
A guarantee of accrued pension benefits to participants at retirement age, regardless of their employment status at that time.

Private pension plans are subject to federal regulation, including vesting rules, under ERISA.[61] **Vesting** is a process that guarantees pension-plan participants will receive their pensions when they reach retirement age, regardless of their employment status at that time. In other words, the benefits cannot be revoked, even if the employee no longer works for the company. Vesting prevents companies from laying off employees before they retire so they are unable to collect their pensions. Under ERISA, all pension plans must provide employees with vested rights to their accrued benefits after they meet a certain minimum years of service—say, 5 years. So, for example, if an employee leaves the company prior to the minimum years of service, that person would lose any money the firm contributed to their pension. However, employers can pay out a departing employee's vested benefits if the present value of the benefit is small.

ERISA also requires minimum funding standards be followed to ensure pension benefits will be available to employees when they retire.[62] Currently, the pensions of many older companies—including GM, Chrysler, U.S. Steel, and Delta Air Lines—are underfunded. In addition, many state and local governments are facing pension funding shortages in the billions of dollars due to the last recession. Equally worrisome are the number of pension plans in danger of failing altogether.

ERISA also created the Pension Benefit Guaranty Corporation (PBGC), a federal government agency. The PBGC ensures that if a plan is terminated, guaranteed minimum benefits are paid to participants. When companies go through bankruptcy proceedings, they often try to cancel their pension obligations, leaving employees to rely on the PBGC for retirement income. Unfortunately for retirees, the monthly pension payments from the PBGC are often significantly less than those promised under a company's original retirement plan. Another growing concern is that the PBGC—which has a $48.2 billion deficit of its own that has been growing annually—will be unable to meet its financial obligations.[63] The PBGC is supported by premiums paid by employers. To improve its funding situation, the agency has asked Congress to allow it to increase the premiums it charges employers.

11.3g Domestic Partner Benefits

More employers are granting benefits to employees who establish *domestic partnerships*, which are relationships involving unmarried same-sex or opposite-sex couples. Viacom, Gannett Company (publisher of *USA Today*), Levi Strauss, Silicon Graphics, Warner Bros., and Stanford University are among the many organizations that offer benefits to domestic partners of employees.

HR decisions about domestic partnership benefits need to take into account local and state laws and how they are being implemented. For example, several California cities, including Berkeley, Los Angeles, Oakland, and San Francisco, have adopted an ordinance that requires all companies with city contracts to extend domestic partner benefits to their employees who reside in the city or who work on contracts for the city.[64]

The definition of a domestic partnership varies from company to company. However, Apple Computer's definition, which is as follows, is typical: A domestic partner, the company says, is "a person over age 18 who shares living quarters with another adult in an exclusive, committed relationship in which the partners are responsible for each other's common welfare." Employers that offer domestic partnership coverage typically require employees to sign an "Affidavit of Domestic Partnership" attesting that they meet certain conditions such as the following:

- A minimum age requirement
- A requirement that the couple live together
- A specification of financial interdependence
- A requirement that the relationship be a permanent one
- A requirement that each not be a blood relative[65]

Organizations that offer benefits to domestic partners are simply extending current benefits, normally full medical and dental plans, to all employees. This is especially important to employees of the LGBTQ community. This is an important distinction because many health plans will not cover medical gender-affirmation surgery or gender dysphoria, for example.[66] JP Morgan made another stride toward equality for the LGBTQ community by making its fertility benefits more expansive. Under the new benefits, employee same-sex couples can receive funding for fertility treatments, so they no longer have to pay out of their own pocket when trying to have a family.[67]

Summary

LO 1 The cost of health care programs has become the major concern in the area of employee benefits. Organizations are taking a variety of approaches to contain health care costs. Included among the factors being considered when developing benefits programs are the relative preference shown for each benefit by managers and employees, the estimated cost of each benefit and the total amount of money available for the entire benefits package, and how it compares to the competition. Through committees and surveys, a benefits package can be developed to meet employees' needs. Through the use of flexible benefit plans, also called cafeteria plans, employees are able to choose the benefits that are best suited for their individual needs.

LO 2 Nearly one-fourth of the benefits package that employers provide is legally required. These benefits include employer contributions to Social Security, unemployment insurance, workers' compensation insurance, and state disability insurance.

Social Security taxes collected from employers and employees are used to pay three major types of benefits: (1) retirement benefits, (2) disability benefits, and (3) survivors' benefits. Payroll deductions and taxes are also legally required to fund Medicare, the government program that provides medical and hospital insurance and prescription drug coverage for people older than age 65.

LO 3 For most professions besides piloting in the United States, there is no mandatory retirement age. The topics covered in retirement planning can include pension plans, health insurance coverage, Social Security and Medicare, personal financial planning, wellness and lifestyle, and the general process of adjusting to retirement. Whether to offer a pension plan is the employer's prerogative. However, once a plan is established, it is then subject to federal regulation under ERISA to ensure that benefits will be available when an employee retires. Two pension plans are available—defined benefit and defined contribution. With a defined benefit plan, the amount an employee receives on retirement is based on years of service, average earnings, and age at time of retirement. Two of the most significant trends are the growth of 401(k) plans and cash balance pension plans, both of which are defined contribution plans.

Key Terms

backup care program
contributory plan
defined benefit plan
defined contribution plan
disease management programs
elder care
employee assistance programs (EAPs)
flexible benefits plans (cafeteria plans)
health maintenance organizations (HMOs)
high-deductible health insurance plan (HDHP)
noncontributory plan
phased retirement
preferred provider organization (PPO)
sabbatical
severance pay
supplemental unemployment benefit (SUB)
vesting
wellness programs
workers' compensation insurance

Discussion Questions

LO 1 Many organizations are concerned about the rising cost of employee benefits and question their value to the organization and to the employees. In your opinion, which benefits are of greatest value to employees? To the organization? Why?

LO 2 Employers are required by law to provide specific benefits to employees. Which laws mandate benefits to employees, and what are the provisions of those laws?

LO 3 Working in teams of three or four, assume your team was hired as a benefits consultant to a small business having 50 to 60 employees. What benefits do you believe this employer should offer, given its limited resources? Justify your reasons for offering these benefits while considering their advantages and disadvantages.

HRM Experience

Understanding Employer Benefit Programs

This exercise will help you more fully understand the benefits discussed in this chapter. Additionally, you will explore, in detail, the benefits and services offered by your employer and other employers in your area.

Assignment

Working in teams of four to six individuals, obtain information on the benefits package offered by your employer or other employers in your area. Once you have gathered this information, identify (1) each benefit offered, (2) what the benefit provides the employee, (3) employee eligibility (if required), and (4) how the benefit is paid for (employer, employee, or a combination of both). Compare benefit packages. Be prepared to discuss your findings with the class.

CASE STUDY 1 Adobe's Family-Friendly Benefits: An Unexpected Backlash

Adobe Consulting Services (ACS), a provider of HR software application systems, prides itself on the variety of benefits it offers employees. In addition to health care, pension, and vacation benefits, the company offers an attractive family-friendly benefits package including flexible schedules, child and elder care assistance, counseling services, adoption assistance, and extended parental leave. Unfortunately, sometimes the company's progressive work–life policy experiences a backlash from some employees, as the following case illustrates.

In March 2019, Teresa Wheatly was hired by Adobe as a software accounts manager. With excellent administrative and technical skills, plus 4 years of experience at Adaptable Software, Adobe's main competitor, Teresa became a valued addition to the company's marketing team. As a single mother with two grade-school children, Teresa received permission to take Fridays off. She was also allowed to leave work early or come in late to meet the needs of her children. Teresa is one of 11 software account managers at Adobe.

The problem for Adobe, and particularly for Janis Blancero, director of marketing, began in the fall of 2019. On September 15, Dorothy McShee, citing "personal reasons"—which she refused to discuss—requested a 4-day workweek for which she was willing to take a 20 percent cut in pay. When Dorothy asked for the reduced work schedule, she sarcastically quipped, "I hope I don't have to have kids to get this time off." On October 3, Juan Batista, a world-class marathon runner, requested a flexible work hours arrangement to accommodate his morning and afternoon training schedule. Juan was registered to run the London, England, marathon in May 2021. Just prior to Juan's request, Susan Woolf asked for and was granted an extended maternity leave to begin after the birth of her first child in December.

If these unexpected requests are not enough, Blancero has heard comments from senior account managers about how some employees seem to get "special privileges," while the managers work long hours that often require them to meet around-the-clock customer demands. She has adequate reason to believe that there is hidden tension over the company's flexible work hours program. Currently, Adobe has no formal policy on flexible schedules. Furthermore, with the company's growth in business combined with the increasing workload of software account managers and the constant service demands of some customers, Blancero realized that she simply cannot grant all the time-off requests of her employees.

Questions

1. Do managers like Janis Blancero face a more complicated decision when evaluating the personal requests of employees versus evaluating employees' individual work performance? Explain.
2. (a) Should Adobe establish a policy for granting flexible work schedules? Explain.

   (b) If you answered yes, what might that policy contain?
3. If you were Janis Blancero, how would you resolve this dilemma? Explain.

CASE STUDY 2 Evaluate the Work–Life Climate in Your Company

What is the quality of the work–life environment in your company? The following survey provided by the Work and Family Connection will help provide a "case analysis" of the climate in your organization. Answers to the 20 questions will provide clear insights about your company's position in the work–life area.

Do you agree or disagree with the following statements?

1. My manager or supervisor treats my work–life needs with sensitivity.
2. It is usually easy for me to manage the demands of both work and home life.
3. My career path at this company is limited because of the pressure of my home-life demands.
4. My job at this company keeps me from maintaining the quality of life I want.
5. My manager or supervisor is supportive when home-life issues interfere with work.
6. My manager or supervisor focuses on results, rather than the time I am at my desk.
7. My manager or supervisor has a good understanding of flexible work hours practices.
8. If I requested a flexible work arrangement, my manager or supervisor would support me.
9. My manager or supervisor is often inflexible or insensitive about my personal needs.
10. I believe my manager or supervisor treats me with respect.
11. My manager or supervisor allows me informal flexibility as long as I get the job done.
12. My manager or supervisor tends to treat us like children.
13. My manager or supervisor seldom gives me praise or recognition for the work I do.
14. My manager or supervisor seems to care about me as a person.
15. I would recommend this company to others.
16. The work I do is not all that important to this company's success.
17. If I could find another job with better pay, I would leave this organization.
18. If I could find another job where I would be treated with respect, I would take it.
19. If I could find another job where I could have more flexibility, I would take it.
20. I am totally committed to this company.

For a perfect score, you should answer "Disagree" to questions 3, 4, 9, 12, 13, 16, 17, 18, and 19 and "Agree" to questions 1, 2, 5, 6, 7, 8, 10, 11, 14, 15, and 20.

To score your responses, begin by giving yourself 20 points. Then deduct one point for every "wrong" response from the total score.

If your score is 18 to 20: Congratulations! Your organization is leading the nation in flexibility and supportiveness.

If your score is 14 to 17: Your organization is probably more supportive and flexible than most, but you have room to grow.

If your score is 11 to 13: You could be open to other job offers in the race for talent.

If your score is 10 or less: Your managers will need help to manage the dynamic and far-reaching twenty-first-century workforce.

Source: Used with permission of the Work and Family Connection, 5195 Beachside Drive, Minnetonka, Minnesota 55343; 1-800-487-7898, http://www.workfamily.com.

Notes and References

1. Kris Alban, "6 Employee Benefits with Exceptionally High Return on Investment," BenefitsPro (January 28, 2021); "Glassdoor's 5 Job Trends to Watch in 2016," Glassdoor Team (January 12, 2016).
2. "Top 20 Employee Benefits & Perks," Glassdoor Team (February 3, 2016).
3. Scott Wooldridge, "Breaking down Benefit Costs: 6 Charts That Show Where the Money Goes," benefitspro.com (January 28, 2019).
4. Careers at Microsoft, https://careers.microsoft.com/us/en/usbenefits.
5. "Total Rewards" is all of the tools available to an employer that may be used to attract, motivate, and retain employees. Total rewards include everything the employee perceives to be of value resulting from the employment relationship.
6. Mark Harbeke, "5 Workplace Committees to Form and Their Business Benefits," Inc.com (January 5, 2011), http://www.inc.com/guides/2011/01/5-workplace-committees-to-form-and-their-business-benefits.html; Lin Grensing-Pophal, "Could You Benefit from an Employee Benefits Committee?" Society for Human Resource Management (February 26, 2009).
7. Heather Garbers, "Why 'One Size Fits All' Is No Longer a Relevant Benefits Strategy," The SHRM Blog (February 25, 2017); Barbara A. W. Eversole, Donald L. Venneberg, and Cindy L. Crowder, "Creating a Flexible Organizational Culture to Attract and Retain Talented Workers Across Generations," *Advances in Developing Human Resources* 14, no. 4 (2012): 607–625.
8. Dave Rietsema, "What Is Employee Self-Service?" HR Payroll Systems (November 07, 2020), https://www.hrpayrollsystems.net/employee-self-service/; Dianna L. Stone, Diana L. Deadrick, Kimberly M. Lukaszewski, and Richard Johnson, "The Influence of Technology on the Future of Human Resource Management," *Human Resource Management Review* 25, no. 2 (2015): 216–231.
9. Stephen Miller, "Employees Value Benefits, Don't Understand Costs," Society for Human Resource Management (April 20, 2011).
10. Kat Greene, "Providence Health to Pay $352M to End ERISA Suit," *Law360* (October 24, 2016).
11. Mark Feffer, "How to Boost Employee Adoption of New HR Tech," Society for Human Resource Management (September 9, 2019); JoAnn Davis, "Communication: It Is More Than Distributing Information," *Employee Plan Benefits Review* 62, no. 1 (2007): 5.
12. "The IKEA Parable: A Primer for Applying Design Thinking to Benefits Communication," Segal Benz (May 15, 2018), https://www.segalbenz.com/blog/use-design-thinking-principles-to-drive-benefits-engagement; Jeremy Smerd, "Tweeting Benefits in 140 Characters or Less," *Workforce Management* (August 2009), http://www.workforce.com.
13. Stephan Miller, "Employers Enhance Emotional and Mental Health Benefits for 2020," Society for Human Resource Management (October 28, 2019).
14. U.S. Department of Health and Human Services, "Health Insurance and Mental Health Services," March 18, 2020, https://www.mentalhealth.gov/get-help/health-insurance.
15. Guin Becker Bogusz, "Health Insurers Still Don't Adequately Cover Mental Health Treatment," National Alliance on Mental Illness, March 13, 2020.
16. Bahaudin G. Mujtaba and Frank J. Cavico, "A Review of Employee Health and Wellness Programs in the United States," *Public Policy and Administration Research* 355, no. 4. (2013): 1–16.
17. "America Outbound: The Free World Has Employees Finding Healthcare Abroad," *Medical Tourism Magazine* (October 2019), https://www.magazine.medicaltourism.com/article/america-outbound-the-free-world-has-employees-finding-healthcare-abroad; Corinne Marie Karuppan, "Employer-Based Coverage and Medical Travel Options: Lessons for Healthcare Managers," *Journal of Healthcare Management* 59, no. 3 (2014): 210–223.
18. Kimberly J. Reid, Kathleen M. Aguilar, Eric Thompson, and Ross M. Miller, "Value-Based Benefit Design to Improve Medication Adherence for Employees with Anxiety or Depression," *American Health & Drugs Benefits* 8, no. 5 (2015): 263–271.
19. The Home Depot Physical Wellness, March 1, 2020, https://thdhomerfund.org/resources/physical-wellness; "The *Fortune* 100 and Their Fitness and Wellness Programs," *Health Fitness Revolution* (August 15, 2015), http://www.healthfitnessrevolution.com/fortune-100-fitness-wellness-programs/.
20. Theresa Agovino, "Companies Seek to Boost Low Usage of Employee Assistance Programs," Society for Human Resource Management (November 21, 2019); Jodi M. Jacobson and Paul Sacco, "Employee Assistance Program Services for Alcohol and Other Drug Problems: Implications for Increased Identification and Engagement in Treatment," *American Journal on Addictions*, 21, no. 5 (2012): 468–475.
21. Charlotte Huff, "Employers Collaborate to Customize Health Coverage," *Workforce* (October 18, 2010), http://www.workforce.com/2010/10/18/employers-collaborate-to-customize-health-coverage/.
22. Kathryn Mayer, "Is COVID-19 a Turning Point for Workplace Mental Health?" *Human Resource Executive* (May 11, 2020),

https://hrexecutive.com/will-covid-finally-make-employers-fix-their-mental-health-problem/.

23. Kathryn Mayer, "COVID-19 Strategy 101: How to Improve Mental Health," *Human Resource Executive* (June 23, 2020), https://hrexecutive.com/covid-19-strategy-101-how-to-improve-mental-health/.
24. "Social Security Program Fact Sheet," December 31, 2020, https://www.ssa.gov/OACT/FACTS/.
25. Since the Social Security Act is continually subject to amendment, readers should refer to the literature provided by the nearest Social Security office for the most current details pertaining to the tax rates and benefit provisions of the act.
26. "Contribution and Benefit Base," Social Security Administration (February 23, 2021), https://www.ssa.gov/oact/cola/cbb.html.
27. "How You Earn Credits," Social Security Administration (2021), https://www.ssa.gov/pubs/EN-05-10072.pdf.
28. As an example, the Social Security Administration manages the Supplemental Security Income (SSI) program, which makes payments to people with low incomes who are age 65 or older, who are blind, or who have disabilities. However, SSI is not paid for by Social Security taxes but rather by the U.S. Treasury's general funds.
29. "How You Earn Credits," Social Security Administration (2020), https://www.ssa.gov/pubs/EN-05-10072.pdf.
30. Ibid.
31. You may think that Medicaid and Medicare are the same. Actually, they are two different programs. Medicaid is a state-run program (with some funding by the federal government) that provides hospital and medical coverage for people with low income and little or no resources. Each state has its own rules about who is eligible and what is covered under Medicaid. Some people quality for both Medicare and Medicaid. For more information about the Medicaid program, contact your local medical assistance agency, social services, or welfare office.
32. "Topic No. 751: Social Security and Medicare Withholding Rates," *Internal Revenue Service* (February 5, 2021), https://www.irs.gov/taxtopics/tc751.html.
33. COBRA, P.L. 99-272, 100 Stat. 82 (1986).
34. "Supersizing ObamaCare Subsidies," *Wall Street Journal* (February 24, 2021), https://www.wsj.com/articles/supersizing-obamacare-subsidies-11614210175.
35. FLMA, P.L. 103-3, 107 Stat. 6 (1993).
36. A "serious health condition" means an illness, injury, impairment, or physical or mental condition that involves any period of incapacity or treatment connected with patient care.
37. Rachel Blakely-Gray, "States with Paid Family Leave," *Patriot*, January 18, 2021; Janet Walsh, "Americans Value Moms, But Policies Don't," *Huffington Post* (May 5, 2011), http://www.huffingtonpost.com.
38. Arthur Wilson, "10 Businesses That Have Mastered Work/Life Balance," *Workstars* (2021); Kathryn Mayer, "7 Benefit Trends to Watch in 2021," *Human Resource Executive* (January 5, 2021).
39. Natalie Hackbarth, Aaron Brown, and Henry Albrecht, "Workplace Well-Being: Provide Meaningful Benefits to Energize Employee Health, Engagement, and Performance," *Quantum Workplace* (2016), https://www.limeade.com/content/uploads/2016/12/Workplace-Well-Being_FINAL.pdf.
40. Ibid.
41. Kristina Haynie, "Child Care in America: 2019 State Fact Sheets," *Child Care Aware of America* (2019), https://www.childcareaware.org/our-issues/research/statefactsheets/.
42. Myelle Lansat and Rebecca Aydin, "20 of the Best Job Perks and Benefits Millennials Have That Their Parents Didn't," *Business Insider* (December 2, 2019), https://www.businessinsider.com/best-job-perks-benefits-for-millennials-2018-8; "Top 20 Employee Benefits & Perks," Glassdoor Team (February 3, 2016).
43. "Caregiving in the U.S.: 2020 Report," AARP and National Alliance for Caregiving (May 2020), https://www.aarp.org/content/dam/aarp/ppi/2020/05/full-report-caregiving-in-the-united-states.doi.10.26419-2Fppi.00103.001.pdf.
44. Ibid.
45. Joanne Sammer, "Improving the Lives of Employee Caregivers Makes Business Sense," Society for Human Resource Management (January 6, 2020), https://www.shrm.org/resourcesandtools/hr-topics/benefits/pages/improving-lives-of-employee-caregivers-makes-business-sense.aspx; Stephen Miller, "Caregiving Benefits Tend to Miss the Mark," Society for Human Resource Management (January 22, 2019), https://www.shrm.org/resourcesandtools/hr-topics/benefits/pages/caregiving-benefits-miss-the-mark.aspx.
46. "Case Study: Home Depot's Employer-Supported Childcare," U.S. Chamber of Commerce Foundation.
47. Bureau of Labor Statistics, U.S. Department of Labor, *Employer Costs for Employee Compensation* (September 2020).
48. John Harrington, "Wouldn't You Like 30 Mandated Days Off? Here Are the Countries with the Most Vacation Days," *USA Today* (July 23, 2019), https://www.usatoday.com/story/money/2019/07/23/paid-time-off-countries-with-the-most-vacation-days-brazil-france/39702323/.
49. Adewale Maye, *No-Vacation Nation, Revised*, Center for Economic and Policy Research (May 2019).
50. Edwin N. Torres, Elizabeth Yost, Giulio Ronzoni, "No Vacation Needed: An Exploration of Why American Hospitality Workers Won't Use up Their Vacation Days," *Journal of Human Resources in Hospitality & Tourism* (January 25, 2021); Oi Ling Siu, Cary L. Cooper, and David R. Phillips, "Intervention Studies on Enhancing Work Well-Being, Reducing Burnout, and Improving Recovery Experiences among Hong Kong Health Care Workers and Teachers," *International Journal of Stress Management* 21, no. 1 (2014).
51. Catherine A. Allen, "Burned Out? You Might Just Need a Reboot Break," *Life Science Leader* (December 1, 2013), http://www.lifescienceleader.com.
52. "No One in the Private Sector Gets Unlimited Vacation and Sick Leave," *Politifact* (January 28, 2011), http://www.politifact.com.

53. Allen, "Burned Out?"
54. Brian O'Connell, "The Business Case for Employee Student Loan Repayment Programs," Society for Human Resource Management (January 25, 2020), https://www.shrm.org/hr-today/news/all-things-work/pages/the-business-case-for-employee-student-loan-repayment-programs.aspx.
55. Ibid.
56. "Types of Retirement Plans," United States Department of Labor (March 8, 2021), https://www.dol.gov/general/topic/retirement/typesofplans.
57. "Worker Participation in Employer-Sponsored Pensions: Data in Brief," Congressional Research Service (December 1, 2020), https://fas.org/sgp/crs/misc/R43439.pdf; William J. Wiatrowski, *The Last Private Industry Pension Plans: A Visual Essay* (Bureau of Labor Statistics, 2012).
58. E. S. Browning, "Boomers Find 401(k) Plans Fall Short," *Wall Street Journal* (February 19, 2011).
59. Jean-Pierre Aubry and Kevin Wandrei, "Have Localities Shifted Away from Traditional Defined Benefit Plans?" *State and Local Pension Plans* 70 (Center for Retirement Research at Boston College, April 2020); Jessica Marquez, "Cash-Balance Plans Make a Comeback," http://www.workforce.com/section/02/feature/25/16/23/index.html.
60. "Cash Balance Pension Plans," U.S. Department of Labor (January 2014), https://www.dol.gov/sites/default/files/ebsa/about-ebsa/our-activities/resource-center/faqs/faq_consumer_cashbalanceplans.pdf.
61. ERISA, P.L. 93-406, 88 Stat. 829 (1974).64
62. Carolyn Hirschman, "Overseeing Pension Management," *HR Magazine* 49, no. 7 (July 2004): 66.
63. *Pension Benefit Guaranty Corporation: A Primer*, Congressional Research Service (January 8, 2021), https://crsreports.congress.gov.
64. "Are California Employers Required to Provide Medical Benefits to Employees' Domestic Partners?" Society for Human Resource Management (January 30, 2020), https://www.shrm.org/resourcesandtools/tools-and-samples/hr-qa/pages/.aspx; "Domestic Partner Benefits: Facts and Background," Employee Benefit Research Institute (February 2009), https://www.ebri.org/pdf/publications/facts/0209fact.pdf.
65. Pay and Leave Administration, U.S. Office of Personal Management, http://www.opm.gov.
66. Stephen Miller, "3 Checklists for Avoiding LGBTQ Discrimination in Your Benefits Programs," Society for Human Resource Management (June 30, 2020), https://www.shrm.org/ResourcesAndTools/hr-topics/benefits/Pages/3-checklists-for-avoiding-LGBTQ-discrimination-in-your-benefit-programs.aspx.
67. Hugh Son, "JP Morgan Is Expanding Fertility Benefits to Help LGBTQ Employees Have Families," CNBC (June 21, 2019), https://www.cnbc.com/2019/06/21/jp-morgan-is-expanding-fertility-benefits-to-help-lgbtq-employees.html.

danchooalex/E+/Getty Images

CHAPTER 12

Promoting Safety and Health

Learning Outcomes

After studying this chapter, you should be able to

LO 1 Summarize the general provisions of the Occupational Safety and Health Act (OSHA).

LO 2 Describe the measures managers and employees can take to create a safe work environment.

LO 3 Describe the programs organizations utilize to build better health among their workforces.

Nearly 90 percent of all companies in the United States use some form of health and safety program. Safety programs are plans of action to prevent accidents or occupational diseases. Health and safety programs are plans of action to encourage the health and wellness of employees. They ensure that employees can continue to work, which lowers costs for the company. However, current research shows that health programs not only save the company money through fewer sick days, less need to pay workers' compensation, fewer disability payments, and less need to replace employees who are injured or killed, but also increase employee productivity. "When you give people the tools and the opportunity to be physically and mentally healthier, it's not just that they're more likely to be at work," says Lamar Pierce, professor at Washington University. "Those employees are also more likely to be productive."[1]

LO1

Summarize the general provisions of the Occupational Safety and Health Act (OSHA).

12.1 Safety and Health: It's the Law

Consider the facts shown in Figure 12.1.

Figure 12.1 Employer-reported Workplace Injuries and Illnesses

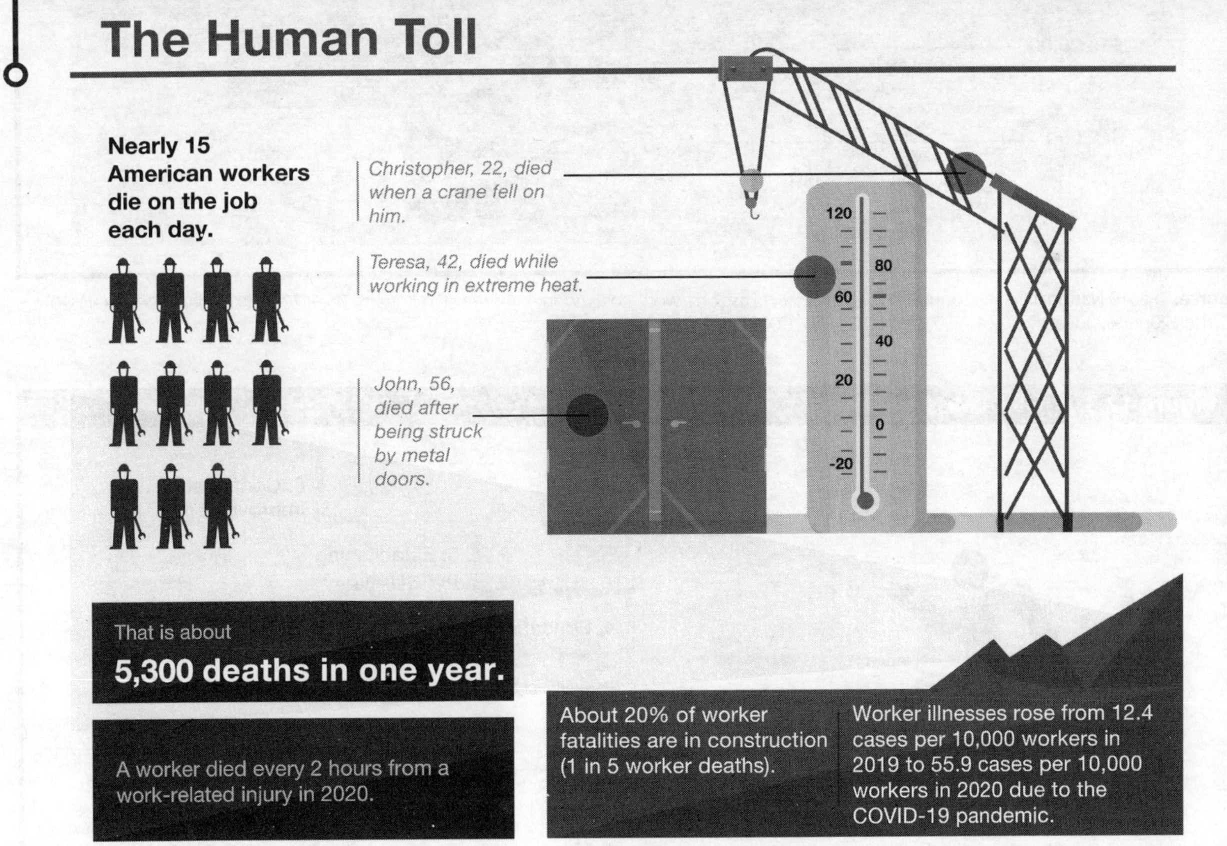

Source: Employer-reported Workplace Injuries and Illnesses—2019, Bureau of Labor Statistics (November 4, 2020) https://www.bls.gov/news.release/archives/osh_11042020.pdf.

The total impact of worker injury and death is roughly $171 billion per year. Figure 12.2 breaks down where these costs occur.

Providing workers with a safe and healthy environment is not just good for business or compliant with the law, it's the right thing to do. In 1970, Congress passed the Occupational Safety and Health Act (OSHA).[2] The mission of OSHA is to "assure the safety and health of America's workers by setting and enforcing standards; providing training, outreach, and education; establishing partnerships; and encouraging continual improvements in workplace safety and health" (see Figure 12.3).

Figure 12.2 Cost of Worker Injury and Death

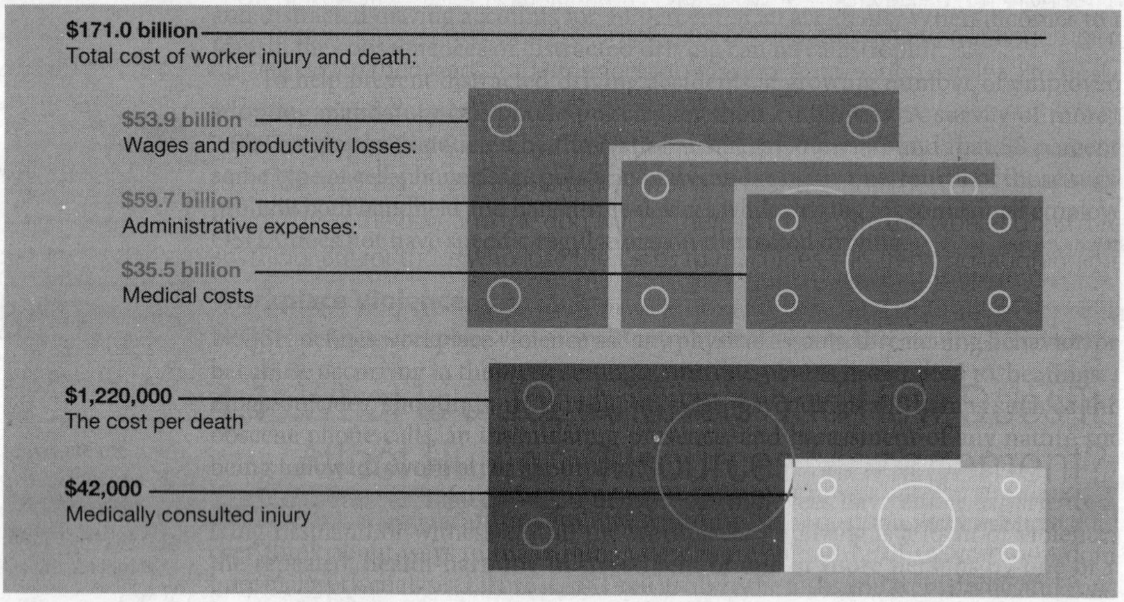

Source: © 2019 National Safety Council. https://injuryfacts.nsc.org/work/costs/work-injury-costs/#:~:text=The%20cost%20per%20worker%20in,cost%20per%20death%20was%20%241%2C220%2C000.

Figure 12.3 OSHA Mission

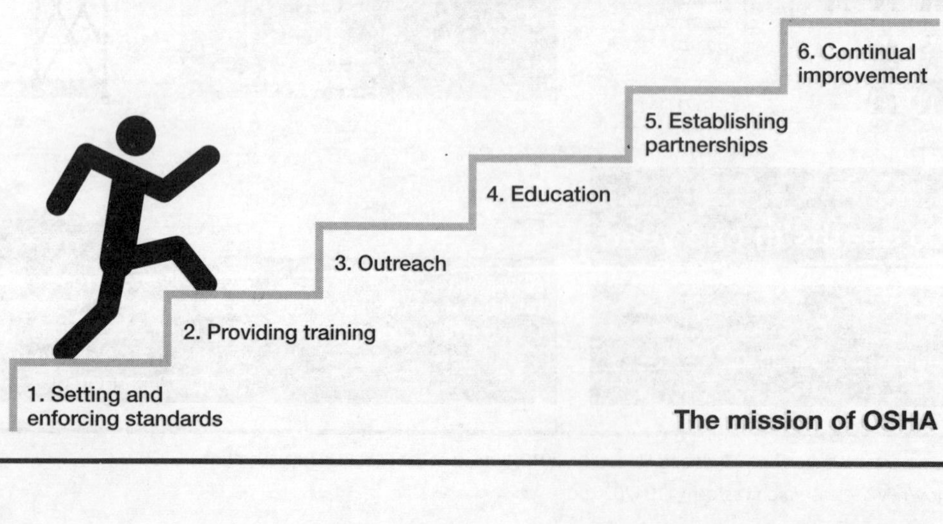

Despite the statistics shown in the infographic, OSHA has been very effective in reducing the number of injuries resulting in lost work time, the incident rate of specific injuries such as back problems, and the number of job-related deaths. Today, most employees report that the safety conditions in their organizations are very good.

12.1a OSHA's Coverage

OSHA covers all private-sector employees and public employees in state and local governments. Self-employed workers are not covered by the law. Federal agencies are required to establish and maintain a safety and health program that is monitored by the Occupational Safety and Health Administration (also called OSHA).

12.1b OSHA Standards

One of OSHA's responsibilities is to develop and enforce mandatory job safety and health standards. These standards cover the workplace, machinery and equipment, materials, power sources, processing, protective clothing, first aid, and administrative requirements. For example, during the COVID-19 pandemic, OSHA issued guidelines requiring employers provide COVID-19–specific prevention programs.[3] To comply with the federal law, employers need to become familiar with those standards that are applicable to their establishments and to ensure that their employees use personal protective gear and equipment when required for safety. Employers can be cited and fined if they do not comply with OSHA standards.[4]

OSHA can begin standards-setting procedures on its own initiative or following a petition from other parties, including the Secretary of Health and Human Services (HHS) and the National Institute for Occupational Safety and Health (NIOSH). Other bodies that may also initiate standards-setting procedures include state and local governments and any nationally recognized standards-producing organization, employer, or labor representative (see Figure 12.4). NIOSH, however, is the major source of standards. As an agency of the Department of Health and Human Services, it is responsible for conducting research on various safety and health problems, including the psychological factors involved in those issues.[5]

Figure 12.4 How OSHA Standards Are Set

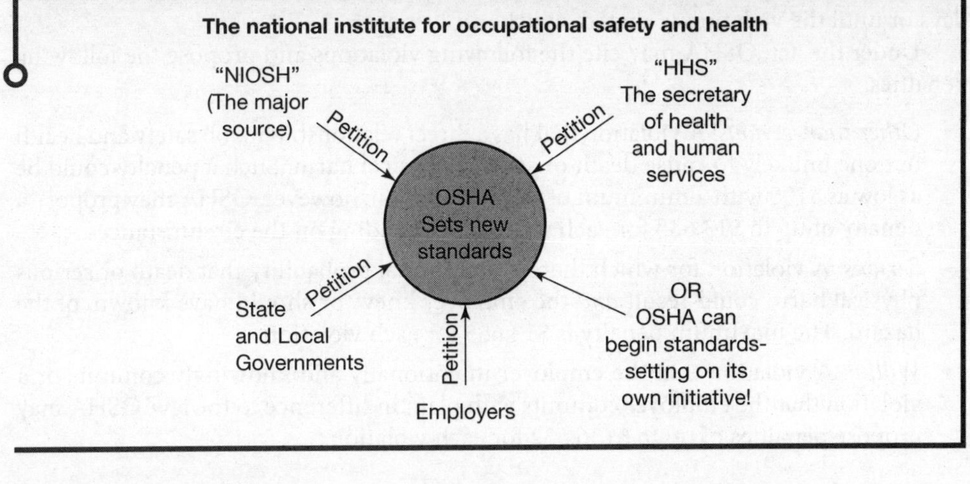

Because it slowed them down, the workers who built New York's skyline in the early 1900s were actually discouraged from using safety devices such as ropes to prevent falls. Not surprisingly, a disproportionately large number of workers fell to their deaths.

12.1c Enforcing OSHA Standards

OSHA is authorized to conduct workplace inspections, issue citations, and impose penalties on employers. In recent years OSHA has stepped up its enforcement activities. In 2019, OSHA conducted 33,393 federal inspections and 42,063 state plan inspections.[6] Figure 12.5 shows the most frequently violated OSHA standards resulting from these federal and state inspections.

Workplace Inspections

Under OSHA, "upon presenting appropriate credentials to the owner, operator, or agent in charge," an OSHA compliance officer is authorized to do the following:

- Enter without delay and at reasonable times any factory, plant, establishment, construction site or other areas, workplace, or environment where work is performed by an employee of an employer; and
- Inspect and investigate during regular working hours, and at other reasonable times, and within reasonable limits and in a reasonable manner, any such place of employment and all pertinent conditions, structures, machines, apparatus, devices, equipment and materials therein, and to question privately any such employer, owner, operator, agent, or employee.[7]

Citations and Penalties

OSHA citations may be issued immediately following the inspection or later by mail. Citations tell the employer and employees which regulations and standards are alleged to have been violated and the amount of time allowed for their correction. The employer must post a copy of each citation at or near the place the violation occurred for three days or until the violation is abated, whichever is longer.

Under the act, OSHA may cite the following violations and propose the following penalties:

- *Other-than-serious:* A violation that has a direct relationship to job safety and health but one unlikely to cause death or serious physical harm. Such a penalty could be as low as $100 with a minimum of $0 per violation; however, OSHA may propose a penalty of up to $13,653 for each violation depending on the circumstances.
- *Serious:* A violation for which there is substantial probability that death or serious physical harm could result *and* the employer knew, or should have known, of the hazard. The maximum penalty is $13,653 for each violation.
- *Willful:* A violation that the employer intentionally and knowingly commits or a violation that the employer commits with plain indifference to the law. OSHA may propose penalties of up to $136,532 for each violation.[8]

Figure 12.5 Most Frequently Violated OSHA Standards

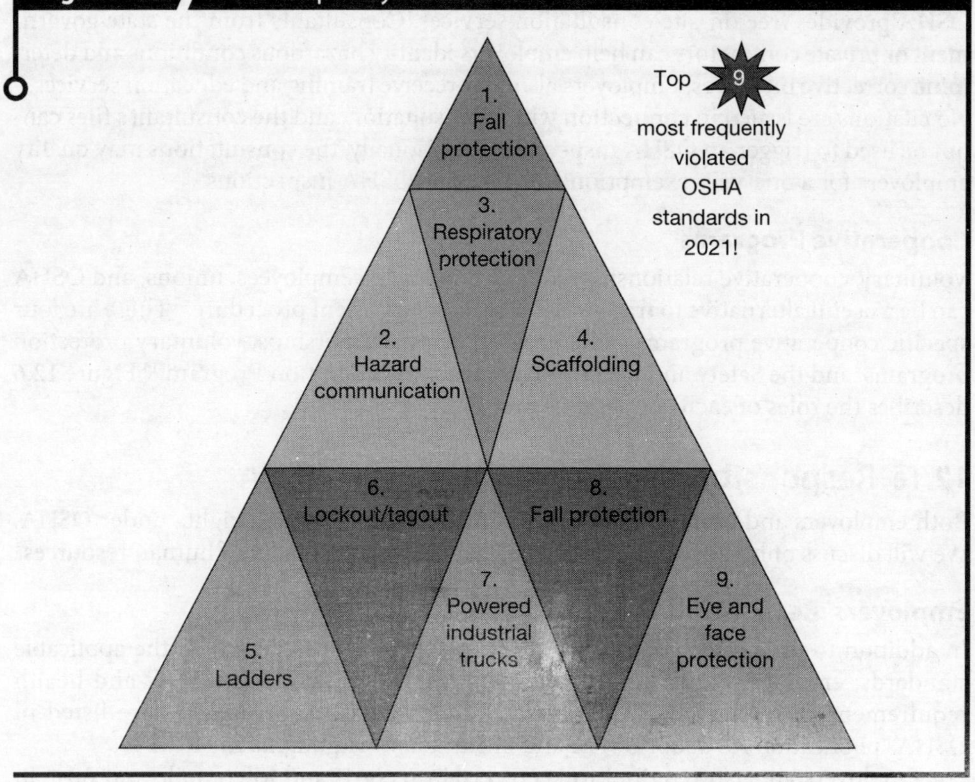

Source: https://www.nsc.org/newsroom/osha-reveals-top-10-violations-for-fiscal-year-202, (March 2, 2021).

If a willful violation results in the death of an employee, OSHA can assess penalties up to $250,000 for an individual or $500,000 for a corporation, imprisonment of up to 6 months, or both. Fines can reach into the millions or tens of millions of dollars. For example, in 2020 OSHA issued $3.5 million in citations to companies for violations related to coronavirus prevention.[9] Amazon was one of these companies, which was found to have "failed to provide effective safety and health training on COVID-19 and procedures to mitigate potential exposure."[10]

OSHA can adjust any penalty downward depending on the employer's good faith (such as demonstrating effort to comply with the act), history of previous violations, and size of business.[11] However, the agency can adjust penalties upward, too. OSHA's Severe Violator Enforcement Program (SVEP) identifies employers with repeated, serious citations and, among other things, subjects them to increased, multi-worksite inspections and higher penalties. OSHA provides an updated directory of all companies on the SVEP for the public to view. Once a company is declared an SVEP, it stays on the list for a minimum of three years, making it difficult to secure loans, attain and retain employees, and develop a favorable reputation.[12]

12.1d OSHA Consultation Assistance

Besides helping employers identify and correct specific hazards, OSHA can help employers develop and implement effective workplace safety and health programs that emphasize preventing worker injuries and illnesses.

On-Site Consultation

OSHA provides free on-site consultation services. Consultants from the state government or private contractors can help employers identify hazardous conditions and determine corrective measures. Employers also may receive training and education services.[13] No citations are issued in connection with a consultation, and the consultant's files cannot be used to trigger an OSHA inspection. Additionally, the consultations may qualify employers for a one-year exemption from routine OSHA inspections.

Cooperative Programs

Voluntary, cooperative relationships among employers, employees, unions, and OSHA can be a useful alternative to traditional OSHA enforcement procedures. There are four specific cooperative programs—alliances, strategic partnerships, voluntary protection programs, and the Safety and Health Achievement Recognition Program.[14] Figure 12.6 describes the roles of each cooperative program.

12.1e Responsibilities and Rights under OSHA

Both employers and employees have certain responsibilities and rights under OSHA. We will discuss only those that relate directly to the management of human resources.

Employers' Responsibilities and Rights

In addition to providing a hazard-free workplace and complying with the applicable standards, employers must inform all their employees about the safety and health requirements mandated by OSHA. Specific employer responsibilities are listed in OSHA's publication *All about OSHA* and illustrated in Highlights in HRM 1.

Employers are also required to keep certain records and to compile and post an annual summary of work-related injuries and illnesses. From these records, organizations can compute their *incidence rate*—the number of injuries and illnesses per 100

Figure 12.6 Cooperative Programs

Cooperative programs:

1. Alliances	2. Strategic partnership programs (SPPs)	3. Voluntary protection programs (VPPs)	4. Safety and health achievement recognition program (SHARP)
Organizations collaborate with OSHA to improve safety health.	Long-term Agreements between Employers and OSHA to improve safety and health.	Try to establish a cooperative relationship between Employers and OSHA (the middle-men) There are 3: 1. Star 2. Merit 3. Demonstration	A certification program that recognizes small employers with exemplary achievements in workplace safety and health.

What Are My Responsibilities under OSHA?

If you are an *employer* that OSHA covers, you must:

- Meet your general duty responsibility to provide a workplace free from recognized hazards that are causing or are likely to cause death or serious physical harm to employees, and comply with standards, rules, and regulations issued under the act.
- Be familiar with mandatory OSHA standards and make copies available to employees for review upon request.
- Inform all employees about OSHA.
- Examine workplace conditions to make sure they conform to applicable standards.
- Minimize or reduce hazards.
- Make sure employees have and use safe tools and equipment (including appropriate personal protective equipment) and that such equipment is properly maintained.
- Use color codes, posters, labels, or signs when needed to warn employees of potential hazards.
- Establish or update operating procedures and communicate them so that employees follow safety and health requirements.
- Provide training required by OSHA standards (hazard communication, lead, etc.).
- Report to the nearest OSHA office within eight hours of any fatal accident or one that results in the hospitalization of three or more employees.
- Keep OSHA-required records of work-related injuries and illnesses, and post a copy of the totals from the last page of OSHA No. 200 during the entire month of February each year. (This applies to employers with 11 or more employees.)
- Post, at a prominent location within the workplace, the OSHA poster (OSHA 2203) informing employees of their rights and responsibilities. (In states operating OSHA-approved job safety and health programs, the state's equivalent poster and/or OSHA 2203 may be required.)
- Provide employees, former employees, and their representatives with access to the Log and Summary of Occupational Injuries and Illnesses (OSHA 200) at a reasonable time and in a reasonable manner.
- Provide access to employee medical records and exposure records to employees or their authorized representatives.
- Cooperate with the OSHA compliance officer by furnishing the names of authorized employee representatives who may be asked to accompany the compliance officer during an inspection. (If none, the compliance officer will consult with a reasonable number of employees concerning safety and health in the workplace.)
- Not discriminate against employees who properly exercise their rights under the act.
- Post OSHA citations at or near the worksite involved. Each citation, or copy thereof, must remain posted until the violation has been abated, or for three working days, whichever is longer.
- Abate cited violations within the prescribed period.

If you are an *employee* whom OSHA covers, you should:

- Read the OSHA poster at the job site.
- Comply with all applicable OSHA standards.
- Follow all employer safety and health rules and regulations, and wear or use prescribed protective equipment while engaged in work.
- Report hazardous conditions to the supervisor.
- Cooperate with the OSHA compliance officer conducting an inspection if the officer inquires about safety and health conditions in your workplace.
- Exercise your rights under the act in a responsible manner.

Source: "OSHA Inspections: OSHA FactSheet," August 2016, https://www.osha.gov/sites/default/files/publications/factsheet-inspections.pdf; *OSH Act, OSHA Standards, Inspections, Citations and Penalties* (Washington, DC: Occupational Safety and Health Administration, May 20, 2011), http://www.osha.gov.

full-time employees during a given year. The standard formula for computing the incidence rate is shown by the following equation, in which 200,000 equals the base for 100 full-time workers who work 40 hours a week, 50 weeks a year:

$$\text{Incidence rate} = \frac{\text{Number of injuries and illnesses} \times 200{,}000}{\text{Total hours worked by all employees during period covered}}$$

It is the employer's responsibility to provide employees with protective equipment when necessary and ensure it is used. Employers must also provide their workers with safety training and be prepared to discipline employees for failing to comply with safety rules. In addition, employers must not discriminate against employees who exercise their rights under the act by filing complaints with OSHA.[15]

Employees' Responsibilities and Rights

Employees are required to comply with all applicable OSHA standards, to report hazardous conditions, and to follow all employer safety and health rules and regulations, including those prescribing the use of protective equipment. Workers have the right to demand safe and healthy conditions on the job without fear of punishment. They also have many rights that pertain to requesting and receiving information about safety and health conditions.[16] For example, most states—and federal law—require that employers provide information to employees about the hazardous chemicals they handle. Commonly known as **right-to-know laws**, these statutes require employers and manufacturers to give employees information about the toxic and hazardous substances they could come into contact with on the job and what the health risks related to those substances are.

right-to-know laws
Laws that require employers to advise employees about the hazardous chemicals they handle.

12.2 Promoting a Safe Work Environment

LO2
Describe the measures managers and employees can take to create a safe work environment.

Typically, a firm's HR department or the industrial relations department is responsible for managing its safety program. The HR department typically coordinates the safety communication and training programs, maintains the safety records required by OSHA, and works closely with managers and supervisors in a cooperative effort to make the program a success.

12.2a Creating a Culture of Safety

Lower-level operational managers and supervisors have traditionally been the bedrock of efforts encouraging health and safety in their organizations.[17] Indeed, one study by the American Institute of Plant Engineers showed that there was a direct correlation between an increase in managers' commitment to safety and a decrease in accidents (see Figure 12.7).

Today, however, firms try to create a "culture" of safety within their organizations that goes beyond managing operational processes and reducing accidents.[18] A culture of safety exists when everyone within an organization consciously works to improve its safety and health conditions. Johnny C. Taylor, president and CEO of the Society for Human Resource Management, has talked about the key role that managers have in this effort. During the COVID-19 vaccination rollout, many companies were deciding whether to mandate vaccinations for their employees. Regardless of which decision they ultimately make, Taylor emphasizes how the right decision should be based on a company's unique culture.[19] Highlights in HRM 2 will help you assess your knowledge and awareness of safety and health issues.

2 Highlights in HRM

Test Your Safety Smarts

Take the following quiz to evaluate your knowledge and awareness of safety and health issues. The answers are found at the end of this chapter.

1. True or False? Employers have the right to be told by an Occupational Safety and Health Administration (OSHA) compliance officer the reason why their workplace is undergoing investigation.
2. True or False? Employers have the legal right to have a company representative accompany OSHA compliance officers on inspections.
3. True or False? OSHA requires employers to give its inspectors access to employees' medical and safety records.
4. True or False? So that they can correct potential health and safety problems, employers have the right to know the name of an employee who files a complaint with OSHA.
5. Which causes more accidents: unsafe actions or unsafe conditions?
6. True or False? Employers are required to provide employee training on OSHA standards.
7. True or False? Employers are required to allow OSHA inspectors on premises for unannounced inspections.
8. True or False? Employers have 24 hours to report to OSHA accidents that result in a fatality.

As part of their culture of safety, some companies periodically conduct **fitness-for-duty evaluations** of their current employees. Fitness-for-duty evaluations are similar to pre-hire physical exams but can performed done any time during employment. They determine an employee's physical, mental, and emotional fitness and are most often used for safety-related or security-sensitive positions. For example, federal rules require nuclear-plant workers to undergo random fitness-for-duty evaluations on the job to determine if they have been using alcohol or drugs.

fitness-for-duty evaluations
Evaluations randomly conducted to determine an employee's physical, mental, and emotional fitness for a job.

Figure 12.7 How Manager Commitment to Safety Reduces Worker Accidents

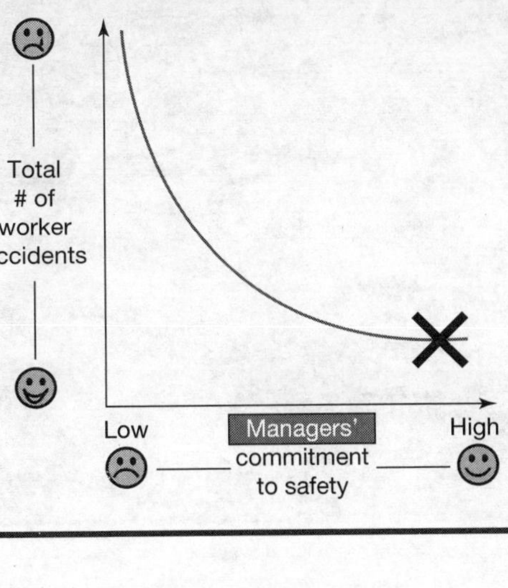

The Key Role of the Supervisor

Like HR managers, supervisors play a key role in their employer's safety programs. One of a supervisor's major responsibilities is to communicate to an employee the need to work safely.[20] Proper work procedures, the use of protective clothing and devices, and potential hazards should be explained thoroughly.[21] Moreover, supervisors must continually observe employees at work, reinforce safe practices, and immediately correct behaviors that are unsafe.[22]

Proactive Safety Training Programs

In certain occupational areas, safety and health training is legally required. For example, employers regulated by a federal agency called the Pipeline and Hazardous Materials Safety Administration are legally required to provide their employees with environmental-safety protection training. When training is mandated, employers must keep accurate records of all employee education. Violations can incur criminal penalties.

Most organizations have a safety awareness program that entails the use of several different media. Safety lectures or courses, paired with printed and audiovisual materials, are common elements of these programs.[23] The use of games has also become an interactive way to provide employees with safety training. Costco and Amazon, for example, have successfully used a product called *Safety Bingo* to motivate employees on a daily basis to create a safety-conscious atmosphere and remind them of their safety goals.[24]

A study published in 2021 tested the effectiveness of traditional instructional safety training against the increasingly popular computer game training. The traditional methods were associated with three limitations: (1) representation of the workplace situation, (2) accessibility for workers who have low literacy, and (3) maintaining the workers'

OSHA regulations mandate the use of protective equipment in recognized hazardous conditions.

Sukanya sitthikongsak/ Getty Images

attention. The study showed that the computer game overcame these limitations while providing the employees with a greater knowledge of the safety procedures.[25]

HR professionals and safety directors in particular advocate employee involvement when designing and implementing safety programs.[26] Employees can offer valuable ideas regarding specific safety and health topics to cover, instructional methods, and proper teaching techniques. Furthermore, employees are more likely to embrace safety training when they feel a sense of ownership over the instructional program.[27]

12.2b Enforcing Safety Rules

Firms communicate specific safety rules and regulations in a variety of ways, including through supervisors, bulletin board notices, employee handbooks, and signs attached to equipment. In addition to safety labels and signs, many companies prominently display in their workplaces the number of consecutive days they have operated without an injury. The idea is to motivate employees to keep the injury-free "streak" going and possibly set new records for injury-free performance.

12.2c Investigating and Recording Accidents

The supervisor and a member of the safety committee should investigate every accident that occurs in the workplace, even those considered minor. Such an investigation may determine which factors contributed to the accident and reveal which corrections are needed to prevent it from happening again.

OSHA requirements mandate that employers with 11 or more employees maintain records of work-related occupational injuries and illnesses.[28] As stated in an earlier section, OSHA also requires each of these organizations to keep a Log of Work-Related Injuries and Illnesses (OSHA Form 300). All recordable cases must be entered in the log. A **recordable case** is any injury or illness that results in any of the following: death, days away from work, restricted work or transfer to another job, or medical treatment beyond first aid. Other problems employers must record as work-related include loss of consciousness or diagnosis of a significant injury or illness by a health care professional.[29] Figure 12.8 shows OSHA's diagram for classifying accidents under the law. For every recordable case written in the log, the organization must complete an Injury and Illness Incident Report (OSHA Form 301). OSHA Form 301 requires the employer to answer a series of questions about the case. Each year OSHA Form 300A, Summary of Work-Related Injuries and Illnesses, must be completed and posted in a conspicuous place or places where notices to employees are customarily posted. However, when completing all OSHA forms, employers must not list the name of an injured or ill employee if the case has "privacy concerns," such as those involving sexual assault, HIV infection, and mental illness.[30]

recordable case
Any occupational death, illness, or injury to be recorded in the log (OSHA Form 300).

Highlights in HRM 3 shows the OSHA poster that employers are required to display at the workplace.

12.2d Safety Hazards and Issues

Workers face many different safety hazards on the job, which differ depending on their occupations. We cannot cover all of them in this chapter, but we will discuss a number of hazards that have been receiving a great deal of attention from HR managers and firms lately.

Job Safety and Health Protection Poster

Figure 12.8 Guide to Recording Cases under the Occupational Safety and Health Act

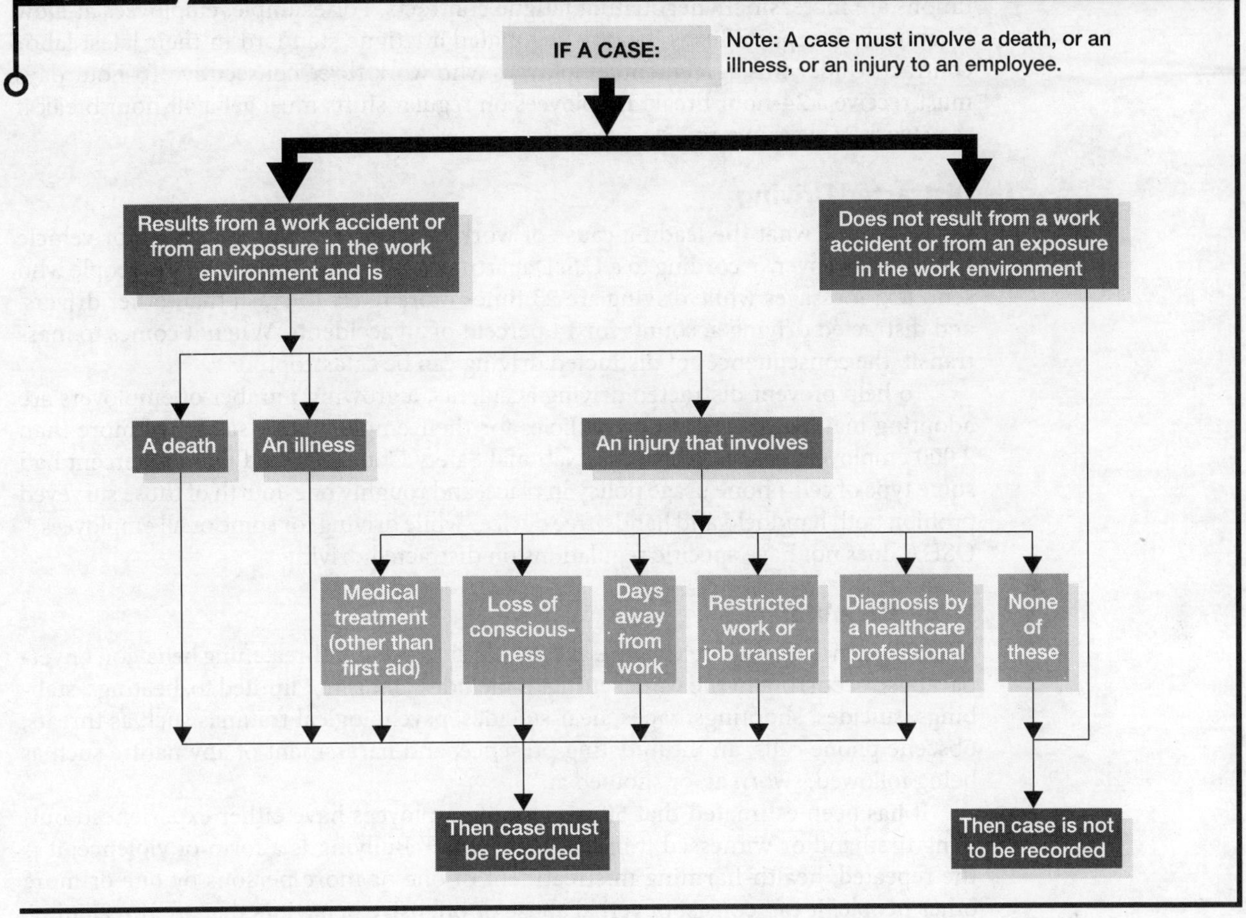

Fatigue

In recent years, few safety issues have been in the news more than employee fatigue. You have probably heard about air traffic controllers who have fallen asleep on the job and could not be awakened by pilots trying to contact them. Fatigue is more of a problem in organizations that operate around the clock or have night shifts. Studies show that 30 to 50 percent of night-shift workers report falling asleep at least once a week while on the job, according to Dr. Charles Czeisler, chief of sleep medicine at Brigham and Women's Hospital in Boston.[31] Not only is there more fatigue on the job, but night shifts also increase the risk of insomnia. The more hours an employee works and the more consecutive shifts they have, the more severe the sleep problems are likely to be.[32]

Fatigue may not result in life-or-death consequences for most jobs. Nonetheless, managers, employees, and the public are concerned about how it affects workplace safety and performance. The regulations in certain industries limit the number of hours employees can work per shift. The airline industry is one such industry. However, even with these limits, workers are finding themselves fatigued. Some experts say downsizing may be a factor, as fewer workers are being asked to cover more shifts. Recently, the U.S. government vowed it would give air traffic controllers an extra hour off between shifts to combat fatigue. Many airlines, including Delta and United, have given their pilots permission to call in and report if they are too fatigued to fly.[33]

Although OSHA currently has no fatigue standard, it is seeking to establish one, and unions are increasingly negotiating fatigue contracts. For example, employees at Dow Chemical's Freeport, Texas, facility negotiated a fatigue standard in their latest labor contract. Under this agreement, employees who work three consecutive 16-hour days must receive a 24-hour break. Employees on regular shifts must get a 48-hour break if they work 21 days in a row.[34]

Distracted Driving

Do you know what the leading cause of worker fatalities each year is? Motor vehicle crashes. Moreover, according to a U.S. Department of Transportation study, people who send text messages while driving are 23 times more likely to crash than other drivers, and distracted driving accounts for 14 percent of all accidents. When it comes to mass transit, the consequences of distracted driving can be catastrophic.[35]

To help prevent distracted driving accidents, a growing number of employers are adopting mandatory cell-phone policies for their employees. A survey of more than 2,000 employers conducted by the National Safety Council found that 58 percent had some type of cell-phone usage policy in place, and roughly one-fourth of those surveyed prohibit both handheld and hands-free devices while driving for some or all employees.[36] OSHA does not have specific regulations on distracted driving.

Workplace Violence

NIOSH defines workplace violence as "any physical assault, threatening behavior, or verbal abuse occurring in the work setting. It includes, but is not limited to, beatings, stabbings, suicides, shootings, rapes, near suicides, psychological traumas such as threats, obscene phone calls, an intimidating presence, and harassment of any nature such as being followed, sworn at, or shouted at."

It has been estimated that 50 percent of employees have either experienced bullying firsthand or witnessed it in the workplace.[37] Bullying is a form of violence; it is the repeated, health-harming mistreatment of one or more persons by one or more other people. It can consist of verbal abuse or offensive behaviors that are threatening, humiliating, intimidating, or interfere with someone's ability to work. For example, bullying can be found when one employee withholds information or resources from another employee, treats the victim in a disrespectful way, interferes with work activities, or prevents someone from expressing themselves. Due to lack of legislation, workplace bullying is currently pursued under Title VII antidiscrimination laws, though only 20 percent of bullying cases involve a direct application of the antidiscrimination laws.[38]

Not only does bullying lead to lower morale among employees, but it can result in deadly suicides, violence, and homicides in the workplace.[39] A number of countries around the world, including France and Sweden, have enacted laws against bullying. All U.S. states have passed some form of antibullying law.[40]

Reducing Workplace Violence

In addition to protecting workers at high risk of on-the-job assaults, OSHA recommends firms analyze their workplaces to uncover areas of potential violence and develop violence prevention programs and training for their employees. To begin, background checks should be conducted for all job applicants to ensure they don't have histories showing a propensity toward aggression or violence.[41] In fact, employers can be sued for negligent hiring if they do not take this step and workplace injury occurs as a result. Managers, supervisors, and employees should also be trained to recognize violence indicators such as those listed in Figure 12.9.

Figure 12.9 Violence Indicators: Know the Warning Signs

The following behaviors should be taken seriously when assessing situations of potential violence:

- Direct or veiled threatening statements
- Recent performance declines, including concentration problems and excessive excuses
- Insubordination and severe reactions to criticism
- Prominent mood or behavior changes; despondence
- Preoccupation with guns, knives, or other weapons
- Deliberate destruction of workplace equipment; sabotage
- Fascination with stories of violence or war
- Reckless or antisocial behavior; evidence of prior assaultive behavior
- Aggressive behavior or intimidating statements; yelling or using profanity
- Written messages of violent intent; exaggerated perceptions of injustice
- Serious stress, legal, or financial problems in one's personal life
- Intruding on other people's privacy by pestering, spying on, or stalking them
- Expressed desire or observable obsession with harming a specific group or person
- Evidence of violence against a family member
- Substance abuse

Sources: Adapted from "Violence in the Federal Workplace: A Guide to Prevention and Response," Interagency Security Committee, 2019; "Understanding Workplace Violence Prevention and Response," Society for Human Resource Management; *Violence in the Workplace: Risk Factors and Prevention Strategies, NIOSH Bulletin #59*; David D. Van Fleet and Ella W. Van Fleet, "Preventing Workplace Violence: The Violence Volcano Metaphor," *Journal of Applied Management and Entrepreneurship* 12, no. 3 (2007): 17; Bella L. Galperin and Joanne D. Leck, "Understanding the Violent Offender in the Workplace," *Journal of American Academy of Business* 10, no. 2 (2007): 114.

Last, but certainly not least, a firm's HR department must effectively communicate to a firm's employees that it has zero tolerance for violence.[42] Organizations such as Garden Fresh (a restaurant chain), Enterprise Rent-a-Car, JetBlue Airways, and Ritz Carlton have formalized workplace violence prevention policies informing employees that aggressive employee behavior will not be tolerated. Employees should encourage other employees to report any possible or observed incidents to their firm's HR departments. Some firms have set up hotlines for employees to report incidents without having to fear repercussions for "getting involved."

Workplace Emergencies

According to OSHA, a workplace emergency is an unforeseen situation that threatens employees, customers, or the public; disrupts or shuts down operations; or causes physical or environmental damage. Emergencies can be natural or humanmade. In addition to workplace violence, they can include the following:

- Floods
- Hurricanes
- Tornadoes
- Fires
- Toxic gas releases
- Chemical spills
- Radiological accidents
- Explosions
- Civil disturbances and terrorism

emergency action plans
A plan developed by an organization that contains step-by-step procedures for dealing with various emergency situations.

OSHA requires companies to have **emergency action plans** to deal with these kinds of incidents. An emergency action plan must include, among other things, procedures for reporting a fire or other emergency, evacuating a facility, and accounting for employees after an evacuation. It must also include procedures for employees who must remain in the facilities to ensure critical plant operations continue, as well as procedures for workers performing rescue and medical duties. A copy of the emergency action plan should be either provided to employees or kept in a convenient location where employees can access it. Organizations with 10 or fewer employees are allowed to communicate their emergency plans orally to employees.

Highlights in HRM 4 shows a readiness-assessment checklist that organizations can complete to determine how prepared they are for an emergency. OSHA Publication 3088, *How to Plan for Workplace Emergencies and Evacuations*, is also a helpful guideline for employers.

Crisis Management Teams

Some organizations have formed crisis management teams. During the COVID-19 pandemic, many organizations found that such teams would have been helpful if they had already been in place before the crisis disrupted their business operations.[43] Crisis management teams and HR managers play a key role when it comes to getting employees back to work and paid on time following an emergency. Crisis management teams are also responsible for disseminating public information and addressing the press.

These teams, which are composed of both hourly and managerial employees, also work in conjunction with HR to conduct initial risk assessment surveys, develop emergency action plans, test them, and perform crisis intervention during emergency events. For example, a crisis management team would investigate a threat reported by an employee. The team's mandate would be to gather facts about the threat, decide whether the organization should intervene, and, if so, determine the most appropriate method of doing so. Figure 12.10 shows what a crisis management team or other manager could do to calm an angry employee, for example.

Figure 12.10 Calming an Angry Employee

If you try to defuse a tense situation, remember that anger frequently results from a person's feeling of being wronged, misunderstood, or unheard. Keep the following tips in mind to guide you:

- Strive to save the employee's dignity during an angry confrontation. Do not attack a person's rash statements or continue a muddled line of thinking.
- Hold all conversations in private. Do not allow employees to create an embarrassing public situation for themselves, yourself, or other employees.
- Always remain calm. Anger or aggressiveness on your part will trigger a similar response in the employee.
- Listen to the employee with an open mind and nonjudgmental behavior. Give the employee the benefit of hearing them out.
- Recognize the employee's legitimate concerns or feelings. Agree that the employee has a valid point and that you will work to correct the problem.
- If the employee is very emotional or if the engagement seems out of control, schedule a delayed meeting so people can calm down.
- Keep the discussion as objective as possible. Focus on the problem at hand, not the personalities of individuals. A cornerstone of conflict resolution is to attack the problem, not the personality.
- If the employee appears overly aggressive, withdraw immediately and seek professional help before any further discussion with the employee.
- If your efforts fail to calm the employee, report the incident to your manager, security, or human resource personnel.

Source: Adapted from professional literature on crisis management and seminars attended by the authors.

Emergency Readiness Checklist

Readiness Assessment

How Prepared Is Your Business for an Emergency?	Yes	No	Unsure
1. Does your business know what kinds of emergencies might affect it—both internally and externally?	❑	❑	❑
2. Does your business have a written, comprehensive emergency plan in place to help ensure your safety and take care of employees until help can arrive?	❑	❑	❑
3. Has your business created and practiced procedures to quickly evacuate and find shelter in case of an emergency?	❑	❑	❑
4. Has your business created a communication plan to communicate with employees in an emergency? (Examples include an established telephone call tree, password-protected page on the company website, email alert or call-in voice recording, and a contact list that includes employee emergency contact information.)	❑	❑	❑
5. Has your business talked with utility service providers about potential alternatives and identified backup options?	❑	❑	❑
6. Has your business determined a plan for resuming key operations, specifically considering which operations need to be up and running first after the emergency?	❑	❑	❑
7. Has your business created a list of inventory and equipment, including computer hardware, software, and peripherals (such as backed-up/protected records and critical data) for business continuity and insurance purposes?	❑	❑	❑
8. Has your business met with your insurance provider to review current coverage in case of an emergency?	❑	❑	❑
9. Does your business promote family and individual preparedness among coworkers (such as emergency preparedness information shared through staff meetings, newsletters, the company intranet, periodic employee emails, and other internal communication tools)?	❑	❑	❑
10. Have emergency shutdown procedures been developed for equipment such as boilers, automatic feeds, or other operations that cannot simply be left running in an emergency evacuation?	❑	❑	❑
11. Has your business worked with your community on emergency planning efforts and helped to plan for community recovery?	❑	❑	❑

Readiness Results

Count your number of "Yes" responses to calculate a score. Your score is a *general reflection* of how much you know about emergency planning efforts at your business and/or how prepared your business may be for an emergency.

❑ If you have 8-11 "Yes" responses, you are well on your way to having a comprehensive and effective plan in place.

❑ If you have 4-7 "Yes" responses, while some aspects of your plan may be in place, you have some work to do to fill gaps.

❑ If you have 1-3 "Yes" responses, get started immediately on developing an emergency plan for your business. This training program is a great first step!

Planning for Emergencies

Source: Planning for Emergencies. © 2007 National Safety Council.

LO3

Describe the programs organizations utilize to build better health among their workforces.

12.3 Creating a Healthy Work Environment

Because of the dramatic impact workplace accidents have, managers and employees sometimes pay more attention to them than to the health hazards present in the work environment. Accidents happen quickly, whereas the effects of health hazards show up only over time. When they do show up, though, they adversely affect workers, their families, and their companies.

12.3a Ergonomics

One way to help eliminate health hazards in the workplace is via ergonomics. Recall that we discussed ergonomics in Chapter 4 when we looked at job design. Ergonomics focuses on ensuring that jobs are designed for safe and efficient work while improving the safety, comfort, and performance of users. Ergonomics also considers the requirements of a diverse workforce, accommodating, for example, people who may lack the strength to operate equipment requiring intense physical force or people who may lack the stature to reach equipment controls.

Ergonomics has proven cost-effective at organizations such as Compaq Computer, 3M, Pratt and Whitney, and the U.S. Postal Service and has eliminated, or at least reduced, many repetitive motion injuries, particularly those related to the back and wrist. The key elements of successful ergonomic programs are shown in Figure 12.11.[44]

12.3b Health Hazards and Issues

At one time, health hazards were associated primarily with jobs found in manufacturing operations. In recent years, however, hazards in jobs outside of plants, such as in offices, health care facilities, and airports, have been recognized, and methods to lessen these hazards have been adopted.

Figure 12.11 Key Elements for a Successful Ergonomics Program

Companies with award-winning ergonomics programs list the following as common elements of success:

- *Provide notice and training for employees.* Implement a well-publicized ergonomics policy or present ergonomic information in safety policies or training programs. Train employees, supervisors, and managers in basic workplace ergonomics.
- *Conduct preinjury hazard assessment.* Survey the workplace and work processes for potential hazards and adopt measures to lessen the exposure to ergonomic risk factors. Answer the question: "Are certain work areas more prone to ergonomic hazards than others?"
- *Involve employees.* Include employees in risk assessment, recognition of musculoskeletal disorder (MSD) symptoms, design of work-specific equipment or tools, and the setting of work performance rules and guidelines.
- *Plan and execute.* Integrate ergonomic responsibilities into the performance plans for all personnel. Demand accountability for program success.
- *File injury reports.* Encourage early reporting of MSD symptoms or injuries. Refer employees to the company's medical facilities or to the employee's personal physician for treatment.
- *Evaluate and assess the ergonomics program.* Periodically review the effectiveness of the ergonomics program. If the program appears to be ineffective, determine the underlying causes for failure and propose corrective changes.

Cumulative Trauma Disorders

Increasing numbers of meat cutters, cooks, dental hygienists, textile workers, violinists, flight attendants, office workers at computer terminals, and others whose jobs require repetitive motion of the fingers, hands, or arms are reporting injuries related to their jobs.[45] Known as **cumulative trauma disorders** or repetitive motion injuries, these musculoskeletal disorders are injuries of the muscles, nerves, tendons, ligaments, joints, and spinal discs caused by repeated stresses and strains. One of the more common conditions is *carpal tunnel syndrome*, which is characterized by tingling or numbness in the fingers and occurs when a tunnel formed by bones and ligaments in the wrist narrows and pinches nerves that reach the fingers and the base of the thumb. Without proper treatment, employees with carpal tunnel syndrome can completely lose feeling in their hands.

Ethan Miller/Staff/ Getty Images News/Getty Images

An ergonomically designed computer workstation like this will reduce the strain on the worker's eyes, neck and shoulders, wrists, and back.

cumulative trauma disorders
Injuries involving tendons of the fingers, hands, and arms that become inflamed from repeated stresses and strains.

Ergonomics techniques have been successfully used to improve or correct workplace conditions that cause or aggravate these kinds of cumulative trauma disorders.[46] Continuous developments in office furniture, video display terminals, tool design, computer keyboards, and adjustable workstations are all attempts not just to make the work setting more comfortable—and, businesses hope, more productive—but also to lessen musculoskeletal disorders. Minibreaks involving exercise and the changing of work positions have been found to be helpful as well.

Computer Workstation Issues

Figure 12.12 provides a checklist of potential repetitive-motion problem areas for employees using computers. Video and computer screens are a particular concern. The problems that managers have to confront in this area fall into three major groups:

1. *Visual difficulties.* Screen operators frequently complain of blurred vision, sore eyes, burning and itching eyes, and glare.[47]
2. *Muscular aches and pains.* Pains in the back, neck, and shoulders are common complaints of screen operators.
3. *Job stress.* Eyestrain, postural problems, insufficient training, excessive workloads, and monotonous work are complaints reported by three-fourth of screen users.

To capitalize on the benefits of computer screens while safeguarding employee health, Dr. James Sheedy, a screen and vision expert, offers these tips on how to minimize the negative effects of computer use on the eyes and body:

- Place the computer screen 4 to 9 inches below eye level.
- Keep the monitor directly in front of you.
- Sit in an adjustable-height chair with lower back support and with feet flat on the floor.

Figure 12.12 Computer Workstation Ergonomics Checklist

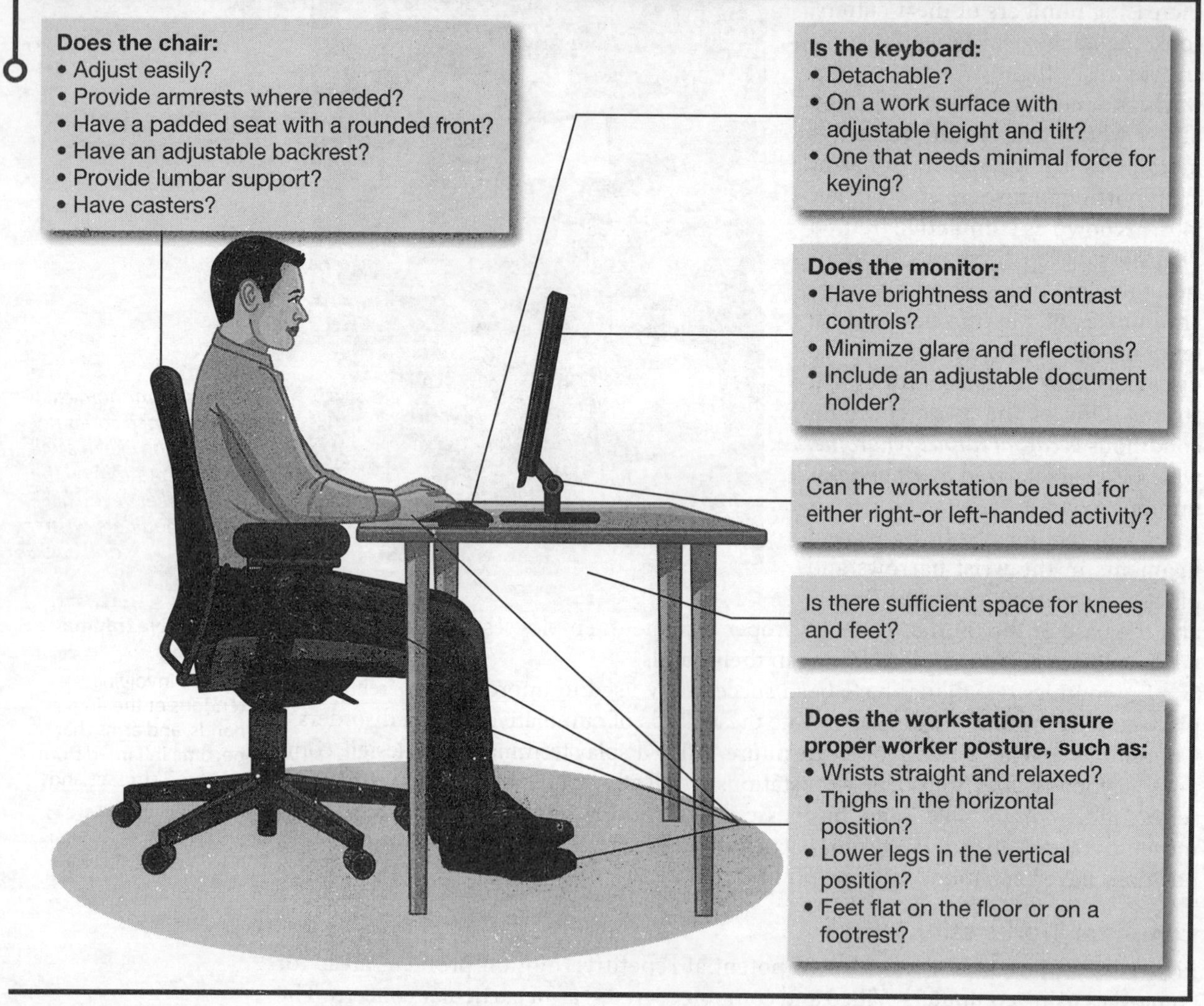

Sources: Melanie Pinola, "7 Things You Need for an Ergonomically Correct Workstation," *The New York Times* (May 14, 2020); National Institute for Occupational Safety and Health, *Elements of Ergonomics Programs: A Primer Based on Workplace Evaluations of Musculoskeletal Disorders* (Washington, DC: U.S. Government Printing Office, March 1997).

- Use shades or blinds to reduce the computer screen glare created by window lighting.
- Keep elbows close to body and supported.
- Place wrist and hands in line with forearms.

Chemical Hazards

The OSHA Hazard Communication Standard (HCS) is the most frequently cited OSHA standard for general industry as well as for the construction industry. This standard is intended to ensure that producers perform adequate testing and evaluation of their chemicals and that users of the chemicals receive appropriate information on the chemical hazards to which they are exposed.

All hazardous chemical containers must be labeled with the identity of their contents and must state any appropriate hazard warnings. OSHA's HCS prescribes a system for communicating these warnings, including the format for **Material Safety Data Sheets (MSDSs)**. MSDSs must include the chemical name of a hazardous substance; all of the risks involved in using it, including any potential health risks; safe handling practices; personal protective equipment needed; first aid in the event of an accident; and information identifying the manufacturer. OSHA-required chemical training includes informing employees of the methods used to detect the presence or release of hazardous chemicals, the physical and health problems posed by hazardous chemicals, and the ways in which employees can protect themselves from chemical dangers.

Material Safety Data Sheets (MSDSs)
Documents that contain vital information about hazardous substances.

Chemical hazards can affect the reproductive health of either women or men. In an important case concerning women, the U.S. Supreme Court ruled in *International Union v. Johnson Controls* (1991) that employers may not bar women of childbearing age from certain jobs because of potential risk to their fetuses.[48] The Court said that such policies are a form of sex bias that is prohibited by federal civil rights law. The decision has made it important for employers to inform and warn female workers about fetal health risks on the job.

Smoking and Tobacco Smoke

Virtually all large organizations, and even some smaller ones, have established smoking policies specifying when and where smoking will be allowed in their organizations, if at all. When developing smoking policies, it is advisable to involve both smokers and nonsmokers.

Pathogens

The advent of the COVID-19 pandemic has brought the dangers of pathogens to the forefront of public awareness, including the need for protective devices such as masks while working in areas where these dangers may lurk. Exposures to blood and other body fluids occur across a wide variety of occupations and can result in employees contracting diseases. The pathogens of primary concern are the human immunodeficiency

Small Business Application

OSHA Resources for Small Businesses

Meeting all of OSHA's requirements can seem like a daunting task for small businesses, especially ones just setting up shop. Fortunately, for business owners and entrepreneurs, OSHA has a wealth of resources and programs designed to help small businesses. The agency estimates that for every dollar a small business invests in safety in health measures, it can reap as much as $4 to $5 in savings in terms of these costs.

Donjon Shipbuilding & Repair (DSR), an Erie, Pennsylvania, a shipbuilding and repair facility, wanted to build a strong safety culture upon its establishment in 2010, so the company's managers contacted the Indiana University of Pennsylvania OSHA Consultation program to help. They were given a full list of hazards to eliminate. After working with the OSHA consulting program for three years, DSR received a Safety & Health Achievement Recognition Program (SHARP) designation, signifying improvement, in January 2020. The company had a measurable reduction in total workplace injuries, which led to increased productivity, morale, and overall success. DSR went from 47 injuries per year to 3 injuries per year with no days away from work. In total, the company went more than 900 days without a lost-time injury.

Source: *Small Business Success Stories* (Washington, DC: Occupational Safety and Health Administration, March 12, 2021), http://www.osha.gov.

virus (HIV), hepatitis B virus (HBV), and hepatitis C virus (HCV). Workers can be exposed to such pathogens through needlestick and other sharp-object injuries, mucous membranes, and skin exposures.

12.3c Building Better Physical and Emotional Health among Employees

Along with improving working conditions that are hazardous to employee health, employers today are cognizant of the physical and emotional health of their employees. Some have chosen to provide their employees with programs to maintain and improve both.

Recall that we discussed employee assistance programs (EAPs) in Chapter 11. EAPs can help employees with a range of problems, including relationship, marital, and family problems; anger, depression, anxiety, and stress; and elder care demands. Workplace issues, addiction, and self-improvement are other areas in which EAPs provide workers with assistance.

Wellness and Weight Issues

In Chapter 11, we also mentioned wellness programs as being available from some employers. For example, Discovery Communication, in Silver Spring, Maryland, provides a wellness center to its employees. The company employs a medical assistant, nurse practitioner, and physician who offer health services, including stress management, consultation and techniques, fitness programs, and podiatry care.[49] Google encourages employee wellness through its "small changes" program, in which employees at Google headquarters are encouraged to ride scooters to meetings, eat healthier food at the cafeteria with portion sizes kept in check, be active and playful with the in-office slide and ping-pong tables, and take advantage of the on-site physical therapist and chiropractor.[50]

We also mentioned weight-related problems and obesity in Chapter 11. As you know, excess weight can affect both the health and productivity of workers. A study by Duke University researchers, who examined the records of nearly 12,000 university employees, found that employees with an unhealthy weight experienced medical costs that were more than five times higher than those of workers with a healthy weight. They also missed eight times the number of workdays, which by some estimates costs companies an estimated $5.5 billion a year in lost productivity.[51] Not surprisingly, employers are launching or improving programs specifically designed to help employees maintain or lose weight by exercising and eating properly.[52] For example, a nutritional component is part of the wellness program of JWT, a New York advertising firm. Nutritional programs address two lifestyle changes: (1) increasing a person's physical exercise (via walking, jogging, bicycling, or other physical activities); and (2) adopting nutritional dietary programs that emphasize eating lots of fruits and vegetables, fish, and low-fat dairy products.[53] Stephanie Pronk, the chief health officer at RedBrick Health, a Minneapolis health technology and services company, notes that employers today are trying to create a "culture of wellness" that makes thinking about maintaining a healthy weight second nature to employees.[54]

Job Stress and Burnout

stress
Any adjustive demand caused by physical, mental, or emotional factors that requires coping behavior.

It is no secret that employees today are more stressed out than they have been in years past. A Gallup poll recently found that 66 percent of employees were dissatisfied with the amount of stress they experience in the workplace.[55] **Stress** is any demand on the individual that requires coping behavior. Stress comes from two basic sources: physical activity and mental or emotional activity. The physical reaction of the body to both types of stress is the same. Psychologists use two separate terms to distinguish between positive and negative forms of stress, even though reactions to the two forms are the same, from a biochemical perspective. **Eustress** is positive stress that accompanies achievement and exhilaration.[56] This type of stress is regarded as a beneficial force that helps us to forge ahead against obstacles. What is harmful is **distress**. Stress becomes distress when we begin to sense a loss of our feelings of security and adequacy. Helplessness, desperation, and disappointment turn stress into distress.

eustress
Positive stress that accompanies achievement and exhilaration.

distress
Harmful stress characterized by a loss of feelings of security and adequacy.

burnout
A severe stage of distress, which manifests as depression, frustration, and loss of productivity.

Burnout is a severe stage of distress. Career burnout generally occurs when a person begins questioning his or her own personal values. Quite simply, the person no longer feels that what he or she is doing is important. Depression, frustration, and a loss of productivity are all symptoms of burnout. Burnout is primarily due to a lack of personal fulfillment in the job or a lack of positive feedback about one's performance.[57] During the COVID-19 pandemic, burnout became rampant. One-third of U.S. employees started "living at work"—with the kitchen table becoming their new office desk. As the pandemic subsided, many of these people were not able to turn off their "always at work" mentality, which created an enormous amount of distress.

To decrease the chance of burnout, managers should provide role clarity, offer opportunities to develop on a personal and professional level, and conduct feedback and goal development sessions with employees on a regular basis.[58] Other potential solutions include making sure you have a manageable workload and having a strong sense of connection to family and friends.[59]

Unfortunately, the causes of workplace stress remain numerous and sometimes overwhelming. According to a study by Luminari, a national health care company, four factors have a major influence on employee stress (see Figure 12.13):

- *High demand:* having too much to do in too short a time
- *High effort:* having to expend too much mental or physical energy over too long a period
- *Low control:* having too little influence over the way a job is done on a day-to-day basis
- *Low reward:* receiving inadequate feedback on performance and no recognition for a job well done

Figure 12.13 Different Factors That Create Stress for Employees

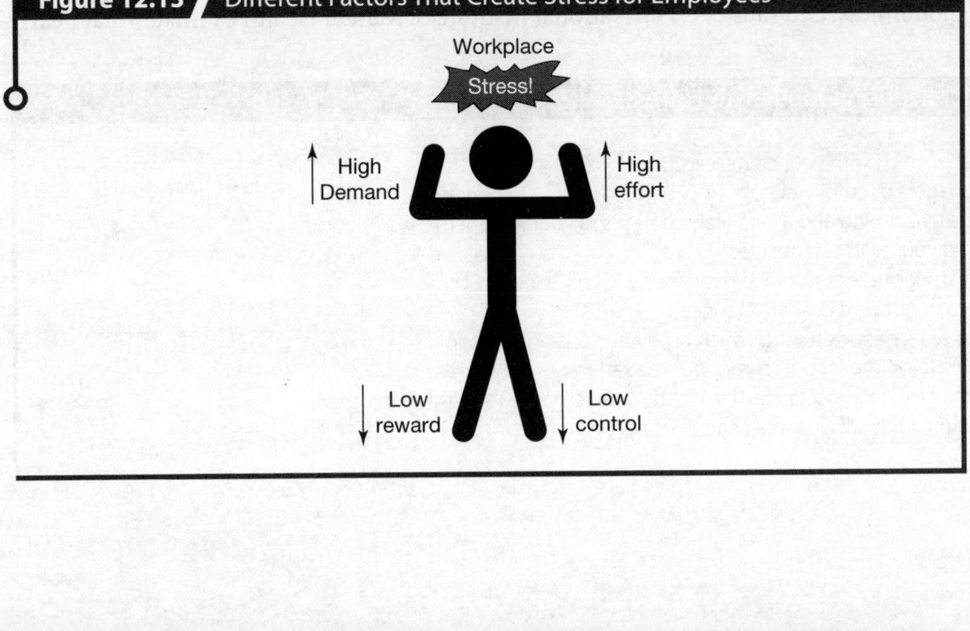

Other job stressors include layoffs and organizational restructuring; disagreements with managers or fellow employees; prejudice because of age, gender, race, or religion; inability to voice complaints; and poor working conditions. Even minor irritations such as lack of privacy, unappealing music, and other conditions can be distressful to one person or another.

Job stress places all kinds of people at risk for fatigue, high blood pressure, cardiovascular problems, depression, and obesity and increases employees' susceptibility to infectious diseases. Studies have shown that work-related stress contributes to injuries and illnesses. All of these factors feed into higher health care costs and can lower productivity, job satisfaction, and retention.[60] Stress is also the most frequently cited reason employees give for why they would leave a company.[61]

HR professionals are well aware of the negative effects of workplace stress on employees' health and job performance.[62] In one study, the top three sources of stress employers identified as negatively affecting the workplace were lack of work–life balance, inadequate staffing, and technologies that expand availability during nonworking hours.[63] Armed with this awareness, many employers have developed stress management programs to teach employees how to minimize the negative effects of job-related stress.[64] A typical program might include instruction in relaxation techniques, coping skills, listening skills, methods of dealing with difficult people, time management, and assertiveness.

All of these techniques are designed to break the pattern of tension that accompanies stressful situations and to help participants achieve greater control of their lives. In addition, organizational techniques, such as clarifying the employee's work role, redesigning and enriching jobs, correcting physical factors in the environment, and effectively handling interpersonal factors, should not be overlooked in the process of teaching employees how to handle stress. Stress management counselors recommend several ways to resolve job-related stress, as described in Figure 12.14.

Depression

depression
A negative emotional state marked by feelings of low spirits, gloominess, sadness, and loss of pleasure in ordinary activities.

Emotional problems and personal crises become organizational problems when they affect people's behavior at work and interfere with their job performance.[65] The most prevalent problems among employees are personal crises involving marital, family, financial, or legal matters.[66] Most personal crises are resolved in a reasonable period of time. Unfortunately, when a personal crisis lingers, it can lead to depression. **Depression** is a decrease in functional activity accompanied by persistent symptoms of low spirits, gloominess, and sadness. The National Institute of Mental Health estimates that nearly

Figure 12.14 Tips for Reducing Job-Related Stress

- Build rewarding relationships with your coworkers.
- Talk openly with managers or employees about your job or personal concerns.
- Prepare for the future by keeping abreast of likely changes in your job's demands.
- Do not greatly exceed your skills and abilities.
- Set realistic deadlines; negotiate reasonable deadlines with managers.
- Act now on problems or concerns of importance.
- Designate dedicated work periods during which time interruptions are avoided.
- When feeling stressed, find time for detachment or relaxation.
- Do not let trivial items take on importance; handle them quickly or assign them to others.
- Take short breaks from your work area as a change of pace.

7 percent of the adult population experience depression each year.[67] Fortunately, with the treatments available today, 80 percent of depressed individuals will significantly improve, usually within a matter of weeks.

Managers are in a good position to identify the signs of depression on the job.[68] Employees with depression may exhibit decreased energy, concentration and memory problems, guilt feelings, irritability, and chronic aches and pains that do not respond to treatment. Managers and supervisors who suspect an employee is depressed are encouraged to express their concerns to the person, actively listen to the employee, and—if the depression persists—suggest professional help.[69] Under no circumstances should managers attempt to play amateur psychologist and try to diagnose an employee's condition.[70] Mood disorders such as depression are complex in nature and do not lend themselves to quick diagnoses. Furthermore, in reviewing such cases, the organization should pay particular attention to workplace safety factors because there is general agreement that emotional disturbances are primary or secondary factors in a large percentage of industrial accidents and incidents of violence.

Alcoholism

Nearly 6 million working Americans bring their alcohol problems with them to the workplace.[71] It has been estimated that business and industry lose more than $20 billion each year because of alcoholism. This disease affects both the young and the old, is prevalent across the sexes, and affects workers in every occupational category.[72]

The first step in helping the employee with alcoholism is to awaken the person to the reality of their situation. A supervisor should carefully document evidence of the person's declining performance on the job and then confront the employee with unequivocal proof to that effect. The employee should be assured that help will be made available without penalty. Because the evaluations are made solely in terms of poor on-the-job performance, a supervisor can avoid any mention of alcoholism and allow such employees to seek aid as they would for any other problem.

Employers must remember that alcoholism is classified as a disability under the Americans with Disabilities Act (ADA—see Chapter 3). Alcoholism is regarded as a disease, similar to a mental impairment. Therefore, a person disabled by alcoholism is entitled to the same protection from job discrimination as any other person with a disability. However, under the ADA, employers can discipline or discharge employees when job performance is so badly affected by alcohol usage that the employee is unable to perform the job.[73]

Drug Abuse

Like alcohol abuse, the abuse of illegal drugs by employees costs businesses billions of dollars annually in terms of safety risks, theft, reduced productivity, absenteeism, and accidents. A wide range of employers, including federal contractors and private and public transportation firms, are subject to regulations aimed at eliminating the use of illegal drugs on the job. Federal antidrug initiatives include the following:

- *The Drug-Free Workplace Act of 1988*, which requires federal contractors and recipients of federal grants to take specific steps to ensure a drug-free work environment. One of the main provisions of this act is the preparation and distribution of an antidrug policy statement.
- *Department of Defense (DOD) contract rules*, which specify that employers entering into contracts with the DOD must agree to a clause certifying their intention to maintain a drug-free workplace.

- *Department of Transportation (DOT) regulations*, which require that employees whose jobs include safety- or security-related duties be tested for illegal drug use under DOT rules.

To help employers benefit from being drug-free and to further its mission to help companies maintain safe, healthy, and productive workplaces, the U.S. Department of Labor has created the Working Partners for an Alcohol- and Drug-Free Workplace. The goal of this initiative is to raise awareness of the impact of substance abuse in the workplace and to provide employers with substance abuse prevention information. Additionally, the Department of Labor's Drug-Free Workplace Advisor provides information to employers about how to establish and maintain an alcohol- and drug-free environment.[74]

The ADA considers an individual with a serious, life-affecting drug problem to be disabled, provided the person is enrolled in a drug treatment program and not currently using drugs. In turn, such a person's employer must make reasonable accommodations for their disability. Reasonable accommodations might include time off from work or a modified work schedule to obtain treatment. As we noted earlier, federal regulations require employers to test their workers for drug use under certain specified conditions.[75]

The abuse of legal drugs can also pose a problem for employees.[76] In fact, unlike cocaine and other illegal drugs, according to Quest Diagnostics, a blood testing company, both employees' prescribed use and misuse of opiates such as hydrocodone and oxycodone have been rising sharply in recent years. Employees who abuse legal drugs—those prescribed by physicians—often do not realize they have become addicted or how their behavior has changed as a result of their addiction. Also, managers should be aware that some employees may be taking legal sedatives or stimulants as part of their medical treatment and that their behavior at work may be affected by their use of these drugs.

Summary

LO 1 The Occupational Safety and Health Act was designed to assure, so far as possible, safe and healthful working conditions for every working person. In general, this act extends to all employers and employees. The Occupational Safety and Health Administration (OSHA) sets health and safety standards, ensures employers and employees comply with them, and provides safety and health consultation and training where needed. Both employers and employees have certain responsibilities and rights under OSHA. Employers not only are required to provide a hazard-free work environment, but also must keep employees informed about OSHA requirements and provide them with protective equipment when necessary and ensure they wear it. Under the "right to know" regulations, employers are required to keep employees informed about hazardous substances present in the workplace and to instruct them in avoiding the dangers presented by those substances. Employees, in turn, are required to comply with OSHA standards, to report hazardous conditions, and to follow all employer-established safety and health regulations.

LO 2 To provide safe working conditions for their employees, employers typically establish a formal safety program, for which their HR departments act as liaison. The program may have many facets, including providing safety knowledge and motivating employees to use it, making employees aware of the need for safety, and rewarding them for safe behavior. Incentives such as praise, public recognition, and awards are used to involve employees in the safety program. Employers also engage their workers by asking them to join safety committees, help develop safety procedures, observe the safety practices of their coworkers, and investigate any accidents. The maintenance of required records from accident investigations provides a basis for information that can be used to create a safer work environment.

LO 3 Along with providing safer and healthier work environments, many employers establish programs that encourage employees to improve their health habits. Wellness programs that emphasize exercise, nutrition, weight control, and avoidance of harmful substances serve employees at all organizational levels.

Key Terms

burnout
cumulative trauma disorders
depression
distress
emergency action plans
eustress
fitness-for-duty evaluation
Material Safety Data Sheets (MSDSs)
recordable case
right-to-know laws
stress

Discussion Questions

LO 1 When OSHA was enacted in 1970, it was heralded as the most important new source of protection for the U.S. worker in the second half of the twentieth century. Based on the information presented in this chapter, what is your opinion about the effectiveness or the ineffectiveness of this act? Should it be expanded, or should businesses have more freedom to determine safety standards for their workers?

LO 2 What steps should management take to increase the motivation of their employees to operate safely?

LO 3 To live a healthier life, medical professionals say we need to identify those things we currently do that either impair or contribute to our health. Discuss with others a way to develop a lifetime program for a healthy lifestyle.

CASE STUDY 1 Deadpool Ends in Death

The facts of the case are straightforward. A shop floor dispute at an automobile parts manufacturing plant in Hamilton, Iowa, ended with one worker killing another. At about 2 p.m., police responded to a report of a fight that erupted between two employees. When members of the Hamilton Police Department's Violent Crime Unit arrived, they found Mark Lomas seriously injured. Lomas, 30, died three hours later at Good Samaritan Memorial Hospital. The other employee, Thomas Waycross, was charged with second-degree murder.

During the investigation of the incident, employees noted that Lomas and Waycross often "bickered" when working together. One employee remarked that Waycross liked to "act tough." Another employee claimed that Waycross had a "Deadpool-type" personality. It was widely known that management had told both employees to "learn to get along" or quit.

When asked about the incident, police spokesperson Kathy Calder remarked, "Employers must be vigilant when monitoring for signs of potential workplace violence." Nancy Lomas, Mark's wife, has filed a negligence lawsuit against the company.

Questions

1. What are some violence indicators an employee might display?
2. What are some actions management can take to help prevent workplace violence?
3. How can employees protect themselves against workplace violence?

Source: Adapted from a case known to one of the authors. All names are fictitious.

CASE STUDY 2 Too Much Fatigue and Stress? You Decide

Job fatigue and stress are significant problems faced by employees and their managers. Unfortunately, when a case of depression arises as a result, trying to resolve the problem may be difficult—sometimes leading to conflict—as this case illustrates.

Donald Knolls was an air traffic control supervisor for International Gateway Airport (IGA), an airport serving a major metropolitan area. Donald began to experience depression-related problems largely due to severe stress and fatigue on the job. A few months later, he requested and was granted a disability leave for treatment of his illness. After eight months, his personal physician, an expert in depression treatment and a licensed consulting psychologist, agreed that he was sufficiently improved to return to his former position.

IGA then sent Donald to the physician it had used when Donald first requested his disability leave. After an extensive evaluation, the doctor concluded that while Donald had made considerable strides in overcoming his depression, he should not be immediately returned to his former supervisory position because the conditions of the job had not changed and he was apt to find the stress too great. Instead, he recommended that Donald be returned to a nonsupervisory position on a six-month trial basis, with the case to be reviewed at the end of that time. IGA followed the advice of its doctor and did not return Donald to a supervisory position. Donald, angered by management's decision, filed a grievance through IGA's alternative dispute resolution procedure, a procedure that could end in binding arbitration.

During several meetings between Donald and management, the employer maintained that it had the right to rely on the medical opinion of "a fair and impartial" doctor who had determined that Donald should not be returned to the position that was the cause of his original stress-related emotional problems. Additionally, management pointed out to Donald that IGA's disability leave provision stated that it "may require appropriate medical documentation if it believes an employee is not fit to return to his or her former position."

Donald responded, through an attorney he hired to represent his position, that the disability leave provisions were clear but, nevertheless, biased against an employee because they completely disregarded the opinion of his physician and psychologist. According to Donald, "Why bother to get expert medical opinions if they are dismissed?" He further noted, "I have never felt better. I'm really ready to get back to my job." Finally, Donald's lawyer contended that Donald was the victim of discrimination based on his former state of depression: "What happened to Donald would not have happened if his illness had been a more conventional physical injury."

Questions

1. When conflicting medical opinions are presented, should the advice of a medical expert count more heavily than the opinion of a general physician? Explain your answer.
2. Is the charge of discrimination presented by Donald's lawyer relevant to this case? Explain your answer.
3. If you were presented with this case, what decision would you reach? Explain.

Source: *Small Business Success Stories* (Washington, DC: Occupational Safety and Health Administration, May 25, 2011), http://www.osha.gov.

Answers to Highlights in HRM 2

1. True
2. True
3. True
4. False
5. Unsafe actions (85 percent of all accidents)
6. True
7. False
8. False (8 hours)

Notes and References

1. Erika Ebsworth-Goold, "Working Well by Being Well: The Bottom Line Benefits of Corporate Wellness Programs," *The Source* (St. Louis: Washington University, August 24, 2016).
2. P.L. 91-596, 91st Congress, S. 2193, December 29, 1970.
3. Allen Smith, "OSHA Issues Worker Safety Guidance for Coronavirus Protection Programs," Society for Human Resource Management (February 1, 2021). https://www.shrm.org/resourcesandtools/legal-and-compliance/employment-law/pages/coronavirus-osha-worker-safety-guidance.aspx.
4. OSHA publishes many pamphlets pertaining to various aspects of the act, such as employee workplace rights and voluntary compliance programs. All OSHA publications can be downloaded at no cost from the agency website at http://www.osha.gov; you may also call 800-321-OSHA or fax a request to 202-693-2498.
5. *All about OSHA*, 12.
6. https://www.osha.gov/oshstats/commonstats.html (March 13. 2021).
7. Occupational Health and Safety Act, 91st Congress, S.2193 (1970) Section 8; *All about OSHA*, 15–16.
8. https://www.osha.gov/penalties/ (January 26, 2021).
9. Allen Smith, "OSHA Gathers More than $3.5 Million in Coronavirus Penalties." Society for Human Resource Management (December 17, 2020). https://www.shrm.org/resourcesandtools/legal-and-compliance/employment-law/pages/osha-gathers-coronavirus-penalties.aspx.
10. Allana Akhtar, "California Just Fined Amazon $1,870 for Poor Workplace Safety during the Coronavirus Pandemic," Business Insider, October 14, 2020.
11. Occupational Safety and Health Administration, *Field Operations Manual*, Chapter 6, Section 17 (April 14, 2020).
12. P. C. Hendershot Cowart, "OSHA Severe Violator Enforcement Program: 5 Things Employers Should Know," March 5, 2019, https://www.oshadefensefirm.com/blog/2019/march/osha-severe-violator-enforcement-program-5-thing/.
13. For a comprehensive list of compliance requirements of OSHA standards or regulations, refer to Title 29 of the *Code of Federal Regulations* at www.osha.gov or call (800) 321-OSHA.
14. *All about OSHA*, 28.
15. *All about OSHA*, 10.
16. Ibid.
17. Roy Maurer, "Making Safety Committees Work," *Society for Human Resource Management* (August 8, 2013): 1.
18. Ibid., 2.
19. Johnny C. Taylor, "Viewpoint: Mandating Vaccinations Should Depend on Company Culture," Society for Human Resource Management (March 25, 2021), https://www.shrm.org/resourcesandtools/hr-topics/employee-relations/pages/viewpoint-mandating-vaccinations-should-depend-on-company-culture.aspx.
20. Ray Prest, "The Supervisor's Crucial Role in Safety Performance," *Occupational Health and Safety* (October 2020); Robert Pater, "Next Level Safety Cultures," *Occupational Health and Safety* (May 2008).
21. Oregon OSHA, "Supervisor Responsibilities," *Health and Safety Resource Magazine* 21 (December 2011): 7.
22. Carol Leaman, "The Future of Safety Training," *Occupational Health and Safety* (September 2013).
23. Ismael E. Garza, "Increasing Safety Awareness in the Workplace: Measuring the Emotional, Cognitive and Rhetorical Effectiveness of Informational Illustrations Used in Safety Documents," *University of Houston–Downtown* (December 2009): 80.
24. "How to Make Safety Training Fun," *Workplace Safety Experts* (June 2011).
25. Lucia Vigoroso, Federica Caffaro, Margherita Micheletti Cremasco, and Eugenio Cavallo, "Innovating Occupational Safety Training: A Scoping Review on Digital Games and Possible Applications in Agriculture," *International Journal of Environmental Research and Public Health* 18, no. 4 (2021): 1868, https://doi.org/10.3390/ijerph18041868.
26. Aruna Vayuvegula, "Learning Activities for Making Safety Training Fun," *CommLab India* (January 2012).
27. E. Kevin Kelloway and Cary L. Cooper, *Occupational Health and Safety for Small and Medium Sized Enterprises* (Edward Elgar Publishing, 2011), 45.
28. OSHA considers an injury or illness to be work-related if an event or exposure in the work environment either caused or contributed to the resulting condition or significantly aggravated a preexisting injury or illness. Work-relatedness is presumed for injuries and illnesses resulting from events or exposure occurring in the work environment. OSHA defines the work environment as "the establishment and other locations where one or more employees are working or are present as a condition of their employment. The work environment includes not only physical locations, but also the equipment or materials used by the employee during the course of his or her work."
29. For complete information on the recording and reporting of illnesses and injuries, see OSHA Publication 3169, *Recordkeeping*, particularly Sections 1904.5 (determination of work-relatedness) and 1904.7 (general recording criteria). See also the OSHA website at http://www.osha.gov.
30. If employers have a "privacy concern case," they may not enter the employee's name on the OSHA 300 log. Instead, they should enter "privacy case" in the space normally used for the employee's name. This will protect the privacy of the injured or ill employee when another employee, a former employee, or an authorized employee representative is provided access to the OSHA 300 log. Privacy cases must be recorded on a

separate confidential list. Employers must consider the following injuries or illnesses to be privacy concern cases: (1) an injury or illness to an intimate body part of the reproductive system; (2) an injury or illness resulting from a sexual assault; (3) mental illnesses; (4) HIV infection, hepatitis, or tuberculosis; (5) needlestick injuries and cuts from sharp objects that are contaminated with another person's blood or other potentially infectious material; and (6) other illnesses, if the employee independently and voluntarily requests that his or her name not be entered on the log.

31. Randolph P. Schmid, "Odd Work Schedules Pose Health Risk," *ABC News* (April 16, 2011), http://abcnews.go.com.
32. S. Lee, J. B. Park, K. J. Lee, et al., "Effects of Work Organization on the Occurrence and Resolution of Sleep Disturbances among Night Shift Workers: A Longitudinal Observational Study," *Scientific Reports* 11 (2021): 5499, https://doi.org/10.1038/s41598-021-85017-8.
33. Alison Duquette, "Fact Sheet:–Pilot Flight Time, Rest, and Fatigue," Federal Aviation Administration. (Accessed May 18, 2021).
34. L. M. Sixel, "Working: Beyond Exhausted, But Still on the Job," *Houston Chronicle* (May 5, 2011), http://www.chron.com; https://www.osha.gov/OshDoc/data_Hurricane_Facts/faq_longhours.html (April 11, 2017).
35. "Traffic Safety Facts: Research Note," DOT HS 812 926, National Highway Traffic Safety Administration (April 2020).
36. Julie Ferguson, "Distracted Driving and Employer's Policies," *HR Web Café* (November 1, 2009), http://www.hrwebcafe.com.
37. Michelle Heath, Erika N. Williams, and Dre Wynn, "Experiential Learning Activity to Ameliorate Workplace Bullying," *Innovative Instructional Classroom Projects/Best Practices* (January 11, 2021).
38. Ibid.
39. Roy Maurer, "Workplace-Bullying Laws on the Horizon?" *Society for Human Resource Management* (July 2013): 3.
40. Deborah Temkin, "All 50 States Now Have a Bullying Law. Now What?" *Huffington Post* (April 27, 2015).
41. W. Barry Nixom and Kim Kerr, *Background Screening and Investigation: Managing Hiring Risk from the HR and Securities Perspectives* (Elsevier, August 2011), 28.
42. S. Hihi and S. Bulut, "The Psychological Causes and Effects of Bullying in the Workplace," *Clinical Psychological Research* 4, no. 1 (2021): 1–5; Marcia K. Korow, "How Reflective Is Our Policy?" *Nursing Management* 39, no. 1 (January 2008): 37; see also Scott R. Gane, "Avoiding Violent Outcomes," *Security Management* 51, no. 6 (June 2007): 140.
43. Tam Harbert, "Which Employees Will You Need?" Society of Human Resource Management (March 13, 2021).
44. John P. Baeseman and Douglas Newhand, "The Ergonomically Correct Workplace," *Document Processing Technology* 15, no. 7 (December 2007): 20.
45. Emil Jacob, "The Future of Computer Ergonomics," *Occupational Health and Safety* (September 2011); see also Joshua S. Berger and Roy Garvin, "Microcentrifuge Tube Ergonomics and the Required Force of Opening," *Occupational Health and Safety* (July 2010).
46. Michael S. Zedalis and Keitha Kessler, "Frequently Asked Questions: Ergonomics and Hand Protection," *Occupational Health and Safety* 76, no. 4 (April 2007): 64.
47. Reid Goldsborough, "Keeping Your Eyes Healthy in Front of a Computer Screen," *TECH Directions* 66, no. 10 (May 2007): 12.
48. The Supreme Court decision in *International Union v. Johnson Controls* may be found in 59 U.S. Law Week 4029.
49. Judy Ashley, "Building a Culture of Wellness the Discovery Way," *Workspan* (July 2007): 43.
50. The Greatest Team, "The 46 Healthiest Companies to Work for in America," *Greatest* (October 2013); see also Joshua Love, "Five Reasons Corporate Wellness Is More Important Than Ever," *Forbes* (September 2013); Mary Lorenze, "7 Habits of Highly Successful Corporate Wellness Programs," *CareerBuilder* (July 2010).
51. Dale Kaplan and Park Dietz, "Use Employee Assistance to Manage Risk," *Occupational Health and Safety* 76, no. 7 (July 2007): 82.
52. Josh Cable, "Shedding Pounds Good for Bottom Line," *Occupational Hazards* 69, no. 10 (October 2007): 18.
53. Jeremy Smerd, "Young and Unhealthy: Urgent Care Required," *Workforce Management* 86, no. 15 (September 10, 2007): 36.
54. "Obesity Programs Are Latest Wellness Focus," *HR Focus* 84, no. 7 (July 2007): 12.
55. "U.S. Workers' Satisfaction with Job Dimensions Increases," *Gallup* (August 29, 2016), http://www.gallup.com/poll/195143/workers-satisfied-job-dimensions.aspx.
56. Kerry Sulkowicz, "Stressed for Success," *Business Week* (May 21, 2007): 18.
57. Gary M. Stern, "Employee Burnout: Around the Corner? Already Here?" *Fortune, CNN Money* (May 2012).
58. "U.S. Workers' Satisfaction with Job Dimensions Increases."
59. Jennifer Moss, "Beyond Burned Out," *Harvard Business Review*, February 10, 2021.
60. http://www.watsonsyatt.com/research/reports.asp.
61. Jenna Goudreau, Gail Edmondson, and Michelle Conlin, "Dispatches from the War on Stress: Business Begins to Recon with the Enormous Costs of Workplace Angst," *Business Week* (August 6, 2007): 74; see also Michael R. Frone, "Are Work Stressors Related to Employee Substance Use? The Importance of Temporal Context Assessments of Alcohol and Illicit Drug Use," *Journal of Applied Psychology* 93, no. 1 (2008): 199.
62. "Will Stress Be Your Next Wellness Target?" *HR Focus* 85, no. 1 (2008): 12.
63. Tower Watson, "2013/2014 Staying@Work Report: U.S. Executive Summary," *National Business Group on Health* 29407 (2013): 6.

64. Ashley Weinberg, Cary L. Cooper, and Dr. Valerie J Sutherland, *Organizational Stress Management: A Strategic Approach* (Palgrave Macmillan, September 2010), 234.
65. Dale Kaplan and Park Dietz, "Use Employee Assistance to Manage Risk," *Occupational Health and Safety* 76, no. 7 (2007): 82.
66. Gary M. Stem, "Not Tonight, Dear," *The Conference Room Review* 44, no. 2 (2007): 38.
67. James Hunter, "Research on Depression," National Institute of Mental Health and PsychCentral (October 2013), https://www.nimh.nih.gov/health/statistics/prevalence/any-anxiety-disorder-among-adults.shtml.
68. "Treating Depression Improves Productivity," *Industrial Engineer* 40, no. 1 (January 2008): 11.
69. "Depression Outreach Can Boost Productivity," *HR Focus* 84, no. 12 (2007): 12.
70. The HR Specialist, "ADA Warning for Bosses: You're Not Qualified to Diagnose Employees' Mental Illness," *Discrimination and Harassment in Human Resources: Business Management Daily* (November 2012).
71. Pearl Jacobs and Linda Scaain, "Alcohol Abuse in the Workplace: Developing a Workable Plan of Action," *Research in Business & Economics Journal* (March 2010): 1.
72. Mindy Chapman, "Drugs and Alcohol Workplace Trends," *Occupational Health and Safety* 76, no. 8 (2007): 32.
73. *The Employer's Legal Handbook*; see the section on preventing discrimination.
74. Information regarding the U.S. Department of Labor's efforts to create a drug-free workplace can be found at http://www.dol.gov.
75. Kathy Gurchiek, "Employer Testing Credited for Lower Drug-Use Rates," *HR Magazine* 52, no. 6 (2007): 36.
76. Andrew Powell, "Prescription for a Hazardous Workplace," *Occupational Health and Safety* (September 2013).

CHAPTER 13

Employee Rights and Discipline

Learning Outcomes

After studying this chapter, you should be able to

LO 1 Explain the concepts of employee rights and employer responsibilities.

LO 2 Differentiate separate sets of disciplinary policies that use progressive and positive discipline approaches.

LO 3 Identify the different types of alternative dispute resolution methods.

In this chapter, we discuss the rights of employees, the privacy they can expect in the workplace, and employee discipline. Companies without clear policies and procedures for dealing with employee rights and discipline can end up losing lots of money and, worst of all, ruining their reputation.

This is where HR managers play a crucial role. To be effective, they must stay abreast of current laws, agency regulations, and court ruling; establish written employment policies based on this information; and educate the staff members in their organizations about them.

13.1 Employee Rights and Privacy

LO1 Explain the concepts of employee rights and employer responsibilities.

Employee rights can be defined as the guarantees of fair treatment that workers expect in return for their services to an employer. These expectations become rights when they are granted to employees by the courts, legislatures, or employers. Included among those rights are the rights of employees to protest unfair disciplinary actions, to question genetic testing, to have access to their personal files, to challenge employer searches and monitoring, and to be largely free from employer discipline for their off-duty conduct.[1]

employee rights Guarantees of fair treatment that become rights when they are granted to employees by the courts, legislatures, or employers.

The evolution of employee rights is a natural result of the evolution of societal, business, and employee interests.[2] However, legal scholars recognize that the protection of employee privacy rights extends only so far; federal and state courts generally view the privacy rights of employees as minimal. As attorney Benjamin J. Cook notes, "Employees may have expectations of privacy, but an employer's policies may eliminate many of those expectations."

For example, consider the issue of camera surveillance. Generally, it is legal to install cameras in the workplace (except in bathrooms and locker rooms), as long as employees are informed about them. However, after pornography was discovered on one of its computers, a California children's home for abused children installed hidden surveillance cameras in an office shared by two employees. The person who had accessed the pornography was never caught. However, the two employees who shared the office later discovered the camera and were upset they were being monitored. They claimed their privacy rights had been violated, but the Supreme Court of California ruled against them, saying that their employer had a legitimate business reason for conducting the surveillance.[3]

13.1a Employee Rights versus Employer Responsibilities

Balanced against employee rights is the employer's responsibility to provide a safe workplace for employees while guaranteeing safe, quality goods and services to consumers.[4] An employee who uses drugs may exercise their privacy right and refuse to submit to a drug test. But should that employee produce a faulty product as a result of drug impairment, the employer can be held liable for any harm caused by that product. Employers must therefore exercise *reasonable care* in the hiring, training, and assignment of employees to jobs.[5] It is in these areas that employee rights and employer responsibilities often come into conflict (see Figure 13.1).

Figure 13.1 Employee Rights versus Employer Rights

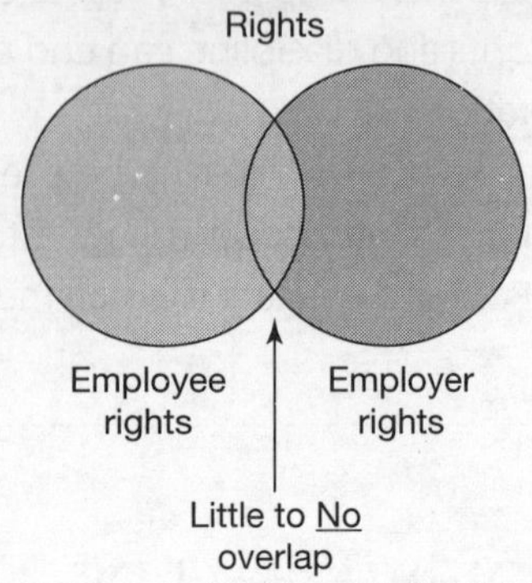

When employers fail to honor the rights of employees, it can result in costly lawsuits, damage the organization's reputation, and hurt employee morale. But the failure to protect the safety and welfare of employees or consumer interests can invite litigation from both groups. There is little to no overlap when it comes to balancing employee rights with employer rights.

13.1b Negligent Hiring

negligence
The failure to provide reasonable care when such failure results in injury to consumers or other employees.

In Chapter 6, we discussed negligent hiring. In law, **negligence** is the failure to use a reasonable amount of care when such failure results in injury to another person. A general responsibility exists for employers to exercise *reasonable care* in preventing employees from intentionally harming other employees during the course of their work.[6]

Unfortunately, when one employee commits a violent act against another employee or an employee willfully defames another employee through email messages communicated at work, the employer may face a negligent-hiring lawsuit claiming that the employer should have used more reasonable care in the hiring of its employees.[7] A negligent-hiring lawsuit can seem like a " Catch-22" situation for an employer. In the remainder of this section, we discuss various rights that employees have come to expect from their employers.

13.1c Job Protection Rights

It is not surprising that employees should regard their jobs as a right that should not be taken away without "just cause" (a good reason) for doing so. However, although employees might believe they have a right to their jobs, there are no laws in the United States guaranteeing them this right, as you will see shortly.

psychological contract
Expectations of a fair exchange of employment obligations between an employee and an employer.

Nonetheless, workers have certain expectations about the employment relationships they have with their employers.[8] This expectation, referred to as the **psychological contract**, is an intangible perception of an employer's and an employee's mutual obligations toward each other.[9] For example, in exchange for their talents, energies, and technical skills, workers expect employers to provide fair compensation, steady work, job training, and promotions.

Employment-at-Will

The employment relationship has traditionally followed the common-law doctrine of employment-at-will. An **employment-at-will relationship** is created when an employee agrees to work for an employer for an unspecified period of time. Because the duration of the employment is indefinite, it can, in general, be terminated at the whim of either party.[10]

employment-at-will relationship
The right of an employer to fire an employee without giving a reason and the right of an employee to quit when they choose.

Does the employment-at-will doctrine give managers and supervisors the unrestricted right of termination? No.[11] First, as emphasized throughout this text, federal and state laws, court decisions, and administrative rulings restrict termination decisions. For example, as you learned in Chapter 3, people cannot be fired because of certain characteristics such as their race, gender, and so forth. Second, in unionized organizations, union collective bargaining agreements limit automatic discharges. These agreements specify the kinds of infractions that can lead to termination.

Not all employers operate on the at-will principle, however. Some have written policies that require good cause to terminate an employee. In any case, despite the at-will doctrine, in today's litigious environment, most employers are very cautious when terminating employees. Barry Roseman, an employment attorney, notes, "Employers increasingly need to operate under the premise that they have to 'prove' that an employee's conduct or action warrants termination, if they hope to prevail in court."

Wrongful Discharge

Approximately 2 million workers are discharged each year.[12] A substantial number of these employees sue their former employers for **wrongful discharge**—that is, a discharge that is illegal. Wrongful discharge suits challenge an employer's right under the employment-at-will concept to unilaterally terminate employees.[13] Various state courts now recognize the following three important exceptions to the employment-at-will doctrine:

wrongful discharge
A discharge, or termination, of an employee that is illegal.

1. *Violation of public policy.* This exception occurs when an employee is terminated for refusing to commit a crime; for reporting criminal activity to government authorities; for disclosing illegal, unethical, or unsafe practices of the employer; or for exercising employment rights. See Figure 13.2 for examples of public policy violations.

Figure 13.2 Discharges That Violate Public Policy

An employer may not terminate an employee for:

- Refusing to commit perjury in court on the employer's behalf
- Cooperating with a government agency in the investigation of a charge or giving testimony
- Refusing to violate a professional code of conduct
- Reporting Occupational Safety and Health Administration (OSHA) infractions
- Refusing to support a law or a political candidate favored by the employer
- Whistle-blowing, or reporting illegal conduct by the employer
- Informing a customer that the employer has stolen property from the customer
- Complying with summons to jury duty

2. *Implied contract.* This exception occurs when employees are discharged despite the employer's promise (expressed or implied) of job security or contrary to established termination procedures. An employer's oral or written statements may constitute a contractual obligation if they are communicated to employees and employees rely on them as *conditions of employment.*[14]
3. *Implied covenant.* This exception occurs when an employer has acted with a lack of good faith and fair dealing. For example, an employer would be violating an implied covenant if it were to terminate a salesperson simply to avoid having to pay them a commission. By inflicting harm without justification, the employer violated the implied covenant between the two parties.

The confusion and conflict between the traditional rights of employers to terminate employees at will and the rights of employees to be protected from unjust discharge are far from resolved. HR specialists recommend firms follow the suggestions given in Figure 13.3.[15] Next, let's look at some situations that can result in wrongful discharge suits.

Whistle-Blowing

whistle-blowing
Complaints to governmental agencies by employees about their employers' illegal or immoral acts or practices.

Employees engage in **whistle-blowing** when they report an employer's illegal actions, immoral conduct, or illegal practices to governmental agencies charged with upholding the law. A number of federal and state laws protect whistle-blowers from retaliation from their employers.[16] In 2020, three Google employees sued Google for not complying with the California state law dealing with allowing and protecting whistle-blowers.[17]

The Sarbanes-Oxley (SOX) Act protects whistle-blowers employed in publicly traded companies.[18] This law encourages whistle-blowing by motivating publicly held companies to promote a more open culture that is sympathetic to employees who have a "reasonable belief" that a law has been violated. Federal employees are covered by the federal Whistleblower Protection Act (WPA).[19] The Notification and Federal Employee

Figure 13.3 Tips to Avoid Wrongful Employment Termination Lawsuits

- *Terminate an employee only if there is an articulated reason.* An employer should have clearly articulated, easily understandable reasons for discharging an employee. The reasons should be stated as objectively as possible and should reflect company rules, policies, and practices.
- *Set and follow termination rules and schedules.* Make sure every termination follows a documented set of procedures. Procedures can be outlined in an employee handbook, a supervisory manual, or even an intraoffice memorandum. Before terminating them, give employees notices of unsatisfactory performance and improvement opportunities through a system of warnings and suspensions.
- *Document all performance problems.* A lack of documented problems in an employee's personnel record may be used as circumstantial evidence of pretextual discharge if the employee is "suddenly" discharged.
- *Be consistent with employees in similar situations.* Document reasons given for all disciplinary actions, even if they do not lead to termination. Terminated employees may claim that exception-to-the-rule cases are discriminatory. Detailed documentation will help employers explain why these "exceptions" did not warrant termination.

BlueBarronPhoto/Shutterstock.com

When Boeing employee O'Hara reported Boeing's actions to an ethics hotline, Boeing HR reported him to management, who quickly fired him. However, federal and state laws protect employees from this kind of retaliation when whistle-blowing.

Antidiscrimination and Retaliation Act (No FEAR Act) requires federal agencies to be more accountable for violations of antidiscrimination and whistle-blower protection laws. The False Claims Act (FCA) and Dodd-Frank Wall Street Reform and Consumer Protection Act protect and financially reward whistle-blowers who expose fraud related to governmental programs and wrongdoing related to consumer financial products or services, respectively. The FCS act protected D. R. O'Hara and rewarded him $4.6 million when he reported Boeing for charging the government for new parts but using recycled ones.[20] The Occupational Safety and Health Administration (OSHA) administers the whistle-blowing provisions in 15 federal statutes protecting whistle-blowers in the airline, nuclear power, and public transportation industries, among others.

Whistle blowing cases can result in embarrassment for employers, harassment for employees, and large fines for employers that are found guilty.[21] To prevent these cases from leading to ugly lawsuits, HR professionals recommend companies implement a whistle-blowing policy that encourages employees to report illegal or immoral conduct internally rather than externally. The policy should provide for the safeguarding of employee rights, a complete and unbiased investigation of the incident, a speedy report of findings, and an appeals procedure for employees who are dissatisfied with the company's findings. Companies may provide websites where employees can blow the whistle internally before they go outside the company to find justice. Such a website may also encourage employees to stop friends from leaking important information. You could say it promotes whistle-blowing on whistle-blowers.[22]

Implied Contract

A majority of Americans work without an employment contract, but under certain conditions these employees may be granted contractual employment rights. This occurs when an implied promise by the employer suggests some form of job security to the employee. Once these explicit or implicit promises of job security are made, courts generally prohibited the employer from terminating the employee without first exhausting the conditions of the contract. The following are some examples of how an implied contract may become binding:

- Telling employees their jobs are secure as long as they perform satisfactorily and are loyal to the organization.
- Stating in the employee handbook that employees will not be terminated without the right of defense or access to an appeal procedure.
- Urging an employee to leave another organization by promising higher wages and benefits, then reneging on those promises after the person has been hired.

Employers can lessen their vulnerability to implied contract lawsuits by implementing prudent managerial practices, training, and HR policies. HR experts recommend the following approaches:

1. Training supervisors and managers not to imply contract benefits in conversations with new or present employees.
2. Including in employment offers a statement that an employee may voluntarily terminate their employment with proper notice and may be dismissed by the employer at any time and for a justified reason.
3. Including employment-at-will statements in all employment documents—for example, employee handbooks, employment applications, and letters of employment[23] (see Highlights in HRM 1).
4. Having written proof that employees have read and understood the employment-at-will disclaimers provided to them. In other words, make sure employees know they are an employment-at-will employee.

Explicit Contracts

Explicit employment contracts are formal written and signed agreements that grant to employees and employers agreed-upon employment benefits and privileges. Such contracts normally state the period of employment, terms and conditions of employment (e.g., salary and benefits), and severance provisions. Explicit contracts are popular with executives, senior managers, and people with highly technical or professional skills and abilities. When an employee has an explicit contract, the employee cannot be dismissed at will.

In today's highly competitive environment, before hiring employees, employers sometimes impose certain restrictions, or provisions, in explicit contracts. The most widely used restrictions including the following options:

- *Nondisclosure of information agreement.* This provision forbids employees from revealing proprietary information outside the company, either during or following their employment. Courts widely enforce these agreements.
- *Intellectual property agreement.* This provision grants to an employer the ownership of an idea, invention or process, or work of authorship developed by the employee during the time of employment. Such an agreement expressly states that the employer retains all rights, titles, and interests in ideas that are subject to patent laws and developed during the employee's period of hire.

1 Highlights in HRM

Examples of Employment-at-Will Statements

Employment handbooks frequently include an opening statement that employees are employed at will—that is, there are no guarantees about the duration of their employment. They also typically state that no supervisors or managers, except specified individuals (i.e., the HR director or company president), have the authority to promise any employment benefit—including salaries and job positions. All handbooks should include a disclaimer that expressly provides that all employment policies and benefits contained in the handbook are subject to change or removal at the sole and exclusive discretion of the employer.

Two examples of at-will statements are as follows:

> I acknowledge that if hired, I will be an at-will employee. I will be subject to dismissal or discipline without notice or cause, at the discretion of the employer. I understand that no representative of the company, other than the president, has authority to change the terms of an at-will employment and that any such change can occur only in a written employment contract.

> I understand that my employment is not governed by any written or oral contract and is considered an at-will arrangement. This means that I am free, as is the company, to terminate the employment relationship at any time for any reason, so long as there is no violation of applicable federal or state law. In the event of employment, I understand that my employment is not for any definite period or succession of periods and is considered an at-will arrangement. That means I am free to terminate my employment at any time for any reason, as is the company, so long as there is no violation of applicable federal or state law.

A cautionary note: Because at-will employment is governed by state laws, for an employer to preserve its at-will status, it must follow the regulations of its jurisdiction. This includes the writing of employment-at-will statements.

- *Noncompete agreement.* This provision prevents ex-employees from either becoming a competitor or working for a competitor for a designated period of time, for example, one or two years.[24] Noncompete agreements are designed to protect confidential information, customer relations, and other valuable assets.[25]
- *Nonpiracy agreements.* These agreements prohibit ex-employees from soliciting clients or customers of former employers for a specific period of time *and* from disclosing or making use of confidential employer information.

Explicit contracts are enforceable in court when either the employee or the employer violates any provisions of the agreement. For example, in 2021, Ralph Lauren sued its vice president of footwear and accessories, Elise Schneider, when she left the company to go work for a competitor, Tory Burch. The company claimed that Schneider had a six-month noncompete agreement in her employment contract.[26]

constructive discharge
An employee's voluntary termination of their employment because of harsh, unreasonable employment conditions placed on the individual by the employer.

Constructive Discharge

It is increasingly common for employees to quit or resign from their jobs because the intolerable acts of their employers left them no choice. This situation is referred to as a **constructive discharge**. In such a case, the employees are "forced" to resign because of intolerable working conditions purposefully placed upon them by the employer.[27]

In a leading constructive discharge case, *Young v. Southwestern Savings and Loan Association*, the court noted:

> The general rule is that if the employer deliberately makes an employee's working conditions so intolerable that the employee is forced into involuntary resignation, then the employer has encompassed a constructive discharge and is as liable for any illegal conduct involved therein as if he had formally discharged the aggrieved employee.

The courts, by formulating the constructive discharge doctrine, attempt to prevent employers from accomplishing covertly what they are prohibited by law from achieving overtly.[28]

Discharge as a Result of Retaliation

Title VII of the Civil Rights Act, the Age Discrimination in Employment Act, the Americans with Disabilities Act, and other employment laws prohibit employers from retaliating against employees when they exercise their rights under these statutes (see Chapter 3). Employees may believe retaliation occurs when managers transfer them to lower-rated jobs, deny them salary increases or promotions, impose on them unrealistic job assignments, or become belligerent or uncommunicative with them after they file discrimination complaints or receive a favorable settlement.[29]

In recent years, retaliation claims have become some of the most costly and frequent workplace disputes. To prevent retaliation charges, employers should implement a separate anti-retaliation policy and train managers and supervisors in acceptable and unacceptable methods to resolve employee complaints.[30] A key component of any anti-retaliation policy is to treat employees with dignity and respect. Other suggestions to reduce retaliation discharges include the following:

- Take no adverse employment actions against employees when they file complaints. Let them know you take their complaints seriously and are looking into them.
- Keep complaints confidential.
- Be consistent and objective in your treatment of employees. Evaluate employees on how well they perform, not on their personalities.
- Harbor no animosity toward employees when they file discrimination lawsuits. Treat every employee the way you would want to be treated—fairly.

Discharges and the WARN Act

In 1989, Congress passed the Worker Adjustment and Retraining Notification (WARN) Act, which requires organizations with more than 100 employees to give employees and their communities 60 days' notice of any closure or layoff affecting 50 or more full-time employees.[31] Notice must be given to collective bargaining representatives, unrepresented employees, the appropriate state dislocated worker agency, and the highest elected local official. Terminated employees must be notified individually in writing. The act allows for several exemptions, including "unforeseeable circumstances" and "faltering businesses."

13.1d Privacy Rights

The right to privacy focuses on freedom from unwarranted government or business intrusion into one's personal affairs. It involves the individual's right to be given personal autonomy and to be left alone.[32] Not surprisingly, employees strongly defend their right

Figure 13.4 The Balance of Employee Rights to Privacy versus Employers' Right to Know

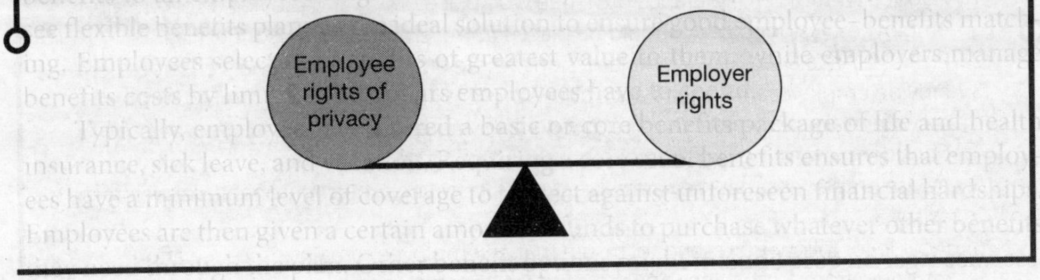

to workplace privacy. Meanwhile, employers defend their right to monitor employees' activities when they directly affect a business, its productivity, workplace safety, and/or morale.[33] So who is right? Employers or employees? (See Figure 13.4.)

In this section, we discuss some of the most pressing privacy issues being debated by employees and employers today and how they are being resolved.

Substance Abuse and Drug Testing

As you learned, in the United States companies can legally test workers for drugs. However, certain restrictions apply. In the private sector, drug testing is largely regulated by individual states. Pro-drug testing states generally permit testing, provided that strict testing procedures are followed.[34] By contrast, states with restrictive drug-testing laws generally prohibit testing for drugs except in very specific circumstances and for drugs listed in state regulations.[35]

Federal regulations and laws restrict drug testing as well. Recall from Chapter 3 that the Equal Employment Opportunity Commission does not allow job applicants to be tested before they are extended offers. Also, companies must recognize that some drugs that would otherwise be illegal, such as opiates and medical marijuana, may be legitimately prescribed for certain conditions.[36]

Safety-Sensitive Positions

Drug testing is most prevalent among employees in sensitive positions within the public sector, in organizations doing business with the federal government, and in public and private transportation companies. Since the passage of the Drug-Free Workplace Act of 1988, applicants and employees of federal contractors have become subject to testing for illegal drug use. Barring state and federal laws that restrict or prohibit drug testing, however, private employers generally have a right to require employees to submit to the tests. The exception is unionized workforces—drug testing programs for these employees must be negotiated by their unions.

Criticisms of Drug Testing

In Chapter 6, we explained that studies have failed to show that drug testing makes the workplace safer and that alcohol appears to create more problems than illicit drugs do.[37] Another criticism of drug tests, including urinalysis and hair tests, is they do not reveal whether a person is currently under the influence of a drug. Illegal substances remain in urine for various periods of time—cocaine for approximately 72 hours, marijuana for 3 weeks or longer.[38] Therefore, an employee can test positive for a drug days or weeks after using it but not be impaired on the job. Alcohol will not show up in a urinalysis

Figure 13.5 Recommendations for a Drug-Free Workplace Policy

1. Adopt a written zero-tolerance drug-free workplace policy and provide a copy to all employees. A signed copy should be placed in the employee's personnel file.
2. Post "We Are a Drug-Free Workplace" signs where employees will widely observe them.
3. Provide employees with substance abuse prevention educational materials. Arrange substance abuse awareness training for employees and managers.
4. Consider performing pre-employment drug testing on all new hires.
5. Advise employees that they are subject to drug testing when "reasonable suspicion" exists.
6. Provide for follow-up testing to ensure that an employee remains drug-free after returning from a substance abuse treatment program.
7. Provide for post-accident drug testing when justified by property loss or damage, serious injury, or death.
8. Use only federally or state-approved/certified labs for analysis.
9. Utilize the services of a medical review officer for all positive drug test results.
10. Maintain strict "need-to-know" confidentiality for all test results.
11. Apply terms of a written policy strictly, fairly, and equally among employees and managers.

or hair test. To test for current alcohol use, a breathalyzer, blood, or saliva test must be used. Thus, the question becomes, Which test should an employer use?

Organizations also have to ensure that any samples taken from employees are properly handled and accredited labs are used to test them. The results of the tests must be kept confidential and provided only to those who need to know—for example, supervisors or HR staff members—and not to other coworkers or disinterested managers.

For all of these reasons, companies have become less aggressive about drug testing than they were in decades past when the tests first found their way into the workplace. Today, most companies test employees only when reasonable suspicion or probable cause exists. Figure 13.5 shows an example of a drug-free workplace policy.

Impairment Testing

impairment testing Also called fitness-for-duty or performance-based testing; testing that measures whether an employee is alert enough to work.

An alternative to drug testing is to evaluate an employee's suitability for work through **impairment testing**. Also called fitness-for-duty or performance-based testing, impairment testing measures whether an employee is alert enough to work. One impairment test requires an employee to keep a cursor on track during a video game–like simulation. Results from such tests, when compared against baseline data gathered earlier on the employee, mimic those of a sobriety test. One advantage of impairment testing is that it focuses on workplace conduct rather than off-duty behavior. Furthermore, it identifies employees who are impaired because of problems that a drug test cannot spot: fatigue, stress, and alcohol use.

13.1e Employee Surveillance

Why do companies use surveillance and other technology to watch what their employees do? One reason is employee theft, such as the stealing of merchandise, supplies, or equipment; the selling of information such as customer lists and trade secrets; embezzlement; and so on.[39] Monitoring quality control, ensuring the safety of employees, and eliminating the amount of time they spend surfing the Web and doing personal business on company time are other reasons.[40] Next, we'll look at some of the most common methods of surveillance, and the employer–employee rights associated with them.

Camera Surveillance

DuPont uses long-distance cameras to watch employees on its loading docks. The Cheesecake Factory uses video surveillance of kitchens, dining rooms, and hostess stations to monitor how workers treat customers and each other. Most high-end hotels have cameras in their facilities to protect both workers and guests. Employers also install cameras in their parking lots and remote workplace areas to help improve safety. Few federal laws protect workers from being watched. In general, employers can train video cameras on their employees without significant legal concerns as long as they have a legitimate business reason for doing so and inform employees they are doing as much. States, however, set their own regulations.

Employers are not the only ones with cameras, though. You might not be surprised to hear that employees' cameras have become an issue firms are dealing with. In just a few seconds, a coworker with a camera phone can take offensive pictures of their coworkers in private or embarrassing situations and disseminate those images around the world via the Web.[41] In 2017, a McDonald's employee was fired for posting a video showing rats running around inside the fast-food chain. The video led to health inspectors closing the restaurant and the employee losing her job.[42]

Small cameras and camera phones can also be used to quickly and efficiently conduct industrial espionage and steal a company's patents and trade secrets. As a result, some employers ban the use of these devices in the workplace unless employees are given special permission to use them. Workers in Apple's testing rooms are required to cover up devices with black cloaks when they are working on them so the company can be assured no "rogue" cameras are being used to take pictures of the products.[43]

sahua d/Shutterstock.com

Many companies ban the use of personal recording devices to prevent the leak of confidential information to the outside world.

Phone Conversations and Text Communications

In general, employers have the right to monitor calls, text messages, and direct messages sent from their telecommunications devices, provided they do so for compelling business reasons and employees have been informed that their communications will be monitored. However, a federal law, the Electronic Communications Privacy Act (ECPA), places some limitations on that right.[44] The ECPA restricts employers from intercepting wire, oral, or electronic communications. For example, under the law, if an employee receives a personal call, the employer must hang up as soon as they realize the call is personal. However, if employees are told *not* to make personal calls or send text messages from their business phones, the ECPA no longer applies, and their communications may be monitored.

Email, Internet, and Computer Use

Many employees are unaware that their employers can monitor what they do online and fire or discipline them based on that information.[45] According to a recent report by the American Management Association, more than one-fourth of employers have fired workers for misusing email, and about one-third have fired workers for misusing the Internet.[46]

Until recently, employers were allowed to monitor any and all email communications their employees sent from work computers. However, court rulings have since limited employer's rights somewhat. For example, some courts have ruled that employers can monitor incoming and outgoing data on their *own* email systems but not email sent via outside email systems such as Yahoo, Google, and AOL systems. One firm discovered this the hard way after monitoring an employee who was planning to go to work for a competitor. She believed her emails sent on her employer's computer, but via a nonwork email system, were private. A New Jersey court agreed with her.[47]

Other privacy issues relate to Internet sites that employees are allowed to access. More and more companies are banning social media at work, after seeing the negative effects it has on productivity and even on their own reputation. For example, Taco Bell took a lot of heat when a photo of an employee licking a taco shell was posted on social media.

As the use of Instagram, SnapChat, TikTok, and other social media platforms continues to grow, their abuse in the workplace is increasing in tandem. According to one study, more than 70 percent of businesses have had to take disciplinary action against employees for misusing social media.[48] (See Figure 13.6 for reasons employees use social media.)

Companies can legally create electronic communication policies that limit employees' Internet use. Blocking employees from accessing sites such as Facebook, eBay, gambling, and pornographic websites has also become a common tactic for firms.

The measures employees need to take to protect their laptops and what they should do if these devices are stolen should also be part of an electronic policy.[49] If they go missing, a mountain of valuable corporate data can fall into the wrong hands. Likewise, organizations are also adopting policies related to electronic storage devices such as USB drives. Studies have shown that people own a lot of USB drives, but are often uncertain of what they contain and where they are always located. Use of USB drives with company network–connected devices can also infect a company's computers and servers with viruses.

Figure 13.6 Why Do Employees Turn to Social Media at Work?

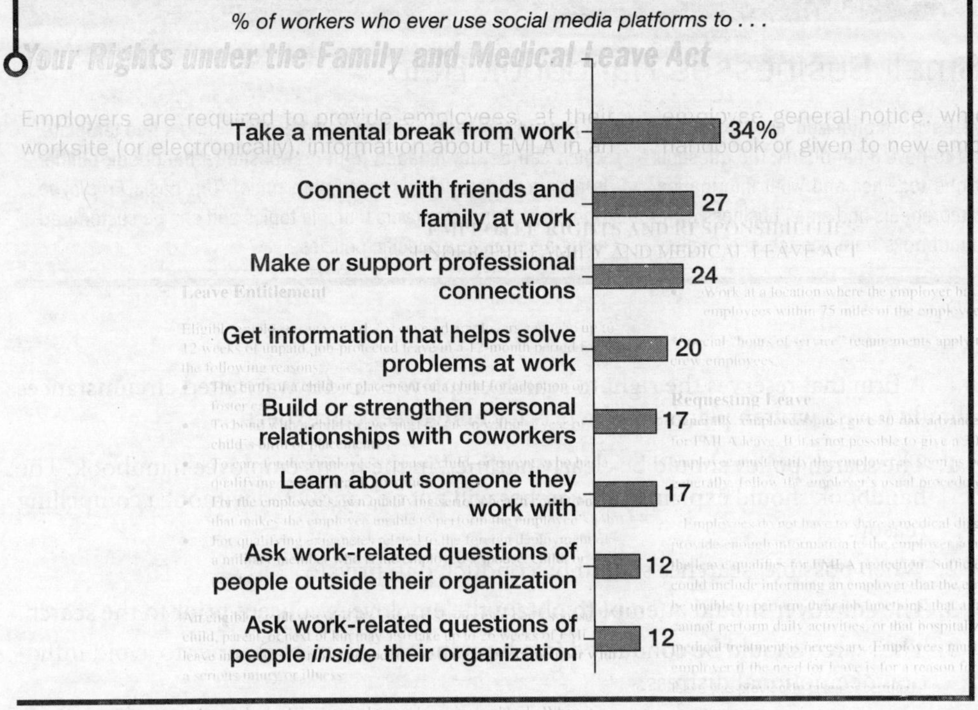

Source: Survey conducted September 11–21, 2014. "Social Media and the Workplace."

Surveillance of Work from Home

The COVID-19 pandemic brought about a new era of work from home (WFH; also called remote work), and along with it arose a new question about employee surveillance: How do employers and supervisors monitor the productivity and work of their employees when they are not in the office? Many companies tried systems that would track mouse movement and keyboard usage.[50] Some are even asking that employees stay on camera all day while they are working. This has created a debate about the appropriateness of policies, as some believe such monitoring is completely legal and reasonable while others say it is unnecessary and an invasion of privacy. One employee working for an e-commerce company decided to go on unpaid leave until she was able to return to the office instead of downloading surveillance software that her company required WFH employees to use.[51]

Searches

Can employers search employees' work lockers, desks, suitcases, toolboxes, and general work areas without their knowledge? Generally speaking, yes. However, random searches of employees' personal belongings without probable cause should be avoided. Even if a firm has probable cause, legal experts advise that a company should first look at the information it has from available sources such as security cameras, timecards, and so forth to see whether the search is truly warranted. Body searches should be performed only under emergency situations. If conducted, the searches should be done by a security officer and a person of the same gender.

Small Business Application

SHRM Offers Small Businesses Handbook Help

Throughout this chapter, we have emphasized how extremely important it is for an employer to have a handbook. The question is, How do you begin to put one together, and what information should it contain? To help entrepreneurs and small business owners avoid having to create handbooks from scratch, the Society for Human Resource Management has developed a free template, which can be downloaded from its website (a handbook builder is also available for a subscription price). The basic *Employee Handbook Template* covers multiple topics and can be customized using a company's specific policies.

A firm that reserves the right to search employees under warranted circumstances should have a written plan as to the privacy employees can expect.

1. The search policy should be clearly outlined in the firm's employee handbook. The handbook should explain that searches will not be conducted without a compelling reason.
2. When possible, searches should be conducted in private.
3. The employer should attempt to obtain the employee's consent prior to the search.
4. The search should be conducted in a humane and discreet manner to avoid infliction of emotional distress.
5. The penalty for refusing to consent to a search should be specified.

Access to Personnel Files

Employees entrust their employers with a wealth of personal information for various purposes, including their Social Security numbers, home addresses, family information, bank account numbers so they can have their paychecks deposited directly, and so forth. Personnel files also generally contain performance appraisal and salary information, background and credit reports, criminal records, and test scores.

HR's Responsibility to Safeguard Personnel Information. A firm's HR department is almost always responsible for maintaining this information and safeguarding its flow to prevent the loss of information and identity theft.[52] The Privacy Rights Clearinghouse, a nonprofit privacy advocate organization, estimates that more than 50 million people have been put at risk as a result of security breaches that revealed their private information. For example, Adobe suffered a data breach in which hackers stole 38 million users' credit card records and login information.[53] In 2021, the California State Controller's Office suffered a breach in which the personal and financial data of thousands of employees were lost to a breach instigated by a phishing email.[54]

HR managers need to take the lead when it comes to safeguarding employee information. Under the Privacy Act of 1974, federal agencies must safeguard the personal information of their employees. Figure 13.7 shows the steps employers can take to safeguard employees' personal information. Also, as you learned in Chapter 3, employees' medical and genetic information must be kept confidential in a separate file from any employee's other personnel information.

Figure 13.7 Guidelines for Safeguarding Personnel Files

- Define exactly what information is to be kept in employee files. Do not collect information from employees or applicants that you do not need or use. Do not collect information that could be viewed as discriminatory or could form the basis for an invasion-of-privacy suit.
- Identify the individuals allowed to view personnel files, and when and why they should be allowed to do so. Keep employee records in a locked and secured area that only qualified personnel can access on a need-to-know basis. Maintain a log that shows who accessed which records and when.
- Specify where, when, how, and under what circumstances employees may review or copy their files.
- Do not use Social Security numbers as employee identifiers. Instead, use random identifiers and keep the Social Security numbers as narrowly distributed as possible. Do not print Social Security numbers on people's paychecks or send documents to employees via mail or email that contain those numbers. The exception are IRS documents mailed at year end for tax purposes.
- Use encryption software that translates personnel data into a code that can be accessed only using a key or password.
- Do not give out information about employees over the phone. The person might claim they are a prospective employer or banker looking to help process a loan for an employee but in reality could be a debt collector, stalker, or person engaging in identity theft. Instead, tell the person to send you a written authorization form signed by the employee that allows you to disclose the information. When you receive the form, verify it with the employee.
- Audit employment records on a regular basis to remove irrelevant, outdated, or inaccurate information.
- Shred and securely dispose of any paper records containing sensitive company and employee information.

Source: Adapted from "Complying with Employment Record Requirements," Society of Human Resource Management (April 4, 2018); "Employee Rights and Identity Theft," Texas Workforce Commission, http://www.twc.state.tx.us (accessed June 2, 2011).

Employee Access to Personnel Files. Legislation at the federal level and various states laws permit employees to inspect their own personnel files. How much access is allowed varies from state to state.[55] The states that grant employees the privilege to see their personnel files generally provide:

- The right to know of the existence of one's personnel file
- The right to inspect one's own personnel file
- The right to correct inaccurate data in the file

Typically, if a state law allows employees to examine their files, employers can insist that someone from HR, or a supervisor, be present to ensure that nothing is taken, added, or changed. Even in the absence of specific legislation, most employers give their employees access to their personnel files. Employment professionals recommend that organizations develop a policy on employee files that includes, at a minimum, the points noted in Figure 13.7.

Off-Duty Employee Conduct

Consider the COVID-19 pandemic and the responsibility employers have in tracking where an employee's positive COVID-19 test originated. This responsibility raises a thorny question: Should companies be able to restrict employees' off-duty behavior, such as travel?[56]

The majority of states (nearly 30) have passed laws that prohibit employers from disciplining or firing employees for activities they pursue offsite on their own time as long as they are legal.[57] However, even when the activities are illegal, court rulings have suggested that this conduct may not, in some circumstances, be a lawful justification for employee discipline. Organizations that want to discipline employees for off-duty misconduct must establish a clear relationship between the misconduct and its negative effect on other employees or the organization.[58] This might be established, for example, in cases in which off-duty criminal misconduct creates a disruptive impact in the workplace. Another example might be when the public nature of the employee's job (such as police or fire department personnel) creates an image problem for the organization. However, before banning specific off-duty behavioral conduct, employers are advised to obtain legal advice.

Off-Duty Employee Speech

Some organizations have social networking and blogging policies that restrict employees from making disparaging remarks about their firms or its supervisors, or otherwise casting their organizations in a bad light. The First Amendment prohibits the government—not private employers—from telling us what we can and cannot say. However, like off-duty conduct, state laws and courts have tried to balance the rights of employees with those of their employers in this regard.[59] In addition, the National Labor Relations Act, which allows workers to form unions, protects the rights of employees to talk to one another about their working conditions.

Meanwhile, employees need to realize that what they say online can put their employers in an awkward situation to which they are going to feel compelled to respond. Moreover, online posts that are racist and/or sexist, demean or harass one's coworkers, and reveal confidential company information are not likely to be legally protected. Such actions will likely be career enders for employees.

Workplace Romances

Workplace romances create a dilemma for organizations. Workplace crushes and romances are so prevalent (54 percent of Americans have had a crush on a coworker and 27 percent have had a romance with a coworker), however, that it is simply illogical to try to prohibit the development of relationships.[60] However, watching such relationships is important because acceptable behavior in a consensual relationship between employees can become harassing behavior if one party to the relationship no longer welcomes the conduct. It may also result in violence should a scorned lover seek violent revenge at the work site. Of particular concern is an employer's liability if a coworker, supervisor–subordinate, or other power-differentiated romance goes sour and leads to charges of sexual harassment.[61] Furthermore, workplace romances can lead to employee charges of favoritism against a coworker involved in a supervisor–subordinate romance. These "reverse harassment" claims are based on preferential treatment given to an employee engaged in a romantic affair. Workplace romances can also create morale problems when other employees feel unfairly treated; such situations can lead to jealousy, resentment, and hard feelings[62] (see Figure 13.8).

Figure 13.8 When Workplace Romance Can Be a Bad Idea

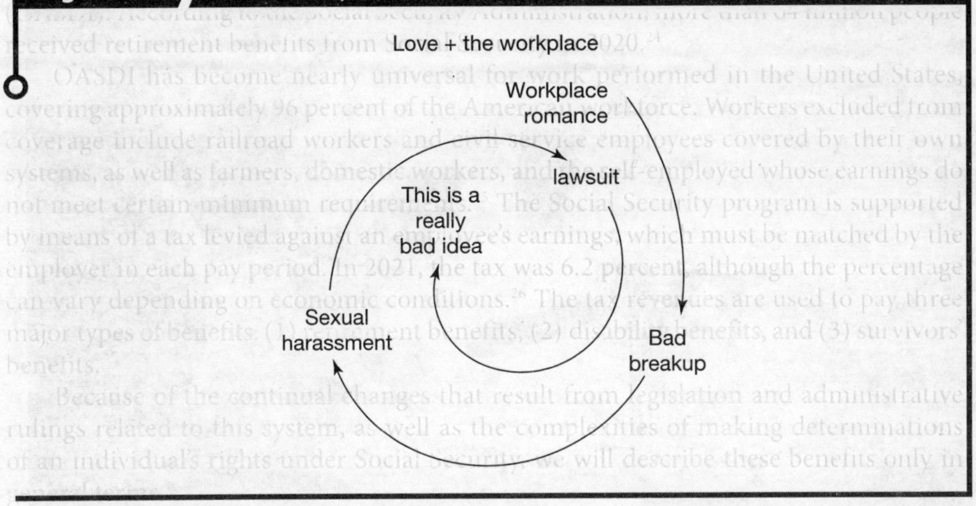

As mentioned in Chapter 3, although some companies have strict anti-fraternization policies, such a policy can lead to lawsuits. Moreover, recall that the rights of companies to control the legal, off-duty conduct of their employees are limited. Sexual harassment policies have become the preferred way to deal with the issues related to workplace romances. Some employers have the dating parties sign *consensual relationship agreements* stating that they will not let their relationship affect the work environment or sue their employer should the relationship go sour.[63]

Body Art, Grooming, and Attire

Tattoos and body piercings are increasingly popular and have become more socially acceptable, with more than one-fourth of the population having at least one tattoo. Nearly half of Millennials (47 percent) and more than one-third of Generation Xers (36 percent) have one or more tattoos. This stands in stark contrast to baby-boomers, only 13 percent of whom have a tattoo.[64]

However, employers have the right to establish reasonable standards for grooming, attire, tattoos, and facial piercings and to require employees to abide by those standards.[65] An at-will employee who does not do so can be let go. However, policies on appearance should reflect the nature of the organization and its industry, takes into account the types of safety concerns it faces, and not impinge on an employee's religious rights.[66]

Matt Stroshane/Getty Images News/Getty Images

A relationship with a fellow astronaut fizzled, and Nowak was later arrested for attempting to kidnap her former lover's new girlfriend. The girlfriend was able to escape unharmed from Nowak, who was later discovered and arrested. NASA didn't institute a nonfraternization policy following the incident, but it did beef up its screening policies to help screen out candidates with psychological issues.

Dean Drobot/Shutterstock.com

According to some, tattoos help Millennials declare their identity with conviction.

LO2

Differentiate separate sets of disciplinary policies that use progressive and positive discipline approaches.

discipline
A tool used to correct and mold the practices of employees to help them perform better, and to ensure they conform to acceptable standards.

13.2 Disciplinary Policies and Procedures

When managers are asked to define the word *discipline*, their most frequent response is that discipline means punishment (see Figure 13.9).

However, in the context of management, **discipline** does not mean punishment. Rather, discipline is a tool used to correct the practices of employees to help them perform better so they conform to acceptable standards. Many organizations, such as Bank of America and Adobe, define *discipline* in their policy manuals as training that "corrects, molds, or perfects knowledge, attitudes, behavior, or conduct." Figure 13.10 lists the more common disciplinary problems identified by managers.

It goes without saying that disciplinary actions should be taken only for justifiable reasons and that employees should be treated fairly and consistently. Good guidelines will help a firm not only avoid lawsuits, but also prevent the development of a poisonous atmosphere at work that can lead to low morale among employees and high turnover.

Figure 13.9 The True Definition of Discipline

Discipline ≠ Punishment
= Constructive Training

Figure 13.10 Common Disciplinary Problems

Attendance Problems
- Unexcused absence
- Chronic absenteeism
- Unexcused or excessive tardiness
- Leaving without permission

Dishonesty and Related Problems
- Theft
- Falsifying employment application
- Willfully damaging organizational property
- Punching another employee's time card
- Falsifying work records

Work Performance Problems
- Failing to complete work assignments
- Producing substandard products or services
- Failing to meet established production requirements

On-the-Job Behavior Problems
- Bullying
- Sexual harassment
- Possessing firearms or other weapons
- Possessing illegal narcotics or alcohol
- Intoxication at work
- Insubordination
- Using abusive or threatening language with supervisors
- Horseplay
- Smoking in unauthorized places
- Fighting
- Gambling
- Failing to use safety devices
- Failing to report injuries
- Carelessness
- Sleeping on the job

13.2a The Result of Inaction

On the one hand, even when it's justified, managers don't generally enjoy disciplining their employees. On the other hand, failing to do so generally can aggravate a problem that eventually must be resolved.

Figure 13.11 presents a disciplinary model that illustrates the areas where provisions should be established. The model also shows the logical sequence in which disciplinary steps must be carried out to ensure enforceable decisions. Should discipline become necessary, the employee's immediate supervisor is the logical person to apply the company's disciplinary procedures and monitor the employee's improvement, although the HR departments should develop disciplinary policies and actions, and ensure they conform to current laws.

Figure 13.11 A Disciplinary Model

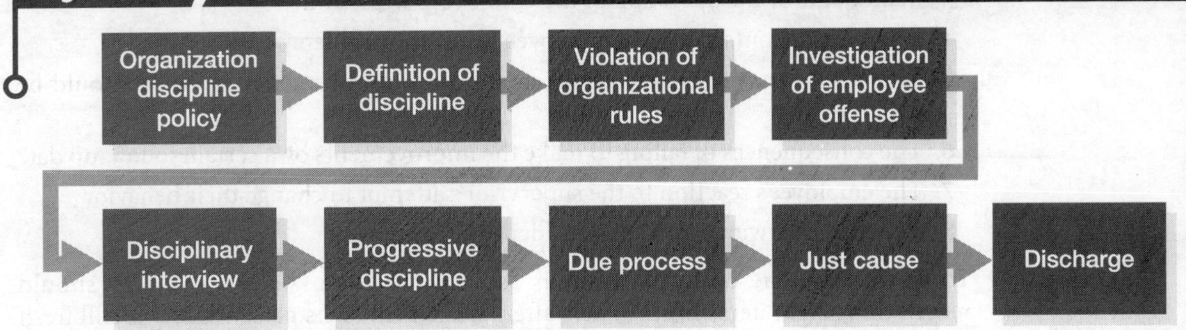

13.2b Setting Organizational Rules

Setting an organization's rules is the foundation for an effective disciplinary system. These rules establish the types of behaviors expected of employees. The following suggestions can help HR managers and their firms when they are considering the rules the organization should adopt and how they should be implemented:

1. The rules must be reasonable and relate to the safe and efficient operation of the organization.
2. The rules as well as the consequences for breaking them should be written down and widely disseminated to all employees. Neglecting to communicate the rules is a major reason why disciplinary actions taken against employees are reversed.[67]
3. The rules should be clearly explained. Employees are more likely to accept a rule if they understand the reason behind it.
4. Employees should sign a document stating that they have read and understood the organizational rules.
5. The rules should be reviewed periodically—perhaps annually—especially those rules critical to work success.

13.2c Investigating a Disciplinary Problem

Figure 13.12 lists seven questions to consider when investigating an employee offense. Attending to each question will help ensure a full and fair investigation while providing reliable information free from personal prejudice.

Documenting Misconduct

When a manager fails to record the misconduct of employees, it can undermine a firm's efforts to deal with the behavior. A manager's records of employee misconduct are considered business documents, and as such they are admissible evidence in arbitration hearings, administrative proceedings, and courts of law.

While the documentation does not need to be lengthy, to be complete it should include the following eight items:

1. The date, time, and location of the incident(s)
2. The behavior exhibited by the employee (the problem)
3. The consequences of that action or behavior on the employee's overall work performance and/or the operation of the employee's work unit
4. Prior discussion(s) with the employee about the problem
5. The disciplinary action to be taken and the improvements expected should be documented
6. The consequences of failing to make the improvements by a certain follow-up date
7. The employee's reaction to the supervisor's attempt to change their behavior
8. The names of witnesses to the incident (if applicable)

To ensure that the documentation is as accurate as possible, a manager should record these eight items immediately after an incident takes place while it is still fresh in their mind.

Figure 13.12 Questions to Consider during Disciplinary Investigations

1. In very specific terms, what is the offense charged?
   - Is management sure it fully understands the charge against the employee?
   - Was the employee really terminated for insubordination, or did the employee merely refuse a request by management?
2. Did the employee know they were doing something wrong?
   - What rule or provision was violated?
   - How would the employee know of the existence of the rule?
   - Was the employee warned of the consequence?
3. Is the employee guilty?
   - What are the sources of facts?
   - Is there direct or only indirect evidence of guilt?
   - Has anyone talked to the employee to hear their side of the situation?
4. Are there extenuating circumstances?
   - Were conflicting orders given by different supervisors?
   - Does anybody have a reason to want to "get" this employee?
   - Was the employee provoked by a manager or another employee?
5. Has the rule been uniformly enforced?
   - Have all managers applied this rule consistently?
   - What punishment have previous offenders received?
   - Were any other employees involved in this offense?
6. Is the offense related to the workplace?
   - Is there evidence that the offense hurt the organization?
   - Is management making a moral judgment or a business judgment?
7. What is the employee's past work record?
   - How many years of service has the employee given the organization?
   - How many years or months has the employee held the present job?
   - What is the employee's personnel record as a whole, especially their disciplinary record?

The Investigative Interview

Before any disciplinary action is initiated, an investigative interview should be conducted to confirm that the employee is fully aware of the organization's rules and aware that they have not followed those rules.[68] This interview should concentrate on how the offense violated the performance and behavior standards expected. Most important, the employee must be given a full opportunity to explain their side of the issue.[69]

Employees do not have the right to have an attorney present during an investigative interview. However, in *NLRB v. Weingarten, Inc.*, the U.S. Supreme Court upheld a National Labor Relations Board ruling in favor of a unionized employee's right to have a union representative with him or her during an investigative interview—if the employee reasonably believes that discipline could result from the interview.[70] Currently, nonunion employees do not have the right to have a coworker present in an investigatory interview that may lead to disciplinary action.

13.2d Approaches to Disciplinary Action

Assuming a thorough investigation shows that an employee has violated a rule, a firm can take one of two approaches to disciplinary action: progressive discipline or positive discipline.

Progressive Discipline

progressive discipline The application of corrective measures by increasing degrees.

Progressive discipline is the application of corrective measures by increasing degrees. It is designed to motivate an employee to correct their misconduct voluntarily. A number of factors must be considered in determining how severe a disciplinary action should be, including the factors listed in Figure 13.12.

The typical progressive discipline procedure includes four steps. From an oral warning (or counseling), the action may progress to a written warning, to a suspension without pay, and ultimately to discharge only as a last resort. When progressive discipline is applied properly:

1. Employees always know where they stand regarding offenses.
2. Employees know what improvement is expected of them.
3. Employees understand what will happen next if improvement is not made.

Positive Discipline

Some HR professionals believe that the intimidating and adversarial nature of progressive discipline keeps it from achieving the intended purpose. For these reasons, organizations such as Saint Alphonsus Regional Medical Center, Ocean Spray, Banner Health, Pennzoil, and Bay Area Rapid Transit have instead used an approach called **positive or nonpunitive discipline**. Positive discipline is based on the concept that employees must assume responsibility for their personal conduct, job performance, and careers.[71]

positive or nonpunitive discipline A system of discipline that focuses on early correction of employee misconduct, with the employee taking total responsibility for correcting the problem.

Positive discipline requires a cooperative environment in which the employee and the supervisor engage in a joint discussion to agree on a way to resolve the performance issue. The employee then bears the sole responsibility for implementing the solution. Rather than reprimands, the supervisor provides the employee with reminders to improve their performance.

Positive discipline is implemented in three steps. The first step is the conference between the employee and the supervisor to find a solution to the problem. If improvement does not occur after this discussion, the supervisor holds a second conference with the employee to determine why the solution agreed to in the first conference did not work. At this stage, however, a written reminder is given to the employee. This document states the new or repeated solution to the problem, with an affirmation that the improvement is the responsibility of the employee and a condition of their continued employment.

When both conferences fail to produce the desired results, the third step is to give the employee a one-day *decision-making leave* (a paid leave). The purpose of this paid leave is for the employee to decide whether they wish to continue working for the organization. Employees given a decision-making leave are instructed to return the following day with a decision either to make a total commitment to improve their performance or to quit the organization. If a commitment is not made, the employee is dismissed with the assumption that they lacked responsibility toward the organization.

13.2e Discharging Employees

Because discharging a worker poses serious consequences for the employee—and possibly for the organization—it should be undertaken only after a deliberate and thoughtful review of the situation.[72] If an employee is fired, they may file a wrongful discharge suit claiming the termination was "without just or sufficient cause," implying a lack of fair treatment by management.

Figure 13.13 "Just Cause" Discharge Guidelines

1. Did the organization forewarn the employee of the possible disciplinary consequences of their action?
2. Were management's requirements of the employee reasonable in relation to the orderly, efficient, and safe operation of the organization's business?
3. Did management, before discharging the employee, make a reasonable effort to establish that the employee's performance was unsatisfactory?
4. Was the organization's investigation conducted in a fair and objective manner?
5. Did the investigation produce sufficient evidence of proof of guilt as charged?
6. Has management treated this employee under its rules, orders, and penalties as it has other employees in similar circumstances?
7. Did the discharge fit the misconduct, considering the seriousness of the proven offense, the employee's service record, and any mitigating circumstances?

How does an employer know if it has just cause to terminate an employee? This question is not easily answered, but standards governing discharges do exist in the form of rules developed in the field of labor arbitration.[73] These rules consist of a set of guidelines that are applied by arbitrators to determine if a firm had just cause for a termination. Such guidelines are normally set forth in the form of questions, like those shown in Figure 13.13. For example, before discharging an employee, did the manager forewarn the person of possible disciplinary action? A "No" answer to any of the seven questions in the figure generally means that just cause was not established and that the decision to terminate was arbitrary, capricious, or discriminatory. The significance of these guidelines is that they are being applied not only by arbitrators, but also by judges in wrongful discharge suits. It is critical that managers at all levels understand the just cause guidelines, including their proper application.

Informing the Employee

Regardless of the reasons for a discharge, it should be done with personal consideration for the employee affected. Every effort should be made to ease the trauma a discharge creates.[74] The employee must be informed honestly, yet tactfully, of the exact reasons for the action. Doing so can help the employee face the problem and adjust to the termination in a constructive way.

To gain confidence, a supervisor might want to discuss, and even rehearse, with workplace peers and an HR manager the upcoming termination meeting to ensure that all important points are covered and presented in the best way possible. Although managers agree that there is no single right way to conduct the discharge meeting, the following guidelines will help make the discussion more effective:

1. Come to the point within the first 2 or 3 minutes, and list in a logical order all reasons for the termination.[75]
2. Be straightforward and firm, yet tactful, and remain resolute in your decision.
3. Make the discussion private, businesslike, and fairly brief.
4. Do not mix the good with the bad. Trying to sugarcoat the problem sends a mixed message to the employee.
5. Avoid making accusations against the employee and injecting your personal feelings into the discussion.
6. Avoid bringing up any personality differences between you and the employee.

7. Provide the employee with any severance pay information, and let the person know about the status of their benefits and coverage.
8. Explain how you will handle employment inquiries from future employers looking to hire the person.[76]

Termination meetings should be held in a neutral location, such as a conference room, to prevent the employee from feeling unfairly treated. The manager should never provoke the employee. Should the employee become belligerent or agitated, or show signs of hostility, the meeting should be stopped immediately and the firm's HR department and security notified.

It is common for managers or security officers to accompany employees back to their work areas to collect their belongings and then escort them off the premises. However, this should be done as discreetly as possible to lessen any embarrassment the employee may experience.

A manager who terminates an employee should keep the details of the termination private and not disparage the person when talking to other people, including other managers, customers, and the person's former coworkers. If such negative comments are shared widely, that gives the terminated employee grounds to sue the manager and firm for defamation.

Due Process

Despite the at-will employment doctrine, most people believe that employees should not be disciplined without the protection of due process. HR managers normally define **due process** as the employee's right to be heard—the right of the employee to tell their side of the story regarding the alleged infraction of organizational rules. Employers risk having their terminations overturned—even when they are justified—when employees are denied due process.

due process
Procedures that constitute fair treatment, such as allowing an employee to tell their story about an alleged infraction and defend against it.

13.2f Alternative Dispute Resolution Procedures

In unionized workplaces, grievance procedures are stated in virtually all labor agreements. In nonunion organizations, however, **alternative dispute resolution (ADR)** methods are often used.[77] ADR methods address employee discharges and complaints outside of court, which is generally faster and cheaper for both parties. Employers often ask workers to sign ADR agreements when they receive their offer letters or sign their employee handbooks.

alternative dispute resolution (ADR)
Any of several different employee complaint or dispute resolution methods that do not involve going to court.

Although the right to require employees to sign ADR agreements is supported by court decisions, to be enforceable, these agreements must be fair and equitable to both employees and employers.[78] Employers can't "stack the deck" against employees by imposing rules on employees that clearly favor the employer. As one legal expert has noted, "As much as possible, the agreement should provide employees with the same rights and remedies that they would have enjoyed had their day in court been available to them."[79] Next we will look at some of the different types of alternative dispute resolution methods organizations use.

Step-Review Systems

step-review system
A system for reviewing employee complaints and disputes by successively higher levels of management.

A **step-review system** is based on a preestablished set of steps—normally four—for the review of an employee's complaint by successively higher levels of management. These procedures are patterned after the union grievance systems we will discuss in

Chapter 14. For example, they usually require that the employee's complaint be formalized as a written statement. Managers at each step are required to provide a full response to the complaint within a specified time period, perhaps 3 to 5 working days.

An employee is sometimes allowed to bypass meeting with their immediate supervisor if the employee fears reprisal from this person. Unlike appeal systems in unionized organizations, however, nonunion appeal procedures ordinarily do not provide for a neutral third party—such as an arbitrator—to serve as the judge of last resort. In most step-review systems, the president, chief executive officer, vice president, or HR director acts as the final authority, and this person's decision cannot be appealed. Some organizations give employees assistance in preparing their complaint cases. For example, an employee who desires it may be able to get advice and counsel from a designated person in the HR department before discussing the issue with management.

Peer-Review Systems

A **peer-review system**, also called a complaint committee, is composed of equal numbers of employee and management representatives. The employees on the committee are normally elected by secret ballot by their coworkers for a rotating term, whereas the managers are assigned, also on a rotating basis. A peer-review system functions as a jury because its members weigh evidence, consider arguments, and, after deliberation, vote independently to render a final decision.

peer-review system
A system for reviewing employee complaints that utilizes a group composed of equal numbers of employee representatives and management appointees. The group weighs the evidence, considers the arguments, and, after deliberation, votes to render a final decision.

The peer-review system can be used as the sole method for resolving employee complaints, or it can be used in conjunction with a step-review system. For example, if an employee is not satisfied with management's action at step 1 or 2 in the step-review system, the employee can submit the complaint to the peer-review committee for final resolution. A benefit of the peer-review system is the sense of justice that it creates among employees.

Open-Door Policy

The idea behind an **open-door policy** is that to facilitate communication and the free exchange of ideas, every manager's office door should be open to every employee. Such a policy is also an old standby method for settling employee complaints. In an organization that has such a policy, an employee is allowed to contact various managers above their immediate supervisor for various reasons, including grievances; these levels may extend as high as a vice president, president, or chief executive officer. The person who acts as "the court of last resort" is the HR director or a senior staff official.

open-door policy
A policy of settling grievances that identifies various levels of management above the immediate supervisor for employee contact.

Open-door policies can lead to some problems, however. For example, some managers do not like to listen honestly to employee complaints. As an employee once told the authors of this text, "My manager has an open-door policy, but the door is only open one inch." Because of this, employees are often reluctant to approach managers with their problems. One way to make an open-door policy work better is to ensure employees with grievances first try to work out their problems with their immediate supervisors before contacting higher-up managers. This way, the chain of command isn't violated, and the supervisor of the employee who aired the grievance does not feel as if they were not given a chance to resolve the issue.

Ombud System

An **ombud** is a designated individual from whom employees may seek counsel for the resolution of their complaints. The ombud listens to an employee's complaint and attempts to resolve it by seeking an equitable solution between the employee and the

ombud
A designated individual from whom employees may seek counsel for resolution of their complaints.

supervisor. Because the ombud has no authority to finalize a solution to the problem, compromises are highly possible, and all parties concerned tend to feel satisfied with the outcome.

To function successfully, the ombud must be able to operate in an atmosphere of confidentiality that does not threaten the security of the managers or subordinates who are involved in a complaint. It is recommended that these personnel have access to high levels of management to ensure that employee complaints receive fair treatment.

Mediation

mediation
The use of an impartial, neutral party to reach a compromise decision in employment disputes.

mediator
A third party in an employment dispute who meets with one party and then the other party, then suggests compromise solutions or recommends concessions from each side that will lead to an agreement.

Along with arbitration, mediation is fast becoming a popular way to resolve employee complaints. During **mediation**, which is also discussed in Chapter 14 in conjunction with labor agreements, a neutral person (mediator) helps employees and managers negotiate and reach a voluntary agreement that is acceptable to both parties. The essence of mediation is compromise. The **mediator** holds a meeting with the employee and management, listens to the position of each side, gathers facts, and then through discussion, suggestions, and persuasion obtains an agreement that satisfies the needs and requirements of both sides.

A mediator serves primarily as a fact finder and as an open channel of communication between the parties. Unlike arbitrators, mediators have no power or authority to force either side toward an agreement. In consequence, they must use their communication skills and the power of persuasion to help the parties resolve their differences (see Figure 13.14). A cornerstone of mediation is that the parties maintain control over the settlement outcome.[80]

Arbitration

Private employers may require that employees settle their disputes through arbitration.[81] Arbitration, which is fully explained in Chapter 14, works like this: The employee and employer present their cases, or arguments, to an arbiter, who is typically a retired judge. The arbiter then makes a decision that the parties have agreed to be bound by. Arbitration is used primarily to resolve discrimination suits related to age, gender, sexual harassment, and race.[82] Other workplace issues, such as promotions, compensation, discipline, and application of company policies, can also be arbitrated if an employer's arbitration program allows it.

While arbitration agreements normally mandate that employees arbitrate their discrimination claims and may prevent workers from suing their employers in court, they cannot prohibit employees from filing discrimination charges with the EEOC and other government agencies in an effort to pursue their statutory rights. In *EEOC v. Waffle House Inc.*,[83] the U.S. Supreme Court ruled that even when an employee has signed a mandatory arbitration agreement, if it chooses to, the EEOC can file a suit in its own name and recover monetary damages for the individual. Writing for the Court,

Figure 13.14 Key to Success

Employer rules + Communication with employee = the 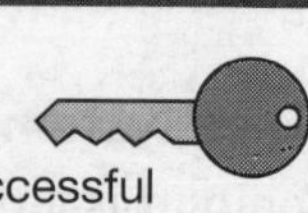 to successful discipline

10'000 Hours/DigitalVision/Getty Images

Discussion and compromise are cornerstones of employment mediation, which is a highly effective method of resolving disputes.

Justice John Paul Stevens noted, "The EEOC has the authority to pursue victim-specific relief regardless of the forum that the employer and the employee have chosen to resolve their dispute."[84]

13.3 Managerial Ethics in Employee Relations

LO3 Identify the different types of alternative dispute resolution methods.

Beyond what is required by the law is the question of organizational ethics and the ethical—or unethical—behavior demonstrated by managers. **Ethics** can be defined as a set of standards of acceptable conduct and moral judgment. Ethics provides cultural guidelines—organizational or societal—that help us decide between proper or improper conduct.[85] How a firm treats its employees largely distinguishes an ethical organization from an unethical one. In an ethical organization, managers are honest in their dealings with employees, and each group has mutual respect for the other.[86]

ethics
A set of standards of conduct and moral judgments that help to determine right and wrong behavior.

As you learned earlier in the book, many organizations have their own codes of ethics that govern how they deal with their employees and the public. These written codes focus attention on an organization's ethical values and provide a basis for its managers to evaluate their plans and actions. HR departments have been given a greater role in communicating an organization's values and standards, monitoring compliance with its code of ethics, and enforcing the standards throughout the organization. Many organizations now have ethics committees and ethics ombuds to provide training in ethics to employees. The ultimate goal of ethics training is to avoid unethical behavior and adverse publicity; to gain a strategic advantage; and most of all, to treat employees in a fair and equitable manner, recognizing them as productive members of the organization.

Summary

LO 1 Workers have certain expectations about the employment relationship they have with their employers, including the mutual obligations they have to each other. Included among those expectations are a certain degree of privacy and fair and equitable treatment while on the job. Employers, however, have the responsibility to monitor the activities of their workers to provide a safe and secure workplace, which is free from harmful employee acts. When the perceived rights of employees differ from the reasonable responsibilities of management, conflict can result.

LO 2 A firm's HR professionals, in combination with other managers, should establish disciplinary policies, or rules, that relate to the safe and efficient operation of the organization. These rules should be written down, explained, widely communicated within the organization, and consistently applied. They should also be revised regularly as laws, regulations, and court rulings change. An investigation of an infraction begins with properly documenting the infraction. To determine the severity of the disciplinary measure, managers need to know whether the employee knew of the rule that was violated, any extenuating circumstances that might justify the employee's conduct, the employee's past work record, and various other factors.

LO 3 Alternative dispute resolution procedures are ways to resolve disputes out of court while ensuring employees receive fair treatment. The most common forms of ADRs are step-review systems, peer-review systems, the open-door system, the ombud system, mediation, and arbitration.

Key Terms

alternative dispute resolution (ADR)
constructive discharge
discipline
due process
employee rights
employment-at-will relationship
ethics
impairment testing
mediation
mediator
negligence
ombud
open-door policy
peer-review system
positive or nonpunitive discipline
progressive discipline
psychological contract
step-review system
whistle-blowing
wrongful discharge

Discussion Questions

LO 1 Explain three areas in which employee rights and employer responsibilities could result in conflict. How might this conflict arise?

LO 2 Discuss why documentation is so important to the disciplinary process. What constitutes correct documentation?

LO 3 What do you think would constitute an effective alternative dispute resolution system? What benefits would you expect from such a system? If you were asked to rule on a discharge case, what facts would you analyze in deciding whether to uphold or reverse the employer's action?

CASE STUDY 1 Discharged for Disrespectful Behavior

At the end of a game with the Dallas Mavericks, Chad Shanks, the official social media manager for the Houston Rockets, sent out the following tweet:

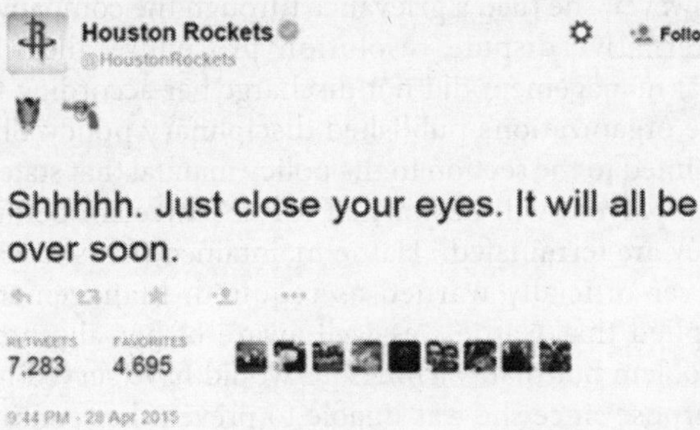

Source: Twitter

After sending out the tweet, he got 7,600 retweets and 5,000 favorites. The Dallas Mavericks, whose mascot is a horse, responded by tweeting, "Not very classy, but we still wish you guys the best of luck in the next round."

Though responses were quite positive from Rockets fans, the Rockets decided to fire Chad for the tweet. The Rockets also apologized for the tweet, saying it was in "very poor taste & not indicative of the respect we have for the @dallasmavs & their fans." After he was fired, Chad followed up with a tweet from his personal account:

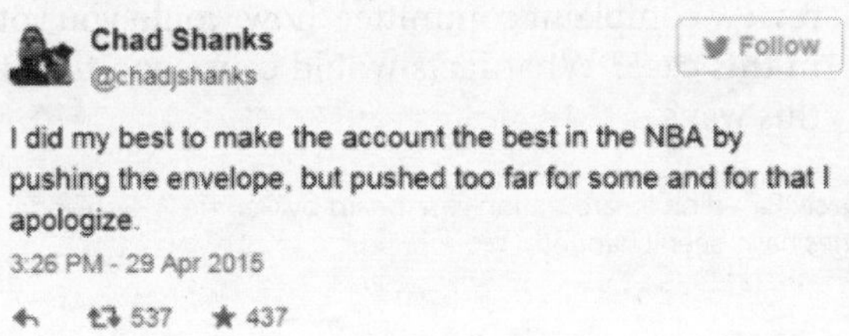

Source: Twitter

In an interview later, Chad commented that "leading up to our series with Dallas, there were some harsh quotes about our team from Mark Cuban and former Rocket Chandler Parsons was returning after saying some negative things about the city, so the rivalry between the two organizations was at an all-time high." He figured this was his chance to take a jab at the Mavs. He meant it to be just a play on taking an old horse out to pasture that would get Rockets fans even more pumped up. He said he was quite confused that people would equate pretend violence on an emoji horse with actual violence on a real horse.

Chad's job was to stir up interest from fans and have fun with social media. His boss told him on numerous accounts that his job was to "take the [twitter] account to subversive places" and do everything he could to give the fans engaging content. Up until this point, Chad was considered one of the best social media experts out there and he had always pulled through for the Rockets. It just didn't seem fair to be fired over this one incident.

Questions

1. Given the facts of this case, should Chad have been discharged? Why or why not?
2. Should the social media manager of a company be held to a higher standard of personal conduct than others in the company? Explain.
3. Should management have considered Chad's past work record before deciding on discharge? Explain.

Sources: Adi Joseph, "Exclusive Q&A: Rockets' Fired Social Media Manager Explains Ill-Fated Tweet," *Sporting News* (April 29, 2015); Calvin Watkins, "Rockets Fire Social Media Manager after Tweet Directed at Mavericks," *ESPN* (April 30, 2015); Mike Foss, "The Houston Rockets Fire Man behind That Creepy Tweet to the Dallas Mavericks," *USA Today* (April 30, 2015).

CASE STUDY 2 You Can't Fire Me! Check Your Policy

Supervisors report that discharging an employee is one of the toughest tasks they perform as managers. Furthermore, termination for absenteeism can be particularly difficult due to the causes of absenteeism and, in some cases, the past work record of the employee. This case illustrates a typical absentee problem faced by management.

Hattie Mae was employed by Beach Electrical Systems for nine years. For the first six years of her employment, she was considered a model employee. Hattie's annual performance reviews were always above average or exceptional, and she was described by her managers as a loyal and dedicated employee. However, things changed rapidly in 2014 when Hattie became, as her current manager stated, "an absentee problem."

According to HR department records, in 2018 and 2019 Hattie was absent 12 percent and 19 percent of the time, respectively. Her worst year was 2020, when she was absent 27.2 percent of the time. However, unlike other absent employees, Hattie was always absent because of genuine and verifiable illnesses or work-related accidents. Hattie's supervisor had talked to her periodically about her attendance problem, but she was never given an official warning notice—oral or written—that she would be fired if her attendance record did not improve.

The incident that caused her termination occurred on Thursday, May 20, 2021. On that day her manager notified all department employees (eight in total) that they would need to work overtime on Saturday, May 22, 2021, to complete a critical order for a highly valued and important customer. All employees agreed to work on Saturday, except Hattie, who cited "personal reasons," which she refused to disclose, for her refusal to work.

On Monday, May 24, 2021, her supervisor, with concurrence from the department manager, terminated her employment for "unsatisfactory attendance." Hattie did not dispute the attendance record; however, she filed a grievance through the company's alternative dispute resolution procedure alleging that management did not discharge her according to the organization's published disciplinary policy. She pointed to the section in the policy manual that states, "Employees will be warned for absenteeism before they are terminated." Hattie maintained that she was never officially warned as required. Management replied that Hattie was well aware of her absentee problem but that warning her would have served no purpose since she was unable to prevent her continued illnesses from occurring. Additionally, her refusal to work overtime on Saturday was a further indication of her lack of concern for her job or the welfare of the company.

Questions

1. What role, if any, should Hattie's past work record play in this case? Explain your answer.
2. Does management have a right to know why employees refuse to work overtime? Why or why not?
3. Evaluate the arguments of Hattie Mae and management in this case.
4. If you were a member of the company's peer-review complaint committee, how would you vote in this case? What facts would cause you to vote this way?

Source: Based on an arbitration case heard by George W. Bohlander. Names have been changed.

Notes and References

1. "Off-Duty Conduct Privacy," United Employees Law Group (March 6, 2017); "How to Get More Control over 'Virtual' Workplace Devices," *HR Focus* 84, no. 6 (2007): 9. See also John D. Canoni, "Location Awareness Technology and Employee Privacy Rights," *Employee Relations Law Journal* 30, no. 1 (2004): 26.
2. Michael Orey, "Fear of Firing," *Business Week* (April 23, 2007): 52.
3. "Managing Workplace Monitoring and Surveillance," Society for Human Resource Management, (March 13, 2019); David J. Walsh, *Employment Law for Human Resource Practice* (Mason, OH: South-Western, 2007), Chapter 17.

4. Jeffery A. Mello, "Introduction: The Evolving Nature of the Employment Relationship: Reconsidering Employee Responsibilities and Rights," *Employee Responsibility and Rights Journal* 15, no. 3 (2003): 99.
5. Mike McKee, "California Supreme Court Narrows Workplace Privacy," *Law.com* (August 5, 2009), http://www.law.com.
6. "Background Checks Are on the Rise," *HR Focus* 84, no. 7 (2007): 51.
7. James B. Sherman, "Landmark Decision Defines Cause of Action for 'Negligent Supervision' of Employees, Personal Liability for Supervisors," Wessels Sherman (May 23, 2019); Maria Greco Danahar, "Retailer Sued over Clerk's Conduct," *HR Magazine* 52, no. 6 (2007): 141.
8. Donna Scimia, "A Common Sense Approach to Reducing Liability in Today's Workplace," *Employee Relations Law Journal* 33, no. 2 (2007): 23.
9. Wilson Wong, "The Psychological Contract Factsheet," Chartered Institute of Personnel and Development (February 4, 2021); Rita Zeidner, "How Deep Can You Probe?" *HR Magazine* 52, no. 10 (2007): 57. See also Jena McGregor, "Background Checks That Never End," *Business Week* (March 20, 2006): 40.
10. Adam Uzialko, "How At-Will Employment Works for You and Your Employees," business.com (November 11, 2020); Robert Del Campo, "Psychological Contract Violation: An Individual Difference Perspective," *International Journal of Management* 24, no. 1 (2007): 43.
11. Ellen Dannin, "Why At-Will Employment Is Bad for Employers and Just Cause Is Good for Them," *Labor Law Journal* 58, no. 1 (2007): 5.
12. "Job Openings and Labor Turnover Summary," Bureau of Labor Statistics (March 16, 2017), https://www.bls.gov/news.release/jolts.nr0.htm.
13. *Adair v. United States*, 2078 U.S. 161 (1908).
14. "How At-Will Employment Is Changing," *HR Focus* 84, no. 10 (2007): 1.
15. Patric J. Cihon and James Ottavio Castagnera, *Employment and Labor Law*, 6th ed. (Mason, OH: South-Western, 2008), 3–4.
16. Lawrence Peikes, "Employer Pays for Reneging on a Promise," *HR Magazine* 49, no. 3 (2004): 109.
17. *Doe v. Google Inc.*, Calif. Ct. App. No. A157097, September 21, 2020.
18. Quiang Lin and Brian H. Kleiner, "New Developments Concerning Termination in Violation of Public Policy" *Management Research Review Feature Edition*, no. 4 (2010): 111; Susan H. Roos, "Fired Fendi Manager Bags over $1 Million," *HR Magazine* 52, no. 6 (2007): 141.
19. David C. Lindsay and Sabrina Rockoff, "State Regulations Update: Beyond Sarbanes-Oxley: State Law Protection in the Era of the Whistleblower," *Employment Relations Today* 34, no. 1 (2007): 69. See also Paul D. Scott, "Whistleblowers Wanted," *Journal of Accountancy* 203, no. 5r (2007): 86.
20. "Boeing Will Pay $25 Million to Resolve Allegations That It Defrauded the DoD in a Contract to Provide Drones: Whistleblower Awarded $4.6 Million," *whistleblowergov.org* (February 8, 2021), https://www.whistleblowergov.org/government-contracts.php?article=boeing-will-pay-25m-to-resolve-allegations-that-it-defrauded-the-dod-in-a-contract-to-provide-drones_184#navbar.
21. U.S.C.S. § 1514A (a) (2002). See D. Bruce Shine, "Pity the SOX Whistleblower: Pity the SOX Lawyer Whistleblower!" *Labor Law Journal* 58, no. 4 (2007): 228.
22. Theresa Agovino, "Whistleblowers: An Early Detection System," Society for Human Resource Management (February 1, 2020); Eugine Kim, "Google Reportedly Has an Internal Site for Employees to Report Whistle-Blowers," *Business Insider* (June 2, 2016).
23. Benisa Berry, "Organizational Culture: A Framework and Strategies for Facilitating Employee Whistleblowing," *Employee Responsibilities and Rights Journal* 16, no. 1 (2004): 1.
24. "*Toussaint v. Blue Cross and Blue Shield of Michigan:* Employee Rights and Wrongful Discharge, 408 Mich. 579, 292 N.W.2d 880 (1980)," *Michigan Bar Journal* (March 2009): 15.
25. Roy Maurer, "Biden Plans to Ban Noncompete, No-Poaching Clauses," Society for Human Resource Management (November 25, 2020); "Employee Handbooks: Have You Updated Yours Lately?" *HR Focus* 83, no. 7 (2006): 5.
26. Kali Hays, "Ralph Lauren Sues Former Footwear Exec over Move to Tory Burch," *WWD* (April 2, 2021).
27. Howard J. Rubin and Gregg A. Gilman, "Will Garden Leaves Blossom in the States," *Employee Relations Law Journal* 33, no. 2 (2007): 3. See also Brian L. Lemer and Jeffrey K. Geldens, "Ensuring Fair Play: Using Common Law to Protect against Unfair Competition from Former Employees," *Employee Relations Law Journal* 32, no. 3 (2006): 41.
28. Steven M. Gutierrez, Joseph D. Neguse, and Steven Collis, "The Human Limits of Human Capital: An Overview of Noncompete Agreements and Best Practices for Protecting Trade Secrets from Unlawful Misappropriation," *Employee Relations Law Journal* (Summer 2010): 64.
29. Stephanie Bornstein, "Disclosing Discrimination," *Boston University Law Review* 101, no. 1 (March 3, 2021): 287; Jonathan A. Segal, "I Quit! Now Pay Me," *HR Magazine* 49, no. 10 (2004): 129.
30. "Preventing Unlawful Workplace Retaliation in California," Society for Human Resource Management (January 10, 2019); Martha Crumpacker, "The U.S. Supreme Court Clarifies Constructive Discharge under Title VII: Responsibilities and Opportunities for Human Resources Practitioners," *Public Personnel Management* 36, no. 1 (2007): 1.
31. 29 U.S.C.A. §§ 2101–2109 (2001); Rebecca M. Archer and Stephen T. Lanctot, "Are Your Hands Tied? A Practical Look at Employee Claims for Retaliation," *Employee Relations Law Journal* 33, no. 1 (2007): 53.

32. "Is There a 'Right to Privacy' Amendment?" findlaw.com (September 30, 2019).
33. "Privacy in Employment," justia.com (September 2018), https://www.justia.com/employment/hiring-employment-contracts/privacy-in-employment/#:~:text=In%20general%2C%20your%20employer%20has,with%20regard%20to%20communications%20technology; Janis Procter-Murphy, employment attorney, interview by author, December 9, 2007.
34. "Balancing HR Systems with Employee Privacy," *HR Focus* 83, no. 11 (2006): 11.
35. Diana Cadrain, "Are Your Employee Drug Tests Accurate?" *HR Magazine* 48, no. 1 (2003): 41.
36. "If You're Asked to Take a Drug Test," *Nolo*, http://www.nolo.com (accessed June 1, 2011).
37. Jeffrey Juergens, "Alcohol and Drugs in the Workplace," Addiction Center (March 24, 2021).
38. Adrienne Santos-Longhurst, "How Long Does Cocaine Stay in Your System?" healthline.com (February 27, 2020); "If You're Asked to Take a Drug Test," *Nolo*, http://www.nolo.com (accessed June 1, 2011).
39. "Constitution Limits Pre-employment Drug Testing by Public Employers," *Venulex Legal Summaries* (2008 Q1): 1; "Drug Testing Is Common and Codified at Many Workplaces," *HR Focus* 83, no. 6 (2006): 9; "New Developments Question the Use of Drug Tests in the Workplace," *Safety Director's Report* 4, no. 9 (2004): 3-6; "Fired for Blogging," http://www.nolo.com (accessed June 3, 2011); Sandy Smith, "What Every Employer Should Know about Drug Testing in the Workplace," *Occupational Hazards* 66, no. 8 (2004): 45–48.
40. T. L. Stanly, "Workplace Drug Testing and the Growing Problem of Methamphetamines," *Supervision* 68, no. 8 (2007): 3.
41. William I. Sauser Jr., "Employee Theft: Who, How, Why, and What Can Be Done," *S.A.M. Advanced Management Journal* 72, no. 3 (2007): 13.
42. Andrea Marvin, "Video Shows Rats Running around McDonald's," *ABCNews* (February 10, 2017).
43. Adrienne Fox, "Caught in the Web," *HR Magazine* 52, no. 12 (2007): 35.
44. "Employee Rights and Identity Theft," Texas Workforce Commission, http://www.twc.state.tx.us (accessed June 2, 2011).
45. Brad Stone and Ashlee Vance, "Apple's Obsession with Secrecy Grows," *The New York Times* (June 22, 2009), http://www.nytimes.com.
46. Electronic Communications Privacy Act, 18 U.S.C. § 2510–2720.
47. Rita Zeidner, "Keeping E-mail in Check," *HR Magazine* 52, no. 6 (2007): 70.
48. "Top Ten Reasons Companies Block Social Media at Work," *Everfi* (November 23, 2020).
49. Allen Smith, "What to Include in Policies Regarding Damage to Equipment," Society for Human Resource Management (October 14, 2020); Mark Szakonyi, "Big Brother at Work," *Portfolio* (February 8, 2010), http://www.portfolio.com.
50. Aiha Nguyen, "On the Clock and at Home: Post–COVID-19 Employee Monitoring in the Workplace," Society for Human Resource Management (2020); Chip Cutter, Te-Ping Chen, and Sarah Krouse, "You're Working from Home, But Your Company Is Still Watching You," *Wall Street Journal* (April 18, 2020).
51. Bobby Allyn, "Your Boss Is Watching You: Work-from-Home Boom Leads to More Surveillance," *NPR* (May 13, 2020).
52. Paul E. Paray, "N.J. Supreme Court Sides with Employee on Email Privacy Case," *Digital Risk Strategies* [blog] (April 5, 2010), http://blog.digitalriskstrategies.com.
53. "Why It's Time to Update Your Privacy Policies," *HR Focus* 84, no. 4 (2007): 3.
54. "Phish Leads to Breach at Calif. State Controller," Krebson Security (March 21, 2021), https://krebsonsecurity.com/2021/03/phish-leads-to-breach-at-calif-state-controller/.
55. Dan Caterinicchia, "Safeguarding HR Information," *HR Magazine* 50, no. 11 (November 1, 2005): 55–59.
56. Jathan Janove, J.D. "6 Burning COVID-19–Related Legal Questions for 2021," Society for Human Resource Management (March 22, 2021), https://www.shrm.org/hr-today/news/hr-magazine/spring2021/pages/six-burning-covid-legal-questions-for-2021.aspx.
57. Lisa Nagele-Piazza, "Can Employees Be Fired for Off-Duty Conduct?" Society for Human Resource Management (October 24, 2017); Diane Cadrain, "Setting the Records Straight," *HR Magazine* 52, no. 6 (2007): 82.
58. Ibid.; "Fired for Blogging," http://www.nolo.com (accessed June 3, 2011).
59. Cynthia F. Cohen and Murray E. Cohen, "On-Duty and Off-Duty: Employee Rights to Privacy and Employers Right to Control in the Private Sector," *Employee Responsibilities and Rights Journal* 19, no. 4 (2007): 235.
60. "Crushing on Your Co-worker? You're Not Alone," Society for Human Resources (February 12, 2020), https://www.shrm.org/about-shrm/press-room/press-releases/pages/new-survey-on-workplace-romance-2020.aspx.
61. Gene Marks, "Employers Can't Forbid Romance in the Workplace—But They Can Protect Workers," *The Guardian* (February 20, 2020); Julianne Pepitone, "Facebook Firing Settled out of Court," *CNNMoney* (February 8, 2011), http://money.cnn.com.
62. Charles A. Pierce, Brandee J. Broberg, Jamie R. McClure, and Herman Aquinis, "Responding to Sexual Harassment Complaints: Effects of a Dissolved Workplace Romance on Decision Making Standards," *Organizational Behavior and Human Decision Processes* 95, no. 1 (2004): 83.
63. Judy Greenwald, "Employers Are the Losers in the Dating Game," *Workforce Management*, http://www.workforce.com/section/09/feature/24/93/98/index.html.

64. Statista Research Department (December 12, 2019); "Tattoo Takeover: Three in Ten Americans Have Tattoos, and Most Don't Stop at Just One," *The Harris Poll* (February 10, 2016).
65. Kathryn Tyler, "Sign in the Name of Love," *HR Magazine* 53, no. 2 (2008): 41.
66. Kathy Gurchiek, "Religion and Work: 'A Hot Topic and Getting Hotter Every Day,'" Society for Human Resource Management (March 17, 2017); "How Companies Are Dealing with Workplace Body Art Issues," *HR Focus* 81, no. 4 (2004).
67. George W. Bohlander and Donna Blancero, "A Study of Reversal Determinants in Discipline and Discharge Arbitration Awards: The Impact of Just Cause Standards," *Labor Studies Journal* 21, no. 3 (1996): 3–18.
68. Jathan W. Janove, "Private Eye 101," *HR Magazine* 49, no. 7 (2004): 127.
69. Danielle Cronquist, "How to Conduct an HR Investigation," BambooHR (February 5, 2020); Mollica Kelly, "Perceptions of Fairness," *HR Magazine* 49, no. 6 (2004): 169.
70. *NLRB v. Weingarten Inc.*, 95 S.Ct. 959 (1975), 402 U.S. 251, 43 L.Ed.2d. 171.
71. Readers interested in the pioneering work on positive discipline should see Randy Pennington, "Viewpoint: Employee Discipline for the New Workplace," Society for Human Resource Management (September 18, 2018); James R. Redeker, "Discipline, Part 1: Progressive Systems Work Only by Accident," *Personnel* 62, no. 10 (1985): 8–12; James R. Redeker, "Discipline, Part 2: The Nonpunitive Approach Works by Design," *Personnel* 62, no. 11 (1985): 7–14.
72. Skye Schooley, "How to Fire an Employee the Right Way," business.com (October 5, 2020); Stephen P. Postalakis, "Avoiding a Sticky Situation: A Guide to Firing an Employee," *Catalyst 2002* (March/April 2007): 22.
73. For an excellent explanation of just cause discharge guidelines, see Frank Elkouri and Edna Asper Elkouri, *How Arbitration Works*, 5th ed. (Washington, DC: Bureau of National Affairs, 1997).
74. Carol MacKinley, "On Firing Well: Four Principles for Easing the Hardest Job in HR," *Human Resource Executive* (January 26, 2021); Jack and Suzy Welch, "The Right Way to Say Goodbye," *Business Week* (March 25, 2007): 144.
75. Elizabeth Agnvall, "Case Closed. Now What?" *HR Magazine* 53, no. 2 (2008): 69.
76. Nancy Hatch Woodward, "Smoother Separations," *HR Magazine* 52, no. 6 (2007): 94.
77. Michael Orey, "The Vanishing Trial: As Court Battles Become More Rare, Some Experts Fear the Effects on the Law," *Business Week* (April 30, 2007): 38.
78. Louise Lamothe, "Avoiding Potholes in Mandatory Arbitration: A Look at Recent California Decisions," *Dispute Resolution Journal* 58, no. 2 (2003): 18. See also D. Diane Hatch, James T. Hall, Mark T. Kobata, and Marty Denis, "Law Firm's Arbitration Procedures Rules Unfair," *Workforce Management* 86, no. 13 (July 23, 2007): 10.
79. Masood Ahmed, "Alternative Dispute Resolution during the Covid-19 Crisis and Beyond," *King's Law Journal* (February 25, 2021); Walsh, *Employment Law for Human Resource Practice*, 19.
80. Ruth D. Raisfeld, "How Mediation Works: A Guide to Effective Use of ADR," *Employee Relations Law Journal* 33, no. 2 (2007): 30.
81. Jennifer J. Froehlich, "The New Company Unions: Mandatory Individual Employment Arbitration Agreements and Section 8(a)(2) of the National Labor Relations Act," *Labor Law Journal* 58, no. 3 (2007): 195.
82. Elizabeth F. R. Gingerich, "Enforcing Arbitration Agreements in Discrimination Claims: Judicial Reconsideration," *Employee Relations Law Journal* 33, no. 4 (2008): 61.
83. *EEOC v. Waffle House Inc.*, 534 U.S. 279 (2002).
84. "EEOC May Sue Even If Arbitration Agreement Exists," *HR Focus* 79, no. 3 (2002): 2.
85. Betsy Stevens, "Corporate Ethical Codes: Effective Instruments for Influencing Behavior," *Journal of Business Ethics* 78, no. 4 (2008): 601.
86. Jennifer Schramm, "Perception on Ethics," *HR Magazine* 49, no. 11 (2004): 176.

Atomazul/Shutterstock.com

CHAPTER 14

The Dynamics of Labor Relations

Learning Outcomes

After studying this chapter, you should be able to

- **LO 1** Describe the process by which unions organize employees and gain recognition as their bargaining agent.
- **LO 2** Discuss the bargaining process and the bargaining goals and strategies of a union and an employer.
- **LO 3** Outline how the labor agreement might establish the issue of management rights and union security agreements, and what these may imply.
- **LO 4** Describe a typical union grievance procedure, including the basis for arbitration awards.
- **LO 5** Identify key challenges that unions face, and discuss how unions might deal with the issues associated with these challenges.

Al Seib/Shutterstock.com

Who knew delivering mail was such a heroic job? During the COVID-19 pandemic, when many people were staying at home, postal workers were able to identify health problems of elderly individuals at home.

Mention Labor Day, and most people think of the start of the football season, shopping Labor Day sales, mourning the unofficial end of summer, or complaining about that one time they needed to renew their driver's license and the DMV closed early. But Labor Day, without all of its modern trappings, is actually a federal holiday honoring the American labor movement and its contributions to worker health, safety, well-being, and productivity.

Mention labor movements and trade unions, and most people will have a more polarized opinion, whether considering the adversarial relationship between employees and higher-ups and strikes, or industrial democracy, fairness, opportunity, and equal representation.[1] And some may wonder if unions are still relevant today, in an era with worker safety laws and globalization. Unions are still active in many areas of U.S. business, influencing policies and helping workers in a range of different ways. For example, unions played a major role in protecting workers' rights during the COVID-19 pandemic.[2] New York nursing homes affiliated with labor unions had fewer COVID-19 deaths and infections than those without union representation.[3] Union postal workers save lives by alerting officials if an elderly person hasn't been collecting his or her mail. Even the TV shows you watch are the product of one of America's most unionized industries.[4]

14.1 The Labor Relations Process

LO1 Describe the process by which unions organize employees and gain recognition as their bargaining agent.

Individually, employees may be able to exercise relatively little power in their relationship with employers. If individual employees believe they are not being treated fairly, then they may organize into unions and bargain with the employer collectively. **Unions** represent an organized association of workers formed to further the interests of the individuals working for an employer. The ability of workers to form a union and collectively bargain with an employer is a legal right granted by the **National Labor Relations Board (NLRB)**.

When workers decide to unionize, the labor relations process begins. As Figure 14.1 illustrates, the **labor relations process** consists of a logical sequence of five events: (1) workers desire collective representation, (2) the union begins its organizing campaign, (3) the NLRB representation procedure begins, (4) collective negotiations lead to a contract, and (5) the contract is administered. Laws and administrative rulings influence each of the separate events by granting special privileges to, or imposing defined constraints on, workers, managers, and union officials.[5]

For example, when Gawker Media workers became tired of the instability of their employment environment, they decided to start an organizing campaign. The campaign was spearheaded by Hamilton Nolan, one of Gawker's senior writers. Even though Gawker is a digital media outlet populated by 20- and 30-something college grads who start with decent salaries of $40,000 to $50,000 per year and great benefits, employees felt that a union could provide a safety net during uncertain times. Once they decided they wanted collective representation, employees had to choose a union to help with the

union
An association of people with a common interest to improve their working conditions.

National Labor Relations Board (NLRB)
The agency responsible for administering and enforcing the Wagner Act. It serves the public interest by reducing interruptions in production or service caused by labor–management strife.

labor relations process
A logical sequence of five events: (1) workers desire collective representation, (2) the union begins its organizing campaign, (3) the NLRB representation process begins, (4) collective negotiations lead to a contract, and (5) the contract is administered.

Figure 14.1 The Labor Relations Process

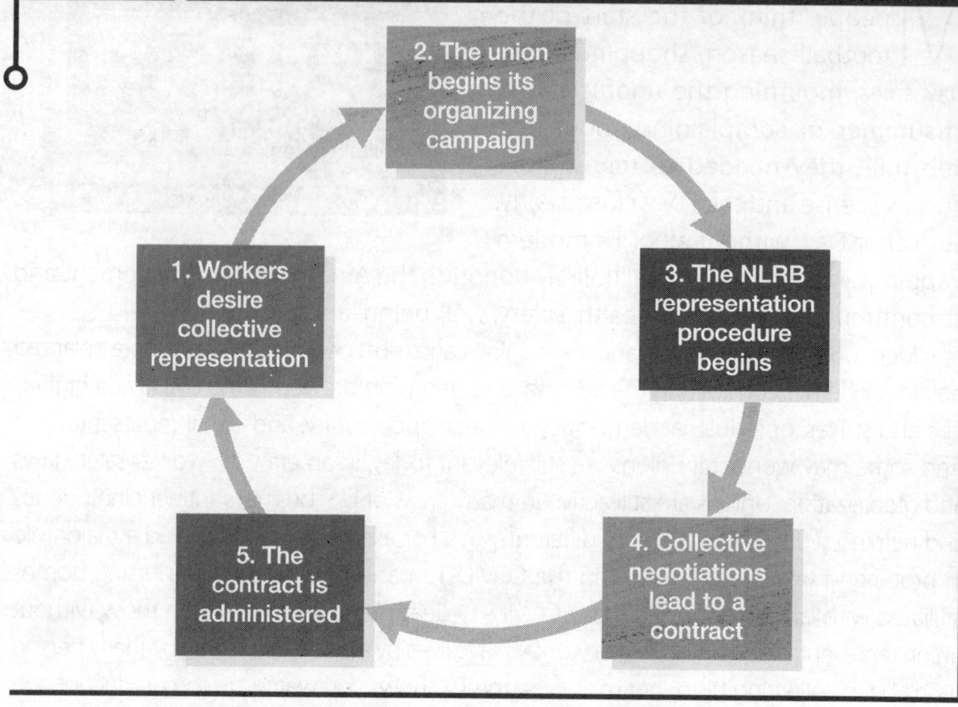

organizing campaign. They chose to work with the Writers Guild of America East to help with the campaign. When the union was finally recognized and formalized through the NLRB representation process, Gawker employees collectively bargained and came up with a contract between the union and the employer.

The new contract didn't necessarily impose many new demands on the employer, but rather formalized the relationship between employees and the employer and made

Lev radin/Alamy Stock Photo

Amazon unionization efforts in Bessemer, Alabama, were due in part to unfair COVID-19 work requirements.

it more difficult for the employer to lay people off. In fact, Gawker employees were not necessarily concerned with their wages, so they did not make wage levels a point of negotiation with Gawker.

Gawker's formation of a union inspired employees at other media companies to do the same. Now, more than 30 media companies have unions among their employees. The media industry is experiencing so much growth and change that employee dynamics are fragile.[6]

14.1a Why Employees Unionize

A surge of support for unions has started up again in the United States. During the "Occupy Wall Street" movement in 2011, many citizens protested against the large sums of bailout money paid to corporate America. They then moved to the "Fight for 15," as the Service Employees International Union supported a series of protests and strikes in a question to increase the U.S. minimum wage to $15 per hour.[7]

While participation in traditional unions has dramatically declined in the last few decades (from 20 percent of all U.S. workers in 1983 to 12.1 percent in 2020,[8] recently alternative collective labor structures have emerged and Millennials have demonstrated a newfound interest in unions (See Figure 14.2 on why employees unionize).[9] Roughly 65 percent of Millennials have been shown to approve of unions, which is a much higher level of appreciation than that found among their older generational peers. Younger employees want work–life balance, a team-oriented work culture, and transparency concerning compensation and promotion—all values similar to those espoused by unions.[10]

- *Dissatisfaction with management*. Employees may seek unionization when they perceive that managerial practices regarding promotion, transfer, shift assignments, or other job-related policies are administered in an unfair or biased manner. Employees cite favoritism shown by managers as a major reason for joining unions. Furthermore, employers' failure to give employees an opportunity to participate in decisions affecting their welfare may encourage union membership.
- *Economic needs*. Dissatisfaction with wages, benefits, and working conditions appears to provide the strongest reason to join a union. According to the Economic Policy Institute, workers who belong to unions have, on average, incomes 11.2 percent higher than those of nonunion workers.[11] Also, 95 percent of union workers have job-related health coverage, compared to 68 percent of nonunion workers.[12]

Figure 14.2 Why Employees Unionize

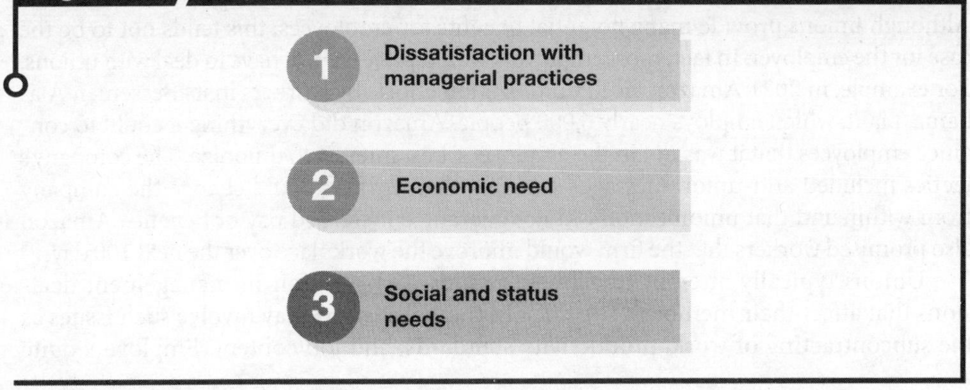

FernandoPodolski/Getty Images

Millennial protestors tackle problems as a collective, which lends way to employees using unions to achieve results that are otherwise unattainable as individuals.

- *Social and status needs.* Employees whose needs for recognition and social affiliation are being frustrated may join unions as a means of satisfying these needs. Through their union, they have an opportunity to fraternize with other employees who have similar desires, interests, problems, and gripes. Such concerns often revolve around job insecurity, broken promises, lack of autonomy, double standards, hopelessness, humiliation, and lack of recognition. Employees (especially Millennials) may join unions to benefit from the equality and teamwork that organization membership may provide. Additionally, the union provides workers with leadership opportunities, such as becoming a **union steward**, which puts their leadership talents to use as officers of the union and representatives of fellow employees.

union steward
An employee who as a nonpaid union official represents the interests of members in their relations with management.

Of the factors mentioned, organizing campaigns around social concerns (e.g., justice, equality, and teamwork) tends to be more successful than basing campaigns on dissatisfaction with management or even economic issues.[13] In other words, employees today are more interested in being treated fairly and working collectively.

14.1b Challenges of Unions to Management

Although unions provide many potential benefits for employees, this tends not to be the case for the employer. In fact, most employers would prefer to not have to deal with unions. For example, in 2021 Amazon faced unionization efforts by workers in its Bessemer, Alabama, plant, which employs nearly 6,000 people. Amazon did everything it could to convince employees that it was not in the employees' best interest to unionize. The company's tactics included anti-union messages stressing that workers could change the company from within and that unionization did not guarantee increased pay or benefits. Amazon also promised workers that the firm would improve the workplace over the next 100 days.[14]

Unions typically attempt to achieve greater participation in management decisions that affect their members. Specifically, these decisions may involve such issues as the subcontracting of work, productivity standards, and job content. Employers quite naturally seek to claim many of these decisions as their exclusive *management prerogatives*— decisions over which management claims exclusive rights.

For example, the terms negotiated by unions can determine what corrective action is to be taken in directing and in disciplining employees. When disciplining employees, supervisors must be certain they can demonstrate *just cause* (see Chapter 13) for their actions. Additionally, specific contract language can also reduce the supervisor's ability to manage in such areas as scheduling, training, transfers, performance evaluation, and promotions. Under provisions of the labor agreement, supervisors may have to promote employees based on seniority rather than on individual merit.

Finally, unions can create divisions between management and workers, making it difficult to foster a team spirit within the organization so that everyone is working for a common organizational cause. To avoid these constraints, many organizations try to ensure the work environment is a place where people are well compensated, management is supportive and collaborative with workers, and all people are treated equally.[15]

14.1c Union Avoidance Practices

There are things companies like Amazon can do from an HRM perspective to decrease the chances that their employees will want to form a union, thereby avoiding the union organizing campaign altogether. Specifically, companies can adopt six practices or principles to decrease the chances of employees wanting to unionize (Figure 14.3).[16]

The first practice has to do with *pay*. As discussed in Chapter 9, not only do above-market wages and benefits increase performance and decrease turnover, but they also decrease the likelihood that employees will want to unionize. For example, very few companies that have above-market wage and benefits policies have unions. One reason the unionization effort at the Amazon Bessemer plant failed is because Amazon was already starting employees at $15 per hour, with full benefits. This was higher than the market wage. In fact, in an effort to reduce future unionization efforts at its other plants, after the failed unionization attempt in the Bessemer plant, Amazon increased its pay rates between $0.50 and $3 per hour for workers across the United States. "This is on top of our already industry-leading starting wage of $15 an hour and the more than $2.5 billion that we invested last year in additional bonuses and incentives for front-line teams," said Darcie Henry, Amazon vice president.[17]

The second practice is to *promote more employees from within* and to do it often. People like to feel that they are progressing and that they have a chance for growth and advancement. Opportunities for career advancement help to bolster hope and a sense of equity in work environments where employees who do a good job are recognized and given chances to better their positions in the organization.

Third, companies can *conduct cultural audits*. As discussed in Chapter 2, cultural audits provide managers with a picture of what the company needs. It tells management how employees feel about what is going on in the organization and the quality of the working environment. Organizations can then take this information and facilitate developmental programs for employees, focus more on employee needs, and correct problems before they become too large. Attitude surveys also provide a venue in which employees can feel they are being listened to. Management must take care with these surveys, however. Organizations that do not respond to or act upon this valuable feedback risk fostering even more discontent in their workforce, as employees will likely perceive that their suggestions are not valued.

The fourth practice is to *offer job rotations and training programs*. In Chapter 7, we discussed effective ways to manage training programs and job rotation assignments. Specifically, job rotations help reduce burnout, which can lead to people either leaving

Figure 14.3 Union Avoidance Practices

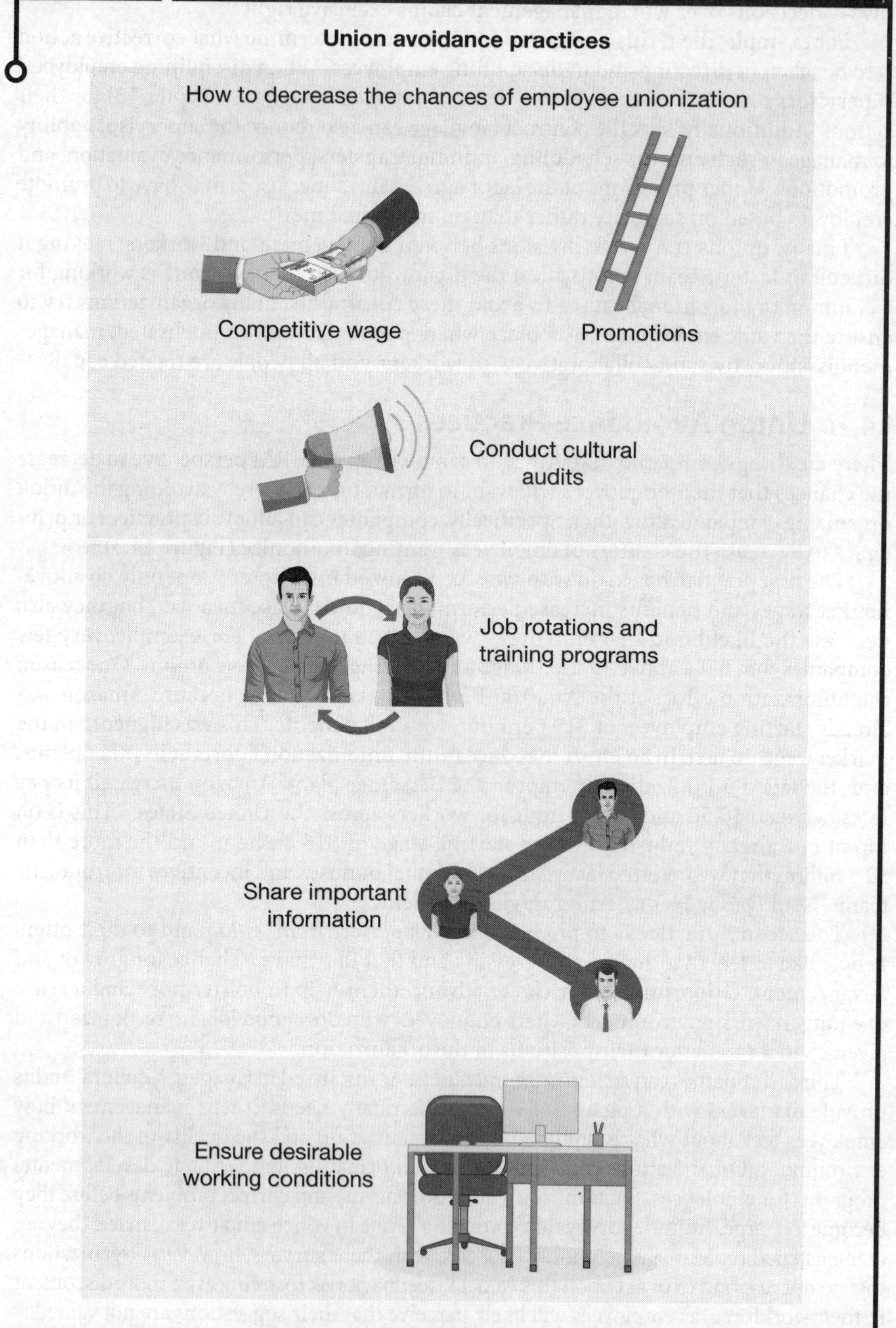

their jobs or feeling trapped and hopeless. Job rotations also lead to increased employee satisfaction. If variety is the spice of life, then job rotation is the spice of work. This leads to increased commitment to the organization.

Fifth, companies can *share information with employees about the state of the organization*. Companies that practice open book management are more likely to earn the trust and commitment of their employees and to avoid push-back from unions and consumers when they face financial troubles.[18] Mike Rose, CEO of Mojo Media Labs, discovered open book management at a conference and immediately began implementing it in his company. He found the advantages were plentiful, especially in creating stronger bonds between the employees and the company.[19] Open book management helps ensure employees understand the management decisions and are less likely to turn to a union when they aren't receiving enough transparency.

Finally, organizations should *make sure they have desirable working conditions*. While it is not feasible to make the working environment pleasant in all industries, an organization should make sure the work environment it creates for its employees is at least as equally desirable as that offered by other firms in the same industry. This means having appropriate and sufficient lighting, ergonomic workspaces, and a non hostile environment. In situations where more people are working remotely from home, this means providing home office set up, mental health support, gym memberships, childcare benefits, meal home delivery and virtual team activities. It is important to recognize that these strategies react to the conditions cited at the beginning of the chapter as the main reasons why workers unionize. Because these conditions are under the direct control of management, they can be changed to help discourage or prevent unionization.

14.1d Organizing Campaigns

Once employees desire to unionize, a formal organizing campaign may be started either by a union organizer or by employees acting on their own behalf.[20] Contrary to popular belief, most organizing campaigns are begun by employees rather than by union organizers. Large national unions such as the United Auto Workers, the United Brotherhood of Carpenters, the United Steelworkers, and the Teamsters, however, have formal organizing departments whose purpose is to identify organizing opportunities and launch organizing campaigns.

Organizing Steps

Terry Moser, former president of Teamster Local 104, identifies the typical organizing campaign as a series of five progressive steps that can lead to employee representation (Figure 14.4).

Step 1 The first step begins when employees and union officials meet up to explore the possibility of unionization. During these discussions, employees investigate the advantages of labor representation, and union officials begin to gather information on employee needs, problems, and grievances. Labor organizers also seek specific information about the employer's financial health, supervisory styles, and organizational policies and practices. To win employee support, labor organizers must build a case *against* the employer and *for* the union.

Step 2 As an organizing campaign gathers momentum, the organizer schedules an initial union meeting to attract more supporters. The organizer uses the information gathered in step 1 to address employee needs and explain how the union can secure these

Small Business Application

Unions and Small Business—Like Water and Oil

While most small businesses are not unionized and prefer it that way, it is not uncommon for employees to unionize even when they are small in number.

Why might employees of small businesses want to unionize? Usually when businesses are small, they are much less formal and more personal. This informality presents advantages in being able to adapt to the environment and devote needed resources to building the business. However, as small businesses grow, the benefits of informality decrease and the costs of having informal relationships increase. Some employees may begin to feel singled out—or worse yet, left out. Such situations sow seeds of discontent. To reduce the threat of unionization among small businesses, employers must consider when to hire an HR specialist to help manage their people and work culture more effectively.

A firm with only a few employees cannot afford a full-time HR specialist to deal with work culture issues. Illustrated here are a few conditions to help you understand when to appoint a specialist to deal with these issues.[21]

However, if these practices don't work and your employees still decide they want to pursue organizing a union, there are things management can do to stop the union from organizing.

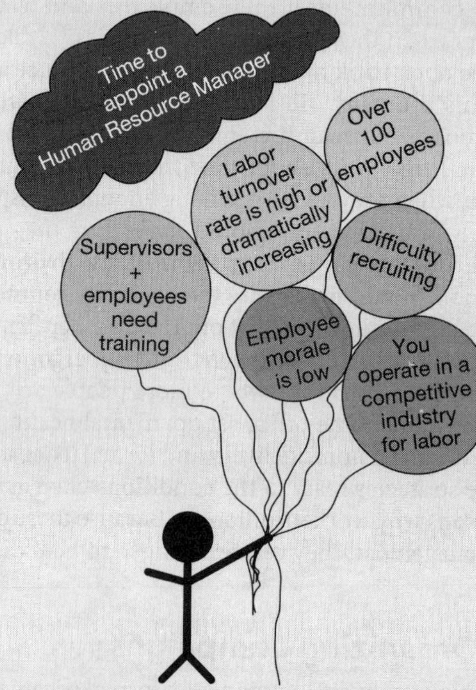

Figure 14.4 The Five Steps to Organizing a Union

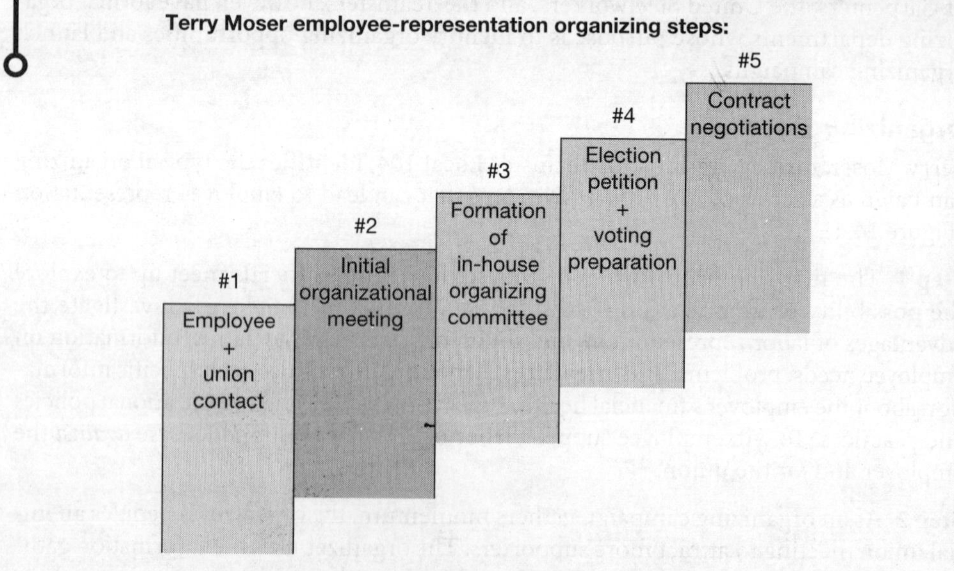

goals. Two additional purposes of organizational meetings are (1) to identify employees who can help the organizer direct the campaign and (2) to establish communication chains that reach all employees.

Step 3 Next, it is important to form an in-house organizing committee composed of employees willing to provide leadership to the campaign. This committee's role is to interest other employees in joining the union and in supporting its campaign. An important task of the committee is to have employees sign an **authorization card** indicating their willingness to be represented by a labor union in collective bargaining with their employer. At least 30 percent of the employees must sign authorization cards before the NLRB will hold a representation election.[22] Highlights in HRM 2 illustrates an authorization card.

authorization card
A statement signed by an employee authorizing a union to act as a representative of the employee for purposes of collective bargaining.

Step 4 If a sufficient number of employees support the union drive, the organizer seeks a government-sponsored election. A representation petition is filed with the NLRB, asking that a secret ballot election be held to determine whether employees actually desire unionization. Before the election, a large publicity campaign is directed toward employees, seeking their support and election votes. This is a period of intense emotions for the employees, the labor organization, and the employer.

Step 5 Union organizing is concluded when the union wins the election. The NLRB "certifies" the union as the legal bargaining representative of the employees. Contract negotiations now begin; these negotiations represent another struggle between the union and employer. During negotiations, each side seeks commitment to employment conditions favorable to its position. Members of the in-plant organizing committee and the union organizer attempt to negotiate the employees' first contract. In about one out of four union campaigns, unions are unable to secure a first contract after winning a representation election.[23] Should the union fail to obtain an agreement within 1 year from winning the election, the Taft-Hartley Act allows the employees to vote the union out through a NLRB "decertification" election.

Organizing Tactics

Unions have developed organizing strategies to compensate for a decline in membership and to counteract employer antiunion campaigns. (Both topics are discussed later in this chapter.) Unions employ the following organizing tactics—in varying degrees—to achieve their goals:

1. *Political involvement*. Unions play an important role in politics. For example, during the 2020 presidential election, many major unions publicly endorsed candidates. While a majority of the largest labor unions endorsed Joe Biden, Donald Trump was able to gain the support of the major police union.[24] Such endorsements reflect unions' perceptions of which political candidates have their best interests at heart.
2. *Neutrality agreements*. Neutrality agreements secure a binding commitment from the employer to remain neutral during the organizing drive. The employer agrees that managers will not campaign against or disparage the union and will only provide facts about the union when questioned by employees. Furthermore, the employer agrees to accept a card check to recognize the union if the union produces sufficient employee-signed authorization cards.[25]

1 Highlights in HRM

Test Your Labor Relations Know-How

1. An auto mechanic applied for a job with an automotive dealership. The applicant was denied employment because of their union membership. Was the employer's action lawful?

   ____________Yes ____________No

2. During a labor organizing drive, supervisors questioned individual employees about their union beliefs. Was this questioning permissible?

   ____________Yes ____________No

3. When members of a union began wearing union buttons at work, management ordered the buttons to be removed. Was management within its rights?

   ____________Yes ____________No

4. While an organizing drive was under way, an employer agreed—as a social gesture—to furnish refreshments at a holiday party. Was the employer acting within the law?

   ____________Yes ____________No

5. A company distributed to other anti-union employers in the area a list of job applicants known to be union supporters. Was the distribution unlawful?

   ____________Yes ____________No

6. During a union organizing drive, the owner of Servo Pipe promised the company's employees a wage increase if they would vote against the union. Can the owner legally make this promise to their employees?

   ____________Yes ____________No

7. Do employees have the right to file unfair labor practice charges against their employer even when the organization is nonunion?

   ____________Yes ____________No

8. The union wishes to arbitrate a member's grievance, which management has demonstrated is completely groundless. Must management arbitrate the grievance?

   ____________Yes ____________No

9. John Green, a maintenance engineer, has a poor work record. Management wishes to terminate his employment. However, Green is a union steward, and is highly critical of the company. Can management legally discharge this employee?

   ____________Yes ____________No

10. During an organizing drive, an office manager expressed strong anti-union beliefs and called union officials "racketeers," "big stinkers," and a "bunch of radicals." The manager told employees who joined the union that they "ought to have their heads examined." Were the manager's comments legal?

    ____________Yes ____________No

Answers are found at the end of this chapter.

3. *Organizer training.* Traditionally, organizing has been a part-time work. Today, the AFL-CIO's Organizing Institute is actively training a new generation of professional, highly skilled, full-time organizers. Organizers who successfully complete the training program are usually hired by local and national unions. They work to assist workers to gain representation, by educating workers about their rights, identifying and developing leadership skills, and running campaigns for union recognition.
4. *Corporate campaigns.* Unions may enlist political or community groups to boycott the product(s) of a targeted company. Other tactics include writing newspaper editorials chastising specific company decisions; filing charges with administrative agencies such as the Occupational Safety and Health Administration (OSHA), the Department of Labor, and the NLRB; and pressuring an organization's financial institution to withhold loans or demand payments.

2 Highlights in HRM

United Food and Commercial Workers International Union Authorization Card

United Food & Commercial Workers International Union

Affiliated with AFL-CIO-CLC

AUTHORIZATION FOR REPRESENTATION

I hereby authorize the United Food & Commercial Workers International Union, AFL-CIO-CLC, or its chartered Local Union(s) to represent me for the purpose of collective bargaining.

(Print Name) (Date)

(Signature) (Home Phone)

(Home Address) (City) (State) (Zip)

(Employer's Name) (Address)

(Hire Date) (Type Work Performed) (Department)

(Hourly Rate) (Day Off) Day Shift ____ Night Shift ____ Full Time ____ Part-Time ____

Would you participate in an organizing committee? Yes ____ No ____

5. *Social media.* Social media is fast becoming an effective union organizing tool. Websites exist that link employees to union literature, union membership applications, and individual union web pages. "Cyberunions" seek to apply computer technology to all aspects of organizing activity.[26] For example, some union organizing efforts have used hashtags to bring attention to their campaigns. The #fightfor15 and #ourwalmart are two examples of effective efforts to bring people together for protests and rallies. Coworker.org also created a platform to gather petitions from low-wage workers who otherwise lack the ability to collectively organize because they are scattered across multiple locations. Finally, another source of support for unions is the Worker's Lab. Launched in 2015, the Worker's Lab is like a venture capital fund for worker organizing movements. The funds are used to support innovative alt-labor movements that will lead to more innovative organized labor unions.[27]

14.1e Employer Tactics Opposing Unionization

Employers use a two-pronged campaign to fight unionization. First, when possible, employers stress the favorable employer–employee relationship they have experienced in the past without a union. Employers may emphasize any advantages in wages, benefits, or working conditions the employees may enjoy in comparison with those provided by organizations that are already unionized. "While you have a right to join a union," the employers may remind their employees, "you also have a right not to join one and to deal directly with the organization free from outside interference."

Geopix/Alamy Stock Photo

Biden won the presidential election with the help of many union workers.

Second, employers emphasize any unfavorable aspects of unionism, including strikes, the payment of union dues and special assessments, and published abuses of members' legal rights, along with any false promises made by the union in the course of its campaign. They also highlight union rules on member conduct, such as being fined for crossing a picket line. In addition, employers may cite government statistics to show that unions commit large numbers of unfair labor practices. Employers may initiate legal action should union members and/or their leaders engage in any **unfair labor practices (ULPs)** during the organizing effort.

unfair labor practices (ULPs)
Specific employer and union illegal practices that deny employees their rights and benefits under federal labor law.

Within the limits permitted by the Taft-Hartley Act, employers can express their views about the disadvantages of being represented by a union. However, when counteracting a union campaign, managers must not threaten employees with loss of their jobs or loss or reduction of other employment benefits if they vote to unionize. Nor may employers offer new or improved employee benefits or higher wages as a means of getting employees to vote "no union." Highlights in HRM 3 lists some of the activities in which managers or supervisors should not engage.[28]

14.1f How Employees Become Unionized

The employees to be organized constitute the bargaining unit to be covered by the labor agreement. The NLRB defines a **bargaining unit** as a group of two or more employees who have common employment interests and conditions and may reasonably be grouped together for purposes of collective bargaining. If an employer and a union cannot agree on who should be part of the bargaining unit, an appropriate bargaining unit will be determined by the NLRB on the basis of a similarity of interests (such as wages, job duties, or training) among employees within the unit. For example, in hospitals, the NLRB has designated separate units for nurses, technicians, doctors, maintenance employees, office clerical personnel, all other nonprofessionals, and security guards.

bargaining unit
A group of two or more employees who share common employment interests and conditions and may reasonably be grouped together for purposes of collective bargaining.

3 Highlights in HRM

Employer "Don'ts" during Union Organizing Campaigns

Union organizing drives are emotionally charged events. Furthermore, labor law, NLRB rulings, and court decisions greatly affect the behavior and actions of management and union representatives. During the drive, managers and supervisors should avoid the following actions:

- Attending union meetings, spying on employee–union gatherings, or questioning employees about the content of union meetings
- Questioning present or current employees about their union sentiments, particularly about how they might vote in a union election
- Threatening or terminating employees for their union support or beliefs
- Changing the working conditions of employees because they actively work for the union or simply support its ideals
- Supplying the names, addresses, and phone numbers of employees to union representatives or other employees sympathetic to the union
- Promising employees improvements in working conditions (wage increases, benefit improvements, and so on) if they vote against the union
- Accepting or reviewing union authorization cards or pro-union petitions because employees' names are listed on these documents

14.1g NLRB Representation Election

If it succeeds in signing up 30 percent of employees within the bargaining unit, the union petitions for an NLRB-conducted election. The petition to hold representation elections usually is initiated by the union, although employers, under certain circumstances, have the right to petition for one (see Highlights in HRM 4). Prior to the election, the NLRB holds a *pre-election hearing* with the employer and the union, or unions, seeking to represent the employees. At this meeting, several important issues are settled, including verification of the authorization cards, the NLRB's jurisdiction to hold the election, determination of the bargaining unit (if contested by the parties), the date of the election, and the voting choice(s) to appear on the ballot. The ballot lists the names of the unions that are seeking recognition and also provides a choice of "no union." See Highlights in HRM 2 for an example of a union authorization card.

After the election is held, the winning party is determined on the basis of the number of actual votes, not on the number of members of the bargaining unit. For example, suppose the bargaining unit at XYZ Corporation has 100 employees, but only 27 employees voted in the election. A union receiving 14 yes votes among the 27 voting (a majority) would be declared the winner, and the union would bargain for all 100 employees. By law, the union would be granted **exclusive representation** over all bargaining unit employees.[29] The union is *certified* by the NLRB as the bargaining agent for at least a year or for the duration of the labor agreement. Once the union is certified, the employer is obligated to begin negotiations leading toward a labor agreement.

exclusive representation
The legal right and responsibility of the union to represent all bargaining unit members equally, regardless of whether employees join the union or not.

An important statistic in labor relations is the win/loss record of unions in certification elections. In 1950, the union win rate in elections held by the NLRB was 74.5 percent. This percentage dropped dramatically to 60.2 percent in 1965 and to 48.2 percent in 1995. For the years 2015–2019, the union win rate increased to 71.9 percent.[30]

Some of the different types of unions include craft unions, industrial unions, and employee associations. **Craft unions** include the International Association of Machinists, United Brotherhood of Carpenters, and United Association of Plumbers and Pipefitters.

craft unions
Unions that represent skilled craft workers.

NLRB Election Poster

NOTICE TO EMPLOYEES

FROM THE National Labor Relations Board

A PETITION has been filed with this Federal agency seeking an election to determine whether certain employees want to be represented by a union.

The case is being investigated and NO DETERMINATION HAS BEEN MADE AT THIS TIME by the National Labor Relations Board. IF an election is held, Notices of Election will be posted giving complete details for voting.

It was suggested that your employer post this notice so the National Labor Relations Board could inform you of your basic rights under the National Labor Relations Act.

YOU HAVE THE RIGHT under Federal Law

- **To self-organization**
- **To form, join, or assist labor organizations**
- **To bargain collectively through representatives of your own choosing**
- **To act together for the purposes of collective bargaining or other mutual aid or protection**
- **To refuse to do any or all of these things unless the union and employer, in a State where such agreements are permitted, enter into a lawful union-security agreement requiring employees to pay periodic dues and initiation fees. Nonmembers who inform the union that they object to the use of their payments for nonrepresentational purposes may be required to pay only their share of the union's costs of representational activities *(such as collective bargaining, contract administration, and grievance adjustments).***

It is possible that some of you will be voting in an employee representation election as a result of the request for an election having been filed. While NO DETERMINATION HAS BEEN MADE AT THIS TIME, in the event an election is held, the NATIONAL LABOR RELATIONS BOARD wants all eligible voters to be familiar with their rights under the law IF it holds an election.

The Board applies rules that are intended to keep its elections fair and honest and that result in a free choice. If agents of either unions or employers act in such a way as to interfere with your right to a free election, the election can be set aside by the Board. Where appropriate the Board provides other remedies, such as reinstatement for employees fired for exercising their rights, including backpay from the party responsible for their discharge.

NOTE:

The following are examples of conduct that interfere with the rights of employees and may result in the setting aside of the election.

- **Threatening loss of jobs or benefits by an employer or a union**
- **Promising or granting promotions, pay raises, or other benefits to influence an employee's vote by a party capable of carrying out such promises**
- **An employer firing employees to discourage or encourage union activity or a union causing them to be fired to encourage union activity**
- **Making campaign speeches to assembled groups of employees on Company time within the 24-hour period before the election**
- **Incitement by either an employer or a union of racial or religious prejudice by inflammatory appeals**
- **Threatening physical force or violence to employees by a union or an employer to influence their votes**

Please be assured that IF AN ELECTION IS HELD every effort will be made to protect your right to a free choice under the law. Improper conduct will not be permitted. All parties are expected to cooperate fully with this Agency in maintaining basic principles of a fair election as required by law. The National Labor Relations Board, as an agency of the United States Government, does not endorse any choice in the election.

NATIONAL LABOR RELATIONS BOARD

an agency of the

UNITED STATES GOVERNMENT

THIS IS AN OFFICIAL GOVERNMENT NOTICE AND MUST NOT BE DEFACED BY ANYONE

FORM NLRB-666 (5-90)

* U.S. Government Printing Office: 1990-270-693/10127

Figure 14.5 Different Types of Unions

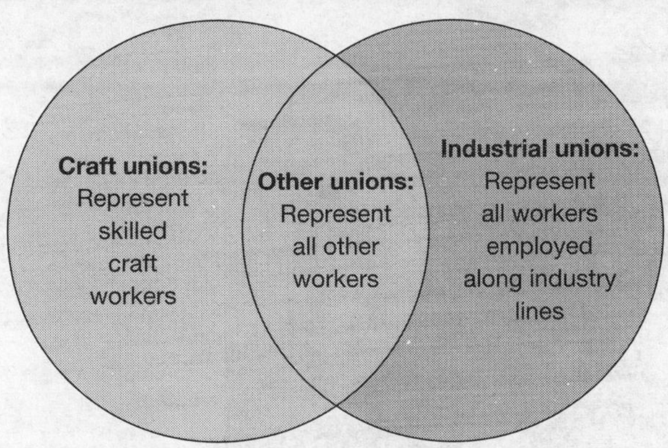

Unions that represent unskilled and semiskilled workers employed along industry lines are known as **industrial unions** (Figure 14.5). The American Union of Postal Workers is an industrial union, as are the United Auto Workers; United Steelworkers; American Federation of State, County, and Municipal Employees; and Office and Professional Employees International Union. While this distinction still exists, technological changes, union mergers, and competition among unions for members have helped reduce it. Today workers of all kinds are being represented by both types of union. For example, the UAW represents workers in diverse industries from auto manufacturing to agriculture, and from health care to higher education.[31]

industrial unions
Unions that represent all workers—skilled, semiskilled, unskilled—employed along industry lines.

While technically not unions, **employee associations** represent various groups of professional and white-collar employees. Examples of employee associations include the National Education Association, Michigan State Employees Association, American Nurses Association, and Air Line Pilots Association. In competing with unions, these associations, for all purposes, may function as unions and become just as resolute as unions in representing their members.

employee associations
Labor organizations that represent various groups of professional and white-collar employees in labor–management relations.

Public Unions

Creation of unions for federal, state, and local government employees has been an area of important activity since the early 1960s. Today, unions represent more than 34.4 percent of all government workers in the United States, compared with just 11 percent in 1960.[32]

LO2
Discuss the bargaining process and the bargaining goals and strategies of a union and an employer.

14.2 The Bargaining Process

Those unfamiliar with contract negotiations often view this process as an emotional conflict between labor and management, complete with marathon bargaining sessions, fist pounding, and smoke-filled rooms. In reality, negotiating a labor agreement entails long hours of extensive preparation combined with diplomatic maneuvering and the development of bargaining strategies. Furthermore, negotiation is only one part of the **collective bargaining process**. (See Figure 14.7 later in the chapter.) Collective bargaining also may include the use of economic pressures in the form of strikes and boycotts by a union. Lockouts, plant closures, and the replacement of strikers are similar pressures used by an employer. In addition, either or both parties may seek support from the general public or from the courts as a means of pressuring the opposing side.

collective bargaining process
The process of negotiating a labor agreement, including the use of economic pressures by both parties.

One of the functions of a union steward is to discuss issues with management as they arise. Here, a steward is discussing a safety issue with the site manager.

Imagesource/Photo Library

14.2a Preparing for Negotiations

Preparing for negotiations includes assembling data to support each side's bargaining proposals and forming the bargaining team. This permits collective bargaining to be conducted on an orderly, factual, and positive basis with a greater likelihood of achieving desired goals. Assuming that the labor agreement is not the first to be negotiated by the parties, preparation for negotiations ideally will start soon after the current agreement has been signed. This practice allows negotiators to review and diagnose weaknesses and mistakes made during the previous negotiations while the experience is still current in their minds.

Typically, each side has four to six representatives at the negotiating table. The chief negotiator for management is the vice president or manager for labor relations; the chief negotiator for the union is the local union president or national union representative. Other members of management's team may include representatives from accounting or finance, operations, employment, legal, or training. The local union president is likely to be supported by the chief steward, various local union vice presidents, and a representative from the national union. Importantly, it is widely accepted that the conduct of the negotiators strongly influences the individual bargaining sessions and the outcomes reached. According to one experienced negotiator, "The conduct of negotiations largely depends on the relationship and attitude of negotiators toward one another. If you want conflict in your bargaining sessions, just start off attacking the other side."

14.2b Gathering Bargaining Data

Employers gather economic data primarily in the areas of wages and benefits. However, internal data relating to grievances, disciplinary actions, transfers, promotions, overtime, and former arbitration awards are useful in formulating and supporting the employer's bargaining position. The supervisors and managers, who must live with and administer the labor agreement, can be very important sources of ideas and suggestions concerning changes that are needed in the *next* agreement.

When negotiating contracts, union bargainers talk about "taking wages out of competition." This term refers to having similar contract provisions—particularly concerning wages and benefits—between different companies so as to prevent one employer from having a favorable labor cost advantage over another. For example, the United Auto Workers, when representing workers at both General Motors and Ford, will seek similar contract provisions. Furthermore, this allows unions to show their members that they are receiving wages and benefits comparable to those of other employees doing similar work. Other negotiated labor agreements, particularly at the local and regional levels, play a significant part in settling the terms of the labor agreement.

14.2c Developing Bargaining Strategies and Tactics

Both management and union negotiators approach bargaining with a defined strategy. In tough economic periods, the employer's strategy might be to seek cost containment or specific reductions in wages or benefits such as health care or pension costs. Conversely, in times of economic growth—when a union strike would harm sales—the employer will be more willing to meet union demands. The employer's strategy should also consider proposals the union is likely to submit, goals the union is striving to achieve, and the extent to which the union may be willing to make concessions or to resort to strike action in an effort to achieve these goals.

At a minimum, the employer's bargaining strategy must address these points:

- Likely union proposals and management responses to them
- A listing of management demands, limits of concessions, and anticipated union responses
- Development of a database to support management bargaining proposals and to counteract union demands
- A contingency operating plan should employees strike

Certain elements of strategy are common to both the employer and the union. Generally, the initial demands presented by each side are greater than the terms it actually hopes to achieve.[33] This is done to provide room for concessions. Moreover, each party usually avoids giving up the maximum it is capable of conceding to allow for further concessions that may be needed to break a bargaining deadlock.

The negotiation of a labor agreement can have some of the characteristics of a poker game, with each side attempting to determine its opponent's position while not revealing its own.[34] Each party normally tries to avoid disclosing the relative importance that it attaches to a proposal so that it will not be forced to pay a higher price than is necessary to have the proposal accepted. As in buying a new car, the buyer and seller employ a lot of strategy to obtain the best outcome possible.

14.2d Negotiating the Labor Agreement

While there is no "exact" way to negotiate a labor agreement, typically each side focuses on one issue or several related issues until agreement is reached.[35] For each bargaining issue to be resolved satisfactorily, the point at which agreement is reached must be within

bargaining zone
An area in which the union and the employer are willing to concede when bargaining.

limits that the union and the employer are willing to accept. In a frequently cited bargaining model, Ross Stagner and Hjalmar Rosen call the area within these two limits the **bargaining zone**. In some bargaining situations, such as the one illustrated in Figure 14.6, the solution desired by one party may exceed the limits of the other party. Thus that solution is outside the bargaining zone. If that party refuses to modify its demands sufficiently to bring them within the bargaining zone or if the opposing party refuses to extend its limit to accommodate the demands of the other party, a bargaining deadlock results.[36] For example, when bargaining for a wage increase for employees, if the union's lowest limit is a 4 percent increase and management's top limit is 6 percent, an acceptable range—the bargaining zone—is available to both parties. If management's top limit is only 3 percent, however, a bargaining zone is not available to either side, and a deadlock is likely to occur. Figure 14.6 shows that as bargaining takes place, several important variables influence the negotiators and their ability to reach agreement within the bargaining zone.

14.2e Good-Faith Bargaining

The Taft-Hartley Act requires an employer to negotiate in good faith with the union's representatives over conditions of employment; the same obligation applies to the union representatives.[37] Good faith requires meetings to be held at reasonable times

Figure 14.6 The Bargaining Zone and Negotiation Influences

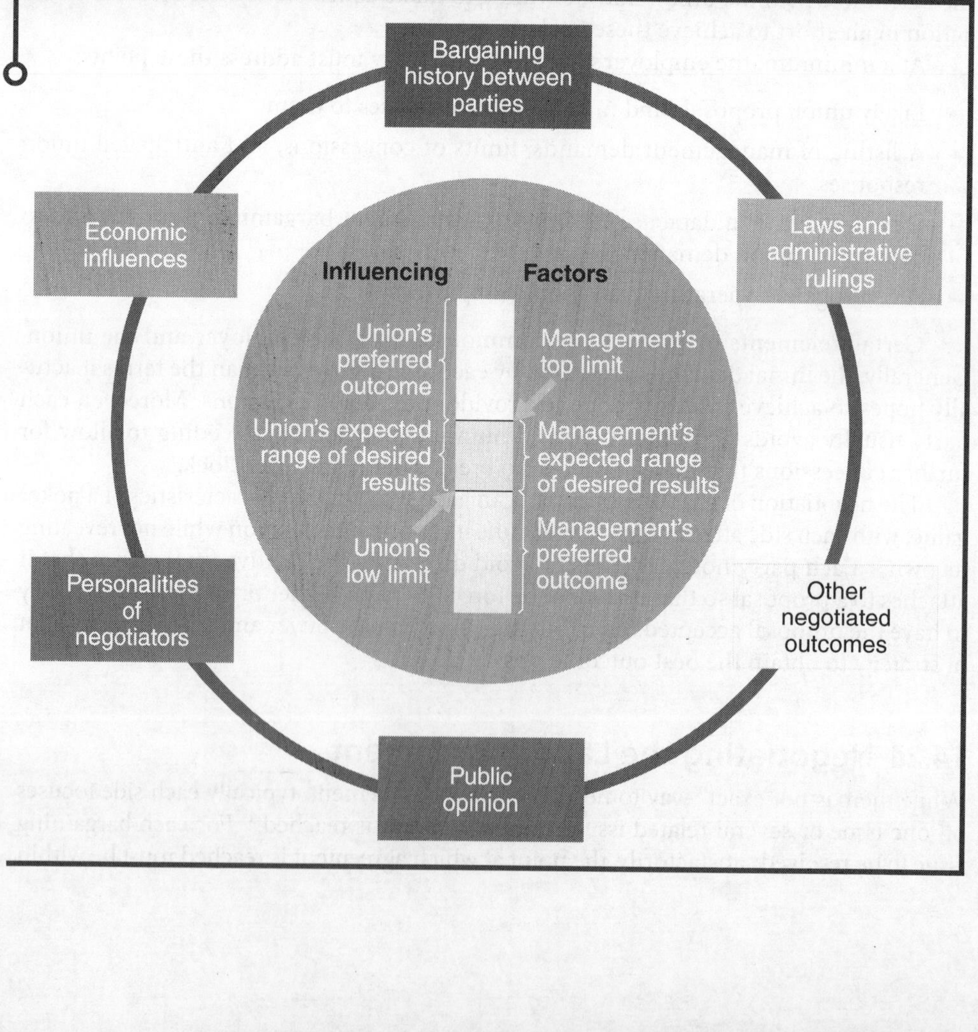

and places to discuss employment conditions. It also requires that the proposals submitted by each party be realistic. In discussing the other party's proposals, each side must offer reasonable counterproposals for those it is unwilling to accept. Finally, both parties must sign the written document containing the agreement reached through negotiations.

14.2f Interest-Based Bargaining

U.S. labor–management negotiations are generally characterized as adversarial. With adversarial bargaining, negotiators start with defined positions, and through deferral, persuasion, trade, or power, they work toward the resolution of individual bargaining demands. Unfortunately, as noted by one labor negotiator, "adversarial bargaining does little to establish a long-term positive relationship based on open communications and trust. By its nature, it leads to suspicion and compromise."[38] To overcome these negative feelings, labor and management practitioners may use a non adversarial approach to negotiating.

Interest-based bargaining is based on the identification and resolution of mutual interests rather than on meeting specific bargaining demands.[39] Interest-based bargaining is a problem-solving process conducted in a way that creates effective solutions while improving the relationship between the parties involved. The focus of the bargaining strategy is to discover mutual bargaining interests with the intent of formulating options and solutions for mutual gain.[40] Rather than using proposals and counterproposals as a means of reaching agreement (as in adversarial negotiations), participants use brainstorming, consensus decision making, active listening, process checking, and matrix building to facilitate the settlement of issues. An underlying goal of interest-based bargaining is to create a relationship for the future based on trust, understanding, and mutual respect.

interest-based bargaining
Problem-solving bargaining based on a win-win philosophy and the development of a positive long-term relationship.

14.2g Management and Union Power in Collective Bargaining

Fortunately, the great majority of labor–management negotiations are settled peacefully. However, should negotiations become deadlocked, bargaining can become highly adversarial, as each side will now wield its bargaining power to achieve its desired ends. The party's **bargaining power** consists of its economic, political, and social influence to achieve its demands at the expense of the other side.

bargaining power
The power of labor and management to achieve their goals through economic, social, or political influence.

Union Bargaining Power

The bargaining power of the union may be exercised by striking, picketing, or boycotting the employer's products or services. A strike is the refusal of a group of employees to perform their jobs. Unions usually seek strike authorization from their members to use as a bargaining ploy to gain concessions that will make a strike unnecessary. A strike vote by the members does not mean they actually want or expect to go out on strike. Rather, it is intended as a vote of confidence to strengthen their leaders' position at the bargaining table.

When a union goes on strike, it pickets the employer by placing people at business entrances to advertise the dispute and to discourage others from entering the premises. Because unions often refuse to cross another union's picket line, the pickets may serve to prevent the delivery and pickup of goods or performance of other services. For example, a Teamster truck driver may refuse to deliver produce to a food store whose employees are out on strike with the United Food and Commercial Workers Union.

Another economic weapon of the union is a *boycott*, which is a refusal to patronize the employer. For example, production employees on strike against a hand tool manufacturer might picket a retail store that sells the tools made by the struck employer. Unions will also use handbills, radio announcements, email campaigns, and newspaper ads to discourage the purchase of the employer's product or service.

Management Bargaining Power

When negotiations become deadlocked, the employer's bargaining power largely rests on being able to continue operations in the face of a strike *or* to shut down operations entirely.

Should employees strike the organization (a practice referred to as an economic strike), employers have the legal right to hire replacement workers. With this right, employers acquire a bargaining weapon equal in force to the union's right to strike. As one observer noted, "The availability of a worker replacement strategy improves management's ability to battle a union head-on in the way that unions have battled employers for decades."[41]

In extreme situations, the employer may elect to lock out its employees. The lockout is a bargaining strategy in which the employer denies employees the opportunity to work by closing its operations. Besides being used in bargaining impasses, lockouts may be initiated by employers to combat union slowdowns, damage to their property, or violence within the organization that may occur in connection with a labor dispute. Employers may still be reluctant to resort to a lockout, however, because of their concern that denying work to regular employees might hurt the organization's image.

14.2h Resolving Bargaining Deadlocks

Unions and employers in all types of industries—sports, transportation, entertainment, manufacturing, communication, and health care—have used mediation and arbitration to help resolve their bargaining deadlocks.[42] As discussed in Chapter 13, mediation is a

A strike is one way union members can exercise their bargaining power.

Al Seib/Los Angeles Times/Getty Images

voluntary process that relies on the communication and persuasive skills of a mediator to help the parties resolve their differences. The federal government is likely to become involved in labor disputes through the services of the Federal Mediation and Conciliation Service (FMCS).

Unlike a mediator, an **arbitrator** assumes the role of a decision maker and determines what the settlement between the two parties should be. In other words, arbitrators write a final contract that the parties *must* accept. Compared with mediation, arbitration is rarely used to settle private-sector bargaining disputes. In the public sector, where strikes are largely prohibited, the use of *interest arbitration* is a common method to resolve bargaining deadlocks. Generally, one or both parties are reluctant to give a third party the power to make the settlement for them. Consequently, a mediator typically is used to break a deadlock and assist the parties in reaching an agreement. An arbitrator generally is called on to resolve disputes arising in connection with the administration of the agreement, called *rights arbitration* or *grievance arbitration*, which will be discussed shortly.

arbitrator
A neutral third party who resolves a labor dispute by issuing a final decision in the disagreement.

Figure 14.7 summarizes the collective bargaining process.

14.3 The Labor Agreement

LO3 Outline how the labor agreement might establish the issue of management rights and union security agreements, and what these may imply.

When negotiations are concluded, the labor agreement becomes a formal *binding* document listing the terms, conditions, and rules under which employees and managers agree to operate. Highlights in HRM 5 shows some of the major articles in a labor

Figure 14.7 The Collective Bargaining Process

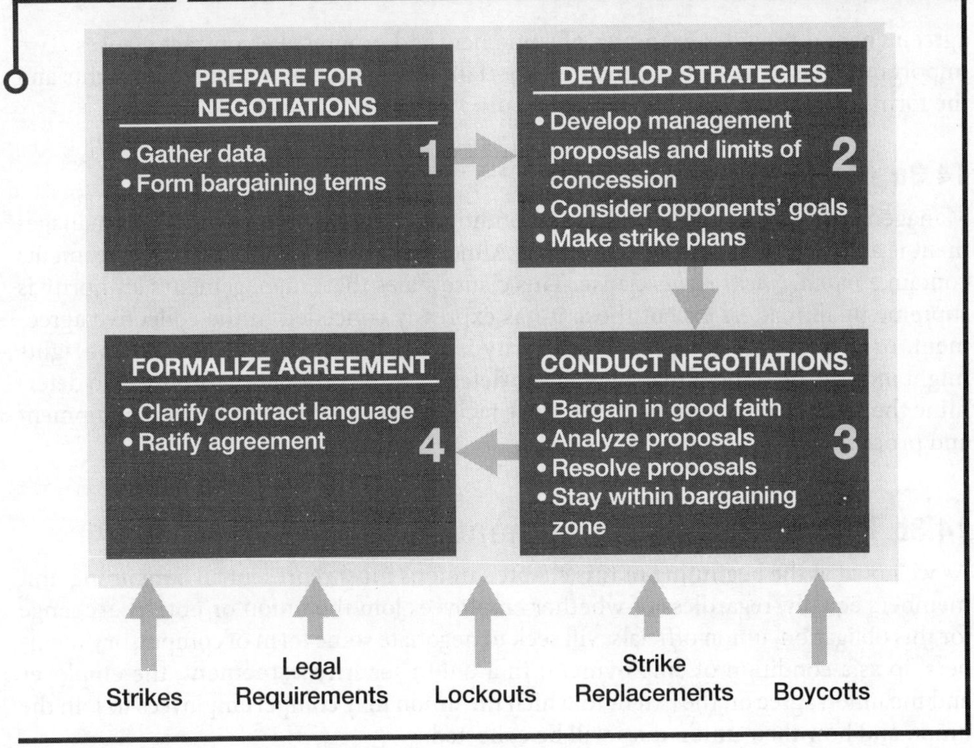

5 Highlights in HRM

Items in a Labor Agreement

Typical clauses will cover:

- Wages
- Vacations
- Holidays
- Work schedules
- Management rights
- Union security
- Transfers
- Discipline
- Training
- Grievance procedures
- No strike/no lockout clause
- Overtime
- Safety procedures
- Severance pay
- Seniority
- Pensions and benefits
- Outsourcing
- Work rules

Progressive clauses will cover:

- Employee access to records
- Limitations on use of performance evaluation
- Elder care leave
- Flexible medical spending accounts
- Protection against hazards of technology equipment (VDTs)
- Limitations against electronic monitoring
- Procedures governing drug testing
- Bilingual stipends
- Domestic partnership benefits
- Employee involvement programs

agreement and provides examples of some new and progressive contract clauses. Two important items in any labor agreement pertain to the issue of management rights and the forms of security afforded to the union.

14.3a Management Rights

Management rights have to do with the conditions of employment over which management is able to exercise exclusive control. Almost without exception, labor agreements contain a *management rights* clause. This clause states that "management's authority is supreme in all matters except those it has expressly conceded in the collective agreement, or in those areas where its authority is restricted by law." Management rights might include the right of management to determine the products to produce, to determine the location of production or service facilities, or to select production equipment and procedures.

union security agreement
An agreement between an employer and the union about the extent to which the union may compel employees to join the union and how the dues will be collected.

14.3b Union Security Agreements

As we noted at the beginning of this chapter, unions must represent all bargaining unit members equally, regardless of whether employees join the union or not. In exchange for this obligation, union officials will seek to negotiate some form of compulsory membership as a condition of employment. In a **union security agreement**, the employer and the union agree on the extent to which the union may compel employees to join the union and how their union dues will be collected.

14.4 Administration of the Labor Agreement

LO4

Describe a typical union grievance procedure, including the basis for arbitration awards.

Negotiation of the labor agreement, as mentioned earlier, is usually the most publicized and critical aspect of labor relations. However, since no agreement could possibly anticipate all forms that disputes might take, the bulk of labor relations activity comes from the day-to-day administration of the agreement. In addition, once the agreement is signed, each side will naturally interpret ambiguous clauses to its own advantage. These differences are traditionally resolved through the grievance procedure.

14.4a Negotiated Grievance Procedures

The **grievance procedure** typically provides for the union to represent the interests of its members (and nonmembers as well) in processing a grievance. It is considered by some authorities to be the heart of the bargaining agreement, or the safety valve that gives flexibility to the whole system of collective bargaining.[43]

grievance procedure
A formal procedure that provides for the union to represent members and nonmembers in processing a grievance.

The grievance procedure is normally initiated by the union—or an individual employee—when it feels management has violated some article of the labor agreement. In one case, the union filed a grievance against a supervisor when it believed the supervisor promoted an employee out of seniority—known as a bypass grievance. A significant benefit of the grievance procedure is that it provides a formal and orderly procedure for the union to challenge the actions of management without resorting to force. One authority has noted that the grievance procedure fosters cooperation, not conflict, between the employer and the union.[44]

14.4b Grievance Arbitration

The function of **rights arbitration** is to provide the solution to a grievance that a union and an employer have been unable to resolve by themselves. As mentioned earlier, arbitration is performed by a neutral third party (an arbitrator or impartial umpire). This third party's decision dictates how the grievance is to be settled.[45] Both parties involved in the dispute are obligated to comply with the decision.

rights arbitration
Arbitration over interpretation of the meaning of contract terms or employee work grievances.

Under the **fair representation doctrine**, unions have a legal obligation to provide assistance to members who are pursuing grievances. Because members can bring suit against their unions for failing to process their grievances adequately, many union officers are reluctant to refuse to take even weak grievances to arbitration.

fair representation doctrine
A doctrine under which unions have a legal obligation to assist both members and nonmembers in labor relations matters.

Arbitration Hearing

In our experience, employees unfamiliar with arbitration find the process confusing and often stressful. This is true for employees in a nonunion setting, as well as those in a union setting. Arbitration hearings have the appearance of a court hearing but lack many of the formalities of a court proceeding. The process begins with the swearing-in of witnesses and the introduction of the *submission agreement*. The submission agreement is a statement of the problem to be resolved. Such a statement might read: "Was the three-day suspension of Alex Hayden for just cause? If not, what is the appropriate remedy?" The parties will then make opening statements, followed by the presentation of facts and evidence, and the oral presentation of witnesses. The hearing concludes with each side making summary statements that are arguments in support of its position.

The arbitrator is responsible for ensuring that each side receives a fair hearing, during which it may present all of the facts it considers pertinent to the case. The primary purpose of the hearing is to assist the arbitrator in obtaining the facts necessary to resolve a human relations problem, rather than a legal one. The arbitrator, therefore, has the right to question witnesses or to request additional facts from either party. After conducting the hearing and receiving post-hearing briefs (should the parties choose to submit them), the arbitrator customarily has 30 days in which to consider the evidence and render an award. In most labor contracts, the costs of arbitration are shared equally by the parties.

Arbitration Award

The arbitration award is a formal written document given to both sides of the dispute (employee and employer). As in grievance procedures, there is no specific format for an arbitration award, but typically it contains five parts: (1) submission agreement, (2) facts of the case, (3) positions of the parties, (4) opinion of the arbitrator, and (5) decision rendered. As might be expected, the decision of the arbitrator is of major importance to the parties. However, the reasoning behind the decision—the opinion—is equally important because it can provide guidance concerning the interpretation of the labor agreement and the resolution of future disputes arising from its administration. In pointing out the merits of each party's position, the reasoning that underlies the award can help lessen the disappointment and protect the self-esteem of those representing the unsuccessful party. The opinion also evaluates the evidence presented by each side in support of its position and, in discipline cases, whether management had just cause for the action taken against an employee. (See Chapter 13 for a discussion of just cause in arbitration.)

Because of the importance and magnitude of arbitration in both the union and nonunion settings, the process by which arbitrators make decisions and the factors that influence those decisions are of continuing interest to managers. Typically, arbitrators use four factors when deciding cases:

1. The wording of the labor agreement (or employment policy in nonunion organizations)
2. The submission agreement as presented to the arbitrator
3. Testimony and evidence offered during the hearing
4. Arbitration criteria or standards (similar to standards of common law) against which cases are judged

In practice, arbitration decision making is not an exact science. In fact, the decisions of arbitrators can be rather subjective. Arbitrators can, and do, interpret contract language differently (e.g., what "just cause discharge" actually means), they assign varying degrees of importance to testimony and evidence, they judge the truthfulness of witnesses differently, and they give arbitration standards greater or lesser weight as they apply to facts of the case. Each of these influences introduces subjectivity into the decision-making process.[46]

LO5

Identify key challenges that unions face, and discuss how unions might deal with the issues associated with these challenges.

14.5 Contemporary Challenges to Labor Organizations

We conclude our discussion of labor relations by highlighting important issues facing unions today: the decrease in union membership, foreign competition, and technological advances.

14.5a Decrease in Union Membership

A major challenge confronting organized labor is to halt the decline in union membership. In 1983, one out of five workers were union members; in 2020, that proportion declined to only one in ten members. This decrease in membership doesn't represent a decrease in concern for the labor market. In fact, labor movements are stronger today than ever—they just aren't translating into union membership.[47] Other reasons for the decline in union membership include the following:

- A shift from traditional unionized industries (manufacturing, mining) to high-technology industries (information technology, health care)[48]
- Growth in the employment of part-time and temporary workers
- Growth in small businesses, in which unionization is more costly and difficult to perform
- Globalization of the workforce, particularly among low-wage employers[49]

What are labor organizations doing to stop the decline in union membership? The answer, according to one union official, is "energized organizing." First, unions are targeting previously ignored service workers such as janitors, housekeeping professionals, food service employees and retail associates. Furthermore, unions see recent immigrants, the fastest-growing segment of working people in the United States, as a potent prospect for union growth.[50]

Second, the AFL-CIO has embraced an aggressive unionization strategy. Richard Trumka, president of the AFL-CIO, has argued that "Republicans, and too many democrats, have rigged our economy to enrich the select few. . . . There is a Wall Street wing that seeks to undermine Donald Trump's promises to workers." Trumka has also pointed out the efforts that unions are taking to organize white-collar workers such as graduate students and technology professionals, as well as hotel and fast-food workers.[51]

Chip Somodevilla/Getty Images

Richard Trumka takes on both political parties, questioning the way politicians have failed to address the inability of future generations to earn as much money as their parents.

14.5b Globalization and Technological Change

The importation of steel, consumer electronics, automobiles, clothing, textiles, and shoes from foreign countries creates a loss of jobs in the United States for the domestic workers who would otherwise produce these products. Furthermore, foreign subsidiaries of U.S. corporations such as Carrier, Westinghouse, and Xerox have been accused by labor unions of exporting the jobs of U.S. workers. As a result, unions are demanding more government protection against imports, seeking to protect U.S. jobs from low-cost overseas producers. Adding to that trend, in recent years the service sector of the U.S. economy has witnessed the outsourcing of white-collar jobs to foreign employers in locations such as India and Indonesia.

offshoring
Work that was previously carried out in one country is moved to another country.

More and more Americans are worried about their jobs being filled by people in other countries. **Offshoring**, defined as shifting work that was previously carried out in one country to another country, has been examined with great fear and trepidation in the last 20 years. The United States is now at a critical crossroads in how we deal with offshoring of American jobs. There is no question that most of the recent growth in U.S. companies has come from outside of the country. Companies argue that to remain competitive against their foreign rivals they must take advantage of lower-cost labor in countries such as India and China—perpetuating the continual loss of union jobs in the United States. Statistics show that between 2001 and 2018, the United States lost 3.7 million jobs to China alone.[52]

To bring back jobs, President Donald Trump renegotiated the North Atlantic Free Trade Agreement (NAFTA) to ensure fewer jobs would go to Mexico and more would stay in the United States. The revised agreement, signed in 2020, is known as the United States–Mexico–Canada Agreement (USMCA). Since this time, President Joe Biden has pointed to the USMCA to improve North American competitiveness and keep jobs from moving to China.

Regardless of these efforts, however, most of the job losses that occur in the United States resulted from technology advances, rather than from globalization.[53] Improvements in computer technology and highly automated operating systems have lowered the demand for certain types of employees while increasing the demand for others. Decline in membership in the auto, steel, rubber, and transportation unions illustrates the job losses from technology, but new jobs in healthcare, software development, data analytics, mental health, digital marketing, and human resource management illustrate that when old jobs die new ones are born. In fact, U.S. workers in 1995 had around a 7.3% chance of losing their jobs in any given quarter. Today, that figure is down below 6%.[54] Instead of trying to slow down technological change to preserve existing jobs, it might make sense for unions to focus on embracing technological change to help create more jobs. . . . and then figure out what this means for unions and employers?

Summary

LO 1 A formal union organizing campaign is used to solicit employee support for the union. Once employees demonstrate their desire to unionize through signing authorization cards, the union petitions the NLRB for a secret ballot election. If 51 percent of those voting in the election vote for the union, the NLRB certifies the union as the bargaining representative for all employees in the bargaining unit.

LO 2 Negotiating a labor agreement is a detailed process. Each side prepares a list of proposals it wishes to achieve while also trying to anticipate proposals desired by the other side. Bargaining teams must be selected, and all proposals must be analyzed to determine their impact on and cost to the organization. Managers establish goals that seek to retain control over operations and to minimize costs. Union negotiators focus their demands on improved wages, hours, and working conditions. An agreement is reached when both sides compromise their original positions and final terms fall within the limits of the parties' bargaining zone.

Traditionally, collective bargaining between labor and management has been adversarial. Presently, there is an increased interest in nonadversarial negotiations—that is, negotiations based on mutual gains and a heightened respect between the parties. What the FMCS calls interest-based bargaining is one form of nonadversarial negotiations.

LO 3 Once the labor agreement is established, it sets up the rules and procedures that must be followed in regard to how labor and management proceed. Two important items in any labor agreement pertain to the issue of management rights and the forms of security afforded to the union. Management reserves the right to make decisions related to work, except for cases where clear guidelines have been negotiated. Likewise, management must cooperate with the union as outlined in the labor agreement.

LO 4 When differences arise between labor and management, they are normally resolved through the grievance procedure. Grievance procedures are negotiated and thus reflect the needs and desires of the parties. The typical grievance procedure consists of three, four, or five steps—with each step having specific filing and reply times. Higher-level managers and union officials become involved in disputes at the higher steps of the grievance procedure. The final step of the grievance procedure may be arbitration. Arbitrators render a final decision on problems not resolved at lower grievance steps.

The submission agreement is a statement of the issue to be solved through arbitration. It is simply the problem the parties wish to have settled. The arbitrator must answer the issue by basing the arbitration award on four factors: the content of the labor agreement (or employment policy), the submission agreement as written, testimony and evidence obtained at the hearing, and various arbitration standards developed over time to assist in the resolution of different types of labor–management disputes. Arbitration is not an exact science, because arbitrators assign varying degrees of importance to the evidence and criteria by which disputes are resolved.

LO 5 A major challenge confronting organized labor is to halt the decline in union membership. Unions have tried to change their tactics by focusing on workers not previously addressed by organizing efforts, such as public agencies, low-wage labor, online platforms, and white-collar workers.

Key Terms

arbitrator
authorization card
bargaining power
bargaining unit
bargaining zone
collective bargaining process
craft unions
employee associations
exclusive representation
fair representation doctrine
grievance procedure
industrial unions
interest-based bargaining
labor relations process
National Labor Relations Board (NLRB)
offshoring
rights arbitration
unfair labor practices (ULPs)
union
union security agreement
union steward

HRM **Experience**

Learn about Unions

Unions, like businesses, are dynamic and varied. Some unions are very large, such as the United Auto Workers (UAW) and the American Federation of State, County and Municipal Employees (AFSCME), and represent workers nationally or even internationally. Others are smaller in size—for example, the Writers Guild of America East (WGAE) and the Air Traffic Controllers Association (ATCA)—and represent only specific groups of employees or organize only in a designated geographic area. This exercise will help you learn more about unions.

Assignment

Working individually or in teams, select four or five different unions or employee associations and report on the following. Vary your selections (large/small, public/private, and so on) to widen your understanding of labor organizations.

- History of the union
- Membership size and type of employees represented
- Mission of the union
- Structure of the union, including its major departments
- National officers
- Names of employers with whom the union has an agreement
- Special benefits the union offers members
- Other interesting or pertinent information

The AFL-CIO website (http://www.afl-cio.org) provides a list of all unions—and their websites—affiliated with the federation. National unions and their locals, along with library research, can also provide information. Be prepared to present your findings during a class discussion.

Discussion Questions

LO 1 Describe what it means for HR managers when employees win an election to unionize. What can HR do at this point to make sure the employees' and company's interests align?

LO 2 Of what significance is the bargaining zone in the conduct of negotiations? What are some influences affecting negotiated outcomes? Suppose the negotiations between Data Services International and its union have become deadlocked: What form of bargaining power does each side possess to enforce its bargaining demands? What are the advantages and disadvantages of each form of bargaining power for both the employer and the union?

LO 3 How might a management rights clause determine which conditions an employer can control in the workplace? What is identified by the union security agreement, and how might it reflect results of the bargaining process?

LO 4 a. What are some of the actions being taken by unions to cope with the contemporary challenges they face?

b. How can companies respond to the labor changes that result from increased technology and globalization?

LO 5 What are unions doing to prevent declines in their membership? How are factors such as foreign competition and technological advances causing issues for unions?

CASE STUDY 1 The New Union Battles: Public Unions vs. Rich World Governments

While private-sector unions may be rapidly declining in the United States, public-sector unions are still strong . . . or at least they were. In 2011, public-sector unions representing teachers, prison guards, police officers, rail workers, and civil servants were dealt a blow by their employers—the government. At the forefront of this battle, which began in Wisconsin, was the issue of collective bargaining.

This was not the first time Wisconsin had been at the forefront of collective bargaining. The Wagner Act of 1934 did not grant public employees the right to collective bargaining. In the 1950s and 1960s, public-sector employees pushed for collective bargaining rights. Finally, in 1959, Wisconsin became the first state to grant this right to public employees. In a dramatic turn of events, Wisconsin is now the first state to repeal collective bargaining rights for its public-sector employees.

After a standoff with state Democrats and pro-union demonstrators, Wisconsin Governor Scott Walker and the state legislature decided that public employees did not have the right to collective bargaining. This set off a chain reaction in other states. For example, in 2017 lawmakers in Iowa proposed a bill to prohibit collective bargaining for state employees. This crackdown on collective bargaining could now act as a model for policymakers to overhaul the federal workforce. Public-sector employees are concerned about their future.

Questions

1. Why are politicians so interested in trying to repeal collective bargaining rights for public-sector employees?
2. What risks does losing their collective bargaining rights hold for public employees?
3. As an elected politician charged with making major cuts in your state budget, how would you negotiate with the public-sector unions? As a public-sector union leader, how would you negotiate with the state legislature?

Sources: Thomas Kochan, "Protective Bargaining: How to Prevent the Labor Wars," *Boston Review* (March 23, 2011), http://www.bostonreview.net/BR36.2/thomas_kochan_wisconsin_labor_wars.php; "The Battle Ahead: The Struggle with Public-Sector Unions Should Be about Productivity and Parity, Not Just Spending Cuts," *The Economist* (January 6, 2011), http://www.economist.com/node/17851305; David Morris, "When Unions Are Strong, Americans Enjoy the Fruits of Their Labor," *Huffington Post* (April 8, 2011), http://www.huffingtonpost.com/david-morris/when-unions-are-strong-am_b_846802.html; Clay Masters, "Iowa Moves to Restrict Collective Bargaining for Public Sector Workers," NPR (February 14, 2017); Associated Press, "Scott Walker's Wisconsin Could Be a Model for Trump on Unions," *The Denver Post* (February 6, 2017).

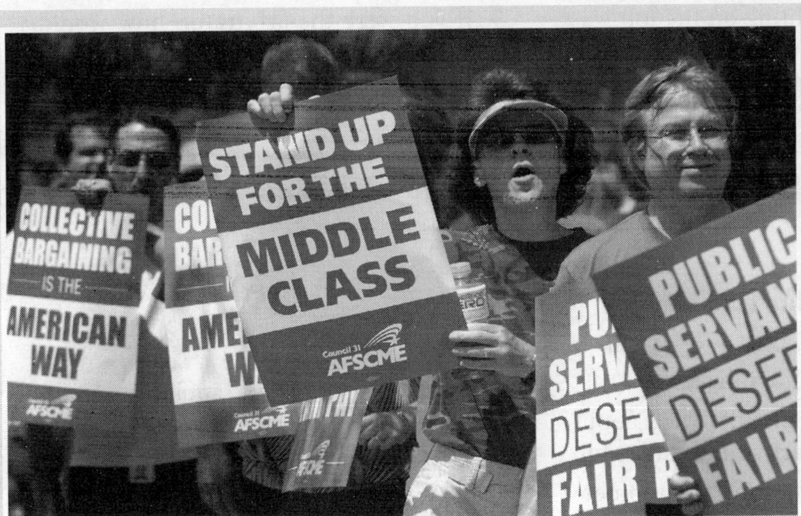

Seth Perlman/AP/Shutterstock.com

AFSCME (American Federation of State, County, and Municipal Employees) union members picket outside the Illinois statehouse in 2011 after their contracted pay raises were cancelled during a state budget crisis.

CASE STUDY 2 The Arbitration Case of Jesse Stansky

At the arbitration hearing, both parties were adamant in their positions. Nancy Huang, HR manager of Phoenix Semiconductor, argued that the grievant, Jesse Stansky, was justly terminated for arguing and hitting a coworker—a direct violation of company policy and the employee handbook. Stansky argued that he had been a good employee during his 10 years of employment.

The submission agreement governing the case read, "It is the employer's position that just cause existed for the discharge of Mr. Jesse Stansky and the penalty was appropriate for the offense committed." Additionally, the employer introduced into evidence the labor agreement, which defined just cause termination as follows:

> Just cause shall serve as the basis for disciplinary action and includes, but is not limited to: dishonesty, inefficiency, unprofessional conduct, failure to report absences, falsification of records, violation of company policy, destruction of property, or possession or being under the influence of alcohol or narcotics.

Stansky was hired as a systems technician on November 20, 2007, a position he held until his termination on October 25, 2021. According to the testimony of Huang, Phoenix Semiconductor strived to maintain a positive and cordial work environment among its employees. Fighting on the job was strictly prohibited. Stansky's performance evaluation showed him to be an average employee, although he had received several disciplinary warnings for poor attendance and one 3-day suspension for a "systems control error." Stansky was generally liked by his coworkers, and several testified on his behalf at the arbitration hearing.

The termination of Stansky concerned an altercation between himself and Gary Lindekin, another systems technician. According to witnesses to the incident, both Stansky and Lindekin became visibly upset over the correct way to calibrate a sensitive piece of production equipment. The argument—one witness called it no more than a heated disagreement—lasted approximately 3 minutes and concluded when Stansky was seen forcefully placing his hand on Lindekin's shoulder. Lindekin took extreme exception to Stansky's behavior and immediately reported the incident to management. After interviews with both Stansky and Lindekin and those who observed the incident, Huang, Samantha Lowry, the employee's immediate supervisor, and Grant Ginn, department manager, decided that Stansky should be terminated for unprofessional conduct and violation of company policy.

Questions

1. Which arguments should be given more weight: those based on company policy, the employee handbook, and the labor agreement or mitigating factors given by the grievant and his witnesses? Explain.
2. How might unprofessional conduct be defined? Explain.
3. If you were the arbitrator, how would you rule in this case? Explain fully the reasons for your decision.

Source: Adapted from an arbitration heard by George W. Bohlander. All names are fictitious.

Answers to Highlights in HRM 1

1. No. Applicants are considered to be employees and, as such, are protected under the law.
2. No. Individual questioning of employees about their union membership or activities is unlawful.
3. No. Except in specific situations (e.g., to promote safety), employees have the right to wear union insignia.
4. Yes.
5. Yes. Blacklisting of job applicants or employees is against labor law.
6. No. During an organizing drive, an employer cannot promise improvements in wages or benefits as a means of defeating the union.

7. Yes. Both nonunion and union employers are subject to unfair labor practice charges.
8. Yes. When a grievance arbitration clause exists in a labor agreement, management must arbitrate cases that seem baseless.
9. Yes. Employees can be disciplined or discharged for work-related misconduct but not solely because of their union affiliations or union sentiments.
10. Yes. Anti-union remarks are not unlawful, provided they are not coercive.

Notes and References

1. Pandej Chintrakam, "Labor Unions and Income Inequality: Evidence from US States," *Journal of Applied Sciences* 11, no. 20 (2011): 3530–3533.
2. Celine McHicholas, Lynn Rhinehart, Margaret Poydock, Heidi Shierholxz, and Daniel Perez, "Why Unions Are Good for Workers—Especially in a Crisis Like COVID-19," Economic Policy Institute (August 25, 2020).
3. Adam Dean, Atheendar Venkataramani, and Simeon Kimmel, "Mortality Rates from COVID-19 Are Lower in Unionized Nursing Homes," *Health Affairs*, September 10, 2020.
4. Donna Brazile, "What Have Unions Done for Us?" CNN (September 4, 2012), http://www.cnn.com/2012/09/04/opinion/brazile-unions/.
5. For an expanded model of the labor relations process, see John Dunlop, *Industrial Relations Systems* (New York: Henry Holt, 1958), Chapter 1. This book is a classic in the labor relations field. Also, those interested in labor relations may wish to explore in greater detail the historical developments of the U.S. labor movement. Much can be learned about the current operations of labor organizations and the philosophies of labor officials from labor's historical context. A brief but comprehensive history of labor unions can be found in undergraduate labor management textbooks such as those listed among the references in this chapter.
6. Marisa Fernandez and Sara Fischer, "More Than 30 Media Companies Have Unionized in the Past 2 Years," *Axios* (April 9, 2019).
7. Kavi Guppta, "Will Labor Unions Survive in the Era of Automation?" *Forbes* (October 12, 2016); Nina Foo, "Millennials Are the Key to Saving Unions," *Organizer* (February 8, 2017); Lydia Saad, "Americans' Support for Labor Unions Continues to Recover," Gallup (August 17, 2015).
8. "Union Members Summary," U.S. Bureau of Labor Statistics (January 22, 2021), https://www.bls.gov/news.release/union2.nr0.htm#:~:text=The%20percentage%20of%20workers%20represented,total%20wage%20and%20salary%20employment.
9. Sara Horowitz, "Will Gawker Employees' Decision to Organize Make Unions Cool Again?" *Fast Company* (April 24, 2015).
10. Lydia Saad, "Labor Union Approval Steady at 15-Year High," Gallup (August 30, 2018), https://news.gallup.com/poll/241679/labor-union-approval-steady-year-high.aspx.
11. Celine McNicholas, Heidi Shierholz, Daniel Perez, Lynn Rhinehart, and Margaret Poydock, "Why Unions Are Good for Workers—Especially in a Crisis Like COVID-19," Economic Policy Institute (August 25, 2020), https://www.epi.org/publication/why-unions-are-good-for-workers-especially-in-a-crisis-like-covid-19-12-policies-that-would-boost-worker-rights-safety-and-wages/.
12. "Union Workers More Likely Than Nonunion Workers to Have Healthcare Benefits in 2019," U.S. Bureau of Labor Statistics (October 28, 2019), https://www.bls.gov/opub/ted/2019/union-workers-more-likely-than-nonunion-workers-to-have-healthcare-benefits-in-2019.htm.
13. Nicole S. Cohen and Greig de Peuter, "New Media Unions: Organizing Digital Journalists," March 25, 2020; Foo, "Millennials Are the Key to Saving Unions"; Saad, "Americans' Support for Labor Unions Continues to Recover"; Kate Bronfenbrenner, "The Role of Union Strategies in NLRB Certification Elections," *Industrial and Labor Relations Review* 50, no. 2 (1997): 195–212.
14. Karen Weise and Noam Scheiber, "Why Amazon Workers Sided with the Company over a Union," *The New York Times*, April 16, 2021.
15. "Challenges Continue for Organized Labor in 2017," *Law 360* (March 15, 2017); Selena Maranjian, "Unions: Good or Bad?" *The Motley Fool* (November 22, 2014).
16. Barbara L. Rau, "The Diffusion of HR Practices in Unions," *Human Resources Management Review* 22, no. 1 (2012): 27–42.
17. Dave Lee, "Amazon Raises US Employee Pay after Bruising Union Fight," *Financial Times*, April 28, 2021.
18. Shad S. Morris, "Book Review of Offshoring of American Jobs," *Human Resource Management* 50, no. 2 (2011): 303–306.
19. Rob Dube, "Why Open Book Management Creates Better Businesses and Stronger Teams," *Forbes*, January 9, 2020.
20. William H. Holley, Kenneth M. Jennings, and Roger S. Wolters, *The Labor Relations Process* (New York: Cengage Learning, 2011).

21. Forbes Human Resources Council, "5 Reasons Your Small Business Needs a Human Resources Professional," *Forbes* (November 3, 2016), https://www.forbes.com/sites/forbeshumanresourcescouncil/2016/11/03/5-reasons-your-small-businessneeds-a-human-resources-professional/#2163c28385f2.
22. "Union Organizing: Authorization Cards: What Steps Should an Employer Take When Presented with Union Authorization Cards?" Society for Human Resources Management (June 1, 2012), https://www.shrm.org/resourcesandtools/tools-and-samples/hr-qa/pages/authorizationcardpresentation.aspx.
23. Neil King Jr., Thomas M. Burton, and Kris Maher, "Political Fight over Unions Escalate," *Wall Street Journal* (February 22, 2011), http://online.wsj.com/news/articles/SB10001424052748703800204576158851079665840.
24. Darragh Roche, "Labor Day 2020: Here's Where Major Unions Stand on Trump vs. Biden Election," *Newsweek* (September 7, 2020), https://www.newsweek.com/labor-day-2020-major-unions-trump-biden-election-1530073.
25. "Organizing Institute: Three-Day Training," AFL-CIO, http://www.aflcio.org/Get-Involved/Become-a-UnionOrganizer/Organizing-Institute/Three-Day-Training.
26. Arthur B. Shostak, *The Cyberunion Handbook: Transforming Labor through Computer Technology* (New York: Routledge, 2015).
27. Kati Sipp, "The Internet vs. the Labor Movement: Why Unions Are Latecomers to Digital Organizing," New Labor Forum (April 23, 2016).
28. Neil Bucklew, Christopher N. Ellison, and Jeffrey D. Houghton, "Shared Governance and Academic Collective Bargaining in American Higher Education: A Potential Model for US Participation in the Global Experience of Works Councils and Codetermination," *Journal of Collective Bargaining in the Academy* 4, no. 1 (2013): 1–13.
29. "Election Report for Cases Closed," *FY 2016* (May 1, 2017): 1.
30. Robert Iafolla, "Unions Win Same Share of 2020 Mail, In-Person Elections," *Bloomberg Law* (October 27, 2020), https://news.bloomberglaw.com/daily-labor-report/unions-win-same-share-of-2020-mail-ballot-in-person-elections.
31. "Union Members Summary," Bureau of Labor Statistics (May 1, 2017).
32. Leigh Thompson, *The Mind and Heart of the Negotiator*, 3rd ed. (Upper Saddle River, NJ: Prentice Hall, 2004).
33. John Valery White, "How to Play Your Hand: Lessons for Negotiators from Poker," *UNLV Gaming Law Journal* 2, no. 2 (2011).
34. Joel Cutcher-Gershenfeld, Thomas Kochan, John-Paul Ferguson, and Betty Barrett, "Collective Bargaining in the Twenty-First Century: A Negotiations Institution at Risk," *Negotiation Journal* 23, no. 3 (July 2007): 249.
35. Ross Stagner and Hjalmar Rosen, *Psychology of Union–Management Relations* (Belmont, CA: Wadsworth, 1965), 95–97. This is another classic in the field of labor–management relations.
36. The National Labor Relations Board offers an excellent book on the National Labor Relations Act. This book discusses good-faith bargaining as well as other important legal issues—for example, employers covered by the law, unfair labor practices, and election procedures. See *Basic Guide to the National Labor Relations Act* (Washington, DC: U.S. Government Printing Office, 1997).
37. Joe Stanley, interview by author, January 5, 2008, Phoenix, AZ.
38. The FMCS has a complete and comprehensive program to train labor and management negotiators in the art and techniques of interest-based bargaining (IBB). Information on the IBB program can be obtained from the FMCS national headquarters at 2100 K Street, N.W., Washington, DC 20427 or from FMCS district offices.
39. Leonard J. Marcus, Barry C. Dorn, and Eric J. McNulty, "The Walk in the Woods: A Step-by-Step Method for Facilitating Interest-Based Negotiation and Conflict Resolution," *Negotiation Journal* 28, no. 3 (2012): 337–349.
40. Roger J. Peters and Deborah Bavarnick Mastin, "To Mediate or Not to Mediate: That Is the Question," *Dispute Resolution Journal* 62, no. 2 (2007): 14.
41. Personal conversation of one of the authors with a head of HR for a large industrial company.
42. *Grievance Guide*, 12th ed. (Washington, DC: BNA Books, 2007); Paul J. Gollan and David Lewin, "Employee Representation in Non-Union Firms: An Overview," *Industrial Relations: A Journal of Economy and Society* 52, no. s1 (2013): 173–193.
43. Vera Riggs, Labor–Management Relations Conference, August 11, 2007, Phoenix, AZ.
44. What are the steps typically found in a grievance procedure? SHRM HR Q&As. (Accessed Nov. 5, 2021).
45. Lawrence Mishel, "Unions, Inequality, and Faltering Middle-Class Wages," *Issue Brief* 342 (2012).
46. Arbitration awards are not final in all cases. Arbitration awards may be overturned through the judicial process if it can be shown that the arbitrator was prejudiced or failed to render an award based on the essence of the agreement.
47. Eli Rosenberg, "Workers Are Fired up. But Union Participation Is Still on the Decline, New Statistics Show," *The Washington Post* (January 23, 2020).
48. Lance Compa, "Labor at a Crossroads: How Unions Can Thrive in the 21st Century," *The American Prospect* (January 27, 2015), http://prospect.org/article/labor-crossroads-how-unions-can-thrive-21st-century.

49. Yuki Noguchi, "AFL-CIO's Trumka Says Both Parties Have Lost Focus on U.S. Workers," NPR (April 4, 2017).
50. Will Kimball and Robert E. Scott, "China Trade, Outsourcing and Jobs," Economic Policy Institute (December 11, 2014), http://www.epi.org/publication/china-trade-outsourcing-and-jobs/.
51. Kimberly Amadeo, "How Outsourcing Jobs Affects the U.S. Economy," *The Balance* (March 30, 2017).
52. Robert E. Scott and Zane Mokhiber. January 30, 2020. Growing China Trade Deficit Cost 3.7 Million American Jobs Between 2001 and 2018. Economic Policy Institute.
53. Robert D. Atkinson and Luke Dascoli. September 13, 2021. Even After COVID-19, the U.S. Labor Market Remains More Stable Than People Think. Information Technology & Innovation Foundation.
54. Ibid.

Nuad Contributor/Shutterstock.com

CHAPTER 15

International Human Resources Management

Learning Outcome

After studying this chapter, you should be able to

LO 1 Explain the political, economic, sociocultural, and technological factors in different countries that HR managers need to consider.

LO 2 Summarize the key differences between domestic and international HRM.

LO 3 Explain how to set up a compensation system that may account for both global and local standards.

LO 4 Explain how labor relations differ around the world.

Have you ever noticed that much of what you buy is not made in the United States? The shirt you are wearing right now was probably made in Bangladesh, Vietnam, Indonesia, or China. The brand, of course, may be American (such as Abercrombie & Fitch, Hollister, or American Eagle), but that just means that the company is headquartered here. In fact, despite antiglobalization sentiments, most companies today are involved in international business in one way or another.

Managing human resources across these international settings may help to leverage specialized skills, provide cheaper labor, or even bring new ideas into the company. However, managing human resources internationally also makes everything even more complicated.[1] Such complications arise because each country possesses unique political policies, economic situations, social and cultural norms, and technological capacities. The first part of this chapter describes some of the environmental factors that affect the work of managers in a global setting. We show how a political, economic, sociocultural, and technological (PEST) analysis can help effectively assess the threats and opportunities facing human resources management (HRM) in a global setting. Just as with domestic operations, the dimensions of the environment form the context in which HRM decisions in foreign countries are made.

Next, we show how companies respond to these environmental complications. We examine the different forms companies may take to help them compete in a global environment—international, multidomestic, global, and transnational. In many respects, these organizational forms influence the kinds of managerial and HR issues a company faces. A major portion of this chapter deals with the various HR activities involved in the recruitment, selection, development, and compensation of employees working abroad. However, as we explain later in this chapter, workers stationed all over the United States are increasingly finding themselves working virtually with people from other cultures who speak different languages. This creates challenges not only for them but also for firms' HR managers.

15.1 Analyzing Your International Environment

LO1

Explain the political, economic, sociocultural, and technological factors in different countries that HR managers need to consider.

In Chapter 1, we highlighted some of the global trends affecting HRM. Because political, economic, social, and technological conditions are constantly shifting across the world, how people are managed in those changing environments will shift as well. To systematically help companies manage in the global environment, a political, economic, sociocultural, and technological (PEST) analysis can be conducted. It acts as an audit of a company's environmental influences to help it determine its strategy and HR response.

Conducting a PEST analysis entails scanning different contextual environments to understand the long-term trends and how they might impact a company.[2] As an HR manager, PEST analysis can help you to (1) spot business or personnel opportunities, and obtain advanced warning of threats; (2) spot trends in the business environment so you can proactively adapt to these changes; (3) avoid implementing HR practices in a particular country where they may fail; and (4) break free of old habits and assumptions about how people should be managed to help bring about innovative ideas for the entire company.

Figure 15.1 PEST Analysis

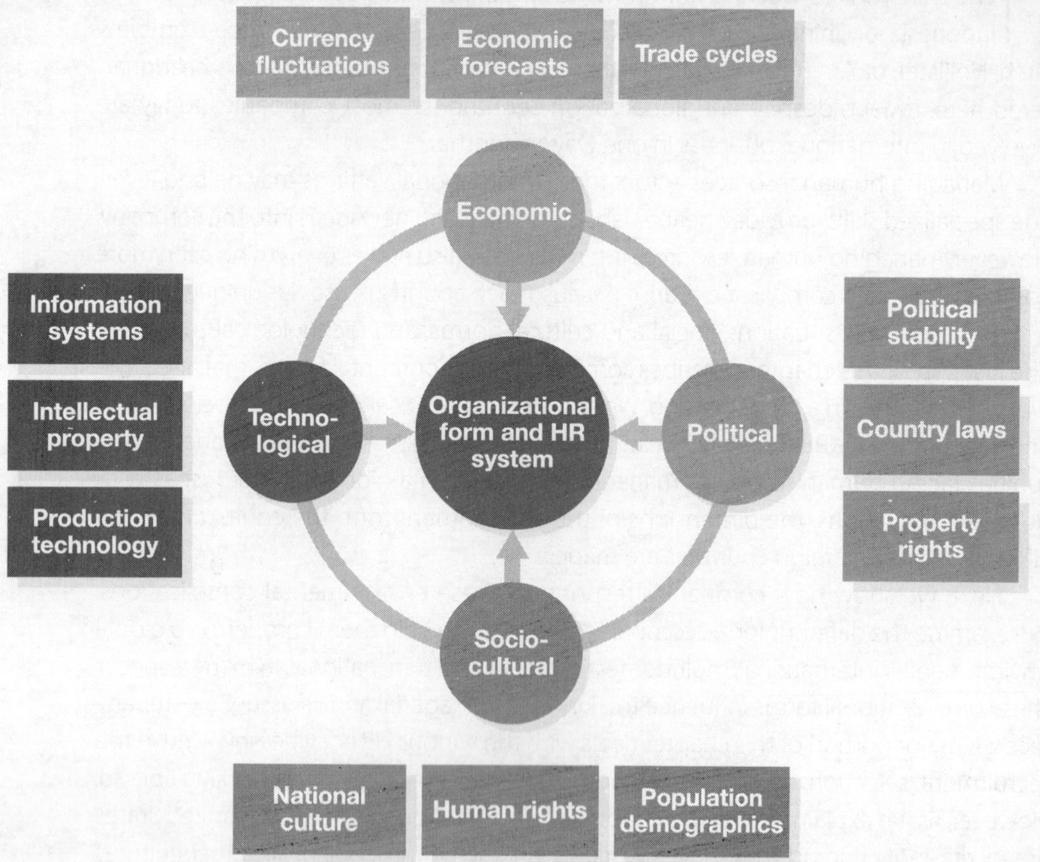

We begin by showing you how to perform a PEST analysis (Figure 15.1)—something completely different from an analysis of the issues you may be facing with household insects and rodents.

15.1a Political Factors

political factors
External factors including labor laws, property rights, and patent processes.

First, **political factors** are assessed by examining a country's labor laws, property rights, and patents. For example, when the Ohio-based welding company Lincoln Electric started operations in Brazil, it was not able to offer its yearly bonus program based on performance because any bonuses paid for two consecutive years become a legal entitlement.[3]

In many countries, particularly those in Africa, property rights are poorly protected by governments. Whoever has the political power or authority can seize others' property with few or no repercussions. Civil unrest can also lead to the poor enforcement of property rights. Companies have less incentive to locate factories or invest in countries experiencing strife. Another issue relates to intellectual property rights—rights related to patents, trademarks, and so forth.

15.1b Economic Factors

Economic factors consist of trends related to market and trade cycles, specific industry changes, customer preferences, and country economic growth forecasts. For example, in 1995, the World Trade Organization (WTO) was formalized as a cooperative forum where country leaders could come together and increase free trade across the world. As of 2021, the WTO member countries included more than 160 nations and covered 98 percent of all international trade.[4] In addition, countries are continually negotiating free trade agreements with each other in hopes of increasing their economic activity and power.

Eric LAFFORGUE/Gamma-Rapho/Getty Images

In 2016, South Africa's parliament approved a bill allowing the government to take land from individual and corporate owners if it is in the public interest. "South Africa Approves Land Expropriation Bill," BBC News, May 26,2016.

As an example, starting in March 2021 China's and Norway's chief trade negotiators began discussing a free trade agreement between the two countries. Norway will gain market access to major exports of China and Indonesia. For China, this agreement will help expand its trade through all of Europe. Their collective goal is to promote economic development, especially in the wake of the global coronavirus pandemic.[5]

economic factors
External factors including the strength or weakness of markets, stability of trade cycles, specific industry conditions, customer preferences, and government's economic policies.

15.1c Sociocultural Factors

Beyond the economic issues just mentioned, a country's **sociocultural factors** (communications, religion, values and ideologies, education, and social structure) also have important implications when it comes to a company's decision about when and how to do business there. Many U.S. companies have found India to be an attractive place to locate their facilities, particularly call centers, because of low labor costs and language similarities, Moreover, the U.S. military's long-term stay in Panama developed economic relationships that have proved valuable for both countries. Now that the Panama Canal has been expanded to accommodate larger freight ships, the United States is looking to take advantage of these close ties.[6]

sociocultural factors
External factors including method and style of communications, religions, values and ideologies, education standards, and social structure.

By recognizing and accommodating different ideologies, religious beliefs, communication styles, education systems, and social structures, managers stand a better chance of understanding the culture of a **host country**—that is, a country in which an international business operates. Even in countries that have close language or cultural links, HR practices can be dramatically different. For example, night shifts may be taboo. Employers might be expected to provide employees with meals while at work and transportation between home and work. In most of the Islamic Middle East, it is completely acceptable to ask coworkers very personal questions about their children, especially their sons, but never about their wives.[7]

host country
A country in which an international corporation operates.

In some countries, like Malaysia, corporate leaders fashion "personnel sharia," which represent human resource rules to ensure that employees exhibit ethical and moral values in their conduct at work.

Odua Images/Shutterstock.com

(Source: P. Sloane-White, "Working in the Islamic Economy: Sharia-ization and the Malaysian Workplace," Sojourn: *Journal of Social Issues in Southeast Asia* 26, no. 2 (2011): 304–334.)

In another example, Netflix has encountered challenges in expanding internationally. In 2015, Netflix had about 30 international employees who were initially uncomfortable with Netflix's culture of bluntness, which was at sharp odds with their home culture of communicating in subtler ways. Netflix is currently working to reconcile the company's culture with some national cultures, which have notably different communication preferences.[8]

15.1d Technological Factors

technological factors External factors pertaining to the technological infrastructure and investments, information systems, manufacturing equipment, and consumer access to technology.

Related to a country's sociocultural norms, where it stands technologically also influences the threats and opportunities that foreign companies face. **Technological factors** refer to the maturity of manufacturing equipment, information systems, technology platforms, research funding, and consumer access to technology. Even in less-developed countries where manufacturing is typically stronger due to a low cost of labor and a high cost of capital-intensive equipment, labor-saving technology is becoming more affordable and accessible. Take, for instance, a textile factory in Vietnam. It is more cost-effective for the factory to purchase high-tech threading equipment to spin the cotton into thread than it is to hire hundreds of people to thread the cotton by hand, even when the average wage for such employees is less than $100 per month.

While advances in technology have pushed some economies toward more service-based jobs, information systems and technology platforms have also increased the rate at which these services can be traded across countries. Along with the creation of the WTO, 1995 also signified the beginning of the Internet era. America Online (AOL) went public in 1995, marking the beginning of integrated technology platforms that could be shared instantaneously across the world. *Integrated technology platforms* comprise common operating systems, such as Microsoft Windows 365, that can be used across multiple computers connected through the Internet. Through these common platforms, work becomes less specific to particular companies and countries.

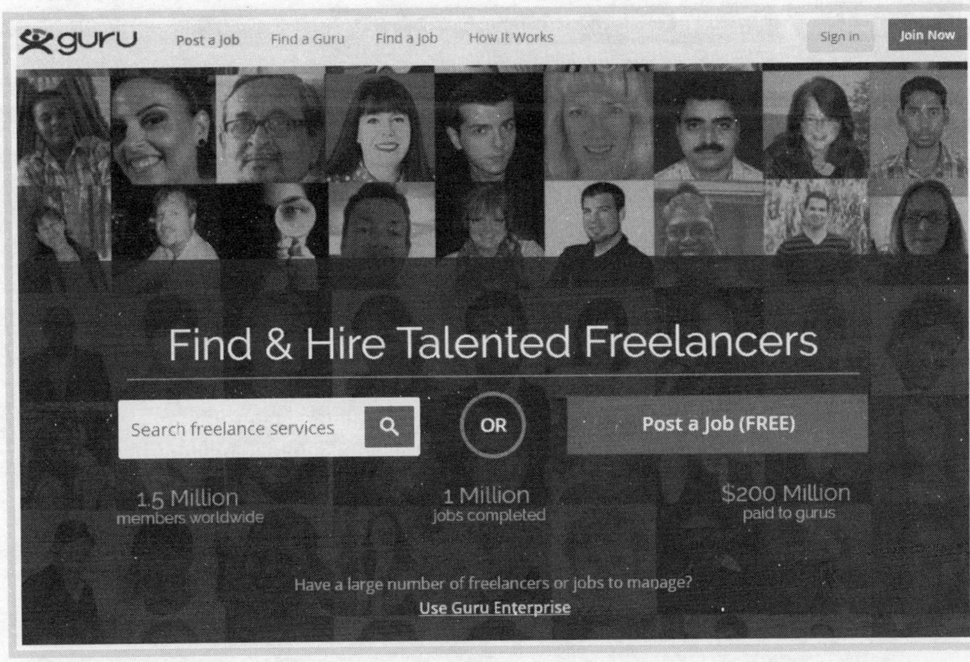

Source: Guru.com

Gig worker platforms like Upwork and Guru help you connect to talent from all over the world.

In this era, employees have become empowered to compete without the need for support from a large company. For example, websites such as those operated by Fiverr and Upwork serve as an online marketplace where individuals can offer various services and compete for business throughout the world. Imagine you are interested in developing a new website for your company. By going to the Internet, you can select various individuals offering these specific services. They may be from Manila, Mumbai, Manhattan, or Munich.

In sum, changes in the PEST factors have altered both the way companies are formed and how they manage their human resources.

15.1e Analyzing Your International Operations

International business operations can take several different forms. A large percentage carry on their international business with only limited facilities in foreign countries. Others, particularly *Fortune* 500 corporations, have extensive facilities and personnel in various countries around the world. Dell, for example, actually employs more people outside the United States than within it. Managing these resources effectively and integrating their activities to achieve global advantage is a challenge to the leadership of these companies.

Figure 15.2 shows four basic types of organizations and how they differ in the degree to which international activities are separated to respond to the local regions and integrated to achieve global efficiencies. The **international corporation** is essentially a domestic firm that builds on its existing capabilities to penetrate overseas markets. Companies such as Honda, General Electric (GE), and Procter & Gamble used this approach to gain access to Europe—they essentially adapted their existing products for overseas markets without changing much else about their normal operations.

international corporation
A domestic firm that uses its existing capabilities to move into overseas markets.

Figure 15.2 Types of Organizations

multidomestic corporation (MDC)
A firm with independent business units operating in multiple countries.

A **multidomestic corporation (MDC)** is a more complex form that usually has fully autonomous units operating in multiple countries. Shell, Philips, and ITT are three typical MDCs. These companies have traditionally given their foreign subsidiaries a great deal of latitude to address local issues such as consumer preferences, political pressures, and economic trends in different regions of the world. Frequently these subsidiaries are run as independent companies without much integration.

global corporation
A firm that has integrated its worldwide operations through a centralized home office.

The **global corporation**, in contrast, can be viewed as a multinational firm that maintains control of its operations worldwide from the country in which it is headquartered. Japanese companies, such as Matsushita and NEC, tend to treat the world market as a unified whole and try to combine their activities in each country to maximize their efficiencies on a global scale. These companies operate much like a domestic firm, except that they view the whole world as their marketplace.

transnational corporation
A firm that attempts to balance local responsiveness and global scale via a network of specialized operating units.

Finally, a **transnational corporation** attempts to achieve the local responsiveness of an MDC while also achieving the efficiencies of a global firm. To balance this global/local dilemma, a transnational corporation uses a network structure that coordinates specialized facilities positioned around the world. Through this flexible structure, the firm provides autonomy to its operations in foreign countries but brings these separate activities together into an integrated whole. For most companies, the transnational form represents an ideal rather than a reality. McDonald's is an example of a transnational corporation. At local restaurants, it often offers culture-specific food items, such as the vegetarian McAloo Tikki in India, the McKebab in Israel, and the Hawaiian Deluxe Breakfast complete with Spam, rice, eggs, and hash browns. With 31,000 restaurants across 119 countries serving 58 million people each day, it makes sense that McDonald's overseas revenue makes up nearly 65 percent of the company's total revenue, and that McDonalds' core burger-fries-and-shakes menu is tweaked to cater to local tastes.[9]

Akhil Wadhwani/IndiaPicture/Alamy Stock Photo

McDonald's McAloo Tikki can be found only in India.

Although various forms of organizations exist, in this chapter we will generally refer to any company that conducts business outside its home country as an international business. Perhaps not surprisingly, with the global environment being filled by companies originating from different countries and operating in multiple cultures, increased pressure is being placed on the HRM function. International HRM is being seen more and more as a key source of competitive advantage for international businesses. In this environment, HR units can no longer operate as separate groups attached only by a common brand and finances. HR managers must more effectively manage and move people across country borders. In the next section, we examine the different HR practices used to manage in these complex circumstances.

expatriates (home-country and third-country nationals)
Employees from the home country or a third country who are on international assignment.

LO2
Summarize the key differences between domestic and international HRM.

15.2 Managing Your International Operations

When a company expands globally, HR managers are generally responsible for ensuring that its operations are staffed with the right people. There are three main ways a company can staff an international operation. First, the company can send people from its home country or from another nonhost country. These employees are often referred to as **expatriates**. Expatriates can be further classified as **home-country nationals**, if they are from the home country, or as **third-country nationals**, if they are from another country that is not the home or host country. Second, the company can hire host-country nationals, natives of the host country, to do the managing. Third, it can hire third-country nationals, natives of a country other than the home country or the host country. Most corporations use all three approaches for staffing their multinational operations.[10] Note, however, that host countries sometimes restrict firms' choices by passing laws and

host-country nationals
Employees who are natives of the host country.

third-country nationals
Employees who are natives of a country other than the home country or the host country.

Figure 15.3 Changes in International Staffing over Time

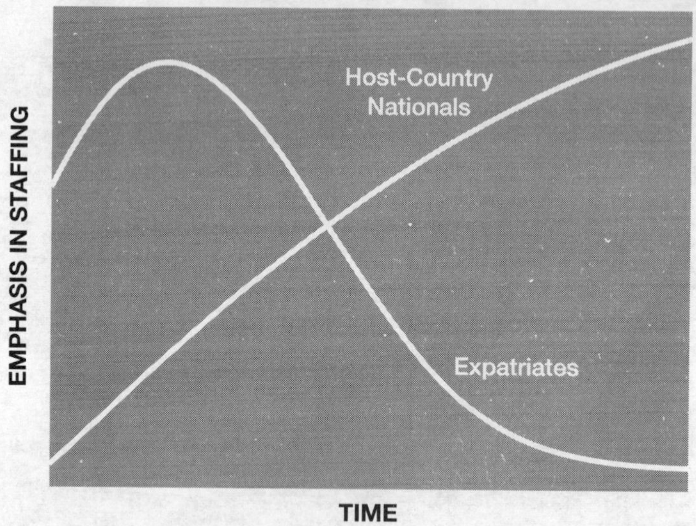

regulations designed to increase employment of host-country individuals. Tax incentives, tariffs, and quotas are all measured frequently implemented by the host country to encourage local hiring.

As shown in Figure 15.3, in the early stages of their international expansion, organizations often send home-country nationals to establish activities (particularly in less-developed countries) and to work with local governments. This is generally very costly. Traditionally, expatriates have received generous salaries, automobiles, full relocation services, private schooling for their children, trips home, and other perks. Collectively, these services may end up costing more than $300,000 yearly, on average, making the cost of a typical 3-year expatriate assignment more than $1 million.

In recent years, there has also been a trend to send expatriates on shorter, project-based assignments (1 to 6 months versus 1 to 3 years) and to shift more quickly toward hiring host-country nationals. This strategy has three main advantages:

- Hiring local citizens is generally less costly than relocating expatriates. Local citizens also know the cultural and political landscape of the country and are often more likely to be able to gain the support of local staff members.
- Since local governments usually want good jobs for their citizens, foreign employers may be required to hire locally.
- Most customers want to do business with companies (and people) they perceive to be local versus foreign.

Because U.S. companies want to be viewed as true international citizens, there has also been a trend away from hiring expatriates to head up operations in foreign countries, especially European countries. ABB, Eli Lilly, and PepsiCo, which have strong regional organizations, have tended to replace their U.S. expatriate managers with local managers as quickly as possible. In addition to hiring local managers to head their foreign divisions and plants, more companies are using third-country nationals. Third-country nationals are often multilingual and already acclimated to the host country's culture—perhaps because they live in a nearby region. Thus, they are also less costly to relocate and sometimes better able to cope culturally with foreign environments.

As part of this trend, companies may use expatriates only when a specific set of skills is needed or when individuals in the host country require development. Typically, expatriate assignments fail when the expatriate is selected because of their technical skills alone, rather than the ability to adapt to the host country. For example, U.S. managers value their time as a commodity, so they tend to focus more intently on productivity and efficiency. However, this kind of manager may be frustrated by—and even frustrating to—host-country nationals in countries such as China, where *quanxi*, or connections, are more important than money.[11] To help their expatriates adapt in Asia and elsewhere, firms are finding it helpful to pair them with local "buddies," or host-country mentors, or even make them complete cultural training before departing.

15.2a Recruiting Internationally

Improved telecommunications and travel have made it easier to match up employers and employees of all kinds worldwide. For example, in 2017 we worked with Microsoft to help this company improve the recruiting and connectedness of its employees located all over the world. The majority of Microsoft's current and potential employees are located outside the United States—which is also the case for most large corporations today.

HR departments must be particularly responsive to the cultural, political, and legal environments both domestically and abroad when recruiting internationally. Companies such as Starbucks, Lockheed Martin, and Honeywell have made a special effort to create codes of conduct for employees throughout the world to ensure that standards of ethical and legal behavior are known and understood. Lockheed Martin has a strong international ethics program to ensure all decisions throughout the company are made with integrity. For example, its vision statement stresses three principles: (1) doing what is right, (2) respecting others, and (3) performing with excellence. All employees are required to undergo business conduct and compliance training. This training helps employees deal with difficult issues related to export control, insider trading, international business practices, kickbacks and gratuities, and the Truth in Negotiations Act. The programs are offered in more than 21 languages.[12]

The regulatory environment outside the United States often differs substantially from that found inside the country. Differences in the regulations faced by international businesses may range from those that cover procedures for recruiting and screening to those governing employees' working conditions, pay and incentives, and retirement provisions. In Japan, for example, criminal background checks on candidates are not allowed. In France, employees can work only 35 hours per week until overtime and rest days start to be required.[13]

In addition, almost all countries have work permit or visa restrictions that apply to foreigners. A **work permit or visa** is a document issued by a government granting authority to a foreign individual to seek employment in that government's country. Since the terrorist attacks of September 11, 2001, getting skilled foreign workers into the United States had generally been difficult for companies. However, in 2017, the U.S. government made it even more difficult for workers to get a work permit or H1B visa. H1B visas were created to import specialized technological and scientific talent that was not sufficiently available in the United States. This was particularly difficult news for companies such as Google, Apple, LinkedIn, and SnapChat, which already have

work permit or visa
A government document granting a foreign individual the right to seek employment.

a difficult time finding qualified tech workers. According to one study, the United States has a shortage of approximately 110,000 computer science jobs annually.[14] Even so, students who come from foreign countries to attend school in the United States are finding it more difficult to get jobs with U.S. companies after they graduate.

To resolve this dilemma, many Indian and Chinese nationals living in the United States are being heavily recruited by companies and governments to return to their home countries and work there. For example, when one former Microsoft employee was denied an H1B visa, he went home to India and started his own company. It's now valued at more than $7 billion. That's a lot of lost tax revenue and jobs for the United States.

Making matters worse, other countries have become less restrictive than the United States in terms of granting foreign residents citizenship and work permits. The United Kingdom, for example, gives graduates of the world's top 50 business schools an automatic right to work there for a year. In addition, the European Union is contemplating introducing a "blue card" system designed to expedite the EU citizenship of talented employees.[15] Whatever the employee's destination, HR managers need to ensure that work permits and visas are applied for early in the relocation process.

To recruit employees at the executive level for their international businesses, companies often use executive recruiting firms such as Heidrick & Struggles in the United States or Spencer Stuart in the United Kingdom. At lower levels, as Chapter 7 explained, companies recruiting abroad often need to advertise their firms and employment "brand" to recruits who are not familiar with it. In countries such as India and China, an employer's reputation is extremely important to candidates' families—sometimes more important than the salary.

Many employers have learned that the best way to find workers in less well-developed countries is through referrals and radio announcements because many people lack sufficient reading or writing skills. Other firms use international recruiting firms to find skilled labor abroad.

A visa is issued to foreign individuals granting them the right to work in that country.

Alex Stojanov/Alamy Stock Photo

Notably, as mentioned earlier, some countries require the employment of locals if adequate numbers of skilled people are available. Specific exceptions are sometimes granted (officially or unofficially) in certain cases, as for Mexican farm workers in the United States and for Italian, Spanish, Greek, and Turkish workers in Germany and the Benelux countries (Belgium, the Netherlands, and Luxembourg). Foreign workers invited to perform needed labor are usually referred to as **guest workers**. Foreign workers with H2B visas can come to the United States for a maximum of 9 months to perform temporary, nonagricultural seasonal work on a one-time basis only. These types of visas are often used in conjunction with recruiting workers for entry-level positions in hotels and restaurants during peak travel seasons.

guest workers
Foreign workers invited to perform needed labor.

Although hiring non-nationals can result in lower direct labor costs for a company, the indirect costs—those related to housing, language training, health services, recruitment, transportation, and so on—can be substantial. Some companies competing in industries with acute talent shortages are nonetheless finding the expenditures worthwhile.[16] Nursing is one such industry. (See the Case Study at the end of the chapter.)

Apprenticeships

A major source of trained labor in European nations is apprenticeship training programs (described in Chapter 7). In Europe, a dual-track system of education directs a large number of youths into vocational training. The German system of apprenticeship training, one of the best in Europe, provides training for office and shop jobs under a three-way responsibility contract between the apprentice, the apprentice's parents, and the organization. At the conclusion of their training, apprentices can work for any employer but generally receive seniority credit with the training firm if they remain in it. France has been able to draw on its "Grandes Écoles" for centuries. Created during the Renaissance to fulfill a need that universities were not meeting at the time, the Grandes Écoles educate prospective engineers up to the equivalent level of master of engineering.

Staffing Transnational Teams

In addition to focusing on individuals, companies are increasingly using transnational teams to conduct international business. **Transnational teams** are composed of members of multiple nationalities who work virtually on projects that span multiple countries. Aware that many products being created in developed economies will have a limited market in developing economies, companies such as P&G, GE, and Tata Motors have turned to transnational teams to help develop low-cost but high-quality products for the poor. For example, Tata Motors developed the Tata Nano, a car priced at only $2,000. Known as the cheapest car in the world, the Tata Nano was developed by a large transnational team, with suppliers in different countries designing specific parts to meet a price-sensitive threshold.[17]

transnational teams
Teams composed of members of multiple nationalities working on projects that span multiple countries.

Teams such as these are especially useful for performing tasks that the firm as a whole is not yet structured to accomplish. For example, they may be used to transcend the existing organizational structure to customize a strategy for different geographic regions, transfer technology from one part of the world to another, and communicate between headquarters and subsidiaries in different countries. Sometimes companies send employees on temporary assignments abroad as part of transnational teams lasting perhaps a few months. This might be done to break down cultural barriers between international divisions or to disseminate new ideas and technologies to other regions. In other instances, employees are transferred for extended periods of time. Years ago, Fuji sent 15 of its most experienced engineers from Tokyo to a Xerox facility in Webster,

New York. Over a 5-year period, the engineers worked with a team of U.S. engineers to develop the "world" copier. This effort led to a joint venture that has lasted for decades. Fuji-Xerox now employs approximately 10,000 people globally at 13 companies around the world.[18]

The fundamental task in forming a transnational team is assembling the right group of people who can work together effectively to accomplish the goals of the team. Many companies try to build variety into their teams so as to maximize responsiveness to the special needs of different countries. Cross-cultural training can benefit transnational teams by helping them overcome any language and cultural barriers they face.

15.2b Selecting Employees Internationally

Selecting employees in a foreign country environment can be difficult. When embarking on a quest to hire employees in a new country, a firm's international HR managers should get to know the local market and customs in hiring. This will help the firm understand what to look for in employees. When GE first entered India, it did not realize that much of the effective hiring was done through family ties and friendship networks. Not wanting to appear biased, GE at first did not allow such practices. However, after struggling to obtain good recruits, GE finally incorporated peer and family referral systems into its selection practices. This led to selection of employees who stayed within the organization much longer.

To better understand the local market, firms can take a few specific steps. First, international HR managers should get to know the universities, technical schools, and primary schools in the area. More than just ensuring their graduates' qualifications, such schools can provide extensive networks of future employees and offer insights on the types of candidates managers would want to select. To work with them effectively, firms must take the time to understand how the local schools operate. In many developing countries, higher education systems are underdeveloped and either do not provide enough future employees or do not prepare employees with suitable skills. For example, Rolls-Royce and Intel have both become involved in the development of school curricula for both managerial and engineering skill development. When partnering with local universities, Rolls-Royce and Intel offer funding and curriculum design to better prepare students for the work environment. Though they come at their own expense, these companies see such costs as investments in future employees as well as a chance to shape the skills they need to run their companies in those countries.

Second, international HR managers should develop networks in the local business and government communities. Because many companies' reputations may not precede them, they must use personal networks to develop trust in the company. An international HR manager's job will not be just to select the right people who come to the office, but also to go out and select the right people within the community. For instance, when Unilever, a large British–Dutch consumer products company, opens up operations in a foreign environment, it often becomes heavily involved in the local community by conducting community feedback meetings, local education programs, and environmental studies. The company's extensive involvement in the local environment helps to rapidly build its local reputation, which increases its knowledge of potential new hires.[19]

Finally, to effectively select employees in a local environment, international HR managers must understand the employees of the firm's competitors. As they map out and get to know key employees in competing organizations, they can develop a better understanding of what to look for in other employees while building up a new pool of applicants to recruit in the future. For example, companies such as Exxon and Marriott, as well as smaller companies, often turn to employees of competing companies because they already know that these employees have the necessary skills and abilities to survive in their own company. This consideration is especially important because more and more domestic companies are hiring away foreign international firms' employees, using the lure of patriotism and staying power of a local company.

Selecting Global Managers

What if an organization cannot find the appropriate talent in the local country? What if a firm is launching operations in a foreign country but needs managers who know the ins and outs of the company or who have company-specific expertise? In this case, organizations need to select managers from one country and move them to another. Levi Strauss has identified the following six skill categories for the **global manager**, or manager equipped to run an international business:

global manager
A manager equipped to run an international business.

- The ability to seize strategic opportunities
- The ability to manage highly decentralized organizations
- An awareness of global issues
- Sensitivity to diversity issues
- Competence in interpersonal relations
- Community-building skills[20]

If a candidate for expatriation is willing to live and work in a foreign environment, an indication of their tolerance of cultural differences should be obtained. Conversely, if local nationals have the technical competence to carry out the job successfully, they should be carefully considered for the job before the firm hires a domestic candidate and sends the person abroad. As we explained, most corporations today realize the advantages to be gained by staffing international operations with host-country nationals wherever possible.

Selecting home-country and third-country nationals for international businesses requires that more factors be considered than when selecting host-country nationals. While the latter must, of course, possess managerial abilities and the necessary technical skills, they have the advantage of familiarity with the physical and **cultural environment** and the language of the host country. Thus, hiring global managers from these three different groups brings different sets of advantages and disadvantages.

cultural environment
The communications, religion, values and ideologies, education, and social structure of a country.

Colgate-Palmolive, Whirlpool, and Dow Chemical have identified a set of **core skills** that they view as critical for success abroad as well as a set of **augmented skills** that help facilitate the efforts of expatriate managers. These two types of skills are shown in Highlights in HRM 1. Many of these skills are not significantly different from the skills managers need to succeed domestically. Although in years past the average U.S. expatriate manager was an American-born Caucasian, more companies today are seeing the advantages of taking ethnicity into account when assigning expatriates to specific locations. But such a decision needs to be considered carefully. For example, an Indian candidate applying for a position in India may never have actually visited the country or may not relate well to the culture. Ultimately, the candidate best qualified for the job should be sent.

core skills
Skills considered critical to an employee's success abroad.

augmented skills
Skills helpful in facilitating the efforts of expatriate managers.

Highlights in HRM 1

Skills of Expatriate Managers

Core Skills

- Experience
- Decision making
- Resourcefulness
- Adaptability
- Cultural sensitivity
- Team building
- Maturity

Augmented Skills

- Technical skills
- Negotiation skills
- Strategic thinking
- Delegation skills
- Change management

In the past, women were overlooked for global managerial positions—perhaps because companies believed they would fare poorly in foreign, male-dominated societies or because they believed women have less desire to go abroad. Today women account for approximately 25 percent of all expatriates.[21] Moreover, multiple studies show that women expatriates perform just as well as men.[22]

Several steps are involved in selecting individuals for an international assignment, and the sequencing of these activities can make a big difference:

Step 1: Begin with self-selection. Employees should begin the process years in advance by thinking about their career goals and how interested they are in working abroad. Companies such as EDS and Deloitte give their employees self-selection instruments to help them consider the pros and cons of international assignments. Performance Program Inc.'s Overseas Assignment Inventory and the International Mobility Assessment test, developed by Tucker International, are two such tests.

Step 2: Create a candidate pool. After employees have self-selected, organizations can build a database of candidates for international assignments. Information in this database might include availability, languages, country preferences, and skills.

Step 3: Assess candidates' core skills. From the short list of potential candidates, managers can assess each candidate in terms of their technical and managerial readiness relative to the needs of the assignment.

Step 4: Assess candidates' augmented skills and attributes. As Figure 15.4 shows, expatriate selection decisions are typically based on the technical competence of candidates as well as their professional and international experience. In addition, organizations are beginning to pay more attention to an individual's ability to adapt to different environments. How well a person adjusts depends on their flexibility, emotional maturity and stability, empathy for the culture, language and communication skills, resourcefulness and initiative, prior international experience, exposure to different cultures, and diplomatic skills. If these skills are lacking, no amount of technical competency is likely to result in a successful assignment.[23]

Figure 15.4 Expatriate Selection Criteria

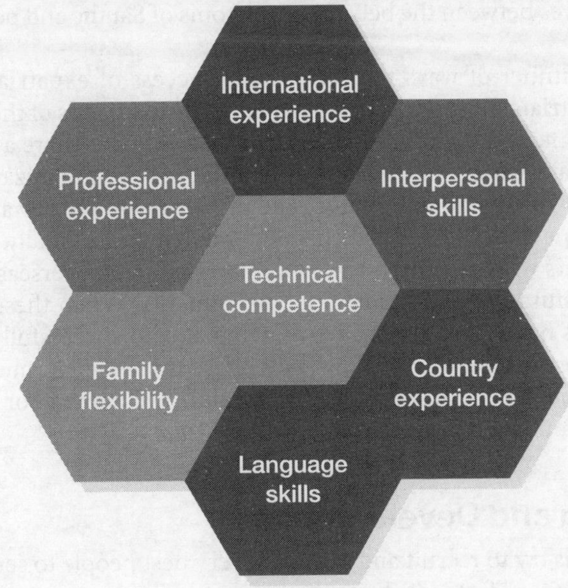

Even companies that believe they have selected the best candidates frequently experience high expatriate **failure rates**. Figure 15.5 shows the major causes of assignment failure. In particular, poor cultural fit is a major reason why assignments fail. For example, although China is among the easiest countries to which to attract Western expatriates, it is also one of the hardest places for them to succeed because the country's culture is so different from Western cultures.

failure rates The percentage of expatriates who do not perform satisfactorily.

A lack of expatriate support from headquarters is another major cause of failure with international assignments. Expatriates often describe themselves as "out of sight and out of mind." This highlights the importance of headquarters maintaining close contact with these employees to see how they are faring.

Yet another big factor is a spouse's inability to adjust to the new surroundings. Today, more companies are preparing families for international relocation by offering them cultural and language training. ARAMCO, a Saudi Arabian corporation, has such

Figure 15.5 Causes of Expatriate Assignment Failure

- Family adjustment
- Lifestyle issues
- Work adjustment
- Bad selection
- Poor performance
- Other opportunities arise
- Business reasons
- Repatriation issues

a program. Its program includes practical information such as how to deal with Saudi Arabia's transportation systems, where to shop, day-to-day finances, and an explanation of the differences between the beliefs and customs of Saudis and people from other cultures.[24]

There are a number of ways to improve the success of expatriate assignments. Ultimately the expatriate must find a way to adjust to the demands of their company, the country environment, and their family needs. Employees who share a common vision with the company are willing to undergo difficulties for the organization. Employees who take the time to understand the culture and market in which they are operating will be better able to cope with unexpected changes and demands. Finally, employees who have family members who are supportive and interested in an overseas assignment are much more successful in their international assignments. When these conditions are in place, expatriates have a greater chance of being able to successfully adjust to their international positions. Figure 15.6 shows how these three factors must be aligned to ensure expatriate adjustment. In addition, training and development for both expatriates and their spouses can have a big impact.

15.2c Training and Development

Although companies try to recruit and select the very best people to send abroad, once they are selected, a critical factor in those employees' success is appropriate training. Not only is this type of training crucial for expatriate managers, but it is also important for the foreign employees they will ultimately supervise. For example, understanding how Japanese or Chinese business people negotiate contracts or how business people from

Figure 15.6 Expatriate Adjustment Factors

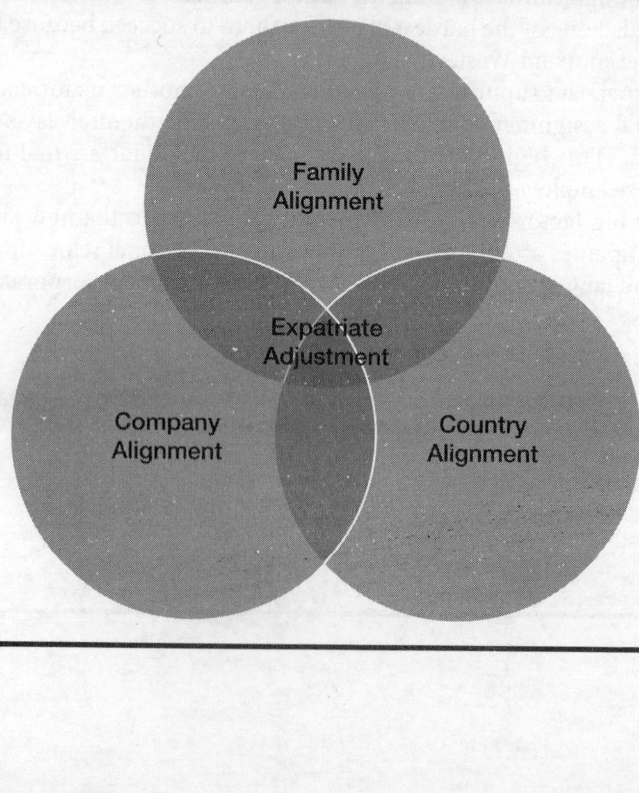

Latin America view the enforcement of meeting times can help expatriate managers and their employees deal with one another more successfully. The biggest mistake managers can make is to assume that people are the same everywhere.

Apart from developing talent for overseas assignments, most companies have found that good training programs also help them attract the employees they need from host countries.

15.2d Content of Training Programs

Lack of training is one of the principal causes of failure among employees working internationally. Those working internationally need to know as much as possible about (1) the country where they are going, (2) that country's culture, and (3) the history, values, and dynamics of their own organizations. Figure 15.7 gives an overview of what someone needs to study for an international assignment. In many cases, the employee and their family can obtain a great deal of general information about the host country, including its culture, geography, social and political history, climate, food, and so on, via the Internet, books, and podcasts.

However, at least five essential elements are needed in training and development programs to prepare employees for working internationally: (1) language training, (2) cultural training, (3) assessing and tracking career development, (4) managing personal and family life, and (5) repatriation—a final, but critical, step.[25]

Language Training

Communication with individuals who have a different language and a different cultural orientation can be extremely difficult. Indeed, most executives agree that it is among the biggest problems for the foreign business traveler. Unfortunately, only a small percentage of Americans are skilled in a language other than English, though this situation is changing. Students who plan careers in international business should start instruction in one or more foreign languages as early as possible. Some companies do their own language training. When ARCO Products, a U.S. firm, began exploring potential business

Figure 15.7 Preparing for an International Assignment

To prepare for an international assignment, one should become acquainted with the following aspects of the host country:

1. Social and business etiquette
2. History and folklore
3. Current affairs, including relations between the host country and the United States
4. Cultural values and priorities
5. Geography, especially its major cities
6. Sources of pride and great achievements of the culture
7. Religion and the role of religion in daily life
8. Political structure and current players
9. Practical matters such as currency, transportation, time zones, and hours of business
10. The language

opportunities in China, its HR department set up a language training class (with the help of Berlitz International) in conversational Mandarin Chinese. Multinational companies as well as businesses that outsource work abroad stand to benefit from this type of training.

Fortunately for most Americans, English is almost universally accepted as the primary language for international business. Particularly when many people from different countries are working together, English is usually the designated language for meetings and formal discourse. Many companies provide instruction in English for their employees who are required to use English in their jobs. Dow Chemical requires that all employees across the globe be fluent in English so that they can communicate more easily with one another. Even with an interpreter, much is missed.

The following list illustrates the complexities of the communication process in international business.

- In England, to "table" a subject means to put it on the table for present discussion. In the United States, it means to postpone discussion of a subject, perhaps indefinitely.
- In the United States, information flows to a manager. In cultures in which authority is centralized (such as Europe and South America), the manager must take the initiative to seek out the information.
- Getting straight to the point is uniquely American. Many Europeans, Arabs, Asians, and others resent the directness of American-style communication.
- In Japan, there are at least 16 ways to avoid saying "no."
- When something is "inconvenient" to the Chinese, it is most likely downright impossible.
- In most foreign countries, expressions of anger are unacceptable; in some places, public display of anger is taboo.
- The typical American must learn to treat silences as "communication spaces" and not interrupt them.
- In general, Americans must learn to avoid gesturing with the hand. A couple of cases in point: When former President Richard Nixon traveled to Brazil in the 1950s, he waved and gave the "A-OK" sign to the country's citizens. But in Brazil, the gesture is considered obscene and insulting. Nonverbal communication training can help businesspeople avoid some of these communication pitfalls. Highlights in HRM 2 illustrates that some of Americans' everyday gestures have very different meanings in other cultures.[26]

Cultural Training

Cross-cultural differences represent one of the most elusive aspects of international business, but when successfully managed, tend to improve the satisfaction and success of expatriates and their employers.[27] Brazilians tend to perceive Americans as always in a hurry, serious, reserved, and methodical, whereas Japanese people view Americans as relaxed, friendly, and impulsive. Why do these different perceptions exist, and how do they affect the way we do business across borders? People's attitudes and behaviors are influenced, in large part, by the culture and society in which they have been educated and trained. Each culture has its own expectations for the roles of managers and employees. An American manager in Asia once complained that meetings held in his foreign place of employment accomplished nothing. He was used to arriving

2 Highlights in HRM

Nonverbal Communications in Different Cultures

Calling a Waiter

In the United States, a common way to call a waiter is to point upward with the forefinger. In Asia, a raised forefinger is used to call a dog or other animal. To get the attention of a Japanese waiter, extend the arm upward, palm down, and flutter the fingers. In Africa, knock on the table. In the Middle East, clap your hands.

Insults

In Arab countries, showing the soles of your shoes is an insult. Also, an Arab may insult a person by holding a hand in front of the person's face.

A-Okay Gesture

In the United States, using the index finger and the thumb to form an "o" while extending the rest of the fingers is a gesture meaning okay or fine. In Japan, however, the same gesture means money. Nodding your head in agreement if a Japanese uses this sign during your discussion could mean you are expected to give him some cash. In Brazil, the same gesture is considered a seductive sign to a woman and an insult to a man.

Eye Contact

In Western and Arab cultures, prolonged eye contact with a person is acceptable. In Japan, however, holding the gaze of another is considered rude. The Japanese generally focus on a person's neck or tie knot.

Handshake and Touching

In most countries, the handshake is an acceptable form of greeting. In the Middle East and other Islamic countries, however, the left hand is considered the toilet hand and is thought to be unclean. Only the right hand should be used for touching.

Scratching the Head

In most Western countries, scratching the head is interpreted as lack of understanding or confusion. To the Japanese, it indicates anger.

Indicating "No"

In most parts of the world, shaking the head left and right is the most common way to say no. But among the Arabs, and in parts of Greece, Yugoslavia, Bulgaria, and Turkey, a person says no by tossing the head up, sometimes clicking the tongue at the same time. In Japan, no can also be said by moving the right hand back and forth.

Agreement

In addition to saying yes, Africans will hold an open palm perpendicular to the ground and pound it with the other fist to emphasize "agreed." Arabs will clasp their hands together, forefingers pointed outward, to indicate agreement.

Source: S. Hawkins, *International Management* 38, no. 9 (1983): 49. Copyright 1983 by Reed Business Information Ltd. Reprinted with permission.

at a final decision during meetings. But to his Asian coworkers, meetings were solely a place in which to share ideas. Decisions were to be made before or after the meeting. As this example suggests, being successful abroad depends on a person's ability to understand the way things are normally done and to recognize that changes cannot be made abruptly without considerable resistance, and possibly antagonism, on the part of local nationals.

A wealth of data from cross-cultural studies reveals that nations tend to cluster along certain cultural dimensions, such as their work goals, values, needs, and attitudes toward work. Using data from eight comprehensive studies of cultural differences, Simcha Ronen and Oded Shenkar have grouped countries into the clusters shown in Figure 15.8. Ronen and Shenkar point out that while evidence for grouping countries into Anglo, Germanic, Nordic, Latin European, and Latin American clusters appear to

Figure 15.8 A Synthesis of Country Clusters

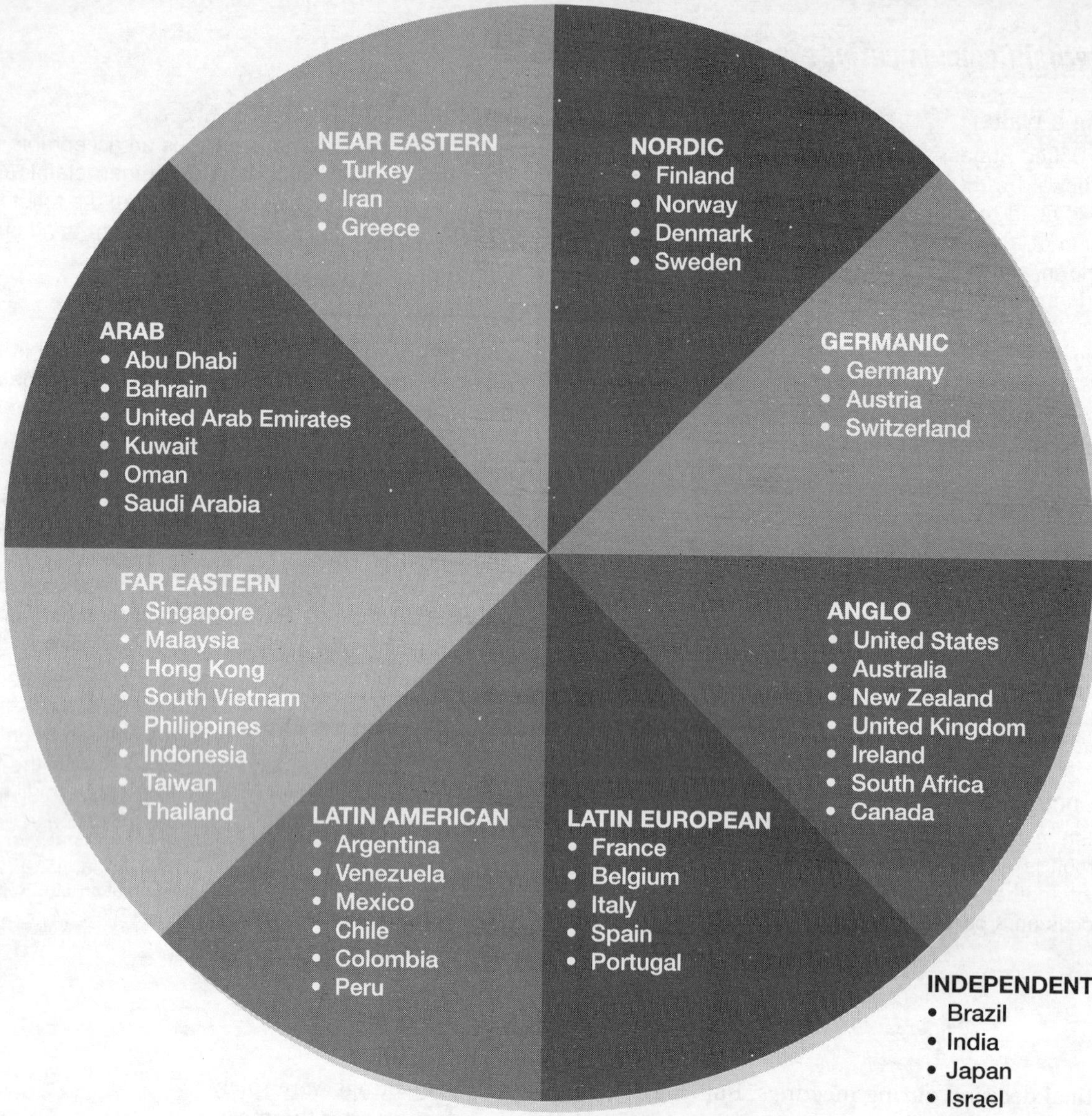

be quite strong, clusters encompassing the Far Eastern and Arab countries are ill defined and require further research, as do clusters of countries classified as independent. Many areas, such as Africa, have not been studied much at all. It should also be noted that the clusters shown in Figure 15.8 do not include Russia and the former satellites of the Soviet Union. Those countries, if added to the figure, would likely fall between the Near Eastern and Nordic categories.

Studying cultural differences can help managers identify and understand work attitudes and motivation in other cultures. Compared with Japanese people, for example,

Americans may feel relatively little loyalty to their organizations. In Japan, employees are more likely to feel a strong loyalty to their company, although this has been changing. Japanese companies no longer universally guarantee an employee a job for life, and layoff decisions are increasingly being made based on merit, not seniority—a practice unthinkable in the country in the past. Latin Americans tend to view themselves as working not only for a particular company, but also for an individual manager. Thus managers in Latin American countries can encourage performance only by using personal influence and working through individual members of a group. In the United States, competition has been the name of the game; in Japan, Taiwan, and other Asian countries, cooperation tends to be the underlying philosophy.[28]

One important dimension of leadership, whether in international or domestic situations, is the degree to which managers invite employee participation in decision making. While it is difficult to find hard data on employee participation across different countries, careful observers report that American managers are about in the middle on a continuum of autocratic to democratic decision-making styles. Scandinavian and Australian managers also appear to be in the middle. South American and European managers, and especially those from France, Germany, and Italy, gravitate toward the autocratic end of the continuum. Japanese managers are at the most participatory end. Because Far Eastern cultures and religions tend to emphasize harmony, group decision making predominates there.[29]

Assessing and Tracking Career Development

International assignments provide some definite developmental and career advantages. For example, working abroad tends to increase a person's responsibilities and influence within the corporation. In addition, it provides a person with a set of experiences that are uniquely beneficial to both the individual and the firm. In this way, international assignments enhance a person's understanding of the global marketplace and offer the opportunity to work on a project important to the organization.[30] Furthermore, research shows that international assignments increase a person's creative problem-solving skills and receptivity to new ideas.[31]

In recent years, U.S. companies have become a melting pot of CEOs. Increasingly, foreign-born CEOs are making up the *Fortune* 500 top slots. Executive recruiters say corporate boards are asking for leaders with experience outside of the United States. Foreign-born expatriates tend to be greater risk takers and harder workers. They are people who have left their home countries and communities to set off on their own.[32]

To maximize the career benefits of a managerial assignment, a candidate should ask two key questions before accepting a foreign post:

- Do the organization's senior executives view the firm's international business as a critical part of their operation?
- Within top management, how many executives have a foreign-service assignment in their background, and do they feel it important for an executive to have overseas experience?

Managing Personal and Family Life

As noted previously, one of the most frequent causes of an employee's failure to complete an international assignment is personal and family stress. **Culture shock**—a disorientation that causes perpetual stress—is often experienced by people who settle overseas for extended periods. This stress is caused by hundreds of jarring and disorienting

culture shock
Perpetual stress experienced by people who settle overseas.

incidents, such as being unable to communicate, having trouble getting the telephone to work, being unable to read the street signs, and a myriad of other everyday matters that are no problem at home. Soon minor frustrations become catastrophic events, and the person feels helpless and drained, emotionally and physically.

As noted in Chapter 5, more and more employers are assisting two-career couples in terms of finding suitable employment in the same location. To accommodate dual-career partnerships, some employers offer spouses career and life planning counseling, continuing education, intercompany networks to identify job openings in other companies, job-hunting or fact-finding trips, and help securing work permits abroad.

Repatriation

repatriation
The process of transition for an employee home from an international assignment.

An increasing number of companies, such as Monsanto, 3M, EDS, and Verizon, have developed programs specifically designed to facilitate **repatriation**—that is, helping employees make the transition back home. Repatriation programs are designed to prepare employees for adjusting to life at home, which at times can be more difficult than adjusting to a foreign assignment.

Unfortunately, not all companies have career development programs designed for repatriating employees or do not do an effective job of it. Employees often lament that their organizations are vague about repatriation, their new roles within the company, and their career progression. In many cases, employees abroad have learned how to run an entire international operation—or at least significant parts of it. When they return home, however, their responsibilities are often significantly diminished. Some surveys have found that as many as 60 percent of expatriates believed their careers had not advanced after returning home.[33] It is also not at all uncommon for employees to return home after a few years to find that there is *no* position for them in the firm and that they no longer know anyone who can help them—their longtime colleagues have moved to

A foreign assignment can be an excellent step in a person's career. But to be successful, expatriates often need extensive training on their host countries' languages, cultural differences, business practices, and other related issues.

View Stock/Alamy Stock Photo

3 Highlights in HRM

Repatriation Checklist

Before They Go:

- Make sure there is a clear need for the international assignment. Develop a clear set of objectives and expectations and time frames in which they should be met.
- Make sure that your selection procedures are valid. Select the employee and also look at and involve the employee's family.
- Provide (or fund) language and cultural training for the employee and the employee's family.
- Offer counseling and career assistance for the spouse.
- Establish career planning systems that reward international assignments and lead to promotion and knowledge sharing.
- Jointly establish a developmental plan that focuses on the goal to be achieved.
- Tie performance objectives to the achievement of the goal.
- Identify mentors who can be a liaison and support person from home.
- Keep communications open so that the expatriate is aware of job openings and opportunities.
- Arrange for frequent visits back home (for the employee and the family). Make certain they do not lose touch with friends and relatives.

When They Come Back Home:

- Throw a "welcome home" party and arrange for a meeting with other former expatriates.
- Offer counseling to ease the transition.
- Arrange conferences and presentations to make certain that knowledge and skills acquired away from home are identified and disseminated.
- Set up an expatriate database to help other employees who go abroad later.
- Get feedback from the employee and the family about how well the organization handled the repatriation process.

Sources: Adapted from Bennet & Associates, Price Waterhouse, and Charlene Marmer Solomon, "Repatriation Planning Checklist," *Personnel Journal* 14, no. 1 (1995): 32; Yamasaki, Yukiko. "Why Do Some Employees Readjust to Their Home Organizations Better Than Others? Job Demands–Resources Model of Repatriation Adjustment" (2016); Charlene Marmer Solomon, "Global HR: Repatriation Planning," *Workforce* (2001), special supplement: 22–23.

different departments or even different companies. This situation frequently leaves the repatriated employee feeling alienated. Wondering about their future also creates stress for them and their families while they are abroad.

Even when employees are successfully repatriated, their companies often do not fully utilize the knowledge, understanding, and skills developed on their international assignments. This hurts the employee, of course, but it also hurts the firm's chances of utilizing the employee's expertise to gain a competitive advantage. Not surprisingly, expatriates frequently leave their companies within a year or two of coming home.

Monsanto's repatriation program is designed not only to smooth the employee's return to the home organization, but also to ensure that the expatriate's knowledge and experience are fully used. As part of this program, returning expatriates get the chance to showcase their new knowledge in debriefing sessions. Some companies also create databases of expatriates to help other employees who go abroad later.[34] Of course, if a firm is able to retain its current repatriates, it will have better success recruiting future expatriates. A repatriation checklist is shown in Highlights in HRM 3.

LO3

Explain how to set up a compensation system that may account for both global and local standards.

15.3 Compensation

One of the most complex areas of international HRM is compensation. Different countries have different norms for employee compensation. For Americans, while nonfinancial incentives such as prestige, independence, and influence may be motivators, money is likely to be the driving force. Other cultures are more likely to emphasize respect, family, job security, a satisfying personal life, social acceptance, advancement, or power. Since there are many alternatives to money, the rule is to match the reward with the values of the culture. In individualistic cultures, such as the United States, pay plans often focus on individual performance and achievement. In contrast, in collectively oriented cultures such as Japan and Taiwan, these plans focus more on internal equity and personal needs.[35]

In general, a guiding philosophy for designing pay systems might be "think globally and act locally." That is, executives should usually try to create a pay plan that supports the overall strategic intent of the organization but provides enough flexibility to customize particular policies and programs to meet the needs of employees in specific locations. After a brief discussion of compensation practices for host-country employees and managers, we will focus on the problems of compensating expatriates.

15.3a Compensation of Host-Country Employees

As shown in Figure 15.9, minimum wages vary dramatically from country to country. Minimum-wage workers in manufacturing positions in Luxembourg make more than $28,000 per year. By contrast, in Mexico, minimum-wage workers earn less than $2,000 per year, on average. Host-country employees are generally paid on the basis of productivity, time spent on the job, or a combination of these factors. In industrialized countries, pay is generally by the hour; in developing countries, pay is generally by the day. The piece-rate method is quite common. In some countries, including Japan, seniority is an important element in determining employees' pay rates. In Italy, Japan, and some other countries, it is customary to add semiannual or annual lump sum payments equal to 1 or 2 months' pay. These payments are not considered profit sharing, but rather an integral part of the basic pay package. Profit sharing is legally required for certain industry categories in Mexico, Peru, Pakistan, India, and Egypt (among the developing countries) and in France (among the industrialized countries).

Employee benefits can vary dramatically from country to country as well. In France, for example, benefits constitute a much higher proportion of people's pay than they do in the United States. In contrast to the average of 10 vacation days in the United States, workers in the United Kingdom, France, and the Netherlands receive about 25 days of paid vacation. Workers in Sweden and Austria receive 30 days. Whereas in the United States most benefits are awarded to employees by employers, in other industrialized countries most of them are legislated or ordered by governments.[36]

Because the largest cost for most companies is labor, it plays a prime role in international HR decision making. However, some people believe that companies are overcapitalizing on worldwide compensation differences. Many firms have generated bad press for charging hundreds of dollars for their individual products while the people who make them earned only a few cents on the dollar. This has led to international political protests, as was mentioned in Chapter 1, and pressure on firms to exercise greater global social responsibility.

Figure 15.9 Hourly Wages in Different Countries

Dataset: Real Minimum Wages

Country	Pay Period Unit Time Hourly Minimum Wage	Annual Dollar 2021 Annual Minimum Wage Earnings
Luxembourg	$13.78	$28,603.91
Australia	$12.14	$23,975.61
Netherlands	$10.44	$23,520.56
Ireland	$9.62	$23,447.04
Belgium	$10.38	$22,133.37
Germany	$10.87	$22,097.86
New Zealand	$11.20	$20,932.45
France	$11.66	$20,903.33
Canada	$9.52	$20,643.41
United Kingdom	$10.34	$20,053.09
South Korea	$6.84	$19,880.75
Israel	$7.94	$17,713.12
Slovenia	$5.72	$15,269.87
United States	$7.25	$15,080
Spain	$5.83	$14,289.76
Poland	$3.35	$13,214.88
Greece	$4.98	$12,128
Hungary	$2.90	$10,669.44
Slovakia	$3.43	$10,518.39
Czech Republic	$5.17	$10,342.44
Portugal	$5.76	$9,584.72
Lithuania	$4.78	$9,365.14
Costa Rica	$3.37	$9,132.30
Latvia	$4.30	$8,969.79
Colombia	$2.66	$7,768.45
Chile	$2.25	$7,319.53
Estonia	$3.40	$7,082.27
Brazil	$2.18	$5,114.28
Russia	$2.27	$4,734.24
Turkey	$1.93	$4,516.20
Mexico	$1.05	$1,193.78

Data extracted on May 18, 2021.

Source: OECD.stat (Data are calculated in terms of purchasing power parity [PPP]).

Kevork Djansezian/Getty Images News/Getty Images

Student protesters put pressure on University of Southern California to stop using sweatshop labor in the manufacturing of USC school apparel.

Nike is just one example of a company that has experienced pressure from groups protesting the treatment of its overseas workers. In the face of these protests, it soon realized it couldn't afford to ignore the problem any longer. Ultimately, the bad press took a toll on Nike's bottom line. As a result, Nike now monitors all its partner factories to ensure that workers are not underage, that pay is competitive, and that working conditions are compliant with international standards. More than 100 full-time staff are dedicated to monitoring these partner factories. While this effort costs Nike approximately $11 million per year, the company has unexpectedly realized additional cost savings, as its monitoring staff are also able to help the factories with streamlining the work processes, training managers, and decreasing corrupt practices.[37]

15.3b Compensation of Host-Country Managers

In the past, the compensation of host-country managers has been based on local salary levels. Today, however, more companies are offering their host-country employees a full range of training programs, benefits, and pay comparable to that provided to their domestic employees back in the country of origin but adjusted for local differences. Such a program is known as a **global compensation system**.

global compensation system
A centralized pay system whereby host-country employees are offered a full range of training programs, benefits, and pay comparable with a firm's domestic employees but adjusted for local differences.

According to a survey by the HR consulting firm Watson Wyatt, companies are split evenly as to whether they have central (global) compensation systems or decentralized (local) systems. Companies with centralized systems report having higher effectiveness and satisfaction levels with their compensation systems, and more companies are saying they are moving toward these systems. Unilever, for example, used to leave the compensation arrangements largely to the boss of a region or a big country. Now brand managers in different countries increasingly compare notes so they see potential discrepancies based on market differences and expatriate assignments. In response, the company moved from a narrow grading structure to five global work levels.[38]

15.3c Compensation of Expatriate Managers

If the international assignment is to be successful, the expatriate's compensation plan must be competitive, cost-effective, motivating, fair, easy to understand, consistent with international financial management, relatively easy to administer, and simple to communicate. To be effective, an international compensation program must:

1. Provide an incentive to leave the United States
2. Allow for maintaining an American standard of living
3. Provide for security in countries that are politically unstable or present personal dangers
4. Include provisions for good health care
5. Reimburse the foreign taxes the employee is likely to have to pay (in addition to having to pay domestic taxes) and help the employee with tax forms and filing
6. Provide for the education of the employee's children abroad, if necessary
7. Allow for maintaining relationships with family, friends, and business associates via trips home and other communication technologies
8. Facilitate the expatriate's reentry back home when the assignment is finished
9. Be put in writing[39]

For short-term assignments, usually those that are project based, expatriates are frequently given per diem (per day) compensation. These managers might reside in hotels and service apartments instead of leasing houses. They are also less likely to bring their family members with them. Such an assignment becomes more like a commuting assignment in which the expatriate spends the week in the host country and returns home on the weekend.

For longer-term assignments, there are two basic types of compensation systems. The first is **home-based pay**, based on the **balance sheet approach**, a system designed to equalize the purchasing power of employees at comparable positions living overseas and in the home country and to provide incentives to offset qualitative differences between assignment locations.[40] The balance sheet approach generally comprises the following steps:

home-based pay
Pay based on the compensation practices used in an expatriate's home country.

balance sheet approach
A compensation system designed to match the purchasing power in a person's home country.

Step 1: Calculate the base pay. Begin with the home-based gross income, including bonuses. Deduct taxes, Social Security, and pension contributions.

Step 2: Figure the cost-of-living adjustment (COLA). Add a cost-of-living adjustment to the base pay. Typically, companies do not subtract when the international assignment has a lower cost of living. Instead, they allow the expatriate to benefit from the negative differential. Often a housing allowance is added in here as well.

Step 3: Add incentive premiums. General mobility premiums and hardship premiums compensate expatriates for separation from family, friends, and domestic support systems. They usually amount to 15 percent of base salary, although in recent years, some companies have reduced this percentage. Oftentimes incentive premiums are paid for hazardous duty or harsh conditions the expatriate might experience while abroad. Expatriates who locate to war zones, for example, can sometimes earn three times their base salary.

Step 4: Add assistance programs. These additions are often used to cover extra costs such as moving and storage, automobile, and education expenses.

The differentials element is intended to correct for the higher costs of overseas goods and services so that in relation to their domestic peers, expatriates neither gain purchasing power nor lose it. It involves a myriad of calculations to arrive at a total differential figure, but in general the expatriate's salary amounts to between three and five times the home-country salary. Fortunately, employers do not have to do extensive research to find comparative data. They typically rely on data published quarterly by the U.S. State Department for use in establishing allowances to compensate U.S. civilian employees for costs and hardships related to assignments abroad.

split pay
A system whereby expatriates are given a portion of their pay in the local currency to cover their day-to-day expenses and a portion of their pay in their home currency to safeguard their earnings from changes in inflation or foreign exchange rates.

host-based pay
Expatriate pay comparable to that earned by employees in a host country.

localization
Adapting pay and other compensation benefits to match that of a particular country.

Recently, **split pay** plans have become popular among companies. Under a split pay system, expatriates are given a portion of their pay in the local currency to cover their day-to-day expenses. The rest of their pay is distributed in their home currency to safeguard their earnings should changes in foreign exchange rates or inflation adversely affect their pay.

Another type of compensation system is **host-based pay**. Many companies are under pressure to move expatriates to this system because it is generally less costly. Host-based pay is compensation that is equivalent to that earned by employees in the country where the expatriate is assigned; it is based on a process called **localization**. When an employee is localized, their compensation is set on par with local standards and practices. Incentive premiums are generally phased out, and the employee pays only local taxes and falls under the social benefit programs established by the government of the host country.

Usually the decision to localize an employee depends on whether that person will ultimately remain abroad or return home. In many companies, the decision depends on whether the employee or the employer is the driving force behind the localization. An expatriate employee with a strong desire to remain in the host country beyond the planned length of assignment (perhaps because they have married a local or simply fallen in love with the country) is likely to be more amenable to localization.

15.3d Performance Appraisal

As we noted earlier, individuals frequently accept international assignments because they know that they can acquire skills and experiences that will make them more valuable to their companies. Frequently, however, it may prove difficult for the home office to evaluate the performance of employees working abroad. Even the notion of performance evaluation is indicative of a U.S. management style that focuses on the individual, which can cause problems in Asian countries such as China, Japan, and South Korea and in Eastern European countries such as Hungary and the Czech Republic. Performance appraisal problems can contribute to failure rates among expatriates and actually derail an individual's career rather than enhance it.[41]

Who Should Appraise Performance?

In many cases, an individual working internationally has at least two allegiances: to their home country (the office that made the assignment) and to the host country in which the employee is currently working. Superiors in each location frequently have different information about the employee's performance and may also have very different expectations about what constitutes good performance. For these reasons, the multiple-rater (360-degree) appraisal discussed in Chapter 8 is popular among global firms. There are exceptions, however. For example, Thai workers do not see it as their business to evaluate their bosses, and Thai managers do not think subordinates are in any way qualified to assess them. Before implementing a different appraisal process, HR managers need to understand how the process is likely to be received in the host country.[42]

imtmphoto/Shutterstock.com

The notion of individual performance evaluation reflects a U.S. management style that does not match the norms of Eastern European and Asian countries.

Home versus Host-Country Evaluations

Domestic managers who have not worked abroad are frequently unable to understand an expatriate's or host-country manager's experiences, value these employees, or accurately measure their contributions to the organization. Geographic distances can create communication problems for expatriates and home-country managers, although email, instant messaging, and other HR information systems technologies have begun to close the gap.[43] Even so, local managers who have daily contact with the employee are more likely to have an accurate picture of their performance. Host-country evaluations can sometimes be problematic, though.

Even if the formal appraisal is conducted in the home office and promotion, and pay and other administrative decisions are made there, most HR experts agree that performance evaluations should try to balance the two sources of appraisal information. If cultural bias is a major concern, it may be possible to have people of the same nationality as the expatriate conduct the appraisal.

Performance Criteria

Because expatriate assignments are so costly, many HR managers are increasingly under pressure to calculate the return on investment (ROI) for these assignments. What did the firm get for the million dollars it spent to send an expatriate abroad? Has the expatriate achieved the goals set forth in the assignment in the appropriate time frame? Obviously, the goals and responsibilities inherent in the job assignment are among the most important criteria used to evaluate an individual's performance, and different goals necessitate measuring different criteria. These criteria are tied to the various reasons employees were sent abroad in the first place—whether it was part of a goal to transfer technical skills or best practices, as a result of a merger or new division, to improve a division's financial performance, or to develop managerial talent.

Calculating the ROI of an assignment involves five steps:

1. Define the assignment's objectives.
2. Agree on the quantifiable measurements for the assignment.
3. Develop an equation that converts qualitative behavior into quantifiable measurements.
4. Evaluate the expatriate's performance against these measurements.
5. Calculate the ROI. (This can be a complex cost accounting or a simple calculation to see if the expatriate covered the cost of keeping them on assignment.)

Companies also look at how well the total cost of the assignment was managed, taking into account any tax efficiencies and whether the right mix of expatriates, third-country nationals, and locals was used to minimize the assignment's costs.[44] The danger with ROI calculations, however, is that there is a temptation to resort to using "easy" criteria such as productivity, profits, and market share to measure an expatriate's performance. These criteria may be valid, but they also may not suffice to capture the full range of an expatriate's responsibility. Other, more subtle factors should be considered as well. Leadership development, for example, involves a much longer-term value proposition. In many cases, an expatriate is an ambassador for the company, and a significant part of the job is cultivating relationships with citizens of the host country.

Providing Feedback

Performance feedback in an international setting is clearly a two-way street. Although the home-country and host-country superiors may tell expatriates how well they are doing, it is also important for expatriates to provide feedback regarding the support they are receiving, the obstacles they face, and the suggestions they have about the assignment. More than in almost any other job situation, expatriates are in the very best position to evaluate their own performance.

In addition to ongoing feedback, an expatriate should have a debriefing interview immediately on returning home from an international assignment. These repatriation interviews serve several purposes:

- They help expatriates reestablish old ties with the home organization and may prove important for setting new career paths.
- The interview can address technical issues related to the job assignment itself.
- The interview can address general issues regarding the company's overseas commitments, such as how relationships between the home and host countries should be handled.
- The interview can be very useful for documenting insights an individual has about the region. These insights can then be incorporated into training programs for future expatriates. However, if the learning is not shared, then each new expatriate to a region may have to go through the same cycle of adjustment.[45]

Figure 15.10 summarizes the pros and cons of using expatriates, host-county nationals, or third-country nationals to manage a firm's overseas operations.

Figure 15.10 Comparison of Advantages in Sources of Overseas Managers

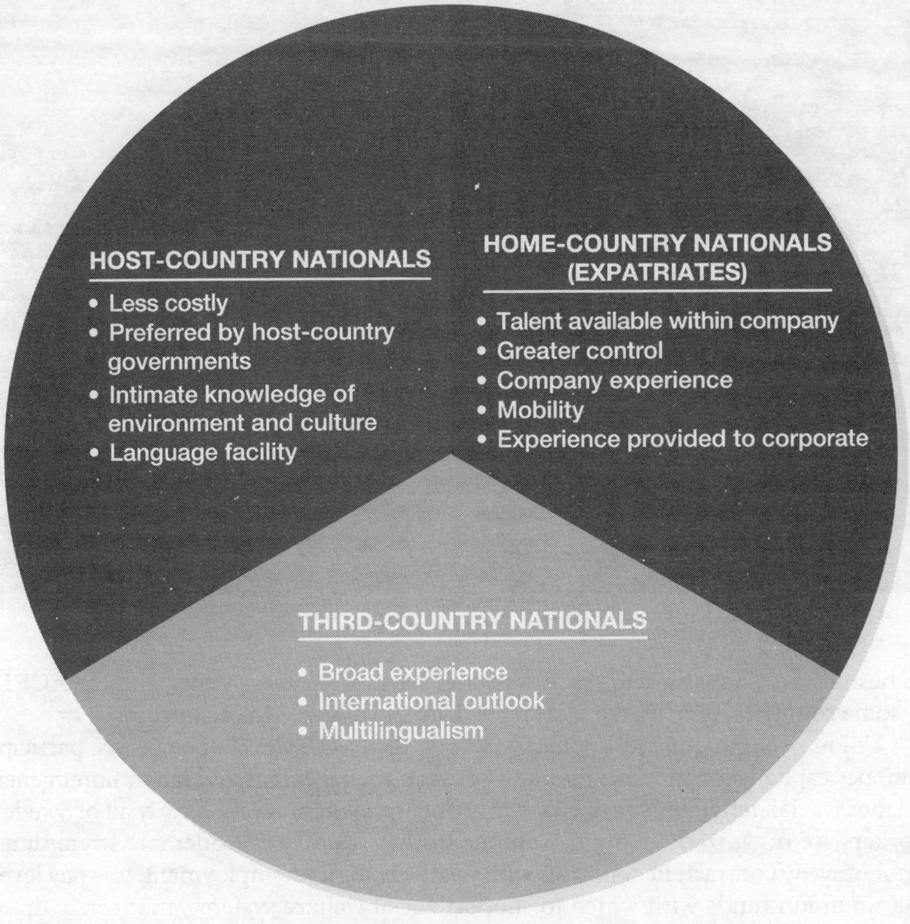

15.4 Analyzing the International Labor Environment

LO4 Explain how labor relations differ around the world.

A country's labor environment plays a large role in international business and HR decisions. As we have said, wages and benefits vary dramatically across the world, as do safety, child, and other legal regulations. In many countries, the regulation of labor contracts is profound and extensive. Labor unions around the world differ significantly as well. Differences exist not only in the collective bargaining process, but also in the political-legal conditions.

For example, the EU prohibits discrimination against workers in unions, but in many other countries, including countries in Central America and Asia, labor unions are illegal. China has only one union, the All-China Federation of Trade Unions (ACFTU), a Communist Party institution that for decades has aligned itself more closely with management than with workers. As Walmart discovered, Western firms that want to

While employees at Walmart and Sam's Club in China have little bargaining power, being part of the ACFTU gives them a collective sense of identity.

STR/AFP/Getty Images

do business in China have to reach collective bargaining agreements with the ACFTU. In some countries, only workers at larger firms are allowed to organize.[46]

Union strength depends on many factors, such as the level of employee participation, per capita labor income, mobility between management and labor, homogeneity of labor (racial, religious, social class), and unemployment levels. Nearly all of Sweden's workers are organized, giving the unions in that country considerable strength and autonomy. By contrast, in countries with relatively high unemployment, low pay levels, and no union funds with which to support social welfare systems, unions are driven into alliance with other organizations: political parties, churches, or governments. This is in marked contrast to the United States, where the union selected by the majority of employees bargains only with the employer, not with other institutions. By contrast, the unions in many European countries (such as Sweden) have a great deal of political power and are often allied with a particular political party. When employers in these countries deal with unions, they are, in effect, dealing indirectly with governments.

In a number of countries, however, including Japan, Germany, New Zealand, and the United Kingdom, unions have been losing some of their power. Ironically, the power of the unions to gain high wages and enforce rigid labor rules has been blamed for hurting competitiveness, particularly in European countries. Laws make it difficult to fire European employees, so workers are hired only sparingly. Unemployment benefits are very generous, so people tend to remain unemployed for longer periods rather than seek work.

15.4a Collective Bargaining in Other Countries

We saw in Chapter 14 how the collective bargaining process is typically carried out in companies operating in the United States. When we look at other countries, we find that the process can vary widely, especially with regard to the role of government.

Collective bargaining can take place at the firm, local, or national levels. In Australia and New Zealand for most of the twentieth century, labor courts had the authority to impose wages and other employment conditions on a broad range of firms (many of which were not even privy to the suits brought before the courts). In the United Kingdom and France, the government intervenes in all aspects of collective bargaining. Government involvement is only natural where parts of industry are nationalized.

In developing countries, the governments commonly have representatives present during bargaining sessions to ensure that unions with relatively uneducated leaders are not disadvantaged when bargaining with skilled management representatives. Even so, in these countries a union may do little more than attempt to increase wages and leave the rest of the employment contract unchanged. In more-developed countries, goals related to other aspects of the employment relationship, such as workweek lengths, safety requirements, and grievance procedures, are more likely to be pursued.

15.4b International Labor Organizations

The most active of the international union organizations has been the International Trade Union Confederation (ITUC), which has its headquarters in Brussels, Belgium. The ITUC is a confederation of 311 national trade union centers, representing 176 million trade union members in 162 countries and territories. The ITUC's mission is to promote worker rights and interests through international cooperation between trade unions, campaigning, and advocacy with governments and global institutions.[47]

Another active and influential organization is the International Labour Organization (ILO), a specialized agency of the United Nations created in 1919. The ILO perhaps has had the greatest impact on the rights of workers throughout the world. It promotes the rights of workers to organize, the eradication of forced and child labor, and the elimination of discrimination. The organization has been effective because it involves nation-states as well as workers and their employers. Agenda 2030 for Sustainable Development places decent work for all at the heart of the ILO's current initiatives.[48]

FABRICE COFFRINI/AFP/Getty Images

Around the world, collective bargaining processes vary widely. The ILO and other international labor organizations promote the rights of workers to organize.

15.4c Labor Participation in Management

In many European countries, provisions for employee representation are established by law. An employer may be legally required to provide for employee representation on safety and hygiene committees, worker councils, or even boards of directors. While their responsibilities vary from country to country, worker councils basically provide a communication channel between employers and workers. The legal codes that set forth the functions of worker councils in France, for example, are very detailed. Councils are generally concerned with grievances, problems of individual employees, internal regulations, and matters affecting employee welfare.

codetermination Representation of labor on the board of directors of a company.

A higher form of worker participation in management is found in Germany, where representation of labor on the board of directors of a company is required by law. This arrangement, known as **codetermination**, is often referred to by its German name, *Mitbestimmung*. While sometimes puzzling to outsiders, the system is fairly simple. Company shareholders and employees are required to be represented in equal numbers on the supervisory boards of large corporations. Power is generally left with the shareholders, and shareholders are generally assured the chairmanship. Other European countries and Japan either have or are considering minority board participation, in which employee representatives at least have a seat at the table.[49]

Each of these differences makes managing human resources in an international context more challenging. But the crux of the issue in designing HR systems is not choosing one approach that will meet all the demands of international business. Instead, organizations facing global competition must balance multiple approaches and make their policies flexible enough to accommodate differences across national borders. Throughout this book we have noted that different situations call for different approaches to managing people, and nowhere is this point more clearly evident than in international HRM.

Summary

LO 1 Analyzing the political, economic, sociocultural, and technological factors affecting your company can help to (1) spot business or personnel opportunities, (2) spot trends in the business environment (3) avoid inappropriate HR practices, and (4) break free of old habits.

LO 2 International HRM consists of managing three different types of employees—expatriates (home-country and third-country nationals), host-country nationals, and third-country nationals. Managing each set of employees requires different approaches to recruitment, selection, training, and compensation.

LO 3 The standards for total compensation, including pay, benefits, and customary practices, vary from country to country. These factors may impact which approach a company needs to take to effectively balance its global company culture and the more decentralized local culture. The way expatriate employees are compensated is also an important issue. Implementing a home-based pay system can establish a standard that can properly take care of these expatriates and ensure a smooth transition to an international assignment.

LO 4 In many European countries—Germany, for one—employee representation is established by law. Organizations typically negotiate the agreement with the union at a national level, frequently with government intervention. In other countries, union activity is prohibited or limited to only large companies. European unions have much more political power than many other unions around the world, although their power has declined somewhat due to globalization forces. The International Confederation of Free Trade Unions and International Labour Organization are among the major worldwide organizations endeavoring to improve the conditions of workers.

Key Terms

augmented skills
balance sheet approach
codetermination
core skills
cultural environment
culture shock
economic factors
expatriates (home-country and third-country nationals)
failure rates
global compensation system
global corporation
global manager
guest workers
home-based pay
host-based pay
host country
host-country nationals
international corporation
localization
multidomestic corporation (MDC)
political factors
repatriation
sociocultural factors
split pay
technological factors
third-country nationals
transnational corporation
transnational teams
work permit or visa

Discussion Questions

LO 1 In recent years, we have observed an increase in foreign production throughout the world. What PEST factors would you consider to be most relevant to H&M's HR managers when trying to figure out if they should open up a plant in Vietnam to make clothes?

LO 2 a. Starbucks is opening new stores abroad every day, it seems. If you were in charge, would you use expatriate managers or host-country nationals to staff the new facilities? Explain your thinking.

b. This chapter places considerable emphasis on the role spouses play in terms of the success of an overseas manager. What other steps should companies take to increase the likelihood of a successful experience for all parties involved?

c. Talk with a foreign student on your campus; ask about their experience with culture shock on first arriving in the United States. What did you learn from your discussion? If the cost of living is lower in a foreign country than in the United States, should expatriates be paid less than they would be at home? Explain your position. Who should ultimately decide whether an employee should be localized or not? If grooming a talented individual for a leadership role is an important outcome of a foreign assignment, how can this be worked into a performance appraisal system? How would a manager assess leadership accomplishments?

LO 3 We understand that different cultures are motivated by different types of compensation. How might this be represented in a U.S. company that employs workers in China?

LO 4 a. What are the major differences between labor–management relations in Europe and those in the United States?

b. Do you believe that codetermination will ever become popular in the United States? Explain your position.

HRM Experience

An American (Expatriate) in Paris

There is often a great deal of work involved in setting up expatriate assignments. The administrative requirements can be far ranging and extend beyond the employee to also include family issues. Suppose you were faced with the following scenario. What would be the most pressing considerations that you would need to address?

The Scenario

You are the head of HR for Sarip International, a consulting firm specializing in hotel and restaurant management. Your firm is opening an office in Paris, France, and Jim Verioti, director of sales and marketing, has been asked to assume responsibilities for the expansion. Jim understands that the expatriate assignment will last 2 to 3 years. Although he has traveled to Europe for work on several occasions, this is his first long-term assignment overseas. He has a lot of questions about what he can expect as well as some personal constraints.

Jim and his wife Betty have just moved into their new home (their mortgage is around $1,750 per month). In addition, Betty is an elementary school teacher and doesn't really know how the move will affect her job security. Their three children, Veronica (14), Reggie (12), and Archie (10), are of an age at which school considerations are very important. A friend told them about the American School in Paris, and this is a consideration. None of the Veriotis speak French.

Assignment

Working in teams of four to six individuals, put together the package that would allow Jim to move his family to Paris while still maintaining his present lifestyle (his current annual salary is $160,000 plus incentives). Address at least the following issues:

1. Visas and permits
2. Relocation allowance and housing
3. Language and culture training
4. Spousal employment concerns
5. Health/medical/insurance issues
6. Compensation and incentives
7. Education for the children

The following websites may be helpful to you, but other resources may prove valuable as well:

- U.S. embassy in Paris (https://fr.usembassy.gov/)
- French consulates in the United States (https://france.visahq.com/)
- Expatica.com (http://www.expatica.com/fr/main.html)
- Americans in Paris (http://www.americansinfrance.net)
- Easy Expat (http://www.easyexpat.com/paris_en.htm)
- Centers for Disease Control and Prevention (http://wwwn.cdc.gov/travel/default.aspx)
- American School in Paris (http://www.asparis.org/about)
- Medibroker (insurance) (http://www.medibroker.com)
- Travlang (currency calculator) (http://www.travlang.com/money/)

CASE STUDY 1 How about a 900 Percent Raise?

Registered nurse Carmen Lopez wants a raise—so she's leaving Mexico and moving to California to take a job at Desert Valley Medical, a hospital near Los Angeles, where her income will increase tenfold. "I was making US$500 a month in Mexico, and in the U.S. I will be making between $25 and $28 an hour," Lopez says. Lopez, upon finishing her U.S. nursing exam, will be joining nine other Mexican nurses at Desert Valley Medical.

As U.S. baby-boomers age, the number of registered nurses in the United States is not keeping up. An estimated 1.2 million nursing vacancies emerged by 2022. Lopez and her colleagues were recruited by MDS Global Medical Staffing in Los Angeles. Roger Viera, cofounder of MDS Global Staffing, says he and his business partner have invested $1 million, and the Mexican government added another $1 million, to open a nurse residency program in Mexico that trains and certifies nurses to work in the United States. "We only recruit qualified nurses. They must have a four-year bachelor of science degree and four years of work experience," Viera says. MDS expects to recruit from Mexico's 12 nursing schools and from Costa Rica.

MDS has also recruited Maria de la Cruz Gonzalez, who says she's excited about this opportunity to emigrate with her husband and work as a nurse in the United States. "The hospitals offer us a two-year contract where our nuclear family can come along to live with us in the U.S.," she says. MDS gives the nurses 3 months of paid rent and transportation, provides placement with client hospitals, and provides training in technology and language. They will be able to work in U.S. hospitals for 2 years under the United States–Mexico–Canada Agreement visa.

Donna Smith, chief nursing officer at Desert Valley Medical, says she is happy to have the Mexican nurses join her staff and believes that they are as qualified as U.S. nurses. But, she says, they will need more technical experience before they can go to work, since technology is different in the hospitals of Mexico. "We will provide them with extra training once they get here," she says.

Questions

1. Is recruiting nurses abroad a good idea for U.S. hospitals facing worker shortages?
2. Can you think of any cultural problems U.S. hospitals might encounter as a result?
3. What long-term recruiting measures should U.S. hospitals strive for?

Sources: Condensed from Aisha Belone, "How About a 900 Percent Raise? Mexican Nurses Head North to Cure the Ballooning U.S. Health Care Labor Shortage," *Latin Trade* 12 no. 7 (2004): 30; Rebecca Grant, "The U.S. Is Running out of Nurses," *The Atlantic* (February 3, 2016).

CASE STUDY 2 A "Turnaround" Repatriate Plan: U.S. Company Moves Indian Workers Back Home

In an unusual move, a seriously ailing Dallas software company, i2 Technologies, resettled 209 Indian engineers, programmers, and managers in their South Asian homeland on a voluntary basis to help stem losses as it laid off thousands of other employees. A series of corporate crises led to the mass repatriation back to India.

Many returnees had worked in Texas, Massachusetts, and California for 5 to 7 years on H1B visas designed for temporary, highly skilled workers, although about 10 percent had acquired permanent residency green cards or U.S. citizenship. They found the company's Move to India Program too good to turn down—even if it meant a pay cut of 50 percent or more. None were pressured by management to return, said Gunaranjan "Guna" Pemmaraju, a 30-year-old engineer, who returned home. The returnees, many graduates of India's top technical universities, were confident of finding other U.S. jobs if i2 laid them off and were prepared to "change industries if need be," he asserted.

"When I left America, I actually kissed the ground," Pemmaraju said. "It helped me grow as an individual, and it enriched my thought process." Significantly, though, Pemmaraju says the quality of life in his middle-class Bangalore neighborhood is comparable—with a few minor downsides that he and his wife are willing to accept. Although their pay shrank in dollar terms, the repatriates are relatively better off in India.

"If we were in the top 25 percent in the United States, we're in the top 5 percent here," said one repatriate.

"We may not have 85-inch TV sets, but we have more of a sense of community and belonging here," another added.

Pemmaraju relies on DSL Internet access, fields morning calls from Dallas colleagues on a cell phone, and watches satellite TV while pedaling his new exercise bike. Instead of a Honda Accord, he drives a much smaller Suzuki Zen sedan.

For i2, the wage and benefit savings are helping it edge toward profitability. The company says the savings have been substantial. At its peak, i2 employed 6,349 people, with about 800 in India. It has since scaled down to 2,500 workers, 1,100 of whom are based in Bangalore.

Pemmaraju's family expresses no regrets about returning, yet they retain fond memories of the United States, a country of "milk and honey"—not to mention seven-layer Taco Bell burritos and Krispy Kreme doughnuts. Pemmaraju was tickled by a recent call to a fast-food restaurant in Bangalore. "A guy answered the phone saying, 'Thank you for calling Pizza Hut. Would that be for delivery or carry out?'" he said. "It's just what they said in Arlington [Texas]!"

Questions

1. Does repatriation represent a good financial strategy for firms with international employees?
2. Besides cost savings, does i2 have anything to gain by repatriating its Indian employees?
3. What type of repatriation preparation training do you think i2's repatriates should receive before going home?

Source: Condensed from Barry Shlachter, "Software Firm Resettles Indian Workers in Turnaround Plan," *Fort Worth Star-Telegram* (via Knight-Ridder/Tribune Business News), June 24, 2004.

Notes and References

1. Shad S. Morris, Daniel Chng, Jian Han, Bi-Juan Zhong, and Oded Shenkar, "Leveraging Local Talent for Global Learning in Multinational Enterprises' Foreign Subsidiaries" [Working Paper], 2017.
2. PESTLE analysis factsheet, Chartered Institute of Personnel and Development (October 15, 2015), https://www.cipd.co.uk/knowledge/strategy/organisational-development/pestle-analysis-factsheet.
3. Jordan Siegel and Barbara Zepp Larson, "Labor Market Institutions and Global Strategic Adaptation: Evidence from Lincoln Electric," *Management Science* 55, no. 9 (2009): 1527–1546.
4. See www.wto.org for more information on the World Trade Organization.
5. Bob Savic, "Norway and China Strive to Complete Free Trade Agreement Negotiations," *China Briefing* (March 14, 2021).
6. "The Panama Canal Expansion: Changes Beyond the Waterway," Knowledge@Wharton (June 3, 2016), http://knowledge.wharton.upenn.edu/article/panama-canal-expansion-changes-beyond-waterway/; Steven Mufson, "An Expanded Panama Canal Opens for Giant Ships," *Washington Post* (June 26, 2016).
7. S. Vollmer, "How to Mind Your Manners in the Middle East: CPAs Who Do Business in the Region Need to Know the Cultural Rules," *Journal of Accountancy* 219, no. 1 (2015): 42; Ruchika Tulshyan, "Quirkiest Cultural Practices from Around the World," *Forbes* (March 18, 2010).
8. Caroline Fairchild, "Netflix Redefined American Company Culture. Will It Do the Same Abroad?" *CNBC* (June 20, 2016), www.cnbc.com/2016/06/20/netflix-redefined-american-company-culture-will-it-do-the-same-abroad.html.
9. Robert Johnson, "17 Awesome McDonald's Dishes You Can't Buy in America," *Business Insider* (June 16, 2011), http://www.businessinsider.com/mcdonalds-meals-around-the-world-2011-6?op=1/#donalds-hawaiian-deluxe-breakfast-12.
10. Carla Joinson, "No Returns," *HRMagazine* 47, no. 11 (2002): 70–77; Frank Jossi, "Successful Handoff," *HRMagazine* 47, no. 10 (2002): 48–52; Steve Bates, "Study Discovers Patterns in Global Executive Mobility," *HRMagazine* 47, no. 10 (2002): 14; Morgan McCall and George Hollenbeck, "Global Fatalities: When International Executives Derail," *Ivey Business Journal* 66, no. 5 (2002): 74–78; Leslie Gross Klass, "Fed up with High Costs, Companies Thin the Ranks of Career Expats," *Workforce Management* 83, no. 10 (2004): 84.
11. Valerie Berset-Price, "Training: The Solution to the Expat Challenge," *Training Magazine* (May 4, 2012), https://trainingmag.com/content/training-solution-expat-challenge.
12. Readers interested in codes of conduct and other ethical issues pertaining to international business might want to read Nadar Asgary and Mark Mitschow, "Toward a Model for International Business Ethics," *Journal of Business Ethics* 36, no. 3 (2002): 238–246; Diana Winstanley and Jean Woodall, "The Adolescence of Ethics in Human Resource Management," *Human Resource Management Journal* 10, no. 4 (2000): 45; J. Brooke Hamilton and Stephen Knouse, "Multinational Enterprise Decision Principles for Dealing with Cross-Cultural Ethical Conflicts," *Journal of Business Ethics* 31, no. 1 (2001): 77–94; Michael Maynard, "Policing Transnational Commerce: Global Awareness in the Margins of Morality," *Journal of Business Ethics* 30, no. 1 (2001): 17–27.
13. Adam Chandler, "Au Revoir to France's 35-Hour Workweek?" *The Atlantic* (March 10, 2016).
14. Michael Solomon, "H1B Visas: Why They're Broken and What We Can Do," *Huffington Post* (March 20, 2017).
15. Ben Wildavsky, "Reverse Brain Drain: How Much Should the U.S. Worry?" *Chronicle of Higher Education* (March 28, 2011); "Keeping out the Wrong People: Tightened Visa Rules Are Slowing the Vital Flow of Professionals into the U.S.," *Business Week* 3902 (October 4, 2004): 90; "Security Delays Hurt U.S. Business," *Legal Times* (August 23, 2004); "Skilled Workers Leave in Reverse Brain Drain," *Fort Worth Star Telegram* (August 25, 2007): 9A.
16. "Society: Affirmative Action? Oui! At Long Last, France Takes a Page from America in Order to Manage Diversity—and Bring Minorities into Elite Schools," *Newsweek International* (April 12, 2004): 30; Leo D'Angelo Fisher, "The Hunt for a New Work Order," *BRW* 30, no. 9 (2008): 46–52.

17. Martin Aschmoneit and Dijana Janevska, "Closing the Gap between Frugal and Reverse Innovation: Lessons Learned from the Case of the Tata Nano," Linköping University Department of Management and Engineering (2013).
18. https://www.linkedin.com/company-beta/163911/ (May 2, 2017); see the Fuji-Xerox website for detailed information about the company, http://www.fujixerox.com/eng/; Andrea Poe, "Selection Savvy," *HRMagazine* 47, no. 4 (2002): 77–83; "Exploiting Opportunity: Executives Trade Stories on Challenges of Doing Business in Global Economy," *Business Mexico* 15, no. 2 (2005): 54–58.
19. https://www.unilever.com/careers/ (May 2, 2017).
20. Sheree R. Curry, "Offshoring Swells Ranks of 'Returnees' Working Back in Their Native Countries," *Workforce Management* 84, no. 2 (2005): 59; Yochanan Altman and Susan Shortland, "Women and International Assignments: Taking Stock—A 25-Year Review," *Human Resource Management* 47, no. 2 (2008): 199–216; Handan Kepir Sinangil and Deniz S. Ones, "Gender Differences in Expatriate Job Performance," *Applied Psychology: An International Review* 52, no. 3 (2003): 461–475; "More Women Sent on International Assignment," *Compensation & Benefits* 39, no. 2 (2007): 14–15.
21. *BGRS Global Mobility Trends Report* (2016), http://globalmobilitytrends.bgrs.com/#/data-highlights.
22. Nina Cole and Yvonne McNulty, "Why Do Female Expatriates 'Fit-in' Better Than Males?" *Cross Cultural Management*, 18, no. 2 (2011); Robert O'Connor, "Plug the Expat Knowledge Drain," *HRMagazine* 47, no. 10 (2002): 101–107; Andrea Graf and Lynn K. Harland, "Expatriate Selection: Evaluating the Discriminant, Convergent, and Predictive Validity of Five Measures of Interpersonal and Intercultural Competence," *Journal of Leadership & Organizational Studies* 11, no. 2 (2005): 46–63.
23. Paula Caligiuri, *Cultural Agility: Building a Pipeline of Successful Global Professionals* (New York: John Wiley & Sons, 2013); Paula Caligiuri, Ibraiz Tarique, and Rick Jacobs, "Selection for International Assignments," *Human Resource Management Review* 19, no. 3 (2009): 251–262; Riki Takeuchi, "A Critical Review of Expatriate Adjustment Research through a Multiple Stakeholder View: Progress, Emerging Trends, and Prospects," *Journal of Management* 36, no. 4 (2010): 1040–1064; Riki Takeuchi, Seokhwa Yun, and Paul Tesluk, "An Examination of Crossover and Spillover Effects of Spousal and Expatriate Cross-Cultural Adjustment on Expatriate Outcomes," *Journal of Applied Psychology* 87, no. 4 (2002): 655–666; Andrea Poe, Iris I. Varner, and Teresa M. Palmer, "Role of Cultural Self-Knowledge in Successful Expatriation," *Singapore Management Review* 27, no. 1 (2005): 1–25; Semere Haile, Marcus D. Jones, and Tsegai Emmanuel, "Challenges Facing Expatriate Performance Abroad," *International Journal of Business Research* 7, no. 5 (2007): 100–105; Margery Weinsten, "China a Double-Edged Sword for Ex-Pats," *Training* 43, no. 11 (2006): 12.
24. "Motorola to Increase Operations in China," *New York Times* (November 8, 2001), C4; Peter J. Buckley, Jeremy Clegg, and Hui Tan, "Knowledge Transfer to China: Policy Lessons from Foreign Affiliates," *Transnational Corporations* 13, no. 1 (2004): 31–73; Neeraj Kataria and Shweta Sethi, "Making Successful Expatriates in Multinational Corporations," *Asian Journal of Business and Economics* 3, no. 3.4 (2013): 1–12.
25. Managers who are interested in setting up a language training program or who wish to evaluate commercially available language training programs should consult the "Standard Guide for Use-Oriented Foreign Language Instruction." This seven-page guide is published by the American Society for Testing and Materials (ASTM), (610) 832–9585, http://www.astm.org. See also "Why Top Executives Are Participating in CEIBS and IESE's Joint Global Management Programme," *PR Newswire* (July 19, 2004); John Okpara and Jean Kabongo, "Cross-Cultural Training and Expatriate Adjustment: A Study of Western Expatriates in Nigeria," *Journal of World Business* 46, no. 1 (2011): 22–30.
26. Jared Wade, "The Pitfalls of Cross-Cultural Business," *Risk Management* 51, no. 3 (2004): 38–43; Semere Haile, Marcus D. Jones, and Tsegai Emmanuel, "Challenges Facing Expatriate Performance Abroad," *International Journal of Business Research* 7, no. 5 (2007): 100–105.
27. Vipin Gupta, Paul Hanges, and Peter Dorman, "Cultural Clusters: Methodology and Findings," *Journal of World Business* 37, no. 1 (2002): 11–15; Jane Terpstra-Yong and David Ralston, "Moving Toward a Global Understanding of Upward Influence Strategies: An Asian Perspective with Directions for Cross-Cultural Research," *Asia Pacific Journal of Management* 19, no. 2 (2002): 373–404; Hsiu-Ching Ko and Mu-Li Yang, "The Effects of Cross-Cultural Training on Expatriate Assignments," *Intercultural Communication Studies* 1 (2011): 158–174.
28. David C. Thomas and Mark F. Peterson, *Cross-Cultural Management: Essential Concepts* (Thousand Oaks, CA: Sage, 2014); Ping Ping Fu et al., "The Impact of Societal Cultural Values and Individual Social Beliefs on the Perceived Effectiveness of Managerial Influence Strategies: A Meso Approach," *Journal of International Business Studies* 35, no. 4 (July 2004): 33; Geert Hofstede, *Culture's Consequences: Comparing Values, Behaviors, Institutions, and Organizations across Nations* (Thousand Oaks, CA: Sage, 2001).
29. Justin Martin, "The Global CEO: Overseas Experience Is Becoming a Must on Top Executives' Resumes, According to This Year's Route to the Top," *Chief Executive* 195 (January–February 2004): 24–31; Alizee B. Avril and Vincent P. Magnini, "A Holistic Approach to Expatriate Success," *International Journal of Contemporary Hospitality Management* 19, no. 1 (2007): 53–64; David C. Thomas and Mark F. Peterson, "The Manager as Decision Maker: Cross-Cultural Dimensions of Decision-Making," in *Cross-Cultural Management: Essential Concepts* (Thousand Oaks, CA: Sage, 2014).

30. David Lipschultz, "Bosses from Abroad," *Chief Executive* 174 (January 2002): 18–21; Denis Lyons and Spencer Stuart, "International CEOs on the Rise," *Chief Executive* 152 (February 2000): 51–53; "U.S. Companies with Foreign-Born Executives," *Workforce Management* 83, no. 7 (2004): 23.
31. A. K. Leung and C. Chiu, "Multicultural Experience, Idea Receptiveness, and Creativity," *Journal of Cross-Cultural Psychology* 41, no. 5–6 (2010): 723–741; W. Maddux and A. Galinsky, "Cultural Borders and Mental Barriers: The Relationship between Living Abroad and Creativity," *Journal of Personality and Social Psychology* 96, no. 5 (2009): 1047–1061.
32. Sharon Gillenwater, "Immigrant CEOs: What Global Citizens Bring to American Business," *Boardroom Insiders* (March 23, 2016).
33. Charles M. Vance, Yvonne McNulty, Yongsun Paik, and Jason D'Mello, "The Expat-preneur: Conceptualizing a Growing International Career Phenomenon," *Journal of Global Mobility* 4, no. 2 (2016): 202–224; Daomi Lin, Jiangyong Lu, Xiaohui Liu, and Xirụ Zhang, "International Knowledge Brokerage and Returnees' Entrepreneurial Decisions," *Journal of International Business Studies* 47, no. 3 (2016): 295–318; Phyllis Tharenou and Natasha Caulfield, "Will I Stay or Will I Go? Explaining Repatriation by Self-Initiated Expatriates," *Academy of Management Journal* 53, no. 5 (2010): 1009–1028; Mark C. Bolino, "Expatriate Assignments and Intra-organizational Career Success: Implications for Individuals and Organizations," *Journal of International Business Studies* 38, no. 5 (2007): 819–835.
34. M. Kraimer, M. Bolino, and B. Mead, "Themes in Expatriate and Repatriate Research over Four Decades: What Do We Know and What Do We Still Need to Learn?" *Annual Review of Organizational Psychology and Organizational Behavior* 3 (2016); 83–109; Lynette Clemetson, "Special Report on Globalization: The Globe Trotters," *Workforce Management* (December 2010); Calvin Reynolds, *Guide to Global Compensation and Benefits* (New York: Harcourt, 2001); Gary Parker, "Establishing Remuneration Practices across Culturally Diverse Environments," *Compensation & Benefits Management* 17, no. 2 (2001): 23–27; Timothy Dwyer, "Localization's Hidden Costs," *HRMagazine* 49, no. 6 (2004): 135–141.
35. Caroline Fisher, "Reward Strategy Linked to Financial Success: Europe," *Benefits & Compensation International* 32, no. 2 (2002): 34–35; "Comparative Analysis of Remuneration: Europe," *Benefits & Compensation International* 31, no. 10 (2002): 27–28; Fay Hansen, "Currents in Compensation and Benefits: International Trends," *Compensation and Benefits Review* 34, no. 2 (2002): 20–21.
36. Donald C. Dowling Jr., "Avoid These Global Compensation and Global Benefits Plan Obstacles," Society for Human Resource Management (April 22, 2014), https://www.shrm.org/resourcesandtools/hr-topics/global-hr/pages/globalcompensation-benefits-plans.aspx; Chao Chen, Jaepil Choi, and Shu-Cheng Chi, "Making Justice Sense of Local–Expatriate Compensation Disparity: Mitigation by Local Referents, Ideological Explanations, and Interpersonal Sensitivity in China–Foreign Joint Ventures," *Academy of Management Journal* 45, no. 4 (2002): 807–817.
37. Richard Locke, "Does Monitoring Improve Labor Standards? Lessons from Nike," *Industrial and Labor Relations Review* 61, no. 1 (2007): 3–31; Greg Distelhorst, Jens Hainmueller, and Richard M. Locke, "Does Lean Improve Labor Standards? Management and Social Performance in the Nike Supply Chain," *Management Science* (2016); Ashley Lutz, "How Nike Shed Its Sweatshop Image to Dominate the Shoe Industry," *Business Insider* (June 6, 2015), http://www.businessinsider.com/how-nike-fixed-its-sweatshop-image-2015-6.
38. Patricia Zingheim and Jay Schuster, "How You Pay Is What You Get," *Across the Board* 38, no. 5 (2001): 41–44; "Benefits for Expatriate Employees: International," *Benefits & Compensation International* 31, no. 10 (2002): 26–27; Steven P. Nurney, "The Long and Short of It: When Transitioning from a Short-Term to a Long-Term Expatriate Assignment, Consider the Financial Implications," *HRMagazine* 50, no. 3 (2005): 91–95.
39. "Designing Global Compensation Systems," Society for Human Resource Management (April 3, 2017), https://www.shrm.org/resourcesandtools/tools-and-samples/toolkits/pages/designingglobalcompensation.aspx; Stephan Kolbe, "Putting Together an Expat Package: As More and More Companies Adopt an International Outlook, They Are Increasingly Sending Staff on Overseas Assignments—Usually Involving a Complex Relocation Package," *International Money Marketing* (September 2004): 33.
40. Nick Royle, "Three Expatriate Compensation Approaches," *The Global Talent Mobility Company* (May 5, 2011), http://msigbs.com/blog/global-compensation-payroll-administration/three-expatriate-compensation-approaches/; the U.S. State Department Index of Living Costs Abroad can be found on the Web at http://www.state.gov/travel.
41. "International Assignment: Performance Management: How Can a Company Manage an Expatriate Employee's Performance?" Society for Human Resource Management (November 30, 2012), https://www.shrm.org/resourcesandtools/tools-and-samples/hr-qa/pages/expatriateperformance.aspx.
42. Paula Caligiuri, "The Big Five Personality Characteristics as Predictors of Expatriate's Desire to Terminate the Assignment and Supervisor-Rated Performance," *Personnel Psychology* 53, no. 1 (2000): 67–88; Calvin Reynolds, "Global Compensation and Benefits in Transition," *Compensation and Benefits Review* 32, no. 1 (2000): 28–38; Charlene Marmer Solomon, "The World Stops Shrinking," *Workforce* 79, no. 1 (2000): 48–51; Stephenie Overman, "Mentors without Borders: Global Mentors Can Give Employees a Different Perspective on Business Matters," *HRMagazine* 49, no. 3 (2004): 83–87; Agnes Slavic, Nemanja Berber, and Bojan Lekovic,

"Performance Management in International Human Resource Management: Evidence from the Cee Region," *Serbian Journal of Management* 9, no. 1 (2014): 45–58.

43. Frank Jossi, "Successful Handoff," *HRMagazine* 47, no. 10 (2002): 48–52; Paula Caligiuri, David Day, and Shirley Puccino, "Worldwide Practices and Trends in Expatriate Compensation and Benefits," *Benefits & Compensation Digest* 44, no. 1 (2007): 34–38; Eric Krell, "Evaluating Returns on Expatriates," *HRMagazine* 50, no. 3 (2005): 60–65.
44. B. Sebastian Reiche, Günter K. Stahl, Mark E. Mendenhall, and Gary R. Oddou, *Reading and Cases in International Human Resources Management*, 6th ed. (New York: Routledge, 2016).
45. Bernhard Ebbinghaus and Jelle Visser, *The Societies of Europe: Trade Unions in Western Europe since 1945* (London: Palgrave Macmillan, 2000); John Pencavel, "Unionism Viewed Internationally," *Journal of Labor Research* 26, no. 1 (2005): 65–98; "Membership Required," *Economist* 87, no. 8591 (2008): 66; Jeremy Smerd, "Unions Reverse Decline," *Workforce Management* 87, no. 2 (2008): 1–3.
46. Randall S. Schuler, Susan E. Jackson, and Ibraiz Tarique, "Global Talent Management and Global Talent Challenges: Strategic Opportunities for IHRM," *Journal of World Business* 46 (2011): 506–516; Christopher Rhoads, "Germany Faces Storm over Tech Staffing—Labor Groups Are Enraged by Proposal to Import Badly Needed Workers," *Wall Street Journal* (March 7, 2000): A23; "European Workplaces Tighten Policies as Countries Struggle to Compete Worldwide," *Pittsburgh (Pennsylvania) Post-Gazette* (via Knight-Ridder/Tribune Business News), November 28, 2004.
47. http://www.ituc-csi.org/ (May 2, 2021).
48. http://www.ilo.org/wcmsp5/groups/public/—dgreports/—dcomm/documents/publication/wcms_374809.pdf (May 18, 2021).
49. Herbert Spiro, "Co-determination in Germany," *American Political Science Review* 48, no. 4 (1954): 1114–1127; Yuko Nishimura, "Reconstructing Minority Identities in 21st Century Japan," *Global Ethnographic Journal for Ethnographic Research* (January 23, 2012), http://oicd.net/ge/index.php/reconstructing-minority-identities_yukonishimura/.

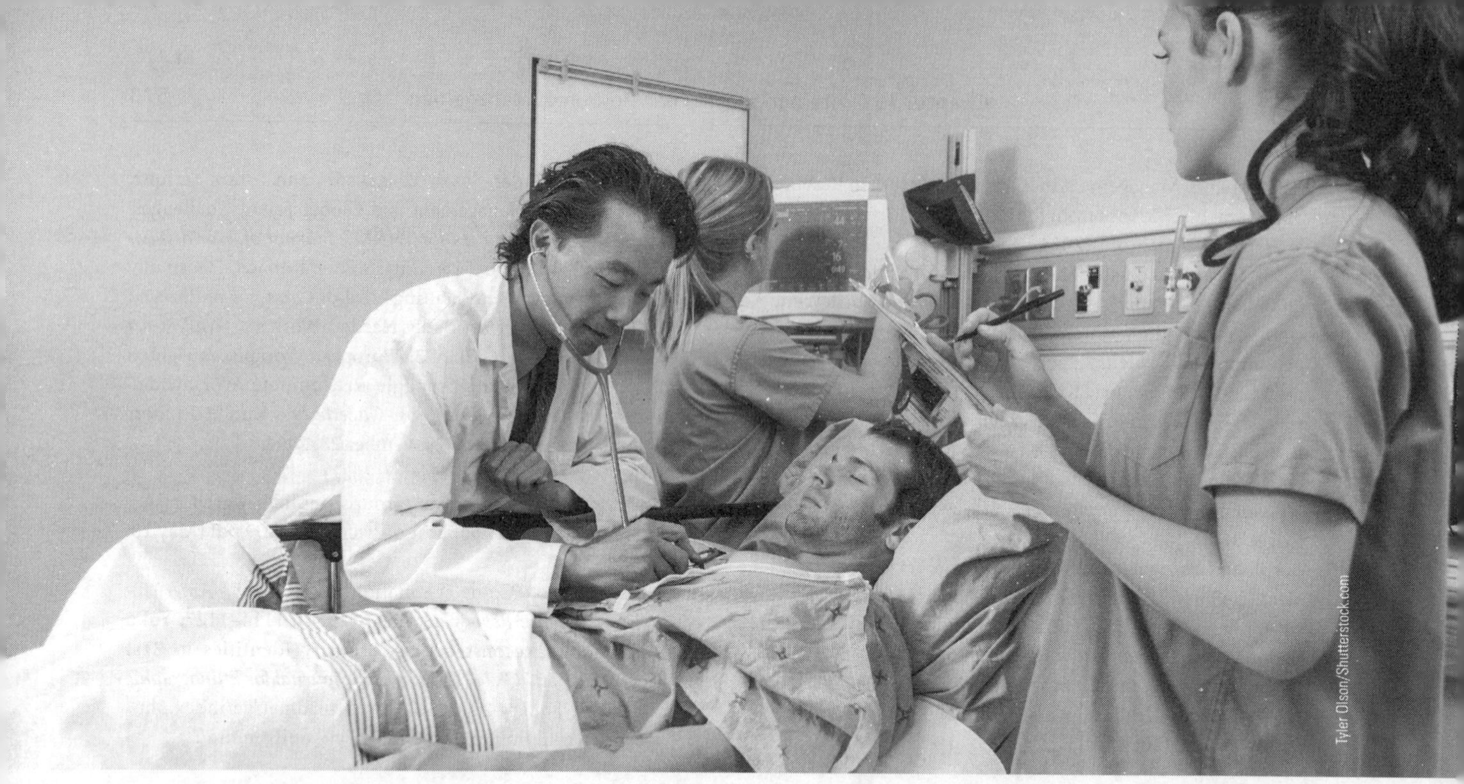
Tyler Olson/Shutterstock.com

CHAPTER 16

Implementing HR Strategy: High-Performance Work Systems

Learning Outcomes

After studying this chapter, you should be able to

LO 1 Discuss how a firm's strategy can be achieved using a high-performance work system and what its fundamental principles are.

LO 2 Describe how a high-performance work system is designed, including the importance of horizontal and vertical alignment.

LO 3 Recommend processes for implementing and evaluating a high-performance work system.

LO 4 Discuss a high-performance work system's potential outcomes for both employees and the organization.

So you have finished reading 15 chapters on HRM. Congratulations—textbooks do not always make for the most gripping reading. But before you close this book, think about the following question: What is more difficult—designing effective HR practices or implementing them as one system?

Most HR textbooks simply end after each individual aspect of HRM is introduced and explained. But in today's competitive environment, many organizations are discovering that it is how the pieces are *combined* together and put into practice that makes all the difference. After all, managers typically do not focus on staffing, training, and compensation practices in isolation from one another. Instead, these HR practices are implemented together as an overall system to enhance employee involvement and performance. So now that we have talked about the individual pieces, let's talk about how they fit together into a **high-performance work system (HPWS)**. Understand that this is not a piece of software. Rather, an HPWS is the combination of HR practices, work structures, and processes specific to a firm that maximizes the knowledge, skills, commitment, flexibility, and resilience of employees, which in turn enhances a firm's competitiveness.

high-performance work system (HPWS)
A specific combination of HR practices, work structures, and processes that maximizes knowledge, skill, commitment, flexibility, and resilience of a firm's employees.

An HPWS can take an organization from being good to great. Consider the Dallas Cowboys. The Cowboys have recruited top talent and paid them top dollar. The owner of the Cowboys, Jerry Jones, has also replaced the Cowboys' coaches multiple times. Although the team has won its division a number of times in recent years, it hasn't (at least at the time of this writing), won a Super Bowl since 1996. Even making the playoffs has been a rare occurrence for the Cowboys. As one HR professional and writer puts it: "Talent might be the fuel of a business's performance, but it's the organization that makes it over the finish line first that really counts."[1] Put another way, it's not enough for organizations to improve just their various HR practices—employee recruitment, rewards, and retention, and so forth. They have to improve their "people processes" as an entire system aligned with their strategies. If some of the "pieces of the puzzle" don't fit, the firm is bound to lose the game.

Figure 16.1 Implementing HR Strategy: High-Performance Work Systems

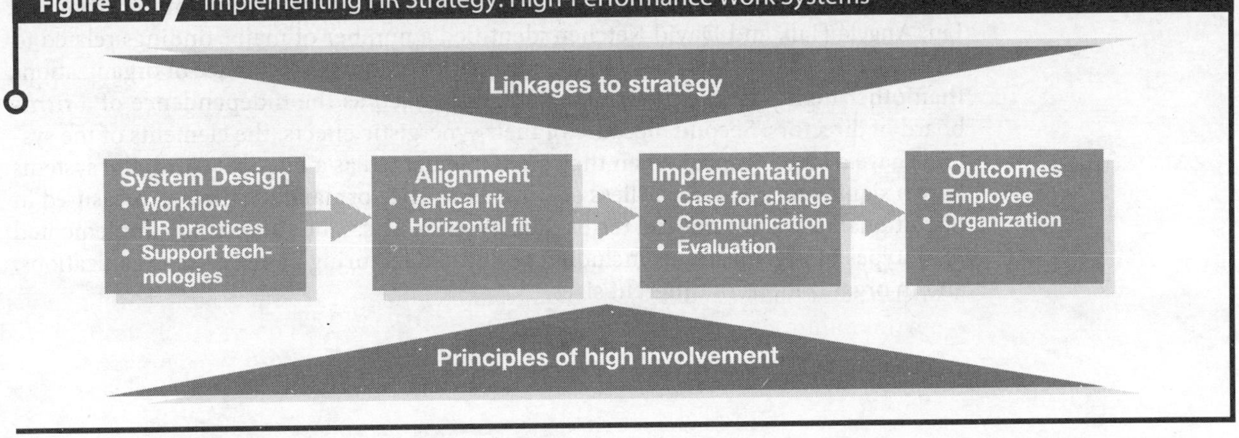

In this chapter, we look at how the various pieces of the HR puzzle fit together to implement a firm's strategy. We start by discussing the fundamental principles that guide the development of HPWSs and the potential benefits that can occur as a result. Then we outline the various components of the system, the workflow design, HR practices, management processes, and supporting technologies (see Figure 16.1). We also describe the ways in which an organization tries to tie together, or align, all the pieces of the system and link them with its strategy. We end the chapter with a discussion of the processes organizations use to implement HPWSs as well as the outcomes that benefit both employees and the organization as a whole.

16.1 Fundamental Principles

LO1

Do you think the fundamental principles of getting employees highly involved with their work provides an adequate context for designing high-performance work systems? What other concerns or guidelines for developing high-performance work systems would you suggest?

In Chapter 1, we noted that organizations face a number of important strategic and competitive challenges such as adapting to global competition, harnessing technology, improving productivity, and containing costs. We also noted some very important employee concerns that must be addressed, such as developing a diverse and inclusive workforce with different educational skills, recognizing employee rights, and adjusting to the new work attitudes of employees and their desire for work–life balance. We now know that the best organizations go beyond simply balancing these sometimes competing demands; they create work environments that blend these concerns to simultaneously get the most from their employees and meet their needs while reaching the organization's short-term and long-term goals.

Four simple but fundamental principles underlie an HPWS (Figure 16.2):

- Egalitarianism and engagement
- Shared information and trust
- Knowledge development
- Performance–reward linkage[2]

These principles are the building blocks for managers who want to create HPWSs. We will use them as a framework for the rest of the chapter.

In addition, it should be noted that in a review and statistical analysis of 92 studies involving more than 19,000 organizations, researchers James Combs, Yongmei Liu, Angela Hall, and David Ketchen identified a number of major findings related to HPWSs. First, the systems have a larger influence on the performance of organizations than other highly visible governance practices, such as the independence of a firm's board of directors. Second, because of their synergistic effects, the elements of the systems have a larger impact when they are implemented as a bundle. Third, the systems have a significant effect regardless of whether the performance of firms is measured in operational terms or financial terms. Finally, HPWSs can be successfully implemented in all types of organizations, including both manufacturing and service organizations, and in organizations of different sizes.

Figure 16.2 Underlying Principles of High-Performance Work Systems

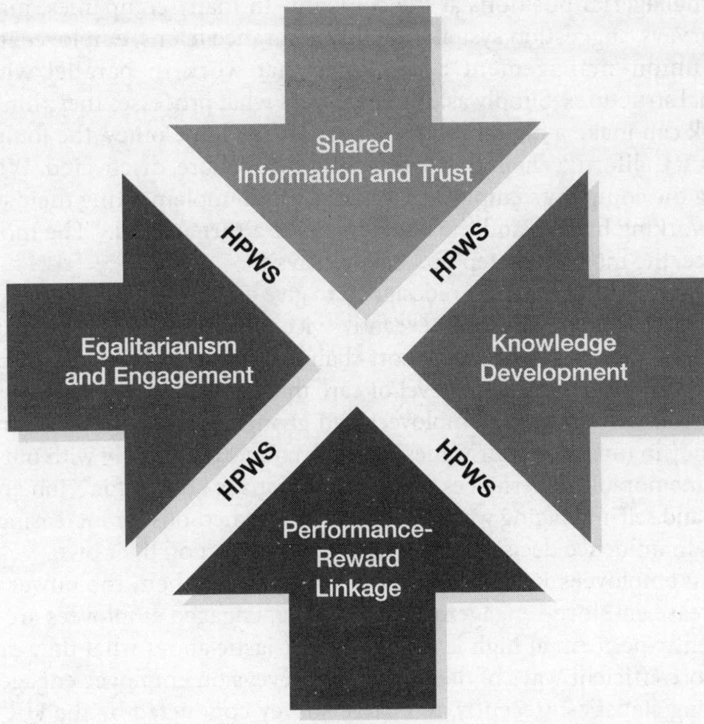

16.1a Egalitarianism and Engagement

Egalitarianism simply means people are treated as equals. People want a sense that they are members, not just workers, in an organization. Status and power differences tend to separate people and magnify whatever disparities exist between them. Today, however, the "us versus them" battles that have traditionally raged between managers, employees, and labor unions are increasingly being replaced by more cooperative approaches to managing work. More egalitarian work environments lessen status and power differences and, in the process, increase collaboration and teamwork. When this happens, productivity can improve if people who once worked in isolation from (or in opposition to) one another begin to work together.

Nucor Steel has nurtured an egalitarian work environment and created remarkable loyalty and productivity among its employees, each of whom is listed alphabetically on the company's annual report. Upper-level managers at Nucor do not enjoy better insurance programs, vacation schedules, or holidays, or have corporate cars, jets, executive dining rooms, or designated parking places. In fact, benefits such as Nucor's profit-sharing plan, scholarship program, employee stock purchase plan, bonus plan, and service awards program are not available to Nucor's officers at all. Similarly, at the Swedish-based company IKEA, hierarchical differences aren't prominent, in part because egalitarianism is a Swedish value. Employees are on a first-name basis and sit side-by-side at IKEA desks in an open-floor arrangement with their managers. Few managers even have business cards.[3]

Moving power downward in organizations—that is, empowering employees—frequently requires structural changes that involve more than just rearranging the furniture and getting rid of executive parking spaces. Recall from Chapter 2 how the online shoe retailer Zappos had to radically restructure its entire operation when it eliminated managerial positions at the company. In many companies, managers use employee surveys, suggestion systems, quality assurance teams, employee involvement groups, or union–management committees that work in parallel with existing organizational structures. Simply asking employees what processes they think work well or don't work can make a big difference. That's what Chip Conley, the founder Joie de Vivre Hotels, a California chain that was teetering on failure, discovered. When Conley began asking the company's employees for advice and implementing their suggestions, they began working harder, and the business made a turnaround. "The more you give people a voice, the more they step up," Conley says.[4]

In addition, workflows can be redesigned to give employees more control and influence over decision making. Ed Evans, executive vice president and chief human resources officer of the Four Seasons hotel and resort chain, attributes the company's success to its employees and culture: "The same level of care that we extend to our guests applies to our people. By empowering our employees and giving them the tools and trust needed to succeed, they in turn carry our values forward, connecting deeply with our guests and creating the memorable experiences that Four Seasons is known for."[5] Job enlargement, enrichment, and self-managing work teams are typical methods for increasing the power of employees to influence decisions, suggest changes, or act on their own.

Involving employees in decision making and giving them the power to act also tends to increase employee engagement. Recall that engaged employees are employees who consistently perform at high levels, are enthusiastic about what they do, and look for better, more efficient ways of doing things. Surveys on employee engagement have yielded varying statistics. Recently, in a large survey conducted by the HR consulting firm Aon Hewitt, only 24 percent of U.S. employees said they were highly engaged on the job; worse yet, 63 percent said they were not engaged at all.

Disengaged employees and employees who are only semi-engaged can cost a company dearly. The French bank Société Générale found this out when a junior-level trader lost billions of the bank's money making illicit trades. Some experts believe that a number of Société Générale employees were perhaps aware of the problem but did not report it, possibly because of poor employee engagement. "There's plenty of evidence that suggests that strategic human resources management and high-performance work systems are foundational in driving employee engagement," says Ellie Maggio, the managing director of Emend Management Consultants in Toronto, Canada. "If an organization is strategic about human resources, they're going to have higher engagement."[6]

16.1b Shared Information and Trust

The principle of shared information is critical to the success of employee empowerment and involvement initiatives in organizations. In the past, employees were hired to do narrowly defined jobs and not given a great deal of information about their firms. One of the underlying ideas of HPWSs is that workers are intimately acquainted with the nature of their own work and, therefore, are in the best position to recognize problems and devise solutions to them. Only individuals and teams can transform an organization. Organizations, cultures, and processes cannot; they can only support or stifle the efforts of individuals and teams that do.[7] However, without timely and accurate information about the business, employees can do little more than simply carry out orders; they will not understand the overall direction of the business or be able to contribute fully to its success.

When employees are given timely information about business performance, plans, and strategies, they are more likely to make good suggestions for improving the business and to cooperate in major organizational changes. They are also likely to feel more committed to new courses of action if they take part in the decision making. And they're likely to be happier, which seems to be at least one key to HPWSs, research shows.[8] They will "know more, do more, and contribute more."[9]

Shared information shifts organizations away from command and control and toward employee commitment. It also shifts the relationship between employers and employees, from one that is merely transactional to one that is more relational. A study of Chinese hospitals found that HPWSs don't work as well when employees and employers view their relationship as merely an exchange of labor for money (transactional). Employees just end up exhausted by the extra demands put on them.

By contrast, when employees and employers have a more relational view—they see the firm's commitment to its employees, and the employees' commitment to the firm, as a long-term relationship—an HPWS is more likely to succeed.[10] Sharing key information with employees indicates you trust them and that your commitment to them is long term. So does having a certain amount of job security, which in turn gives employees confidence to experiment with new ideas and products without having to worry about getting fired if they fail. Thus, trust can make the difference between firms like Apple that are able to innovate and adapt to change versus firms that are merely able to improve their productivity, quality, or cost savings.[11]

16.1c Knowledge Development

Knowledge development is the twin sister of information sharing. As Richard Teerlink, former CEO of Harley-Davidson, noted, "The only thing you get when you empower dummies is bad decisions faster." High-performance work systems depend on the shift from touch labor to knowledge work. Employees today need a broad range of technical, problem-solving, and interpersonal skills to work either individually or in teams on cutting-edge projects. Because of the speed of change, knowledge and skill requirements must also change rapidly. In today's work environment, employees must learn continuously. Stopgap training programs may not be enough.

Companies have found that employees in HPWSs need to learn in "real time," on the job, using innovative new approaches to solve novel problems. At Ocean Spray's Henderson, Nevada, plant, making employees aware of the plant's progress has been a major focus. A real-time scoreboard on the Henderson plant floor provides workers with streaming updates of the plant's vital stats, including average cost per case, case volumes filled, filling speeds, and injuries to date. When people are better informed, they do better work. "We operate in real time, and we need real-time information to be able to know what we have achieved and what we are working towards," says an Ocean Spray manager.

16.1d Performance–Reward Linkage

It is not uncommon for employees to intentionally or unintentionally pursue outcomes that are beneficial to them but not necessarily to the organization as a whole. A corollary of this idea, however, is that things tend to go more smoothly when there is some way to align the interests of an organization and its employees. When companies reward their employees based on their performance, workers naturally pursue outcomes that are mutually beneficial to themselves and the organization. When this happens, some amazing things can result. For example, supervisors do not have to constantly watch to make sure that employees do the right thing. Instead, employees are more likely to go out of their way—above and beyond the call of duty—to make certain that their coworkers are getting the help they need, systems and processes are functioning efficiently, and the firms' customers are happy.

As Case Study 2 at the end of the chapter explains, every 4 weeks, the natural foods grocer Whole Foods calculates the profit per labor hour for every team in every store. Teams that exceed a certain threshold get a bonus in their next paycheck. Performance-based rewards such as these ensure that employees share in the gains that result from any performance improvement. This also ensures fairness and tends to focus employees on the organization.

LO2 Although achieving both horizontal and vertical fit are important for high-performance work systems, which do you consider more critical and why?

16.2 Designing High-Performance Work Systems

No two firms, even those that compete against each other, are exactly the same. However, despite companies' differences, there are some clear trends in work design, HR practices, leadership roles, and information technologies that tell us what HPWSs look like.[12] Some of these are summarized in Figure 16.3.

16.2a Workflow Design and Teamwork

High-performance work systems frequently begin with the way work is designed. Reengineering, Lean Six Sigma, Kaizen, Agile management, and the like have driven many organizations to redesign their work flows. Firms are focusing on the key business processes that drive customer value—and then creating teams that responsibility for those processes. Recall that this is the idea behind self-directed work teams.

For example, UPS redesigned its delivery process to give truck drivers responsibility for scheduling their own routes and for making necessary changes quickly. UPS drivers work together as a team to identify bottlenecks and solve problems that slow delivery. To facilitate this collaboration, an advanced telematics system (called ORION) was installed in the delivery trucks to help teams of drivers balance routes among those with larger or lighter loads.[13] By redesigning the workflow around key business processes, companies such as UPS have been able to establish a work environment that facilitates teamwork, takes advantage of its employees' skills and knowledge, empowers employees to make decisions, and provides them with more meaningful work.[14]

In most cases, a "homegrown" process and procedures developed by a firm's managers and employees will work better than one adopted from elsewhere. Each organization has unique circumstances, and parties are more likely to commit to procedures they create and own. Homegrown processes can also give a firm a competitive advantage because they are harder for competitors to imitate.

A common mistake organizations make is focusing on either top-down changes driven by executives or bottom-up changes cultivated by the employees. Firms such as Champion International, now a part of International Paper, and ASDA, a low-cost British retailer, are among the many companies that have found that the best results occur when managers and employees work together.[15] At MTS, a telecommunications company based in the Canadian province of Manitoba, unions and company managers design, select, and implement new procedures together.

Figure 16.3 Design Aspects of High-Performance Work Systems

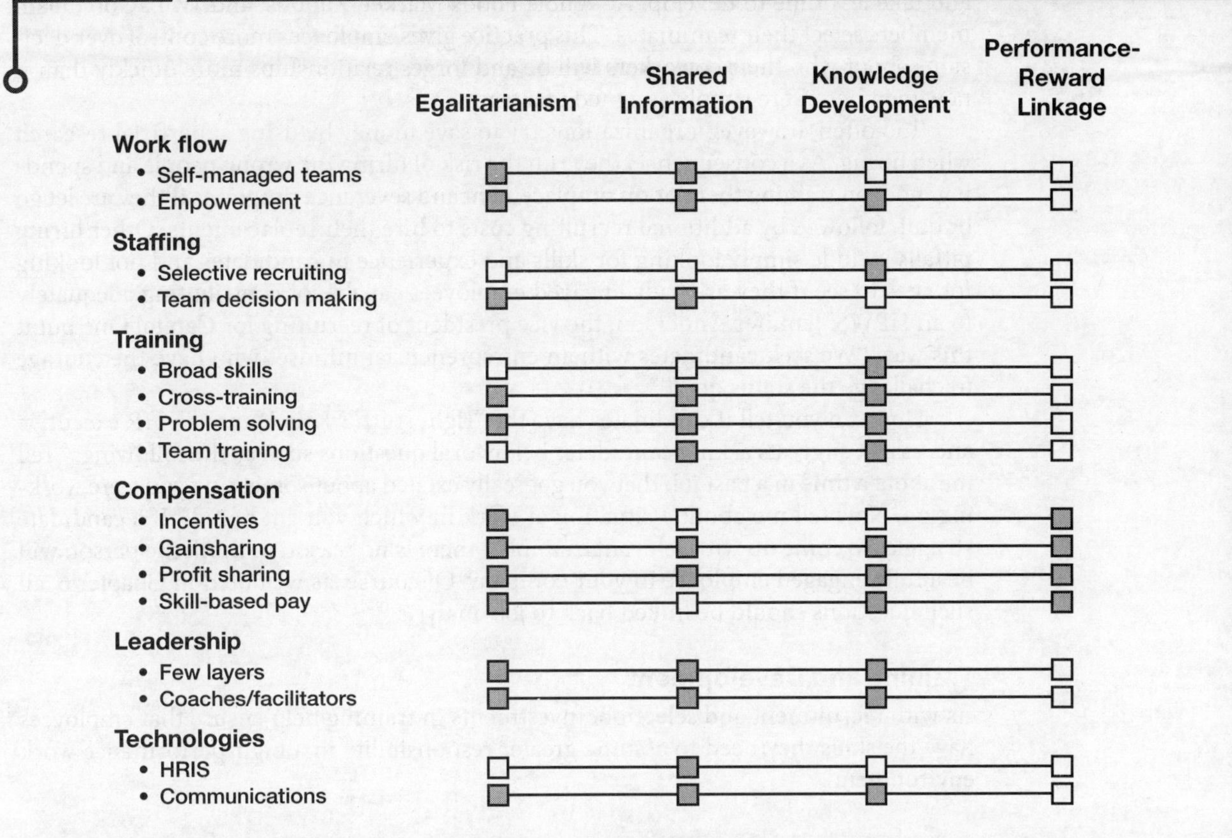

HR personnel need to be intimately involved with the development of new procedures, too. Most HR managers have a good idea of what works in a particular firm and what does not. Thus, the recruiting, evaluation, and reward systems devised by a firm's HR department can have a huge impact on how well HPWSs are implemented.

16.2b Complementary Human Resources Policies and Practices

Work redesign, in and of itself, does not result in an HPWS. Neither does reengineering or Lean or Six Sigma. Instead, other supporting elements of HRM are needed to reach the organization's goal. For example, several studies suggest that both the performance of employees and their satisfaction are much higher when organizations combine their changes in workflow design with HR practices that encourage skill development and employee involvement.[16] Next, let's look at some of these key HR practices.

Staffing Practices

Many HPWSs begin with highly selective recruitment and staffing practices. The recruitment tends to be both broad and intensive to obtain the best pool of candidates from which to choose. Human resources information systems have made it easier for firms to compile an inventory of their talent and search for employees with the specific skills they need. Talented, high-potential employees "come up to speed" more quickly and take less time to develop. At Whole Foods Market, Zappos, and W. L. Gore, team members select their teammates. This practice gives employees more control over decisions about who their coworkers will be and forges relationships more quickly than if new members were simply assigned to a team.[17]

Too often, however, organizations try to save money by using superficial research when hiring. As a consequence, they run the risk of hiring the wrong people and spending more on training them or on outplacement and severance programs if they are let go or quit, followed by additional recruiting costs to hire their replacements. Other hiring pitfalls include simply looking for skills and experience in candidates and not looking for cues to see if they are truly engaged employees capable of contributing adequately to an HPWS. Jennifer Anderson, the vice president of recruiting for Capital One put it this way: "We seek candidates with an entrepreneurial mindset who have the courage to challenge the status quo."[18]

How can you tell if candidates have the "right stuff"? Kris Dunn, an HR executive and writer, suggests asking candidates behavioral questions such as the following: "Tell me about a time in a past job that you got really excited about something you were working on. Now tell me about a situation at work in which you got bored." If a candidate struggles to come up with relevant examples, there is no reason to think the person will be a fully engaged employee in your company. Of course, as we noted in Chapter 6, all such questions should be linked back to job analysis.[19]

Training and Development

As with recruitment and selection, investments in training help ensure that employees have the skills they need to assume greater responsibility in a high-performance work environment.

Abdul Razak Latif/Shutterstock.com

High-performance work systems have helped many auto manufacturers improve their production and quality.

Schindler Elevator, the world's second-largest manufacturer of elevators, provides a 60-hour prehire training program of instruction and testing in such subjects as orientation/company history, safety, plant policies and procedures, just-in-time (JIT) techniques, and basic shop math. The company also has an apprenticeship program. Schindler's emphasis on teamwork, engagement, and continuous improvement requires employees to develop a broader understanding of work processes performed by others around them, rather than rely on just knowing their own jobs.[20]

Recall that cross-training involves training employees in jobs in areas closely related to their own. Cross-training is very important for an HPWS. For example, nurses in the perinatal unit of Cincinnati-based TriHealth implemented cross-training to facilitate teamwork and cooperation across units; the training also helps nurses identify trouble spots that can occur in several of the jobs and allows them to suggest areas for improvement.

In the end, training and development programs help to reinforce (at least) three of the four core principles of HPWFs. First, they help create a more egalitarian environment, where employees are engaged and empowered. Second, they reinforce shared information and trust. Third, they nurture ongoing knowledge development. The fourth principle, performance–reward linkage, is illustrated in the next section.

Compensation and Benefits

The compensation package is another important piece of an HPWS. Because HPWSs ask many different things from employees, it is difficult to isolate one single approach to setting pay rates that works for everyone. As a consequence, many companies are experimenting with alternative compensation plans. To link pay and performance, HPWSs often include some type of employee incentives. Pushing decision making down to front-line roles usually requires higher compensation for two reasons: Leaders often need to pay more to attract highly skilled people, and the higher pay can be used to reward high performance, says Alec Levenson, senior research scientist at the Center for Effective Organizations at the University of Southern California in Los Angeles.[21] At Henry Ford Health System, a Detroit-area hospital network, employees' monetary performance incentives are tied to the system's strategic plan. If the system exceeds its financial targets, and if a business unit also achieves its targets and budget, then employees are awarded commensurately.[22] In 2010, Hilcorp Energy, a Houston firm, awarded every employee either a new car or $50,000 for meeting a five-year challenge for doubling the firm's value, production rate, and oil and gas reserves. When employees doubled Hilcorp's numbers again in 2015, each one of them received $100,000.[23]

Other organizational incentives such as gainsharing, profit-sharing plans, and employee stock ownership plans, focus employee efforts on outcomes that benefit both themselves and the organization as a whole. The Scanlon plan, Rucker plan, and improshare—three systems discussed in Chapter 10—have been used by companies to elicit employee suggestions and reward them for contributions to productivity.

High-performance work systems can also incorporate skill-based pay plans. By paying employees based on the number of different job skills they have, organizations such as Shell Canada and Honeywell have created both a broader skill base among employees and a more flexible pool of people to rotate among interrelated jobs. Both of these qualities are beneficial in a high-performance work environment and may justify the extra compensation.[24]

Lastly, more companies are connecting their firm's corporate responsibility goals with their compensation systems. Whole Foods, the retailer Marks & Spencer, and Tesco (a global grocer and merchandiser) are among the companies that incorporate sustainability targets into their performance goals. Whole Foods and Tesco's goals include community-involvement initiatives as well.[25]

Recall that in addition to linking pay and performance, HPWSs are based on the principle of egalitarianism. This principle encourages employees to be more involved and committed.[26] At Henry Ford Health System, each staff member within a business unit—including physicians—gets the same incentive reward if the unit's goals are met, which in a recent year averaged about $800.[27] At Tesco, the bonuses staff members and executives receive are tied to meeting the company's corporate social responsibility goals, as is the pay for the firm's board of directors.[28] Open pay plans that allow employees to know what everyone else makes are another compensation system used to create a more egalitarian environment.

Of course, not every company can afford to offer its employees incentive pay or profit sharing, let alone a car or a $100,000 bonus. As we have explained, every company has to develop its own practices. To better match their HR practices with their workforces and retain lower-wage workers in high-turnover industries, some firms utilize programs that motivate employees by offering them more flexibility and other work–life benefits. Kaiser Permanente and Marriott have implemented a range of practices geared toward this end, such as giving employees flexible starting and ending times to their work shifts and the ability to take paid time off for a few hours to take care of their personal business rather than having to take an entire day off if they don't need it.[29] Lyft and other companies are utilizing ATM-like systems that allow workers to cash out their pay as soon as they earn it, rather than waiting for a paycheck.[30]

Management Processes and Leadership

Organizations such as Motorola, Doubletree Hotels, American Express, and Reebok International found that the success of any HPWS depends on first changing the roles of managers and team leaders. With fewer layers of management and a focus on team-based organization, the roles of managers and supervisors are substantially different in the HPWS environment. Specifically, managers and supervisors are seen more as coaches, facilitators, and integrators of team efforts.[31] Rather than autocratically imposing their demands on employees and closely monitoring workers, managers share responsibility for decision making with employees, help them become better decision makers, and troubleshoot and innovate on their own. Typically, the term *manager* is replaced by the term *team leader.* In a growing number of cases, leadership is shared among team members. It's not uncommon to rotate team leaders at various stages in team development. That way, different individuals can assume functional leadership roles when their particular expertise is needed most.

16.2c Supportive Information Technologies

Communication and information technologies are yet one more piece that has to be added to the framework of HPWSs. Technologies of various kinds create an infrastructure vital for communicating and sharing information. During the COVID-19 pandemic, virtually every organization scrambled to make certain that employees working remotely had access to the technology they needed to perform their jobs well. This went beyond access to communication and video conferencing, and included secure access to data and information required for decision making and performing the required functions of their work. Many organizations found that, when the right adjustments were made, employee productivity did not suffer with this model of working.

But information technologies need not be high tech. Even in a hybrid work environment, the richest communication still occurs face to face. The important point is that HPWSs cannot succeed without timely and accurate communications and data. (Recall the principle of shared information.) Typically, the information shared needs to be about business plans and goals, unit and corporate operating results, incipient problems and opportunities, and competitive threats.[32]

16.3 Strategic Alignment

Each of these practices we have discussed highlights the individual pieces of an HPWS. As we discussed in Chapter 2, careful planning helps ensure that the pieces fit together and are linked with the overall strategic goals of the organization. Figure 16.4 summarizes the internal and external linkages needed to fit HPWSs together.

16.3a Ensuring Horizontal Fit

Chapter 2 noted that **horizontal fit**, or alignment, occurs when all *internal* elements of a work system—HR practices, work designs, management processes, and technologies—reinforce one another. The synergy achieved through overlapping work and HR practices is at the heart of what makes a high-performance system effective.

horizontal fit
The situation in which all the internal elements of the work system reinforce one another.

Figure 16.4 Achieving Strategic Alignment

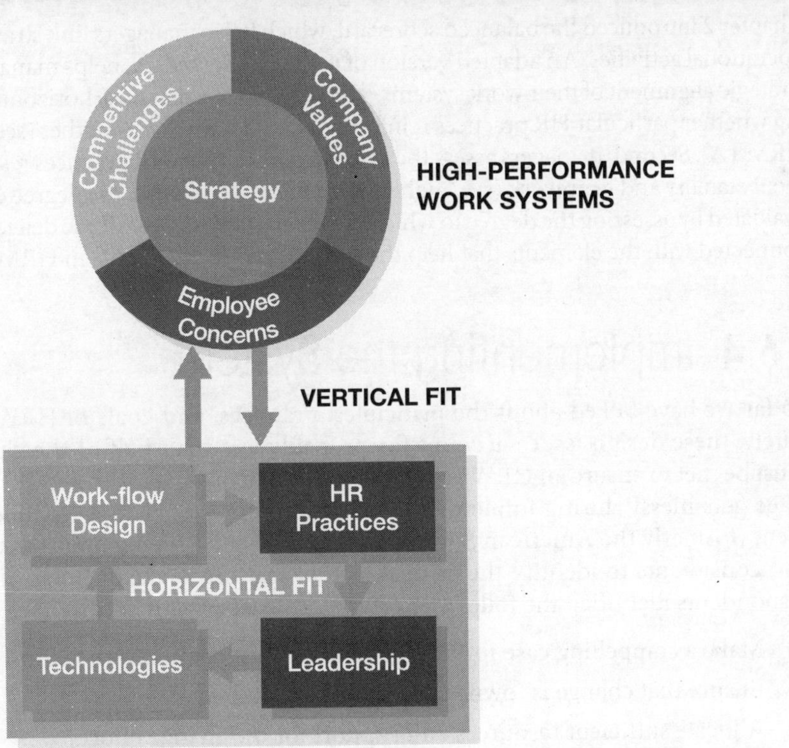

For example, a training program that encourages teamwork may be of no use if it is accompanied by a compensation system that reinforces individual performance. The two components might be working at cross purposes. Moreover, changes in one component will affect all of the other components because the pieces are interdependent.

16.3b Establishing Vertical Fit

vertical fit
The situation in which the work system supports the organization's goals and strategies.

To achieve **vertical fit**, or vertical alignment, HPWSs must support the organization's strategies given its external competitive challenges, its organizational values, and the concerns of employees.[33]

UPS uses a planning process known as "Eyes on the Enterprise," which begins with a statement of corporate vision, values, strategies, and key capabilities for investment. These priorities establish clear goals for the organization. In turn, each business unit establishes annual objectives based on these goals, and the process cascades down through every level of management. Ultimately, each employee within UPS has a clear "line of sight" to the strategies and goals of the organization, so they can see how individual effort makes a difference.[34]

Efforts such as these help focus the design of HPWSs on a firm's strategic priorities. Objectives such as innovation, faster speed to market, cost containment, quality enhancement, and better customer service directly influence what is expected of employees and the skills they need to be successful. High-performance work systems are designed to link employee initiatives to those strategies.

16.3c Assessing Strategic Alignment: The HR Scorecard

Chapter 2 introduced the balanced scorecard, which helps managers link strategic goals and operational activities. An adapted version of it, the HR Scorecard, helps managers assess the strategic alignment of their work systems.[35] First, managers diagnose horizontal fit by assessing whether particular HR practices reinforce or conflict with one another (see Highlights in HRM 1A). Second, managers assess the extent to which their HR practices result in employment stability and teamwork (see Highlights in HRM 1B). Third, the degree of vertical fit is evaluated by assessing the degree to which the results that the workforce delivers are actually connected with the elements that help the firm excel (see Highlights in HRM 1C).

LO3

This chapter emphasizes the processes required to implement a high-performance work system. What are the most critical steps to successfully implementing one?

16.4 Implementing the System

So far we have talked about the principles, practices, and goals of HPWSs. Unfortunately, these design issues account for probably less than half of the challenges that must be met to ensure an HPWS is successful. Much of what looks good in the planning stage gets messy during implementation. When the Association for Talent Development (formerly the American Society for Training and Development) asked managers and consultants to identify the critical factors that can make or break an HPWS, the respondents identified the following actions as necessary for success (see Figure 16.5):

- Make a compelling case for change linked to the company's business strategy.
- Ensure that change is "owned" by senior and line managers.
- Allocate sufficient resources and support for the change effort.
- Ensure early and broad communication of the effort.

1A Highlights in HRM

Diagnosing Horizontal Fit

This chart estimates the degree to which the various HR management subsystems work together. Think of the degree of fit and internal consistency as a continuum from −100 to +100, and assign a value in that range to each relationship. Examples of the extremes and midpoints on that continuum are as follows:

−100: The two subsystems work at cross purposes.

0: The two subsystems have little or no effect on one another.

+ 100: Each subsystem is mutually reinforcing and internally consistent.

DNK: Don't know or have no opinion.

	HR Planning	Recruiting and Selection	Training and Development	Performance Management and Appraisal	Compensation and Benefits	Work Organization (e.g., Teams)	Communication Systems	HR Performance Measurement	
								Cost	Value Creation
HR planning	—	−30	0	−20	0	0	0	0	0
Recruiting and selection		—	0	−10	−20	−30	0	30	−40
Training and development			—	0	0	0	0	30	−10
Performance management and appraisal					0	−30	20	0	−20
Compensation and benefits					—	−50	0	40	0
Work Organization (e.g., teams)						—	0	0	0
Communication systems							—	0	0
HR performance measurement									

Source: Brian Becker, Mark Huselid, and Dave Ulrich, *The HR Scorecard* (Cambridge, MA: Harvard University Press, 2001).

- Ensure that teams are implemented in a systemic way.
- Establish methods for measuring the results of the change.
- Ensure continuity of leadership and appoint "champions" of the initiative.[36]

16.4a Building a Business Case for Change and Engaging Stakeholders

Change can be threatening because it asks people to abandon the old ways of doing things and accept new approaches that—to them at least—are untested. Figure 16.6 shows how to "build a bridge" with the firm's stakeholders such as its employees, the

1B Highlights in HRM

Testing the Alignment of the HR System with HR Deliverables

Indicate on a scale of −100 to +100 the degree to which the following HR system elements facilitate the HR deliverables shown. Examples of the extremes and midpoints on that continuum are as follows:

−100: This dimension is counterproductive for enabling this deliverable.

0: This dimension has little or no effect on this deliverable.

+100: This dimension significantly enables this deliverable.

DNK: Don't now or have no opinion.

	HR Planning	Recruiting and Selection	Training and Development	Management and Appraisal	Compensation and Benefits	Work Organization (e.g., Teams)	Communication Systems
Employment stability	0	0	0	0	−50	−20	0
Team-based behaviors	0	0	−30	−20	−40	0	0
Strategy-focused behaviors	0	0	0	0	40	0	0
High-talent staffing level	0	−50	0	−50	0	0	0

1C Highlights in HRM

Testing the Alignment of HR Deliverables

Indicate on a scale of −100 to +100 the degree to which each HR deliverable in the following chart enables each strategic driver. Empty cells indicate this is not a key deliverable for a particular driver. Examples of the extremes and midpoints on that continuum are as follows:

−100: This deliverable is counterproductive for enabling this driver.

0: This deliverable has little or no effect on this driver.

+ 100: This deliverable significantly enables this driver.

DNK: Don't know or have no opinion.

		HR Deliverable			
	Strategic Performance Drivers	Employment Stability among Senior R&D Staff	Team-Based Behaviors	Strategy-Focused Performance	High-Talent Staffing Level
1.	Shorten product development times	−80	−30	30	
2.	Enhance customer focus and responsiveness	−20		−20	
3.	Enhance productivity		−10	−50	−40
4.	Develop and successfully manage joint ventures	−10	−50		

Figure 16.5 Implementing High-Performance Work Systems

unions it works with, and other groups when implementing HPWSs.[37] One way to forge a partnership is to show the groups where the business is today—its current performance and capabilities. Then show them where the organization needs to be in the future. The gap between today and the future represents a starting point for discussion. For example, when executives at TRW wanted to make a case for changing to an HPWS, they used employee attitude surveys and data on turnover costs. The data provided enough

Figure 16.6 Building Cooperation with Stakeholders

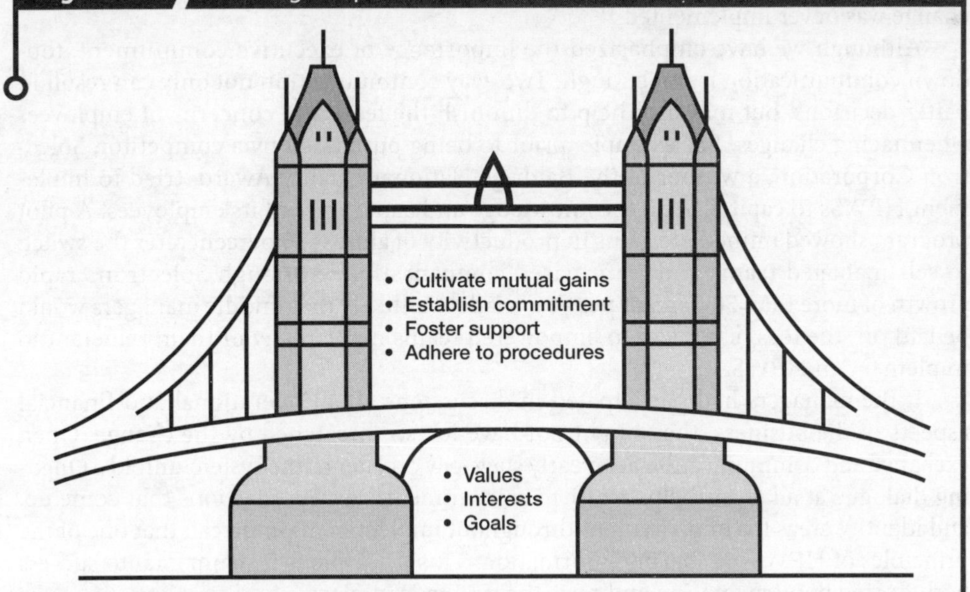

Source: Adapted from the Conference Board of Canada.

momentum to get a conversation going about needed changes and sparked some suggestions about how they could be implemented.

Some research studies have found that unions can be a barrier to HPWSs, perhaps because unions are concerned that the efficiencies achieved might be so great that workers' jobs would be eliminated.[38] To help get unions on board, managers should try to create "win-win" situations in which all stakeholders, including unions, gain from the implementation of HPWSs. Organizations such as Shell and Novartis have found that "interest-based" (win-win) approaches work best.

16.4b Establishing a Communications Plan

Building support for an HPWS and implementing such a system will be more readily accomplished if a top manager champions or promotes the system. This person should spend a substantial amount of time communicating with employees about the change and the reasons for it, and then, along with other top managers, work closely with middle managers to make it happen. Because middle managers operate in the trenches of an organization amid both its people and its processes, they can have a big impact on a firm's performance and how fast changes take place.[39]

Nonetheless, the burden of making major transformations should not be shouldered only by middle managers. It should be clear to employees that the CEO and senior managers are also intimately involved with and committed to the change. When Harley-Davidson executives tried to institute employee involvement groups without first demonstrating their own personal commitment to the program, employees were apathetic about it. They concluded that the changes were just "another program" put in place by HR. Similarly, the CEO of a business consulting company was adamant that his vice presidents understand a new initiative and give a short speech about it at an introductory session. On the day of the program's launch, however, the CEO himself did not show up. The message to the vice presidents was clear: The CEO did not think the change was important enough to become an active participant. Not surprisingly, the change was never implemented.[40]

Although we have emphasized the importance of executive commitment, top-down communication is not enough. Two-way communication not only can result in better decisions, but may also help to diminish the fears and concerns of employees when facing changes. For example, prior to being purchased by a competitor, Solectron Corporation, a winner of the Baldrige National Quality Award, tried to implement HPWSs to capitalize on the knowledge and experience of its employees. A pilot program showed immediate gains in productivity of almost 20 percent after the switch to self-managed teams and team-based compensation. Although Solectron's rapid growth of more than 50 percent per year made it unlikely that middle managers would be laid off, the loss of control to empowered teams made many of them reluctant to implement an HPWS.

If the managers had participated in discussions about operational and financial aspects of the business, they might not have felt so threatened by the change. Open exchange and communication at an early stage pay off later as the system unfolds. Ongoing dialogue at all levels helps reaffirm commitment, answer questions that come up, and identify areas for improvement throughout implementation. Recall that one of the principles of HPWSs is sharing information. This principle is instrumental to success both during implementation and once the system is in place.

Navigating the Transition to High-Performance Work Systems

Different organizations implement HPWSs in different ways. In startup firms, managers have the advantage of being able to put everything in place at once. However, when organizations have to be retrofitted, the process can be a bit more involved. For example, when Honeywell switched to an HPWS in one of its plants, employees attended training programs and participated in the redesign of their jobs while the plant was shut down and being reequipped with new technology. When the new plant was reopened, self-managing teams were put in place, and a new pay system was implemented for the high-performance workforce.[41]

Not every organization has the luxury of suspending operations while changes are put in place. For example, in existing organizations, the pieces of the system often have to be changed incrementally rather than as a total program. Establishing an implementation plan that provides a timetable for redesigning the workflow and training employees can keep the effort from bogging down.

Adhering to New Procedures

Following the new procedures required to implement an HPWS is often the hardest part of the job. As one HR executive puts it, "Procedure is the 'rug' on which alliances [a firm's stakeholders] stand. Pull it out by making a unilateral management determination or otherwise changing the rules of the game, and the initiative will falter. Procedure keeps the parties focused."[42]

HR managers are in a good position to help employees in transition handle what they are going through in terms of changes. When the old ways of doing things are abandoned, many experienced employees can feel like beginners again on the job. This disruption to their lives can be stressful and sometimes polarizes employees. To cope, many people, including managers, are likely to revert to older routines. Ford and Texas Instruments created special units to facilitate their transitions to HPWSs. The consumer-goods maker Unilever created a team of senior line and HR managers to help prevent relapses.[43]

16.4c Evaluating and Sustaining the Success of the System

Once HPWSs are in place, they need to be monitored and evaluated over time. First, the organization needs to conduct a **process audit** to determine whether the system has been implemented as it was designed and whether the principles of HPWSs are being reinforced. Employee-related questions such as the following might be included in this audit:

process audit
Determining whether the high-performance work system has been implemented as designed.

- Are employees actually working together, or is the term "team" just a label?
- Are employees getting the information they need to make empowered decisions, and are they engaged?
- Are training programs helping employees develop the knowledge and skills they need?
- Are employees being rewarded for good performance and useful suggestions?
- Are employees treated fairly so that power differences are minimal?
- Are quality-of-life goals being achieved for employees?

To determine whether the HPWS is succeeding, managers should look at metrics such as the following:

- Are the behaviors the organization desires being exhibited on the job?

- Are quality, productivity, flexibility, and customer service objectives being met?
- Is the organization more competitive than it was in the past?

Implementing an HPWS is one thing; sustaining it is another. As with any change activity, there will undoubtedly be missteps during the system's implementation for any number of reasons. Xerox Corporation found that when it implemented teams without also changing its compensation system to support teamwork, it got caught in a bad transition. The teams actually performed worse than employees working alone. In other words, building and fostering HPWSs can't be a piecemeal approach.

Because the work teams in an HPWS are performing at their peak, burnout can be a problem among employees. If there aren't enough staff members to manage the volume of work, a high level of stress is almost guaranteed. Employee poaching by competitors can occur, too. Motorola's Indian division strategically recruited its employees and put together an HPWS, only to have them be hired away by a competitor. Consequently, Motorola had to look for new ways to motivate and retain the division's workforce.

Small Business Application

Are Your Employees Engaged, or Do You Need an HPWS?

Companies with disengaged workforces suffer from problems that do not seem to get better, including excessive employee turnover, lower productivity, and profits. When employees are engaged, however, the results can be much different. One Gallup study reported that firms with top engagement scores had 18 percent higher productivity and 16 percent higher profitability. Another study found that engaged employees outperform other employees and are far less likely to leave their organizations. In a small business, engagement can have an even bigger impact because the margin for error when it comes to success or failure is so thin.

As a small-business owner, how do you know if your employees are engaged or not? One way would be to survey them. Gallup has come up with a 12-question survey designed to gauge employee engagement that includes the following items:

- Do you have the materials and equipment you need to do your work right?
- At work, do you have the opportunity to do what you do best every day?
- In the last seven days, have you received recognition or praise for doing good work?
- Does your supervisor, or someone at work, seem to care about you as a person?
- Is there someone at work who encourages your development?
- At work, do your opinions seem to count?

Business author Barb Taylor Krantz has another idea about how to measure engagement: Just talk to your employees. A CEO of a large company can't talk to all of the firm's employees, but a small-business person can. What motivates them to achieve, which aspects of their jobs are most satisfying, and how can they contribute more in those areas? What challenging goals can they set for their own development? If your employees can't answer these questions, chances are good they are not engaged.

So how can you increase the engagement of employees other than by asking them to work harder than they already are? Simply looking for a quick fix to engagement won't work, says HR blogger Gautam Ghosh. "For world-class companies like Southwest Airlines, employee engagement is a way of life that's taken them years to build into their cultures. It's not a strategy or program to them. It's just part of their corporate DNA."

To improve employees' engagement, you may have to take a deep dive, by looking at your firm's culture, rethinking how you operate, and implementing the concepts in this chapter. Two other good publications that can help a small business implement an HPWS are *The HR Scorecard: Linking People, Strategy, and Performance* and *The Power of Full Engagement: Managing Energy, Not Time, Is the Key to High Performance and Personal Renewal.*

Sources: Duckjung Shin and Alison M. Konrad, "Causality between High-performance Work Systems and Organizational Performance," *Journal of Management* 43, no. 4 (2017): 973; Barb Krantz Taylor, "Are Employees Going Above and Beyond?" *The Bailey Group* (July 10, 2009), http://www.thebaileygroup.com; "The Backlash against Employee Engagement," RiseSmart (April 2, 2010), http://www.risesmart.com.

Finally, HPWSs should be periodically reevaluated in terms of new organizational priorities and initiatives. Because an HPWS is built to deliver value to customers and thereby increase a firm's strength, as their needs change, so too should the system. When change occurs, it should be guided by a clear understanding of the business needs and exhibit a close alignment with strategy.

16.5 Outcomes of High-Performance Work Systems

LO4 Do high-performance work systems always result in a win-win situation for employers and their employees? Why or why not?

Organizations achieve a wide variety of outcomes from successful HPWSs and effective HR management. We have categorized these outcomes in terms of either *employee concerns*, such as quality-of-work-life issues and job security, or *competitive challenges*, such as the firm's performance, productivity, and profitability. Throughout this text, we have emphasized that the best organizations find ways to achieve a balance between these two sets of outcomes and pursue activities that improve both.

16.5a Employee Outcomes and Quality of Work Life

When properly implemented, managed, and monitored, HPWSs offer employees numerous potential benefits. Many of these benefits relate to the intrinsic motivation created by work that is more interesting and engaging, leading to higher quality of work life. Because the systems emphasize learning, people have an opportunity to improve themselves and try new things. Oftentimes, employees are empowered to take more risks, and even make mistakes, which in turn can actually lead to generating new ideas, products, services, and markets. As Richard Carlton, a former executive of 3M, put it, "You can't stumble if you're not in motion."[44] Because employees are more informed and have more latitude to decide how to achieve their goals, they are likely to feel they have a bigger role to play and that their opinions and expertise are valued more. As a result, they are more likely to be satisfied on the job and to find that their career-growth needs are being met. In addition, workers are likely to have more job security because their skills are higher and their potential to contribute to the organization is greater. This makes them more marketable to other organizations.

Conversely, when employees are underutilized, the performance of an organization suffers, and employees develop poor work attitudes and habits. Some years ago, Land Rover, a manufacturer of four-wheel-drive vehicles, found itself saddled with a notorious reputation for poor quality and productivity. In response, it sought to implement a fundamental transformation. The company instituted extensive training (including giving every employee a personal training fund to be used on any subject), implemented more team-based production methods, reduced the number of separate job classifications, developed more cooperative relations with organized labor, and began a total quality program. As a result of these changes, productivity, quality, and the company's sales soared.[45]

16.5b Organizational Outcomes and Competitive Advantage

Several desirable organizational outcomes can also result from using HPWSs. These outcomes include greater innovation for a firm, greater flexibility, higher productivity, lower costs, better responsiveness to customers, and higher revenues and profits. For example, a study of 962 firms in multiple industries showed that HPWSs resulted in an annual increase in profits of more than $3,800 per employee. Another study of 62 automobile plants showed that those implementing HPWSs had 47 percent better quality and 43 percent better productivity.[46]

However, although benchmarks such as these are indicative of success, they may not be enough to sustain an organization's competitive advantage. Recall that in Chapter 2 we said that organizations can create a sustainable competitive advantage through people if they focus on four criteria. These same criteria also hold for HPWSs:

- *Valuable:* High-performance work systems increase value by establishing ways to increase innovation and efficiency, decrease costs, improve processes, and provide something unique to customers.
- *Rare:* High-performance work systems help organizations develop and harness skills, knowledge, and abilities that are not equally available to all organizations.
- *Difficult to imitate:* High-performance work systems are designed around team processes and capabilities that cannot be transported, duplicated, or copied by rival firms.
- *Organized:* High-performance work systems combine the talents of employees and rapidly deploy them in new assignments with maximum flexibility.[47]

These criteria clearly show how HPWSs, in particular, and HR management, in general, are instrumental in achieving competitive advantage through people.

However, for all their potential, implementing HPWSs is not an easy task. The systems are complex and require close partnering among all of a firm's stakeholders. Ironically, this very complexity can lead to a competitive advantage. The ability to integrate business and employee concerns is indeed rare, and doing it in a way that adds value to customers is especially noteworthy. Organizations such as Google, Marriott, and Southwest Airlines have been able to achieve this feat over an extended period of time, and as a result they enjoy a competitive advantage.

Land Rover vehicles were notorious for their poor quality until a company-wide transformation resulted in better quality and productivity.

John Henderson/Alamy Stock Photo

Summary

LO 1 High-performance work systems are specific combinations of HR practices, work structures, and processes that maximize the knowledge, skills, commitment, and flexibility of employees. These systems are based on the principles of shared information and trust, knowledge development, performance–reward linkages, and egalitarianism and employee engagement.

LO 2 High-performance work systems are composed of several interrelated components. Team members are carefully selected, undergo extensive training, including cross training, and often share leadership duties. Integrated information systems can help ensure that employees have the information they need to make timely and productive decisions. To align the interests of employees with those of the organization, the reward systems associated with HPWSs are performance-based and often include group and organizational incentive pay and sometimes skill-based pay. When all the pieces of the system support and complement one another, the HPWS can achieve horizontal fit. When such a system is aligned with the competitive priorities of the organization as a whole, it can achieve vertical fit as well.

LO 3 Implementing HPWSs within existing organizations often has to be done in stages. The implementation is much more likely to go smoothly if a business case is first made for the HPWS and fully communicated to employees. Gaining the support of the firm's various stakeholders is essential. A company's HR department can be an invaluable partner when it comes to implementing an HPWS. HR personnel can also help establish a transition structure to shepherd the implementation through its various stages and reassure employees they will be successful working in the new system. Once the system is in place, it should be evaluated in terms of its processes, outcomes, sustainability, and ongoing fit with the organization's strategic objectives.

LO 4 When implemented effectively, HPWSs benefit both employees (who enjoy more interesting work and better quality of work life) and their organizations (which realize improved productivity, customer value, innovation, and agility), and can provide a company with a sustainable competitive advantage.

Key Terms

high-performance work system (HPWS)

horizontal fit

process audit

vertical fit

Discussion Questions

LO 1 Do you think the fundamental principles of getting employees highly involved with their work provide an adequate context for designing high-performance work systems? What other concerns or guidelines for developing high-performance work systems would you suggest?

LO 2 Although achieving both horizontal fit and vertical fit is important for high-performance work systems, which do you consider more critical and why?

LO 3 This chapter emphasizes the processes required to implement a high-performance work system. What are the most critical steps to successfully implementing such a system?

LO 4 Do high-performance work systems always result in a win-win situation for employers and their employees? Why or why not?

HRM Experience

Assessing the Strategic Fit of High-Performance Work Systems

High-performance work systems are potentially powerful tools. However, ensuring all HR practices support one another and the principles of an HPWS is not always easy. Some HR practices might support the HPWS, while others work against it. It takes only one misaligned practice to crash the whole system. Recall that the HPWS principles include the following:

- Egalitarianism and engagement
- Shared information and trust
- Knowledge development
- Performance–reward linkage

Assignment

The following figure lists the main HR practices used at Egan Clothiers, Ltd. Working in teams of four to six, assess the extent to which you believe each HR practice supports (or works against) each of the HPWS principles.

1. For each cell in the matrix, insert a number indicating the extent to which you believe the HR practice supports the principle or is counterproductive. The scale runs from –5 (strongly counterproductive) to +5 (very supportive). Zero indicates neither support nor detriment.
2. When you are done filling in each cell, add the numbers across each row to determine how supportive each HR practice is of all of the principles. Which HR practice is the most supportive? Which HR practice is the least supportive?
3. Add each column to see how the overall set of HR practices supports each principle. Which principle is most strongly supported? Which principle is the biggest concern?
4. Add the rows and/or columns to see how well the HPWS is supported overall. What changes would you recommend to improve the system?

Note: This figure corresponds to the integrative case on Egan Clothiers, Ltd., in the back of the text. The exercise can be used in conjunction with the case, or you may simply refer to the case as background reading.

EGAN CLOTHIERS, LTD.

HPWS PRINCIPLES

HR PRACTICES	Egalitarianism	Shared Information	Knowledge Development	Performance-Reward Linkage		
STRUCTURE						
• Cross-functional team						Row 1
• Department rotation						Row 2
STAFFING						
• Select for experience						
• Promote from within						
TRAINING						
• Retail selling skills						
• Customer service						
REWARDS						
• Results appraisal						
• Forced distribution						
• Individual incentives						
TECHNOLOGY						
• HR information system						
• Post performance						
	Column 1	Column 2	Column 3	Column 4	TOTAL	

SCORING KEY

5 = strongly supports the principle
0 = neutral
–5 = strongly counterproductive

CASE STUDY 1 How Implementing an HPWS Fortified the Snack-Food Maker Snyder's-Lance

When Greg Flickinger became the director of manufacturing for the snack-food maker Snyder's-Lance's facility in Charlotte, North Carolina, he was determined to build from scratch the kind of high-performance workforce he had led when he worked for a competing firm. Many organizations take piecemeal approaches to improving their firms. But Flickinger knew that one-off plans for improvement would not result in sustained improvements for the plant—especially given the fact that nearly 1,000 employees worked at the Charlotte site producing more than 500 types of products. What the Charlotte plant needed was an all-encompassing high-performance work system.

The first step in developing the HPWS was to create a vision for it that could be defined succinctly and communicated easily to all staff members. Ultimately the vision was defined as follows: "To nurture a transition from a traditional work system to an employee-centric high-performance work system (HPWS) with a cultural foundation rooted in total employee involvement and focused on continuous improvement."

The details inherent in the vision then shaped the foundation of a formal but very simple and direct mission: "Take care of your people and deliver your numbers." This statement was front and center in every meeting, every communication, and every initiative that was undertaken. It provided the rallying cry and aligned everyone across the site with a concept that was easily translated into something real that people could get their minds around, says Flickinger.

To implement the HPWS, the company completely restructured the way the plant was led. The hierarchical structure of supervisors, department managers, and superintendents was eliminated, and replaced with team leaders, line leaders, and technical support leaders. The line leadership concept was the most critical role in the development of the plant's culture of accountability. A line leader was assigned to each line and was responsible for all of its inputs and outputs—from raw materials and ingredients in the door through to the finished products out the door. In essence, each line leader owned the success of all aspects of their line 24 hours a day. This created a single point of accountability. The technical support leaders became the support group for line leaders by providing them with expertise in areas such as reliability engineering, system engineering, line changeovers, and sanitation.

Another milestone in the development of the HPWS was cross-training everyone, including salaried employees. Employees had one month to learn all the jobs and determine who would work what job. They had to learn to work together as a team in a very different way than they had ever worked before. This gave everyone on the line an opportunity to walk in the shoes of everyone else and take another step forward toward building trust and respect among salaried and hourly employees.

After the HPWS was completely implemented, the Charlotte plant experienced financial results no one thought were possible:

- A 40 percent reduction in waste
- A 41 percent reduction in incidents
- A 52 percent reduction in consumer complaints

These metrics signaled that the HPWS had been effective. Moreover, the improvements were sustained in following years. What made these gains even more significant was that the performance improvements were made with negligible capital investment. Put simply, the results were driven through a focus on people and processes.

Implementing an HPWS isn't an easy process, though, says Flickinger. Sustained results do not come overnight. Above all, empowering an organization at the individual level doesn't mean that a firm's managers can walk away from their guidance, prioritization, and, above all, support roles, he says. "As a leader, you have to make sure the effort touches every employee individually and in a real way. Make the tough decisions to ensure you are taking care of your people, and remember, above all else, sustained success begins and ends with them."

Questions

1. Identify how Synder's-Lance engages its employees.
2. Why might it be more effective to implement an entire new system like an HPWS rather than make incremental changes at a production facility like the one in Charlotte? Couldn't the large-scale changes create chaos in a plant its size?

Sources: Adapted from Greg Flickinger, "How Snyder's-Lance Transformed Its Plant into a High Performance Work System," *Food Processing* (2011), http://www.foodprocessing.com.

CASE STUDY 2 Whole Foods Market Faces Whole New Challenge

In this chapter we talked about how hierarchical, command-and-control types of organizational structures are giving way to high-performance work systems—systems characterized by egalitarianism, knowledge and information sharing, employee empowerment, and reward and performance linkages. That description pretty well sums up the approach taken by Whole Foods Market, the world's leading natural and organic foods grocer. Whole Foods started out in 1980 with one small store in Austin, Texas. In 2017, Amazon acquired Whole Foods for $13.7 billion. Today this company employs more than100,000 employees in more than 500 stores in North America, Canada, and the United Kingdom.

Whole Foods' HR practices have been a big part of its success, and some have wondered what Amazon might do to that legacy. Since its earliest days, Whole Foods hasn't been "run" in a hierarchical way, with top-down directives being issued by executives and store managers. Instead, the company embraces empowerment by in-store teams. In fact, managers are referred to as "team leaders." Each team takes responsibility for one area of the store, such as baked goods, meat, poultry, and so forth, and is authorized to make product, pricing, and staffing decisions. This high degree of decentralization allows the stores to better tailor their offerings and services to meet the needs of their local communities, which helps them be more competitive.

The decentralized approach begins with hiring. The company found that centralized, online recruiting left local stores awash with resumes but not much knowledge about applicants. Applicants can still submit resumes online, but now each location has its own in-store kiosks where applicants can apply. Many interviews at Whole Foods Markets are conducted by teams of employees. And even after an applicant is hired, the importance of teamwork continues to be emphasized. New employees are assigned to one of the store's teams for a trial period, after which the team members vote to determine if the person deserves a full-time spot on the team. The same process is used at the corporate level for employees who want to join the firm's marketing, human resources, finance, and IT departments.

The voting is crucial in part because it affects workers' paychecks. The teams are treated as separate profit centers and rewarded with monthly bonuses if their labor costs are under budget. Stores sometimes offer prizes for competing teams. Consequently, nobody wants to vote in a slacker. Not surprisingly, the company does not do a lot of monitoring of its employees—the employees do it themselves. "We don't have lots of rules handed down from headquarters in Austin," John Mackey, the founder of the company and former CEO, has said. "Peer pressure enlists loyalty in ways that bureaucracy doesn't."

To encourage a more egalitarian environment, Mackey instituted a salary cap on executive pay. Originally, senior executives could make no more than 14 times the average annual salary of a full-time employee. Although that number has risen as the company has become larger, employees still have an equal footing. For example, employees vote on company-wide initiatives, and the company provides full-timers with full health care benefits as well as access to a company-funded wellness account.

To encourage learning and knowledge sharing that can help employees learn about products, the company instituted a mentoring program and developed an online portal called "Whole Foods Market University" to aid in training. Nearly 8 out of 10 employees say that the training Whole Foods offers has helped them advance professionally. Employees are encouraged to pursue continuing education through the company's online training portal or certifications such as the American Cheese Society Certified Cheese Professional exam, green recycling classes, cooking seminars, and work-related field trips. Invariably, Whole Foods lands on *Fortune*'s 100 Best Companies to Work For list each year. "I love working at Whole Foods, and I hope to grow with this company for years and years to come," says one of its employees. "This company empowers me and makes me feel valued and valuable."

The current challenge for Whole Foods is sustaining that environment—and the firm's success. Recently the company has been facing greater competition from lower-priced grocers like Trader Joe's and regional grocers that sell organic food, putting pressure on

Whole Foods' growth and profitability. The company responded by streamlining operations, creating efficiencies in purchasing and merchandising, and fine-tuning functions like technology and human resources. The goal was to improve customer and employee experiences by enabling regional operations to focus on running the stores and to better define team members' roles, growth opportunities, and paths for advancement. Whole Foods has also undertaken initiatives geared toward lowering its prices, creating a customer loyalty program, and, thanks to its relationship with Amazon, collaborating with Amazon Prime to blend its in-store operations with online purchasing. Although the biggest growth has been in its online business, Whole Foods has reinvigorated growth in its in-store sales as well. Even during the COVID-19 pandemic, the company created more than 10,000 new jobs.

However, some industry analysts think that, despite the positive news, the changes in Whole Foods' business model may be harming the "secret sauce" that has made the company so distinctive. "What's happened in the natural food sector is that the world has changed very fast around it," says Joe Dobrow, a health food writer and book author. "Now there isn't very much that is unique to Whole Foods anymore."

Questions

1. Why don't all companies treat their employees like Whole Foods does? Are there downsides of doing so?
2. Do you think Whole Foods will have to change its HR practices to better compete? Are the practices no longer vertically or horizontally aligned with the firm's strategy? Or does the firm's strategy need to change?

Sources: Russell Redman, "Whole Foods Market to Consolidate Some Operations: Specialty Grocer Outlines Changes and Growth Plans in Company Memo," *Supermarket News*, May 14, 2021; Dana Burkus, "Are Whole Foods' Smiling Cashiers and Friendly Baristas Replaceable?" Society for Human Resource Management, September 18, 2017; David Burkus, "Why Whole Foods Builds Its Entire Business on Teams," *Forbes*, June 8, 2016; Alexandra Stevenson, "Whole Foods Pressured by Activist Investor Jana Partners," *The New York Times*, April 10, 2017; Tom Philpott, "Employees Are Bitter as Whole Foods Chops Jobs and Wages," *Mother Jones* (October 3, 2015), http://www.motherjones.com; "Celebrating Great Workplace Cultures," *Great Place to Work Institute* (2013), http://www.greatplacetowork.com; "Whole Foods Market Named to 2013 'World's Most Ethical Companies' List," *MarketWatch* (March 6, 2013), http://www.marketwatch.com; Gary Hael and Bill Breen, "Creating a Community of Purpose: Management Innovation in Action," Harvard Business School Press, 2007; "Whole Foods Market's Unique Work Culture and Practices," ICMR (2006), http://www.icmrindia.org; Frank Roche, "HR Lessons from Whole Foods," KnowHR, http://www.knowhr.com.

Notes and References

1. Diane Landsman, "Talent Management at the Best Workplaces," *Talent Management* (April 4, 2007), http:/talentmgt.com.
2. James Combs, Yongmei Liu, Angela Hall, and David Ketchen, "How Much Do High-Performance Work Practices Matter? A Meta-Analysis of Their Effects on Organizational Performance," *Personnel Psychology* 59 (2006): 501–528; Rebecca R. Kehoe and Patrick M. Wright, "The Impact of High-Performance Human Resource Practices on Employees' Attitudes and Behaviors," *Journal of Management* 39, no. 2 (2013): 366–391; D. A. Nadler and M. S. Gerstein, "Designing High-Performance Work Systems: Organizing People, Work, Technology, and Information," in *Organizational Architecture* (San Francisco: Jossey-Bass, 1992), 195–208; E. Lawler III, Susan Albers Mohrman, and Gerald E. Ledford, *Creating High Performance Organizations: Practices and Results of Employee Involvement and Total Quality Management in* Fortune *1000 Companies* (San Francisco: Jossey-Bass, 1995); Edward Lawler III, Susan Albers Mohrman, and George Benson, *Organizing for High Performance: Employee Involvement, TQM, Reengineering, and Knowledge Management in the* Fortune *1000: The CEO Report* (San Francisco: Jossey-Bass, 2001). See also David Nadler, Michael Tushman, and Mark Nadler, *Competing by Design: The Power of Organizational Architecture* (New York: Oxford University Press, 1997); Jody Gitell Hoffer, "Relationships and Resilience," *Journal of Applied Behavioral Science* 44, no. 1 (2008): 25–47.
3. Beth Kowitt, "At Ikea, No Ranks, No Rancor," *Fortune* (March 15, 2016): 202.
4. Verne Harnish, "Five Ways to Keep Employees Excited," *Fortune* (December 3, 2012), 40.
5. Murielle Tiambo, "To Be a Successful Independent, You Need to Empower Your Employees and Let Them Know They Are Critical to Success," *Forbes*, February 19, 2019; Tae-Youn Park and Jason D. Shaw, "Turnover Rates and Organizational Performance: A Meta-Analysis," *Journal of Applied Psychology* (2013): 98(2): 268; J. B. Arthur, "Effects of Human Resource Systems on Manufacturing Performance

and Turnover," *Academy of Management Journal* 37 (1994): 670–687; M. Huselid, "The Impact of Human Resource Management Practices on Turnover, Productivity, and Corporate Financial Performance," *Academy of Management Journal* 38 (1995): 635–672; Mark A. Youndt, Scott A. Snell, James W. Dean, Jr., and David P. Lepak, "Human Resource Management, Manufacturing Strategy, and Firm Performance," *Academy of Management Journal* 39, no. 4 (1996): 836–866; John F. Tomer, "Understanding High-Performance Work Systems: The Joint Contribution of Economics and Human Resource Management," *Journal of Socio-Economics* 30, no. 1 (2001): 63; Kris Dunn, "Rules of Engagement," *Workforce Management Online* (July 2008).

6. Arnold B. Bakker, Evangelia Demerouti, and Ana Isabel Sanz-Vergel, "Burnout and Work Engagement: The JD-R Approach," *Annual Review of Organizational Psychology and Organizational Behavior* 1, no. 1 (2014): 389–411; Rasha Mourtada, "Bosses Fan the Flames of Burnout," *Globe and Mail* (June 8, 2011), http://www.theglobeandmail.com.
7. Zixiang Ma, Yaping Gong, Lirong Long, and Yong Zhang, "Team-Level High-Performance Work Systems, Self-Efficacy and Creativity: Differential Moderating Roles of Person–Job Fit and Goal Difficulty," *International Journal of Human Resource Management* 32, no. 2 (2021): 478–511; "Developing and Sustaining High-Performance Work Teams," Society for Human Resource Management (July 23, 2017), https://www.shrm.org.
8. Linda Anderson, "A Little Something for the Weekend," *Financial Times* (June 3, 2011), http://www.ft.com.
9. Carlton P. McNamara, "Making Human Capital Productive," *Business and Economic Review* 46, no. 1 (1999): 10–13; Meagan Stovel and Nick Bontis, "Voluntary Turnover: Knowledge Management—Friend or Foe?" *Journal of Intellectual Capital* 3, no. 3 (2002): 303–322.
10. M. Zhang, C. Zhu, P. Dowling, and T. Bartram, "Exploring the Effects of High-Performance Work Systems (HPWS) on the Work-Related Well-Being of Chinese Hospital Employees," *International Journal of Human Resource Management* 24, no. 16 (2013): 3196–3212.
11. Hui Zhang and Lanyun Wang, "The Description and Evaluation on the Modern Mechanism of High-Performance Work Systems," *Modern Management* 3, no. 5 (2013): 135–140.
12. Steven D. Silver, "Designing Technology for Managing the Information Exchange of Decision Making Teams," *Decision Support Systems* 61 (2014): 136–146; Martin Eppler and Oliver Sukowski, "Managing Team Knowledge: Core Processes, Tools and Enabling Factors," *European Management Journal* 18, no. 3 (2000): 334–341; Andrea Foote, "One in a Million: Ocean Spray Henderson Has Parlayed Hard Work and Dedication into a Remarkable Operations Milestone," *Beverage World* 122, no. 8 (August 15, 2003): 22–29; Rick Frattali, "The Company That Teaches Together Performs Together," *T + D* 61, no. 7 (2007), http://www.astd.org.
13. K. J. Carrig and S. A Snell, *Strategic Execution: Driving Breakthrough Performance in Business* (Palo Alto, CA: Stanford University Press, 2019).
14. Mark Chen, "Applying the High-Performance Work Teams to EPC," *AACE International Transactions* (2002): PM61PM67; Valerie Sessa, "Supporting Work Team Effectiveness: Best Management Practices for Fostering High Performance," *Personnel Psychology* 53, no. 2 (2000): 457–460.
15. Amina Malik, Laxmikant Manroop, and Pankaj C. Patel, "An Empirical Examination of the Relationship between HPWS and Firm Performance," *Academy of Management Proceedings* 2016, no. 1 (2016); Martha Gephart and Mark Van Buren, "Power of High Performance Work Systems," *Training & Development* 50, no. 10 (1996): 21–36; Michael Beer, "How to Develop an Organization Capable of Sustained High Performance: Embrace the Drive for Results–Capability Development Paradox," *Organizational Dynamics* 29, no. 4 (2001): 233–247.
16. Karina Van De Voorde and Susanne Beijer, "The Role of Employee HR Attributions in the Relationship between High-Performance Work Systems and Employee Outcomes," *Human Resource Management Journal* 25 no. 1 (2015): 62–78; Lawler, Mohrman, and Ledford, *Creating High Performance Organizations*; Eileen Appelbaum, Thomas Bailey, Peter Berg, and Narne Kalleberg, *Manufacturing Advantage: Why High-Performance Work Systems Pay Off* (Ithaca, NY: Cornell University Press, 2000); Gil Preuss and Brenda Lautsch, "The Effect of Formal versus Informal Job Security on Employee Involvement Programs," *Relations Industrielles* 57, no. 3 (2002): 517–539; Wendy S. Becker, "*Manufacturing* Advantage: Why High-Performance Work Systems Pay Off," *Personnel Psychology* 56, no. 2 (2003): 549–553.
17. Liang-Chih Huang et al., "High Performance Work Systems, Employee Well-being, and Job Involvement: An Empirical Study" *Personnel Review* 45, no. 2 (2016): 296–314; Laurie J. Bassi and Mark E. Van Buren, "Sustaining High Performance in Bad Times," *Training & Development* 51, no. 6 (1997): 32–42; Michael J. Stevens and Michael A. Campion, "Staffing Work Teams: Development and Validation of a Selection Test for Teamwork Settings," *Journal of Management* 25, no. 2 (1999): 207–228.
18. Christopher Tkacyz, "Tips from Recruiters at the 100 Best Companies," *Fortune* (March 15, 2016): 90.
19. Bruce Horowitz, "Twelve Unconventional Interview Questions That Recruiters Should Ask," *HR Magazine*, June 11, 2021; Carolee Coleter, "To Build a Productive Team, Interview Effectively," *Natural Foods Merchandiser* 25, no. 12 (2004): 27; Kris Dunn, "Rules of Engagement," *Workforce Management Online* (July 2008).
20. Agam Shah, "Going Up? The Elevator-as-a-Service Business," *Wall Street Journal*, October 19, 2019; "We Elevate Training: We Invest in You," Schindler, https://www.schindler.com/us/internet/en/careers/why-schindler/training.html#button.

21. Alec Levenson, "The Value of High Performance Work Design," *Talent Economy* (November 7, 2017), http://www.talenteconomy.io.
22. Jake Rosenfeld, "Paying Workers Based on Performance Is Harder Than It Looks," *Wall Street Journal*, March 17, 2021; Douglas McCarthy, Kimberly Mueller, and Jennifer Wrenn, "Henry Ford Health System: A Framework for System Integration, Coordination, Collaboration, and Innovation," Commonwealth Fund (August 2009), http://www.commonwealthfund.org.
23. Chris Matthews, "This Company Gave Every One of Its Employees a $100K Christmas Bonus," *Fortune* (December 11, 2015), http://fortune.com; Erica Frey, "Hilcorp Energy," *Fortune* (August 12, 2013), 14.
24. Jake Rosenfeld, "You're Not Paid Based on Your Performance," *Harvard Business Review*, February 23, 2021; Rosemary Batt and Lisa Moynihan, "The Viability of Alternative Call Centre Production Models," *Human Resource Management Journal* 12, no. 4 (2002): 14; Frank Giancola, "Skill-Based Pay: Issues for Consideration," *Benefits & Compensation Digest* 44, no. 5 (2007): 1–15.
25. Rod Newing, "Targets Are Linked to Pay by Early Adopters," *Financial Times* (June 7, 2011), http://www.ft.com.
26. David Paper, James Rodger, and Parag Pendharker, "A BPR Case Study at Honeywell," *Business Process Management Journal* 7, no. 2 (2001): 85–93. See also Robert McNabb and Keith Whitfield, "Job Evaluation and High Performance Work Practices: Compatible or Conflictual?" *Journal of Management Studies* 38, no. 2 (2001): 293–312; Leslie A. Weatherly, "Performance Management: Getting It Right from the Start," *HR Magazine* 49, no. 3 (2004): S1–S11.
27. Douglas McCarthy, Kimberly Mueller, and Jennifer Wrenn, "Henry Ford Health System: A Framework for System Integration, Coordination, Collaboration, and Innovation," Commonwealth Fund (August 2009), http://www.commonwealthfund.org.
28. Newing, "Targets Are Linked to Pay by Early Adopters."
29. Rachel Emma Silverman, "For Hourly Jobs, White-Collar Perks," *Wall Street Journal* (October 8, 2011), B8.
30. Stacy Cowley, "New Payday Options for Making Ends Meet," *The New York Times* (July 4, 2016), https://www.nytimes.com.
31. Peter Gahan, Max Theilacker, Mladen Adamovic, Daejeong Choi, Bill Harley, Joshua Healy, and Jesse E. Olsen, "Between Fit and Flexibility? The Benefits of High-Performance Work Practices and Leadership Capability for Innovation Outcomes," *Human Resource Management Journal* (August 2020); Clinton Longenecker, "Building High Performance Management Teams," *Industrial Management* 43, no. 6 (2001): 21–26; Wendy S. Becker, "Manufacturing Advantage: Why High-Performance Work Systems Pay Off," *Personnel Psychology* 56, no. 2 (2003): 549; Srivastava Pallavi and Jyotsna Bhatnagar, "Turnaround at Motorola India: Mobile Devices Business through the HR Lever," *Journal for Decision Makers* 33, no. 1 (2008): 119–129.
32. Alexandar Samuel, "How to Manage the New Hybrid Workplace," *Wall Street Journal*, March 21, 2021; W. Randy Evans and Walter D. Davis, "High-Performance Work Systems as an Initiator of Employee Proactivity and Flexible Work Processes," *Organization Management Journal* 12, no. 2 (2015): 64–74; Keith Newton, "The High Performance Workplace: HR-Based Management Innovations in Canada," *International Journal of Technology Management* 16, no. 1–3 (1998): 177–192; Georg Von Krogh, Kazuo Ichijo, and Ikujiro Nonaka, *Enabling Knowledge Creation: How to Unlock the Mystery of Tacit Knowledge and Release the Power of Innovation* (New York: Oxford University Press, 2000); Lawler, Mohrman, and Benson, *Organizing for High Performance*.
33. Patrick M. Wright and Scott A. Snell, "Toward a Unifying Framework for Exploring Fit and Flexibility in Strategic Human Resource Management," *Academy of Management Review* 23, no. 4 (1998): 756–772; Clair Brown and Michael Reich, "Micro-Macro Linkages in High-Performance Employment Systems," *Organization Studies* 18, no. 5 (1997): 765–781; S. A. Snell, M. Shadur, and P. M. Wright, "Human Resources Strategy: The Era of Our Ways," in M. A. Hitt, R. E. Freeman, and J. S. Harrison (eds.), *Handbook of Strategic Management* (London: Blackwell, 2002), 627–649.
34. Carrig and Snell, *Strategic Execution: Driving Breakthrough Performance in Business*; Björn Michaelis, Joachim D. Wagner, and Lars Schweizer, "Knowledge as a Key in the Relationship between High-Performance Work Systems and Workforce Productivity," *Journal of Business Research* 69, no. 5 (2015): 1035–1044; Van Buren, M.E and Werner, J.M. "High Performance Work Systems," High performance work systems," *Business and Economic Review*, 43, no. 1 (1996): 15–23; Gilbert Probst, Steffen Raub, and Kai Romhardt, *Managing Knowledge: Building Blocks for Success* (New York: Wiley, 2000). For a similar example of horizontal fit within European firms, see Sue Hutchinson, John Purcell, and Nick Kinnie, "Evolving High Commitment Management and the Experience of the RAC Call Center," *Human Resource Management Journal* 10, no. 1 (2000): 63–78.
35. Brian Becker, Mark Huselid, and Dave Ulrich, *The HR Scorecard: Linking People, Strategy, and Performance* (Cambridge, MA: Harvard Business School Press, 2001).
36. Tom Harbert, "How to Manage Change: HR Can Play a Critical Role in Helping the Workforce Evolve to Meet Future Needs," *HR Magazine*, March 11, 2021; Jongwook Pak and Seongsu Kim, "Team Manager's Implementation, High Performance Work Systems Intensity, and Performance: A Multilevel Investigation," *Journal of Management* (2016): 0149206316646829; Arup Varma, Richard W. Beatty, Craig Eric Schneier, and David O. Ulrich, "High Performance Work Systems: Exciting Discovery or Passing Fad?" *Human Resource Planning* 22, no. 1 (1999): 26–37.

37. Sarah Jensen Clayton, "An Agile Approach to Change Management," *Harvard Business Review,* January 11, 2021; Greg Satell, "4 Tips for Managing Organizational Change," *Harvard Business Review*, August 27, 2019; Takao Katom, Hideaki Miyajima, and Hideo Owan, *Does Employee Stock Ownership Work?* Research Institute of Economy, Trade and Industry (RIETI; 2016); Louise Clarke and Larry Haiven, "Workplace Change and Continuous Bargaining," *Relations Industrielles* 54, no. 1 (1999): 168–191; Ruth Wright, "Forging Sustainable Alliances in a New Economy," *Canadian Business Review* (Summer 1995): 20–24; Sukanya Sengupta, "The Impact of Employee-Share-Ownership Schemes on Performance in Unionised and Non-Unionised Workplaces," *Industrial Relations Journal* 39, no. 3 (2008): 170–190.
38. Akhtar Mahmood, Muhammad Kashif Khurshid, and Usman Ali, "The Impact of High Performance Work System on Employees' Attitude: The Mediating Role of Human Resource Flexibility," *Journal of Contemporary Management Sciences* 2, no. 1 (2017): 83–124; Wenchuan Liu, James P. Guthrie, Patrick C. Flood, and Sarah Maccurtain, "Unions and the Adoption of High Performance Work Systems: Does Employment Security Play a Role?" *Industrial & Labor Relations Review* 63, no. 1 (2009): 109.
39. Ethan R. Mollick, "People and Process, Suits and Innovators: The Role of Individuals in Firm Performance," *Social Science Research Network* (June 27, 2010), http://papers.ssrn.com.
40. Karina Van De Voorde and Susanne Beijer, "The Role of Employee HR Attributions in the Relationship between High-Performance Work Systems and Employee Outcomes," *Human Resource Management Journal* 25, no. 1 (2015): 62–78; Varma, Beatty, Schneier, and Ulrich, "High Performance Work Systems," 26–37; Gephart and Van Buren, "Power of High Performance Work Systems"; "Making Change Work—for Real," *HR Focus* 80, no. 1 (January 2003): S1.
41. Man Cao, Yixuan Zhao and Shuming Zhao, "Facilitating the Implementation Process of High-Performance Work Systems," *Frontiers in Psychology* (September 25, 2020); Judith A. Neal, Cheryl L. Tromley, Ernie Lopez, and Jeanne Russell, "From Incremental Change to Retrofit," *Academy of Management Executive* 9, no. 1 (1995): 42–54.
42. Wright, "Forging Sustainable Alliances," 20–24; Hannele Rubin, "How CEOs Get Results," *Chief Executive* (February 2001): 8.
43. Randa A. Wilbur, "Making Changes the Right Way," *Workforce* (March 1999): S12–S13; Gephart and Van Buren, "Power of High Performance Work Systems"; Irena St. John-Brooks, "CEOs See HR as Helping to Lead Organizational Efforts: USA," *Benefits & Compensation International* 32, no. 1 (2002): 73–74; "Human Resources Role Transformed at Deutsche Bank," *Human Resource Management International Digest* 10, no. 5 (2002): 12–14; Michael Svoboda and Silke Schroder, "Transforming Human Resources in the New Economy: Developing the Next Generation of Global HR Managers at Deutsche Bank AG," *Human Resource Management* 40, no. 3 (2001): 261–273; "HR Advice: Manage Transition—Not Just Change," *HR Briefing* (November 15, 2002): 1–2; "HR Must Seize Major Role over Change Management," *Personnel Today* (May 20, 2003): 8.
44. Liang-Chih Huang et al., "High Performance Work Systems, Employee Well-Being, and Job Involvement: An Empirical Study," *Personnel Review* 45, no. 2 (2016): 296–314; "How to Take the 'Non' out of Your Non-Performers," *Human Resource Department Management Report* (February 2005): 1–5; Paul Lukas and Maggie Overfelt, "3M, a Mining Company Built on a Mistake, Stuck It out until a Young Man Came along with Ideas about How to Tape Those Blunders Together as Innovations—Leading to Decades of Growth," *Fortune* (April 1, 2003), http://money.cnn.com/smallbusiness.
45. Andrew Biladeu, Gerry Yemen, Michael Lenox, and Jared Harris, "Tata Motors Limited: Ratan's Next Step," Darden Business Publishing, UVA-S-0184, 2013; Ian Rowley and Nandini Lakshman, "Can Tata Rev up Jaguar?" *BusinessWeek.com*, March 26, 2008, Jeffrey Pfeffer, "When It Comes to 'Best Practices'—Why Do Smart Organizations Occasionally Do Dumb Things?" reprinted from *Organizational Dynamics* (Summer 1996), with permission from Elsevier; Cordelia Brabbs, "Rover's White Knight," *Marketing* (May 18, 2000): 28; Georg Auer, "Burela to Instill Quality Culture at Land Rover," *Automotive News* 75, no. 5902 (2000): 32x–32z; Ronald W. Pant, "Land Rover History Lesson," *Truck Trend* 8, no. 3 (2005): 12; Bradford Wernle, "Solihull Must Do 'a Halewood' to Survive; Jaguar Plant Is the Example Land Rover Factory Must Follow," *Automotive News Europe* 9, no. 19 (September 20, 2004): 39.
46. P. Kumar, "High Performance Work Systems and Organizational Success," *Journal of Human Resource* 2, no. 6 (2014): 1–14; Gephart and Van Buren, "The Power of High Performance Work Systems."
47. John Purcell, "Best Practice and Best Fit: Chimera or Cul-de-Sac?" *Human Resource Management Journal* 9, no. 3 (1999): 26–41; Snell, Shadur, and Wright, "Human Resources Strategy: The Era of Our Ways," 627–649; Patrick M. Wright, Benjamin Dunford, and Scott A. Snell, "Human Resources and the Resource-Based View of the Firm," *Journal of Management* 27, no. 6 (2001): 701–721.

Integrative Cases

Case 1

Time for Realignment: Developing a Culture of Transparency at MX

Introduction

Nate drew himself forward in his chair and surveyed the job candidate on the other end of the Zoom call: "Here at MX, we're trying to empower the world to be financially strong. What values does it take to empower the world to be financially strong?" Nate often includes this question when looking to hire new talent at MX. Creating a transparent and open culture where people are excited about their jobs means that everyone in the company must embody the values required to improve the financial lives of individuals. At least, this is what Nate Gardner believes.

Nate Gardner is the chief customer officer (CCO) of MX. He started working for the company in this role in 2012, after working as the CEO of Costa Vida, where he helped build a restaurant brand that expanded to 25 branches and led to a multimillion-dollar exit. In his time at MX, Nate has been involved in both the contraction and expansion of MX. By 2016, he and other members of the executive team realized that the organically grown culture of MX had strayed from its foundation. Ryan Caldwell had founded the company in 2010 with the idea that people should be able to manage their finances through banks and other financial institutions more easily; that if they could see exactly where their money was going and be given some easier-to-use tools in managing their finances, perhaps they could avoid many of the financial problems he had seen his own friends and family make—problems that sometimes led to unanticipated debt, unnecessary fees, and even financial ruin. Knowing that more than 80 percent of the U.S. population lives from paycheck to paycheck, Ryan decided that if he could simply create solutions for end users and their banks to more effectively visualize and track their finances, he could help those individuals become financially stronger.

Today, MX helps financial institutions and fintechs utilize their data more effectively to outperform the competition in a rapidly evolving industry. The company provides software solutions to enable people and organizations to quickly and easily collect, enhance, analyze, present, and act on financial data. Using a method in which software tools are

As one of the fastest growing fintech companies in the United States, MX has learned that sustainable growth comes from a focus on its people making good product with a purpose to make the world financially strong.

delivered and licensed online via subscription, rather than bought and installed on individual computers (Software as a Service), MX provides organizations with mobile banking apps, financial visualization for banking customers, analytics and marketing of internal data, and data aggregation for customers who want to focus more on their core business of banking and financial services and have someone else ensure the customers have a seamless experience dealing with their banking or financial transactions online.

Alignment Problems

By 2016, however, MX had started to become a victim of its own success. It started hiring experienced senior leaders who were more familiar with the financial sector. It looked first and foremost to a person's resume—years of experience and technical competencies—with little acknowledgment of their fit with MX's foundation. It didn't take too long for Ryan, Nate, and other members of the executive team to realize that this was a mistake. The new senior hires were extremely good at what they did and quickly started to steer the culture more toward profits, processes, and privacy. But people were now losing a sense of why they were there. People were also being fired for mysterious reasons, and doubt started to set in. They started to doubt the organization: What was its purpose? They doubted the senior leadership team: Who are they going to fire next? How do I perform and show that I'm valuable to the company? What are the criteria? What once felt like a small, open company was now turning into a large, closed culture with no common vision or common way of working. If something wasn't done fast, MX stood to lose everything its employees had worked for. MX would be counted among the many tech startups that saw a surge in growth but was not able to adapt to that growth.

Alignment Solutions

From Nate's perspective, he saw two options. First, the company could acknowledge this shift in the culture and build in rigid processes to ensure that people were doing what they were supposed to be doing. In this case, MX would move to a more professionalized model—something that happens at a lot of companies when they start to grow and bring on new senior leaders who are familiar with large organizations. Second, the company could fight back against this shift and go back to its foundational roots. But going back to its roots didn't seem like an option for a maturing company. How could the firm maintain an open and transparent culture while also supporting major growth?

One day Nate was reading Laszlo Block's *Work Rules*, which described how Google had developed a startup culture in a large organization. He realized that if Google could do it with thousands of employees, then MX could do it with just hundreds employees. Even before finishing the book, he called up Ryan: "You've got to read this book. I think it's the key to our alignment problem." Desperate for a solution, Ryan read the book and quickly agreed. Ryan then distributed copies of the book throughout the organization. "We need to get everyone thinking like founders," Ryan said. "Having a founder's mindset means that regardless of title, we are empowered to act on our ideas to compose world-changing solutions to our customers and our MX team."

This triggered something inside of Nate. He thought, "We need to start with the problem, not with the solution—what problem are we trying to solve and what kinds of values are needed to solve this problem."

"Someone interested in climbing to the top of Mt. Everest only has to go online and look at some pictures of Mt. Everest to get a sense of what kinds of values will be needed to make it to the top," says Nate. "Looking at Mt. Everest, you see that this is going to take some real grit and preparation. It will attract a certain type of individual. Climbing Mt. Everest is not for everyone."

Nate started by calling the executive team together to discuss the "mountain" they were all trying to climb—to empower the world to be financially strong. Once they agreed on the challenge, they were then able to focus on what should be most valuable in the company. These values would act as guidelines for the company's aspirations. Through multiple iterations and after talking with key stakeholders in the organization, the team put together a rough list of seven core values for the company. These values were then presented in a town hall meeting to everyone in the company as a rough draft of what the company values should be. The executive team asked everyone in the company to give feedback on the core values and to help make changes to those values. Many changes were made, and a final set of values was constructed. But this was just the beginning.

Once the mission and values were created, the team laid out a plan to realign the culture. The next step was to embed these values in everything they did. They started by transforming the hiring process. Up to this point, hiring was random and done by managers alone. They quickly developed a hiring process that democratized hiring using behavioral science. They turned to behavior-based interviews, in which key questions asked about the job candidate's commitment to the core values. Moreover, the manager was only one piece of the hiring puzzle. All team members had an equal vote in the hiring process as well, and all were involved in interviewing. This was the first point of changing the culture because it acted as a gatekeeper to what kind of people were let into the organization in the first place.

The next area for change was the performance management system. Up to this point, there was no transparency in how employees were evaluated and developed. To ensure MX stayed true to its roots of meritocracy, the company leaders provided consistency in how people were given feedback and how promotions and salary decisions were made. They also made everyone's performance (including the executive team) in the organization completely transparent and contingent on the company values.

Next, they hired Brandon Woolf, who had worked at Google for nine years, as the "Chief People Officer." Brandon helped put together a transparent OKR (objectives and key results) system that aligned with the MX values. OKRs represent a framework for defining and tracking objectives and their outcomes. They were first popularized at Google, where this approach to management and goal setting became central to the company's culture. In fact, Larry Page, cofounder of Google, credited OKRs with helping Google achieve its 10-times growth rate.

Brandon worked with the executive team to develop unique OKRs for MX that fit and are aligned with the company's core values. Brandon also teamed up with a business intelligence company to create a dashboard that allowed for ongoing monitoring of these objectives and key results throughout the company, ensuring the values were embedded in everything people do at MX.

Even with all of this, the lasting power of this cultural shift would be put to the test soon.

Going Forward

In 2021, MX was at about 700 employees and was continuing to grow at exponential rates. Could the more organic structure that relied on its core values to govern how people were hired, developed, and managed maintain the strong culture amidst this rapid growth? Moreover, due to the COVID-19 pandemic of 2020–2021 many of its employees continued to work much of their time remotely. Nate was a bit worried. "I think the strength of our realigned culture will be put to a true test in the next year few years as we continue to grow in the virtual workspace," he commented. "I wonder what else we need to do to make sure this culture will stick?"

Questions

1. How can hiring people with lots of experience be dangerous to a company?
2. How would a virtual work culture be different from a culture established for employees in an office or facility?
3. Consider the development of MX's new performance management system. Does it seem like an effective system?

Case 2 Trains and Training at BNSF Railway

By its nature, the railroad industry can be a dangerous one in which to work. Consequently, railway workers must be equipped with the knowledge, tools, focus, and skills to work safely. At BNSF Railway, safety is of the utmost importance. As new hires come on board, BNSF provides training through multiple methods, including on-the-job training in the field with input from experienced employee mentors and safety assistants or safety coordinators. Formal training is provided for many positions at the company's Technical Training Center (TTC) in Overland Park, Kansas, as well as in the field.

Newly hired conductors at BNSF, for example, have an interim period before they are officially hired. Candidates must successfully respond to a panel interview. During the interview, BNSF's interviewers communicate the challenges of working for a railroad, along with BNSF's safety vision. Candidates also must pass safety and rules exams, and complete either a 13- or 15-week intensive training program (depending on the location), which includes both classroom and on-the-job training. The program culminates in a final exam that, when passed, qualifies students as conductors.

United Transportation Union (UTU) training coordinators help with the first week of training and pair students with experienced conductors who mentor students during the on-the-job training segment. Once the new hires are paired, the experienced conductors play a significant role in conductor training, teaching 9 to 10 weeks of the 13- to 15-week program. "I particularly focus on deadly decisions—and consequences of at-risk behaviors," says one of the UTU's training coordinators.

To further integrate a new conductor, a division's UTU training coordinators provide enhanced safety training specific to the conductor's location. This includes an overview of the local terrain and environmental extremes that a potential employee is likely to encounter. In Montana, for example, trainers help employees understand the challenges of operating through the mountains and in winter conditions.

Of course, the training at BNSF isn't just for new hires. For those on a managerial track, the company offers mentoring, safety leadership training, and an annual company-wide initiative called "People Leader Training." It is designed to develop the leadership capabilities of employees via a competitive railroad simulation and a 12-week online program that utilizes case studies, social learning, and gamification principles. BNSF also cross-trains its transportation trainers. They become qualified to train locomotive engineers and conductors, as well as provide training on simulators and rules and remote train control. This effectively increases BNSF's training capacity while also expanding individual trainers' areas of specialty.

Questions

1. What methods does BNSF use as part of its comprehensive training system for new hires? How do the methods differ for employees on a managerial track?
2. Explain the company's team approach to training. How does cross-training the company's trainers benefit BNSF?
3. What is the purpose of explaining, during interviews, BNSF's safety practices and on-the-job working challenges?

Sources: Excerpted/adapted from "Trainers Carry Forward BNSF's Safety Vision to New Hires," *Railway* (Spring 2011): 16–17; "Additional 2016 Best Award Winners," Association for Training and Development (October 5, 2016), https://www.td.org.

Case 3

Job Analysis and Hiring Decisions at Ovania Chemical Company

Background

Ovania Chemical Corporation is a specialty chemicals producer of polyethylene terephthalate (PET) thermoplastic resins, which are primarily used to make containers for soft drinks and bottled water, as well as packaging for food and pharmaceutical products. Although it's smaller than other chemical producers that operate on a global scale, Ovania has competed successfully in the specialty chemical business. Its main plant is located in Steubenville, Ohio, along the Ohio River midway between Pittsburgh, Pennsylvania, and Wheeling, West Virginia.

Over the years, advances in technology have altered the nature of chemical production. Like other firms in the industry, Ovania Chemical is constantly taking steps to stay abreast of these changes. Not surprisingly, the technological changes have been accompanied by redesign of employee jobs. In fact, over the last 3 years, there have been drastic changes in both the number and the kinds of jobs being performed by employees. The latest change at the Steubenville plant involves the job transformation of the system analyzer position.

The System Analyzer

Because chemical production involves highly integrated process technologies, someone is needed who can monitor all of the individual components simultaneously. The system analyzer is primarily responsible for this monitoring function. It is one of the most prestigious nonmanagerial jobs in the entire plant, and its importance is likely to grow.

Formerly, this position was classified as that of a semiskilled maintenance technician. As the plant has become more automated, however, the requirements for the system analyzer job have become much more extensive. Knowledge of pneumatics, hydraulics, information technology, programming, scheduling, and electrical wiring are all increasingly critical aspects of this job. The three men who currently hold the position admit that they will be incapable of performing adequately in the future. It is estimated that within 2 years, the tasks, duties, and responsibilities of the system analyzer will have changed by more than 70 percent. For these reasons, the decision was made to recruit and select three new people for the rapidly transforming position.

Job Analysis and New Position Analysis

The selection committee consisted of Ovania's Steubenville plant manager, Ravi Sarabe; the HR manager, Emily Claire; and two senior engineers, Dave Packley and Mary Young. With the help of two consultants, they first conducted a job analysis for the new position of system analyzer. Although they had to make some predictions about what the nature of the job would be in the future, they collectively felt they had created an accurate depiction of the requirements for someone who would occupy the position. Figure 3.1 shows a list of the major performance dimensions of the job and a subsample of specific tasks characteristic of each dimension.

From this list of tasks, the selection committee then delineated a set of 12 KSAOs required for anyone in the system analyzer position (shown in Figure 3.2). The numbers beside each ability indicate the tasks (see Figure 3.1) to which it is related. The abilities marked with an asterisk (*) were considered by the committee to be "critical." Any applicant not scoring well on each of the critical dimensions would be considered unqualified for the job.

Figure 3.1 Performance Dimensions (Duties and Tasks)

Maintaining Spares and Supplies
1. Anticipates future need for parts and supplies and orders them.
2. Stocks parts and supplies in an orderly fashion.
3. Maintains and calibrates test equipment.
Troubleshooting
4. Applies calibration standards to verify operation by subjecting the system to known standards.
5. Decides whether the problem is in the sensor, in the processor, in the process stream, and/or in the sample system.
6. Uses troubleshooting guides in system manuals to determine the problem area.
7. Uses test equipment to diagnose the problem.
8. Makes a general visual inspection of the analyzer system as a first troubleshooting step.
9. Replaces components such as printed circuit boards and sensors to see if the problem can be alleviated.
Handling Revisions and New Installations
10. Makes minor piping changes such as size, routing, and additional filers.
11. Makes minor electrical changes such as installing switches and wires and making terminal changes.
12. Uses common pipefitting tools.
13. Uses common electrical tools.
14. Reads installation drawings.
Record-Keeping
15. Maintains system files showing the historical record of work on each system.
16. Maintains loop files that show the application of the system.
17. Updates piping and instrument drawings if any changes are made.
18. Maintains Environmental Protection Agency records and logbooks.
19. Disassembles analyzers to perform repairs on site or back in the shop.
20. Replaces damaged parts such as filters, electronic components, light source, lenses, sensors, and values.
21. Uses diagnostic equipment such as oscilloscopes, ohmmeters, and decade boxes.
22. Tests and calibrates repaired equipment to ensure that it works properly.
23. Reads and follows written procedures from manuals.
Routine Maintenance
24. Observes indicators on systems to ensure that there is proper operation.
25. Adds reagents to systems.
26. Decides whether the lab results or the system is correct regarding results (i.e., resolves discrepancies between lab and analyzer results).
27. Performs calibrations.

Figure 3.2 Abilities and Tasks

Numbers represent tasks cited in Figure 3.1. Asterisks indicate abilities considered critical by the committee.

Skills	Task Numbers
*Finger dexterity	3, 4, 7, 9, 10, 11, 12, 13, 19, 20, 21, 22, 25, 27
*Mechanical comprehension	3, 5, 6, 7, 8, 9, 10, 11, 12, 13, 14, 17, 19, 20, 22, 23, 24, 27
*Numerical ability	3, 4, 10, 11, 12, 13, 14, 21, 24, 27
*Spatial ability	2, 4, 5, 9, 10, 11, 14, 19, 20
*Visual pursuit	3, 4, 5, 6, 7, 8, 9, 10, 11, 14, 16, 17, 19, 20, 21, 22, 27
*Detection	2, 3, 5, 6, 7, 8, 9, 10, 14, 19, 20, 23
Oral comprehension	1, 2, 5, 6, 7, 8, 9, 19, 21, 25, 26
Written comprehension	1, 15, 16, 17, 18
Deductive reasoning	1, 2, 3, 5, 6, 7, 8, 9, 10, 11, 19, 21, 20, 22, 26, 27
Inductive reasoning	1, 2, 3, 5, 6, 7, 8, 9, 10, 11, 19, 21, 20, 22, 26, 27
Reading comprehension	3, 6, 7, 9, 14, 22, 23, 21, 27
Reading scales and tables	2, 3, 4, 6, 7, 8, 9, 14, 21, 23, 24, 27

Anticipated Selection Process

The committee hoped to find the best available talent for the job, so they wanted to recruit externally for it. However, Ovania's top managers were also deeply committed to promoting from within. Ultimately, the committee decided to recruit both internally and externally for the new position. The committee also decided to encourage the firm's current system analyzers to reapply for the job.

Because there was a 2-year lead time before the newly transformed position would be put in place, the committee was very careful not to include in the selection battery any skills or knowledge that could reasonably be trained for within that 2-year period. Only aptitude or ability factors were incorporated into the selection process rather than achievement tests.

The three present system analyzers were White males. However, since Ovania Chemical had a rather unenviable history of employment discrimination charges, the decision was made to have applicants undergo a battery of tests but not look at their previous experience. The committee believed this would encourage underrepresented groups, including women, to apply for the new position regardless of their prior experience in the field.

However, there was some concern about prejudice if a woman or a member of an underrepresented group were to get the job. Several employees at the company said they wondered if a woman would be willing to get into the treatment tanks to check gauge readings. All of these factors, taken together, made for a very sensitive selection process. Ovania's managers, however, were dedicated to making the procedures and decisions fair and objective.

Fifty-six employees applied for the new position of system analyzer. Twenty-one were female; fifteen were Black. Only two of the three current system analyzers reapplied for the new position. The company decided that an overall total score of 800 on the 12 tests would be the cutoff score for an applicant to be seriously considered for the system analyzer position. This criterion resulted in the primary pool of 20 candidates shown in Figure 3.3. It should be noted that although each of the aptitude tests has been published, standardized (100 points possible for each test), and validated for other jobs, the same was not true of the system analyzer job because it is a new position. Therefore, whether the tests are predictive depends on content validity judgments made by the managers of the company. The final cutoff scores and methods for combining the multiple predictors are problematic for the selection committee as well.

Figure 3.3 Primary Pool of Candidates

Name	Race	Sex	External/ Internal	Test Scores: Finger Dexterity	Mechanical Comprehension	Numerical Ability	Spatial Ability	Visual Pursuit	Detection	Oral Comprehension	Written Comprehension	Deductive Reasoning	Inductive Reasoning	Reading Comprehension	Reading Scales and Tables		
Baldwin, T.	W	M	I	83	76	78	76	69	71	90	70	74	72	88	92	=	941
Bittner, D.	W	M	E	92	62	88	89	96	85	90	94	93	89	97	87	=	1062
Bohlander, G.	W	M	E	67	78	74	70	76	62	80	69	71	76	78	82	=	883
Buffett, J.	B	M	E	87	97	89	61	94	93	75	90	85	96	85	80	=	1032
Denny, A.	B	F	I	92	88	72	72	78	79	69	76	81	83	81	78	=	949
Egan, M.	W	F	E	93	80	76	98	76	88	93	92	93	78	81	92	=	884
Granger, D.	W	F	I	82	82	79	75	77	73	72	80	81	77	70	80	=	856
Haney, H.	W	M	E	82	76	76	71	69	80	62	76	75	74	78	67	=	810
Kight, G.	W	F	E	65	75	72	67	80	74	62	47	66	67	60	80	=	815
Kovach, S.	W	M	E	82	87	85	85	83	88	81	80	80	83	84	80	=	998
Laukitis, T.	B	F	E	87	97	63	89	93	90	91	85	86	96	88	89	=	1054
Lesko, B.J.	B	F	I	83	84	89	91	80	82	86	88	85	84	90	89	=	1031
Rom, D.	B	M	I	80	60	67	66	67	62	74	80	67	72	75	66	=	835
Sara, E.	W	F	I	89	91	77	93	90	91	88	78	98	80	80	76	=	1021
Sauder, C.	W	F	E	76	72	78	81	80	72	73	77	75	79	82	82	=	927
Sherman, A.	W	F	I	91	82	78	93	92	94	89	77	95	77	81	92	=	1041
Snell, J.	W	M	E	80	85	84	81	81	80	89	88	84	86	81	82	=	1001
Timothy, S.	W	F	E	82	78	76	71	69	80	62	76	76	70	71	67	=	878
Whitney, J.	W	M	I	67	71	70	76	76	62	81	69	71	76	78	82	=	815
Wright, P.	W	M	I	80	60	57	56	57	62	74	80	69	72	75	65	=	887

Questions

1. How would you go about conducting a job analysis for a job that does not yet exist?
2. What reasons did the selection committee have for selecting only those factors that could not be acquired in a 2-year training program?
3. Should the concern for women getting down into the dirty treatment tanks have been a selection issue?
4. Would the test battery and selection procedure decided on be defensible in court?

Case 4 Ill-Fated Love at Centrex Electronics

Juanita Hernandez-Canton never imagined she would lose her job at Centrex Electronics Corporation (CEC). Unfortunately, after 6 years of employment, the last 2 as a senior product engineer in CEC's military/space division in Atlanta, Hernandez-Canton made a mistake: she fell in love.

CEC is highly regarded as a quality employer in the electronics industry. It is a multinational corporation with engineering services and production facilities in Spain, Canada, Hong Kong, Mexico, and Germany. With more than 12,000 employees in the United States, the firm has been named as one of the country's top 100 organizations to work for by several studies. It is known as a top-paying corporation with proactive employee relations policies.

Kathryn Garner, the vice president of human resources for CEC, is credited with establishing many positive employee rights policies, including those covering electronic communications, drug testing, search and surveillance, access to employee records, same-sex partner benefits, and off-duty conduct. The corporation allows employees to marry except in cases where one employee is in a direct reporting relationship with the other.

Hernandez-Canton joined CEC shortly after graduating from Georgia State University in 2012. At that time she was married to Tom Canton, her college sweetheart. In 2015, Canton died suddenly. As a single parent, his widow then became dependent upon her job for the majority of her family's support.

Hernandez-Canton enjoyed rapid promotions through various engineering positions. She also had been awarded the firm's Engineering Distinction Award for her research and development work in metallography. But in January 2017, a week after receiving a significant raise, she was called into the firm's HR department. The question from the military/space division manager was clear and direct: "Are you dating Mike Domzalski?" Domzalski was a former CEC senior engineer who in 2015 had gone to work for International Technologies, a direct competitor of CEC. There was no denying the romance. The two had dated while Domzalski was with CEC, and he still remained friends with other CEC engineers. It was widely known among Hernandez-Canton's friends that she was "extremely fond" of Domzalski.

Now, chastised for her involvement, Hernandez-Canton was ordered to forget about Domzalski or be demoted. After the meeting, she told a friend, "I was so socialized in CEC culture and so devoted to my job that I thought seriously about breaking up with Mike." As she later testified in court, however, she never got the chance because she was dismissed the day after the meeting with her manager.

At the root of Hernandez-Canton's dismissal was a corporate policy regarding the leaking of confidential product information. This policy seeks to avoid situations where an employee of CEC might be compromised and forced into providing sensitive or confidential information to an employee of a competing organization. Hernandez-Canton's work in research and development made her subject to the following CEC policy:

> Employees performing jobs where they have access to sensitive or confidential information which could benefit competitors are prohibited from being married to or from having a romantic relationship with individuals employed by competing organizations.

Since Domzalski's work at International Technologies was similar to Hernandez-Canton's work at CEC, the corporation believed their "romantic relationship" made her discharge appropriate. Feeling aggrieved, Hernandez-Canton engaged the services of an attorney specializing in employee rights claims. In preparing her wrongful discharge suit, the attorney told her that given the nature of her case, he believed she could win the lawsuit. While gathering background information for the trial, the attorney discovered something that her former division manager did not know. Shortly before her discharge, the chairman of CEC had declared: "CEC employees are responsible for their own off-the-job behavior. We are concerned with an employee's off-the-job conduct only when it reduces the employee's ability to perform normal job assignments."

A jury trial in state court upheld the wrongful discharge suit and awarded Hernandez-Canton $425,000 in back pay and punitive damages. Like all trials, however, this one took its toll on the parties involved. "I couldn't function for 4 or 5 months after the trial, I was so emotionally upset and drained," Hernandez-Canton said. She is now employed as an engineer for a medical-device maker; she and Domzalski are no longer dating. "It was a bad experience all around," she says. "There was a real sense of belonging and a feeling of personal job worth at CEC. If I had my way, I'd take my old job back today."

Questions

1. What exceptions to the employment-at-will doctrine would the attorney have used to file the lawsuit?
2. Comment on the confidential information policy adopted by Centrex Electronics. Do you agree with the way it is used? Explain.
3. Is dating a "romantic relationship"? Explain.

Source: This case is adapted from an actual situation known to the authors. All names are fictitious.

Case 5 Pepper Construction Group: Change in Safety Leads to Decline in Injuries and Illnesses

Dave Pepper, the third-generation owner of Pepper Construction, met with his insurance group to review the group's annual summary of safety performance. To his surprise, Pepper Construction's experience modification rate (EMR) placed the company in the bottom third of the group. The EMR compares the frequency and severity of workers' compensation claims between companies of similar size operating in the same type of business and reflects the degree to which a particular company's experience is better or worse than the industry as a whole. At the time, Pepper Construction Group's EMR was 0.71, nearly 30 percent better than the national average for general contractors—but two-thirds of the insurance group members were even better. Safety performance was good, but not good enough.

The Solution

Pepper Construction had begun to develop a long-range strategic planning initiative. The initial goals set by the company's leaders were related to business growth—profit, efficiency, information technology, and production—but not one mentioned safety. Pepper reminded his team members that the company's most valuable asset has always been its people, and he encouraged them to shift their focus. It was as if a light went on within his management group. They fully embraced the commitment to safety and saw that it would protect the company's greatest asset—their people. The strategic plan shifted, and safety became the first priority. Their initial goals remained, but safety was now the foundation on which profit, growth, and productivity would be built.

Senior management, along with a newly formed safety committee, developed the following TEAM safety mission statement to communicate the company's commitment to an accident-free workplace:

- Training for all employees.
- Empowerment where everyone has the authority to say "no" to unsafe conditions.
- Action—the commitment to taking the steps necessary to protect employees and continuously strive to improve the safety program.
- Motivation—making sure the safety of the company's people is the top priority, above all else.

The challenge was to communicate the safety mission through the entire company, from the hourly craftsmen through the executive level. Previous annual safety seminars included every craftsman in the company, with often more than 600 people in the same lecture hall listening to lectures and generic training topics. To emphasize their commitment to safety, Pepper and Ken Egidi, the president of Pepper Construction Company, held much smaller meetings limited to no more than 40 people. They took the time to shake every employee's hand and made it very clear that everyone had the right, and responsibility, to work safely.

Pepper and his team worked hard to ensure all employees knew the company was serious about safety. They put in place additional resources to support this goal. For example, the company hired a new corporate safety director, increased training opportunities, and formed trades safety committees.

Pepper Construction now offers safety training in Spanish, including an OSHA-developed training program that consists of a 10-hour course and first-aid training. The company also provides comprehensive safety orientations on every job site. In addition, the company provides safety seminars for the trades.

These seminars include up to 4 hours of training specific to the skills needed by the craftspeople, such as powered lift training, fall protection, and emergency response. Almost 90 percent of the company's current craftspeople have completed OSHA's 30-hour construction safety course.

Pepper Construction has also worked through OSHA's cooperative programs to improve its safety performance. The company is a gold-level participant in OSHA Region V's Strategic Partnership with the Builders Association. The goals of this strategic partnership include reducing injuries, illnesses, and fatalities in construction by addressing key industry hazards, promoting recognition for construction safety excellence, and sharing best practices. Gold-level participants must meet a number of requirements, including the implementation of a comprehensive safety and health management program and maintaining an injury/illness rate at least 10 percent lower than the Bureau of Labor Statistics (BLS) rate for their industries.

Pepper Construction is also a participant in the OSHA Challenge Program, a three-stage process to implement an effective system to prevent fatalities, injuries, and illnesses. An electronic tool that breaks down the actions, documentation, and results desired is provided by OSHA to participating companies as well. Pepper Construction is also applying for recognition under OSHA's Voluntary Protection Programs (see Chapter 12).

The Impact

Since the strategic planning initiative and subsequent restructuring of its safety and health program, Pepper Construction Company has seen a dramatic decrease in its OSHA-recordable injury and illness rates. The firm is now well below the national average incidence rate in the construction industry.

When asked about the return on investment, Pepper has said the biggest benefit is the improved company culture: "Our workers are looking after each other, watching out for hazards and eliminating them—and really caring for their fellow employees." Pepper's improved safety culture has also spread to its subcontractors. When Pepper Construction bids out jobs, it reviews each subcontractor's safety and health records. All subcontractors are prequalified, and no bids are awarded to subcontractors that do not meet the company's safety performance standards.

As a result of Pepper Construction's increased scrutiny of its subcontractors' safety records, it has removed contractors from its list of prequalified contractors because of poor safety performance. For example, several years ago, an iron worker was observed standing on the rail of an aerial lift without proper fall protection. Because the steel erecting company officials did not consider this a serious safety problem, they were removed from the job site and did not work on another Pepper Construction site for 4 years. After this contractor initiated an intensive safety management program, its performance improved; the contractor is currently applying for reinstatement to Pepper Construction's prequalified contractors list.

Questions

1. How does the Pepper Construction's "TEAM" mission help keep the company on track toward better safety?
2. Why should Pepper Construction be concerned about the safety of its subcontractors?

Source: Paul Flentge, "Change in Safety Culture at Pepper Construction Group Leads to Dramatic Decline in Injuries and Illnesses," *Success Stories and Case Studies* (Washington, DC: Occupational Safety and Health Administration, July 2010), http://www.osha.gov/.

Case 6

Qualtrics after SAP: Shaping the Future of Employee Experience

Introduction

When you're the go-to experience management company for the lion's share of *Fortune* 500 companies, how much higher can you climb? Quite a bit, as it turns out. Over the past two decades, Qualtrics has made a name for itself expanding the definition of what a company's relationship between its customers and employees can be. In 2018, Qualtrics made a quantum leap in market share via its acquisition by commerce giant SAP, to the tune of $8 billion. The German juggernaut has prided itself on latching onto burgeoning tech companies for nearly three decades. But the question on the lips of everyone in tech was this: Why did SAP pay a king's ransom to acquire Qualtrics, and then three years later spin the company off through an initial public offering (IPO), pushing up the value of Qualtrics to more than $21 billion? Before diving into what the strategy should be for Qualtrics and SAP now that Qualtrics has gained more autonomy through this IPO—that is, how do both companies ensure that they continue as they have become an insta-global company—let's look at the two companies.

SAP

SAP is an enterprise software company founded in 1972. The company's name is an initialism for "Systems, Applications and Products in Data Processing." Since its earliest days, SAP's influence has extended to nearly every corner of the globe from its headquarters in Walldorf, Germany. Boasting more than 425,000 employees in 180 countries, SAP has risen far from its humble origins as a startup by former IBM employees who were told to give up on the project that would become SAP's flagship software. By 1973, SAP had released a financial accounting program—the first of many products in its lineup—and the basis of the software module system that would come to be called SAP R/1. This remained the basis of the company's software offerings until the development of SAP R/2, which would remain essentially unchanged until the release of SAP R/3 in 1992. Currently a financial powerhouse, SAP began trading publicly in 1988 on the Frankfurt and Stuttgart stock exchanges. At this point, SAP had migrated from mainframe computing to client/server services. Recognizing the Internet's enormous potential, mySAP.com brought the company into the twenty-first century.

Perhaps the greatest shift in SAP's focus began in 2012, when the company started acquiring cloud product–based companies, spending billions to compete with rival Oracle. In 2014, SAP reunited with its former parent at IBM in a partnership to develop and provide cloud technology. A partnership with Microsoft further emphasizes SAP's collaborative view of its future. At present, SAP software affects more than three-fourths of all transactions conducted around the globe. The 2018 acquisition of Qualtrics only served to underline the company's vision of having fingers in all the worlds' pies.

Qualtrics

Qualtrics is an experience management company founded in 2002. Headquartered in Provo, Utah, the firm has made a global name for itself providing a subscription-based software program that companies can use to monitor customer, employee, brand, and product experiences. While it initially landed on the map thanks to its flagship survey platform, Qualtrics has, in recent years, dedicated much of its talent and resources to developing a full suite of feedback products designed for the express purpose of capturing the most complete experience information available, commonly referred to as X-data.

The company's first big financial gambit of 2018 involved a bid to go public, with the firm's owners filing an IPO to the tune of $200 million. However, before these plans were finalized, SAP made Qualtrics an offer it couldn't refuse—$8 billion and autonomy to maintain the company culture that Qualtrics had been known for. As the global pioneer of experience management (XM) software, Qualtrics is helping companies move into the experience economy.

Experience Economy

The experience economy describes the next big wave in the economy, following the agrarian economy, where growing food was king; the industrial economy, where products were king; and the more recent service economy, where human services were king. In the experience economy, businesses orchestrate memorable events for their customers, and that memory or "experience" itself becomes the product.

Today, customers and employees desire experiences more than products and even services. An experience occurs when a company uses services and goods to engage individual customers in a way that creates a memorable event. Sometimes these experiences can be as bizarre as hotels where guests sleep on blocks of ice or inside prison cells, restaurants that serve stir-fried scorpions or coconut tree grubs, or race events where participants crawl through muddy pools of water littered with electric wires or swim across rivers with alligators.

While some of these experiences might seem to be for only young and impulsive adrenaline junkies, they are actually consumed by people from all walks of life. People want these experiences because they are "collectible," not necessarily pleasurable. As stated by Anat Keinan at Harvard Business School, "[People] want to collect as many memorable experiences as possible to build their experiential resume." Indeed, in the end people are beginning to eschew high-value products and even time-saving services for experiences that they can remember, that can provide more sustenance to what is becoming a more leisurely existence, that can help to define who they are.

Most recently, this experience economy has begun to hit the workplace. Employees, like customers, want to feel as if they are getting value for their work. Value is not just money, but also includes things like flexibility, office environments where people can talk openly, feedback, and a feeling that employees are contributing to something that will make a difference for society. The employee experience isn't just about making sure employees have the resources and managerial oversight needed to do their jobs; instead, it is more about helping them have continual experiences at work that provide more sustenance, that help define them. This includes providing meaningful mentorship, offering lifestyle benefits, and knowing the individual needs of people. By knowing their needs, companies can provide a menu of benefits that take into account what is most meaningful to each person—flexible hours, quality teams, open office space, time at work to unwind and recharge, opportunities to give back to the community, employee wellness, gym memberships, meal plans, and better ways to include others.

Qualtrics and SAP: Combining Forces

In the new experience economy, companies not able to engage with and track the employee experience are doomed. This juncture is where Qualtrics and SAP joined forces. Qualtrics makes experience software that allows companies to capture experience data of employees, and SAP services many of the world's employees. One of the biggest challenges companies face is knowing how their employees are responding to something like a new HR program or a redesigned website. What did they like about it and what didn't they like?

Answering these questions is not as simple as sending out a survey. Qualtrics provides a platform that enables companies to easily collect, report, and analyze the data in real time, and then publish those results to managers so they can immediately act on the information. By combining Qualtrics' platform for understanding employee experiences with SAP's operational platform that helps track a company's success factors, Qualtrics and SAP offer a solution that can help their clients understand and respond to the employee experience. As stated by Ryan Smith, CEO of Qualtrics:

> "Our mission is to help organizations deliver the experiences that turn their customers into fanatics, employees into ambassadors, products into obsessions, and brands into religions. Supported by a global team of over 95,000, SAP will help us scale faster and achieve our mission on a broader stage. This will put the XM Platform everywhere overnight."

Bill McDermott, former CEO of SAP, noted: "SAP already touches 77 percent of the world's transactions. When you combine our operational data with Qualtrics' experience data, we will accelerate the XM category with an end-to-end solution with immediate global scale. For Qualtrics, this introduces a dynamic new partner with the belief, passion, and scale to bring experience management to millions of customers around the world."

Going Forward

With the global platform that SAP provides, Qualtrics has been successful in delivering on SAP's expectations. As SAP CEO Christian Klein pointed out, "Qualtrics beat our expectations." Even with SAP taking Qualtrics public, "we are and will be fully committed to experience management and Qualtrics being a key element of our Intelligent Enterprise Strategy," Klein said. So the big question is, now that Qualtrics has more freedom to attract and compensate talent while still reaping the benefits of SAP's customer base, what should it do now to ensure its culture moves back a bit, so that it starts to feel like an agile tech company again? How can the company get its teams to feel as if Qualtrics is still in the global game and supported by its majority shareholder, SAP, while being young and scrappy again?

Questions

1. What is important about Qualtrics keeping an agile tech company feel?
2. Are surveys the best way to measure employee experience?
3. What role does an HR manager have in the experience economy?

References

http://healthland.time.com/2010/11/22/the-business-of-weird-why-people-pay-for-bizarre-experiences/
https://www.computerworld.com/article/3428040/six-months-in--how-is-qualtrics-fitting-in-at-sap-.html
https://joshbersin.com/2018/11/why-did-sap-pay-8-billion-to-acquire-qualtrics/
https://hbr.org/1998/07/welcome-to-the-experience-economy
http://www.strategyfocusedhr.com/experience-economy-includes-employees/

Case 7 The Last Straw for Aero Engine

The meeting lasted only 10 minutes, since all those present quickly agreed that Tom Kinder should be fired. According to management, Kinder had caused the company numerous problems over the last 18 months, and the incident on Saturday was "the straw that broke the camel's back." Plant managers believed they had rid themselves of a poor employee, one whom the company had offered many opportunities for improvement. It seemed like an airtight case, which the union could not win if it was taken to arbitration.

Tom Kinder had worked for the Aero Engine Company for 14 years prior to being terminated. He was initially employed as an engine mechanic servicing heavy-duty diesel engines. For his first 9 years with Aero Engine, he was considered a model employee by his supervisors and plant management. Kinder was also well liked by his fellow employees. His performance appraisals were always marked "exceptional," and his personnel folder contained many commendation letters from customers and supervisors alike. Supervisor Chen Lee described Kinder as "devoted to his job of building and repairing engines." Through company-sponsored training classes and courses taken at a local trade school, Kinder had acquired the knowledge and experience to build and repair specialty engines used in arctic oil exploration.

The Aero Engine Company, with headquarters in the Midwest, was engaged primarily in the production and maintenance of specialty engines used in drilling, heavy manufacturing, and diesel transportation. The company had experienced very rapid growth in its sales volume, the number of products it produced, and the size of its workforce since 2015. (At the time of Kinder's termination, the company employed about 1,700 employees.) Aero Engine avoided hiring new personnel and then laying them off when they were no longer needed. Company policy stated that layoffs were to be avoided except in extreme circumstances. When heavy workloads arose, the natural solution to the problem was to schedule large amounts of overtime and to hire temporary employees through one of the local temporary help services.

Kinder's work problems had begun approximately 5 years prior to his discharge, when he went through a very emotional and difficult divorce. He was a devoted family man, and the divorce was a shock to his values and his way of life. The loss of custody of his children was particularly devastating to his mental well-being. He became sullen, withdrawn, and argumentative with his supervisors. Several of his close friends said they thought he was depressed. Aero Engine has a comprehensive employee assistance program (EAP) for employees experiencing personal challenges. Kinder's supervisor, Gordon Thompson, had recommended the services of the EAP to him, but it was unknown if he had used counseling since the EAP program is voluntary and confidential. Management professes that it took a very proactive and humanistic approach toward Kinder, an employee whom the company valued and respected. However, regardless of the company's concern for Kinder, his work performance had become problematic.

An absenteeism problem developed and continued until his discharge. Over the 18 months prior to this termination, Kinder was absent 27 complete days and 9 partial days and was tardy 19 times. Twelve months before termination, he had been given a written warning that his attendance must improve or he would face further disciplinary action, including possible discharge. Unfortunately, his attendance did not improve; however, he received no further disciplinary action until his discharge on Monday.

Management had experienced problems other than absenteeism with Kinder. The quantity and quality of his work had decreased to only an acceptable level of performance. His supervisor had discussed this with him on two occasions, but no disciplinary action was ever instituted. Furthermore, during heavy production periods Kinder would either refuse to work overtime assignments or, once assigned, would often fail to report for work. It was an incident that occurred during a Saturday overtime shift that caused his discharge.

The Saturday prior to his discharge, Kinder was assigned to a high-priority project that required him to build a specialty engine for a large and loyal customer. The big new engine was needed to replace a smaller engine that had exploded on an Alaskan drilling rig. The engine was being built in a newly constructed plant building located one-half mile from the company's main production facilities. At approximately 9:15 a.m. that Saturday, Gordon Thompson had walked over to the new building to check on the progress of the engine. As Thompson passed by a window, he noticed Kinder sitting at a desk with his feet up, reading a magazine. The supervisor decided to observe him from outside the building. After about 25 minutes, Kinder had not moved, and Thompson returned to the plant to report the incident to Glenn Navarro, the plant production manager. Neither the supervisor nor the production manager confronted Kinder about the incident.

At 8:15 the next Monday morning, supervisor Thompson and production manager Navarro met with the director of human resources to review Kinder's total work performance. After this short meeting, all those present decided he should be fired. His discharge notice read, "Terminated for poor work performance, excessive absenteeism, and loafing." At 10:15 that morning Kinder was called into Navarro's office and discharged. Navarro then handed him his final paycheck, which included 8 hours of work for Monday.

Questions

1. Comment on the handling of this case by the supervisor, production manager, and director of human resources.
2. How much concern should organizations show for employees before taking disciplinary action related to work performance that has suffered due to mental health challenges? Explain.
3. To what extent were consistent discipline and due process applied prior to the discharge?
4. If Kinder's discharge went to arbitration, how would you decide the case? Why? Which arguments would labor and management present to support their respective positions?

Source: This case is based on an actual arbitration. All names are fictitious.

Case 8 Employee Selection and Training at Meadowbrook Golf and Golf Ventures West

Meadowbrook Golf, headquartered in Championsgate, Florida, is a leader in golf course management, maintenance, and supplies in the United States. Today the organization is composed of four companies that meet the demands of the market: Meadowbrook Golf provides the management, International Golf Maintenance provides the maintenance, and Golf Ventures East and West are the golf supply arms of the business.

Ron Jackson is the CEO of Meadowbrook. The turf business is a highly specialized, tight-knit industry. The company's strong reputation was built on its expertise in providing superior products and services to golf courses and municipalities. Jackson knew the only way he could take the company to the next level was to not only find the right people with the specific experience they needed, but also find a way to keep those employees happy and motivated so they would stay.

Jackson learned about a behavioral assessment tool called Predictive Index, produced by the Wellesley, Massachusetts–based management consulting company PI Worldwide, and brought it into Meadowbrook as a way to help the managers understand what motivated their employees to come to work every day. Meadowbrook also realized that its top performers possessed very similar behavioral characteristics. Using the lessons from the behavioral assessments, Meadowbrook was able to incorporate this information into its hiring process.

Golf Ventures West (GVW), the supply division of Meadowbrook in the western United States, offers equipment that ranges from a string trimmer to a $70,000 rotary motor, along with fertilizer, seed, and specialty products. Mike Eastwood, the president of GVW, had the best talent in the industry, long-time clients, and very low turnover. While it all seemed idealistic, Eastwood had a problem: he needed his team to sell more. The challenge was to identify which specific sales training they needed.

When sharing his concerns with Jackson, Eastwood learned that the publishers of the Predictive Index also offered a selling training tool that identified the strengths of salespeople and areas for their development as well as offered customer-focused sales (CFS) training. To explore the tool further, he and his senior management team took the assessment themselves. The results accurately identified Eastwood's selling style. His general managers, most of whom had more than 30 years in the industry, scored in the mid-to-high range.

Next, Eastwood gave his sales team members the assessment. However, their overall scores were in the mid-to-low range. Eastwood quickly realized that despite the talent of his sales team, 80 percent of them did not really know how to sell. The results of the assessment showed that most sales representatives were not asking enough investigative questions when speaking with their clients. This was a huge breakthrough. Eastwood's team members then took the CFS workshop to learn how to think like customers do and investigate and uncover their needs.

The results? "My most senior and successful salesperson followed the CFS process and closed a $40,000 deal with a customer that had only purchased from our competitor for the last 10 years," says Eastwood. In another instance, Eastwood had a salesperson who was underperforming but knew he had the potential to be successful. This salesperson went through the sales training and was moved to a new territory. "In 4 months he has sold more in his new territory than he had in a year in his original territory," says Eastwood. Apparently, the training is paying off. Even though golf courses, in general, have been struggling in recent years, Golf Ventures West has expanded its operations to a number of new locations across the country.

Questions

1. Why did Eastwood and his general managers take PI's competency assessment prior to administering it to the company's other salespeople?
2. How did the assessment help uncover the skills gap that was holding back Golf Ventures West's salespeople?
3. What does the case indicate about the training "readiness" of the company's salespeople?

Source: Adapted from "Hire Smart, Develop Selling Skills and Manage for Individual and Team Success," PI Worldwide, http://www.piworldwide.com.

Case 9 Newell's Decision to Downsize: An Ethical Dilemma

A particular issue in business ethics is: "What exactly does the term *ethics* mean?" Various writers have described ethics as rules that govern behavior, desired societal values such as respect for justice, or accepted principles of right or wrong. One author noted, "While laws concern what we must do, ethics concerns what we should do."[1]

In the practice of HR, managers and supervisors are continually faced with ethical dilemmas regarding the fair and equitable treatment of employees. Ethical choices abound in areas such as recruitment and selection, employee privacy, whistle-blowing, sexual harassment, and diversity or affirmative action. An important ethical dilemma faced by managers today is the fair and correct way to downsize organizations. The decisions involved in downsizing a workforce are complex and, as one manager stated, "gut-wrenching."

The Need to Downsize

Newell Corporation is a medium-sized manufacturer of navigational systems for commuter and larger airplanes. The company operates two plants—one in Atlanta, Georgia, and the other in Norwood, California. In 2020, the Norwood plant employed 273 employees, most of them engaged in the manufacture and technical support of company products.

Newell is regarded as an excellent place to work by its employees and within the surrounding communities. Employee morale and loyalty have always been high, and job satisfaction studies conducted by the company consistently rate the organization as a fair and equitable place to work. The company's HR policies can be described as proactive and progressive. With its positive reputation, Newell has been able to select new employees from a large pool of job applicants.

One cornerstone of HR policy has been to use the principle of seniority when training, assigning, transferring, and promoting employees. Additionally, with Newell's emphasis on employee retention, employees have experienced and come to expect long and steady employment. Prior to 2018, Newell had never downsized its workforce. Employment growth at the Norwood facility had been moderate and steady.

The racial composition of the company has been predominantly White, for two reasons. First, the racial composition of the company's local labor market has historically been predominantly White. A review of the company's federally required EEO-1 report showed that Newell had few employees in each of the racial-ethnic minority categories listed. This is true for both hourly and managerial positions. However, since then, the demographic characteristics of the local labor market have changed dramatically to include more Hispanics and Latinx, African Americans, and Asian Americans.

In 2014, Newell experienced a large increase in the demand for its products. To meet customer orders, the Norwood plant hired 27 new manufacturing assemblers and 14 new technical support technicians. With the increased diversity of the external labor force, plus the desire to increase the diversity of its internal workforce for both business and ethical reasons, 34 of the 41 new hires were members of underrepresented groups. The following is an excerpt from Newell's statement of vision and values published in July 2019:

> Newell Corporation believes that a work environment that reflects a diverse workforce, values diversity, and honors the worth of its employees benefits the company, its customers, and its employees. Employment decisions will be made on these principles while also considering the efficient and effective operation of the organization.

1. Terry Halbert and Elaine Ingulli, *Law and Ethics in the Business Environment*, 7th ed. (Mason, OH: Cengage Learning, 2011).

Because many of the new employees from underrepresented groups needed to be trained to do the company's manufacturing and technical jobs, the firm spent approximately $1.7 million on entry-level skills training. The integration of these employees into the Norwood facility was seamless and without racial tension.

In 2019, sales for Newell's products once again followed historical patterns. Unfortunately, sales then unexpectedly took a sharp downturn: a 12 percent decline in 2020 and a 23 percent decline in 2021. The causes for the decline in sales were attributed to the COVID-19 global pandemic. The fear of traveling hit the entire world at once; travelers weren't traveling, airline companies either weren't filling flights or weren't flying them at all. In turn, there was a decline in the market demand for the products made by Newell and its competitors.

In February 2021, Tom Malcom, Norwood's director of HR; Steven L. Davis, corporate vice president for manufacturing; and Mary Umali, Norwood's plant manager, decided to downsize the workforce at the Norwood facility. Specifically, they decided to lay off 37 manufacturing employees and 11 technical support personnel. The difficult question faced by senior management was how to lay off employees in a manner that would be fair and equitable to individuals and legally defensible while maintaining the integrity of Newell's HR policies and the productivity of the Norwood plant.

Questions

1. What is the ethical dilemma faced by management in this case? Explain.
2. What specific problems might Newell face in its downsizing decision?
3. What options might Newell employ in its downsizing decision? Explain.
4. How would you downsize the workforce at the Norwood facility? Explain.

Source: This case was adapted from an actual case known to the authors. All names are fictitious.

Case 10

Someone Has to Go: A Tough Layoff Decision

Located in the Los Angeles area, Aero Performance, with 27 employees, is a sales and maintenance company that provides equipment upgrades and general aircraft maintenance to regional airlines, corporate aircraft, and small international carriers. When Aero Performance was founded 2 years ago, the company faced little competition, and the robust airline market seemed to present unlimited potential for growth. Unfortunately, industry economics coupled with cost-cutting measures by airlines and new competition from similar airline service companies meant that Aero's business performance leveled off, and the company even experienced losses in certain specialized areas. Airline companies as well as the owners of corporate jets delayed the purchase and installation of Aero's advanced electronic equipment.

Mike Martinez, manager of the technology upgrade unit, faces a tough decision. With a significant downturn in his unit's work, he must lay off one employee. This decision is particularly difficult because all of the employees in the unit are qualified employees with average or better work records. Additionally, each employee has a unique personal background directly affecting their work life. A summary of the background and work record of each of the four employees follows.

Gary Meadors is married and has two children in high school. He lives modestly to send his kids to college. His wife works evenings at a convenience store to assist with family expenses. Meadors has worked 9 years with Aero Performance: 6 years in airline maintenance, and 3 years in the technology upgrade unit. He has learned airline technology largely through technical articles, trade journals, and on-the-job experience. His performance evaluations are average, and he is considered a consistent and reliable employee. His attendance and company loyalty are exceptional.

Brenda Baldwin is the only woman in the technology upgrade unit. She is a single mother with a child in elementary school. Brenda has 3 years of service with Aero Performance, all in Martinez's unit. She joined the company after obtaining an airline technology degree from a well-respected 4-year university. Brenda continues to take evening classes in her field and seems to have, according to Martinez, "the most potential for growth in the company." However, her performance has slipped the past year, and she has been counseled for an attendance problem. She has felt somewhat resented as a female in a traditionally male-dominated industry.

Udit Chopra is a dedicated employee. In fact, everyone says he is "married to his job." He will work long hours to complete technical installations and is regarded as a perfectionist. Udit has a college degree in marketing but has found his home in airline technology. He possesses an excellent ability to persuade Aero Performance customers to upgrade their technology systems. Udit drives a new BMW and is believed to come from a wealthy family.

Craig Cottrell joined Aero Performance 3 years ago, having been hired away from a competitor. He has a total of 12 years of experience in the airline service industry. Craig has a complete understanding of airline technology. Cottrell's work performance the first 2 years with Aero Performance was barely average; however, his work record the past year was evaluated as very high. Currently, he is the top performer in the unit. There has been work friction between him, Baldwin, and Chopra over the selection and installation of cockpit instruments.

	Seniority (Years)	Salary	Performance 2018	2019	2020	2021
Gary Meadors	9	$74,250	Average	Good	Average	Average
Brenda Baldwin	3	$81,190		High	Good	Average
Udit Chopra	5	$78,500	Average	Good	Good	Good
Craig Cottrell	3	$75,960		Average	Average	High

Mike Martinez must make his decision by this Friday. Aero Performance will grant the laid-off employee a severance package to assist in transition to other employment. Martinez is committed to aiding his employee in finding another job in the airline service industry.

Questions

1. What criteria should be used to determine potential layoff candidates? What emphasis, if any, should be given to non-job-related factors such as personal problems or a spouse's need to work? Explain your answer.
2. What should be included in a severance package for laid-off employees? How long should the severance package last?
3. Are there any potential legal implications of Martinez's decision?
4. How would you handle the termination interview?

Glossary

A

Acceptance rate The percentage of applicants who accept a firm's jobs after being offered them.

Adventure-based learning The use of adventures, such as games, trust activities, and problem-solving initiatives, to further the personal and social development of participants.

Adverse impact A concept that refers to the rejection of a significantly higher percentage of a protected class for employment, placement, or promotion when compared with the successful, nonprotected class.

Affirmative action A policy that goes beyond equal employment opportunity by requiring organizations to comply with the law and correct any past discriminatory practices by increasing the numbers of underrepresented groups in specific positions.

Agility A firm's ability make quick changes to gain a competitive advantage.

Alternative dispute resolution (ADR) Any of several different employee complaint or dispute resolution methods that do not involve going to court.

Applicant tracking system (ATS) A system recruiters use to post job openings, screen resumes and uploaded profiles, contact (via email) potential candidates for interviews, and track the time, costs, and other metrics related to hiring people.

Apprenticeship training A system of training in which a worker entering the skilled trades is given thorough instruction and experience, both on and off the job, in the practical and theoretical aspects of the work.

Arbitrator A neutral third party who resolves a labor dispute by issuing a final decision in the disagreement.

Assessment center test A process by which managerial candidates are evaluated at an assessment center as they participate in a series of situations that resemble what they might need to handle on the job.

Augmented skills Skills helpful in facilitating the efforts of expatriate managers.

Authorization card A statement signed by an employee authorizing a union to act as a representative of the employee for purposes of collective bargaining.

Automated interview Interviews in which the questions are administered to applicants via computers. The interviews can be conducted at a firm's facilities, using kiosks, online, or via phone.

B

Backup care program A benefit program whereby an employer provides or subsidizes temporary care for its employee's elders or children when their regular arrangements fall through.

Balance sheet approach A compensation system designed to match the purchasing power in a person's home country.

Balanced scorecard (BSC) A measurement framework that helps managers translate strategic goals into operational objectives.

Bargaining power The power of labor and management to achieve their goals through economic, social, or political influence.

Bargaining unit A group of two or more employees who share common employment interests and conditions and may reasonably be grouped together for purposes of collective bargaining.

Bargaining zone An area in which the union and the employer are willing to concede when bargaining.

Behavior modeling A learning approach in which work behaviors are modeled, or demonstrated, and trainees are asked to mimic them.

Behavior modification A technique that operates on the principle that behavior that is rewarded, or positively reinforced, will be exhibited more frequently in the future, whereas behavior that is penalized or unrewarded will decrease in frequency.

Behavior observation scale (BOS) A behavioral approach to performance rating that measures the frequency of observed behavior.

Behavioral description interview (BDI) An interview in which an applicant is asked questions about what they actually did in a given situation.

Behaviorally anchored rating scale (BARS) A behavioral approach to performance rating that consists of a series of vertical scales, one for each important dimension of job performance.

Benchmarking The process of looking at your practices and performance in a given area and comparing them with those of other companies.

Blended learning The use of both in-person classroom learning and online learning.

Bona fide occupational qualification (BFOQ) Suitable defense against a discrimination charge only when age, religion, sex, or national origin is an actual qualification for performing the job.

Bonus An incentive payment that is supplemental to the base wage.

Branding A company's efforts to help existing and prospective workers understand why it is a desirable place to work.

Broadbanding A pay system that collapses many traditional salary grades into a few wide salary bands.

Burnout A severe stage of distress, which manifests as depression, frustration, and loss of productivity.

Business environment Factors in the external environment that a firm cannot directly control but that can affect its strategy and performance.

Business necessity A work-related practice that is necessary to the safe and efficient operation of an organization.

C

Calibration A process whereby managers meet to discuss the performance of individual employees to ensure their employee reviews are aligned with one another.

Career paths Lines of advancement in an occupational field within an organization.

Career plateau A situation in which for either organizational or personal reasons the probability of moving up the career ladder is low.

Charge form A discrimination complaint filed with the EEOC by employees or job applicants.

Chief Diversity Officer (CDO) A top executive responsible for implementing a firm's diversity efforts.

Chief ethics officers A high-ranking manager who is directly responsible for fostering the ethical climate within the firm.

Chief learning officer A high-ranking executive who is responsible for fostering employee learning and development within the firm.

Codetermination Representation of labor on the board of directors of a company.

Collective bargaining process The process of negotiating a labor agreement, including the use of economic pressures by both parties.

Combined salary and commission plan A compensation plan that includes a straight salary and a commission.

Compensation scorecard Displays the results for all the measures that a company uses to monitor and compare compensation among internal departments or units.

Compensatory model A selection decision model in which a high score in one area can make up for a low score in another area.

Competence-based pay Pay based on an employee's skill level, variety of skills possessed, or increased job knowledge.

Competency assessment An analysis of the sets of skills and knowledge needed for decision-oriented and knowledge-intensive jobs.

Competitive environment Consists of a firm's specific industry, including the industry's customers, rival firms, new entrants, substitutes, and suppliers.

Concurrent validity The extent to which the test scores of current employees correlate with their job performance.

Construct validity The extent to which a selection tool measures a theoretical construct or trait.

Constructive discharge An employee's voluntary termination of their employment because of harsh, unreasonable employment conditions placed on the individual by the employer.

Consumer Price Index (CPI) A measure of the average change in prices over time in a fixed "market basket" of goods and services.

Content validity The extent to which a selection instrument, such as a test, adequately samples the knowledge and skills needed to do a particular job.

Contrast error A performance rating error in which an employee's review is biased either upward or downward because that employee is compared with another employee just previously evaluated.

Contributory plan A pension plan in which contributions are made jointly by employees and employers.

Cooperative training A training program that combines practical on-the-job experience with formal educational classes.

Core capabilities Integrated knowledge sets within an organization that distinguish it from its competitors and that deliver value to customers.

Core skills Skills considered critical to an employee's success abroad.

Core values The strong and enduring beliefs and principles that guide a firm's decisions and are the foundation of its corporate culture.

Corporate social responsibility The responsibility of the firm to act in the best interests of the people and communities affected by its activities.

Craft unions Unions that represent skilled craft workers.

Criterion-related validity The extent to which a selection tool predicts, or significantly correlates with, important work behaviors.

Critical incident method A job analysis method used to identify both desirable and undesirable behaviors that resulted in either a very good outcome or a very bad outcome on the job.

Cross-training The process of training employees to do multiple jobs within an organization.

Cross-validation Verifying the results obtained from a validation study by administering a test or test battery to a different sample (drawn from the same population).

Cultural audits Audits of the culture and quality of work life in an organization.

Cultural environment The communications, religion, values and ideologies, education, and social structure of a country.

Culture shock Perpetual stress experienced by people who settle overseas.

Cumulative trauma disorders Injuries involving tendons of the fingers, hands, and arms that become inflamed from repeated stresses and strains.

Customer evaluations A performance evaluation that includes evaluations from a firm's external and internal customers.

D

Defined benefit plan A pension plan in which the amount an employee is to receive on retirement is specifically set forth.

Defined contribution plan A pension plan that establishes the basis on which an employer will contribute to the pension fund.

Dejobbing The process of structuring organizations not around jobs, but rather around projects that are constantly changing

Demotion A downward transfer that moves an individual into a lower-level job that can provide developmental opportunities.

Depression A negative emotional state marked by feelings of low spirits, gloominess, sadness, and loss of pleasure in ordinary activities.

Differential piece rate A compensation rate under which employees whose production exceeds the standard amount of output receive a higher rate for all of their work than the rate paid to those who do not exceed the standard amount.

Disabled individual Any person who (1) has a physical or mental impairment that substantially limits one or more of the person's major life activities, (2) has a record of such impairment, or (3) is regarded as having such an impairment.

Discipline A tool used to correct and mold the practices of employees to help them perform better, and to ensure they conform to acceptable standards.

Disease management programs Programs that provide patients and their caregivers with information on monitoring and treating medical conditions, while coordinating communication between them, their health care providers, their employers, and insurers.

Disparate treatment A situation in which protected class members receive unequal treatment or are evaluated by different standards.

Distress Harmful stress characterized by a loss of feelings of security and adequacy.

Downsizing The planned elimination of jobs.

Due process Procedures that constitute fair treatment, such as allowing an employee to tell their story about an alleged infraction and defend against it.

E

Economic factors External factors including the strength or weakness of markets, stability of trade cycles, specific industry conditions, customer preferences, and government's economic policies.

Elder care Care provided to an elderly person by an employee who remains actively at work.

E-learning Learning that takes place via electronic media.

Emergency action plans A plan developed by an organization that contains step-by-step procedures for dealing with various emergency situations.

Employee Assistance Programs (EAPS) Services provided by employers to help workers cope with a wide variety of problems that interfere with the way they perform their jobs.

Employee associations Labor organizations that represent various groups of professional and white-collar employees in labor–management relations.

Employee empowerment Giving employees the power to initiate change, thereby encouraging them to take charge of what they do.

Employee engagement A situation in which workers are enthusiastic and immersed in their work to the degree that it improves the performance of their companies.

Employee leasing The process of dismissing employees, who are then hired by a leasing company (which handles all HR-related activities), and contracting with that company to lease back the employees.

Employee profiles Profile of workers developed by studying an organization's top performers to recruit similar types of people.

Employee rights Guarantees of fair treatment that become rights when they are granted to employees by the courts, legislatures, or employers.

Employee stock ownership plans (ESOPS) Stock plans in which an organization contributes shares of its stock to an established trust for the purpose of stock purchases by its employees.

Employee team A group of employees working together toward a common purpose, in which members have complementary skills, members' work is mutually dependent, and the group has discretion over tasks performed.

Employment-at-will relationship The right of an employer to fire an employee without giving a reason and the right of an employee to quit when they choose.

Environmental scanning Systematic monitoring of the major external forces influencing the organization.

Environmental, social, and governance (ESG) Factors used to evaluate an organization's collective conscientiousness for social and environmental sustainability.

Equal Employment Opportunity (EEO) The treatment of individuals in all aspects of employment—hiring, promotion, training, and so on—in a fair and nonbiased manner.

Equal Employment Opportunity Commission (EEOC) The EEOC's work consists of formulating EEO policy and approving all litigation involved in maintaining equal employment opportunity. The EEOC's guidelines are not federal law but administrative rules and regulations published in the *Federal Register*.

Ergonomics The process of studying and designing easy-to-use equipment and systems so the physical well-being of employees is not compromised and work gets done more efficiently.

Error of central tendency A performance rating error in which all employees are rated about average.

Escalator clauses Clauses in labor agreements that provide for quarterly cost-of-living adjustments in wages, basing the adjustments on changes in the consumer price index

Essay method A trait approach to performance rating that requires the rater to write a statement describing an employee's behavior.

Ethics A set of standards of conduct and moral judgments that help to determine right and wrong behavior.

Eustress Positive stress that accompanies achievement and exhilaration.

Exclusive representation The legal right and responsibility of the union to represent all bargaining unit members equally, regardless of whether employees join the union or not.

Exempt employees Employees not covered by the overtime provisions of the Fair Labor Standards Act.

Expatriates (home-country and third-country nationals) Employees from the home country or a third country who are on international assignment.

Experiential learning The process of learning by "doing," reflecting on it, critically analyzing it, and applying it in new situations or settings.

F

Failure rates The percentage of expatriates who do not perform satisfactorily.

Fair employment practices (FEPS) State and local laws governing equal employment opportunity that are often more comprehensive than federal laws and apply to small-business employers.

Fair representation doctrine A doctrine under which unions have a legal obligation to assist both members and nonmembers in labor relations matters.

Fitness-for-duty evaluations Evaluations randomly conducted to determine an employee's physical, mental, and emotional fitness for a job.

Flexible benefits plans (cafeteria plans) Benefit plans that enable individual employees to choose the benefits that are best suited to their particular needs.

Flextime Flexible working hours that give employees the option of choosing their daily starting and quitting times, provided that they work a set number of hours per day or week.

Forced distribution A performance ranking system whereby raters are required to place a certain percentage of employees into various performance categories.

Forced-choice method A trait approach to performance rating that requires the rater to choose from statements designed to distinguish between successful and unsuccessful performance.

Four-fifths rule A rule of thumb followed by the EEOC in determining adverse impact for use in enforcement proceedings.

Functional job analysis (FJA) A job analysis approach that utilizes an inventory of the various types of work activities that can constitute any job.

Furloughing A situation in which an organization asks or requires employees to take time off for either no pay or reduced pay.

G

Gainsharing plans Programs under which both employees and the organization share financial gains according to a predetermined formula that reflects improved productivity and profitability.

Global compensation system A centralized pay system whereby host-country employees are offered a full range of training programs, benefits, and pay comparable with a firm's domestic employees but adjusted for local differences.

Global corporation A firm that has integrated its worldwide operations through a centralized home office.

Global manager A manager equipped to run an international business.

Graphic rating scale method A trait approach to performance rating whereby each employee is rated according to a scale of characteristics.

Grievance procedure A formal procedure that provides for the union to represent members and nonmembers in processing a grievance.

Guest workers Foreign workers invited to perform needed labor.

H

Hay profile method A job evaluation technique using three factors—knowledge, mental activity, and accountability—to evaluate executive and managerial positions.

Health Maintenance Organizations (HMOs) Organizations of physicians and health care professionals that provide a wide range of services to subscribers and their dependents on a prepaid basis.

High-deductible health insurance plans (HDHPS) A medical insurance plan characterized by high deductibles but lower premiums for workers and a health spending account to which employers contribute funds employees can keep should they leave the organization.

High-performance work system (HPWS) A specific combination of HR practices, work structures, and processes that maximizes knowledge, skill, commitment, flexibility, and resilience of a firm's employees.

Home-based pay Pay based on the compensation practices used in an expatriate's home country.

Homeshoring The practice of outsourcing work to domestic workers who work out of their homes.

Horizontal fit The situation in which all the internal elements of the work system reinforce one another.

Host-based pay Expatriate pay comparable to that earned by employees in a host country.

Host country A country in which an international corporation operates.

Host-country nationals Employees who are natives of the host country.

Hourly work Work paid on an hourly basis.

Human capital The knowledge, skills, and capabilities of individuals who have economic value to an organization.

Human capital readiness The process of evaluating the availability of critical talent in a company and comparing it to the firm's supply.

Human Resource Planning (HRP) The process of anticipating and providing for the movement of people into, within, and out of an organization.

Human resources information system (HRIS) A computerized system that provides current and accurate HR-related data for the purposes of control and decision making.

Human Resources Management (HRM) The process of managing human talent to achieve an organization's objectives.

I

Impairment testing Also called fitness-for-duty or performance-based testing; testing that measures whether an employee is alert enough to work.

Improshare A gainsharing program under which bonuses are based on the overall productivity of the work team.

Independent contractors Workers who are self-employed and do project work on a contract basis for different organizations.

Industrial engineering A field of study concerned with analyzing work methods and establishing time standards.

Industrial unions Unions that represent all workers—skilled, semiskilled, unskilled—employed along industry lines.

Instructional objectives The desired outcomes of a training program.

Interest-based bargaining Problem-solving bargaining based on a win-win philosophy and the development of a positive long-term relationship.

Internal labor markets Labor markets in which workers are hired into entry-level jobs and higher-level jobs are filled from within.

International corporation A domestic firm that uses its existing capabilities to move into overseas markets.

J

Job An activity people do for which they get paid, particularly as part of the trade or occupation they occupy.

Job analysis The process of obtaining information about a job by determining its duties, tasks, or activities.

Job characteristics model A job design theory that purports that three psychological states (experiencing meaningfulness of the work performed, responsibility for work outcomes, and knowing the results of the work performed) result in a jobholder's improved work performance, internal motivation, and lower absenteeism and turnover.

Job classification system A system of job evaluation in which jobs are classified and grouped according to a series of predetermined wage grades.

Job crafting A naturally occurring phenomenon in which employees mold their tasks to better fit their individual strengths, passions, and motives.

Job description A statement of the tasks, duties, and responsibilities of a job to be performed

Job design An outgrowth of job analysis that improves jobs through technological and human considerations so as to enhance organization efficiency and employee job satisfaction.

Job enlargement The process of adding a greater variety of tasks to a job.

Job enrichment Enhancing a job by adding more meaningful tasks and duties to make the work more rewarding or satisfying.

Job evaluation A systematic process of determining the relative worth of jobs to establish which jobs should be paid more than others within an organization.

Job progressions The hierarchy of jobs new employees might experience, ranging from a starting job to jobs that successively require more knowledge and/or skill.

Job ranking system The simplest and oldest system of job evaluation, in which jobs are arrayed on the basis of their relative worth.

Job rotation The process whereby employees rotate in and out of different jobs.

Job sharing An arrangement in which two part-time employees do a job normally held by one full-time employee.

Job specifications A statement of the specific knowledge, skills, and abilities that a person who is to perform a job needs.

Just-in-time training Electronic training delivered to trainees when and where they need it to do their jobs.

K

Knowledge workers Workers whose responsibilities extend beyond the physical execution of work to include planning, decision-making, and problem-solving.

L

Labor relations process A logical sequence of five events: (1) workers desire collective representation, (2) the union begins its organizing campaign, (3) the NLRB representation process begins, (4) collective negotiations lead to a contract, and (5) the contract is administered.

Learning Management System (LMS) Online system that provides a variety of assessment, communication, teaching, and learning opportunities.

Leniency or strictness error A performance rating error in which the appraiser tends to give employees either unusually high or unusually low ratings.

Line managers Non-HR managers who are responsible for overseeing the work of other employees.

Localization Adapting pay and other compensation benefits to match that of a particular country.

M

Management by objectives (MBO) A philosophy of management that rates the performance of employees based on their achievement of goals set mutually by them and their managers.

Management forecasts The opinions (judgments) of supervisors, department managers, experts, or others knowledgeable about the organization's future employment needs.

Manager and/or supervisor evaluation A performance evaluation done by an employee's manager and often reviewed by a manager one level higher.

Markov analysis A method for tracking the pattern of employee movements through various jobs in a firm.

Material Safety Data Sheets (MSDSs) Documents that contain vital information about hazardous substances

Mediation The use of an impartial, neutral party to reach a compromise decision in employment disputes.

Mediator A third party in an employment dispute who meets with one party and then the other party, then suggests compromise solutions or recommends concessions from each side that will lead to an agreement.

Mentors Individuals who coach, advise, and encourage employees of a lesser rank.

Merit guidelines Guidelines for awarding merit raises that are tied to performance objectives.

Microlearning Training sessions that take place in a very short time frame, usually five minutes or less.

Mission The basic purpose of the organization as well as its scope of operations.

Mixed-standard scale method A trait approach to performance rating that is similar to other scale methods but based on a comparison with (better than, equal to, or worse than) a standard.

Mobile recruiting The process of recruiting candidates via their mobile devices.

Multidomestic corporation (MDC) A firm with independent business units operating in multiple countries.

Multiple cutoff model A selection decision model that requires an applicant to achieve some minimum level of proficiency on all selection dimensions.

Multiple hurdle model A selection decision model in which only those applicants with the highest scores at an initial test stage go on to subsequent stages.

N

National Labor Relations Board (NLRB) The agency responsible for administering and enforcing the Wagner Act. It serves the public interest by reducing interruptions in production or service caused by labor–management strife.

Nearshoring Occurs when a firm relocates jobs abroad to nations closer to its domestic market.

Negligence The failure to provide reasonable care when such failure results in injury to consumers or other employees.

Negligent hiring The failure of an organization to discover, via due diligence, that an employee it hired had the propensity to do harm to others.

Nepotism A preference for hiring the relatives of current employees.

Nine-box grid A comparative diagram that includes appraisal and assessment data to allow managers to easily see an employee's actual and potential performance.

Noncontributory plan A pension plan in which contributions are made solely by the employer.

Nondirective interview An interview in which the applicant is allowed the maximum amount of freedom in determining the course of the discussion, while the interviewer carefully refrains from influencing the applicant's remarks.

Nonexempt employees Employees covered by the overtime provisions of the Fair Labor Standards Act.

O

Offshoring The business practice of sending jobs to other countries.

Offshoring Work that was previously carried out in one country is moved to another country.

Ombud A designated individual from whom employees may seek counsel for resolution of their complaints.

Onboarding The process of systematically socializing new employees to help them get "on board" with an organization.

On-the-Job Training (OJT) A method by which employees are given hands-on experience with instructions from their supervisor or other trainer.

Open-door policy A policy of settling grievances that identifies various levels of management above the immediate supervisor for employee contact.

Organization analysis An examination of an organization's environment, goals, strategies, performance, and resources so as to determine what training it should do.

Organizational culture The shared values, beliefs, and assumptions people in an organization have.

Orientation The formal process of familiarizing new employees with the organization, their jobs, and their work units.

Outplacement services Services provided by organizations to help terminated employees find a new job.

Outsourcing Contracting outside the organization to have work done that formerly was performed by internal employees.

P

Panel interview An interview in which a board of interviewers questions and observes a single candidate.

Passive jobseekers People who are not looking for jobs but could be persuaded to take new ones given the right opportunity.

Pay equity An employee's perception that compensation received is equal to the value of the work performed.

Pay grades Groups of jobs within a particular class that are paid the same rate.

Pay rate compression Compression of pay between new and experienced employees caused by the higher starting salaries of new employees; also the differential in pay between hourly workers and their managers.

Pay-for-performance standard A standard by which managers tie compensation to employee effort and performance.

Peer evaluation A performance evaluation done by one's fellow employees, generally on forms compiled into a single profile for use in the evaluation meeting conducted by the employee's manager.

Peer-review system A system for reviewing employee complaints that utilizes a group composed of equal numbers of employee representatives and management appointees. The group weighs the evidence, considers the arguments, and, after deliberation, votes to render a final decision.

Performance management The process of creating a work environment in which people can perform to the best of their abilities.

Performance reviews A process in which a manager evaluates an employee's performance relative to the requirements of their job and uses the information to show the person where improvements can be made and how.

Perquisites Special nonmonetary benefits given to executives; often referred to as perks.

Person analysis The process of determining the specific individuals who need training in an organization.

Phased retirement A program that allows employees to gradually cut their hours at work before retiring.

Piecework Work paid according to the number of units produced.

Point system A quantitative job evaluation procedure that determines the relative value of a job based on the total points assigned to it.

Political factors External factors including labor laws, property rights, and patent processes.

Position Analysis Questionnaire (PAQ) A questionnaire that identifies approximately 300 different tasks to determine the degree to which each is involved in doing a job.

Positive or nonpunitive discipline A system of discipline that focuses on early correction of employee misconduct, with the employee taking total responsibility for correcting the problem.

Predictive validity The extent to which candidates' test scores match criterion data obtained from them after they have been hired and on the job for a period of time.

Preemployment test An objective and standardized test used to gauge a person's knowledge, skills, abilities, and other characteristics relative to those of other individuals.

Preferred Provider Organization (PPO) A network of physicians who establish an organization that guarantees lower health care costs to employers and their employees.

Process audit Determining whether the high-performance work system has been implemented as designed.

Profit sharing Any procedure by which an employer pays, or makes available to all regular employees, special current or deferred sums based on the organization's profits.

Progressive discipline The application of corrective measures by increasing degrees.

Promotion A change of assignment to a job at a higher level in the organization.

Protected classes Individuals of an underrepresented race, women, older people, and individuals with disabilities who are covered by federal laws on equal employment opportunity.

Psychological contract Expectations of a fair exchange of employment obligations between an employee and an employer.

Q

Quality of fill A metric designed to measure how well new hires who fill positions are performing on the job.

R

Real wages Wage increases larger than rises in the consumer price index; that is, the real earning power of wages.

Realistic Job Preview (RJP) Informing applicants about all aspects of the job, including both its desirable and undesirable facets.

Reasonable accommodation An attempt by employers to adjust, without undue hardship, the working conditions or schedules of employees with disabilities or religious preferences.

Recency error A performance rating error in which the evaluation is based largely on the employee's most recent behavior rather than on their behavior throughout the evaluation period.

Recordable case Any occupational death, illness, or injury to be recorded in the log (OSHA Form 300).

Recruitment Process Outsourcing (RPO) The practice of outsourcing an organization's recruiting function to an outside firm.

Red circle rates Payment rates above the maximum of the pay range.

Reliability The degree to which an interview, test, or other selection procedures result in consistent information about a candidate.

Remote or virtual interviews Interviews conducted via videoconferencing or over the Web.

Repatriation The process of transition for an employee home from an international assignment.

Replacement charts Listings of current jobholders and people who are potential replacements if an opening occurs.

Re-recruiting The process of keeping track of and maintaining relationships with former employees to see if they would be willing to return to the firm.

Reverse discrimination The act of giving preference to members of protected classes to the extent that unprotected individuals believe they are suffering discrimination.

Reverse mentoring A program whereby younger employees are called on to mentor older employees and executives about social media trends, new technology, and marketplace trends.

Rights arbitration Arbitration over interpretation of the meaning of contract terms or employee work grievances.

Right-to-know laws Laws that require employers to advise employees about the hazardous chemicals they handle.

S

Sabbatical An extended period of time (four or more weeks) in which an employee leaves an organization to pursue other activities and later returns to their job.

Salary plus bonus plan A compensation plan that pays a salary plus a bonus achieved by reaching targeted sales goals.

Scanlon plan A bonus incentive plan managed by employee and management committees, with the aim of attaining cost-reduction improvements.

Selection The process of choosing individuals who are qualified to fill existing or projected job openings.

Selection ratio The number of applicants compared with the number of people to be hired.

Self-evaluation A performance evaluation done by the employee being evaluated, generally on an evaluation form completed by the employee prior to the evaluation meeting.

Sequential interview A format in which a candidate is interviewed by multiple people, one right after another.

Severance pay A one-time payment sometimes given to an employee who is being involuntarily terminated.

Sexual harassment Unwelcome advances, requests for sexual favors, and other verbal or physical conduct of a sexual nature in the working environment.

Similar-to-me error A performance rating error in which an appraiser inflates the review of an employee because of a mutual personal connection.

Situational interview An interview in which an applicant is given a hypothetical incident and asked how they would respond to it.

Skill inventories Files of personnel education, experience, interests, skills, and so on that allow managers to quickly match job openings with employee backgrounds.

Sociocultural factors External factors including method and style of communications, religions, values and ideologies, education standards, and social structure.

Split pay A system whereby expatriates are given a portion of their pay in the local currency to cover their day-to-day expenses and a portion of their pay in their home currency to safeguard their earnings from changes in inflation or foreign exchange rates.

Spot bonus An unplanned bonus given for an employee's effort unrelated to an established performance measure.

Spot rewards Programs that award employees on the spot when they do something particularly well during training or on the job.

Staffing table A table that shows a firm's jobs, along with the numbers of employees currently occupying those jobs and future (monthly or yearly) employment requirements.

Stakeholders Key people and groups that have an interest in a firm's activities and that can either affect them or be affected by them.

Standard hour plan An incentive plan that sets rates based on the completion of a job in a predetermined standard amount of time.

Step-review system A system for reviewing employee complaints and disputes by successively higher levels of management.

Straight commission plan A compensation plan based on a percentage of sales.

Straight piecework An incentive plan under which employees receive a certain rate for each unit produced.

Straight salary plan A compensation plan that permits salespeople to be paid for performing various duties that are not reflected immediately in their sales volume.

Strategic human resource management The pattern of human resources deployments and activities that enable an organization to achieve its strategic goals.

Strategic planning Procedures for making decisions about the organization's long-term goals and strategies.

Strategic vision A statement about where the company is going and what it can become in the future.

Stress Any adjustive demand caused by physical, mental, or emotional factors that requires coping behavior.

Structured interview An interview in which a set of standardized questions having an established set of answers is used.

Subordinate evaluation A performance evaluation of a superior by an employee, which is often used for developmental rather than for administrative purposes.

Succession planning The process of identifying, developing, and tracking key individuals for executive positions.

Supplemental Unemployment Benefits (SUBS) A plan that enables an employee who is laid off to draw weekly benefits from the employer, which draws from a fund created for this purpose, in addition to state unemployment compensation.

Sustainability Doing business in a way that does as little harm to the environment and depletes as few natural resources as possible.

T

Talent reviews Strategic meetings to determine if a company has the human resources it needs to compete in the future.

Task analysis The process of determining a training program's content by studying the tasks and duties a job involves.

Task inventory analysis An organization-specific list of tasks and their descriptions used as a basis to identify components of jobs.

Team evaluation A performance evaluation that recognizes team accomplishments rather than individual performance.

Team incentive plan A compensation plan in which all team members receive an incentive bonus payment when production or service standards are met or exceeded.

Technological factors External factors pertaining to the technological infrastructure and investments, information systems, manufacturing equipment, and consumer access to technology.

Telecommuting Working remotely; the use of personal computers, networks, and other communications technology to do work in the home that is traditionally done in the employer's workplace.

Third-country nationals Employees who are natives of a country other than the home country or the host country.

360-degree evaluation A performance evaluation done by different people who interact with the employee, generally on forms compiled into a single document for use in the evaluation meeting conducted by the employee's manager.

Time-to-fill Metrics that refer to the number of days from when a job opening is approved to the date a person accepts the job and begins it.

Transfer The placement of an employee in another job for which the duties, responsibilities, status, and pay and benefits are approximately equal to those of the previous job the person held.

Transfer of training The effective application of principles learned to what is required on the job.

Transnational corporation A firm that attempts to balance local responsiveness and global scale via a network of specialized operating units.

Transnational teams Teams composed of members of multiple nationalities working on projects that span multiple countries.

Trend analysis A quantitative approach to forecasting labor demand based on a factor such as sales.

U

Unfair Labor Practices (ULPs) Specific employer and union illegal practices that deny employees their rights and benefits under federal labor law.

Uniform Guidelines on Employee Selection Procedures A procedural document published in the *Federal Register* to help employers comply with federal regulations against discriminatory actions.

Union An association of people with a common interest to improve their working conditions.

Union security agreement An agreement between an employer and the union about the extent to which the union may compel employees to join the union and how the dues will be collected.

Union steward An employee who as a nonpaid union official represents the interests of members in their relations with management.

V

Validity The degree to which a test or selection procedure actually measures or predicts a person's ability to do a job.

Value creation What a firm adds to a product or service by virtue of making it; the amount of benefits provided by the product or service once the costs of making it are subtracted.

Variable pay Tying pay to some measure of individual, group, or organizational performance.

Vertical fit The situation in which the work system supports the organization's goals and strategies.

Vesting A guarantee of accrued pension benefits to participants at retirement age, regardless of their employment status at that time.

Video résumés Short video clips that highlight applicants' qualifications beyond what they can communicate on their resumes.

Virtual job fair Job fairs conducted online.

Virtual teams Teams that utilize telecommunications technology to link team members who are geographically dispersed—often worldwide, across cultures and across time zones.

W

Wage and salary survey A survey of the wages paid to employees of other employers in the surveying organization's relevant labor market.

Wage curve A curve in a scattergram representing the relationship between relative worth of jobs and pay rates.

Wellness programs Employer-sponsored programs designed to encourage employees to maintain and improve their health and well-being by getting regular checkups, eating properly, exercising, and managing their stress levels so as to prevent costly and protracted illnesses.

Whistle-blowing Complaints to governmental agencies by employees about their employers' illegal or immoral acts or practices.

Work permit or visa A government document granting a foreign individual the right to seek employment.

Work valuation A job evaluation system that seeks to measure a job's worth through its value to the organization.

Workers' compensation insurance State-mandated insurance provided to workers to defray the loss of income and cost of treatment due to work-related injuries or illness.

Workforce (HR) analytics The process of gathering and analyzing data to improve a firm's human resources management.

Workforce utilization analysis A process of classifying protected-class members by number and by the type of job they hold within the organization.

Wrongful discharge A discharge, or termination, of an employee that is illegal.

Y

Yield ratio The percentage of applicants from a particular source who make it to the next stage in the selection process.

Name Index

Organization Index

W

X

Y

Z

Subject Index

P

Q

R

S

T

U

V

Notes and References